RISE OF THE AMERICAN NATION:
John Carroll Edition

This edition of RISE OF THE AMERICAN NATION *has been prepared for the Catholic high schools of the United States. Emphasizing the importance of individual action, the text treats American history as the story of people, the record of their direct participation in the life of the nation. Students follow the lives of many of the great men and women who helped shape America's destiny, through their own speeches and writings, or through those of their contemporaries.* RISE OF THE AMERICAN NATION *is truly an American history textbook for the 1960's.*

THE TEXTBOOK AUTHORS ARE WELL QUALIFIED, BOTH AS TEACHERS AND AS WRITERS

Lewis Paul Todd, who for many years taught high school American history as well as college-level methods courses in the teaching of social studies on the secondary school level, is editor of *Social Education,* the official journal of the National Council for the Social Studies.

Merle Curti is a leading American historian an writer, whose many books include *The Growth of American Thought,* f ᵇ he was awarded the Pulitzer Prize for History in 1943. He is ᵗson Turner Professor of American History at the Univ

John T. Farrell, Professor of Americ atholic University of America in Washington, D. C. r for 25 years. Dr. Farrell has published various a *ⁱc Historical Review* and his participation in the *A* ord Series is the legal diary of William Samuel John

Sister M. Peter Sanz, O.P. (classiᵥ or), brings to this textbook many years of experience in teaching A ican history in the high school classroom. Holding degrees from the University of Illinois and from The Catholic University of America, she is presently Instructor in History at Rosary College, River Forest, Illinois.

HARCOURT, BRACE & WORLD, INC.
Catholic Department Offices: New York and Burlingame

THE ORGANIZATION FACILITATES TEACHING AND STUDYING

RISE OF THE AMERICAN NATION: John Carroll Edition, is divided into four *parts,* each of which represents a major period of American history. Part introductions dramatize to the student, however, that these periods of American history have occurred within four overlapping lifetimes. Representing the four lifetimes are Thomas Jefferson, Abraham Lincoln, Theodore Roosevelt, and the American people today.

The four parts are divided into *units* — 12 in all — each a major idea breaking at a natural point in history.

Within each unit are from two to five *chapters,* either "chronological" or "analytical" chapters or both. Chronological chapters follow generally the order of time, with pauses for anecdote and analysis. Analytical chapters — signaled by an emblem and termed "Changing Ways of American Life" — take one or more important themes and provide necessary background, explanation, or interpretation.

Each chapter contains *sections,* a total of 166 sections in the textbook.

THE FLEXIBILITY OF THE ORGANIZATION MAKES POSSIBLE A VARIETY OF TEACHING PLANS

Each of the chapter sections develops an idea which contributes to the understanding of the larger chapter and unit ideas. These sections, averaging 1500 words, provide reading assignments of reasonable length and are followed by Section Surveys which help the student to review and test himself (e.g., pages 214, 251, 589). Readily adaptable to the typical school year, these 166 sections can be used in planning individual lessons or as parts of larger units of study.

THOROUGH AND VARIED STUDY HELPS FOLLOW CHAPTERS AND UNITS

Each of the 41 chapters ends with: (1) a "Chapter Survey" which contains interesting "Points to Discuss" and a developmental map-skills program called "Using Maps and Charts," and (2) "Tracing the Main Ideas," which summarizes major developments of the chapter (e.g., pages 90, 246, 484, 521, 725, 772).

Each of the 12 units concludes with: (1) "Outstanding Events" (a convenient list of dates and events), (2) "Then and Now" comparisons, (3) "Extending Your Horizon" (guides with specific references for deeper study), (4) suggested "Individual Activities," (5) suggested "Group

Activities," and (6) bibliographies for student reading (e.g., pages 203-4, 283-4, 581-2, 746-7.

THE WRITING IS EXCEPTIONAL FOR INTEREST AND CLARITY

With the authors' fluent style of writing, their skillful use of transitions to help students bridge sections and chapters, and their careful explanations of difficult terms, RISE OF THE AMERICAN NATION is well within the grasp of senior high school students. Difficult words are defined in context; moderately difficult words in footnotes.

SPECIAL FEATURES ARE ILLUMINATING AND ENTERTAINING

The 125 "Special Features" provide a special kind of insight into people, events, and ideas that are part of America's heritage. An excellent source for student projects, they are also a constant reminder of entertaining and instructive bypaths of American history (e.g., pages 63, 101, 219, 225, 381, 763).

THE MAPS ARE UNUSUALLY CLEAR AND INSTRUCTIVE

RISE OF THE AMERICAN NATION contains more than 70 interpretative maps, all of them done especially for the book and placed at the spot where the student needs them. The use of color and symbols, especially in the maps of war campaigns, is particularly effective in making the maps easy to read and understand (e.g., pages 128, 243, 289, 323, 327, 800).

THE NATION'S TWO GREATEST DOCUMENTS
ARE AN INTEGRAL PART OF THE TEXT

The Declaration of Independence and the Constitution are included in full at that point in the running text when they are studied. A full section of the text explains the four major elements of the Declaration, and the Constitution is presented with an annotated study guide (pages 122-4 and 174-202).

STUDENTS ARE INTRODUCED
TO OTHER IMPORTANT DOCUMENTS

Positioned at appropriate places throughout the text are excerpts from selected American "documents," ranging from memorable speeches to significant charters (e.g., pages 76, 347, 397, 736). Each of these documents — as well as others — is presented at greater length or in full in an accompanying book of "Living American Documents."

A SPECIAL ATLAS OF MAPS AND CHARTS
IS PROVIDED FOR REVIEW AND REFERENCE

A 32-page historical atlas of the United States, often referred to in study questions in the text has great value for reference throughout the course. The maps and charts also provide students with a convenient over-all view of various aspects of America's growth (pages 816-47).

A CHRONOLOGICAL PRÉCIS OF AMERICAN HISTORY
IS PROVIDED FOR ORIENTATION AND REVIEW

A 10-page section, "Chronology of Events in American History," summarizes the main events of each presidential administration and is accompanied by two continuous graphs, which trace the ups and downs of business from 1789 to the present and the development and tenure of office of political parties during the same years (pages 850-9).

A COMPREHENSIVE PROGRAM OF TEACHING AIDS
IS AVAILABLE

A most comprehensive teaching aids program accompanies RISE OF THE AMERICAN NATION: JOHN CARROLL EDITION.

teacher's manual and resource guide—of 256 pages, including suggestions for teaching each assignment section in the text; procedures and questions for motivating learning; activities; and answers to questions in the text. George J. Gill, Chairman of the History Department at Regis High School in New York City, is the author responsible for this teacher's manual for the JOHN CARROLL EDITION. A teacher of history for many years, Dr. Gill was recently awarded a Ph.D. in American history from Fordham University.

book of documents — a hardbound book containing extended or complete versions of the excerpts of selected American documents in the text, as well as other documents not included in the text.

phonograph record album — two 12-inch, 33⅓ RPM recordings containing such selections as a dramatization of the Peter Zenger trial and readings on the Revolutionary War and the War Between the States, and the actual voices of Will Rogers, Franklin D. Roosevelt, Harry S. Truman, Dwight D. Eisenhower, and many others.

RISE OF THE AMERICAN NATION

JOHN
CARROLL
EDITION

Rise of the
AMERICAN
NATION

LEWIS PAUL TODD · MERLE CURTI

and for the John Carroll Edition **JOHN T. FARRELL**

CLASSROOM EDITOR
SISTER M. PETER SANZ, O.P.
Department of History, Rosary College, River Forest, Illinois

Maps by **HAROLD K. FAYE**   *Charts by* **RUDOLF MODLEY**

900
TO

HARCOURT, BRACE & WORLD, INC.   *New York   Burlingame*

THE AUTHORS

Lewis Paul Todd is known among social studies teachers for his textbook writing and for his articles and editorials in social studies periodicals. He has made several contributions to the Yearbooks of the National Council for the Social Studies (NCSS). In 1947 he became editor of *Social Education,* the official journal of the NCSS. Since 1950 he has written weekly editorials for the *Civic Leader,* a publication of the Civic Education Service. In addition to his collaboration on *Rise of the American Nation,* he is co-author of a series of social studies textbooks for elementary schools.

Merle Curti is Frederick Jackson Turner Professor of American History at the University of Wisconsin and was recently Visiting Professor of History at the University of Tokyo. He has also lectured in India and at Cambridge University in England. He was formerly Professor of American History at Teachers College, Columbia University. ¶ In 1960 Professor Curti received the award of the American Council of Learned Societies for particularly distinguished scholarship. He has been president of the American Historical Association. The long list of books he has written includes *The Social Ideas of American Educators, The Making of an American Community,* and *The Growth of American Thought,* for which he won the Pulitzer Prize for History in 1943.

John T. Farrell is Professor of American History at The Catholic University of America in Washington, D.C. He was formerly an associate professor of American history at the College of New Rochelle, New Rochelle, New York. The legal diary of William Samuel Johnson is his contribution to the American Legal Record Series. Dr. Farrell has published various articles in *The Catholic Historical Review.* He has been president of the Catholic Historical Association, and presently he is a member of the American Historical Association, Catholic Historical Association, and the Connecticut Historical Society.

ACKNOWLEDGMENTS

EDITORIAL ASSISTANTS AND ADVISERS: *Ralph H. Gabriel,* Sterling Professor of History, Emeritus, Yale University; *Paul Ledbetter,* Teacher of American History, Dallas, Texas; *Isidore Starr,* Teacher of American History, New York City; *Robert D. Torrey,* Director of Curriculum and Instruction, Larkspur, California; *Helen Yeager,* Supervisor of Social Studies in the Secondary Schools, Cincinnati, Ohio.

COVER PHOTO: San Xavier Mission near Tucson, Arizona. Photo by Henderson from Rapho-Guillumette.

TITLE PAGE PHOTO: The White House in Washington, D.C. Photograph by Arnold Newman. Reprinted by special permission from *Holiday,* copyright 1959 by The Curtis Publishing Company.

DRAWINGS: Chapter opening drawings by Ray Houlihan; text drawings by Witold Mars. (Other acknowledgments appear on page 880.)

CONTENTS

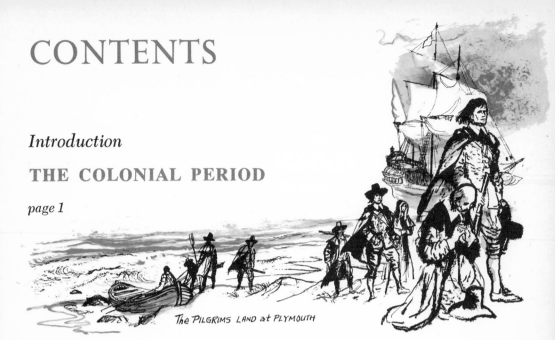

The PILGRIMS LAND at PLYMOUTH

v

Part 1

CREATING A NEW NATION

page 93

ARRIVAL OF DELEGATES CONSTITUTIONAL CONVENTION ~ PHILADELPHIA 1787

Part **2**

THE NATION DIVIDED

page 285

LINCOLN AND DOUGLAS DEBATING
DURING THE SENATORIAL CONTEST–1858

UNIT FOUR: THE RISE OF SECTIONALISM (1820's–1860's), 286

Part **3**

THE NATION REUNITED

page 405

RAILROAD YARD · 1880's

Part 4

THE NATION AS A WORLD LEADER

page 583

BUILDING THE PANAMA CANAL —

MAPS AND CHARTS

TEXT MAPS

TEXT CHARTS

HISTORICAL ATLAS

OF THE UNITED STATES

ELEVATION PROFILE

SPECIAL FEATURES

Introduction   THE COLONIAL PERIOD

Part 1   CREATING A NEW NATION

Part 2   THE NATION DIVIDED

Part 3   THE NATION REUNITED

Part 4   THE NATION AS A WORLD LEADER

LIVING AMERICAN DOCUMENTS

THE COLONIAL PERIOD

UNIT ONE

Building the Colonies

1450–1763

Colonel George Washington of the Virginia Militia, painted by C. W. Peale   **3**

Europeans Settle in the New World

ENGLISH ATTACK
SPANISH ARMADA at CALAIS

EUROPEANS called the fleet the "Invincible Armada" when it sailed from Spain. As for the Spanish admiral, he hoped and prayed for victory as he gazed thoughtfully at the long lines of fighting ships under his command.

The vessels rose and fell upon the long swells, rolling slowly from port to starboard and back again as the seas swept under them. The admiral could see flags and pennants whipping in the wind, sailors clinging to the rigging, soldiers lining the rails, and the muzzles of cannon bristling from the gun ports.

The fleet was entering the English Channel. To the north, off the port quarter, was England, the land that the admiral intended to invade and conquer for his king. From the decks of their ships, the Spaniards could see smoke signals rising from the shore and tiny figures on horseback racing along the coastal roads. They knew that the alarm had been sounded and that the English would be waiting for them.

The momentous day was Saturday, July 30, the year, 1588.

The attack begins. On Sunday the English fleet sailed out to attack. The English ships were smaller than the lumbering Spanish men-of-war—smaller and swifter and manned by better-trained sailors and better gunners.

The Spanish ships sailed majestically up the Channel, keeping formation, their officers and crews confident of victory. But the English vessels swept in and out, picking off stragglers, firing broadsides, and then retreating outside the range of the Spanish guns.

The Spaniards were furious. They waved their swords and shouted at the Englishmen, daring them to come alongside and fight like men.

The Englishmen knew better. They were outnumbered two to one, and outgunned, and they had no intention of making a frontal attack on the Spanish fleet. To be sure, the famous sea rover Sir Francis Drake, who had only contempt for the Spaniards, would have attacked boldly. But Drake was only second in command. First was the English admiral, Lord Howard of Effingham,

1450   1500   1550   1600   1650   1700   1750   1975

who scorned Drake's tactics. "We'll pluck them feather by feather," he said.

The running battle continued for nearly a week. On Saturday evening after a long, slow sail up the English Channel, the Spanish fleet anchored in the harbor of Calais (kal-AY) on the coast of France. The English ships took station just outside the entrance to the harbor and waited for the Spaniards to come out and continue the fight.

The Spanish admiral was in no hurry. England was only twenty miles away across the Channel. In spite of the English attack, his fleet was still in fighting order, and he had reason to expect victory. But fate ruled otherwise.

The Spaniards meet disaster. On Sunday night the English set fire to a number of old vessels and headed them under full sail toward the Spanish fleet anchored in the harbor. Picked crews of English sailors stayed with the blazing ships until they reached the very mouth of the harbor, then took to open boats and returned to their own vessels.

It was an old trick, but it worked. The Spaniards were terrified at the sight of the fire ships bearing down upon them. Word swept through the fleet that the burning vessels were loaded with explosives. The Spanish admiral gave the fatal order for his ships to cut their anchor cables and escape as best they could. Out of the harbor they fled, not in battle formation, but in wild disorder.

The Englishmen were waiting for them. Into the Invincible Armada the English gunners poured broadside after broadside. They kept firing until their guns were almost too hot to touch and their powder was gone.

What was left of the Spanish fleet fled to the north around Scotland, then turned south. The Spaniards were trying to escape, but a great storm came up and wrecked many of the remaining vessels. It was a shattered and broken fleet that finally returned to Spain.

History makes a turn. The defeat of the Spanish Armada by the Englishmen was one of the decisive moments in world history—and in the history of the land that later became the United States of America. For nearly a hundred years, Spain had been growing rich and powerful from trade and plunder in the New World. Unchecked, Spain might have gone on to build strong colonies along the Atlantic seaboard of North America from what is now Maine to Florida.

The conflict between England and Spain that erupted in the English Channel in 1588 marked the turning point of Spain's fortunes in the New World. Spanish power continued strong for many years. But Englishmen soon went ahead to build permanent colonies in North America.

To understand why the famous sea battle of 1588 was so decisive a moment in the beginnings of our country, we must trace events that preceded and followed it. These explain the discovery, exploration, and settlement of the Americas.

AS THE STORY DEVELOPS

1. Europeans search for an all-water route to far-off Asia.
2. Columbus leads Europeans to explore the New World.
3. Spain grows powerful by exploiting its New World colonies.
4. England nibbles, then smashes, at Spanish sea power.
5. England finally gains a foothold in North America.

1 Europeans search for an all-water route to far-off Asia

Most men dream of discovering something new. Christopher Columbus was no exception. Almost one hundred years before the defeat of the Spanish Armada, Columbus dreamed of discovering a new all-water trade route between Europe and Asia. Like other men of his day, Columbus also dreamed of the riches and honors that would be his if he succeeded.

The problem Columbus dreamed of solving was troubling people through-

(*Continued on page 8*)

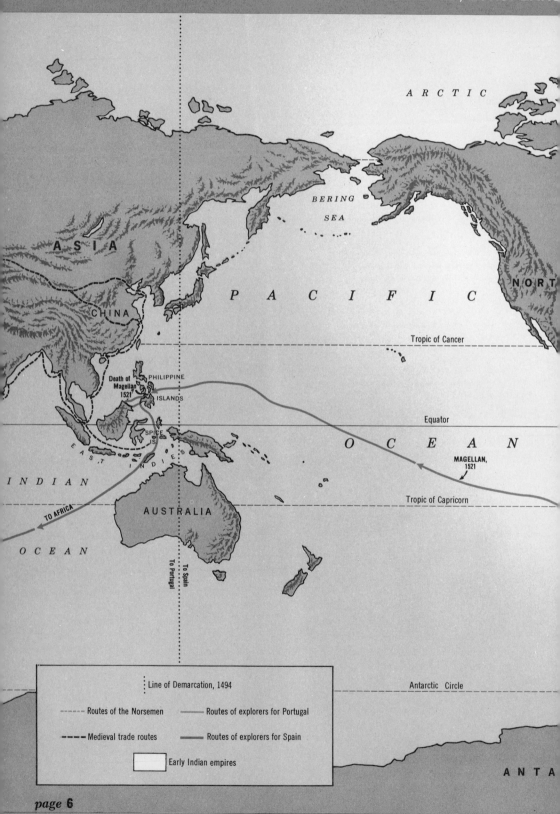

ARCTIC

BERING

SEA

ASIA

CHINA

PACIFIC

NORT

Tropic of Cancer

Death of
Magellan
1521

PHILIPPINE

ISLANDS

SPICE
IS.

Equator

EAST

INDIES

OCEAN

MAGELLAN,
1521

Tropic of Capricorn

INDIAN

AUSTRALIA

TO AFRICA

OCEAN

To Spain

To Portugal

Antarctic Circle

Line of Demarcation, 1494

Routes of the Norsemen   Routes of explorers for Portugal

Medieval trade routes   Routes of explorers for Spain

Early Indian empires

ANTA

ARCTIC OCEAN

GREENLAND

Arctic Circle

ICELAND

NORSEMEN, ABOUT 1000

"WINELAND"?

NEWFOUNDLAND

AMERICA

ATLANTIC

NORWAY

SWEDEN

ENGLAND

EUROPE

NETH.

FRANCE

PORTUGAL

SPAIN

Genoa

Venice

ITALY

Mediterranean Sea

Damascus

Baghdad

PERSIA

ASIA

INDIA

ARABIA

Calicut

COLUMBUS, 1492

BAHAMA IS.

TEC

MAYA

BALBOA, 1513

PANAMA

CABRAL, 1500

AFRICA

DA GAMA, 1498

OCEAN

SOUTH AMERICA

INCA

BRAZIL

VESPUCCI, 1501

DA GAMA, 1497

DIAZ, 1486-88

INDIAN

To Portugal

To Spain

Cape of Good Hope

OCEAN

MAGELLAN'S SHIP "VICTORIA," 1522

MAGELLAN, 1520

TIERRA DEL FUEGO

Strait of Magellan

TICA

NORTH AMERICA

ARCTIC OCEAN

GREENLAND

ASIA

CHINA

ATLANTIC

EUROPE

OCEAN

AFRICA

The world as known to Europeans before Columbus' voyage, 1492 out Europe in the latter half of the 1400's. Europeans needed new and better ways of trading with Asia. Many of Europe's keenest traders, indeed, were trying to solve this problem when Columbus was still a child in his father's small wool-combing shop in the Italian seaport of Genoa.

Importance of trade. For more than two hundred years Europeans had been getting products from Asia—sugar and glass and steel and cutlery from Damascus and Baghdad, rugs from Persia, pepper from India, cloves and cinnamon and nutmegs from the Spice Islands of the East Indies, porcelain and silks from China. Since the days of the Crusades to the Holy Land (1096–1272), Europeans had learned to want these and many other articles that they could not produce for themselves. To pay for these products, Europeans had been sending woolen goods and tin and gold and silver back along the trade routes.

Europeans needed the products they got from Asia. They needed the tough Damascus steel for their swords and armor. They needed rugs and porcelain and glass to make their cold, damp castles and manor houses more livable. More than anything else, perhaps, they needed spices, especially pepper, which they sometimes called "black gold." Spices gave variety and flavor to their coarse food, particularly to their meat.

Difficulty of trade. The old trade routes (see map, pages 6–7) had always been difficult, dangerous, and expensive. It took months, sometimes years, for a box of spices or a bale of cloth to travel from Asia to Europe. Products moving overland from China and central Asia were carried by camel caravans across vast wastelands and high mountain passes. Goods moving from the East Indies along the sea-land route made a long sea voyage westward across the Indian Ocean, then were carried over the burning Arabian Desert by plodding camel caravans. Next came another sea voyage, this time across the Mediterranean Sea on ships bound for the Italian cities of Genoa or Venice, whose merchants° held a *monopoly*° on trade between the eastern Mediterranean and Europe. Finally, the much-wanted products of Asia were sold in Europe.

The search for new routes. The growing demand for products from Asia had a direct bearing on the discovery of America. Portugal and Spain resented the virtual control of east-west trade that the Venetians and Genoans enjoyed. It naturally occurred to the Portuguese and Spanish, and later to Frenchmen, Englishmen, and Dutchmen of the Netherlands, that it might be possible to get goods from Asia more cheaply by discovering new ocean routes to the Far East.

Thus it was, while Columbus was growing up in Genoa and spending his spare time playing around the wharves, that a search was under way for a new all-water route between Europe and the Far East. Before the search ended, explorers had pushed back the frontiers of the known world. This expansion of trade out of the Mediterranean into world sea lanes is sometimes called the Commercial Revolution.

Portugal finds a way. Portuguese seamen led the search for an all-water route to Asia. They were financed by Prince Henry of Portugal, also known as Prince Henry the Navigator.

Prince Henry was interested in exploration. On the coast of Portugal he built a shipyard and a school for navigators. There he and his followers experimented with new types of ships and sails, building vessels seaworthy enough to brave the open waters of the Atlantic Ocean. He and his men also experimented with new methods of navigation, new maps, and new instruments for determining latitude, longitude, and direction—such instruments as the compass and astrolabe.

••

° *merchant:* one who buys and sells goods. In earlier times the term usually meant a businessman who carried on large-scale trade with foreign countries. Today it usually means a storekeeper.
° *monopoly:* exclusive control over the supply of a commodity or service, free from competition.

La Salle at the mouth of the Mississippi

CHRISTENDOM AND AMERICA

Europeans who brought faith and civilization to America had a term for the formative society from which they came, the term *Christendom*. Shaped by the Catholic Church in the Middle Ages, Christendom included the people of the old Roman Empire as well as the Germanic people of northern Europe who had overrun the ancient world.

One direction in which Christendom expanded was into the peninsula where Spain and Portugal developed, and from there it got its start toward lands overseas. When the Portuguese began to explore the Atlantic Ocean and the coast of Africa, their astronomers and navigators were drawn from all over Europe.

Missionaries traveled with the explorers.

Over the next three centuries—from the 1400's to the 1700's—Christendom was gradually broken up into political subdivisions. But this was also a time so rich in progress, not only in the greater knowledge of geography but as well in art and literature, that it has deserved the term *Renaissance* (REN-uh-sahns), a French word meaning "new birth." The discovery and exploration of America occurred in this interval, when the forces which had made Christendom were still strong and when the cultural enrichments of the Renaissance were new. These influences were a tremendous endowment with which to furnish a new world.

But Prince Henry was not content merely to experiment. He sent one expedition after another down along the unexplored coast of Africa (see map, pages 6–7). After his death in 1460, men of Portugal continued to explore the African coastline, trading as they went and pushing farther and farther southward with every expedition. Finally, in 1488, Bartholomeu Diaz (DEE-ahs) and his crew rounded the southern tip of Africa. Diaz wanted to continue toward Asia but his men, weary from months at sea and fearful of the unknown, refused to go farther. So Diaz turned back. But ten years later, in 1498, Vasco da Gama, also from Portugal, followed

Diaz's route around the Cape of Good Hope and continued across the Indian Ocean to Calicut in far-off India.

The achievements of Diaz and Da Gama were enormously important to the little kingdom of Portugal and to the future of the world. Within a few years Portuguese vessels were sailing back and forth along the new, all-water route to India and the Spice Islands.

In 1494 a treaty between Portugal and Spain established a *Line of Demarcation* 370 leagues west of the Cape Verde Islands. Newly found lands to the west of this line were to belong to Spain, and those to the east were to belong to Portugal (see map, pages 6–7).

1. Why were the products of Asia so important to European life?
2. Discuss the roots of Christendom which underlie our American culture.
3. In the latter half of the 1400's, why did some of the nations of Europe become interested in an all-water route to Asia?
4. Describe the contributions of Prince Henry, Diaz, and Da Gama to the discovery of an all-water route to Asia.
IDENTIFY: Crusades, monopoly, spices, Commercial Revolution, Spanish Armada, Renaissance, Line of Demarcation; Columbus; 1488, 1498.

2 Columbus leads Europeans to explore the New World

While Portuguese seamen were groping their way around Africa, Columbus set out in 1492 under the flag of Spain on the first of his four great voyages. But unlike the other explorers, who believed that the best all-water route to Asia was around the southern tip of Africa and eastward, Columbus headed westward. Knowing that the earth was round, a knowledge shared by informed people of his day, Columbus was certain that if he sailed far enough he would come to Asia. In trying to prove his point, Columbus started what has been called the Geographic Revolution.

Columbus finds a new world. Instead of reaching Asia, Columbus landed at an island off the coast of an unknown new world. Columbus thought that he had reached Asia because his calculations showed the westward distance from Europe to Asia to be much shorter than it actually is.

On the morning of October 12, 1492, Columbus and his crew went ashore on the island, which they called San Salvador. The island where they landed is now believed to be Watlings Island in the Bahamas (see map, pages 6–7). Once on shore, they thanked God for leading them safely across the sea. But

not a man among them dreamed that he had discovered a new world.

Columbus tried again and again and still again to discover an all-water route to the Spice Islands and the riches of Asia. He failed and returned from his fourth voyage a poor, lonely, broken-hearted man. He died in 1506 without the comfort of knowing that the world that he had discovered would, in time, have more influence upon Europe than all the riches that he had dreamed of finding in Asia.

Balboa finds a new ocean. Columbus had discovered and started to explore a new world. A few years after his death, a Spaniard named Vasco Nuñez de Balboa (NOON-yehs deh bal-BOH-ah) discovered a new ocean.

We pick up Balboa's story in the year 1513 as he starts on an expedition across the Isthmus of Panama (see map, pages 6–7). He is seeking gold that the Indians tell him lies to the west. Indian guides lead him and his men through a hot, steaming forest. After many hardships they finally reach the foot of a small mountain. Balboa climbs the mountain and catches his first glimpse of the great "South Sea," or what we now call the Pacific Ocean. It lies below him, a vast body of water stretching to the south and the west as far as the eye can see. Is it another great ocean? Balboa can only guess. If he is right, then Asia lies far to the west.

Magellan circles the earth. Ferdinand Magellan proved that Balboa's guess was indeed correct. Magellan's story begins in 1519 as he sets sail from Spain on what turns out to be one of the greatest voyages in human history. Magellan, a Portuguese, is sailing under the flag of Spain. A year after his departure, he is leading his small fleet through a narrow waterway, now called the Strait of Magellan, at the southern tip of South America (see map, pages 6–7).

For more than a month Magellan sails westward through the strait. Snow-covered mountain peaks loom on either side. At night the slopes of the mountains twinkle with the campfires of Indians, so that Magellan calls the land "Tierra del Fuego" (tih-EHR-uh del foo-EH-goh), or Land of Fire. At last he passes through the strait and an ocean opens out before him—a sea so vast and calm that he names it the Pacific Ocean.

Is this the great "South Sea" that Balboa had seen from the mountain in Panama? There is only one way to find out. Sail on and discover the truth.

Two years later, in September 1522, a small vessel with the appropriate name *Victoria* sails into a Spanish harbor. The 18 men in the crew are all that remain alive of 237 who sailed with Magellan from Spain three years earlier. These 18 men have done what no one else has ever done before—they have sailed around the world. But Magellan, the original leader, is not among them. Killed in a battle, he lies buried in the Philippine Islands, half a world away.

Magellan's expedition proved to even the most stubborn European that the lands Columbus had discovered were indeed part of a new world. The expedition also gave Spain its claim to the Philippine Islands. In the years that followed, Spain sent soldiers to conquer the Filipinos, missionaries to convert them to Christianity, and merchants to open up trade. So the Philippine Islands became a Spanish *colony*.°

Explorers and conquerors. After Columbus discovered the New World, other daring men began to explore its coastline and interior. Among the early ones were Pedro Alvares Cabral (PEH-droh AHL-vah-rehs cah-BRAHL), Amerigo Vespucci (ah-meh-REE-goh ves-POO-chi), and Ponce de León (POHN-seh deh leh-OHN).

Cabral, sailing around Africa to India under the Portuguese flag, was blown off his course and in the year 1500 landed on the shores of what is now Brazil (see map, pages 6–7). He claimed this territory for Portugal.

In 1501 Amerigo Vespucci, a Floren-

° *colony:* a settlement or territory created by a group of people who have left their native land, but who continue to live under the control of their mother country.

■ This portrait of Christopher Columbus, by an artist who lived at the same time, now hangs in the Metropolitan Museum in New York City.

tine, sailed on a Spanish expedition along the coast of what is now South America. When he returned to Europe, he wrote a letter in which he expressed the bold opinion that what he had seen was a new continent. News of Vespucci's conclusion reached a famous geographer, who proposed that the newly discovered lands be called America in honor of Amerigo Vespucci. And so Columbus missed even the honor of having the new lands named after him.

A few years later, in 1513, Ponce de León, a Spanish nobleman, sailed along the coast of land which he named Florida (see map, page 13). On a later voyage, while marching inland at the head of a band of soldiers and a pack of savage dogs, he was killed when an Indian's arrow pierced his body.

Hernando Cortez (KOR-tez), another Spaniard, was more fortunate. Cortez landed on the coast of Mexico in the year 1519. Then, burning his ships behind him, he led his men into the interior, determined to conquer the Aztec Indians and their leader Montezuma—or die in the attempt. He conquered, winning glory and gold.

Several years later, in 1531–35, another Spaniard, Francisco Pizarro (pi-ZAR-ro), led an expedition southward from the Isthmus of Panama into the country of the powerful Inca Indians. After sailing along the coasts of what are now the countries of Ecuador and Peru, Pizarro landed and marched into the interior. His march led him upward through the passes of the towering Andes Mountains and into the heart of the Inca Empire. There he and his men conquered the Incas and seized an immense treasure of gold and silver.

The conquests of Cortez and Pizarro were more than personal triumphs. They gave the Spaniards control of the strategic parts of Mexico, Central America, and South America. For a time treasure from the Aztecs and the Incas and gold and silver from the mines of Mexico and Peru made Spain the wealthiest and most powerful nation in Europe.

Exploring northward. The treasure that Cortez and Pizarro had discovered fired men's imagination. Other Spaniards, known as *conquistadores* (kon-KWIS-tuh-DO-rehs), or conquerors, set out in search of similar fame and fortune. Among them were Hernando de Soto and Francisco Vásquez de Coronado (VAS-kehs deh ko-ro-NA-do).

In 1539 De Soto, clad in golden armor, set out to explore the southeastern part of what is now the United States, where he discovered the Mississippi River, the "Father of Waters" (see map, page 13). But De Soto's expedition ended in 1542, when he died and his body was weighted with stones and lowered into the muddy water of the great river that he had discovered.

Meanwhile, in 1540, Coronado set out northward from Mexico, hoping to find the "Seven Cities of Cibola." According to reports the streets of these fabled cities were paved with gold and the walls of the buildings were studded with rubies and other gems. For months

Coronado and his men explored what is now the southwestern part of the United States. One of his lieutenants discovered the Grand Canyon of the Colorado River. Coronado himself marched eastward, crossing what is now the panhandle of Texas and reaching what is now the eastern part of Kansas. He explored an immense territory before returning to Mexico, but discovered neither golden cities nor treasure in this area.

England stakes a claim. Meanwhile, the English were also establishing claims to large areas of the New World.

In 1497 John Cabot, a Venetian sea captain commissioned by King Henry VII, sailed to North America out of the harbor of Bristol, England. Little is known about Cabot as a person, and even less about his famous voyage. It appears that, on this voyage and another he made in the following year, he sailed along the coasts of what are now Newfoundland, Nova Scotia, New England (see map, opposite page), claiming this land for England in the name of King Henry. It also appears that for this work the thrifty king rewarded Cabot with a gift of ten pounds and an annual pension of twenty pounds. This was small reward indeed for the explorer who gave England its first claim to a large part of the North American continent.

France enters the contest. French claims to a share of North America were based on the voyages of Giovanni da Verrazano (joh-VAHN-ee dah vehr-raht-SAH-noh) and Jacques Cartier (kar-TYEH). Verrazano set out in 1524 in search of a water route through America to Asia. He failed, to be sure, but his explorations (see map, opposite page) added something to man's knowledge of the world and gave the French their first claim to new lands overseas.

Ten years later, in 1534, Cartier made the first of three voyages to the lands across the Atlantic. On the first voyage he explored the Gulf of St. Lawrence. On his second and third voyages he explored the St. Lawrence River as far

(*Continued on page 14*)

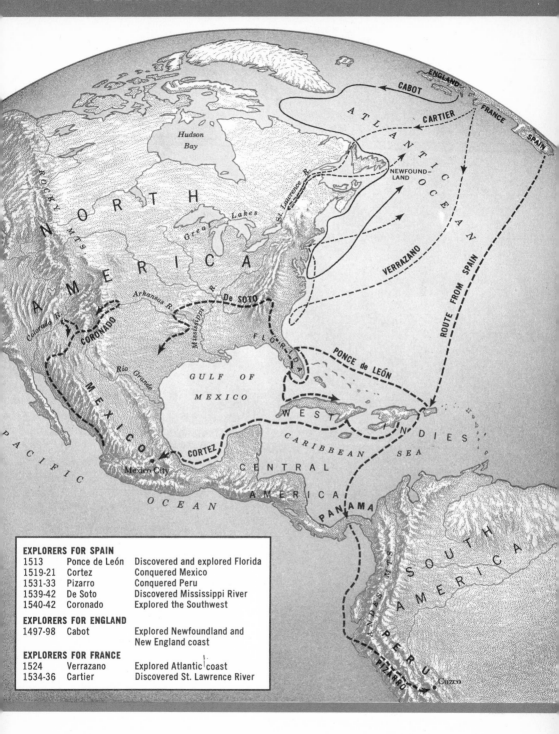

EXPLORERS FOR SPAIN
1513	Ponce de León	Discovered and explored Florida
1519-21	Cortez	Conquered Mexico
1531-33	Pizarro	Conquered Peru
1539-42	De Soto	Discovered Mississippi River
1540-42	Coronado	Explored the Southwest

EXPLORERS FOR ENGLAND
| 1497-98 | Cabot | Explored Newfoundland and New England coast |

EXPLORERS FOR FRANCE
| 1524 | Verrazano | Explored Atlantic coast |
| 1534-36 | Cartier | Discovered St. Lawrence River |

■ The explorers whose routes are shown above greatly expanded the limits of the known world. The Spaniards, given a head start by Columbus, claimed vast areas in both North and South America. Early English and French claims extended primarily along the North Atlantic coast. These claims played a vital role in the early history of the United States.

COLUMBUS WAS NOT FIRST

The first "Americans" probably came from Asia many thousands of years ago across what is now Bering Strait off Alaska. They had bows and arrows, stone knives and axes, and probably dogs. Through thousands of years, these people moved southward and eastward, settling in all parts of the Americas. Their descendants were the Indians.

Norsemen sailing from northern Europe also discovered the New World. Sometime in the late 900's, Eric the Red and his followers landed on Greenland and built a settlement called Brattahild. In the year 1000, Eric's son, Leif the Lucky, was returning to Greenland from a visit to Norway. He and his crew were blown off course and finally made a safe landing on the northeast coast of North America. They called the country "Wineland the Good" after the wild grapes they found growing there. Then they made their way back to Brattahild. Other Norsemen also went to Wineland. Then they stopped coming, and records of their deeds were handed down to later generations by wandering minstrels.

Other Europeans may also have "discovered" the New World before Columbus. If so, no written records have remained. In any case, Columbus was not first. It is more nearly correct to say that he "rediscovered" the New World. The important thing is that after Columbus' great voyage the Americas stayed discovered.

as the present site of Montreal and tried to build a colony on a spot not far from where Quebec now stands. The colony was not a success, but the work of Cartier helped to strengthen French claims to what is now Canada.

Filling in the world map. And so, between 1492 and 1542, a period of only 50 years, these and other explorers carried the flags of Spain, Portugal, England, and France to the New World. During these years the outlines of the American continents began to take shape on maps men were drawing in Europe. Each new discovery, each new expedition, further aroused European interest in the lands across the sea.

SECTION SURVEY

1. Explain how Balboa and Magellan "proved that the lands Columbus had discovered were indeed part of a new world."
2. Why did European nations continue to send explorers to the New World?
3. By 1542 which areas of the New World were claimed by Spain, Portugal, France, and England?
4. On whose explorations did each of these four countries base its claims?

IDENTIFY: colony, conquistadores, Aztecs, Incas; Cabral, Vespucci, Ponce de León, Cortez, Montezuma, Pizarro, De Soto, Coronado, Cabot, Verrazano, Cartier; October 12, 1492, 1513, 1519–22.

3 Spain grows powerful by exploiting its New World colonies

Settlers seeking new homes, as well as explorers and conquerors, traveled from Europe to the New World during the 1500's. Men and women from Portugal settled along the coast of what is now Brazil. Spaniards settled in other parts of South America, in Central America, in Mexico, and on islands in the Caribbean Sea.

Spanish-speaking people also settled in what is now the southern part of the

United States. The first Spanish settlement was St. Augustine, Florida, which was founded in 1565. Later, in 1609, Spaniards settled at Santa Fe, New Mexico. During this same period Spaniards built numerous ranches and missions in what is now the northern part of Mexico and the southwestern part of the United States.

Old ways in the New World. To their American colonies the Portuguese and Spaniards brought domestic animals, plants, and seeds never before seen in the New World. In pens and crates on the decks of their ships, they transported horses, donkeys, cattle, pigs, sheep, goats, and poultry. Using barrels cut in half and filled with earth, they carried fruit and nut trees—olive, lemon, orange, lime, apple, cherry, pear, fig, apricot, almond, walnut, and chestnut. In bags they brought seeds of wheat, barley, rye, rice, peas, lentils, and flax. They also transplanted sugar cane and flowers.

By 1580 the Portuguese and the Spaniards had built prosperous farms, ranches, and cities in the New World. They were digging gold and silver from old Indian mines in Mexico and in Central and South America. They were operating seaports that served as centers of a vigorous trade between the Old World and the New. They were printing books in the New World and educating at least some of their youth in newly built colleges. Churches and missions dotted the land. Toward the end of the 1500's, more than 150,000 Spaniards were living in the New World.

Colonies for the king. All of the Spanish colonies belonged to the king of Spain. He ruled Spain and the Spanish colonies with the help of advisers, but he could ignore the advisers if he wished, for his was the final word. Because the Spanish rulers had complete, or absolute, power, they are sometimes called *absolute kings* or *absolute monarchs*. And because the people living in Spain or in the Spanish colonies had almost no voice in the government, we sometimes say that they were "subjected" to the king's will, or, more brief-

■ In the public square, where the activity of St. Augustine, Florida, flourished, St. Augustine's Church stands prominent.

ly, that they were the king's "subjects."

The Spanish rulers claimed that God had given them the right to rule Spain. They claimed that they were God's representatives on earth and were responsible only to God for their actions. This theory of government, which was common in Europe during this period, was called the *divine right of kings*.

In the New World itself, viceroys,° appointed by the king, ruled in his name with complete authority. For them, as for the humblest Spanish subject, His Majesty's orders were law. In brief, the Spanish king regarded the colonies as *his* personal possessions. The land was his, the people were his subjects, and the wealth of the New World was his to use as he pleased. And use it he did. He rewarded his loyal friends and advisers, nobles of Spain, with rich gifts—gold and silver, large grants of land, trading privileges, and the right to operate the gold and silver mines.

Crest of Spanish power. The gold and silver of the New World were carried to Spain in great "treasure fleets." A treasure fleet was an imposing sight. In the center of the fleet were treasure-laden

••

° *viceroy:* a person appointed by the king to rule a country or colony as the deputy of the king. The word is French: *vice,* meaning "in place of," plus *roi,* meaning "king."

SPAIN AND AMERICAN HISTORY

No greater treasures ever rewarded conquerors than those acquired by the Spaniards. But the Spaniards were more than robbers; they were builders, pioneers, and missionaries.

On the northern limits of their New World empire was a borderland along which a great deal of the history of the United States was to be made. The southern colonies and, later, states such as Florida and Alabama were formed out of the eastern part. In these areas agriculture owed much to Spanish pioneering in the West Indies. Cotton, sugar cane, indigo, rice, and "tropical" fruits were first produced in the Spanish islands, after the original plants had been brought from Mediterranean lands. Even the southern plantation economy, with Negro slavery, was first organized in Spanish colonies—after the Dominican Father Las Casas foresaw that it was a lesser evil than the working to death of the Indians.

Florida and the whole Gulf Coast attracted American traders—as well as land-grabbers, pirates, and gamblers—from colonial times to the era of Davy Crockett and Andrew Jackson.

Texas, the Santa Fe trail, and California's gold fields marked a later path of empire for the United States. Silver dollars, merino sheep, longhorn cattle, mission architecture, and a Spanish-speaking population have long distinguished the southwestern territories and states. But before there was any United States, this border had been a "Rim of Christendom," for the Spaniards, a new Spain, within which they were laying out cities, building cathedrals, founding universities.

galleons. These were huge vessels for their day, slow and clumsy, but heavily armed. Surrounding them in a great circle was a protecting convoy of smaller, swifter war ships. Year after year these fleets moved the wealth of the New World to the Old.

And then, in 1580, Spain had another stroke of good fortune. King Philip II of Spain became ruler of Portugal as well. The two kingdoms were united. In the New World Portugal's thriving colonies were joined to those of Spain. Portugal's rich trade with India and the Spice Islands of the East Indies brought still greater wealth to Spain. Spanish power seemed unbeatable. And yet, as you know, Spain's power finally declined throughout the world.

The Spaniards themselves were partly responsible for their failure to keep Spain the strongest nation in Europe. Easy money helped to ruin them. Instead of building industries to produce goods at home, they used gold and silver from America to buy from other countries the goods that they needed. As a result, when the flow of gold and silver diminished, Spaniards could neither pay for the goods that they needed, nor produce such goods for themselves.

1. Describe four ways in which Spain improved living conditions in its colonies.
2. Summarize Spanish contributions to American culture.
3. Justify this statement: Despite Spain's great wealth in the New World, Spanish power was bound to decline.

IDENTIFY: subject, divine right of kings, viceroy, galleon; St. Augustine, Santa Fe, Philip II, Rim of Christendom; 1565.

4 England nibbles, then smashes, at Spanish sea power

Spain's power in the world started on a long decline when Englishmen and Dutchmen called "sea dogs" began nibbling at Spanish treasure ships in the Caribbean Sea.

Hawkins pesters the Spaniards. John Hawkins was the first famous English "sea dog." Today we would call him a "pirate"; the Spaniards, indeed, called him just that. But his fellow Englishmen and his queen, Elizabeth I, looked upon him as something of a hero.

In the 1560's Hawkins began to transport slaves from Africa to the Spanish West Indies. This was against Spanish law, but Spanish noblemen who owned estates in the New World conveniently forgot the law and traded with the daring Englishman. Before long, however, Hawkins discovered an easier—if riskier —way to make money. He began to raid Spanish seaports and to attack Spanish treasure ships.

Drake infuriates King Philip. Other daring "sea dogs" followed Hawkins' example. Among the boldest of them all was Francis Drake. In 1577 Drake left England with a fleet of swift, heavily armed vessels. He headed southward and sailed through the Strait of Magellan into the Pacific Ocean (see map, page 18). Then he headed northward, skirting the western coast of South America. In the coastal waters between Peru and Panama, he found exactly what he wanted—unprotected vessels loaded with treasure. The Spaniards were not expecting an enemy in these remote waters and saw no need to provide convoys for their merchant ships.

Before long, Drake had seized all the plunder he could carry. He continued northward—not daring to return by the way he had come—and spent the winter on the coast of what is now California. When spring came, he sailed boldly across the Pacific in the *Pelican,* his only remaining vessel, across the Indian Ocean, around the southern tip of Africa, and up through the Atlantic Ocean to England, arriving home in the autumn of 1580.

King Philip of Spain was furious, for he knew that neither Drake nor the other English "sea dogs" could set sail without Queen Elizabeth's permission. He also knew that much of the plunder went into the English royal treasury. Philip therefore demanded that Queen Elizabeth punish Drake for his "piracy." Instead, Elizabeth welcomed Drake as a hero and, to show her gratitude, knighted him on the deck of his ship, now renamed the *Golden Hind.*

Queen Elizabeth's action was a direct challenge to the Spanish king. Philip was quick to meet the challenge. He gave orders to assemble a mighty fleet to invade and conquer England.

England gains freedom at sea. As you have seen, Spain's attempt in 1588 to conquer England ended in disaster. The year 1588, therefore, was a turning point in history. Spain, with its powerful fleet destroyed, and torn by troubles at home, began to decline in power. To be sure, for many years Spanish power remained strong in both the Old World and the New. But Spain was no longer the most feared nation in Europe.

While Spain became weaker, England and France and the Netherlands grew stronger. In time the English Royal Navy won for England the title of "Mistress of the Seas." Even as early as the end of the 1500's, no power on earth could prevent Englishmen from build-

ENGLAND DEFEATS
SPANISH ARMADA, 1588

ENGLAND

NEWFOUNDLAND

ATLANTIC

AFRICA

RALEIGH'S EXPEDITION

DRAKE, 1571

SPAIN

NORTH
AMERICA

DRAKE, BACK TO
ENGLAND, 1579

VIRGINIA

ROANOKE ISLAND
(RALEIGH'S COLONY,
1585)

SPANISH TRADE ROUTE

OCEAN

DRAKE, 1580

SPANISH ROUTE

WEST INDIES

CARIBBEAN SEA

PACIFIC

SPANISH

TO THE PHILIPPINES

PANAMA

DRAKE CAPTURES
SPANISH SHIPS

TERRITORY

SOUTH AMERICA

PACIFIC OCEAN

DRAKE

Strait of
Magellan

ing colonies in the New World. And by this time many Englishmen were eager to do just that.

Englishmen learn about America. All through the 1500's Englishmen had been as interested as other Europeans in the New World. They repeated over and over again the stories that they had heard about the strange new lands and peoples across the Atlantic.

Some of these stories came from fish-ermen. Beginning at least as early as 1504, fishing boats from Europe made regular yearly trips to the Grand Banks off Newfoundland. Now and then the fishermen landed on the nearest coast to get fresh water and to dry and salt their catch. They met Indians and some-times traded for furs. Although few of the fishermen could read or write, they did talk, and their stories made the rounds of European seaports.

Far more exciting were the exploits of the "sea dogs" and the reports of the explorers. In the 1580's an English geographer named Richard Hakluyt (HAK-loot) began gathering and editing these reports. From them, Englishmen gained a wealth of information about the New World.

Two early colonies fail. Even before the defeat of the Spanish Armada, two Englishmen tried unsuccessfully to build colonies in America. Sir Humphrey Gilbert sailed across the Atlantic in 1583, intending to settle on the site of what is now St. John's, Newfoundland. But the expedition failed when Sir Humphrey and all his shipmates were lost in a storm.

The following year Queen Elizabeth gave permission to handsome, dashing Sir Walter Raleigh to build colonies in the New World, at his own expense. Raleigh spent a fortune in the attempt —and failed.

Raleigh's grant of land included all of eastern North America north of Spanish Florida. He named the land Virginia. With the backing of a number of men, he organized an expedition to explore the Atlantic coast. The expedition returned with good reports, and in 1585 Raleigh sent out his first group of colonists. They landed on Roanoke Island, off the coast of what is now North Carolina (see map, page 18).

The first Roanoke colony failed, however, and in 1587 Raleigh sent out a second group of colonists, who also settled on Roanoke Island. Unfortunately, the Spanish attempt to invade England in 1588 prevented Raleigh from sending fresh supplies. And when, in 1591, a relief expedition finally reached Roanoke, the settlers were gone. To this day, the fate of this little band of colonists remains a mystery.

Although Raleigh failed to build a colony, his efforts helped to strengthen England's interest in the New World. And Raleigh himself never lost faith: "I shall yet live to see it an English nation," he predicted of the land that he called Virginia.

RICHARD HAKLUYT, GEOGRAPHER

Now and again scholars who collect and edit material have as great an influence in shaping history as kings, soldiers, and statesmen. So also do promoters and advertisers—men who publicize events and make people want to do one thing rather than another. Such a man was Richard Hakluyt (1552?–1616).

From the time that he was a small boy, Hakluyt was interested in the voyages of discovery and exploration that had been taking place since Columbus had made his first voyage to the New World. Hakluyt said that he read "whatever printed or written discoveries and voyages I found . . . either in Greek, Latin, Italian, Spanish, Portuguese, French, or English languages." In 1582 he published his first great collection, extending it in later editions, under the title *The Principal Navigations, Voyages, and Discoveries of the English Nation.*

Hakluyt's *Voyages* were widely read in England and stimulated the English government and people to challenge other nations who had staked out claims in the New World. The collection contains actual reports by such men as Cabot, Hawkins, Drake, Frobisher, Davis, and Raleigh. For this reason, the *Voyages* are what the historians call primary sources. The language is quaint, but each report is a great adventure story.

SECTION SURVEY

1. Why did England decide to challenge Spanish sea power?

2. How did Hawkins, Drake, and Hakluyt help to arouse Englishmen's interest in the New World?

3. Trace early attempts of England to establish colonies in the New World.

4. Why is the year 1588 considered one of the great turning points in world history?

IDENTIFY: sea dog, primary sources; Elizabeth I, Sir Humphrey Gilbert, Raleigh, Roanoke; 1577–80.

5 England finally gains a foothold in North America

Sir Walter Raleigh had tried, on a small scale, to start a colony on Roanoke Island and had lost his fortune in the attempt. The next colonial venture was made by a large business organization in which hundreds of Englishmen had invested money, hoping to profit from colonial trade and development.

The famous charter of 1606. In 1606 King James I of England gave a single *charter*° to two groups of men. One group, which centered in Plymouth, England, was known as the Plymouth Company. The other, which centered in London, was known as the London Company. The map on page 21 shows the land that King James granted to each of these companies in the large area that was then called Virginia.

The charter was important for another reason: It included a promise by King James that all who settled in the English colonies would retain their *rights and privileges* as Englishmen. In

••
° **charter:** an official document granting certain rights, powers, or privileges to a specific person or group; a written contract.

■ In ships like these, built to celebrate the 350th anniversary of Jamestown, Virginia, the first permanent English settlers journeyed to America.

the words of the charter, they were to "have and enjoy all liberties, franchises, and immunities . . . as if they had been abiding and born within this our realm of England, or any other of our said dominions." In later years, as you will see, the English colonists again and again reminded the English government of its promise to respect their rights and privileges. Thus, the early colonists helped to strengthen the idea of *self-government*.

Jamestown makes a poor start. It was Christmas time in the year 1606 when three small ships of the London Company weighed anchor and moved with the outgoing tide down the Thames River and out upon the wintry sea. The London Company had wasted no time putting its share of the charter to use.

From the beginning the expedition was in trouble. In their ignorance the men did almost everything wrong. They took a roundabout way to America, following Columbus' route, and 16 of the 120 men died on the long voyage.

When the colonists finally reached Virginia, in the spring of 1607, they began to build a settlement, which they called Jamestown in honor of the king (see map, page 21). They picked the poorest possible location for their settlement—a low, wooded area on the banks of a river, which they called the James, near a marsh infested with malaria-carrying mosquitoes. The men did not take time to dig wells, but chose instead to drink the dirty river water. They built the flimsiest kind of shelters, in which they were drenched by rain in summer and half-frozen by cold when winter came.

The directors make mistakes. Not all the fault for their early failure lay with the settlers. The directors of the London Company, back in England, made a number of mistakes.

For one thing, the Company, remembering Spain's rich discoveries, insisted that the settlers hunt for gold. The settlers were quite willing to do so, but, of course, there was none to be found in the area. As a result, the men wasted valuable time that would have been better spent in building houses and cultivating crops.

To make matters worse, everything that the men secured from trade or produced from the land had to go into a common storehouse, under rules worked out in London. The settlers were to own nothing, and received only as much food and clothing as they needed.

But the worst mistake of all, perhaps, was the failure of the directors to enlist enough real workmen to settle the colony. In the original group of 120 settlers that landed at Jamestown, there were only 12 laborers and skilled workmen. The rest were listed as "gentlemen"—men who had never done a day's work with their hands.

Bad times for Jamestown. It is not surprising that by the end of the first year only 53 of the settlers were still alive. They, too, might have perished if it had not been for John Smith.

Smith set himself up as a leader of the colony. He ordered the men to dig wells, build better shelters, clear the land, and plant corn and other crops. During this period Smith made a number of trips to Indian villages to get corn and meat.

John Smith was a harsh ruler. Every morning he marched the men into the fields to cultivate the crops or into the forest to cut wood. They marched to and from their jobs to the beat of a drum. They grumbled and complained, but the rule was "No work, no eat." So the men worked. And, thanks to John Smith, the colony survived.

When Smith returned to England, however, matters went from bad to worse. The winter of 1609–10 was terrible beyond belief. In later years the survivors called it "the starving time." When spring came, the sick, half-starved colonists were prepared to abandon Jamestown. Fortunately, just at this time a number of ships arrived from England with new settlers and fresh supplies, giving the colonists new hope.

In 1609 the king granted a new charter, which gave more land to the Virginia colony (see map, this page).

PLYMOUTH COMPANY GRANT, 1606

OPEN TO BOTH COMPANIES, 1606

LONDON COMPANY GRANT, 1609*

LONDON COMPANY GRANT, 1606

Lake Ontario

NORTHWEST

James R.

Jamestown — Point Comfort

ROANOKE I.

WEST

Scale of miles   0   200

*"Land 200 miles north and south of Point Comfort, lying from seacoast up into the land from sea to sea, west and northwest."

Conditions improve. Slowly, after 1610, conditions began to improve. Much to the surprise of everyone, it was tobacco that saved the colony.

Europeans first learned about smoking tobacco from the American Indians. By the early 1600's the habit of smoking was spreading over Europe. King James I of England tried to stop it. He said that smoking was "loathsome to the eye, hateful to the nose, harmful to the brain, dangerous to the lungs. . . ." But in spite of King James's objections, more and more people started smoking tobacco.

ADVICE TO PIONEERS

"Those leaving for Virginia," an English statement of 1622 read, "must provide themselves with the following tools for a family of six:

"4 hoes, 3 shovels, and 2 spades
"2 broadaxes, 5 felling axes
"2 steel hand-saws, 2 two-hand saws
"1 whipsaw with file and set
"2 augers, 6 chisels
"2 pickaxes, one grindstone
"Nails of all sorts."

It is interesting to compare this list with the tools and other equipment a pioneer family might take to a homestead in Alaska today.

Until Jamestown was settled, all of the tobacco that Englishmen and other Europeans smoked came from the Spanish West Indies. Then, around 1612, John Rolfe (who later married the Indian princess Pocahontas) learned how to grow and cure tobacco in Virginia. Within a few years the colonists were shipping large quantities of this valuable product to England.

By 1619 there were more than 1000 men in the Virginia colony, and most of them were making a living by raising tobacco. They were growing tobacco on every inch of cleared land. Their farms dotted the banks of the James River for a distance of twenty miles beyond the original settlement.

There were, however, other reasons for the growth of Jamestown. Among the new settlers were many skilled workmen—carpenters, masons, blacksmiths, farmers, fishermen. Also, the London Company abandoned the idea of the common storehouse. Starting in 1618,

each man who paid his own way to Jamestown was given fifty acres of land. The colonists could now work their own fields and sell their own products.

Self-government begins. In 1619 the London Company took another big forward step by giving the colonists the right to share in their own government.

July 30, 1619, is a memorable date in American history. On that date twenty-two *burgesses,* or representatives, two from each of the settled districts along the James River, met in Jamestown. Each of the burgesses had been elected by the voters of his own district. The House of Burgesses, as this lawmaking body came to be called, represented the men who owned land in the new colony. The first meeting was a short one, but extremely important, for it marked the first step toward *representative government* in the New World.

The colony grows. The date 1619 is memorable for other reasons. In that year the directors of the London Company sent 60 women to Virginia. The women, all unmarried, could pick and choose the husbands they wanted from the colony of more than 1000 bachelors. They were quickly married and, as the directors had foreseen, exercised a steadying influence upon the men.

In 1619, also, a Dutch vessel brought the first Negro slaves to the colony. But the slaves, 20 in number, represented only a very small part of the labor supply of Virginia. As you will see, many years passed before slavery became an important part of the life of the colony.

The directors of the London Company, encouraged by the growing prosperity of Virginia, began to send out hundreds of new settlers. Following orders from the company, some of the new settlers started an iron works on the James River. Others planted olive trees and laid out vineyards. But most of the newcomers cleared a piece of land and began to grow tobacco.

Then disaster struck. Alarmed by the rapid growth of the colony, neighboring Indians went on the warpath. In 1622, on a night that the survivors never forgot, the Indians swooped down upon the outlying farmhouses, killing many of the settlers and burning most of the buildings. But Virginia quickly recovered from this blow. After striking back at the Indians, the colonists rebuilt their houses and started again. Between 1620 and 1624 about 4000 men, women, and children arrived as settlers in the colony.

Virginia becomes a royal colony. In spite of the growth of the colony, King James I decided that it had been badly managed. In 1624 he withdrew the charter from the London Company and took over the management of the colony. From that time on, Virginia was a *royal colony,* ruled directly by the king.

Virginia was now the property of the Crown, that is, of the English king. But its government was not as restrictive as that of the Spanish colonies to the south and west, where the king of Spain and his viceroys still held absolute power. The king now appointed the governor and gave him power to veto, or reject, any laws. He also appointed a *council,* consisting of 12 members, to assist the governor. But King James I did not attempt to wipe out the House of Burgesses. The House of Burgesses continued to make the laws, subject to the approval of the governor and of the king. The settlers continued to elect the members of the House of Burgesses.

SECTION SURVEY

1. What important promise did King James I make to the colonists in the charter of 1606?

2. (a) Note five conditions that almost caused the Jamestown colony to fail. (b) What factors led to its final success?

3. Describe three important events (political, social, and economic) that occurred in 1619.

4. Why is the establishment of the House of Burgesses regarded as one of the landmarks of representative government in America?

IDENTIFY: charter, London Company, royal colony, Magna Carta, Parliament, legislature; John Smith, John Rolfe; 1607, July 30, 1619.

BACKGROUNDS OF ENGLISH GOVERNMENT

In the year 1215 a group of English barons banded together against their monarch, King John, a harsh ruler who had been making excessive demands for money from the barons, and ignoring their traditional rights. The barons forced King John to sign *Magna Carta,* or the Great Charter.

The Great Charter was important because it contained the idea that government should be "constitutional," or conducted according to law. Limits were set on what the king could demand from the barons. Some provision was made to protect the interests of clergymen, merchants, and townsmen, but the peasants were not affected. Nevertheless, when Englishmen of the 1600's and 1700's wanted to uphold what they called the "rights of Englishmen," they looked back to *Magna Carta* as the foundation on which those rights rested.

With the establishment of the "Parliament," or lawmaking body, in 1265, Englishmen took another step toward assertion of their rights through *representative government.* The English Parliament did not meet regularly for many, many years. In time, however, it did win the right to meet regularly and to help write the laws, or *legislation.* Long before the 1600's, England's Parliament had divided into two bodies—the House of Lords (or the "upper house") and the House of Commons (or the "lower house"). The House of Commons consisted of elected *representatives.*

The men who settled the American colonies carried the English type of government with them to the New World. Every colony had its *legislature,* or lawmaking body. The colonial legislatures, like the English Parliament, were divided into two houses—an upper house and a lower house—and the representatives in the lower house were elected by the voters themselves. The lower houses of the legislatures had different names in different colonies—the "House of Burgesses" in Virginia and "The Assembly" in a number of other colonies.

Points to Discuss: 1. Explain this statement: Columbus, by a historic mistake, opened a vast new world to exploration.

2. Why were the Italians not interested in sending navigators to search for an all-water route to Asia?

3. The motives for the exploration and settlement of the New World have been summed up by three words: Glory, Gospel, and Gold. Do you agree?

4. Investigate and report on the role of Bartolomé de las Casas, Spanish missionary.

5. Discuss the pattern of government in Virginia after it became a royal colony.

Using Maps: 1. Using the map on pages 6 and 7, answer the following questions: (a) How many medieval trade routes are shown? (b) If you had been a trader in the Middle Ages, which of the trade routes would you have preferred? (c) If Magellan were making his famous voyage today, what short cuts could he use? (d) Identify the Italian cities that were most important in trade with the East. (e) Compare the importance of the voyage of Diaz with that of Da Gama. (f) Which parts of the world were known to Europeans about 1500? Which were still unexplored? (g) What is the significance of the Line of Demarcation of 1494?

2. Using the maps on pages 13 and 18, show why the route from Peru and Mexico to Spain was dangerous for Spanish ships.

3. Study the map on page 21. What future problems can you foresee as an outcome of the London Company Grant?

4. What famous explorers might you wish to add to the list of explorers found with the map on page 13?

Consulting the Sources: For interesting documents concerning early exploration rights and for accounts of early Spanish activity in the New World, see John Tracy Ellis (ed.), *Documents of American Catholic History* (hereafter referred to as Ellis, *Docs.*), Nos. 1–15.

■ TRACING THE MAIN IDEAS

Men have always lived in a changing world. There have been certain periods in history, however, when changes came with such speed and transformed so many different aspects of life that they were truly revolutionary. Such an age was the one that you have been reading about in this chapter.

The "revolutions" began in Europe. There was the revolution now called the Renaissance, or rebirth, in which men became increasingly curious about the world around them. There was the Commercial Revolution in which traders from Spain, Portugal, England, and other nations facing the Atlantic discovered new all-water routes to Asia and so destroyed the monopoly of the Italian traders of Genoa and Venice. There was the Geographic Revolution in which European explorers, led by Columbus, discovered a New World far across the Atlantic.

And, finally, there was in England a growing spirit of independence. Englishmen had been insisting since the 1200's that they had a "right" to share in the government, to be "represented" in the lawmaking body that they called Parliament. This movement stretched over too long a period to be called a "revolution." But it was in full swing by the 1600's, and the changes it was destined to bring in the way that men lived and governed themselves were nothing short of revolutionary.

In such an age—an exciting age in which new ideas and new ways of living were transforming the everyday affairs of life in Europe—Englishmen planted their first permanent New World settlement and brought to it the principle of representative government.

As you will see in the next chapter, Englishmen soon carried the same principle of representative government to all the other settlements and colonies built along the Atlantic seaboard.

The British Colonies Grow Strong

The PILGRIMS LAND at PLYMOUTH

I F Europe had been a happier place in the 1600's, the attractions of the New World would not have been so compelling. But Europe was not a happy place, at least not for many people, and for this reason the lands across the sea became doubly attractive.

Men and women who had little hope of ever living better in Europe looked to America with new hope. Here was a rich but empty land, almost unexplored, waiting for the ax and the plow of the pioneer. Here was opportunity, almost limitless, for men and women bold enough to seize it.

And so they came, first to Jamestown, then to New England, and then in ever-growing numbers to other wild and lonely places along the Atlantic seaboard. By 1733, when Georgia was started, European settlers had built thirteen colonies. And the boldest of the settlers, true pioneers, were pushing westward through the forest, clearing land and building homes for themselves in the wilderness.

Out of such simple beginnings a new country was born.

In this chapter and in Chapter 3 you will review the major events that took place in the building of the colonies up to the 1760's. Later, in Chapters 4 and 5, you will read in greater detail about everyday life in the English colonies. You will see how the new ways of life helped to stimulate new ideas and new ideals.

AS THE STORY DEVELOPS

1. Many Englishmen seek fresh starts in North America.
2. New England is settled by Pilgrims and Puritans.
3. Diverse peoples immigrate to the Middle Colonies.
4. Southern planters create a distinctive way of life.

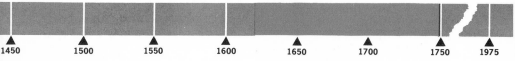

| 1450 | 1500 | 1550 | 1600 | 1650 | 1700 | 1750 | 1975 |

1 Many Englishmen seek fresh starts in North America

Opportunity! That was the great attraction. Like a magnet, opportunity drew men and women from Europe to the New World. But even so, people would not have come in such numbers if conditions in Europe had been better.

Conflict over religion. During the 1500's and 1600's Europe was torn by religious strife. The conflict broke out shortly after Columbus discovered the New World. At that time virtually all Europeans were members of the Roman Catholic Church. The conflict began when a group of men in the Church began to question some of its practices and beliefs. One of these men was Martin Luther in Germany. Another was John Calvin in France.

These men and others who shared their feelings finally broke away from the Roman Catholic Church and established Protestant, or "protesting," religious organizations. Roman Catholics called this movement the Protestant Revolt. Protestants called it the Reformation. By whatever name it was called, this religious conflict was not just a battle of words and ideas. Armies marched, wars were fought, and thousands died in battle or were burned at the stake in the name of religion.

England made a break with the Roman Catholic Church in 1534. At this time King Henry VIII established the Anglican Church, sometimes called the Church of England. The head of the Anglican Church was the king of England. Every English citizen, regardless of his own religious belief, was required by law to belong to this Church and to pay taxes for its support.

Search for religious freedom. In spite of the law, large numbers of Englishmen raised objections to the Anglican Church. Many Roman Catholics insisted upon their right to continue worshiping as they always had. Among the Protestants there were some people, called Dissenters, who felt that the Anglican Church was too much like the Roman Catholic Church.

One group of Dissenters was willing to belong to the Anglican Church, but tried in every way to reform, or "purify," it. These Protestants were known as Puritans.

Other groups of Protestant Dissenters refused to have anything to do with the Anglican Church. These people broke away and formed their own religious organizations. For this reason, they were called Separatists, or Independents, or Nonconformists. The Pilgrims were one of these groups.

Life in England was never easy for Dissenters. At times conditions became especially difficult. Men and women were persecuted by their neighbors, fined by the government, and sometimes sent to jail. It is not surprising, then, that at the height of persecution thousands of people left England in the hope of finding greater *religious freedom* in the New World. As they built their colonies, they were joined by religious refugees, both Catholics and Protestants, from other European countries.

Search for political freedom. The desire to be free from political persecution also drove many Englishmen—as well as people from other European countries—to the New World. For a period of nearly a hundred years, many Englishmen had hardly dared to express an opinion on the subject of politics.

Political problems in England came to a head during the reign of the first of the Stuart kings, James I, who ruled during the years from 1603 to 1625. King James I tried both to make and enforce laws without the consent of Parliament, the established legislature, or lawmaking body, of England. James believed in the "divine right of kings" (page 15) and insisted that he was responsible to no earthly power for his actions. Most members of Parliament refused to accept this theory of government. As a result, an intense quarrel broke out between James I and Parliament.

The quarrel became even more intense after Charles I became king in 1625. For eleven years, from 1629 to 1640, Charles I ruled without Parliament. During these years his word was law. Then, in 1642, a civil war called the Puritan Revolution broke out. The war ended in 1649 when Charles I was beheaded. For the next eleven years, England was ruled by a group of Puritans with Oliver Cromwell as their leader until his death in 1658.

During this long period of political controversy, whoever was in power was often intolerant toward those not in power. To escape this intolerance, many Englishmen moved to the New World.

Widespread unemployment. Religious persecution and lack of political freedom were only two of the problems troubling many Englishmen during the years when the colonies were being started. One of the biggest problems was unemployment.

During the 1500's and 1600's many of the owners of large estates in England drove tenant farmers from their land, turned the plowed fields into pastures, and raised large flocks of sheep. The landowners did this because they could make more money by selling wool than they could by collecting rent.

Many of the displaced farmers moved to English towns and cities where they found jobs. But there were not enough jobs for all of them, and large numbers had no place to go and no way to earn a living. Many of these unfortunate people became beggars, wandering up and down the country roads, eating when they could find food, and sleeping wherever they could lay their heads.

The more desperate of these displaced people became criminals—highwaymen, pickpockets, thieves. Many were caught. Some were hanged on gallows beside the road as a warning to their fellow criminals. Others were shipped to the colonies to work off their sentences at hard labor. Still others were thrown into prison.

Not all of the people in England's crowded jails were criminals as we un-

NOVA BRITANNIA.
OFFERING MOST
Excellent fruites by Planting in
VIRGINIA.

Exciting all such as be well affected to further the same.

LONDON
Printed for SAMVEL MACHAM, and are to be sold at his Shop in Pauls Church-yard, at the Signe of the Bul-head.
1609.

■ A pamphlet advertising Virginia to prospective settlers appeared in London in 1609. Can you read its cover? The letters f and s look alike.

derstand that term today. Many were there for the sole reason that they could not pay their debts, no matter how small. There they remained until the debts were paid—or until they were sent to one of the English colonies overseas to work off the money they owed.

But only a small proportion of the unemployed men and women turned to crime or ended up in a debtor's prison. Most of them continued to look for work. And we may be sure that when America was mentioned they listened with rapt attention. Many of these people were willing to risk anything to get a fresh start in life. Large numbers of them signed contracts called *indentures*. Under these indentures they promised to work in America without wages for a period varying from two to seven years in return for free transportation to that land of opportunity. People who signed indentures were called *indentured servants*. Others, called *redemptioners*, were sold on landing for their passage money and a fee to the ship's captain.

Economic ferment. These were difficult times in England, not only for the unemployed, but also for thousands of other people. Prices were rising, and it was difficult to make ends meet.

When this happens today, we call it *inflation*. During a period of inflation, with prices soaring, a fixed amount of money will buy fewer and fewer goods. People who have only a limited amount of income find it harder and harder to buy food and clothing.

One of the reasons for rising prices in England—and for that matter throughout Europe—was the flow of gold and silver from the Spanish colonies of the New World. This gold and silver poured into the hands of Spaniards who used it to buy products from other countries. Because of the increased demand for their products, farmers and manufacturers in other countries were able to secure higher prices. The rising prices created hardships for thousand of people.

But higher prices also helped to bring prosperity to a considerable number of Englishmen, particularly to businessmen—merchants, traders, and manufacturers. Thus, some of the treasure of the New World flowed through Spain and into the hands of English businessmen. And as their fortunes grew, the businessmen began to look for profitable ways to invest their money. Many bought shares in overseas trading ventures. The boldest among them began to think of financing colonies in the New World.

A dam about to burst. In the late 1500's and early 1600's, then, conditions in England favored colonization. Thousands of people longed for freedom to worship as they pleased. Thousands were eager to escape from political unrest and persecution. Poor people, many of whom were unemployed, wanted jobs and the opportunity to earn a better living. Businessmen had money to invest in promising colonial ventures.

England in the opening years of the 1600's was like a dam behind which the water was rising higher and higher. When the dam finally burst, a flood of people poured out to populate the colonies overseas.

▱ **SECTION SURVEY**

1. Describe the religious conditions in England that drove people to the New World.
2. What political events caused people to leave England?
3. Show how economic conditions led Englishmen to seek opportunities in the New World. What does inflation mean?

IDENTIFY: Protestant Reformation, Anglican Church, Dissenters, Puritans, Separatists, Pilgrims, Puritan Revolution, indentured servants, inflation; Stuart kings, Cromwell; 1534, 1642–49.

2 New England is settled by Pilgrims and Puritans

On November 11, 1620, a small, storm-battered ship sailed in from the ocean and dropped anchor off the tip of Cape Cod, a wind-swept neck of land jutting out from the mainland of North America. The passengers, called Pilgrims, were about to start the first permanent colony in New England. At this time there was only one other English settlement along the entire Atlantic seaboard, the struggling colony of Jamestown, Virginia.

The "why" of the Pilgrim story. Why had the Pilgrims come to this wild and lonely spot? Not one of the 102 passengers could have answered for all the others. Many had come because they wanted to be free to worship in their own way, for, being Separatists, they refused to follow the practices of the Church of England.

But not all of the passengers were Separatists. John Alden, for instance, was a young cooper, or barrelmaker, who had helped to get the *Mayflower* ready for its voyage and who had decided to make the long journey out of the spirit of adventure. Others joined the little band for reasons of their own, not necessarily religious reasons. Some of the passengers had been living for a number of years in the Netherlands, where the government had allowed them to worship in their own way. They had been treated well by the Dutch, but they did not want their children to grow up speaking Dutch and living like Dutchmen rather than Englishmen.

Whatever their reasons for coming— and the religious motive was dominant —the passengers on board the *Mayflower* were firmly agreed on one thing: they intended to establish new homes and a new way of life for themselves and their children in the New World.

The Mayflower Compact. The first job the Pilgrims tackled was that of organizing a new government. The London Company (see page 20) had given the Pilgrims a grant of land south of the Hudson River. But storms had blown them off their course, with the result that in November the Pilgrims found themselves off New England, where they had no legal right to land and settle. Nor did they have any plans for governing the colony once they landed.

And so, while the crew furled the sails, the Pilgrim leaders gathered in the cabin. There, after much deliberation, they wrote and signed what we now call the Mayflower Compact. In this compact, or agreement, they promised "all due submission and obedience" to the laws that they themselves would pass.

The Mayflower Compact was not a plan of government. Nor did it commit the Pilgrims to a democratic way of life. Nevertheless, this short document marked an important step along the road to self-government in the New World, as you will see in Chapter 5.

Plymouth is settled. By the time the Pilgrims finished signing the compact,

The Mayflower Compact (1620): EXCERPT

We whose names are underwritten, . . . having undertaken . . . a voyage to plant the first colony in the northern parts of Virginia, do by these presents solemnly and mutually in the presence of God, and one another, covenant and combine ourselves together into a civil body politic; . . . and by virtue hereof do enact, constitute, and frame such just and equal laws, ordinances, acts, constitutions, and offices, from time to time, as shall be thought most meet and convenient for the general good of the colony unto which we promise all due submission and obedience . . .

it was too late in the day to lower a boat and row ashore. The next day was Sunday. Restraining their impatience to set foot on land, the Pilgrims remained on board the ship and devoted the day to prayer and worship. Early Monday they landed at what is now Provincetown, Massachusetts.

The Pilgrims spent more than a month looking for a place to settle, and finally selected a location on the other side of what is now called Cape Cod Bay (see map, page 37). This spot had been visited in earlier years by English explorers, who had named it Plymouth and marked it on the map.

Plymouth had a number of advantages, including a small but good harbor, a brook of clear fresh water, and a hill easily defended against attack. The Pilgrims were also attracted to it because it had once been the site of an Indian village and for that reason was surrounded by cleared fields.

The Pilgrims sailed into Plymouth harbor late in December and, as William Bradford, one of the leaders, noted in his journal, "The twenty-fifth day began to erect the first house. . . ." Those who were able to work toiled through the cold, cheerless winter months. Many sickened and died. Be-

JESUITS AND INDIANS

From France in the early 1600's came a remarkable set of missionaries, few in number but strong in faith. Take St. Isaac Jogues, for example. From study and talk with learned men in Europe, he turned to a mission for Indians in America. These Indians had no words in their own language to use in a catechism. And of all the Indians within reach, the savage Mohawks were the least friendly. Jogues met martyrdom; but there were others to whom the Indians afterwards listened, until many, including the holy Katherine Tekakwitha, accepted the Catholic faith.

Among the more friendly Hurons, whole tribes were baptized and the "blackrobes" won their loyalty. No wonder, therefore, that the Jesuits were able to reveal so many secrets of North America. All this, along with the manners and customs of the Indians, the missionaries described in their reports.

fore spring arrived, half of the little band had perished. But not one of the survivors abandoned the colony when in April the *Mayflower* started back to England.

Those who were still alive might not have survived much longer had it not been for the help of friendly Indians, and of one in particular who bore the name of Squanto. Squanto taught the little group of English country people how to make the most effective use of the resources of forest, sea, and soil. Perhaps most important of all, he brought them seeds of native plants—pumpkin, squash, beans, and Indian corn—and showed them how to grow these crops in the cleared fields.

In November 1621 the Pilgrims celebrated their first year in the New World by setting aside a period of several days for recreation and thanksgiving. They were joined in the celebration by nearly a hundred Indians and by more than thirty new settlers who had just arrived on a ship from England.

This ship, the *Fortune,* was the first of several in the following years that carried men and women and children across the Atlantic to the Plymouth colony. As the years passed, Plymouth grew a little in size, while other small villages sprang up nearby.

The settlers earned most of their livelihood by farming, although fish and game remained for many years an important source of food. They also carried on some trade with England. The products they shipped back to the Old Country included furs and lumber.

Faith, courage, hard work, and an intense desire to be free enabled the Pilgrims to survive the first desperate period and plant a permanent colony on the shores of New England. But they were never able to attract any considerable number of new settlers. Finally, under a charter granted in 1691, Plymouth became a part of its larger neighbor to the north, Massachusetts Bay Colony.

The roots of Massachusetts. The Puritans of Massachusetts Bay Colony, like most of the Pilgrims of Plymouth, moved to the New World largely for religious reasons. As you have seen, the Puritans were willing to remain members of the Anglican Church, but they wanted to change some of its practices. Charles I, who became king of England in 1625, would have none of this. As the years passed, he made life increasingly difficult for the Puritans. Finally, a number of prominent Puritan leaders, among them John Winthrop and Sir Richard Saltonstall, decided to form a company and plant a colony in America. In 1629 they secured a charter from the king and organized the Massachusetts Bay Company.

Fortunately for the Puritans, the men

■ The earliest New England shelters were crude, as shown by these modern reconstructions at Salem, Massachusetts. Notice the bark-covered hut (right), and shelters of upright palings. Later pioneers learned from Swedish settlers how to build the more familiar log cabin.

who wrote the charter neglected to name the place where the directors of the company were to hold their annual meeting. The directors, who were shrewd men, made the most of this oversight. They voted to take the charter and move to the New World, where they would be free to run the company as they pleased. So it was that Massachusetts became a *self-governing colony,* for many years almost independent of the English king and Parliament.

The Puritans arrive. The Puritans began to arrive in large numbers during the summer of 1630—nearly a thousand men, women, and children aboard seventeen ships. Unlike the Pilgrims, who had come as nearly penniless refugees, the new settlers were well provided with food, clothing, tools, and other necessary equipment. Among the colonists were skilled workmen—carpenters, masons, blacksmiths, shipwrights, and men trained in other trades. Some, like the first governor, John Winthrop, who kept a journal that was published later as a history of New England, were educated men, graduates of Cambridge and Oxford, England's leading universities.

One by one the ships unloaded their cargoes, and the people began immediately to build a number of villages along the coast north of Plymouth. Some settled at Shawmut, later called Boston (see map, page 37). Others settled in small villages nearby that are now important suburbs of Boston. A few settled at Naumkeag (NOM-keg), later called Salem, which had been a fishing and trading village since 1626.

The Indians, whose watchful eyes missed nothing, must have been astonished at this sudden burst of building activity. But this was only a beginning. During the next few years shipload after shipload of passengers joined the early settlers. By 1640, more than 20,000 Englishmen were living in Massachusetts Bay Colony.

Government in Massachusetts. The daily affairs of religion and of government were closely intermingled in Massachusetts Bay Colony. On the ship that carried him to the New World, John Winthrop had warned his fellow passengers that the Lord "will expect a strict performance" from us. He and the other leaders intended to see that the settlers remained true to their Puritan beliefs, and to this end they established the Puritan Church as the only recognized church in the colony. They, the leaders, planned to keep control of the government, as well as the church, in their own hands. In order to do this, they limited to a small select group of the settlers the right to vote, called the *suffrage,* and to hold public office.

But from the· start, some of the settlers rebelled against the strict rule. They demanded the right to participate in the government. As a result of this demand, Winthrop and the other leaders were soon forced to loosen their hold. They granted the right to vote to all Puritan men in good standing in their churches. They also granted each town the right to send *representatives* to the legislature of the colony, called the General Court. So it was that very early in its history, Massachusetts, like the colony of Jamestown, began to operate under a *representative form of government*.

Roger Williams founds Rhode Island. Of all the settlers who came to Massachusetts Bay Colony in the early years, none created more of a stir than Roger Williams. He landed in the colony in 1631, a young man in his middle twenties, and soon became pastor of a church in Salem.

Roger Williams taught that the colonists had no right to their land unless they bought it from the Indians. He insisted that every individual had the *right to worship* as he pleased, that each man had the right to believe and say what he liked. He argued, in effect, that the church and the state° should be separate and that government should be based upon the will of the people.

Regarding Roger Williams as a menace to the peace and well-being of Massachusetts Bay Colony, the Puritan authorities decided to send him back to England. Williams escaped in the nick of time, fleeing for safety through the wilderness to his friends, the Narragansett Indians. He lived with them for several months. Then, in the spring of 1636, with a group of his old friends from Massachusetts, he founded the village of Providence at the head of Narragansett Bay (see map, page 37).

Other exiles from Massachusetts, among them Mrs. Anne Hutchinson, soon started other settlements along the shores of Narragansett Bay. In 1643 Roger Williams returned to England where, in 1644, he secured a charter for the colony of Rhode Island, which then included Providence and two other settlements, those at Newport and Portsmouth.

· ·

° *state:* This term is often used in American history with two different meanings. It may refer to the government of any country or colony, as it does here. Or it may refer to one of the "states" of the United States.

From the beginning the government of Rhode Island rested upon the *consent of the governed*—in this instance upon the right of all adult males to vote and in other ways to have a voice in the way that they were governed. The settlers were also guaranteed the right to worship as they pleased.

A later charter, granted in 1663, deprived more than half of the adult males of their right to vote by requiring that a man must own a certain amount of property before he could vote. These so-called "property qualifications" on the right to vote caused much discontent, not only at that time, but also in later years. Even with this restriction on the right to vote, however, Rhode Island offered more freedom to more settlers than any of the other New England colonies. The charter of 1663 placed no restrictions on religious freedom, as you will see in Chapter 5. For this reason, Rhode Island attracted settlers of many religious faiths.

Westward to Connecticut. Connecticut, like Rhode Island, was an offshoot from the older colony of Massachusetts. But the men and women who settled Connecticut were not exiles. They were sturdy pioneers, the first of many, many thousands who during the course of American history moved out to the *frontier*° in search of larger opportunities for themselves and their children.

In 1635 the Reverend Thomas Hooker and nearly all of the members of his church in Newtown (later Cambridge), Massachusetts, decided to move farther out. With the permission of the General Court, they moved southwest in the spring of 1636, traveling with all their property through the wilderness and planting their first settlement at Hartford, Connecticut (see map, page 37).

· ·

° *frontier:* In American history the frontier was a region that, at any given time, lay just beyond the last line· of settlements. (In the U.S. Census of 1890, the frontier was defined as a region having from two to six inhabitants per square mile.) Beginning in early colonial times, pioneers from the settled communities pushed farther and farther inland and created new settlements; as a result, the frontier gradually moved westward.

Clothing of the Puritans

Other pioneers started neighboring settlements. Among the new settlements were Windsor and Wethersfield, which in 1639 joined with Hartford and adopted a plan of government. This plan was called the Fundamental Orders of Connecticut.

More than twenty years later, in 1662, after fifteen towns had been settled, Connecticut secured a charter from King Charles II. This charter extended the boundaries of the Connecticut colony to include a number of small settlements along Long Island Sound. The most important of these was New Haven. The charter also gave the settlers the right to govern themselves, thus making legal a practice that they had followed from the days of the first settlement at Hartford. The charter of 1662 proved so satisfactory that the citizens of Connecticut kept it as their state constitution° after they won their independence from Great Britain in the Revolutionary War.

New Hampshire and Maine. While Connecticut was growing from a few

....
° *constitution:* the system of principles and laws under which a government is organized. A constitution may or may not be written down in a single document.

small villages into a self-governing colony, pioneers were pushing northward from Massachusetts into the area that later became the states of New Hampshire and Maine.

The right to settle this territory had been granted to John Mason and Sir Ferdinando Gorges (GOR-jez) as early as 1622. In 1629 the two men divided the land between them, Gorges taking the territory north of the Piscataqua (pis-KAT-ah-kwah) River, Mason the southern portion. Both men tried to build colonies, but succeeded only in planting a few small settlements, which for a number of years remained little more than trading posts.

By the late 1630's settlers in substantial numbers were moving northward from Massachusetts and building settlements on the land claimed by Mason and Gorges. The Puritan authorities, who were watching this development with keen interest, decided to claim the territory for Massachusetts. By the 1650's Massachusetts had managed to gain control over both New Hampshire and Maine. It was able to hold control over Maine until 1820 when, more than thirty years after the Constitution of the United States had been adopted, Maine

Matchlock musket

PAN FOR GUNPOWDER

MATCH HOLDER

SHIELD →

SERPENTINE

became the twenty-third state to enter the Union. But New Hampshire broke away from the Puritan colony in 1679, when it received a charter from Charles II and became a royal colony.

New England in the 1750's. Although the New England Colonies had their own governments and were completely independent of one another, they all developed along much the same lines.

By the 1750's thriving towns and cities had been built around all of the good harbors along the New England coast. Boston had a population of about 15,000. All of the seaport towns were busy, thriving places.

The country back from the coast was dotted with small towns and villages. From the beginning New England farmers had settled together in small communities rather than on remote farmsteads. There were good reasons for the development of community life in New England. Among these reasons were religion, the Indians, and geography.

Many of the New England communities had been started by groups of friends and neighbors who belonged to the same church. Hartford, Connecticut, you will recall, was started in this way. The first thing these people did when they reached the place that they intended to settle was to plan a new town. The plan usually included a "common," or central area, lots for homes around the common, a piece of land for the church and the town hall, and nearby farm land for each of the settlers. Surplus land was held by the original settlers for sale to newcomers.

The need for defense, as well as the desire to be near the church and the town hall, also prompted the settlers to build compact communities. Out on the frontier itself, where the danger from Indian attack was greatest, the first settlers also built a fort or blockhouse.

The settlers also adopted universal military training and organized a *militia.* The militia was a group of citizens trained for military service but not on active duty except in times of emergency. By law each man eighteen years of age or older had to own a matchlock musket "not under three foot nine inches in length," a pound of gunpowder, twenty bullets, and "two fathom of match."° The militia drilled regularly on the common, or "the village green" as it was often called. In times of danger, the men would take turns mounting guard.

Geography also influenced the spread of small farming communities in New England. In many places the soil was shallow and filled with rocks and boulders, the land hilly and covered with forests. For this reason, it was not often possible for a man to clear a large amount of land and build a big farm.

•••

° *match:* a kind of cord which, when lit, was used to fire the gunpowder in a musket.

⌐ SECTION SURVEY

1. What reasons led the Pilgrims to come to the New World?

2. Compare patterns of representative government as practiced in Massachusetts and in Rhode Island.

3. Why did the Puritans disapprove of Roger Williams?

4. New England became a region of small farming communities. Show how religion, geography, and the Indians influenced this development.

IDENTIFY: Mayflower Compact, self-governing colony, consent of the governed, frontier, constitution, militia; Bradford, Squanto, John Winthrop, Anne Hutchinson, Hooker, Mason and Gorges; 1620, 1630, 1639.

3 Diverse peoples immigrate to the Middle Colonies

The first settlements in the Middle Colonies (see map, page 37) were planted by people from the Netherlands and Sweden. In 1609, only two years after Jamestown, Virginia, had been started, Henry Hudson, an Englishman sailing in the service of the Dutch East India Company of the Netherlands, explored the river that ever since has borne his name.

During the next few years Dutch traders made a number of voyages to the Middle Atlantic coast. As a result of the favorable reports that they turned in, a group of investors secured a charter from the government of the Netherlands and organized the Dutch West India Company. The charter gave the company control over all trade and colonies in the New World. This charter was in conflict, of course, with the charter granted by James I to the London Company, which founded Jamestown.

The rise of New Netherland. The members of the Dutch West India Company acted promptly to secure the trade of the entire Middle Atlantic coast. They called the land they claimed New Netherland (see map, page 37). Around a fort that they built on the lower tip of Manhattan Island, they planted the settlement of New Amsterdam, now New York City. They also established other forts and trading posts on the Hudson River at the present site of Albany, on the Connecticut River near the present site of Hartford, and on the Delaware River below the present site of Philadelphia.

In an effort to build the colony of New Netherland, the Dutch West India Company in 1629 offered huge areas of land to any member of the company who, within four years, would settle at least 50 tenants on his estate. A number of the members accepted the offer. These landowners, or *patroons,* had an enormous amount of power, similar to the power of feudal lords in Europe during the Middle Ages.

Most Dutch citizens, who were free men, were not interested in moving to the New World to live under a feudal lord. As a result, New Netherland grew very slowly. Under the control of the Dutch West India Company it never had more than 10,000 inhabitants. The settlers, most of whom were located in the trading center of New Amsterdam, came from a number of nations. In 1646 it was reported that eighteen languages could be heard in this seaport.

The Dutch threat to the English. From the beginning New Netherland was a threat to the English colonies. From their strategic naval base at New Amsterdam, Dutch war ships were able to

■ New Amsterdam, under the Dutch, was pictured thus before 1650. Notice the crane for weighing cargo (center), windmill, fort, and barracks (left rear) and large houses (right rear). From this point today one sees the skyscrapers of New York City's financial district.

strike at English ships bound to and from New England and the Southern Colonies. From New Amsterdam the Dutch also controlled the trade of three vital river valleys—the Hudson, the Connecticut, and the Delaware (see map, opposite page). This control was strengthened when, in 1655, the Dutch seized New Sweden, a small group of settlements which had been built along the Delaware River.

Particularly valuable was the Dutch control of the Hudson River. From a point north of Fort Orange (now Albany), the Mohawk Valley provided a route through the mountains into the Great Lakes region and the interior of the continent. Dominating this route was the formidable league of Indians known as the Five Nations. These Indians were friendly with the Dutch. They served as middlemen, bringing furs from the Great Lakes region to the Dutch posts on the Hudson River. But since the settlers in New England also desired this rich fur trade, Dutch control of the Hudson River was a continual source of friction.

The English seize New Netherland. It was Dutch expansion eastward along Long Island and northward in the Connecticut Valley that finally brought matters to a head. This expansion plunged the Dutch into conflict with traders and settlers from New England who were pushing down into the same territory. Through fear of the Dutch and also for other reasons, the colonies of Massachusetts, Plymouth, Connecticut, and New Haven decided in 1643 to unite their military forces in the New England Confederation.° But it was not merely New England that was threatened. The future of Maryland and Virginia to the south was also at stake. Obviously, the showdown between the English and the Dutch could not be long delayed.

The end came suddenly for the Dutch when, in 1664, an English fleet

•••
° *confederation:* a political league in which members retain most of their powers, while a central governing body takes care of problems, like foreign affairs, common to all.

sailed into the mouth of the Hudson River. Overwhelmed by the superior strength of the English, Peter Stuyvesant, the Dutch governor, was forced to haul down his nation's flag from above the ramparts of New Amsterdam. In this way, without a shot fired, the Netherlands was eliminated as a colonial power in North America.

New Jersey is founded. Charles II, then king of England, presented all the territory that had once been New Netherland to his younger brother James, the Duke of York. Charles's gift included not only the land between the Connecticut and the Delaware Rivers, but also Long Island, the islands of Nantucket and Martha's Vineyard, and all of Maine east of the Kennebec River. This enormous territory became the property of the thirty-year-old Duke of York.

James gave the name New York to part of the former Dutch colony. The land between the Hudson and the Delaware Rivers was called New Jersey (see map, opposite page). Then James began to hand out princely gifts of land to his friends. The largest gift, the entire colony of New Jersey, went to Lord John Berkeley and Sir George Carteret.

At the time, in 1664, New Jersey was almost a total wilderness, with only a few hundred settlers. There were several small settlements earlier established by Dutch and Swedish colonists along the banks of the Delaware River, and a handful of tiny villages in the north that had been settled by men and women from New England. Berkeley and Carteret tried to get more settlers, but with limited success. Finally, in 1702, after the property had changed hands many times, the king of England stepped in and claimed New Jersey as a royal colony.

New York under English rule. The newly created colony of New York had a much different history from that of New Jersey. From the beginning the young Duke of York took a direct and personal interest in the former Dutch colony. One of his first acts, and one of

(*Continued on page 38*)

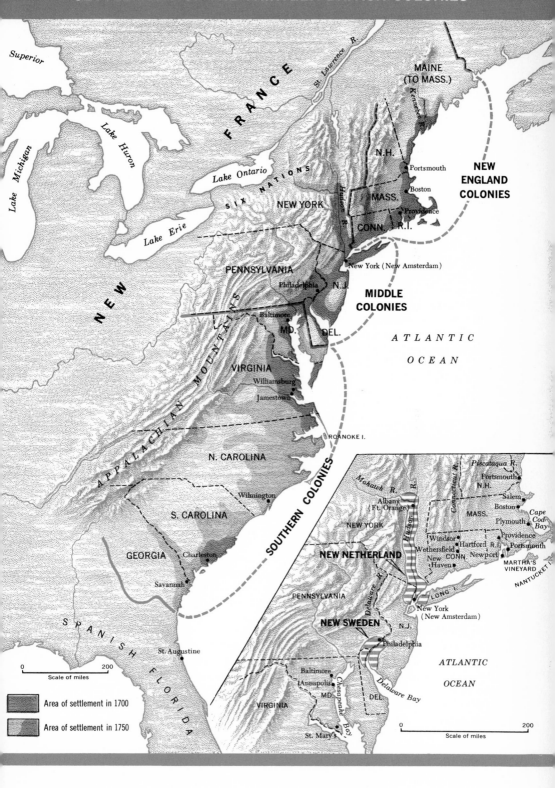

Superior

Lake Michigan

Lake Huron

F R A N C E

St. Lawrence R.

Lake Ontario

Lake Erie

MAINE
(TO MASS.)

Kennebec R.

N.H.

Portsmouth

NEW
ENGLAND
COLONIES

S I X   N A T I O N S

NEW YORK

MASS.

Boston

Hudson R.

CONN.   R.I.

Providence

N E W

PENNSYLVANIA

New York (New Amsterdam)

Philadelphia   N.J.

MIDDLE
COLONIES

Baltimore

MD.   DEL.

A T L A N T I C

O C E A N

A P P A L A C H I A N   M O U N T A I N S

VIRGINIA

Williamsburg

Jamestown

ROANOKE I.

N. CAROLINA

SOUTHERN COLONIES

Wilmington

S. CAROLINA

GEORGIA   Charleston

Savannah

S P A N I S H   F L O R I D A

St. Augustine

0   200
Scale of miles

Area of settlement in 1700

Area of settlement in 1750

Inset map

Mohawk R.

Piscataqua R.

Portsmouth
N.H.

Albany
(Ft. Orange)

Connecticut R.

Salem

Boston

NEW YORK

MASS.

Plymouth   Cape
Cod
Bay

Hudson R.

Windsor   Providence

NEW NETHERLAND

Wethersfield   Hartford   R.I.

New   CONN.   Newport

Haven

MARTHA'S
VINEYARD

NANTUCKET I.

PENNSYLVANIA

LONG I.

New York
(New Amsterdam)

NEW SWEDEN

N.J.

Delaware R.

Philadelphia

A T L A N T I C

O C E A N

Baltimore

Annapolis

Chesapeake Bay

MD.   DEL.

Delaware Bay

VIRGINIA

St. Mary's

0   200
Scale of miles

THOMAS DONGAN
AND NEW YORK PROVINCE

When the English took New Netherland from the Dutch in 1664, they found it in bad condition. No definite boundaries existed for the province; the Indians of the Hudson Valley were on the warpath; and the people generally lacked experience in self-government. The Duke of York gave the province a new name— New York—and a set of laws—the Duke's Laws. But there was no representative government until, in 1682, the Duke sent over as governor an Irish Catholic gentleman, Colonel Thomas Dongan (1634–1713). The first legislature New York ever had met at Dongan's call in October 1683. It adopted a Charter of Liberties which embodied the rights of Englishmen according to Magna Carta and the Petition of Right.

Before he was removed as governor in 1688, Dongan continued constitutional government; established the bounds of New York; made the Iroquois accept the king of England as their sovereign; and fortified a northern frontier against the French. He gave to New York City and to Albany their first charters and assisted private schools with grants of land. He retired in 1688 to a private estate on Long Island, but the next year had to flee because of anti-Catholic measures taken by Jacob Leisler's revolutionary regime. He spent the remainder of his life in poor circumstances in England.

the wisest of his career, was to order his colonial officials to treat the Dutch with "humanity and gentleness." He also allowed the Dutch to continue using their own language and worshiping in their own churches.

But in the long run the Duke proved to be a hard ruler. He levied heavy taxes without the consent of the people and, except for a brief two-year period (1683–85), he refused to allow them any voice in the government.

Arbitrary rule is overthrown. The Duke wanted to be an absolute ruler, and his chance to realize this wish came in 1685 when he became King James II of England. A year later, in 1686, he combined New Jersey, New York, and the New England Colonies under a form of government called the Dominion of New England. He then abolished representative government in these former colonies and appointed Sir Edmund Andros as governor of the Dominion.

This period of *arbitrary rule*° lasted a little over two years. Citizens in England resented James's harsh methods of ruling as much as the colonists resented his governor, Andros. In 1688 people in England arose in a revolt called the Glorious Revolution, drove James II from the throne, and, in 1689, adopted a Bill of Rights ° which included the right to representative government. The new king, William of Orange, restored the colonial charters, and the *colonial representative assemblies* resumed their meetings.

Pennsylvania and Delaware. One of the most remarkable of all the Englishmen to found colonies, and certainly one of the most successful, was William Penn. As a youth he enjoyed many advantages, including an excellent college education. His father was a prominent admiral in the Royal Navy. In these early years Penn seemed destined for a career in the fashionable life of the English court. But then, in 1667, at the age of twenty-two, he heard a Quaker sermon on the text, "There is a faith that overcometh the world." The sermon converted Penn. For the remainder of his life, he was a member of the Society of Friends, often called Quakers.

Penn's father, the admiral, was shocked and angry when he heard the news of his son's conversion, for the Quakers were at this time one of the most disliked religious groups in Eng-

....

° *arbitrary rule:* government by a ruler with unlimited power, unrestrained by laws.
° *bill of rights:* a list, or bill of particulars, stating certain rights and liberties that are guaranteed to every citizen by the government.

land. But Penn went his own way. His father finally forgave him and left him a large inheritance.

Part of Penn's inheritance was a debt that Charles II had owed his father. In place of the money, the king in 1681 gave Penn a charter making him *proprietor* of a huge grant of land in the New World. On this land Penn founded a colony to which the king gave the name Pennsylvania. As a proprietor, Penn had power over this *proprietary colony* almost as great as the king's power over the royal colonies.

Pennsylvania had no coastline. Penn solved this problem in 1682 by asking for, and receiving, another grant of land to the south, on the west bank of Delaware Bay. This new grant, later called Delaware (see map, page 37), was for many years referred to as "the lower counties." Until the Revolutionary War both grants remained in the hands of the Penn family, which governed them as separate colonies.

Pennsylvania, which Penn liked to call the "Holy Experiment," attracted many settlers. One of Penn's first acts was to write and publish in English, French, Dutch, and German a pamphlet describing the colony he proposed to build. In the pamphlet he invited honest, hard-working settlers to come, promising them religious toleration, representative government, and cheap land. To every settler who would establish his home and family in the colony, Penn offered 500 acres of free land, with the right to buy additional land at one shilling an acre.

Settlers poured in by the thousands—Quakers from England, Wales, and Ireland; Scotch-Irish Presbyterians; Swiss and German Protestants; Catholics and Jews from many countries of Europe. Penn kept his promises to the settlers, and he also treated the Indians fairly and as equals. For these and other reasons, Pennsylvania developed more rapidly than any of the other colonies.

The Middle Colonies in the 1750's. By the 1750's the Middle Colonies—Pennsylvania, Delaware, New Jersey, and New York—were among the most prosperous in the New World. Philadelphia, on the Delaware River, was the

■ Philadelphia in 1702 was the largest town in the colonies. Notice the two large warehouses and numerous imposing homes. William Penn's planning is shown by the careful placement of the wharves and the straight streets. At the upper left is a village of friendly Indians.

largest and busiest seaport in America. New York was a close second.

From the beginning agriculture was the major way of making a living. But the people did not settle in farming villages, as the New Englanders had done. Except on the western frontier, there was no real danger from the Indians, and the newcomers were therefore free to scatter over the countryside. Because the soil was fertile and the land gently rolling, men could cultivate fairly large farms. On these farms they produced not only food for themselves and their families, but also a surplus for sale. Indeed, the Middle Colonies soon came to be known as the "breadbasket" of the New World. The harbors of Philadelphia and New York were always filled with ships loading flour, meat, and other foodstuffs for sale in England and the West Indies.

Perhaps the most striking characteristic of the Middle Colonies was the great variety of occupations. Although most of the people were farmers, the colonies were famous for their iron mines, their shipyards, and their manufacture of glass, paper, and textiles. And from the beginning these colonies were true "melting pots" of people from many different nations with different religious backgrounds—much more so than any of the other colonies.

SECTION SURVEY

1. Give three reasons why the Dutch were regarded as a threat to the English colonies.

2. (a) What made the colony of Pennsylvania so attractive to European settlers? (b) Why was the colony so successful?

3. Explain why the Middle Colonies can be described as "melting pots."

4. What role did geography play in making the Middle Colonies different from the New England Colonies?

IDENTIFY: Dutch West India Company, patroon, Five Nations, New England Confederation, Dominion of New England, Glorious Revolution, Bill of Rights, proprietary colony; Hudson, Stuyvesant, John Berkeley, Carteret, Andros; 1664.

4 Southern planters create a distinctive way of life

Virginia, the first Southern Colony, started with the struggling settlement at Jamestown, as you have seen. By 1632, when Maryland was chartered, Virginia was firmly established.

Maryland is founded. Sir George Calvert, the first Lord Baltimore, had been a member of the Virginia Company and shared the colonizing fever which ran among aristocrats and courtiers in the reign of James I. After he became a Roman Catholic, he had to resign his offices at court, but retained the royal favor. He first tried unsuccessfully to plant a colony in frigid Newfoundland. Later, as an immigrant to Virginia in 1628, he discovered he was unwelcome because of his religion. He returned to England and made application for a charter which granted him and his heirs what is now Maryland, plus a portion including Delaware Bay, which his descendants afterward had to surrender to William Penn. By the time the charter was issued, in 1632, George had died and been succeeded by Cecilius Calvert, his son and the second Lord Baltimore.

From the time of the first settlement, at St. Mary's in 1634, Maryland prospered. There had been enough learned from the Virginia experience so that starving times were avoided, and an economy much like that of Virginia was soon flourishing along the tidewater rivers emptying into lower Chesapeake Bay. But the colony was to be notable for reasons other than material prosperity. It was the first successful proprietary colony, one in which the proprietor stood in relation to the colonists as a king to his subjects. Besides, it was a successful venture in religious toleration, at that time a very radical and unpopular ideal.

George and Cecilius Calvert were determined that their colony would be a place of toleration. They were required to support this ideal with a large fortune because colonization was very expensive. Fewer Catholics than Protestants came forward as settlers, and those who were Catholics, along with the Jesuit missionaries who accompanied them, were exposed to the gravest calamities if the experiment should fail.

Until major difficulties came from the disturbances of the Puritan Revolution in England, no legislation to ensure toleration was necessary. The proprietor was the absolute lord who made policy and told the legislative assembly what to do; and he required his appointed officials to punish anyone who abused another for religious reasons. But about ten years after Maryland was founded, it seemed that a loss of the charter was threatened by Puritans in power in England. In Maryland still other Puritans—who had originally come into the colony as refugees from Virginia—threatened to take over the government.

At this juncture, Lord Baltimore authorized the assembly to pass a Toleration Act, as was done in 1649. That it limited toleration to Christians only, and that it made blasphemy a capital offense, are attributable to the Puritans in the Assembly. These zealots continued their efforts to overthrow the proprietor and to make Maryland a Protestant commonwealth like Massachusetts. They had almost succeeded, when the restoration of monarchy in England in 1660 enabled Lord Baltimore to regain full control.

The Carolinas are created. Maryland was about thirty years old when, in 1663, Charles II gave a charter for Carolina to eight English noblemen as proprietors of the colony. The grant of land included all of the territory between Virginia and Spanish Florida and westward to the "south seas."

With the aid of John Locke, a young English philosopher, the proprietors drew up a constitution for the colony they proposed to build. This constitution was probably the most unrealistic plan of government ever prepared for an English colony in the New World. It provided an elaborate system of *social*

Westover

WILLIAM BYRD II

William Byrd II (1674–1744) is remembered as a statesman, planter, businessman, scholar, and one of the first of a long line of distinguished American leaders bearing the name of Byrd. Born in Virginia in 1674 and educated in England, he began his career in government when, at the age of eighteen, he was elected to the Virginia House of Burgesses. From then until his death, he served his colony with distinction in a number of high offices.

William Byrd II lived a rich and full life. He inherited a great estate, Westover, on the banks of the James River, not far from Williamsburg. The mansion is still standing, and Virginians count it as one of their great historic treasures. Byrd's personal library numbered 3600 volumes. He helped to survey the dividing line between Virginia and North Carolina, and his report of this project is one of the most colorful pieces of colonial writing that has come down to us from those early days.

Byrd also kept a diary. The following entry, dated May 10, 1740, when he was sixty-six years old, gives us a glimpse of his love of learning and of the active life he led: "I rose about five, read Hebrew and Greek. I prayed and had tea . . . I played billiards and settled several accounts and walked till dinner and then ate fish. After dinner I put several things in order. L-N-R and Mrs. D. came over and told me all was well. I talked with my people and prayed."

classes for the colony. At the top of the social ladder were to be eight hereditary nobles (the proprietors), each with at least a 48,000-acre estate. Below the top nobility in descending order of importance were lesser nobles to whom Locke gave such outlandish titles as landgraves, caciques, barons, and lords of manors. At the bottom of the ladder were the rank and file of colonists.

The plan was doomed from the beginning. Geography and the desires of the settlers, not a project drawn on paper, determined the course of Carolina history. From the first days of settlement, the colony divided naturally into two parts (see map, page 37).

The northern section, North Carolina, was settled mostly by pioneers from Virginia. They built cabins, cleared the land, and grew their own food and a "cash crop"° of tobacco for sale in England. Many of them also earned a livelihood from the pine forests, which supplied them with lumber and naval stores—tar, pitch, rosin, turpentine—products all needed by England's Royal Navy and the growing fleet of English merchant ships.

The southern section, South Carolina, proved more attractive to settlers from overseas. Through the seaport of Charles Town (later shortened to Charleston), settlers of many different faiths from many different nations

....

° *cash crop:* a crop which is raised primarily for sale, since it can be sold readily and converted into money.

Hauling tobacco for shipment

passed on their way to new homes in the New World. There were Anglicans and other religious groups from England; Scots in considerable numbers; French Huguenots (ʜʏoo-guh-nahts), who were Protestants fleeing persecution in France; Germans; emigrants from the West Indies; and, as the years passed, growing numbers of Negro slaves. Many of the settlers managed to build large and prosperous rice plantations on the rich coastal lowlands. Others gained a livelihood from the production of naval stores and, on the frontier itself, from the fur trade.

During the early years the colonists waged a continuing struggle for a larger voice in the government. Finally, in 1729, the proprietors sold their rights to the king, and North and South Carolina became royal colonies with representative assemblies.

Georgia is founded. In 1732, three years after North and South Carolina became royal colonies, the king granted a charter for Georgia (see map, page 37). The British° government was pleased to see a colony started so close to Spanish Florida, for it would serve as a "buffer state" protecting the settled areas farther north in the event of Spanish attack.

But the compelling motive for starting the colony of Georgia had nothing to do with politics or business. Georgia was born out of the love of man for his fellow men. It was started by a group of prominent Englishmen to provide a place in which unfortunate English debtors could make a new start in life.

James Oglethorpe, the leader of the group of founders, arrived in Georgia in 1733 with the first group of debtors. They settled at Savannah, each man receiving 50 acres of land free and clear. Slavery and the sale of rum were not to

....

° *British:* In 1707 the separate countries of England and Scotland were united into a single country which is properly called Great Britain. In common usage throughout the colonial period, however, the words "England" and "English" are often used to mean "Great Britain" and "British."

■ **An orderly ground plan, home plots and a city palisade, guardhouse and wharf were the beginnings of Savannah.**

the Atlantic coastal plains. Farther south the luxurious homes of wealthy rice planters were scattered over the coastal lowlands. There were no large towns in the South at this time except Charleston with a population of 10,000 and Baltimore with 5000.

A distinguishing characteristic of the Southern Colonies was slavery. The plantations, whether growing tobacco or rice, required large numbers of workmen. With plenty of land available to them on the frontier, free men would not work for wages on the plantations. As a result, the planters began to rely more and more upon slaves. By the 1750's the system of slave labor was firmly fixed in all of the Southern Colonies except Georgia, and it was beginning to become established there.

If slaves could have been used profitably on the farms of the Middle Colonies or on the much smaller farms of New England, no doubt slavery would have become established there as well as in the South. In colonial times few people anywhere objected to slavery as such. Slavery was either profitable or unprofitable. In the Southern Colonies it was profitable, and slaves were used in ever-increasing numbers.

Although the planters set the pattern of southern life, most southern people lived in the back country—the inland areas that lay "back" from the seacoast. These people—pioneers and small farmers—lived much like pioneers in New England and the Middle Colonies.

be allowed in the colony.

Oglethorpe and the other trustees also tried to recruit other settlers, offering liberal grants of land to all who immigrated to the colony. During the next few years a small number of immigrants arrived, among them several groups of New Englanders, a number of Germans, and some Scots. In 1752 the trustees, as required by their charter, turned Georgia over to the king as a royal colony.

The effort to settle Georgia was not a fruitless one. Because of Oglethorpe and his fellow trustees several thousand Englishmen were saved from debtor's prison and given a fresh start in life. And later, of course, Georgia became an active and prosperous state.

The Southern Colonies in the 1750's. By the 1750's the Southern Colonies—Maryland, Virginia, North and South Carolina, and Georgia—had all developed their own special ways of living. The great tobacco plantations in Maryland, Virginia, and North Carolina covered the rich tidewater lands near the ocean, and extended farther inland on

✍ **SECTION SURVEY**

1. What were the motives for the settlement of (a) Maryland, (b) the Carolinas, and (c) Georgia?

2. Contrast economic features of tidewater lands and back country.

3. There had been religious toleration in the Maryland colony from its founding. What happened to make it needful to pass a formal toleration act in 1649?

IDENTIFY: tidewater river, cash crop, French Huguenots; Lord Baltimore, Locke, Oglethorpe; 1649, 1733.

■ CHAPTER SURVEY   (For review, see Section Surveys, pages 28, 34, 40, 43.)

Points to Discuss: 1. The study of American history is a continuation of the study of European history in a new setting. Discuss the truth or falsity of this.

2. If Europe had been a happier place in the 1600's, the attractions of the New World would not have been so compelling. Explain this statement with reference to the religious, political, and economic conditions in Europe at that time.

3. Life in the colonies was characterized by democratic and undemocratic elements. Support this statement by evidence.

4. Show how the New England Colonies, the Middle Colonies, and the Southern Colonies differed from one another geographically, economically, and socially.

Using Maps: 1. Using the map on page 37, answer the following: (a) Identify the Southern, Middle, and New England Colonies. (b) In which colonies do we find the largest area of settlement in 1750? (c) Name and locate the oldest settlement in the United States. (d) Why was the St. Lawrence River important to New France? (e) Identify the mountain range which had to be crossed first in westward expansion.

2. Using the inset map on page 37, answer the following: (a) Why did Baltimore, Philadelphia, New York, and Boston become important cities? (b) Explain the settlement of a large number of small towns in New England.

3. Geography influences people. Using maps in Chapters 1 and 2, show the relationships between inland waterways, oceans, and the location of settlements.

Consulting the Sources: For excerpts from the Maryland Charter and interesting sources about toleration attitudes in the colonies, see Ellis, *Docs.*, Nos. 25–35.

■ TRACING THE MAIN IDEAS

English settlement began at Jamestown, and a few years later at Plymouth, with the vanguard of settlers. As the years passed, settlers came in ever-growing numbers, and every good harbor along the Atlantic coast became a point of debarkation and the beginning of "the great adventure" for men and women from overseas.

One of the most impressive features of the colonial world was its almost infinite variety. The settlers, men and women alike, came to the New World for many different reasons, bringing with them the love of their own language and their own ways of life.

But everywhere, in all the colonies, regardless of the backgrounds or the beliefs of the settlers, there was a burning desire to win in the New World larger opportunities than could be found in the Old.

These were the colonial beginnings of the American nation—and of "the American way of life." You will learn more about them in Chapters 4 and 5. But the colonies did not grow undisturbed. As you will see in the next chapter, both the Spaniards and the French—and especially the French—threatened for a time to seize the English colonies and win for themselves control of the entire North American continent.

Great Britain Wins New Territory

FORT NIAGARA
BUILT BY THE FRENCH IN 1726

By the middle of the 1700's, a map of the land and sea areas of the world could be drawn with reasonable accuracy. Spread out on the map were vast colonial territories claimed by Portugal, Spain, the Netherlands, France, and Great Britain. These colonial areas were prizes for which each of the contending nations was ready to sacrifice blood and effort. Thus, during most of the 1600's and 1700's these European nations were engaged in almost constant warfare.

In the New World the British flag waved proudly over thirteen colonies along the Atlantic seaboard. War ships of His Majesty's Royal Navy stood guard over the 1300-mile coastline and the nearly 1,500,000 men, women, and children who lived in the colonies. The war ships were needed, for Great Britain had powerful enemies.

To the south were the Spaniards. They had built a series of forts and missions that stretched from Florida to California along what is now the south-ern boundary of the United States. But during the 1600's and the 1700's Spain's power had been declining steadily. In 1754 the British did not think of Spain as a major threat.

To the north and west was New France. And this was a different story. The French were strong, and growing stronger, not only in Europe, but in all their far-flung colonies—including New France. Between the British colonies and New France there was bitter rivalry and fear and an uneasy peace.

This is the story of the growth of New France, of British victory in the French and Indian War, and of trouble-some policies adopted by Great Britain in controlling its American territory.

AS THE STORY DEVELOPS

1. New France grows and threatens the British colonies.
2. Great Britain smashes French power in North America.
3. Trouble looms between the colonies and Great Britain.

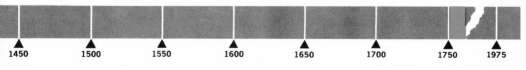

1450   1500   1550   1600   1650   1700   1750   1975

QUEBEC

A. The Fort
B. The Recollet
C. The Platform
D. The Jesuits
E. The Cathedra
F. The Seminar
G. The Hotel Die
H. The Bishops
I. The Redoubt
K. The Hospital

■ As early as 1733, Quebec was well established. On top of the hill were a large fort and a cathedral. Halfway up (center) was the bishop's imposing residence. Alongshore were wharves, warehouses, and settlers' homes. Within 30 years, the British won this site.

1 New France grows and threatens the British colonies

French claims to North America were based, as you have seen (page 12), on the early voyages of Verrazano (1524) and Cartier (1534–42). But it was Samuel de Champlain who planted the first successful French settlements in the New World.

French claims in North America. Champlain made his first voyage to the New World in 1603. Before he died in 1635, he had built a permanent settlement at Quebec, had won for France the friendship of the powerful Algonquin Indians, and had explored the greater part of the St. Lawrence Valley (see map, page 49).

Other Frenchmen pushed up the St. Lawrence River, explored the Great Lakes, and paddled their frail canoes into the very heart of the North American continent. Among the hundreds of explorers and missionaries in this immense wilderness area were Marquette, Joliet (JO-li-ET), and La Salle.

In 1673 Father Marquette, S.J., and Louis Joliet, a fur trader, crossed the Great Lakes and paddled down the Mississippi River as far as the mouth of the Arkansas River. Eight years later, in 1681–82, La Salle followed the same route to reach the Gulf of Mexico (see map, page 49). He claimed the entire Mississippi Valley for France, and called it Louisiana in honor of King Louis XIV. Later, in 1718, France built the settlement of New Orleans at the mouth of the Mississippi River.

By the early 1700's, then, the French controlled the two major gateways into the heart of North America. Their fortified settlement at New Orleans gave them control of the southern entrance to the entire Mississippi Valley. Their fortified settlements at Quebec and Montreal gave them control of the St. Lawrence River.

Combined with the Great Lakes, the St. Lawrence River provided a natural water route into the interior of the continent. By paddling and by easy portages° of only a few miles, the explorers

••
° *portage:* overland transport of boats and equipment between two bodies of water.

46

and traders could drop their canoes into the waters of the Mississippi River or one of its tributaries, and the entire region between the Appalachians and the Rockies was open to them.

French settlements. The rulers of France hoped to fill New France with large estates owned by nobles and worked by peasants. They expected that the peasants would live in compact farming villages on the estates.

Because of the St. Lawrence River the hope of building compact French farming villages in the New World was never realized. Each noble, or *seigneur* (seh-NYER), wanted his estate to front on the river, which was the only source of transportation—a smooth ribbon of ice in the winter, a water route in the summer. And when the seigneur brought tenants, called *habitants* (a-bee-TAHN), to work his estate, each habitant insisted upon water frontage. As a result, the settled area of New France consisted of two rows of farmhouses stretching along the banks of the St. Lawrence from Quebec to Montreal and up the Richelieu (RISH-uh-loo) River.

The fur trade. Beyond the settled areas lay the immense wilderness partly explored by Marquette, Joliet, La Salle, and other bold Frenchmen. The most easily exploited resource of this great area was furs.

From the earliest days much of the wealth of New France came from the fur trade. The lure of furs drew adventurous Frenchmen into the forested wilderness of the New World. Courageous *coureurs de bois* (koo-RUR duh BWAH), or runners-of-the-woods, launched their canoes, paddled far into the interior, wintered with friendly Indian tribes, and in the spring triumphantly guided their Indian allies to the trading center at Montreal. They reached Montreal about the same time that cargo ships from France sailed into the harbor.

For several weeks bedlam reigned on the banks of the river below the city. Indians exchanged their furs for goods from Europe—blankets, cloaks, cloth, beads, metal, ornaments, copper and iron kettles, awls, spoons, knives, hatchets, guns, powder, and liquor. Only when the last cask of brandy had been emptied did the carnival come to an end. One morning, as quickly as they had come, the Indians and the *coureurs de bois* loaded their canoes and paddled away into the forests from which they had come. The French ships weighed anchor and started on the hazardous voyage back to Europe with their cargoes of furs.

The weakness of New France. On the map New France was an imposing domain. It included Canada and the immense area of the Mississippi Valley (see map, page 49).

But the map was misleading. It told only part of the story. Except for Quebec and Montreal the settled areas of Canada consisted, as you have seen, of farmhouses strung along the St. Lawrence River like beads on a string. And beyond the settled areas a chain of small forts and trading posts stretched

■ Some British colonists, like the French, traded with the Indians for furs. This price list of 1703 shows that values were based upon beaver skins.

ONe yard Broad Cloth, *three* Beaver skins, *in season*.
One yard & half Gingerline, *one* Beaver skin, *in season*
One yard Red or Blew Kersey, *two* Beaver skins, *in season*.
One yard good Duffels, *one* Beaver skin, *in season*.
One yard & half broad fine Cotton, *one* Beaver skin, *in season*
Two yards of Cotton, *one* Beaver skin, *in season*.
One yard & half of half thicks, *one* Beaver skin, *in season*.
Five Pecks Indian Corn, *one* Beaver skin, *in season*
Five Pecks Indian Meal, *one* Beaver skin, *in season*.
Four Pecks Pease, *one* Beaver skin, *in season*.
Two Pints of Powder, *one* Beaver skin, *in season*.
One Pint of Shot, *one* Beaver skin, *in season*.
Six Fathom of Tobacco, *one* Beaver skin, *in season*.
Forty Biskets, *one* Beaver skin, *in season*.
Ten Pound of Pork, *one* Beaver skin, *in season*.
Six Knives, *one* Beaver skin, *in season*.
Six Combes, *one* Beaver skin, *in season*.
Twenty Scaines Thread, *one* Beaver skin, *in season*.
One Hat, *two* Beaver skins, *in season*.
One Hat with Hatband, *three* Beaver skins, *in season*.
Two Pound of large Kettles, *one* Beaver skin, *in season*.
One Pound & half of small Kettles, *one* Beaver skin, *in season*
One Shirt, *one* Beaver skin, *in season*.
One Shirt with Ruffels, *two* Beaver skins, *in season*.
Two Small Axes, *one* Beaver skin, *in season*.
Two Small Hoes, *one* Beaver skin, *in season*.
Three Dozen middling Hooks, *one* Beaver skin, *in season*.
One Sword Blade, *one* & *half* Beaver skin, *in season*.

in a long arc through the Great Lakes and the upper Mississippi Valley. Only the Indians and an occasional *coureur de bois* disturbed the age-old solitude of the forest.

The fur trade was one of the major reasons for the weakness of the French empire in the New World. To be sure, the fur trade provided a livelihood for thousands—for manufacturers and workmen in the mother country, for shipowners and merchants, for traders, for *coureurs de bois,* and for the Indians of New France. But the fur trade also made it almost impossible for the French to strengthen the settled areas along the St. Lawrence River. The carefree life of the *coureur de bois* drew the young and strong into the forests.

French and British power. In 1754, on the eve of the French and Indian War, the British colonists had certain advantages over their French rivals to the north. For one thing, as you know, the British colonies were well estab-

France and Great Britain at War, 1689–1763

Conflicts in Europe and elsewhere

War of the League of Augsburg,
  1689–1697
War of the Spanish Succession, 1702–1713
War of the Austrian Succession,
  1740–1748
Seven Years' War, 1756–1763

Conflicts in America

King William's War, 1689–1697
Queen Anne's War, 1702–1713
King George's War, 1744–1748
French and Indian War, 1754–1763

lished by the 1750's. For another, the British colonists outnumbered the colonists of New France by 23 to 1. For still another, most of the British settlements were confined to a fairly narrow belt of

FRENCH INFANTRYMAN

BRITISH STAFF OFFICER

BRITISH GENERAL OFFICER

BRITISH INFANTRYMAN

FRENCH COLONEL

IROQUOIS INDIANS

COUREURS DE BOIS

Uniforms— French and Indian War

48

land along the coast, whereas the French were scattered over half the continent (see map, this page).

But the French also enjoyed advantages. In the first place, New France itself was united under a single government and could act quickly when action was necessary. In contrast, the British colonies had separate governments, and they seldom acted together, even when co-operation was needed.

In the second place, the French won the support of many Indians. The reason was simple. French fur traders did not destroy forests and drive away game as British settlers did when they cleared land for new farms. There was, however, one important exception. The Iroquois, who lived in what is now New York state, refused to ally themselves with the French.

In the third place, France in the early 1750's was the most powerful European nation. French armies were second to none, and French naval forces competed with the British for control of the seas.

Between 1689 and 1748 rivalry between France and Great Britain had

49

THE REMARKABLE IROQUOIS

No Indians in all North America were more greatly feared by their enemies or respected by their friends than the members of the Iroquois Confederation. The Finger Lakes of New York state bear the proud names of the five original tribes—Mohawk, Seneca, Oneida, Cayuga, and Onondaga. After 1700, when the Tuscaroras of North Carolina joined the Confederation, the Five Nations, as they were called, became the Six Nations.

According to legend, the Iroquois Confederation was organized by two great leaders—Deganawidah and Hiawatha. For more than two centuries the Confederation was highly successful.

The legendary Deganawidah was a man of magnificent vision. He dreamed of a day when the Confederation would include *all* Indians, war would be abol-

ished, and peace would reign across the face of the earth. We catch a glimpse of this noble ideal in the Iroquois "constitution," passed on by word of mouth from generation to generation: "I, Deganawidah, and the Confederated Chiefs now uproot the tallest pine tree, and into the cavity thereby made we cast all weapons of war. Into the depths of the earth, deep down into the underearth currents of water flowing to unknown regions, we cast all weapons of strife. We bury them from sight and plant again the tree. Thus shall the Great Peace be established."

Deganawidah's ideal was shattered when the Europeans began to settle the New World. Allied with the British, the organization that had been created as an instrument of peace became, for a time, a formidable instrument of war.

kept them at war with each other off and on for a combined total of nearly 25 years. Among other things, they were fighting for control of the seas and possession of distant colonies. In each of the wars the North American continent was only one of several prizes the British and French hoped to win. Armed forces of the two powers clashed on the seas and in Europe, Asia, and North America. But none of the wars was decisive. (See table, page 48.)

In 1754 the clouds of war were gathering once again. The two European giants were about to lock horns in another test of strength. This was to be the struggle that would decide the fate of North America.

⌇ SECTION SURVEY

1. How did Champlain, Marquette and Joliet, and La Salle lay the basis for France's claim to Canada and the Mississippi Valley?

2. Show how the St. Lawrence River played a vital role in the development of New France.

3. Explain why the fur trade was New France's greatest strength and greatest weakness.

4. Draw a chart consisting of two columns headed "New France" and "British colonies." Compare the two rivals with reference to (a) population, (b) type of settlement, (c) government, (d) relations with the Indians, and (e) military strength.

IDENTIFY: Algonquin, seigneur, *coureurs de bois*.

2 Great Britain smashes French power in North America

The world-wide conflict that finally decided the destiny of the North American continent started in the valley of the Ohio River. It started in 1754 when the expanding empires of France and Great Britain clashed in the land beyond the Appalachian Mountains in the contest that came to be called the French and Indian War, or the Seven Years' War.

The first clash. A group of wealthy Virginians were responsible for the first of a series of events that led to the French and Indian War. For business reasons and with no thought of the fateful consequences, these men formed a company and secured from the British king a huge grant of land in the upper Ohio Valley. They intended to make a profit from this land by dividing it into small farms, and then selling these farms to settlers.

The French, alarmed at these real estate activities on what they considered to be French territory, sent an expedition to strengthen France's claim to the land. In 1753 the French started constructing a chain of forts connecting Lake Erie with the Ohio River (see map, page 52).

George Washington, a twenty-one-year-old surveyor of Virginia whose brother had invested in the Ohio real estate venture, was sent by the governor of Virginia to warn the French that the land belonged to the British. (The land had been originally granted to the colony of Virginia by the charter of 1609. See map, page 21.) The French ignored the warnings of George Washington.

The following year Washington, this time a major at the head of a force of militia, returned to the frontier and constructed Fort Necessity, a few miles south of the French Fort Duquesne (doo-KAYN). Fort Duquesne itself was situated at the strategic point where the Monongahela and Allegheny Rivers join to form the Ohio River—the present site of Pittsburgh (see map, page 52). A small force of French and Indians defeated Washington in a battle which was fought at Fort Necessity on July 4, 1754.

The colonies fail to unite. The French were now entrenched along a line of scattered points from the Great Lakes south to the Ohio River, with outposts in the Allegheny Mountains. As a result, the entire northern frontier of the British colonies was exposed to attack from Indians, and the western country was closed to both British traders and British settlers.

At this critical moment delegates from seven of the British colonies met at Albany, New York, to discuss common measures of defense against the French and their Indian allies. They were joined there by Indian representatives from the Six Nations.° The Six Nations,

∙∙

° Earlier the Five Nations (page 50).

Military uniforms of Virginia

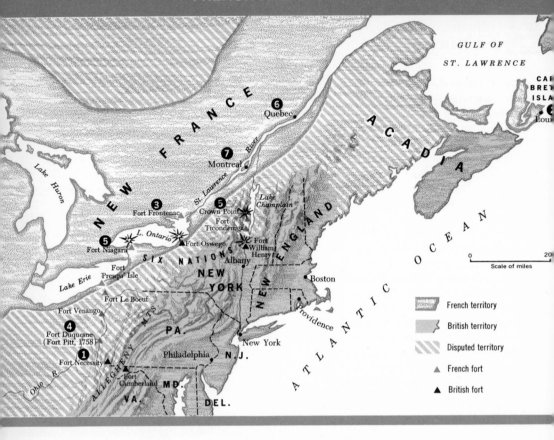

sometimes called the Iroquois Confederation, occupied most of the area that is now central New York. Armed first by the Dutch and then by the English, they were the most powerful group of Indians in North America. And they were long-standing enemies of the French and of the Indians who were friendly to the French. Needless to say, their representatives were more than welcome at the Albany congress.

Shortly after the meeting opened, Benjamin Franklin made a proposal that the British colonies in America unite for defense in a permanent union. Franklin's proposal of 1754—known as the Albany Plan of Union—was rejected by both the British officials and the colonists. The colonists rejected it because they feared that they would lose their right to act independently. The colonists also rejected a somewhat similar proposal by officials of the British government. Although these proposals were rejected, they were important because they caused many colonists to think about the advantages of united action.

British disasters. It was only a few months after the failure of the Albany congress that General Edward Braddock arrived from England with regiments of British regulars, or "redcoats." The British redcoats and a strong force of Virginia militiamen advanced through the wilderness toward the French forces at Fort Duquesne (see number 1 on map, this page). They were ambushed when only ten miles from their goal.

Braddock and 63 of his 89 officers were killed. More than half of his men were casualties—killed, wounded, or captured. The disaster would have been even greater if George Washington and the Virginia militia had not fought back, in Indian fashion, from the cover of trees and rocks.

Braddock's disaster left the 350-mile length of the Pennsylvania, Maryland, and Virginia frontier exposed to Indian attack. Matters went from bad to worse when British expeditions against the French forts at Niagara and Crown Point also failed, and the French captured Forts Oswego and William Henry (see map, opposite page). In Great Britain discouragement set in. "We are undone," cried an English nobleman. "We are no longer a nation."

Pitt rallies the British. Fortunately for Great Britain, William Pitt, a man of enthusiasm and organizing ability, became the leader of the British government in the fall of 1756. Pitt determined to reverse the course of the struggle and to win complete victory for British arms. He was a strong leader, a man of intense enthusiasm, enormous energy, and supreme self-confidence. "I know that I can save England, and that nobody else can," he is reported to have said.

Under Pitt's leadership the British Empire rallied. He discharged officials—military and civil—whose only claim to office was birth, wealth, or influence, replacing them with men of merit. He gave colonial officers ranks equal to those in the king's own troops. He strengthened the British navy and moved more troops to America. He took the offensive throughout the British Empire, relying in America on able leaders like Jeffrey Amherst, James Wolfe, George Howe, and John Forbes.

British victories. The territory of New France was like a tree. Its roots were the lines of communication for transporting soldiers, supplies, and messages across the Atlantic. Its trunk was the St. Lawrence River. Its spreading limbs and branches were the French-controlled waterways of the Great Lakes and the Mississippi Valley, with forts and trading posts scattered along them like leaves.

In 1758 the British destroyed the roots of the tree when a combined naval and land force under General Amherst cap-

NORTH AMERICA IN 1763

DISPUTED AND UNEXPLORED

Hudson Bay

MIQUELON & ST. PIERRE (FR.)

Mississippi R.

LOUISIANA

THE THIRTEEN COLONIES

ATLANTIC OCEAN

New Orleans

Gulf of Mexico

FLA.

CUBA

(FR.)

WEST

INDIES

Caribbean Sea

GUADELOUPE (FR.)

MARTINIQUE (FR.)

British

Spanish

(Fr.) French

tured Louisburg, a powerfully armed French fort on Cape Breton Island (see number 2 on map, page 52.) The fall of Louisburg doomed New France, because the victory provided the British navy with an operating base from which it could cut off French reinforcements and supplies being sent to America. During this same year the British also captured Fort Frontenac on Lake Ontario (see number 3 on map, page 52). This victory weakened the French line of communications to Fort Duquesne, which the French promptly abandoned, permitting General Forbes to occupy it without a struggle (see number 4 on map, page 52). Fort Duquesne was renamed Fort Pitt.

During the year 1759 the British won even more sweeping victories. Amherst forced the French to retreat from their

53

forts at Crown Point and Ticonderoga. Some of Amherst's forces seized Fort Niagara (see number 5 on map, page 52). This latter victory forced the French to abandon their forts in the upper Ohio Valley. And in September 1759 the British captured Quebec (see number 6 on map, page 52).

The fortress of Quebec had been considered impregnable because of its location on heights called the Plains of Abraham overlooking the St. Lawrence River. For more than two months a powerful British fleet under Admiral Charles Saunders and a landing party under General James Wolfe besieged the fort, which was commanded by the Marquis de Montcalm. Finally, in the gray dawn of a September morning, a daring landing party scaled the rocky cliffs, surprised the defenders on the Plains of Abraham, and then fought their way into the city.

The battle of Quebec was a magnificent victory for the British. The year 1759, indeed, is called by British historians "the wonderful year," for it brought Great Britain sweeping successes in America, in Europe, in the Mediterranean, and in India.

The following year, 1760, the French surrendered Montreal to General Amherst after only slight resistance (see number 7 on map, page 52). And in 1762, fearful of British victory, Spain entered the world-wide conflict on the side of France. But Spanish aid was both too little and too late. The British kept winning on distant battle fronts all over the world. They completed their string

■ In this old print, British forces under General Wolfe are shown going ashore, climbing cliffs, and meeting French forces under the command of the Marquis de Montcalm. To the left of Quebec, in the background, is the fortress which was the object of the British attack.

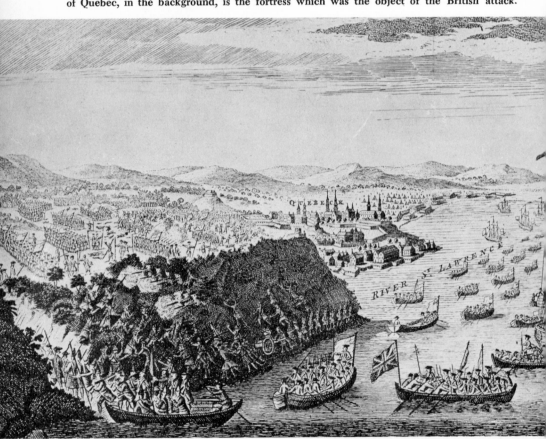

of victories by seizing the Philippine Islands and Cuba from Spain, the West Indies sugar islands of Martinique (mar-ti-NEEK) and Guadeloupe (gwah-duh-LOOP) from France, and French territory in India.

The spoils of war. Out of the world-wide struggle for trade, colonial empire, and naval supremacy the British emerged victorious over all their enemies. Meeting in Paris, representatives of Great Britain, France, and Spain drew up the Treaty of Paris in 1763. By the terms of the treaty, Great Britain secured most of India and all of North America east of the Mississippi River, except the city of New Orleans on the east bank.

France, on the other hand, lost nearly all its possessions in India and in America. The British allowed France to keep only four relatively unimportant islands in the New World. Two of these, St. Pierre (san PY'EHR) and Miquelon (me-KLON) off the coast of Newfoundland, were needed by the French for fishing purposes. The two others were the sugar islands of Guadeloupe and Martinique.

Spain, having entered the war as an ally of France, had to give up Florida to Great Britain. The French compensated the Spaniards for this loss by giving them New Orleans and the vast, almost unexplored territory of Louisiana west of the Mississippi River (see map, page 53). The British also restored Cuba and the Islands of the Philippines to Spain.

How war influenced the colonies. The American colonists, as well as Great Britain, profited from the long contest with their colonial rivals. Out of the school of armed conflict, they acquired experience in warfare. Equally important, the colonists learned that only by co-operating with one another could they hope to defend themselves.

But in 1763 colonial Americans were still far from being united. It took the American Revolution, and the years of unrest that followed, to teach them the absolute necessity for co-operation.

■ The Marquis de Montcalm, a distinguished general at the age of 47, led the French troops at the Battle of Quebec. James Wolfe, equally distinguished at the age of 32, commanded the British troops. Both died on the battlefield. Today this monument to their memory stands at Quebec. Its Latin inscription, translated, reads: "Their courage led them to the same fate; History to the same fame; Posterity to the same monument."

SECTION SURVEY

1. Explain this statement: "The world-wide conflict that finally decided the destiny of the North American continent started in the valley of the Ohio River."

2. Why do British historians refer to 1759 as "the wonderful year"?

3. (a) State the terms of the Treaty of Paris of 1763. (b) What was the significance of this treaty?

4. The New England Confederation (page 36), the Albany Plan of Union, and the French and Indian War were steps toward unification of the colonies. Do you agree? Justify your position.

IDENTIFY: The Iroquois Confederation; Franklin, Braddock, Pitt, Amherst, Wolfe, Montcalm; 1754, 1763.

3 Trouble looms between the colonies and Great Britain

In 1763 Great Britain's steadily growing empire included a total of thirty-three different colonies. Only thirteen of these colonies, as you know, were located along the Atlantic seaboard of North America. The others were scattered over the face of the earth.

Why were British leaders—and the leaders of other European countries—so eager to win colonies? For the answer to this question, we must understand the mercantile system of trade.

The mercantile system of trade. There was nothing new about the mercantile system of trade or, as it is often called, *mercantilism.* Nor was it peculiar to the British Empire. It had been developed during the 1600's and the 1700's by the Dutch, the Spaniards, the Portuguese, and the French, as well as by the British.

Mercantilism, briefly, is an economic and political policy whereby a nation tries to gain greater wealth and power than its rivals. The specific purpose of mercantilism in the 1600's and 1700's was to build up a powerful, self-sufficient empire in a world full of religious wars and bitter commercial rivalry. Under the mercantile system the government of a nation tried to gain greater power than its rivals by building a larger army and navy. To build greater military power, the nation needed money. In order to get more money, a nation sought to sell its goods abroad, and to sell more goods than it needed to buy from other countries. It sought, in other words, to build a *favorable balance of trade.* A nation gains a favorable balance of trade when it is able to *export,* or sell abroad, more of its own products than it has to *import,* or buy from other nations.

If a nation could manage to secure a highly favorable balance of trade, it could (1) be self-sufficient, (2) become wealthy, and (3) build up a powerful army and navy. Colonies were an essential part of the plan. From the British point of view, colonies would strengthen Great Britain in three ways. They would, in the first place, provide the raw materials without which the small island kingdom could not supply its own needs. They would, in the second place, provide markets for goods produced in Great Britain, particularly manufactured goods. Finally, the colonies would help to make Great Britain powerful. They would encourage the growth of a strong merchant fleet, which would serve as a training school for the Royal Navy. They would provide bases from which the Royal Navy could operate.

To apply the mercantile theory of trade, the British Parliament enacted many laws during the 1600's and 1700's.

Restrictions on manufacturing. One series of laws restricted nearly all the manufacturing of the British Empire to England. For example, in 1699 Parliament passed legislation forbidding the colonists to export wool, raw or manufactured, even to a neighboring colony. In 1732 another law forbade the colonists to manufacture beaver hats. In 1750 still another law forbade them to manufacture iron products. The British government also did everything within its power to prevent skilled mechanics from leaving Great Britain, fearing they would help the colonists to start their own manufacturing plants.

These restrictions on manufacturing were not particularly burdensome to the American colonists, who at this time had neither the money nor the skilled labor to establish industries.

Restrictions on shipping. Beginning as early as 1651, another series of laws, known as the Navigation Acts, restricted all trade within the empire to British ships. These acts forbade the importation of goods from Africa, Asia, and the non-British colonies of America into any port of the British Empire except in British ships.

Under the encouragement of this legislation, a powerful merchant fleet was soon plying the seas between the colonies and the mother country. The American colonists, being British citizens, were of course permitted to build, operate, and man their own vessels. They benefited greatly. In the late 1760's and early 1770's fortunes were being made by many American colonial merchants, and colonial shipyards were producing one third of all merchant vessels sailing under the British flag.

Restrictions on selling. The Navigation Act of 1660 listed, or "enumerated," specific colonial products that should be shipped only to England. Among these *enumerated goods* were such important products as tobacco, cotton, and sugar. The colonists therefore could not sell these products on the mainland of Europe, where they might have secured higher prices.

But by the 1700's the British government was paying *bounties* on some enumerated goods. Bounties are payments that governments sometimes make to stimulate production of certain goods. Bounties on tar, resin, turpentine, and hemp stimulated the production of these so-called naval stores, which were urgently needed by the merchant fleet and the Royal Navy. Bounties on whale oil and fish stimulated the growth of a colonial fishing fleet, from which the British secured both ships and men for naval forces in times of war.

Restrictions on buying. A new Navigation Act passed by Parliament in 1663 compelled the colonists to buy most of their goods from Great Britain. Further, all European goods headed for the colonies had to be sent first to England, where an import *duty*° was collected, and then reshipped in British vessels. One purpose of these requirements was to enable the Royal Navy to protect merchant shipping between Great Britain and America from enemy ships and pirates. Another purpose was to protect British manufacturers from the competition of their European rivals.

••

° *duty:* a sum of money that is collected by law on the import or export of goods; also called a *tariff.*

WILLIAM PHIPS, MERCHANT OF MASSACHUSETTS

One must search far to find a success story to match that of William Phips (1651–95), a poor boy who, in a brief life span of forty-four years, won great fortune and high honors.

William Phips was born on the New England frontier. At eighteen he was apprenticed to a ship carpenter. He taught himself to read and write, married the well-to-do widow of a Boston merchant, built his own trading vessels, and in the winter of 1687 discovered a sunken Spanish treasure ship in the West Indies.

For two months his men dived, raked, and grappled, hauling from the depths of the sea dripping baskets of jewels, silver ingots and bars, and silver and gold coins. By law, part of this treasure went to the British Crown, and as a reward King James II knighted Phips. A few years later, the king appointed Sir William Phips "Captain-General and Governor-in-Chief of the Province of Massachusetts Bay in New England."

With all his wealth and titles, Sir William remained, as one biographer put it, something of a roughneck. He continued to hobnob with ship carpenters and other friends of his early days. And his two-year term as governor was less than a success. On at least two occasions he publicly brawled with Royal officials, once beating a captain in the Royal Navy with his cane. While in London, standing trial for his misconduct, he died, bringing to an end one of colonial America's most interesting rags-to-riches stories.

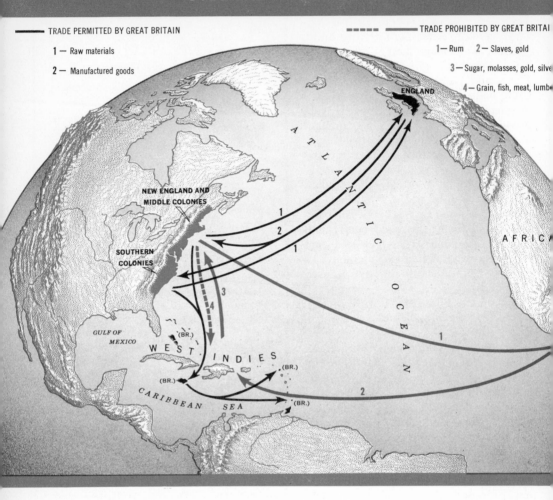

TRADE PERMITTED BY GREAT BRITAIN
1 — Raw materials
2 — Manufactured goods

TRADE PROHIBITED BY GREAT BRITAI
1— Rum   2— Slaves, gold
3— Sugar, molasses, gold, silve
4— Grain, fish, meat, lumb

ENGLAND

ATLANTIC

NEW ENGLAND AND
MIDDLE COLONIES

AFRICA

SOUTHERN
COLONIES

OCEAN

GULF OF
MEXICO

(BR.)

W E S T   I N D I E S

(BR.)

(BR.)

CARIBBEAN   SEA

(BR.)

Mercantilism creates friction. By numerous acts of legislation, then, the British government applied the system of mercantilism. Since other colonial powers followed similar practices, the world in colonial times was divided into a number of competing empires. As you have seen, this competition was one of the basic causes of the colonial wars. But the mercantile system also created friction within the British Empire itself, especially in the relations between Great Britain and its colonies in North America.

When the mercantile system was first being developed, it seemed to threaten the prosperity of New England and the Middle Colonies. These colonies produced goods similar to those produced by British farmers and workers—grain, lumber, fish, cloth, iron, and other products. The people of Great Britain did not need the products of these colonies, and actually enacted laws barring them from Great Britain.

Fortunately, the New England and Middle Colonies soon established new markets for their goods. As a result, the mercantile legislation did not seriously disturb them.

Colonial trade routes. The map on this page shows one of the major sources of income for the colonial merchants—the *triangular trade* involving

Africa, the West Indies, and the colonies.

Leaving colonial ports, vessels set sail for Africa on the first leg of the triangle, their decks and holds piled high with kegs of rum produced in colonial distilleries. On the west coast of Africa, they exchanged the rum for slaves or gold. From Africa the vessels sailed on the second leg of their voyage. This took them to the West Indies, where the slaves were exchanged for molasses, sugar, or money. The final leg of the triangular trade route brought the ships home to the colonies loaded with sugar or molasses, for making more rum, and a balance of gold and silver.

Another busy trade route, also shown on the map, was that which directly connected the colonies with the islands in the Caribbean Sea. Ships from New England and the Middle Colonies sailed southward with cargoes of grain, fish, meat, cloth, soap, lumber, shingles, knocked-down shacks for the slaves, and casks for molasses and sugar. On the return voyage the ships were freighted with the usual cargo of sugar, molasses, and money.

Colonists evade the laws. Most of this trade was perfectly legal. But some of it was in direct violation of British laws. One of the most widely violated laws was the Molasses Act of 1733.

The Molasses Act had been pushed through Parliament by planters in the British West Indies. It was intended to force the American colonists to buy their sugar and molasses from the British West Indies. Supplies purchased from the French, Dutch, or Spanish islands could be imported into the colonies only after the payment of a very high duty. Since the British West Indies could supply only about one eighth of the molasses needed by the colonists, the act almost compelled colonial merchants to evade the law.

Had the government of Great Britain really enforced the Molasses Act, many colonial merchants and businessmen would have been ruined, most of the rum distilleries would have been forced to close, and numerous workers would have been thrown out of jobs.

But for a long time Great Britain did not seriously attempt to enforce the Molasses Act. Instead, the government followed a policy that British statesmen referred to as *salutary neglect*. The government was content, as one British statesman, Robert Walpole, expressed it, "to let sleeping dogs lie."

Trouble lies ahead. In 1763, however, the British government needed money to pay its war debt. It needed money for the defense of its large and growing empire. It needed money to pay the officials required to govern the scattered colonies.

How could the British government secure this money? One way was to adopt a new mercantile policy. The major purpose of the earlier mercantile laws had been to regulate trade. The major purpose of the new laws was to raise revenue.

When the British government began, after 1763, to develop this new policy, it ran head on into real trouble. The conflict, as you will see in Unit Two, did not end until the thirteen colonies declared and won their independence from Great Britain.

✔ SECTION SURVEY

1. What were the main purposes of the mercantile system of trade?

2. Show how British mercantile policy placed restrictions on colonial (a) manufacturing, (b) buying, and (c) selling.

3. Would you have favored British mercantilism if you had been a colonial (a) shipowner, (b) shipbuilder, (c) fisherman, or (d) manufacturer of beaver hats and iron products? Give reasons.

4. How did the New Englanders profit from the triangular trade?

5. Why did the British shift in 1763 from a policy of "salutary neglect" to one of revising its mercantile laws?

IDENTIFY: favorable balance of trade, self-sufficiency, Navigation Acts, enumerated goods, bounty, import duty, Molasses Act, salutary neglect; 1733.

Points to Discuss: 1. Explain this statement: The rivalry between New France and the British colonies was part of their world-wide struggle.

2. Compare the respective advantages and disadvantages of the French and British as they began the Ohio Valley conflict.

3. In what ways did geography influence the course of the French and Indian War? What other factors might account for early defeats suffered by the British?

4. It has been said that the American Revolution began with the close of the French and Indian War. Discuss this.

5. Summarize the important features of the British mercantile system. Consider all the reasons why Great Britain felt a need to review and revise her mercantile policy after 1763. In what ways did her success against the French give her new "burdens" in America?

Using Maps: 1. Using the map on page 49, (a) compare the areas of settlement of the British and French in 1750; (b) how were the explorations of Champlain, Marquette and Joliet important to France?

2. Using the map on page 52: (a) Locate and identify British and French posts. (b) Locate and discuss the major victories which proved to be decisive.

3. Using the map on page 53, indicate the territory (a) won by Great Britain, (b) given to Spain, and (c) left to France by the Treaty of Paris, 1763.

4. Using the map on page 58, (a) explain Great Britain's mercantilist policies and (b) describe the triangular trade.

Consulting the Sources: See Ellis, *Docs.*, No. 17, for an account of Isaac Jogues; Nos. 16, 18, 20, 21 for accounts of other missionaries.

■ TRACING THE MAIN IDEAS

During the 1600's and the 1700's the Indian war whoop on the lonely frontier of Georgia or New England echoed the larger conflict going on in the Western world. Powerful European nations struggled for supremacy. They were driven by the rising spirit of nationalism, the desire for colonial empires, and the competition for trade.

By 1763 Great Britain was victorious. The Dutch and the French had been expelled from the mainland of North America. The Spanish had been pushed west of the Mississippi River, holding only New Orleans on the east bank. Victory had also crowned the efforts of British forces in other parts of the world, notably in India, and the British flag waved above a large and growing empire.

But victory brought new problems as well as glory to the British people. One of the major problems was that of governing the rapidly growing empire. Great Britain, like the other colonial powers of Europe, had tried to bind the colonies and the mother country together with a series of laws that, taken together, were known as the "mercantile system." As its empire grew, Great Britain found it increasingly necessary to adopt new regulations.

As you will see in Chapter 6, Great Britain's efforts to reorganize its empire during the years after 1763 antagonized people living in the colonies along the Atlantic seaboard and in 1775 plunged the colonists and the mother country into the Revolutionary War.

But the quarrel that led to armed conflict cannot be fully understood without some knowledge of everyday life in the colonies. In their efforts to adapt themselves to the New World environment, the colonists developed ideas and ways of living different from those of people living in Great Britain. This steadily increasing spirit of "Americanism" is explained in Chapters 4 and 5.

The Colonists Gradually Become Americans

CHANGING WAYS

OF AMERICAN LIFE

IN 1751 Benjamin Franklin, then forty-five years of age, asked for and secured from the British government an appointment as Postmaster General of the American colonies. Franklin wanted this position in part for personal reasons. But most of all, he wanted to be Postmaster General because he was eager to have the colonies united in a confederation, and for this purpose he knew that a good postal service was a necessity. He realized that the colonies could never unite unless they had a better system of communication.

Even before Franklin received the appointment, he made a tour of the post roads north of Philadelphia. Post roads were the routes over which mail was carried either by a rider on horseback or by stagecoach. Ten years later, in 1763, Franklin made a much longer trip of more than 1600 miles, traveling over nearly every post road in America.

As a result of his travels, Benjamin Franklin knew how Americans lived and what they were thinking. He had visited southern planters. He had lived with the townspeople. He had stopped overnight with farmers. He had talked with frontiersmen.

In the next few pages you are going to look at each of these four groups of people. And you will see, as Franklin saw, that on many matters they were sharply divided one from another. But you will also see, as Franklin saw, that by the 1750's and 1760's from one end of the British colonies to the other many people were beginning to think of themselves as "Americans."

AS THE STORY DEVELOPS
1. **The southern planter seems more English than American.**
2. **The townspeople mix English with American ideas.**
3. **The pioneer farmer gradually becomes less English.**
4. **The frontiersman becomes the first true American.**

Home of a southern planter

1 The southern planter seems more English than American

On Franklin's travels through the Southern Colonies in 1763 he saw few towns or cities. Baltimore, Maryland, which had been started in 1729, contained only a few thousand people. Charleston, South Carolina, the largest and wealthiest seaport in the entire Southland, had not yet reached the ten thousand mark.

Southern population. By the 1760's there were more than 2,000,000 people in all the British colonies along the Atlantic seaboard. About half of these people lived in the five Southern Colonies—Maryland, Virginia, North Carolina, South Carolina, and Georgia.

Throughout the colonies the majority of the people lived in the country, but in the South the proportion of country dwellers was especially high. Most of the southern people lived on small farms similar to those in New England and the Middle Colonies. Some lived on the frontier in small clearings cut from the forest. The wealthy planters lived on the fertile coastal plains. A few of these great planters owned plantations several thousand acres in size.

The planter. The southern planter drew his wealth from agriculture. Although he raised most of the food used on the plantation, his riches usually came from a single crop. In the Carolinas and Georgia, especially in South Carolina, rice was the important product. In Maryland, Virginia, and North Carolina tobacco was the chief cash crop. The wealthy planters lived much like English country gentlemen.

The plantation. The large plantation was a complete economic unit. In the center, looking out upon broad acres, stood the mansion, usually a large brick home of the Georgian style of architecture then popular among the wealthy country gentlemen of England. Behind the mansion were the simpler homes of the overseer, or supervisor, and the necessary artisans, or skilled workers. On Washington's estate at Mount Vernon, Virginia, for example, there were homes for the carpenters, bricklayers, masons, blacksmiths, millers, and weavers. Then there were the cabins of the slaves, who numbered about 200.

Each plantation was almost self-sufficient—independent, that is, of the rest of the world. Meat was butchered from herds of cattle and hogs. Other foods and clothing were secured from the land. Business ability was required to organize and to administer an enterprise of this kind. This task fell upon the shoulders of the planter and his wife. Theirs was a luxurious way of life, but it carried heavy responsibilities.

English economic ties. Most of the planter's luxuries came, of course, from England, for even as late as the 1750's the American colonists produced few manufactured goods. Every year on the tobacco plantations slaves rolled the large hogsheads of tobacco to the wharves, where they were loaded on vessels usually owned by northern merchants. Frequently the planter sent with his shipment a list of goods that he wished his agent in London to purchase for him. The agent sold the tobacco, rice, or indigo; bought the articles desired by the planter; and shipped these, together with a financial statement, to his client in America.

Social life. In this way the planters filled their homes with luxuries from the Old Country—table silver, furniture, clothes, tapestries, wines, and books.

Since the plantations were more or less isolated from one another, visits were frequently exchanged by the planters. Washington, during two months in 1768, entertained guests on twenty-nine different days and dined out on seven other occasions. The dinners were splendid affairs. After dinner the evenings were spent in conversation or at cards. Out of this custom of social visiting, there developed the tradition of southern hospitality that has continued to this day.

FRANKLIN IMPROVES THE POSTAL SERVICE

Before Benjamin Franklin became Postmaster General, the postal service in the British colonies was a sorry business. The postriders, who carried the mail on horseback, were poorly paid and often dishonest. The person to whom a letter was addressed paid the postage, making it easy for a dishonest postrider to charge any fee he wanted and to pocket the extra money.

Worst of all was the lack of privacy. No one could be sure that the letter he sent would not be opened and read by other people. Government officials, businessmen, and others often opened and read mail addressed to friends and neighbors.

In some cases, when letters arrived, they were spread out on a table in a tavern. One reporter described such a scene in 1751, the same year Franklin applied for his appointment. The reporter saw a man pick up a letter and read the address on the envelope. "Egad," the man said, "I must know the contents of it," and he rushed out of the room with someone else's mail clutched in his hand.

Franklin quickly changed all this. He required everyone who handled the mails to keep careful accounts. He also started new postal routes. By providing this better means of communication, Franklin helped to unite the colonies for the struggles that lay ahead.

Like the other planters Washington was proud of his horses and his pack of hounds. Dressed in scarlet hunting clothes from England, he took pleasure in riding to the hounds. In his diary we read that during January and February 1769 he went fox hunting on fifteen different occasions.

Many of the richer planters also

owned town houses in Charleston, Williamsburg, or Annapolis, where they spent several months each year. During this period they enjoyed dancing, music, art, dramatics, and lectures. They also spent much time playing cards, watching cockfights, racing horses, and fox hunting.

English influence. The plantations of the South reminded visitors of country estates in England. They were, in a sense, part of England carried overseas to the New World. The wealthy planters dressed and talked and acted much like country gentlemen back in the mother country. Indeed, they had more in common with Englishmen in the Old Country than they had with the small farmers and the frontiersmen who lived only a short distance farther inland.

And yet, as you will see, when the break with England finally came, some of the southern planters were among the first to take up arms to fight for independence. A southern planter, Richard Henry Lee, offered the resolution that the United Colonies "are, and of right ought to be, free and independent states." Another planter, Thomas Jefferson, wrote most of the Declaration of Independence. Still another planter, George Washington, led the American armies to victory.

But it is also true that when the Revolution broke out some of the wealthy planters remained loyal to England, as did some of the wealthy people in the New England and Middle Colonies. Their economic as well as social ties with the mother country were too strong to break.

✔ **SECTION SURVEY**

1. "The large plantation was a complete economic unit." Explain.
2. What is meant by the statement that the riches of the plantation owner usually came from a single crop?
3. Describe the different social groups that lived in the South.
4. What economic ties bound the southern planter to England?

2 The townspeople mix English with American ideas

Like the southern planters the wealthier townspeople in all the colonies dressed and acted like wealthier Englishmen in the Old Country. This is not surprising. Most of the colonial cities and towns were seaports, and their ties with England were close indeed. All travel and trade between the Old World and the British colonies flowed through these seaports.

By the 1750's, with a population of 20,000, Philadelphia was the largest city in the British colonies in America. In one year, 1754, a total of 471 trading vessels entered and left its busy harbor. New York and Boston were a close second and third in importance. Charleston, South Carolina, and Baltimore, Maryland, were the only towns of considerable size south of Pennsylvania.

Social divisions. By the 1760's merchants were the most influential citizens in all of the large northern towns. This was true even in New England, where in earlier years clergymen had been the leaders. The merchants, together with lawyers and the official families of the royal governors from England, set the fashions for the wealthier people. They drew their wealth from trade and from buying and selling land. Some of them owned country estates worked by tenant farmers.

Far below the merchants on the social ladder were the numerous household servants—white indentured servants and Negro slaves. Between the merchants and the servants were the majority of the town inhabitants, the free artisans and laborers.

These three classes—the wealthy townspeople, the skilled workmen, and the servants and slaves—compared to similar classes in England.

Influence of the Old World. The influence of the Old World could be seen in many other features of town life. Some of the wealthy townsmen built houses similar to those which they had seen on their visits to the Old World. Sometimes they even brought the bricks from England. Lower New York, originally settled by the Dutch, resembled an Old World port.

Like the wealthy southern planters, the wealthy townspeople imported much of their furniture and household equipment from England. The interiors of their houses, as well as the exteriors, reminded visitors of the Old World.

Like that of well-to-do people in England, the social life of the wealthy townsmen centered in the banquet hall and in elaborate dances. They rode to these festive occasions in gleaming coaches, drawn by white horses with silver trappings, driven by coachmen and outriders in blue coats and yellow capes.

Many well-to-do townspeople also enjoyed card playing, horse racing, cockfighting, and the theater. In Boston, however, strict Puritan ideas still prevailed, and such recreation was frowned upon or forbidden by law.

This brilliant social life was confined, of course, to a handful of the townspeople. The household servants usually lived in simply furnished rooms over the family quarters. The artisans often lived in quarters behind their small shops that fronted on the streets.

A visit to Philadelphia. Imagine for a moment that we are back in colonial America, strolling through the seaport of Philadelphia in, say, 1754. In other colonial towns the streets meander this way and that, following the early cowpaths and farm lanes. Philadelphia is different. Here William Penn's careful planning has proved worthwhile. The streets run neatly north and south, east and west. Some are paved with cobblestones, others are merely hard-pressed earth, and as we walk on these our feet raise little clouds of dust. We have seen the homes of the wealthy—red brick and white stone houses surrounded by gardens and lawns. Now we pass the small shops of the artisans—ship chandler, baker, butcher, tailor, cobbler, blacksmith, dyer, and leather worker.

We look up at the sound of a bell and pause to listen as the town crier, introducing his news with "Hear ye, hear ye," announces a sale of indentured servants just arrived on a ship from England.

On our way to the water front we see the market house and join throngs of housewives and servants who, with baskets on their arms, crowd around the stalls. Farmers from the surrounding countryside are displaying their produce—butter, cheese, poultry, beef, mutton, and vegetables.

Philadelphia street scene

Colonial shipbuilding

Along the water front. Reaching the water, we continue along Dock Street, which parallels the Delaware River. The noise of hammers and saws attracts our attention, and we see a shipyard with the skeleton of a small vessel rising from the ways. Next to it, from a tiny sloop, a group of fishermen are heaving their day's catch upon the planks of the wharf. Beyond, its masts reaching toward the sky, lies the English ship we have come to see.

Approaching its mooring place, we find ourselves in the midst of bustle and confusion. Men with boxes and bales on their shoulders are pushing their way toward the nearby warehouse. At one side a knot of colonists surrounds a sailor, plying him with questions, eager for the latest news from the Old World. And on the deck, looking bewildered and unhappy, are the indentured servants, or redemptioners.

The wealthy colonists, easily distinguished by their dress and self-assurance, pass among the servants, their eyes open for a good bargain. Now and then a sale is made, and we watch the owner and his new servant leave the ship, the one in front leading the way, the other following with his belongings in a sack over his shoulder.

English ways of life. As we retrace our steps into the town, it would be easy to think that we are walking the streets of an English city. Passing the open door of a merchant's "counting house," we see clerks on tall stools painstakingly recording business transactions in their ledgers. Across the street is a tavern. In front of the tavern are a row of hitching posts and a hollow log to serve as a watering trough for horses.

We have not seen the town hall nor the jail with its pillory and stocks nor the several churches that we know are an important part of the city. But we have seen enough to learn that life in the colonial towns is in many ways similar to life in English towns. The people dress and talk like Englishmen. The houses and public buildings look like English houses and public buildings. There are the same social divisions that we could see in any English town.

The American "melting pot." But in some ways the colonial towns are different from the towns of England. Even though some people may want to do so, they cannot carry all the Old World ways to the New World.

For one thing, people from many different nations are learning to live together in colonial America. The colonial towns, as well as the frontier and the farming areas, are "melting pots." The section of Philadelphia known as Germantown is filled with settlers from far-off Germany. On the streets we pass men and women from Ireland and Scotland, many of them on their way to frontier lands of the west. And if we listen carefully, we hear the accents of people from France, Switzerland, Sweden, and many other European countries.

The "melting pot" of colonial America is also producing a new American vocabulary. English travelers who visit the colonies hear words they never hear in England. The colonists are speaking what Samuel Johnson, the famous English dictionary maker, in 1756 called the "American dialect." By the 1760's the new American vocabulary has borrowed many words from other languages. From the Indians it has borrowed *skunk, hickory, squash, raccoon, canoe, toboggan, moccasin, tomahawk,* and *wigwam.* From the Dutch it has borrowed *cruller, stoop, waffle, scow, boss,* and *cookie.* From the French it has borrowed *bureau, gopher, chowder, bogus, portage,* and *prairie*. And the colonists have invented many new words, among them *bullfrog, eggplant, snowplow, cold snap, trail, popcorn, shingle,* and *backlog*.

Building the towns. The colonists are also trying to solve in their own way problems faced by all townspeople. They are trying to solve problems of water supply, sewage, sanitation, health, and police and fire protection. They are learning to work together, to co-operate, in an effort to solve these problems. In Philadelphia, Benjamin Franklin is one of the leaders, keeping up a steady stream of articles about these problems in his newspaper, the *Pennsylvania Gazette*. Largely because of his efforts, Philadelphia is one of the first cities in the world to have paved streets, street lights, police and fire departments, and a public library. To be sure, Europeans are also working for these same improvements in their cities. But the colonists take special pride in the cities that they have built with their own hands.

Opportunity for all. The greatest difference between English and American towns can be summed up in the word "opportunity." There is plenty of work for everyone in Philadelphia, New York, Boston, or in any of the other colonial towns. No one need remain a servant for very long. And if the town itself does not seem to offer enough opportunity, there is always the chance to move west. Many do move west. They stay in the town only long enough to save a little money; then they are off over the roads that lead to a new way of life.

SECTION SURVEY

1. What were the chief occupations of the townspeople in the colonies?

2. Describe five ways in which wealthy townspeople imitated the life of the well-to-do in England.

3. Show how an "American dialect" grew out of the American melting pot.

4. Explain the fact that the greatest difference between English and American towns was "opportunity."

Cotton Mather

THE INOCULATION BATTLE

Citizens of Boston shuddered when they recalled the terrible summer and fall of 1721. An epidemic of smallpox had struck the city. By the time it had run its course, more than half of the 10,000 inhabitants had been stricken, more than 800 had died, and hundreds of others had been disfigured. Physicians knew of no way to fight this dread disease. They could only quarantine the patient—and hope for the best.

The Reverend Cotton Mather, one of the most learned men in the colonies, was not content merely to hope. He had heard about a method of fighting smallpox from an African slave. Later, in his wide reading, he had come across a report that Turkish doctors had controlled the disease by a method known as inoculation. This consisted of taking matter from the blisters of a sufferer and inserting it into the skin of a healthy person. The healthy person contracted the disease, of course, but as a mild case, and after he recovered, he was forever immune. Such, at least, was the theory. But it had never been tried in America.

Only one Boston physician, Dr. Zabdiel Boylston, was willing to try the new method—and did. The other physicians, and many townspeople, called Mather and Boylston "murderers." But when the epidemic was over, the record showed that inoculation, dangerous though it was, had been effective. For the next 80 years, until Dr. Edward Jenner of England discovered how to prevent smallpox by vaccination, inoculation was widely used throughout the colonies and Western Europe.

3 The pioneer farmer gradually becomes less English

Although townspeople and even wealthy planters were slowly growing away from England, the area of America that was most different from the Old World lay back from the seacoast. Here, in the country, lived more than 90 per cent of all the colonists.

Farming villages. Not far from the coast, and particularly in New England, New Jersey, and Pennsylvania, there were many small farming villages of 50 or 100 families, with a church or meetinghouse, a school, and several shops. The villagers might go to a cobbler to have their shoes made, to a blacksmith to have their wagons fixed, to a doctor for medical attention, or to a general store to buy sugar, spices, or English fabrics for dresses. Traveling barbers also came to the villages to cut hair and pull teeth. At regular intervals a candlemaker stopped to pour each settler's tallow into large tin molds.

To pay for these services, the farmers of the village and the surrounding territory sold their surplus tobacco, grain, cattle, and hogs in the nearest seaboard or river-port town.

Before they returned home, the farmers often stopped to make purchases in the shops displaying goods from England—furniture, tableware, silver and pewter vessels, fine cloth, and other luxuries. Thus, the settlers who lived in areas where it was possible to market their surplus produce were able to live better than their more isolated fellows.

Moving into new homes. People married young in colonial America. Some couples settled on a portion of their father's land. More often the newly married couple became pioneers and moved farther inland where land was cheaper. It was a common sight to see a couple pass through a village on their way to a new home. The husband strode along, rifle in hand, knife in belt. Beside him walked his wife. Behind, in a small cart pulled by an ox or a horse, were a few boxes with all their belongings. Bringing up the rear, tied to the cart by a rope, was a scrawny cow.

Pioneer shelters. Many of the settlers lived at first in caves along the riverbanks or in shallow pits roofed with branches and covered with sod to keep out the rain. Others built wigwams; in the South these were often covered with palmetto leaves; in the North, with bark. Frequently the newcomers put up three-sided log shelters with the open side

■ This picture, drawn in 1853, shows several details characteristic of a pioneer farm: the clearing, with stumps, surrounded by a split-rail fence; corn growing behind the small barn; the log house at the left. The farmer is about to shoot a bear out of a tree.

facing away from the prevailing winds. Sooner or later those who stayed to farm the land built a full log cabin, a practical type of architecture for forested country, introduced into the colonies by Swedish settlers.

These cabins were usually crude, one-room affairs, with a dirt floor, no windows, and a door hung on leather hinges. Their most important feature was the huge fireplace around which the settlers huddled for warmth, and in which they cooked their food. Later, if the pioneers prospered, they improved the cabin. They laid a wooden floor, cut windows in the walls, and covered the openings with waxed paper or glass. They built a loft for the children to sleep in, added new rooms, and, if all went well, finally nailed clapboards on the outside walls over the rough logs.

The pioneers rose at dawn and went to bed at dusk. There were few books, even for those who could read, and the pioneers felt little need to light the cabins at night. Usually the glow from the fireplace furnished the only illumination. When more light was needed, people used large splinters of pine wood, which they thrust into cracks in the wall where they burned with a bright, smoky flame. They used candles only on special occasions, for tallow was hard to get. Only wealthy townspeople used candles and oil lamps to any extent.

Household equipment. The fireplaces furnished the only heat in the early log cabins, and the pioneers shivered as the winter winds swept through the cracks between the logs or down the drafty chimney. It is no wonder that people put warming pans in their beds, went to bed early, and bundled themselves in layers of blankets. And it is no wonder that every family that could afford to do so bought one of the stoves Benjamin Franklin had invented.

The fireplace also furnished the means of cooking. The pioneers boiled vegetables, soups, and stews in large copper or iron kettles—prized possessions in any household—which hung from a pole in the throat of the chimney. They baked in Dutch ovens beside the fireplaces.

The furniture, especially in the early years of any settlement, was homemade and crude. Beds were little more than wooden bunks placed along the wall. Logs, hewn smooth with an ax, were used for chairs and benches. Tables were smooth boards placed on trestles. Since planks were hard to get, the colonists often broke up packing boxes from England and used the boards for table tops. Only well-to-do settlers owned tablecloths.

Eating utensils were simple and few. On pioneer farms settlers often used wooden trenchers for dishes. These were slabs of wood ten or twelve inches square and two or three inches thick with a hollow place in the center to hold the food. The pioneers whittled spoons out of wood. They drank from gourds that they grew themselves or from tankards that they made from wood, leather, or the horns of cattle. As the settlers grew more prosperous, they bought pewter and silver utensils.

Food for the pioneers. Once colonial Americans learned to make use of the abundant resources of the New World, they never lacked food and drink. The rivers and lakes were alive with fish, and the forests were filled with game. Deer in herds of several hundred or more were often seen near the forts in the early days. Turkeys as heavy as thirty pounds were found in all the colonies, although the settlers rapidly wiped them out. We read that pigeons were so plentiful from Virginia northward that they sometimes darkened the sky and broke the limbs of trees in which they roosted. Wild rabbits and squirrels destroyed so many crops that bounty payments were offered for their pelts.

Pioneer clothing. The pioneer farmers also made their own clothing, having brought with them from the Old World the skills of spinning and weaving. They made thread from the wool of their own sheep and from the flax they grew in their own fields. The women and girls spun the thread, wove it into cloth, and cut and sewed dresses for their own use.

THE PIONEER AND HIS AX

The ax and the rifle—without them the early Americans could not have conquered the wilderness and pushed the frontier steadily westward. Of the two, it was the ax that proved to be the Indian's greatest enemy. It was the ax that leveled the forests, destroyed the Indian's hunting grounds, and prepared the way for the plow of the farmer.

The pioneer's ax was a dozen tools in one. He held the axhead in the palm of his hand, and used it as a plane. He tapped the axhead with a block of wood, and had a chisel. He nicked the handle every inch, and had a measure. When need arose, he made the ax serve as a substitute for a knife.

But it was when he hefted the ax in his two hands, placed his feet firmly on the ground, and tackled a giant tree that the man and the tool seemed to become a single instrument.

"Watching an axman is like watching magic," one observer wrote. "These men of the woods sleep with their axes under their beds at night, and every minute of the day they are swinging their blades with such sure strokes that they can just look at a tree and know how many strokes will fell it."

They also tanned deerskin and fashioned it into moccasins, shoes, and jackets.

Social life and recreation. Life on a pioneer farm was hard, and there was little time or energy for recreation. Nevertheless, the settlers did manage on occasion to combine work and play.

When a newcomer was ready to build his log cabin or when he had felled the trees and was ready to drag them from the land to clear a field, his neighbors came to help him with the heavy work. "House-raisings" sometimes lasted for several days. In the morning the men lifted the logs into place to form the cabin walls. Meanwhile, the women pre-

pared a dinner of great piles of cornbread and an entire beef or deer barbecued over an open fire. After dinner there were sports, such as wrestling, foot racing, and shooting contests. In the early evening they danced.

People who lived in areas that had been settled for some years had more chances to be neighborly. In these areas church establishments were the basis of the community, around which the social order was constructed. During the week, at appropriate seasons, they met to help one another with cornhusking, sheep-shearing, sewing, and quilting. A wedding was always an occasion for a celebration. There were also election days, on which all work ceased, and training days, on which the local militia drilled in an open field and then spent the afternoon in sports and conversation.

Self-sufficiency. The pioneer farmer was a jack-of-all-trades. Give him a gun, an ax, a knife, a hoe, a sickle, and a kettle or two and he could, with the help of his wife and children, clear the land, build a house, and raise the crops. When all is said and done, however, most pioneer farmers lived a harsh existence. They were self-sufficient from necessity, not from choice. For the great majority there were no doctors, no schools, and few churches. They usually had a roof over their heads, enough to eat, and freedom from oppressive laws and heavy taxes, but they paid for these advantages with lives of back-breaking labor.

Patterns among pioneers. In the minds of these self-reliant pioneer farmers, certain ideas began to take root and grow. The pioneers were free men, who by their own efforts had created homes in the wilderness. They were individualists, for a man's success depended on his own strength and skill. They believed in the value of co-operation, for only by helping one another could they clear the enormous trees from their land and erect their houses. They felt themselves to be the equals of other men, for they saw most of their neighbors living the same kind of life that they were living. Finally, they were optimists, for all around them they saw the forests yielding to their axes, homes and villages springing up, and men who had started with nothing raising their families in security and growing comfort.

Those pioneer farmers who were of English descent still thought of themselves as Englishmen, but the ties between this group of settlers and the mother country were few. More and more, they were beginning to think of themselves as "Americans."

 SECTION SURVEY

1. Compare the life of a pioneer farmer in colonial times with that of a farmer today with reference to (a) shelter, (b) household equipment, (c) food, (d) clothing, (e) social life and recreation.

2. Explain this statement: "The pioneer farmer was a jack-of-all-trades."

3. Why did many of the pioneer farmers begin to think of themselves as "Americans" rather than as Englishmen?

4 The frontiersman becomes the first true American

Most "American" of all the colonists were the frontiersmen. The frontier, or forest land to the west of settled communities, was essentially a man's world, and mainly a young man's world at that. Every year, in all the colonies, hundreds of adventurous youths left home to find excitement in the western forests.

Life on the frontier. With the first plunge into the wilderness, men shed many traces of European civilization. All that they owned they carried in their hands or wore on their backs—a hunting knife, a long rifle, powder, and shot. Yet with this meager equipment they managed to survive. For clothing they shed their European dress in favor of coonskin caps, buckskin shirts and trousers, and moccasins of deerskin. Game,

fish, nuts, and berries furnished much of their food. They slept beneath the stars, in caves, or in crude log shelters.

Some frontiersmen built cabins, cleared patches of land, married, and raised families. But most of these men were trappers and hunters who preferred the lonely life of the forests to the ties of a home. Now and then they made their way to a trading post to exchange a few furs for new supplies of powder, shot, and perhaps a little corn. Many frontiersmen never returned from their travels in the woods, for it was a wild, dangerous life, in which men matched their wits and forest skills against Indians and the forces of nature.

Recreation. Now and then the frontiersmen for miles around gathered together for companionship and sport. Their recreation reflected the hard, rough life that they led. Hunting was both a necessity and a pleasure, and they were crack shots with the rifle. Shooting matches were common.

Games of sheer physical strength also furnished much of their fun. They held foot races, wrestling matches, jumping contests, and demonstrations of hurling the tomahawk and flinging a heavy wooden fence rail.

In the evenings, before a crackling log fire, they swapped colorful tales of forest adventure and told jokes at the expense of newcomers to the wilderness.

A new kind of talk. The "tall tales," full of a highly exaggerated boasting, contained many new words and phrases that the frontiersmen borrowed from the Indians or coined to describe new objects and experiences. From the Indians the frontiersmen learned such words and phrases as *powwow, peace pipe,* and *burying the tomahawk.* To describe strange features of the land, they adopted such new words as *water gap, barrens, salt lick, underbrush,* and *bluffs.* Seaboard folk began to talk of the *back country,* of *backwoodsmen,* and of *taking to the woods.*

Frontier independence. These were the men who explored the "no man's land" between civilization and savage-

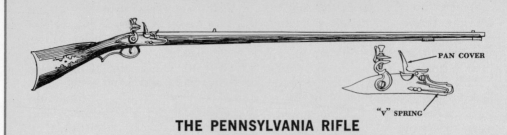

PAN COVER

"V" SPRING

THE PENNSYLVANIA RIFLE

The Pennsylvania rifle, sometimes called "the long rifle," was developed by German gunsmiths who settled in and around Lancaster, Pennsylvania, in the early 1700's. They had learned how to make rifles back in their homeland, but these were not good enough for the frontier. On the frontier a man needed a gun that would shoot straight and true. A hunter could carry only so many bullets with him, and he had to make each shot count, even if the target was only a rabbit or squirrel for his next meal. And no man alone in the wilderness knew when a single shot might save his life.

By 1750, Pennsylvania gunsmiths were making rifles of amazing accuracy. Up to a range of 100 yards, they were about as accurate as an ordinary rifle is today. These rifles helped Americans to conquer the wilderness. With the rifle, the ax, and the Conestoga wagon—also invented in Pennsylvania—Americans pushed the frontier steadily westward.

Did the Pennsylvania rifle win the Revolutionary War that presently broke out between the American colonists and Great Britain? Maybe not. But it played a big part in the victory. In the reports they sent back to England, British generals referred to the "terrible guns of the rebels." Against the Pennsylvania rifle, the British—with a few exceptions—had only clumsy, smoothbore muskets with which a man could hardly expect to hit a target at more than 150 feet.

ry, who discovered the fertile valleys and the passes through the mountains. They were individualists, brimming with the spirit of independence, self-reliance, and initiative. But their individualism was co-operative as well as competitive, for there were times on the frontier when an additional pair of strong arms and an extra rifle meant the difference between life and death.

And in the forest the idea of equality —which is the core of democracy—took root and grew swiftly. A man was judged, not by fine clothes, eloquent language, or titles after his name, but by his skill in woodcraft and his knowledge of the wilderness.

Down the whole length of the frontier, from New France to Spanish Florida, men lived pretty much the same sort of life. The German, Scotch-Irish, or English on the Virginia frontier had more in common with the Massachusetts frontiersmen than they had with the rich planters in the tidewater regions of their own colony, or with the wealthy townsmen of the colonial seaports. Frontier life was a wonderful process of mixing many people with different backgrounds into a new, independent kind of person.

SECTION SURVEY

1. Show how the life of a frontiersman differed from that of a planter, townsman, and pioneer farmer.

2. Choose five words or phrases used by frontiersmen and explain the meaning of each.

3. What typically American ideas developed on the frontier?

4. Explain this statement: "Frontier life was a wonderful process of mixing many people with different backgrounds into a new, independent kind of person."

Points to Discuss: 1. In what ways did the social life of the planter resemble that of an English country gentleman?

2. Describe the various jobs that were available for young people in the colonies.

3. In what ways was the outlook of the frontiersman and the pioneer farmer different from that of the merchant and planter?

4. Why was the frontier so attractive to young men and women?

5. American history cannot be explained without an understanding of geography. Support this statement by referring to life in the colonies between 1607 and 1763.

Using Maps: 1. Geography influences people, and people influence geography. (See pages 818–19.) What geographic factors led to differences in the way of life in New England, in the South, and in the Middle Colonies?

2. Using the map on pages 838–39, compare the means of travel between Savannah and Boston in 1790 with those of today.

Consulting the Sources: For first-hand narrative accounts of colonial life see H. S. Commager and A. Nevins (eds.), *The Heritage of America*, "Life in the American Colonies," pages 48–85.

■ TRACING THE MAIN IDEAS

When the settlers arrived in the New World, they were European in language, dress, customs, and ways of thinking and acting. They naturally tried to reproduce the everyday ways of life with which they had been familiar in the Old World. This, of course, proved to be impossible. They quickly changed the material aspects of their ways of life—houses, clothing, tools, weapons—to meet their needs. More slowly, they began to change the ideas and practices that they had brought with them from the Old World.

The southern planters and the wealthy townsmen changed more slowly than the other colonial groups. Because their ties with England were so close, they continued in some ways to be more English than they were American.

The pioneer farmers and the frontiersmen changed much more rapidly. Because they had so few ties with England, they became much more American

than they were English. As Frederick Jackson Turner, a famous historian, once said, there was on the frontier "a steady movement away from the influence of Europe, a steady growth of independence on American lines."

There was another important fact about these four groups of colonists. They were growing apart. Many of the merchants and planters felt, as many people in England did, that family background or wealth made them "better" than the rank and file of people and entitled them to special privileges. The farmers and frontiersmen, on the other hand, were becoming more and more democratic in their ways of living and thinking.

In the next chapter you will see how the new ideas and ideals of the colonists influenced the development of colonial schools, churches, and government. You will see the beginnings of what we call "the American way of life."

Democratic Ideas Take Root in Colonial America

CHANGING WAYS

OF AMERICAN LIFE

Roger Williams, Puritan clergyman, fleeing through the snow-covered forests to seek refuge with his friends, the Narragansett Indians . . .

Lord Baltimore, liberal founder of Maryland, enforcing in his colony a policy of toleration . . .

William Penn, Quaker, standing defiantly, hat clamped firmly on his head, before the wigged and robed judges in an English courtroom . . .

John Peter Zenger, editor of the *New York Weekly Journal,* a lonely figure in a cold and cheerless prison cell writing articles for his paper . . .

They form a proud company, these

and other colonial leaders who battled for man's right to be free. And there were others—many others—for from the earliest days of settlement a substantial number of the colonists struggled for freedom—for the right to worship as they pleased, for the right to secure an education, for the right to speak their minds freely, for the right to participate in government. When people possess these rights and others, we say that they live in a "democratic society," or simply in a "democracy."

In Chapter 2 you saw how the colonists built their settlements along the Atlantic seaboard. In this chapter you will see how they began to carry the idea of freedom into their churches, schools, and government. This, the idea of freedom, lies at the root of what we now call "the American way of life."

AS THE STORY DEVELOPS

1. Religious tolerance spreads through the colonies.
2. Freedom to learn and freedom to think strike fertile soil.
3. The colonists acquire valuable experience in self-government.
4. Colonial legislative assemblies gain power in America.

1 Religious tolerance spreads through the colonies

When settlers first began to build colonies on the American continents, there was little or no religious freedom in the Old World. Each of the European nations had set up, or "established," an official state church. The government collected taxes to support the official state church. The government required every citizen to pay these taxes and to join the *established church.*

Old World religious beliefs. Naturally enough, the first settlers brought the idea of the established state church to the Americas. In the French, Spanish, and Portuguese colonies the religion of the Roman Catholic Church was the state religion. In part of New York and in the Southern Colonies of Georgia, North and South Carolina, Virginia, and Maryland (after 1692), the Anglican Church was established. In New England the colonies of Massachusetts, Connecticut, and New Hampshire made the Congregational Church the official religion. In the Middle Colonies, on the other hand, there were so many different religious groups that no single church was established except, as you have seen, in part of New York.

To the New World colonies the settlers also brought the bitter religious conflicts and rivalries of the Old World. There was almost constant border warfare, as you know, between the British colonists and the Roman Catholics of New France. These clashes were mainly over economic and political differences, but they were aggravated as well by religious differences. Many of the border conflicts with Spain in the south were also aggravated by religious differences.

Even within the colonies themselves the various religious groups often persecuted one another severely. Most of the colonists who came to the New World in search of religious freedom were thinking only of freedom for themselves. Plymouth was for Separatists,

HYSTERIA IN SALEM

During the colonial period many people in both Europe and the colonies believed in the evil power of witches. In the spring of 1692, fear of witches threw the village of Salem, Massachusetts, into a panic.

The panic started when several young women and girls listened to the witchcraft stories of Tituba, a slave belonging to the village minister, the Reverend Samuel Parris. The girls presently began to fall to the ground in fits, shrieking with pain. They claimed they were being pierced with pins by a savage demon. When questioned further, they named certain women in the community as their "tormentors."

The Reverend Mr. Parris called in ministers from neighboring towns. All but one agreed the girls were victims of witchcraft. The governor of Massachusetts then appointed a commission which arrested and tried several hundred persons during the summer. Nineteen, who refused to confess that they were witches, were hanged. No one knew who would be accused next. Terror walked the streets of Salem.

By October the trials and executions had gone to such lengths that even the most rabid witchhunters were getting uneasy. Judge Samuel Sewall, who had taken a prominent part in the trials, confessed that he had been mistaken. Others also confessed that they had been wrong. The government of Massachusetts officially expressed regret at the role it had played.

Belief in witchcraft lingered on for many years, both in Europe and in America. But it finally died, and the dreadful affair in Salem was never again repeated in any of the British colonies in the New World.

Rhode Island Charter (1663): EXCERPT

𝔑o person within the said colony at any time hereafter shall be any wise molested, punished, disquieted, or called in question for any differences in opinion in matters of religion ... all and every person and persons may, from time to time, and at all times hereafter, freely and fully have and enjoy his and their own judgments and consciences in matters of religious concernments ...

Maryland Toleration Act (1649): EXCERPT

𝔅e it ... enacted ... that no person or persons ... professing to believe in Jesus Christ shall from henceforth be any ways troubled, molested, or discountenanced for, or in respect of, his or her religion, nor in the free exercise thereof within this province ...

Pennsylvania Charter of Privileges (1701): EXCERPT

𝔍 do hereby grant and declare that no person or persons, inhabiting in this province or territories, who shall confess and acknowledge *One* almighty God ... shall be in any case molested or prejudiced in his or their person or estate, because of his or their conscientious persuasion or practice ...

Massachusetts Bay Colony for Puritans. Men and women who refused to accept the official religious beliefs, or doctrines, were often thrown into jail or driven from the colony.

Roger Williams and a new idea. Roger Williams, as you have seen, was one of those rebellious spirits who dared to battle against intolerance. From his pulpit in a church in Salem, Massachusetts, he denied that the government had the right to coerce a man's conscience. Hearing that the Puritan authorities planned to send him back to England, he escaped from the colony and founded Providence, Rhode Island.

The colony of Rhode Island was small in size, but large in significance. It became a symbol of religious freedom for America and the whole world. There were no taxes for the support of the church, no laws requiring men to attend church, no religious qualifications for voting. All men might worship as they pleased, and all men might speak their minds freely.

Lord Baltimore and William Penn. Lord Baltimore and William Penn also won notable victories for the principle of religious toleration. In both Maryland and Pennsylvania this principle was written into the basic law.

Maryland, as you have seen, was settled originally as a haven for persecuted Catholics, as well as for economic reasons. From the beginning the leaders admitted both Catholics and Protestants. But friction developed, and Lord Baltimore secured passage of the Toleration Act of 1649.

The Toleration Act provided that no one "professing to believe in Jesus Christ shall from henceforth be any ways troubled, molested, or discountenanced for, or in respect of, his or her religion, nor in the free exercise thereof within this province." The Maryland act, however, did not overthrow public support of religion, as it was overthrown in Rhode Island; and the Maryland law gave no protection to Jews and those who did not profess belief in Jesus Christ.

In Pennsylvania, the legislative basis was broader than it was in Maryland, but not as broad as in Rhode Island. Any person could settle in Pennsylvania if he believed that "one Almighty and Eternal God" was the "Creator, Upholder, and Ruler of the World," but only Christians could take part in the government.

The growth of toleration. With Rhode Island, Maryland, and Pennsylvania leading the way, all of the colonies eventually grew more tolerant in matters of religion. As the years passed, it became

■ These three men played leading parts in planting and nurturing the roots of religious liberty in colonial America. Lord Baltimore (left) established the principle in Maryland; William Penn (center), in Pennsylvania; Roger Williams (right), in Rhode Island.

increasingly difficult for any single religious group to regulate the lives of all the settlers.

An important exception occurred in Maryland after 1689 when the Protestants finally overthrew the government of the Catholic proprietor. Under royal government from 1690 until 1715, the Catholics were deprived of the toleration benefits which their leaders had made a basic principle of the colony's government since 1634. The harsh laws passed against Catholics in the interval of royal rule were not repealed when a Protestant heir to the title of Lord Baltimore was restored to his rights in 1715, and Maryland again became a proprietary colony. Not until the American Revolution brought the overthrow of the established Anglican Church did Catholics in Maryland recover full religious liberty.

Church and state. The idea of tolerance, strained and retarded, struck at the foundations of the official state churches. If all religious groups were allowed to worship as they pleased, why should the state collect taxes for the support of a church to which many of the taxpayers did not belong?

Thus, as the years went by, the state churches in the British colonies lost more and more of their power. They became weaker than the state churches in England, the Scandinavian countries, the Netherlands, Germany, France, Spain, and Portugal. Although they continued to exist in New England and in the Southern Colonies until after the Revolutionary War, the movement that was to destroy their privileged position gathered strength in colonial America.

Thus the colonists began to order religious freedom in the American way. By the 1760's the roots had taken firm hold. One of America's great democratic ideals was slowly but steadily being transformed from a dream into a reality.

1. When settlers first came to America, there was almost no religious freedom in Europe. Why was this so?

2. "Most of the colonists who came to the New World in search of religious freedom were thinking only of freedom for themselves." Give facts to support this.

3. Justify this statement: Roger Williams had the most advanced ideas about democracy in New England.

4. What happened to toleration benefits for Catholics in Maryland in 1689 when the Catholic proprietor's government was ousted?

IDENTIFY: established church, Maryland Toleration Act, religious freedom, separation of church and state; 1649.

2

Freedom to learn and freedom to think strike fertile soil

Freedom to learn, to think, to speak, and to publish—as well as religious freedom—are among the essentials of the democratic way of life. People who do

■ In this crudely drawn but interesting early print, the building of Dartmouth College is halted while a professor gives a lesson.

not have these freedoms cannot vote intelligently or reach solutions to the problems, public and personal, with which they are confronted from day to day.

Dictators know this only too well. It is no accident that dictators who in our time have gained power have promptly seized control of all educational institutions, the radio and other means of communication, and the newspapers and other publications.

In the 1600's and 1700's freedom to learn, to think, to speak, and to publish was severely limited throughout most of Europe.

Old World ideas about education. Europeans in general accepted the idea that only wealthy men needed a formal education. There were, to be sure, exceptions to the general rule, and now and then an unusually able boy from a poor home received an education and rose to prominence. On the whole, however, it was the men of wealth who made the laws and ran the governments. It was accepted that they should have the best education money could provide. But most Europeans believed that this kind of education would be wasted on the ordinary people—the farmers, wage earners, and skilled workers.

The settlers brought these Old World ideas about education to the New World. The wealthy townsmen and planters hired tutors for their sons. They could also afford to buy books, pamphlets, and newspapers. The planters were able to spend time in the towns, where they had the opportunity to meet and talk with educated men from England and other countries. Wealthy colonists could send their sons to private schools and universities in England. If an English education was beyond their means, they could always send their sons to one of the nearby colonial colleges.

Nine colonial colleges were started before the Revolutionary War. These colleges were founded by men who had attended the older British institutions. They taught most of the same subjects as the older colleges in England. Latin and Greek were required subjects.

Changing ideas in education. Before long, however, the well-to-do colonists began to realize that their children needed a different kind of education. In the first place, the planters, who secured their income from exports to England, were forced to take an active part in business. As a result, unlike the country gentlemen of England, the Americans did not look down upon men who earned their living from trade. Indeed, many of the early planters' sons became prosperous and respected merchants.

In the second place, the well-to-do colonists were more concerned with education than were the country gentlemen of England. The Americans realized that in the rural, isolated society of the colonies it would be easy for their children to grow up in ignorance, no better educated than the masses of people whom the wealthy colonists considered their inferiors.

In the third place, as the merchants grew in numbers and influence, they began to ask the schools and colleges to provide more than the classics in their courses of study. Before the colonial period was ended, some of the schools were giving courses in navigation, geography, modern languages, accounting, commercial law, and other subjects more immediately useful to businessmen than Greek and Latin.

Finally, the scarcity of books in the colonies led many of the merchants to organize societies for the purpose of establishing libraries. Libraries of this type were, of course, open only to the members of these societies. In all sections of the country, however, civic-minded persons won enough support to get a few small public libraries established.

In these and other ways the environment of the New World modified the traditional ideas about education that the wealthy colonists had brought with them from England.

The first public schools. Money to buy books, to travel, to hire tutors, and to attend private schools and colleges was not available to most of the people—the small farmers living near the villages,

THE BEGINNINGS OF
HIGHER EDUCATION

During the colonial period, nine institutions of higher learning were started that have endured until the present, although the names of several have been changed. They are listed below with the dates of their founding, their present names, and their locations.

1636. Harvard University, Cambridge, Massachusetts.
1693. College of William and Mary in Virginia, Williamsburg, Virginia.
1701. Yale University, New Haven, Connecticut.
1740. University of Pennsylvania, Philadelphia, Pennsylvania.
1746. Princeton University, Princeton, New Jersey.
1754. Columbia University, New York City.
1764. Brown University, Providence, Rhode Island.
1766. Rutgers University, New Brunswick, Newark, and Camden, New Jersey.
1769. Dartmouth College, Hanover, New Hampshire.

Colonial school children

the frontiersmen, and the tradesmen and artisans of the towns. Most of their energy went into the hard job of earning a living. Yet a great many colonists learned to read, write, and do simple arithmetic. Even on the frontier, where neither schools nor churches existed, some children learned to read at the knees of their mothers. And in the towns some children, while learning a trade as apprentices, also learned to read and write and do simple arithmetic through the kindness of their master or his wife. And in all of the colonies, there were at least a few elementary schools that children of poorer families could attend.

In the Middle and Southern Colonies some schools were run by the various churches. But these schools were few and far between. South of Delaware the children of farmers and other workmen had only limited opportunities to go to school.

In the New England Colonies it was easier to get an education. The Puritan leaders believed that the people were more likely to become God-fearing and law-abiding citizens if they could read the Bible and sermons.

In 1647 the Massachusetts government passed a law requiring that all towns except very small ones must provide schools for the children. This was the first law of its kind passed in the colonies or in Europe. The law began by stating that in the past it had been "one chief point of that old deluder, Satan, to keep men from a knowledge of the Scriptures . . . by keeping them [the Scriptures] in an unknown tongue. . . ."

That the Scriptures were said to have been kept in an unknown tongue was deception. The Bible had been written in the chief written language of Europe at that time, Latin. The Reformation did much to hasten the need for translation of the Scriptures and all the truths of the Faith into the vernacular, the language of the people. One of the more famous translations was the King James Version of the Bible. It was published in England in 1611, about the time the colonists began to leave. The vernacular Bible was the basic reader from which New England developed literacy.

To encourage reading and to prevent learning from "being buried in the grave of our fathers," the Massachusetts law ordered (1) that every town having 50 householders or more should at once appoint a teacher of reading and writing and pay him out of town funds, (2) that every town having 100 householders or more must provide a school good enough to prepare young men for entering a college or pay a penalty for failure to do so.

The "Old Deluder Law," as it has been called, was not popular everywhere. Towns sometimes neglected to provide the education ordered by the law. Nevertheless, the law was a landmark in the history of education, for it expressed a new and daring idea about education.

The town schools of colonial New England have been rightly regarded as one of America's greatest contributions to modern civilization—public responsibility for education of all the people. And education, public or private, however paid for, has been and remains essential to our society and one of democracy's strongest roots.

The quality of schooling. Even where colonial schools existed, the quality of the education that they provided was not always high. The teachers, in many cases, were not much better educated than the children who sat before them. Often, especially in New England, the teacher was an elderly housewife, who heard the children's lessons while she did her washing and baking. Sometimes the village preacher conducted the classes.

In many schools indentured servants did the teaching. Although some of the indentured servants were able scholars of excellent character, others were inferior in every way.

The equipment of the colonial schools was most often of the simplest kind. Classes were usually held in a church, a town hall, or a private home. As a rule children of all ages sat in the same room and were taught by the same teacher. The terms were short. Attendance was irregular, for at any time a child might have to stay at home to plant or harvest crops, or to cut wood.

Blackboards, slates, paper, and crayons were seldom to be had. Textbooks were rare. The one exception was the *New England Primer*, which was widely used in the northern colonies. This little book first appeared about 1690, and more than 3,000,000 copies were sold during the 1700's. The primer was more than a reader. From it children were taught to be obedient, to be law-abiding citizens, and to worship God.

G	As runs the Glass, Our Life doth pass.
H	My Book and Heart Must never part.
I	J o b feels the Rod,— Yet bleffes GOD.
K	Proud Korah's troop Was fwallowed up
L	L o t fled to *Zoar*, Saw fiery Shower On *Sodom* pour.
M	Moses was he Who *Ifrael's* Hoft Led thro' the Sea.

■ The Bible was taught along with reading. Notice "M" in the *New England Primer* (above) and "The Lord's Prayer" (below), printed on paper, mounted in a hornbook, and covered by a sheet of transparent horn.

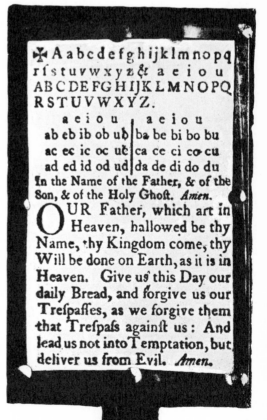

✠ A a b c d e f g h i j k l m n o p q r ſ s t u v w x y z & a e i o u
A B C D E F G H I J K L M N O P Q R S T U V W X Y Z.

a e i o u	a e i o u
ab eb ib ob ub	ba be bi bo bu
ac ec ic oc uc	ca ce ci co cu
ad ed id od ud	da de di do du

In the Name of the Father, & of the Son, & of the Holy Ghoft. *Amen.*

OUR Father, which art in Heaven, hallowed be thy Name, thy Kingdom come, thy Will be done on Earth, as it is in Heaven. Give us this Day our daily Bread, and forgive us our Trefpaffes, as we forgive them that Trefpafs againft us : And lead us not into Temptation, but deliver us from Evil. *Amen.*

Education on farms and frontier. The education of the plain folk in the colonies was not entirely limited to what they could learn at their mothers' knees, in the classroom, or as apprentices to a master craftsman. For the most part, the education of the frontiersmen and the pioneer farmers came from the practical school of experience. Face to face with problems for which they had no experience to guide them, men learned to think for themselves and to work out their own solutions. On the farm and frontier the individual had to be practical, inventive, self-sufficient, and versatile in his thinking. This was a new kind of education and, as you will see, it was to have a profound influence upon the development of American democracy.

Few books reached the frontier, but many of the pioneer farmers owned copies of the Bible and much-thumbed almanacs. The almanacs contained a wide variety of information, from advice on medicine, recipes, planting, and harvesting to discussions of politics and religion. The almanacs also contained selections from the great European writers and numerous homely maxims urging the farmers to be content with their lot, obedient, respectful, thrifty, and industrious. The farmers also received some intellectual stimulation from public meetings and from Sunday sermons.

■ The almanac of Benjamin Franklin ("Poor Richard") was widely read. Its weather data might serve "from Newfoundland to South Carolina."

Education in the towns. The plain folk in the towns—owners of small shops, artisans, longshoremen, fishermen, and others—had larger opportunities than the farmers or frontiersmen to secure an education. In addition to the regular schools, there were by the 1700's an increasing number of private evening schools where students might learn mathematics, accounting, modern languages, and other subjects useful to a man interested in business.

Reading material was also easier to secure in the towns. There were Bibles, almanacs, a few books, pamphlets, and, by the 1700's, a growing number of newspapers. People who could not afford to buy the newspapers could always read them or hear them read at a nearby tavern. The papers contained news, sermons, and articles contributed by readers. The townsmen also picked up news and ideas from public meetings, informal gatherings at the taverns, and debating societies that they sometimes organized. In these ways, the workers who lived in the colonial towns learned to think for themselves and to express their opinions.

Victory for a free press. From the earliest days many colonial leaders looked with misgivings at the growing spirit of independence. These leaders were clinging to an old idea that it was dangerous to educate men and women

---

Poor Richard, **1733.**

A N

Almanack

For the Year of Chrift

1 7 3 3,

Being the Firft after LEAP YEAR.

And makes fince the Creation	Years
By the Account of the Eaftern *Greeks*	7241
By the Latin Church, when ☉ ent. ♈	6932
By the Computation of *W.W.*	5742
By the *Roman* Chronology	5682
By the *Jewifh* Rabbies.	5494

Wherein is contained

The Lunations, Eclipfes, Judgment of the Weather, Spring Tides, Planets Motions & mutual Afpects, Sun and Moon's Rifing and Setting, Length of Days, Time of High Water, Fairs, Courts, and obfervable Days.

Fitted to the Latitude of Forty Degrees, and a Meridian of Five Hours Weft from *London*, but may without fenfible Error, ferve all the adjacent Places, even from *Newfoundland* to *South-Carolina*

By *RICHARD SAUNDERS*, Philom.

PHILADELPHIA:
Printed and fold by *B. FRANKLIN*, at the New Printing-Office near the Market

or allow them to read freely. They were afraid that education would encourage the rise of what they called a "barbarous, rude, or stubborn" class of servants who would prove to be "pests instead of blessings to the country." This point of view was expressed in unmistakable terms by William Berkeley, governor of Virginia, who on one occasion boasted that there were neither free schools nor printing presses in Virginia while he was governor.

Many colonists held a directly opposite point of view. These colonists believed that people should be free to learn, to think, and to express their opinions. They also believed that printers should be free to print and distribute their own thoughts and the thoughts of others.

One colonial printer, John Peter Zenger, dared to publish articles criticizing the royal governor of New York. His victory in a famous trial in 1735 marked a long step forward toward freedom of the press. From this beginning in colonial times, freedom of speech and of the press has developed into one of the strongest roots of the democratic way of life.

SECTION SURVEY

1. (a) What Old World ideas about education did the colonists bring with them to the New World? (b) Describe four conditions in the colonies that helped to change these ideas.

2. Why was the Massachusetts education law of 1647 a landmark in the history of education?

3. How did education in the towns compare with schooling on pioneer farms and on the frontier?

4. Why did some colonists object to free public education?

5. Why was the trial of John Peter Zenger a landmark of American democracy?

IDENTIFY: "Old Deluder Law," *New England Primer*, almanac, freedom of speech, freedom of the press; William Berkeley; 1735.

PETER ZENGER'S TRIAL

The famous trial of John Peter Zenger took place in August 1735, in a warm, crowded courtroom in the city of New York. The evidence was all against Zenger. He had been arrested in the autumn of 1734 for printing criticisms of the governor in his newspaper, the *New York Weekly Journal.* Under British law, this made him guilty of criminal libel, even if the criticisms were true.

Zenger's only hope was the jury. Among the members were several of his friends and neighbors. He knew that some of them believed the law was bad. He knew that some of them believed that a newspaper should be allowed to print the truth, even if the truth offended the governing authorities. But would the members of the jury have the courage to ignore the instructions of the judges?

Fortunately for Zenger, he was defended by one of the ablest lawyers in America, Andrew Hamilton of Philadelphia. Hamilton addressed the jury with force and passion. When you decide this case, he said, you will be deciding far more than the fate of a poor printer. You will be deciding the fate of every free man in the British colonies. Peter Zenger, he continued, has been fighting for the right to speak and write the truth. He has been fighting for liberty. Set him free, and you will take your places by his side.

Hamilton's magnificent plea won the day. When the jury filed back into the room and the foreman announced the verdict "Not guilty," the spectators burst into a roar of applause. John Peter Zenger, editor and publisher, walked out of the courtroom a free man. With the brilliant aid of lawyer Andrew Hamilton, he had helped to establish the principle of freedom of the press.

3 The colonists acquire valuable experience in self-government

In their colonial governments, as well as in religion and education, the colonists fought for a larger measure of freedom. During the course of their struggle, they gained experience in politics and firmly planted the roots of representative government.

Virginia led the way in 1619, as you have seen, with the creation of the House of Burgesses. The House of Burgesses gave the colony of Virginia the first representative government in the New World. It also provided an example for the other colonies England planted along the Atlantic seaboard.

Types of colonial governments. England established three types of colonies in America, as you know. There were royal colonies belonging to the English Crown, proprietary colonies belonging to proprietors, and self-governing colonies practically independent of English control. Each colony had a governor, a council, and a representative assembly.

In a royal colony—and by the 1760's eight of the thirteen colonies were royal colonies—the governor and his councilors, appointed by the king, administered the laws, sat as a high court of justice, and acted as the *upper house* of the legislature. The *lower house,* or assembly, was elected by the qualified voters. Although the lower house helped to make the laws, its actions could be vetoed by the king or the king's representatives.

In proprietary colonies—including, by the 1760's, Maryland, Pennsylvania, and Delaware—the proprietor was granted a large amount of power by the king of England. The proprietor in turn appointed the governor and, in the case of Maryland, the councilors who formed the upper house of the legislature. The lower house was elected by the voters, just as it was in the eight royal colonies. In Pennsylvania there was only one house—the assembly—in the legislature.

The two remaining colonies, Rhode

■ In this famous building at Williamsburg, the Virginia House of Burgesses met after 1705. Its red brick walls, tower, dormers, and evenly spaced windows mark it as a forerunner of the Georgian style of architecture, widely used in England and America by the mid-1700's.

Island and Connecticut, were self-governing. Each was almost completely independent of England. The voters elected the governor and the representatives in both the upper and lower houses of the legislature.

Connecticut's written constitution. Connecticut had the further distinction of being the first colony to adopt a *written constitution.*° This constitution, or plan of government, was known as the Fundamental Orders of Connecticut. As you have seen, it was adopted in 1639, only three years after Thomas Hooker and his fellow settlers arrived on the banks of the Connecticut River. Its eleven "orders," or laws, provided a detailed guide for the organization of the government and the election of officers.

With the adoption of the Fundamental Orders, the Connecticut settlers established a *government under written law.* When disputes arose, it was the written law that would provide the answer, not the opinions of the members of the legislature. The principle of government under a written constitution, a principle adopted in 1639 by the little colony of Connecticut, became one of the cornerstones of American representative government.

It is important to remember, however, that neither in Connecticut nor in any of the other colonies were the people thinking of what we now call democracy. Most of the settlers probably had never even heard this word. Representative assemblies were organized in each of the English colonies because the principle had already been established in England with the House of Commons, the lower house of Parliament. Thomas Hooker and his followers wrote the Fundamental Orders because they had an immediate problem to solve, the problem of governing them-

....

° *written constitution:* Constitutions may be in the form of written documents like the Constitution of the United States. Some constitutions are referred to as unwritten because the principles of government are not listed in a single document, as, for example, in Great Britain.

selves in a new community, and this seemed to be the best way to solve it.

Limitations on self-government. Regardless of the reason, the fact remains that from the beginning the people had a voice in the government of each of the British colonies along the Atlantic seaboard. But in the colonies, as well as in England at that time, it was a somewhat limited voice.

The right to vote was limited in several ways. In the first place, it was limited to adult males who owned a specified amount of property. To vote, a man had to prove that he owned a farm or town lot of a stated size or that he had an income and paid taxes of a stated amount. These *property qualifications* existed even in the self-governing colonies of Connecticut and Rhode Island.

In the second place, *religious qualifications* kept many people from voting. In many colonies, particularly during the 1600's, men who did not belong to the established state church were not permitted to vote.

In addition to the people who were not permitted to vote, there were many who might have voted, but who were too indifferent to take the trouble. Some of these people had never enjoyed political rights in the Old World, and when they came to the colonies, they did not concern themselves with political problems. Finally, the isolation in which so many of the frontiersmen

BACON'S REBELLION

"Mr. Drummond, you are welcome," Governor William Berkeley of Virginia said when one of the ringleaders of Bacon's Rebellion was brought before him. "I am more glad to see you than any man in Virginia. Mr. Drummond, you shall be hanged in half an hour." Mr. Drummond *was* executed. So, too, were 36 other leaders of the rebellion.

Such was the end of the rebellion that broke out in Virginia in 1676. For many years the frontiersmen and small farmers had been dissatisfied with the rule of Governor Berkeley. They claimed that the plain folk of the colony were not adequately represented in the legislature. They further claimed that Governor Berkeley and the wealthy planters along the coast had deliberately refused to crush an Indian uprising, not wishing to anger the Indians, with whom many of the planters carried on a profitable fur trade.

Goaded to desperation by the massacre of white settlers in the outlying regions of Virginia, a number of small farmers, led by Nathaniel Bacon, took matters into their own hands. Several hundred of them marched to the frontier and killed more than 150 Indians. They then turned upon the rulers of the colony, seized Jamestown, secured control of the legislature, and passed a number of laws favorable to the plain folk.

But the rebellion was short-lived. The leader, Nathaniel Bacon, died as a result of exposure. Berkeley and the great planters recovered power and crushed the remnants of the resistance. But Bacon's Rebellion was an example of growing unrest in the colonies.

lived kept many of them from voting and from otherwise participating in the government.

The qualifications for election to the assemblies were even higher than the qualifications for voting. These qualifications varied from colony to colony. In some colonies they were very high. In South Carolina, for example, an assemblyman had to own 500 acres of land and ten slaves or land, houses, and other property worth a substantial sum of money. Because of these and other qualifications, the representatives elected to the colonial assemblies were generally men of considerable wealth and influence.

The struggle over the assemblies. The ordinary people of the colonies quite naturally resented this concentration of political power in the hands of the well-to-do people. The resentment of these people led to continued antagonism and occasional outbreaks of violence.

This conflict between the well-to-do and the plain folk, most of whom were farmers, is sometimes referred to as the conflict between the seaboard and the frontier. The wealthy people on the seaboard—great planters on the fertile tidewater land, rich town merchants, and influential lawyers—controlled the assemblies and voted for those laws that would advance their own interests. The ordinary people—artisans, pioneer farmers, and frontiersmen—with only a limited voice in the assemblies, had no legal means by which to protect themselves from laws harmful to their interests. Nor could they secure passage of laws that would provide them with ready cash, lower taxes, lower interest rates on the mortgages° on their homes and farms, and lower fees for deeds° to land.

••

° *mortgage:* When anyone borrows money to buy real estate, he signs a mortgage agreeing to turn the property over to the moneylender if the money, plus interest, is not repaid within a definite time.

° *deed:* a legal document proving ownership of land.

Out of their long-continued struggle for control of the colonial legislatures, the colonists acquired practical experience in politics. It was in their local governments, however, and especially in New England communities, that the colonists enjoyed the greatest opportunity to practice the art of self-government.

The need for local government. From the very beginning every community, large or small, had to establish rules, or laws, for the conduct of the everyday affairs of community life. In many of the early communities, defense against Indian attack was one of the most serious problems. For all of the communities, there were problems of fire and police protection, sanitation, schooling, the settlement of disputes between citizens, and scores of other practical matters.

No one questioned the need for local government. There was, however, a big question to be answered in all the colonies. Who would make and enforce the laws for the local community?

New England local government. The Pilgrims anticipated this question even before they set foot on the shores of New England. As you have seen, on November 11, 1620, shortly after they anchored in what is now the harbor of Provincetown, the Pilgrims drew up the Mayflower Compact. The men who signed this document agreed to make "such just and equal laws . . . as shall be thought most meet and convenient for the general good of the colony." They also promised that they would obey these laws.

The significance of the Mayflower Compact lay in the fact that in it a group of ordinary people took part in making an agreement under which they were to live. For this reason, the document marked an important milestone along the road to government of and by and for the people.

After they settled at Plymouth, and with the Mayflower Compact as their guide, the Pilgrims established a form of local government that other New England communities later adopted. This new form of local government came to be called the *town meeting*.

On "town meeting" days all of the citizens of the community gathered in the town hall to discuss town problems, levy taxes on themselves, and elect town officers. The discussions sometimes became heated, for every citizen had the right to say what he thought.

The principal town officers were the "selectmen," usually three in number, who administered the laws that the voters adopted in the town meeting. Only the men voted, and in the early days the right to vote was limited by religious and property qualifications. Nevertheless, the New England town meetings provided larger opportunities to participate in government than the citizens enjoyed in either the Middle or the Southern Colonies.

Local government in Southern and Middle Colonies. The town meeting type of government met the needs of the people who lived in the compact farming villages and towns of New England. In the Southern Colonies, where most people lived on large plantations or on more or less isolated farms, local government had to cover a much larger area than a town. In the South, therefore, the people established the *county* as the unit of local government. Some southern counties included several hundred square miles.

The chief officers of the county were the "justices of the peace." These officers administered the laws, acted as judges in legal disputes, levied and collected taxes, provided for roads, and distributed county funds to widows, orphans, and other people unable to take care of themselves. There was also a "county lieutenant," who was responsible for defending the county against Indian uprisings and against civilian disturbances of any sort. All of these officers were usually appointed by the governor, but he chose them from people living in the county itself.

The Middle Colonies adopted a mixture of both the town and the county type of local government. In New York the town was more apt to be the unit

Elected colonial assemblymen   *Royal governor and aides*

of local government; in Pennsylvania the county was more important.

Growing spirit of independence. The local governments, regardless of the type, dealt with everyday problems of immediate concern to the people. It was at the local level, therefore, that most citizens received their first lessons in self-government. And, as you will see, the experience and confidence that they gained in local and colonial government strengthened their determination to exercise a larger measure of control over the royal and proprietary governors.

☞ **SECTION SURVEY**

1. Discuss the similarities and differences among the three types of colonial government.

2. Why are the Mayflower Compact and the Fundamental Orders of Connecticut regarded as landmarks of American democracy?

3. There were many undemocratic practices in colonial America. Illustrate this fact by referring to restrictions on voting and office holding.

4. In the colonies a struggle developed for control of the colonial assemblies. Explain.

5. Show how the types of local government served as "schools of practical experience" for the colonists.

IDENTIFY: upper house, lower house, written constitution, "government under written law," Bacon's Rebellion, town meeting, county; 1639.

4 Colonial legislative assemblies gain power in America

The struggle for a larger voice in the colonial governments was only one of the continuing conflicts of the colonial period. In the royal colonies, as you have seen, the British king appointed the governors and the councilors; in the proprietary colonies the British proprietors, who usually lived in England, appointed the governors and councilors. Except in the self-governing colonies of Rhode Island and Connecticut, then, the colonial governments were really split into two parts. The governor and the councilors represented the interests of Great Britain and the Empire as a whole. The assembly, on the other hand, represented the interests of the colonies.

Attitude of British officials. Because of this divided control the storms of political controversy in the colonies centered on the royal governors. Most of these officials were selected from the ruling group in England—politicians, lawyers, and soldiers—although now and then a privileged colonist was favored by the Crown with an appointment as royal governor of one of the colonies.

In making appointments to the royal colonies, the Crown did not necessarily look for men with ability. Sometimes royal favorites were given jobs as a reward for services rendered to, or friendship for, the king and his companions. Some of the royal governors were excellent administrators who tried to balance British and colonial interests. A few were narrow-minded, shortsighted men who had little qualification, by training or experience, for the offices to which they were appointed.

Sir William Berkeley, who governed Virginia from 1642 until 1653, and again from 1658 to 1677, was charged, somewhat unjustly, with using his power to gain privileges for himself and friends at the expense of others. But whether good, bad, or indifferent, the governors used their position to increase their own fortunes, and they were sometimes willing to pay handsomely to secure the jobs.

The military officers and clerks who served the royal governors were, as a rule, no better than their superiors. They were often appointed merely because they happened to be friends of the governor or his family.

Bad as these practices were, we should remember that they prevailed in England as well as in the colonies. We should also remember that there were many able men in positions of authority in the colonies. The fundamental problem, as you know, was that the royal officials believed that the colonies existed chiefly to serve the interests of the mother country, or the interests of the Empire as a whole.

Growing power of the assemblies. The majority of the colonists, speaking through their representatives in the assemblies, held the opposite point of view. Why, they asked, should they pay taxes to furnish high salaries to countless outsiders from England, many of whom were lazy and incompetent? And what right had anybody to say that the interests of the colonists were less important than the interests of Englishmen in the mother country?

Fortunately for the colonists, they possessed one extremely powerful weapon with which to curb the authority of the royal governors. They controlled the purse strings. That is, the colonial assemblies had the power to vote all grants of money to be spent by the colonial governments.

Suppose the governor asked for money with which to pay the salaries of ten new clerks whom he wished to appoint. The assembly could immediately say, "Yes, we'll grant you the money—provided you allow us to name the men whom you appoint to these offices." Or, to take another instance, suppose the governor requested money to pay his official expenses. The assembly could say, "Yes, we'll grant the money—provided you *first* submit an itemized statement explaining in detail how the money will be spent."

On other occasions the assemblies refused to grant funds for the governors' salaries until the end of each year. In this way, the colonists served notice upon the governors that they would do well to rule wisely. "Let us keep the dogs poor," one member of the New Jersey legislature disrespectfully remarked, "and we'll make them do what we please."

The governors hated these limitations upon their power, but they were unable to do much about them. They needed money to carry on the everyday business of the colonies, and they wanted good salaries for themselves. This money could come only from the assemblies. Even before the Revolutionary War, the colonial assemblies were, in most respects, practically their own masters. They had, to a considerable extent, won their freedom from control by the British government.

✔ **SECTION SURVEY**

1. Explain this statement: During the colonial period, "the colonial governments were really split into two parts."

2. If you had been a colonist in Virginia, what criticism could you have made concerning the royal governor and his appointees?

3. Show how the colonial assemblies used their control of the purse strings to limit the power of the royal governors.

■ **CHAPTER SURVEY** (For review, see Section Surveys, pages 78, 83, 88, 89.)

Points to Discuss: 1. The environment of the colonies gradually made changes in ideas and ways of life brought from the Old World. Compare and discuss Old World and New World ideas of political, economic, and social aspects of life.

2. Freedom of thought and expression has been called the basic freedom of democracy. Do you agree? Why?

3. Compare education in colonial times with education today.

4. Curtis P. Nettels, an authority on colonial history, has said: "The basic institutions of American government and the prevailing political philosophies of today were shaped in large measure during the colonial period." Support this statement by relating specific developments in the colonial period to present-day institutions or patterns.

5. What connection can you see between the rise of local self-government and the spirit of independence that led to the American Revolution?

Using Maps: 1. Geographical factors were an important influence in determining the forms that local government took in the New England, Middle, and Southern Colonies. Discuss.

2. Geographic differences between the Piedmont and seaboard areas in the South also led to political differences. Explain this statement, using the map on pages 818–19.

Consulting the Sources: Read the account of Bacon's Rebellion in Commager and Nevins, *The Heritage of America*, pages 53–61.

■ **TRACING THE MAIN IDEAS**

The first small roots of democracy struck fertile soil in the British seaboard colonies. The colonists brought with them from Europe the idea of a class system. They accepted, at first, the Old World restrictions on individual freedom in regard to religion, education, and the right to vote and hold public office. But discontent began to grow, slowly during the early years of colonization, then more rapidly.

Stimulated by the growth of freedom in England itself and even more by the environment of the New World, the set-

tlers began to demand larger freedom for themselves. During the course of their struggles, they gained practical experience in politics and self-government. They established the principles of religious toleration, free public education, and representative government.

As you will see in Chapter 6, the colonists in the process of developing their own way of life had grown much further away from Great Britain by 1763 than the British realized. This lack of understanding led to controversies, and finally, in 1775, to armed conflict.

Unit Survey (Reread "Tracing the Main Ideas," pages 24, 44, 60, 73, 90.)

OUTSTANDING EVENTS

1492 Columbus discovers America.
1497–98 John Cabot's explorations.
1498 Vasco da Gama's voyage.
1513 Balboa discovers Pacific Ocean.
1519 Cortez lands in Mexico.
1519–22 Magellan's men circle earth.
1534 Cartier makes first voyage.
1588 English defeat Spanish Armada.
1603 Champlain makes first voyage.
1607 Jamestown is founded.
1609 Hudson explores Hudson River.
1619 House of Burgesses meets.
1619 First slaves brought to Virginia.
1620 Pilgrims reach Cape Cod.
1620 Mayflower Compact.
1630 Massachusetts Bay Colony founded.
1639 Fundamental Orders of Connecticut.
1643 New England Confederation formed.
1647 Massachusetts passes school law.
1649 Maryland Toleration Act.
1651–63 Principal Navigation Acts.
1664 English take over New Netherland.
1673 Exploration by Marquette, Joliet.
1681–82 Exploration of Mississippi River by La Salle.
1686 Dominion of New England created.
1733 Molasses Act.
1735 Zenger trial.
1754 French and Indian War starts.
1754 Albany Plan of Union proposed.
1759 British capture Quebec.
1763 Treaty of Paris.

THEN AND NOW

1. Why is Columbus Day, October 12, celebrated today in three different countries: the United States, Spain, and Italy?

2. What is the historical explanation of the Thanksgiving holiday in November?

3. In what ways are the problems of space travel today like problems faced by explorers more than 300 years ago?

EXTENDING YOUR HORIZON

1. Prepare a report from the *Dictionary of American Biography* on Michel Guillaume de Crèvecœur. Read his 18th-century account "What Is an American?" in H. S. Commager (ed.), *America in Perspective*.

2. Read Chapter 1 of Ellis, *American Catholicism*, "The Church in Colonial America," and prepare a report on the Maryland settlement or a report on Spanish and French missionary activities in North America. (Good source material for such reports may be found in Ellis, *Documents of American Catholic History*.)

3. For the story of the extreme heroism of a French missionary, see Robert L. Reynolds, "The Ultimate Courage of Jean de Brebeuf," *American Heritage*, October 1959.

4. If you are interested in medicine, read the article of Laurence Farmer, M.D., "When Cotton Mather Fought the Smallpox," in *American Heritage*, August 1957.

INDIVIDUAL ACTIVITIES

1. Maps can often tell interesting as well as useful things. A map of the United States, for example, shows that many American cities, rivers, and mountains have names that are French, Spanish, Dutch, or Indian. Using maps of the United States, such as those on pages 818–19 and 846–47, see whether you can support that statement about American place names.

2. On an outline map of the world (sketch one if you wish), show in different colors the routes followed by the Portuguese, Spanish, French, and English explorers from 1450 to 1700.

3. Draw a time line five inches long and label each inch as follows: 1450, 1500, 1550, 1600, 1650, 1700. Along this line insert the discoveries of the Spanish, Portuguese, French, and English explorers.

GROUP ACTIVITIES

1. Select a class committee to prepare a wall chart on the original colonies using these headings: Colony, Date, Founders, Motives, Significant Names and Events.

2. Have a committee make a bulletin board "pin" or "yarn" map of the United States. Use rotating committees to keep the map up to date through use of appropriate material. The use of three-dimensional figures is effective.

3. Let panels prepare reports for the class on life in the New England, the Middle, and the Southern Colonies. Be sure to compare and contrast the economic, politi-

cal, and social developments as these were influenced by climate and geography.

4. Let a committee prepare a time line for classroom display covering the period 1450 to 1763. Above the line indicate important events in the American colonies; below the line insert important events in Europe.

SUGGESTED FURTHER READING

Books for more mature students are starred in this and later reading lists.

GENERAL REFERENCE BOOKS

The following books may be useful throughout the study of American history.

ADAMS, JAMES T., *Album of American History,* Scribner, 4 vols. Pictorial.

——, *Dictionary of American History,* Scribner, 6 vols.

ANGLE, PAUL M., *The American Reader,* Rand McNally. Selected primary sources.

COMMAGER, HENRY STEELE, ed. *Documents of American History,* Appleton-Century-Crofts. Comprehensive primary sources.

COMMAGER, HENRY STEELE, and ALLAN NEVINS, *The Heritage of America,* Little, Brown. Selected primary sources.

ELLIS, JOHN TRACY, *American Catholicism,* Univ. of Chicago Press.

——, ed., *Documents of American Catholic History,* Bruce.

GABRIEL, RALPH H., *The Pageant of America: A Pictorial History of the United States,* Yale Univ. Press, 15 vols.

JOHNSON, ALLEN, ed., *Dictionary of American Biography,* Scribner, 22 vols.

MORRIS, RICHARD, *The Encyclopedia of American History,* Harper. Valuable for ready reference.

STARR, ISIDORE, L. P. TODD, and M. CURTI, *Living American Documents,* Harcourt, Brace. Selected primary sources.

BIOGRAPHY

EATON, JEANETTE, *Lone Journey: The Life of Roger Williams,* Harcourt, Brace.

GALT, THOMAS, *John Peter Zenger,* Crowell.

°MORISON, SAMUEL ELIOT, *Admiral of the Ocean Sea,* Little, Brown. About Columbus.

——, *Christopher Columbus, Mariner,* Little, Brown; New American Library (Mentor Books).

NOLAN, JEANNETTE, *La Salle and the Grand Enterprise,* Messner.

SHIPPEN, KATHERINE, *Leif Eriksson: First Voyager to America,* Harper.

WOOD, WILLIAM C., *Elizabethan Sea Dogs,* Yale Univ. Press.

OTHER NONFICTION

ANDREWS, C. M., *Colonial Folkways,* Yale Univ. Press.

——, *Fathers of New England,* Yale Univ. Press.

BOULTON, HERBERT E., *Spanish Exploration in the Southwest, 1542–1706,* Barnes and Noble.

COLLIER, JOHN, *Indians of the Americas,* New American Library (Mentor Books).

FISHER, SYDNEY, *Quaker Colonies,* Yale Univ. Press.

JOHNSTON, MARY, *Pioneers of the Old South,* Yale Univ. Press.

LAMB, HAROLD, *New Found World,* Doubleday.

LANGDON, WILLIAM C., *Everyday Things in American Life,* Scribner.

°MATTINGLY, GARRETT, *The Armada,* Houghton Mifflin.

MUNRO, WM. B., and G. M. WRONG, *Adventures in New France,* Yale Univ. Press.

PARKMAN, FRANCIS, *The Parkman Reader,* Ed. by Samuel Eliot Morison, Little, Brown. Selected from classic work on French-English conflict in North America.

——, *The Discovery of the Great West: La Salle,* Ed. by William R. Taylor, Rinehart (paper).

——, *Jesuits in North America,* Little, Brown.

STARKEY, MARION LENA, *The Devil in Massachusetts,* Knopf.

HISTORICAL FICTION

CATHER, WILLA, *Shadows on the Rock,* Knopf. Colonial life in French Canada.

COOPER, JAMES FENIMORE, *The Last of the Mohicans,* Dodd, Mead; and others. Indian fighting.

FORBES, ESTHER, *Paradise,* World Book. Life on the Massachusetts frontier.

HAWTHORNE, NATHANIEL, *The House of the Seven Gables,* Macmillan; and others.

——, *The Scarlet Letter,* Dodd, Mead; and others. Psychological novel.

JOHNSTON, MARY, *To Have and to Hold,* Houghton Mifflin; Pocket Books. Novel of romance in the colonies.

——, *The Slave Ship,* Little, Brown.

ROBERTS, KENNETH, *Northwest Passage,* Doubleday. French and Indian War.

PART 1

CREATING A NEW NATION

When Thomas Jefferson was born in 1743 on the frontier of Virginia, the thirteen American colonies were part of the British Empire. From New Hampshire south through Georgia, there was a thin line of settlement along the Atlantic coast. The people, nine out of ten of whom were farmers, looked eastward to Great Britain for political leadership.

During his lifetime, Jefferson took a leading part in a far-reaching political revolution. When he died in 1826, the United States was a proudly independent nation, a federal union of 24 states, and the advancing frontier had crossed the Mississippi River.

As late as the 1820's, however, nearly nine out of every ten Americans were still living on farms or in rural areas. The Industrial Revolution that was to transform America from an agricultural to an industrial nation was only beginning when Thomas Jefferson was carried to his final resting place.

UNIT TWO

Winning Independence

1763–1789

New Tensions Strain Old Loyalties

NEW YORK—
FROM THE EAST RIVER 1760's

FORT GEORGE

The BATTERY

OLD DUTCH CHURCH

TRINITY CHURCH

CITY HALL

THE year 1763 was one of the proudest in Great Britain's history. Victorious over all its rivals, Great Britain had established claims to an empire that circled the globe. British harbors were jammed with shipping. Battered units of the British navy and weatherworn transports rode in on the incoming tides, bringing the fighting men of Great Britain back to their homes and families. Other vessels weighed anchor and sailed out of the harbors carrying government military personnel to the far-flung outposts of the empire.

To the average Britisher the future appeared brighter than it had for many years. But thoughtful men in Great Britain and in other countries realized that the British Empire faced a number of new and troublesome problems, particularly in the American colonies of the New World. One of these thoughtful observers was the French statesman Count Vergennes (ver-ZHEN).

Vergennes predicted a speedy end to Great Britain's moment of glory. "The American colonies stand no longer in need of England's protection," he said. "She will call on them to help contribute toward supporting the burden they have helped to bring on her, and they will answer by striking off all dependence."

Vergennes proved to be an accurate prophet. Just thirteen years after his prediction, the British colonies along the Atlantic seaboard declared their independence from Great Britain.

AS THE STORY DEVELOPS

1. Great Britain faces problems in governing its empire.
2. Taxation without representation inflames the colonists.
3. Tension increases between Great Britain and the colonies.
4. The clash of interests in America leads to a deadlock.

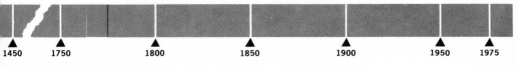

1450   1750   1800   1850   1900   1950   1975

1 Great Britain faces problems in governing its empire

The peace that came with victory in 1763 brought no rest to the governing officials in Great Britain. Candles and lamps in government offices burned late into the night as the British leaders wrestled with the problems of reorganizing the rapidly growing empire.

Need for new taxes. One problem was the need for more money. The British, as you know, had fought four costly wars between 1689 and 1763. In the last of these conflicts, known in Europe as the Seven Years' War and in America as the French and Indian War, British troops had fought in Europe, Asia, and Africa, as well as in America. The wars left Great Britain heavily in debt. To make matters worse, the British government now needed even more money to maintain the military and naval defenses of its world-wide empire.

British leaders quite naturally expected the American colonists—who were also subjects of the king—to help pay the war debts and the cost of defense, especially of their own defense. In short, the British government now had to collect more taxes from the colonists.

Florida and Canada. Another troublesome problem was that of the newly acquired holdings in North America. The governments of Florida and Canada had to be completely reorganized. Spaniards and Frenchmen in these areas, long-time enemies of Great Britain, were now British subjects. But they were British subjects in name only. How could they be made loyal subjects?

What kind of government would work best in these newly acquired regions?

The western lands. No less troublesome was the problem of organizing a government for the wilderness beyond the Appalachian Mountains. With the defeat of the French, all semblance of law and order had vanished from this region. Fearful that colonial farmers would pour over the mountains and destroy their hunting grounds, the Indians went on the warpath. The uprising known as Pontiac's Conspiracy started in 1763 under the able leadership of Pontiac, chief of the Ottawa Indians and a formidable foe. For nearly a year death and destruction raged along the western frontier (see map, opposite page). Settlers fled eastward as the flames of their burning cabins lighted the surrounding forest and the war whoops of the Indians rang in their ears.

To add to the confusion, the British themselves did not agree as to what should be done with the lands west of the Appalachians. One group, led by the Hudson's Bay Company, was interested solely in the fur trade. This group urged the government to keep settlers from moving across the mountains into the western lands. Another group, including most of the colonists, urged the government to do all it could to develop the western lands as a farming region.

Even more complicated was the question of the ownership of the lands beyond the Appalachian Mountains. As the map shows on the opposite page, several colonies claimed land in this region. These claims were based on the original colonial charters, several of

Fort Boonesborough, later Boonesboro, Kentucky

Pontiac's Conspiracy, 1763

Proclamation Line of 1763

Western lands claimed by the colonies

Added to Quebec by Quebec Act, 1774

which had granted territory "from sea to sea." In theory, that is, some of the colonial claims reached to the Pacific Ocean! But, as the map also shows, some of the colonies claimed the same land. Here was another problem with which the British had to wrestle.

Weakness of British leaders. War debts and defense costs, the government of Florida and Canada, and the question of ownership of the western lands—these were only a few of the serious problems facing the British government in 1763.

In order to solve these problems, Great Britain needed the wisest of statesmen—men with ideals, men broadly educated, men who could understand the needs of the colonies and therefore reconcile them with the needs of Great Britain. But men of this type were not in power at the time. George III, who was king from 1760 to 1820, was a stubborn, narrow-minded individual who viewed the colonies as mere dependencies° of Great Britain. When he became king, he surrounded himself with "yes men"—ministers, that is, whose first thought was always to please their master.

The stage set for trouble. In 1763 it was clear to everyone concerned that there were serious differences of opinion between British officials and American colonists. The British pointed out that they had saved the colonists from the French and Indian menace. They also pointed out that the colonists were being protected by the British army and navy. The British believed, therefore, that it was only fair for the colonists to help pay part of the cost of protecting the empire and themselves.

To this view many of the colonists replied that the war was now over and that they wanted to be left alone. Farmers, frontiersmen, merchants, and manufacturers were anxious to pursue their own interests without being bothered by the problems of keeping an empire together. Southerners, New Englanders, middle colonists, although many were Englishmen, had begun to look upon themselves as having problems quite different from those of England.

••

° *dependency:* a territory or region subject to the control of a more powerful country, but not considered as part of that country.

SECTION SURVEY

1. "The peace that came with victory in 1763 brought no rest to the governing officials in Great Britain." Describe the problems of reorganization which victory had brought to plague the British officials.
2. Indicate several reasons why the question of what to do with lands west of the Appalachians was difficult to solve.
3. (a) Imagine that you are a British official living in the American colonies in 1763. What arguments could you use to persuade the colonists that they ought to pay taxes to the British government? (b) As an American colonist, how might you reply to these arguments?

IDENTIFY: dependency, Pontiac's Conspiracy; 1763.

2 Taxation without representation inflames the colonists

Starting in 1763, the British government began to adopt a series of measures designed to put its empire on a sound footing. The person responsible for these measures was George Grenville, who became prime minister, or leader of the British government, in 1763. To the surprise of Grenville and other British officials, as well as to George III, all of their efforts to reform colonial administration met with strenuous opposition from the colonists. The root of the trouble was rising resentment among the colonists over laws passed by a Parliament in which they were not represented. Step by step the gap between the mother country and the American colonies grew wider.

The Proclamation of 1763. As a first move in the new colonial program, George III announced in the Proclamation of 1763 that all lands west of the Appalachian Mountains in the area formerly claimed by France now belonged to the British Crown. In this official declaration the king also ordered all settlers to withdraw temporarily to the east of a line along the crest of the Appalachian Mountains (see map, page 97). This measure, prompted by Pontiac's uprising, attempted to reduce friction between the settlers and the Indians by reserving certain areas of land for the Indians. Royal control was extended over the fur trade of the entire western region, and no trader was permitted to cross the mountains without the permission of British officials.

To the average Britisher the measure appeared reasonable. At last Great Britain had recognized the need for a uniform policy in regard to the Indians, the fur trade, and the disposal of western lands. The temporary prohibition against settlement and trade in the western lands would give the British government an opportunity to develop a long-range policy without the distraction of conflicts between settlers and Indians.

But American fur traders and colonists who looked forward to settling on the western lands were filled with resentment. So, too, were colonial merchants who outfitted the traders and real estate speculators who had already acquired land beyond the Alleghenies.

The Sugar Act of 1764. While the tempers of the colonists were still inflamed by the Proclamation of 1763, Parliament landed another stinging blow with the passage of the Sugar Act of 1764. By this measure Parliament hoped to raise money, or revenue, to be applied toward the expenses of "protecting and securing" the colonies against attack. The Sugar Act provided that the money would be raised by a duty on molasses, sugar, and other products imported from places outside the British Empire. A similar law, called the Molasses Act, had been enacted in 1733 (page 59), but the duty of 1733 was so high that the colonists had openly violated the law by smuggling.

Parliament was determined to enforce the new measure and collect the money the government needed. In an effort to make smuggling less profitable, the new duty on molasses was set at only half— and in 1766 at only one sixth—of what it had been under the Molasses Act of 1733. To secure obedience, British officials began to enforce the new law by every means at hand. Naval patrols began to inspect ships entering colonial harbors. Royal inspectors started to search warehouses and even private residences, looking for smuggled goods. The revenue collectors also tried to enlist the aid of the colonists themselves by offering any citizen a share of the confiscated goods if he reported that his friends or neighbors were smuggling.

Parliament hoped that the Sugar Act of 1764 would relieve British taxpayers, who until now had borne the main burden of defense costs. Parliament also hoped that the act would benefit the planters of the British West Indies.

Despite the lower duty on molasses, the Sugar Act interfered severely with

Barrelmaking at sea

the business of colonial merchants, shipowners, and distillers of rum, all of whom had been earning profits on duty-free molasses and other goods smuggled in from the French, Dutch, and Spanish islands in the Caribbean. Angry colonial merchants began to organize committees to discuss means of resistance.

The Currency Act of 1764. Soon after the passage of the Sugar Act, Parliament enacted another law forbidding the colonies to issue paper money. Coupled with this measure was the provision that in the future all taxes must be paid in gold or silver coin rather than in paper money.

This regulation, called the Currency° Act of 1764, antagonized many colonists, and particularly the colonial merchants. Money had been scarce enough before Parliament passed the new measure. Since 1750 the balance of trade between Great Britain and the colonies had shifted in favor of Great Britain. To equalize the balance, colonial merchants had to send large amounts of currency, in addition to trade goods, to Great Britain. These currency ship-

••

° *currency:* This term refers to money that is "current" or that is used at any given time as the legal medium of exchange. Currency may be in the form of *coins,* that is, pieces of gold, silver, or other metals stamped and issued by the government. It may also take the form of printed or engraved paper, usually called *paper money.*

ments were draining away the supply of currency in the colonies. Where, then, could the colonists find the money to carry on their business activities and pay their taxes?

The Quartering Act. In 1765, while colonial tempers were running high, Parliament adopted still another inflammatory piece of legislation known as the Quartering Act. This act, requested by General Thomas Gage, commander in chief of the British forces in America, required the colonial authorities to provide barracks and supplies for British troops stationed in America.

The Stamp Act of 1765. In the midst of growing agitation in the colonies, Parliament adopted the Stamp Act of 1765. The Stamp Act, like the Sugar Act, was designed to raise revenue for the defense of the colonies. But the new act was a far more sweeping measure. Taxes were levied on licenses of all kinds, on college diplomas, playing cards, newspapers, advertisements, and

■ As tension mounted around Boston, this handbill was circulated, urging townspeople not to buy from a local merchant who was probably importing British goods.

WILLIAM JACKSON,

an *IMPORTER*; at the

BRAZEN HEAD,

North Side of the TOWN-HOUSE,

and *Opposite the Town-Pump, in*

Corn-hill, BOSTON.

It is defired that the SONS and DAUGHTERS of *LIBERTY,* would not buy any one thing of him, for in fo doing they will bring Difgrace upon *themfelves,* and their *Pofterity,* for *ever* and *ever,* AMEN.

legal documents such as deeds to land and mortgages on property. The act got its name from the fact that all such documents and materials had to bear a stamp showing the tax had been paid.

The British government was astonished at the angry outburst with which many of the colonists greeted the Stamp Act. After all, the colonists had always paid taxes for the support of the empire. But these taxes were what many of the colonists now began to call *indirect,* or external, taxes—duties, for example, collected on goods that entered colonial ports. The duties were finally paid only by those people who bought the merchandise on which duty had been collected. In many cases, people were not aware that they were paying these duties because they were hidden in the price of the merchandise. These duties, the colonists insisted, had been levied as a means of regulating trade.

The stamp tax was different. It was a *direct,* or internal, tax. Unlike an indirect tax, which is hidden in the price of the merchandise, a direct tax is one which individuals must pay directly to the government. Up to this time, as you will recall, the colonial assemblies had increasingly taken into their own hands the power of the purse in the colonies (page 89). Direct taxes had been levied by the colonial assemblies, and the colonists were used to this kind of taxation. The stamp tax, however, was a direct tax levied, not by a colonial assembly, but by a Parliament in which the colonists had no representatives.

Without the colonists' having any voice in the matter, the Stamp Act threatened to take money directly from their pockets. The settler who bought a few acres of land on the frontier would be compelled to pay a special tax on the deed to his property. Small farmers would have to pay taxes on warehouse receipts for tobacco or grain. Artisans in the towns would be required to pay taxes for their playing cards, newspapers, and other purchases. And, of course, planters, merchants, lawyers, and editors would be paying taxes every time they turned around. This "vicious" tax, the colonists insisted, violated their right to tax themselves since it was levied without the consent of their own representatives. Here, indeed, was "taxation without representation."

Many colonists refused to listen to the British argument that Parliament actually represented all British subjects, including the colonists. True, British spokesmen admitted, colonial representatives did not sit in Parliament. But there were other large groups of Britishers not directly represented in Parliament by men for whom they voted. In the new, rapidly growing English cities of Manchester and Birmingham, for example, there were many thousands of men who did not vote. What did the colonists mean by "no taxation without representation"? To these arguments the colonists turned deaf ears.

Opposition to the Stamp Act. With the passage of the Stamp Act of 1765, Parliament suddenly found that it had stumbled into a hornet's nest. Resolutions condemning the measure poured into England from the colonies. Colonial lawyers, merchants, and publishers met in protest. Colonial assemblies declared that all taxes were illegal except those levied by representatives of the people in their own legislatures.

In October 1765 delegates from nine colonies met in New York. This group of delegates was called the Stamp Act Congress. After asserting their loyalty to the king and promising "all due subordination" to Parliament, the delegates vowed resistance to all taxes levied without the consent of their own colonial legislatures.

Many colonial merchants, joined by other leading citizens, went a step further than the Stamp Act Congress by signing *nonimportation agreements*. In these agreements they promised not to buy or import British goods. Within a few months products made in Great Britain almost vanished from colonial stores and warehouses.

Some of the townsmen took even more direct action. Organized in soci-

A tax stamp

STAMP MASTERS

Few of the stamp masters appointed by the British ever sold a single stamp. Most took one look at the crowds of Patriots and promptly resigned. Those who hesitated soon learned the virtue of travel and took to the road, usually with a crowd in hot pursuit.

When Zachariah Hood of Maryland refused to resign, colonists leveled his store to the ground, burned him in effigy, and began to mutter threats against his life. Attempting to escape, Hood rode so hard that he killed a horse. He sought safety among the British troops in New York, but a crowd gathered around the garrison and threatened the redcoats themselves. Hood then fled to Long Island, only to find that he had been followed by his determined pursuers. He finally resigned.

The stamp master for New Hampshire, George Meserve, had to pass through Boston on his way from Europe. He was quickly persuaded that it was to his best interest to resign. But when he reached New Hampshire, the patriots insisted that a mere resignation was not good enough. They would settle for nothing less than the burning of his commission. Meserve gladly surrendered the dangerous paper. "I did not know," he later wrote, "whether I should have escaped from this mob with my life, as some were for cutting off my head, others for cutting off my ears and sending them home with my commission."

THE RIGHTS
OF ENGLISHMEN

In opposing the policies of the British government after 1763, the colonists were continuing to assert what they believed to be their rights as Englishmen. Beginning as far back as Magna Carta in 1215, as you know, Englishmen had been recording these rights in formal documents. Two of the most important of these documents—the Petition of Right and the Bill of Rights—had been written in England during the 1600's, while the colonists were struggling to build English colonies in North America. Following are excerpts from these famous documents:

English Petition of Right (1628)

They [your subjects] do therefore humbly pray your most excellent majesty that no man hereafter be compelled to make or yield any gift, loan, benevolence, tax, or such like charge without common consent by act of Parliament; ... and that your majesty would be also graciously pleased, for the further comfort and safety of your people, to declare your royal will and pleasure that in the things aforesaid all your officers and ministers shall serve you according to the laws and statutes of this realm ...

English Bill of Rights (1689)

Levying of money for or to the use of the crown ... without grant of Parliament ... is illegal.

It is the right of the subjects to petition the king ...

The raising or keeping a standing army within the kingdom in time of peace, unless it be with the consent of Parliament, is against law.

Election of members of Parliament ought to be free.

The freedom of speech and debates or proceedings in Parliament ought not to be ... questioned in any court or place out of Parliament.

Excessive bail ought not to be required, nor excessive fines imposed, nor cruel and unusual punishments inflicted ...

eties called Sons of Liberty, these exuberant colonists rioted in the large towns, destroyed the offices of stamp tax collectors, burned stamps in the streets, pillaged the houses of royal officials, and applied tar and feathers to citizens sympathetic to Great Britain.

The Stamp Act is repealed. Englishmen listened with mixed feelings to the news of colonial resistance to the Stamp Act. George III was shocked. "It is undoubtedly the most serious matter that ever came before Parliament," he exclaimed.

British merchants were also shocked, although for somewhat different reasons than George III. The colonial nonimportation agreements had brought British-American trade almost to a standstill. Many British merchants faced financial ruin. To prevent this, they demanded that Parliament repeal the Stamp Act. They were joined in this demand by a number of influential Britishers who sympathized with the colonists. Edmund Burke, a statesman and writer, expressed his pride in men who would thus oppose an "illegal" measure. William Pitt, a member of Parliament who later became prime minister, declared, "I rejoice that America has resisted."

Under such heavy pressure Parliament backed down and repealed the Stamp Act in March 1766. News of the repeal brought wild rejoicing in the colonies and sighs of relief from British businessmen and friends of the colonists. Some of the more excitable colonists prepared to erect statues to George III and William Pitt. In New York City, Sons of Liberty erected a huge flagpole, called a liberty pole, around which they gathered to celebrate the repeal and to pledge their devotion to the cause of liberty. In Great Britain members of Parliament turned upon George Grenville, the prime minister responsible for the measures imposed on the colonies between 1763 and 1765, and forced him to resign.

The Declaratory Act of 1766. In the midst of all the excitement, most people paid little attention to another measure enacted by Parliament. This was the so-called Declaratory Act of 1766, which Parliament passed in connection with the repeal of the Stamp Act. In the Declaratory Act, Parliament asserted its "full power and authority to make laws to bind the colonies and people of America . . . in all cases whatsoever."

And so, despite rejoicing in the colonies, the basic issue dividing the colonists from the mother country remained unsettled. Did the British Parliament have the right to make laws for the colonists and to tax them when they had no elected representatives in Parliament? This was the basic question.

⌄ **SECTION SURVEY**

1. Why did the Proclamation of 1763 make sense to the British, but not to the colonists?
2. How did the Currency Act of 1764 add to an already existing problem?
3. Compare the Molasses Act of 1733 with the Sugar Act of 1764. Explain why the act of 1764 was resented more.
4. Why did the colonists consider that the Stamp Act violated one of their fundamental rights as Englishmen? Indicate four ways in which they showed their opposition.
5. Was the Stamp Act repealed more because of British pressure or American pressure? Justify your answer.

IDENTIFY: revenue, Quartering Act, indirect taxes, direct taxes, duty, nonimportation agreement, Sons of Liberty, Declaratory Act; Grenville; 1765.

3 Tension increases between Great Britain and the colonies

Money! This was Great Britain's crying need in 1766. Money to raise and maintain the armed forces needed to guard the far-flung outposts of the British Empire. Money to build and maintain the war ships that guarded the sea lanes to and from the colonies. Money to pay the war debts left over from the Seven Years' War.

This was not a new problem, as you know. It was the same problem that the British government had faced in 1763. It was the same problem that the members of Parliament had tried to solve with the passage of the Stamp Act of 1765. But, as you have seen, the Stamp Act was so unpopular that Parliament finally repealed it. In 1766 the problem remained unsolved.

The Townshend Acts. In 1767, under the leadership of Charles Townshend, Parliament decided once again to try to raise revenue in America. But the members of Parliament still had painful memories of the Stamp Act. They knew how deeply the colonists resented "direct" taxes. They decided, therefore, to return to the long-accepted method of collecting duties on goods entering the seaports. Since the colonists had always paid duties, or "indirect" taxes, of this kind, Parliament hoped the new duties would not cause any trouble.

The Townshend Acts levied import duties on articles of everyday use in America—tea, lead, glass, and colors for paint. If Parliament had stopped at this point, the colonists might not have objected. But Parliament wanted to be sure that the new law would be enforced. In an effort to put teeth into the law, they legalized what were then called *writs of assistance.*

Writs of assistance. Writs of assistance were search warrants. "Writ" is an old word meaning "written." Writs of assistance, then, were written statements giving a government official the legal right to search a man's ship, his business establishment, or even his home. The writs of assistance of colonial times were not, however, anything like the search warrants with which we are now familiar.

Today, before a man's house can be entered and searched, the officers of the law must first procure a search warrant. But to secure this search warrant, the officers must present reasonable evidence before a judge that the *specific object* (or objects) for which they are searching is in a *particular place.* And when the search warrant is issued, it must state specifically the article sought and the premises to be searched. By this means citizens of the United States are protected from meddling officials.

The writs of assistance used in colonial times were quite different from present-day search warrants. Armed with one of these general search warrants, a British customs official could enter any vessel or warehouse or home in America, at any time, to ransack the place with the bare hope that he might find smuggled goods.

For many years American colonial merchants had been arguing that use of the writs was illegal, and an invasion of their "rights as Englishmen." As recently as 1761, when Boston customs officials had applied for a writ against a group of merchants, the merchants had taken their case to court. James Otis, their attorney, had more than once denounced the writs in fiery language. "What a scene does this open," he cried in one speech. "Every man, prompted by revenge, ill humor, or wantonness to inspect the inside of his neighbor's house, may get a writ of assistance."

Now, in 1767, the hated writs were legalized by an act of Parliament. Neither Otis nor any other colonist could alter this fact. But they could and did protest, heaping their anger and contempt upon a Parliament that dared to do this thing to British citizens. Nor was it any comfort to the colonists to know that the writs were also being used in England. Indeed, John Wilkes, a member of Parliament, had to flee to France for his life because he dared to oppose this dictatorial method of search.

Arguments and resolutions. The colonists expressed their resentment against the Townshend Acts, including the much-hated writs of assistance, in a number of ways. New Yorkers refused to provide living quarters for British soldiers sent to enforce the law. Parliament promptly punished the colony by suspending its assembly, in this way depriving New Yorkers of their right to representative government.

Other colonists picked up their pens and began to write. They poured out their resentment° in a flood of angry pamphlets, resolutions, and petitions. Under the leadership of Samuel Adams, the legislature of Massachusetts drafted and adopted a letter to the other colonies, urging them to unite for resistance. The assemblies of Maryland, South Carolina, and Georgia promptly endorsed the letter. Parliament replied to this challenge by forbidding the legislatures of these four colonies to meet.

The American case was summarized in a set of resolutions adopted by the Virginia House of Burgesses. The resolutions began with an introductory statement by George Washington in which he referred to "our lordly masters in Great Britain." The resolutions then went on to repeat the American claim that only colonial legislatures had the right to levy taxes on the colonists.

Direct action—and violence. While many colonial leaders protested with resolutions and petitions, other colonists decided to act. They signed new nonimportation agreements in which they promised not to import or buy British goods. The earlier agreements at the time of the Stamp Act of 1765 had almost ruined British merchants and had forced Parliament to repeal the measure. The agreements had worked then, and they would work again. So reasoned many of the colonists.

But the more exuberant Americans were not content with these agreements. Once again mobs poured into the streets. They boarded and smashed revenue cutters,° attacked British customs officials, and freely applied tar and feathers to anyone who dared to inform on smugglers. Even the British soldiers who were landed to keep order were sometimes attacked.

In Boston crowds taunted the soldiers, calling them "lobsters," "redcoats," and "bloody backs." Now and then some of the more irresponsible

....
° *revenue cutter:* an armed boat used to enforce customs laws and to arrest smugglers.

BRITISH TROOPS LAND IN BOSTON

Shortly after the British troops arrived in Boston in 1768, Paul Revere made an engraving (see above) in which he pictured the landing.

In his description of the arrival of the ships of war and transports, he wrote that they came with "their Cannon loaded . . . as for a regular Siege. At noon on Saturday, October the 1st, the fourteenth and twenty-ninth Regiments, a detachment from the 59th Reg^t and Train of Artillery, with two pieces of Cannon, landed on the Long Wharf; there Formed and Marched with insolent Parade, Drums beating, Fifes playing, and Colours flying up King Street, Each Soldier having received 16 rounds of Powder and Ball."

members of a crowd hurled stones and snowballs at the soldiers. Every month friction between the citizens and the soldiers became more intense. Thoughtful colonial leaders and British commanders alike did everything they could to avoid more serious trouble. But in spite of all their efforts, the incident they dreaded finally occurred.

The Boston Massacre. On March 5, 1770, a large crowd gathered in Boston around a detachment of the 29th British Regiment. The crowd yelled insults and threw snowballs. All this had happened many times before. And then suddenly the soldiers fired into the crowd, killing three civilians and mortally wounding two others. The city went wild with anger. A "massacre," the people called the affair, and demanded that the British withdraw all troops from the city.

Later, when passions had cooled somewhat, the soldiers were tried for murder. They were defended by Josiah Quincy, Jr., and John Adams, who later became the second President of the United States. Neither of these men had any sympathy for the British, but they insisted that every individual was entitled to a fair trial. All except two of

■ In this famous engraving of the Boston Massacre by Paul Revere, British troops are shown as being ordered to fire at Americans. We do not know how accurate the picture is. Revere, a leading Boston patriot, may have been picturing the British in the most unfavorable light.

the soldiers were acquitted. These two were convicted of manslaughter, but were soon released.

Repeal—and continued unrest. The gap between Great Britain and the American colonies was wide indeed when Lord Frederick North became prime minister of Great Britain in 1770. The new prime minister urged Parliament to repeal the Townshend Acts. As he pointed out, the nonimportation agreements were once again ruining the business of many British merchants, and the cost of enforcing the law was proving to be much too heavy.

In 1770 Parliament repealed the Townshend Acts, which had imposed duties on so many articles of everyday use in the colonies. Parliament also allowed the Quartering Act to expire. But the British government insisted that a small import duty on tea be retained in a new law as a symbol that Parliament could tax the colonists. As George III put it, there must "always be one tax to keep up the right."

The repeal of the Townshend Acts brought a temporary end to much of the unrest in the colonies. But an occasional act of violence reminded the British that the basic issue remained unsettled.

One of these outbreaks occurred in June 1772 when several boatloads of men attacked and burned the British revenue ship *Gaspee* a few miles south of Providence, Rhode Island. From the colonial point of view, an alarming thing about the *Gaspee* affair was the announcement by British officials that the suspected persons would be sent to England for trial. This decision threatened to weaken the practice of self-government in Rhode Island.

Even more alarming, because it seemed to show how the wind was blowing, was an announcement made at this same time by the royal governor of Massachusetts. From now on, Governor Thomas Hutchinson declared, the salaries of the governor and the Massachusetts judges would be paid by the Crown. This would free the governor

106

and the judges from all dependence upon the Massachusetts legislature.

Committees of Correspondence. The colonists reacted promptly to these new threats to their freedom. Led by Samuel Adams, citizens of Boston met in a special town meeting and created a "Committee of Correspondence" consisting of twenty-one members, with James Otis as chairman. This committee had the job of keeping other colonies —and "the World"—informed about what was happening in Massachusetts. The idea worked so well that during the next few months other colonies organized similar committees. Many of the most prominent leaders in the colonies served on these committees. In Virginia, for example, the committee included Thomas Jefferson, Patrick Henry, and Richard Henry Lee.

In the absence of any central government where leaders from the various colonies could meet, the Committees of Correspondence performed an important service by keeping each colony informed of events and opinions in the other colonies. And, as it turned out, the colonists organized this new method of communication none too soon, for in 1773 Parliament adopted another measure that really started tempers boiling, as you will see.

⮕ **SECTION SURVEY**

1. Compare the Townshend Acts with the Stamp Act as to aims and means.

2. (a) What were the writs of assistance, and why did the colonists resent them? (b) How did the colonists express their protest against the Townshend Acts?

3. Describe the steps leading to the Boston Massacre. Who do you feel was to blame? Justify your answer.

4. Was the repeal of the Townshend Acts a complete colonial victory? Explain.

5. What was the function of the Committees of Correspondence set up by Samuel Adams?

IDENTIFY: revenue cutter, *Gaspee;* Townshend, Otis, Samuel Adams, Josiah Quincy, Jr., John Adams, Lord North; March 5, 1770.

4 The clash of interests in America leads to a deadlock

The series of events that brought the American colonies to the verge of rebellion started in 1773 with the passage of a new law called the Tea Act. Parliament passed this measure in an effort to help the British East India Company, a well-established trading company with headquarters in England.

The Tea Act of 1773. The British East India Company was in trouble. To put the matter simply, it had 17 million pounds of unsold tea piled up in its warehouses—and no buyers. If the tea were not sold, and quickly, the company would be wiped out.

Part of the company's difficulties arose from the refusal of many American colonists to buy tea. When the Townshend Acts were repealed, as you know, duties on all goods imported into the colonies had been removed except a small duty on tea, which the British government had retained as a symbol of its power to tax the colonies. The tax was a small one, but many colonists would have none of it. They refused to buy tea imported from England.

Faced with this desperate situation, the British East India Company turned to Parliament for help. The members of Parliament, many of whom owned stock in the company, quickly worked out what they thought was a reasonable solution to the problem.

First, the members of Parliament granted the company a large loan of public money. They then passed a law that made it possible for the company to lower its price on tea without losing any of its profits. Under the Navigation Act of 1663, as you recall, trade goods, like tea from India, had to be shipped to England to be taxed before they could be reshipped and sold in the colonies. But Parliament's new law, called the Tea Act, permitted the British East India Company to sell tea directly to the colonists without the payment of the duties usually collected at the ports of Great Britain. As a result, the company was able to reduce the price of tea that it sold in the colonies. The members of Parliament figured that the colonists would buy the tea now that the price was lowered—and the British East India Company would be saved.

Why the colonists objected. Why, given the chance to buy tea at lower prices, did the colonists protest? For one thing, as you know, a small import duty was still collected on each pound of tea entering American ports, and by now the colonists were opposed to *all* taxes imposed by Parliament.

In the second place, the new Tea Act would enable the British East India Company to undersell all of its competitors, even those who were smuggling tea into America without paying import duties. In effect, this would give the company a monopoly on the sale of tea in America. Thus, many colonial middlemen, or merchants, who had been sharing in the profits of the tea trade would be driven out of business.

The tea merchants were joined in their resistance by nearly all colonial businessmen. True enough, only tea was affected by the act. But if a monopoly were granted to one British company, was it not reasonable to expect that other monopolies would soon be granted to other British companies? As

one American merchant wrote: "Would not the opening of an East India House in America encourage all the great companies in Great Britain to do the same? If so, have we a single chance of being anything but *Hewers-of-Wood and Drawers-of-Water* to them?"

Violence breaks out again. Faced with this threat to their businesses, the colonists reacted swiftly. Crowds rioted on the colonial streets. Most of the colonists now refused to buy tea. The British East India Company could not sell a single pound. In Charleston tea was stored in damp cellars to rot. In Annapolis a ship and its cargo of tea were burned. Philadelphians and New Yorkers refused to allow British ships carrying tea to enter their harbors.

In Boston, late in 1773, colonists disguised as Indians boarded ships and heaved the cargo into the water, destroying in one wild night 342 chests of tea valued at thousands of dollars. The Boston Tea Party, as it was called, attracted widespread attention. Many of the colonists approved, but others, who were loyal to the king and to British institutions, were shocked at such violence.

The Intolerable Acts of 1774. British officials and merchants were furious. It had been bad enough for the colonists to refuse to pay taxes. It was far worse for them to destroy property.

Colonial merchant shipping

By overwhelming majorities Parliament passed four measures designed to discourage further violence and to strengthen the power of British officials over the colonists. The colonists called these measures the Intolerable Acts. One measure closed the port of Boston to all shipping until the colonists paid for the tea they had destroyed there. A second measure revoked the Massachusetts charter of 1691 and forbade Massachusetts colonists to hold town meetings. A third measure, a new Quartering Act, required the colonists to provide food and housing for British soldiers sent to America to enforce the laws. A fourth measure provided that British officials in Massachusetts charged with crimes committed while enforcing British laws could have their cases tried, not in that colony, but in England.

The Quebec Act of 1774. While passing the Intolerable Acts, Parliament also passed a fifth measure, called the Quebec Act. The purpose of the Quebec Act was to establish order in Canada, which, as you recall, the British had won by treaty from the French in 1763.

The Quebec Act, which greatly enlarged the province of Quebec, established the southern boundary of Canada at the Ohio River and the western boundary at the Mississippi River (see map, page 97). French laws were to continue in Canada, and French Canadians, most of them Roman Catholics, were guaranteed religious freedom.

Parliament had no thought of punishing the American colonists when it passed the Quebec Act. Indeed, the act was a sound piece of legislation. But it came at the same time as the Intolerable Acts, and the colonists regarded it as another attempt to punish them, by destroying the claims of Massachusetts, Connecticut, and Virginia to the western lands, and by strengthening the Catholicism which they disliked.

Reaction to the Intolerable Acts. It soon became clear that Great Britain meant to enforce the Intolerable Acts. General Gage, leader of the British

THE WOMEN ALSO REBEL

Ladies as well as men expressed indignation at the Tea Act. Throughout the colonies, groups of women met and pledged themselves to drink no more tea until the hated act had been repealed. The following verse, which appeared in colonial newspapers, summarized the attitude of many of the ladies:

A Lady's Adieu to Her Tea-Table

Farewell the Teaboard with your gaudy attire,
Ye cups and saucers that I did admire;
To my cream pot and tongs I now bid adieu;
That pleasure's all fled that I once found in you . . .
No more shall my teapot so generous be
In filling the cups with this pernicious tea,
For I'll fill it with water and drink out the same,
Before I'll lose Liberty that dearest name . . .
Before she shall part I will die in the cause,
For I'll never be govern'd by tyranny's laws.

armed forces in America, was now named governor of Massachusetts and was given reinforcements to help him maintain order. The colonists had defied the royal authority with physical force. Very well, Great Britain would uphold the laws with physical force.

"The New England governments are in a state of rebellion," George III declared. "Blows must decide whether they are to be subject to this country or independent."

Many colonists had no intention of submitting. Great Britain, thinking only of punishing Massachusetts and warning the other colonies, had succeeded in arousing antagonism throughout America. "Dined at Colonel Harrison's," one traveler in Virginia noted in his diary on May 30, 1774. "Nothing talked of but the blockade of Boston

Declaration and Resolves of the First Continental Congress (1774): EXCERPT

𝕿he good people of the several colonies ... declare ... that the inhabitants of the English colonies in North America, by the immutable laws of nature, the principles of the English constitution, and the several charters or compacts, have the following rights:

Resolved,

¶ That they are entitled to life, liberty, and property, and they have never ceded to any sovereign power whatever, a right to dispose of either without their consent.

¶ That our ancestors, who first settled these colonies, were at the time of their emigration from the mother country, entitled to all the rights, liberties, and immunities of free and natural-born subjects, within the realm of England ...

¶ That the foundation of English liberty, and of all free government, is a right in the people to participate in their legislative council ...

Harbor. The people . . . talk as if they were determined to dispute the matter with the sword."

There was, indeed, a lot of sword-rattling in the colonies at this time. But most of the colonists apparently believed that the British government would back down in the face of protests and repeal the Intolerable Acts, as it had repealed the Stamp Act and the Townshend Acts.

The First Continental Congress. Many of the colonists remained completely loyal to Great Britain. They believed that the colonies should obey the laws of Parliament without protesting. Other colonists tried to think of ways to persuade the British to compromise.

On September 5, 1774, delegates from all of the colonies except Georgia assembled in Philadelphia to discuss such measures at a meeting called the First Continental Congress. The delegates quickly adopted a number of resolutions. Denying any thought of independence, the delegates nevertheless demanded an immediate change in British policies. They solemnly asserted their rights to "life, liberty, and property"; to "all the rights, liberties, and immunities" of Englishmen; to the "free and exclusive power of legislation in their own several legislatures." They pledged each other mutual support. They revived the nonimportation agreements against British products. They agreed not to sell goods to Great Britain or the British West Indies if, by January 1775, the British had not made compromises. They resolved to create local "committees of safety and inspection" to secure firm and uniform action against the British government.

Finally, the delegates to the First Continental Congress disbanded with the understanding that they would meet again in the spring of 1775 to take further steps if Parliament had not by then withdrawn the Intolerable Acts.

Both sides hold out. The winter of 1774–75 found Great Britain and the colonies, or at least many leaders on both sides, lined up firmly against each other. Parliament refused to repeal the Intolerable Acts until the colonists paid for the tea they had destroyed. Among the colonists, those now in control of the situation refused to pay for anything until Great Britain repealed the Intolerable Acts.

⌐ **SECTION SURVEY**

1. Why did so many of the colonists object to the Tea Act even though it lowered the price of tea in the colonies?

2. How did the colonists express their opposition to the Tea Act?

3. Give four reasons why the colonists objected to the Intolerable Acts of 1774.

4. Why did the colonists consider the Quebec Act of 1774 as "another attempt to punish them"?

5. What actions did the First Continental Congress take?

IDENTIFY: British East India Company, monopoly, Boston Tea Party; General Gage; 1773, September 5, 1774.

Points to Discuss: 1. Explain the principles of mercantilism and the meaning of "favorable balance of trade."

2. Describe how the British applied the principles of mercantilism by means of (a) the Navigation Acts, (b) the Molasses Act of 1733, (c) restrictions on colonial manufacturing, (d) the Proclamation of 1763, and (e) the Currency Act of 1764.

3. Explain why colonial opposition to British policies increased after 1763.

4. Explain why "taxation without representation" became one of the basic issues dividing the colonies from Great Britain.

5. It has been said, "Only the wisest of men could have reconciled the differing interests of the mother country and the colonies in the 1760's." Do you agree? Why?

6. In what ways did the year 1763 mark a turning point in Britain's relations with her colonies?

Using Maps: 1. Using the maps on pages 21 and 97, explain the reasons for the conflicting claims of certain colonies to western lands.

2. Using the map on page 97, answer the following: (a) Where did Pontiac's Conspiracy cause the greatest damage? (b) What was the purpose of the Proclamation of 1763? (c) Why did the Quebec Act of 1774 arouse the indignation of the British colonists?

3. Referring to the map on page 58, summarize the aims of British mercantilism and the importance of the triangular trade to the colonists.

Consulting the Sources: For the provisions of the Quebec Act and for interesting reactions of the Continental Congress to the act, refer to Ellis, *Docs.*, Nos. 40 and 42.

■ TRACING THE MAIN IDEAS

British victory in the Seven Years' War, called in America the French and Indian War, made Great Britain the leading colonial power in the world. British citizens had paid in blood and treasure to win their great empire. By 1763 the struggle was finally settled. France had been defeated. Peace had come at last.

But peace brought new problems. During the long years of colonial warfare, the American seaboard colonies had been growing away from the mother country. The people who settled these colonies had learned to think of America as *their* land, as a place apart from England. They learned to love the new country that had brought most of them better lives than they or their fathers had known in the Old World. They began to think of themselves as Americans, although they did not ordinarily use the word "American" until after the Revolutionary War and although, until 1776, nearly all of them continued to think of themselves as loyal citizens of the British Empire.

A new way of life was developing in America. It was now about 150 years since the first English settlers had come to America, and the peoples of the Old World and the New were finding it more and more difficult to understand each other.

The gap was wide indeed in 1763 when Great Britain decided to adopt a new policy and to make the colonies obey the laws which had been passed in London.

Step by step, between 1763 and 1775, the mother country and its colonies moved further apart. Yet by 1775 it was perhaps not too late to reconcile the differences. As you will see in Chapter 7, however, the reconciliation never came. Instead, the colonists declared their independence and won their freedom on the battlefield.

The Colonies Win Their Independence

*VILLAGERS DRILLING
on LEXINGTON GREEN*

JOHN HOWE, a private in the army of King George III, was a spy. Fortunately for him, he did not look like a spy. The people he met as he walked along the Massachusetts roads took him for an honest Yankee workingman. He even sounded like a Yankee. His regiment had been stationed in Boston long enough for him to learn how Yankees talked—and even, in some cases, what they were thinking about.

General Gage, British commander in Boston, had heard that the New Englanders were .collecting arms and ammunition. He sent Private Howe and other spies out into the surrounding countryside to learn the truth. And John Howe was learning fast. He learned where the powder and shot were stored. He also learned that the Yankees were ready to fight. At a farmhouse near Lexington, he stopped to talk to an old man. The old man was cleaning a gun. Howe asked him what he intended to shoot. "A flock of redcoats at Boston," the man replied.

It was the same story everywhere Howe went. He saw rebellious colonists—by now called Patriots—cleaning their guns and drilling openly on village greens. In taverns and public buildings he saw lists posted bearing the names of people who remained loyal to the king. He heard of Loyalists who had been tarred and feathered and of other Loyalists whose homes had been burned because they dared to defend the British point of view.

"The king is openly cursed," one observer wrote in the winter of 1775, "and his authority is set at defiance." John Howe, British spy, knew that this was true. He had heard it and seen it firsthand in his travels through the New England countryside.

This was the report John Howe carried back to General Gage in Boston. General Gage, who had heard the same story from other British spies, decided the time had come to act. By acting promptly he might, perhaps, nip the bud of rebellion. He decided to seize the powder and shot that the colonists were storing nearby at Concord and at several other towns.

AS THE STORY DEVELOPS

1. British-American differences break out in open war.
2. The colonists decide to fight for their independence.
3. American Patriots wage and win the Revolutionary War.
4. The victorious Americans gain a favorable Treaty of Peace.

| 1450 | 1750 | 1800 | 1850 | 1900 | 1950 | 1975 |

British-American differences break out in open war

General Gage could no more hide his plans from the colonists than they could hide their activities from the eyes of his spies and informers. In the spring of 1775, the Patriots in Boston were watching the British closely. They knew something was brewing. What is more, they made arrangements to warn the surrounding countryside if, and when, the British troops should march.

Lexington and Concord. Late at night on April 18, along the banks of the Charles River across from the sleeping city of Boston, a man paced restlessly in the darkness. Suddenly the feeble rays of a lantern shone from a window in the steeple of the Old North Church in Boston. The restless man saw the flickering light, looked again to be sure that it was the signal he had been watching for, and then leaped into the saddle of his waiting horse and galloped off into the darkness—and into the pages of history.

The man, of course, was Paul Revere. He and a fellow Patriot, William ("Billy") Dawes, Jr., rode through that fateful night, pounding on farmhouse doors, shouting their cry of alarm. Behind them, as the hoofbeats of their horses faded into the distance, lamps winked on in kitchens. Wives, their eyes filled with worry, hastily prepared food while their menfolk hurriedly pulled on clothes and lifted their muskets and powder horns from the pegs on the wall. Then the men were off across the fields to join their friends and neighbors at the appointed meeting place.

British troops, meanwhile, had rowed across the Charles River and were marching down the road toward Concord (see map, page 114). They reached Lexington at dawn on April 19, 1775. The "minutemen"—members of the militia who had promised to be ready for action at a minute's notice—were there before them, gathered in ranks on the village green. Major Pit-

A BRITISHER'S TRIBUTE TO THE MINUTEMEN

On April 20, with the cruel memories of the long march from Lexington to Boston still fresh in his mind, one of the British commanders paid a tribute to the courage and skill of the colonial minutemen:

"Whoever looks upon them as an irregular mob will find himself very much mistaken," Hugh Earl Percy wrote in a letter to England. "Nor are several of them void of a spirit of enthusiasm as we experienced yesterday, for many of them concealed themselves in houses and advanced within ten yards to fire at me and other officers, though they were morally certain of being put to death themselves in an instant."

cairn, commander of the British patrol, ordered the colonists to drop their guns and leave the green. The colonists kept their guns, but started to leave when someone fired a shot. Immediately, without waiting for orders, the British troops fired several volleys. When the smoke cleared away, eight colonists lay dead, and ten others were wounded.

The British troops went on to Concord, where they cut down a liberty pole, set fire to the courthouse, and destroyed several gun carriages and a few tools. After encountering armed Patriot forces at Concord's North Bridge, the British started back toward Boston. But the country was swarming with angry colonists. From behind stone walls and the shelter of buildings, the colonists fired steadily upon the redcoats as

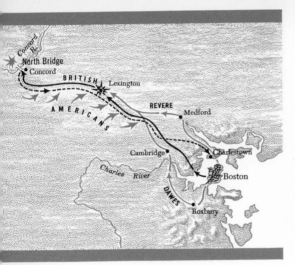

■ **War Breaks Out: April 19, 1775**

delegates to the First Continental Congress had agreed the previous year to assemble again if the British government did not meet their demands.

Some delegates to the Second Continental Congress, like Samuel Adams of Massachusetts and Patrick Henry of Virginia, were now ready to take *radical* action—to declare independence, seize British officials, and ask France and Spain for help. But most of the delegates were more *conservative*. They were reluctant to urge extreme changes in the relations between the colonies and the mother country.

The conservatives won. Led by John Dickinson of Pennsylvania, they assured the king that they had "not raised armies with ambitious designs of separating from Great Britain." With this plea for reconciliation, however, the delegates coupled a stern message. They made it clear that they would resist tyranny ° with force if that were necessary. And to show that they meant business, they appointed George Washington of Virginia as commander in chief of the Continental Army. In this way, the armed Patriots around Boston became, in name at least, an army.

∙∙∙

° **tyranny:** the exercise of absolute and arbitrary power without regard for law and justice.

they made their death march down the long road back to the safety of Boston. During that march the British casualties amounted to 73 killed, 174 wounded, and 26 missing.

The redcoats reached Boston late in the day. Curious townspeople saw haggard faces, bloody bandages, and men in tattered uniforms stumbling under the weight of wounded comrades. When night fell, the lights of numerous campfires twinkled like fireflies around the rim of the city. These were the fires of rebellion, fed by a goodly number of the 16,000 minutemen from the surrounding countryside.

Ticonderoga and Crown Point. The days slipped by. Within a month, in May, came news that the "Green Mountain Boys," a small colonial force commanded by Ethan Allen of what is now Vermont, had seized the British forts at Ticonderoga and Crown Point on Lake Champlain (see map, opposite page). Most welcome of all was news that powder and shot from the captured forts was on its way to Boston.

The Second Continental Congress. Meanwhile, delegates to a Second Continental Congress had been making their way to Philadelphia, where they met on May 10, 1775. As you recall,

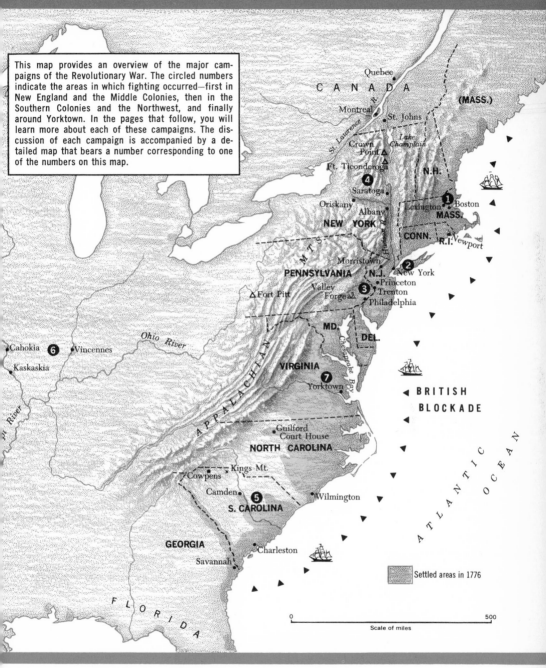

This map provides an overview of the major campaigns of the Revolutionary War. The circled numbers indicate the areas in which fighting occurred—first in New England and the Middle Colonies, then in the Southern Colonies and the Northwest, and finally around Yorktown. In the pages that follow, you will learn more about each of these campaigns. The discussion of each campaign is accompanied by a detailed map that bears a number corresponding to one of the numbers on this map.

Quebec

C A N A D A

(MASS.)

Montreal

St. Johns

St. Lawrence R.

Lake Champlain

Crown Point

Ft. Ticonderoga

N.H.

④ Saratoga

Oriskany

Lexington ❶ Boston

Albany

MASS.

NEW YORK

CONN.

R.I. Newport

Morristown

M T S.

PENNSYLVANIA

N.J. ❷ New York

Princeton

△ Fort Pitt

Valley Forge

❸ Trenton

Philadelphia

MD.

DEL.

Chesapeake Bay

•Cahokia ⑥ •Vincennes

Ohio River

Kaskaskia

VIRGINIA

❼

Mt. River

Yorktown

A P P A L A C H I A N

B R I T I S H
B L O C K A D E

•Guilford Court House

A T L A N T I C   O C E A N

NORTH CAROLINA

•Cowpens •Kings Mt.

Camden• ⑤

•Wilmington

S. CAROLINA

GEORGIA •Charleston

Savannah•

Settled areas in 1776

F L O R I D A

0   500

Scale of miles

■ As you read the text and examine each numbered map in the pages that follow, look frequently at the map above so that you will understand the progress of the war and the relationships among the various campaigns. On all of the detailed maps, red stands for American forces, black for British forces. The following symbols are used on the detailed maps:

⟶   American Advance   ⟶   British Advance

------▸   American Retreat   ------▸   British Retreat

✷   American Victory   ✸   British Victory

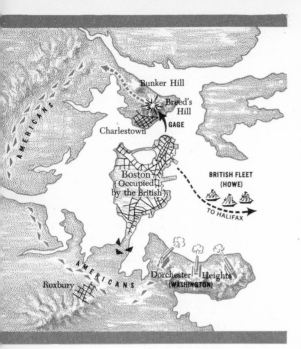

① Fighting Around Boston: June 1775–March 1776

The British evacuate Boston. The Second Continental Congress promptly took further steps to strengthen the colonial position. The Congress sent diplomatic agents to request aid from several European countries, including France, Spain, and the Netherlands. Late in 1775 the Congress also sent a military expedition to Canada in two columns, one under Richard Montgomery of New York, the other under Benedict Arnold. The colonists hoped that these two expeditions would encourage the French Canadians to rise against the British. But the French Canadians did not show much sympathy, and the expedition failed.

Early in 1776, however, the colonists were cheered by other news. In a surprise move at night, Washington occupied Dorchester Heights overlooking Boston, where the British fleet lay anchored in the harbor (see map 1, this page). The British, literally caught napping, awakened the next morning to find themselves looking across the bay into the mouths of cannon.

The British general, Sir William Howe, who had replaced Gage as the commanding officer, decided it was now useless to try to hold Boston. The British fleet lifted anchor and sailed out of the harbor on March 17, 1776. With the fleet went the entire British garrison, as well as about a thousand Loyalists.

The Battle of Bunker Hill. Before Washington reached Massachusetts to take command of the minutemen in the Boston area, blood had again been shed. General Gage, the British commander, decided to make a frontal attack on the armed New Englanders who were encamped at Charlestown, overlooking Boston harbor. On June 17, 1775, in three bold assaults the redcoats attacked the Americans on Breed's Hill, mistakenly called Bunker Hill (see map 1, this page). Both sides lost heavily. Finally, the Patriots, their ammunition exhausted, retreated with a loss of almost 450 men. But the British left more than 1000 of their men dead upon the battlefield.

Shocked at news of this disaster, George III clamped a tight naval blockade° on all the colonies and proclaimed the colonists rebels. He also hired 10,000 German soldiers, called Hessians (HESH-unz), to help force the Americans into obedience to the Crown.

∙∙

° *naval blockade:* in war an attempt by enemy ships to close a harbor or coast line.

🖝 **SECTION SURVEY**

1. Why did the British march on Lexington and Concord?

2. Justify this statement: Most of the delegates to the Second Continental Congress took a conservative rather than a radical view of relations with Great Britain.

3. What was the military importance of (a) the Battle of Bunker Hill and (b) the seizure of Dorchester Heights?

IDENTIFY: Patriots, Loyalists, minutemen, "Green Mountain Boys," radical, conservative, tyranny, blockade, Hessians; General Gage, Revere, Dawes, Major Pitcairn, Allen, Patrick Henry, Arnold, Dickinson, Sir William Howe; April 19, 1775, June 17, 1775.

2 The colonists decide to fight for their independence

Up to the spring of 1776, most of the colonists refused to admit that they were fighting a war. In their opinion, they were merely resisting unjust acts of Parliament.

Reasons for caution. A few Patriots, as you know, had already urged the colonists to declare their independence. Most of the colonists, however, were reluctant to make the final break. For one thing, the law, order, and stability maintained by the British government were prizes that no thoughtful people would cast lightly aside.

But there were more immediate reasons why the colonists hesitated to declare their independence. First, if they revolted and failed to win, they could be executed for treason.

To this sobering prospect was coupled the fear of revolution and anarchy° within the colonies themselves. Colonial leaders had seen mobs in action against tax collectors, British revenue officers, and Americans who were sympathetic toward king and Parliament. They did not wish to exchange the tyranny of Great Britain for the still worse tyranny of colonial mobs.

Finally, as long as the colonists were merely resisting specific acts of Parliament, they could count upon powerful support from friends in Great Britain. Britishers like Edmund Burke, William Pitt, John Wilkes, and Isaac Barré (ba-REH) had joined British merchants in their demand that Parliament repeal objectionable legislation. But the Americans knew that the moment that they began to talk of separation from Great Britain, their friends in the mother country would turn against them and unite with all other Britishers in a fight to preserve the British Empire. Indeed, many men and women in the colonies,

••
° *anarchy:* disorder resulting from lack of government control.

perhaps most, were loyally devoted at this time to the British Empire.

Reasons for independence. Two bitter facts offset these arguments against a break with Great Britain. First, the British government had committed acts that many colonists believed violated their rights as Englishmen. Second, colonists had already shed their blood in defense of these rights.

In this explosive atmosphere Thomas Paine's pamphlet *Common Sense* was like a spark dropped in a keg of gunpowder. Paine was a former British political writer, a friend of Benjamin Franklin. He sympathized with the colonial cause and came to America in 1774. His widely read pamphlet appeared in January 1776.

"I offer nothing more than simple facts, plain arguments, and common sense," Paine wrote. In ringing words he pointed out that America had grown into a new and different nation with

■ Throughout the war, Thomas Paine continued writing pamphlets encouraging the patriots to fight on for independence. His words were widely read.

interests of its own. ". . . the period of debate is closed. Arms, as the last resource, must decide the contest. . . . I challenge the warmest advocate for reconciliation to show a single advantage that this continent can reap by being connected with Great Britain. . . . Everything that is right or reasonable pleads for separation. The blood of the slain, the weeping voice of nature cries, *'Tis Time to Part!*" The stirring words of Paine and other Patriots helped to kindle the spirit of independence.

In the debate over a declaration of independence, colonial Americans took opposite sides on the basis of deep and sincere convictions. But, as Thomas Paine pointed out, there were immediate practical advantages to be had from a declaration of independence.

First, as citizens of an independent nation, captured Patriot soldiers might

■ The committee on the writing of the Declaration of Independence included Franklin of Pennsylvania, Jefferson of Virginia, Adams of Massachusetts, Livingston of New York, and Sherman of Connecticut.

claim the treatment of prisoners of war and avoid being shot as rebels. Second, the Patriot governments could confiscate the property of all Americans who remained loyal to the Crown. Third, the Patriots would have a better chance of winning foreign aid. The French and Spanish kings, for example, might look with favor upon a war that promised to weaken the British Empire by detaching from it the American colonies.

Independence declared. Under the pressure of these arguments, colonial sentiment began to shift in favor of separation from Great Britain. On June 7, 1776, Richard Henry Lee of Virginia introduced a resolution in the Second Continental Congress declaring that "these United Colonies are, and of right ought to be, free and independent states." On June 11, before voting on Lee's resolution, the Congress appointed a committee of five men to write a formal Declaration of Independence. These five men were Thomas Jefferson, Benjamin Franklin, John Adams, Robert R. Livingston, and Roger Sherman. Jefferson was asked by the other four members of the committee to do the actual writing.

On June 28 the committee presented Jefferson's Declaration—with a few changes by Franklin and Adams—to Congress. Congress did not at once discuss the Declaration itself. Instead, it debated Lee's resolution and, by adopting it on July 2, officially declared the new United States of America to be independent of Great Britain. Then Congress turned to Jefferson's statement, which they continued to discuss on July 3.

On July 4, after making several alterations, Congress adopted the Declaration of Independence. In bold strokes John Hancock of Massachusetts, president of the Congress, signed the document. Then the other delegates signed. Copies were immediately prepared and rushed to the legislatures of the newly created states. Finally, on July 8, the Declaration was read and officially proclaimed in Philadelphia.

■ As the Declaration is read from the courthouse balcony at New York, cheering Patriots have built a bonfire in which they are about to burn King George's coat of arms and other symbols of royal authority. Scenes like this took place throughout the thirteen colonies.

Reactions to the Declaration. Many Americans—the Patriots or Whigs°—greeted this news with wild rejoicing. Bells rang. Men sang and danced around bonfires and held banquets to celebrate the stirring occasion. The long period of indecision had ended.

Other Americans greeted the news with indifference. These people—and there was a substantial number of them in every colony—were not much concerned one way or the other.

A third group—the Loyalists or Tories°—refused to have anything to do with the celebrations. Some sat in silence behind closed doors and barricaded windows. They did not want to separate from Great Britain. Moreover,

....

° **Whig:** the name of a major political party in Great Britain which, among other policies, was opposed to taxing the colonies. For this reason, the Patriots in America were sometimes called Whigs.

° **Tory:** the name of another major political party in Great Britain that opposed the Whigs. Since this party believed strongly in the power of the king, American colonists loyal to the king were sometimes called Tories.

for them the bonfires were omens of terror. They had witnessed enough violence during the past ten years to know what to expect—neighbor against neighbor, beatings, tar and feathers, burning houses, flight for safety to Canada or the British West Indies or England. And the Tories, who were now regarded as traitors in their own land, included a high proportion of people with wealth and influence—merchants, lawyers, landowners, former officers of the king, members of the clergy.

The Declaration of Independence. The document in which Thomas Jefferson and his fellow Patriots declared American independence has become one of history's most cherished statements. For nearly 200 years freedom-seeking people all over the world have been inspired by its noble ideas and remarkable eloquence. Our admiration for the Declaration, however, should not obscure the fact that it was a practical document with three major purposes. As you read about these three purposes, turn also to the text of the

In the Pennsylvania State House, now Independence Hall, the Declaration and the Constitution were signed. The statue is of John Barry, Irish-American naval hero of the War for Independence.

Declaration of Independence (pages 122–24) and read the passages that correspond to the three following headings.

1. Preamble and reasons for separation. In the first place, the Declaration was an attempt to win public support for the cause of independence. This appeal to the public of both Europe and America was contained in the "preamble," or introduction, and in the twenty-seven "reasons for separation" from Great Britain. The king was pictured as an evil ruler who intended to establish an absolute tyranny over the colonies. Each grievance was a harsh indictment of George III. "He has forbidden . . . he has plundered . . . he has refused . . . he has constrained . . ." In contrast, the colonists were pictured as patient, submissive, long-suffering citizens. "We have petitioned . . . we have warned . . . we have reminded . . . we have appealed . . ."

2. A new theory of government. The second major purpose of the Declaration of Independence explains why it remains today one of the most influential documents ever written. It has lived because it outlined an inspiring theory of government.

In the opening lines of the second paragraph of the Declaration of Independence, Thomas Jefferson clearly and simply stated the basic principles of what today we call democracy. ". . . all men are created equal," he wrote. ". . . they are endowed by their Creator with certain unalienable rights; . . . among these are life, liberty, and the pursuit of happiness." "Unalienable rights" are rights which cannot be taken away from the people—not by any government, not even by the people themselves.

What is the purpose of government? Jefferson replied that governments exist "to secure these rights." Where do governments obtain this authority? They derive "their just powers from the consent of the governed." What happens when a government begins to act like a tyrant? "It is the right of the people to alter or to abolish it, and to institute new government."

The Declaration of Independence, in this passage, clearly stated the right of the American colonists to revolt against their British rulers. It stated this idea in terms familiar to many people in both Europe and America. More than that, the theories outlined in the Declaration were an invitation to all men, in all times, to assume the right to rule themselves and to accept as truth that knowledge to which their reason had guided them.

3. A formal declaration of war. The third major purpose of the Declaration, which is contained in the final paragraph, was to announce formally that war existed. As Thomas Paine had predicted, this announcement had certain practical advantages for the Patriots. But it could also have grave consequences. If the Patriots failed to make good their claim to independence, the leaders of the revolution could be judged guilty of treason against the British Crown, and could be executed as traitors.

The words in which the delegates pledged "our lives, our fortunes, and our sacred honor" to the successful outcome of the struggle were not idle words. Every delegate who bent to sign the document must have done so with a deep sense of anxiety. They were pledging everything to the cause. Failure would mean ruin.

The ringing of the Liberty Bell in the State House, later known as Independence Hall, at Philadelphia heralded the colonists' separation from the British Empire. But the simple, clear, precise prose of the Declaration of Independence heralded a development of far greater significance—the determination of free men to rid themselves forever from the tyranny of unwanted rulers.

SECTION SURVEY

1. Give four reasons why most of the colonists hesitated to make a final break with Great Britain in the spring of 1776.

2. What three important arguments did Thomas Paine present in favor of a declaration of independence?

3. How did the colonists react to the Declaration of Independence?

4. Show how the Declaration of Independence was (a) an appeal for public support, (b) a statement of theory for a new kind of government, and (c) a declaration of war. Quote from the document.

IDENTIFY: anarchy, *Common Sense,* Whigs, Tories, unalienable rights, contract theory of governments; Barré, Burke, Pitt, Richard Henry Lee, Jefferson, Locke, Hancock; July 4, 1776.

"UNALIENABLE RIGHTS"

No other public document has been so important to the *conscience* of American citizens as the Declaration of Independence. There, in stirring words, Jefferson stated the purpose of all government, namely, to secure these unalienable rights: Life, Liberty, and the Pursuit of Happiness. Over the next century of our history, and extending into our own lifetime—from the disputes over the first state laws to the present excitements about civil rights—the Declaration has been a challenge. Shall we take risks, and suffer some inconvenience, to do justice to all? Often there is some reason in fear or laziness to make us turn away from the challenge. But the cost of ignoring injustice can disturb a conscience which is reminded of the Declaration of Independence. From what we know of Thomas Jefferson, he probably meant it to be that way.

Where did Americans of Jefferson's time get their idea of unalienable rights? They lived some fifteen hundred years after the early Christians who, by refusing to worship Rome's emperors, had refused to render unto Caesar what belonged to God. Jefferson may never have realized that this was the greatest battle of conscience in our history. He got his notion of "self-evident" truths after many others, before his time, had established the standards of freedom. That all of us, ruler and ruled alike, enjoy moral equality, because we are all created to the one end of union with God, had to be established first. Only this truth makes the others "self-evident." Once this truth is established, there are good reasons to criticize any ruler who denies men the liberty such created beings deserve, and good reasons why some who enjoy liberty must not deny it to others.

THE DECLARATION OF INDEPENDENCE

In Congress, July 4, 1776

PREAMBLE

When, in the course of human events, it becomes necessary for one people to dissolve the political bands which have connected them with another, and to assume, among the powers of the earth, the separate and equal station to which the laws of nature and of nature's God entitle them, a decent respect to the opinions of mankind requires that they should declare the causes which impel them to the separation.

A NEW THEORY OF GOVERNMENT

We hold these truths to be self-evident: that all men are created equal, that they are endowed by their Creator with certain unalienable rights, that among these are life, liberty, and the pursuit of happiness.

That, to secure these rights, governments are instituted among men, deriving their just powers from the consent of the governed; that whenever any form of government becomes destructive of these ends, it is the right of the people to alter or to abolish it, and to institute new government, laying its foundation on such principles, and organizing its powers in such form, as to them shall seem most likely to effect their safety and happiness. Prudence, indeed, will dictate that governments long established should not be changed for light and transient causes; and accordingly all experience hath shown that mankind are more disposed to suffer while evils are sufferable, than to right themselves by abolishing the forms to which they are accustomed. But when a long train of abuses and usurpations, pursuing invariably the same object, evinces a design to reduce them under absolute despotism, it is their right, it is their duty, to throw off such government, and to provide new guards for their future security.

REASONS FOR SEPARATION

Such has been the patient sufferance of these colonies; and such is now the necessity which constrains them to alter their former systems of government. The history of the present king of Great Britain is a history of repeated injuries and usurpations, all having in direct object the establishment of an absolute tyranny over these states. To prove this, let facts be submitted to a candid world.

He has refused his assent to laws the most wholesome and necessary for the public good.

He has forbidden his governors to pass laws of immediate and pressing importance, unless suspended in their operation till his assent should be obtained; and when so suspended, he has utterly neglected to attend to them.

He has refused to pass other laws for the accommodation of large districts of people, unless those people would relinquish the right of representation in the legislature, a right inestimable to them, and formidable to tyrants only.

He has called together legislative bodies at places unusual, uncomfortable, and distant from the depository of their public records, for the sole purpose of fatiguing them into compliance with his measures.

He has dissolved representative houses repeatedly, for opposing, with manly firmness, his invasions on the rights of the people.

He has refused, for a long time after such dissolutions, to cause others to be elected; whereby the legislative powers, incapable of annihilation, have returned to the people at large for their exercise; the state remaining, in the mean time, exposed to all the dangers of invasion from without and convulsions within.

He has endeavored to prevent the population of these states; for that purpose obstructing the laws of naturalization of foreigners, refusing to pass others to encourage their migration hither, and raising the conditions of new appropriations of lands.

He has obstructed the administration of justice, by refusing his assent to laws for establishing judiciary powers.

He has made judges dependent on his will alone for the tenure of their offices, and the amount and payment of their salaries.

He has erected a multitude of new offices, and sent hither swarms of officers to harass our people and eat out their substance.

He has kept among us, in times of peace, standing armies, without the consent of our legislature.

He has affected to render the military independent of, and superior to, the civil power.

He has combined with others to subject us to a jurisdiction foreign to our constitution and unacknowledged by our laws, giving his assent to their acts of pretended legislation:

For quartering large bodies of armed troops among us;

For protecting them, by a mock trial, from punishment for any murders which they should commit on the inhabitants of these states;

For cutting off our trade with all parts of the world;

For imposing taxes on us without our consent;

For depriving us, in many cases, of the benefits of trial by jury;

For transporting us beyond seas, to be tried for pretended offenses;

For abolishing the free system of English laws in a neighboring province, establishing therein an arbitrary government, and enlarging its boundaries, so as to render it at once an example and fit instrument for introducing the same absolute rule into these colonies;

For taking away our charters, abolishing our most valuable laws, and altering, fundamentally, the forms of our governments;

For suspending our own legislature, and declaring themselves invested with power to legislate for us in all cases whatsoever.

He has abdicated government here, by declaring us out of his protection and waging war against us.

He has plundered our seas, ravaged our coasts, burned our towns, and destroyed the lives of our people.

He is at this time transporting large armies of foreign mercenaries to complete the works of death, desolation, and tyranny already begun with circumstances of cruelty and perfidy scarcely paralleled in the most barbarous ages, and totally unworthy the head of a civilized nation.

He has constrained our fellow-citizens, taken captive on the high seas, to bear arms against their country, to become the executioners of their friends and brethren, or to fall themselves by their hands.

He has excited domestic insurrections among us, and has endeavored to bring on the inhabitants of our frontiers the merciless Indian savages, whose known rule of warfare is an undistinguished destruction of all ages, sexes, and conditions.

In every stage of these oppressions we have petitioned for redress in the most humble terms; our repeated petitions have been answered only by repeated injury. A prince whose character is thus marked by every act which may define a tyrant is unfit to be the ruler of a free people.

Nor have we been wanting in attention to our British brethren. We have warned them, from time to time, of attempts by their legislature to extend an unwarrantable jurisdiction over us. We have reminded them of the circumstances of our emigration and settlement here. We have appealed to their native justice and magnanimity; and we have conjured them, by the ties of our common kindred, to disavow these usurpations, which would inevitably interrupt our connections and correspondence. They, too, have been deaf to the voice of justice and of consanguinity. We must, therefore, acquiesce in the necessity which denounces our separation, and hold them, as we hold the rest of mankind, enemies in war, in peace, friends.

We, therefore, the representatives of the United States of America, in General Congress assembled, appealing to the Supreme Judge of the world for the rectitude of our intentions, do, in the name and by authority of the good people of these colonies, solemnly publish and declare, that these united colonies are, and of right ought to be, free and independent states; that they are absolved from all allegiance to the British crown, and that all political connection between them and the state of Great Britain is, and ought to be, totally dissolved; and that, as free and independent states, they have full power to levy war, conclude peace, contract alliances, establish commerce, and to do all other acts and things which independent states may of right do. And, for the support of this declaration, with a firm reliance on the protection of Divine Providence, we mutually pledge to each other our lives, our fortunes, and our sacred honor.

John Hancock (MASSACHUSETTS)

NEW HAMPSHIRE
Josiah Bartlett
William Whipple
Matthew Thornton

MASSACHUSETTS
Samuel Adams
John Adams
Robert Treat Paine
Elbridge Gerry

NEW YORK
William Floyd
Philip Livingston
Francis Lewis
Lewis Morris

NEW JERSEY
Richard Stockton
John Witherspoon
Francis Hopkinson
John Hart
Abraham Clark

DELAWARE
Caesar Rodney
George Read
Thomas McKean

MARYLAND
Samuel Chase
William Paca
Thomas Stone
Charles Carroll
  of Carrollton

NORTH CAROLINA
William Hooper
Joseph Hewes
John Penn

SOUTH CAROLINA
Edward Rutledge
Thomas Heyward, Jr.
Thomas Lynch, Jr.
Arthur Middleton

RHODE ISLAND
Stephen Hopkins
William Ellery

CONNECTICUT
Roger Sherman
Samuel Huntington
William Williams
Oliver Wolcott

PENNSYLVANIA
Robert Morris
Benjamin Rush
Benjamin Franklin
John Morton
George Clymer
James Smith
George Taylor
James Wilson
George Ross

VIRGINIA
George Wythe
Richard Henry Lee
Thomas Jefferson
Benjamin Harrison
Thomas Nelson, Jr.
Francis Lightfoot Lee
Carter Braxton

GEORGIA
Button Gwinnett
Lyman Hall
George Walton

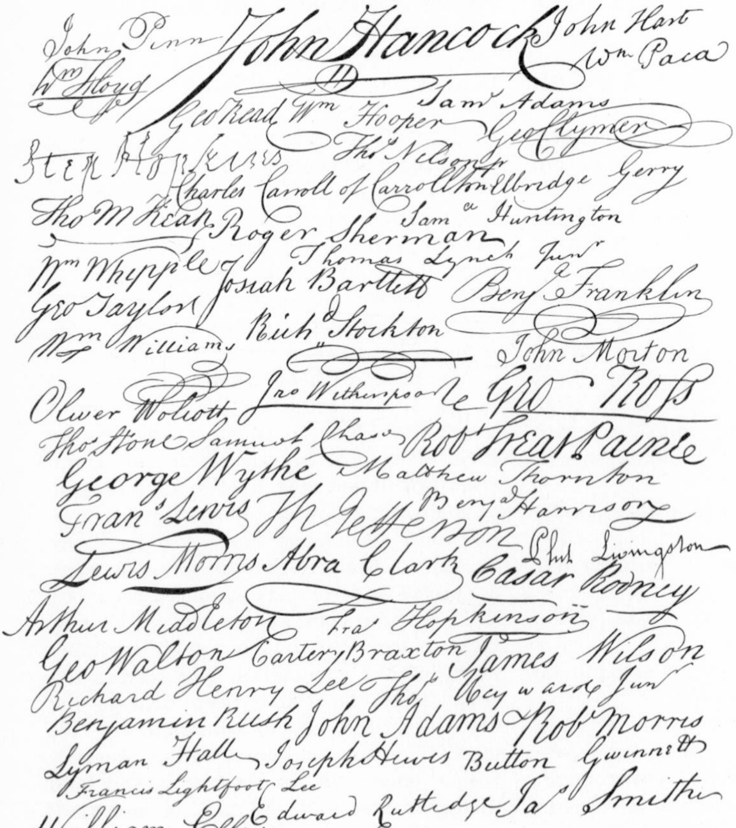

3 American Patriots wage and win the Revolutionary War

In the spring of 1776, while the colonists were debating the question of independence, General Washington moved the Continental Army from Boston to New York. Washington was sure that the British would try to seize New York City and use it as a base of operations for their land and naval forces. By July Washington had nearly 30,000 men guarding the city.

Fighting around New York City. On July 2, the same day that the Second Continental Congress voted to declare the colonies independent, General Sir William Howe sailed into New York harbor and began to land British and Hessian troops on Staten Island (see map 2, this page). A few days later his brother, Admiral Lord Richard Howe, sailed into the harbor with powerful naval reinforcements and a fleet of more than 100 transports. By the end of August, British forces in the New York area numbered more than 30,000 men, of whom more than 8000 were Hessian soldiers hired by the British to fight in America.

Late in August General Howe landed about 20,000 men on Long Island, where General Washington had stationed the bulk of the Continental Army. Howe's troops forced the Americans back to Brooklyn Heights.

The Americans were now caught in a trap. The British army was in front of them. The British fleet was behind them, ready to sail into the East River to cut their only avenue of escape.

Fortunately for Washington, General Howe did not attack immediately. Under cover of fog and darkness, the Americans crossed the East River in small boats and reached the temporary safety of Manhattan Island.

But the British fleet controlled the water around Manhattan Island, and Washington was unable to hold the city. After several sharp engagements he

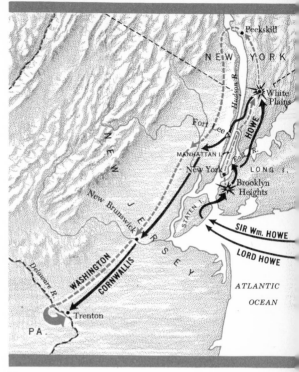

❷ War Around New York: July–December 1776

withdrew northward to White Plains, leaving the British in command of New York City and its splendid harbor.

Retreat across New Jersey. By late October 1776 Washington's position was becoming increasingly desperate. Winter was approaching. The Americans had lost heavily in men and supplies. The army was rapidly melting away as the men, faced with what seemed inevitable defeat, picked up their guns and returned to their homes.

Faced with this difficult situation, General Washington decided to retreat across New Jersey and into Pennsylvania. Once in Pennsylvania, he would have the Delaware River between himself and the British, and he would gain time to regroup his battered forces.

During the retreat across New Jersey, men continued to slip away from the army. By the time Washington reached the Delaware River, he had only about 3000 troops under his command. Weary and discouraged, the soldiers combed

125

British reinforcements under Cornwallis rushed to the Trenton area, reaching there on January 2, 1777. Cornwallis, certain that he had Washington in a trap, prepared to attack in the morning. During the night the American troops slipped quietly away, leaving their campfires burning brightly to deceive the British into thinking that they were still there.

Instead of retiring to the safety of the west bank of the Delaware River, Washington struck inland, badly cut up three British regiments at Princeton, and withdrew swiftly to the hills around Morristown in northern New Jersey (see map 3, this page). There he was in a position to make raids upon the British lines of communication and supply between New York, New Brunswick, and Trenton. Since the latter cities were no longer of any particular value to the British, Howe pulled his troops out of New Jersey.

Washington's victories at Trenton and Princeton ruined British plans for ending the war in the winter of 1776–77. "All our hopes were blasted by that unhappy affair," declared Great Britain's colonial secretary. In contrast, American spirits began to revive. The Americans now had reason to believe they could actually win battles against British regulars. During the next few months volunteers began to swell the ranks of the Continental Army.

Washington had taken great chances, but he had won the gamble. One year after the war had officially opened, the British held only New York City, and Newport, Rhode Island.°

British disaster at Saratoga. Aroused to more vigorous efforts by their defeats at Trenton and Princeton, the British now determined to end the war in 1777. They decided upon a plan that would separate New England from the rest of the colonies.

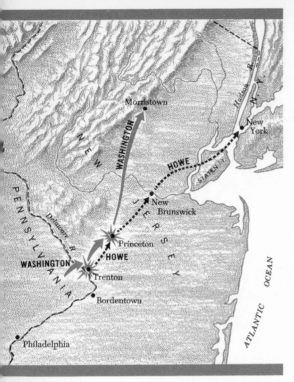

❸ New Jersey Campaigns: Winter of 1776–77

the river for small boats, which they then rowed across to the Pennsylvania side (see map 2, page 125). There Washington's troops went into a cold and cheerless winter encampment.

Victories at Trenton and Princeton. Confident that the war was almost won, General Howe prepared to celebrate Christmas in New York. To keep a watch upon the remnants of the American army, General Charles Cornwallis, commanding the British forces in the field, stationed 1300 Hessians at Trenton and a second force a few miles farther south.

Howe's Christmas celebration was rudely interrupted. Opening a campaign that Frederick the Great of Prussia later called one of the most brilliant in military history, Washington and his troops crossed the ice-choked Delaware on Christmas night. Early the next morning they surprised the Hessians and took more than 1000 prisoners.

· ·

° Early in the war after the British seized New York City, they also captured Newport, an important seaport at the mouth of Narragansett Bay.

126

■ General Benedict Arnold received a leg wound as he and his American troops attacked a position held by Hessian soldiers (in tall helmets) at the Battle of Saratoga. American forces, under Arnold and other generals, won the victory, which became a turning point in the War for Independence. Arnold, a brilliant general, later turned traitor to the American cause and finally died in London, despised by Americans and Britishers alike.

Lieutenant Colonel Barry St. Leger (SEHNT LEJ-ur) was to lead an expedition, with some Indian allies, from Fort Oswego (oz-WE-go) on Lake Ontario through the Mohawk Valley to the Hudson River (see map 4, page 128). General John Burgoyne was to lead a second expedition from Canada down the Richelieu River–Lake Champlain route. General Howe was to lead a third expedition from New York City up the Hudson River. These three forces were to meet at Albany and crush the American forces.

The plan looked beautifully simple to the men who sat in the warmth and comfort of the London War Office and drew lines on the map. What they did not know, or ignored, was that these lines crossed lakes, swamps, mountains, and trackless forests inhabited by hostile Indians and swarming with militiamen ready to defend their homes, villages, and farms.

St. Leger reached the Mohawk Valley on schedule and laid siege to Fort Stanwix, where American forces were stationed. If the fort fell, St. Leger would have a clear road open before him to Albany. General Nicholas Herkimer of New York and a force of German-American militiamen tried to reach Fort Stanwix and reinforce it, but a party of Tories and Indians ambushed them near Oriskany (o-RIS-kah-ny).

General Herkimer, himself badly wounded and soon to die, had no choice but to retreat eastward, leaving the greatly outnumbered garrison in Fort Stanwix to make out as best it could. The situation for the Americans was desperate when, suddenly, word spread

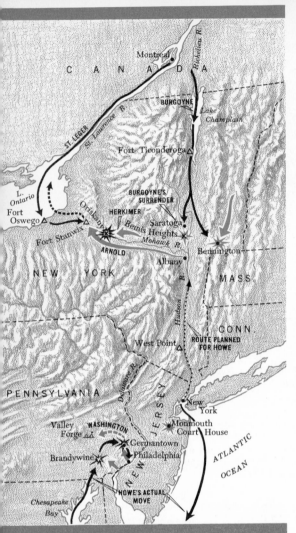

4 Saratoga and Philadelphia Campaigns: 1777-78

mont, where they were destroyed at Bennington by General John Stark and a force of New England militiamen.

Burgoyne's position was now difficult, if not impossible. His provisions were almost gone, his lines of supply were stretched to a dangerous length from Canada through the forests, and the militia of New England and New York were swarming around him like angry bees. Moreover, Howe had failed to join him. Nevertheless, Burgoyne chose to advance.

At Bemis Heights near Saratoga, on the upper reaches of the Hudson River, Burgoyne met the main body of the American forces in the area. Outnumbered by more than two to one and outmaneuvered by the American leaders—Philip Schuyler of New York, Horatio Gates of Virginia, Benjamin Lincoln of Massachusetts, Daniel Morgan of Virginia, and Benedict Arnold of Connecticut—Burgoyne surrendered his entire force of more than 4000 men at Saratoga on October 17, 1777.

An unexplained blunder. Burgoyne might have been saved had the planned British expedition up the Hudson River appeared in time. But it never did appear. Instead of marching northward from New York City, Howe embarked his troops and sailed southward. American scouts followed his progress down the coast. Much to their surprise, he passed the mouth of the Delaware River, sailed to the head of Chesapeake Bay, and disembarked. Then he marched to Philadelphia, overcoming Patriot resistance in the battles of Brandywine Creek on September 11 and Germantown on October 4 (see map 4, this page). Once he was in Philadelphia, Howe settled down for the winter of 1777-78, while Washington went into encampment at Valley Forge, about eighteen miles west of the city.

Why Howe failed to carry through his part of the plan to split the colonies remains uncertain. Perhaps the British War Office blundered and neglected to send the orders in time. Perhaps Howe took matters into his own hands, decid-

through St. Leger's forces that Benedict Arnold was approaching with a large American army. St. Leger's Indians deserted, and he had to retreat to Canada.

Meanwhile, a second British force was moving southward from Canada down the difficult Richelieu River–Lake Champlain route. General Burgoyne, its leader, was just as ignorant of the American wilderness as were his superiors in England. He reached and occupied Fort Ticonderoga without serious opposition. Then his troubles began. In an effort to secure additional supplies, he sent a small raiding party of about 500 Hessian troops into what is now Vering that Burgoyne could handle the situation without help. For whatever reason, Howe's failure to proceed up the Hudson River contributed to the British disaster at Saratoga.

Americans went wild with joy at the news of Burgoyne's defeat. Frenchmen, who were sympathetic to the American cause, celebrated as though they, too, had won a victory. But the British Parliament, sobered by the news, sent commissioners to the Continental Congress with an offer to suspend the Intolerable Acts and pardon the Patriots. Unfortunately for the British, their concessions came nearly two years too late.

France joins in. Aware of what was going on in England, Benjamin Franklin, one of the American commissioners to France, began some shrewd bargaining. His skillful negotiations were crowned with success. France, which from the beginning had been secretly aiding the Americans, now declared war on Great Britain. France hoped by

■ "Yankee Doodle," a British song meant to ridicule Americans, was adopted as a popular American song. New Yorkers prize this "Doodletown" legend.

this means to weaken its long-time rival and to secure revenge for the crushing defeat that the French had suffered in the Seven Years' War.

On February 6, 1778, France and the United States of America signed two treaties. In the first, a commercial

■ General Washington and the young Marquis de Lafayette stand in a biting wind at Valley Forge while tattered American troops try to warm themselves and make some hot food around a fire. Not far away, in Philadelphia, British officers and troops were living in comfort.

JOHN PAUL JONES

John Paul Jones (1747–92), a sandy-haired Scotsman who measured only five feet five inches in his stocking feet, became one of America's great naval heroes during the Revolutionary War.

Born in Scotland, John Paul (the "Jones" came later) first went to sea at the age of thirteen. By the time he was twenty-one he had risen to command of his own vessel. During the next few years his business ventures turned out so well that, by 1773, he was able to retire, if he wished, with a modest income. Then misfortune struck. Forced while in the West Indies to kill a man in self-defense, he escaped with his life only by fleeing to the American colonies under an assumed name—the name of Jones.

In 1775, when the American navy was being organized at Philadelphia, John Paul Jones offered his services and received a commission as a lieutenant. He quickly demonstrated his ability, and in 1776 was given his own command. He won a number of victories in the North Atlantic. In 1778, while cruising off the coasts of Ireland and Scotland in his ship the *Ranger*, he sank a number of enemy ships, and captured a British sloop of war, H.M.S. *Drake*.

Jones' most memorable victory—considered by some naval historians as the greatest naval victory of the war—took place in 1779. Cruising in British waters in an old French ship which he had renamed the *Bonhomme Richard*, he engaged H.M.S. *Serapis*. With his own warship about to sink, Jones lashed the two ships together, and in desperate fighting, much of it hand-to-hand, finally won the victory. It was at the height of this battle, when asked to surrender, that he made his famous defiant statement, "I have not yet begun to fight."

treaty, the two nations agreed to give each other favored treatment in matters of trade. In the other, a treaty of alliance, France agreed to recognize the independence of the United States of America and to wage war upon Great Britain until America was free. America promised to defend the French West Indies. Both countries promised not to make a separate peace with Great Britain.

French co-operation was announced none too soon. Despite the victory at Saratoga, the Americans were in bad shape. Washington's army at Valley Forge was reduced to a handful of poorly equipped, sick, hungry men. But the glad news that they now had a powerful ally filled the Patriots with new hope. Recruits began again to fill the thinned ranks of the army.

Foreign aid arrives. In addition to French aid, Spain and the Netherlands both supported the American cause, and volunteers from a number of European countries came to America. From Prussia came Baron von Steuben, who carried the main burden of organizing and drilling the Continental Army. From Poland came Casimir Pulaski (KAZ-uhmeer pu-LAS-ky) and Thaddeus Kosciusko (koz-ee-USS-ko), who planned the American defenses of West Point on the Hudson River and Bemis Heights near Saratoga. From France came the German-born officer, Baron de Kalb, and the young Marquis de Lafayette, who arrived in America with twelve other officers just before the Battle of Brandywine. After entering the war, France sent gold, powder, shot, equipment, a fleet, and a considerable number of troops to aid the American forces.

The British revise their plans. French intervention forced the British to revise their plans for conquering their former colonies. As a first step, they replaced General Howe with Sir Henry Clinton.

Clinton had orders to strike the next blow at the southern states. Before doing this, however, he withdrew the British troops from Philadelphia and set out across New Jersey toward New York City. Washington pursued the British and overtook them at Monmouth Court House (see map 4, page 128). The battle was indecisive, with about 350 casualties on each side, and the British continued their withdrawal to New York.

From then on, all major military activities ended in the north, although occasionally British raiding parties swept down on towns near New York City.

War in the south. In shifting the attack to the south, Great Britain hoped to profit from the aid of the Tories who were reported to be especially numerous in the southern states.

As in the north, the British had no great trouble occupying any seaports they wished. In December 1778 they seized Savannah, Georgia. In May 1780 they forced General Benjamin Lincoln to surrender Charleston, South Carolina, with 5000 troops—practically the entire American army south of the Potomac River. From these bases General Cornwallis, who now commanded the British armies in the southern states, was able to move where and when he pleased. Under General Cornwallis and Lieutenant Colonel Banastre Tarleton, a daring cavalry leader, British forces

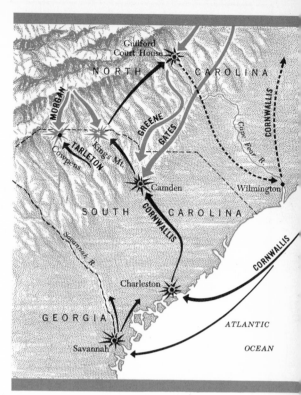

5 War in the South: 1778–81

raided the country, plundering and burning in an effort to terrorize the Patriots. and force them into submission.

But for every Tory who rallied to the British, there was a Patriot who sprang up in opposition. In South Carolina guerrilla bands of farmers and hunters, under the command of southern leaders .like Francis Marion, called "the Swamp Fox," Andrew Pickens, and Thomas Sumter, swarmed about the British forces. To aid these guerrilla bands, Congress sent a small army under the command of General Horatio Gates. Gates, however, was badly defeated at Camden, South Carolina, in August 1780 (see map 5, this page).

It now seemed as though the south were lost to the Patriot cause. But in October 1780 a band of frontiersmen led by Isaac Shelby, John Sevier, and others defeated a party of Tories at Kings Mountain, near the boundary be-

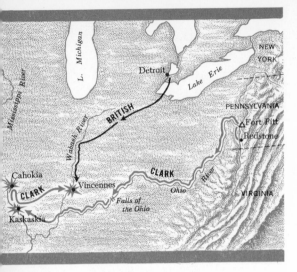

Court House, North Carolina (see map 5, page 131). Although Cornwallis won, his losses were so great that he finally abandoned the entire campaign and withdrew to the security of the coast.

And so by 1781 the British were back where they had been in 1778. They held only the city of New York and a few southern seaports. The campaign in the south had been no more successful than the earlier northern campaigns.

Campaign in the Northwest. Meanwhile, Lieutenant Colonel George Rogers Clark of Virginia had been clearing the western lands of British troops. From Virginia, whose claim to this territory went back to the charter of 1609, Clark secured money and supplies for the expedition. With a small band of hardened frontiersmen, he made his way down the Ohio River and up the Mississippi in the summer of 1778, won the aid of Indians, and surprised the British forts at Kaskaskia, Cahokia, and Vincennes (see map 6, this page). In December, however, Clark suffered a setback when the British recaptured Vincennes. But then in February 1779, in the dead of winter, Clark accomplished what seemed impossible by marching 170 miles eastward through the wilderness to surprise and overwhelm the British garrison at Fort Vincennes. This bold blow cleared the entire western lands of British forces.

tween the Carolinas. At the same time Nathanael Greene of Rhode Island replaced Gates as commander of the American forces in the south.

Although General Greene won no major battles, he and General Daniel Morgan of Virginia, supported by the guerrillas, made the British occupation of inland regions extremely costly. In January 1781 Morgan defeated Tarleton's British force at Cowpens, in South Carolina. Two months later, in March, the Americans struck a serious blow against Cornwallis' forces at Guilford

American uniforms—Revolutionary War

The British surrender. During the summer of 1781, the war proceeded swiftly to a conclusion. Cornwallis moved northward into Virginia and based his army at Yorktown on the peninsula between the York and James Rivers (see map 7, this page). He was supplied by the British fleet operating out of New York harbor. A small American army under Generals Lafayette, Von Steuben, and Anthony Wayne of Pennsylvania watched the British closely, but the American forces were too weak to attack. Washington and a number of American and French soldiers remained at White Plains, New York, to keep an eye upon the British garrison under General Clinton in the city of New York.

This was the situation when a messenger from Admiral de Grasse, commander of the French fleet operating in the West Indies, arrived one day at Washington's headquarters. De Grasse reported that the fleet could be spared for a few months. Where, he asked, could Washington use it most effectively?

With skill and dispatch Washington quickly formulated and carried out a brilliant plan. Following Washington's instructions, De Grasse placed his fleet across the mouth of Chesapeake Bay, thereby cutting off Cornwallis from his sources of supplies and reinforcements. The American army in White Plains then feinted at New York, leading General Clinton to believe that an attack upon the city was imminent. Instead of striking at New York, however, Washington made a forced march to Chesapeake Bay, where he and his army embarked on a fleet of transports and joined the French and American forces, including the southern militia, in front of Yorktown (see map 7, this page).

Cornwallis was hopelessly trapped. Behind him was the French fleet. Before him was a greatly superior force of Americans, reinforced by 6000 French troops under General Jean Rochambeau (roh-shahn-BO). After a British squadron failed to break the French blockade, Cornwallis was ready to admit

7 War Around Yorktown: August–October 19, 1781

defeat. He surrendered his entire army of 7000 men on October 19, 1781. Although the formal treaty of peace was not signed until 1783, all serious fighting on the American continent ceased with the American victory at Yorktown.

⌗ SECTION SURVEY

1. Why were Washington's victories at Trenton and Princeton so important?

2. Explain why the Battle of Saratoga has been called the turning point of the American Revolution.

3. How did the following contribute to American victory: (a) Treaty of Alliance with France in 1778, (b) Von Steuben, (c) Pulaski, (d) Kosciusko, (e) De Kalb, (f) Lafayette, (g) George Rogers Clark?

4. Why did the British campaign in the south fail?

IDENTIFY: commercial treaty; Burgoyne, Schuyler, Gates, Cornwallis, Francis Marion, Daniel Morgan, Greene, De Grasse, John Paul Jones; 1777, 1778, 1781.

4 The victorious Americans gain a favorable Treaty of Peace

Why did Great Britain lose the war? Both sides—the United States of America and Great Britain—faced serious problems during the eight long years of the war. In the end, however, the British problems proved to be more formidable than those of the Americans.

American weaknesses. In their struggle toward victory, the Americans had to overcome several severe handicaps.

One major American weakness was the lack of any really effective central government. Until 1781 when, as you will see, the Articles of Confederation went into effect, the Americans fought under the weak leadership of the Second Continental Congress. The delegates to the Continental Congress, who were chosen by the legislatures of the states, had no real authority. They did make George Washington commander in chief of all the military forces, but they had no power to create an army for Washington to lead. They could only ask each of the states to furnish a certain number of men and supplies—and if the states refused, that ended the matter.

Another important weakness of the Americans was the relatively small number of men who were willing to fight or to take any active part in the war. Many Americans were indifferent as to the outcome of the conflict and devoted their efforts to making the war as profitable for themselves as possible. Some merchants charged high prices for shoddy goods, flour infested with weevils, and other inferior materials that they sold to the American armies. Some farmers sold their produce where it would bring the greatest profit, indifferent as to whether it reached American or British hands. As a result of this indifference and selfishness, Washington and his small band of faithful troops starved and froze at Morristown in the winter of 1776–77 and at Valley Forge in the winter of 1777–78, while in Philadelphia, the British soldiers lived in comfort and luxury.

Nor did the Continental Congress have power to raise money by taxation. The Congress could—and did—borrow money from foreign countries and from American citizens. And it could ask the states for money—but if the states refused, Congress was helpless. In the end, Congress financed most of the cost of the war by issuing paper money known as "Continental currency."

Because of these problems the American military effort was weak and disorganized. Except for the first few weeks of the war, in the summer of 1776, Washington never had more than 16,000 troops under his command at any one time, and he was never sure how many of these he could rely on. After each victory volunteers poured in; after each defeat the army melted away. "What we need is a good army, not a

■ The problem of keeping American forces in action inspired this poster pleading for militia support.

IN COUNCIL OF SAFETY,

PHILADELPHIA, *December 8*, 1776.

SIR,

THERE is certain intelligence of General Howe's army being yesterday on its march from Brunswick to Princetown, which puts it beyond a doubt that he intends for this city.—This glorious opportunity of signalizing himself in defence of our country, and securing the Rights of America forever, will be seized by every man who has a spark of patriotic fire in his bosom. We entreat you to march the Militia under your command with all possible expedition to this city, and bring with you as many waggons as you can possibly procure, which you are hereby authorized to impress, if they cannot be had otherwise—Delay not a moment, it may be fatal and subject you and all you hold most dear to the ruffian hands of the enemy, whose cruelties are without distinction and unequalled.

By Order of the Council,

DAVID RITTENHOUSE, Vice-President.

To the COLONELS *or* COMMANDING OFFICERS *of the respective* Battalions *of this* STATE.

TWO O'CLOCK, P.M.

THE Enemy are at Trenton, and all the City Militia are marched to meet them.

large one," Washington once bitterly remarked. He was destined to have neither. And yet his faith and courage never faltered. It was this faith combined with the unselfish devotion of many soldiers and citizens that finally carried the Patriots to victory.

Geography handicaps the British. Fortunately for the Americans, the British were confronted with even more difficult problems. One of these was the problem created by geography.

When the war started, the Americans occupied the enormous territory from Canada to Florida. The only foothold the British had in this area was the seaport of Boston. In order to win the war, the Americans needed only to hold on to what they had. The British, on the other hand, had to try to regain control of this enormous territory. And in order to regain control, they had to send troops and supplies 3000 miles across the Atlantic in slow sailing ships. A number of British military experts were certain that the task was hopeless, and the Adjutant General of the British army called it "as wild an idea as ever controverted common sense."

Handicapped by the problem of supply, the British were never able to conquer and hold any sizable inland area. Although the Royal Navy controlled the seas and could conquer any seaport it wished at any time, the Americans could always move temporarily inland, where it was difficult for the British to supply a regular army.

British blunders. The British government was guilty of many blunders and much mismanagement. No great effort was made to concentrate an overwhelming force against the Americans. To use an American expression, the British War Office "sent a boy to do a man's errand."

Great Britain's major asset was its professional army. Well organized, well trained, well equipped, and well fed, the British regulars were more than a match for the Patriot troops in any engagement on open, unforested land. But the British regulars were often used badly, for their superiors in England

MONEY FOR THE WAR

It takes money, as well as munitions, to fight a war. Three patriots who helped to bolster the finances of the Continental Congress were Haym Salomon, Gabriel Manigault, and Robert Morris.

Haym Salomon arrived in New York from Poland in 1772. A quiet, thoughtful, dignified man, he quickly established his reputation as a financier whose word was as good as his bond. When the Revolution broke out, he proved himself a true friend of his newly adopted country. Arrested as a spy by the British and condemned to death, Salomon escaped and fled to Philadelphia. There, during the remainder of the war, he continued to lend financial support to the Continental Congress. When the war ended, his country owed him more than $650,000. This debt was never paid.

Gabriel Manigault of South Carolina, the son of a French Huguenot, made a fortune from trade and from his extensive rice plantation. One of the richest men in America, he owned more than 47,000 acres of land. A staunch supporter of the American cause, he enlisted in the Revolutionary forces at the age of seventy-five. During the war he lent the South Carolina Revolutionary Government $220,000, only $40,000 of which was ever repaid.

Robert Morris, a highly successful merchant and businessman of Philadelphia and a signer of the Declaration of Independence, handled the banking business for the Continental Congress. A man of great daring and far-ranging imagination, he resorted to many expedients to raise money for Washington's armies. Although the risks he took often brought him personally to the verge of bankruptcy, he never flagged in his efforts. It is questionable whether Washington's armies could have continued the struggle without the support that Robert Morris was able to provide.

often revealed a hopeless ignorance of the land and the people of America.

One of Great Britain's major mistakes was its reliance upon the so-called Hessian soldiers hired by George III. Many of these unfortunate Germans had been seized forcibly by their rulers, who received payment for them from George III, and shipped them to America. Bewildered and homesick, they knew nothing about the war and cared less. As a result, they made poor soldiers.

The Loyalists or Tories who served under British colors, estimated at from 50,000 to 60,000, fought bitterly and even savagely, as is common when former neighbors face each other in civil war. But they, too, were untrained and unorganized, and their presence in the British ranks served to arouse the fighting spirit of the American Patriots.

Leaks in the blockade. The Royal Navy expected to sweep all enemy ships from the sea and by a tight blockade to cut off resources that the Americans would need to fight the war. But since America was a self-sufficient agricultural region, the blockade was an inconvenience rather than a disaster to the Americans.

Then, too, the Americans did have a navy. During the war more than 50 ships were built and commissioned by the Continental Congress and commanded by such men as John Paul Jones. All of the states except Delaware and New Jersey also constructed and manned their own naval vessels. Although these ships were small, it cost the British time and effort to track them down and destroy them.

More difficult for the British to cope with were the American *privateers.* Privateers were privately owned ships whose owners were authorized by the Continental Congress or the state governments to attack enemy shipping. Slipping through the British blockade in fog or darkness, the privateers would strike at defenseless British merchant vessels or small men-of-war. The money from the sale of captured ships and cargoes was divided among owners, captains, and crews. Since fortunes could quickly be made, this risky business attracted thousands of adventurous colonists. "Probably as many as 90,000 Americans were, first and last, engaged in these voyages," wrote one historian. The American privateers ranged far and wide searching for British ships. British losses were so heavy that marine insurance rates soared, even for shipping in the bays and inlets of the British Isles themselves.

The British antagonize other nations. The British fleet interfered with the shipping of neutral nations. Angered by the interference, several of these nations formed the League of Armed Neutrality. Before the war ended, this league included Russia, Sweden, Denmark, Prussia, Portugal, Naples, and several other European countries. In addition, France, Spain, and the Netherlands were openly at war with Great Britain. Throughout the later years of conflict, the war ships of these Euro-

An American privateer

pean nations, combined with the American navy and privateers, placed a heavy drain upon Great Britain's resources. As a result, the war became increasingly unpopular in Great Britain.

British opposition to the war. In fact, many leaders in Great Britain were opposed to the war effort. The situation was so bad that some British politicians and officers exulted at the news of an American victory, and some officers actually refused to serve overseas in America. British merchants, shipowners, and businessmen were losing heavily.

Great Britain could have continued to fight after Cornwallis' defeat at Yorktown in 1781. The British might have concentrated overwhelming forces against the Americans and, by a strict and long-continued blockade, might have finally worn them out to the point where they would have asked for peace. But the price of continuing the war was heavier than most of the British people were willing to pay.

The peace treaty of 1783. There were many difficult questions that had to be settled in the peace treaty following the war. Negotiations began soon after the surrender of Cornwallis in October 1781, but the final treaty, called the Treaty of Paris, was not completed until September 3, 1783.

As the treaty was finally written, the four American commissioners—Benjamin Franklin, John Jay, John Adams, and Henry Laurens—could hardly have secured better terms. By the terms of the treaty, the Americans secured (1) independence, (2) all the land between the Appalachian Mountains and the Mississippi River from the Great Lakes south to Florida,° and (3) the right to fish in the Gulf of St. Lawrence and off Newfoundland (see map, this page).

One of the thorniest problems arose when Great Britain demanded the restoration of all property and land confis-

° Florida, which Spain had turned over to Great Britain in 1763, was now returned to Spain. The northern boundary of Florida was not clearly defined and remained a source of friction between the Spaniards and the Americans until 1795 (see page 216).

The United States
British
Spanish
French (Fr.)
Disputed areas

cated from the Tories, as well as full payment of all debts owed by Americans to Britishers. Franklin and the other American commissioners insisted that this was impossible. The Tory property had been seized by the different states and had long since been sold. Many of the large estates had been divided into numerous pieces. The Continental Congress had no money with which to purchase these properties and return them to their former Tory owners.

Finally, after a long deadlock, the peace commissioners agreed to "recommend" that the new states allow persons with claims to use the American courts to recover their property.

The commissioners also agreed to make a similar recommendation in regard to the private debts. Although the recommendations were meaningless, since Congress could not compel the states to open their courts to Tory claims, the British made the best of the

■ Benjamin Franklin, here shown being introduced at the court of Louis XVI, secured French aid to support the colonies. He is given credit for the tact that did much to secure the peace and the future of the thirteen colonies.

situation and signed the treaty. Astonished at the liberal terms, the French foreign minister, Vergennes, declared, "The English do not make peace; they buy it."

The French, who were not represented in the peace talks until these decisions had been reached, were angry as well as surprised at the discovery that the United States and Great Britain had agreed upon peace terms. It took all of Franklin's arts of persuasion to smooth the ruffled feelings of the French leaders. His success in negotiating the treaty was a tribute to his skill as a diplomat.

It was fortunate for the Americans that they were represented by Franklin. It was even more fortunate that the peace commissioners decided to negotiate directly with Great Britain. Spain wanted to confine the United States of America to the land between the Atlantic and the Appalachians. Had the American commissioners been forced to sit around a peace table with the representatives from Spain, France, and Great Britain, the thirteen colonies would have won only their independ-ence—nothing more. As it was, by making the most of Great Britain's desire for a quick end to the war, Franklin secured for America a number of liberal concessions and a vast expanse of land west of the Appalachians.

✔ SECTION SURVEY

1. List the advantages that Great Britain had over the Americans at the start of the war.

2. Show how each of the following contributed to the American victory: (a) geography, (b) British military policy, (c) American navy and privateers, (d) British problems in Europe, and (e) British problems at home.

3. Summarize the terms of the Treaty of Paris of 1783.

4. Explain what the French foreign minister meant when he declared, "The English do not make peace; they buy it."

5. Describe the part that Benjamin Franklin played in winning the war and making the peace.

IDENTIFY: "Continental currency," privateer, League of Armed Neutrality; Jay, John Adams, Laurens, Salomon, Manigault, Morris.

Points to Discuss: 1. Compare the attitudes of the radicals and conservatives toward Britain in May 1775. Though the conservatives opposed extreme steps, how did they show firmness toward Britain?

2. Thomas Paine's pamphlet *Common Sense* was "like a spark dropped in a keg of gunpowder." Explain what this means.

3. State the economic and political causes of the American Revolution.

4. Discuss the role of each of the following in the history of the Declaration of Independence: (a) John Locke, (b) Thomas Paine, (c) Richard Henry Lee, (d) Thomas Jefferson.

5. John Adams said that "the American Revolution was effected before the war commenced. It was in the minds and hearts of the people." Discuss his contention.

6. It has been said that the Revolution was the work of a willful and courageous minority. Offer evidence to support this.

7. Why may the Declaration of Independence be called the "birth certificate of the American nation"?

Using Maps: 1. (a) Using the map on page 115, indicate the strategic importance of each of the campaigns in New England, the Middle Colonies, the South, and the Northwest. (b) Indicate the area included in the British naval blockade.

2. Locate each of the following: Saratoga, Yorktown, King's Mountain, Valley Forge, and Vincennes.

3. (a) Which color on the war maps in this chapter is associated with the American forces? Which with the British forces? (b) What symbols are used to show the routes of the American and the British armies?

4. (a) Using the map on page 116, reconstruct the fighting around Boston, 1775–76. Check your views with the text. (b) Using the map on page 125, reconstruct the fighting around New York in 1776.

5. (a) Using the map on page 137, describe the boundaries of the United States after the Treaty of Paris of 1783. (b) Summarize the land claims of the European nations in North America at this time.

Consulting the Sources: For evidence of the role of Father Pierre Gibault, frontier French missionary, in aiding the American cause in George Rogers Clark's western campaign, see Ellis, *Docs.*, No. 45. See also Commager and Nevins, *The Heritage of America*, Nos. 33–41, for contemporary accounts of such expeditions.

■ TRACING THE MAIN IDEAS

From the day the first English settlers in the New World began to adapt themselves to life in a strange environment, they began to grow away from their mother country. By 1763 the gap between the colonies and Great Britain was indeed wide. British efforts to draw the colonies into a firmer position in the British Empire, and to get them to help pay for the cost of running the empire, served only to antagonize the colonists. By the spring of 1775, the situation had become exceedingly tense.

Then the explosion went off. With the bloodshed at Lexington and Concord on April 19, 1775, and later at Bunker Hill, all hope of compromise vanished.

In their Declaration of Independence, the American colonists broke their ties with Great Britain and proclaimed their message of freedom to the entire world. On the battlefields of America, aided by French troops and by French naval forces in the Atlantic, the Americans finally succeeded in wearing down the British and winning their independence.

With the Treaty of Paris in 1783, the world recognized that a new nation had been born. It was the first nation in the modern world to break the ties that bound it to another nation and to launch out on its own as an independent country.

As you will see in the next chapter, however, the people of the new nation faced many problems. The most important of these was the problem of organizing an effective government around which Americans could rally with confidence and pride.

8 1775–1787

The States Unite in a Confederation

A LEGISLATIVE MEETING DURING CONFEDERATION

"THE American war is over," one of America's leaders declared in 1783, "but this is far from being the case with the American Revolution."

The speaker was Dr. Benjamin Rush, a prominent physician of Philadelphia and one of the signers of the Declaration of Independence. Dr. Rush knew— as did Thomas Jefferson and many other Americans—that it was easier to outline a new theory of government, as Jefferson had done in the Declaration of Independence, than it was to build a government that really worked.

Many problems faced the now independent American people. One of the most serious of these problems was whether the thirteen states, which for seven years had joined hands in rebellion against British rule, would remain

united now that the crisis was over. ". . . A long time, and much prudence, will be necessary to reproduce a spirit of union and . . . reverence for government," David Ramsay of South Carolina declared.

Actually, as it turned out, the American people developed a "spirit of union" and "reverence for government" in an amazingly short time. But even so, as you will see, there were moments between 1783 and 1787 when the future looked dark.

AS THE STORY DEVELOPS

1. The former colonies create new state governments.
2. The states unite under the Articles of Confederation.
3. The Confederation lacks power to solve important problems.

1450   1750   1800   1850   1900   1950   19

The former colonies create new state governments

In 1775, even before the actual fighting in the American Revolution started, the long-established governments of the colonies began to crumble. After the fighting at Lexington and at Bunker Hill, a number of the royal governors and their advisers returned to England. The more conservative members of the colonial legislatures also returned to their homes. By 1776 nearly all colonial government had disappeared. Only the local governments, most of them now in the hands of the Patriots, continued to meet and carry on business.

From old governments to new. The members of the Second Continental Congress were alarmed at this situation. They themselves had no power to act as a government for any one or for all of the colonies. On the other hand, they knew that *someone* had to do something to prevent lawlessness and disorder from ripping the colonies to shreds. And so, on May 10, 1775, the delegates to the Second Continental Congress adopted a resolution urging the colonies to organize new governments to replace the colonial governments. John Adams, one of the delegates from Massachusetts, called this "the most important resolution that was ever taken in America."

The legislatures of New Hampshire and South Carolina, both of which were controlled by Patriots, had already written new state constitutions. During the next few months all the other states except Connecticut, Rhode Island, and Massachusetts adopted new state constitutions. As you recall, Connecticut and Rhode Island had been self-governing colonies from the time that they came into existence. The colonial charters of these two self-governing colonies worked so well that Connecticut and Rhode Island continued to use them as state constitutions until well into the 1800's. Massachusetts, however, operated under a temporary government until near the end of the war.

DR. RAMSAY ON GOVERNMENT

Dr. David Ramsay, a physician of Charleston, South Carolina, was one of the leaders of the American Revolution. During the war he offered his services as surgeon in the army. He was captured and spent some time in a British prisoner-of-war camp. From 1782 to 1786, he was a member of Congress, serving for one year as its president.

Dr. Ramsay was a learned and wise statesman. After the American Revolution had ended, he offered the following advice to his countrymen: "To overset an established government unhinges many of those principles which bind individuals to each other. A long time, and much prudence, will be necessary to reproduce a spirit of union and that reverence for government without which society is a rope of sand."

Although the people were fighting for the right to govern themselves, most of them had little or nothing to do with the writing of the new constitutions. In most of the states, the legislatures prepared the constitutions without consulting the people themselves.

This method of organizing the new governments did not suit Massachusetts and New Hampshire. As a result, both of these states held constitutional conventions at which specially elected delegates drafted the constitutions. When the delegates finished their work, the voters themselves had a chance to accept or reject the proposed constitutions.

Governments under law. The democratic ideas expressed in the Declaration of Independence also helped to shape

Virginia Statute for Religious Freedom
(1786): EXCERPT

Whereas Almighty God hath created the free mind . . . all attempts to influence it by temporal punishments . . . tend only to beget habits of hypocrisy and meanness; . . . to compel a man to furnish contributions of money for the propagation of opinions which he disbelieves is sinful and tyrannical; . . . truth is great and will prevail if left to herself . . .

¶ . . . no man shall be compelled to frequent or support any religious worship . . . whatsoever; . . . all men shall be free to profess . . . their opinion in matters of religion; . . . the same shall in no wise diminish, enlarge, or affect their civil capacities . . .

the new state constitutions. The first objective of the men who wrote the new state constitutions was to secure iron-clad guarantees of the "unalienable rights" of "life, liberty, and the pursuit of happiness." As a result, each of the new state constitutions began with a *bill of rights.* Included in these bills of rights were guarantees of religious freedom, the right to free speech and a free press, the right to assemble, the right to a fair trial by jury, and equality of all citizens before the law.

It was significant that the framers of the new state constitutions put the guarantees into *written constitutions,* in this way making the guarantees part of the fundamental law of each of the states. In the future, when any individual had a question as to his rights under the law, all he had to do was to turn to the written law itself. The law, not the opinion of a hereditary ruler, would provide the answer. And the important thing was that the law would give the same answer, the same rights, to every man. Under these written state constitutions, the new American states were adopting *"government of laws, and not of men."*

In order to establish a government of laws, the new constitutions provided for what is called "separation of powers" among the different departments of government. The constitution of Massachusetts provided that "In the government of this commonwealth, the legislative department shall never exercise the executive and judicial powers or either of them: the executive shall never exercise the legislative and judicial powers or either of them: the judicial shall never exercise the legislative and executive powers or either of them: to the end it may be a government of laws, and not of men." Although other state constitutions did not provide for such a clear separation of powers as that of Massachusetts, all the states did limit the power of the executive department.

Other democratic victories. One of the important steps taken by the people of the states was to strengthen the principle of the separation of church and government. When the Revolutionary War broke out, the people of nine of the thirteen colonies were required by law to pay taxes for the support of an official state church. As you have seen (page 75), the people had to pay these taxes even if they belonged to another church. By 1787, however, official churches existed in only three of the states—New Hampshire, Massachusetts, and Connecticut. In all the other states the official churches had been abolished, or "disestablished." The people were free to contribute to the church of their own choice.

From that time on, the principle that the church and the state should be separate, that all individuals should be free to support the church of their own choice and to worship as they pleased, has remained one of the cornerstones of American democracy.

While Americans were strengthening the principle of religious freedom, they were also taking steps to provide more humane treatment for criminals. During the colonial period, under the "criminal code" of English law, there were more than 200 crimes for which a per-

142

son might be executed. When the Revolutionary War broke out, several of the states replaced most of these harsh laws with more humane legislation.

Moving toward democracy. While the Revolutionary War was going on, then, Americans continued to strengthen the roots of democracy that they had already planted during the colonial period. But the democratic way of life did not emerge full blown from the Revolutionary War. Slavery remained. The right to vote continued to be limited to some extent by religious and property qualifications. The state continued to collect taxes to support the Congregational Church in New Hampshire, Massachusetts, and Connecticut. The right to hold office in the state governments was denied to members of certain religious denominations.

Because of these restrictions on the freedom of individuals, the ideals set forth in the Declaration of Independence were only partially realized in the 1780's. But the men and women who fought the Revolutionary War had taken a long step toward the democratic way of life, and it was evident in 1783 that they were about to take other steps. This is what Dr. Benjamin Rush had in mind when he wrote, "The American war is over, but this is far from being the case with the American Revolution."

SECTION SURVEY

1. In what ways did the Declaration of Independence help to shape the new state constitutions?

2. Explain the meaning of the "separation of powers" by referring to the provisions of the Massachusetts constitution.

3. (a) What is meant by the separation of church and state? (b) What states still retained official churches after 1787?

4. (a) Summarize the gains for democracy in the period of writing the new state constitutions. (b) Give examples of undemocratic practices which still prevailed.

IDENTIFY: bill of rights, "government of laws, and not of men."

---

2 The states unite under the Articles of Confederation

By the summer of 1776, when independence was declared, the thirteen former British colonies had become thirteen separate and independent states.

The need for unity. To be sure, each of the state legislatures had sent leaders to Philadelphia as delegates to the Second Continental Congress. But the Continental Congress had no power to act for all the states. The members of the Continental Congress met day after day and carried on long discussions and debates. When some action needed to be taken, the delegates passed a resolution urging each of the states to act. The delegates then sent this recommendation along to their own state governments. If a state government refused to accept the recommendation, the Continental Congress had no power to compel that state to fall into line.

The problem of unity. The delegates to the Continental Congress could, and did, agree that it was necessary for the thirteen states to unite. But in what kind of union? And what kind of central government should they create?

A number of the delegates, including Benjamin Franklin, wanted to build a strong central government. These delegates wanted the central government to be stronger than any of the states.

Most of the delegates objected to the proposal to create a strong central government. These delegates pointed out that the states were fighting a war to win their independence. Why, then, the delegates wanted to know, should the states deliberately create an American government that might turn out to be as tyrannical as British rule had been?

A plan for confederation. After long debate the delegates to the Continental Congress agreed that unity of some kind among the states would be necessary to fight the war. Accordingly, on June 11, 1776, the Continental Congress

(*Continued on page 145*)

Notice the regions numbered 1 to 4 on the map above. As people moved into the unsettled lands in these numbered regions west of the Appalachian Mountains, new states were created and admitted to the Union. The following states were created out of the four regions north and south of the Ohio River:

❶ These states were carved out of the Northwest Territory: Ohio (1803), Indiana (1816), Illinois (1818), Michigan (1837), Wisconsin (1848), and part of Minnesota (1858).

❷ Originally claimed by Virginia; admitted as state of Kentucky in 1792.

❸ North Carolina and South Carolina claims ceded to federal government in 1792; admitted as state of Tennessee in 1796.

❹ Georgia claims relinquished by 1802; became part of Mississippi Territory; admitted as states of Mississippi (1817) and Alabama (1819).

appointed a committee to propose a workable plan of union.

A month later, on July 12, the committee, headed by John Dickinson of Pennsylvania, presented its report to the Continental Congress. The report bore the title "Articles of Confederation and Perpetual Union." For more than a year, the members of the Continental Congress debated these "Articles" sentence by sentence. Finally, on November 15, 1777, the delegates voted to adopt the Articles of Confederation.

The Articles of Confederation created a *confederation*, or league, of free and independent states known as "The United States of America." The central government of the league was to consist of a Congress having from two to seven delegates from each state. Each state delegation was to have only one vote in the Congress.

But this was only the first step in the process of forming a union. Before the Articles of Confederation could become effective, each of the thirteen states had to *ratify*, or accept, the proposal.

The Confederation is adopted. It was not until 1781 that all the states agreed to enter the Confederation. Maryland was the last.

During the discussion over the Confederation, the delegates from Maryland had insisted that all the states with claims to land lying between the Appalachian Mountains and the Mississippi River (see map, page 97) surrender their claims in this area to the Confederation.

Maryland based its proposal on two arguments. First, the British were in actual possession of the western lands. In order to conquer this territory, the common effort of all the states was needed. But, the Maryland delegates argued, it was only fair that if all the states helped to free the western lands, then all the states should share the fruits of victory.

Maryland advanced a second argument. Look into the future, the men from Maryland urged. What will happen when the western lands are filled

Articles of Confederation (1777): EXCERPT

Article 1. The style of this confederacy shall be "The United States of America."

Article 2. Each state retains its sovereignty, freedom, and independence, and every power, jurisdiction, and right, which is not by this confederation expressly delegated to the United States, in Congress assembled.

Article 3. The said states hereby severally enter into a firm league of friendship with each other for their common defense, the security of their liberties, and their mutual and general welfare, binding themselves to assist each other against all force offered to, or attacks made upon them, or any of them, on account of religion, sovereignty, trade, or any other pretense whatever . . .

with thriving towns and prosperous farms? The answer is clear. The states that own these lands will be great and powerful. They will overwhelm by sheer size and population the small states confined to the Atlantic seaboard. And when that time comes, the Confederation will be a league of states unequal in power and influence. This being true, the Maryland delegates declared, we shall not join the Confederation until the states who own western lands surrender their claims.

Maryland's stand provoked heated debates, not only in the Continental Congress, but throughout the country. Finally, in 1781, after all the states with claims to western land had agreed to surrender their claims, Maryland ratified the Articles of Confederation, and the new league of states came into existence.

Land—the first problem. Control of the vast expanse of country west of the mountains gave the Confederation its first real power and a great responsibility. Now, in 1781, the Confederation faced the same fundamental problems that Great Britain and other colonial

145

powers had faced when they first secured colonies in the New World.

Settlers were already beginning to move into the wilderness between the Appalachian Mountains and the Mississippi River. Nothing was more certain than that the tide of settlers would swell.

How was the land to be distributed among the men and women who "colonized" America's frontier? Who was to profit from the sale of the land—a few influential speculators or the settlers? Who was to make laws for the towns and cities and states that would one day appear—the government of the Confederation or the settlers?

These were real problems. The future of the new nation depended to a large extent upon the answers.

Nature of the land problem. Great Britain had never developed a satisfactory land policy for all of its American colonies. As a result, the methods by which new settlers secured land varied from colony to colony.

In colonial New England, for example, a fairly orderly system had been worked out. There, a person wishing to move west joined others of like mind and secured from the colonial assembly a grant of land which was carefully *surveyed*, or measured.

In other colonies, especially in Virginia, individuals generally went out into the new country, selected whatever land appealed to them, and settled on it. Naturally they took the choice land, leaving vacant all that looked less desirable. Settlements were therefore thinly spread out, and the danger of Indian attacks was increased. This method of settlement also led to frequent quarrels over boundaries.

The government of the Confederation decided that it was necessary to provide some systematic method by which individuals could get clear *titles,* or guarantees of ownership, to the western lands on which they settled. The government also decided to provide a system by which settlements could be made more compact and easier to defend against Indian raids.

The Land Ordinance of 1785. The system of land settlement worked out by the government of the Confederation was written down in the Land Ordinance of 1785. This ordinance, or law, was based in part on the New England system for settling new lands. It outlined the method of westward expansion that was employed, with some changes, until it was replaced by the Homestead Act of 1862 (page 397).

The Land Ordinance of 1785 provided for government survey of squares of land six miles long and six miles wide to be known as *townships.* Each township was further surveyed and divided into 36 smaller squares of 640 acres, or one square mile, to be known as *sections.* One section in every township, section number 16, was to be set aside for the support of public schools. Four other sections were reserved for the United States. The remaining 31 sections were to be sold by the government at a price of not less than one dollar an acre. (See chart, page 147.)

There were several advantages in this plan for the regular, systematic development of the western lands. Since settlements would be closer together, the problem of defense against the Indians would be less difficult. Moreover, disputes over boundaries and titles would be largely eliminated, for the exact location of every section would be determined in advance of settlement by government surveyors and land officers. Finally, the sale of lands in this fashion would provide the treasury of the Confederation with funds much needed to meet current expenses and to pay off part of the Revolutionary War debt.

Government of new lands. After it adopted a systematic plan for the settlement of the western lands, the Confederation turned to another problem. How should the western lands be governed?

If the Americans had followed the example of the British Empire, they would have regarded the whole western area as a colony. But Americans remembered how keenly they had resented the British point of view. They could hardly

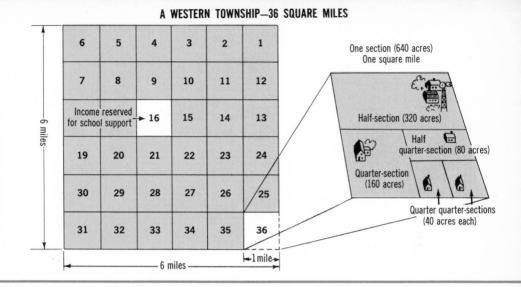

A WESTERN TOWNSHIP—36 SQUARE MILES

One section (640 acres)
One square mile

Half-section (320 acres)

Half quarter-section (80 acres)

Quarter-section (160 acres)

Quarter quarter-sections (40 acres each)

■ From an airplane, many parts of the United States show a neat pattern of farms and roads. This orderliness goes back to the township system of land survey first adopted in 1785. Income from Section 16 was for school support, but the school might be built elsewhere.

forget their recent war, waged in part against the mercantile theory of trade under which colonies were governed for the benefit of the mother country. For this reason, the government of the Continental Congress had already adopted, in 1780, a resolution promising that any new western states could come into the Confederation equal in all respects to the older Atlantic seaboard states.

This decision had been hastened by other developments. Before the Revolutionary War daring men like Daniel Boone had been penetrating the mountain passes and making settlements in what are now Kentucky and Tennessee (see map, page 144). This westward movement had, of course, been checked by the Proclamation of 1763 and the Quebec Act of 1774, which forbade the Americans to hunt, trade, or settle west of the Appalachians. Once the Revolution began, however, more and more people crossed the mountains to enter the forbidden land. For these people the problem of government had to be settled as quickly as possible.

Land speculators were also eager for the Confederation to adopt a plan for the government of the western country. These speculators stood a better chance of selling the land if they could assure prospective settlers that the government had adopted a program for the orderly development of the western lands.

The Northwest Ordinance of 1787. In 1787 the government of the Confederation fulfilled its earlier promise in part by passing the Northwest Ordinance. This ordinance provided for the governing of the Northwest Territory, an area of land shown on the map on page 144.

In the beginning the Northwest Territory was to be ruled by a governor and three judges appointed by the Congress of the Confederation in Philadelphia. Later on, when the population included a total of 5000 free males of voting age, the settlers might elect a legislature to pass laws for themselves, and they might also appoint a delegate to speak for them, but not to vote, in the Congress at Philadelphia. Still later, when the population of any part of the North-

147

Northwest Ordinance (1787): EXCERPT

Article 1. No person ... shall ever be molested on account of his mode of worship or religious sentiments ...

Article 2. The inhabitants of the said territory shall always be entitled to the benefits of the writ of *habeas corpus* and of the trial by jury ...

Article 3. Religion, morality, and knowledge being necessary to good government and the happiness of mankind, schools and the means of education shall forever be encouraged. The utmost good faith shall always be observed toward the Indians ...

Article 6. There shall be neither slavery nor involuntary servitude in the said Territory otherwise than in the punishment of crimes ...

west Territory reached a total of 60,000 free inhabitants, the people could draft a constitution. Once this constitution had been approved by Congress, that part of the Northwest Territory became a state, equal in every respect to the older states. Not less than three nor more than five states were to be carved out of the Northwest Territory.

Democratic achievements. The Northwest Ordinance of 1787 became famous for two other provisions, each of which contributed to the growth of democracy. The first of these encouraged public education. According to the general belief of the fathers of the country, public education was a necessary condition for the successful working of representative government. As a result, the Northwest Ordinance declared that "Religion, morality, and knowledge being necessary to good government and the happiness of mankind, schools and• the means of education shall forever be encouraged." This provision stimulated the public support of schools and colleges in the Northwest Territory. A second provision barred slavery from all the land which composed the Northwest Territory.

The policy developed in the Northwest Ordinance was the most democratic colonial policy the modern world had known. It provided the machinery by which newer, less settled areas were to become, as they developed, equal members with parent communities. Under this general plan, almost all of the new land that the United States was to acquire in its march to the shores of the Pacific Ocean and beyond would be admitted to the Union—first as *Territories,* later as *States.*

The inhabitants in the western Territories sometimes felt that they had many grievances against the national government. With one or two exceptions, however, no Territory ever seriously considered leaving the Union, for the people knew that, sooner or later, they would be admitted as equal members. And they also knew that, as their population grew, their influence on government policy would become more effective.

Years after the Northwest Ordinance was adopted, Daniel Webster gave his sober opinion of its importance: "I doubt whether one single law of any lawgiver, ancient or modern, has produced effects of more distinct, marked, and lasting character than the Ordinance of 1787."

SECTION SURVEY

1. The Articles of Confederation were ready for adoption in 1777, but did not go into effect until 1781 on account of Maryland. Discuss the reasons why Maryland withheld its ratification until 1781.

2. Give the provisions of the Land Ordinance of 1785. What advantages can you see to this important law?

3. State the provisions of the Northwest Ordinance of 1787. Offer arguments to prove that this bill was both a democratic achievement and a measure of truly enduring value.

IDENTIFY: central government, Confederation, ratify, title to land, ordinance, township, section, land speculator, Northwest Territory; John Dickinson, Boone.

DANIEL BOONE, MAN AND MYTH

"Were you ever lost?" a friend asked Daniel Boone. "No," Boone replied, "but I was _bewildered_ once for three days."

One can multiply such stories by the hundreds. Which are true, which fiction, it is hard to say, for Boone lives in history as part man, part myth.

Daniel Boone (1734–1820) was indeed a remarkable character. Born near the town of Reading, Pennsylvania, he became a hunter at the age of twelve. When only seventeen, he settled at Buffalo Lick in the Yadkin Valley of North Carolina. But he spent most of his life in the wilderness, and it is a testimony to his skill and intelligence—as well as a measure of his luck—that he lived to celebrate his eighty-sixth birthday.

Boone's age was remarkable. For most pioneers, life was exciting—and brief! In 1780, for example, a group of 256 settlers in what is now Tennessee signed their names to a "constitution" they had drawn up for their new community. Ten years later, all but a dozen of these men were dead—and only one had died a natural death!

Boone is best known as the bold pioneer who, in a few years before the Revolutionary War, blazed the Wilderness Trail through the Appalachians into the "dark and bloody ground" south of the Ohio River. There were others equally bold, among them James Robertson and John Sevier, who, about the same time, opened up the country that was to become Tennessee. But Boone had the good fortune to have what could be called a "publicity agent."

Boone was approaching his fiftieth year when he sat down with a writer, John Filson, to recall the memorable events of his life. Probably Boone colored the stories he told author Filson. Filson himself added much to the telling. Thus, the man who finally emerged from the pages of the book bore only a limited resemblance to the rough-and-ready pioneer who lived, fought, and died on the frontier of the growing nation.

149

3 The Confederation lacks power to solve important problems

The government created by the Articles of Confederation was able, as you have seen, to solve a number of important problems facing the new nation. But there were a number of other problems the leaders of the new government could not solve.

The problem of weakness. Many Americans insisted that the central government was too weak. Actually, the men who wrote the Articles of Confederation had organized an effective "league of friendship." The trouble was that a mere league, or confederation, of independent states was not strong enough to solve all the critical problems confronting the newly independent states.

On paper the Confederation appeared to have certain powers. It could regulate weights and measures. It could create post offices. It could borrow money and coin money. It could direct foreign affairs and declare war and make peace. It could build and equip a navy. It could ask the states to provide men and money for an army.

These powers looked well enough on paper. But the states, each jealous of

its own rights, had carefully guarded the exercise of these powers. The delegates who sat in Congress had no real authority. They voted as their state legislatures directed them to vote. The delegation from each state was entitled to only one vote in Congress. Rhode Island, smallest of the states, had as much influence in deciding national issues as did the larger states of Virginia, New York, and Massachusetts.

No matter of importance could be settled without the consent of at least nine states, and changes in the Articles required the unanimous vote of the thirteen states. Finally, there was neither an executive, like our President now, with power to enforce measures adopted by Congress, nor a central national court, like our Supreme Court, to protect the rights of citizens.

The problem of money. Money would have been a serious postwar problem for the people even if the Articles of Confederation had created a stronger central government. As it was, the weakness of the Confederation made the problem more difficult to solve.

To illustrate the problem, let us imagine a scene in a colonial store. The date is 1783. The customer has just chosen some goods. He reaches into his pocket to pay his bill. Out on the counter he tumbles a pile of coins and paper money. There are French, Spanish, English, Dutch, German, and Portuguese coins. There are pennies coined in Vermont, Massachusetts, Connecticut, New Jersey, and Pennsylvania. There is paper money issued by the Continental Congress during the opening years of the Revolutionary War and paper money issued by several of the states.

Some of the coins have been "clipped." That is, someone has scraped gold or silver from the edges. Some of the money may be counterfeit. The paper money is almost worthless, "not worth a Continental," as the people themselves say contemptuously. Both the storekeeper and the customer would willingly exchange $1000 of paper money issued by the Continental Con-

■ The paper money which was issued by the Continental Congress could be exchanged, as you see, for "Spanish milled dollars, or the value thereof in gold or silver."

gress for one dollar's worth of silver.

Obviously, only a government with authority to regulate finances in all of the thirteen states could hope to bring order out of such chaos. But the states, each fearful of losing some of its newly won power, had not given this authority to the government of the Confederation. The Confederation could coin its own money. But it had no way of securing gold and silver to be coined. The Confederation could levy taxes on the states, but it had no power to compel the states to pay the taxes. Less than one fourth of the money requested by Congress was ever raised.

No wonder the Confederation could not pay even the interest on the war debts. No wonder Europeans made bets as to how long the United States could survive.

The problem of interstate trade. Europeans had other reasons for looking with scorn upon the new nation. The colonists had rebelled against Great Britain in part, at least, because they wanted to regulate their own trade. Now, with independence won, each state proceeded to make regulations designed to benefit its own citizens.

New York, for example, levied duties on products entering the state from New Jersey and Connecticut. New Jersey got even with New York by heavily taxing a lighthouse built on its soil by New York to guide ships into the Hudson River. And in Connecticut, whose firewood had been taxed at the New York border, a group of merchants agreed not to sell goods to New York for a period of twelve months.

The confusion that resulted from such activities led many Americans to think that perhaps the British had been right when they insisted that only a central authority could regulate trade to the best advantage of all concerned. Merchants who were opposed in theory to central control began to suggest that even the danger of tyranny was preferable to the confusion resulting from control of trade by the separate states. Here and there businessmen demanded that the Confederation be given power to regulate interstate trade.°

The problem of foreign trade. American merchants also found that it was difficult to carry on foreign trade in the years immediately following the peace treaty of 1783. This, too, was in large part the result of the war. The profitable trade that merchants of the New England and Middle Atlantic States had formerly enjoyed with the British West Indies was now denied them by Great Britain. The British, regarding the Americans as a foreign people, no longer gave them bounties and favored treatment in British ports.

Among the people who suffered from the government's lack of power to control foreign trade were the small but growing number of men concerned with manufacturing. During the Revolutionary War, when the British naval blockade made it difficult for Americans to import manufactured goods, Americans started to develop their own industries. But once the fighting stopped, British merchants flooded American markets with manufactured goods produced at low cost by well-established British industries.

American manufacturers blamed this situation on the government. They began to talk about a central government with power to levy import duties on manufactured goods from Great Britain and other countries. Such duties, added to the cost of imported goods, would make the prices of foreign goods and of American goods more nearly equal.

Friction with Great Britain. To add to the confusion, the Confederation did not have the power to enforce its own treaties. When John Adams, who in 1785 was sent to Great Britain as minister from the United States, tried to negotiate a commercial treaty, the British only smiled. What value was a treaty, they politely inquired of Adams, when any one of the thirteen states could ignore it? No, the British said, under the

•••
° *interstate trade:* trade between the people of different states. "Intrastate trade" is trade between people within a single state.

151

system of government operating in America not one, but thirteen, treaties would have to be adopted.

The British were right, of course. American leaders like John Jay were forced to admit that every day the peace treaty of 1783 was being "violated . . . by one or other of the states." Britishers found it impossible to collect the debts owed them by Americans. Tories found it impossible to secure compensation for their property confiscated during the Revolution.

Quite naturally, Britishers grew increasingly angry at the failure of the Americans to pay the Tories. Using this failure as an excuse, the British refused to withdraw from the forts and trading posts in the Northwest Territory (see map, page 144), as they had agreed to do in the treaty of 1783.

Lack of military power. Great Britain's refusal to leave the western forts aroused the indignation of the Americans who lived beyond the Alleghenies. The freedom-loving, independent westerners felt that the new government of the United States should drive the British away. The westerners were asking for a display of military power. This was a request that the government of the Confederation could not meet.

Also as a result of its lack of military strength, the Confederation was powerless to solve, or even partly solve, the Indian problems inherited from colonial times. The Indians continued to be troublesome. They resisted the advance of the whites, who, in cutting forests and making farms, ruined the game and furs on which the Indians depended. Conflict was inevitable.

To make matters worse, reckless Spanish and British officers in North America sometimes encouraged the Indians to attack western settlers. From the forts that they held in the Northwest Territory, the British supplied the Indians with guns and ammunition. The Spaniards, who owned Florida and Louisiana, including all of the land west of the Mississippi River, also supplied the Indians with guns and ammunition.

As you have seen, John Adams failed to obtain a British promise to give up the forts in the Northwest Territory. Nor were other Americans able to get the Spaniards to make any concessions.

In spite of all American efforts, the Spaniards refused to give westerners the right to use the port of New Orleans (see map, page 144). This port was very important to settlers living in the Ohio Valley and in the land east of the Mississippi River. There were no roads over which these settlers could carry their products across the mountains to the markets and the seaports along the Atlantic coast. The only possible way they could sell their produce was to float it down the Mississippi River to New Orleans. There they could load it on seagoing vessels and ship it to the Atlantic ports or to Europe. Unfortunately for the western settlers, the Spaniards who controlled New Orleans refused to guarantee Americans the right to use this seaport, and the American government was not strong enough to force Spain to grant this right.

The threat of civil war. By 1786 the country had sunk into the depths of an economic slump—what we now call a *depression* or *recession.*

The farmers of Massachusetts were especially hard-hit. Before the Revolutionary War much of their cash income had come from the sale of their farm produce to the British West Indies. After the break with Great Britain, this market was, of course, closed to them, and they found it increasingly difficult to get money to pay their taxes and the interest on their mortgages. To make matters worse, merchants and businessmen, mostly from Boston, controlled the state legislature. These men managed to pass new laws that shifted the burden of taxation onto the farmers. Among these taxes was a heavy tax on land.

During the summer of 1786, farmers met in hastily assembled gatherings and in special town meetings to demand relief. "We beg to inform your Honors," one petition to the government read, "that unless something takes place more favorable to the people, in a little time at least, one half of our inhabitants in our opinion will become bankrupt. . . . Surely your Honors are not strangers to the distresses of the people, but do know that many of our good inhabitants are now confined in jail for debt and taxes; many have fled, others wishing to flee to the state of New York or some other state."

But the Massachusetts legislature refused to act, and, as farm after farm was seized for nonpayment of taxes or interest on the mortgage, some of the farmers took matters into their own hands.

Shays' Rebellion. Led by Daniel Shays, who had been a captain during the Revolution, a number of Massachusetts farmers banded together and demanded an end to foreclosures° and a larger representation in the state legislature. They surrounded courthouses and insisted that the judges stop foreclosing mortgages and seizing farm property. A group under Shays also tried to seize the arsenal at Springfield in an effort to secure guns, but his men were too poorly armed to succeed.

° *foreclosure:* the legal action by which a person's mortgaged property is seized when he cannot pay his debts.

◼ The farmers led by Shays were poorly armed and exhausted from marching through snow to Springfield. Even so, they twice charged well-armed militia. Although their rebellion was crushed, it alarmed thoughtful citizens throughout the Confederation.

An Indian raid

Frightened by this defiance of the law, a group of citizens of Boston raised funds to equip a militia to put down Shays' Rebellion. The troops hunted Shays and his men through the snowy woods, killing many and driving some across the state boundary into what is now Vermont. The rebellion was crushed.

But it had been a narrow escape from civil war, and many Americans were thoroughly alarmed. Armed revolt threatened to destroy law and order and the very foundations of society. "There are combustibles in every state which a spark might set fire to," George Washington declared.

Signs of returning prosperity. Not all of the difficult problems that the country faced in the 1780's could be blamed, however, on the weaknesses of the Articles of Confederation. Hard times would have followed the war even with a stronger government in the saddle. After all, property had been destroyed, long-established trade connections had been broken, commerce and business in general had been seriously dislocated.

Even as early as 1785, only two years after the war ended, there were signs of better times ahead. By that date American ships were once again busily engaged in trade with countries outside the British Empire. The profits from this growing trade were being enjoyed by sailors, shipowners, merchants, farmers, and manufacturers. Many of the interstate barriers to trade were not enforced. As a result, American products continued to cross state lines in considerable quantities.

By 1785 some Americans were satisfied with the government under the Articles of Confederation. They were pleased with the signs of returning prosperity. They were satisfied with the wise policy that the Confederation was developing for the western lands.

Despite these gains the fact remained, as you have seen, that the central government was too weak to solve many of the problems facing the new country. It was not strong enough to establish a sound financial system, to regulate trade, to enforce treaties, and to exert military force when force was needed. These weaknesses of the government disturbed certain groups of Americans—merchants and manufacturers, workmen of the cities, and westerners, who needed a strong central government to protect them from the Indians and from the Spaniards and the British in the Mississippi Valley.

✔ SECTION SURVEY

1. List five weaknesses of the government under the Articles of Confederation.
2. (a) What was a serious financial problem for the local colonial storekeeper or merchant? (b) Why was the Confederation unable to solve this problem?
3. Discuss the major difficulties of the Confederation government in its dealings with England and Spain. Indicate what were the chief causes of friction.
4. What signs in 1785 led some Americans to be satisfied with the new government?
5. Why did other groups still think the central government was too weak?

IDENTIFY: interstate trade, foreclosure, Shays' Rebellion; 1786.

Points to Discuss: 1. Benjamin Rush said at the end of the Revolutionary War: "The American war is over but this is far from being the case with the American Revolution." What did he mean?

2. The early state governments provided written constitutions, "government of laws, and not of men." What special values do you see in this type of government?

3. Consider and evaluate the arguments proposed by Maryland for the surrender of western lands by the states to the central government.

4. The Articles of Confederation government proved to have important weaknesses. Do you think it might have been possible for the colonies to have established a stronger central government in 1777? Why?

5. The Articles of Confederation were said to have established "a government by supplication." Explain with examples.

6. Estimate the successes and failures of the Confederation government in its efforts to solve its "western problems." What was undoubtedly the great achievement of the Confederation government?

7. Do you feel it is fair to blame all the postwar difficulties on the weaknesses of the Articles of Confederation? Explain.

8. John Fiske, historian, has called this period the "critical period in American history." Offer evidence to support or disprove his contention.

Using Maps and Charts: 1. Using the map on page 144, (a) give the boundaries of the old Northwest Territory. (b) Locate the British posts and explain why they were permitted on American soil. (c) Point out the Cumberland Gap and indicate its importance. (d) Name and locate the new states formed out of the Northwest Territory. (e) Name and locate the new states formed out of the territory south of the Ohio River and east of the Mississippi River. (f) Identify two areas in New England with conflicting land claims.

Consulting the Sources: See Ellis, *Docs.*, No. 44, for excerpts from state bills of rights concerning religious freedom principles and prejudices.

■ TRACING THE MAIN IDEAS

Early in 1775, more than a year before the colonists declared their independence, the old colonial governments began to crumble. British officials began to leave the colonies. Tories, loyal to the British king and Parliament, began to flee to Canada, the British West Indies, and Great Britain. By 1776 the Americans faced the problem of creating new state governments and a new central government.

The state constitutions that Americans wrote during the Revolutionary War reflected the people's deep-seated desire for a voice in their own government. All of the new governments were based upon written constitutions. All of the new constitutions contained bills of rights guaranteeing freedom to every citizen.

During the Revolutionary War Americans also tackled the problem of building a central government. In their first efforts to govern themselves at the national level, the leaders of the thirteen free states wrote the Articles of Confederation. This experiment with a league of more or less independent states was only partially successful.

There were two basic problems. First, there was the problem of dividing powers between the states and the central government. To this problem the Confederation had given no answer. Second, the Confederation could not establish uniform laws binding upon the states and the people of the states.

Even before 1787 a number of leaders in America had become convinced that only a strengthened central government could secure order in the new nation. Once this conclusion had been reached, many of America's leaders began to take steps to change the existing form of government. As you will see in Chapter 9, these steps led to the drafting and adoption of the Constitution of the United States of America.

The States Create a Federal Union

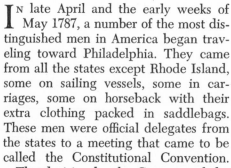

ARRIVAL of DELEGATES. CONSTITUTIONAL CONVENTION - PHILADELPHIA 1787

In late April and the early weeks of May 1787, a number of the most distinguished men in America began traveling toward Philadelphia. They came from all the states except Rhode Island, some on sailing vessels, some in carriages, some on horseback with their extra clothing packed in saddlebags. These men were official delegates from the states to a meeting that came to be called the Constitutional Convention.

The decision by the Congress of the Confederation to call this convention arose from a meeting at Annapolis, Maryland, in 1786. The major purpose of this meeting had been to discuss a uniform system of trade regulations among all of the states.

Only five states were represented at the Annapolis meeting. The delegates decided that it would be useless to try to accomplish anything with such a slim representation. Instead, they petitioned Congress to call another meeting of all the states, not only to discuss commercial problems, but also to study the weaknesses of the Confederation. Congress was slow to act on this proposal, but finally called the meeting for "the sole and express purpose of revising the Articles of Confederation. . . ."

The delegates to the Constitutional Convention soon decided to go beyond their instructions and to write a wholly new Constitution, one that would do more than correct the weaknesses of the Articles of Confederation. Between May and September of 1787, as you will see, they drafted a written Constitution which presently became, and still is, the foundation upon which all government in the United States is built. It has also become a model for builders of representative government throughout the world.

AS THE STORY DEVELOPS

1. State delegations reach agreements and compromises.
2. After strenuous debate the states ratify the Constitution.
3. The Constitution establishes a workable form of government.
4. The Constitution separates, checks, and balances powers.
5. The Constitution safeguards individual liberty.
6. The Constitution is a flexible, living document.

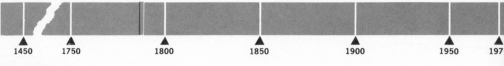

1450   1750   1800   1850   1900   1950   197

1 State delegations reach agreements and compromises

On the morning of May 14, 1787, the date scheduled for the opening of the Constitutional Convention, Philadelphia's State House (later known as Independence Hall) was open and waiting for the delegates. Only two delegations appeared—one from Pennsylvania, the other from Virginia. By May 25, however, delegates from seven states—a majority—were present, and the most famous convention in American history began.

The delegates. The delegates to the Constitutional Convention were a remarkable cross section of American leadership. Most of the delegates had taken active part in the government of their states. Many were learned in history and political philosophy. More than half had been members of Congress. Eight of them had signed the Declaration of Independence, and nearly all had taken part in the American Revolution. Several had been diplomatic representatives from the United States to the governments of Europe. These men understood the problems their country faced.

Most of the delegates were relatively young men. Benjamin Franklin was an exception. Now 81 years old, he was the "elder statesman" of the convention. He was deeply respected by the other delegates and on a number of occasions helped to smooth ruffled tempers. George Washington, unanimously chosen presiding officer of the Convention, was one of the older members at the age of fifty-five. Among the more active leaders, James Madison of Virginia was thirty-six, James Wilson of Pennsylvania was forty-five, Alexander Hamilton of New York was only thirty.

Several of the important men who had helped win the struggle for independence were not present at the Convention. Patrick Henry of Virginia refused to attend, saying that he "smelled a rat." He was afraid that the Convention would take away some of the power of the states, and he was convinced that this would be a setback for free government. Samuel Adams of Massachusetts had not been chosen as a delegate. Thomas Jefferson and Thomas Paine were in Europe.

Meeting in secrecy. The Convention was held in secret. Guards stood watch at every door. Each delegate agreed not to discuss Convention business with outsiders. Indeed, lest the aged and talkative Franklin give away important secrets at the dinner parties that he liked to attend, he was accompanied by a discreet member who was to restrain him if he absent-mindedly began to talk about the Convention's affairs.

Why all this secrecy? The delegates, being practical men, realized that the news of what they were doing would plunge the country into strong argument. They also knew that it is easier to iron out differences of opinion in a private conference room than in a public debate. It would be better, they felt, to agree among themselves before presenting their proposals to the public.

The Convention did keep official notes of the proceedings, but these notes were not released until 1818. James Madison also kept a record. He jotted down his notes during the course of the meetings and then labored far into the night writing them out with a quill pen. Madison's notes, which were far more complete than the official record, were kept secret until after his death in 1836.

Areas of agreement. Although they represented different sections of the country with different interests, the delegates to the Constitutional Convention agreed from the beginning on a number of important matters. They agreed, first of all, that mere revision of the Articles of Confederation would not solve the nation's problems, that an entirely new Constitution was needed.

Most of the delegates believed that the country needed a strong central government, but none of them favored a government with unlimited power. Because of the wide range of differences between sections of the country and groups of people, they knew too that they must construct a government in which no single section or group could dominate the rest. They agreed that they must build a *republican* form of government—that is, a government in which the sovereign power rested in the voters, who would elect the men to run the government for them. The delegates also agreed that a government was needed in which the executive, legislative, and judicial powers would be separated. They knew that property rights had to be protected. They recognized that the new government would be respected only if it had the power to tax, to raise an army, and to regulate commerce. These lessons they had learned under the Articles of Confederation.

But there were sectional differences and economic problems that had to be solved. Had the men who sat in the Convention refused to compromise their differences, the writing of the Constitution would have been impossible. Fortunately for later generations, most of the delegates at Philadelphia made generous concessions time and again.

The Great Compromise. One of the most serious conflicts of the Convention was a struggle between the large and small states over representation in Congress. Early in the meetings Governor Edmund Randolph of Virginia, a large state, presented a plan of government that is now called the Virginia Plan. This plan provided among other things that the population of each state would determine the number of representatives that it could send to Congress. William Paterson of New Jersey, speaking for the small states, presented what is now called the New Jersey Plan. Under this plan, each state was to have equal representation in Congress.

Speaking against the Virginia Plan, Paterson protested, "New Jersey will never confederate on the plan before the committee. She would be swallowed up," he cried.

Speaking for the larger states, James Wilson of Pennsylvania threw back a challenging question: "Are not the citizens of Pennsylvania equal to those of New Jersey? Does it require one hundred and fifty of the former to balance fifty of the latter? No," Wilson warned, "if the small states will not confederate on this plan, Pennsylvania . . . would not confederate on any other."

After a month of debate, the delegates finally adopted what has come to be called the Great Compromise. It is also sometimes called the Connecticut Compromise, since it was first proposed by Roger Sherman of Connecticut. By a narrow margin the Convention voted for a Congress of two houses, a Senate and a House of Representatives. Each state, large or small, was to be represented by two Senators, thereby guaranteeing that each state would have equal power in the Senate. In the House, however, representation was to be based upon population.

The three-fifths compromise. Some equally complicated differences arose during the Convention between delegates from the northern and the southern states. These differences arose basically from a conflict between the economic interests of northern merchants and southern planters.

One dispute arose over the counting of slaves. Southerners wanted to count slaves in determining the number of representatives to be elected to the House of Representatives, but they did not want to count slaves for purposes of direct taxation. Northerners, on the other hand, thought that slaves should be counted for purposes of taxation, but not for representation. As a compromise, northerners and southerners agreed to count three fifths of the slaves for purposes of both representation and taxation. For example, if the total population of a state included 100,000 free men and 100,000 slaves, the population would be listed as 160,000.

The commerce compromises. Another clash between the economic interests of the South and North arose over the

■ This painting by J. B. Stearns was made to commemorate the signing of the Constitution by the delegates in September 1787. George Washington, chairman, is standing on the dais. Standing and facing him, center, is the youthful James Madison. At the left, with hands on cane, is Benjamin Franklin. Most of the delegates, despite powdered wigs, were young.

regulation of trade. The specific problems that troubled the delegates were control of commerce and the regulation of the slave trade.

Northern merchants wanted the central government to regulate commerce with foreign nations and among the states. Southern planters opposed this proposal because they feared that the government might pass tariff laws and other legislation unfavorable to their interests. For example, the income of planters came largely from tobacco, which they shipped to Europe and the northern states. The finished goods that they bought—household furnishings, farm equipment, and many other things —came either from Europe or the northern states. If Congress imposed tariffs, or duties, on exports, planters would be forced to raise the price of tobacco and would lose customers. Tariffs on imported goods, on the other hand, would raise the prices of the things the planters purchased. Under the circumstances, the southern delegates were opposed to

all tariffs, and, therefore, opposed giving Congress unlimited power to regulate trade.

The delegates finally solved the problem by reaching a compromise that was acceptable to both the North and the South. This compromise gave Congress the power "To regulate commerce with foreign nations, and among the several states," including the power to levy tariffs on imports. But Congress was denied the power to levy tariffs on exports of any kind.

The southern planters were troubled, however, by another problem. Since Congress was given the power to regulate commerce and to tax imports, would it not be possible for Congress to prohibit the slave trade by law or to tax the importation of slaves?

At the conclusion of a vigorous discussion, the Convention agreed that until 1808, or for twenty years, Congress should be denied the power to forbid the importation of any persons, such as slaves, that the states might wish to ad-

159

A CATHOLIC GENTLEMAN SPEAKS

The date was September 29, 1787, just twelve days after the signing of the Constitution. Thomas FitzSimons, wealthy merchant of Philadelphia and a civic leader, was speaking of the proper action of the Constitutional Convention in drafting a new and altogether improved Constitution, rather than trying to patch up the Articles of Confederation. He said:

"Has the gentleman ever looked at the new constitution? If he has, he will see it is not an alteration of an article in the old, but that it departs in every principle from the other. It presupposes, Sir, that no confederation exists; or if it does exist, it exists to no purpose, as it can answer no useful purpose; it cannot provide for the common defense, nor promote the general welfare. Therefore, arguments that are intended to reconcile one with the other, or make the latter an appendage to the former, are but a waste of words. Does the gentleman suppose that the convention thought themselves acting under any provision made in the confederation for altering its articles? No, Sir, they had no such idea. They were obliged, in the first instance, to begin with the destruction of its greatest principle, *equal representation*. They found the confederation without vigor, and so decayed, that it was impossible to graft a useful article upon it; nor was the *mode*, Sir, prescribed by that confederation, which requires alterations to originate with Congress. They found, at an early period, that no good purpose could be effected by making such alterations as were provided by the first articles of union. They also saw that what alterations were necessary could not be ratified by the legislatures, as they were incompetent to ordaining a form of government. They knew this belonged to the people only, and that the people only would be adequate to carry it into effect."

mit. During these years no import tax could be levied in excess of ten dollars per person. By this compromise the southerners had won the right to import slaves without interference for about a generation and northerners had secured the right to regulate the slave trade in the future.

The Constitution is completed. Finally, as the summer months passed and as agreements were reached, the Constitution was completed. Time and again the Convention was near failure. Time and again men with angry voices threatened to leave unless they were given what they wanted. But in the end sober counsel prevailed, and the delegates always found a way to compromise the differences that threatened to divide the country.

✔ **SECTION SURVEY**

1. Why was the Constitutional Convention held in secret?

2. How do we know what happened during the convention?

3. Although there were differences of opinion among them, "the delegates to the Constitutional Convention agreed from the beginning on a number of important matters." Explain.

4. The delegates compromised their differences of opinion on three important issues. (a) Describe each issue, (b) present the different points of view, and (c) explain the resulting compromise.

IDENTIFY: Annapolis convention, Independence Hall, Great (or Connecticut) Compromise, the three-fifths compromise; Franklin, Washington, Madison, James Wilson, Edmund Randolph, William Paterson, Thomas FitzSimons.

2 After strenuous debate the states ratify the Constitution

On September 17, 1787, after thirty-nine delegates had signed the document on which they had worked during the long hot summer, the members of the Constitutional Convention met for a farewell dinner. The next day they began to leave Philadelphia. Each delegate was in a hurry to return to his own state, for the really big struggle was yet to be waged—the struggle over ratification, or acceptance, of the Constitution.

Differing opinions about the Constitution. The delegates had arranged that printed copies of the new Constitution be sent to each of the states. The legislatures of the states would then call special state conventions made up of elected delegates. The men who were elected to attend these conventions would decide whether or not to ratify the Constitution. The Constitution would become effective when nine of the thirteen states had ratified it.

Most of the men who left Philadelphia in September were prepared to lead the battle for ratification. These men believed that what they had done was good for the country. They believed that a strong federal government° would be helpful to all the people, that it would establish law and order at home and command the respect of foreign governments. A few of the delegates, however, had refused to sign the Constitution.

In general, the American people divided into two groups in their thinking about the Constitution. One group favored the Constitution because they wanted a strong federal, or national, government. They were called the Federalists. The other group, called the Anti-Federalists, were against the Constitution because they did not favor a

．．．

° *federal government:* This term is used in the United States to refer to the *national* government as opposed to the separate governments of the individual states.

strong federal government and wished to protect the rights of individual states. All over the country, people debated the issues heatedly, and began to bring pressure on the ratifying conventions.

Opponents raise objections. During the debate over ratification by the state conventions, the opponents raised a number of strong objections.

First, many Americans were afraid that the states were being asked to surrender too much of their power to the new federal government. These delegates and their followers preferred a constitution like the Articles of Confederation, in which the states would retain most of their powers and the federal government would have little direct freedom of action.

Second, these opponents believed that the new Constitution did not give the voters enough control over the men who would be running the new federal government. Under the Constitution, the decision as to who could vote was being left to the states. As you know, in some of the states there were property restrictions on voting, and in several states there were religious restrictions. To begin with, then, many people in the country would be excluded from taking part in the election of officials for the new federal government.

To be sure, the Constitution did create a republican, or representative, form of government. But under the Constitution the influence of even the voters was restricted. Choice of the President and Vice-President was to be made by a group of men called *electors*. These men were to be selected, not by the voters, but "in such manner" as each state legislature should direct. As for Senators, they were to be chosen by the state legislatures. Only the members of the House of Representatives would be elected directly by the voters.

A third serious objection to the Constitution was the lack of a "bill of rights." Many Americans feared that this omission would make it possible for the new federal government to deprive them of their hard-won rights as

BENJAMIN FRANKLIN AND THE RISING SUN

By the middle of September 1787, the final draft of the Constitution had been completed. The time had come for the 42 members still remaining at the convention to sign or not to sign. At this point, Benjamin Franklin offered the following advice to his fellow delegates:

" 'Mr. President,' he began, 'I confess that there are several parts of this Constitution which I do not at present approve, but I am not sure I shall never approve them. For, having lived long, I have experienced many instances of being obliged, by better information or fuller consideration, to change opinions, even on important subjects, which I once thought right but found to be otherwise. It is, therefore, that the older I grow, the more apt I am to doubt my own judgment and to pay more respect to the judgment of others. . . .

" 'On the whole, sir, I cannot help expressing a wish that every member of the Convention who may still have objections to it would with me, on this occasion, doubt a little of his own infallibility and, to make manifest our unanimity, put his name to this instrument. . . .' "

James Madison, from whose notes these words have been quoted, went on to say that "Whilst the last members were signing, Dr. Franklin, looking towards the president's chair at the back of which a rising sun happened to be painted, observed to a few members near him that painters have found it difficult to distinguish, in their art, a rising from a setting sun. 'I have,' said he, 'often and often, in the course of the session and the vicissitudes of my hopes and fears as to its issue, looked at that [painting] behind the president without being able to tell whether it was rising or setting; but now, at length, I have the happiness to know that it is a rising and not a setting sun.' "

individuals. A number of states ratified the Constitution with the reservation that an adequate bill of rights be added. As you will see, this demand was later met with the first ten amendments.

Eleven states ratify. The small state of Delaware won the honor of being the first state to ratify the Constitution, when its delegates voted unanimously in convention on December 7, 1787. Before the end of the year, New Jersey and Pennsylvania followed Delaware's example. Georgia and Connecticut ratified early in 1788.

In February 1788 Massachusetts, one of the larger, crucial states, ratified the Constitution after a spirited battle. A change of only ten votes in the Massachusetts convention would have defeated ratification in that state. Next came Maryland and South Carolina, also in the spring of 1788, and finally New Hampshire in June. Now the count stood at nine, the number needed.

Meantime, however, the attention of people all over the country was focused on the ratification struggles going on in Virginia and New York. The new government could hardly hope to succeed without the participation of these large and important states.

The battles in Virginia and New York were fought with much feeling on both sides. The final victory for those who favored the Constitution was very close. A change of only six votes in Virginia and of two votes in New York would have defeated ratification in these states. The victory in Virginia was largely due to the enormous influence of George Washington. The victory in New York was to a large extent a personal triumph for Alexander Hamilton, James Madison, and John Jay. These three men defended the Constitution in a series of brilliant essays that were printed in the newspapers and widely read. Later, the essays were collected and published in a famous volume known as *The Federalist*.

The nation celebrates. When Virginia and New York ratified the Constitution, there were eleven states in the Union, and the new government could be started with some degree of confidence. Now only two states remained outside the Union. North Carolina did not enter until November 1789, and Rhode Island delayed until the spring of 1790.

The fight over ratification had been a bitter one. The margin of victory was close. Nevertheless, it was a victory, and during the summer and fall of 1788 the country celebrated with bonfires and public demonstrations. The old government was ended. The new government was ready to start.

The first election. When all the states except North Carolina and Rhode Island had accepted the Constitution, elections were held in accordance with its provisions. George Washington was unanimously elected President, and John Adams Vice-President. Elections for the new Congress of the United States did not arouse much enthusiasm. In general, the members who were elected had favored the Constitution either in the Convention, or during the struggle for ratification, or both.

Traveling over the bad roads, the new Senators and Representatives slowly gathered in New York, which had become the temporary capital of the nation. They awaited the coming of President-elect Washington and the inauguration of the new government.

SECTION SURVEY

1. How was the new Constitution to be ratified?
2. (a) Present the arguments that you, as a Federalist living in 1787, would give in support of the new Constitution. (b) How might your anti-Federalist neighbor reply in opposing ratification?
3. Since only nine states had to ratify the Constitution, why was it considered essential to have Virginia and New York ratify it? What men aided the cause of ratification in each of these states?
4. What two states had still not accepted the Constitution by 1788?

IDENTIFY: federal government, electors; Hamilton, Madison, Jay, John Adams, *The Federalist*; 1789.

Washington en route to New York

3 The Constitution establishes a workable form of government

The form of government created under the Constitution is based upon four fundamental principles. Of these, one is the principle of *federalism*, or the division of powers between the national government and the state governments.

A federal union is created. The relations between the national government and the state governments had been a thorny problem under the Articles of Confederation. Under the Confederation most of the power was left in the hands of thirteen free and equal states. The national government held no real authority over the states or over the people themselves. The delegates to the Constitutional Convention had seen the weaknesses of this form of government.

From the outset, therefore, most of the delegates agreed that only a *federal union* would be strong enough to establish an orderly society. By creating a federal union, in which each state delegated some of its "sovereignty," or power, to the national government, the framers of the Constitution were able to remedy most of the weaknesses of the Articles of Confederation.

163

SOME FRAMERS
OF THE CONSTITUTION

During the Constitutional Convention, Major William Pierce, a Georgia delegate, jotted down his impressions of some of the men with whom he worked in Philadelphia during the summer of 1787. The excerpt below and those that follow in this chapter are drawn from a few of his character sketches. Although Major Pierce was quite candid in his remarks, it is interesting to observe that, on the whole, he had the highest regard for the character and intelligence of the framers of the Constitution. These were, of course, Major Pierce's own impressions, so that in his estimates of the delegates' ages he was sometimes in error.

Virginia's
James Madison
(1751–1836)

"Mr. Madison is a character who has long been in public life, and what is very remarkable, every person seems to acknowledge his greatness. He blends together the profound politician with the scholar. In the management of every great question, he evidently took the lead in the Convention, and though he cannot be called an orator, he is a most agreeable, eloquent, and convincing speaker.... The affairs of the United States, he perhaps has the most correct knowledge of, of any man in the Union.... Mr. Madison is about thirty-seven years of age, a gentleman of great modesty, with a remarkable sweet temper. He is easy and unreserved among his acquaintance, and has a most agreeable style of conversation."

Individuals and the law. Having agreed to organize a federal union, the delegates were faced with another troublesome question. How could the federal, or national, government enforce the laws that it enacted? Suppose, for example, that a citizen of the state of New York refused to obey a federal law? Should the federal government ask New York to punish the offender? If this procedure were followed and if the state refused to comply, would it not be necessary for the federal government to have the power to maintain its authority?

The longer the delegates debated this question, the more convinced they became that if trouble between the states and the federal government was to be avoided, all laws passed by the federal government *must apply equally to every individual* within the union. To insure obedience to these laws, the delegates decided that the federal government should have the power to reach into the states themselves to punish individuals who violated federal laws.

As a result of this decision, the people of the United States have always lived under two governments and two systems of law—federal and state. They have two citizenships, since they are citizens both of the United States and of the state in which they live. The Tenth Amendment, adopted in 1791, specifies that there are three groups of powers—(1) those delegated to the federal government, (2) those reserved for the states, and (3) those retained by the people.

Specific powers delegated to the federal government. The decision to give the federal government power to enforce its laws led the convention to another difficult problem. What laws should the federal government be allowed to pass? Or, in different words, what powers should the states delegate, or surrender, to the federal government?

After long debate the delegates decided to give the Congress of the United States a number of specific powers. All of these powers, known as *delegated* or *enumerated* powers, are listed in the Constitution. Among them are the power "To lay and collect taxes . . . To borrow money . . . To coin money . . . To regulate commerce with foreign nations, and among the several states . . . To raise and support armies . . . To provide and maintain a navy."

From that listing of powers, it is clear that the delegates gave the federal government authority only over those matters of common concern to the people of all the states. It is also evident that, in their selection of powers to be delegated to the federal government, the framers of the Constitution were trying to correct major weaknesses of the Articles of Confederation—lack of financial power, lack of power to regulate commerce, and lack of military power.

Powers reserved for the states. Under a federalist form of government, the member states still retain freedom to act on matters not assigned to the federal government or expressly forbidden to the states. The states, in turn, commonly assign some of their powers to local governments. In an effort to guarantee this independence of action to the states, the delegates listed several powers that could not be exercised by the federal authorities. For example, the federal government is forbidden to levy any "tax or duty . . . on articles exported from any state."

By implication all powers not specifically granted to the federal government, nor denied to the states, were retained by the states. But to insure against any misunderstanding, the Ninth and Tenth Amendments were adopted in 1791. The Tenth Amendment leaves no room for doubt: "The powers not delegated to the United States by the Constitution, nor prohibited by it to the states, are reserved to the states respectively, or to the people." Those powers retained by the states are known as *reserved* or *residual* powers. They include state control over voting, marriage, and divorce.

Shared powers. There are certain powers that every government must possess, simply in order to exist and function effectively. All governments, for example, must have the power to raise money and to enforce law and order. Both the federal government and the states use the same methods to raise money—taxation and borrowing. Both governments also have police forces to maintain order. In addition, both governments have court systems in which to try people who violate laws.

These powers that are shared by the federal government and the states are called *concurrent* powers. They exist concurrently with, or at the same time as, powers delegated to the federal government, on the one hand, and powers reserved for the states, on the other.

The Constitution as the supreme law. The men who drafted the Constitution realized that conflict might arise between federal and state laws. In an attempt to settle such conflicts, the framers of the Constitution inserted this statement in the Constitution: "This Constitution, and the laws of the United States which shall be made in pursuance thereof, and all treaties made, or which shall be made, under the authority of the United States, shall be the supreme law of the land. . . ." By including this statement, the Founding Fathers proclaimed that, in cases of conflict, the Constitution and the laws of the federal government should rank higher than state constitutions and state laws.

🖝 **SECTION SURVEY**

1. In what ways does a federal union differ from a confederation?

2. Contrast the relationship of the federal government to the states under the Confederation and under the Constitution.

3. The people of the United States live "under two governments and two systems of law—federal and state." Explain this.

4. Define the following terms and give three examples of each: (a) delegated powers, (b) reserved powers, and (c) concurrent powers.

IDENTIFY: federalism, enumerated powers.

4 | The Constitution separates, checks, and balances powers

The first of the basic principles upon which our government is built, as you know, is that of federalism, in which powers are divided between the federal, or national, government and the state governments. A second fundamental principle is the *separation of powers,* with "checks and balances," within the federal government.

Separation of powers. The framers of the Constitution were determined to protect the country from the tyranny of a military dictator or a small group of power-mad individuals. They had not forgotten the troubled years before the Revolutionary War. Even closer to their memories were recent attempts to establish a military dictatorship over the people of the thirteen states. In 1782, for example, a number of officers in the army had offered the title of king to General Washington. If Washington had been ambitious for dictatorial power, the history of the United States would have been different.

To prevent a military dictatorship and to guarantee against the seizure of power by small groups of people, the delegates agreed that the legislative, executive, and judicial powers of the government must be separated.

In developing this principle, the Founding Fathers were much influenced by a book entitled *The Spirit of the Laws,* written by a famous Frenchman, Montesquieu (mohn-tes-KYOO). In his book Montesquieu stressed that "men entrusted with power tend to abuse it." He believed the best form of government was one in which the powers of government were divided among a number of governmental agencies.

With this idea in mind, the delegates called for the establishment of three separate branches of the government, each having certain powers. To Congress they gave the legislative, or law-making, power (Article 1). To the Chief Executive, or President, they entrusted the power to execute or carry out the laws (Article 2). To the judiciary—that is, the federal courts—they granted the power to interpret the laws.

In addition to separating the powers of the legislative, executive, and judicial

■ The Declaration, Constitution, and Bill of Rights are on display today in Washington, D.C.

branches of the federal government, the delegates wrote into the Constitution a system of *checks and balances*. Each branch of the government was given certain powers that it could use to restrain, or balance, the powers of another branch if the other branch tried to abuse or exceed its powers.

Congress checks the President. If a President disregards the provisions of the Constitution, he can be *impeached,* or accused of unlawful acts, by Congress; if he is found guilty, he can be removed from office. A President can make a treaty, but a two-thirds vote of the Senate is necessary for its ratification. A President's power to appoint important officers is limited by the requirement that the Senate must confirm such appointments by a majority vote. Since Congress has control over taxes and expenditures, it can interfere with any Presidential policy that requires expenditures of money. Finally, a two-thirds vote of Congress can overrule the President's *veto,* or rejection, of legislation proposed by Congress.

The President checks Congress. The President, in turn, can check and balance the powers of Congress. Perhaps his most important check is his power to veto Congressional legislation. In addition, he can influence the thinking of many Congressmen through his annual "State of the Union" message and special messages to Congress. He can also exert pressure on Congress by calling a special session and asking for the passage of specific laws.

The President can also exert his influence by focusing public attention on specific issues at press conferences or by speaking directly to the people. If a press conference or a public address results in a barrage of letters and telegrams to Congress, the President may win his points.

Checks by and on the judiciary. The federal judiciary—the Supreme Court and the lower federal courts—interprets the laws. As you will see later, the federal judiciary has the power to declare that a law passed by Congress and ap-

Pennsylvania's James Wilson (1742–1798)

"Mr. Wilson ranks among the foremost in legal and political knowledge. . . . Government seems to have been his peculiar study; all the political institutions of the world he knows in detail, and can trace the causes and effects of every revolution from the earliest stages of the Grecian commonwealth down to the present time. No man is more clear, copious, and comprehensive than Mr. Wilson; yet he is no great orator. He draws the attention not by the charm of his eloquence, but by the force of his reasoning. He is about forty-five years old."—Major William Pierce, page 164.

proved by the President is "unconstitutional."

However, this power of the Supreme Court and of other federal courts can itself be checked in several ways. Congress can impeach federal judges. Congress also determines by law the number of justices on the Supreme Court. At different times laws have provided for as few as five and as many as ten justices.

The President, in turn, appoints all federal judges, with the consent of the Senate. The President's desire for a certain interpretation of the Constitution may sometimes be in conflict either with the Congress or the Supreme Court. If he appoints justices to the Supreme Court who are friendly to his point of view, and if he can get the consent of the Senate to his appointments, he is checking or balancing the power of Congress, of the judiciary, or of both. The President has a further check on the judiciary in his power to grant pardons and reprieves ° to persons who had been convicted of crimes in the federal courts.

Criticism and defense of checks and balances. The separation of powers with checks and balances in the federal government has sometimes been criticized for slowing down the processes of government. Important measures may be needed, but a President belonging to one party and a Congress dominated by another party may not be able to agree on a law. As a general rule, however, the system has worked well and has fulfilled the intentions of the men who wrote the Constitution.

In time of war or other crisis, Congress usually declares that a national emergency exists and grants special powers to the President so that he can act quickly. When the emergency is over, the special Presidential powers are withdrawn.

The principle of the separation of powers with checks and balances was written into the Constitution as a safeguard for the future. It was meant to protect the liberties of the people.

••

° *reprieve:* a warrant authorizing postponement of punishment.

✓ **SECTION SURVEY**

1. (a) What is meant by "separation of powers with checks and balances"? (b) Why did the framers of the Constitution adopt this principle?
2. List five ways in which (a) Congress can check the President and (b) the President can check Congress.
3. (a) Explain how the federal judiciary can check Congress and the President. (b) How can Congress and the President check the federal judiciary?
4. Although our system of separation of powers with checks and balances has been criticized, it has worked well. Justify this statement.

IDENTIFY: Montesquieu's *The Spirit of the Laws,* legislative, executive, judicial, impeach, veto, unconstitutional, pardon, reprieve.

5 The Constitution safeguards individual liberty

A third fundamental principle of government written into the Constitution by its framers is *protection of the liberties of individuals.*

For a long time Americans, and their English ancestors, had insisted upon protection of their rights as individuals against the powers of government—that is, protection of their *civil liberties.* The separation of powers with checks and balances is one way in which the Constitution protects the rights of individuals. And there are many other safeguards. Some appear in the Constitution itself. Others were written into the first ten amendments, known as the Bill of Rights. Still others have been added in later amendments.

Guarantees in the original Constitution. Among the important guarantees of civil liberty in the original Constitution are prohibitions against *ex post facto* laws and bills of attainder. An *ex post facto* law—that is, a law passed "after the deed"—is one that prescribes a penalty for an act that was legal at the time it was committed. A bill of attainder is a legislative measure that punishes a person by fine, imprisonment, or confiscation of property without permitting him to have a trial in court. The Constitution provides that punishment for wrongful acts can be imposed only by the courts, and then only in accordance with the duly established law. To prevent arbitrary convictions by judges, the Constitution also provides that "The trial of all crimes . . . shall be by jury."

The Constitution also guarantees that "The privilege of the writ of *habeas corpus* shall not be suspended, unless when in cases of rebellion or invasion the public safety may require it." The writ of *habeas corpus* is a legal document that forces a jailer to release a person from prison unless he has been formally charged with, or convicted of, a crime.

The Constitution gives special protection to an individual accused of *treason*. The men who drafted the Constitution knew that the charge of treason was an old device that arbitrary rulers often used to get rid of persons they did not like. Such rulers had brought the charge of treason against persons who merely criticized the government, as well as against those who actually helped to prepare an armed uprising against the government. To prevent the arbitrary use of this charge, the Constitution carefully defines treason, stating that "Treason against the United States shall consist only in levying war against them, or in adhering to their enemies, giving them aid and comfort. No person shall be convicted of treason unless on the testimony of two witnesses to the same overt act, or on confession in open court."

The Constitution also gives protection to innocent relatives of a person accused of treason. Only the convicted person can be punished, and no penalty can be imposed upon his family or relatives because of his wrongdoing.

These are only a few of the guarantees of personal rights that the Founding Fathers wrote into the Constitution. They are important examples of the way that the Constitution establishes a common standard of law for every American citizen, old and young, rich and poor alike.

The Bill of Rights. Despite the safeguards written into the Constitution itself, a number of states at first refused to ratify the Constitution because it did not offer greater protection to the rights of individuals. They finally agreed to ratification after they had been promised that a bill of rights would be added to the Constitution by amendment when Congress met.

Writing the Declaration of Independence in 1776, Jefferson had declared: "We hold these truths to be self-evident: that all men are created equal, that they are endowed by their Creator with certain unalienable rights, that among these are life, liberty, and the pursuit of happiness."

In 1789–90 the first Congress of the

South Carolina's John Rutledge (1739–1800)

"Mr. Rutledge is one of those characters who was highly mounted at the commencement of the late Revolution; his reputation in the first Congress gave him a distinguished rank among the American worthies. He was bred to the law, and now acts as one of the chancellors of South Carolina. This gentleman is much famed in his own State as an orator, but in my opinion he is too rapid in his public speaking to be denominated an agreeable orator. He is undoubtedly a man of abilities and a gentleman of distinction and fortune. Mr. Rutledge was once Governor of South Carolina. He is about forty-eight years of age."
—Major William Pierce, page 164.

United States wrote these ideals into the Bill of Rights, the first ten amendments to the Constitution. The Bill of Rights protects individuals against any action by the federal government that may deprive them of life, liberty, or property without "due process of law."

Among the guarantees of liberty in the Bill of Rights, several are especially important. The First Amendment guarantees freedom of religion, speech, press, assembly, and petition. The Fourth Amendment upholds the principle that "a man's home is his castle" by prohibiting unreasonable searches and seizures. The Fifth, Sixth, and Eighth Amendments protect accused persons from arbitrary arrest and punishment by the federal government.

The Bill of Rights, including these and other guarantees of individual liberty, was ratified by the states in 1791. From that time it has remained one of the best-known features of the Constitution. The American people have turned to it for support whenever they have feared that their rights as individuals were in danger. No document in American history except, perhaps, the Declaration of Independence, has been cherished more deeply by the people.

Interpreting individual rights. Although the Constitution, Bill of Rights, and later amendments guarantee certain rights equally to all Americans, individual rights are not absolute. The rights of an individual exist in relation to the rights of others. In guaranteeing freedom of speech and of the press, for example, the Bill of Rights does not grant an individual the right to say or print anything he likes at any time. For example, laws forbid the individual to say or print anything that may defame an innocent person's character. Freedom of speech and of the press, as well as all the other rights guaranteed by the first ten amendments, must be interpreted by the courts to have any real meaning.

When does freedom degenerate into license and end in anarchy? This was the big question the Founding Fathers wrestled with when they started the United States down the path of self-government more than a century and a half ago. The question has remained for each generation of Americans to answer in its own way.

✔ SECTION SURVEY

1. Explain and give an example of (a) an *ex post facto* law and (b) a bill of attainder.
2. (a) How does the Constitution define the crime of treason? (b) Why is this crime defined in the Constitution?
3. What connection can you see between the Declaration of Independence and the Bill of Rights?
4. (a) Explain this statement: "Individual rights are not absolute." (b) Give a practical example of the statement involving one of your rights.

IDENTIFY: civil liberties, writ of *habeas corpus,* "a man's home is his castle."

6 The Constitution is a flexible, living document

The famous British statesman William E. Gladstone once referred to the Constitution of the United States as "the most wonderful work ever struck off at a given time by the brain and purpose of man." This was high praise indeed. But the most convincing testimonial to the effectiveness of the Constitution is the fact that it has weathered the test of time. It stands today, as it has stood for more than a century and a half, as "the supreme law of the land."

The Constitution has survived the years as the supreme law of the land because it is a "living" document, flexible enough to meet the changing needs of a growing nation. By a number of means, as you will see, Americans have been able to adapt the Constitution to changing ways and changing times. So it is that the Constitution works as well today for an industrialized nation of fifty states and about 180,000,000 people as it once worked for an agricultural nation of thirteen states and 4,000,000 people.

The fourth fundamental principle of our Constitution, then, is its *adaptability* to changing times and changing circumstances.

Provision for amendments. The men who drafted the Constitution were as wise in what they did not write as in what they did write. They wrote down only the fundamental laws for the nation, leaving it to Congress to pass supplementary laws as these might be needed. Each time Congress meets, it passes such laws.

But even so the framers of the Constitution anticipated that changes in the fundamental law might have to be made from time to time. Accordingly, they wrote Article 5, which tells how the Constitution may be amended.

Because the amending process is slow and laborious, it is seldom actually used unless the need for change appears to be acute. Some people think the process is too slow and difficult. Others think it wise that no changes should be made in the "supreme law of the land" until the pro's and con's have been thoroughly debated.

In any event, only twenty-two amendments have been adopted since 1789, including the first ten amendments of the Bill of Rights.

The "elastic clause." The delegates to the Constitutional Convention provided still greater flexibility to the Constitution by inserting what has come to be known as the *elastic clause*. To the specific powers granted to Congress, this clause adds the additional power "To make all laws which shall be necessary and proper for carrying into execution the foregoing powers. . . ."

The elastic clause has been the subject of much debate in our history whenever Congress has stretched it to pass legislation not specifically authorized in the Constitution. Congress, for example, has stretched its power to regulate commerce so that it includes the power to improve rivers and harbors.

Whenever Congress has stretched its powers in this way, a question has arisen over which branch of the government shall decide whether a law is "necessary and proper." The Constitution does not clearly state how this question shall be answered. In 1803, however, Chief Justice Marshall established the tradition that this power rests in the Supreme Court (page 227).

The Supreme Court as referee. The power of the Supreme Court to decide whether or not a law or a treaty violates the Constitution has come to be known as the power of *judicial review*. When the Supreme Court exercises this power, it acts as a referee.

Every government needs a referee whose decision is binding. In dictatorships the word of the dictator or of the political party controlling the nation is final. In Great Britain Parliament makes the final decision. In the United States this responsibility rests with the Supreme Court.

Connecticut's Roger Sherman (1721–1793)

"Mr. Sherman exhibits the oddest-shaped character I ever remember to have met with. He is awkward, unmeaning, and unaccountably strange in his manner. But in his train of thinking there is something regular, deep, and comprehensive . . . he deserves infinite praise—no man has a better heart or a clearer head. . . . In the early part of his life he was a shoemaker, but . . . he turned almanac maker, and so progressed upwards to a judge. He has been several years a member of Congress and discharged the duties of his office with honor and credit to himself and advantage to the State he represented. He is about sixty."—Major William Pierce, page 164.

When the Supreme Court speaks, its word is final. But the Supreme Court can—and sometimes does—reverse one of its earlier decisions. And the people can, by the process of amendment, alter the Constitution itself.

The "unwritten Constitution." The Constitution, then, has proved to be a flexible, but durable, instrument. Amendments have altered certain provisions of the Constitution and added others. Court decisions and acts of Congress, especially under the elastic clause, have clothed certain provisions with new meanings.

Other changes in the operation of American government have come about by custom. For example, nothing was said in the Constitution about political parties, which Washington and others looked upon with disfavor as likely to lead to factional quarrels. Neither did the Constitution provide for regular meetings of the heads of the executive departments concerned with defense, foreign affairs, the postal system, finances, and other matters. Such meetings, called cabinet meetings, nevertheless take place and have become an important part of the executive system. Nor did the original Constitution place a limit on the number of terms to which a President might be elected to office. Washington's refusal to accept a third term, however, fostered the two-term tradition which was followed until 1940, when President Franklin Delano Roosevelt was elected to a third term. With the adoption of the Twenty-second Amendment in 1951, the two-term tradition became part of the Constitution.

Custom has established other important practices in the operation of the federal government. When the President, for example, needs to appoint a federal official to work in a state, he commonly seeks the advice of the Senators of that state, provided that they are from his own party. This custom is called "senatorial courtesy." Custom and the pressure of work have also led Congress to use an elaborate system of committees in its lawmaking procedures.

Practices such as these, growing out of custom and tradition, are sometimes called our *unwritten Constitution.* The Constitution does not refer to them, but they are so firmly established that for practical purposes they can be thought of as unwritten laws.

The admission of new states. The delegates, as you have seen, had drawn up a Constitution in which power was distributed between the states and the federal government. By making it possible for new states to enter the Union with a minimum of difficulty, they added still further flexibility and strength to the new government.

Since it was evident that the population would grow rapidly in the western lands, it was especially important to provide in advance for the easy admission of new States. So long as a western area remained a Territory, Congress was responsible for its government. But when the population of the Territory became large enough, the Territory could apply for admission to the Union as a State. In general, the laws passed to govern the admission of new States were the same as those established under the Articles of Confederation in the Northwest Ordinance (pages 147–48).

SECTION SURVEY

1. "The amending process is slow and laborious." Explain this statement by referring to Article 5 of the Constitution.
2. (a) Quote the "elastic clause." (b) Why can this clause also be called the "implied powers" clause? (c) How has this clause made the Constitution flexible?
3. What is the power of judicial review? How did the Supreme Court get this?
4. List four practices which are now considered to be a part of the "unwritten constitution." Give an example of a tradition which has become part of the Constitution.

IDENTIFY: senatorial courtesy.

■ CHAPTER SURVEY

(For review, see Section Surveys, pages 160, 163, 165, 168, 170, 172.)

Points to Discuss: 1. The delegates to the Constitutional Convention were a remarkable cross section of American leadership. Support this statement.

2. It has been said that the Constitution is a bundle of compromises. Do you agree or disagree? Defend your position.

3. Montesquieu has written that "men entrusted with power tend to abuse it." Give examples from history to support his contention. Discuss how the framers of the Constitution sought to avoid this danger.

4. Present the arguments which you might have given if you had been a delegate to one of the state conventions called to ratify the Constitution.

5. What is the nature or essence of federal government? Do you believe that the

separation of powers between the federal and state governments has been wisely made? Justify your answer.

6. By and large, the system of separation of powers with checks and balances has well served the intentions of the men who wrote the Constitution. Give your opinion of this statement and defend your position by explaining how the government has dealt with a particular current problem.

7. Americans have a "living Constitution" sensitive to changing times. Name four features which you believe have helped to make the Constitution a flexible instrument.

8. What does the last amendment provide?

Using Charts: In the pages that follow, the complete text of the Constitution and its amendments are printed in black. Notes on the meaning of the text are printed in red. Some of the more important passages are illustrated by charts. As you read these pages, develop answers to the following questions based upon the charts.

1. Study the chart on page 180. (a) Why are there so many steps in the passage of a bill? (b) What steps can you or any other citizen take to influence the introduction of a bill or the passage of a bill? (c) In your opinion, which step in the passage of a bill is the most critical? Why? (d) How does the Rules Committee play a most important role in the progress of a bill? (e) What is the purpose of the Joint Conference Committee? (f) State the three courses of action that a President can follow when he receives a bill.

2. Compare the charts on page 185 and page 188. What is the difference in the meaning of the terms "division of powers" and "separation of powers"?

3. Turn to the chart on page 185. (a) Which, in your opinion, is the most important delegated power? the most important reserved power? the most important concurrent power? Why? (b) Explain why certain powers were denied to both the federal and state governments. (c) In your opinion, what is the most important advantage of the federal system of government? the most serious disadvantage?

4. Turn to the chart on page 175. (a) What is the basic function of each of the main branches of the federal government? Explain each function. (b) Choose five independent federal agencies and explain the importance of each today. (c) Name the present members of the President's Cabinet and the department they head. (d) What is the reason for two groups of courts in the Judicial Branch?

5. Turn to the chart on page 188. (a) Which of the three branches of government seems to have the most powerful check over the other two? Why? (b) What is Congress' most powerful check over the Executive Branch? over the Judicial Branch? (c) How can the combined powers of the President and the Congress check the Judiciary?

6. Turn to the chart on page 192. State four different methods which can be used in amending the Constitution.

7. Turn to the chart on page 197. (a) How many Presidential electors did your state have in the last election? (b) Why are the November Presidential election results unofficial? (c) What was the minimum number of electoral votes required to win the last Presidential election?

■ TRACING THE MAIN IDEAS

The delegates who met in the spring of 1787 to revise the Articles of Confederation included many of the ablest men in America. Convinced that the Confederation was not strong enough to bring order and prosperity to their country, they abandoned all thought of revision and proceeded to draw up a completely new constitution. Out of their long political experience, out of their keen intelligence, out of their great learning, the framers of the Constitution fashioned a blueprint for the United States of America. Revised, modified, and amended, the Constitution has served the American people for more than 170 years. It stands as a lasting tribute to the wisdom and foresight of the founding fathers.

The Constitution created a republican form of government. It did not, however, create the nation. In Chapter 10 you will see how men and women from many walks of life began to work at the task of unifying their country and of establishing it as a respected member of the family of nations.

THE CONSTITUTION OF THE UNITED STATES

(The text of the Constitution is printed in black; the commentary in red. Portions of the text printed in brackets have gone out of date or been changed by amendment.)

PREAMBLE

We, the people of the United States, in order to form a more perfect Union, establish justice, insure domestic tranquillity, provide for the common defense, promote the general welfare, and secure the blessings of liberty to ourselves and our posterity, do ordain and establish this CONSTITUTION for the United States of America.

¶ In addition to stating the purposes of the Constitution, the Preamble makes it clear that the government is established by consent of the governed. "We, the people, . . . ordain and establish" the government. We, the people, have supreme power.

Article 1. LEGISLATIVE DEPARTMENT

SECTION 1. CONGRESS

All legislative powers herein granted shall be vested in a Congress of the United States, which shall consist of a Senate and House of Representatives.

¶ By separating the functions of government among branches concerned with lawmaking (Article 1), law executing (Article 2), and law interpreting (Article 3), the framers of the Constitution were applying the principle of separation of powers, and developing a system of checks and balances, as a defense against dictatorship. ¶ Practice has modified the provision that all lawmaking power granted in the Constitution shall be vested in Congress. For example, such administrative agencies as the Interstate Commerce Commission (p. 495) can issue regulations which in some ways have the force of laws.

SECTION 2. HOUSE OF REPRESENTATIVES

1. *Election and term of members.* The House of Representatives shall be composed of members chosen every second year by the people of the several states, and the electors in each state shall have the qualifications requisite for electors of the most numerous branch of the state legislature.

¶ The members of the House of Representatives are elected every two years by the "electors" (voters) of the states. Except for the provisions of Amendments 15 and 19, the individual states decide who may or may not vote in elections.

2. *Qualifications.* No person shall be a Representative who shall not have attained to the age of twenty-five years, and been seven years a citizen of the United States, and who shall not, when elected, be an inhabitant of that state in which he shall be chosen.

¶ *Qualifications for a Representative:* (1) At least 25 years of age. (2) A United States citizen for at least 7 years. (3) Residence in the state in which elected. (Custom has added the requirement of residence in the Congressional district from which a Representative is elected.) Each state is divided into Congressional districts for the purpose of electing Representatives to the House; each district elects one. ¶ TERM OF OFFICE: 2 years

3. *Apportionment of Representatives and direct taxes.* Representatives [and direct taxes] shall be apportioned among the several states which may be included within this Union, according to their respective numbers, [which shall be determined by adding

THE THREE BRANCHES OF THE FEDERAL GOVERNMENT

LEGISLATIVE BRANCH

HOUSE OF	SENATE
REPRESENTATIVES	Two Senators
Membership based	from each state
on state populations	

Article 1 establishes
the Legislative Branch.

Standing Committees

of the House
Agriculture
Appropriations
Armed Services
Banking and Currency
District of Columbia
Education and Labor
Foreign Affairs
Government Operations
House Administration
Interior and Insular Affairs
Interstate and Foreign Commerce
Judiciary
Merchant Marine and Fisheries
Post Office and Civil Service
Public Works
Rules
Un-American Activities
Veterans Affairs
Ways and Means

of the Senate
Agriculture and Forestry
Appropriations
Armed Services
Banking and Currency
District of Columbia
Finance
Foreign Relations
Government Operations
Interior and Insular Affairs
Interstate and Foreign Commerce
Judiciary
Labor and Public Welfare
Post Office and Civil Service
Public Works
Rules and Administration

Joint Committees of the House and Senate

Atomic Energy
Defense Production
Disposition of Executive Papers
Economic Reports
Immigration and Nationality Policy
Internal Revenue Taxation

Library of Congress
Navaho-Hopi Indian Administration
Printing
Reduction of Nonessential Federal
  Expenditures

EXECUTIVE BRANCH

Article 2 establishes
the Executive Branch.

Executive Departments
*Heads of these departments
form the President's Cabinet.*
Department of State
Department of the Treasury
Department of Defense
Department of Justice
Post Office Department
Department of the Interior
Department of Agriculture
Department of Commerce
Department of Labor
Department of Health, Education,
  and Welfare

The Executive Office
Bureau of the Budget
Council of Economic Advisers
National Security Council
Central Intelligence Agency
Office of Defense Mobilization
Operations Coordinating Board

Independent Federal Agencies

United States Civil Service Commission
Interstate Commerce Commission
Federal Reserve Board
Federal Trade Commission
Federal Power Commission
United States Tariff Commission
Veterans Administration
Federal Deposit Insurance Corporation
Tennessee Valley Authority
Export-Import Bank
Federal Communications Commission
Securities and Exchange Commission

National Labor Relations Board
Civil Aeronautics Board
Atomic Energy Commission
Indian Claims Commission
Federal Mediation and Conciliation
  Service
General Services Administration
Federal Civil Defense Administration
Subversive Activities Control Board
Small Business Administration
United States Information Agency

JUDICIAL BRANCH

Article 3 establishes
the Judicial Branch.

THE SUPREME COURT

Courts of Appeals

District Courts

Special Courts
Court of Claims
Territorial District Courts
Court of Customs and Patent Appeals
Tax Court
Court of Military Appeals

to the whole number of free persons, including those bound to service for a term of years, and excluding Indians not taxed, three-fifths of all other persons.] The actual enumeration shall be made within three years after the first meeting of the Congress of the United States, and within every subsequent term of ten years, in such manner as they shall by law direct. The number of Representatives shall not exceed 1 for every 30,000, but each state shall have at least 1 Representative; [and until such enumeration shall be made, the state of New Hampshire shall be entitled to choose 3; Massachusetts, 8; Rhode Island and Providence Plantations, 1; Connecticut, 5; New York, 6; New Jersey, 4; Pennsylvania, 8; Delaware, 1; Maryland, 6; Virginia, 10; North Carolina, 5; South Carolina, 5; and Georgia, 3.]

¶ The bracketed portion of this clause beginning on line 3 forms what came to be called the three-fifths compromise (p. 158). Amendment 13 and Section 2 of Amendment 14 overruled this provision. ¶ Originally, each state was entitled to one Representative in Congress for every 30,000 people. Later, membership was limited by law to 435. A census of the population is taken every ten years to determine the number of Representatives to which each state is entitled. Congress can change the number of members, as it did temporarily when Alaska and Hawaii were admitted to the Union before the 1960 census had determined the new number of Representatives for each state. Note that each state, regardless of its population, is entitled to at least one Representative.

4. *Filling vacancies.* When vacancies happen in the representation from any state, the executive authority thereof shall issue writs of election to fill such vacancies.

5. *Officers; impeachment.* The House of Representatives shall choose their Speaker and other officers; and shall have the sole power of impeachment.

¶ *Clause 4.* The "executive authority" refers to the governor of the state; a "writ of election" is an order for a special election to fill the vacant seat. ¶ *Clause 5.* In actual practice, it is the majority party—the political party having the largest number of members in the House—which chooses the Speaker (chairman) of the House and other officials (clerk, doorkeeper, sergeant at arms, postmaster, and chaplain). The Speaker is the only official chosen from among the members of the House. ¶ The House, by a majority vote, can impeach (accuse) certain officers of the Executive Department or a federal judge. The trial of the impeached official takes place in the Senate.

SECTION 3. SENATE

1. *Number of members and term of office.* The Senate of the United States shall be composed of two Senators from each state, [chosen by the legislature thereof,] for six years, and each Senator shall have one vote.

¶ Under the provisions of Amendment 17, the 100 Senators are now elected directly by the voters of the states in the same manner as the Representatives. The former method, by which the state legislatures chose Senators, was considered undemocratic.

2. *Classification; filling vacancies.* [Immediately after they shall be assembled in consequence of the first election, they shall be divided as equally as may be into three classes. The seats of the Senators of the first class shall be vacated at the expiration of the second year, of the second class at the expiration of the fourth year, and of the third class at the expiration of the sixth year, so that one-third may be chosen every second year; and if vacancies happen by resignation, or otherwise, during the recess of the legislature of any state, the executive thereof may make temporary appointments until the next meeting of the legislature, which shall then fill such vacancies.]

¶ One third of the Senate comes up for election every two years. This procedure was established in the first Senate, whose Senators were divided into three groups. One group was to serve for two years, the second for four years, and the third for six years. As a result, the terms of Senators today overlap, making the Senate a "continuing" body, in which two thirds of the members are "carried over" through every election. In contrast, the total membership of the House of Representatives is elected every two years. ¶ If a Senator resigns or dies, the governor of the state is authorized under Amendment 17 to call a special election to fill the vacancy. The state legislature, however, may give the governor power to make a temporary appointment until the next election.

3. *Qualifications.* **No person shall be a Senator who shall not have attained to the age of thirty years, and been nine years a citizen of the United States, and who shall not, when elected, be an inhabitant of that state for which he shall be chosen.**

¶ *Qualifications for a Senator:* (1) At least 30 years of age. (2) A citizen for at least 9 years. (3) Residence in the state in which elected. ¶ TERM OF OFFICE: 6 years

4. *President of the Senate.* **The Vice-President of the United States shall be president of the Senate, but shall have no vote, unless they be equally divided.**

5. *Other officers.* **The Senate shall choose their other officers, and also a president** *pro tempore,* **in the absence of the Vice-President, or when he shall exercise the office of President of the United States.**

¶ *Clause 4.* To serve as President of the Senate is the only duty which the Constitution assigns to the Vice-President. He votes as a Senator only in case of a tie. After the illness of President Eisenhower in 1956 and 1957, the Vice-President undertook additional duties at the President's request. He attended Cabinet meetings, traveled abroad on good will tours, and carried out ceremonial duties such as entertaining leading officials from abroad and representing the government at important events. ¶ *Clause 5.* "Other officers" include a secretary, chaplain, and sergeant at arms. These officers are not members of the Senate. *Pro tempore* means "for the time being," or "temporarily."

6. *Trial of impeachments.* **The Senate shall have the sole power to try all impeachments. When sitting for that purpose, they shall be on oath or affirmation. When the President of the United States is tried, the Chief Justice shall preside; and no person shall be convicted without the concurrence of two-thirds of the members present.**

¶ Only the President, Vice-President, Cabinet officials, and federal judges are subject to impeachment and removal from office. Members of the House and Senate cannot be impeached, but they can be censured and even removed from office by the members of their respective houses. ¶ Officials may be impeached only for committing "treason, bribery, or other high crimes and misdemeanors" (see Article 2, Section 4). The Chief Justice of the United States presides at the impeachment trial of a President. The Vice-President presides over all other impeachment trials. The Senate can find an impeached official guilty only if two thirds of the Senators present agree on the verdict. (A majority of the Senate must be present.) ¶ The only President impeached was Andrew Johnson, in 1867 (p. 417); he was saved from conviction by one vote. In all, the Senate has sat as a court of impeachment in twelve cases. A verdict of guilty was found in four of these.

7. *Penalty for conviction.* **Judgment in cases of impeachment shall not extend further than to removal from office, and disqualification to hold and enjoy any office of honor, trust, or profit under the United States; but the party convicted shall nevertheless be liable and subject to indictment, trial, judgment, and punishment, according to law.**

¶ The punishment for conviction in impeachment cases can consist only of removal from office and disqualification from holding any other federal office, but the convicted person may also be tried for the same offense in a regular court of law.

SECTION 4. ELECTIONS AND MEETINGS

1. *Holding elections.* **The times, places, and manner of holding elections for Senators and Representatives shall be prescribed in each state by the legislature thereof; but the Congress may at any time by law make or alter such regulations, except as to the places of choosing Senators.**

2. *Meetings.* **The Congress shall assemble at least once in every year, [and such meeting shall be on the first Monday in December,] unless they shall by law appoint a different day.**

¶ *Clause 1.* Under this provision, Congress has passed a law stating that, unless the constitution of a state provides otherwise, Congressional elections must be held on the Tuesday following the first Monday in November of even-numbered years. (In Maine, elections are held in September.) Congress has also ruled that Representatives must be elected by districts, rather than by the state as a whole, and that secret ballots (or voting machines, where required by state law) must be used. ¶ *Clause 2.* This clause has been changed by Amendment 20. Today, Congress meets on January 3, unless it sets another day by law.

SECTION 5. RULES OF PROCEDURE

1. *Organization.* Each house shall be the judge of the elections, returns, and qualifications of its own members, and a majority of each shall constitute a quorum to do business; but a smaller number may adjourn from day to day, and may be authorized to compel the attendance of absent members, in such manner, and under such penalties, as each house may provide.

2. *Proceedings.* Each house may determine the rules of its proceedings, punish its members for disorderly behavior, and with the concurrence of two-thirds, expel a member.

¶ *Clause 1.* Each house of Congress may disqualify elected candidates and prevent them from taking office on the grounds of public policy. On one occasion the House refused to admit to membership an elected candidate who had violated the criminal laws. On another occasion the Senate refused to seat a victorious candidate whose election campaign had been characterized by "fraud and corruption." ¶ A *quorum* is the minimum number of persons required to be present to transact business; a majority of the House or Senate constitutes a quorum. In practice, business is often transacted with less than a quorum present, and may go on as long as no Congressman objects to the lack of a quorum. ¶ *Clause 2.* Each house has extensive rules of procedure. Each house can censure, punish, or expel a member. Expulsion requires a two-thirds vote.

3. *Journal.* Each house shall keep a journal of its proceedings, and from time to time publish the same, excepting such parts as may in their judgment require secrecy; and the yeas and nays of the members of either house on any question shall, at the desire of one-fifth of those present, be entered on the journal.

4. *Adjournment.* Neither house, during the session of Congress, shall, without the consent of the other, adjourn for more than three days, nor to any other place than that in which the two houses shall be sitting.

¶ *Clause 3.* Each house is required to keep a journal of its activities. These journals, called the *House Journal* and the *Senate Journal,* are published at the end of each session of Congress. A third journal, called the *Congressional Record,* is published every day that Congress is in session, and furnishes a daily account of what Representatives and Senators do and say. ¶ If one fifth of those present insist on a roll call of the members' votes, the vote of each member must be recorded in the proper house journal. ¶ *Clause 4.* Both houses must remain in session for the same period of time and in the same place.

SECTION 6. PRIVILEGES AND RESTRICTIONS

1. *Pay and privileges.* The Senators and Representatives shall receive a compensation for their services, to be ascertained by law and paid out of the Treasury of the United States. They shall in all cases except treason, felony, and breach of the peace, be privileged from arrest during their attendance at the session of their respective houses, and in going to and returning from the same; and for any speech or debate in either house, they shall not be questioned in any other place.

¶ In 1955 the salary of a Congressman was set by law at $22,500 a year. ¶ The provision concerning privilege from arrest establishes the principle of "Congressional immunity." According to this principle, Congressmen cannot be arrested or brought into court for what they say in speeches and debates in Congress. The aim of this provision is to enable members of Congress to speak freely. Congressmen are subject to arrest, however, if they commit a crime, and, under the laws governing slander and libel, they are liable for any false or defamatory statements they may make outside Congress.

2. *Restrictions.* **No Senator or Representative shall, during the time for which he was elected, be appointed to any civil office under the authority of the United States, which shall have been created, or the emoluments whereof shall have been increased, during such time; and no person holding any office under the United States shall be a member of either house during his continuance in office.**

¶ This clause emphasizes the separation of powers in the federal government. Legislators cannot, while they are members of Congress, hold positions also in the Executive or Judicial Departments. Nor can a legislator resign his post and accept a position which was created during his term of office. Thus, Con- gressmen cannot set up jobs for themselves in the executive or judicial branches of the gov- ernment. Furthermore, if a Congressman re- signs and is appointed to an existing executive or judicial position, he cannot profit from any increase in pay in this position that was voted during his term in Congress.

SECTION 7. METHOD OF PASSING LAWS

1. *Revenue bills.* **All bills for raising revenue shall originate in the House of Rep- resentatives; but the Senate may propose or concur with amendments as on other bills.**

¶ All revenue, or money-raising, bills must be introduced in the House of Representatives. This provision grew out of a demand that the popularly elected branch of the legislature should have the "power of the purse." (Until Amendment 17 was ratified, the House of Representatives was the only popularly elected branch.) It was also felt that the voters had more control over Representatives, who are elected for two-year terms, than over Sena- tors, who are elected for six-year terms; thus, Representatives would be more careful in considering revenue bills. Since the Senate can amend any bill, however, it can amend a revenue bill in such a way as actually to in- troduce a revenue bill of its own.

2. *How a bill becomes a law.* **Every bill which shall have passed the House of Rep- resentatives and the Senate, shall, before it become a law, be presented to the Presi- dent of the United States; if he approve, he shall sign it, but if not, he shall return it, with his objections to that house in which it shall have originated, who shall enter the objections at large on their journal, and proceed to reconsider it. If after such recon- sideration two-thirds of that house shall agree to pass the bill, it shall be sent, together with the objections, to the other house, by which it shall likewise be reconsidered, and, if approved by two-thirds of that house, it shall become a law. But in all such cases the votes of both houses shall be determined by yeas and nays, and the names of the per- sons voting for and against the bill shall be entered on the journal of each house respec- tively. If any bill shall not be returned by the President within ten days (Sundays excepted) after it shall have been presented to him, the same shall be a law, in like manner as if he had signed it, unless the Congress by their adjournment prevent its re- turn, in which case it shall not be a law.**

¶ The process under which a bill becomes a law is shown in the chart on page 180. ¶ If the President does not approve of a bill, there are several things he may do. (1) He may veto, or refuse to sign, the bill. (2) He may permit the bill to become a law without his signature by holding it for 10 days (not count- ing Sundays) while Congress is in session. (3) Toward the end of a Congressional session, he may hold the bill in the hope that Congress will adjourn within 10 days or less. In that case, the bill fails to become a law, just as though the President had formally vetoed it. This type of veto is called a "pocket veto." ¶ A bill vetoed by the President can become a law despite his objections if two thirds or more of both houses vote for the bill a second time. When this happens, Congress is said to have "overridden the Presidential veto."

3. *Presidential approval or veto.* **Every order, resolution, or vote to which the con- currence of the Senate and House of Representatives may be necessary (except on a question of adjournment) shall be presented to the President of the United States; and before the same shall take effect, shall be approved by him, or being disapproved by him, shall be repassed by two-thirds of the Senate and House of Representatives, ac- cording to the rules and limitations prescribed in the case of a bill.**

A typical successful bill follows this course on its way to becoming a federal law. A group of citizens or private organizations may have requested it; or the President may have recommended it; or a group in Congress, in either the House or Senate, may have believed it was needed and agreed to introduce it. The bill is drafted by one or more Congressmen and introduced in the appropriate house —in this case the House of Representatives. Bills pertaining to the raising of money must originate in the House of Representatives; other bills may originate in the House or Senate.

1. Bill is introduced in House of Representatives.

HOUSE OF REPRESENTATIVES

SENATE

SENT TO SENATE

2. Clerk of the House
  a. Congressman submits bill to Clerk, who places it in a box called a "hopper."
  b. Title of bill read to House, number assigned, bill printed, sent by Speaker of the House to committee concerned with the subject of the bill.

6. Clerk of Senate
  a. Clerk sends bill to presiding officer of the Senate (usually the Vice-President).
  b. Presiding officer assigns bill to appropriate committee for study.

3. House Committee
  a. Committee or one of its subcommittees studies bill. May hold hearings, amend, rewrite, kill, or approve.
  b. If bill approved, committee reports bill favorably, and it is placed on the "calendar."

7. Senate Committee
Procedure is similar to that in House (step 3).

4. Rules Committee
Rules Committee may push important bills ahead; may "block" bills it does not approve.

Conference Committee

Irons out differences that may occur between House and Senate and returns revised bill for approval in both House and Senate.

8. Senate Floor
  a. Procedure is similar to that in House (step 5).
  b. If Senate disagrees with House version, bill is sent to Conference Committee of House and Senate.
  c. When passed in same form as in House, bill goes to President.

5. Floor of the House
  a. Bill read and debated.
  b. Amended, or returned to House committee for revision, or approved.
  c. If House approves bill by majority vote, it is read again and passed.

PASSED BY HOUSE

Cabinet Member
May be asked to advise on bill.

9. President
  a. President signs or vetoes bill or allows it to become law without signing it.
  b. Congress can overrule veto by ⅔ vote of both houses.

10. Secretary of State
  a. Affixes Great Seal of the United States.
  b. Proclaims that bill is now Law of the Land.

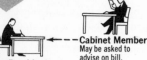

¶ A *joint resolution* results from declarations passed by both houses of Congress on the same subject. It becomes a law in the same manner as a bill. A Congressional declaration of war takes the form of a joint resolution. ¶ A *concurrent resolution* represents only an expression of opinion on the part of either house of Congress. It does not have the force of law and, therefore, does not require Presidential approval. The process of amending the Constitution may start with a concurrent resolution. A vote of both houses on an expression of sympathy may take the form of a concurrent resolution.

SECTION 8. POWERS DELEGATED TO CONGRESS

The Congress shall have power

1. To lay and collect taxes, duties, imposts, and excises, to pay the debts and provide for the common defense and general welfare of the United States; but all duties, imposts, and excises shall be uniform throughout the United States;

¶ Section 8 places important powers in the hands of Congress, indicating that the framers of the Constitution were aware of the weaknesses of the Congress under the Articles of Confederation. This section lists eighteen powers granted to Congress—the *delegated* or *enumerated powers*. The first seventeen are "express" powers because they clearly designate specific areas in which Congress may exercise its authority. The eighteenth power is contained in the famous "elastic clause," from which has come the doctrine of "implied" powers. The elastic clause permits the "stretching" of the other seventeen powers.

¶ *Clause 1*. This clause gives Congress the power to levy and collect taxes, duties or tariffs (taxes on imported goods collected at customhouses), and excises (taxes on goods produced, sold, or consumed within the country). The term "imposts" includes duties and excise taxes. Notice that these taxes must be uniform throughout the United States. According to this clause, the power to tax may be used for two purposes only: (1) to pay the government's debts, and (2) to provide for the common defense and general welfare. The Social Security tax on payrolls (p. 706) is a present-day use of the power to tax.

2. To borrow money on the credit of the United States;

3. To regulate commerce with foreign nations, and among the several states, and with the Indian tribes;

4. To establish a uniform rule of naturalization, and uniform laws on the subject of bankruptcies throughout the United States;

5. To coin money, regulate the value thereof, and of foreign coin, and fix the standard of weights and measures;

6. To provide for the punishment of counterfeiting the securities and current coin of the United States;

¶ *Clause 2*. The power granted in Clause 2 enables the government to borrow money by issuing bonds for sale, on which the government pays interest. This clause, extended by Clause 18, has also given Congress the power to establish national banks and the Federal Reserve System (p. 564). ¶ *Clause 3*. Clause 3, included to remedy one of the major weaknesses of the Articles of Confederation, gives Congress direct control over interstate and foreign commerce. And this provision has been extended, by the use of Clause 18, to give Congress control over transportation, communication, and navigation. In order to exercise this broad power, Congress has set up various administrative agencies, such as the Interstate Commerce Commission and the Federal Communications Commission. ¶ *Clause 4*. Clause 4 provides the power to regulate the methods by which aliens become citizens of the United States and to form rules regarding bankruptcy. ¶ *Clause 5*. Clause 5 permits Congress to coin money, to determine the gold and silver content of money, and to order the printing of paper money. It also permits Congress to set up uniform standards for measuring weights and distances. ¶ *Clause 6*. Under Clause 6, the Treasury Department is authorized by Congress to investigate counterfeiting of money or government bonds.

7. To establish post offices and post roads;

8. To promote the progress of science and useful arts by securing for limited times to authors and inventors the exclusive right to their respective writings and discoveries;

9. To constitute tribunals inferior to the Supreme Court;

10. To define and punish piracies and felonies committed on the high seas and offenses against the law of nations;

11. To declare war, [grant letters of marque and reprisal,] and make rules concerning captures on land and water;

¶ *Clause 7.* Clause 7 grants Congress the power to control post offices and the mail service. Through its power to appropriate money to run the various government departments, including the Post Office Department, Congress can also determine the postal rates. ¶ *Clause 8.* Clause 8 shows that the framers of the Constitution were eager to promote the progress of science and the arts. Under this power, Congress has passed laws providing that inventors be granted *patents* (exclusive rights to manufacture and sell their inventions for 17 years) and that authors and composers be granted *copyrights* (exclusive rights to control the publication or performance of their works for a 28-year period, renewable for an equal length of time). ¶ *Clause 9.* Clause 9 granted Congress the power to establish the federal district courts, the Courts of Appeals, and other special courts. ¶ *Clause 10.* Empowered by Clause 10, Congress protects and controls citizens and ships of the United States when they are out of the country. Congress may also punish counterfeiting in the U.S. of bonds and notes of a foreign government. ¶ *Clause 11.* Clause 11 gives Congress the power to declare war. Although Congress alone has this power, there have been instances when Presidents took military action without prior consent of Congress. In 1846 President Polk sent troops into an area which was claimed by both the United States and Mexico (p. 330). In 1950 President Truman ordered American troops into Korea to stop Communist aggression (p. 790). ¶ "Letters of marque and reprisal" were licenses issued by the government to privateers (armed ships, privately owned), allowing them to attack enemy ships during wartime. In the War of 1812, many of these licenses were issued, and American privateers took advantage of them to do extensive damage to British trade. Today, this practice is outlawed by international agreement.

12. To raise and support armies, but no appropriation of money to that use shall be for a longer term than two years;

13. To provide and maintain a navy;

14. To make rules for the government and regulation of the land and naval forces;

15. To provide for calling forth the militia to execute the laws of the Union, suppress insurrections, and repel invasions;

16. To provide for organizing, arming, and disciplining the militia, and for governing such part of them as may be employed in the service of the United States, reserving to the states, respectively, the appointment of the officers, and the authority of training the militia according to the discipline prescribed by Congress;

¶ *Clause 12.* The two-year limit in Clause 12 on money appropriations for the army was included to keep the major military power under strict civilian control. ¶ *Clause 13.* Notice that appropriations for the navy were not limited. An air force, of course, was not dreamed of when the Constitution was written. ¶ *Clause 14.* Under the power granted in Clause 14, Congress has established rules and regulations governing military discipline and the procedure of courts-martial. ¶ *Clauses 15, 16.* The term "militia" now refers to the National Guard units of the states. These units may now be called up by the President to keep law and order. They can become part of the United States Army in emergencies.

17. To exercise exclusive legislation in all cases whatsoever, over such district (not exceeding ten miles square) as may, by cession of particular states, and the acceptance of Congress, become the seat of government of the United States, and to exercise like authority over all places purchased by the consent of the legislature of the state in which the same shall be, for the erection of forts, magazines, arsenals, dock-yards, and other needful buildings;—and

¶ The power in Clause 17 enables Congress to exercise control over the District of Columbia, as well as over forts, arsenals, federal courthouses, post offices, dockyards, and other installations owned and operated by the federal government in the various states.

18. To make all laws which shall be necessary and proper for carrying into execution the foregoing powers, and all other powers vested by this Constitution in the government of the United States, or in any department or officer thereof.

¶ "Necessary and proper" are the key words in Clause 18, the so-called *elastic clause.* Only by combining the power granted in this clause with one of the other seventeen powers can Congress make use of the implied powers granted to it in the Constitution. Laws based on this clause are, of course, subject to review by the judicial branch.

SECTION 9. POWERS DENIED TO THE FEDERAL GOVERNMENT

1. [The migration or importation of such persons as any of the states now existing shall think proper to admit shall not be prohibited by the Congress prior to the year 1808; but a tax or duty may be imposed on such importation, not exceeding $10 for each person.]

¶ Section 9 limits the powers of Congress. ¶ *Clause 1.* "Such persons" refers to slaves. This provision grew out of the commerce compromises at the Constitutional Convention (p. 158). It was agreed that Congress would not prohibit the importation of slaves prior to 1808, and that it would not impose an import tax of more than $10 per slave. The importation of slaves into the United States was stopped in 1808.

2. The privilege of the writ of *habeas corpus* shall not be suspended, unless when in cases of rebellion or invasion the public safety may require it.

3. No bill of attainder or *ex post facto* law shall be passed.

¶ *Clause 2.* The guarantee of the writ of *habeas corpus* (meaning "you may have the body, or person") has been called the most important single safeguard of personal liberty known to Anglo-American law. It protects a person against being held in jail on insufficient evidence or no evidence at all. The lawyer of a person who is arrested can readily obtain a writ, or court order, which requires that the arrested person be brought before a judge who is to determine whether there are sufficient grounds to hold him in jail. If there are not enough grounds the person must be set free ¶ *Clause 3.* A "bill of attainder" is a legislative measure which condemns a person and punishes him without a jury trial. Such measures were used in England where Parliament could, by law, declare a person guilty of treason and punish him by death and confiscation of property. Under the Constitution, Congress cannot by law single out certain persons and inflict punishment on them. The power to punish belongs to the judiciary. ¶ An *ex post facto* law was a law which punished a person for doing something which was legal before the law was passed, or which increased the penalty for earlier actions. Because of this clause, the Lindbergh Kidnapping Law of 1932, for example, cannot be applied to persons who committed the crime of kidnapping before 1932.

4. No capitation or other direct tax shall be laid, unless in proportion to the census or enumeration herein before directed to be taken.

5. No tax or duty shall be laid on articles exported from any state.

6. No preference shall be given by any regulation of commerce or revenue to the ports of one state over those of another: nor shall vessels bound to, or from, one state, be obliged to enter, clear, or pay duties in another.

¶ *Clause 4.* A "capitation tax" is a direct tax imposed on each person, such as the poll tax on persons voting. This provision was inserted to prevent Congress from taxing Negro slaves per poll, or per person, for the purpose of abolishing slavery. Amendment 16 overrules this clause as far as income taxes are concerned. ¶ *Clause 5.* Clause 5 also resulted from the commerce compromises. The southern states wanted to make sure that Congress could not use its taxing power to impose taxes on southern exports, such as cotton and tobacco ¶ *Clause 6.* Clause 6 declares that the United States is an open market in which all states have equal trading and commercial opportunities.

7. No money shall be drawn from the Treasury, but in consequence of appropriations made by law; and a regular statement and account of the receipts and expenditures of all public money shall be published from time to time.

8. No title of nobility shall be granted by the United States; and no person holding any office of profit or trust under them, shall, without the consent of the Congress, accept of any present, emolument, office, or title, of any kind whatever, from any king, prince, or foreign state.

¶ *Clause 7.* This clause concerns the all-important "power of the purse." Since Congress controls expenditures, it can limit the powers of the President by limiting the amount of money he may spend to run the government. This clause has been described as the single most important curb on Presidential power in the Constitution. Furthermore, the requirement to account for money spent and received helps to protect the public against misuse of funds. ¶ *Clause 8.* This clause prohibits the establishment of a nobility in this country. It also helps to keep United States officials from accepting bribes from foreign governments.

SECTION 10. POWERS DENIED TO THE STATES

1. No state shall enter into any treaty, alliance, or confederation; grant letters of marque and reprisal; coin money; emit bills of credit; make anything but gold and silver coin a tender in payment of debts; pass any bill of attainder, *ex post facto* law, or law impairing the obligation of contracts, or grant any title of nobility.

2. No state shall, without the consent of the Congress, lay any imposts or duties on imports or exports, except what may be absolutely necessary for executing its inspection laws; and the net produce of all duties and imposts, laid by any state on imports or exports, shall be for the use of the Treasury of the United States; and all such laws shall be subject to the revision and control of the Congress.

3. No state shall, without the consent of Congress, lay any duty of tonnage, keep troops, or ships of war in time of peace, enter into any agreement or compact with another state, or with a foreign power, or engage in war, unless actually invaded, or in such imminent danger as will not admit of delay.

¶ According to Section 10, states cannot: (1) Make treaties. (2) Coin money. (3) Pass either bills of attainder or *ex post facto* laws. (4) Impair obligations of contract. (5) Grant titles of nobility. (6) Tax imports or exports without the consent of Congress. (7) Keep troops or war ships in time of peace. (8) Deal with another state or foreign power without the consent of Congress. (9) Engage in war unless invaded. ¶ *Clause 1.* Because Shays' Rebellion (p. 153) was still fresh in the minds of the delegates to the Constitutional Convention, and since several of the states at that time were being urged to pass legislation relieving debtors from the payment of their debts, the delegates decided to protect creditors once and for all by denying states the right to pass laws that would impair obligations of contract. During the Great Depression which began in 1929, and the New Deal period (1933–45), the Supreme Court upheld state laws relieving debtors or mortgagees from paying their debts on the due dates, but payments were simply postponed, not cancelled. *Clause 3.* States may enter into agreements or compacts with each other, provided Congress approves. There have been many such arrangements among states on problems concerning port development, conservation, minimum wages, crime prevention, flood control, the pollution of rivers, lakes, and harbors, and other matters.

Article 2. EXECUTIVE DEPARTMENT

SECTION 1. PRESIDENT AND VICE-PRESIDENT

1. *Term of office.* The executive power shall be vested in a President of the United States of America. He shall hold his office during the term of four years, and together with the Vice-President, chosen for the same term, be elected as follows:

¶ This provision gives the executive power to the President. He may use all of the means at his disposal to carry out the laws. The power and prestige of the Presidency depend to some extent, of course, on the personality of the man who holds the office.

2. *Electoral system.* Each state shall appoint, in such manner as the legislature thereof may direct, a number of electors, equal to the whole number of Senators and

THE FEDERAL SYSTEM

DIVISION OF POWERS

FEDERAL GOVERNMENT

FEDERAL AND STATE GOVERNMENTS

STATE GOVERNMENTS

Important "enumerated" powers "delegated" to the Congress:

- To regulate interstate and foreign commerce
- To declare war
- To establish laws governing citizenship
- To coin money
- To control the postal system
- To regulate patents and copyrights
- To establish lower courts
- To establish and support the armed forces

Also there are "implied" powers provided by the so-called "elastic clause" (Art. 1, Sec. 8, clause 18) granting the power to pass all laws necessary and proper to carry out the enumerated powers.

Important "concurrent" powers shared by Federal and State Governments:

- To tax
- To borrow money
- To establish penal laws
- To charter banks
- To take property for public purposes with just compensation (This power is called "eminent domain.")

Important "residual" or "reserved" powers retained by the state governments:

- To regulate suffrage
- To maintain a system of public education
- To establish marriage and divorce laws
- To establish laws governing corporations
- To establish traffic laws
- To regulate intra-state commerce

Also, according to the 10th Amendment, all powers (1) not delegated to the federal government or (2) not prohibited by the Constitution are reserved to the states or to the people.

PROHIBITED POWERS

Powers denied the Federal Government:

- To suspend the writ of habeas corpus (except in cases of rebellion or invasion)
- To give preferential treatment in commerce or revenue to the ports of any state
- To draw money from the Treasury except by appropriation under a specific law
- To levy taxes on exports
- No person holding federal office can accept a gift from a foreign country without consent of Congress.

Powers denied the Federal and State Governments:

- To pass bills of attainder
- To pass ex post facto laws
- To grant titles of nobility

Powers denied the State Governments:

- To enter into treaties with other nations or with other states without the consent of Congress
- To coin money
- To impair obligations of contract
- To place a tax on imports or exports except to carry out its inspection laws
- To keep troops or ships in time of peace without consent of Congress

This chart describes the division of powers in the original Constitution. Additional limitations on the powers of the Federal Government are enumerated in the Bill of Rights.

Representatives to which the state may be entitled in the Congress; but no Senator or Representative, or person holding an office of trust or profit under the United States, shall be appointed an elector.

3. *Former method of using the electoral system.* [The electors shall meet in their respective states, and vote by ballot for two persons, of whom one at least shall not be an inhabitant of the same state with themselves. And they shall make a list of all the persons voted for, and of the number of votes for each; which list they shall sign and

certify, and transmit sealed to the seat of the government of the United States, directed to the president of the Senate. The president of the Senate shall, in the presence of the Senate and House of Representatives, open all the certificates, and the votes shall then be counted. The persons having the greatest number of votes shall be the President, if such number be a majority of the whole number of electors appointed; and if there be more than one who have such majority, and have an equal number of votes, then the House of Representatives shall immediately choose by ballot one of them for President; and if no person have a majority, then from the five highest on the list the said House shall in like manner choose the President. But in choosing the President the votes shall be taken by states, the representation from each state having one vote. A quorum for this purpose shall consist of a member or members from two-thirds of the states, and a majority of all the states shall be necessary to a choice. In every case, after the choice of the President, the person having the greatest number of votes of the electors shall be the Vice-President. But if there should remain two or more who have equal votes, the Senate shall choose from them by ballot the Vice-President.]

¶ *Clauses 2, 3.* These clauses established the electoral system, but very little that the Founding Fathers decided about electing a President has survived in the form they intended. The delegates to the Constitutional Convention, still fearful of popular rule, decided that the President and Vice-President ought to be elected by a small group of men called "electors," chosen according to a method determined by each state legislature. Until Andrew Jackson's Presidency, electors were chosen by state legislatures. Since then, the people have voted directly for the electors. Some changes in the method of electing a President have been made by formal amendment, as in Amendment 12; other changes have resulted from political practice. (The method of electing a President today is shown in the chart entitled "How a President is Elected" on page 197.

4. *Time of elections.* The Congress may determine the time of choosing the electors, and the day on which they shall give their votes; which day shall be the same throughout the United States.

5. *Qualifications for President.* No person except a natural-born citizen, [or a citizen of the United States, at the time of the adoption of this Constitution,] shall be eligible to the office of President; neither shall any person be eligible to that office who shall not have attained to the age of thirty-five years, and been fourteen years a resident within the United States.

¶ *Qualifications for President:* (1) He must be a native-born citizen of the United States. (2) He must be at least 35 years of age. (3) He must have been for at least 14 years a resident of the United States. ¶ TERM OF OFFICE: 4 years

6. *Filling vacancies.* In case of the removal of the President from office, or of his death, resignation, or inability to discharge the powers and duties of the said office, the same shall devolve on the Vice-President, and the Congress may by law provide for the case of removal, death, resignation, or inability, both of the President and Vice-President, declaring what officer shall then act as President, and such officer shall act accordingly, until the disability be removed, or a President shall be elected.

¶ If a President dies or is removed from office, the Vice-President replaces him. John Tyler, in 1841, was the first Vice-President to succeed to the Presidency. By assuming the office of President and not simply serving as an acting President, he established a precedent that has since been followed. ¶ Under the Presidential Succession Act of 1947, if both the President and the Vice-President die or are removed from office, the order of succession is as follows: (1) Speaker of the House, (2) President *pro tempore* of the Senate, and (3) the Cabinet members in the order in which their offices were created.

7. *Salary.* The President shall, at stated times, receive for his services, a compensation, which shall neither be increased nor diminished during the period for which he shall have been elected, and he shall not receive within that period any other emolument from the United States, or any of them.

8. *Oath of office.* **Before he enter on the execution of his office, he shall take the following oath or affirmation:—"I do solemnly swear (or affirm) that I will faithfully execute the office of President of the United States, and will to the best of my ability, preserve, protect, and defend the Constitution of the United States."**

¶ *Clause* 7. In 1949 the President's salary was set by law at $100,000 a year, plus a $50,000 expense account and a nontaxable fund for travel and official entertainment limited to $40,000. The Vice-President's salary was set, in 1955, at $35,000 a year, plus a $10,000 expense allowance. ¶ *Clause* 8. The President assumes his office officially only after taking the oath of office, which is administered by the Chief Justice of the United States.

SECTION 2. POWERS OF THE PRESIDENT

1. *Military powers.* **The President shall be Commander in Chief of the Army and Navy of the United States, and of the militia of the several states, when called into the actual service of the United States; he may require the opinion, in writing, of the principal officer in each of the executive departments, upon any subject relating to the duties of their respective offices, and he shall have power to grant reprieves and pardons for offenses against the United States, except in cases of impeachment.**

¶ The important point in this provision is that it places the armed forces under the control of a civilian. The President is a civilian, but he is superior in military power to any military officer. ¶ The words "principal officer in each of the executive departments" are the basis for the creation of the President's Cabinet. Each Cabinet member is the head of one of the executive departments. The President chooses his own Cabinet, with the consent of the Senate. He can remove any Cabinet official without asking Senate approval.

2. *Treaties and appointments.* **He shall have power, by and with the advice and consent of the Senate, to make treaties, provided two-thirds of the Senators present concur; and he shall nominate, and by and with the advice and consent of the Senate, shall appoint ambassadors, other public ministers and consuls, judges of the Supreme Court, and all other officers of the United States, whose appointments are not herein otherwise provided for, and which shall be established by law; but the Congress may by law vest the appointment of such inferior officers, as they think proper, in the President alone, in the courts of law, or in the heads of departments.**

¶ The President makes treaties with the advice and consent of two thirds of the Senate. A treaty ratified by the Senate becomes the supreme law of the land. The President can also enter into executive agreements with foreign governments. Although such agreements may have the same force as treaties, they do not require Senate approval. ¶ With consent of the Senate, the President can ap- point diplomatic officials, federal judges, military officers, and members of administrative agencies. "Inferior officers" are those subordinate to the Cabinet members or to federal judges. ¶ At the present time, a majority of the positions in the federal government are filled by candidates who have passed examinations given by the United States Civil Service Commission (pp. 437–38).

3. *Filling vacancies.* **The President shall have power to fill up all vacancies that may happen during the recess of the Senate, by granting commissions which shall expire at the end of their next session.**

¶ If a vacancy in an important position occurs while Congress is not in session, the President can fill it with an interim appointment. When Congress meets again, this appointment, or a new appointment, must be submitted to the Senate for approval.

SECTION 3. DUTIES OF THE PRESIDENT

He shall from time to time give to the Congress information of the state of the Union, and recommend to their consideration such measures as he shall judge necessary and expedient; he may, on extraordinary occasions, convene both houses, or either of

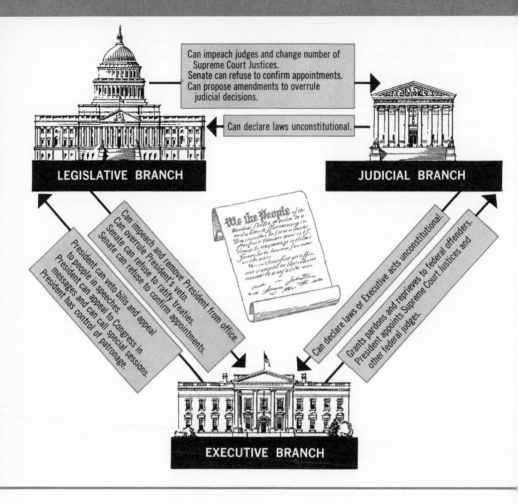

Can impeach judges and change number of Supreme Court Justices.
Senate can refuse to confirm appointments.
Can propose amendments to overrule judicial decisions.

Can declare laws unconstitutional.

LEGISLATIVE BRANCH

JUDICIAL BRANCH

Can impeach and remove President from office.
Can overrule President's veto.
Senate can refuse to ratify treaties.
Senate can refuse to confirm appointments

President can veto bills and appeal to people in speeches in messages and can call special sessions.
President can appeal to Congress in messages and can call special sessions.
President has control of patronage.

Can declare laws or Executive acts unconstitutional.

Grants pardons and reprieves to federal offenders.
President appoints Supreme Court Justices and other federal judges.

We the People

EXECUTIVE BRANCH

them, and in case of disagreement between them, with respect to the time of adjournment, he may adjourn them to such time as he shall think proper; he shall receive ambassadors and other public ministers; he shall take care that the laws be faithfully executed, and shall commission all the officers of the United States.

¶ The President's duties include: (1) *Legislative duties:* delivering annual and special messages to Congress; calling special sessions of Congress; approving or vetoing bills (see Article 1, Section 7). (2) *Diplomatic duties:* receiving (or refusing to receive) ambassadors or ministers of foreign countries to indicate that the United States "recognizes" (or refuses to "recognize") the governments of these countries. The President can also send home the ambassador of a foreign country as a sign that the United States is breaking off diplomatic relations with that country. (3) *Executive duties:* executing all the laws. Actually, the laws are carried out by the various government departments, commissions, and administrative agencies; but the President is responsible for seeing that they are carried out. (4) *Military duties:* commissioning all officers of the United States armed forces.

SECTION 4. IMPEACHMENT

The President, Vice-President, and all civil officers of the United States, shall be removed from office on impeachment for, and conviction of, treason, bribery, or other high crimes and misdemeanors.

Article 3. JUDICIAL DEPARTMENT

SECTION 1. FEDERAL COURTS

The judicial power of the United States shall be vested in one Supreme Court, and in such inferior courts as the Congress may from time to time ordain and establish. The judges, both of the Supreme and inferior courts, shall hold their offices during good behavior, and shall, at stated times, receive for their services a compensation, which shall not be diminished during their continuance in office.

¶ By authorizing the establishment of a system of federal courts, Article 3 creates the judicial power—the power to hear and decide cases. The lack of a federal court system was one of the weaknesses of the government under the Articles of Confederation. Under the judicial power granted by the Constitution, the courts have declared unconstitutional certain laws of Congress, acts of the President, laws of the state legislatures, and decisions of the state courts. ¶ Only the Supreme Court is established by the Constitution itself, but the Constitution gives Congress the authority to establish the lower courts which exist today. Since the Constitution does not state the number of justices to be appointed to the Supreme Court, Congress decides the number by law. At first, the Supreme Court had six justices. Congress has set the number at as many as ten and as few as five. ¶ Congress has created two types of lower courts. One type includes 84 federal district courts and 11 Courts of Appeals, which review cases sent up by the district courts. District courts and Courts of Appeals are called "constitutional courts" because they are general courts deriving their power directly from the Constitution. The second type of courts deals with cases of a specialized nature. The Court of Claims, the Tax Court, and the Court of Customs and Patent Appeals are included in this second group. ¶ The framers of the Constitution wanted to make sure that our federal judges would be independent of political influence. Accordingly, federal judges are appointed for life, subject to good behavior, and their pay cannot be reduced by law during their term of office.

SECTION 2. JURISDICTION OF FEDERAL COURTS

1. *General jurisdiction.* The judicial power shall extend to all cases, in law and equity, arising under this Constitution, the laws of the United States, and treaties made or which shall be made, under their authority; to all cases affecting ambassadors, other public ministers and consuls; to all cases of admiralty and maritime jurisdiction; to controversies to which the United States shall be a party; to controversies between two or more states; [between a state and citizens of another state;] between citizens of different states; between citizens of the same state claiming lands under grants of different states, and between a state, or the citizens thereof, and foreign states, citizens, or subjects.

¶ Here the words "law" and "equity" have special meanings. "Law" means the common law—the laws that originated in England and that have been based on centuries of judicial decisions. "Equity" refers to principles of justice also developed in England to remedy wrongs in situations in which the common law was inadequate. Today, in the United States, law and equity are applied by the same judges in the same courts. ¶ The power of the federal courts extends to two types of cases: (1) those involving the interpretation of the Constitution, federal laws, treaties, and laws relating to ships on the high seas and navigable waters; and (2) those involving the United States government itself, foreign diplomatic officials (ambassadors, public ministers, and consuls), two or more state governments, and citizens of different states when the sum involved is $3000 or more; also cases involving a state or its citizens versus foreign countries or citizens of foreign countries.

2. *Supreme Court.* In all cases affecting ambassadors, other public ministers and consuls, and those in which a state shall be a party, the Supreme Court shall have original jurisdiction. In all the other cases before mentioned, the Supreme Court shall have appellate jurisdiction, both as to law and fact, with such exceptions, and under such regulations as the Congress shall make.

¶ "Original jurisdiction" means the right to try a case before any other court may hear it. "Appellate jurisdiction" means the right of a court to try cases appealed from lower courts. Most of the cases tried by the Supreme Court come up as a result of appeals from lower federal and state courts. Cases involving foreign diplomats and any of the 50 states, however, may be started directly in the Supreme Court.

3. *Conduct of trials.* **The trial of all crimes, except in cases of impeachment, shall be by jury; and such trial shall be held in the state where the said crimes shall have been committed; but when not committed within any state, the trial shall be at such place or places as the Congress may by law have directed.**

¶ Every person accused of a federal crime is guaranteed a jury trial near the scene of the crime. But the accused may give up this privilege, if he wishes. ¶ The provisions of this clause have been expanded by Amendments 5, 6, and 7.

SECTION 3. TREASON

1. *Definition.* **Treason against the United States shall consist only in levying war against them, or in adhering to their enemies, giving them aid and comfort. No person shall be convicted of treason unless on the testimony of two witnesses to the same overt act, or on confession in open court.**

¶ Treason is the only crime specifically defined in the Constitution. To be found guilty of treason, a person must be shown to have helped wage war against the United States, or to have given aid and comfort to its enemies. The facts must be proved either by the testimony of two witnesses to the same overt act, or by confession in open court.

2. *Punishment.* **The Congress shall have power to declare the punishment of treason, but no attainder of treason shall work corruption of blood or forfeiture except during the life of the person attainted.**

¶ The punishment for treason, as determined by Congress, is death or a fine of $10,000 and imprisonment for not less than five years. This clause further states that the punishment for treason cannot be extended to the children of a traitor. They cannot be deprived of their rights and their property—as had been done in England.

Article 4. **RELATIONS AMONG THE STATES**

SECTION 1. OFFICIAL ACTS

Full faith and credit shall be given in each state to the public acts, records, and judicial proceedings of every other state. And the Congress may by general laws prescribe the manner in which such acts, records, and proceedings shall be proved, and the effect thereof.

¶ The purpose of this provision is to make sure that the official records of one state are respected in all the other states. Official records of this kind include birth, marriage, and death certificates; corporation charters, wills, and court decisions. This provision also protects a citizen's rights to collect money that has been awarded him by a court decision in one state, even if the person who owes him the money moves to another state.

SECTION 2. PRIVILEGES OF CITIZENS

1. *Privileges.* **The citizens of each state shall be entitled to all privileges and immunities of citizens in the several states.**

2. *Extradition.* **A person charged in any state with treason, felony, or other crime, who shall flee from justice, and be found in another state, shall on demand of the executive authority of the state from which he fled, be delivered up, to be removed to the state having jurisdiction of the crime.**

3. *Fugitive slaves.* **[No person held in service or labor in one state, under the**

laws thereof, escaping into another, shall in consequence of any law or regulation therein, be discharged from such service or labor, but shall be delivered up on claim of the party to whom such service or labor may be due.]

¶ *Clause 1.* The terms "privileges" and "immunities" simply mean the rights of citizens. Thus, a state cannot discriminate against citizens of other states in favor of its own citizens, except in certain very special areas—such as voting, for example. A state can impose residence requirements for voting, so that a citizen of another state will have to reside in the state for a specified period before he may exercise his right to vote as a citizen of his new state. ¶ *Clause 2.* This provision prevents a prisoner or a person charged with a crime from escaping justice by fleeing across a state line. It provides that a criminal be returned by the state in which he is captured to the state where the crime was committed—a process known as "extradition." A governor of a state cannot be forced to extradite, or return, a prisoner, however, if the governor feels that such action will result in injustice to the accused person. ¶ *Clause 3.* Since the ratification of Amendment 13 in 1865 brought an end to slavery, this clause is now of historical interest only.

SECTION 3. NEW STATES AND TERRITORIES

1. *Admission of new states.* **New states may be admitted by the Congress into this Union; but no new state shall be formed or erected within the jurisdiction of any other state; nor any state be formed by the junction of two or more states, or parts of states, without the consent of the legislatures of the states concerned as well as of the Congress.**

¶ The Northwest Ordinance of 1787 (p. 147) provided that new states be admitted to the Union on completely equal footing with the original thirteen states. Although the Constitution declares here that new states may not be created within the territory of any other state without its consent, in 1863 West Virginia was formed within the state of Virginia. This exception occurred during the War Between the States, and West Virginia received permission from the loyal, rather than the secessionist, government of Virginia.

2. *Power of Congress over territories and other property.* **The Congress shall have power to dispose of and make all needful rules and regulations respecting the territory or other property belonging to the United States; and nothing in this Constitution shall be so construed as to prejudice any claims of the United States, or of any particular state.**

¶ Under this provision, Congress has the power to control all property belonging to the federal government. It can set up governments for Territories and colonies of the United States. It can grant independence to a colony, as it did to the Philippines in 1946. It can set aside land for national parks and build dams for flood control.

SECTION 4. GUARANTEES TO THE STATES

The United States shall guarantee to every state in this Union a republican form of government, and shall protect each of them against invasion; and on application of the legislature, or of the executive (when the legislature cannot be convened) against domestic violence.

¶ If the President finds that public property is being destroyed and the public safety is endangered in a state, he may decide to send troops into that state without the request of local authorities. He may even proclaim martial law in a state.

Article 5. METHODS OF AMENDMENT

The Congress, whenever two-thirds of both houses shall deem it necessary, shall propose amendments to this Constitution, or, on the application of the legislatures of two-thirds of the several states, shall call a convention for proposing amendments, which, in either case shall be valid to all intents and purposes, as part of this Constitution, when ratified by the legislatures of three-fourths of the several states, or by

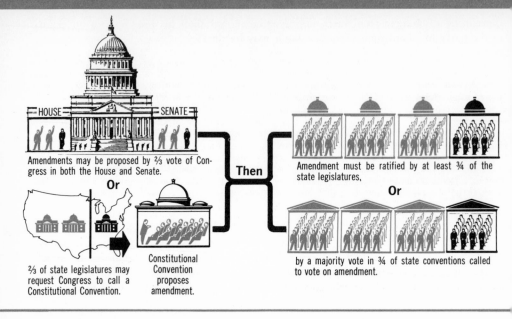

HOUSE — SENATE

Amendments may be proposed by ⅔ vote of Congress in both the House and Senate.

Or

⅔ of state legislatures may request Congress to call a Constitutional Convention.

Constitutional Convention proposes amendment.

Then

Amendment must be ratified by at least ¾ of the state legislatures,

Or

by a majority vote in ¾ of state conventions called to vote on amendment.

conventions in three-fourths thereof, as the one or the other mode of ratification may be proposed by the Congress; provided that [no amendments which may be made prior to the year 1808 shall in any manner affect the first and fourth clauses in the Ninth Section of the First Article; and that] no state, without its consent, shall be deprived of its equal suffrage in the Senate.

¶ One of the most important features of the Constitution is that it can be amended, or changed. This adaptability is one of the four main principles of the Constitution. ¶ An amendment must first be *proposed*, and then *ratified*. There are four methods of amending the Constitution (see chart, above). So far, all amendments have been proposed by Congress and ratified by state legislatures, except Amendment 21, which was ratified by the convention method. ¶ The fact that only 22 amendments have been adopted since 1789— and only 12 since 1791—indicates that it is not easy to change the Constitution, and that changing it is a serious matter, requiring much thought and discussion in Congress, in the state legislatures, and among the people. ¶ Notice that there are two areas in which the Constitution cannot be amended. The first exception is obsolete because it refers to the period before 1808. The second exception is still very important because it guarantees that every state shall have equal representation in the Senate.

Article 6. GENERAL PROVISIONS

1. *Public debts.* All debts contracted and engagements entered into, before the adoption of this Constitution, shall be as valid against the United States under this Constitution, as under the Confederation.

¶ This provision was important because it announced to all that the new government would assume and pay back all debts incurred by the government under the Articles of Confederation. It was one of several actions advocated by Alexander Hamilton and undertaken by Congress in order to establish the credit of the new government.

2. *The supreme law.* This Constitution, and the laws of the United States which shall be made in pursuance thereof, and all treaties made, or which shall be made, under the authority of the United States, shall be the supreme law of the land; and the judges in every state shall be bound thereby, anything in the constitution or laws of any state to the contrary notwithstanding.

¶ This is the famous "supremacy clause" of the Constitution. It declares that the "supreme law of the land" is: (1) the Constitution, (2) the laws of the United States passed under this Constitution, and (3) the treaties made under the authority of the United States.

¶ According to the supremacy clause, the national government is superior in power to the states, provided its actions are in accordance with the Constitution. The Supreme Court determines whether the actions of the President and Congress are constitutional.

3. *Oaths of office.* The Senators and Representatives before mentioned, and the members of the several state legislatures, and all executive and judicial officers, both of the United States and of the several states, shall be bound by oath or affirmation, to support this Constitution; but no religious test shall ever be required as a qualification to any office or public trust under the United States.

¶ No religious qualification shall ever be required as a condition for holding public office. This provision results from the fact that in the United States there is separation of church and state, and that a man's religion is considered a private, and not a public, matter.

Article 7. RATIFICATION

The ratification of the convention of nine states shall be sufficient for the establishment of this Constitution between the states so ratifying the same.

¶ The Constitutional Convention was summoned by the Congress under the Articles of Confederation for the purpose of amending the Articles. According to the Articles of Confederation, amendments had to be approved by all thirteen states. Instead of amending the Articles, however, the delegates to the Constitutional Convention drafted an entirely new plan of government. And realizing that it would be difficult to get the approval of all the states—Rhode Island, for example, had not even sent delegates to Philadelphia—the Founding Fathers provided that the Constitution would go into effect after ratification by only nine states, instead of thirteen. As a result, some of the opponents of the Constitution argued that it had been adopted by revolutionary means.

DONE in Convention by the unanimous consent of the States present the seventeenth day of September in the year of our Lord one thousand seven hundred and eighty-seven and of the independence of the United States of America the twelfth. In witness whereof we have hereunto subscribed our names,

G Washington—President and deputy from Virginia

NEW HAMPSHIRE
John Langdon
Nicholas Gilman

MASSACHUSETTS
Nathaniel Gorham
Rufus King

CONNECTICUT
William Samuel Johnson
Roger Sherman

NEW YORK
Alexander Hamilton

NEW JERSEY
William Livingston
David Brearley
William Paterson
Jonathan Dayton

PENNSYLVANIA
Benjamin Franklin
Thomas Mifflin
Robert Morris
George Clymer
Thomas FitzSimons
Jared Ingersoll
James Wilson
Gouverneur Morris

DELAWARE
George Read
Gunning Bedford
John Dickinson
Richard Bassett
Jacob Broom

MARYLAND
James McHenry
Daniel of St. Thomas Jenifer
Daniel Carroll

VIRGINIA
John Blair
James Madison

NORTH CAROLINA
William Blount
Richard Dobbs Spaight
Hugh Williamson

SOUTH CAROLINA
John Rutledge
Charles Cotesworth Pinckney
Charles Pinckney
Pierce Butler

GEORGIA
William Few
Abraham Baldwin

AMENDMENTS TO
THE CONSTITUTION

Amendment 1. FREEDOM OF RELIGION, SPEECH, PRESS, ASSEMBLY, AND PETITION (1791)

Congress shall make no law respecting an establishment of religion, or prohibiting the free exercise thereof; or abridging the freedom of speech, or of the press; or the right of the people peaceably to assemble, and to petition the government for a redress of grievances.

¶ Amendment 1 protects five great civil liberties: (1) Freedom of religion means that Congress cannot interfere with the right to worship as one sees fit. The Supreme Court, however, has ruled that Congress can require "conscientious objectors" to bear arms during wartime. Congress has, however, made special provisions to permit conscientious objectors to participate in war work without bearing arms. (2) Freedom of speech means the right to speak out privately and publicly. However, this right does not permit anyone to slander people (make false and malicious remarks about them), and under the Smith Act of 1940 (p. 742), no one can advocate the overthrow of the government by force and violence. Furthermore, the Supreme Court has declared that freedom of speech can be limited by the federal government if there is a "clear and present" danger that what is said may injure the general welfare. (3) Freedom of the press gives newspapers and magazines the right to print whatever they wish provided they do not libel people (publish false and malicious remarks about them) or advocate the violent overthrow of the government. Also, the use of the United States mails may be denied to those publications which spread indecent and fraudulent ideas. (4) Freedom to assemble is the right to attend meetings and join clubs. (5) The right to petition for redress of grievances means the opportunity to express complaints to any official of the federal government.

Amendment 2. RIGHT TO KEEP ARMS (1791)

A well-regulated militia, being necessary to the security of a free state, the right of the people to keep and bear arms shall not be infringed.

¶ The purpose of this amendment was to prevent Congress from depriving people of the right to bear arms in order to resist a tyrannical government. Congress and many of the states, however, have forbidden the carrying of concealed weapons.

Amendment 3. QUARTERING OF TROOPS (1791)

No soldier shall, in time of peace, be quartered in any house, without the consent of the owner; nor in time of war, but in a manner to be prescribed by law.

¶ This amendment was designed to prevent the national government from requiring private homeowners to house and feed troops. The quartering of troops in private homes by the British government had been a source of friction before the American Revolution.

Amendment 4. SEARCH AND SEIZURE; WARRANTS (1791)

The right of the people to be secure in their persons, houses, papers, and effects, against unreasonable searches and seizures, shall not be violated; and no warrants shall issue but upon probable cause, supported by oath or affirmation, and particularly describing the place to be searched, and the persons or things to be seized.

¶ Amendments 3 and 4 are based on the important principle that "a man's home is his castle." With the hated "writs of assistance" (p. 103) still fresh in their minds, the supporters of this amendment aimed to limit issuance of search warrants to the following conditions: (1) the warrant must be issued by a judge; (2) there must be a good reason for its use; (3) the officer who asks for a search warrant must take an oath in support of his reasons for demanding the warrant; and (4) the warrant must describe the place to be searched and the persons or things to be seized.

Amendment 5. RIGHTS OF ACCUSED PERSONS (1791)

No person shall be held to answer for a capital, or otherwise infamous, crime, unless on a presentment or indictment of a grand jury, except in cases arising in the land or naval forces, or in the militia, when in actual service in time of war or public danger; nor shall any person be subject for the same offense to be twice put in jeopardy of life or limb; nor shall be compelled, in any criminal case, to be a witness against himself; nor be deprived of life, liberty, or property, without due process of law; nor shall private property be taken for public use, without just compensation.

¶ This amendment lists the rights of an accused person: (1) A person accused of a capital crime (one for which the death penalty may be imposed) or any other serious crime must first be accused by a grand jury (a jury of 12 to 23 persons) before he can be brought to trial. An "indictment" or "presentment" by a grand jury is merely a formal accusation. (2) A person cannot be tried twice for the same crime. (3) A person cannot be required to give testimony incriminating himself in a courtroom or before a grand jury or Congressional committee. However, under the Immunity Act of 1954, a witness can be required to testify in cases involving subversion (conspiracy to overthrow the government), with the promise that he will not be tried on the basis of the evidence that he has furnished about himself. (4) A person cannot be deprived of life, liberty, or property without due process of law—or according to the law of the land. (5) Congress cannot take private property for public use without paying a fair price for it. This provision, an important protection of the property rights of individuals, establishes what is known as the principle of "eminent domain." ¶ Members of the armed forces are tried by military courts and commissions and are not subject to the provision calling for indictment by a grand jury.

Amendment 6. RIGHT TO SPEEDY TRIAL (1791)

In all criminal prosecutions, the accused shall enjoy the right to a speedy and public trial, by an impartial jury of the state and district wherein the crime shall have been committed, which district shall have been previously ascertained by law, and to be informed of the nature and cause of the accusation; to be confronted with the witnesses against him; to have compulsory process for obtaining witnesses in his favor, and to have the assistance of counsel for his defense.

¶ This amendment continues the rights of an accused person. Notice that all witnesses against an accused person must appear on the witness stand, and that the government must help the accused to produce favorable witnesses. If an accused person cannot afford to hire a lawyer, the judge will assign one, and the government will pay the lawyer's fee.

Amendment 7. JURY TRIAL IN CIVIL CASES (1791)

In suits at common law, where the value in controversy shall exceed twenty dollars, the right of trial by jury shall be preserved, and no fact tried by a jury shall be otherwise re-examined in any court of the United States than according to the rules of the common law.

¶ This amendment provides for a jury trial in federal civil cases (trials where one person sues another) involving more than $20. By custom, however, people do not go to federal courts unless a more substantial sum of money is involved.

Amendment 8. BAIL, FINES, PUNISHMENTS (1791)

Excessive bail shall not be required, nor excessive fines imposed, nor cruel and unusual punishments inflicted.

¶ A person accused of a crime and awaiting trial may be permitted to leave jail if he or someone else posts "bail"—a sum of money serving as a guarantee that the accused will appear at his trial. The courts determine the amount of bail asked for. Cruel and unusual punishments, such as torture and beheading, are prohibited.

195

Amendment 9. POWERS RESERVED TO THE PEOPLE (1791)

The enumeration in the Constitution, of certain rights, shall not be construed to deny or disparage others retained by the people.

¶ The Constitution does not describe specifically all the rights to be retained by the people. This amendment was added to guarantee that those fundamental rights not enumerated in the Constitution shall be respected by the national government.

Amendment 10. POWERS RESERVED TO THE STATES (1791)

The powers not delegated to the United States by the Constitution, nor prohibited by it to the states, are reserved to the states respectively, or to the people.

¶ This is known as the "Reserved Power Amendment." Powers delegated to the national government are listed in Article 1, Section 8. Powers prohibited to the states are found in Article 1, Section 10. Amendment 10 makes it clear that all other powers—the so-called "reserved powers"—are left to the states or to the people.

Amendment 11. SUITS AGAINST STATES (1798)

The judicial power of the United States shall not be construed to extend to any suit in law or equity, commenced or prosecuted against one of the United States, by citizens of another state, or by citizens or subjects of any foreign state.

¶ This is the first amendment to our Constitution which was designed to overrule a Supreme Court decision. In the case of *Chisholm v. Georgia* (1793), the Supreme Court ruled that two citizens of South Carolina could sue Georgia in a federal court for property that Georgia had confiscated. The states objected, arguing that since the states were sovereign, it was undignified to permit a state to be sued by a citizen of another state in a federal court. As a result of this amendment, a citizen who wishes to bring suit against a state must introduce his case in the courts of the state being sued.

Amendment 12. ELECTION OF PRESIDENT AND VICE–PRESIDENT (1804)

The electors shall meet in their respective states, and vote by ballot for President and Vice-President, one of whom, at least, shall not be an inhabitant of the same state with themselves; they shall name in their ballots the person voted for as President, and in distinct ballots the person voted for as Vice-President, and they shall make distinct lists of all persons voted for as President, and of all persons voted for as Vice-President, and of the number of votes for each, which lists they shall sign and certify, and transmit, sealed, to the seat of government of the United States, directed to the President of the Senate; the President of the Senate shall, in the presence of the Senate and House of Representatives, open all the certificates and the votes shall then be counted; the person having the greatest number of votes for President shall be the President, if such number be a majority of the whole number of electors appointed; and if no person have such majority, then from the persons having the highest numbers not exceeding three on the list of those voted for as President, the House of Representatives shall choose immediately, by ballot, the President. But in choosing the President, the votes shall be taken by states, the representation from each state having one vote; a quorum for this purpose shall consist of a member or members from two-thirds of the states, and a majority of all the states shall be necessary to a choice. [And if the House of Representatives shall not choose a President whenever the right of choice shall devolve upon them, before the fourth day of March next following, then the Vice-President shall act as President, as in the case of the death or other constitutional disability of the President.] The person having the greatest number of votes as Vice-President, shall

TIME SEQUENCE		

REPUBLICAN NATIONAL CONVENTION

SUMMER OF ELECTION YEAR

A convention of party representatives from every state nominates candidates for President and Vice-President.

DEMOCRATIC NATIONAL CONVENTION

A convention of party representatives from every state nominates candidates for President and Vice-President.

BEFORE ELECTION

STATE REPUBLICAN HEADQUARTERS

The Republican Party in your state chooses electors* who promise to vote for the party's candidates for President and Vice-President.

STATE DEMOCRATIC HEADQUARTERS

The Democratic Party in your state chooses electors* who promise to vote for the party's candidates for President and Vice-President.

ELECTION DAY (NOVEMBER)

BALLOT BOX

In voting for a Presidential nominee, the voters actually vote for the electors of the nominee's party. This is the Popular Vote.

IF PARTY WINS...   **IF PARTY WINS...**

DECEMBER

The electors of the victorious party of each state assemble at their state capital and vote separately for their party's Presidential and Vice-Presidential candidates. This is the Electoral Vote.

Certified copies of these electoral votes are sent to the President of the United States Senate.

JANUARY

The President of the Senate counts the electoral votes in the presence of both houses of Congress.

President   Vice-President

To be elected, a candidate must receive at least a majority of the Electoral Vote.

*Each political party in each state is entitled to choose as many electors—delegates to the Electoral College—as it has Representatives and Senators in Congress.

be the Vice-President, if such number be a majority of the whole number of electors appointed, and if no person have a majority, then, from the two highest numbers on the list, the Senate shall choose the Vice-President; a quorum for the purpose shall consist of two-thirds of the whole number of Senators, and a majority of the whole number shall be necessary to a choice. But no person constitutionally ineligible to the office of President shall be eligible to that of Vice-President of the United States.

¶ This amendment alters Article 2, Section 1, Clause 3. Before the passage of this amendment, the electors each voted for two persons, without designating which was to be President, and which Vice-President. As a result, in 1796 the people elected a Federalist President (John Adams) and a Republican Vice-President (Jefferson) (p. 219). In 1800 the electors of the victorious Republican Party each cast one vote for Jefferson, whom they wanted to be President, and one vote for Burr, whom they wanted to be Vice-President. The result, of course, was a tie (p. 224). Amendment 12, which instructs electors to cast separate ballots for President and Vice-President, prevents such situations.

Amendment 13. SLAVERY ABOLISHED (1865)

SECTION 1. Neither slavery nor involuntary servitude, except as a punishment for crime whereof the party shall have been duly convicted, shall exist within the United States, or any place subject to their jurisdiction.

SECTION 2. Congress shall have power to enforce this article by appropriate legislation.

¶ Amendments 13, 14, and 15 resulted from the War Between the States. Amendment 13 freed the slaves, Amendment 14 made Negroes citizens, and Amendment 15 forbade the states to deny Negroes the right to vote. ¶ Amendment 13 forbids slavery, and, under Section 2, Congress has the power to enforce this order.

Amendment 14. RIGHTS OF CITIZENS (1868)

SECTION 1. *Citizenship defined.* All persons born or naturalized in the United States and subject to the jurisdiction thereof, are citizens of the United States and of the state wherein they reside. No state shall make or enforce any law which shall abridge the privileges or immunities of citizens of the United States; nor shall any state deprive any person of life, liberty, or property, without due process of law; nor deny to any person within its jurisdiction the equal protection of the laws.

¶ This section contains a number of important provisions. By the definition of citizenship given here, Negroes were granted citizenship. The second sentence, forbidding states to abridge the privileges and immunities—the rights—of citizens, meant that the states could not interfere with the right of Negroes and other citizens to live a peaceful, useful life, or to travel. ¶ This amendment, like Amendment 5, contains a "due process of law" clause. Amendment 5 denies to Congress and Amendment 14 denies to the states the power to deprive any person of life, liberty, or property without "due process of law." This amendment, originally intended to protect Negro citizenship, has been broadly interpreted by the courts as a protection for corporations. Corporations, under this interpretation, are considered as "persons." Their property cannot be taken away except by fair, legal methods. Thus, for example, the Interstate Commerce Commission can fix railroad rates only after giving the railroad corporations an opportunity to present their side of the case. ¶ The "due process" clause also protects individuals from unfair actions by their state governments. It protects freedom of religion, speech, press, petition, and assembly against state action. It prevents a state, in the exercise of its police power (the power to do everything to protect the lives, health, morals, and safety of its people), from depriving anyone of civil liberties, except during a national emergency. ¶ The last provision of Section 1 prevents a state from denying to any person within its jurisdiction the equal protection of the laws. In 1954, in the case of *Brown v. Board of Education of Topeka*, the Supreme Court interpreted this provision to mean that segregation in public schools is unconstitutional.

SECTION 2. *Apportionment of Representatives.* **Representatives shall be apportioned among the several states according to their respective numbers, counting the whole number of persons in each state, excluding Indians not taxed. But when the right to vote at any election for the choice of electors for President and Vice-President of the United States, Representatives in Congress, the executive and judicial officers of a state, or the members of the legislature thereof, is denied to any of the male inhabitants of such state, being twenty-one years of age and citizens of the United States, or in any way abridged, except for participation in rebellion, or other crime, the basis of representation therein shall be reduced in the proportion which the number of such male citizens shall bear to the whole number of male citizens twenty-one years of age in such state.**

¶ This section was intended to guarantee that Negroes would be given the right to vote. If a state prevented any male citizen, 21 years of age or over, from voting, then the state's representation in Congress was to be reduced proportionately.

SECTION 3. *Disability for engaging in insurrection.* **No person shall be a Senator or Representative in Congress, or elector of President and Vice-President, or hold any office, civil or military, under the United States, or under any state, who, having previously taken an oath, as a member of Congress, or as an officer of the United States, or as a member of any state legislature, or as an executive or judicial officer of any state, to support the Constitution of the United States, shall have engaged in insurrection or rebellion against the same, or given aid or comfort to the enemies thereof. But Congress may, by vote of two-thirds of each house, remove such disability.**

¶ This section aimed to punish the leaders of the Confederacy for having broken their oath to support the Constitution of the United States. All officials who had taken this oath and who later joined the Confederacy in the War Between the States were disqualified from holding federal or state offices. Although many southern leaders were excluded under this section from holding office after the war, by 1872 most of them were permitted to return to political life. In 1898 all others were pardoned.

SECTION 4. *Public debt.* **The validity of the public debt of the United States, authorized by law, including debts incurred for payment of pensions and bounties for services in suppressing insurrection or rebellion, shall not be questioned. But neither the United States nor any state shall assume or pay any debt or obligation incurred in aid of insurrection or rebellion against the United States, [or any claim for the loss or emancipation of any slave;] but all such debts, obligations, and claims shall be held illegal and void.**

¶ This section makes three important points: (1) The public debt of the United States incurred in fighting the War Between the States was valid and could never be questioned by southerners. (2) The Confederate debt was void. It was illegal for the federal government or the states to pay any money on Confederate debts. This provision was meant to serve as a harsh lesson to all who had invested money in Confederate bonds. (3) No payment was to be made to anyone for the loss of former slaves.

SECTION 5. *Enforcement.* **The Congress shall have power to enforce, by appropriate legislation, the provisions of this article.**

Amendment 15. RIGHT OF SUFFRAGE (1870)

SECTION 1. **The right of citizens of the United States to vote shall not be denied or abridged by the United States or any state on account of race, color, or previous condition of servitude.**

SECTION 2. **The Congress shall have power to enforce this article by appropriate legislation.**

¶ The purpose of this amendment was to extend the *franchise*, or the right to vote, to Negroes. Thus, a person who meets all of the qualifications for suffrage in a state cannot be deprived of the right to vote simply because of his race or color.

Amendment 16. INCOME TAX (1913)

The Congress shall have power to lay and collect taxes on incomes, from whatever source derived, without apportionment among the several states, and without regard to any census or enumeration.

¶ In 1894, as part of the Wilson-Gorman Tariff (p. 442), Congress passed an income tax law. The following year, in the case of *Pollock v. Farmers' Loan and Trust Company*, the Supreme Court declared this tax law unconstitutional. The Court stated that the income tax was a direct tax and, therefore, according to the Constitution (Article 1, Section 2, Clause 3; Article 1, Section 9, Clause 4) should have been apportioned among the states according to their population. This decision was unpopular because it prevented the government from taxing people on the basis of their incomes in order to pay for government expenses, which were already large, and growing larger. Amendment 16 overruled the Supreme Court decision and gave Congress the power to tax incomes from any source, and without apportionment among the states according to population. Today, income taxes are the federal government's major source of income.

Amendment 17. ELECTION OF SENATORS (1913)

SECTION 1. *Method of election.* The Senate of the United States shall be composed of two Senators from each state, elected by the people thereof, for six years; and each Senator shall have one vote. The electors in each state shall have the qualifications requisite for electors of the most numerous branch of the state legislatures.

SECTION 2. *Filling vacancies.* When vacancies happen in the representation of any state in the Senate, the executive authority of such state shall issue writs of election to fill such vacancies: *Provided* that the legislature of any state may empower the executive thereof to make temporary appointments until the people fill the vacancies by election as the legislature may direct.

[SECTION 3. *Not retroactive.* This amendment shall not be so construed as to affect the election or term of any Senator chosen before it becomes valid as part of the Constitution.]

¶ Before the passage of this amendment, Senators were chosen by the state legislatures (see Article 1, Section 3, Clause 1). There was a great deal of dissatisfaction with this method because it gave the voters little control over the Senate. Amendment 17 provides for the direct election of Senators by the voters of a state, a method which helps to make Senators responsive to the will of the voters.

Amendment 18. NATIONAL PROHIBITION (1919)

[SECTION 1. After one year from the ratification of this article the manufacture, sale, or transportation of intoxicating liquors within, the importation thereof into, or the exportation thereof from, the United States and all territory subject to the jurisdiction thereof for beverage purposes is hereby prohibited.

SECTION 2. The Congress and the several states shall have concurrent power to enforce this article by appropriate legislation.

SECTION 3. This article shall be inoperative unless it shall have been ratified as an amendment to the Constitution by the legislatures of the several states, as provided in the Constitution, within seven years from the date of the submission hereof to the states by the Congress.]

Amendment 19. WOMAN SUFFRAGE (1920)

SECTION 1. The right of citizens of the United States to vote shall not be denied or abridged by the United States or by any state on account of sex.

SECTION 2. Congress shall have power to enforce this article by appropriate legislation.

¶ This amendment, extending the right to vote to all qualified women, marked the greatest single step in extending the suffrage. The struggle to win this basic right for women began many years before the ratification of the nineteenth amendment.

Amendment 20. "LAME DUCK" AMENDMENT (1933)

SECTION 1. *Beginning of terms.* The terms of the President and Vice-President shall end at noon on the 20th day of January, and the terms of Senators and Representatives at noon on the 3d day of January, of the years in which such terms would have ended if this article had not been ratified; and the terms of their successors shall then begin.

SECTION 2. *Beginning of Congressional sessions.* The Congress shall assemble at least once in every year, and such meeting shall begin at noon on the 3d day of January, unless they shall by law appoint a different day.

SECTION 3. *Presidential succession.* If at the time fixed for the beginning of the term of the President, the President-elect shall have died, the Vice-President-elect shall become President. If a President shall not have been chosen before the time fixed for the beginning of his term, or if the President-elect shall have failed to qualify, then the Vice-President-elect shall act as President until a President shall have qualified; and the Congress may by law provide for the case wherein neither a President-elect nor a Vice-President-elect shall have qualified, declaring who shall then act as President, or the manner in which one who is to act shall be selected, and such person shall act accordingly until a President or Vice-President shall have qualified.

SECTION 4. *Filling Presidential vacancy.* The Congress may by law provide for the case of the death of any of the persons from whom the House of Representatives may choose a President whenever the right of choice shall have devolved upon them, and for the case of the death of any of the persons from whom the Senate may choose a Vice-President whenever the right of choice shall have devolved upon them.

[SECTION 5. *Effective date.* Sections 1 and 2 shall take effect on the 15th day of October following the ratification of this article.

SECTION 6. *Time limit for ratification.* This article shall be inoperative unless it shall have been ratified as an amendment to the Constitution by the legislatures of three-fourths of the several states within seven years from the date of its submission.]

¶ When the Constitution was written, the means of transportation and communication were so slow that it was decided that a new President and new Congressmen elected in November could not reach the capital to take office until March 4. However, since sessions of Congress began in December, a session including newly elected Congressmen could not be held until 13 months after their election. Thus, even if a Congressman running for re-election were defeated in November, he would serve in the session of Congress which began the month after his defeat, and continue to serve for several months. Since defeated candidates had been politically rejected by the voters, they were called "lame ducks," suggesting that their "political wings" had been clipped. One of the purposes of Amendment 20 was to limit the term and power of "lame duck" Congressmen.

Amendment 21. REPEAL OF PROHIBITION (1933)

SECTION 1. The eighteenth article of amendment to the Constitution of the United States is hereby repealed.

SECTION 2. The transportation or importation into any state, territory, or possession of the United States for delivery or use therein of intoxicating liquors, in violation of the laws thereof, is hereby prohibited.

[SECTION 3. This article shall be inoperative unless it shall have been ratified as an amendment to the Constitution by conventions in the several states, as provided in the Constitution, within seven years from the date of the submission hereof to the states by the Congress.]

¶ This amendment, which repealed Amendment 18, was the only amendment ratified by special state conventions instead of state legislatures. Congress felt that a popular referendum (vote) would give the people a better chance to voice their opinions on prohibition. As in Amendments 18 and 20, Congress placed a 7-year limit on ratification.

Amendment 22. TWO–TERM LIMIT FOR PRESIDENTS (1951)

SECTION 1. No person shall be elected to the office of the President more than twice, and no person who has held the office of President, or acted as President, for more than two years of a term to which some other person was elected President shall be elected to the office of the President more than once. [But this Article shall not apply to any person holding the office of President when this Article was proposed by the Congress, and shall not prevent any person who may be holding the office of President, or acting as President, during the term within which this Article becomes operative from holding the office of President or acting as President during the remainder of such term.]

[SECTION 2. This article shall be inoperative unless it shall have been ratified as an amendment to the Constitution by the legislatures of three-fourths of the several states within seven years from the date of its submission to the states by the Congress.]

¶ The original Constitution placed no limit on the number of terms a President could be elected to office. Washington and Jefferson, however, set a two-term precedent. In 1940 this tradition was broken when Franklin D. Roosevelt was elected for a third term, and in 1944, when he won a fourth term. The purpose of this amendment was to write the two-term precedent into law. The bracketed portion was included so that the amendment would not apply to President Truman, who held office when it was ratified.

Unit Survey (Reread "Tracing the Main Ideas," pages 111, 139, 155, 173.)

OUTSTANDING EVENTS

1763 Proclamation of 1763.
1764 Sugar Act, Currency Act.
1765 Stamp Act Congress meets.
1767 Townshend Acts.
1770 Boston Massacre.
1773 Boston Tea Party.
1774 Intolerable Acts.
1774 First Continental Congress.
1775 Fighting at Lexington, Concord.
1775 Second Continental Congress.
1776 Paine's *Common Sense* appears.
1776 Declaration of Independence.
1777 Burgoyne surrenders at Saratoga.
1778 Treaty of alliance with France.
1778–79 Clark takes the Northwest.
1781 Cornwallis surrenders.
1781 Articles of Confederation go into effect.
1783 Treaty of Paris; United States independence recognized.
1785 Land Ordinance.
1787 Northwest Ordinance.
1787 Constitution drafted.
1788 George Washington elected President.
1789 Washington inaugurated as President.

THEN AND NOW

1. What similarities and differences can you observe between the United Nations today and the American government under the Articles of Confederation?

2. Between 1945 and the present, a number of colonies inspired by American example have won freedom from their mother countries. Give examples.

3. Read the two introductions in D. W. Brogan, *The American Character*, Vintage (paper). It will provide a good "then and now" contrast for you which should prove of value throughout your entire study of American history.

EXTENDING YOUR HORIZON

1. The more ambitious student can add to his understanding of the roots of the Constitution by reading Chapter I, "The Founding Fathers: An Age of Realism," in Richard Hofstadter, *The American Political Tradition and the Men Who Made It*, Vintage. For a good summary of the events of

1787 in Philadelphia read Robert L. Schuyler, "The Framing and Adopting of the Constitution," in *The Declaration of Independence and the Constitution*, a pamphlet in *Problems of American Civilization*, "Amherst Series" (Heath).

2. For an interesting account of the roles of Molly Corbin and Molly Pitcher in the American Revolution read Fairfax Downey, "The Girls Behind the Guns," *American Heritage*, December 1956.

3. Read and prepare a report on John Dos Passos, "Lafayette's Two Revolutions," in *American Heritage*, December 1956.

4. Benjamin Franklin played an important diplomatic role in the American Revolution. Prepare a report for the class based on the article by Helen Augur, "Benjamin Franklin and the French Alliance," *American Heritage*, April 1956.

INDIVIDUAL ACTIVITIES

1. Choose any military campaign of the American Revolution and show how geography influenced American and British strategy.

2. Sketch a map of the United States and indicate in color the provisions of the Treaty of Paris of 1783. Label and mark off the area included in the provisions of the Northwest Ordinance of 1787.

3. Draw a time line of the period 1763–83 and indicate all important events.

4. Consult Commager's *Documents of American History*, No. 86, for Hamilton's proposed Plan of Union. Compare his proposals with the actual provisions in the Constitution. What does Hamilton's plan reveal about his ideas of government?

GROUP ACTIVITIES

1. Let a committee plan a class reading of the Declaration of Independence, assigning solo parts and deciding where choral reading will be most effective.

2. Appoint a research committee to present reports on the life and contributions to the American Revolution of the following: Lafayette, Von Steuben, Pulaski, Kosciusko, and Father Pierre Gibault.

3. Plan a class debate or discussion on this topic: Could Great Britain have prevented the American Revolution? Helpful material will be found in *The Causes of the American Revolution,* especially Chapters 1, 5, 6, and 7, in *Problems in American Civilization,* "Amherst Series."

4. Let a committee make plans for a thorough class discussion on the drawing up of the American Constitution in 1787. Investigate the roles of the leading figures and give arguments for and against the secrecy maintained. Valuable sources of information include Saul K. Padover's *The Living Constitution,* Mentor (paper); accounts of members found in the *Dictionary of American Biography* which can be compared to estimates of these delegates by a fellow delegate, Major William Pierce; Max Farrand, *The Fathers of the Constitution,* and *The Framing of the Constitution;* and the pamphlet in the "Amherst Series," *The Declaration of Independence and the Constitution.*

SUGGESTED FURTHER READING

GENERAL REFERENCE BOOKS

ADAMS, JAMES T., *The Epic of America,* Little, Brown.

ANGLE, PAUL M., *By These Words, Great Documents of American Liberty,* Rand McNally. Selected sources.

HEFFNER, RICHARD D., *A Documentary History of the United States,* Mentor (paper).

NEVINS, ALLAN, ed., *Times of Trial,* Knopf (reprints from *American Heritage*).

BIOGRAPHY

BAKELESS, JOHN, *Background to Glory,* Lippincott. About George Rogers Clark.

BOWEN, CATHERINE DRINKER, *John Adams and the American Revolution,* Little, Brown; Grosset & Dunlap (Universal).

BOWERS, CLAUDE G., *The Young Jefferson,* Houghton Mifflin.

CRANE, VERNER WINSLOW, *Benjamin Franklin and a Rising People,* Little, Brown.

CUNLIFFE, MARCUS, *George Washington: Man and Monument,* Little, Brown.

EATON, JEANETTE, *Young Lafayette,* Houghton Mifflin.

*FORBES, ESTHER, *Paul Revere and the World He Lived In,* Houghton Mifflin.

FRANKLIN, BENJAMIN, *Autobiography,* Dutton; and others.

HOLBROOK, STEWART, *Lost Men of American History,* Macmillan.

MAUROIS, ANDRÉ, *Washington: The Life of a Patriot,* Oxford Univ. Press [Toronto].

MEADE, ROBERT D., *Patrick Henry: Patriot in the Making,* Lippincott.

PADOVER, SAUL K., *Jefferson,* New American Library (Mentor Books).

SCHACHNER, NATHAN, *Alexander Hamilton: Nation Builder,* McGraw-Hill.

——, *Thomas Jefferson: A Biography,* Yoseloff, 2 vols.

VAN DOREN, CARL, *Benjamin Franklin,* Viking.

WOODWARD, W. E., *Tom Paine: America's Godfather,* Dutton.

OTHER NONFICTION

ALDEN, JOHN RICHARD, *The American Revolution: 1775–1783,* Harper (text ed.).

BECKER, CARL, *The Declaration of Independence: A Study in the History of Political Ideas,* Knopf (Vintage Books); Peter Smith.

——, *The Eve of the Revolution,* Yale Univ. Press.

CATTON, BRUCE, ed. *American Heritage Book of the Revolution,* Simon and Schuster. Pictorial.

COYLE, DAVID CUSHMAN, *The United States Political System and How It Works,* New American Library (Mentor Books).

*MILLER, JOHN C., *Origins of the American Revolution,* Little, Brown.

——, *Triumph of Freedom,* Little, Brown.

MONTROSS, LYNN, *Rag, Tag, and Bobtail,* Harper. About the Continental Army.

MORRIS, RICHARD B., *The American Revolution: A Short History,* Van Nostrand (Anvil Books).

MURRAY, JOHN COURTNEY, S.J., *We Hold These Truths,* Sheed & Ward.

PADOVER, SAUL, *The Living Constitution,* New American Library (Mentor Books).

PECKHAM, HOWARD, *The War for Independence: A Military History,* Univ. of Chicago Press (paper).

VAN DOREN, CARL, *The Great Rehearsal,* Viking. The Constitutional Convention.

HISTORICAL FICTION

BOYD, JAMES, *Drums,* Scribner.

EDMONDS, WALTER D., *Drums Along the Mohawk,* Little, Brown. Indian raids.

LANCASTER, BRUCE, *Guns of Burgoyne,* Lippincott.

——, *From Lexington to Liberty.* Doubleday.

ROBERTS, KENNETH, *Arundel,* Doubleday. A soldier on Arnold's expedition.

——, *Oliver Wiswell,* Doubleday. Tories.

——, *Rabble in Arms,* Doubleday.

*Building
the Nation*

1789–1845

The Nation Makes a Strong Start

WASHINGTON'S INAUGURATION at FEDERAL HALL – NEW YORK

IT is April 30, 1789. At New York City, the temporary capital of the nation, a crowd has gathered in Wall Street for the inauguration of the first President of the United States. Above the crowd, on the balcony of Federal Hall, stands George Washington. Robert R. Livingston, Chancellor of the State of New York, administers the oath of office. For a moment there is silence. Then a roar of applause breaks from the crowd.

What thoughts may have passed through Washington's mind as he gazed down on the sea of faces and as the waves of sound rose around him?

Perhaps Washington weighed in his mind the chances for success of the new government. He knew that most people still thought of themselves as citizens of New York, Delaware, or Virginia, and not yet as citizens of the United States. The people might hail him as President of the United States, but Washington was fully aware that the United States was as yet a nation in name only.

Indeed, many of Washington's close associates were pessimistic about the future of the new nation. John Adams, newly elected Vice-President, feared the Republic would not last beyond his own lifetime. Alexander Hamilton thought that the Constitution was "frail and worthless." Washington himself thought of the United States as an "experiment entrusted to the hands of the American people."

For better or worse, however, the experiment was now under way.

AS THE STORY DEVELOPS

1. The new federal government is organized and started.
2. Congress deals successfully with money problems.
3. The national government adopts a foreign policy.
4. Political parties become active in government.
5. President Adams struggles with a divided party.
6. Federalist ideas and methods persist under the Republicans.

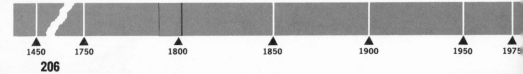

1450   1750   1800   1850   1900   1950   1975

The new federal government is organized and started

Washington's trip from Mount Vernon, his home in Virginia, to New York City had been a triumphal pageant. All along his route crowds turned out to watch him pass, to cheer him, to scatter flowers in his path. The welcome he received in New York City had been overwhelming.

But now the celebrations were over. President Washington and the other elected officials—Vice-President John Adams; the Senators, two from each of the states; and the 59 Representatives—had taken the oath to uphold the Constitution. Now they had to face the task of organizing the new government, and making it work.

Basic problems. The newly elected officials had as a guide the general principles written into the Constitution and the experience gained from their work in the various colonial governments. They had to build everything from the ground up.

There were, as yet, no federal laws, no courts, no law-enforcement officers. Serious financial problems had to be met, but there was no federal treasury and no method for collecting taxes. Worse still, there was little money in the country with which the people could pay the taxes that the new government would certainly have to levy. And on top of all the other problems facing the officials, the new government owed a large debt that it had inherited from the Revolutionary War and from the government under the Confederation.

Difficult problems lay ahead for the new nation in its relations with other nations. The President had to work out a foreign policy acceptable to the Congress, appoint ambassadors, and instruct them in their duties. If trouble should arise, there was little military strength to call upon. The navy built by the Continental Congress had been decommissioned and the army, by this time, consisted of only some 600 officers and enlisted men.

The new government had the power under the Constitution to deal with these and other problems. But dealing with them successfully called for hard work and statesmanship on the part of the President and Congress. For there were, as you will see, strongly opposing views in the nation about how such problems should be dealt with.

Congress goes to work. One of the first and most important measures Congress adopted was the Judiciary Act of 1789. This act provided for a Chief Justice and five Associate Justices of the Supreme Court. The first Chief Justice appointed by the President and approved by the Senate was John Jay.

The Judiciary Act also established thirteen district courts and three circuit courts, carrying out the power of Congress under Article 1 of the Constitution "To constitute tribunals inferior to the Supreme Court."

The Judiciary Act further provided that all disputes over the meaning of the Constitution, federal laws, and treaties must, in the last resort, be settled by the Supreme Court. If this power—the power of judicial review—had not been granted to the Supreme Court, each state would have been free to place its own interpretation on federal laws, and we would have had a league of sovereign or independent states, not a federal union. For this reason, the Judiciary Act was essential to the establishment of the federal system.

The first Congress also took several other important steps. It sent the Bill of Rights to the states for ratification. It re-enacted, or passed for a second time, the Northwest Ordinance providing a government for the Northwest Territory. Mainly to raise money, or revenue, it adopted a small tariff on imports.

The "cabinet" is created. The Congress also created three executive departments to help the President with his work. These three departments were the Department of State to help the President handle foreign and other af-

Painting by Charles Willson Peale

GEORGE WASHINGTON

If a man ever deserved the title "Father of His Country," that man was George Washington (1732–99). Such was the conclusion of Douglas Southall Freeman of Virginia, who, in the ten years before his death in 1953, wrote a famous six-volume biography of this great American.

"Washington, and probably Washington alone, kept the revolution alive," historian Freeman once wrote in a letter. "He was the only man who combined military experience with infinite patience, inflexible determination, a sound sense of organization, absolute integrity, regard for civil rights, and a justice so manifest in every act that even his rivals had to admit his superiority of character. . . ."

Throughout our history, Washington has been an inspiration to Americans from all walks of life. He had no desire for personal glory or power. When, in the closing years of the Revolutionary War, some of his officers urged him to accept the title of king, he indignantly rejected the offer.

After the war Washington gave up his command of the army to return to the life of a private citizen at Mount Vernon, the 8000-acre Virginia plantation he loved. "How much more delightful," he wrote to a friend in 1788, "is the task of making improvements in the earth than all the vainglory which can be acquired by ravaging it by the most uninterrupted career of conquests." He was acquainted with the best agricultural practices of the day and managed his plantation with skill. He took great pleasure in hunting, in entertaining, and in community affairs.

Only a sense of duty led Washington to take part in the Constitutional Convention in 1787. Only that same stern sense of duty led him to accept the responsibilities of the first President of the United States of America.

Washington's home, Mount Vernon

fairs, the Department of the Treasury to deal with financial problems, and the Department of War to manage military matters.

The heads of these departments soon came to be known as the President's "cabinet,"° although the Cabinet as we know it today was not officially recognized by law until 1907. The heads of these departments, called Secretaries, met with the President for informal conferences, although their function was purely advisory. The responsibility for making final decisions in the Executive Department rested then, as it does now, with the President alone.

President Washington filled his first "cabinet" by appointing Thomas Jefferson as Secretary of State, Alexander Hamilton as Secretary of the Treasury, and Henry Knox as Secretary of War.

Washington also appointed Samuel Osgood as Postmaster General. Postal affairs were then administered by the Treasury Department, for the Post Office Department was not created until 1829. Finally, Washington chose Edmund Randolph to fill the position of Attorney General. Randolph, who became the fourth member of Washington's cabinet, advised the President on matters of law. The Attorney Generalship was at first a part-time job, for the Department of Justice was not created until 1869.

∙∙∙

° *cabinet:* This term, which has come to mean a group of advisers, originally referred to a "cabinet," or private office, in which advisers gathered for conferences.

✔ SECTION SURVEY

1. (a) What basic problems faced our young republic in 1789? (b) Compare these problems with those which our country faces today.

2. Describe three measures adopted by the first Congress in its effort to solve important problems.

3. Who were our first "cabinet" officers, and what positions did they hold?

IDENTIFY: Judiciary Act, re-enact, cabinet; Jay, Jefferson, Hamilton, Knox, Osgood, Edmund Randolph; April 30, 1789.

2 Congress deals successfully with money problems

Among the many problems that the new government had to solve, the most urgent was that of money. The government needed money to pay salaries, to build and maintain the army and navy, to operate the post offices, and to carry on other activities. It also needed money to repay the debt owed to foreign countries and to American citizens.

The problem of finances. During the first year or two of its operation, the govment's problem of securing the money that it needed was exceptionally difficult. To be sure, the Constitution stated that Congress had the power "To lay and collect taxes. . . ." As you have seen, the first Congress used this power when it adopted a small tariff on articles imported into the United States. But Congress knew that the money secured from this tariff would not even begin to pay the expenses of running the new government. More money would have to come from some other tax or taxes. But what kinds of taxes?

There was another big question: Where would American citizens get the gold and silver coin or the paper money with which to pay their taxes? In 1789 there was very little currency in the United States. Although the Constitution gave Congress the power "To coin money," this was easier said than done. Where were the gold and silver to come from?

Looking for solutions to these and other financial problems, the members of Congress turned to the new Secretary of the Treasury, Alexander Hamilton. "Give us a plan for solving the nation's financial problems," they said in effect.

In turning to the Secretary of the Treasury for this help, the first Congress was setting an important precedent. While Congress is responsible for passing laws, it has always relied heavily on the Executive Department for advice.

ALEXANDER HAMILTON

Alexander Hamilton (1757–1804) was second only to Washington in his influence upon the new government in its early years. Only thirty-two years of age when he became Secretary of the Treasury, he had already carved an amazing career for himself. He was born on the West Indian island of Nevis in humble circumstances, but even when he was a child, his brilliance and ambition lifted him above his fellows. At seventeen, while attending King's College in New York (now Columbia University), he ably defended the colonial cause in public speech and writing. At twenty, he was serving on General Washington's staff. At twenty-six, he was one of the country's leading lawyers. He was influential in calling the Constitutional Convention, and attended it as a delegate from New York.

In spite of Hamilton's devotion to the nation, he made no secret of his opinion that monarchy was the ideal form of government. But realizing that his fellow Americans would not accept a king, he supported the Constitution, which created a republican, or representative, form of government as "better than nothing." But he was convinced that the federal government should be as strong as possible. In fact, he would have abolished the states.

Hamilton's fear that representative government would give the great body of the people too much political power did not prevent him from supporting the Constitution. Indeed, it was Hamilton's financial genius and flawless integrity that helped to establish the new government on a solid foundation.

Repaying the war debt. In a series of reports to Congress, Hamilton proposed a program which would put the nation's finances on a sound basis. In his first report Hamilton asked the legislators to build a solid foundation under the new government by establishing its credit. He knew that a nation, like an individual, must pay its debts, or lose the respect and trust of its neighbors and find it impossible to borrow in the future.

The United States and the separate states owed a combined war debt of more than $80,000,000—a staggering sum for those days. Hamilton proposed to repay all of this debt.

Everybody agreed that the United States should pay $12,000,000 that it owed to France, the Netherlands, and Spain. However, many Congressmen objected to Hamilton's proposal to repay $44,000,000 that the Continental Congress had borrowed from American citizens during the Revolutionary War. The Continental Congress had borrowed this money by issuing paper money and selling *government bonds.* Government bonds are certificates issued by a government in exchange for a loan of money. The certificate is a promise that the loan, plus interest, will eventually be repaid. But, as you know, the credit of the government during and after the war was so low that its paper money was "not worth a Continental," and its bonds were equally low in value.

By now many of the people who originally held the government bonds and the paper money had long since sold them to speculators for a fraction of their original, or "face," value. Hamilton was now proposing that these bonds and paper money be redeemed, or paid off, at their face value. But why, Hamilton's opponents asked, should the entire country pay out its hard-earned money for the benefit of a small group of speculators? However, Hamilton convinced Congress that a debt must be paid if the nation's credit was to be established.

The remainder of the total debt, about $25,000,000, was owed by several of the states to American citizens. Hamilton recommended that the federal government take over this debt and redeem every penny the states owed. This proposal started a violent argument. States with small debts and states that had already paid their war debts argued that it was unfair to expect them to shoulder, or "assume," their neighbors' burdens. Southerners protested that most of the state bonds, like the bonds of the Continental Congress, had passed into the hands of speculators, who would again profit at the expense of the people.

Defeat appeared to be certain, but at the last moment a compromise was arranged. The southerners, led by Thomas Jefferson, agreed in the so-called Assumption Bill that the government should assume the debts of the states. In return, the northerners, led by Hamilton, agreed to vote for a bill that would locate the new national capital along the banks of the Potomac River on land donated by Virginia and Maryland.°

Hamilton's bank proposal. Equally brilliant was Hamilton's proposal to Congress that it pass a bill calling for the creation of a *national bank* to be called the Bank of the United States. What Hamilton had in mind was not just one bank, but a banking system. The system would consist of a large central bank, with branch banks located in the major cities of the country.

This was a far-reaching proposal, almost a revolutionary proposal. At the time, in the early 1790's, there was no centralized banking system in the United States. There were only small local banks, chartered by the different states.

Hamilton took pains to point out the advantages of a national banking system. The branch banks would provide safe places for tax officials to deposit the money they collected from the people. When the government wanted to transfer money from one part of the country to another, the branch banks could do this by sending checks rather than by going to the risk and inconven-

ience of actually shipping gold and silver. Moreover, a banking system of this kind would be large enough to lend money to the government as well as to private individuals. When the central bank did not have as much money to lend as the government might wish to borrow, it could always turn to one or more of its branch banks for help.

Finally, the Bank of the United States would provide what Hamilton called "a sound, uniform currency," that is, currency that would have the same value in all parts of the country. People would have faith in the paper money, or *bank notes*, that bore the name of the Bank of the United States. People would prefer these bank notes to the paper money printed by small local or state banks. As a result, Hamilton predicted, small shaky banks would close down, while others would make every effort to win the confidence of the public. All of this would be good for business—and for the country as a whole.

The bank proposal is adopted. Hamilton's arguments in favor of a Bank of the United States were sound. Nevertheless, his opponents, led by Jefferson, objected vigorously. They too had telling arguments. First, according to Hamilton's proposal, the Bank of the United States would sell 25,000 shares of stock at $400 each, amounting to a total *capital stock*, or money value, of $10,000,000. The gov-

■ This building in Philadelphia became headquarters for the Bank of the United States. It symbolized the new stability of the federal government.

° The government was moved to the new capital, Washington, D.C., in 1800.

ernment would buy one fifth of all the shares. The other four fifths would be bought by private investors, who would, of course, be the wealthy people of the country. This would have the effect, Jefferson maintained, of giving the wealthy people a monopoly of the money power of the country.

Jefferson also protested that a national bank would have an unfair advantage in competition with the local or state banks. Again he was right. All government funds would be deposited in the Bank of the United States and its branches, where they could be lent to individuals at a profit to the national bank. Private banks would have no opportunity to earn profits on the deposit and loan of government funds.

Finally, Jefferson claimed that the bank would be unconstitutional. As he pointed out, the Constitution did not give the federal government power to create a bank. In reply Hamilton pointed to the "elastic clause" of the Constitution, in which Congress was given the right "To make all laws which shall be necessary and proper for carrying into execution the foregoing powers . . ." including the power "To lay and collect taxes . . ." and "To borrow money on the credit of the United States." Was it not "necessary and proper," Hamilton asked, for Congress to create an institution to aid in its responsibility of collecting taxes and borrowing money?

Thus the arguments ran for and against Hamilton's recommendation. But, in spite of a violent debate in the cabinet, Washington leaned toward Hamilton's side, and in 1791 a bill granting a charter to the Bank of the United States was passed by Congress over strenuous opposition.

Hamilton's tariff proposal. Hamilton also urged Congress to pass another tariff law. As you have seen, one of the first acts of Congress had been the adoption of a law levying a small tariff on imported goods. Congress had passed this measure mainly with the thought of raising revenue for the new government. But when Hamilton proposed a new tariff law, he was thinking of what we call a "protective" tariff.

The difference between a "revenue" tariff and a "protective" tariff is one of purpose and therefore of rates. If, for example, the tariff, or duty, on a blanket manufactured in England were very low, English manufacturers would be able to pay the duty and still compete with American manufacturers for American trade. This would be a *revenue tariff*. But if the tariff were very high on each blanket, say as high as 100 per cent of its value, then the English blanket would have to be sold in the United States for twice what it cost the English manufacturer to make it. As a result, the English manufacturer could not hope to sell blankets in America in competition with American manufacturers. A tariff of this kind would not bring in revenue to the government, since the English manufacturer would abandon his American markets. But it would "protect" the American manufacturers from competition and would be called a *protective tariff*.

The tariff act that Congress had already adopted, while mainly for revenue, had mild protective features. But Congress did not even consider Hamilton's recommendation of a truly protective tariff. Nevertheless, the recommendation illustrates how clearly Hamilton had thought through his program for binding the wealthy people, in this case the manufacturers, to the government by ties of self-interest. This recommendation also reveals how well Hamilton understood the needs of the young nation. He saw that the United States could become truly independent only when it was able to produce most of the goods that it needed.

The Whisky Rebellion. In a fourth recommendation Hamilton urged Congress to levy a tax on distilled liquors. The tax he had in mind was an *excise tax*° which the distiller himself would have to pay for every gallon of liquor that he produced and sold.

....

° *excise tax:* a tax levied upon goods produced within the country where they are consumed.

■ An unknown artist has later imagined this scene during the Whisky Rebellion. Indignant citizens have tarred and feathered a tax collector and are "riding him on a rail." Whether or not such an event took place, the federal government put down the rebellion.

Hamilton could hardly have hoped to secure much revenue from a tax of this kind. That was not his goal. He wished to impress the frontiersmen with the power of the federal government. What better way than to reach into the back country and pluck money from the pockets of the freedom-loving frontiersmen by taxing them for every gallon of whisky that they distilled?

In order to understand why this proposal was so important, remember what the frontier was like in the 1790's. The frontiersmen were almost isolated from the settled areas along the Atlantic coast. Travelers could move back and forth only over the roughest of trails through the forests. As a result, the frontiersmen could not hope to transport the corn that they grew to markets in the settled areas. And corn was their most important crop. But they could and did distill the corn into whisky. Then they loaded the jugs or kegs of whisky onto the backs of mules and drove the mules eastward to market. Whisky, in short, was the most important source of cash for many farmers who lived on the frontier. The excise tax would hit them hard.

Hamilton knew that the tax would cause resentment. Indeed, this was exactly what he wanted, for it would give the new government a chance to demonstrate its power. As he expected, the frontiersmen rebelled. They refused to pay the tax, and the "Whisky Rebellion" broke out on the frontiers of western Pennsylvania in 1794. But the rebellion melted away when 15,000 militiamen were sent to the scene by the federal government. The militiamen were accompanied by the Secretary of the Treasury himself and commanded by "Light-Horse Harry" Lee of Virginia. No lives were lost, but the federal government had demonstrated its strength.

Hamilton's program succeeds. Hamilton's financial program proved a great success. By paying off the debt it owed, the new government demonstrated that it intended to meet its obligations honestly and punctually. The centralized banking system provided a sound, uniform currency. The excise tax brought in a small amount of much-needed revenue. More important, it extended the influence of the government to the frontier.

To be sure, Hamilton's financial program put money into the pockets of the well-to-do. Americans who owned government bonds, who invested in the Bank of the United States, and who needed a sound, uniform currency were delighted—and became staunch supporters of the new government.

But Hamilton's financial program did not benefit only the well-to-do. It was important to all Americans, for it gave the United States a workable money system and a credit reputation that few of the older nations of Europe enjoyed.

1. For what purposes did Washington's administration need money?

2. Explain Hamilton's policies with reference to (a) the foreign debt of the United States, (b) the domestic debt of the United States, (c) the debts of the separate states, (d) a national bank, and (e) excise taxes.

3. Why were some people opposed to Hamilton's debt policies? Explain.

4. (a) Give Hamilton's arguments in favor of a national bank. (b) Give Jefferson's arguments in opposition to the bank.

5. How did Hamilton's policies help to establish the credit of the United States?

IDENTIFY: government bonds, Assumption Bill, bank note, revenue tariff, protective tariff, excise tax, Whisky Rebellion; "Light-Horse Harry" Lee; 1791, 1794.

3

The national government adopts a foreign policy

The United States was born in a world torn by revolution and warfare. This situation enormously complicated the problems of the new government.

The French Revolution. Even while the first American Congressmen were gathering to organize the government in the spring of 1789, a revolution of the common people and a few nobles and churchmen broke out in France. Fighting under the slogan "liberty, equality, and fraternity," the French revolutionists shared some of the ideas expressed in the American Declaration of Independence. But they were divided in their viewpoints and more violent than the American revolutionists in their insistence upon their ideas.

Within a few years after the outbreak of trouble, the revolutionists gained complete power in France. They mobbed and beheaded thousands of people in the French upper classes and nobility, including King Louis XVI and Queen Marie Antoinette. Thousands of other upper-class Frenchmen escaped to England and other neighboring countries. There, safe from the sharp blade of the guillotine, they laid plans to regain control of France.

Europeans looked at the French Revolution with mixed feelings. Many people, and particularly the ruling classes, were filled with horror. They were fearful that the example set by the French revolutionists might spread to their countries. As a result, they were eager to see the revolution crushed. By 1793 the new government of France, called the Republic, was at war with Great Britain and other European countries.

Americans become involved. It was impossible for American citizens to remain untouched by the fires of revolution, counterrevolution, and warfare raging in Europe and at sea. The French seized American ships carrying goods to Great Britain or its possessions. The British seized American ships carrying goods to France or its colonies and *impressed,* or kidnaped, American sailors to serve in the British navy. Most of these sailors were citizens of the United States, but some were, in fact, deserters from the British navy.

In the United States citizens took sides. Hamilton and his followers were for Great Britain. Jefferson and his followers favored France and the French Revolution. Social gatherings often broke up in vigorous arguments.

The United States chooses neutrality. The position of the United States was indeed critical. The United States, as you recall, was obliged by its treaty with France in 1778 to take up arms in defense of the French West Indies. But if the United States went to the aid of France, it would find itself at war with Great Britain. War would be suicidal, for the new nation was not prepared for armed conflict on either land or sea.

It was a grave situation that confronted President Washington in April 1793, when Edmond Genêt (zhuh-NEH), minister from the French Republic, arrived in the United States. Genêt did not insist that the United States come to the defense of the French West Indies, but he did demand that it open its seaports

THE BATTLE OF FALLEN TIMBERS

Little Turtle, Black Wolf, Blue Jacket, Tecumseh, Turkey Foot, and many other Indian chiefs, with from 1500 to 2000 warriors at their sides, were confident of victory. Twice before they had routed American armies from the Northwest Territory. Now, in the summer of 1794, they were well supplied with British guns and powder and shot, and the position they held was a natural fortress. Some years earlier, a tornado had roared along the crest of a hill, leaving behind it a two-mile swath of torn and twisted trees. In this wild tangle the Indians took shelter and waited for the attack.

General ("Mad Anthony") Wayne was also confident of victory. Among the 2000 troops he had trained and now commanded were several hundred mounted Kentucky riflemen, tough frontiersmen with long experience in Indian warfare. On August 20 the Americans struck swiftly, firing a volley and then charging with bayonets. In an hour the battle was over, and the Indians scattered.

The Battle of Fallen Timbers brought an end to almost twenty years of Indian warfare. For the first time since the Revolutionary War, peace came to the frontier. And when the British finally withdrew from the forts they had been holding in American territory, the extensive tracts of land beyond the Appalachians were open to settlement.

to French naval vessels and privateers.

Many Americans welcomed Genêt with enthusiasm and called upon the President to honor the American obligation to France. Others, friendly to Great Britain, urged Washington to break all relations with France.

Backed unanimously by his cabinet, the President ignored the popular clamor and on April 22, 1793, issued a Proclamation of Neutrality. The proclamation forbade American citizens to take part in any hostilities on land or sea with any of the belligerent states. Congress endorsed the President's action by passing a neutrality act.

War with Great Britain avoided. In spite of the neutrality act, the United States still stood on the brink of war. Indeed, in 1793, conflict with Great Britain seemed certain.

To save its West Indian colonies from starvation, France for the first time allowed Americans to carry on trade with the French West Indies. The British promptly seized American ships, on the ground that trade not permitted in time of peace could not be carried on in time of war.

As American ships were confiscated and American sailors were impressed into the British navy, many Americans became increasingly angry. Men began to drill on village greens, to fortify entrances to harbors, and to build war ships.

Washington's Farewell Address (1796):
EXCERPT

The great rule of conduct for us in regard to foreign nations is, in extending our commercial relations, to have with them as little political connection as possible. So far as we have already formed engagements, let them be fulfilled with perfect good faith . . .

Europe has a set of primary interests which to us have none or a very remote relation. Hence she must be engaged in frequent controversies, the causes of which are essentially foreign to our concerns . . .

It is our true policy to steer clear of permanent alliances with any portion of the foreign world, so far, I mean, as we are now at liberty to do it . . .

In an effort to prevent war, President Washington sent Chief Justice John Jay of the Supreme Court to London to try to settle the outstanding differences between Great Britain and the United States. Jay was only partly successful. The British won the best of the bargain. They secured the right to trade freely in all American ports. In return for this privilege, they did promise to withdraw their troops by 1796 from certain forts they still occupied on the northwestern frontier. At the same time they insisted upon the right of British fur traders to carry on their business in American territory.

The treaty, known as the Jay Treaty, greatly disappointed many Americans. Some of Jefferson's more hotheaded followers said that Hamilton and the government had "sold out" to Great Britain. Mobs burned Jay in effigy and threw stones at Hamilton.

In the end, however, when the name-calling and the arguments died away, most Americans had to agree that the Jay Treaty had accomplished its major purpose: It had helped to prevent war with Great Britain. It had also prodded the Spaniards into action that proved extremely helpful to the United States.

Differences with Spain are settled.
News of the Jay Treaty came as a blow to Spain. The Spanish government had just signed an agreement with the French Republic. As a result of this agreement, the Spaniards faced the possibility of war with Great Britain. Under the circumstances, Spain was eager to insure American neutrality. When the United States and Great Britain settled their differences, the Spanish government decided that it was time to act.

In 1795, in the Pinckney Treaty, the Spaniards granted the United States everything that Americans had been demanding from Spain since 1783. The treaty finally settled the long-standing dispute between the United States and Spain over boundaries of Florida and Georgia (see map, pages 822–23). Spain also agreed to curb Indian attacks upon settlements in Georgia and the frontier regions between the Appalachians and the Mississippi River. An even more important concession, however, was the right freely to navigate the Mississippi River. This right included the privilege of transferring goods at New Orleans from river boats to ocean-going vessels without payment of duties to Spain.

This right, known as the *right of deposit*, was especially important to the western farmers. Although they sent bundles of furs and jugs of whisky eastward over the mountain trails on the backs of mules and donkeys, settlers in the western lands could not send heavy or bulky products to the eastern markets by pack trains. Instead, they floated their products down the Ohio and the Mississippi to New Orleans. There they sold their products to shipmasters bound for Europe or for one of the Atlantic coast ports. After the sale had been completed, the men broke up their rafts and sold the lumber.

Although this was a clumsy way of carrying on trade, it was cheaper than sending goods by pack train directly to eastern markets. The Pinckney Treaty assured westerners that Spain would no longer threaten to close their vital trade route, the Mississippi River.

Washington against foreign alliances.
In 1796 President Washington, refusing to serve a third term, prepared to leave office and return to Mount Vernon. During his two terms he had helped to establish the new nation on a solid foundation. His administration had organized the machinery of government. It had managed to avoid war with Great Britain and France. It had settled the long-standing argument with Spain. These were solid accomplishments.

Nevertheless, Washington was troubled. He was troubled about the sharp, often bitter arguments between Hamilton and his followers and Jefferson and his followers. He was also troubled about United States relations with other countries.

As one of his last public acts, President Washington wrote his Farewell Address to Congress and to his fellow citizens. In this address Washington urged the American people to remain devoted to the Union and to avoid the formation of political parties. He also warned them to avoid "permanent alliances" with "any portion of the foreign world" on the ground that such alliances might tie the hands of the infant nation and prevent the government from acting in its own best interests.

☞ **SECTION SURVEY**

1. (a) Why did France expect our aid in 1793? (b) Should we have helped France? Give reasons to support your opinion.
2. What conditions led Washington to issue his Proclamation of Neutrality in 1793?
3. (a) Give the provisions of the Jay Treaty. (b) Why did this treaty disappoint many Americans?
4. (a) State the provisions of the Pinckney Treaty. (b) Why was this treaty especially important to the westerners?
5. Summarize Washington's advice to the American people in his Farewell Address.

IDENTIFY: impressment of seamen, neutrality, right of deposit; Genêt; 1793, 1795, 1796.

4 Political parties become active in government

The development of political parties deeply troubled President Washington. But by September 1796, when Washington wrote his Farewell Address and warned against "the danger of parties," a two-party system already existed, and the names Federalist and Republican were being applied to the two opposing parties.

The two-party system arises. The Constitution said nothing about the formation of political parties. Many Americans besides George Washington hoped that party divisions and party disagreements could be avoided. It soon became apparent that this was impossible.

As early as the Presidential election of 1792, two major parties appeared in American politics. Washington was re-elected by unanimous vote. Vice-President John Adams was also re-elected, but against considerable opposition. He was opposed by George Clinton of New York, a candidate sponsored by Thomas Jefferson and his followers.

Hamilton's followers came to be known as Federalists. The Federalist Party included many wealthy merchants, manufacturers, lawyers, and clergymen. John Adams, himself a Federalist, said they represented "the rich, the well-born, and the able." Among them were many people who had no faith in the ability of the average person to play an intelligent part in government. The Federalist Party was strongest in New England and along the Atlantic seaboard.

The opposition party was led by Thomas Jefferson. Known at first as the Anti-Federalists, the members of this party soon took the name Democratic-Republicans. Before long, they dropped the first part of the name and called themselves simply Republicans. Although some wealthy people were Republicans, most of Jefferson's supporters were the owners of small farms or wage earners in the growing towns.

Party differences. Thomas Jefferson's beliefs were quite different from Hamilton's. Hamilton had little faith in the ability of the average people to govern themselves. Jefferson, on the other hand, had great faith in the average man's ability to take an effective part in the government. Jefferson put this faith into words in the Declaration of Independence, in his statement that all governments should secure their power from "the consent of the governed."

Hamilton, distrusting average people, proposed to keep wealthy people in power by creating a strong federal government under their control. Since a *strict,* or literal, interpretation of the Constitution would not permit the creation of a sufficiently strong federal government, Hamilton chose to read his own meaning into the Constitution by a *loose* interpretation.

Jefferson, on the other hand, wanted the people, particularly the small farmers who made up 90 per cent of the total population, to exercise controlling power in the country. Therefore, he favored the weakest possible federal government, strong state governments, and ironclad guarantees of individual liberties. He believed that the Constitution *as written* gave sufficient power to the government. When a question arose as to the meaning of the Constitution, Jefferson chose a *strict* interpretation.

Hamilton and Jefferson had frequent clashes of opinion because of their differing beliefs and the resulting differences in their interpretations of the Constitution. For example, in 1791, as you recall, disagreement arose when Hamilton proposed the creation of the Bank of the United States. Jefferson, insisting on a "strict" interpretation of the Constitution, argued that Congress had no authority to create the bank because there was no mention of banks or banking in the Constitution. Hamilton, interpreting the Constitution "loosely," had a ready answer. The Constitution did give Congress power to regulate money, he argued, and since a national bank was needed to secure this regulation, Congress therefore had the power to create such a bank.

■ Political cartoons, often extremely bitter, have been used throughout American history. In this detail from a cartoon of 1796, a cartoonist favorable toward the Federalists shows Jefferson and colleagues holding back the progress of the government under George Washington.

By 1794 most of the voters had chosen the political party to which they wished to belong. From that day to this, the political life of the United States has revolved around the *two-party system,* with "third parties" developing from time to time to press for policies they felt the major parties were neglecting.

Nominating candidates. On March 4, 1797, President John Adams, a Federalist, took the oath of office. A few minutes later Thomas Jefferson, a Republican, was sworn in as Vice-President.

A Federalist President, a Republican Vice-President! How did this curious political situation develop? The answer lies in the election of 1796. In the answer is an example of how custom helped to shape our political institutions.

Both the Federalists and the Republicans entered the election year determined to win. President Washington had announced his intention of retiring, and the Presidency and the Vice-Presidency were wide open.

The Constitution, as you know, gave no directions for nominating candidates for the Presidency and Vice-Presidency. Because the Constitution was silent on this subject, the political leaders of the two parties were free to choose their own methods. As a result, they kept political power in their own hands by holding Congressional conferences, later called *caucuses,* in which they chose the candidates. The voters at large had nothing to say about the nomination of candidates.

Months before election day the Federalists in Congress met in one of these private conferences, or caucuses. The Congressmen who gathered at this meeting chose John Adams and Thomas Pinckney, who had drawn up the Pinckney Treaty, as the Federalist candidates for the Presidency and the Vice-Presidency. The Republican Congressmen, meeting in a similar party conference, chose as their candidates Thomas Jefferson and Aaron Burr. In this way the leaders of the political parties selected the men that they, the leaders, wanted to run for office. But in the 1790's the

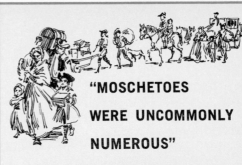

"MOSCHETOES WERE UNCOMMONLY NUMEROUS"

In September 1793, Philadelphia was almost a ghost town—Philadelphia, the most populous and prosperous city in the United States and the temporary capital of the nation. The members of Congress had packed up and left. President Washington had left. Every day, carts, wagons, and coaches rolled out of the city carrying entire families to safety in the country.

An epidemic of yellow fever had broken out suddenly in August. People who contracted the disease usually died within three or four days. No one knew what caused it. No one knew how to combat it. The physicians were helpless.

In mortal fear, people remaining in the city barred their doors and windows. When they had to venture outside, they covered their noses and mouths with cloths soaked in vinegar or camphor and walked down the middle of the streets. They burned fires in the streets "to purify the air," fired guns, and rang church bells.

Late in October, after more than 4000 persons had died, the epidemic ended as suddenly as it had begun. People began to return to the city. President Washington returned. Congress re-assembled. Shops opened. By December, life was back to normal.

During the next hundred years, yellow fever epidemics ravaged city after city, especially in the South. Finally, in 1900, Dr. Walter Reed of the U.S. Army Medical Corps proved that yellow fever was transmitted from man to man by the bite of the *Stegomyia* mosquito.

At the height of the 1793 epidemic, one of Philadelphia's leading physicians, Dr. Benjamin Rush, observed that "moschetoes were uncommonly numerous." He never knew how close he had come to discovering the source of the dread disease.

final decision rested, not with the political parties nor with the voters, but with a group of men called "electors."°

Role of the electors. When election day arrived, voters all over the country traveled to the polling places and voted for officials to serve them in local, state, and federal government. The voters did *not*, however, vote for the President and the Vice-President. Instead, they voted for electors who, in turn, were to cast *electoral votes* for President and Vice-President.

After the election, the winning electors in each state gathered together in their own states, and each elector then voted, as the Constitution provided, "by ballot for two persons." They then forwarded the result of their vote to the President of the Senate who, in the presence of the Senate and the House of Representatives, opened all the returns and had them counted.

There was nothing in the Constitution to say that the electors had to vote for the candidates previously nominated by the two political parties. According to the Constitution, the electors were completely free to vote for whomever they wished. It was felt that this small, select group of men would be better informed and therefore able to choose more wisely than the voters at large.

But the men who framed the Constitution had not foreseen that the country would divide into two major political parties. They had not foreseen that the electors might choose a President representing one political party and a Vice-President representing another. In 1796, however, this happened.

The election of 1796. When the electors chosen in the November elections gathered in their respective states to vote for the President and the Vice-President, they had before them four names —the Federalist candidates, John Adams and Thomas Pinckney, and the Republi-

....

° The group of Presidential electors in each state has come to be known as an Electoral College. Sometimes the entire body of electors in the United States is referred to as the Electoral College.

can candidates, Thomas Jefferson and Aaron Burr.

It was expected that the electors would choose either *both* Federalist candidates or *both* Republican candidates. But a number of leading Federalists, among them Alexander Hamilton, did not like John Adams. These Federalists worked out a plan that would give Pinckney the Presidency and put Adams in as Vice-President. But the plan backfired. When the electoral votes were counted, John Adams had the largest number of votes, Thomas Jefferson the next largest. As a result, the United States had a Federalist President and a Republican Vice-President.

Custom changes the Constitution. It was custom, rather than law, that prevented a similar situation from recurring in the future. Gradually, after 1796, electors came to understand that they were expected to vote only for the previously nominated candidates. The Federalist electors, for example, understood that they were expected to vote for the Federalist candidates. Likewise, the Republican electors understood that they were to vote for the Republican candidates. This custom became part of our "unwritten Constitution."

↙ **SECTION SURVEY**

1. (a) Identify the leaders of the Federalist Party and the Republican Party. (b) What economic groups supported each party?

2. Compare the two parties with regard to (a) views on strong federal government versus states' rights, (b) interpretation of the Constitution, and (c) views on the national bank.

3. Who were the candidates in the election of 1796?

4. The election of 1796 was the only one in American history in which a President and Vice-President belonging to different political parties were elected. How did this happen? Why is it unlikely that it will happen again?

IDENTIFY: two-party system, caucus, electoral votes, Electoral College; Thomas Pinckney, Burr.

5 President Adams struggles with a divided party

President John Adams was not pleased at having a Republican Vice-President in his administration. But he had little time to worry about this situation, for when he took office, the United States was threatened by war with France.

On the verge of war with France. American relations with France had grown steadily worse since 1793. The French resented American treatment of their minister Genêt, America's refusal to aid France by honoring the Treaty of 1778, and the American Proclamation of Neutrality of 1793. The French also resented the Jay Treaty, which France regarded as pro-British.

As a result of this friction, France had become increasingly hostile during Washington's second administration. The French navy had seized ships flying the American flag and prevented them from reaching British ports. The French Directory, a committee of five men who governed France after 1795, had refused to receive the minister whom President Washington sent to Paris. President Adams regarded this as an insult to the United States. France, he said, had "treated us neither as allies nor as friends nor as a sovereign state." Nevertheless, he decided to make one more effort to preserve peace.

The XYZ Affair. Early in 1797 President Adams sent three Americans to Paris to try to reach an agreement with France. The three American commissioners were John Marshall, Elbridge Gerry, and Charles C. Pinckney. The French government refused to receive the Americans officially. While waiting for an official reception, the Americans were visited by three Frenchmen.

The Frenchmen, who were later identified by President Adams as merely "X, Y, and Z," made three insulting demands. First, the American government must apologize publicly to France for some remarks Adams had made in a re-

John Adams, second President of the United States, faced many problems and was not widely popular, but his reputation has increased through the years.

cent speech to Congress; second, the United States must grant a loan to France; and third, the American envoys must pay a bribe of $250,000 to the five members of the French Directory.

When news of this insult reached America, large numbers of Americans demanded war. Rallying around the slogan "Millions for defense, but not one cent for tribute," Americans began war preparations. In 1798 the government created the Navy Department and authorized construction of war ships and fortification of harbors. The government also strengthened the army and recalled former President Washington from Mount Vernon to assume chief command, with Hamilton as his first subordinate. Although war was not officially declared, a state of war actually existed. Within a few months American war ships captured more than 80 vessels flying the French flag.

President Adams avoids war. At this moment President Adams committed one of the most courageous acts of his career. Although many members of his own party were clamoring for a declaration of war, Adams tried once again to secure peace. In 1799 he sent another group of commissioners to Paris.

By the time the Americans arrived, Napoleon had overthrown the corrupt Directory and made himself dictator of France, with the title of "First Consul." Napoleon was as eager as Adams to reach a settlement with the United States, for he wanted to begin his rule free from conflicts with foreign nations.

For this reason, the Americans and the French quickly reached an agreement. Both countries agreed to abandon the old treaty of 1778. The United States agreed to drop its claims against the French for illegal seizure of American ships. Nevertheless, a major source of friction remained, for the French continued to seize American ships that attempted to trade with the British.

In spite of the shortcomings of the agreement, President Adams had succeeded in avoiding full-scale war with France. Like Washington before him, Adams believed that the infant nation could endure only if it avoided being drawn into European conflicts.

By safeguarding America's interests in this crucial period of its history, President Adams deliberately sacrificed any popularity that he might have enjoyed with his own party.

The Alien and Sedition Acts. While anti-French feeling was running high, the Federalist majority in Congress enacted in 1798 a series of laws designed, they said, to unite the country. It was generally understood, however, that the laws would also weaken the Republican Party.

This legislation, often called the Alien and Sedition Acts, actually included four different laws—(1) the Naturalization Act, (2) the Alien Act, (3) the Alien Enemies Act, and (4) the Sedition Act. Congress passed these laws against the advice of Adams and other Federalist leaders.

The Naturalization Act extended from 5 to 14 years the length of time an alien, or foreigner, had to reside in the United States before he could become a naturalized citizen. Congress justified the act on the grounds that it would help protect the country from enemy aliens in wartime. But since most newcomers joined the Republican Party as soon as they secured their citizenship papers, the partisan implications of the measure were apparent. The Federalists wished to remain in office.

The Alien Act authorized the President "to order all such aliens as he shall judge dangerous to the peace and safety of the United States . . ." or those concerned in any plots against the government to leave the country. The Alien Enemies Act authorized the President, in time of war or invasion, to imprison or banish any foreigners he believed to be a menace to the public security. These two acts were defended by the Federalists as necessary war precautions, but it was evident that they could also be employed to stifle anti-Federalist agitation. After all, it was a Federalist President who would decide which aliens were "dangerous to the peace and safety of the United States."

The Sedition Act was intended to silence American citizens themselves. Sedition means, among other things, the use of language to stir up discontent or rebellion against a government. Under the Sedition Act punishment by fine and imprisonment could be used to silence anybody who wrote, said, or printed anything "false, scandalous and malicious . . . against the government of the United States, or either house of the Congress . . . or the President of the United States, with intent to defame the said government. . . ."

If all of these laws had been enforced, they would have effectively ended opposition to the Federalist Party. The Naturalization Act went into effect at once. The Alien Act and the Alien Enemies Act were not enforced, but the mere threat of imprisonment or deportation by the government drove many fearful Frenchmen from the country. Although the Sedition Act was used to silence only about ten Republican editors and printers who had expressed opposition to the government, the fear of punishment undoubtedly kept many others from making critical comments.

DEDHAM'S LIBERTY POLE

One day, during the height of the agitation over the Alien and Sedition Acts, a liberty pole suddenly appeared in Dedham, Massachusetts. Attached to the pole was a placard which read as follows: "No stamp act, no sedition and no alien acts, no land tax. Downfall to the tyrants of America: peace and retirement to the President: long live the Vice-President and the minority." A crowd quickly gathered. Federalists and Republicans exchanged heated words, then blows. The Federalist partisans won the tussle, pulled down the liberty pole, and tore up the placard.

Federalists demanded punishment for the person who had committed this outrage. The guilty man was David Brown, a veteran of the Revolutionary War, who had seen much of the world as a sailor and who liked to discuss politics at the village store. Brown was arrested, held in jail, and eventually tried. Judge Samuel Chase of the United States Circuit Court presided at the trial, where Brown surprised everyone by saying he was sorry for what he had done. But when the Court demanded that he give the names of those who had worked with him, he refused.

Judge Chase had no sympathy for "radicals" like David Brown. He sentenced Brown to the heaviest penalty that any American was ever given for violating the Alien and Sedition Acts— 18 months in prison and a $450 fine. Since Brown had no money to pay the fine, he remained in prison for two years, until Thomas Jefferson became President and pardoned him.

Virginia and Kentucky Resolutions. The Republicans were furious at these measures, which they claimed destroyed free speech and greatly strengthened the power of the federal government, particularly the power of the President. They voiced their protest in the Kentucky and Virginia Resolutions.

The Kentucky Resolutions, prepared by Thomas Jefferson, were adopted by the legislature of the new state of Kentucky in 1798 and 1799. The Virginia Resolutions, prepared by James Madison, were adopted by the legislature of Virginia in 1798. Together, these resolutions outlined the *states' rights,* or *compact,* theory of the Constitution. There were several points in this theory: (1) the federal government had been created by the states; (2) the federal government was merely an agent for the states, operating under a "compact," or agreement, which had delegated to the federal government certain specific responsibilities and no more; (3) the federal government, or its agent, could be criticized by its creators, the states, if it committed unauthorized acts. And who was to determine when an act was unauthorized, or unconstitutional? Why, the states, of course.

Carried to an extreme, the states' rights, or compact, theory of the Constitution would have given the states power to declare null and void° any act of

....

° *null and void:* not legal and therefore not binding on anyone.

Congress that the states considered unconstitutional. The theory could lead to *secession*, or withdrawal, of one or more states from the Union—which, as you will see, was precisely what did happen in 1861. This interpretation of the Constitution was, of course, a complete contradiction of the views expressed by Hamilton and the Federalists, who claimed that the government had been created by the people, not by the states, and that the Supreme Court was the sole judge of the constitutionality of an act of Congress.

The Kentucky and Virginia Resolutions were sent to the other state legislatures with the hope that they might receive favorable action. In this respect Jefferson and Madison were disappointed. Federalist majorities controlled most of the state governments, and the Resolutions were "tabled"; that is, action on them was indefinitely postponed. Nevertheless, the Resolutions proved to be extremely effective political weapons. They offered the voters a choice between a strong federal government and a decentralized union in which the power held by the states would be greater than the power held by the federal union.

✔ SECTION SURVEY

1. President John Adams' effort to avoid war with France has been called "one of the most courageous acts of his career." Describe this effort, and indicate the final settlement with Napoleon.

2. (a) Why did the Federalists enact the Alien and Sedition Acts? (b) Give the provisions of these acts. (c) Give the provisions of the Naturalization Act.

3. The reaction to the Alien and Sedition Acts led to the Kentucky and Virginia Resolutions. Explain the compact theory of the Constitution which these resolutions proposed. How did this theory conflict with Federalist views of the Constitution?

IDENTIFY: XYZ Affair, "Millions for defense, but not one cent for tribute," alien, naturalized citizen, sedition, null and void; Napoleon; 1798.

6 Federalist ideas and methods persist under the Republicans

By the time President Adams' administration was drawing to a close, the Federalists had lost much of their earlier influence. Many Americans, including members of the Federalist Party, were dissatisfied with the high taxes made necessary by preparations for war. Most damaging to the Federalists, however, was the public's angry reaction to the Alien and Sedition Acts.

The election of 1800. When election year 1800 rolled around, Congressmen of both parties met in conferences, or caucuses, as they had done in 1796, to select candidates for office. The Federalists chose President John Adams to run for a second term, with Charles C. Pinckney as his running mate for the Vice-Presidency. The Republicans again chose Thomas Jefferson for President. For Vice-President they again selected Aaron Burr, who was a brilliant New York lawyer and one of the top-ranking leaders of the Republican Party.

The Republicans won the election, gaining control of the Executive Department and of both houses of Congress. In spite of their victory, however, the Republicans and the country at large faced an extremely serious situation. There were even rumors of civil war.

The problem was that Jefferson and Burr had both received the same number of electoral votes. The understanding had been that the candidate receiving the largest number of electoral votes would be President; the candidate with the second largest number of votes, Vice-President. Now there was a tie.

At first glance, this problem seemed easy to solve. The Constitution clearly stated that in the event of a tie the final decision would be made by the House of Representatives, voting by states, with the total representation from each state having a single vote. Ordinarily, the House would have given the Presidency to Jefferson, for he had been

THOMAS JEFFERSON

Thomas Jefferson (1743–1826) enjoyed a long and brilliant career. As a young man, he served in the Virginia House of Burgesses. With Samuel Adams and others, he helped to organize the Committees of Correspondence, and his opposition to Great Britain was so vigorous that he was denounced as a traitor to be hanged when caught. While serving as a member of the Continental Congress, he was responsible for writing the Declaration of Independence. He was governor of Virginia (1779–81), minister to France (1785–89), Secretary of State (1790–93), Vice-President (1797–1801), and President of the United States (1801–09).

Jefferson was a scholar as well as a statesman. He admired the writings and philosophies of ancient Greece and Rome. He was himself a brilliant writer and profound student whose work in political science, history, and the physical sciences was widely acclaimed in Europe as well as in America.

Jefferson was as much interested in practical affairs as he was in scholarship. As an architect, he designed the University of Virginia and his own lovely home, Monticello. From his friend, David Rittenhouse, the skilled clockmaker of Philadelphia, he learned the art of clockmaking. He designed folding doors, a circular filing cabinet for his music, a revolving chair, the first dumbwaiter in America, a new type of plow that was much better than any in use at that time, and many other devices.

Jefferson had great faith in the ability of the rank and file of people to govern themselves wisely. His faith in the individual and in the value of widespread education is revealed in the simple epitaph that he wrote for his own tombstone: "Here lies Thomas Jefferson, Author of the American Declaration of Independence, of the Statute of Virginia for Religious Freedom, and Father of the University of Virginia."

Jefferson's Home, Monticello

■ When Jefferson was inaugurated in 1801, only the right wing of the National Capitol had been completed. It housed the Senate, the House of Representatives, and the Supreme Court. In the background, down Capitol Hill, are the beginnings of Washington, D.C.

nominated for this position by the Republican caucus. But some of the Federalists in the House preferred Aaron Burr. Burr was a Republican, but was not as staunch in support of Republican principles as Jefferson was.

The Federalists did not have enough voting strength to win the office for Burr, but for thirty-five successive ballots they were able to prevent Jefferson from winning a majority of the votes. Finally, on February 17, 1801, when Inaugural Day was little more than two weeks away, the deadlock broke and Jefferson won on the thirty-sixth ballot.

As a result of this confusion in the election of 1800, Congress drew up the Twelfth Amendment and sent it to the states for ratification. Finally ratified in 1804, the amendment stated that electors must vote on separate ballots for President and Vice-President.

The midnight appointments. Having lost control of the executive and legislative branches of the government, the Federalists began, as soon as the elections were over, to strengthen their grasp on the judicial branch. During the four months between Election Day and Jefferson's inauguration on March 4, 1801, the Federalist majority in the old

Congress passed a new Judiciary Act. This act of 1801 increased the number of judges in the federal courts by 16.

President Adams promptly appointed Federalists to these positions. Because the President labored until late in the evening of his last day in office signing the commissions of the new judges, his appointees were given the scornful name of "midnight judges."

Adams appoints John Marshall. As it developed, the most significant of Adams' appointments—though not one of his midnight appointments—was that of John Marshall of Virginia to the position of Chief Justice of the Supreme Court of the United States. Probably no single act of President Adams' administration was more far-reaching in its consequences.

John Marshall's reputation remains to the present day one of the greatest among America's Chief Justices. A staunch Federalist, he largely dominated the other justices on the Supreme Court during the thirty-four years he served, from 1801 to 1835. In a series of more than 500 opinions that came from his mind and pen, Chief Justice Marshall helped to mold the political and economic structure of the new nation.

Marshall establishes basic principles.
During his long term as Chief Justice, John Marshall established three basic principles of American law. These three principles became foundation stones of the federal union.

(1) In the first place, Marshall stated that the Supreme Court has the power to determine when an act of Congress is unconstitutional. Although this principle—the power of judicial review—had been foreshadowed in the Judiciary Act of 1789, it was not made clear until John Marshall handed down in 1803 the first of his long series of decisions, *Marbury v. Madison*. In this decision Marshall declared that part of the Judiciary Act passed by Congress in 1789 was unconstitutional. "It is emphatically the province and duty of the judicial department to say what the law is," Marshall stated. Jefferson and those who shared his views were shocked at this interpretation of the Constitution. As Jefferson expressed it, Marshall made the Constitution "a mere thing of wax in the hands of the judiciary, which . . . [they] may twist and shape into any form they please."

In later decisions (page 257) Marshall established two other fundamental principles. He declared (2) that the Supreme Court had the power to set aside laws of state legislatures when these laws were contrary to the federal Constitution, and (3) that the Supreme Court had the power to reverse the decision of a state court.

Significance of Marshall's work. In these decisions Marshall strengthened the federal government at the expense of the states by weakening the legal basis for the states' rights, or compact, theory of government. In this way, he helped to shape the loose collection of states into a *national* union of the people.

As the years passed, and as the Supreme Court handed down its decisions, Jefferson's alarm increased. From his home in Monticello, in Virginia, he wrote these words: "The great object of my fear is the federal judiciary. That

body . . . ever acting, with noiseless foot . . . gaining ground step by step, and holding what it gains, is engulfing insidiously the special [state] governments. . . ."

Despite his fears Jefferson was powerless to alter the course of events. In decision after decision, the Supreme Court broadened the meaning of the Constitution. Owing largely to John Marshall's efforts, the federal government became increasingly powerful.

◣ **SECTION SURVEY**

1. Like the election of 1796, the Presidential election of 1800 was one of the most unusual in our history. Explain.

2. Show how the Twelfth Amendment remedied the conditions that made possible the unusual elections in 1796 and 1800.

3. Despite their many achievements the Federalists lost the election of 1800. Give three reasons why you might have voted against them in 1800.

4. Although the Federalists lost the election of 1800, their influence continued through the rulings of Chief Justice John Marshall. Discuss his three basic principles which "became foundation stones of the federal union."

IDENTIFY: "midnight judges," judicial review, *Marbury v. Madison;* 1801–35, 1803.

(For review, see Section Surveys, pages 209, 214, 217, 220, 224, 227.)

Points to Discuss: 1. Why was Washington the wisest choice for the first President?

2. In one stroke Hamilton succeeded in establishing the country on a solid financial basis, greatly strengthened the national government, and lined up the wealthy groups behind the new government. Explain.

3. (a) Contrast the fundamental differences between Hamilton and Jefferson and show how these gave rise to the first American political parties. (b) Can it be said that the contributions of both helped us to achieve balanced government? Justify your answer.

4. Compare the action of the federal government during Shays' Rebellion with its action during the Whisky Rebellion.

5. (a) Discuss the reasons for the rise and the decline of the Federalist Party. (b) What were the lasting contributions of this party to domestic and foreign policy?

6. If Washington were alive today, do you think he would approve of permanent alliances? Justify your answer.

7. (a) Evaluate the importance of the Pinckney Treaty of 1795. (b) Despite the opposition to it, what was accomplished by the Jay Treaty with Britain?

8. Show how the Twelfth Amendment resulted from the Presidential elections of 1796 and 1800.

9. Explain how the compact theory of government set forth in the Kentucky and Virginia Resolutions might be said to have foreshadowed a national problem which would be finally settled only by war.

Using Maps and Charts: 1. Using the charts on page 820, give the area of the United States in 1783. Compare the relative size of that area with the area of the United States today.

2. Using the charts on pages 824–25, indicate the approximate population of the United States in 1790 and the percentages of this population living in urban and rural areas. Compare these statistics with those of today.

3. Using the map on pages 818–19, indicate the importance of the Mississippi River to the settlers living west of the Appalachian Highlands. Indicate the connection between the dependence on the Mississippi River and the Pinckney Treaty.

4. Referring to the same map, explain why the farmers of western Pennsylvania preferred to transport whisky rather than grain to the eastern markets.

Consulting the Sources: See Commager and Nevins, *The Heritage of America*, No. 45, for an eyewitness account of the inauguration of George Washington in 1789.

■ TRACING THE MAIN IDEAS

Between 1789 and 1800 the Founding Fathers breathed life into the Constitution. During these years they organized a new government and welded the more or less independent states into a union.

Under President Washington and President John Adams the Federalists made important strides. They set the machinery of government into motion and successfully launched the United States into the current of world affairs.

These early years of life under the Constitution had been full of peril for the young nation. More than once a false step would have torn the "frail fabric" of the new republic into shreds. But when President Adams and most of the Federalist Congressmen left office on March 4, 1801, they could look with pride upon a growing nation in which the people were slowly being knit together.

Americans were still a divided people, not yet sure of themselves and of their future, but the division was more and more between national political parties. State boundaries were becoming less and less important, while the national government was steadily increasing in strength. The American nation was beginning to take form.

In the next chapter you will see how the new nation acquired a vast new territory beyond the Mississippi River, survived the strain of war, and grew in strength and unity of purpose.

The Nation Grows in Size and Power

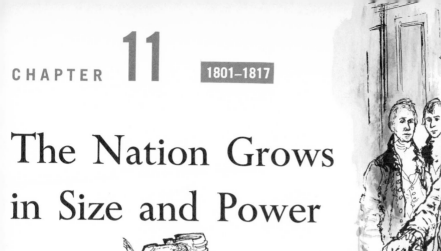

JEFFERSON INTERVIEWING LEWIS AND CLARK

ON March 4, 1801, John Adams, the outgoing President, left the "President's House" in the early morning too troubled in mind to pay Thomas Jefferson, the newly elected President, the courtesy of remaining for his inaugural ceremony. A staunch Federalist, Adams feared that the victory of Jefferson and the Republican Party meant the end of the new nation.

While Adams was jolting northward in his carriage, over the rough road that led out of Washington, D.C., Jefferson was reading his Inaugural Address in the Senate chamber of the partly finished Capitol building. In his address, Jefferson tried his best to quiet the fears of Federalists who shared with John Adams the belief that a revolution was about to sweep across the country. He pledged himself to "the honest payment of our debts" and promised to preserve "the general government in its whole constitutional vigor." The best government, he said, is "a wise and frugal government, which shall restrain men from injuring one another, shall

leave them otherwise free to regulate their own pursuits of industry and improvement, and shall not take from the mouth of labor the bread it has earned." This, he said, "is the sum of good government."

Jefferson's quiet, moderate statement pleased the Federalists. Alexander Hamilton accepted it as "a pledge . . . that the new President will not lend himself to dangerous innovations, but in essential points will tread in the steps of his predecessors."

The inauguration of Thomas Jefferson marked the beginning of a long period of Republican control. During these years the United States more than doubled in size, fought a war to protect its rights, and emerged from the war stronger than it had ever been.

AS THE STORY DEVELOPS

1. Thomas Jefferson strengthens and expands the nation.
2. The United States tries to secure the freedom of the seas.
3. Americans again fight the British in the War of 1812.

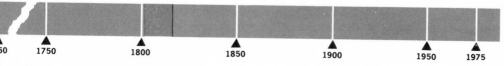

50   1750   1800   1850   1900   1950   1975

1 Thomas Jefferson strengthens and expands the nation

Thomas Jefferson's pledge that the Republicans would act with moderation did not prevent him from exercising vigorous leadership as President. Immediately upon taking office, he urged Congress to repeal a number of Federalist laws that he felt were harmful to the best interests of the country. He also did not hesitate to use the armed forces to protect American rights. And when the opportunity came to double the size of the United States, he acted quickly and efficiently, even though he was not at all sure that the Constitution gave him the power to take the action he did.

Federalist laws repealed. The Alien and Sedition Acts of 1798, which Jefferson strongly opposed, had expired before he took office. But one of them, the Naturalization Act, also passed in 1798, was still in effect, and Congress, at Jefferson's urging, promptly repealed it. Congress also repealed the excise tax on whisky, which Jefferson regarded as unconstitutional. Congress likewise repealed the Judiciary Act of 1801 so that the "midnight judges" whom President Adams had appointed on the eve of Jefferson's inauguration were not permitted to assume office.

Jefferson then turned his attention to the army and the navy, persuading Congress to cut their appropriations and to reduce them in size. He was opposed to a strong military establishment because it greatly strengthened the federal government. Moreover, by reducing the armed forces, Jefferson could operate the government more economically.

By repealing Federalist laws and reversing Federalist policies, the Republicans were in a real sense putting their own principles into practice.

Federalist programs continued. The Republican Party, however, did not wipe out all the work of the Federalists. Jefferson acted with moderation. During his administration he continued much of the Federalist program and kept many Federalists in office.

Hoping to relieve the bitterness of feeling between the Federalists and Republicans, Jefferson said in his Inaugural Address: "We are all Republicans, we are all Federalists." By his subsequent actions he proved that he meant what he said and revealed his desire to bring greater unity to the nation.

Although Jefferson had argued that the Bank of the United States was unconstitutional, he could do nothing to disturb it, for its charter ran until 1811. And even though Jefferson had also opposed Hamilton's plan to have the federal government assume the state debts, his Secretary of the Treasury, Albert Gallatin, paid off installments on the public debt as rapidly as possible.

Defending American rights. In a war with the pirates of North Africa, Jefferson actually pushed forward the Federalist ideal of a strong federal government. The Mohammedan rulers of the Barbary States of North Africa—Morocco, Algiers, Tunis, and Tripoli—had long made a habit of seizing the ships of Christian nations and holding their crews for ransom. Instead of declaring war on the pirates, the European governments had concluded that it was cheaper to secure protection by the yearly payment of tribute, or bribes. Since 1783 the United States, whose merchants traded with the Mediterranean countries, had also been paying tribute to the pirates of North Africa. But when the rulers of Algiers and Tripoli made exorbitant demands upon the United States, Jefferson decided that the time had come to fight.

War ships dispatched by Jefferson to the Mediterranean won honor for the American navy. Not even the daring exploits of John Paul Jones during the Revolutionary War were more courageous than the deed of Lieutenant Stephen Decatur. On a night in February 1804, Decatur rowed into the harbor of Tripoli with a handful of men and boarded the *Philadelphia,* an American war ship that had previously been captured by the Tripolitans (see map, this page). He and his men surprised the pirate crew, set fire to the ship, and rowed back to their own vessel through a hail of gunfire from the shore.

Americans rejoiced in this and other exploits. New heroes, shared in common by people from every section of the United States, stimulated love of the nation. And when the war ended early in 1805, Americans had won the right to sail the Mediterranean free from the payment of tribute. More than that, by crushing the power of the Mediterranean pirates, the United States performed a real service to the maritime, or seafaring, nations of Europe and raised the United States in the estimation of the rest of the world.

A nearby threat arises. While Jefferson was defending American rights against the Mediterranean pirates, the United States became involved in a far more serious conflict with France. In 1800 Napoleon, the ruler of France, secured from Spain the territory of Louisiana, which Spain had held since 1762.

In the early 1800's Louisiana was not the area that we know by that name to-

BARBARY STATES

day; it was an enormous expanse of land stretching westward from the Mississippi River to the Rocky Mountains and northward to Canada (see map, page 232). Some people believed that it included Texas. Whatever its boundaries might be, both Spain and France tried to keep the transfer of this vast area secret from the rest of the world. But rumors of the deal reached the United States Department of State.

Reasons for concern. Jefferson was alarmed. As long as the mouth of the Mississippi River had been held by a rapidly declining power such as Spain, the United States had not been especially concerned. France, on the other hand, was a mighty nation, with a steadily growing empire. French control of the Caribbean Sea and of the mouth of the Mississippi River would deprive Americans of the "right of deposit" at New Orleans and bottle up the trade of the westerners in the valleys of the Mississippi and Ohio Rivers. French possession of Louisiana would check American expansion into the interior of the continent. It would also place France, a powerful and aggressive nation, upon the western border of the United States.

Moreover, the President was interested in the western country. Unlike many Federalists, who were concerned with shipping and finance, the Republican Jefferson believed that the

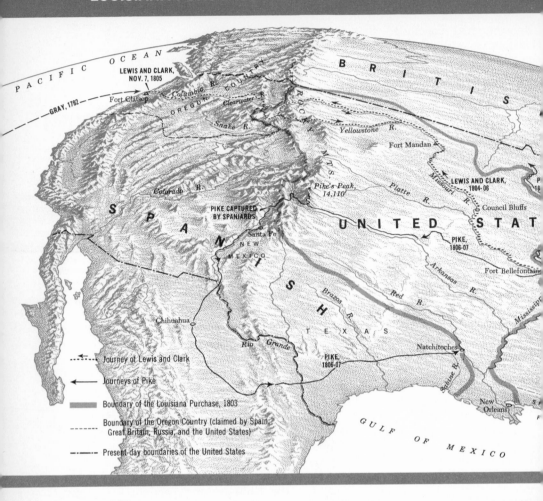

strengthening of western lands was desirable and necessary. He believed that the westerners would be loyal and contented citizens only if the federal government insured a free outlet for their goods into the Gulf of Mexico.

Jefferson warns France. Accordingly, the President wrote to Rufus King, the United States minister in England, that, if the rumors about Louisiana were true, it would be necessary to "marry ourselves to the British fleet and nation." These were strong words from a man who only a few months earlier had promised in his Inaugural Address to promote "peace, commerce, and honest friendship with all nations, entangling alliances with none." Nevertheless, to keep France from controlling the Mississippi River and the great American West, Jefferson was prepared to form an alliance with the British government.

But Jefferson did not assume that war with France was inevitable. He urged the American minister to Paris, Robert R. Livingston, to offer Napoleon as much as $10,000,000 for the land on which the city of New Orleans was located and for West Florida—an area immediately to the east of New Orleans. This would guarantee American control of the Mississippi River and provide the western farmers with an outlet for their products. To aid Livingston, Jefferson sent James Monroe to Paris.

Napoleon sells Louisiana. When the American commissioners made their offer to Napoleon's representative, there was a moment of silence. Then the Frenchman smiled. How much would you pay for *all* of Louisiana? he asked. The Americans tried to conceal their astonishment. After some discussion it was agreed that the United States would pay the equivalent of about $15,000,000 for the entire area. The transaction, probably the largest land transaction in history, was negotiated early in 1803.

Why did Napoleon sell this valuable French territory? The answer to this question is plain to see on the map on this page. Notice particularly the West Indian island of Santo Domingo. Before France could hope to take possession of Louisiana, French forces had to establish a strong naval base in the West Indies. From such a base French war ships would be in a position to dominate the South Atlantic and the Caribbean Sea. With this in mind, Napoleon had decided to reconquer Haiti, a former French colony on the western half of the island of Santo Domingo. The Haitians, led by Toussaint L'Ouverture (too-SAN loo-ver-tyur), had earlier seized the opportunity provided by the French Revolution to rise in revolt and win their independence.

Napoleon had failed in his attempt to put down the revolt and to conquer the entire island of Santo Domingo. For one thing, the Haitians had put up fierce resistance. For another, yellow fever had wiped out many of Napoleon's troops. Without control of Santo Domingo, Louisiana was useless to France. Moreover, in 1802 Napoleon was laying plans for the conquest of all Europe, which would mean, of course, a renewal of war between Great Britain and France. He knew that the British navy, once war broke out, could easily seize his overseas possessions, including those in the New World. Therefore, he decided to save what he could, and $15,000,000 was better than nothing.

Purchase despite complications. Napoleon's offer to sell Louisiana pleased Jefferson. But the offer also troubled him.

Jefferson, as you know, had always opposed giving the federal government any powers not specifically granted by the Constitution. The Constitution said nothing about the right of the government to buy territory from a foreign nation. Jefferson therefore thought that an amendment to the Constitution would be necessary before the purchase could be made. But his advisers warned him that this would take time and that while the amendment was being adopted Napoleon might change his mind. Jefferson therefore sent the treaty of purchase to the Senate for its approval, although he later admitted that he had been inconsistent and had "done an act beyond the Constitution."

In the Senate, Jefferson's political enemies, the Federalists, strongly objected to the treaty. They declared that $15,000,000 was too high a price for an empty wilderness. They frankly expressed their fear that when so large a western territory was filled with farmers, the eastern commercial interests in Congress would be outvoted. If this occurred, how could the Federalists expect to get through Congress any measures designed to help eastern commerce and finance?

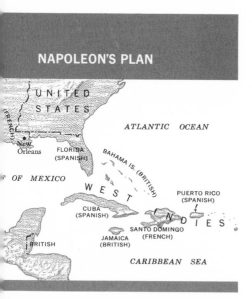

NAPOLEON'S PLAN

UNITED STATES (FRENCH)

New Orleans

FLORIDA (SPANISH)

ATLANTIC OCEAN

BAHAMA IS. (BRITISH)

OF MEXICO

WEST

PUERTO RICO (SPANISH)

CUBA (SPANISH)

INDIES

JAMAICA (BRITISH)

SANTO DOMINGO (FRENCH)

BRITISH

CARIBBEAN SEA

BEYOND
THE
MISSISSIPPI

If Catherine II, Empress of Russia, hadn't stopped him, a reckless Connecticut Yankee might have been the first American to explore the vast territory beyond the Mississippi. At least he would have been the first to die trying! John Ledyard, the Yankee, was on a business trip to Europe when he decided to return home by way of Siberia, the Pacific Ocean, and the unexplored wilderness of the North American continent. He was on his way, well into Siberia, before Catherine called a halt to his bold adventure.

As it turned out, the honor of first crossing the western half of North America fell to a U.S. Army expedition led by Meriwether Lewis and William Clark. The party of about 30 men left the Mississippi at St. Louis on May 14, 1804, and traveled up the Missouri River to its headwaters. There they hired Indian guides and horses, and journeyed 300 miles over perilous mountain trails to the headwaters of the Clearwater River. Then they built canoes by hollowing out tree trunks, and made their way down the Clearwater and the Columbia to the Pacific.

The expedition was marked by good luck as well as good management. During the first winter Lewis and Clark hired a French-Canadian fur trader and his Indian wife, Sacajawea, to serve as guides and interpreters. At the headwaters of the Missouri, the leader of the first Indians they met turned out to be Sacajawea's brother!

On September 23, 1806, the party returned to St. Louis. Only one man had died on the trip. Even Sacajawea's son, only two months old when he started, made the trip safely.

Meanwhile, other bold explorers, including Zebulon Pike, were pushing into the Southwest. These early expeditions gave Americans their first real knowledge of the country beyond the Mississippi.

To strengthen their arguments, most Federalists insisted that the Constitution did not give the federal government power to buy territory. The Federalists' arguments were as inconsistent as those of Jefferson, for the Federalists had claimed that the Constitution should be broadly interpreted and that it gave the federal government all powers not specifically denied to it.

The stand that Jefferson and the Federalists took on the Louisiana issue illustrates how ideas change as interests and situations change. Despite Federalist objections, the treaty of purchase was finally approved, and in 1803 Louisiana, or the Louisiana Purchase, became part of the United States.

Significance of the purchase. Nobody knew what the boundaries of Louisiana were or what lay within the territory. When Robert R. Livingston asked Napoleon's representative what the United States had acquired, the Frenchman is reported to have replied, "I do not know. You have made a noble bargain for yourselves, and I suppose you will make the most of it."

As the years passed, Americans realized that they had indeed made a "noble bargain." The Louisiana Purchase provided an immense area into which the growing nation could expand its western frontiers.

The purchase of Louisiana was one of the outstanding events in American history. It was a guarantee that the new nation would one day become one of the leading world powers. As Robert R. Livingston observed when the treaty was signed, "From this day the United States take their place among the powers of the first rank."

The election of 1804. During their first term in office, the Republicans had greatly strengthened their following among the voters. As a result, they entered the Presidential election confident of victory. Thomas Jefferson was reelected and, with George Clinton of New York as Vice-President, assumed the duties of the Chief Executive for a second term.

1. (a) Describe four important changes that Jefferson and the Republicans made in the Federalist program. (b) What Federalist policies were retained?

2. Why did Napoleon's acquisition of Louisiana upset Jefferson? How did Jefferson look upon the western lands?

3. What led Napoleon to decide to sell Louisiana so soon after he had acquired it? Describe the negotiations.

4. In what ways did the purchase of Louisiana seem to involve a violation of Jefferson's own principles?

5. Show how the Louisiana Purchase led Federalists and Republicans to reverse their earlier positions on loose versus strict interpretation of the Constitution.

IDENTIFY: tribute, Barbary States, entangling alliances; Gallatin, Decatur, Livingston, Toussaint L'Ouverture, Lewis and Clark, Pike; 1803.

2 The United States tries to secure the freedom of the seas

By 1803 Napoleon felt strong enough to begin his conquest of Europe. By 1807, after a series of brilliant victories, Napoleon had almost attained his goal. But he still had some formidable obstacles. To the east stood Russia. To the west, across the English Channel, stood Great Britain. British troops had been driven from the European mainland, but the British navy was powerful at sea, and Napoleon knew that Great Britain might put its troops back on European soil at any moment.

Americans profit from the war. One of Napoleon's desperate problems was that of supply. The British navy controlled the seas across which France had to bring products from its overseas possessions and from neutral countries, particularly the United States. France's position was made worse by the economic chaos that the war had created throughout Europe.

America was an important source of supply to both France and Great Britain, but especially to France. Great Britain could send its merchant fleet to any part of the world to secure imports, but France had few ships and therefore relied upon merchant vessels from the United States. American merchants and others profited handsomely from the European war. From 1789 to 1805 the tonnage, or carrying capacity, of the American merchant marine increased enormously, from a little more than 100,000 tons to nearly 1,000,000 tons. During this same period the total of American imports and exports increased four times. A large part of this trade was with France and its colonies.

Interference with America's trade. For two major reasons, Great Britain was determined to destroy America's trade with France. First, it was obvious that American goods strengthened Napoleon in his life-or-death struggle with Great Britain. Second, the expansion of the American merchant fleet threatened to make the United States a formidable competitor with British merchants and shipowners.

The British not only watched, they also acted. In a series of measures called Orders in Council, the British in 1807 forbade American vessels to enter any ports under Napoleon's control, either in Europe, the West Indies, or India.

While Great Britain was trying to shut off all trade with France, Napoleon attempted to blockade, or seal off, the British Isles. In a series of Orders, including the Berlin Decree of 1806 and the Milan Decree of 1807, he forbade all nations, the United States included, to carry on trade with the British. He further warned that he would confiscate every vessel that entered French ports after stopping at Great Britain or any of the British colonies. Moreover, he threatened to seize every ship that submitted to inspection by British cruisers or that paid duties to the British government.

For many months American merchants chose to match wits with the

GABRIEL RICHARD, FRONTIER PASTOR

Born in the south of France, trained as a Sulpician to teach in a seminary, Father Richard (1767–1832) never expected to become priest to the raw frontier area of Detroit in 1798. But persecution of the clergy in France in 1791 caused his superiors to send him to Bishop John Carroll in Baltimore. From there he went to the Illinois country and finally to Detroit.

Father Richard helped to rebuild Detroit after fire destroyed all but the military post in 1805. Afterward, by founding schools, he made himself the single force for education in the community. He also won the affection of the Indians. His loyalty to the United States kept others loyal during the War of 1812 and led to his being made a prisoner of war by the British.

In 1809 Father Richard founded the first press in Detroit. In 1817 he joined with others to found the University of Michigan. Chosen as the Territory's delegate to Congress, he was the first and only priest to sit in that body. His zeal in promoting a road from Detroit to Chicago led to Congressional authorization for it. It was a fitting end to Father Richard's apostolate that he died from cholera, contracting it from the sick he served in an epidemic. His Bishop's counsel, "To do toward the Protestants all that might draw them to the Catholic church," was the principle of his life.

French and British naval commanders by engaging in the dangerous but highly profitable practice of blockade running. The profits attracted so many merchants and seamen that in 1807 the foreign trade of the United States soared to the highest level in the nation's history. Profitable as this risky trade was to the merchants, it involved the United States in constant conflict with both the British and the French.

The Embargo Act of 1807. As Jefferson saw it, the only reasonable alternative to this defiance of Great Britain and France by American merchants was the withdrawal of all American ships from the high seas. With this in mind and with the approval of his entire cabinet, Jefferson urged Congress to vote for an *embargo*, that is, a law forbidding Americans to trade with any foreign nation, including, of course, Great Britain and France. Following this suggestion, Congress late in December 1807 voted for the Embargo Act, which forbade American vessels to leave for foreign ports.

It was apparent from the outset that the Embargo Act could not be fully enforced. Americans smuggled goods across the border to Canada. A number of merchants kept their vessels abroad, where, sailing under British or French licenses, they continued to earn large profits for their owners. Nevertheless, American trade suffered badly.

New England merchants, the first to feel the pinch, angrily demanded repeal of the Embargo Act, claiming that the measure was a deliberate scheme by which Jefferson hoped to ruin New England's commerce. Unemployed sailors and farmers, the latter unable to sell their crops to foreign buyers, joined the merchants in town meetings and adopted resolutions urging repeal. Even western farmers and farmers in other parts of the country were hard hit.

Reluctantly, Jefferson gave in to the growing demand for repeal. On March 1, 1809, three days before he left office, Congress ended the embargo by repealing the Embargo Act.

The country drifts toward war. Following the precedent started by George Washington, Jefferson refused to run for a third term. In the Presidential election of 1808, James Madison of Virginia won by a substantial vote, and George Clinton was re-elected to the Vice-Presidential office.

Madison was a quiet, scholarly man. For eight years before his election to the Presidency, Madison had served as Jefferson's Secretary of State. He shared Jefferson's views, and was determined to gain respect by peaceful means for American rights on the high seas. However, during his first administration the country moved toward war.

Madison tries diplomacy. In place of the Embargo Act, Congress in 1809 substituted the Non-Intercourse Act. Under this arrangement American merchants were not permitted to do business with Great Britain or France, although trade with other nations was allowed. But the British and French trade was precisely the trade that Americans demanded. As a result of continued pressure from the merchants, Congress in 1810 allowed the Non-Intercourse Act to expire. As far as Congress was concerned, American ships could now sail where and when they pleased. American shipowners and their captains were back once more in the dangerous business of blockade-running.

Still searching for some way to avoid trouble with Great Britain and France, President Madison on May 1, 1810, signed a new law known as Macon's Bill No. 2. The new law urged Great Britain and France, the belligerent nations, to withdraw their restrictions against American shipping, promising that when either power did this the United States would promptly refuse to trade with the other power.

Napoleon outwits Madison. President Madison was playing a dangerous game, one that might easily involve the United States in war. If the United States refused to trade with one of the warring nations, that nation would accuse Americans of taking sides against it.

The keen-witted Napoleon recognized this fact and in August 1810 announced that France was revoking all restrictions against American shipping. Madison was warned by the British government and several of his own advisers that Napoleon could not be trusted. Madison ignored these warnings and issued orders prohibiting trade with Great Britain.

Madison's policy failed, for Napoleon continued to interfere with American ships. The policy had won the United States little, if anything, from France. On the other hand, it had antagonized Great Britain.

Great Britain meets Madison's demands. War with Great Britain might have come at once, but, fortunately for the United States, the British were facing a serious economic depression. During the winter of 1811–12, the British grain crops failed, prices of food became high, trade slumped, factories closed, and men were thrown out of work.

Under pressure from British merchants, businessmen, and workers, Parliament at last decided to withdraw the Orders in Council that had interfered with American trade. Parliament suspended these orders on June 16, 1812. Great Britain's need for American trade had forced the British government to meet President Madison's demands.

SECTION SURVEY

1. In what way did the United States profit from the Napoleonic wars?

2. (a) Why did Great Britain wish to destroy American-French trade? (b) How was America caught between British and French devices to check its trade?

3. (a) Explain the purpose and terms of the Embargo Act. (b) Why was there a strong demand for its repeal?

4. Describe the Non-Intercourse Act and Macon's Bill No. 2.

5. (a) How did Napoleon mislead Madison? (b) What led Great Britain to yield to Madison?

IDENTIFY: Orders in Council, Berlin and Milan decrees, blockade-running, embargo; 1807, 1809, 1810.

3 Americans again fight the British in the War of 1812

On June 18, 1812, two days after Parliament agreed to withdraw the Orders in Council, Congress declared war on Great Britain. Why?

First, there was no Atlantic cable or radio in those days, and Americans had not yet heard of the action of the British Parliament. But the War of 1812 was not fought solely over the issue of neutral rights on the high seas. If it had been, Congressmen from the eastern states with their interests in trade would have been strongly in favor of the war, while Congressmen from other parts of the country would have been opposed to it. Actually, Congressional votes from the eastern states were divided, while the great majority of southern and western Congressmen were in favor of the war. How can this be explained? What were the underlying causes of the war?

Land hunger. Land hunger on the part of westerners was an old story. Pioneer farmers quickly exhausted the fertility of their soil and then took up the westward march in search of new lands, which they cleared, planted, and soon wore out. By 1812 they had almost reached the end of the forested areas.

The northwestern farmers did not want to move into the treeless *prairies* (see map, pages 818–19). They needed timber for houses and fences. Many of them had mistaken ideas about the great treeless acres of prairie land. Some farmers believed that the soil was poor, and all knew that the tough prairie sod would be difficult to plow. They preferred to move northward into the rich, wooded sections of lower Canada.

The farmers living in Tennessee, western Georgia, and what is now northern Alabama longed for the lands of Spanish Florida bordering the Gulf of Mexico (see map, page 243). They wanted this land not only for farming, but also because it was being used as a safe hiding place by runaway slaves and by Indians who kept attacking American settlements along the frontier. People from this section of the country, led by influential leaders like John Sevier and Felix Grundy of Tennessee, clamored for the conquest of Florida. A war with Great Britain would provide an excuse for this conquest, for Spain was virtually an ally of the British since Napoleon had invaded Spain.

National pride. The rising spirit of pride in the new nation was also a cause of the War of 1812. Americans resented impressment of American sailors and insults to the flag. Many Americans had come to believe that the United States was destined to expand until the American flag flew over the entire Western Hemisphere from the North Pole to the Strait of Magellan. At the very least, they said, Canada and Mexico and the land as far as the Pacific Ocean should belong to the United States.

American uniforms—War of 1812

ARTILLERYMAN

INFANTRYMAN

INFANTRYMAN

STAFF OFFICER

SEAMAN

NAVAL CAPTAIN

■ At the Battle of Tippecanoe, General William Henry Harrison is shown on horseback as he advances with his troops against the Indians. The artist has tried to picture the battle at the point where the Indians, after fighting bravely, finally broke and fled.

Indian troubles. The Indian problem was another reason why westerners demanded war against Great Britain. The Indians of the northwestern areas had been persuaded or forced to give up more and more of their land to the advancing white Americans. Time after time, they had been promised that this was the last land they would be forced to relinquish. And every time the promise had been broken.

Encouraged by Canadian fur traders, a great Indian leader named Tecumseh decided to make a final stand against white expansion. He began to form a confederation of Indian tribes in both the northwest and the southwest.

As the influence of Tecumseh and his brother, "the Prophet," began to spread along the frontier, westerners became alarmed. Why not seize Canada, they asked, and thus end once and for all the dangers of an alliance between the British and the Indians?

In the Congressional elections of 1810, citizens who lived in the frontier regions helped to elect several young men to Congress. Among these men were Henry Clay of Kentucky, John C. Calhoun of South Carolina, Felix Grundy of Tennessee, and Peter B. Porter of western New York. Known as

"War Hawks," these young Congressmen helped to whip up war spirit in Congress. "Is it nothing to us," demanded Henry Clay of Kentucky, "to extinguish the torch that lights up savage warfare? Is it nothing to acquire the entire fur trade connected with that country and to destroy the temptation and opportunity of violating your revenue and other lands?"

As a result of western demands, in the late autumn of 1811, General William Henry Harrison, the Governor of Indiana Territory, led American troops against Indians under the leadership of Tecumseh. These were encamped where the Tippecanoe River flows into the Wabash River (see map, page 243) in what was soon to become the state of Indiana. The Indians fought bravely, and Harrison lost many men. When he left the battlefield, he was in doubt about the outcome. But the Indians had also suffered badly, and they quickly fled northward. Harrison was somewhat surprised to discover that he had actually won the battle. Although the Battle of Tippecanoe was not a decisive victory, it helped to establish Harrison's reputation as a frontier military hero and, as you will see, paved the way for his election to the Presidency in 1840.

239

CHARLES CARROLL OF CARROLLTON

Charles Carroll of Carrollton (1737–1832) was the grandson of the first Carroll who came to Maryland in search of religious freedom. Because the Protestants had taken over the colony by the time Charles was born, there was to be little religious liberty for Catholics until the American Revolution. His early education was with other boys of Catholic families, at a school kept quietly by the Jesuits; but the Carroll family was wealthy enough to send to Europe not only Charles, but also his cousin John, who in 1790 became the first American bishop. At that time Charles could not have acquired in America his remarkable education in letters, which he received in France, and in law, derived from attending London's Inns of Court.

On returning to America, Charles accepted his rich landed inheritance, and then became active in defense of America's right to self-government. His published writings against taxation without representation brought him election in 1774 to the colony's convention for considering grievances. This event marked a great change in the situation of Catholics, who thereafter were to enjoy full political rights. As the Revolution proceeded, Charles became a member of the Continental Congress and a signer of the Declaration of Independence. Later, from 1826 to 1832, he enjoyed the distinction of being the sole survivor of this body.

Charles Carroll was probably the person most influential in drafting the first Maryland constitution. He supported ratification of the federal Constitution in 1788. Afterward, in Congress, he helped secure the location of the nation's capital on the banks of the Potomac. A great friend and admirer of George Washington, and a Federalist, he became less active after the election of Thomas Jefferson in 1800.

The war begins. There were, then, a number of reasons for the War of 1812—land hunger, national pride, Indian troubles, and the fur trade. But in his war message to Congress, President Madison chose to emphasize a different reason—the British government's refusal to allow Americans the *freedom of the seas.* Madison emphasized to Congress the seizure of American ships and the impressment of American seamen.

And so, as you know, Congress declared war on the British Empire on June 18, 1812, two days after the British Parliament had suspended the Orders in Council, President Madison's major reason for advocating the war. Many Americans, among them Henry Clay, believed that the Kentucky militia could conquer Canada in three weeks. However, the war dragged on for more than two years.

The election of 1812. In May, only a few weeks before war was declared, leaders of the Republican Party by unanimous vote nominated Madison for a second term. The Federalists nominated De Witt Clinton of New York. Although Madison won the election by a comfortable margin, Clinton carried all the New England and Middle Atlantic states, except Vermont and Pennsylvania. Moreover, the Federalists made heavy gains in the Senate and House of Representatives.

The election of 1812 clearly revealed that many Americans were opposed to the war. This feeling was especially strong in New England.

The war divides the country. Even after the conflict started, many Federalists continued to feel that it was unnecessary. The merchants realized that war with the British would drive the last remnant of their shipping from the seas. Furthermore, they looked with grave suspicion on proposals to annex Canada and Florida to the United States, for they saw clearly that additional land would greatly increase the power of the farmers. Why, the Federalist merchants asked, should we fight a war that will serve only to weaken our influence in the federal government?

Even some Republicans shared these misgivings about the war. John Randolph of Virginia, for instance, raised an issue that would haunt the halls of Congress for many years and finally lead to the War Between the States. He declared that the annexation of Canada would increase the strength of that part of the United States in which slavery did not exist and weaken the power of the southern states in the federal government. Randolph also feared that a war would so increase the powers of the federal government that the traditional rights of the states would be endangered.

Handicaps to the war effort. The opposition of the Federalists and a minority of Republicans weakened the war effort in other ways as well. Governors of New England states refused to permit the state militia to leave the boundaries of their states in order to invade Canada. When Congress debated the question of a compulsory draft law in order to provide an adequate number of men for the army, the New England Federalists denounced the measure.

Daniel Webster, a gifted young orator from Massachusetts, declared in Congress that compulsory military service was unconstitutional. "Where is it written in the Constitution?" Webster cried. "In what article is it contained that you may take children from their parents and parents from their children and compel them to fight the battles of any war in which the folly or the wickedness of the government may engage it?" Others joined Webster when he insisted that such an act was tyranny. New Englanders in general, and Federalists in particular, contemptuously referred to the War of 1812 as "Mr. Madison's War."

When the war dragged on without success and American ships were swept from the seas, New England Federalists became increasingly bitter. Finally, on December 15, 1814, a group met in secret session at Hartford, Connecticut, in what was known as the Hartford Convention, to discuss the situation and to

■ Samuel Wilson, of Troy, New York, in the War of 1812, supplied the army with provisions stamped "U.S.," meaning United States. The initials became attached to Wilson's name as "Uncle Sam." It may be that Wilson's nickname gave cartoonists their name for the figure symbolizing the United States.

formulate remedies. After some discussion they proposed a number of amendments to the Constitution. These amendments were designed to increase the influence and power of the commercial sections of the country.

Perhaps most significant of all, the delegates to the Hartford Convention proclaimed that when any minority within the country considered laws of the federal government unconstitutional, the minority had the right to declare such laws null and void. This was a restatement of the Virginia and Kentucky Resolutions (page 223). But this time the statement came from Federalists, not from Republicans. As it turned out, however, the Hartford Convention met too late to have any effect upon the war.

Although most southerners and westerners were in favor of the war, they too were divided. Southerners had their hearts set on the conquest of Florida; westerners were just as eager to conquer Canada. As a result, it was difficult for the military leaders to plan and carry out a strategy that would please even those who supported the war effort.

241

Lack of preparation. The country was not prepared for war. The navy's small fleet of a dozen ships was helpless before the more than 800 war ships of the British Royal Navy.

The army and the militia were no better situated than the navy. The army consisted of fewer than 7000 men at the outbreak of the war. Its commanders frequently were well-meaning but aged Revolutionary War veterans who proved no match for superior British commanders. Another weakness was the American failure to appoint a single commander in charge of the whole strategy and direction of the war effort. Moreover, the militia on which the Americans chiefly depended was, on the whole, poorly equipped and trained.

In both the army and the navy many American officers and men fought gallantly in the War of 1812 and made great sacrifices in blood and suffering. Nevertheless, courage and valor on the part of individuals could not compensate for lack of preparedness.

The war ends in a stalemate. The primary objective of the United States was the invasion and conquest of Canada. Despite several attempts the Americans failed to achieve this goal.

On the other hand, by securing control of Lake Erie, the Americans did succeed in preventing a Canadian force from occupying American territory for any length of time. Lake Erie was secured in 1813 through the victory of Captain Oliver H. Perry and his small naval force. His report of the victory, "We have met the enemy and they are ours," is still remembered as part of the tradition of the American navy. Equally important was the victory of Captain Thomas Macdonough on Lake Champlain, near Plattsburg, New York, in 1814. With this victory Macdonough prevented a British invasion from Canada by way of the Champlain Valley.

■ The United States entered the War of 1812 with a plan for a three-pronged drive into Canada. The three attacking forces, composed mainly of poorly trained militia, were to start their drives from Detroit (1), the Niagara area (4), and Plattsburg (7).

1812—The year 1812 brought a series of disasters for the American side. In July, General William Hull crossed the Detroit River into Canada (1). Then, fearing his lines of communication would be cut by a strong force of British and Indians, Hull withdrew from Canada and surrendered Detroit without firing a shot. Farther west, the American garrison at Fort Dearborn, where Chicago now stands, was wiped out. Later in the year, the British repulsed two feeble attacks across the Niagara River (4). And in November, a drive launched from Plattsburg (7) against Montreal ended on the Canadian border when the American militia refused to leave United States territory.

1813—The situation improved somewhat in 1813. In April a combined naval and military expedition sailed from Sackett's Harbor, raided York (now Toronto), and, contrary to orders, burned the public buildings of that city before withdrawing. Some months later, Captain Perry's naval victory on Lake Erie (2) forced the British to abandon Detroit. General William Henry Harrison pursued the retreating troops and their Indian allies, overtook them at Moravian Town on the north bank of the Thames River (3), and on October 5 won a decisive victory. With the death of their leader Tecumseh, who was killed in this battle, the Indians who had been helping the British deserted the British cause.

1814–1815—In 1814, with the defeat of Napoleon in Europe, the British were able to send strong forces to America. Before the reinforcements arrived, however, an American army under General Jacob Brown had crossed the Niagara River (4) and on July 5 had defeated the British troops in the Battle of Chippawa. A second battle, fought on July 25, near the Canadian village of Lundy's Lane, ended in a draw.

The British, in 1814, launched three campaigns. A powerful British invading force of more than 10,000 regular troops was stopped by Captain Macdonough's victory on Lake Champlain (7). A second invading force landed on the Potomac below Washington, marched into the city against only token resistance, and burned the public buildings before retiring (5). This same force was prevented from landing at Baltimore by the fierce resistance put up by the troops manning Fort McHenry—when Francis Scott Key wrote "The Star-Spangled Banner" (6). The third invading force, which landed near New Orleans (8), was decisively defeated by American troops commanded by Major General Andrew Jackson, in a battle fought two weeks after a peace treaty had been signed.

■ At the Battle of New Orleans, General Andrew Jackson directs his troops as they fire from behind fortification at the advancing British forces. Jackson's troops include frontiersmen in coonskin caps, as well as regular soldiers. British transports lie offshore.

The one outstanding American military victory of the War of 1812 was that of General Andrew Jackson at New Orleans. Jackson, born near the border between North and South Carolina, had already won fame as a vigorous Indian fighter in the Tennessee country into which he had moved. When he heard of British operations near New Orleans, he hastened to the spot. In a large-scale encounter with General Pakenham, he defeated the British. This victory did much to promote the future political fortunes of General Jackson and to give the Americans the impression that the War of 1812 ended in an American victory.

The truth is that the victory at New Orleans had little if any effect upon the outcome of the war. Negotiations for a peace treaty had been in progress between the Americans and the British at Ghent in Belgium for some time. The five American commissioners were John Quincy Adams, Henry Clay, Albert Gallatin, Jonathan Russell, and James A. Bayard. An agreement between these men and the British commissioners had been reached before the battle of New Orleans was fought. Lack of modern means of communication prevented this news from reaching New Orleans in time to stop the battle.

The Treaty of Ghent. The Treaty of Ghent, signed on Christmas Eve, 1814, did not itself settle any of the major points of conflict between the United States and Great Britain. Nothing was said about the impressment of American seamen or about neutral rights on the high seas. Neither country acquired any territory as a result of the war.

The treaty, however, did restore peace, which was by now badly wanted by both sides. It provided for the release of all prisoners of war and for the restoration of all occupied territory. It also provided for the appointment of a commission to settle certain disputes over the boundaries between the United States and Canada.

Settling disputes peaceably. The decision to create a commission to negotiate and settle the dispute over the northeast boundary had far-reaching consequences. Shortly after the war ended, the United States and Great Britain created a number of other commissions to tackle the long-standing problems of trade, furs, and fishing rights along the North Atlantic coast.

The labors of these commissions produced worthwhile results. One commission which finished its work in 1815 did away with trade discriminations, and American ships were permitted to sail to all British ports except those in the West Indies. Another commission gave Americans the right to fish along the Canadian coast and to dry their fish on Canadian shores.

The Rush-Bagot Agreement. While commissions provided for in the Treaty of Ghent were at work, the United States and Great Britain signed another treaty of even greater significance.

Immediately after the war, both the United States and Canada had begun to build war ships on the Great Lakes to defend their frontiers. Statesmen in the United States, Canada, and Great Britain felt that this was a needless expense and an invitation to trouble in the future. Because they shared this feeling, the statesmen were able to meet in the friendliest of spirits and to draft the famous Rush-Bagot Agreement. This agreement, which was approved in 1818, provided that the United States and Canada would maintain only a few small vessels for police purposes on Lake Champlain and the Great Lakes. In the same year a commission established the boundary between the United States and Canada extending from the Lake of the Woods, west of Lake Superior, to the Rocky Mountains.°

The principle of settling disputes by negotiation and of limiting armaments along the Canadian–United States border was one of the enduring products of the War of 1812. It is in large part responsible for the friendship that has characterized Canadian–United States relations during the past century and a quarter.

The war as a turning point. The creation of commissions to settle disputes by peaceful means and the adoption of the Rush-Bagot Agreement were only two of the consequences of the War of 1812. Actually, the war marked a turning point in American history.

From 1789 to 1815, events in Europe had helped to shape United States policies, especially in regard to foreign affairs. After the Treaty of Ghent, the United States became much more independent of Europe. Equally important, the nations of Europe treated with growing respect the young country that had not hesitated to go to war with the greatest naval power in the world.

Great Lakes sailing ships

In the long run, the most significant result of the war was the fact that it freed the United States from involvement in European affairs and allowed Americans to concentrate upon the job of developing their own country. After 1815 the American people as a whole turned their backs upon Europe and tackled with renewed vigor the exciting task of opening up the western lands.

⚓ SECTION SURVEY

1. Explain how each of the following led to the War of 1812: (a) land hunger, (b) national pride, (c) Indian troubles, (d) fur trade, (e) desire for freedom of the seas, and (f) impressment of American seamen.

2. Why did most Federalists and even some Republicans oppose the war?

3. What was the purpose of the Hartford Convention?

4. Explain why it can be said that the Treaty of Ghent proved that the war ended in a stalemate.

5. Explain the significance of the Rush-Bagot Agreement.

IDENTIFY: "War Hawks," "Mr. Madison's War," Webster-Ashburton Treaty; Tecumseh, "the Prophet," William Henry Harrison, Perry, Macdonough, Jackson; 1812, 1814, 1818, 1842, 1846.

° The northeastern boundary from the Atlantic Ocean to the Lake of the Woods was later settled by the Webster-Ashburton Treaty of 1842. The boundary from the Rocky Mountains to the Pacific Ocean was fixed by treaty in 1846 (see map, pages 822–23).

■ **CHAPTER SURVEY** (For review, see Section Surveys, pages 235, 237, 245.)

Points to Discuss: 1. The epitaph on Jefferson's tombstone reads: "Here lies Thomas Jefferson, Author of the American Declaration of Independence, of the Statute of Virginia for Religious Freedom, and Father of the University of Virginia." (a) In what way can each of these be considered contributions to American democracy? (b) In writing Jefferson's epitaph, which achievements would you list?

2. Summarize the important changes introduced by the Jefferson administration when it took office in 1801.

3. Show how the economic struggles between the French "tiger" and the English "shark" (1806–1812) affected America, and discuss America's policies of retaliation.

4. (a) Since both Jefferson and Madison were opposed to war, how do you account for the War of 1812? (b) The War of 1812 has been called a war for free seas and it has been called a war for free land. Support either position with adequate evidence.

5. How might the decision at the Treaty of Ghent to appoint a commission for the settlement of boundary disputes be said to be its most important provision?

Using Maps and Charts: 1. Turn to the map on page 232. (a) Compare the extent and importance of the explorations of Lewis and Clark with those of Pike. (b) How were those of Lewis and Clark of special importance to the future history of the United States?

2. Using the map on page 231 and a modern world map, indicate what countries now compose the area once ruled by the Barbary pirates.

3. Using the map on page 233, describe Napoleon's plans for North America.

4. Using the map on page 243, indicate the scenes of America's most important victories. Why were these important?

5. Referring to the charts on page 820, compare the area of the original United States with that of the Louisiana Territory. Was your state one of those carved out of this Territory?

Consulting the Sources: See Commager's *Documents,* No. 114, for Madison's war message of June 1, 1812. Compare the reasons listed by Madison for going to war with England with the causes of the war as you know them.

■ TRACING THE MAIN IDEAS

Between 1801 and 1815 the young, struggling United States doubled in size, adding the vast territory of Louisiana to its domain. The Louisiana Purchase was one of Thomas Jefferson's outstanding accomplishments as President. By 1815 the Indians had been driven from the northwestern frontier, and the way was open for the advance of pioneers into the unsettled lands of the Mississippi Valley.

During this period the United States became involved in the violent Napoleonic Wars which plunged Europe and the rest of the Western world into turmoil between 1796 and 1815. Although the United States failed to maintain for itself the freedom of the seas, and although it failed to stay out of war, it emerged from the conflict without loss of territory or national strength. The War of 1812 marked a turning point in the relations between Canada and the United States. Despite bitterness generated by armed conflict, the way was paved for the peaceable settlement of disputes in the future.

Finally, the troubles that Americans faced in this period of turmoil helped to draw them together into a united nation. They emerged from the War of 1812 with a strong feeling of unity.

In the next chapter you will see how the growing nation undertook to become economically as well as politically independent of Europe and to stand on its own feet as an equal member of the family of nations.

The Unified Nation Commands Respect

ON THE CUMBERLAND ROAD IN MARYLAND – LATER THE NATIONAL ROAD TO THE WEST

THE War of 1812 marked a turning point in American affairs. Freed at last from involvement in the affairs of Europe, Americans in 1815 were able, for the first time, to turn their full attention to the task of developing their own country.

The war itself had greatly stimulated a feeling of national pride. So strong was this feeling during the years from about 1817 to 1825, and so united were Americans in their determination to strengthen the growing nation, that this period came to be known as the "Era of Good Feelings."

As you will see, however, the term "Era of Good Feelings" was not entirely accurate. The spirit of "sectionalism" was also gaining strength as different sections of the country began to develop in different ways. The Northeast, particularly New England, was being reshaped by the Industrial Revolution. The South, primarily an agricultural region, was devoting more and more of its effort to the cultivation of cotton. The

"West," which most Americans still thought of as the land between the Appalachian Mountains and the Mississippi River, was attracting growing numbers of pioneer settlers.

The men who held positions of leadership in Washington—the President and the members of Congress—faced the problem of welding these three sections of the rapidly growing country—the Northeast, the South, and the West—into a unified whole. As you will see, they solved this problem, at least temporarily, by means of a program they called the "American System."

AS THE STORY DEVELOPS

1. **The Industrial Revolution reaches the United States.**
2. **New national leaders develop the "American System."**
3. **The growing nation faces new and complex problems.**
4. **The United States becomes a guardian of the Western Hemisphere.**
5. **American education and arts reveal national pride.**

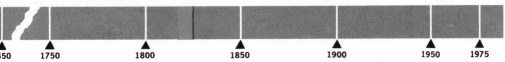

450   1750   1800   1850   1900   1950   1975

1 The Industrial Revolution reaches the United States

Samuel Slater arrives. Samuel Slater landed in New York in 1789, the year George Washington was inaugurated. Slater was one of many inventors and skilled workmen of his time whom we may call pioneers of the Industrial Revolution. By 1789 this revolution in manufacturing and industry was well under way in England. Slater, who became known as the "Father of the American Factory System," lived to see the Industrial Revolution begin to transform life in the United States.

Samuel Slater was a fugitive from England. To be sure, he was not a criminal in the sense we are apt to apply the term. As a textile worker he had violated English law by slipping out of the country without permission.

Although he was only twenty-one when he left England, Slater was al-

■ Water power had been used for many years for grinding grain, as shown here. Samuel Slater adopted the underlying principle to bring power to textile machinery.

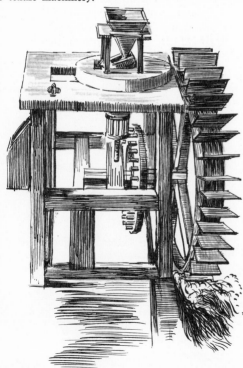

ready a highly skilled mechanic. He had worked for a number of years in a cotton textile mill. He knew as much, perhaps, as any living person about the new spinning and weaving machines that British inventors had built. What is more, he knew that British businessmen wanted to keep the secrets of these new machines from other countries. For this reason, the British government had forbidden the sale of the machines and the emigration of textile workers.

Slater arrived in New York with empty hands and almost empty pockets. But he had ideas. He knew how to build power-driven machines for spinning and weaving cloth.

Factories begin to replace home industries. Samuel Slater went to Providence, Rhode Island, and then to nearby Pawtucket. There, with the financial aid of Moses Brown, a Quaker merchant, Slater reproduced from memory the machines he had used in England. Indeed, he built even better machines.

Before long, Slater was operating a successful cotton factory in Rhode Island with water power to turn the spindles. At first the new mills did nothing more than spin thread with power-driven machines. The thread was then distributed to homes scattered over the surrounding countryside according to the so-called "putting out system." Working at hand looms in their own homes, women wove the thread into cloth, which they then returned to the mill owner. Within a few years, however, mills began to weave the cloth as well as spin the yarn, and the "putting out system" began to disappear. During the early 1800's less and less work was done in the home; more and more work was done in the new textile mills.

But the power-driven machines and the buildings to house them were too costly to be purchased by most individual craftsmen. As a result, *capitalists°* like Moses Brown built the factories, installed the machinery, purchased raw

°°
° *capitalist:* a person who invests money or other possessions in a business with the hope of earning profits.

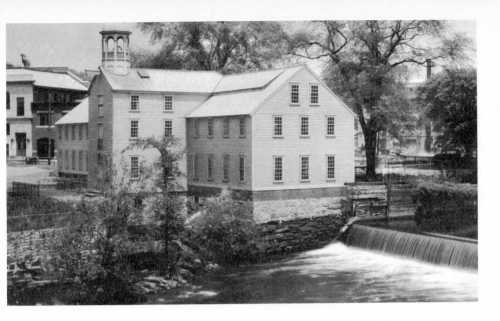

■ Samuel Slater's mill, still standing in Pawtucket, Rhode Island.

materials, hired workers, and distributed the finished products. Starting with the textile industry, the Industrial Revolution spread rapidly to the manufacturing of other products, among them firearms, clocks, and watches.

The Industrial Revolution would have come to America even if Samuel Slater had never been born. As it turned out, however, he was a pioneer in the development of the *factory system.*

The search for laborsaving machines. From the days of the earliest settlements, there was never enough manpower in either the towns or the countryside to develop the seemingly limitless natural resources of the New World. Slowly but steadily, pioneer men and women pushed westward. With so much unoccupied land available, they preferred to own their own farms rather than work as hired hands. Faced with this problem of a labor shortage, American farmers put their numerous sons and daughters to work at an early age.

The older sections of the country also faced the problem of a labor shortage. There was much more work to be done in the growing towns than there were men and women to do it. This scarcity of labor stimulated men to invent laborsaving machinery, to install it in factories and on farms, and to provide better working conditions and higher wages than in Europe.

The government encourages inventors. Under these circumstances, it was not surprising that the government took steps to encourage inventors. The first of these steps had been taken in 1790 when Congress enacted a law granting inventors, as well as authors, exclusive rights to the profits from their ideas for 14 years. This law meant that the new tool or the new machine or the new book belonged to the inventor or author and that during a period of 14 years it could be produced and sold only with his permission.°

New sources of power. Another important development in the Industrial Revolution was the discovery and application of new sources of power to run machinery. The textile machinery first used in Great Britain was driven by water power. In 1769, however, James Watt, a Scotsman, took out a patent for a successful steam engine. By the 1790's steam power was rapidly replacing water power in British mills.

• •

° Inventions can now be "patented" for 17 years. Publications can be "copyrighted" for 28 years, and the copyright may be renewed for an additional 28 years.

AMOS LAWRENCE:

Merchant, Manufacturer,

Philanthropist

Amos Lawrence was born on a farm in Groton, Massachusetts, in 1786. He was a delicate boy, too frail to help with the farm work. When he was fourteen, his father apprenticed him as a clerk to a country storekeeper. When he became twenty-one, he took his total savings of $20 and moved to Boston. There he obtained enough credit to start a drygoods store.

Amos prospered as a merchant, clearing $1500 the first year. In partnership with his younger brother, Abbott, he quickly accumulated a large fortune. In 1813, for example, the brothers made a profit of more than $40,000. After the War of 1812, Amos Lawrence, like a number of other farsighted merchants, began to invest in American manufacturing enterprises. He and Abbott pioneered in the development of New England's cotton textile industry.

From 1831 until his death in 1854, Amos Lawrence devoted his efforts to philanthropy, feeling that it was his religious duty to give generously to worthy causes. During the Irish famine of 1846–47, he took the lead in organizing a relief ship that carried food to the starving people. He assisted needy students, professors, and ministers. He gave generously to Williams College, Wabash College, Kenyon College, and Groton Academy. He helped Harvard establish a scientific school, which was later named for him.

Amos Lawrence, a self-made businessman, helped establish the American pattern of philanthropy—a pattern which has distinguished many well-to-do Americans and, indeed, Americans as a whole.

Although Americans in the 1790's knew about steam engines and were in fact building some of their own, steam power did not come so quickly to the United States as it did to Great Britain. By 1812, for instance, there were only 10 steam-powered mills in the new nation. The reason was not that Americans were uninterested in steam as a source of power, but simply that they had in their rivers and streams, especially in New England, more than enough water power to operate their first factories.

Interchangeable parts. It was Eli Whitney, a Connecticut resident, who hit upon the idea of building machines with *interchangeable parts*. Without this development, *mass production* would have been impossible.

Whitney's great discovery grew out of his work with guns. Before the early 1800's all guns were manufactured by gunsmiths who hammered out each part separately and assembled the parts by hand. When any part of a gun was damaged, a new part had to be made by hand to replace it.

In 1798 Eli Whitney decided to manufacture guns using a new principle of production. "I should like," he wrote to the Secretary of the Treasury from his home in Connecticut, "to undertake the manufacture of 10,000 or 15,000 stand of arms. I am persuaded that machinery moved by water, adapted to this business, would greatly diminish the labor and facilitate the manufacture of this article. Machines for forging, rolling, floating, boring, grinding, polishing, etc., may all be made use of to advantage."

Although Whitney's was an unusual request, he got his contract from the government, partly because Thomas Jefferson, then Vice-President, was an inventor himself. But when more than two years had passed, people began to think that Whitney's project was a failure.

Then the young inventor made a trip to Washington. Before a group of skeptical officials, he unpacked a box containing the parts of ten identical guns.

At Whitney's request an official selected one part from each of the piles scattered about the table. The first gun was then assembled. This process was repeated until all ten guns had been assembled and fired. Those present at the demonstration witnessed what actually was the beginning of mass production.

A look ahead. Not even the most farsighted of these Americans ever dreamed that the developments that he saw taking place were only the first steps in a revolution that was destined to change life everywhere.

In years to come, the Industrial Revolution would help to unite the American people. It would help to solve the problem of transportation by binding the nation together with a web of steel rails. It would help to solve the labor shortage, providing Americans with labor-saving devices beyond the wildest imaginations of men living in the opening years of the nation's history. It would help Americans to conquer the wilderness, to make use of the rich resources of forest and sea and soil, and to transform the United States into the wealthiest country on the face of the earth. The Industrial Revolution would, through the work of the scientists and the engineers who fathered it and nourished it with their ideas, help people to conquer disease, to solve many of the problems of community life, and to build a better way of life.

SECTION SURVEY

1. Why is Samuel Slater considered "a pioneer in the development of the factory system" in the United States?

2. What conditions led to the growth of the Industrial Revolution in our country during the early 1800's?

3. How did our government try to encourage inventors?

4. Describe Eli Whitney's contributions to our industrial development.

5. List four ways in which the Industrial Revolution has influenced the history of our country.

IDENTIFY: capitalist, patent, interchangeable parts; Moses Brown.

2 New national leaders develop the "American System"

The men who tackled the job of running the new nation in the years following the War of 1812 were, for the most part, new on the national scene. The older men who had led the American people through the Revolutionary War and the opening years of the nation's history were passing from the scene.

The famous three. Three of the new leaders who were replacing the older statesmen were particularly outstanding. They were destined to play prominent roles in the nation's history during the next thirty-five years. Each came from a different section of the country.

Henry Clay, a Republican of Kentucky, entered Congress in 1811. It was Clay and his youthful colleagues who had clamored for war with Great Britain in 1812 and who, as you know, were sometimes called "War Hawks." Trained in the law and striking in appearance, Henry Clay became an impressive orator and the acknowledged spokesman for the western parts of the country.

John C. Calhoun of South Carolina also entered Congress in 1811. He, too, was a lawyer, a persuasive speaker, and a Republican. Like Clay, he had also favored the War of 1812. With his keen mind and his devotion to politics, Calhoun began his career as a spokesman for the nation at large, but soon became the major spokesman for the southern part of the country and for the doctrine of states' rights.

Daniel Webster of Massachusetts entered Congress in 1813. He was born on a farm in New Hampshire. Like Clay and Calhoun, Webster became a lawyer, practicing first in New Hampshire and later in Boston, Massachusetts. Like Clay and Calhoun, Webster was a powerful speaker. In Congress, which he entered as a Representative of the Federalist Party, he quickly became the outstanding spokesman for the northeastern part of the country. At first Webster

■ These three men had a profound influence on their times. Daniel Webster (left) became a spokesman for northern interests. John C. Calhoun (right) became a champion of southern interests. Time and again, Henry Clay (center) found compromises between their interests.

worked for low tariffs. But as industrial interests in the Northeast replaced shipping interests, he became a defender of high protective tariffs.

The elections of 1816 and 1820. It was one of the older statesmen, however, who won the Presidential election of 1816. James Monroe, Republican, who had served as Secretary of State under President Madison, easily defeated the Federalist candidate, Rufus King, winning the election by a vote of 183 to 34 in the Electoral College. King, a brilliant and able Senator from New York, represented a dying party. By 1816 the Federalists were so weakened that they won only three states—Massachusetts, Connecticut, and Delaware. When President Monroe toured New England after his inauguration in 1817, even a Boston publication, the *Columbian Centinel*, said that the times would prove to be an "Era of Good Feelings."

This phrase pleased the new President, and, as the years passed, it did seem to describe the life of the nation. The different groups in the country began to work together on common problems. The Federalist Party disappeared, and for more than ten years there was only one political party in the United States, the Republican Party, originally founded by Thomas Jefferson.

By 1820 the political harmony was so widespread, at least on the surface, that President Monroe actually ran for reelection without any opposition. When the electoral votes were counted, he received all but one—and the elector from New Hampshire who cast the single negative vote did so only because he felt that the extraordinary honor of a unanimous election should remain with George Washington.

The American System. In 1816, even before President Monroe was elected for the first time, the Republicans took a number of steps to strengthen the growing nation. In so doing they did not hesitate to increase the powers of the federal government at the expense of states' rights. To justify their actions, they used a "loose" interpretation of the Constitution, like the one favored earlier by Alexander Hamilton and the Federalists. This was one reason for the disappearance of the Federalist Party. By 1816 the Republicans were doing many things the Federalists had been advocating for years.

Nationally minded statesmen, like Henry Clay of Kentucky, insisted that

252

the nation could be strengthened only by developing a sound economic program that would enable the United States to become independent of the rest of the world. The economic program that the Republicans adopted in 1816 came to be called the *American System*, a term later used by Henry Clay in a speech in Congress.

In his speech, Clay included in the American System only a protective tariff and improved transportation. Actually, the economic program the Republicans developed rested on three major foundations: (1) a national bank to provide a sound, uniform financial system; (2) a protective tariff to provide a wall behind which American factories could grow and prosper; and (3) a transportation system to bring the northeastern manufacturers and the western and southern farmers together for their mutual advantage.

The second Bank of the United States. To help promote the economic well-being of the nation, the Republicans borrowed from the Federalists the idea of a national bank. Congress approved this idea and in 1816 granted a charter to the second Bank of the United States.

In order to understand why the Republicans took this action, we must go back to the year 1811. In that year the charter of the first Bank of the United States expired. State legislatures, especially those in the western areas of the country, immediately granted new charters permitting private individuals to organize and operate banks.

Between 1811 and 1816 the number of banks chartered by the states nearly tripled. In many cases, these state banks were subject to only a limited amount of regulation. Under the circumstances, it was not surprising that some of the banks issued far more paper money than they could back up with gold or silver. And inevitably the value of this paper money declined. As a result, the Treasury of the United States found itself accepting for taxes a growing amount of almost worthless bank notes.

It was this unhealthy financial situation that caused the Republicans to recall Alexander Hamilton's Federalist belief that a national bank was essential to the economic well-being of the nation.

The protective tariff of 1816. With the enactment of a protective tariff in 1816, the Republicans adopted another of Hamilton's basic ideas and made it part of the American System. During the first decade of the 1800's, and even more during the war years from 1812 to 1815, Americans had found it difficult to get manufactured goods from Europe. As a result, new factories had sprung up on American soil. But when the War of 1812 ended, British manufacturers naturally were eager to drive their American competitors out of business.

The ink was hardly dry on the Treaty of Ghent before British vessels began to arrive in American ports to unload their cargoes of factory-made goods. The British manufacturers were resorting to a practice known to businessmen as "dumping"—that is, they were selling large quantities of their goods below cost in order to drive rival manufacturers out of business. Once American factories closed, the British manufacturers would raise the price of their products and recover their earlier losses, knowing that they would have little competition from the ruined Americans.

The owners of American factories had no intention of being driven out of business. They demanded protection against their British rivals. As a result, Congress adopted the Tariff Act of 1816, which levied high duties on manufactured goods shipped into the United States. The new tariff was designed to protect the so-called *infant industries*.

In 1816 most Americans favored the protective tariff. Even Thomas Jefferson believed it was desirable. John C. Calhoun of South Carolina, later to become an arch foe of tariffs, supported the Tariff Act of 1816 on the assumption that the South would develop industries of its own. In protecting its infant industries, the young nation was looking forward to becoming self-sufficient and economically independent of England.

What evidence can you give to explain why the period from about 1817 to 1825 is known as the "Era of Good Feelings"?

2. Explain the financial conditions that led to the chartering of the second Bank of the United States.

3. Discuss the reasons for the Tariff Act of 1816.

IDENTIFY: American System, "dumping," infant industries; Clay, Calhoun, Webster, Monroe; 1816.

3 The growing nation faces new and complex problems

The new nation was growing by leaps and bounds. Soon after the Constitution went into effect, four new states were added to the original thirteen—Vermont (1791), Kentucky (1792), Tennessee (1796), and Ohio (1803). Between 1810 and 1820 the population west of the mountains more than doubled, from about one million to more than two million, and five new states entered the Union—Louisiana (1812), Indiana (1816), Mississippi (1817), Illinois (1818), and Alabama (1819).

Demand for better transportation. Until shortly after the War of 1812 ended, the western settlers had to depend almost entirely upon the rivers or upon very poor roads for transportation. They shipped their surplus produce in flatboats or on rafts down the Ohio and other rivers into the Mississippi and down the Mississippi to New Orleans.

But it was almost impossible to use flatboats or rafts to transport manufactured goods upriver, and keelboats, which were invented for this purpose, were laborious and slow. As a result, most manufactured products from the eastern parts of the country reached the western areas by means of rough roads across the mountains. Transporting goods by wagon over these roads was costly and time-consuming.

The solution to this problem was an improved system of roads and the building of canals. Indeed, it became increasingly evident that a good transportation system was as essential to the new nation as a good Constitution and a strong federal government. Westerners needed roads and canals to carry their products to eastern markets. Northeastern manufacturers needed roads and canals to move their manufactured goods into the sparsely settled areas of the country. And southerners were also interested in having something done. As John C. Calhoun of South Carolina put it, "We are greatly and rapidly—I was about to say fearfully—growing. This is our pride and our danger, our weakness and our strength. . . . Let us, then, bind the republic together with a perfect system of roads and canals."

First steps by private enterprise. The need for better transportation had been apparent for many years. In 1785, even before the Constitution was adopted, George Washington had helped to organize a company to build a canal around the Great Falls of the Potomac River, near the present site of Washington, and extending into the western areas of Maryland (see map, page 289).

During the 1790's and early 1800's businessmen throughout the country organized other companies to build roads and canals. The first important road project, begun in 1791, was the building of the Lancaster Turnpike between Philadelphia and Lancaster, Pennsylvania. Soon roads were being constructed in other states. By 1811 New York, for example, had granted 137 charters to private companies, and businessmen had built more than 1400 miles of improved toll roads° in New York state alone.

Nearly all of the new roads and canals built by the early 1800's started in the coastal cities—Boston, New York, Philadelphia, Baltimore, Charleston—and ran into the surrounding country.

°°°

° *toll road:* a road on which a toll, or fee, is collected from users to meet the costs of maintenance or construction. Also called a *turnpike.*

The roads and canals made it possible for farmers living in the surrounding areas to transport their produce to market and to secure manufactured goods from the eastern factories.

The new roads and canals financed by private companies during the late 1700's and early 1800's helped to meet the demand for improved transportation in the coastal areas. But the improved roads and canals did not run into the sparsely settled regions in the western parts of the seaboard states, and not one penetrated the Appalachian Mountains. Men who had money to invest were not willing to gamble on the possible returns from a transportation system reaching into thinly populated areas.

"Internal improvements" at public expense. Such was the situation that prompted a growing number of citizens to demand that the federal government finance and construct the needed highways and canals. During President Jefferson's administration Albert Gallatin, Secretary of the Treasury, actually recommended a sweeping plan whereby the federal government would construct a network of highways covering the entire United States. Congress did not adopt Gallatin's ambitious proposal. It did, however, appropriate money in 1806 for the construction of a road to be built from Cumberland, Maryland, across the mountains into what is now West Virginia.

Construction was begun in 1811. Within a few years this road, which came to be called the Cumberland Road or the National Road, was pushed westward from Cumberland as far as Ohio. (Later, between 1822 and 1838, Congress made several additional grants of money, as a result of which the National Road was extended across Ohio and Indiana to Vandalia, Illinois—see map, page 289. As each section was finished the federal government turned it over to the states through which it ran.) Thousands of men and women poured into the western country over the National Road, particularly after the War of 1812.

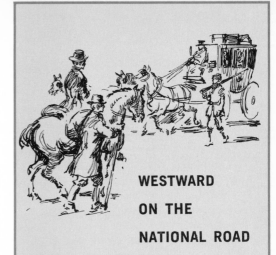

WESTWARD ON THE NATIONAL ROAD

In the spring of 1817, Morris Birkbeck, an Englishman, started westward on the National Road. The stagecoach on which he and several other passengers were traveling went only as far as McConnel's Town, Pennsylvania.

"So here we are," he wrote in his journal, "nine in number, one hundred and thirty miles of mountain country between us and Pittsburgh. We learn that the stages which pass daily from Philadelphia and Baltimore are generally full and that there are now many persons at Baltimore waiting for places. No vehicles of any kind are to be hired, and here we must either stay or *walk* off. The latter we prefer, and separating each our bundle from the little that we have of traveling stores, we are about to undertake our mountain pilgrimage—accepting the alternative most cheerfully after the dreadful shaking of the last hundred miles by stage. . . .

"Old America seems to be breaking up and moving westward. We are seldom out of sight, as we travel on this grand track towards the Ohio, of family groups, behind and before us. . . .

"To give an idea of the internal movements of this vast hive, about twelve thousand wagons passed between Baltimore and Philadelphia in the last year. . . . Add to these the numerous stages, loaded to the utmost, and the innumerable travelers on horseback, on foot, and in light wagons, and you have before you a scene of bustle and business, extending over a space of three hundred miles, which is truly wonderful."

In 1816, with the National Road progressing westward, John C. Calhoun introduced in Congress the so-called Bonus Bill° asking for additional *internal improvements* at federal expense. Calhoun's plan was approved by Congress early in 1817. But President Madison objected. Before leaving office he vetoed the Bonus Bill, not because he disapproved of internal improvements, but because he felt that the Constitution did not give Congress the power to spend money in this way. President Monroe shared Madison's convictions, and Congress' plans for further internal improvements at public expense collapsed.

Even so, the economic program adopted by Congress during Madison's administration had accomplished a great deal. It had given financiers and people in general a national bank that provided them with a reasonably sound currency. It had given the manufacturers a protective tariff. It had helped to open up the

∙∙

° *Bonus Bill:* Calhoun's plan was called the Bonus Bill because it recommended that internal improvements be financed by using the $1,500,000 bonus that the second Bank of the United States was to pay for its charter, as well as all future dividends the government would receive from the Bank stock it owned.

western areas by pushing the National Road farther westward. In general, it had strengthened the different sections and drawn them closer together.

The Panic of 1819. By 1818 all sections of the country were enjoying a large measure of prosperity. Conditions were so prosperous, in fact, that various groups began to indulge in *overspeculation.°* Southerners, tempted by rising prices for cotton, were buying land at exorbitant prices. Settlers in the western areas, tempted by rising prices for grain and meat, were also scrambling to buy land. Manufacturers in the northeastern states, eager to take advantage of the general prosperity, were building new plants and factories.

All of these groups were borrowing money to finance their enterprises. And the banks, instead of making it difficult to borrow money, actually encouraged the frenzy of speculation by lending money too freely on the flimsiest of security. For a time even the directors of the Bank of the United States failed to apply brakes to the increasingly serious

∙∙

° *overspeculation:* excessive, risky investment in land, commodities, stocks, and the like, with the hope of earning large profits.

■ The Conestoga wagon, originally developed in Pennsylvania in the early 1700's, came into wide use as the road system of the nation was improved. Thousands of these wagons carried freight over the National Road and other roads. This photograph was taken about 1890.

overspeculation and inflation.

Then the crash came. Late in 1818 the directors of the Bank of the United States ordered all their branch banks not to renew any personal mortgages. In addition the directors ordered the branch banks to present all state bank notes to the state banks for immediate payment in gold or silver or in national bank notes. State banks, unable to meet their obligations, closed their doors. Farmers and manufacturers, unable to renew their mortgages, lost their property.

By the middle of 1819, the Bank of the United States had acquired by foreclosure huge areas of land in the South and West and large numbers of business enterprises in the East. People ruined by foreclosure turned against the bank, blaming it for their troubles, and calling it "The Monster."

The Supreme Court strengthens the federal government. In the midst of the financial panic and the bitter denunciation of the Bank of the United States, Chief Justice Marshall of the Supreme Court handed down one of his most significant decisions in the case of *McCulloch v. Maryland*. The state legislature of Maryland had levied a heavy tax upon the bank notes of all banks in Maryland that had not been chartered by the state legislature. This tax fell, of course, upon the Baltimore branch of the Bank of the United States. When the bank refused to pay the tax, the case went first to the state Court of Appeals and finally to the Supreme Court.

Three major issues were involved: (1) Does the federal government or do the states have the sovereign power? (2) Does the Constitution give Congress power to create a national bank? (3) If Congress does have this power, does the state have the right to tax the bank?

In 1819 Marshall decided all these issues in favor of the federal government. In reference to the first point, he declared: "The government of the Union, then . . . is emphatically and truly a government of the people"—that is, a government created by the people, not the states, and whose power is supreme.

In reference to the second point, Marshall admitted that Congress had only limited powers. But, he went on to say, "Let the end be legitimate, let it be within the scope of the Constitution, and all means which are appropriate, which are plainly adapted to that end, which are not prohibited, but consist with the letter and spirit of the Constitution, are constitutional." Since Congress had the power to levy and collect taxes and to borrow money, it followed, according to Marshall, that Congress also had the right to create a national bank to carry out these financial powers.

In reference to the third point, Marshall declared that "the power to tax involves the power to destroy" and that no state had the power to destroy a national institution. It followed that Maryland, or any other state, had no right to tax the Bank of the United States.

Marshall's continuing influence. In 1819, the same year that John Marshall handed down his famous decision in the case of *McCulloch v. Maryland,* he wrote another decision of far-reaching consequences. In the case of *Trustees of Dartmouth College v. Woodward,* Marshall set aside an act of the New Hampshire legislature. The original charter under which Dartmouth College operated had been granted by George III in 1769. In 1815 the New Hampshire legislature drafted a law altering this charter. The trustees claimed that the new law was unconstitutional. When the case came before the Supreme Court, John Marshall supported the trustees. In his argument Marshall pointed out that a charter was a valid contract guaranteed by the Constitution and that no state had the power to interfere with such a contract.

This decision was important for two reasons. First, it asserted the right of the Supreme Court to set aside state laws when such laws were contrary to the Constitution. Second, it guaranteed that corporations operating under state charters would not be subjected to the whims of state legislators. For this reason, the Dartmouth College Case is sometimes referred to as the "Magna Carta" of the corporation.

Five years later, in 1824, in the case of *Gibbons v. Ogden,* Marshall declared another state law unconstitutional. The case involved an attempt by the New York legislature to give Robert Fulton and his business associates a monopoly over all steamboat traffic on the Hudson River. Marshall argued that the power to regulate interstate commerce had been granted by the Constitution to the federal government. Since navigation on the Hudson River involved interstate commerce, the monopoly granted by the state legislature was unconstitutional.

In the course of his argument, Marshall greatly broadened the definition of interstate commerce. As a result, his decision in 1824 paved the way for later federal control of such "interstate commerce" as telegraph, telephone, radio, and television, as well as kidnaping and the theft of automobiles, provided that the criminals crossed state lines.

In these and other decisions John Marshall did much to strengthen the powers of the federal government. And so, while Congress through the American System was seeking to build a stronger and more unified nation, John Marshall on the Supreme Court bench was moving toward the same end.

Rifts in the spirit of unity. As you will see later, however, bitterness growing out of the Panic of 1819 and directed especially against "The Monster," the Bank of the United States, helped to bring about upheavals that by 1829 put Andrew Jackson, representative of the frontier areas of the country, into the White House. And, as you will also see later, differences over the question of slavery and the admission of Missouri into the Union hung like a dark cloud over the nation even during the "Era of Good Feelings."

The Jacksonian upheavals and the issue concerning Missouri are discussed in later chapters. It is necessary now to see how the United States, through the Monroe Doctrine, asserted its growing power in foreign affairs.

✒ **SECTION SURVEY**

1. "A good transportation system was as essential to the new nation as a good Constitution and a strong federal government." Do you agree? Give reasons to support your opinion.

2. Why did Calhoun's plan for internal improvements at public expense fail?

3. Explain the causes of the Panic of 1819.

4. (a) What three issues were involved in the case of *McCulloch v. Maryland?* (b) How did John Marshall treat each issue? (c) Why was his decision significant?

5. How did Marshall's decisions in the Dartmouth College Case and in *Gibbons v. Ogden* help to strengthen the federal government?

IDENTIFY: toll road (turnpike), Cumberland (National) Road, Bonus Bill, overspeculation; 1819, 1824.

4 The United States becomes a guardian of the Western Hemisphere

After the War of 1812, as you have seen, the growing spirit of national pride and the growing fact of national power began to have a strong influence on developments within the United States. These new feelings of pride and strength also influenced foreign policy.

At this time the Spanish- and Portuguese-speaking peoples south of the United States, called Latin Americans, were struggling to win their independence from Spain and Portugal. Remembering their own recent struggle for independence in the Revolutionary War, many American citizens sympathized with the struggles for independence going on in these areas. As for actual foreign policy, the United States government began taking steps to secure Florida from Spain and to prevent European countries from expanding their influence anywhere in the New World.

Revolution in Latin America. In the early 1800's, as you know, Napoleon was trying to secure mastery over all of Europe. In 1808 he conquered Spain. This

258

was the signal for Latin Americans to rise in revolt.

The enormous South American continent is broken into fragments by mighty mountain barriers, such as the Andes, and by impenetrable rain forests, such as those of the Amazon River Valley. As a result, the Latin-American struggle for independence took place in a number of separate revolutions (see map, page 261).

The Latin-American armies, separated though they were, all fought for essentially the same objectives: freedom and independence. In South America they were ably commanded by men like Francisco Miranda; Simón Bolívar (see-MON bo-LEE-vahr), "the George Washington of South America"; Bernardo O'Higgins; and José de San Martín (ho-SEH deh sahn mahr-TEEN). In Mexico, including the southwestern borderlands of what is now the United States, the leaders were Miguel Hidalgo (me-GEL e-DAHL-go), José María Morelos (ho-SEH mah-REE-ah mo-REH-lohs), and, later, Augustín de Iturbide (ah-goos-TEEN deh e-toor-BEE-deh).

By 1822 the American continents were almost free of foreign control. Russia still claimed the vast unexplored territory of Alaska. Great Britain still ruled Canada, British Honduras, British Guiana (gee-AHN-uh), and a number of West Indian islands. Spain still ruled Cuba and Puerto Rico. France and the Netherlands still ruled French and Dutch Guiana and several of the islands in the Caribbean. But Europeans were on their way out. The growing forces of democracy and the drive toward national independence were remaking the map.

The United States wins Florida. The revolutions in Mexico and other Latin-American countries were of immediate concern to the United States. Many citizens of the United States viewed the struggle of their Latin-American neighbors as a continuation of their own earlier struggle for independence. Some of them supplied the revolutionists with arms and munitions in spite of repeated Spanish and Portuguese protests. Other

CANADA WINS SELF-GOVERNMENT

Like the other people of the Americas, Canadians had a growing desire to be free from the tight bonds that held them to the mother country—in their case, Great Britain. This spirit of Canadian nationalism was stimulated by the War of 1812. It continued to grow, reaching a climax in 1837 when a group of French Canadians, led by Louis Joseph Papineau, and a group of English-speaking Canadians, led by William Lyon Mackenzie, took up arms in efforts to obtain more self-government than the British were willing to grant.

With memories of the American Revolution in mind, the British government sent a commission to investigate the cause of the unrest. Led by the Earl of Durham, the commission arrived in 1838, studied the problem, and reported its findings. It recommended an immediate union of French-speaking Lower Canada (now Quebec) and English-speaking Upper Canada (now Ontario). Lord Durham also recommended the ultimate union of all the Canadian provinces and a grant of self-government. The first of these recommendations was adopted, and in 1840 an Act of Union joined Upper and Lower Canada under one Parliament. In 1849 the new union was given the right to control its own domestic affairs.

The Parliament of the new union of Upper and Lower Canada was in continual difficulty, however, largely because it was composed of about equal numbers of French Canadians from Quebec and English Canadians from Ontario. Many Englishmen and Canadians believed that only a union of all the Canadian provinces would solve the problem. After extended conferences, the federal union of Canada was born by act of the British Parliament on July 1, 1867. Thus, Canada became the first self-governing dominion in the world-wide British Empire.

citizens of the United States saw in the conflicts an opportunity to settle long-standing border disputes with Spain and to secure additional territory for the United States.

The American government officially took a position of neutrality in the conflicts between Spain and Portugal, on the one hand, and their colonies, on the other. However, between 1810 and 1813 the United States annexed the territory known as West Florida (see map, pages 822–23). The Spaniards protested, but they were powerless to act.

A few years later, in 1818, Andrew Jackson and an American military force, hotly pursuing a group of marauding Seminole Indians, invaded East Florida, seized the Spanish forts of Pensacola and St. Marks, and hanged two British subjects accused of furnishing military supplies to the Indians. Once again the Spanish, deeply involved in the attempt to regain control of their former colonies in Latin America, were powerless to act. But Jackson's invasion convinced Spain that the United States would not rest until all of Florida was under the Stars and Stripes. Spain wisely decided to sell while it still held the territory.

After a period of negotiations, the two countries signed the Adams-Onés Treaty in 1819, giving the United States all the land east of the Mississippi River, together with any claims that Spain might have to the Oregon country (see map, pages 822–23). In return the United States agreed to assume claims totaling $5,000,000 that American citizens held against Spain for damages to American shipping during the Napoleonic Wars. More important in the long run was the agreement by the United States to abandon its claim to Texas as part of the Louisiana Purchase.°

Great Britain favors the revolutions. Great Britain favored the revolutionists

••

° The southwestern boundary of the United States at this time was placed along the Sabine River, from its headwaters north and west to the 42nd parallel, and along the 42nd parallel to the Pacific (see map, pages 822–23).

of Latin America. The British did not want land, but, like the United States, they were looking forward to increasingly profitable trade with a Latin America no longer tied economically to Spain and Portugal. They were determined to retain the trade of Latin America, which, since the beginning of the revolutions against Spain, had been carried largely in British ships. If the Spanish colonies were restored to Spain, the Spanish mercantile system would be re-established, and the Spanish-American trade would again move overseas to Spain in Spanish ships.

Europe interferes in the Americas. Other nations did not join the British and the Americans in their support of the revolutions in Latin America. Until 1815, when Napoleon was finally defeated at the Battle of Waterloo, the nations of Europe were too occupied with their own problems to take an active part in the affairs of Latin America. With the fall of Napoleon and the breakup of his once mighty empire, however, Russia, Prussia, and Austria formed the Holy Alliance, with the avowed purpose of crushing revolutions.

As long as the Holy Alliance confined its activities to the Old World, it aroused no concern in the United States. But when, strengthened by the addition of France, the Holy Alliance announced its intention of restoring the former Spanish colonies to Spain, Americans became concerned.

To make matters worse, the tsar of Russia in 1821 issued an order warning the vessels of other nations to avoid the Pacific coast from Alaska southward to the 51st parallel. This order barred American vessels from the Oregon coast, which the United States claimed jointly with Great Britain. The Oregon country was already a useful port of call for Yankee traders, who gave trinkets to the Indians in exchange for furs from which big profits were made in China and elsewhere (see page 296). For this reason, the American government could not permit the tsar's order

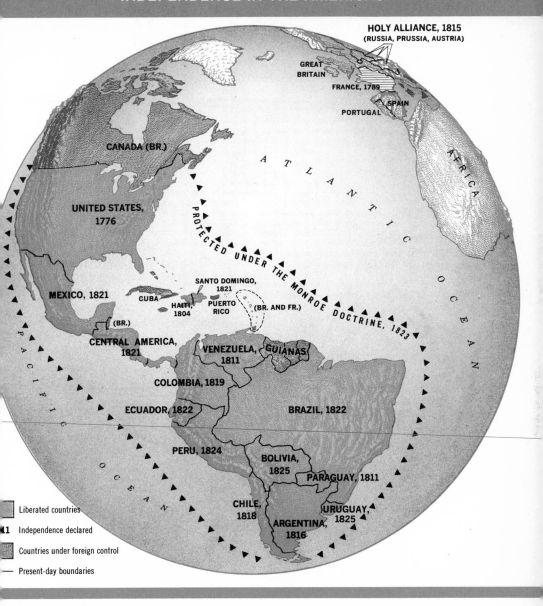

HOLY ALLIANCE, 1815
(RUSSIA, PRUSSIA, AUSTRIA)

GREAT
BRITAIN

FRANCE, 1789

SPAIN

PORTUGAL

CANADA (BR.)

A T L A N T I C   O C E A N

AFRICA

UNITED STATES,
1776

PROTECTED UNDER THE MONROE DOCTRINE, 1823

MEXICO, 1821

CUBA

SANTO DOMINGO,
1821

HAITI,
1804

PUERTO
RICO

(BR. AND FR.)

(BR.)

CENTRAL AMERICA,
1821

VENEZUELA,
1811

GUIANAS

COLOMBIA, 1819

ECUADOR, 1822

BRAZIL, 1822

PERU, 1824

BOLIVIA,
1825

PARAGUAY, 1811

P A C I F I C   O C E A N

CHILE,
1818

URUGUAY,
1825

ARGENTINA,
1816

Liberated countries

Independence declared

Countries under foreign control

Present-day boundaries

to go unchallenged. The United States had to take some action in response to the Russian decree and the intentions of the Holy Alliance in Latin America.

America's reply: the Monroe Doctrine. The United States met the challenge by three specific actions. First, the government addressed a strong note of protest to Russia, bluntly asserting American rights to sail the Pacific waters. Second, the United States recognized the independence of the revolutionary governments of Latin America. Third, President Monroe, in his annual message to Congress delivered on December 2, 1823, announced an American foreign policy that came to be known as the Monroe Doctrine.

The Monroe Doctrine (1823): EXCERPT

The American continents ... are henceforth not to be considered as subjects for future colonization by any European powers ... We owe it, therefore, to candor and to the amicable relations existing between the United States and those powers [Holy Alliance] to declare that we should consider any attempt on their part to extend their system to any portion of this hemisphere as dangerous to our peace and safety. With the existing colonies and dependencies of any European power we have not interfered and shall not interfere. But with the governments who have declared their independence and maintained it, and whose independence we have ... acknowledged, we could not view any interposition for the purpose of oppressing them, or controlling in any other manner their destiny, by any European power in any other light than as the manifestation of an unfriendly disposition toward the United States ...

Our policy in regard to Europe, which was adopted at an early stage of the wars which have so long agitated that quarter of the globe, nevertheless remains the same, which is, not to interfere in the internal concerns of any of its powers ...

In this famous message President Monroe made four clear declarations: (1) The Western Hemisphere was no longer open to colonization by European powers. (2) Any attempt by any European country to establish colonies in the New World or to gain political control of any American country would be viewed "as the manifestation of an unfriendly disposition toward the United States." (3) The United States would not meddle in European affairs or in the affairs of American colonies already established. (4) In return, Europe must not in any way disturb the political status of any free American country.

Enforcing the Doctrine. With the Monroe Doctrine the United States proclaimed a policy of "America for Americans." The important question, of course, was whether the United States could enforce the Monroe Doctrine.

Fortunately, the Americans were supported by the Latin Americans to the south, as well as by Great Britain. Although the Latin Americans recognized that the United States was acting in its own self-interest, they realized that the Monroe Doctrine practically guaranteed their independence from Europe.

But it was Great Britain, and more specifically the British navy, that gave the Doctrine its real strength. In 1823 and, in fact, until well into the 1900's, the British fleet controlled the Atlantic sea lanes. It was only with British consent that the ships of any nation, including the United States, moved between Europe and the Americas. It was America's good fortune that British merchants were keenly interested in preserving the independence of the countries of Central and South America. At the first hint of interference from the Holy Alliance, Great Britain sided with the Americas.

Significance of the Doctrine. The Monroe Doctrine was a direct warning to Russia, to France, to Spain, and to other European powers that the United States was vitally concerned in the affairs of all the nations in North, Central, and South America. It became a cornerstone of United States foreign policy.

The Monroe Doctrine also revealed the growing spirit of American strength and unity. In 1823 it meant that President Monroe spoke for a united people, grown in numbers to more than 10,000,000 citizens. He spoke for a nation that was becoming increasingly conscious of its own strength. He spoke for a nation that was determined to retain its hard-won independence from Europe and to decide its own policies in its own way.

✔ **SECTION SURVEY**

1. Why were the people of the United States interested in the revolutions of Latin America?

2. (a) Describe how the United States acquired all of Florida. (b) What territorial concessions did we make to Spain?

3. Explain why the actions of Russia and the Holy Alliance led to the issuance of the Monroe Doctrine.

4. (a) List the provisions of the Monroe Doctrine. (b) Why were they important?

5. "It was Great Britain, and more specifically the British navy, that gave the Doctrine its real strength." Discuss this quotation.

IDENTIFY: Holy Alliance; Miranda, Bolívar, O'Higgins, San Martín, Hidalgo, Morelos, Iturbide; 1823.

5 American education and arts reveal national pride

With development of the American System, Americans revealed their intention of becoming *economically* independent of Europe. With the Monroe Doctrine Americans declared their complete *political* independence from Europe, thereby bringing to a logical conclusion the struggle that they started with the Revolutionary War. Both of these developments were long steps forward in the growth of the new nation. So, too, was another development which, because it took a less dramatic form, is apt to go unnoticed.

This third step in the growth of the nation was the development of truly American education, art, and literature. With this new development, the United States began to become *culturally* independent of Europe. To be sure, not all of the educators, artists, and writers of this period revealed in their work the growing spirit of *nationalism*, of national pride. But those who did reveal this spirit helped to unite the nation fully as much as the businessmen and the political leaders who were working for economic and political independence.

A national university proposed. It was pride in the new nation that prompted a number of Americans to speak out in favor of a national university. Many citizens shared the view of George Washington, who believed that a national university would help to train people for public service, as well as provide the nation with a growing body of educated citizens. During the early years of the country's history, this proposal received considerable support. John Quincy Adams, who became President in 1825, was only one of many men who tried, although unsuccessfully, to establish such an institution.

Noah Webster—author and educator. Another illustration of the growing spirit of independence was Noah Webster's project for molding a national "American" language, distinct from English. "America," Webster had declared in 1783, "must be as independent in *literature* as she is in *politics*, as famous for *arts* as for *arms*." With this in mind, Webster labored at the tremendous task of publishing a dictionary—*An American Dictionary of the English Language*—in which the British spelling of many words was simplified. When his dictionary was finally published in 1828, Webster hoped that it would help Americans to achieve a standardized language.

Webster also prepared a spelling book. It was published as early as 1783 and was used in nearly every elementary school in America. By the time Webster died in 1843, more than 15,000,000 copies had been sold, and nearly 100,000,000 copies were sold before the book went out of general use. Like the dictionary, the spelling book helped Americans to develop a uniform national language.

American history and geography. In addition to his work on the dictionary and the spelling book, Webster edited a famous school reader, *An American Selection of Lessons in Reading and Speaking*. One of the major purposes of this book was to arouse the spirit of national pride by instilling reverence for American heroes. In order to realize this purpose, Webster devoted more than half of his school reader to material from American history. Webster later

OLD BONES—
AND
NATIONAL PRIDE

Pride in the new nation, as well as a keen sense of curiosity, led artist Charles Willson Peale from his home in Philadelphia to a farm near Newburgh, New York, to dig—of all things—for a collection of old bones.

The French naturalist Georges Louis Leclerc Buffon was partly responsible for the expedition. The famous Frenchman had once remarked that something about America prevented animals from reaching a large size. A number of Americans, including Peale, disagreed. They knew that huge bones had been unearthed in Ohio. They were certain that some day someone would discover the complete skeleton of a giant animal. Indeed, the American Philosophical Society, of which Peale was a member, appointed a "bone committee" to find such a skeleton.

News that a farmer near Newburgh had discovered some enormous bones in a swamp filled Peale with excitement. In June 1801 he journeyed to the farm, took one look at the bones, and paid the farmer $300 for the right to dig.

President Jefferson lent Peale a navy pump to drain the swamp and an army tent to shelter the workers. Peale hired twenty-five men, and by the end of the summer they had unearthed hundreds of bones. Peale had them shipped to Philadelphia, and there he spread them out on the floor of his museum. Then he began the apparently impossible task of reconstructing the skeleton. There was no one to whom he could turn for advice, for the only prehistoric skeleton ever assembled up to that time was in Spain. After months of painstaking effort, Peale succeeded—and he had *two* giant skeletons of mammoths to show for his efforts. The mammoths stood 11 feet high at the shoulders. They were 15 feet long with 11-foot tusks.

So America had no large animals! Here in Peale's museum was proof to the contrary.

wrote other books entirely concerned with the study of American history.

Meanwhile, another scholar, Jedidiah Morse, was introducing American youth to the geography of their own country. Morse, like Webster, stated that one of his purposes was to teach American history, and his geographies were largely devoted to the story of American life.

Books for the study of the nation's history were prepared by a number of other writers. Before the "Era of Good Feelings" came to an end, the study of American history had become an accepted part of the curriculum of many of the elementary schools of the new nation. One indication of the rising spirit of national pride was legislation passed in 1827 by Massachusetts and Vermont requiring all the larger schools in these states to teach American history.

The arts. During the early years of the nation's growth, a number of artists were also influenced by the spirit of nationalism. This influence showed in the work that they did.

There were, for instance, the architects who designed the nation's capital. Although a French engineer, Major L'Enfant (lahn-FAHN), planned the city of Washington, American architects played a large part in its design and construction. Thomas Jefferson, for example, actually drew a plan for the Capitol. His plan did not win acceptance, but the architects did accept his proposal for the locations of the Capitol and the White House. Another American, William Thornton, and Benjamin Latrobe, an Englishman with a Pennsylvania-born mother, designed the Capitol. As the city of Washington grew, it helped to give American citizens a feeling of permanence, a growing conviction that the new nation was solidly planted and destined to endure.

During this same period, painters like Charles Willson Peale, Gilbert Stuart, and John Trumbull began to devote much of their time to painting portraits of the nation's leaders. Although these men lacked sufficient originality and technical skill to be great artists, they

One of the famous portrait painters of the early nation was Gilbert Stuart, who undertook but never quite finished the celebrated picture of George Washington shown above. Another was John Trumbull, born in 1756, who painted a picture of himself when a young man.

helped to direct attention to the nation's founders. Their influence is shown by the fact that even today the portraits that they painted of Washington, Jefferson, and other early leaders of the United States still look down upon young people in classrooms all over America.

Writers. During the early 1800's a number of writers began to draw upon the American environment for the material in their stories. Some, like Mason Locke Weems, better known as Parson Weems, who published a biography of the first President of the United States, wrote in glowing terms about the fathers of the nation.

Other writers, among them Washington Irving and James Fenimore Cooper, began to write about America itself. Irving turned to the Dutch society of the Hudson Valley, producing such works as "The Legend of Sleepy Hollow," "Rip Van Winkle," the *Knickerbocker History of New York*, and many others. In his early novels Cooper turned to the Indians and the frontier. The *Leather-stocking Tales,* a series of novels, are only a few of the books that he produced.

A new feeling of unity. The ideal of national unity, or of nationalism, was one of the forces that helped to shape American life during the first thirty or more years of the nation's history. This ideal stimulated rich and poor alike in all sections of the country. It stimulated the frontiersmen who were hewing their way through the forests, the businessmen in the growing cities, and the statesmen in Washington. It stimulated educators, artists, and writers as well as the men, women, and children who listened to their ideas and read their books and looked at their paintings. So the new nation became stronger and more unified as the years went by.

✔ SECTION SURVEY

1. Describe the contribution to American education of (a) Noah Webster and (b) Jedidiah Morse.

2. Explain how American architects and painters in the early 1800's helped to make the United States culturally independent of Europe.

3. What would you say have been the chief influences on American culture of Washington Irving and James Fenimore Cooper?

IDENTIFY: nationalism; L'Enfant, Thornton, Latrobe, Charles Willson Peale, Stuart, John Trumbull, Weems; 1827.

■ CHAPTER SURVEY

(For review, see Section Surveys, pages 251, 254, 258, 262–63, 265.)

Points to Discuss: 1. Describe the part played by each of the following men in the Industrial Revolution: (a) Samuel Slater, (b) Moses Brown, and (c) Eli Whitney.

2. Explain how each of the following contributed to the growth of industry: (a) the War of 1812, (b) scarcity of labor, and (c) the government.

3. (a) The War of 1812 stimulated a feeling of nationalism or national pride. Explain this statement. (b) Indicate the connection between the feeling of nationalism and Clay's American System.

4. Explain how each of the following revealed the growing spirit of American nationalism: (a) the protective tariff, (b) the national bank, (c) internal improvements at national expense.

5. Explain why the Republican Party adopted Hamilton's Federalist program during the "Era of Good Feelings."

6. Describe the world situation which led to the Monroe Doctrine.

7. Compare the isolation policies of Washington, Jefferson, and Monroe.

8. Explain how Marshall's decisions strengthened the powers of the federal government.

9. What evidence do we have of the spirit of American nationalism in literature, art, architecture, and education?

Using Maps and Charts: 1. Referring to chart number 1 on pages 832–33, summarize the factors that contributed to the start of the Industrial Revolution.

2. Using chart 4 on page 841, compare the tariffs of 1789 and 1816. Explain the difference in rates.

3. Referring to the map on page 261, explain the reasons for the issuance of the Monroe Doctrine.

Consulting the Sources: For text of the Monroe Doctrine and background, see Commager, *Documents*, Nos. 126–27.

■ TRACING THE MAIN IDEAS

The desire for independence and for national unity reached a peak in the United States during the decade following the War of 1812. Because the people were so united in their efforts to strengthen the new nation, the period from about 1817 to 1825 was called the "Era of Good Feelings."

During the "Era of Good Feelings," Americans from all walks of life worked at the task of making their nation strong and independent of the rest of the world. Congress, supported by many businessmen and farmers, adopted the so-called American System. This system was designed to make the United States economically independent and self-sufficient. It consisted of a national bank to provide a sound financial system, a high tariff for the protection of American industry, and a national transportation system to connect the East and the West.

Meanwhile, President Monroe and his advisers took steps to make the United

States politically independent of Europe. The means they used for this purpose was the Monroe Doctrine.

During these same years educators, artists, and writers were devoting their efforts to American themes and American heroes, thus helping to make the United States culturally independent of Europe.

But the "Era of Good Feelings" was near its end. Beneath the surface, divisive forces were at work. As a result, the new nation was soon split by sectional controversy that in time plunged the country into four terrible years of warfare.

Before turning to the story of sectional controversy, however, it is necessary to look at another important development. During the years that the American people were building a new nation, they were also strengthening the spirit and practices of democracy. This is the story told in the next chapter.

CHAPTER **13**   1825–1845

The Nation Becomes More Democratic

=SIDENT-ELECT JACKSON EN ROUTE To WASHINGTON ~ 1829

B Y 1824 it was clear that the so-called "Era of Good Feelings" was drawing to a close. The Republican Party and the American public in general were divided over a number of important developments. One of these developments, which you will read about in Unit Four, was the growing rivalry among the three major sections of the new nation—the North, the South, and the West. Another development was the rapidly growing strength of democracy.

What is *democracy?* Abraham Lincoln partly defined it later when he referred to "government of the people, by the people, for the people." The right of every qualified person to vote and hold office—that is, to participate in his own government—is sometimes called *political* democracy. But we know that there is more than this to democracy. We sometimes speak of *economic* and *social* democracy, by which we mean a society in which all people have an equal opportunity to secure an education, to choose the careers that they wish to follow, and to live from day to day as free men, equal in the eyes of the law to all their neighbors.

As you have seen, this larger conception of democracy had begun to develop roots in the early years of America's history. And yet, even political democracy was limited when the Constitution was adopted. The right to vote and to hold public office was restricted in varying degrees in different states.

During the early years of the nation's history, however, political democracy began to make gains, slowly at first, and then with ever-growing speed. Starting in the western states, and then in the older states along the Atlantic seaboard, most of the restrictions were removed. By the late 1820's political democracy was rapidly gaining ground. In 1828 it scored a major victory with the election of Andrew Jackson as President.

AS THE STORY DEVELOPS

1. Andrew Jackson emerges as "the people's choice."
2. The people take a more active part in government.
3. Jackson fights the "money power" of the Northeast.
4. Congressional compromise averts a threat to the Union.
5. The Jacksonian era ends in an economic depression.

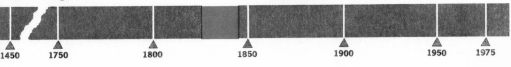

| 1450 | 1750 | 1800 | 1850 | 1900 | 1950 | 1975 |

1 Andrew Jackson emerges as "the people's choice"

The growing power of the rank and file of people, as well as the rivalry between the major sections of the country, was clearly revealed in the political struggles from 1824 to 1828. During these years the Democratic Party began to take shape—the party, that is, that bears that name today.

The election of 1824. In 1824 there were four candidates for the Presidency, and all four called themselves Republicans. At least three of them were *favorite son* ° candidates, nominated to represent different sections of the country. John Quincy Adams of Massachusetts—the son of John Adams, the second President—represented the northeastern states. William H. Crawford of Georgia represented the southern states. Andrew Jackson of Tennessee represented the western states. Henry Clay thought of himself as a national leader, although he came from Kentucky, then a "western" state.

Among the four candidates only Henry Clay had a definite program. Clay urged support for the American System that he had done so much to develop during President Monroe's administration. In the American System, as you have seen, Clay and other leaders in Congress tried to balance the interests of the different sections of the country. Even in these early years of his famous career, Clay was beginning to establish himself in the role of "the Great Compromiser"—a role he was to play many times in the years ahead. The other three candidates hedged on most of the specific issues, including the tariff and such internal improvements as the development of roads.

When the electoral votes were counted, Jackson had 99, Adams had 84,

----

° *favorite son:* In present usage, the term usually refers to a candidate placed in nomination on the first ballot by his state's delegation —as an honor, but with little chance of being nominated.

Crawford had 41, and Clay had only 37. No one candidate had the 131-vote majority of all the electoral votes that was needed for election. In such a situation, according to the Twelfth Amendment to the Constitution, the House of Representatives was required to choose the President from the top three candidates. Clay, who was automatically eliminated, being the fourth candidate, persuaded his followers in the House to vote for Adams. Adams therefore won. John C. Calhoun of South Carolina became Vice-President.

Jackson battles against Adams. The new President, John Quincy Adams, appointed Henry Clay to the position of Secretary of State. Jackson and his followers claimed that this was part of a "corrupt bargain." They maintained that Clay had promised to support Adams in exchange for the top post in the Cabinet.

The charge of a "corrupt bargain" was false. Both Clay and Adams had acted in what they considered were the best interests of the country. But Jackson believed the charges were true. He was especially bitter because, as he pointed out, the electors had given him the largest number of votes.

Jackson was so angry that he resigned from the United States Senate in 1825 and began a three-year campaign to win the Presidential election of 1828. During the course of this three-year battle, both Adams and Jackson called themselves Republicans. Adams, however, referred to himself as a National-Republican, while Jackson called himself a Democratic-Republican.

As the months passed, some of the people who supported Jackson, including Vice-President Calhoun, began to call themselves Democrats. In those days the word "Democrat" was a radical term. Jackson avoided it publicly, although he did not hesitate to use it in private conversation and letters. By the 1830's, however, Jackson's party was frankly calling itself the Democratic Party. Jackson's opponents organized as the Whig Party in 1834, taking the name of their party from the old Whig Party in England which had opposed the tyranny of George III. For twenty years the Democrats and Whigs were the two major political parties in the country.

The election of 1828. By 1828, as you will see later, the right to vote had been granted to most white adult men. Many of the new voters considered Jackson to be their leader. They made much of the fact that he had been born in a log cabin and had risen by his own efforts.

Under these circumstances, Jackson won a sweeping victory, receiving 178 electoral votes to 83 for Adams. Adams' strength was chiefly in New England and New Jersey. Jackson won every state west of the Appalachian Mountains and south of the Potomac River. Jackson also won in Pennsylvania and New York. John C. Calhoun was re-elected to the Vice-Presidency.

Americans differed violently in their reactions to the election. Noting that the votes of average people had figured decisively in an election for the first time, many Americans of wealth and influence, including President Adams, felt that "King Mob" had triumphed.

Other Americans were jubilant. As they interpreted the election, democracy had triumphed, and the rank and file of people were entering a new era.

Jackson's first inauguration. On March 4, 1829, political democracy celebrated its greatest victory up to that time. All over the land average men and women rejoiced at the inauguration of Andrew Jackson. As one writer said, "It was the people's day, and the people's President, and the people would rule." The nation's tiny capital on the banks of the Potomac was jammed with 10,000 visitors. "A monstrous crowd of people is in the city," Daniel Webster wrote. "I never saw anything like it before. Persons have come five hundred miles to see General Jackson, and they really seem to think that the country is rescued from some dreadful danger."

The inaugural celebration was itself a symbol of a new era. After his Inaugural Address the new President held open house in the Executive Mansion—the White House. Jackson's followers jammed in to greet him and to enjoy refreshments. Men with muddy boots climbed on chairs and tables to get a better view, furniture was broken, trays of food were knocked over, fights broke out, and women fainted.

The President himself narrowly escaped bodily injury at the hands of the well-meaning but riotous crowd, and he escaped only by flight from the mansion. The exuberant guests were finally dispersed by the simple expedient of placing bowls of punch and other refreshments on the lawns of the White House. Dignified citizens who witnessed the scene from a safe distance were filled with horror. "The reign of King Mob seemed triumphant."

Jackson: the man. What was he like, this man who aroused such conflicting emotions?

■ Andrew Jackson, an impressive man, was hated by some Americans, idolized by many more. His strong personality left an indelible stamp on the office of the American Presidency.

A FRENCHMAN LOOKS AT AMERICAN DEMOCRACY

In the spring of 1831, during Andrew Jackson's first term as President, a twenty-six-year-old Frenchman arrived in the United States. Alexis de Tocqueville had been sent by his own government to study the prison system in America, but he did not confine his attention to prisons. In his extensive travels, this keen reporter observed the manners and habits, the industries and occupations, the daily life of the people. When he returned to France, he described what he had seen in a volume entitled *Democracy in America*. This book remains today one of the most penetrating studies ever made of the young American nation.

De Tocqueville was enormously impressed with the rapid expansion of the new nation and the vitality of the people. "This gradual and continuous progress of the European race toward the Rocky Mountains has the solemnity of a providential event;" he wrote, "it is like a deluge of men rising unabatedly, and daily driven onward by the hand of God!"

But the fact that struck De Tocqueville most forcefully was the lack of class distinctions. "Amongst the novel objects that attracted my attention during my stay in the United States," he wrote, "nothing struck me more forcibly than the general equality of conditions. . . .

"It is evident to all alike that a great democratic revolution is going on amongst us; but there are two opinions as to its nature and consequences. To some it appears to be a novel accident, which as such may still be checked; to others it seems irresistible, because it is the most uniform, the most ancient, and the most permanent tendency which is to be found in history. . . ."

Andrew Jackson was in many ways representative of "the people." Born on the Carolina frontier in 1767, the son of immigrant parents from northern Ireland, he grew up without the benefit of formal schooling. Like other Americans, he moved west with the advancing line of settlement, and as a youth settled in Tennessee. Honest, loyal, and industrious, he succeeded in becoming a well-to-do southern planter.

Although Jackson had represented Tennessee in both houses of Congress, his fame rested largely on his military career. He had led the American forces, as you know, in their victory over the British at New Orleans in 1815, and had won a reputation as a hard-hitting Indian fighter by his defeat of the Creek Indians in Mississippi and Alabama and the Seminoles in Florida.

Jackson's opponents sneered at him, claiming that he could not spell, that he told rough stories, smoked an old pipe, chewed tobacco, and lounged around in worn clothes. Whether or not these statements were ever true, they certainly did not apply to Jackson's later life. As he became a wealthy planter and achieved a national reputation, Jackson cultivated the manners of a gentleman. Tall, slender, with a shock of white hair, he presented a striking and distinguished appearance. His followers often called him "Old Hickory."

Significance of the election. Jackson's inaugural celebration in 1829 was different indeed from that of the first inauguration in 1789, when President Washington held a formal reception for his friends. Fundamental changes had clearly taken place in the country since the days of President Washington and the Federalists. For one thing, political power was more evenly divided between well-to-do people and people of average circumstances. Before 1829 all the Presidents had come from surroundings of wealth and refinement. In contrast, Andrew Jackson had been born into poverty and had risen through his own efforts to a position of influence. He was identified with the hopes and ambitions of a majority of the people, and they claimed him for their own.

In the second place, Jackson's election indicated that the western section of the country was a new force to be reckoned with in national politics. Andrew Jackson was from Tennessee. He was the first President to come from a state that did not border on the Atlantic. All of his predecessors had come from the seaboard states. Now for the first time a frontiersman, a westerner, sat in the Executive Mansion.

But Jackson's followers were not all westerners. To be sure, western frontiersmen had voted for him because he had been a frontiersman, because he had carved for himself an enviable reputation as an Indian fighter. Frontiersmen felt that he would understand their problems. But great numbers of small farmers everywhere voted for him for the same reason. Many southern planters also voted for him because, as a planter himself, he owned slaves and would understand the slaveowner's point of view. Many city workers voted for him because they believed he would help them to get certain laws that they wanted, as you will see later. It is possible that Jackson might not have been elected in 1828 without the support of many of the city workers.

✔ SECTION SURVEY

1. Show why the election of 1824 was one of the most unusual in our history.
2. Explain the reasons for the split in the Republican Party.
3. How did the election of Andrew Jackson in 1828 illustrate the growing strength of political democracy?
4. Explain why some people felt that with Jackson's victory, "The reign of King Mob seemed triumphant."
5. Some historians have described Jackson's election as the "Revolution of 1828." What facts can you give to support this view?

IDENTIFY: "corrupt bargain" charge, National-Republicans, Democratic-Republicans, Democrats, Whigs; John Quincy Adams; 1824, 1828.

2 The people take a more active part in government

Andrew Jackson, the new President, brought to his office in 1829 no carefully developed political program. It is doubtful if he ever attempted to outline a set of political principles.

Yet despite his lack of a clear-cut program, Jackson held three convictions with stubborn persistence. First, he believed in political democracy. He believed that the government belonged to all the people, and he was determined that the majority must rule. Second, Jackson believed in the Union—the United States as a whole. The new nation must be preserved at any cost. Third, Jackson believed in the power of the Presidency.

Jackson extends the "spoils system." One of the President's first steps was to remove many of his political opponents from public office and to replace them with people who had supported his candidacy. "No . . . rascal who made use of an office or its profits for the purpose of keeping Mr. Jackson out of power is entitled to the least leniency save that of hanging," cried one ardent Jacksonian.

The *spoils system,* as it was called, was a practice by which public offices were at the disposal of a victorious political party, to be given to supporters of the party, often without regard for their fitness to hold public office. The name "spoils system" for this practice came from the common expression "to the victors belong the spoils." The spoils system had become common practice in some northern and western states. It had also been used to some extent in the federal government, but Jackson applied it more vigorously than ever.

In general, Jackson removed everyone that he suspected of having supported his political opponents. Older, experienced men were replaced by younger and often poorly qualified men. Although Jackson actually replaced only

PIERRE JEAN DE SMET

Traditions of early Jesuit missions were renewed by Father De Smet (1801–73). Just before the settlers were beginning to respond to another "western fever," before the covered wagons began to roll over the plains, the Jesuits in St. Louis heard from distant Indians of the great West. These asked for a "blackrobe." They had heard of such missionaries from eastern Indians, grandsons and daughters of Hurons and Iroquois to whom Jesuits had brought baptism many years before. Ready for this new effort was Father De Smet, born in Belgium, who had come to America with a desire for mission work.

He was a big man in every way, and a great traveler. Starting with the Plains Indians, he extended mission stations from Iowa to Oregon. He interrupted his teachings only to go to Europe to raise money and gather priests and nuns to return with him. Before the American settlers reached Oregon in large numbers, he had arranged to take over the mission stations from the Canadians. Then he turned inland to found missions among Flat Heads and Blackfeet. He persuaded them all to "bury the tomahawk" and stop fighting among themselves. But it was much harder to keep them at peace with the white men.

Among the Sioux of the Dakotas, great hatred of the whites raged from about 1858 until well after the War Between the States. They had many grievances. In 1868 the War Department sent peace commissioners to seek out Sitting Bull and his warriors. Only Father De Smet, who had been persuaded to go along, had any hope of reaching the Indian camp without being massacred. He showed his great influence over the Indians by journeying alone and unarmed to them and getting them to agree to peace.

about one fifth of all federal officeholders, he established a precedent in the use of the spoils system that later Presidents followed with drastic results.

Jackson defends the spoils system. Jackson maintained that he was actually improving the government by applying the spoils system on a large scale. He claimed that one man was as good as another. "The duties of all public officers are, or at least admit of being made, so plain and simple that men of intelligence may readily qualify themselves for their performance," Jackson stated.

Jackson also believed that it was sound policy to keep changing officeholders. He felt that a man who remained too long in office became indifferent to the public welfare, and forgot that he was a servant of the people.

Still more important, in Jackson's mind, was the fact that it was good democratic procedure to give as many men as possible the opportunity to learn by experience how the government functioned. He maintained that the more people who held office at one time or another during any given generation, the more the government would be responsive to the changing needs of the people.

Jackson's policies in regard to public office brought politics into the range of the average man. Even a poor man could risk devoting his time to political activities if he could hope for a job as a reward for faithful service.

Defects of the spoils system. As a result of Jackson's policies, however, political parties came to be led and supported by officeholders who were paid by the government, and who contributed a certain percentage of their salaries or wages to maintain their political organizations.

The spoils system also encouraged many individuals to look upon the public payroll as a sort of trough where they could gorge themselves at the taxpayer's expense. It was during this period, as you will see later, that the professional politician and the "city boss" were born. Many professional politicians have labored unselfishly for the nation, but some have used their positions largely for self-interest and have brought reproach upon our political system.

These political abuses were not entirely the responsibility of Andrew Jackson, but, by extending the spoils system, he helped to open the door through which such abuses entered national politics.

Nominating conventions begin. During Jackson's administration political democracy gained an important victory with the increasing use of *nominating conventions* for choosing candidates for federal office. Until this time, as you know, candidates for federal office had been selected by legislators gathered in closed meetings, or caucuses, and the people at large had enjoyed little if any voice in the nominating process. In the meantime, however, a different practice had been developing at the local level. Groups of voters, meeting in their own communities, chose delegates for county conventions, which in turn nominated men for county offices.

This practice gradually spread upward into state politics and eventually into national politics. In 1831, for example, the Anti-Masonic Party held a national convention in Baltimore, nominated a candidate for the Presidency, and adopted a *platform,* or statement of political policies. Later in the year, the National-Republicans held a convention, also in Baltimore, and, as you will see, nominated Henry Clay for the Presidency. Still later, in May 1832, the Democratic Party, following these earlier examples, held a convention in Baltimore and nominated Andrew Jackson to run for re-election. By 1832 the present practice of nominating the President and Vice-President in nominating conventions had been firmly established.

Jackson's "kitchen cabinet." Andrew Jackson adopted still another device to bring the government and the people closer together. In addition to his regular cabinet, he surrounded himself with

Andrew Jackson at political convention

a group of unofficial advisers. Jackson's political enemies dubbed these advisers the "kitchen cabinet," implying that they entered the White House by a back door and met in secret.

Some members of the "kitchen cabinet" were newspaper editors. Jackson recognized the importance of friendly relations with the press, and he placed a number of prominent editors in public office. In return, they helped him to mold public opinion, to secure publicity, and to win support for his policies.

Jackson speaks for the people. On most of the great issues of his time, Jackson spoke for the people. By 1830 the three sectional divisions of the country were becoming more sharply defined. Each section had its outstanding champion. Daniel Webster of Massachusetts represented the dominant interests of the Northeast—the merchants, manufacturers, financiers, bankers, and men of property in general. John C. Calhoun of South Carolina was the spokesman for the planters of the South. Thomas Hart Benton of Missouri, vigorous and forthright, became the advocate of the West, especially of western farmers and land speculators, whose primary interest was to secure cheap, or even free, public land. Henry Clay of Kentucky, the Great Compromiser, tried to discover a formula for balancing the interests of the three sections and, in the process, to become President.

Andrew Jackson seemed to speak for the plain people everywhere. He placed himself, as he said, at the head of "the humbler members of society—the farmers, mechanics, and laborers who have neither the time nor the means" to secure for themselves the things that they want from the government.

⌐ SECTION SURVEY

1. What three convictions or beliefs determined Jackson's actions as President?
2. (a) Jackson claimed that his use of the spoils system was in the interests of democracy. Explain. (b) Show how the use of the spoils system helped to lead to political corruption.
3. How did the use of nominating conventions for choosing federal officeholders bring the government and the people closer together?
4. What was Jackson's aim in using his "kitchen cabinet"?
5. In what ways did Jackson help to strengthen political democracy?
IDENTIFY: party platform, Anti-Masonic party; Thomas Hart Benton.

3 Jackson fights the "money power" of the Northeast

One of Jackson's bitterest fights was against the Bank of the United States. Many small businessmen, farmers, and workmen had fought this battle since the original bank was created by Alexander Hamilton in 1791. President Jackson, in his first message to Congress early in 1829, opened his attack against the second Bank of the United States. As the months passed, he became more and more vigorous in his opposition.

Jackson opposes the Bank. The Bank of the United States, Jackson stated, was a "money power"—a monopoly which "the rich and powerful" used to their own advantage. He pointed out that a majority of the shares of bank stock were owned by wealthy investors living in the Atlantic seaboard states from Maryland through New England and by people of like mind living in Europe. The handful of investors living west of the Appalachians owned only a small fraction of the stock.

Why, the President asked, should the government continue to grant control of the Bank to a small group of wealthy individuals, most of them from one section of the country? "Many of our rich men," he declared, ". . . have besought us to make them richer by acts of Congress. By attempting to gratify their desires, we have in the results of our legislation arrayed section against section, interest against interest, and man against man, in a fearful commotion which threatens to shake the foundations of our Union."

The President's followers were delighted by these words. But Nicholas Biddle, president of the second Bank of the United States, called Jackson's statement "a manifesto of anarchy."

To his charge that the Bank was a tool of the rich easterners, Jackson added the serious charge that it engaged in questionable political activities. He charged, for example, that by granting loans to Congressmen the Bank was able to influence legislation. There is little doubt that it did, at least after Jackson made his accusation—an accusation which many people considered unfair. Once the directors of the Bank were convinced that the President intended to destroy their institution, they fought back with every weapon at their command. "This worthy President," Biddle angrily stated, "thinks that because he has scalped Indians . . . he is to have his way with the Bank. He is mistaken."

Jackson also claimed that the mere existence of the Bank was unconstitutional. In so doing he ignored the Supreme Court decision of 1819 in *McCulloch v. Maryland* that had ruled to the contrary (page 257). Jackson indicated that he did not intend to be bound by verdicts of the Supreme Court. "Each public officer who takes an oath to support the Constitution swears that he will support it as he understands it, and not as it is understood by others . . ." Jackson bluntly asserted. "The opinion of the judges has no more authority over Congress than the opinion of Congress over the judges, and, on that point, the President is independent of both."

Many Americans joined Jackson in his opposition to the Bank. Some people who wanted to borrow from the Bank were angry if the Bank refused to lend money unless they could give adequate security in money or goods as a pledge of repayment. From a banker's point of view, this was sound business. Bankers could and did point out that they had no right to lend money that did not belong to them without adequate guarantee that the borrower could repay the loan. It was not only farmers and wage earners who wanted easy credit, and who resented the sound banking policies of the second Bank of the United States. More influential were rising business interests which, being refused easy credit by the Bank of the United States, turned to private and state banks. These felt themselves unduly restricted by the Bank of the United States, which was denounced in the popular slogans of the day as a monstrous monopoly.

The Bank becomes an election issue. Angered at the opposition, the supporters of the Bank, including Henry Clay, decided to bring matters to a head. They persuaded Nicholas Biddle to apply for a renewal of the Bank's charter. The bill passed both houses of Congress in the summer of 1832, four years before the charter was due to expire.

Henry Clay and the National Republicans deliberately raised the issue at this time. They hoped that Jackson would veto the bill. If he did, the National Republicans could make the Bank a major issue in the election of 1832.

President Jackson did what Clay and the National Republicans hoped he would do. In forceful terms, he vetoed the measure intended to recharter the Bank.

The National Republicans nominated Henry Clay for the Presidency late in 1831. During the following months Clay and his followers campaigned in favor of rechartering the Bank. Andrew Jackson, running for re-election as the candidate of the Democratic Party, continued his vigorous opposition. Although there were other issues in the campaign, the Bank question was the major one.

Jackson won the election, with Martin Van Buren of New York as his Vice-President. Clay and the National Republicans suffered a crushing defeat at the polls. The electoral vote was 219 to 49. Under these circumstances, everyone understood that the Bank charter would not be renewed in 1836.

Jackson destroys the Bank. Not content to wait for the Bank to die a natural death in 1836, Jackson destroyed it by the simple process of gradually withdrawing all federal deposits. Federal funds were now deposited in certain state banks. These so-called "pet banks" were selected, Jackson's enemies claimed, on the basis of their loyalty to Jackson and his party.

The Bank of the United States, now deprived of federal deposits, was badly crippled, but it managed to survive until 1836, when its charter expired.

For Andrew Jackson and those who supported him, the outcome of the struggle with the Bank was a victory over monopoly of the money power by wealthy easterners and over special privilege in government. In their opinion, this was another triumph for democracy.

SECTION SURVEY

1. (a) What proof did Jackson present to support his charge that the second Bank of the United States was a monopoly and "money power"? (b) Would you have agreed with him?

2. On what grounds did Jackson base his charge that the Bank (a) engaged in political activities and (b) was unconstitutional?

3. Which groups sided with Jackson in his opposition to the Bank?

275

4. Why did the National Republicans decide to make the Bank an issue in the election of 1832?

5. What were Jackson's reasons for placing federal funds in "pet banks"?

IDENTIFY: Biddle, Van Buren; 1832, 1836.

4 Congressional compromise averts a threat to the Union

In his fight with the Bank of the United States, Andrew Jackson flatly stated that he, as President, did not intend to have his hands tied by a decision of the Supreme Court. But this statement did not indicate any lack of respect for the federal Union established by the Constitution of the United States. Indeed, beginning in 1830 Jackson took such a fighting stand in support of the Union that southern champions of states' rights, who had been supporters of Jackson, were thrown into confusion. The issue that forced Jackson into his firm position was a revolt of South Carolina planters against a high protective tariff.

Rising tariffs. When America's source of manufactured goods was cut off by the Embargo Act of 1807 and the War of 1812, the United States, as you know, was forced to build its own factories. When the war ended in 1815, British manufacturers tried to drive their new rivals from the scene by "dumping" British goods in America. The United States then tried to encourage its own manufacturers by the protective tariff of 1816. The tariff rates of 1816 were raised in 1824 and again in 1828.

Southern reaction. The Tariff Act of 1828, called by its enemies the "Tariff of Abominations" because of the high rates it imposed, was passed by such a large majority in Congress that the planters of the South became alarmed. Reflecting their alarm, John C. Calhoun, the Vice-President, wrote—but did not sign—a pointed statement in which he expressed his views about the tariff and the larger issue of states' rights. The legislature of South Carolina adopted this statement, which came to be known as the "South Carolina Exposition and Protest," together with a set of eight resolutions in which the tariff was termed unconstitutional and unjust. Georgia, Mississippi, and Virginia adopted similar resolutions.

The "South Carolina Exposition and Protest" echoed the compact theory of government originally stated in the Kentucky and Virginia Resolutions of 1798 and 1799 (page 223). The substance of Calhoun's argument was that the separate states had the right to *nullify,* or refuse to obey, any act of Congress that they believed to be unconstitutional.

Webster defends the Union. Calhoun's doctrine of states' rights provoked bitter debate in Congress. The southern point of view was clearly expressed in January 1830 by Senator Robert Y. Hayne of South Carolina, who argued that southern opposition to the tariff was "resistance to unauthorized taxation." In this famous debate Hayne restated Calhoun's views on states' rights and nullification.

The northern viewpoint was eloquently expressed by Daniel Webster of Massachusetts in one of the most famous speeches ever given in the Senate. Webster repudiated the theory that the United States was a mere league, or compact, of states. He argued that it is "the people's Constitution, the people's government, made for the people, made by the people, and answerable to the people." No state had the power to declare an act of Congress unconstitutional, Webster insisted. If a state could do this, if each state were to obey only those laws it chose to accept, Webster declared, the Union would become "a mere rope of sand."

Webster maintained that there was only one agency empowered to decide upon the constitutionality of acts of Congress. That agency, he said, was the Supreme Court of the United States. In thunderous words he flung out his challenge to Calhoun and Hayne and all who accepted the doctrine of states' rights and nullification: "Liberty *and* Union, now and forever, one and inseparable!"

Jackson upholds the Union. On which side would the President take his stand? The answer was not long in coming.

At a Jefferson Day dinner in April 1830 President Jackson rose from his chair, fixed his eyes upon Vice-President Calhoun, held his glass in the air, and proposed a toast: "Our Federal Union— It must and shall be preserved!"

A long moment of silence followed Jackson's toast. Then the fiery Calhoun, spokesman for the southern planters, rose to his feet and threw back a defiant challenge: "The Union—next to our liberty, the most dear! May we always remember that it can only be preserved by respecting the rights of the states. . . ."

The issue was joined, and the leaders of both sides were able fighters who were reluctant to compromise when principles were at stake.

The conflict smoldered for two years. Then, in 1832, Congress adopted a new tariff measure. The Tariff Act of 1832 provided somewhat lower rates than the "Tariff of Abominations." But the new act was still a protective tariff and therefore, from the southern point of view, no better than the old. Convinced that the advocates of a protective tariff controlled Congress, South Carolina decided to act.

South Carolina threatens to secede. In November 1832 South Carolina called a convention which, by a vote of 136 to 26, adopted the Ordinance of Nullification. Declaring the tariff acts of 1828 and 1832 "null, void, and no law," and not "binding upon this state, its officers, or citizens," the ordinance expressed defiance of the government of the United States. It closed with a solemn warning that if the federal authorities attempted to enforce the tariff law after February 1, 1833, South Carolina would secede from the Union, and take its place as a sovereign power among the nations of the world.

JOHN C. CALHOUN

John Caldwell Calhoun (1782–1850) was born on a plantation in South Carolina. His Scotch-Irish father, a successful planter, gave the boy every educational advantage, and young Calhoun made the most of his opportunities. After graduation from Yale in 1804, he studied law at Tapping Reeve's famous law school in Litchfield in Connecticut. Returning to South Carolina, he served one term in the state legislature and then, in 1811, entered Congress as one of the "War Hawks." His vigorous support of the War of 1812 led admirers to refer to him as "the young Hercules who carried the war on his shoulders."

For a number of years after the war, Calhoun strongly supported legislation designed to strengthen the Union. By the end of the 1820's, however, changing ways and changing times had transformed Calhoun's point of view. In his South Carolina Exposition, written in opposition to the tariff of 1828, he clearly stated the doctrine of states' rights and nullification. From this time on, he became the acknowledged leader of the southern section of the country.

John C. Calhoun was one of the principal statesmen of his day. Although he was lacking in a sense of humor, his enormous intellectual capacity and his inflexible devotion to duty won him the respect of all who knew him, including his opponents. For about forty years, from 1811 to 1850, he served his country and the southern cause in one high office after another, twice as Vice-President of the United States. When he died in 1850, one of the most influential figures in American history passed from the scene.

The President acts. The President now moved into the spotlight. As Chief Executive of the United States, he was charged with enforcing the laws. He acted promptly. In "off-the-record" statements he lived up to his reputation as a fighting man, warning that he was prepared to "hang every leader . . . irrespective of his name or political or social position. . . . Tell them," he said to a Congressman, "that they can talk and write resolutions and print threats to their hearts' content. But if one drop of blood be shed there in defiance of the laws of the United States, I will hang the first man of them I can get my hands on to the first tree I can find."

For the public record Jackson was more moderate. In a long, carefully worded statement he repeated his belief in the Union and his determination to uphold it at whatever cost, but he left the way open for a peaceable solution.

Calhoun was out on a limb. The other southern states had refused to follow South Carolina along the road to secession, and Calhoun and his followers stood alone against the full might of the United States. With the possibility of violence facing the country, political leaders proposed to end the crisis by means of a compromise tariff.

Compromise saves the day. Under the leadership of Henry Clay, the Great Compromiser, Congress adopted a compromise measure, the Tariff Act of 1833. Under this act, tariff rates were to be reduced gradually to the level of 1816, which Calhoun had once supported. This reduction was part of what the South demanded. But the reductions in the rates were to take place over 10 years. During this time manufacturers would be better able to adjust to the lack of high tariff protection.

Along with the compromise tariff act, Congress in 1833 also adopted the Force Act, specifically authorizing the President to enforce the federal tariff laws by the use of military power.

War had been averted. "Old Hickory," as Jackson was called, became a symbol of a strong, united nation.

1. (a) What was the purpose of Calhoun's "Exposition and Protest"? (b) Summarize Webster's arguments in answer to Calhoun and Hayne.
2. How did the debate over the tariff reflect the different economic interests of the major sections of the country?
3. Explain (a) the purpose and (b) the provisions of the South Carolina Ordinance of Nullification of 1832.
4. What was Jackson's position during this crisis?
5. Show how Clay's compromise satisfied the South, the North, and Jackson.

IDENTIFY: Tariff of Abominations, nullify, doctrine of states' rights, Force Act; 1828, 1830, 1832, 1833.

5 The Jacksonian era ends in an economic depression

In March 1835 Andrew Jackson passed the midpoint of his second term as President and paused to take stock of his accomplishments and to consider the future. From Jackson's point of view, his administration had been a great success. He had won every major battle with his political opponents. His supporters were devoted to him. One of them expressed a widely held opinion when he wrote that "General Jackson may be President for life if he wishes." But Jackson was ready to retire, and he made this clear to his friends.

The election of 1836. In 1835, after Jackson had announced his intention not to run for a third term, the Democratic Party held a nominating convention in Baltimore. At the convention the party chose Martin Van Buren of New York as its Presidential candidate.

Martin Van Buren had served in Jackson's first administration as Secretary of State, and in his second as Vice-President. Van Buren was a shrewd politician who was sometimes called the "little magician" or even the "sly fox." He entered the race for the Presidency with the strong support of Jackson.

The Whig Party, which, as you know, had been organized in 1834, was made up of assorted groups of people who were united chiefly by their dislike of "King Andrew" Jackson and the policies of the Democratic Party.

The Whigs did not choose to unite behind a single candidate. They chose instead to use the same "favorite son" strategy that had been employed twelve years earlier in the election of 1824. In each section of the country, the Whigs selected a "favorite son" to run for the Presidency. They hoped by this means to divide the total vote and prevent Van Buren from getting a majority. This would throw the election into the House of Representatives, where the Whigs hoped to have enough strength to choose one of their own candidates.

The Whig strategy failed. Van Buren won a majority of the electoral votes.

On March 4, 1837, the new President took the oath of office. He rode to the inaugural ceremony in a carriage drawn by four gray horses. Jackson, the retiring President, sat beside him, tall and straight despite his almost seventy years, his shock of white hair bared to the sunlight.

In his Inaugural Address, Van Buren announced that he intended to follow in Jackson's footsteps. He soon discovered that this was impossible. He was hardly in office before the nation plunged into an economic depression.

The roots of the depression. The depression of 1837 had its roots in events that occurred largely during Jackson's administration. After his victory at the polls in 1832, as you know, Andrew Jackson gradually withdrew federal funds from the Bank of the United States and then deposited this money in "pet banks," many of them in the west. With the federal money as security, the "pet banks" printed large amounts of their own bank notes. In many cases the "pet banks" were also "wildcat banks" which issued bank notes far in excess of the federal funds on deposit. Because they were so plentiful and had so little real value, these bank notes were easy to borrow. People borrowed this "easy money," often with a minimum of security, to buy land and to invest in the nation's growing transportation system. For a time it seemed to more cautious observers as though almost everyone in the country was speculating with borrowed money.

Land speculators were especially active. Between 1830 and 1836 yearly federal income from the sale of public land rose from less than $2,000,000 to about $24,000,000. Much of this money

Street scene in Jacksonian era

THE ANTI-RENT WAR IN THE HUDSON VALLEY

During the years from 1839 to 1846, the Hudson Valley was torn by an outbreak of violence that came to be called the Anti-Rent War.

The roots of the trouble reached back two hundred years to the time when the Hudson Valley was part of New Netherland. In those early days great landowners, or patroons, were given perpetual title to huge tracts of land. They leased this land to tenants. In return for the use of the land, the tenants paid yearly tribute to the owners—tribute in the form of farm produce, free labor, and money. Farmers whose families had lived on the same land for generations were never able to enjoy the pride of ownership.

In 1839 the growing discontent burst into open revolt when the owners of the enormous Van Rensselaer estates tried to collect about $400,000 in back dues. The farmers resisted. Disguised as Indians, they tarred and feathered the sheriffs who tried to collect the dues. Finally, in 1845, after a deputy sheriff had been murdered, the Governor proclaimed the area "in a state of insurrection."

In the end, however, the farmers won their battle. The Governor himself urged the legislature to pass laws more favorable to the farmers. And in 1846 New York adopted a new constitution in which the old Dutch type of land ownership was abolished.

was in the form of "wildcat" bank notes. The United States Treasury was flooded with this unsound currency.

In July 1836 President Jackson acted to check the wave of speculation that was sweeping across the country by issuing what came to be known as the "Specie Circular." In this Executive Order he forbade the Treasury to accept as payment for public land anything except gold or silver, which were known as *specie,* or bank notes backed by specie.

The Panic of 1837. Shortly after Jackson issued his order, the trouble began. The sale of public land dropped off sharply because few people had gold or silver coins with which to pay for the land. Persons holding bank notes supposed to be redeemable in gold or silver began to ask the banks to exchange the bank notes for the gold or silver itself. Many banks were unable to redeem their own bank notes. As a result, banks began to fail. By the end of May 1837, soon after President Van Buren took office, every bank in the United States had suspended specie payment. Before the panic ended, hundreds of banks had gone out of business.

As the banks failed and sound money disappeared from circulation, business began to suffer. Factories closed. Construction work ended on buildings and on the growing system of transportation. Thousands of wage earners lost their jobs. Hungry people rioted in the streets of New York and Philadelphia.

It did not occur to President Van Buren or to other leaders of his day that the government could or should do anything to try to stop the depression. Van Buren believed, and had so stated, that "The less government interfered with private pursuits, the better for the general prosperity." Under the circumstances, he was forced to sit back and watch the depression run its course.

The depression was only one problem President Van Buren faced during the years from 1837 to 1841. But it was the depression more than anything else that cost him the election of 1840.

The election of 1840. In December 1839 the Whig Party held a nominating convention at Harrisburg, Pennsylvania. The members of the convention sniffed victory in the air. They did not attempt to publish a platform. Instead, they chose to fight the campaign entirely on the issue of the depression, which they of course blamed on Van Buren and the Democrats. To lead the fight, they nominated a hero of the War of 1812 and the Indian Wars, General William Henry Harrison of Ohio, with John Tyler of Virginia as his running mate.

The campaign of 1840 was one of the most boisterous in American history. General Harrison, who owned a prosperous 2000-acre farm, was nevertheless pictured as a poor but honest man who lived in a log cabin and earned his daily bread in the hardest way. The Whigs built log cabins for headquarters and entertained the crowds at political rallies with barrels of hard cider. Recalling General Harrison's battle with the Indians on the banks of the Tippecanoe River in 1811, the Whigs aroused enthusiasm for their candidates by shouting, "Tippecanoe and Tyler too." To ridicule their opposition, the Whigs shouted, "Van, Van is a used-up man."

The Whigs won an overwhelming victory. Harrison and Tyler received 234 electoral votes to 60 for Van Buren.

But General Harrison did not live to enjoy his triumph. He died shortly after he took office, and Vice-President John Tyler, a states' rights Democrat who intensely opposed Jackson and his friends, succeeded to the Presidency.

A look ahead. During President Tyler's administration and that of his Democratic successor, James K. Polk, who was inaugurated in 1845, the boundaries of the nation were carried to the Pacific Ocean. During these same years the growing differences between the North and South became increasingly serious.

What was happening in the North, the South, and the West to create these conflicts? As you will see in Unit Four, two strikingly different ways of living and working had been developing in the northern states and the southern states. Out of these different ways of life arose tensions that became increasingly severe from the 1820's to the 1860's and finally led to the tragic War Between the States.

■ Candidate Harrison, former Governor of Indiana Territory and a well-to-do man, was pictured in 1840 as a hard-working, cabin-dwelling farmer.

SECTION SURVEY

1. Show how each of the following contributed to the depression of 1837: (a) "pet" and "wildcat" banks, (b) land speculation, and (c) the "Specie Circular."

2. "The depression of 1837 had its roots in events that occurred largely during Jackson's administration." Justify this statement.

3. Describe the various ways in which the depression of 1837 affected the country.

4. With reference to the election of 1840, give (a) the parties and their candidates, (b) the campaign issues, and (c) the famous slogans.

IDENTIFY: specie; William Henry Harrison, Tyler; 1836, 1837, 1840.

■ CHAPTER SURVEY

(For review, see Section Surveys, pages 271, 274, 275–76, 278, 281.)

Points to Discuss: 1. For the elections of 1800 and 1824, compare (a) the candidates, and (b) the method of choosing the President.

2. Explain the relationship of the Democratic and Whig Parties to the first political parties.

3. Why have some historians referred to the elections of 1800 and 1828 as revolutions?

4. (a) In what ways did the growth of democracy contribute to the election of Jackson in 1828? (b) In what ways did Jackson as President promote the growth of democracy?

5. Comment on the accuracy of this statement: On most of the great issues of his time, Jackson spoke for the people.

6. Explain the connections between the Kentucky and Virginia Resolutions, the Hartford Convention, and the South Carolina Exposition and Protest.

7. Describe the circumstances under which the following famous statements were made: (a) Webster—"Liberty *and* Union, now and forever, one and inseparable." (b) Jackson—"Our Federal Union: it must and shall be preserved." (c) Calhoun—"The Union: next to our liberty, the most dear."

8. Jackson's enemies called him "King Andrew" while his friends called him "a man of the people." Explain.

Using Maps and Charts: 1. (a) Using the map on pages 822–23, locate the frontier in 1790 and in the 1830's. (b) What were the national boundaries when Jackson was President?

2. (a) Using chart 4 on page 841, compare the tariffs of 1789, 1816, and 1828. (b) Account for the increasing rates.

3. Referring to the chart entitled "Business Activity" (pages 850–59), compare the panics of 1819 and 1837 for their (a) duration, (b) causes, and (c) results. See index for further information.

Consulting the Sources: See Ellis, *Docs.*, No. 72, for impressions of Alexis de Tocqueville on the relationship of American Catholics and democracy. No. 70 gives Bishop England's account of his own address before the U.S. Congress in 1826.

■ TRACING THE MAIN IDEAS

The Jacksonian era ended with the triumph of the Whigs in the inauguration of General Harrison on March 4, 1841. During most of the years between 1824 and 1841, Andrew Jackson occupied the center of the national stage. During these years Jackson stood as a symbol of democracy and national unity.

But Jackson was far more than a symbol. He firmly believed that the people should share in the task of government. He firmly believed that the Union established by the Constitution was a national Union. In the eight years of his administration, he did much to make the government more democratic. He brought the people into closer touch with the government. During the tariff controversy he fought to maintain national unity.

The depression that started in 1837 and continued through the administration of Jackson's successor, the Democrat Martin Van Buren, gave the Whigs a chance to win control of the government. They made the most of their opportunity in the campaign of 1840, sending General Harrison to the White House. With the Whig victory, a colorful era came to an end.

But the democratic impulse continued strong. Democracy is more than the right to vote and to hold public office. It is, in a larger sense, a way of life that offers every person an equal opportunity to live and work as a free individual. This democratic impulse helped to send Andrew Jackson to the Presidency in 1829. It also set in motion a wave of reforms that affected many phases of American life.

As you will see in Unit Four, these reforms were taking place side by side with the division of the nation into three distinct sections—the North, the South, and the West.

Unit Survey (Reread "Tracing the Main Ideas," pages 228, 246, 266, 282.)

OUTSTANDING EVENTS

1790 John Carroll consecrated as first Catholic bishop of the United States.

1792 George Washington re-elected President.

1793 Proclamation of Neutrality.

1796 John Adams elected President.

1798 Alien and Sedition Acts.

1798–99 Kentucky and Virginia Resolutions.

1800–01 Thomas Jefferson elected President.

1803 *Marbury v. Madison.*

1803 Louisiana Purchase.

1804–06 Lewis and Clark expedition.

1804 Jefferson re-elected President.

1807 Embargo Act.

1808 James Madison elected President.

1812 Madison re-elected President.

1812 War of 1812 begins.

1814 Hartford Convention meets.

1814 Treaty of Ghent restores peace.

1815 Battle of New Orleans.

1816 Second Bank of United States chartered.

1816 Protective tariff adopted.

1816 James Monroe elected President.

1818 Rush-Bagot Agreement approved.

1819 Treaty gives Florida to U.S.

1820 Missouri Compromise.

1820 Monroe re-elected President.

1823 Monroe Doctrine proclaimed.

1824 John Quincy Adams elected President.

1828 "Tariff of Abominations."

1828 Andrew Jackson elected President.

1830 Webster-Hayne debate.

1832 Ordinance of Nullification.

1832 Jackson vetoes renewal of charter for Bank of United States.

1832 Jackson re-elected President.

1836 Martin Van Buren elected President.

1837 Panic; economic depression begins.

1840 William Henry Harrison elected President.

1841 Harrison dies, and John Tyler becomes President.

THEN AND NOW

1. The American capital was originally at New York. Explain the circumstances that brought it to Washington, D.C.

2. Why will there never be another election with the results of that in 1800? How has the 22nd Amendment made Eisenhower's position as President in his second term a unique one?

3. Summarize Washington's key ideas on foreign policy after reading his Farewell Address. What do you think would be his view today of American foreign policy? Justify your answer.

EXTENDING YOUR HORIZON

1. For a deeper insight into Jeffersonian and Jacksonian democracy, read Chapters 2 and 3 in Richard Hofstadter, *The American Political Tradition* [Knopf (Vintage)].

2. For a fuller understanding of the positions taken by Hamilton and Jefferson on the constitutionality of the First National Bank, read the letters of each to President Washington as found in Chapter 3 of Heffner, *A Documentary History of the United States* (Mentor).

3. Read "The Letter that Bought an Empire," *American Heritage,* April 1955. Report to the class.

INDIVIDUAL ACTIVITIES

1. Make one or more cartoons showing Jackson as seen by his friends and enemies. Collect political cartoons as you find them in your daily paper.

2. On an outline map, indicate the major areas added to our country on the basis of treaties made between 1783 and 1842.

GROUP ACTIVITIES

1. Let two committees prepare signs, slogans, and cartoons which might have been used to win votes in the election of 1800, with one committee working for Adams, and the other for Jefferson. Campaign speeches in favor of the respective candidates might also be prepared. In a Presidential campaign year, committees can create similar materials for candidates of that year.

2. Have a group of students study Chapter II, "Catholics as Citizens 1790–1852" in John T. Ellis, *American Catholicism.* Then, let them present to the class a discussion of the character of American Catholicism in this period under these headings: nationalism; the Church as an Ameri-

canizing institution; nativist opposition; the role of Roman Catholics in public affairs.

SUGGESTED FURTHER READING

BIOGRAPHY

BAKELESS, JOHN, *Lewis and Clark: Partners in Discovery*, Morrow.

*BOWERS, CLAUDE G., *Jefferson and Hamilton*, Houghton Mifflin.

——, *Jefferson in Power*, Houghton Mifflin.

*HACKER, LOUIS M., *Alexander Hamilton in the American Tradition*, McGraw-Hill.

LOTH, DAVID, *Chief Justice Marshall and the Growth of the Republic*, Norton.

MILLER, JOHN C., *Alexander Hamilton: Portrait in Paradox*, Harper.

MIRSKY, JEANETTE, and ALLAN NEVINS, *The World of Eli Whitney*, Macmillan.

*MORRIS, RICHARD B., ed. *Basic Ideas of Alexander Hamilton*, Pocket Books.

PADOVER, SAUL K., *Jefferson*, New American Library (Mentor Books).

RICHARD, L. E., *Abigail Adams and Her Times*, Appleton-Century-Crofts.

*SCHLESINGER, ARTHUR M., JR., *Age of Jackson*, Little, Brown; New American Library (Mentor Books).

WALTERS, RAYMOND, JR., *Albert Gallatin*, Macmillan.

OTHER NONFICTION

ADAMS, HENRY, *The United States in 1800*, Cornell Univ. Press (paper).

BEIRNE, FRANCIS F., *The War of 1812*, Dutton.

*CORWIN, EDWARD, *John Marshall and the Constitution*, Yale Univ. Press.

DANGERFIELD, GEORGE, *The Era of Good Feelings*, Harcourt, Brace.

DE VOTO, BERNARD, *Across the Wide Missouri*, Houghton Mifflin. Treats the fur trade.

FORESTER, C. S., *The Age of the Fighting Sail*, Doubleday. Naval war of 1812.

HAMILTON, ALEXANDER, and others, *The Federalist Papers*, Dutton (Everyman's Library); and others. Essays on government and politics. Best known are numbers 10, 78, 84.

KROUT, JOHN ALLEN, and DIXON RYAN FOX, *The Completion of Independence*, Macmillan. Social and cultural history, 1790–1830.

PADOVER, SAUL K., *Thomas Jefferson on Democracy*, New American Library (Mentor Books).

PRATT, FLETCHER, *The Heroic Years*, Random House. The years 1801–1815.

TURNER, F. J., *The Rise of the New West*, Peter Smith.

VAN DEUSEN, GLYNDON G., *The Jacksonian Era, 1828–1848*, Harper.

HISTORICAL FICTION

ADAMS, SAMUEL HOPKINS, *Canal Town*, Random House; and others. Building of the Erie Canal.

ATHERTON, GERTRUDE, *The Conqueror*, Lippincott. About Hamilton.

BENÉT, STEPHEN VINCENT, *Thirteen O'Clock*, Heinemann (London). Stories recalling American legends.

BUSBEE, JAMES, JR., *Yankee Mariner*, Hearst (Avon Books). About the War of 1812.

CARMER, CARL, *Genesee Fever*, Doubleday. About land speculation.

CHURCHILL, WINSTON, *Richard Carvel*, Macmillan. Eighteenth-century Britain and America.

DOBIE, FRANK J., *The Mustangs*, Bantam. Tales of old Texas.

EVANS, MARY ELLEN, *The Seed and the Glory*, McMullen.

FORBES, ESTHER, *Johnny Tremain*, Houghton Mifflin. Historical novel of American Revolution.

FORESTER, C. S., *Captain from Connecticut*, Little, Brown.

GABRIEL, GILBERT W., *I, James Lewis*, Doubleday. Fur empire in Oregon.

HALE, EDWARD EVERETT, *The Man Without a Country*, Houghton Mifflin; Revell. An American classic.

LANCASTER, BRUCE, *Phantom Fortress*, Little, Brown. Revolutionary War in the South.

PAGE, ELIZABETH, *The Tree of Liberty*, Rinehart. The years 1750–1800.

ROBERTS, KENNETH, *Captain Caution*, Doubleday. Novel about War of 1812.

——, *The Lively Lady*, Doubleday. Novel about War of 1812.

——, *Lydia Bailey*, Doubleday. Barbary pirates and revolution in Haiti.

STONE, IRVING, *The President's Lady*, Doubleday. Novel about Rachel Jackson.

PART 2

THE
NATION
DIVIDED

The major themes in Part One of this book were the political developments that transformed the British colonies along the Atlantic seaboard into an independent nation and strengthened democracy by greatly extending the right to vote. Thomas Jefferson (1743–1826) was one of many Americans who lived through these creative years.

Abraham Lincoln was seventeen years old when Jefferson died. Jefferson, the elderly statesman, had lived to see the nation born. Lincoln, the youth, lived to see the Union tested by fire and sword in one of the most tragic conflicts in history.

Lincoln also lived to see revolutionary changes in the economic life of the nation. When he was born in a log cabin in 1809, nine out of ten Americans were living on farms, and the frontier had not yet reached the Mississippi River. When he died in 1865, the Industrial Revolution was in full swing, and the smoking factory chimney was replacing the farmhouse as the symbol of the nation's economy.

The Rise of Sectionalism

1820's–1860's

The Northern States Build New Industries

CHANGING WAYS

OF AMERICAN LIFE

By the 1840's the Industrial Revolution was moving steadily ahead in the United States. "I visited the . . . factory establishment at Waltham, within a few miles of Boston," Harriet Martineau, an English traveler, wrote of a trip she made in 1834–35. "Five hundred persons were employed at the time of my visit."

The Waltham textile plant was one of the largest in the country, but there were many others, most of them only a few years old. The mills and factories, simple structures of wood or stone or brick, stood on the banks of swift-flowing rivers and streams, from which they secured their power. Nearby were the small houses of the workers and the larger houses of the owners.

Factories and the towns that were springing up around them were becoming an increasingly important part of American life by the 1840's, particularly in the northeastern states. They were the visible evidence of the changes that were slowly beginning to alter life in the Northeast and that would, in time, affect the entire nation.

In her travels the English visitor also saw other signs of change—the new roads, new canals, and new railroads that were connecting the growing towns with one another and with the surrounding countryside, and that were reaching across the Appalachians to the farms and towns in the growing western regions. The rapidly developing transportation system and the new mills and factories were part of the Industrial Revolution that was beginning to transform the United States from an agricultural to an industrial nation.

AS THE STORY DEVELOPS

1. The nation develops a better transportation system.
2. Businessmen of the northern states grow more powerful.
3. Wage earners help create the early industrial system.
4. Rising immigration adds to the country's population.

287

1 The nation develops a better transportation system

The United States would never have been able to expand westward across the Appalachian Mountains, then to the Mississippi River, and finally to the Pacific coast without the development of a good system of transportation. Just as the Constitution gave the American people a strong federal union of the states, so roads, canals, railways, and steamboats made it possible for people in different parts of the country to exchange both material products and ideas and to work together for the common good.

Roads and highways. The development of better roads and highways was well under way by the 1820's. Private companies, as you have seen (page 254), had built hundreds of miles of good roads and turnpikes, especially in the eastern part of the country. In order to open up the western region, state legislatures had financed the construction of state-owned roads leading into the interior. Pennsylvania, for example, had built an extension to the Lancaster Turnpike, carrying the new state road through the mountain passes to Pittsburgh at the headwaters of the Ohio River (see map, opposite page). The Philadelphia-Pittsburgh Turnpike was completed in 1818.

But the most important road project, as you have seen, was the building of the National Road, on which construction had been started in 1811. Financed by the federal government, the National Road had cut across state boundaries and progressed slowly westward. By 1833 the road was open to traffic as far as Columbus, Ohio. By 1852 it reached Vandalia, Illinois, not far from the Mississippi River (see map, opposite page). In 1853 the 834 miles of the National Road were turned over to the states.

By 1860 Americans would look with pride at the system of roads and highways that crisscrossed the eastern half of the nation. In 1790, according to estimates of the Bureau of the Census, there had not been a single important stretch of hard-surfaced road in the entire United States. By 1820 over 9000 miles of surfaced roads had been completed; by 1860, more than 88,000 miles.

Effect of the roads. The roads built with private, state, and federal money began to change the lives of many thousands of Americans. Farmers in the outlying parts of the eastern states and in the sparsely settled country west of the Appalachian Mountains were at last able to buy and sell in the city markets of the East. The roads were crowded with freight wagons and other traffic.

Moving produce by wagon cost less than carrying it on the backs of horses or mules, but wagon transportation was not inexpensive. In 1817, for instance, it still cost $13 to transport a barrel of flour from Pittsburgh to Philadelphia—and this was over one of the best highways in the United States! Even on the best of the hard-surfaced roads, bulky products like corn, wheat, and flour could not be transported profitably by wagon over distances of more than 150 miles. Farmers, businessmen, and others began to demand less expensive means of transportation.

The Erie Canal. The construction of canals was one answer to the demand for cheaper methods of transportation. As early as the 1780's and the 1790's, leaders of the state of New York had begun agitating for a canal to be built between Albany and Buffalo. Such a canal,

STAGECOACH

CONESTOGA WAGON

LIGHT WAGON

Along the National Road

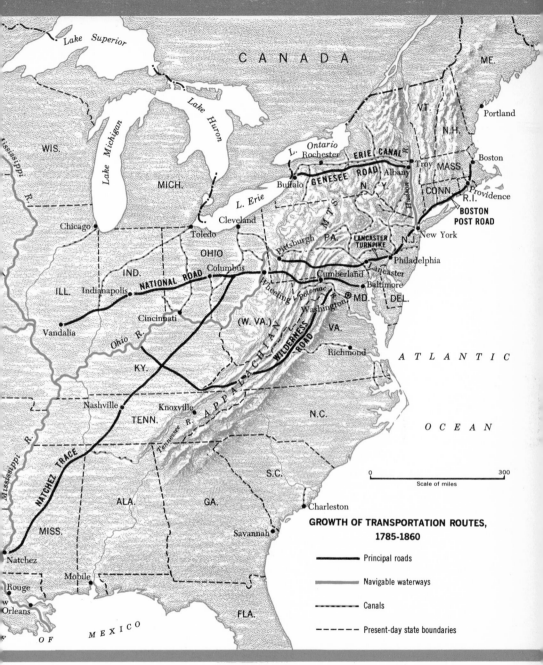

GROWTH OF TRANSPORTATION ROUTES, 1785-1860

———— Principal roads

———— Navigable waterways

----------- Canals

- - - - - - Present-day state boundaries

flowing into the Hudson River at Albany, would provide inexpensive water transportation from New York City to the Great Lakes.

Agitation for the canal grew stronger when the National Road was started. It then became clear to New Yorkers that

Baltimore, connected with the western areas by the only highway through the mountains, had a good chance of becoming the most important commercial port on the Atlantic coast. Thoroughly alarmed, the legislature of New York, acting under the leadership of Governor

289

De Witt Clinton, authorized the construction of the Erie Canal.

In 1817 the dirt began to fly in one of the major engineering feats in American history. Immigrants, many from Ireland, did most of the hard work. When the canal was finished, a man-made waterway, 42 feet wide and at least 4 feet deep, stretched westward for 363 miles from the Hudson River at Troy to Lake Erie at Buffalo (see map, page 289). A series of 83 locks lifted the boats over a total rise of more than 500 feet on the east-west journey and lowered them on the return trip.

It is no wonder that the opening of the canal on October 26, 1825, was an occasion for wild rejoicing. When the official procession of canal boats started from Lake Erie, a relay of cannon placed twelve miles apart boomed the news down the whole length of the canal to Albany and down the Hudson River to New York City. The official procession, including Governor Clinton, moved slowly down the new waterway, stopping for celebrations at towns and settlements along the way. Ten days later Governor Clinton ended his voyage at the mouth of New York harbor where, in a solemn ceremony, he poured a cask of Lake Erie water into the Atlantic Ocean to symbolize the joining of the Great Lakes and the Atlantic.

The Erie Canal was an immediate success. Horses and mules, urged along by a driver who walked behind them on a towpath that bordered the canal, drew the heavy barges through the water. At the stern of each barge stood a helmsman. Passengers rode in luxurious barges with gaily colored curtains at the windows.

Cities began to grow along the route, among them Utica, Syracuse, and Rochester. The city of New York became the "gateway to the West" and the leading commercial port of the nation, doubling its population within a decade after the opening of the canal. Cheap transportation had accomplished all this. Because a horse could pull fifty times as much weight in still water as he could pull over a road, freight rates dropped to a new low. Before the canal was completed, it had cost more than $100 to transport a ton of goods by road from Buffalo to New York; after the canal was finished, the same ton of goods could be carried through the canal for as little as $5 to $10.

The canal-building era. As money began to flow into the pockets of New York businessmen and as the population of New York City began to swell, businessmen of other commercial cities like Philadelphia and Baltimore decided that they, too, would have to build canals. Pennsylvania, eager to secure a share of the traffic with the western regions, constructed a canal through the Allegheny Mountains to connect Philadelphia with the headwaters of the Ohio River (see map, page 289).

Other states also built frantically. By the 1830's canals were being dug throughout the country. When the depression of 1837 settled upon the country, more than 3000 miles of canals had been built in the United States, most of them in the northern part of the country. With the depression, however, the enthusiasm for canal building came to an abrupt end, partly because railroads were becoming increasingly important, partly because the states were unable or unwilling to invest in canal projects. Several states defaulted on their canal bonds, failing to repay money that people had invested in them. Some states sold the state-owned canals to private companies. Others continued to operate the canals they had built. But for some time, state development of transportation facilities was ended.

River steamboats. Another essential link in the new transportation system was the steamboat. Before 1800 a number of inventors in both Europe and America had built steam-driven boats. But it was Robert Fulton's demonstra-

---

■ A visiting French artist painted this colorful scene of steamboats along the New Orleans riverfront. The boats were ungainly but efficient.

BISHOP HUGHES
AND A SCHOOL CRISIS

Bishop Hughes, who became New York's first Archbishop in 1850, was spokesman for thousands of Irish Catholics who landed, poverty-stricken, in that city. They were refugees from hardship and religious discrimination, but eager to acquire an education.

The city's schools were run by the Public School Society, a group of fiery Protestants. The Society had all the available money from the state for support of "free" schools. The books used in teaching bitterly criticized the Catholic Church. Protestant bibles were distributed. Every effort was made to make orphans Protestants. The Irish found the situation much like that in the British-dominated Ireland they had left; but in New York they had political freedom to resist it. After a severe contest, with many disorders, Bishop Hughes and the Catholics welcomed the demise of the Public School Society in 1842.

New York state's Governor William H. Seward had supported the Catholics in this battle. He and Bishop Hughes would have preferred to have the state continue to grant money to private groups to use in education; and if the Catholics got their share, the others would have no good reason to complain. But this was not to be. In New York and elsewhere, after the fight over the Public School Society, only city authorities ran the schools; and no religion at all was to be taught. The Catholics therefore had to begin *parochial schools* in order to combine religious and other instruction. Thus, while Catholics are taxed like others for public schools, from which they get indirect benefits, they also have to support their own schools, which are, also indirectly, of benefit to all.

tion of the *Clermont,* on the Hudson River in 1807, that first attracted widespread attention in the United States.

Fulton and his business associates realized that immense profits could be earned in the western areas. Up to this time, as you know, river boats could not navigate economically upstream. In 1811 Fulton and his associates built a steamboat at Pittsburgh and took it down the Ohio River to the Mississippi. Called the *New Orleans,* it ran successfully up and down the Mississippi until July 14, 1814, when it ripped its hull on a snag near Baton Rouge and sank. Other boats were soon built, however, and by the 1820's steam-driven vessels were a fairly common sight on the Mississippi and Ohio Rivers and their tributaries.

From the 1820's to the 1860's, river steamers transported most of the cargo of the Mississippi Valley. They chugged up and down the Mississippi and threaded their ways east and west to villages and towns on the numerous tributaries. By 1840 four fifths of all the traffic in the Mississippi Valley was carried by steamboats, and steamers were appearing on the Great Lakes.

Construction of railroads. Like the early roads and canals, the railroads grew out of commercial rivalry among the cities along the Atlantic seaboard. Baltimore led the way. Construction of the first section of the Baltimore and Ohio Railroad began on July 4, 1828, the fifty-second anniversary of the Declaration of Independence.

Present at the start of construction in Baltimore was Charles Carroll, at ninety-one years of age the only surviving signer of the Declaration of Independence. The famous patriot said that this occasion was the greatest event of his life. Even Carroll, however, could not have visualized the importance of the ceremony in which he was taking part. As the years went on, roads, canals, and steamboats were vital in the development of the United States, but it was the railroad more than any other part of our transportation system that made possible the development of the

Map legend:
━━━━━━ Railroads in 1850
━━━━━━ Railroads built between 1850 and 1860
------ Present-day state boundaries

Scale of miles: 0 — 300

greatest industrial nation in the world.

In 1828 only men with consuming optimism dared hope for the successful development of railroads. The first locomotive on the Baltimore and Ohio—the *Tom Thumb*, built by Peter Cooper of New York—was a crude, undependable contraption. The rails on which the engine ran were wooden timbers with thin strips of metal along the top. With much clanging of metal, fearsome showers of sparks, and loud hissing of steam, the *Tom Thumb* could reach a maximum speed of a little more than 10 miles per hour.

Despite these feeble beginnings the Baltimore and Ohio Railroad and other railroads more than justified the faith of their promoters. In spite of violent opposition from the stagecoach lines, progress was rapid. Rival seaports began to construct rail lines into the interior. By 1833 merchants of Charleston, South Carolina, had financed a 136-mile railroad into the interior of the state as far as Hamburg (see map, this page). At

293

■ In the 1830's, a long covered bridge carried a highway and the Baltimore and Ohio Railroad across the Potomac River into Harper's Ferry, Virginia. In the right foreground is a stretch of the Chesapeake and Ohio Canal. With some exceptions, the canals were put out of business by the railroads.

the time it was the longest railway line in the world under a single management. Other cities, such as Boston, New York, and Philadelphia, followed suit. Better locomotives were developed. Rails made entirely of iron replaced the wooden ones with their metal strips. Cars were improved. By 1840 nearly 3000 miles of track had been laid; by 1850 the total had grown to more than 9000 miles. By 1860, 30,000 miles of rails linked the East and the western regions as far as the Mississippi River (see map, page 293).

Effects of improved transportation. It was a difficult and costly job for the young nation to push its transportation system from the Atlantic coast, through the Appalachian Mountains, and out to the great water system of the Mississippi Valley. But the job was done—by roads, canals, steamboats, and railroads.

As each new stage of the transportation system was completed, new areas of the western regions were linked with the eastern seaboard. The products of eastern factories began moving west in ever-growing volume, stimulating the development of the eastern factories.

The new means of transportation also stimulated the development of the western regions. Pioneer settlers could now travel to these promised lands more easily than ever. Once settled, the pioneers could send their surplus crops to the eastern cities. The improved system of transportation brought the western farms and eastern factories closer together.

At the same time small villages in the western regions began growing into large towns and even cities. At first these communities served mainly as centers of trade between western farms and eastern factories. But by 1860 the towns and cities west of the mountains—what we now call the Middle West—were developing thriving industries of their own.

📖 **SECTION SURVEY**

1. Explain the importance of the National Road.

2. State the reasons for building the Erie Canal.

3. What was the importance of the Erie Canal to (a) New York state and (b) the nation?

4. In your opinion, which was most important in the development of our country: (a) roads, (b) canals, (c) steamboats, or (d) railroads? Give reasons for your choice.

5. Show the relation between improved transportation and the industrial growth of our country.

IDENTIFY: default, *Clermont, Tom Thumb;* Clinton, Fulton, Peter Cooper; 1807, 1817–25.

2 Businessmen of the northern states grow more powerful

The Industrial Revolution, stimulated in the United States in the 1790's by Samuel Slater and others and developed still more by the War of 1812, continued to gain momentum between 1820 and 1860. Many new factories were built. Some of these new factories, like textile mills and ironmaking plants, were built in the South. An increasing number of industries began to develop also in the rapidly growing cities of the Middle West. But most of the new industries were established in New England and the Middle Atlantic states.

The developing transportation system made it possible for manufacturers to sell their goods over a larger and larger area of the country. At the same time their new industries were protected from European competition by a tariff wall (see page 276). Although the upward trend of the tariff was checked after 1832, the manufacturers continued to receive some tariff protection.

The growing nation. Manufacturers also benefited from a rapidly growing nation. In 1790 there had been only 13 states in the new nation. By 1840 the number had grown to 26. By 1860 it reached a total of 33.

The population was also increasing. From about 4,000,000 in 1790, it grew to more than 17,000,000 in 1840. By 1860 it swelled to more than 31,000,000.

The overwhelming majority of these people earned their living as farmers, as their fathers and grandfathers had done in the 1790's. In 1840 nearly 9 out of every 10 Americans still lived in rural areas.

But the towns were growing both in number and in size. In 1790 there had been only 12 towns with populations larger than 2500. In 1840 the census takers reported 85 towns and cities with more than 2500 inhabitants, a number of them west of the Appalachian Mountains. By 1860 there were 229.

By 1840 the United States was no longer a small nation. It was a big nation, and it was growing bigger every year. Its growing population needed the products of the new industries.

Investment of capital. Where did the manufacturers get the money, or in other words the capital, to invest in the new mills and factories?

A large part of the necessary capital came from European investors, but much of it came from well-to-do Americans—especially from merchants. This was especially true during the period of the Embargo Act (1807–09) and the War of 1812, for American money as well as ships was "unemployed" in these years. By 1820 $50,000,000 had been invested in manufacturing in the United States. By 1850 the amount had risen to

■ In 1844 Samuel F. B. Morse successfully demonstrated the telegraph he had invented. Within two or three years, it was relaying news of the Mexican War. This new means of communication was also vital in the development of the railroads.

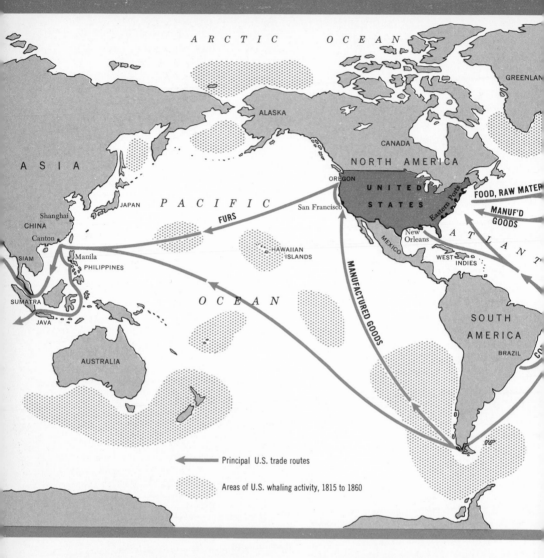

ARCTIC OCEAN

GREENLAN

ALASKA

CANADA

ASIA

NORTH AMERICA

OREGON

UNITED STATES

FOOD, RAW MATER

JAPAN

PACIFIC

San Francisco

Eastern Ports

MANUF'D GOODS

Shanghai
CHINA
Canton

FURS

New Orleans

A T L A N T

SIAM

Manila
PHILIPPINES

HAWAIIAN ISLANDS

MEXICO

WEST INDIES

SUMATRA

JAVA

O C E A N

MANUFACTURED GOODS

SOUTH AMERICA

AUSTRALIA

BRAZIL

Co

Principal U.S. trade routes

Areas of U.S. whaling activity, 1815 to 1860

$500,000,000. By 1860 it totaled more than $1,000,000,000.

Most of the manufacturing establishments constructed with this money were small, *individually owned* factories or mills. Frequently the owner was also the manager, who hired and directed the workers and worked side by side with them. Sometimes larger businesses were organized as *partnerships,* in which two or more men shared in the ownership and operation of the business. Widespread use of the *corporation* as a form of business organization was still to come (Chapter 23).

The merchant marine. While industry was growing, American seamen were carrying the American flag and American goods to the far ends of the earth. Even before 1800 Yankee sailing vessels had been familiar sights in the ports of China, Java, Sumatra, Siam (now Thailand), India, and the Philippines. The vessels left their home ports with cargoes of beads, knives, gunpowder, cotton goods, pottery, and rum. Stopping at harbors in the Pacific Northwest, the captains traded these goods with the Indians in exchange for furs. The furs were then carried to China and sold.

EUROPE

MEDITERRANEAN SEA

AFRICA

Calcutta
INDIA

Aden

INDIAN

OCEAN

TEA, SILKS, SPICES

From the 1820's to the 1860's, American merchants kept building larger and faster sailing ships to add to the American merchant marine. In these larger and faster vessels American seamen continued to carry the American flag to the far ends of the earth. They carried passengers and supplies to California in the days of the Gold Rush of 1849 and later. Trade with China and other Asiatic countries continued to flourish. By 1860 Americans had secured more than half of all the commerce to and from the great Chinese port of Shanghai; American seamen were trading along the Yangtze (YANG-tsee) River in China; and American whalers were likely to appear for water and provisions in almost any port of the world (see map, these pages).

Yankee seamen were equally successful on the Atlantic. As early as 1824 they had secured most of the traffic in passengers and freight between Liverpool, England, and the ports of Boston and New York. An Englishman explained how the Yankees achieved this success. "The reason will be evident to anyone who will walk through the docks at Liverpool," he said. "He will see the American ships, long, sharp built, beautifully painted and rigged, and remarkable for their fine appearance and white canvas. He will see the English vessels, short, round, and dirty, resembling great black tubs."

Clipper ships. During the 1840's and 1850's sailing ships of American merchants became world-famous. The celebrated "clipper ships" were the pride and glory of the seas. One of the clippers, the *James Baines*, made the crossing from Boston to Liverpool in 12 days. The activities of the merchant fleet kept American shipyards busy, and the fortunes made from commerce helped to finance America's growing factories and railroads.

But at this time the British, who for half a century had been outdistanced by the Yankee sailors and shipbuilders, were busily constructing ocean-going

Returning, the vessels brought tea and other luxuries to the United States.

This long voyage was dangerous, but enormously profitable if successful. In a few hours of trading, one captain secured 560 otter skins from the Indians of the Pacific Northwest in exchange for goods that had cost him only $2. He sold the otter skins in Canton, China, for $22,400. In 1797 a group of thirty boys and young men, the oldest twenty-eight years of age, took their vessel around the world, returning with a net profit of more than $50,000 on an initial investment of less than $8000.

(*Continued on page 299*)

The clipper Zephyr *in Messina harbor, Sicily*

CLIPPER SHIPS

No sailing ships ever built could match the Yankee clippers in speed or beauty. Even their names—*Zephyr, Flying Cloud, Herald of the Morning*—suggest swift and graceful motion.

The clippers were distinctly American. Plans for these streamlined vessels came from the drawing boards of American designers. From Maine to Baltimore, clippers slid down the ways of American shipyards and into the trade lanes.

The clipper's era of glory came in the first half of the 1800's. During these years clippers sailed the seven seas, outdistancing every other ship afloat. They made the run from China to New York in as little as 75 days, thereby capturing the rich Orient trade from slower vessels that required nearly a year to make the same trip. Clippers captained by shrewd Yankees wrested much of the lucrative London–East India trade from their British rivals.

The California gold rush further boosted the prestige of the clipper ship. Gold-hungry prospectors demanded bookings on the speedy clippers, which made the run around Cape Horn in 80 days, cutting months from the best time of their competitors.

The clipper had its beginnings during the American Revolution when the struggling nation needed fast ships capable of outmaneuvering Britain's heavily armed vessels. In the 1790's the first Secretary of the Treasury, Alexander Hamilton, ordered ten schooner clippers to serve as the nation's first Coast Guard. Merchants and shipbuilders perfected the design.

Today, one of the few clipper-type vessels still in service belongs to the United States Coast Guard. The *Eagle*'s trim hull—steel-plated as a concession to modern times—slices the waters of the Atlantic each year carrying cadets on a training cruise. Her towering masts and vast expanse of white sail are a monument to the proud clippers that once displayed America's flag in the far ports of the earth.

steamships. By 1860 steamships had demonstrated their superiority over sailing vessels. During the War Between the States, American shipowners lost much of their already dwindling business, and the decline in the United States merchant marine continued until the 1900's.

✓ **SECTION SURVEY**

1. "By 1840 the United States was no longer a small nation." Justify this statement.

2. Where did businessmen get the capital to invest in new industries during this period?

3. What were the reasons for the success of our merchant marine during the first half of the nineteenth century?

4. Why did our merchant marine decline?

IDENTIFY: partnership, clipper ship.

3 Wage earners help create the early industrial system

As more and more factories were built, mainly in the northern part of the country, manufacturers had to find workers to run the machines and do other work in the new industrial plants. Where did they find these workers?

Early labor supply. Until about 1830 the wage earners were mostly native-born American women and children. In 1831, for instance, children under 12 years of age made up about 40 per cent of all the wage earners in the cotton textile mills of Rhode Island. In other industries and other areas the percentage of child labor was not so high, but everywhere children performed a substantial number of the factory tasks.

Women were quite willing to work in the textile factories. After all, the women reasoned, since they were used to spinning and weaving in their own homes, what did it matter if the work were transferred to a factory? As for the children, they did whatever their parents told them to, at a time when it was commonly believed that labor was good for children.

During the early 1800's factory owners often contracted for the labor of an entire family. Advertisements like the following, which appeared in the Providence, Rhode Island, *Manufacturers' and Farmers' Journal* for January 14, 1828, were frequently inserted in the newspapers of the industrial towns: "Families Wanted—Ten or twelve good respectable families, consisting of four or five children each, from nine to sixteen years of age, are wanted to work in a cotton mill in the vicinity of Providence." Of course, employers also hired individual men and women.

Conditions of labor. The family system of labor recruitment had certain advantages for the workers. The family was kept together, for example, instead of being split up to work in different factories or even in different towns. The work was not always difficult. Machinery ran much more slowly than it does today, and the children did the lighter tasks. In a textile mill, for example, children might be assigned such jobs as carrying boxes containing bobbins, or spools, and mending broken threads. Although the hours were long—12 to 14 hours a day six days a week—the workday was no longer than that on the farm, which lasted from sunrise to sunset.

British labor compared. Workers in American factories during the first thirty or forty years of the 1800's were never forced to endure the evil, degrading conditions of their fellows in Great Britain. During the early 1800's young children in Great Britain were taken from orphanages and poorhouses to do hard work in factories, mills, and mines. As late as 1830, a Parliamentary investigating committee reported that children as young as eight and nine years of age were taxing their strength from dawn to dusk or even longer, under the most unsanitary and harsh conditions. The committee produced evidence of children chained to benches, of other children being driven with whips, and of women crawling on hands and knees to haul mine cars through narrow tunnels.

As a result of this report, Parliament in 1833 passed a "factory act" placing certain limits on the working hours of children. Later acts passed during the next few years helped to eliminate the worst evils, but throughout the 1840's conditions in British factories were grim compared to those in the United States.

Most Americans would never have stood for such conditions, not because Americans were essentially different from British workers, but because in America there was a means of escape. If conditions became too bad, the Americans could return to their farms or perhaps take up new land on the frontier.

Moreover, unlike in Great Britain, labor was scarce in the United States; a ruthless employer would soon find himself with an empty building and idle machines. The realization of this fact, plus in many cases a genuine desire to treat the workers decently, prompted some American employers to try to provide good working conditions.

The Waltham system. A notable but short-lived experiment was the one worked out at Waltham, Massachusetts, beginning in 1813. Only persons of good character were employed in the Waltham textile plant. The women and girls were required to live in company-owned boarding houses, run much like college dormitories of today, with matrons in charge to see that certain rules were observed. Employees were discharged for lying, profanity, and laziness. All employees were required to attend church. Educational programs, lectures, debates, and social gatherings were organized. The factories were clean and cheerful, with flower boxes at the windows and pictures above the looms.

The Waltham system spread to several other factories. For a while it worked well. Women and girls, as well as men, welcomed a chance to leave home and get an education, which was often unavailable on the farm. By 1840, however, the system was beginning to break down as factories grew in size, and, as you will see, employers began to hire immigrants who had begun to stream into the country during the 1830's.

Discontent arises. Although working conditions in the earlier American factories were in general far better than those in Great Britain, by the 1830's and 1840's growing numbers of American workers were laboring under extremely harsh conditions. Many workers were forced to toil as much as 16 hours a day in the squalid, dirty, crowded tenement areas of cities like Boston, New York, and Philadelphia. This situation existed particularly in the clothing industries, where workers, mostly women and children, labored in the dark, dirty, upper stories of buildings, called lofts. Equally depressing was the plight of women and children who picked up unfinished garments from a central plant and took them to their slum lodgings to complete the sewing, receiving a small payment for each finished garment.

As time passed, the common argument that child labor was good for children began to break down. More and more people, including the workers themselves, began to demand educational opportunities for children on the ground that democracy was unworkable among illiterate people. In an effort to meet these demands, some manufacturers opened Sunday schools and evening schools for the boys and girls. But these efforts were unsuccessful, for children who had worked long hours six days a week were in no condition to attend classes in their few hours of free time.

Early labor organizations. The wage earners' discontent with many features of the new industrial economy led them to form workingmen's organizations for the improvement of wages and working conditions—the earliest American labor unions. Thus, the growth of the labor movement in the United States paralleled the growth of industry.

The labor movement was especially active during the late 1820's and the early 1830's. It furnished support for Andrew Jackson and the Democratic Party in the years of Jackson's Presidency.

During these years of unusual labor activity, the newly organized local unions even thought of a great national union of all workers. If such a union could be created, one observer commented, "the rights of each individual would then be sustained by every workingman in the country, whose aggregate wealth and power must be able to resist the most formidable oppression."

By 1834, when representatives of labor met in their first national convention, there were probably more than 300,000 organized workers in the United States. In this same year a group of workmen organized the National Trades Union. The National Trades Union never became powerful, but it did hold three national conventions and passed several resolutions that represented a significant development in the beginnings of labor organization and labor thinking.

The workers' demands. The workers' organizations made a number of demands, with higher wages heading the list. Hand in hand with this demand went agitation for a 10-hour working day. The workers won partial success in 1840 when President Martin Van Buren established the 10-hour day for all government workers.

But the wage earners looked upon shorter hours not merely as desirable ends in themselves, but also as a means to even more important ends. What many workers wanted was equality of educational opportunity. This meant that children working 12 to 14 hours daily for six days a week must be released from manual toil and given the chance to attend school. And this, in turn, meant that schools must be built with public funds in all parts of the country. By their demands for the education of their children, the wage earners helped to speed the development of tax-supported public schools.

AMERICAN INGENUITY

In 1790 the first U.S. Patent Office opened for business in New York City. Every inventor applying for a patent was required to submit a working model of his invention. American ingenuity being what it was, the models poured in. In 1802 the Patent Office was installed in the Department of State in Washington, D.C., but was soon removed to larger quarters in Blodgett's Hotel.

By 1836 more than 7000 models had been filed. There were models of "self-propelling boats," steam engines, bridges, saw mills, steam mills, fire engines, threshing machines, and dozens of plows. All these models and all the Patent Office records were consumed in a fire which on December 15, 1836, burned Blodgett's Hotel to the ground.

Applications and models continued to pour into the new Patent Office from inventors in every section of the country and every walk of life. In 1870, overwhelmed by the problem of storage, Congress dropped the requirement that inventors submit models with their applications. Models then on file (there were almost 200,000) ranged from such practical inventions as the telegraph, the Gatling gun, and the first egg beater to novelties such as a hen house on which, when the chicken went out to scratch, a sign appeared with the inscription, "I'm out. You may have my egg."

Wage earners also demanded an end to the practice of throwing a man into prison when he could not pay his debts. By the early 1840's nearly all of the states had abolished this penalty.

By the 1830's and 1840's organized labor had begun to take shape as a new force in American life. Workers had begun to develop the idea of unions and of *collective bargaining*—bargaining, that is, between union representatives and employers over wages, hours, and working conditions. Unions had begun to develop the *strike* when union members refused to work until their employer met their demands, and the *picket line* when union members paraded outside a plant during a strike and persuaded other workers not to take their jobs.

Weakness of organized labor. Although the American labor movement was beginning to take root, it was not yet strong enough to win many of the things that the wage earners demanded. There were several reasons for the weakness of the American labor movement in these early years of its history.

In the first place, many wage earners had not yet become aware that they were a new and growing group in the economic life of the nation and that they had interests in common. This feeling was partly the result of tradition. From the earliest days of settlement, most Americans had been farmers, and the early factories and mills drew most of their labor supply from the farms. The Americans' strong spirit of independence, of individualism, made it difficult for labor organizations to draw workers into unions. Wage earners continued to think of themselves as individuals who could look after their own interests. They were reluctant to follow the rules laid down by a union.

In the second place, cheap land was always available. This cheap land did not actually attract many dissatisfied workers, who preferred town to country life, but it did draw westward thousands of farmers who might otherwise have turned to the cities for employment.

In the third place, until 1842, labor unions were nowhere recognized by law. In that year Chief Justice Lemuel Shaw of the Supreme Court of Massachusetts handed down a decision (*Commonwealth v. Hunt*) recognizing the legal right of labor unions to exist in Massa-

chusetts. This decision set a precedent, but wage earners had to struggle in one state after another for the right to organize, and the struggle was a long one.

In the fourth place, the depression of 1837 threw thousands of men out of work. These unemployed workers could not afford to pay union dues and had to grasp at any job in desperation, regardless of what it paid. This situation helped to slow down the advance of the labor movement.

Finally, immigrants began to come to the United States in large numbers during the 1830's, as you will see. Many of these immigrants were willing to work for low wages. Immigration, therefore, forced down the wages of many native-born American workers and almost brought the labor movement to a halt.

■ This remarkable picture of 1847 shows crowds of immigrants debarking at New York City. They were fleeing famine in Ireland, and seeking a new life in America. At the left is a Chinese junk, thought to have been the first Chinese vessel to visit the eastern United States.

✔ SECTION SURVEY

1. Discuss the conditions of labor and the early sources of labor supply in the United States in the early 1800's.

2. (a) Compare working conditions in America then with those existing in England. (b) Describe the harsh conditions which came to prevail in America after 1830.

3. What reasons lay behind the early attempts at labor unions? List the aims and demands of these early unions.

4. Explain why early attempts at labor organization were only partly successful.

IDENTIFY: Waltham system, National Trades Union, collective bargaining, strike, picket line, *Commonwealth v. Hunt;* 1842.

4 Rising immigration adds to the country's population

Between 1790 and 1830 the population of the United States more than tripled, increasing, as you have seen, from about 4,000,000 to nearly 13,000,000. Nearly all of this growth was the result of births in the United States itself. During these years fewer than 400,000 immigrants entered the country.

Immigration grows. In the 1830's, however, the small stream of immigration swelled to a great flood. From 1830

303

to 1840, more than half a million immigrants poured into the United States (see chart, page 824). Forty-four per cent came from Ireland, 30 per cent from Germany, 15 per cent from Great Britain, and the remainder from various other countries of Europe. Between 1840 and 1850, a million and a half immigrants arrived in the United States, 49 per cent of them from Ireland.

Irish immigrants. The Irish came in search of relief from terrible conditions in their homeland. In Ireland during these years, many of the people worked as tenants on the estates of landlords who lived in England. The landlords did little or nothing to improve the conditions of their tenants, who barely managed to make a living. And then, in 1846, a terrible famine struck Ireland. Thousands died during the "Potato Famine," as it was called. Other thousands fled to America.

The people who fled Ireland were attracted to the United States, rather than elsewhere, for several reasons. They avoided Canada because they shared the dislike of the British Empire that was common at that time among native-born Americans. They liked what they heard about American democracy. They were thrilled at the reports of plenty in the United States. Moreover, American contractors encouraged them to come and work on the roads, canals, and railroads, and manufacturers attracted them into the new mills and factories.

Hardships of immigration. The immigrants endured hardships almost beyond belief in their efforts to reach the United States. The following news item that appeared in the *Edinburgh Review* of July 1854 gives a glimpse of the sufferings of the people who crossed the Atlantic as immigrants in those days:

"Liverpool was crowded with emigrants, and ships could not be found to do the work. The poor creatures were packed in dense masses in ill-ventilated and unseaworthy vessels, under charge of improper masters, and the natural result followed. Pestilence [disease] chased the fugitive to complete the work of famine. Fifteen thousand out of ninety thousand emigrants . . . in British bottoms [ships] in 1847 died on the passage or soon after arrival. The American vessels, owing to a stringent passenger law, were better managed; but the hospitals of New York and Boston were nevertheless crowded with patients from Irish estates. . . ."

Poor, unable to move to the western lands, many of the Irish immigrants who came in this period settled in the slums of the growing cities. Large groups of Irish people found homes in cities like New York, Boston, Albany, Baltimore, St. Louis, Cincinnati, and New Orleans. Many of the men went to work as unskilled laborers on the roads, canals, and railroads. Many of the women took jobs in the factories, displacing the native-born American wage earners.

German immigrants. Although people from many countries came to America during these years, the Germans formed the second largest group, outnumbered only by the Irish. Between 1845 and 1860 more than 1,300,000 Germans landed in the United States.

Many Germans came because, after 1815, Europe (and Germany in particular) was controlled by rulers who were opposed to democracy. Thousands of Germans who took part in revolutions that broke out in 1830 and 1848 fled when the revolutions failed. Other Germans came to earn a better living. Naturally, in seeking freedom from political persecution and economic hardship, they turned to the United States, the land of free men and cheap farms.

Most of the German immigrants settled on land in the Middle Western states—Ohio, Indiana, Illinois, Wisconsin, Iowa, and Missouri. Able, thrifty farmers, they built prosperous farms on the fertile soil. Many also moved to the cities, and by the 1860's formed a substantial proportion of such communities as Buffalo, Detroit, Cleveland, Cincinnati, Chicago, and St. Louis.

Immigrants resented. Most of the immigrants quickly became American citzens. Because many had come to the

United States in search of political freedom, they helped to strengthen political democracy. Because they were eager to work, they contributed to the wealth of the growing nation. But in spite of these contributions, the immigrants were resented by many native-born Americans, who were afraid that large numbers of "foreigners" would change the older ways of living in America.

Some Germans, for instance, aroused suspicion. They organized their own clubs, gathered in social halls to talk and sing, established their own churches and schools, published their own newspapers, and continued to use their own language. Native-born Americans viewed all these activities with grave misgivings.

It was the Irish who, on religious and nationalist grounds, at this time became the main target of resentment. Naturally, they wished to settle near their acquaintances and their growing churches. As a result, clusters of Irish people kept growing in the cities. Many of them dressed for a time as they had in Ireland. Their accent was strange to other Americans. Because they were different, older settlers at first looked upon them with suspicion. Suspicion of this kind, of course, has been the fate of every large immigrant group.

Feeling against the immigrants often led to friction and violence. Riots broke out in several cities. Feeling ran higher and higher as the number of immigrants increased. In 1845 a national organization of native-born Americans was started. A year later, this society was reorganized as a secret order called the Supreme Order of the Star-Spangled Banner or the Sons of the Sires of '76. Members solemnly pledged themselves to oppose foreigners and to support only American-born Protestants for public office. When asked about the society, a member would answer, "I know nothing." Because of such answers the organization came to be known as the Know-Nothing Party.

During the early 1850's the Know-Nothing Party, officially called by now the American Party, was very strong in American political life. In the election of 1854, for example, it polled one fourth of the total vote of New York and two fifths of Pennsylvania's vote. In Massachusetts it elected every state officer and nearly the entire legislature. In Baltimore the Know-Nothings organized the "Plug-Uglies," so-called because they attended the polls carrying carpenter's awls to "plug" voters who did not give a secret password. However, the election of 1854 was the high tide of the movement. In the national convention of the Know-Nothing Party in 1855, southern and northern members split over the question of slavery, and the Know-Nothing Party gradually lost its strength.

Changing ways of life. From the 1830's to the 1860's, older Americans were bewildered and upset as they saw familiar, traditional ways of life replaced by new and unfamiliar ways. The older Americans did not usually realize that it was machines, factories, and an *urban,* or city, life that were chiefly responsible for the revolution that was taking place. The foreigner was only one of many new elements in the changing pattern of American society. But like minorities in other times and other places, the immigrant became a scapegoat upon whom many native-born Americans heaped the blame for all their troubles, real and imaginary.

✔ **SECTION SURVEY**

1. From which countries did most of the immigrants come between 1830 and 1850?

2. (a) Compare the reasons why the Irish and the Germans emigrated during these years. (b) Where did each group settle?

3. What economic and religious factors were involved in native resentment toward the immigrants? (b) What was the aim of the Know-Nothing Party?

4. Describe some of the forms which native American opposition to the immigrants tended to take.

IDENTIFY: Potato Famine, urban.

■ CHAPTER SURVEY (For review, see Section Surveys, pages 294, 299, 303, 305.)

Points to Discuss: 1. The development of better methods of transportation was as important in uniting the country as the Constitution itself. Do you agree? Why?

2. Estimate the importance of the National Road and the Erie Canal in promoting the development of the interior of the country.

3. Summarize conditions which led to the promotion of manufacturing before 1860.

4. (a) The growth of the labor movement paralleled the growth of industry. Comment on the accuracy of this statement. (b) What obstacles confronted the early labor movement?

5. (a) Compare reasons for immigration in colonial times with reasons for immigration 1830–50. (b) Why did the immigrant become "a scapegoat upon whom native-born Americans heaped the blame for all their troubles"? (See articles pertaining to the Know-Nothing Movement in the *Dictionary of American History*.)

6. How did industrialization promote democracy and help to unite the nation?

Using Maps and Charts: 1. Use the map on page 289 to answer the following: (a) Estimate the length of the Erie Canal and the National Road. (b) How many canals are indicated? How many roads?

2. Using the map on page 293, answer the following: (a) What period is covered by the map? (b) Explain why there are fewer railroads located in the South.

3. Using the map on pages 296–97, answer the following: (a) Indicate the short cuts now available to world shipping that were not available up to 1860. (b) Indicate the chief exports and imports of the United States during the period covered by the map.

4. Refer to the charts on pages 824–25 to answer the following: (a) Compare population in the United States in 1830 with that in 1850. (b) Compare immigration for the same periods, and draw appropriate conclusions. (c) By 1850, what percentage of the total population consisted of foreign-born residents?

Consulting the Sources: See Ellis, *Docs.*, No. 80, for the constitution of a native American group formed in the year 1842. Nos. 81–84 provide interesting information on Catholicism and immigrants in rural and frontier areas. For an interesting document concerning the early years of Notre Dame University, see No. 88.

■ TRACING THE MAIN IDEAS

The Industrial Revolution between the 1820's and the 1860's has been the big story in this chapter. There was no large part of the United States that did not feel the influences of industry. Even in the South, textile mills, ironmaking plants, and other industrial establishments began to appear. But for the most part industrial developments were concentrated in New England, New York, Pennsylvania, and in the growing cities of the Middle West. It was in the North and Middle West that the immigrants mainly settled, seeking opportunities provided by railroad building and other industrial enterprises, as well as by farming.

The industrial towns and cities with their factories, their whirring machines, and their manufacturers, financiers, and wage earners were becoming a major influence in America. Industrialism strengthened democracy by making it possible for the people to buy goods never before available to them and by raising their standards of living. It strengthened national unity by binding the nation together with a network of roads, canals, and railroads.

But industrialism also created new problems. Wage earners, more and more dependent for their daily bread upon forces beyond their individual control, began to join together in labor unions; conflict between workers and owners became increasingly common. Finally, industrialism transformed the North into a new and distinct section of the country, creating serious differences between the North and the South.

The Southern States Create a Cotton Economy

CHANGING WAYS

OF AMERICAN LIFE

"COTTON is king," southerners often said in the 1840's and 1850's. They meant by this expression that cotton was very important to a great majority of the people who lived in the southern states. Indeed, by the 1850's, the cotton grown, shipped, and sold by southerners was worth more than all the rest of America's exports put together.

But in referring to the importance of "King Cotton," southerners were not thinking of themselves alone. They knew that countless other people—in the northern states, in Europe, and around the world—depended upon southern cotton for their living. They were thinking of merchants who traded and shipped in cotton and of the sailors who manned the ships, of the owners of cotton textile factories and of the workers in them, of storekeepers and traders who sold cotton shirts and trousers and

dresses in the United States, in Europe, in Africa, in India—wherever, in fact, they could find buyers.

Southerners could ask in the 1840's and 1850's: "What other product grown by man and fashioned into finished articles affects so many people in so many different parts of the world?" The answer was, "None."

What had happened in the southern states since the 1790's? When the Constitution was ratified, tobacco was the most important crop grown in the South. At that time also, Thomas Jefferson and many other people, in the South as well as in the North, thought that slavery would soon disappear in the United States. Now "cotton was king" and there were almost 4,000,000 slaves in the South.

In tracing the reasons for the profound changes that occurred in southern ways of life, you will learn why the southern states and the northern states were beginning to grow apart, along with some of the reasons why, in the 1860's, they were to fight a bitter war over the issues that divided them.

AS THE STORY DEVELOPS

1. The southern states become the "Cotton Kingdom."
2. Various groups help build the "Cotton Kingdom."
3. Planters exert leadership in the southern states.

307

1 The southern states become the "Cotton Kingdom"

The southern states, by the 1840's and 1850's, embraced a vast area of land stretching southward from Maryland and the Ohio River to the Gulf of Mexico. Included in this great cotton-growing region were also the states of Louisiana, Arkansas, and Texas.

The farm lands. Travelers in the South at this time were most impressed, of course, by the endless acres of cotton fields. But they also saw large plantings of other staple crops,° such as tobacco, rice, and sugar cane. In Virginia, North Carolina, Kentucky, Tennessee, and Missouri, the climate and soil were most favorable for tobacco growing; here the fields were green with broad, flat tobacco leaves. Rice fields flourished in the swampy coastal areas of South Carolina and Georgia. To the west, in the delta of the Mississippi River, huge stands of sugar cane swayed and ripened in the warm winds that swept in from the Gulf of Mexico. Travelers in Virginia might see large fields of wheat and corn. In Texas they could see enormous herds of cattle.

••
° *staple crop:* the principal commodity grown in a locality.

Ginning cotton

From their great staple crops—mainly cotton, tobacco, rice, and sugar cane—southerners received much of their cash income. Most, though not all, of these staple crops were grown, as you will see, on large plantations.

But travelers in the South also saw many small *subsistence farms,* much like those in the North and Middle West, where families raised food crops and livestock for their own use. And there were in the South, as there were elsewhere in the United States, large stretches of woodland, areas of rich soils, and important variations from one place to another in weather and rainfall.

Towns and industries. In an area so predominantly rural and agricultural as the South, industries and towns naturally grew more slowly than in the North. But there were many towns and a few important cities, among them Richmond, Virginia; Charleston, South Carolina; and New Orleans, Louisiana.

In the southern towns and cities tradesmen and skilled workers rubbed shoulders with professional workers—doctors, lawyers, clergymen, and teachers. Along the wharves and on the streets one could see sawmills, paper mills, brickyards, leather tanneries, blacksmith shops, turpentine and whisky distilleries, and a few cotton mills.

In the 1830's, as you have seen, a railroad was built from Charleston, South Carolina, into the interior. By 1860 about 10,000 miles of railroad tracks had been laid throughout the southern states. Along the rivers and coastlines hundreds of steamboats were kept busy exporting the staple crops of the South and importing manufactured goods.

By the 1850's some leading southerners like James De Bow of New Orleans were urging further development of southern industry and commerce. The southern economy, in short, was varied and complex. But overriding all other developments and efforts was the ever-present fact that "cotton was king."

The cotton economy grows. In the late 1700's, as you know, British inventors and manufacturers developed power-

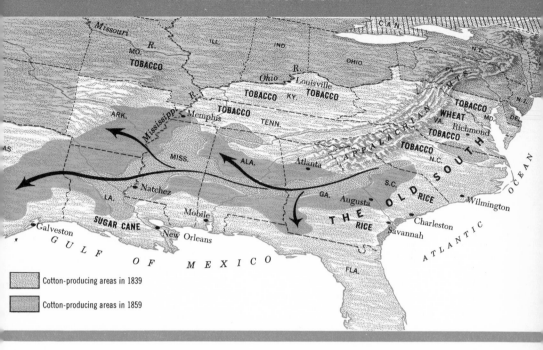

Cotton-producing areas in 1839

Cotton-producing areas in 1859

driven machinery for spinning thread and weaving cloth. Before long, Samuel Slater and others were operating similar machinery in textile mills in the New England and Middle Atlantic states. The new textile mills began to produce cloth in growing quantities, and mill owners on both sides of the Atlantic began clamoring for raw cotton fiber.

Eli Whitney, inventor of interchangeable gun parts (see page 250), also invented in 1793 a machine called the *cotton gin* (*engine*) that broke a bottleneck in the production of raw cotton fiber. The heart of the cotton plant, called the boll, is a tangle of fibers and seeds. Whitney's new machine could separate the seeds from the fibers much faster than this could be done by hand.

Along the South Atlantic coast grew a kind of cotton, called "sea-island cotton," whose long fibers could be separated from the seed fairly rapidly by hand. But only a limited amount of this cotton could be grown along the coast. The "upland cotton," grown in the interior, had shorter fibers that clung so tightly to the seed that a man could separate by hand only about a pound of

cotton fiber a day. As a result, prior to Whitney's invention, cotton could be grown profitably only along the coast.

Whitney's cotton gin, when operated by hand, made it possible for one man to separate 50 pounds of upland cotton a day. And when power was used to operate the cotton gin, a man operating the machine could separate more than 1000 pounds a day.

More and more southern farmers now began to raise and sell cotton, first in Georgia and South Carolina, and later in the rich soils of the Gulf coast states and the Mississippi Valley. The big 500-pound bales of raw cotton fiber flowed in ever larger volume to the textile mills of New England, the Middle Atlantic states, and Great Britain.

The cotton market expands. Meanwhile, by the middle years of the 1800's, new methods of long-distance transportation were being developed—notably the steamship and the railroad. Mill owners in the United States and Europe were therefore able to sell their finished products to more and more people in markets ever more distant. Cotton cloth became cheaper, and before long the

309

■ In later years the famous lithographers, Currier and Ives, imagined this scene on a southern plantation. The planter and his wife (foreground) are directing the work of picking the cotton and hauling it away. Farther back a wagonload of cotton is waiting to be "ginned." The steamboat may have stopped at the plantation wharf for a load of cotton bales.

whirring looms of Great Britain and the northeastern United States were supplying peoples at the ends of the earth with bolts of cotton cloth to be made into clothing. Before long, clothing manufacturers began selling ready-made dresses, shirts, and trousers in worldwide markets.

In 1791 total American production of cotton fiber had been only 400 bales. By 1810 it had risen to 171,000 bales. By 1830 it had jumped to 731,000 bales. In 1860 the figure stood at more than 5,-000,000 bales, two thirds of the world's total production of cotton. Cotton alone represented about two thirds of the value of the entire nation's exports in the year 1860.

Cotton and slavery. From 1800 to 1860, southern prosperity became increasingly dependent on cotton. Textile manufacturers needed more and more cotton. As a result, they paid higher and higher prices for the supply that was often too small to meet their needs. Rising prices tempted southern planters to clear more land in order to grow more cotton.

With the increasing demand for bigger supplies of cotton, the rich soils of the Gulf states and the Mississippi Valley beckoned cotton growers. Planters, the sons of planters, small farmers, and others saw a chance to get ahead by moving west, clearing the soil, and starting cotton plantations. Thus, to the original southern states there were added, by 1845, the states of Louisiana, Mississippi, Alabama, Arkansas, Florida, and Texas.

In order to clear the land and grow cotton, a large supply of inexpensive labor was needed. The northern Europeans who were migrating to the United States preferred to find work in the North. Cotton planters relied, instead, on slaves. The number of slaves in the southern states rose from approximately 1,000,000 in 1800 to 1,643,000 in 1820 and to about 4,000,000 in 1860.

By the late 1850's the cotton economy had reached the height of its power. The cotton lands, or cotton belt, stretched in a long crescent from North Carolina in the east to Texas in the west (see map, page 309). Travelers journeying in the autumn along the dusty roads throughout this region saw the major wealth of the South in every field—ripe cotton bolls, white in the hot sunlight, ready to be picked, cleaned of seed, packed in bales, and shipped to mills in New England and Great Britain.

(see map, page 309).

✏ **SECTION SURVEY**

1. What were the chief crops and industries in the South before 1860?

2. Discuss the importance of Whitney's cotton gin.

3. Describe the factors that enabled the South to become the world's greatest cotton-producing area between 1800 and 1860.

4. Show the relation between cotton production and westward expansion.

5. Explain the relation between cotton production and slavery.

IDENTIFY: "King Cotton," staple crop, subsistence farm, cotton fiber; 1793.

2 Various groups help build the "Cotton Kingdom"

Who were the people who lived in the South? In what respect was life in the southern states different from life in the North and the western regions?

Numbers and social groups. By 1860 the population of the South had risen to approximately 12,000,000. About 4,000,-000 were slaves. The rest were, for the most part, descendants of pre-Revolutionary settlers. Those of English and Scotch-Irish ancestry predominated, but people of French origin were located in the coastal plains of the Carolinas and around New Orleans.

There were German settlements in Texas, but on the whole, European immigrants were not attracted to the South. More than 4,000,000 immigrants were living in the United States by 1860, but only 13.5 per cent of these immigrants lived in the southern states. Most of the immigrants up to this time had come from countries of northern Europe, like Ireland and Germany. The climate and ways of living in the northern states were more familiar to them than were the warmer climate and ways of living in the South. As they entered the United States through the chief ports of entry in the North, they tended to settle in the northern cities and on the farms of the Midwest.

In the South as, indeed, in other parts of the country, the population was divided into a number of social and economic groups. Except for the Negroes, energetic and ambitious men were continually moving from lower to higher economic groups. In the words of one southern historian, a man could mount "from log cabin to plantation mansion on a stairway of cotton bales. . . ."

What were the major economic and social groups in the South in 1860?

The slaves. The 4,000,000 slaves were engaged in a wide variety of occupations. Many worked in the homes of the planters, cooking the meals, doing the

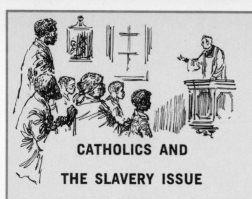

CATHOLICS AND
THE SLAVERY ISSUE

From 1830 to 1860, the Union was shaken by quarrels over Negro slavery. Far from being active in these matters, Catholics were more concerned with threats to their own freedom, which was under attack by agitators who looked upon "Popery" as un-American. Most Catholics were Irish or German immigrants who had settled in the North, where there were few Negroes and slavery had long been abolished. Some Catholics in Maryland and Louisiana owned slaves, but the Church was not strong in the South; chiefly, the complaints made within the Church were about the lack of priests to give sacraments and religious instruction to slaves.

If you had asked a bishop or a priest whether slavery was right or wrong around 1850, the answer would have been, "Slavery must not be abolished if the result would be to destroy society; meanwhile, all who own slaves must see that they learn their religion as a means to salvation." When Catholics differed as to political measures before Congress, like the Kansas-Nebraska Act, no matter of faith was involved. Few Catholics were on the side of anti-slavery however. It was often true that abolitionists were strongly anti-Catholic, and so they had few friends, for example, among New York Irish.

Many Protestant church organizations suffered divisions, beginning in the 1840's, over slavery. But even the War Between the States did not disrupt the religious unity of Catholics. On both sides they fought bravely, while priest chaplains and nursing Sisters won praise. Except for the tragic loss of Negro Catholics after emancipation, the Catholic Church in America was stronger after the War Between the States.

housekeeping, and tending the children.

Some of the slaves became skilled workers. Women learned to spin, weave, and sew. Some became cooks, maids, laundresses, dairymaids, and nurses. Men became blacksmiths, painters, shoemakers, jewelers, and silversmiths. A few learned to do the carpentry, bricklaying, and other tasks required to build a house. A limited number were able not only to build a house, but also to make the necessary plans, draw up contracts, and complete the entire structure.

The great majority of the slaves on the cotton, rice, and sugar cane plantations were laborers who did the hard work in the fields. They planted the cotton, corn, and wheat in the spring; cultivated the growing crops during the summer; picked cotton, harvested grain, and slaughtered livestock in the fall; mended fences and cleared new land in the winter.

The free Negroes. By 1860 there were about 250,000 free Negroes in the South. They were for the most part former slaves who had been set free by their owners. Some, of course, were men and women who had never known slavery, being the children of free Negroes. These people were largely concentrated in Virginia and in the towns and cities of the other southern states.

After a slave uprising in Virginia in 1831, legislatures of all the southern states passed a variety of laws restricting the movements and privileges of free Negroes. They could not testify in court in their own behalf; they often had to register and post bonds for good behavior; they were in other instances forbidden to assemble or to learn to read and write. In practice, however, these laws were not always rigidly enforced.

The poor whites. The "poor white" group of southerners, which probably was not more than 10 or 12 per cent of the white population, was looked down on by other whites and called, in different parts of the South, "hillbillies," "crackers," or "piney woods folks." For the most part, these people were stranded frontier families, many of whom lived in log cabins. Their standard of living was low, at least in part because they lived on the poorer soils, called "pine barrens," or along the rugged Appalachian mountainsides and other hilly areas that were hard to cultivate. These people often suffered from poor health, but they had pride and a fierce independence.

Laborers and tenants. In the southern agricultural economy there were also a large number of white farm laborers and tenant farmers. The farm laborers were hired during the harvest season or, in some instances, to do work regarded as too dangerous for the expensive slaves. The tenant farmers rented and tilled fields that were usually worn out from overuse. These tenant farmers were generally in debt to the planter or to the crossroads storekeeper.

The small farmers. There were also many small independent farmers who owned several acres of productive land and who lived much like small farmers in other parts of the country. These people, often called "yeomen," lived in rudely constructed but reasonably comfortable frame houses, considerably better than the one-room log shelters of the poor whites in the pine barrens and in the mountains. Each year they sold a bale or two of cotton as a cash crop. Their food came largely from the corn, potato, and vegetable patches around their houses. They were almost self-sufficient and had in addition a small cash income of perhaps $100 or more a year. Some, of course, owned more land and were fairly prosperous.

The small slaveowners. Some of the small farmers who prospered were able to buy a slave or two, or perhaps a slave family. A really prosperous small farmer might have 8 or 10 slaves.

When a small farmer acquired a few slaves, his scale of living did not usually change. He continued, often, to work in the fields, shoulder to shoulder with his newly purchased slaves. Although his cash income did increase to perhaps several hundred dollars a year, he remained a member of a distinct social

Baling cotton

group, separated from the large rich planters on the one hand and the poor whites on the other. Some of these small farmers lived in the cotton belt, with only a fence separating them from the plantations. However, most of them lived to the north of the cotton belt and in the fertile valleys of the Appalachian Mountains.

The planters. The most influential people in the South—the planters—were also the fewest in number. According to the Bureau of the Census, a southern "planter" was a person engaged in agriculture who owned 20 or more slaves. In 1860 there were fewer than 50,000 of these planters in the South.

But the planters did not represent a closed circle. A considerable number of small slaveowners acquired more slaves and land, and became planters.

SECTION SURVEY

1. Why did few European immigrants settle in the South?
2. List the different types of work performed by the slaves.
3. Compare the life of (a) the poor whites, (b) the white farm laborers, (c) the tenant farmers, and (d) the small independent farmers.
4. Explain this statement: "The planters did not represent a closed circle."

IDENTIFY: free Negro, yeoman.

Planters exert leadership in the southern states

As a general rule, it was the planters who held the leading political positions in the South and who spoke for the southern states as Senators and Representatives in the Congress of the United States. They held these positions in part because their wealth made it possible for them to devote their time to politics, in part because their education commended them to their fellow citizens, in part because the political system of the southern states gave them control of the machinery of government.

Who were the planters? Many of the planters were descendants of the wealthy colonial planters of the eastern seaboard states. Many others were self-made men who had made their way up the economic and social ladder and established themselves as leaders of their community and of their section of the country. For example, Joseph Emory Davis, a brother of Jefferson Davis, was producing 3000 bales of cotton each year on Mississippi land that he had carved out of frontier wilderness. Among the southern men who started life as small farmers and rose to positions of influence were such prominent leaders as John C. Calhoun of South Carolina, Alexander H. Stephens of Georgia, Joseph E. Brown of Alabama, Albert Gallatin Brown of Mississippi, and Andrew Jackson of Tennessee.

The plantation home. Travelers who journeyed through the South in the 1850's occasionally passed an imposing mansion set well back from the road with close-clipped lawns sweeping down to a river. The house itself, shaded by tall trees and surrounded by formal gardens, looked cool and inviting with its wide verandas and its white Grecian pillars supporting the roof.

Many of these mansions, often having twelve or fifteen luxuriously furnished rooms, were places of distinction and beauty. These were the homes of the wealthy planters, who might own from 100 to 500 slaves or more. However, fewer than 2500 planters, even as late as 1860, could afford such luxury.

The planter who owned from 20 to 100 slaves lived well but in more modest circumstances. His home might have as many as eight or ten rooms, with wide halls and deep verandas surrounded by spacious, shaded grounds. The furnishings of a home of this type were usually comfortable but not luxurious, for most of the planter's wealth was tied up in land and slaves, and he could not afford to import expensive household goods.

Educational leadership. For the most part, the well-to-do planters and their families enjoyed a high level of education. This in itself helps to explain the large influence they exerted. Believing as they did in the importance of education, they hired private tutors for their children or sent the boys to private schools. A high proportion of the older boys went to college. Most attended William and Mary College, the University of Virginia, or another of the numerous southern institutions, but many went north to Yale, Harvard, Princeton, West Point, and Annapolis. Hundreds of brilliant men graduated from southern and northern colleges and rose to positions of leadership.

Political leadership. The form of local government that prevailed throughout the South made it possible for the planters to occupy the leading political positions in the southern states and to represent their section in the Congress of the United States. This form of local government had been introduced into Virginia by the first settlers from Eng-

---

■ When war came between North and South, many southern mansions were destroyed or later fell into decay. But some survived and may be seen today. One is Greenwood in Louisiana (right, above), a home of beautiful proportions in the Classic tradition. Many southern mansions had formal gardens, like the one at Evergreen in Louisiana (opposite, left). Interiors were elegant. A drawing room (opposite, right) has been reproduced in miniature and may be seen at the Art Institute of Chicago.

315

land and in later years had spread through the southern states.

The county was the most important political unit, and the most important officers of the county were the justices of the peace. These men—in varying numbers up to 35—were named by the governor of the state, who was usually one of the wealthy planters. The justices had broad powers. They levied taxes. They provided for the construction of roads, bridges, and schoolhouses. They appointed sheriffs to enforce the law.

The justices met once a month as a judicial body to try cases in law. The justices also met informally and unofficially to choose candidates for election to the state legislature and to the Congress of the United States. Without their approval it was difficult if not impossible for any southerner to win an election for county, state, or national office.

Duties of the planter. When the planter was not away from home on public business, his life was comfortable but not easy. An endless number of details engaged his attention.

In addition to supervising the work on the plantation itself, the planter had to keep records of his business transactions. Since he carried on most of his business by means of correspondence, he had to write numerous letters to shipowners and bankers and to agents who sold his cotton to the textile mills.

In terms of money in the bank, the planter was not usually a rich man. He shipped his cotton in care of an agent in the North Atlantic states or in Great Britain, instructing him to sell the cotton and ship back agricultural implements, clothing, books, and household furnishings. Frequently, after his cotton was sold and his purchases were made, he was in debt to the agent who handled his business for him on commission.

Even more time-consuming was the day-by-day routine of managing the plantation. Each morning the slaves had to be assigned to particular jobs—tending the cotton, hoeing corn, cultivating other food crops, cutting wood, hauling water, feeding livestock, and doing household chores. There was always much work to be done, for a cotton grower also raised most of the food eaten by his family and slaves.

One visitor to a Virginia estate wrote that "during three hours or more in which I was in company with the proprietor, I do not think there were ten consecutive minutes uninterrupted by some of the slaves requiring his personal direction or assistance. He was obliged, three times, to leave the dinner table."

Treatment of the slaves. Students of slavery have been handicapped by a lack of adequate records in their effort to decide how slaves were treated. Generally speaking, they have records, diaries, and journals only for the large plantations. There is some evidence, however, that the slaves on the small plantations and farms were in general more humanely treated than on the large plantations.

On large plantations the slaves usually worked in gangs under the management of an overseer, whose job it was to get as much work out of the labor force and as big crops as possible. The treatment of slaves on plantations where the owner was frequently absent and where an overseer was in charge was likely to be most severe. It was hard to secure men who were willing to serve as overseers, and some of those who did become overseers were harsh, brutal men. On the other hand, there is some evidence that on the big plantations of the lower South the slaves often had more food, better quarters, and superior medical care than did those belonging to small owners.

Many planters provided for their slaves as carefully as they did for members of their own families and in turn won the love of the slaves. Thomas Jefferson, for example, belonged to this group of planters. When Jefferson returned to his hilltop home at Monticello after a long absence, his slaves honored him by meeting his coach at the foot of the hill, unhitching the horses, and pulling the coach by hand up the long grade.

Many planters treated their slaves well because they were valuable property. For example, imagine a planter who owned 50 able-bodied slaves. Allowing from $1000 to $1500 for each slave, a fair enough price in the 1850's, his investment in slaves was from $50,-000 to $75,000. Death of even a single slave meant a serious financial loss; illness of a slave was a setback. Any illness or injury resulting from ill-treatment was contrary to the planter's interests. To protect his investment, therefore, the planter was apt to keep his slaves adequately fed, clothed, and housed.

Was slave labor profitable? It is impossible to say whether or not slave labor was really profitable for the planter of cotton and other staple crops or for the small farmer-owner. Many planters and most small farmers did not keep accurate accounts and therefore did not know from one year to the next just how much they had earned or lost.

Some southerners at the time believed that slave labor was becoming less profitable than hired labor. In 1837 George Tucker, a professor at the University of Virginia, argued in a book entitled *The Laws of Wages, Profits, and Rents* that slavery was an inefficient system of labor. To support this argument, Tucker and others pointed to the high cost of buying slaves; to the fact that unwilling workers were usually poor workers; to the expensive supervision that was required to keep slaves at work; to the cost of food, clothing, and shelter, which continued even when, for one reason or other, slaves could not work; and to the losses caused by disability or death.

But after 1840 such arguments were heard less frequently. Many southerners had come to feel by this time that slavery was not only necessary, but that it was also profitable. Thus bitter southern disapproval was expressed when, in 1857, a New York publisher issued a book by a North Carolina small farmer, or yeoman, which attempted to prove that the South was economically inferior to the North because of the ineffi-

EDMUND RUFFIN

Governor James H. Hammond of South Carolina had only the highest praise for Edmund Ruffin (1794–1865). He was, said Hammond, "one of the few benefactors of mankind whose services have been appreciated by the world while [he was] still living."

The Virginia-born Edmund Ruffin won this praise the hard way. For many years his neighbors called him a crackpot because he insisted that the soil of the South, ruined by the unscientific cultivation of tobacco and other crops, could be restored to rich, productive farm land. But while they laughed, Ruffin continued his experiments with the use of lime and different types of fertilizer, better plowing, improved methods of drainage, and other practices.

The success of many of his experiments astonished even Ruffin, and he began to publicize them through speeches and articles in newspapers, books, and a monthly farm journal, the *Farmer's Register*. He became one of the leading agricultural scientists of his day, and has since been called the "father of soil chemistry in America."

One of Ruffin's most effective demonstrations was carried out on a run-down plantation which he bought and transformed into a model farm. The first year he lost money. Within five years he was reaping profits equal to 20 per cent of his investment. Farmers came from all over the South, were convinced that Ruffin knew what he was doing, and returned home to improve their own farm practices.

ciency of slavery. The author was Hinton Rowan Helper; his book was called *The Impending Crisis*. Feeling in the South ran so high against Helper that he found it wise to move North.

Actually, there is evidence that the large rice, sugar, and cotton plantations were often profitable to their owners at certain times, depending in part upon weather conditions and market prices and in even greater part on managerial skill. On the other hand, some planters were regularly in debt, and many were just barely breaking even.

The pro-slavery argument. Whether or not slavery was a profitable system of agricultural labor, it became a firmly established institution on all of the plantations and many of the small farms of the southern states during the first half of the 1800's. And as slavery grew and spread, it became the subject of increasingly bitter controversy between southerners and northerners. In defense of their way of life, southerners developed what has come to be called "the pro-slavery argument."

The pro-slavery argument was developed by such men as Thomas R. Dew, a professor at the College of William and Mary, George Fitzhugh, a Virginian, and John C. Calhoun of South Carolina, the South's most brilliant political leader until his death in 1850. The arguments that these men and others developed in defense of slavery were popularized throughout the South by leaders at political rallies, by newspaper editors, by novelists and short-story writers, and by preachers.

The pro-slavery argument declared, in part, that slavery was necessary so that southern planters would have an adequate labor supply. Going beyond necessity, the argument held that the institution of slavery was of positive value to the slaves themselves. It provided them with shelter, clothing, and food; it took care of them in sickness and old age; it gave them many of the benefits of civilization.

The champions of slavery often contrasted the secure life of the slave with the uncertain lot of white wage earners in the mills, factories, and mines of the North and of Europe. These white workers, it was argued, were exploited mercilessly by their employers, who had no concern for their well-being, who paid them barely enough to live on, who laid them off when there was no work to do, and who discarded them when they were too ill or too old to toil.

The argument in favor of slavery was mainly advanced by, or on behalf of, the large plantation owners. But the pro-slavery argument was also widely accepted by small planters who were ambitious to become large planters, and by small farmers who owned no slaves, but who hoped in time to acquire some. Insofar as the argument reached the poor whites, it added to their sense of solidarity and pride in being members of the white society of the South.

Most of the plain people of the South, then, as well as wealthy southerners, spurned the anti-slavery arguments of men like Hinton Rowan Helper. Southern people, that is, largely accepted the leadership of the great plantation owners and the institution of slavery itself. They identified slavery with the distinctive southern way of life. Any criticism of slavery, or any efforts to restrict it, they regarded as hostile to their homes, their land, and their way of life.

✓ **SECTION SURVEY**

1. Explain the conditions that enabled the large planters to hold many of the leading political positions in the South.

2. The life of the planter was "comfortable but not easy." Do you agree? Justify your opinion.

3. What conclusions can you reach concerning the treatment of slaves in the South?

4. State the arguments that were presented to show that slavery was unprofitable.

5. Summarize the main points of the pro-slavery argument.

IDENTIFY: county, *The Laws of Wages, Profits, and Rents; The Impending Crisis;* Tucker, Helper.

Points to Discuss: 1. Give evidence of the variety and complexity of the southern economy before 1860.

2. The Industrial Revolution helped to create the Cotton Kingdom. Cite evidence to support this statement.

3. Describe the social and economic groups in the South before 1860.

4. Compare the life of a southern slave with that of a northern factory worker.

5. The treatment of slaves varied from plantation to plantation, depending largely upon the character of the master or the overseer. Explain this statement.

6. Why was it that poor whites and small farmers who owned no slaves chose to fight on the Confederate side when war broke out between North and South?

Using Maps and Charts: 1. Using the map on page 309, (a) explain the shift of cotton-producing areas between the 1830's and the 1850's, and (b) locate the Old South and Mason and Dixon's line.

2. Name the two least populated southern states in 1860 (see page 827).

3. (a) If you had been a cotton planter living in the 1830's who planned to buy a new plantation, and you had before you the map on pages 818–19, in which area would you have decided to buy land? Why? (b) Now turn to the map on pages 830–31, and decide whether your choice was wise.

4. Consulting chart 1 on pages 832–33, indicate which of the technological advances were most helpful to the South, to the North, and to the West, before 1850.

5. Explain the nature of American exports in 1850. See Chart 2 on page 840.

Consulting the Sources: A southern debate on slavery can be found in A. B. Hart, ed., *American History Told by Contemporaries,* Vol. IV, Nos. 169 and 175.

■ TRACING THE MAIN IDEAS

The South, as well as the Northeast, was greatly influenced by the Industrial Revolution that began in England in the late 1700's and soon spread to many other countries in the Western world. The invention of power-driven machines for spinning and weaving yarn created a growing demand for cotton fiber. The invention of the cotton gin gave planters an effective machine for cleaning the seeds from cotton. The invention and development of better methods of transportation made it possible for planters to ship their cotton to the new factories in England and the Northeast.

Except for the cotton gin, however, machines were not much used in the South. It was the slaves who cleared the land, plowed the fields, planted the seeds, and harvested the white and fluffy crop of cotton. As the years passed and larger areas of the South were planted in cotton, slaves became increasingly numerous and increasingly valuable.

To be sure, only a small percentage of the southerners owned slaves. But the slaveowners were the wealthiest, in general the best educated, and the most influential men in the South. They were the political leaders who ran the governments in the southern states and who represented the South in the Congress of the United States. These men—and their wives and families—created a way of living different from that in any other section of the country.

You have now seen how distinctive ways of living and working developed in the North and the South. We turn now to the third section of the United States—that vast and rapidly expanding region known as the West. As you will see, it too was being transformed during the first half of the 1800's.

The Westward Movement Reaches the Pacific

CHANGING WAYS

OF AMERICAN LIFE

"FIFTY-FOUR FORTY or fight!" "The re-annexation of Texas and re-occupation of Oregon!" Such were the spirited slogans of the Democrats as they went to the polls in the election of 1844.

When the Democratic candidate, James K. Polk, won the Presidential election, it was clear that the United States was about to attain its "manifest destiny"—that a majority of its people were determined that the nation should occupy all the vast area between the Mississippi River and the Pacific Ocean.

From the 1820's to the 1860's, Americans continued to bring under cultivation those farm lands that had not already been taken up between the Appalachian Mountains and the Mississippi River. But many restless pioneers were casting eager eyes on lands farther west. In 1821 Missouri, west of the Mississippi, was admitted to the Union —the first state to be carved out of the Louisiana Purchase after Louisiana itself. In the 1820's and 1830's pioneers also crossed the Mississippi into what became Iowa Territory in 1838.

Immediately ahead lay the Great Plains, known to the pioneers as the Great American Desert. This vast, almost treeless expanse, covered with grass and sagebrush, did not appeal to the pioneers until a later time.

But beyond the Rockies, far to the northwest, Oregon beckoned—a fertile and forested land, well watered. To the south lay the magnet of Texas, a rich land thinly settled by Spaniards and Mexicans. Far to the west of Texas and even more thinly settled by Spaniards and Mexicans was California.

From the 1820's to the 1860's, as you have seen, the Industrial Revolution was creating a distinctive way of life in the northern states, while the growing of cotton was creating a different way of life in the southern states. In this chapter you will learn how the third great section of the United States—the "West" as we know it today—was added to the nation. Later, in Chapter 18, you will learn how a struggle developed over whether the northern or southern way of life was to prevail in the new territories and states west of the Mississippi.

AS THE STORY DEVELOPS

1. Fur traders and settlers expand into the Oregon country.
2. American settlers create the Lone Star Republic of Texas.
3. War with Mexico adds the entire Southwest to the nation.
4. A surge of migration brings California into the Union.

■ To remote outposts like Fort Laramie, Wyoming, Indians and "Mountain Men" brought their bundles of furs to trade for guns, ammunition, clothing, and other articles. Within the fort the trader and his assistants kept a sharp eye on Indians and Mountain Men alike.

1 Fur traders and settlers expand into the Oregon country

Far to the northwest of Missouri, beyond the Rocky Mountains, lay an enormous area of towering mountains, magnificent forests, and fertile valleys drained by rivers teeming with fish—the area now called the Pacific Northwest. This rich area, known in history as the Oregon country or simply as Oregon, stretched northward from the 42nd parallel, the northern border of California, to the parallel of 54° 40′, the southern boundary of Alaska (see map, page 323). Until the early 1820's the Oregon country was claimed simultaneously by four nations—Spain, Russia, Great Britain, and the United States.

Conflicting claims. The Spanish claim to the Oregon country was originally based on an agreement reached in 1494 by Spain and Portugal (page 9). Spain, however, gave up its claim in 1819, under the same treaty in which Spain ceded Florida to the United States (page 260).

Russia based its claims to the Oregon country on the explorations of Vitus Bering, a Dane who had explored the area for Russia in 1741. Russian missionaries and fur traders, following Bering's explorations, established missions and trading posts in the Aleutian Islands, on the mainland of Alaska, and finally southward along the Pacific coast as far as northern California.

It was increasing Russian pressure in this area after 1815, as you recall, that prompted the United States to issue the famous Monroe Doctrine of 1823, warning Russia and other nations of Europe that the United States would not tolerate any further colonization in the Western Hemisphere. The Russian tsar decided not to force the issue and in 1824 the Russians withdrew their claims to all land south of the 54th parallel.

Great Britain based its claim to the Oregon country on voyages made to the Pacific by Francis Drake in 1577–80 and by Captain James Cook in 1776–78. Like Russia, Great Britain encouraged fur traders to trade with the Indians of the area for the valuable pelts of beavers and other animals. The British fur trade was controlled by the Hudson's Bay Company, with its western headquarters at Fort Vancouver, now Vancouver, Washington. This fort was presided over by Dr. John McLoughlin, a shrewd, capable, and picturesque Canadian.

The United States had established claim to the Oregon country in 1792, when a merchant sea captain from Boston, Captain Robert Gray, discovered the Columbia River, and began trading for furs. The United States claim was strengthened when, as you will see, American fur traders traveled overland to the Oregon country following the Lewis and Clark Expedition of 1804–06 (page 234).

In 1818 Great Britain and the United States signed a treaty agreeing to joint occupation of the Oregon country for a period of ten years. Ten years later, after Spain and Russia had given up their claims, Great Britain and the United States renewed this treaty.

American fur traders. The story of the fur trade is one of the most colorful in the history of North America. The American interest in the far western fur trade began in earnest after Lewis and Clark returned in 1806 from their expedition. Centering in St. Louis, the western trade was gradually organized by enterprising business concerns like the Rocky Mountain Fur Company. This company outfitted rugged "Mountain Men" who penetrated up the Missouri River, along the Platte River, and overland into the Rocky Mountains. During the trapping season the Mountain Men lived like the Indians and traded with them. In the spring they returned to St. Louis, where their employers paid them for their loads of pelts. The pelts were then marketed in the East and in Europe.

In their exploration of the Rockies, the Mountain Men discovered trails and passes which were later used by settlers moving west. The most important of these passes, the South Pass in what is now Wyoming, led to a trail which crossed the Continental Divide and went from there through the Snake and Columbia River Valleys to the Pacific Ocean. In the 1830's it was found that covered wagons could be driven over this route. Later, the route came to be known as the Oregon Trail (see map, opposite page).

Rivalry for furs. An even more important business venture than the Rocky Mountain Fur Company was the American Fur Company formed in 1808 in New York by John Jacob Astor, a German immigrant. Throughout the vast area of the North American fur trade, Astor engaged in bitter contests with his American and British rivals. In 1811 he built a fort and trading post at Astoria, near the mouth of the Columbia River in the Oregon country.

By the 1820's the American Fur Company controlled most of the American trade in the Upper Mississippi Valley, in the Rockies, and in the Oregon country. Astor's sales organization included offices in St. Louis, New York, England, France, Austria, and China. In 1832 the company sold 25,000 beaver skins, nearly 50,000 buffalo hides, about 30,000 deerskins, and other pelts.

Rivalry between the different fur trade companies, and their greed for profits, often led to unfair dealings and trouble with the Indians. The federal government tried for a while to deal with these problems by regulating prices. But the government gave up its effort in 1823, largely because of pressure from the private traders.

Missionaries arrive. The fur trade, as you have seen, led to the exploration of the river routes over the Great Plains, the mountain passes, and the Oregon country itself. It also led in the 1830's and 1840's to the settlement by American farmers and traders of that part of the Oregon country south of the Colum-

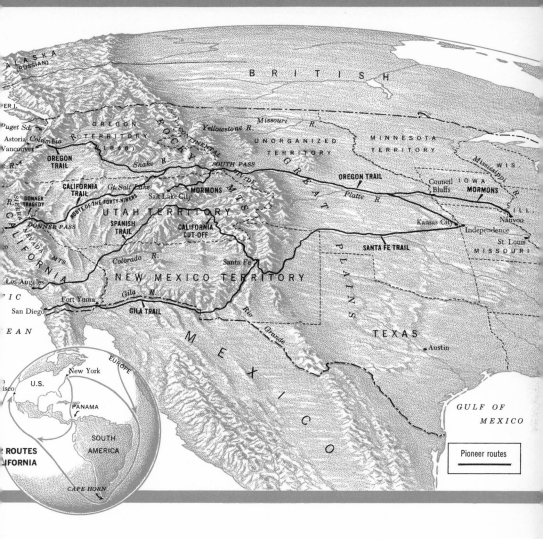

bia River. The surge of settlement was stimulated by missionaries, by New England businessmen interested in trade and fishing, and by such enthusiasts as Hall Jackson Kelley, a writer of schoolbooks and a surveyor.

The first missionaries traveled to the Oregon country with fur traders. Jason Lee, a Methodist, built a mission and a school for Indian children in the fertile Willamette Valley in 1834. Samuel Parker, a Presbyterian minister, followed him a year later. In 1836 Marcus Whitman and H. H. Spalding, both Presbyterians, made the long overland journey with their young brides. In

1840, Father Pierre De Smet, S.J., priest, missioner, educator, and explorer, arrived in the Oregon country.

The early settlers. All of these religious leaders sent back east for more settlers. By the 1840's pioneers were entering the Oregon country at the rate of a thousand a year. They migrated largely in groups, partly as a measure of safety in the Indian country, following the Oregon Trail through the South Pass and along the Snake and Columbia Rivers into the Oregon country.

From the beginning the settlers felt the need of government. In 1843 a committee of nine gathered in the barn of

323

MOUNTAIN MEN

Of all the Mountain Men, that hardy breed of free trappers who for a generation roamed the Far West in search of beaver, none surpassed Jedediah Smith (1798–1831) in courage, skill, and ingenuity. We know little of his early life, except that he was born in New York state and at the age of thirteen was working as a clerk on a Lake Erie freighter.

We catch our first clear glimpse of him as a young man of twenty-four in St. Louis, the center of the western fur trade. There, in 1822, he joined a party of trappers and hunters that, under the leadership of General William Ashley and Major Andrew Henry, was heading up the Missouri River. On this expedition Smith swiftly demonstrated his remarkable qualities as a trapper, hunter, and leader. Within a year he was put in charge of one of Ashley's parties. Within two years he was Ashley's partner. By 1826 he and two fellow trappers had bought out Ashley, and owned an enterprise that dominated the Rocky Mountain beaver trade.

The Mountain Men were as rough a group of men as one could find in America, yet their outstanding leader, Smith, did not himself swear or use tobacco, and drank only on formal occasions. Deeply religious, Smith excelled by virtue of sheer ability and raw courage. In a few brief years he explored more of the Far West than any white man had ever done before. He was the first white American to cross the desert into California. But in 1831, at the age of thirty-three, he met death at the hands of a band of Comanche Indians.

Jedediah Smith and other Mountain Men ranked with Lewis and Clark and Zebulon Pike as explorers of the Far West and the "Shining Mountains." Within a few years the trails they blazed and the passes they discovered became well-established routes for the pioneer settlers.

(The picture above shows some of the clothing and equipment used by Mountain Men: a deerskin jacket, snowshoes, a bowie knife, a large bear trap, and a smaller beaver trap. The tomahawks and trinkets were traded for furs.)

the Methodist mission on the Willamette River and drew up a resolution which said in part: "We the people of Oregon territory, for the purposes of mutual protection and to secure peace and prosperity among ourselves, agree to adopt . . . laws and regulations, until such time as the United States of America extend their jurisdiction over us. . . ."

Oregon becomes a Territory. Congress could not extend its jurisdiction over the Oregon country because the British also claimed the territory. Yet something had to be done to settle the rival claims, for friction was growing between the Hudson's Bay Company and the American settlers. It was clear by the early 1840's that some solution would have to be found to supplement the treaty of joint occupation made in 1818 and renewed in 1828.

Americans living in the East, as well as American settlers in the Oregon country, were demanding that the British withdraw all claims to the land south of the line 54° 40′. This issue got into politics. In the Presidential election of 1844, the Democrats, under the leadership of James K. Polk of Tennessee, made western expansion the keynote of their campaign, using the slogan "Fifty-four forty or fight!"

Fortunately, calmer minds prevailed. In 1818 the United States and Great Britain had arrived through compromise at a treaty which established an unfortified boundary between the United States and Canada as far west as what is now Montana (page 245). Through further compromise Great Britain now agreed, in the Treaty of 1846, to give up its claims to the Oregon country south of the 49th parallel (see map, page 323). Thus, by 1846, a boundary without fortifications existed between the United States and Canada from the Atlantic to the Pacific Ocean. It has remained unfortified ever since.

In 1848 that part of the Oregon country which now clearly belonged to the United States was organized as Oregon Territory.

✔ **SECTION SURVEY**

1. (a) Why was there a dispute over the Oregon country? (b) Why did the United States and Great Britain at first agree on joint occupation of the Oregon country?
2. Show how each of the following helped to lay the basis for our claims to the Oregon country: (a) Captain Gray, (b) Lewis and Clark Expedition, (c) "Mountain Men," (d) Astor, (e) missionaries, and (f) settlers.
3. In the election of 1844, why did the Democratic Party adopt the slogan "Fifty-four forty or fight!"?
4. How did the United States finally acquire the Oregon country?
IDENTIFY: Hudson's Bay Company, Treaty of 1818 (with Great Britain), South Pass, American Fur Company, Treaty of 1846 (with Great Britain); Bering, Marcus Whitman, Father De Smet; 1804–06, 1844.

2 American settlers create the Lone Star Republic of Texas

In the early 1820's, when Americans were beginning to be interested in the Oregon country as a place in which to trade and settle, a stream of other traders and settlers was already moving southwestward into lands originally explored and partly settled by Spaniards. As the traders and settlers moved in, they set in motion a chain of events that led to the acquisition by the United States of the area now occupied by the states of Texas, New Mexico, Arizona, California, Nevada, and Utah, as well as parts of Colorado and Wyoming.

Spanish settlements. Spanish claims to this vast country were based upon the exploring expeditions in the 1540's of De Soto and Coronado (page 12).

In the 1600's and 1700's the Spaniards began to spread thinly northward from Mexico City—the heart of their New World empire. In 1609, as you know, they established Santa Fe, in what is now New Mexico. For a long time Santa Fe remained their chief northern outpost. In the 1700's, fearful of French encroachments from Louisiana and of possible British threats, the Spaniards began to renew their colonizing efforts. Throughout the present states of Texas, New Mexico, Arizona, and California, they established forts which were called *presidios* (preh-SEE-dyos), missions, villages called *pueblos* (PWEH-blohs), towns called *villas* (VEE-lyahs), and scattered ranches of enormous size.

The missions. The missions were an important part of the Spanish colonizing system. A Spanish colony would be a Christian colony, for the missioners, mostly Franciscans, would travel directly with the explorers. The purposes of the missions were to convert the Indians to Catholicism, teach them civilized ways of life, and make them loyal subjects of the Spanish Crown. Many such missions were successfully established.

The center of each mission, of course, was the church, usually a beautiful structure built of stone or adobe.° In addition, the mission included living quarters for the priests and workshops in which the Indians learned weaving, silverworking, blacksmithing, and other crafts. Generally the main buildings were enclosed within an adobe or a stone wall. Around the mission were farming areas where the priests and the Indians grew grain, grapes, and other crops and sometimes raised cattle. After the Indians had become converted to Christianity and had learned Spanish ways of living, they might be given farm lands of their own near the mission.

It was the hope of the Spaniards that strong communities would develop around the missions, with each mission as the center of community life. In many cases this goal was only partly realized, but the missions exercised a strong influence along what is now the southern border of the United States from Texas to California and northward

••

° *adobe* (*uh-*DOH-*bee*): large bricks of clay, baked in the sun.

in California to the vicinity of San Francisco Bay. To this day these areas are dotted with what remains of the old missions—some still in use as churches, some preserved for visitors and some in ruins.

Attitude toward outsiders. Thus for almost two centuries after the founding of Santa Fe in 1609, while the British colonies and later the United States were confined to the land between the Atlantic and the Mississippi, the Spanish occupied or claimed much of what has become, roughly, the southwestern quarter of the United States.

Then, after the Louisiana Purchase of 1803, the tide of westward advance began to lap at Spanish frontiers. The Spanish authorities tried to protect themselves from unwelcome visitors by forbidding all trade with the Americans. American explorers and traders, such as Zebulon Pike, were seized when they entered the Spanish lands south and west of the Louisiana Purchase. But the Spanish policy of excluding aliens began to weaken late in 1820. At that time Moses Austin, a Connecticut-born pioneer, received permission to settle a colony of a few hundred families in what is now Texas, with the understanding that they would become loyal subjects of Spain.

Revolt opens the door. Moses Austin died in 1821 before he could recruit the colonists that he had received permission to settle in Texas. Also, in 1821 the people of Mexico revolted against Spanish rule and established the Republic of Mexico (page 261). The new government of Mexico adopted a more liberal attitude toward traders and settlers.

Soon a flourishing overland trade developed between Independence, in Missouri, and Santa Fe. Long trains of American wagons—loaded with all sorts of manufactured goods, from pins and needles to rifles—set out from Independence on the long and dangerous Santa Fe Trail (see map, page 323). In Santa Fe they traded their goods for silver, gold, or hides, and then began the long journey home. Hostile Indians—especially the Comanches—harassed the traders.

Settlers move into Texas. In addition to letting down barriers against trade, the new government of Mexico also opened its doors to settlers. It gave Stephen F. Austin, the son of Moses Austin, a renewal of the grant of land that his father had received from the former Spanish authorities. Stephen Austin, a well-educated man noted for fairness, good judgment, and organizing ability, began in 1821 to build a vigorous American colony in Texas. Austin's "Old Three Hundred" settlers were a hand-picked group of pioneers.

Other settlers soon followed. By 1830 more than 20,000 men and women had entered Texas, many of them southerners. Slavery had been abolished by that time in Mexico so that it was technically illegal for the southerners to take their slaves with them into Texas. Mexican authorities, however, were lax in enforcing this law, so that many of these southerners were able to bring their slaves along.

The Mexican authorities soon saw that their liberal policies were actually encouraging the growth of an American community, or even an American state, within Mexico itself. Convinced that too many Americans were entering and that the newcomers were too independent in spirit, the Mexican government began to close its doors to further settlement. In 1830 it passed a law in which it attempted to restrict further settlement in the Mexican states bordering on the United States. In this law Mexico also reaffirmed its earlier prohibition of slavery. Land grants not already taken up were cancelled. To enforce these laws and others, Mexican army posts were strengthened throughout Texas.

Texas fights for independence. The Americans in Texas protested vigorously against these and other restrictions of what they believed to be their individual rights. Repeated attempts to get the Mexican authorities to reconsider ended in failure. After several clashes with Mexican officials, fighting broke out.

An event sometimes referred to as "the Lexington of Texas" took place on October 2, 1835. The commander of the Mexican troops stationed at San Antonio tried to seize a cannon at Gonzales (gon-zah-leez) that had been given to the settlers for defense against the Indians (see map, this page). A group of Texans blocked his efforts, and he was forced to return to San Antonio without the cannon.

Later, a band of Texas volunteers led by Ben Milam defeated a large Mexican force in desperate house-to-house fighting in San Antonio. Prisoners taken in the battle were permitted to return to Mexico.

Infuriated by this defeat, the dictator president, General Antonio López de Santa Anna, promptly led a large army back into Texas. The Mexican army besieged a force of almost 200 Texans in the Alamo, a fortified mission at San Antonio (see map, this page). Among the defenders were a number of famous

327

Texans, including James Bowie and William B. Travis, the joint commanders, aided by the newcomer David Crockett. They refused to surrender despite overwhelming odds and died to the last man when Santa Anna stormed the fort on March 6, 1836. On March 27, another force of Texans was massacred at Goliad after it had surrendered and laid down its arms.

But the desperate Texans rallied under the cry of "Remember the Alamo! Remember Goliad!" Led by Sam Houston, the Texans destroyed Santa Anna's army at San Jacinto (sahn ha-SEEN-to) on April 21, 1836, and Santa Anna was captured. A secret treaty was then signed, as a result of which Santa Anna was released with the understanding that he would use his influence to secure Mexican recognition of the independence of Texas, with its southern boundary at the Rio Grande.

Texas becomes independent. Back in March, while the defenders of the Alamo were still holding off the Mexicans, a group of delegates assembled in convention at Washington-on-the-Brazos (BRAH-sohs), then a small village of ten or twelve rude dwellings. There, in a cold, drafty hut, the delegates on March 2, 1836, unanimously adopted a declaration of independence. They also drafted a constitution for a new Republic of Texas, often called the Lone Star Republic. Sam Houston, a former governor of Tennessee and a friend of Jackson, became the first regularly elected president of the Republic of Texas.

Annexation of Texas is delayed. During the revolution American sympathy was, of course, with the Texans. Volunteers, recruited in the United States, crossed into Texas and fought against Santa Anna. But when the new republic petitioned to be admitted to the United States, strong opposition developed. Since Texas wanted to permit slavery, northerners in Congress feared that its admission would increase unduly the strength of the southern states in Congress. Others feared that to admit Texas would be to invite war with

Mexico, which had not recognized Texas' independence. For these reasons, as you will see, the admission of Texas was delayed until 1845.

SECTION SURVEY

1. Why did the Spanish set up missions? Describe Indian life on these missions.
2. Explain the significance of the loss at the Alamo in the Texas War. Evaluate the role of Sam Houston in Texas' independence.
3. What factors delayed the annexation of Texas by the U.S. until 1845?

IDENTIFY: presidio, pueblo, villa, adobe, Comanches, San Jacinto, Lone Star Republic; Moses Austin, Stephen F. Austin, James Bowie, David Crockett, Santa Anna; 1821, 1836, 1845.

3 War with Mexico adds the entire Southwest to the nation

The annexation of Texas in 1845 moved the United States one step closer to war with Mexico. But there were other reasons for the Mexican War, which finally broke out in 1846.

Sources of friction. At the root of the conflict was the fact that two different ways of life met and clashed in the vast region west of Texas and merging into the Mexican area known as Upper California (the California we know today). Mexico's claim to all this territory, a claim inherited from the Spaniards, dated back to 1494, more than a century before the first English settlement appeared on the Atlantic coast. As you have seen, forts, ranches, missions, mines, and even a few towns, such as Santa Fe, dotted the land. Spanish law, Spanish architecture, Spanish customs, and the Spanish language prevailed.

Against this frontier of Spanish cul-

■ Through these wrought-iron gates, visitors today may enter to visit the Alamo. The Alamo was originally one of several missions around San Antonio.

ture with its leisurely tempo of life pressed an irresistible tide of energetic, land-hungry men and women from the United States. These Americans shared a belief that it was the "manifest destiny" of the United States to expand to the Pacific Ocean.

In the 1830's and early 1840's ill feeling between Mexico and the United States steadily mounted. During most of these years, the Republic of Mexico was torn by a series of revolutions, and its government was often corrupt and irresponsible. As a result, Americans— whom the Mexican authorities were now trying to keep from settling on Mexican soil—were often thrown into Mexican jails and mistreated. Indeed, in 1835 a group of 22 Americans suspected of plotting a revolution were executed without a trial.

Debts owed by the Mexican government to citizens of the United States also contributed to the ill feeling. During Mexico's struggles to win its independence from Spain and finally establish its own government in 1821, the property of many Americans living in Mexico had been damaged or destroyed. In 1839 an international commission examined the American claims and awarded the United States citizens a little more than $2,000,000. By 1845 Mexico had paid only three installments on its debt.

Mexicans also had reasons to feel aggrieved. They were bitter about American expansion into Texas and the Texas revolution of 1836, which they blamed on the United States. They feared that this was only the beginning and that the United States wanted to win control of the entire Southwest.

The war fever rises. American naval and military commanders in the Pacific area had standing orders to seize Upper California if war broke out between the United States and Mexico. In 1842 Commodore Thomas Ap Catesby Jones, hearing a false rumor that war had been declared, sailed swiftly to Upper California, seized the capital at Monterey, hauled down the Mexican flag, and

raised the Stars and Stripes. The next day, learning that he had made a mistake, Commodore Jones apologized profusely and withdrew in haste.

In the Presidential election of 1844, the Democrats demanded the annexation of Texas, as well as Oregon, to the nation. When the Democrats won the election, Congress and the out-going President, John Tyler, took steps immediately to admit Texas to the Union.

For Mexico, which had never recognized the Republic of Texas, the obvious intention of the United States to annex Texas was the final blow, equivalent to a declaration of war. The Mexican government broke off diplomatic relations with the United States.

Texas was finally admitted to the Union in December 1845. Meantime, the new President, James K. Polk, was eager also to acquire for the United States the whole vast area stretching from Texas to the Pacific Ocean. But he hoped to do so by peaceful means. In November 1845 he sent Ambassador John Slidell to the Mexican government with an offer to buy Upper California and New Mexico. Having severed diplomatic relations, the Mexican government refused to receive Slidell, and he returned to Washington empty-handed.

War breaks out. President Polk was now sure that Mexico would never willingly give up its control of Upper California and New Mexico, nor its claim to Texas. However, he intended that the United States should occupy the vast area and was ready to declare war to get it. Several members of his cabinet urged him to delay, pointing out that if he waited long enough Mexico would probably commit some act that would justify a declaration of war by the United States.

In January 1846, however, Polk dispatched troops under General Zachary Taylor from the Nueces (NWEH-sehs) River to the north bank of the Rio Grande. Ever since Texas had declared its independence from Mexico, Texans had claimed that their southern border lay on the Rio Grande, but Mexicans

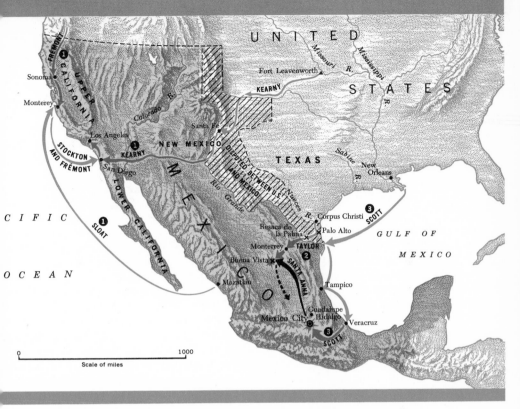

had insisted that it must stop at the Nueces River (see map, this page). By sending troops into this disputed area, Polk could claim that he was acting defensively; but the Mexicans could claim that the United States was acting aggressively.

Weeks passed, with President Polk's impatience mounting daily. Finally, on May 9, the President notified his cabinet that he intended to recommend war with Mexico within a few days. But that very night the news came for which he had long been waiting. Mexican troops had crossed the Rio Grande and had fought with American forces.

Convinced that the American people would approve his action, Polk sent his war message to Congress on May 11. "But now after reiterated menaces," he declared, "Mexico has passed the boundary of the United States, has invaded our territory and shed American blood upon American soil. . . . War exists, and notwithstanding all our ef-

forts to avoid it, exists by the act of Mexico herself. . . ."

Two days later, on May 13, Congress declared war. On the day that Congress made its formal declaration, Polk told his cabinet that "in making peace with our adversary, we shall acquire California, New Mexico, and other further territory, as an indemnity° for this war, if we can."

Who started the war? Many people at the time and many people since have regarded the Mexican War as one of aggression on the part of the United States. One person who questioned the actions of the United States was Abraham Lincoln, a young Illinois lawyer then serving his only term in Congress. In 1847 he introduced in Congress his famous Spot Resolutions, questioning whether the "spot" on the north bank of the Rio Grande where American

....

° *indemnity:* compensation for expenditures or losses.

JOHN
CHARLES
FRÉMONT

John C. Frémont (1813–90)—soldier, explorer, and politician—was born in Savannah, Georgia. He attended Charleston College and later served in the navy, resigning to become an officer with the U.S. Army Topographical Corps. In 1841 he married Jessie Benton, the daughter of Missouri's famous Senator, Thomas Hart Benton.

Frémont took an active part in the Mexican War, helping in the capture of Los Angeles and accepting the surrender of the Mexicans in California. In 1856 he was the Presidential candidate of both the Republican and the Know-Nothing Parties. He served with the Union forces as a major general during the War Between the States; ran again for the Presidency in 1864 (but withdrew his name in September); and was Territorial governor of Arizona from 1878 to 1883.

Frémont's greatest contribution to the nation, however, was as an explorer during the years from 1838 to 1847. Allan Nevins, author of *Frémont, the West's Greatest Adventurer*, called him "the first distinctively scientific explorer produced by the United States." And Kit Carson, who served with Frémont from 1842 to 1847, had only the highest praise for "The Pathfinder."

In addition to his scientific knowledge, Frémont had a talent for writing. Aided by his wife, an author in her own right, he produced reports that were of literary excellence as well as great scientific value. It was Frémont more than any other individual who exploded the myth of the "Great American Desert," and who published the first detailed descriptions of the Great Basin of the Rockies, lying between the Wasatch range on the east and the Sierra Nevada range on the west.

blood had been shed was really United States soil.

On the other hand, some historians have maintained that Mexico deliberately sent troops across the Rio Grande, hoping to start a war that it thought it could win.

Despite the great difference in size between the United States and Mexico, it is true that many Mexican military leaders did not fear a war with the United States. The Mexican leaders were full of confidence. They had expelled the Spaniards in 1821 and had overthrown revolutionists in their own country since that time. Thus they were boastful of their military abilities. They also hoped that Great Britain, which had looked forward to developing its own trade with the Republic of Texas and had therefore opposed its annexation to the United States, would come to the aid of Mexico. The Mexicans believed, too, that the people of the United States would never support a war.

As events turned out, Mexican hopes were misplaced. The Mexicans did not have the necessary military power. Great Britain did not come to their support. Although some northerners feared the expansion of slavery into the vast area that might be acquired as a result of the conflict, the war was in general supported by the American people.

Military operations. Armed forces of the United States operated in three different areas (see map, page 331). One area included Upper California and New Mexico. Upper California fell almost without a struggle. Even before news reached Upper California that war had been declared, a few dozen Americans led by William B. Ide began to plot against Mexican rule. They carried on their discussions in the camp of Captain John C. Frémont, famous explorer, who had arrived in California the previous autumn with an expedition of sixty-two men picked for their marksmanship. At Sonoma on June 14, 1846, Ide and a band of American settlers proclaimed the Republic of California, or the Bear Flag Republic, and hoisted a red flag with a bear and a star painted on it as a symbol of independence.

On July 7 Commodore J. D. Sloat of the United States Navy, hearing of the outbreak of war, landed naval forces at Monterey on the California coast, raised the American flag, and proclaimed California a part of the United States. Frémont then enlisted most of the Americans, including the Bear Flaggers, in a "California battalion," and, with Commodore Robert F. Stockton, moved south and captured Los Angeles. At the same time an overland expedition led by Brigadier-General S. W. Kearny left Fort Leavenworth on the Missouri River, occupied Santa Fe, and thereby secured control of New Mexico. Kearny then continued into California.

Meanwhile, in a second area south of the Rio Grande, an expedition under General Zachary Taylor won victories at the battles of Palo Alto and Resaca de la Palma (reh-SAH-kah deh lah PAHL-mah) on May 8 and 9, 1846, before war was actually declared. Taylor then went on to capture Monterrey, Mexico, in September 1846, and to check the main Mexican forces under Santa Anna at Buena Vista (BWEH-nah VEE-stah) in February 1847.

Despite these defeats the Mexicans continued to fight, and Polk ordered a third expedition to advance against Mexico City, the capital of Mexico, over the route once traveled by Cortez. Under the leadership of General Winfield Scott, an expeditionary force including marines was landed from naval ships on the shores of Mexico near Veracruz on the Gulf of Mexico. Nearly every step of the long, mountainous road to the "Halls of Montezuma" was bitterly contested. Hard battles were fought at several places, but on September 14, 1847, American troops entered Mexico City as conquerors.

Treaty of Guadalupe Hidalgo. By 1848 Upper California, New Mexico, and the entire Southwest were in American hands. General Taylor's troops held northern Mexico, and General Scott's forces walked the streets of the Mexican capital. Mexico was hopelessly defeated and had to end the war on American terms as written down in the Treaty of Guadalupe Hidalgo (gwah-dah-LOO-peh ee-DAL-goh) in 1848.

From the Mexican point of view, these terms were harsh indeed. Mexico was forced to acknowledge the American title to Texas, New Mexico, and Upper California—two fifths of Mexico's land. In return for this huge area, called the Mexican Cession (see map, pages 822–23), the United States gave Mexico $15,000,000 and agreed to assume debts, then totaling about $3,250,-000, that Mexico owed to Americans.

As a result of the Mexican War, President Polk's dream came true. The southwestern boundary of the United States was extended to the Pacific, and the chief objective of those who had cried "manifest destiny" had been realized. Finally, in 1853, Congress approved a payment to Mexico of $10,000,000 for the Gadsden Purchase (see map, pages 822–23), an area of land south of the Gila River needed to construct a southern transcontinental railroad. The purchase was named for James Gadsden of South Carolina who, as minister to Mexico, negotiated the purchase. Except for Alaska, the Gadsden Purchase rounded out the present continental boundaries of the United States.

SECTION SURVEY

1. What were the reasons for the Mexican War from (a) the American point of view? (b) the Mexican point of view?
2. In your opinion, was the war justified? Give reasons.
3. Describe the three major military campaigns of the war.
4. (a) Give the terms of the Treaty of Guadalupe Hidalgo. (b) What was the significance of this treaty in American history?
5. Indicate the importance of the Gadsden Purchase.

IDENTIFY: "manifest destiny," Spot Resolutions, Bear Flag Republic, "Halls of Montezuma"; Jones, Polk, Slidell, Taylor, Ide, Sloat, Kearny, Scott; 1845, 1846–48, 1848, 1853.

4 A surge of migration brings California into the Union

While government officials in the United States, Canada, Great Britain, Mexico, and Texas were wrestling with the problems created by American expansion into the Oregon country and the Southwest, settlers continued to cross the Great Plains in long caravans and thread their way through the passes to the Rocky Mountains and beyond.

The Mormons and Utah. One of the largest groups was the Mormons. The Mormon Church, or the Church of Jesus Christ of Latter-Day Saints, had been founded in western New York in the 1820's by young Joseph Smith. Smith announced that he had found golden plates on which sacred scriptures were engraved. When translated, these became the "Book of Mormon." Thousands of converts joined the new religious faith.

In three different places—Kirtland in Ohio, Independence in Missouri, and Nauvoo in Illinois—Mormons attempted to build an ideal society where they could live and worship in their own way. Each time, they were driven away by hostile neighbors who did not understand them and who disliked their idea that they were a chosen people with a special revelation of truth. Also, in Missouri, the fact that most Mormons were of "Yankee" background and did not favor slavery called forth the opposition of the pro-slavery Missourians. The open acceptance of polygamy by the Mormons at Nauvoo was a further cause of disapproval.

The Nauvoo community prospered above the other two. By 1844 it had become a thriving town of 15,000 persons. In that year, however, nearby communities organized against the Mormons. Joseph Smith and his brother were thrown into jail and then lynched by a mob. Once again the Mormons were forced to move.

Under the able leadership of Brigham Young, the Mormons moved out of Nauvoo. Their long caravan of loaded wagons moved westward across the plains, through the towering Rockies, and finally came to a halt in 1847 on the southwestern shore of Great Salt Lake (see map, page 323). There the Mormons plowed and irrigated the fields, learning many lessons about desert farming which they passed on to later western settlers. They laid out Salt Lake City on the Jordan River, and erected a famous temple. The Mormons also sent missionaries to the ends of the earth and organized ways of transporting converts to their new community in Utah.

For a number of reasons, Utah was not admitted to the Union until 1896. By that time it was a settled and prosperous region, born out of a desire similar to that which had driven the Pilgrims, Roger Williams, and others to worship God in their own way.

Spaniards rule California. Beyond the Great Salt Lake, hidden by the towering ramparts of the Sierra Nevadas, lay Upper California. Neither Spain nor Mexico had ever been strong enough to exploit the rich treasures of this land, far removed from Mexico City and even farther from the Spanish homeland.

From the beginning the ruling authorities in Mexico City had looked upon Upper California as an outpost of their empire, a defense against invaders from the north, but for a long time there was little threat from that direction. The Spaniards became concerned in the 1700's, however, when Russians began to establish fur trading posts in the Oregon country and when Russian vessels began to appear off the coast of northern California. To make their claims good, the Spaniards dispatched soldiers and missionaries in 1769 to build forts and missions at San Diego, Monterey, and wherever else they might be needed.

Led by Gaspar de Portolá and Father Junípero Serra (hu-NEE-peh-ro SEH-ra), a Franciscan priest, Spaniards moved northward along the Pacific coast until they discovered San Francisco Bay. For the next fifteen years Father Serra labored to strengthen the authority of the Spanish Crown and the Catholic Church in California. Before his death in 1784, Father Serra, aided by other Franciscans, had constructed a chain of missions in the fertile valleys along the coast from San Diego to San Francisco Bay.

After Father Serra's death other devoted friars continued the work. Indians gathered around the missions to till the fields, to learn handicrafts, and to be instructed in the ways of God. Along with the missions were a few forts or *presidios*. There were also a few small towns, among them San Diego, Los Angeles, Monterey, and Yerba Buena, where San Francisco now stands. Scattered sparsely over this immense territory were the estates of powerful Spanish landowners.

In this rich land of rare beauty, of vast distances, of unbelievable contrasts of climate and topography, life moved at a slow and leisurely tempo. Trade with the outside world and even with Mexico itself was negligible. The Californians sold some hides, mostly to American trading vessels that stopped now and then at the ports, but on the whole each ranch and each mission was self-sufficient.

Mexicans rule California. Neither Spain before 1821, nor Mexico after 1821, exercised strong control over this area. Mexico's strongest hold in California was weakened when in 1834 it passed an act that forced the Church to sell its mission lands to private owners. After this happened, the Indians began to leave the missions, drifting back into the interior. One by one the missions closed.

In 1846, when the Bear Flag Revolt was staged by a handful of Americans, there were not more than 4000 Mexicans in all of California. The entire Mexican army in control did not exceed 500 soldiers, who were scattered among half a dozen forts. The forts themselves and their armament were obsolete.

(*Continued on page 338*)

FATHER JUNÍPERO SERRA

In 1730 Spanish-born Miguel José Serra, then seventeen years old, became a member of the Order of St. Francis. After several years of intense study, he became a doctor of theology and had every reason to look forward to a brilliant career in the country of his birth. But his dreams were elsewhere. He longed to devote his life to the Indians of New Spain.

In 1749 Father Serra arrived in Mexico City. For a number of years, he carried on missionary work among the Indians of old Mexico and of what is now Texas. But the work by which he was to win a lasting place in history began when he journeyed to the wild, beautiful, almost unexplored country of Upper California.

In 1769 Father Serra established a mission at San Diego. This was the first of twenty-one missions that he and his followers built in the next fifty-three years. Before he died in 1784, he had established a chain of missions that stretched along the coast as far north as what is now San Francisco. Among them were San Gabriel, San Luis Obispo, San Antonio de Padua, San Carlos de Monterey, San Juan Capistrano, Santa Clara, and San Buenaventura.

Father Serra and his devoted followers baptized some six thousand Indians. They also taught the Indians to raise livestock and to grow grain, vegetables, and grapes.

Father Serra was completely self-sacrificing. Although of frail physique, he lived on a meager diet and slept on boards to remind himself that the material things of this world were of little importance and that only the spirit was eternal. The missions he built, worn by time but beautiful even when in ruins, stand as monuments to a devoted man of God who gave freely of himself for the welfare of others.

The movement of settlers into the American West was one of the great migrations of history. Wagon trains, moving a few miles a day, took months to creep over the Great Plains, across shallow but treacherous rivers, through winding mountain passes. Much easier was a trip by clipper ship like the *Eagle Wing* around South America.

MERCHANTS' EXPRESS LINE OF CLIPPER SHIPS FOR SAN FR
Passages 106 & 117 Days.

THE WELL-KNOWN   EXTREME CLI

EAGLE WIN

For Freight, apply at once to
Agents in San Francisco, Messrs. DE WITT, KITTLE & CO.
LINNELL, Commander, is now loading at Pier 16 E. R.
RANDOLPH M. COOLEY, 88 Wall St., Te

Going overland, pioneers met Indians of many tribes, as, for example, the Mandans pictured below left, in a large hut. As settlement progressed, the cowboy appeared on the scene. This western figure was painted (extreme left, below) by Frederic Remington, an artist who was himself a cowboy. In the course of settlement, the famous Concord coach became the only means of public transportation, filling this role until the railroads were built. The coach shown below operated between Hangtown, California, and Carson City, Nevada.

■ In this photograph taken in 1850 along Pine Creek in the California gold fields, men are shoveling gold-bearing gravel into a sluice that they have built. The swift water washes away sand and gravel, leaving the gold particles behind in traps called riffles, from which they are collected when the water is closed off at the head of the sluice.

Even though Spanish and Mexican control over California was weak, to this day the influence of Spanish culture is apparent on every hand. Many towns, rivers, and mountains have Spanish names, and in some places the Spanish language is still spoken. Traces of Spanish laws, customs, and architecture are still found in the life of California.

American settlers arrive. A region of such wealth and beauty as Upper California could not long be hidden from the eyes of restless Americans pressing steadily westward. In 1841 a party of men, women, and children set out from Missouri led by John Bidwell, "the prince of California pioneers." Their trip to California across the plains and mountains, as revealed in the journal of their leader, is a tribute to human courage, endurance, and faith. "We

knew only," Bidwell wrote, "that California lay to the west."

The Bidwell pioneers were followed by many other parties, including the Donner party. Caught in 1846 in the Sierra Nevada mountains by the icy grip of an early winter, the Donner party built crude shelters and struggled to survive. Soup made of boiled leather and powdered bones became a luxury. Of the 79 persons who started, 34 died before an expedition out of California rescued the survivors.

Other settlers also filtered into California. Among them were sailors who deserted from the ships that occasionally stopped for water and food before they continued their trading voyages to the Hawaiian Islands and China. By 1848 several hundred Americans had settled in California.

The Gold Rush. Among the early pioneers in California was John A. Sutter from Switzerland, whose sawmill and fort at Sacramento were the center of bustling activity. On the morning of January 24, 1848, one of his employees, James W. Marshall, detected flakes of yellow metal at the bottom of a stream where a new mill was being built. The shining substance was gold. Despite Sutter's desire to keep the discovery secret until a new mill was built, the news spread like wildfire. The small flow of California settlers swelled into a powerful flood. In 1849, a year after the discovery of gold, it seemed as though the entire male population of the eastern half of the United States was moving to the Pacific coast.

Stories of huge fortunes made overnight circulated all through the older parts of the nation. Some of these stories were true; most were false. True or false, the stories stirred men's imaginations. By the thousands they sold all they owned and joined the mad rush of the "Forty-Niners" to the gold fields of California.

The gold fever even reached Europe. In France holders of winning tickets in "lotteries of the golden ingot" were rewarded with free passage to the fabulous gold fields of far-off California.

By three routes the adventurers from Europe and the eastern United States converged upon California (see map, page 323). The longest but the safest and most comfortable route, as comfort went in those days, was by sailing around Cape Horn.

The quickest, most crowded, and most expensive route was by ship to Central America, by land across the Isthmus of Panama, and by another ship from there to San Francisco. Every old ship that could float was pressed into service. Crowds of men in bright shirts and slouch hats, armed with bowie knives and pistols, fought one another to get across the bottleneck of the Isthmus and on to one of the few ships plying between Panama and California.

A third route, fit only for the rugged and the brave, led men across the Great Plains and through the passes of the mountains, along the routes of the Bidwell and Donner parties. It took the wagon trains of the "Forty-Niners" five months to make the trip from the eastern seaboard. Often trails over the plains and through the mountain passes were lined with household goods thrown away to lighten the load and with dead bodies of beasts and men struck down by Indians, disease, hunger, thirst, cold, or heat.

The first wave of "Forty-Niners" jammed into raw, lawless mining camps. Some found riches beyond their wildest dreams. Most found only disappointment. As the months passed, two streams of travelers passed on the trails and roads leading from San Francisco to the mining regions. Going one way were newcomers eager for fortunes; returning were disappointed gold seekers who had given up the search.

Statehood for California. Gradually the uproar subsided as men turned their efforts to the construction of houses, hotels, stores, and shops in the rapidly growing towns and cities or settled on the land and began to farm. Settlers built schools and churches. In 1849 they established a Territorial government.

No other state passed from Territorial government to statehood as quickly as California did. In 1850 California entered the Union and the thirty-first star was added to the American flag.

⌕ SECTION SURVEY

1. Why were the Mormons persecuted?
2. The influence of Spanish culture on California is still very strong. Justify this statement.
3. What three routes were used by the "Forty-Niners" to get to the gold fields in California?
4. Explain this quotation: "No other state passed from Territorial government to statehood as quickly as California did."

IDENTIFY: Donner expedition, "Forty-Niners"; Joseph Smith, Brigham Young, Junípero Serra, Bidwell, Sutter; 1848, 1849, 1850.

Points to Discuss: 1. Compare the meaning and significance of the word "frontier" in American history and in the history of European countries.

2. Explain the meaning of the term "manifest destiny."

3. Give the basis for claims to the Oregon territory by (a) Spain, (b) Russia, (c) Great Britain, and (d) United States.

4. The northwestern boundary of the United States is 49° North latitude. Tell the story behind this boundary line.

5. Compare American pioneer life in the Pacific Northwest with that in Texas.

6. Review the facts of American acquisition of Florida, Texas, and Oregon. Seek to account for the different methods of settlement with Spain, Mexico, and Great Britain.

7. The Democratic slogan in the election of 1844 was "Re-annexation of Texas and Re-occupation of Oregon!" Explain its meaning.

8. Justify or criticize the United States for the Mexican War.

Using Maps and Charts: 1. Using the map on page 323, answer the following:

(a) If you had been living in St. Louis in the 1840's and wanted to go West, which area would you have chosen for settlement? Why? (b) Describe the route which you would have followed. (c) Which route to the West would you have taken if you had been living on the east coast?

2. Referring to the map on pages 822–23, locate the area in dispute between the United States and Mexico and explain the reason for the dispute.

3. Use the map on page 331, and indicate the major objectives (a) of the military moves by Frémont, Sloat, and Kearny; (b) of the expeditions of Taylor and Scott.

4. Refer to chart 2 on page 820, and answer the following: (a) Compare the area, in square miles, of Texas with that of the Mexican Cession. (b) What percentage of the present United States area did these two constitute? (c) What states were formed out of the acquisition of Texas and the Mexican Cession?

Consulting the Sources: For accounts of Catholic missionary activities in both the Northwest and the Southwest, see Ellis, *Docs.*, Nos. 77, 78, 90, 92–94.

■ TRACING THE MAIN IDEAS

The "Westward Movement" began with the first settlers along the eastern seaboard of North America. Driven by the excitement of exploring the unknown and by the desire for land, generation after generation of pioneers followed the setting sun across the vast, untamed continent.

By the early 1800's the frontier had advanced beyond the Mississippi River. By 1850 bold pioneers had crossed the 2000-mile stretch of plains and mountains and were building new homes in Oregon and California on the Pacific coast. Other venturesome pioneers had moved into Texas and the Southwest. Only the plains and mountains remained to be settled. "Manifest destiny"—by which men meant that it was written in the stars that the United States should possess the land from sea to sea—had been fulfilled.

This immense area reaching from the Mississippi Valley to the Pacific coast was populated by people whose means of livelihood and ideas about government were in many respects different from those of people who lived in the North and in the South. The differences were less important, however, than the fact that the West was growing rapidly in population and in political strength.

Both the North and the South tried to win western support for the laws that they wished Congress to adopt. This struggle for control of the West is one of the keys to an understanding of American history during the generation before the War Between the States.

As you will see in the next unit, men fought the battle in Congress as well as on the western plains. Before turning to this story, however, you will read in the next chapter about some of the developments that were transforming American life during these years.

Ideas of Reform Stir the American People

CHANGING WAYS

OF AMERICAN LIFE

THE verb "to ferment" means "to be inwardly active, agitated, or excited; to seethe mentally or emotionally. . . ."

It would be difficult to find a more accurate term than "ferment" to describe the activities of the American people in the years from the 1820's to the 1860's. The United States was, indeed, in ferment during these years. Changes were taking place with bewildering speed.

The very appearance of America was changing. Industrialism was transforming the North. Cotton growing was bringing prosperity to large areas of the South. Land-hungry pioneers were pushing the frontiers across the Great Plains, through the Rocky Mountains, and into the fertile valleys of the Pacific Northwest and sunny California. In outward appearance the United States by the 1830's and 1840's was a much differ-

ent country from the United States of the 1790's.

The ideas of the people were also changing. By the time Andrew Jackson became President in 1829, all men (with the exception of the slaves and the mentally unfit) had won the right to vote. Now some women were demanding the same right. And a great number of both men and women were trying to make the ideals of democracy work more effectively in the everyday affairs of life.

During the period from the 1820's to the 1860's, reformers were seeking to improve almost every aspect of society. Millions of Americans were "inwardly active, agitated, or excited."

"We are all a little wild here with numberless projects of social reform," Ralph Waldo Emerson, the New England writer and philosopher, wrote to a friend in England.

The story of this period of reform, this age of "ferment," is told in this chapter.

AS THE STORY DEVELOPS
1. **Women gain a more important place in American life.**
2. **Reformers strive to improve conditions of American life.**
3. **Free public education makes a promising start.**
4. **A strong movement develops to abolish slavery.**
5. **Spokesmen for democracy preach faith in the individual.**

341

1 Women gain a more important place in American life

From the earliest days women worked together with men in the development of America. They shared the loneliness, the dangers, the desperately hard work involved in settling the wilderness and transforming it into a land of prosperous farms and thriving towns and cities.

The status of women. But there was this difference: even as late as the 1830's, women had legal rights hardly better than those of children. A married woman had almost no right to own property. When a woman married, all the property she owned went to her husband. If, after her marriage, she earned money or inherited property, this too belonged to her husband.

Moreover, a married woman had almost no claim to her own children. The husband controlled his sons and daughters while he lived. He, not both parents, decided what the children should do. Indeed, if a man wished, he could leave a will placing his children under a guardian after his death, even though their mother were still alive. Actually,

---

LIVING AMERICAN DOCUMENTS

The Seneca Falls Declaration of Sentiments and Resolutions (1848):
EXCERPT

We hold these truths to be self-evident: that all men and women are created equal . . . Now, in view of entire disfranchisement of one half the people of this country, their social and religious degradation—in view of the unjust laws above mentioned, and because women do feel themselves aggrieved, oppressed, and fraudulently deprived of their most sacred rights, we insist that they have immediate admission to all the rights and privileges which belong to them as citizens of the United States . . .

---

however, men rarely used their full legal rights over their wives and children.

As for the practice of politics, that was entirely a man's job. Women often exercised a large influence over husbands and friends, but the right to vote and hold office was a man's right only.

A declaration of women's rights. Even during colonial days a number of women had protested against the limitations on the rights of women. In 1774, for example, Abigail Adams sent a letter to her husband John, who was in Philadelphia attending the First Continental Congress: "We are determined to foment a rebellion," she wrote, perhaps with a twinkle in her eye, "and will not hold ourselves bound by any laws in which we have no voice or representation."

The rebellion Abigail Adams warned her husband about did not come in her lifetime. By the 1820's and 1830's, however, women were raising their voices in defiant protest against their lowly place in society. Leaders appeared, women with deeply rooted convictions.

During these years women frequently tried to force their way into men's meetings, even into political conventions. The men, astonished at this unladylike conduct, usually turned the women away.

A few of the leaders came from Europe, where a similar women's rights movement was under way. Among the Europeans who traveled across the Atlantic to help the American women in their struggle for equal rights with men were Ernestine L. Rose of Poland, Frances Anne Kemble of England, and Frances Wright of Scotland.

But American women bore the brunt of the struggle. Among the American leaders were Lucretia Mott and Elizabeth Cady Stanton. These two women were in large part responsible for organizing the first women's rights convention, held at Seneca Falls, New York, in July 1848. At the convention the women adopted a Declaration of Sentiments, which said, "All men and women are created equal . . ." and went on to list demands for political, social, and economic equality with men. But decisive gains in these fields did not come until the latter half of the 1800's. Most of the early victories were confined to the field of education.

Education for women. Back in the days when Abigail Adams was warning her husband that women would rebel if they did not receive a larger share of rights, a Boston clergyman wrote to a friend: "We don't pretend to teach the female part of the town anything more than dancing, or a little music perhaps."

By the 1820's, however, education for girls and women was getting well started. Emma Hart Willard opened the Troy Female Seminary in 1821 at Troy, New York, and began to teach mathematics, science, history, and other subjects. During the next few years Catharine Esther Beecher, Mary Lyon, and other dedicated women opened schools for girls.

The movement grew most rapidly in the Middle West. The first college to open its doors to women was Oberlin Collegiate Institute in Ohio, which admitted women four years after it was founded in 1834. This action, and the fact that Oberlin also admitted Negroes, led many Americans to look upon the institution as "radical." But other colleges in the Middle West also began to admit women students. In 1856 the University of Iowa attracted attention as the first state university to open its doors to women.

Early achievements. Slowly, and against strong opposition, women began to win places for themselves in what, until this time, had been considered a "man's world." Dr. Elizabeth Blackwell, the first woman to win a medical diploma in the United States, began to practice medicine in New York City in 1850. She founded the first school of nursing in the United States and in 1875 became a professor in the London School of Medicine for Women.

Antoinette Louisa Blackwell, the first fully ordained female minister in the

MOTHER SETON

For truly heroic virtue there were few great women of the nineteenth century to equal Elizabeth Ann Bailey Seton (1774–1821). Her early years in a family of colonial aristocrats, in New York, coincided with the beginnings of the Republic. She was married in 1794 to a New York gentleman and became the mother of five children. Business reverses and poor health caused William Seton to go with his wife and their eldest daughter to Italy, where Seton himself died.

At the time she was in Pisa, and on her sad journey home to America, Elizabeth was drawn to the Catholic faith, with the result that she became a convert at old St. Peter's Church on Ash Wednesday in 1805. A widow, and almost penniless, she had a very difficult time with her Protestant relatives until she answered the request of Bishop Carroll that she come to Baltimore and open a school. She began her educational work, and conceived the idea of a religious community in that city in 1808.

Thanks to the encouragement of Church authority, with spiritual direction by Sulpician priests and with a gift of money from another convert, Mother Seton was able to begin a school at Emmitsburg, Maryland, and to provide for the other women who were the first members of her Daughters of Charity. Meanwhile, she had to see to the upbringing of her own sons and daughters. There were grave hardships and her spirit was severely tested before she died in 1821; but, by that time, her Daughters of Charity had become firmly established under a rule originally provided for religious women by St. Vincent de Paul.

United States, became minister of the Congregational Church at South Butler, New York, in 1852.

Other women won distinction as writers and editors. Louisa May Alcott was the author of a number of children's books, among them *Little Women,* which was translated into several languages. Harriet Beecher Stowe wrote *Uncle Tom's Cabin* (page 351). Margaret Fuller preceded Ralph Waldo Emerson as editor of *The Dial,* a philosophical and literary magazine. She also served for a time as literary critic for the *New York Tribune.*

Dorothea Lynde Dix. Another woman who exerted an enormous influence was Dorothea Lynde Dix. For a number of years, Miss Dix ran a boarding school in Boston, and during these years wrote a highly successful textbook, *Conversations on Popular Things.* Ill health forced her to close her school, but in 1841, after inspecting the East Cambridge jail near Boston, she began a new career of institutional reform that made her famous at home and abroad.

Miss Dix was horrified by conditions in the jail. It was cold, bare, and filthy. The sane and the insane lived side by side. Determined to do something about the situation, she laid the facts before the Massachusetts legislature, but the men were indifferent to her remarks.

Goaded to further action, Dorothea Dix made up her mind to visit every jail and poorhouse in Massachusetts, to collect an overwhelming amount of data, and to present them to the legislature. She packed notebook after notebook with records of horrors almost beyond belief. In all of the jails and poorhouses, she found old men, young girls, the poor, and the mentally ill thrown together in cold, dirty prisons. Some were chained to walls, beds, or floors. Some wore iron collars or strait jackets. Some were confined in cages for years.

Finally, Miss Dix went again to the Massachusetts legislature with her evidence. This time the legislators listened. They began to pass laws to improve conditions in jails and poorhouses.

Other states watched these developments with interest. During the next few years Miss Dix repeated her reform work in Connecticut, New York, Pennsylvania, and Kentucky. Moreover, her efforts to improve the treatment of the poor and the insane attracted the attention of European reformers and helped to improve conditions in European jails and institutions for the poor and insane.

By the 1850's, in large part as the result of the work of Miss Dix and others who shared her views, important reforms had been made in the United States. The death penalty had been abolished for a number of crimes, and a growing number of people were demanding the "complete abolition of capital punishment." Most states had outlawed the whipping of prisoners. Imprisonment for debt had been ended. Men and women were confined in separate sections of prisons, and the mentally ill were separated from other prisoners. More attention was given to the individual criminal, and more effort was made to reform rather than to punish.

Dorothea Dix lived to the age of eighty-five. When she died in 1887, a famous English doctor said, "Thus has died and been laid to rest in the most quiet and unostentatious way the most useful and distinguished woman that America has ever produced."

SECTION SURVEY

1. Even as late as the 1830's, women had legal rights far inferior to those of men. Discuss this statement.

2. What was the significance of the Seneca Falls Convention of 1848?

3. How do you explain the fact that the first victories of the women's rights movement were in the field of education?

4. Describe three notable accomplishments by women during this period.

5. What important reforms did Dorothea Lynde Dix help to introduce?

IDENTIFY: reformer, capital punishment; Lucretia Mott, Elizabeth Cady Stanton, Emma Hart Willard, Elizabeth Blackwell, Antoinette L. Blackwell, Louisa May Alcott, Margaret Fuller; 1821, 1848.

2 Reformers strive to improve conditions of American life

The struggle for equal rights for women was only one of many reforms Americans were working for in the period from the 1820's to the 1860's.

Crusade against alcohol. One of the reform movements in which women as well as men took an active part was the battle against excessive drinking. This battle, known as the "temperance movement," got under way on a national scale in 1833 when advocates of temperance held a convention in Philadelphia. More than 400 delegates from 22 states attended. Before the convention adjourned, the delegates organized the United States Temperance Union. The members of the organization included many businessmen who argued that drinking was physically harmful and caused many accidents. Most of the reformers, however, joined the movement because they believed drinking was a sin.

The temperance movement grew rapidly. In 1836 several groups, including a Canadian organization, joined to form the American Temperance Union. Politicians, hoping to attract votes, took up the cause. Children joined clubs bearing titles such as "The Cold Water Army." Men formed numerous societies, among them the "Sons of Temperance" and "Teetotalers Hall." The reformers flooded the country with literature, some for adults, much of it for children.

Some reformers were not satisfied to fight for moderation, or temperance, in drinking. Insisting that any drinking was harmful and sinful, they demanded state laws prohibiting the manufacture and sale of all alcoholic drinks.

As a result of this widespread agitation, the temperance and prohibition movements began to produce results. In 1846 the state of Maine adopted a prohibition law. Within a few years a number of other states followed suit.

There was strong opposition to these laws, of course, much of it from brew-

Mother Cabrini symbolizes the charitable social work of the Church. Here she contacts a family of immigrants on New York's east side.

ers and distillers of alcoholic drinks. Other citizens protested that the states had no power to decide what a man should or should not drink.

Vigorous though the temperance and prohibition movements were, they did not bring an end to drinking. An unexpected by-product of the prohibition laws was that sales rose sharply for patent medicines with a high alcoholic content. But the efforts of reformers did bring beneficial results. Drinking among women almost ceased. In many communities a drunken man on the street became an object of curiosity or contempt.

Efforts to end war. During the years from about 1820 to 1860, many persons both in the United States and in Western Europe began to devote their efforts to the peace movement. Although Quakers in the United States had always opposed the use of force, except when necessary for police purposes, it was not until after the War of 1812 that a strong anti-war movement developed in America. Numerous local peace societies sprang up, and in 1828 the local organizations joined together to form the American Peace Society.

"THIS IS NO HUMBUG"

On October 16, 1846, the surgical amphitheater of the Massachusetts General Hospital was crowded with people who listened attentively while Dr. John Collins Warren, Professor of Surgery at Harvard Medical School, explained the experiment they were about to witness.

"About five weeks ago," he said, "Dr. Morton, a dentist of this city, informed me that he had invented an apparatus for the inhalation of a vapor, the effect of which was to produce a state of total insensibility to pain. . . . He has wished for an opportunity to test its power in a surgical operation, and I have agreed with him as to the propriety of such an experiment." At this moment, Dr. William Morton arrived. Dr. Warren turned to him. "Well sir," he said, "your patient is ready." Dr. Morton began to administer the anesthetic. Three minutes later he turned to the surgeon: "Dr. Warren, *your* patient is ready."

Dr. Warren performed a major operation on the patient's neck. By the time it was completed, the patient, who had appeared to be unconscious, had begun to mutter incoherently. "Did you feel any pain?" Dr. Warren asked.

"Feel's if m'neck's been scratched," the patient mumbled.

"Is that all?" Dr. Warren asked.

"That's all," replied the patient.

The attendants wheeled the man from the room. No one moved. No one said a word. Finally, the surgeon broke the silence. "Gentlemen," he said, his voice husky with emotion, "this is no humbug."

On November 18, 1846, the *Boston Medical and Surgical Journal* printed an article in which the use of ether as an anesthetic was formally announced to the medical world.

Although Dr. Morton usually is credited with the discovery of ether, a Georgia physician, Dr. Crawford Williamson Long, had been using it in a number of successful operations as early as 1842. Dr. Long, however, did not publish his findings until 1849.

The opponents of war insisted that armed conflict was anti-Christian, inhumane, and uneconomical.

Elihu Burritt, a self-educated Connecticut blacksmith, was another of the leaders of the peace movement. He developed a pledge card against war and secured the signatures of more than 40,000 persons in America and England. He also organized an exchange of letters between workers in British and American cities. With the co-operation of William Ladd, a sea captain and farmer known as the "apostle of peace," he urged the nations of the world to form an international organization, and to create a world court for the settlement of international disputes.

Efforts to build ideal communities. Not all the people who longed for a better world became reformers. Some men and women decided to withdraw from the world around them and build *utopian* (yoo-TOH-pian), or ideal, communities.

Robert Owen, a wealthy British manufacturer, helped to arouse interest in this type of experiment when, in 1825, he started a utopian community at New Harmony in Indiana. New Harmony lasted only a few years, but its failure did not discourage other experiments. "Not a reading man but has a draft of a new community in his waistcoat pocket," Ralph Waldo Emerson once remarked. Two of the well-known, but short-lived, experiments were Brook Farm, near Boston, and the Oneida (oh-NIH-duh) Community in New York.

✓ SECTION SURVEY

1. (a) Describe the growth of the temperance movement at this time. (b) What were the results of this movement?

2. What proof do we have that people at this time were interested in the abolition of war?

3. Why were so many utopian communities started during this period?

IDENTIFY: American Temperance Union, prohibition, American Peace Society; Burritt, Ladd, Robert Owen; 1825, 1828.

3 Free public education makes a promising start

Horace Mann on Education (1848):
EXCERPT

*E*ducation then, beyond all other devices of human origin, is a great equalizer of the conditions of men—the balance wheel of the social machinery . . . it gives each man the independence and the means by which he can resist the selfishness of other men. It does better than to disarm the poor of their hostility toward the rich: it prevents being poor . . .

One of the most important of all the reform programs of the period from the 1820's to the 1860's was the movement for free public schools.

The problem of education. In colonial times New England towns were required by law to provide elementary schools. These New England schools were not entirely free. All parents who could afford to do so paid tuition fees for their children; the town itself paid only for the poor.

By the opening years of the 1800's, however, these so-called "common" schools of New England had reached a very low level. Buildings were inadequate, and the quality of teaching was poor. Conditions were even worse in the Middle Atlantic states and in the southern states, where the people were more dispersed. Indeed, in many areas schools run by churches provided almost the only chance most children had to get an elementary school education.

By the 1820's and the 1830's this situation was beginning to change. A growing number of people began to demand public, tax-supported schools.

Leaders in the movement. Many people, including large numbers of wage earners, joined in the struggle for free public education. Among the leaders were Horace Mann and Henry Barnard.

Horace Mann turned from a brilliant legal and political career to become a crusader for public schools in Massachusetts. When the state legislature of Massachusetts created a state Board of Education in 1837, Mann became its first secretary. He used his growing power and influence to establish *normal schools* for training teachers. He also began to organize the local school districts into a state-wide system of education.

Henry Barnard did for Connecticut and Rhode Island what Horace Mann was doing for Massachusetts. As a result of his leadership, Henry Barnard won national recognition. In 1867 he became the first United States Commissioner of Education.

The work of these and other leaders, among them Calvin E. Stowe of Ohio and Caleb Mills of Indiana, helped to set the pattern of free public education throughout the United States.

Objections to public education. The struggle for free, tax-supported elementary schools was not easily won. Churches that had already established religious schools, or that hoped to do so, objected strenuously. Private schools, both religious and secular, were vigorous in their opposition. Many taxpayers objected to using tax money to pay for schools.

Labor organizations opposed the prejudice against using public funds to educate the children of the poor. Workingmen in some of the larger cities, shoemakers, carpenters, and stonemasons, tried in the 1820's to make this a political issue. Besides urging legislation to guarantee wages on time and in "hard money," they agitated for laws that would provide for free elementary education. By the time of the election of Andrew Jackson, many of these groups had joined the Democratic Party and made free education one of its aims.

Early victories. In spite of the prejudice against "book learning," in spite of the organized opposition, the movement for tax-supported elementary schools

■ By the 1830's public education in America was still limited but was showing new signs of strength. A few cities, mostly in New England, were beginning to build high schools. Some smaller places were also beginning to spend more money on education. In 1830 the town of Vergennes, Vermont, built the small brick school shown above. (In recent years the school has been moved to a museum at Shelburne, Vermont.) But in many places and for many years, much American schooling went on in simpler wooden schools. Winslow Homer, a famous American artist, in 1872 showed such a school (below) in his painting called "Snap the Whip."

began to gain strength. While opponents argued, the people voted. In 1832 New York City established a system of free public elementary schools. Four years later, in 1836, Philadelphia followed suit. Gradually, other cities and towns fell into line. By the 1850's nearly all children, at least in northern cities, could secure a free elementary education.

Meanwhile, strong efforts had been made to provide for free high school education. New England led the way. The first public high school in America, the English High School of Boston, opened in 1821. Six years later, in 1827, the Massachusetts legislature passed the first state law requiring towns with 500 or more families to provide a high school education at public expense.

In response to this law and to the growing demand on the part of voters, a number of Massachusetts towns established high schools. Other towns in other states began to follow the example set by Massachusetts, but the movement gained strength only slowly. By 1850 there were only 55 public high schools in the entire United States. In this same year there were more than 6000 private high schools, or *academies,* as they were called. A high school education was still beyond the reach of most American boys and girls.

The educational ladder. The democratic system of free public education in the United States has been called "a great educational ladder." By the 1860's the "ladder" was beginning to be erected. All children could expect to receive an elementary school education. Boys and girls in the larger towns could attend free public high schools. And by the end of the 1850's, 16 states had established universities supported in large part by public funds.

Alongside this system of free public schools was the older system of private educational institutions—private elementary schools, academies, and more than 100 church-supported colleges. Most of these colleges were small, with from one to three hundred students and from six to twelve professors. But the

fact that there were so many of them shows how deeply Americans believed in the importance of education.

Equally significant was the fact that the principle of the separation of church and state (page 142) was being written into all of the state constitutions. By the 1830's no person could be compelled to pay taxes for the support of any church or of any school that taught particular religious doctrines.

The democratic ideal—equal educational opportunity for everyone, rich and poor alike—was beginning by the 1860's to take solid form.

✔ **SECTION SURVEY**

1. Describe the contributions made by (a) Horace Mann and (b) Henry Barnard to American education.
2. What opposition was there to free public education?
3. List four achievements attained by the supporters of free public schools.
4. Show why political democracy depends on free public schools.

IDENTIFY: normal school, academy; Calvin E. Stowe, Mills; 1821, 1827, 1867.

4 A strong movement develops to abolish slavery

By far the most vigorous of the reform movements of the period from the 1820's to the 1860's was the anti-slavery, or *abolition,* crusade. No single development did more to drive a wedge between the North and the South.

Like the other reform movements of this period, the abolition movement was an active force on both sides of the Atlantic Ocean. American abolitionists cooperated closely with their fellows in the British Anti-Slavery Society. Indeed, Americans were encouraged by the success of the British abolitionists, who managed by 1833 to outlaw slavery throughout the British Empire.

Early efforts to abolish slavery. In colonial days there were only a few Americans who objected to slavery, among them Benjamin Franklin and John Woolman, a Quaker. But the Declaration of Independence, maintaining that "all men are created equal," gave the opponents of slavery a stronger argument than they had had before. By the 1780's several anti-slavery societies were active in the North.

Sentiment against slavery was also growing in the South during these years. It was a Virginian, Thomas Jefferson, who wrote "all men are created equal." But even Jefferson was slow to act on his beliefs. He left a will freeing his own slaves, but did not free them during his lifetime. He and other southerners who shared his concern over slavery, among them George Washington, believed that it would imply criticism of their fellow planters if they were to free their own slaves. They also doubted that it was fair to the slaves themselves to set them free and let them shift for themselves. But Washington, like Jefferson, provided in his will for the freeing of his slaves.

In the 1790's many people believed that the only solution to slavery was to abolish it—to do away with it. At that time this solution was a reasonable one to expect. Those who believed that slavery was wrong were finding allies among men who felt that slavery was no longer profitable. The great southern tobacco plantations, which for generations had drawn their wealth from tobacco raised by slaves, were facing an uncertain future. Land on which tobacco was planted year after year lost its fertility and much of its value, while the cost of feeding, clothing, housing, and caring for the slaves remained the same.

Eli Whitney's invention of the cotton gin in 1793 completely altered the problem of slavery. The textile mills that were springing up in the North and in Great Britain needed cotton, as you have seen, and Whitney's invention made it possible for southern planters to meet their demands. Within a few years southerners were shifting from to-bacco to cotton planting and searching for new land to the southwest. The demand for slaves grew by leaps and bounds.

Abolition in the 1820's. But the renewed value of slavery did not stop the abolition movement. Among the leaders of this movement in the 1820's was Benjamin Lundy, a mild-mannered Quaker. In 1821 Lundy began to publish a periodical, called the *Genius of Universal Emancipation,* in which he urged freedom for all men.

More positive actions were taken by the American Colonization Society, which had been founded in 1817. Supported largely by slaveowners of Kentucky, Maryland, and Virginia—where cotton was not a profitable crop—the American Colonization Society set out to purchase slaves and send them as free men to colonize Sierra Leone and Liberia in Africa. Lack of funds prevented the American Colonization Society from making important contributions to the problem. By 1831 the society had been able to set free only 1420 slaves, about the same number as were being born into slavery every four months in the southern states at that time.

The plan of the American Colonization Society to buy and free slaves was impractical. The society could not possibly raise enough money to solve the problem. Between 1820 and 1860 the value of the average slave rose from $400 to $1000 or even $1500. The number of slaves increased during these years from 1,500,000 to 4,000,000. With each year that passed, slavery was rooting itself more deeply in the cotton planting areas of the South.

Abolition becomes militant. In 1831, however, the opposition to slavery suddenly entered a new and more vigorous phase. The opening attack came from the pen of William Lloyd Garrison of Massachusetts. In the first issue of his paper, the *Liberator,* published in Boston on January 1, 1831, Garrison wrote: "I shall strenuously contend for the immediate enfranchisement of our slave population . . . On this subject I do not wish to think, or speak, or write, with moderation. . . . I am in earnest —I will not equivocate—I will not excuse—I will not retreat a single inch— AND I WILL BE HEARD. . . ."

Garrison's demand for action rallied many men and women to the anti-slavery movement. Quakers and members of the Methodist and Baptist churches joined in large numbers. Sarah and Angelina Grimké of South Carolina freed their slaves, moved to Philadelphia, became Quakers, and devoted their lives to the anti-slavery movement. The Grimké sisters were exceptional, however. Few southerners followed their example. The abolition movement was largely confined to the northeastern and midwestern states where people had no investment in slaves.

Lecturers and authors. As the abolition movement gained momentum, some well-known lecturers and writers joined its membership. Lucretia Mott was one of several women who lectured against slavery, speaking wherever she could find an audience. Theodore Parker of Boston, one of the eminent preachers of his day, became a leader in the movement. The Quaker poet John Greenleaf Whittier wrote verses against what he called the "crime" of slavery. James Russell Lowell, Wendell Phillips, and Ralph Waldo Emerson, all of Massachusetts, lectured and wrote in favor of abolition.

One of the most phenomenal effects of writing upon history occurred later, in 1852, when Harriet Beecher Stowe of Brunswick, Maine, published *Uncle Tom's Cabin*. This melodramatic novel about slavery inflamed the emotions of many people in the North, who failed to recognize its distortions. Mrs. Stowe's book, which has been called "the most influential novel in all history," gave new impetus to the abolition movement.

The movement spreads. During the 1830's and 1840's the abolition movement spread throughout the northeastern states and westward to the states north of the Ohio River. Theodore Dwight Weld, for example, spoke from

Clothing of the 1830's

one end of Ohio to the other, carrying the arguments for abolition into small churches and rural areas.

In 1833 the movement gained new strength with the formation of the American Anti-Slavery Society, a counterpart of the British Anti-Slavery Society. At the height of the American abolition movement, according to one estimate, there were about 2000 local anti-slavery societies with a combined membership of about 200,000.

Abolitionist activities. The abolitionists used various methods to arouse public opinion. They were well organized; they talked, lectured, and wrote. They also poured petitions into state legislatures and into Congress.

Some abolitionists took more direct action when they organized the "underground railroad." Slaves who learned about the "railroad" might slip into the woods until the pursuit died down, and then flee north to Mason and Dixon's line (see map, page 362).

Crossing Mason and Dixon's line, however, did not bring the slaves their freedom. According to a Fugitive Slave Law passed by Congress in 1793, the owner of a runaway slave could recover his slave merely by appearing before any magistrate and declaring that the slave in question belonged to him. For this reason, fugitive slaves were not safe until they reached Canada.

Once across Mason and Dixon's line, however, runaway slaves hoped to get in touch with an "agent" of the underground railroad, who would take them in charge and arrange for their escape. Hiding in attics and haylofts by day and taken to the next "station" by night, the slaves slowly made the long trip northward. In time, with good luck, the hazardous journey was completed and the slaves found freedom in Canada.

Political weakness. Despite their vigorous activities the abolitionists never managed to muster any important political strength. In their first attempt at political action, the organization of the Liberty Party in 1840, their Presidential candidate, James G. Birney, who had been "converted" to abolitionism by the preaching of Theodore D. Weld, polled only about 7000 votes. In the election of 1844, after four years in which to perfect their political organization, the abolitionists polled only 62,300 of the 2,500,-000 votes cast in the country.

Northern opposition. Lack of political support did not mean, however, that people in general were not concerned over the abolition movement. The abolitionists aroused bitter opposition north as well as south of Mason and Dixon's line. Abolitionist preachers were sometimes driven from their pulpits. Prominent citizens like Wendell Phillips of Boston, a well-known lecturer and writer, were barred from clubs and social gatherings. Elijah P. Lovejoy, an abolitionist editor of Alton, Illinois, was murdered by a mob.

Northern wage earners, fearing the job competition of free Negroes, often broke up anti-slavery meetings. Northern businessmen in general frowned upon the abolitionists, fearful that their activities could only be harmful to trade between North and South. Indeed, a crowd including a number of businessmen once forced William Lloyd Garrison to flee for safety to a Boston jail. Garrison remarked on one occasion that he "found contempt more bitter, opposition more stubborn, and apathy more frozen" in New England than in the South.

■ Operators of the "underground railroad" developed many ingenious ruses to help runaway slaves escape. Besides attics and haylofts, there were underground hideouts where slaves concealed themselves during the day. This tunnel was an escape route from one such hideout at Cleveland, Ohio. From here, slaves might go by boat to freedom in Canada.

Southern reactions. But southerners, of course, were most embittered by the anti-slavery movement. In 1831 Nat Turner, a slave, led an uprising in Virginia that cost the lives of 55 white people. This rebellion quickened southern fears of more widespread uprisings of the slaves. Southerners claimed that the abolitionists in general, and William Lloyd Garrison in particular, were responsible for this rebellion. And as losses from runaway slaves became increasingly serious, slaveowners became furious.

In an effort to prevent further rebellion and to protect their property, southerners enacted laws, sometimes called "slave codes," that placed slaves under the strictest supervision. Southern postmasters refused to deliver abolitionist literature. Southern members of the House of Representatives secured in 1836 the passage of a so-called "gag rule" preventing any Representative from reading a petition urging the abolition of slavery in the District of Columbia.

The "gag rule" was repealed after eight years, mainly through the efforts of former President John Quincy Adams, after he became a member of the House of Representatives.

SECTION SURVEY

1. Discuss the aims of the American Colonization Society. Why did it fail?
2. Describe the contributions to the abolition movement of (a) Garrison, (b) the Grimké sisters, (c) Parker, (d) Whittier, (e) Harriet Beecher Stowe.
3. How did each of the following increase sectional bitterness? (a) the *Liberator*, (b) "underground railroad," (c) Turner's Revolt, (d) the "gag rule."
4. Describe (a) northern opposition to the abolitionist crusade, and (b) the southern reaction to it.

IDENTIFY: abolition, the *Liberator*, American Anti-Slavery Society, Mason and Dixon's line, Fugitive Slave Law of 1793, Liberty Party; Lundy, Lucretia Mott, James Russell Lowell, Phillips, Emerson, Birney, Lovejoy, Weld; 1831, 1840, 1852.

---

5 Spokesmen for democracy preach faith in the individual

Michel Chevalier, a French visitor to the United States in the year 1834, was deeply impressed by the vigor of the young nation. "All is here . . . boiling agitation," he commented. "Experiment follows experiment. . . . Men change their houses, their climate, their trade, their condition, their sect; states change their laws, their officers, their constitutions."

All of this activity—the mental activity as well as the physical activity—was reflected in the work of writers and scholars.

Henry David Thoreau (1817–62). Henry David Thoreau hated the industrial society that he saw arising in the United States. To Thoreau, machines were unnecessary gadgets that complicated life. "Nature is sufficient," Thoreau declared. To prove his point, he lived alone for more than two years in a cabin that he built with his own hands on the banks of Walden Pond near Concord, Massachusetts. There, free from the burden of machines and from institutions that he believed imprisoned the human spirit, he wrote the classic book entitled *Walden*.

Thoreau feared the power of the national government as much as he feared the new industrial economy. In 1849 Thoreau, then thirty-two years old, wrote his famous essay, "Civil Disobedience," in which he contended that men were born to be free and that the individual should seek above all else to remain free.

Looking ahead through the years, Thoreau foresaw two grave dangers to human liberty: one, industrialism, with its concern for the material things of life and its disregard for the individual; the other, the national state, with its indifference to the individual and its glorification of power.

Ralph Waldo Emerson (1803–82). Thoreau and Ralph Waldo Emerson

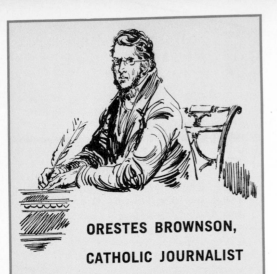

ORESTES BROWNSON, CATHOLIC JOURNALIST

Before he became a famous editor of his own magazine, *Brownson's Quarterly Review*, Orestes Brownson (1803–76) had been a minister in more than one Protestant church. Born in a Presbyterian family and brought up to believe that very few of us can be saved, he turned to preaching in a Universalist pulpit to declare that everyone goes to heaven. Then he took up reform in politics and education in order to try to bring about a heaven on earth in the form of socialism. For a while he thought the Unitarians had the right ideas, so he began preaching for them around Boston. He influenced followers of his friend Emerson, the New England reformers; but then he astonished all who knew him when, in 1844, he was received into the Catholic Church.

Orestes Brownson never ceased to advocate the cause of human rights. He had begun publishing his *Review* in 1838, and soon it became the most influential of the radical, democratic magazines. He attacked special interests, privileged corporations, and the money power generally. Politicians feared his support almost as much as his opposition. When he became a Catholic, his list of subscribers fell off. He continued to publish, but did so now in defense of the faith. He was always read with respect by Catholics, but they had reason to think him harsh and, at times, disagreeable. Among his books were *The Convert*, an honest account of his life, and *The American Republic*, written during the War Between the States, in which he lost two sons.

were close friends. They both lived in Concord, Massachusetts. They both believed in the supreme importance of individual freedom.

Emerson started his career as a Unitarian minister. But he left his pulpit in 1832, at the age of twenty-nine, to become a "preacher to the world." For the greater part of the 50 years he was yet to live, Emerson wrote and lectured. He traveled widely, especially during the period before 1860, and wherever he went he urged men to stand on their own feet, to free themselves from ignorance and prejudice, to think for themselves, and to respect their fellow men. Democracy with its free institutions will not work, he said, if the individuals in a democratic society are not free.

Emerson had a deep faith in America, in democracy, in the ability of men and women to solve the problems that they faced and to build an even better world. He did not share Thoreau's fear of industrialism and of the growing power of the national government.

Nor was Emerson troubled, as many Americans were, by the swelling tide of immigration. Welcome the immigrants, he urged, for "The energy of Irish, Germans, Swedes, Poles, and Cossacks, and all the European tribes—and of the Africans, and of the Polynesians—will construct a new race, a new religion, a new state, a new literature, which will be as vigorous as the new Europe which came out of the smelting-pot of the Dark Ages. . . ."

Walt Whitman (1819–92). One day in 1855 Emerson received a copy of a newly published volume of poems that bore the title *Leaves of Grass*. Much impressed with the writing, he sent a note to the author, Walt Whitman: "I greet you," he wrote, "at the beginning of a great career."

In *Leaves of Grass*, which is still widely read, Whitman "sang" the praises of the growing nation. Like Emerson, he had a deep and abiding faith in democracy and in the ability of the people to build an ever-better way of life for themselves and for their children. "The old

At Brook Farm, a utopian community near Boston, Emerson was a frequent visitor, as were other thinkers and writers like W. H. Channing and Margaret Fuller. The farm, jointly owned and operated by its members (one was Nathaniel Hawthorne), flourished from 1841 to 1847.

and moth-eaten systems of Europe have had their day," he wrote in 1848 when he was working on a newspaper, the Brooklyn *Eagle*. "Here [in America], we have planted the standard of freedom, and here we will test the capacities of men for self-government."

Like Emerson and unlike Thoreau, Whitman did not fear industrialism. On the contrary, he hailed science and industry as liberating forces which would lift from men's backs the age-old burdens of superstition and toil. In his "Carol of Occupations," he glorified the working people and the machines they operated:

"Stave-machines, planing-machines,
  reaping-machines, ploughing-
machines, thrashing-machines, steam
  wagons,
The cart of the carman, the omnibus,
  the ponderous dray . . ."

In "Pioneers! O Pioneers!" he challenged his fellow Americans to share his faith in the future. "We must march . . ." he wrote,

"We the youthful sinewy races, all the
  rest on us depend,
    Pioneers! O Pioneers! . . ."

The larger meaning. Emerson, Thoreau, Whitman—theirs were powerful voices raised in praise of freedom and the democratic way of life. But theirs were by no means the only voices. Those Americans who had no gift for words, and many newcomers to America who did not yet speak the English language,

or spoke it only haltingly, also shared this faith.

This faith in the individual, in democracy, lay at the roots of the reform movements you have read about in this chapter.

Years earlier, in 1776, Thomas Jefferson had expressed the same faith in the words: "We hold these truths to be self-evident: that all men are created equal, that they are endowed by their Creator with certain unalienable rights, that among these are life, liberty, and the pursuit of happiness. . . ."

Emerson, Thoreau, Whitman, the reformers you have been reading about, and many others were trying to apply the principles of the Declaration of Independence to the everyday affairs of life. Small wonder, as the French visitor Michel Chevalier observed, that the nation was filled with "boiling agitation" during the 1830's, 1840's, and 1850's.

SECTION SURVEY

1. (a) What two major developments did Thoreau fear as threats to human liberty? (b) In your opinion, was his fear justified?
2. (a) Why did Emerson think of himself as a "preacher to the world"? (b) Summarize the main ideas of his "message."
3. Contrast Thoreau's and Whitman's views on industrialism.
4. Explain the meaning of Whitman's idea that Americans are "pioneers" who must march forward.

IDENTIFY: *Walden*, "Civil Disobedience," *Leaves of Grass*.

355

(For review, see Section Surveys, pages 344, 346, 349, 353, 355.)

Points to Discuss: 1. Humanitarian striving was a characteristic of the new democratic spirit. Give evidence of humanitarian striving during the Jacksonian period in the fields of education, women's rights, temperance, and the treatment of the criminal and the mentally ill.

2. "Eli Whitney's invention of the cotton gin in 1793 completely altered the problem of slavery." Discuss fully.

3. With reference to the abolitionist crusade it has been said, "No single development did more to drive a wedge between the North and South." Discuss the influence of the abolitionist activity in the North as a factor in stimulating the proslavery views of the South.

4. Which writer, Thoreau, Emerson, or Whitman, do you think was the best spokesman for the American spirit at this time? Support your opinion.

5. The years 1828–50 have been described as the era of "The Rise of the Common Man." How can you support this?

6. Reread the Preamble to the Constitution (page 174). What steps toward the fulfilling of ideals stated in the Preamble were taken during the Jacksonian era?

Using Charts: 1. Referring to chart 8 on page 825, explain the movement of people from the country to the city.

2. Using chart 6 on page 824, explain the increase in life expectancy between 1790 and 1850.

Consulting the Sources: See A. B. Hart, *American History Told by Contemporaries,* III, Nos. 174 and 176, for an interesting contrast between the article by Garrison in the *Liberator* of January 1, 1831, and the account of a New York antislavery meeting.

■ TRACING THE MAIN IDEAS

From the 1820's to the 1860's, new developments began to transform the United States with bewildering speed. Factories and factory towns sprang up in the northern states. Slavery became increasingly important in the cotton-growing areas of the South. New means of transportation stimulated trade and sped the westward movement of land-hungry pioneers. Immigrants in steadily mounting numbers poured into the growing cities and out upon the farm lands.

The French visitor Michel Chevalier looked at America in this period and described it as a place of "boiling agitation." Chevalier was referring to the intense physical activity of the American people as they plunged headlong into the job of building the nation. He was also referring to their enthusiasm for new ideas and their desire to make democracy work.

This faith in democracy stimulated wave after wave of reform movements —among them the struggle for woman suffrage, for more humane treatment of criminals and the mentally ill, for equality of educational opportunity, for the abolition of slavery.

As you have seen, democracy made large advances during these years. But, as you will see in the next unit, the problem of slavery became increasingly acute, reaching a bitter climax in armed conflict between North and South.

Unit Survey (Reread "Tracing the Main Ideas," pages 306, 319, 340, 356.)

OUTSTANDING EVENTS

1789 Slater brings knowledge of power-driven machines to United States.
1793 Eli Whitney invents cotton gin.
1809 Daughters of Charity founded.
1810 First meeting of American bishops.
1825 Erie Canal opens.
1831 First issue of the *Liberator*.
1834 Burning of Ursuline Convent by nativists in Massachusetts.
1836 House passes "gag rule."
1836 Texas declares its independence.
1837 Horace Mann starts school reform.
1842 Massachusetts recognizes legal right of labor unions to exist.
1842 Webster-Ashburton Treaty.
1844 "Gag rule" is repealed.
1845 Texas enters Union.
1846 Treaty settles Oregon boundary.
1846 Sewing machine is patented.
1846 Irish potato famine.
1848 Treaty ends Mexican War; gives United States Mexican Cession.
1848 Women's rights convention.
1848 Diplomatic relations established between United States and Papal States.
1849 Gold rush to California.
1852 *Uncle Tom's Cabin* is published.
1853 Gadsden Purchase approved.

THEN AND NOW

1. Compare the rights of women today with their rights in the 1830's.
2. Compare the life of a factory worker in the 1830's with that of a factory worker today; consider hours of work, factory conditions, wages, collective bargaining, and political influence.

EXTENDING YOUR HORIZON

1. Information on Irish immigration can be found in the article by Leonard Patrick Wibberly, "The Coming of the Green," *American Heritage*, August 1958.
2. Seek to discover the interesting role of Eli Whitney in North-South relations by reading the article by Arnold Whitridge, "Eli Whitney: Nemesis of the South," *American Heritage*, April 1955.
3. For interesting insight into the career of Daniel Webster, see Gerald W. Johnson, "Great Man Eloquent," *American Heritage*, December 1957.

4. The ambitious student will profit through reading and comparing the essays on Andrew Jackson and John C. Calhoun in Richard Hofstadter, *The American Political Tradition* (Vintage), Chapters III and IV.
5. A valuable source of information on the nativist movement is Ray Allen Billington's article "The Know-Nothing Uproar," *American Heritage*, February 1959.

INDIVIDUAL ACTIVITIES

1. (a) On an outline map of the United States, show the following boundary settlements: Pinckney Treaty (1795), Canadian border (1818), Florida Treaty line (1819), Canadian border in the northeast (1842), Canadian border in the northwest (1846), Mexican border (1848) and (1853). (b) Show also the territorial growth of the United States from 1783 to 1853 by indicating the following: the original United States, Louisiana Purchase, Florida, Texas, Oregon, Mexican Cession, Gadsden Purchase.
2. *America in Perspective*, edited by Henry Steele Commager [New American Library (Mentor)], contains interesting views of American life at this period as seen by Alexis de Tocqueville and Harriet Martineau.
3. Accounts of frontier life suitable for oral reports may be found in Chapters 19, 20 of *The Heritage of America*.
4. Consult the *Dictionary of American Biography* for material on the activities of Father Gabriel Richard, Father Samuel Mazzuchelli, and Father Pierre de Smet.
5. Investigate and report on the activities of such humanitarian reformers as William Lloyd Garrison, Dorothea Dix, Arthur Tappan, Wendell Phillips.

GROUP ACTIVITIES

1. Select a suitable group of students to prepare a panel discussion on the pattern by which the nationalism of the Era of Good Feelings gave way to a growing sectionalism. Utilize all material in text. Other worthwhile sources to consult include Richard D. Heffner's *A Documentary History of the United States*, Chapters 8 through 11; Arthur M. Schlesinger, Jr.,

"The Southern Dilemma" in *The Making of American History*, Book One, edited by Donald Sheehan (Dryden); and Richard Hofstadter's essay on Calhoun in *The American Political Tradition*.

2. Plan a round table discussion on the immigration movement and its effects on American life at this period. Consult the pamphlet *Immigration, An American Dilemma*, in Problems in American Civilization, "Amherst Series" (Heath); Carl Wittke, *We Who Built America* (Prentice-Hall); Marcus Lee Hansen, "The Flight from Hunger" in Sheehan's *The Making of American History*, Book One. See also Samuel P. Orth, *Our Foreigners* (Yale Univ. Press); and Chapter III of Ellis, *American Catholicism*. Seek to relate immigration to the nativist movement.

SUGGESTED FURTHER READING

BIOGRAPHY

BEALS, CARLETON, *Stephen Austin*, McGraw-Hill.

°COIT, MARGARET, *John C. Calhoun: An American Portrait*, Houghton Mifflin.

°CURRENT, RICHARD N., *Daniel Webster and the Rise of National Conservatism*, Little, Brown.

DANA, R. H., *Two Years Before the Mast*, Macmillan; and others. Seaboard life.

GRANT, DOROTHY FREMONT, *John England; American Christopher*, Bruce.

JAMES, MARQUIS, *Andrew Jackson: The Border Captain*, Bobbs-Merrill.

——, *Andrew Jackson: Portrait of a President*, Bobbs-Merrill.

KEYES, NELSON BEECHER, *The American Frontier*, Hanover House.

MARGARET, HÉLÈNE, *Giant of the Wilderness*, Bruce. Father Charles Nerinick.

NEVINS, ALLAN, *Frémont, Pathmarker of the West*, Longmans, Green.

NYE, RUSSELL B., *William Lloyd Garrison and the Humanitarian Reformers*, Little, Brown.

ROURKE, CONSTANCE, *Davy Crockett*, Harcourt, Brace.

SCHLESINGER, ARTHUR M., JR., *Orestes A. Brownson: A Pilgrim's Progress*, Little, Brown.

SYRETT, HAROLD C., *Andrew Jackson*, Bobbs-Merrill.

OTHER NONFICTION

BILL, A. H., *Rehearsal for Conflict*, Knopf.

BILLINGTON, RAY A., *The Far Western Frontier: 1830–1860*, Harper (text ed.).

BILLINGTON, RAY A., with JAMES B. HEDGES, *Westward Expansion*, Macmillan.

BINKLEY, W. E., *American Political Parties*, Knopf.

DODD, WILLIAM E., *The Cotton Kingdom*, Yale Univ. Press. The plantation system.

°FISH, CARL R., *Rise of the Common Man*, Macmillan. Democratic innovations of Jacksonian period.

FRANKLIN, JOHN HOPE, *From Slavery to Freedom: A History of American Negroes*, Knopf.

FULLER, EDMUND, *Tinkers and Genius: The Story of the Yankee Inventors*, Hastings House.

HANSEN, MARCUS LEE, *The Atlantic Migration, 1607–1860*, Harvard Univ. Press; Oxford Univ. Press.

——, *The Immigrant in American History*, Harvard Univ. Press.

HART, A. B., *Slavery and Abolition*, Harper (American Nation Series).

HULBERT, A. B., *The Paths of Inland Commerce*, Pocket Books.

LANGDON, W. C., *Everyday Things in American Life, 1776–1876*, Scribner.

MACY, JESSE, *The Anti-Slavery Crusade*, Yale Univ. Press.

MAYNARD, THEODORE, *The Story of American Catholicism*, Macmillan.

SCHLESINGER, ARTHUR M., JR., *The Age of Jackson*, Little, Brown; New American Library (abridged version).

STEPHENSON, NATHANIEL W., *Texas and the Mexican War*, Yale Univ. Press.

THOMPSON, HOLLAND, *The Age of Invention*. Yale Univ. Press.

TOCQUEVILLE, ALEXIS DE, *Democracy in America*, New American Library (Mentor).

TURNER, FREDERICK JACKSON, *The Frontier in American History*, Holt.

°WEBB, WALTER P., *The Great Plains*, Ginn.

HISTORICAL FICTION

BRESLIN, HOWARD, *The Tamarack Tree*, McGraw-Hill. New England politics.

CATHER, WILLA, *Death Comes to the Archbishop*, Knopf.

EDMONDS, WALTER D., *Rome Haul*, Random House (Modern Library). Erie Canal.

——, *Erie Water*, Little, Brown.

HOUGH, EMERSON, *The Covered Wagon*, Dutton; Pocket Books. About pioneers.

RICHTER, CONRAD, *The Trees*, Knopf. Struggles of a pioneer family.

STONE, IRVING, *Immortal Wife*, Doubleday. Jesse and John Frémont.

UNIT FIVE

The Nation Torn Apart

1845–1865

Sectional Strife Becomes Acute

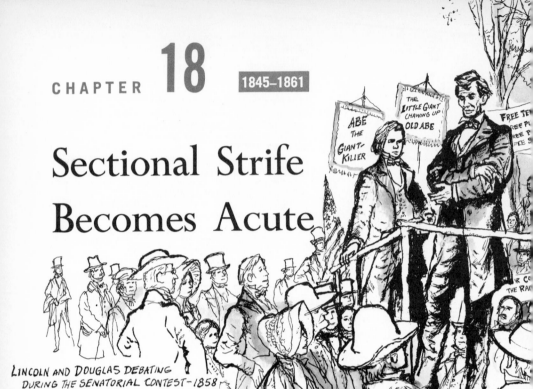

LINCOLN AND DOUGLAS DEBATING DURING THE SENATORIAL CONTEST—1858

THE growing conflict among the three sections of the country—North, South, West—this is the large and tragic theme of American history during the years preceding the War Between the States. The story that unfolds as we review this unhappy period of the nation's development is one of compromise, of brief intervals of uneasy balancing of interests, of breakdowns of compromise, of growing conflict, and of ever more desperate attempts to restore harmony among the sections of the country.

The basic problem was that the North and South and West had developed along very different lines. The industrial North, with its growing factories and towns; the agricultural South, with its increasing dependence upon the single crop of cotton; the wild, untamed West, with its restless pioneers pressing against ever new frontiers—here were three radically different ways of life.

Given these differences, it is not surprising that men from each of these sections should hold radically different views about such issues as internal improvements at federal expense, tariffs, banking and currency, public lands, and the question of slavery.

In order to sense the rising tensions among the three sections of the country, it is necessary to begin with a review of events that had been taking place between the administrations of President Monroe and President Polk.

AS THE STORY DEVELOPS

1. Northerners and southerners maintain an uneasy political balance.
2. Mounting tensions are relaxed by the Compromise of 1850.
3. The long period of compromise comes to an end.
4. The North and the South move steadily toward war.
5. Southern states withdraw from the Union, and the war begins.

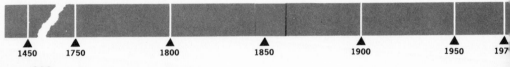

1450 1750 1800 1850 1900 1950 197

Northerners and southerners maintain an uneasy political balance

The first serious clash between the sections—in this case the North and the South—had arisen in 1819–20, when President Monroe was in office, over the question of admitting Missouri to the Union. At times the controversy had become so heated that men talked boldly of "disunion" and "civil war." Former President Thomas Jefferson, following the debates from the peace and quiet of his hilltop home, wrote that the quarrel "awakened and filled me with terror. I considered it at once as the death knell of the Union."

The dispute about Missouri. In order to understand the reasons for Jefferson's grave concern, we must turn back to the opening weeks of the year 1819, when the United States was composed of 11 free states and 10 slave states. Alabama was about to be admitted to the Union as the eleventh slave state. With Alabama in the Union, the North and the South would each have 22 Senators.

Such was the situation when the Territory of Missouri, in which slavery already existed, asked to be admitted to the Union. If Missouri were allowed to enter as a state in which slavery was permitted, the balance of power in the Senate would be upset, with the South having 24 votes to the North's 22.

Tallmadge's explosive proposal. On February 13, 1819, before Alabama was admitted, Representative James Tallmadge of New York rose on the floor of the House to present an amendment to Missouri's application. In his amendment Tallmadge proposed to prohibit the further introduction of slaves into Missouri. He also proposed to free all children born into slavery in Missouri after its admission as a state. This, however, was to be done gradually; the children were to become free only when they reached their twenty-fifth birthday.

Tallmadge and other Congressmen who supported his proposal argued that Congress had the power to prohibit slavery in any Territory of the United States. They pointed out that Congress had prohibited slavery in the Northwest Territory when it adopted the Northwest Ordinance (page 147). They argued that, since Missouri was a Territory and would remain a Territory until Congress approved its application for statehood, Congress should follow the precedent established when it prohibited slavery in the Northwest Territory.

The Missouri Compromise. The House of Representatives, where the North held a majority of the seats, adopted the Tallmadge Amendment by a close vote. But the Senate rejected it by a vote of 22 to 16.

Why, with 11 free states and only 10 slave states represented in the Senate at this time, was the South able to win this victory? (Four Senators had not voted, but, even if their votes had gone to the North, the amendment would have been defeated.) The answer, obviously, is that certain northern Senators voted with the southern *bloc* ° to defeat the amendment. In other words, although in 1819 the issue of slavery had been raised, the lines between North and South had not yet been sharply drawn.

But Congress was now deadlocked, with the House in favor of the amendment, and the Senate opposed. At this point, a group led by Henry Clay of Kentucky proposed a compromise.

At this time the people of Maine were also petitioning Congress to become a state. The admission of Maine would increase the number of free states in the Union. Clay therefore proposed that both Maine and Missouri be admitted— one as a free state and the other without restrictions on slavery. As he pointed out, if this were done, the balance of power between the North and the South in the Senate would not be disturbed. With Alabama, Missouri, and Maine in the Union, each section would have 24 votes.

••

° *bloc:* a group of legislators united on one or more issues.

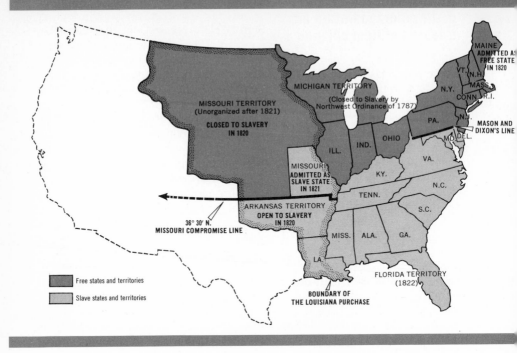

MAINE ADMITTED AS FREE STATE IN 1820

MICHIGAN TERRITORY
(Closed to Slavery by Northwest Ordinance of 1787)

MISSOURI TERRITORY
(Unorganized after 1821)
CLOSED TO SLAVERY IN 1820

VT. N.H.
N.Y. MASS.
CONN. R.I.
PA. N.J.
MASON AND DIXON'S LINE
MD. DEL.

ILL. IND. OHIO
VA.

MISSOURI ADMITTED AS SLAVE STATE IN 1821
KY.
N.C.
TENN.

36° 30' N.
MISSOURI COMPROMISE LINE

ARKANSAS TERRITORY OPEN TO SLAVERY IN 1820
S.C.

MISS. ALA. GA.

LA.
FLORIDA TERRITORY (1822)

Free states and territories

Slave states and territories

BOUNDARY OF THE LOUISIANA PURCHASE

Congress agreed to Clay's compromise proposal in 1820. As part of this compromise, however, slavery was prohibited in all remaining parts of the Louisiana Purchase north of latitude 36° 30' (see map, this page).

So the crisis of 1819–20 had passed. But thoughtful men realized that a period of grave danger lay ahead of the young nation. "This is a reprieve only, not a final sentence," Jefferson declared. And John Quincy Adams wrote in his diary that the conflict over Missouri was "a mere preamble—a title page to a great, tragic volume."

The tariff issue. During the years from 1828 to 1832, as you have seen, conflicting views on the tariff question brought the United States perilously close to division (page 276). In its Ordinance of Nullification of 1832, South Carolina declared the Tariff Law of 1828—the "Tariff of Abominations"— "null, void, and no law, not binding upon this state, its officers, or citizens. . . ." When South Carolina threatened to secede from the Union, fiery-tempered President Jackson talked of

sending armed forces into the state at the first sign of resistance to the federal customs officers. This crisis also passed, however, when both the North and the South agreed to another compromise proposed by Henry Clay, the Tariff Act of 1833, which provided for a gradual reduction of tariff rates. At the same time, however, Congress passed the Force Bill, giving the President power to use federal forces, if necessary, for the collection of customs duties.

Abolitionists gain strength. Meanwhile, the shadow of the slavery issue continued to darken the land. As you have seen, William Lloyd Garrison published the first number of his paper, the *Liberator,* on January 1, 1831, and in so doing launched the abolitionist movement. In spite of opposition, in the North as well as the South, the abolitionist movement grew. By 1836 more than 500 abolitionist societies were active in the North. In 1840 the abolitionists, who now numbered more than 150,000, organized the Liberty Party and, as you know, nominated James G. Birney for the Presidency.

The deadlock over Texas. As the shadow of the slavery issue grew larger and more ominous, the struggle for control of the western areas became more intense. Every time a Territory applied for admission to the Union northern and southern Congressmen marshalled their forces for a struggle.

In 1836 and 1837 Congress admitted Arkansas and Michigan into the Union without any controversy, for one was slave and the other free, and the balance between the North and the South was unchanged. But when the newly organized Republic of Texas (pages 325–28) applied for admission in 1837, Congress was once again confronted with a problem. Slavery already existed in Texas, and much of the undeveloped land there was suitable for the cultivation of cotton. Congress would therefore have to admit Texas as a state in which slavery was allowed, thereby upsetting the balance between the North and the South.

As it happened, President Van Buren and leaders on both sides of Congress were eager at this time to keep the slavery issue out of politics. With the depression that started in 1837 on their hands (page 279), Congressmen had enough problems to handle without coming to grips with the issue of slavery. So Congress did nothing. As a result, in October 1838, Texas formally withdrew its application for admission.

But Texans could not afford to let the matter rest. The population of the Lone Star Republic numbered only fifty thousand white people. If Mexico, with its population of six to seven millions, decided to reconquer its former territory, Texas would be in serious difficulty. What Texans needed was a powerful ally who would protect them against Mexico. Faced with this situation, the Republic of Texas sent diplomatic agents to Europe. These agents negotiated treaties with France, Belgium, the Netherlands, and Great Britain.

For several years the issue of Texas hung in the balance. Mexico refused to recognize Texas' independence. Great Britain and France, on the other hand, continued to reveal their interest in having Texas remain independent. And American opinion remained divided.

The election of 1844. Such was the situation that the United States faced in the election year of 1844. Henry Clay, the Whig candidate, tried to avoid the issue. James G. Birney, again the candidate for the abolitionist Liberty Party, was firmly opposed to the admission of Texas. But James K. Polk of Tennessee, the Democratic candidate, came out, as you know, for "The re-annexation of Texas and re-occupation of Oregon!" and for "Fifty-four forty or fight!"

The Democratic Party's 1844 slogans were clever politics. With these slogans the Democrats shifted the focus from the troublesome issue of slavery to the popular issue of expansion. Northerners and southerners alike were eager to see their country expand westward.

Polk won the election. In February 1845, shortly before he took office, Congress by a joint resolution voted to admit Texas into the Union. The resolution included the following provisions: (1) With the consent of Texas, a total of five states could be carved out of the territory. (2) If Texas did divide, the land north of the 36° 30' line would be closed to slavery. (3) The United States would take over the boundary dispute with Mexico. (4) Texas would retain its lands and pay its own debts.

Texas voted to accept these terms. In December 1845 Texas entered the Union. With the entry of Texas, the balance between southern and northern states swung by one state in favor of the South. It had already swung in favor of the South when Florida entered the Union in March 1845. But the balance was restored by the admission of Iowa in 1846 and Wisconsin in 1848, both free states. Moreover, in 1846 the United States and Great Britain reached an agreement on the northern boundary of the Oregon country (page 325). Northerners and southerners knew that it was only a matter of time before the huge Territory of Oregon applied for admission as one or more free states.

For more than twenty-five years, from the Missouri Compromise of 1820 to the year 1846, Congress had walked a tightrope. By a series of neat compromises, the North and the South had managed to resolve the troublesome problems that time and again had threatened to split them apart. So matters stood in 1846 when, as you know, the United States went to war with the Republic of Mexico.

↙ SECTION SURVEY

1. Why did Missouri's application for admission to the Union create a crisis?
2. (a) State the terms of the Missouri Compromise of 1820. (b) What points did the North and the South each gain by this compromise?
3. Although Texas applied for admission to the Union in 1837, it was not admitted until 1845. Account for this delay. What is meant by a "joint resolution"?
4. Give the parties, candidates, issues, and results of the election of 1844.
IDENTIFY: Tallmadge Amendment, South Carolina Ordinance of Nullification, "The re-annexation of Texas and re-occupation of Oregon!" "Fifty-four forty or fight!"; Clay, Garrison.

2 Mounting tensions are relaxed by the Compromise of 1850

On February 2, 1848, the United States brought the Mexican War to a victorious conclusion with the signing of the Treaty of Guadalupe Hidalgo. In this treaty, as you know, Mexico ceded to the United States a huge area of land in the Southwest—the so-called Mexican Cession.

American pride over the acquisition of this great new area of land was tempered by the sobering thought that the Mexican Cession created a serious problem. Would slavery be permitted or prohibited in the states that were to be carved out of this new area?

Division over the Southwest. In general, Americans divided along four different lines in their views as to what should be done with the land acquired from Mexico.

First, President Polk and a substantial number of citizens felt that the best way to settle the problem was to build upon the Missouri Compromise of 1820. As you recall, the Missouri Compromise prohibited slavery in all remaining areas of the Louisiana Purchase, north of latitude 36° 30′. The solution now proposed by Polk and others was to extend this line to the Pacific, prohibiting slavery north of the line and allowing slavery south of the line.

A second anti-slavery point of view was expressed in the Wilmot Proviso. In August 1846, shortly after the Mexican War started, David Wilmot, a Democratic Representative from Pennsylvania, presented a resolution to Congress. The Wilmot Proviso, as it was called, flatly declared that "neither slavery nor involuntary servitude shall ever exist" in the lands acquired from Mexico. All but one of the northern states adopted resolutions approving the Wilmot Proviso.

Southerners took a third point of view in resisting the Wilmot Proviso. John C. Calhoun, the most influential spokesman for the South, insisted that Congress had no right to prohibit slavery in the Southwest. Indeed, he insisted, Congress had a duty to protect the rights of slaveowners in *all* the Territories.

A fourth group, led by Senator Lewis Cass of Michigan and Senator Stephen A. Douglas of Illinois, argued that the right to decide whether or not slavery should exist in a Territory belonged to the people of the Territory itself. This proposed solution came to be known as "popular sovereignty" or "squatter sovereignty."

Whigs and Democrats straddle the issue. The problem of slavery in the Territories was the burning issue in 1848 when the voters were called upon to elect a new President. But both major parties refused to take a stand on this issue, for both parties included southerners as well as northerners, and any strong stand would have split each party in two.

President Polk, exhausted by his four years in office, refused to run for re-election on the Democratic ticket. During his four-year term he had consistently worked from sixteen to eighteen hours a day and had been absent from Washington only six weeks. With Polk out of the running, the Democrats turned to Lewis Cass of Michigan, one of the authors of the doctrine of "popular sovereignty."

The Whigs placed their hope of victory in General Zachary Taylor, who, as a military hero in the Mexican War, had earned the title "Old Rough and Ready." General Taylor was a southerner, but he had never been seriously involved in politics, and his views on the major political questions were virtually unknown.

The Free-Soil Party splits the vote. The efforts of the Whigs and Democrats to straddle the slavery question drove many northerners into a newly formed third party—the Free-Soil Party. The Free-Soilers, opposing any further extension of slavery into the Territories, adopted the slogan "Free Soil, Free Speech, Free Labor, and Free Men," and nominated former President Martin Van Buren of New York.

Van Buren had the support of three major groups of voters: (1) members of the abolitionist Liberty Party, (2) a number of anti-slavery Whigs and Democrats, and (3) the reform wing of the Democratic Party in New York whose members were called "Barnburners." They received this uncomplimentary name because they had the reputation of going to any length to win their objectives and their opponents compared them to a foolish farmer who burned down his barn in order to get rid of rats.

Van Buren and the Free-Soilers had considerable influence on the election, even though they failed to carry a single state for the Presidency. By capturing a number of Democratic votes, especially in the state of New York, Van Buren unintentionally helped to throw the election to the Whig candidate, General Zachary Taylor. More important, the Free-Soilers managed to win 12 seats in the House of Representatives. Otherwise the House was almost evenly divided between Whigs and Democrats. The Free-Soil Party therefore held the balance of power in the lower house.

Another crisis arises. During and following the election northern and southern tempers were on edge, and the Congress that assembled in December 1849 was torn by dissension. In fact, the controversy was so bitter that the members of the House of Representatives had to vote 63 times before they were able to elect a Speaker of the House and get down to business.

One of the issues before Congress was the application of California for admission to the Union as a new state. Southerners refused to consider the application, for California's constitution already prohibited slavery. If California entered the Union as a free state, the existing balance of 15 slave and 15 free states would be upset in favor of the North.

Another issue before Congress was the controversy between the state of Texas and the newly acquired but as yet unorganized territory of New Mexico. Texas, where slavery was permitted, claimed that its boundary extended westward into country that the federal government had recognized as belonging to New Mexico. Anti-slavery men in Congress naturally tried to confine Texas to the smallest possible limits. Southerners just as naturally resented northern attempts to limit the area of Texas. Matters were complicated still further when Texas claimed that the federal government should assume its war debt, incurred while Texas was fighting for independence from Mexico.

Arguments over other issues echoed through the halls of Congress. Southerners sternly resisted a proposal to abolish slavery in the District of Columbia. They also resisted a proposal to organize New Mexico and Utah into Territories without any mention of slavery. Many northerners, on the other hand,

■ Henry Clay, the Great Compromiser, here stands before the Senate proposing the terms of the Compromise of 1850. In this great effort to preserve the Union, he said, "I know no South, no North, no East, no West to which I owe allegiance."

were just as strongly opposed to a southern proposal to enact a new fugitive slave law. According to the original Fugitive Slave Law, adopted in 1793, state and local officials were responsible for capturing runaway slaves and returning them to their owners. In 1842, however, the Supreme Court had ruled that law enforcement officers in the states were not obliged to help federal officials to capture and return runaway slaves to their southern owners. The proposed new law required that state officials assist in capturing runaway slaves.

All of these issues were loaded with political dynamite. Any one could lead to a break between the North and South. In the opening months of 1850, the United States stood on the brink of war.

Clay proposes a compromise. Such was the situation when Henry Clay of Kentucky rose on the floor of the Senate to offer a compromise proposal. Clay, whose compromises had saved the Union from disasters in 1820 and again in

1833, was known and respected as "the Great Compromiser." Now, in 1850, ill and weary from years of devoted effort to hold the Union together, he stood before the Senate to plead once more for reason and moderation.

Clay's proposals included: (1) The admission of California as a free state. (2) The organization of New Mexico as a Territory without restrictions as to slavery. In return for abandoning all claim to New Mexico, Texas would receive a payment of $10,000,000 from the United States. (3) The abolition of the slave trade—that is, of the buying and selling of slaves—but not of slavery itself in the District of Columbia. (4) The organization of the land acquired from Mexico (except California) into Territories on the basis of "popular sovereignty," so that the settlers in each of the Territories might decide for themselves whether or not they wanted slavery in their Territory. (5) The enactment of a more effective fugitive slave law, one that would compel state and local law enforcement officials to co-operate with federal officials in the capture and return of runaway slaves.

The Great Debate. Clay's proposals provoked one of the most critical and tense debates in American history. Daniel Webster—like Clay, a veteran Whig leader—supported Clay's compromise by arguing that slavery was not likely to prosper in the newly acquired lands. For this reason, Webster declared, it would be unnecessary and unwise for the North to insist on the exclusion of slavery from this area.

Stephen A. Douglas of Illinois, who had argued for "popular sovereignty," supported Webster and Clay. But many northerners, angry with Webster for taking the position that he did, claimed he was betraying the cause of freedom.

John C. Calhoun of South Carolina spoke for the South. He opposed the principle of "popular sovereignty" and all other compromises on the question of slavery. Calhoun was an old man. Like Webster and Clay, he had served his country in the halls of Congress for almost forty years. He was at the point of death, so weak that he had to be carried into the Senate, where a colleague read his speech condemning the compromise. Calhoun insisted, as he had always done, that a slaveowner had the right to take his property anywhere in any of the Territories and that Congress had the duty to protect him in this right. Most southern Senators supported Calhoun.

But others, Whigs and Democrats alike, strongly opposed Calhoun. Among this group were Thomas Hart Benton of Missouri, Salmon P. Chase of Ohio, William H. Seward of New York, and others, who sternly denied that the Constitution recognized slavery. These men resisted the proposed fugitive slave law and urged Congress to exclude slavery from the Territories. Many of them agreed with Seward when he argued that there is "a higher law than the Constitution" and insisted that "all legislative compromises [are] radically wrong and essentially vicious."

Victory for compromise. As it turned out, the extremists in both the North and South were minorities. Most Americans were in favor of compromise, and in September 1850 Congress adopted all of Clay's compromise measures by substantial majorities.

John C. Calhoun, who had fought so long and so hard for the South, was not alive to see the outcome of the Great Debate. He died in March, leaving a great gap in the ranks of southern leadership. Nor did President Taylor live to see the outcome. After he died in July, his successor, President Millard Fillmore of New York, signed the compromise bills and made them law.

So compromise, sometimes called "the essence of politics," once again saved the day. Throughout the nation Americans gathered in public meetings and hailed the work of Clay and his colleagues as a great triumph for national unity. Businessmen spoke enthusiastically for it, expressing their fear that continued controversy between the North and South would ruin business in both sections of the country.

Would the compromise endure? This was the major question on the lips of many Americans in the fall of 1850.

SECTION SURVEY

1. (a) How did the 1848 victory over Mexico aggravate the slavery issue? (b) Discuss the four proposals made for handling the issue of the Mexican Cession.

2. Compare the candidates, parties, and issues in the election of 1848. Estimate the importance of the Free Soil Party in determining the result of this election.

3. "In the opening months of 1850, the United States stood on the brink of war." What issues led to this situation?

4. State the terms of Clay's Compromise of 1850. Describe the scene of the great debate and indicate the respective positions taken by Webster and Calhoun.

IDENTIFY: Wilmot Proviso, "popular sovereignty," Free-Soil Party, "Barnburners"; Cass, Taylor, Douglas, Seward, Fillmore; 1848, 1850.

The long period of compromise comes to an end

The Compromise of 1850 lasted about four years. As you will see, however, the period from 1850 to 1854 was merely the lull before the storm.

Prosperity and growth. Prosperity and growth—these were two of the striking characteristics of the United States during the early 1850's. The South prospered as the price of cotton rose and the annual production of cotton more than doubled. The Northeast prospered as new factories and a growing demand for manufactured products provided plenty of jobs at good wages for everyone, including the scores of thousands of immigrants who were pouring into the country. The Middle West prospered and expanded as railroads opened up the fertile prairie lands and made it possible for the farmers to transport and sell their products. The population of California was growing rapidly.

The railroads were becoming a vital part of the nation's growing economy. In 1847, for example, there were only 660 miles of railway track in all of Ohio, Michigan, Indiana, Illinois, and Wisconsin; by 1861 there were 7653 miles of track in these states. During these same years railroad mileage in the United States as a whole increased from about 9000 to more than 30,000 miles. Most of the new railway lines reached from the Northeast into the Middle West and helped to bind these two areas together (see map, page 293). As a result, when war did come in 1861, the South faced a much more powerful combination than it would have faced had war broken out in 1850 or earlier.

Because the attention of Americans both in the North and South had shifted from the problem of slavery to prosperity and growth, the election of 1852 was uneventful. In their political platforms both of the major parties condemned any further argument over the slavery question; both accepted the Compromise of 1850 as final. When the votes were counted, the Democratic candidate, Franklin Pierce of New Hampshire, had won 27 states; his rival, the Whig candidate, General Winfield Scott, who won fame in the Mexican War, had won only 4 states.

Ominous undercurrents. In his Inaugural Address, President Pierce urged

Clothing of the 1850's

the people to continue to work for national harmony. But national harmony was being undermined by dissension.

The publication of Harriet Beecher Stowe's *Uncle Tom's Cabin* in 1852 (page 351) infuriated southerners, who insisted that her picture of slavery was a vicious falsehood. Many northerners, on the other hand, accepted the picture as truth. From the book and from the play based on the book, they came to think of slavery, not in abstract terms, but as the institution responsible for the suffering of saintly Uncle Tom.

The Fugitive Slave Law of 1850, which was part of the Compromise of 1850, also helped to keep the issue of slavery before the people. Ralph Waldo Emerson, highly regarded as a philosopher and writer in Europe as well as in the United States, expressed the feelings of northern extremists when he wrote in his journal, "This filthy enactment was made in the nineteenth century by people who could read and write. I will not obey it . . ." Northern extremists who shared Emerson's hatred of the law openly defied it.

Southern extremists also helped to fan the flames of fear and misunderstanding when they talked of securing new slave territory to compensate for the votes of California, which, under the Compromise of 1850, had entered the Union as a free state.

The Ostend Manifesto. The Spanish colony of Cuba seemed especially attractive. Indeed, in 1848 President Polk had tried to buy the island for $100,-000,000. Spain had refused to consider the offer. But a number of southerners continued to cast longing eyes at Cuba. Finally, in 1854, the American ministers to Great Britain, France, and Spain met in Ostend, Belgium, and issued a statement that has come to be known as the "Ostend Manifesto."

In this statement the ministers declared that, if Spain refused to sell Cuba to the United States, the United States would have every right to seize Cuba by force. President Pierce promptly disavowed this statement. But the fat was

in the fire. Northern anti-slavery men pointed out that southerners were obviously prepared to risk involving the whole nation in war in order to add new slave territory to the Union.

The Kansas-Nebraska Act. In 1854, while undercurrents like these were undermining national unity, Senator Stephen A Douglas of Illinois sponsored and carried through Congress the Kansas-Nebraska Act. This act had the effect of repealing the Missouri Compromise.

In 1820, you will recall, the Missouri Compromise had established the 36° 30' parallel of latitude from the Mississippi River to the Rocky Mountains as the boundary between slave and free territory, Missouri being the only exception. The Kansas-Nebraska Act created two new organized Territories in the west —Kansas and Nebraska (see map, page 371). Both of these Territories were north of the old 36° 30' line and, therefore, closed to slavery. But the Kansas-Nebraska Act of 1854 abolished the 34-year-old dividing line, declaring it

---

BALANCE BETWEEN FREE AND SLAVE STATES BEFORE COMPROMISE OF 1850

THIRTEEN ORIGINAL STATES

Free States	Slave States
Pennsylvania	Delaware
New Jersey	Georgia
Connecticut	Maryland
Massachusetts	South Carolina
New Hampshire	Virginia
New York	North Carolina
Rhode Island	

STATES ADMITTED 1791–1819
(before Missouri Compromise)

Vermont (1791)	Kentucky (1792)
Ohio (1803)	Tennessee (1796)
Indiana (1816)	Louisiana (1812)
Illinois (1818)	Mississippi (1817)
	Alabama (1819)

STATES ADMITTED 1820–48
(before Compromise of 1850)

Maine (1820)	Missouri (1821)
Michigan (1837)	Arkansas (1836)
Iowa (1846)	Florida (1845)
Wisconsin (1848)	Texas (1845)

STEPHEN
DOUGLAS
MISCALCULATES

Stephen A. Douglas (1813–61), the five-feet-tall senior Senator from Illinois, had enormous energy, a sharp intellect, and a gift for oratory. Referred to on occasions as "The Little Giant" or a "steam engine in britches," he was the undisputed leader of the northern wing of the Democratic Party.

It was no secret that Douglas disliked slavery. Why, then, did he sponsor a bill that opened to slaveowners land that had been closed to slavery for 34 years?

A compelling fact was Douglas' interest in a transcontinental railroad across the Great Plains and mountains to California. Several routes had been proposed. Douglas, a northerner, favored a route that started in the North and ran through the central part of the country.

There was, however, a major objection to the central route that Douglas wanted. It passed through unorganized territory. But once organized with a government of its own, the territory would become attractive to settlers, the value of land would rise, and there would be more reasons to build a railroad through it.

An earlier attempt to organize the central Great Plains as the Territory of Nebraska had been defeated by southern votes. Douglas thought he saw a way to win southern approval without at the same time antagonizing the North. He proposed a compromise solution—the division of the central Great Plains into two Territories, Kansas and Nebraska, leaving the decision about slavery to the inhabitants of the Territories.

Douglas considered the proposed Kansas-Nebraska Act a statesmanlike piece of legislation that would prove attractive to northerners and southerners alike, and would benefit the entire nation. But he was wrong, for the Kansas-Nebraska Act plunged the whole nation into violent controversy.

"inoperative and void" and stating that the Territories were now "perfectly free to form and regulate their domestic institutions in their own way. . . ."

Northern reaction. The major political parties were both split by the Kansas-Nebraska Act. Southern Democrats and southern Whigs both voted for the bill. Northern Democrats joined northern Whigs to vote against it. From 1854 until 1861, when war broke out, neither of the two major parties was able to reunite its northern and southern wings.

Indeed, the Kansas-Nebraska Act plunged the entire nation into new arguments over the slavery question. Out in Illinois an obscure lawyer, Abraham Lincoln, protested against opening the new Territories to slavery. And up in Boston, the day after the Kansas-Nebraska Act was passed, armed forces had to be called out to prevent disorder over the Fugitive Slave Law. A battalion of United States artillery, four platoons of marines, and a sheriff's posse were called out to escort a runaway slave from the courthouse to the ship waiting to carry him back to the South. Crowds of booing spectators were held back by 22 companies of state militia. .

Everywhere throughout the North the issue of slavery once again became a major subject of discussion. The Fugitive Slave Law became increasingly difficult to enforce. And in "anti-Nebraska" meetings men denounced Douglas for reopening the slavery dispute. Douglas himself said that he might have traveled from Boston to Chicago by the light of his own burning effigies.

The race for Kansas. Senator Charles Sumner of Massachusetts was one of many extreme anti-slavery people who believed that the Kansas-Nebraska Act would plunge the country into serious trouble. "It puts freedom and slavery face to face and bids them grapple."

And "grapple" they did, on the plains of the new Territory of Kansas.

The ink was hardly dry on the Kansas-Nebraska Act before northerners and southerners began the race to settle

Kansas. Northerners formed an "Emigrant Aid Company" and sent anti-slavery settlers into Kansas. These men and women founded Lawrence, Topeka, and other settlements. Meanwhile, pro-slavery settlers from Missouri began to move over the border into Kansas. The pro-slavery settlers started the towns of Atchison, Leavenworth, and Lecompton (see map, this page).

Feeling between southerners and northerners was running high in Kansas when the time came for the settlers to draw up a constitution and organize a Territorial government. Was slavery to be allowed in Kansas or not? This was the question. The pro-slavery forces answered it by rushing voters from Missouri over the border and electing a pro-slavery legislature, which promptly began to pass laws favoring slaveowners. The anti-slavery forces then drafted a constitution forbidding slavery and

elected an anti-slavery legislature. As a result, by the end of 1855, the Territory of Kansas had two different governments—one pro-slavery, one anti-slavery.

Dilemma in Washington. Back in Washington, Congressmen watched the struggle with dismay—and no one with greater dismay than the author of the Kansas-Nebraska Act, Stephen A. Douglas. When Douglas had argued for the principle of "popular sovereignty," he had maintained that it would take the issue of slavery in the Territories out of the heated atmosphere of Congress and place it in the Territories themselves for the settlers to decide.

Obviously, Douglas had been mistaken. Congress now had to take sides and recognize either the pro-slavery or the anti-slavery government of Kansas. President Pierce urged Congress to accept the pro-slavery government. But Douglas, who believed that a majority

371

of Kansans were in favor of a free Territory, opposed the President's recommendation. Congress, hopelessly divided, could reach no decision.

"Bleeding Kansas." Meanwhile, violence began to rage in what men called "bleeding Kansas." Northerners and southerners began to pour arms and ammunition into the Territory. An armed group of pro-slavery men marched on the town of Lawrence, center of the free settlers, and burned a part of it. In revenge, a fanatical abolitionist, John Brown, gathered another armed group, including his own sons, and one night murdered five helpless pro-slavery men in cold blood.

The violence over the slavery issue was heightened by conflicts between the pro-slavery and anti-slavery forces over townsites and land claims. At least two hundred citizens lost their lives in the bitter strife. Neither side was guiltless. In the end it was necessary to bring in federal troops to restore order.

The Republican Party is formed. One immediate result of the Kansas-Nebraska Act and the struggle for control of Kansas was the formation of a new political party. Neither of the two major parties, the Whigs and the Democrats, dared take a stand on Kansas or on any other issue involving slavery. Each party needed the support of its members in the Middle West, where the Kansas-Nebraska Act was popular. For this reason, anti-slavery men in both parties decided that the time was ripe for the organization of a new party pledged to prevent the further expansion of slavery in the Territories.

Many towns and cities in the Middle West claim to be the birthplace of the Republican Party. It was at a convention in Jackson, Michigan, on July 6, 1854, however, that the delegates voted to adopt the old label of Thomas Jefferson's party for their new organization, and to call themselves "Republicans."

The election of 1856. By 1856 the Republican Party was strong enough to enter the Presidential contest. At a nominating convention held in Phila-

delphia, the Republicans chose John C. Frémont of California, famous explorer of the west, to head their ticket. The Democrats nominated James Buchanan of Pennsylvania. The Whigs and the American, or "Know-Nothing," Party nominated Millard Fillmore of New York.

When the election returns were counted, it was clear that sectional lines were rapidly stiffening in the nation. The Whigs, who had tried to avoid the slavery issue and be all things to all men, came in a poor third, with only 8 electoral votes (those of Maryland, a slave state). The Democrats, who had come out squarely for the Compromise of 1850 and the Kansas-Nebraska Act "as the only sound and safe solution of the slavery question," came in first with 174 electoral votes (14 slave and 5 free states). The Republicans, who had come out just as squarely against any further expansion of slavery, gave their opponents a good race. Running under the slogan "Free Soil, Free Speech, Free Men, and Frémont," the new Republican Party collected 114 electoral votes (11 free states). It was significant that Buchanan won 14 southern states and only 5 northern states, whereas Frémont's electoral votes all came from 11 northern states. The new Republican Party was obviously a purely sectional political organization.

North against South—this, in substance, was the conclusion to be drawn from the election of 1856. The long period of compromise had come to an end.

📖 **SECTION SURVEY**

1. There were "ominous undercurrents" in the prosperous years 1850–1854. Describe the effects on North and South of (a) the book *Uncle Tom's Cabin*, (b) Fugitive Slave Law, and (c) the Ostend Manifesto.

2. (a) Give the terms of the Kansas-Nebraska Act. (b) Explain how this act revived the dangerous slavery issue.

3. What were the significant political consequences of the Kansas-Nebraska Act?

4. In the form of a chart, compare the parties, candidates, issues, and consequences in the elections of 1852 and 1856.

IDENTIFY: "bleeding Kansas," Republican Party; Pierce, Winfield Scott, John Frémont, James Buchanan; 1854.

The North and the South move steadily toward war

By 1857 the prospect of compromising the struggle between the North and the South seemed remote. From 1857 to 1861, the nation moved toward war.

The Dred Scott decision. On March 6, 1857, two days after President Buchanan took the oath of office, the Supreme Court handed down an explosive decision.

The decision involved Dred Scott, a slave whose owner had taken him from Missouri into Illinois, a free state, and into Minnesota Territory, which was free under the terms of the Missouri Compromise. His owner then took him back into Missouri. A few years later, a group of anti-slavery people brought the Dred Scott case into court, claiming that since Scott had lived in a free state and in free Territory he was a free man. The case went through two lower courts, one of which decided for Scott, the other against. Eventually, the case reached the Supreme Court.

The Supreme Court ruled that Dred Scott (and therefore all slaves or their descendants) was not a citizen of the United States or of the State of Missouri. Therefore, he had no right to sue in either a state or a federal court.

Had the Supreme Court stopped at this point, the Dred Scott case probably would have gone almost unnoticed by the general public. But the Supreme Court, by a vote of six to three, with Chief Justice Roger B. Taney voting with the majority, went on to rule that the Missouri Compromise was unconstitutional because Congress had no power to exclude slavery from the Territories.

WILLIAM GASTON, CATHOLIC SOUTHERNER

Because his mother was a Catholic and his Protestant father was killed in the War of Independence, William Gaston (1778–1844) was brought up as a Catholic in North Carolina. The Church had no priests or schools in that area, so William was the first student of Georgetown College—now Georgetown University—when it opened in 1791. He completed his studies at Princeton and, back in North Carolina, took up law and politics. Twice he was elected to Congress, serving from 1813 to 1817, but the Federalist Party to which he belonged was dying out. He then served in the North Carolina Senate, and in 1832 was appointed a judge of his state's Supreme Court.

What made all this remarkable was the provision of the North Carolina constitution which barred anyone not a Protestant from holding office. In 1835, as a delegate to the state's constitutional convention, Gaston sought to have the religious test abolished. He failed, but the wording of the provision was changed from "Protestant" to "Christian" to make Catholics elegible for office.

In the same convention Gaston fought hard to preserve for free Negroes the right to vote, but he was altogether unsuccessful. As a judge, however, he rendered, in important cases, decisions which recognized that even a slave had *some* rights, for instance, the right to defend himself against unwarranted assaults by a white man. Judge Gaston remained a highly respected member of the North Carolina Supreme Court to the end of his life.

The Court based this decision on the Fifth Amendment, which prohibited Congress from depriving any person of ". . . property, without due process of law."

The Dred Scott decision, the first since the famous case of *Marbury v. Madison* in 1803 in which the Supreme Court had declared an act of Congress unconstitutional, was decidedly unpopular with many northerners. According to the Dred Scott decision, the major plank in the platform of the new Republican Party—the exclusion of slavery from the Territories—was unconstitutional.

The anti-slavery forces in the northern states were severely jolted by the Dred Scott decision. If the Supreme Court continued to hold the position that it had taken, only an amendment to the Constitution could keep slavery out of the Territories. But an amendment had to be ratified by three fourths of all the states. In view of the number of existing southern states, such a majority was out of the question. Moreover, in electing the Democratic candidate Buchanan, the majority of the voters in 1856 had apparently approved the repeal of the Missouri Compromise, which alone had barred the extension of slavery into Territories north of the famous 36° 30′ line.

Anti-slavery men determined to gain strength and win the election of 1860.

A new leader appears. The contest for the office of United States Senator from Illinois in 1858 turned out to be a prelude to the general election of 1860.

Stephen A. Douglas was running for re-election as a Democrat. He knew that, if he won the senatorial race in 1858, he had a good chance of winning the Democratic nomination for the Presidency in 1860.

In opposition to Douglas, the Illinois Republicans put up Abraham Lincoln, a former Whig who had served in the Illinois legislature and who had been in Congress for one term (1847-49). Born in a log cabin in Kentucky, Lincoln was a self-made man. Gifted with a down-to-earth sense of humor and with much

political shrewdness, Lincoln was a match for Douglas in wit, in logical argument, and in general ability.

Lincoln was not an abolitionist. However, he believed that slavery was morally wrong, and he steadfastly accepted the basic principle of the new Republican Party that slavery must not be extended any further. In his acceptance of the nomination for the senatorship, he declared: "A house divided against itself cannot stand. I believe this government cannot endure permanently half slave and half free. I do not expect the Union to be dissolved—I do not expect the house to fall—but I do expect it will cease to be divided. Either the opponents of slavery will arrest the further spread of it, and place it where the public mind shall rest in the belief that it is in the course of ultimate extinction, or its advocates will push it forward till it shall become alike lawful in all the states, old as well as new, North as well as South."

The Lincoln-Douglas debates. Confident of his position and of his ability to defend it, Lincoln challenged Douglas to a series of debates. Throngs of people came to the seven Illinois towns in which Lincoln and Douglas vigorously debated the main political issues of the day. Newspapers in every section of the land reported the debates. Lincoln made a great impression on those who heard him and on many who read what he said.

In the debates Lincoln asked Douglas how he could reconcile his principle of "popular sovereignty" with the Dred Scott decision. This put Douglas in a tight spot. The Supreme Court had ruled in the Dred Scott decision that slaveowners had the right to introduce slavery into any Territory. Douglas, on the other hand, had argued for the principle of "popular sovereignty," under which the people in each Territory would make their own decision about slavery. If Douglas answered Lincoln by stating that he believed in the Dred Scott decision, he would win the support of southerners, but lose the support of northerners. If he continued to argue in favor of "popular sovereignty," he would lose the support of southerners, but win many northern votes. With his eye on the Presidency in 1860, what could Douglas say that would please both northerners and southerners?

Douglas was a brilliant politician. He thought quickly, then answered Lincoln with a clever reply that became known as the Freeport Doctrine, after the Illinois town of Freeport in which the debate took place. Douglas replied that the legislature of a Territory could refuse to enact a law supporting slavery and thus in effect could exclude slavery from the Territory. Douglas' statement was clear enough in Illinois to win him the senatorship. Nevertheless, the Freeport Doctrine weakened Douglas in the South. Southerners began to realize that Douglas, despite his devotion to "popular sovereignty," was no champion of the expansion of slavery.

John Brown's raid. In the fall of 1859, John Brown undertook to start a rebellion of slaves in Virginia. With money obtained from a number of New England and New York abolitionists, Brown armed a party of eighteen men. On October 16 he seized the federal arsenal at the town of Harper's Ferry, in what is now West Virginia. He planned to seize the guns stored in the arsenal, hand them out to slaves nearby, and lead the slaves in what he hoped would be a widespread rebellion.

It was a wild idea, certain to fail. Brown and his followers were captured by Colonel Robert E. Lee of the United States Army in command of a unit of marines. After a trial that Brown admitted was more fair than he had reason to expect, he was hanged for "murder, criminal conspiracy, and treason against the Commonwealth of Virginia."

Many southerners believed that Brown's action represented northern opinion and concluded that slavery was no longer safe from direct attack. As a matter of fact, northern politicians and the majority of northerners were shocked at the news of John Brown's

■ The trial of John Brown had the eyes of all America turned upon it. "Osawatomie Brown" to some was a martyr; to others, a murderer.

raid and quickly condemned it. But extreme abolitionists regarded Brown as a heroic martyr. Emerson declared that Brown was a "new saint" who would "make the gallows glorious like the cross."

Southern newspapers quoted this small minority of abolitionist opinion as typical of what the whole North was thinking. To southerners John Brown's raid was convincing evidence that the North was determined to abolish slavery. By 1860 the ties binding the two sections had almost disappeared.

↙ SECTION SURVEY

1. Summarize (a) the facts of the Dred Scott case and (b) the decision of the Supreme Court.

2. Why did the Supreme Court decision arouse widespread opposition in the North?

3. (a) What was the occasion of the Lincoln-Douglas debates? (b) Explain why the Freeport Doctrine antagonized the South.

4. Describe the reactions of northerners and southerners to John Brown's raid.

IDENTIFY: Taney; 1857, 1858, 1859.

5 Southern states withdraw from the Union, and the war begins

By 1860 most of the ties binding the North and the South together had been broken. The Methodist, Presbyterian, and Baptist churches had split over the issue of slavery. Although many business ties still existed, the political parties were badly divided. This fact became clear when the national political parties met to draw up platforms and to nominate candidates for the Presidency.

The Whig Party disappears. The Whigs had virtually disappeared by 1856, when most southern Whigs went over to the Democrats and most northern Whigs joined the Republicans. In 1860 what was left of the old Whig Party met in Baltimore at a nominating convention. There they nominated John Bell of Tennessee for the Presidency. Changing their name to the Constitutional Union Party, they adopted a platform which called upon all who loved the nation to recognize "no political principles other than the Constitution of the country, the Union of the states, and the enforcement of the law."

The Democratic Party divides. The Democratic Party split wide open in 1860. One group, consisting mostly of southerners, took a strong pro-slavery position. This group nominated John C. Breckinridge of Kentucky for the Presidency and demanded federal protection for slavery in the Territories, as well as other measures designed to secure the interests of the southern minority in the federal government. The other group, mostly northern Democrats, nominated Stephen A. Douglas for the Presidency and took the position that "popular sovereignty" should decide the slavery question in the Territories.

The Republicans gain strength. The Republicans, meeting in Chicago, determined to make the most of the split in the Democratic Party. It was expected that the Republicans would nominate Governor William H. Seward of New York for the Presidency. He lost the nomination, however, partly because he seemed to be identified with eastern "money interests" and partly because a candidate from the Middle West was more likely to win the election. The convention named Abraham Lincoln as its candidate.

The Republican platform was a purely sectional platform, designed to win the support of northern industrialists and wage earners and of farmers, particularly those in the Middle West. The platform came out for protective tariffs, internal improvements, and a railroad to the Pacific. It promised free land to settlers in the new western Territories. And it opposed the extension of slavery into the new Territories.

Four parties—four views. Thus, four political parties entered the Presidential race in 1860. The Republicans, with Lincoln at their head, represented northern industrialists and midwestern farmers and opposed any further extension of slavery. Opposed to the Republicans in the North were the northern Democrats led by Douglas, who were joined by a few Democrats south of Mason and Dixon's line. The Douglas Democrats stood for keeping things much as they were. Douglas urged the people to vote for him on the ground that, if Lincoln were elected, the South would leave the Union.

In the South the contest was between the moderate Constitutional Unionists, led by Bell, and the southern Democrats, led by Breckinridge. The southern Democrats made it clear that they would regard the election of Lincoln as proof that the North was using its superior strength in the nation to encroach upon the rights and interests of the South.

Results of the election. Lincoln won the election, receiving 180 electoral votes, all from the northern free states. Breckinridge mustered 72 electoral votes, all from the southern slave states. Douglas drew 12 electoral votes, winning Missouri and 3 of New Jersey's 7 votes. Bell received 39 electoral votes,

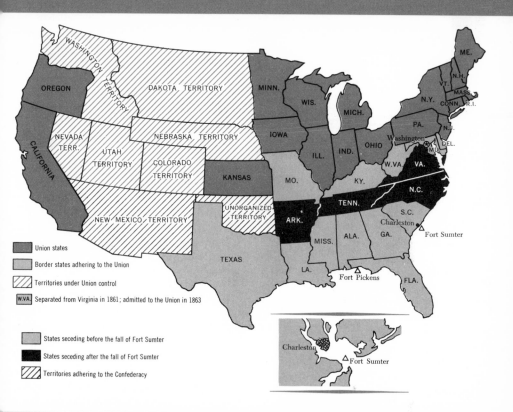

Union states

Border states adhering to the Union

Territories under Union control

W.VA. Separated from Virginia in 1861; admitted to the Union in 1863

States seceding before the fall of Fort Sumter

States seceding after the fall of Fort Sumter

Territories adhering to the Confederacy

winning Virginia, Kentucky, and Tennessee.

The count of the popular vote showed that Lincoln had polled 40 per cent, Douglas 29 per cent, Breckinridge 18 per cent, and Bell nearly 13 per cent. Lincoln was elected President, but by a minority of the popular vote.

Thoughtful observers noted with alarm that in both the North and the South the extremists, Lincoln and Breckinridge, won more votes than the moderates, Douglas and Bell. Did this mean that the southern states would carry out their threat to secede?

Southern states leave the Union. The fateful answer came quickly. Shortly after the November election the legislature of South Carolina called a special convention to consider secession. When the convention met, the delegates unanimously voted that South Carolina was no longer a state of the Union. Other states in the South, not without some opposition, followed the example of South Carolina and seceded from the Union (see map, this page).

Early in 1861 delegates from six of the seven seceding states met at Montgomery, Alabama, and drafted a constitution for the Confederate States of America. The Confederate Constitution resembled the Constitution of the United States. It created a federal government. But there were some important differences. The Confederate Constitution stressed "the sovereign and independent character" of each state. It also guaranteed the right to own slaves.

The Montgomery convention elected as President of the Confederacy Jefferson Davis, a Mississippi planter who had formerly served as United States Senator and Secretary of War. The delegates also elected Alexander H. Stephens of Georgia as Vice-President.

377

Buchanan's inaction. And while southern states were seceding from the Union, what did President Buchanan do to save the situation? The answer is that he did almost nothing. Following the advice of his Attorney General, he announced in his annual message that no state had the right to secede. But he also expressed the opinion that the federal government had no power to hold any state in the Union against its will. So it was that for four months, from Lincoln's election in November 1860 until his inauguration on March 4, 1861, the only efforts made to meet the crisis came in the form of several halfhearted proposals for compromise, all of which were quickly brushed aside by leaders of both the North and the South.

In fairness to Buchanan, it should be said that his policy did avert the war for several months and gave the compromise proposals a chance to be heard. It should also be noted that, having been voted out of office, he may have concluded that the incoming President and his administration should be allowed to settle the problem in their own way.

War begins at Fort Sumter. During this time Confederate troops occupied —without resistance—all but two of the forts and navy yards in the states that had seceded from the Union. By the time Lincoln was inaugurated, on March 4, 1861, only Fort Pickens at Pensacola, Florida, and Fort Sumter at Charleston, South Carolina (see map, page 377), remained in the hands of the federal government. Southerners—or at least those southerners with the most extreme point of view—claimed that these forts belonged to the Confederate States of America, not to the United States of America. Confederate troops surrounded these two forts, but did not attack.

In March, Major Robert Anderson, commanding Fort Sumter, notified the War Department in Washington that his supplies were almost gone. This situation presented President Lincoln with a major problem. If he sent new supplies and reinforcements to Fort Sumter, the Confederacy would consider this to be an act of war. If he failed to send supplies, the fort would pass into Confederate hands. Were this to happen, many people would conclude that the United States government had recognized the right of the southern states to secede.

Finally, toward the end of March and against the advice of the majority of his cabinet, Lincoln gave orders for a relief expedition to be sent to Fort Sumter. When the Confederate government heard this news, it notified General Pierre Beauregard (BOH-ruh-gahrd), commander of the Charleston district, to fire upon the fort if that were necessary to prevent reinforcements from reaching it.

On April 12 at 4:30 in the morning, the Confederate guns around the harbor opened fire on Fort Sumter. Major Anderson, in command of the fort, promptly returned the fire while the relief expedition, unable to pass the Confederate batteries, lay helpless outside the harbor. Two days later, on Sunday afternoon, April 14, Major Anderson led his men out of the fort, which then passed into Confederate hands.

News of the fall of Fort Sumter ended all hope of compromise. Men in the North and the South rushed to join the armed forces. The war had begun.

SECTION SURVEY

1. In the form of a chart, compare the parties, candidates, issues, and results in the election of 1860.

2. It can be said that Lincoln was elected President by a minority of the popular vote, and a sectional minority at that. Explain this statement.

3. In the election of 1860, "the extremists . . . won more votes than the moderates." Justify this statement.

4. Why did the southern states secede in 1860–61?

5. In what ways did the Confederate Constitution differ from the Constitution of the United States?

IDENTIFY: Constitutional Union Party, Fort Sumter; Bell, Breckinridge, Davis, Stephens, Anderson, Beauregard; 1861, April 12, 1861.

■ CHAPTER SURVEY

(For review, see Section Surveys, pages 364, 367, 372–73, 375, 378.)

Points to Discuss: 1. What political and economic factors made the issue of territorial expansion such a vital one for southern plantation owners?

2. John Quincy Adams called the conflict over Missouri in 1820 "a title page to a great, tragic volume." Why?

3. Charles Sumner referred to the Kansas-Nebraska Act as "at once the worst and best bill on which Congress ever acted." What did he mean?

4. How did each of the following increase sectional bitterness? (a) Mexican War, (b) Wilmot Proviso, (c) Garrison, (d) Harriet Beecher Stowe, (e) Compromise of 1850, (f) Kansas-Nebraska Act, (g) Dred Scott case, (h) John Brown's Raid.

5. Why did the South accept the Kansas-Nebraska Act in 1854 and reject its doctrine of "popular sovereignty" in 1857?

6. How did Douglas' "Freeport Doctrine" aid him in 1858 and hurt him in 1860?

7. Compare Jackson's action in regard to South Carolina in 1832–33 with that of Buchanan in 1860. What disadvantage did Buchanan face?

Using Maps and Charts: 1. (a) See the map on page 362 and give the terms of the Missouri Compromise. (b) Which section gained most by the compromise?

2. (a) Using the map on page 371, show the lines that divided free and slave states across the continent. (b) Explain how each of these lines was agreed upon.

3. Using the maps on pages 362 and 371, show how the Kansas-Nebraska Act affected the Missouri Compromise.

4. Use the map on page 377 to identify (a) border states, (b) those southern states seceding before and those seceding after the fall of Fort Sumter, (c) Union states.

Consulting the Sources: For reflections of Chief Justice Taney on slavery in August 1857, see Ellis, *Docs.*, No. 100. In No. 106, Patrick Lynch, a southern Catholic bishop, presents a southerner's case for secession.

■ TRACING THE MAIN IDEAS

Why did the North and South go to war in 1861? What was the immediate cause of the tragic conflict?

There is no easy way to answer these questions. Historians have studied the problem and recorded their conclusions in scholarly volumes that today fill row after row of library shelves. Some historians stress basic differences in the economic and social systems of the North and South, differences that grew greater as the years passed. Other historians point to differences of opinion over the tariff, over internal improvements at public expense, over money and banking, and over the disposal of public lands. Others stress the conflict over slavery. Still others emphasize the issue of states' rights.

These are only a few of the ways in which historians explain the war. It seems at times as though there were as many explanations as there are historians.

This does not mean that the scholars are wrong. Each has put his finger on one or more of the many factors that led to armed conflict.

The thoughtful historian does not attempt to give a short and simple explanation of the war between the North and South. All he can safely do is to explain why northern extremists and southern extremists, a minority in each section, felt and acted as they did. He can only point out that the great majority in the North held that the benefits of the Union were too important and the sentiment of patriotism was too precious to permit the Union to be destroyed. He can only indicate that many in the South who loved the Union and would have preferred to stay in it supported the Confederacy out of loyalty to the principle of states' rights, out of determination to protect their homes, and out of consideration for the position taken by kinfolk, neighbors, and friends.

Americans Endure the Strains of War

BOMBARDMENT of FORT SUMTER –
CHARLESTON, SOUTH CAROLINA

O N Monday, April 15, 1861, two days after Fort Sumter was evacuated by Federal troops, President Abraham Lincoln declared that the government of the United States was confronted with an armed revolt against its authority, and called for 75,000 men to volunteer for three months' service in the army.

In all of the northern states, men enthusiastically answered Lincoln's call to arms. From all walks of life, they rushed to join the colors—Republicans and Democrats, native-born Americans and newly arrived immigrants who had not yet learned to speak the language of their adopted country. For the time being, the North was united as it had never been before.

The poet Walt Whitman remembered the opening weeks of the war and managed to recapture in verse the feeling of unity that gripped northern people in those trying days:

"Beat! beat! drums!—blow! bugles! blow!
Through the windows—through doors—
    burst like a ruthless force,

Into the solemn church, and scatter the congregation;
Into the school where the scholar is studying;
Leave not the bridegroom quiet—no happiness must he have now with his bride;
Nor the peaceful farmer any peace, ploughing his field or gathering his grain;
So fierce you whirr and pound, you drums—so shrill you bugles blow."

In the South as well as in the North, the beat of drums and the shrill voice of the bugle summoned men to arms.

AS THE STORY DEVELOPS

1. North and South, each with advantages, develop their strategies.
2. After four years of war, the Union emerges victorious.
3. The war brings severe hardships to the southern people.
4. Life behind Union lines undergoes important changes.
5. The Union deals with political problems at home and abroad.

| 1450 | 1750 | 1800 | 1850 | 1900 | 1950 | 197 |

1 North and South, each with advantages, develop their strategies

On April 15, 1861, when President Lincoln called for Union volunteers, there were only seven states in the Confederate States of America, or the Confederacy. They were South Carolina, Georgia, Florida, Alabama, Mississippi, Louisiana, and Texas. With Lincoln's call to arms, however, every state in the Union had to make its fateful choice.

The states choose sides. Virginia, on April 17, became the eighth state to join the Confederacy. When Virginia left the Union, the United States Army lost several of its ablest officers. Most famous of all the Virginia officers to take up arms for the South was Robert E. Lee, to whom President Lincoln had offered command of the Union forces. Arkansas, Tennessee, and North Carolina soon followed Virginia into the Confederacy. By May 20, five weeks after Fort Sumter fell, there were eleven states in the Confederacy (see map, page 377).

The mountainous counties in the northwestern part of Virginia did not follow the rest of the state into the Confederacy. In 1863 these counties were admitted to the Union as the state of West Virginia. Control of this area, part of which lay on the Ohio River, was important to the North because it helped to keep open the lines of communication between the Northeast and the Mississippi River.

The "border states"—Delaware, Maryland, Kentucky, and Missouri—were also important to the Union, but for a time it was touch and go whether some of them would fight on the side of the North or the South.

Maryland was especially important, for if it joined the Confederacy, Washington, the Union capital, would have been isolated from the northern states. For a time the fate of Maryland hung in the balance. Many Marylanders were sympathetic to the Confederacy, and on April 19 a mob of angry citizens at-

ROBERT E. LEE

Of all the leaders of the Confederacy, none emerged from the war more honored by his countrymen, northerners and southerners alike, than Robert E. Lee (1807–70). His life, in the words of one historian, had "the breadth, the dignity, the majesty, the round and full completeness of a Miltonic epic, none the less inspiring because it had a tragic end."

Lee, who came from a distinguished Virginia family, attended West Point, graduating in 1829 with a perfect record. Two years later he married a great-granddaughter of Martha Washington. With his marriage, he acquired the estate of Arlington, where the famous national military cemetery is now located. Although Lee might have lived a life of leisure, he chose instead to remain in the United States Army, where for the next thirty years he served with distinction.

When war broke out in 1861, President Lincoln asked Lee to command the Union armies. Lee reluctantly refused. Two months before, when war seemed likely, Lee had said to friends: "If Virginia stands by the old Union, so will I. But if she secedes . . . I will follow my native state with my sword, and, if need be, with my life." The decision to break with the Union was a heartbreaking one for Lee to make, and it was a great loss to the North. One leading northern general said that when the North lost Lee, it lost the equivalent of 50,000 men.

Throughout the war, although consistently outnumbered in men and equipment, Lee fought brilliantly, winning victories that were little short of miraculous. A man of tact, human understanding, and unblemished character, he inspired respect in friend and foe alike, and won the deepest affection from all who knew him.

tacked the Sixth Massachusetts Regiment as it passed through Baltimore on its way to Washington. In an effort to prevent the passage of Union troops and to avoid further bloodshed, Maryland authorities burned the railroad bridges connecting Baltimore with Philadelphia and Harrisburg. But Lincoln, determined to hold Maryland in the Union, sent Federal troops into the state and arrested the leading Confederate sympathizers. Anti-southern leaders then rose to power, and Maryland remained in the Union.

The other border states—Delaware, Kentucky, and Missouri—also decided to join the Union cause. Delaware never hesitated. At first Kentucky refused to obey Lincoln's call for volunteers and tried to remain neutral. But when the Confederate army invaded Kentucky in September, the state declared for the Union. The government of Missouri was in the hands of southern sympathizers. After several battles had been fought, however, the state officially lined up with the North.

"The North" included the Pacific coast states of California and Oregon. After West Virginia had joined the Union in 1863, there was a total of twenty-four states fighting on the northern side.

In every state, especially in the border states, families were torn apart as some members enlisted with the Confederacy, others with the Union. Three of Mrs. Lincoln's brothers fought and died for the South. Robert E. Lee's nephew commanded Union naval forces on the James River in Virginia while his famous uncle was fighting Union forces not many miles away. Caleb Huse, a northerner, was the South's ablest representative in Europe; Senator Robert J. Walker, a former southerner, was the North's ablest European representative. The division within families and the breakup of lifelong friendships were some of the tragic results of the war.

Northern advantages. The North had overwhelming material advantages in the War Between the States. It was greatly superior to the South in population, in manufacturing, agricultural and natural resources, in finances, and in transportation facilities. Northern strength had recently been increased by the admission of three new states to the Union—Minnesota (1858), Oregon (1859), and Kansas (1861).

The population of the twenty-four northern, western, and border states totaled 22,000,000. To this total may be added about 800,000 immigrants who entered the United States during the war years. About 400,000 foreign-born men served in the Union armies.

The varied economic resources of the North—industrial, commercial, financial, agricultural—gave the North an enormous advantage over the predominantly agricultural South. When the war began, the North had 92 per cent of the nation's industries and almost all of the known supplies of coal, iron, copper, and other metals. The North also owned most of the nation's gold, which could be used to buy war materials abroad, whereas the Confederate wealth was largely in land and slaves.

The transportation facilities of the North were also far superior to those of the South. Most of the railroad lines in the country were located in the North and the Middle West. This made it possible for the North to move men and supplies around almost at will, and to transport food from the midwestern farm lands to workers in the eastern cities and to the armed forces in the field. Moreover, with control of the navy and a large part of the mechant marine, the North was able to carry on trade with nations overseas.

Southern advantages. The eleven states of the Confederacy had a combined population of only about 9,000,000—of whom 3,500,000 were slaves. White southerners were outnumbered by northerners, therefore, by more than four to one. But the South took comfort from the fact that other outnumbered people had managed to win wars against seemingly hopeless odds.

Southerners also felt confident be-

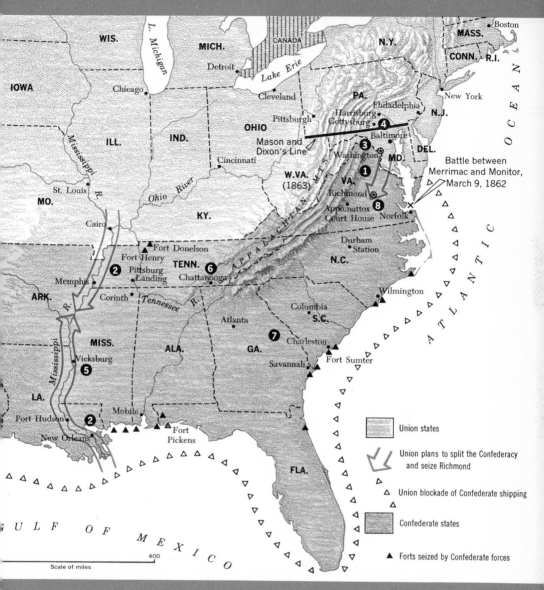

Battle between Merrimac and Monitor, March 9, 1862

Union states

Union plans to split the Confederacy and seize Richmond

Union blockade of Confederate shipping

Confederate states

Forts seized by Confederate forces

This map provides an overview of the major campaigns of the War Between the States, and shows the main points of Union strategy. The circled numbers indicate the areas in which fighting occurred. In the pages that follow, you will learn more about each of these campaigns. The discussion of each campaign is accompanied by a detailed map that bears a number corresponding to one of the numbers on this map. As you read the text that follows and examine each numbered map, look frequently at the map above so that you will understand the sequence of the war and the relationship of each campaign to the over-all Union strategy. On the map above and on the detailed maps, Union states appear in a lighter shade, Confederate states in darker. On all of the detailed maps, red symbols stand for Union forces, black symbols for Confederate forces. The following symbols are used:

⟶	Union advance	⟶	Confederate advance
┄┄➤	Union retreat	┅┅➤	Confederate retreat
✳	Union victory	✴	Confederate victory

Union flag   *First Confederate flag*

cause they had "the immense advantage," as Confederate General Pierre Beauregard put it, of "the interior lines of war." Beauregard meant that, in order to win, the South needed only to fight a defensive war, to protect its territory until the North tired of the struggle. The North, on the other hand, had to penetrate and conquer an area almost as large as Western Europe.

Southerners were also fighting for things that men cherish most—for their homes and families, for their independence, and the right to govern themselves. Northerners, on the other hand, were fighting for a much more intangible thing, for an idea—the preservation of the Union.

The Confederacy also had the advantage that many of its ablest officers had graduated from West Point and had long years of experience in the United States Army. Also, southerners were used to outdoor living, and were, on the whole, more familiar with firearms and horses than men from the Northeast, many of whom had been raised in cities.

Another reason for the optimism of southerners was their conviction that "cotton was king." They believed that the textile mills of Great Britain and France were so dependent on raw cotton that these countries would have to come to the aid of the Confederacy.

War aims and strategy. The major aim of the South in the war never varied. Southerners fought to win their independence.

The North had two major aims. For the first two years President Lincoln insisted that the only purpose of the North in fighting was to restore the Union. After 1862 freedom for the slaves became a secondary objective of the North.

The over-all strategy of the South was as clear and simple as its war aim. Southerners proposed to fight a defensive war, holding the North at arm's length until northerners grew war-weary and agreed to peace on southern terms. The only exception to this strategy of defense was a plan to seize Washington and strike northward through the Shenandoah Valley into Maryland and Pennsylvania. By this plan the South hoped to drive a wedge between the Northeast and the Middle West, disrupt Union lines of communication, and bring the war to a speedy end.

Over-all northern strategy included three different plans of attack: (1) to cripple the South by blockading the Confederate coastline; (2) to split the Confederacy in two by seizing control of the Mississippi River and interior railroad lines; (3) to seize Richmond, Virginia, which had become the Confederate capital in May 1861, and then to drive southward and finally link up with Union forces driving eastward from the Mississippi Valley.

Such were the war aims and war plans of the two opposing sides. In the spring of 1861, as the northern "Boys in Blue" and the southern "Boys in Gray" trudged down the muddy or dusty roads to their first battlefield, no one could be sure of the outcome of the war. As it turned out, four long, cruel years of fighting lay ahead.

SECTION SURVEY

1. (a) Name the states that joined the Confederacy. (b) Name the four "border states."

2. In the form of a chart, compare the North and South with respect to (a) population, (b) number of states, (c) industrial development, (d) transportation facilities, (e) financial resources, and (f) naval power.

3. If you had been a southern sympathizer in 1861, why would you have thought that the Confederacy might win the war?

4. Compare the war aims and military strategy of the North and the South.

IDENTIFY: "Boys in Blue," "Boys in Gray"; Robert E. Lee.

2 After four years of war, the Union emerges victorious

The first important battle of the War Between the States was fought on July 21, 1861, at Manassas Junction, near a stream called Bull Run in northern Virginia (see map 1, this page). In this engagement, called the First Battle of Bull Run, the Confederates defeated the northern recruits, who fled in confusion to Washington.

Results of Bull Run. Northerners were stunned. Had the Confederate commanders been able to take advantage of their victory, they could easily have captured Washington. But the Confederate troops, elated by their victory, scattered pell-mell to celebrate.

The outcome of the First Battle of Bull Run surprised both the North and the South. Northerners, shocked by defeat, began to prepare for a long war. Southerners, misled by what now seemed to them an easy victory at Bull Run, became overconfident. As one observer wrote, "The Confederate army was more disorganized by victory than that of the United States by defeat."

The Union blockade. Meanwhile, Union war ships and other vessels hastily converted into naval service had moved into assigned positions to blockade the 3550 miles of Confederate coastline stretching from Virginia around Florida and the Gulf of Mexico to southern Texas (see map, page 383).

As the months passed, the blockade became increasingly effective. For example, in 1860, the year before war broke out, 6000 ships entered and left southern ports, whereas during the first year of the war only about 800 ships managed to slip through the blockade. Daring Confederate sea captains kept trying throughout the war to "run the blockade," but, as the years wore on, fewer and fewer ships slipped through.

The blockade was a severe handicap to Confederate plans. The South had counted on the export of cotton, tobac-

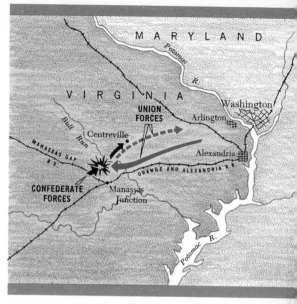

❶ First Battle of Bull Run: July 21, 1861

co, sugar, and other products to provide money for military equipment and manufactured goods from Europe. As the blockade tightened, European products vanished from southern stores. Southern manufacturers could not begin to make up the deficiencies.

As products became increasingly scarce, the prices of southern goods shot skyward, and patriotic southern women turned to the problem of making substitutes. Old looms and spinning wheels were brought down from dusty attics, and busy hands began to spin and weave fabrics for clothing and uniforms. Before the war ended, southerners were melting church bells to make cannon.

The war at sea. Although the Confederacy failed to break the Union blockade, daring seamen of the Confederate Navy managed to make the sea lanes dangerous for northern shipping. During the five and one half months between Lincoln's election and the fall of Fort Sumter, the South seized a number of United States vessels then in southern harbors. During the war they also purchased in England the *Alabama*, the *Florida*, and 17 other war ships. These few vessels were no serious threat to the

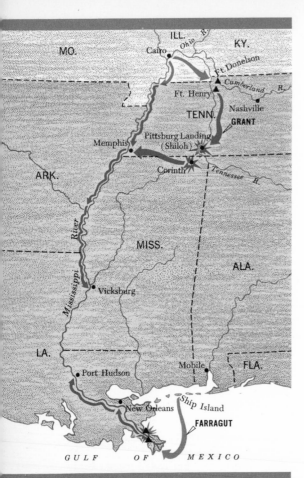

❷ War in the West: 1862

by the Union navy. In spite of these precautions by the South, Union forces captured New Orleans and several forts along the Atlantic coast.

The Union begins the offensive. The Appalachian Mountains divided land operations into two major theaters of war—the eastern and western theaters.

Shortly after the Union disaster at the First Battle of Bull Run, President Lincoln gave General George B. McClellan command of the eastern theater of war. A graduate of West Point, the thirty-four-year-old McClellan was highly popular with his men, who among themselves referred to him as "Little Mac." McClellan, a superb organizer, quickly turned a mob of untrained volunteers into the highly effective Army of the Potomac. In November 1861 Lincoln elevated McClellan to General-in-Chief of all the Union armies. But McClellan was overly cautious, refusing to attack until he was thoroughly prepared, and the saying "All quiet along the Potomac" became a public joke. Even Lincoln finally commented, "If General McClellan does not want to use the army, I would like to *borrow* it."

While the Army of the Potomac was marking time in the east, Union forces in the western theater were engaged in a number of small skirmishes in Missouri in an effort to prevent that state from joining the Confederacy. By 1862, however, Missouri was secure, and General Henry W. Halleck, in command of the western theater, opened a drive into Tennessee.

The war in the west opens. Beginning in western Kentucky where the Tennessee River empties into the Ohio River, an infantry unit under the command of General Ulysses S. Grant—one of General Halleck's subordinate officers—moved southward. On February 6, 1862, Grant captured Fort Henry on the upper Tennessee River, and on February 16 he captured Fort Donelson on the Cumberland River (see map 2, this page). But General Nathan Bedford Forrest, one of the South's great generals, escaped and continued to prove so

United States Navy. Nevertheless, before the war ended, they managed to sink more than 250 merchant ships.

More important to the outcome of the war was the ever-present possibility of a Union naval attack on a southern harbor and the landing of a Union army behind Confederate lines. Fortunately for the South, all of its important harbors had been heavily fortified long before the war. Early in 1861 the Confederacy seized these fortifications, among them Fort Sumter, and continued to man them throughout the war. But this also meant that many thousands of Confederate troops who were badly needed on the fighting front had to remain in the coastal fortresses to guard against an attack dangerous that Union General William Tecumseh Sherman later ordered his men to hunt Forrest down "if it costs ten thousand lives and bankrupts the federal treasury."

In the operations along the Tennessee, the Union infantry was assisted by gunboats, small war ships capable of steaming along the shallow waters of the rivers. Indeed, both in this campaign and in the Mississippi River campaign, gunboats of various types proved extremely useful to both sides.

With Fort Donelson in Union hands, Grant continued southward along the Tennessee River to Pittsburg Landing, sometimes called Shiloh (SHY-loh), in Tennessee. Here he was completely surprised by General Albert S. Johnston of Texas, Confederate commander in the west, and suffered a serious reverse. But with the death of Johnston and the arrival of reinforcements, Grant again took the offensive and after desperate fighting finally drove the Confederate army from the field. At the end of May, Union forces occupied Corinth, in northern Mississippi.

Meanwhile, other Union forces were fighting to the south and north to gain control of the Mississippi River. On the night of April 23, Flag Officer (later Admiral) David G. Farragut of Tennessee ran his gunboats past the forts guarding New Orleans and captured the city. In the meantime, a combined naval and land expedition under Commodore A. H. Foote and General John Pope was moving southward down the Mississippi. In June this expedition seized Memphis, Tennessee, and then continued as far south as Vicksburg, Mississippi (see map 2, page 386).

Thus, by the summer of 1862, Union forces in the western theater had almost succeeded in splitting the Confederacy in two along the Mississippi. Casualties had been enormous on both sides, for the Confederate armies made the Union troops pay dearly for every foot of ground they won. But Union armies had driven the Confederate troops out of Kentucky and western Tennessee, and

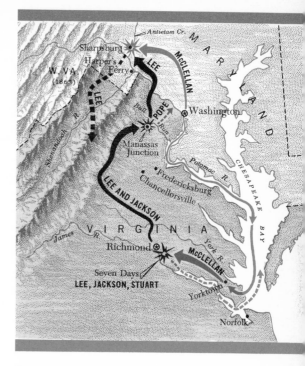

❸ War in the East: 1862

only a short length of the Mississippi River between Vicksburg, Mississippi, and Port Hudson, Louisiana, remained in Confederate hands.

The war in the east. Union victories in the western theater during 1862 were more than balanced by Confederate victories in the eastern theater.

In April 1862 General McClellan, after repeated orders to move against the Confederate capital at Richmond, Virginia, finally started the long-awaited offensive. Leaving General Irvin McDowell with 40,000 men to guard Washington, McClellan transported an army of more than 100,000 troops down the Potomac River, seized Yorktown, Virginia, and began a slow, cautious advance up the peninsula between the York and the James Rivers (see map 3, this page). By the middle of May, McClellan's troops were within a few miles of the Confederate capital. This was the high-water mark of their advance, for here McClellan paused to wait for reinforcements.

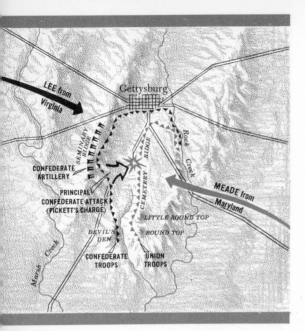

❹ Battle of Gettysburg: July 1–3, 1863

The reinforcements did not arrive, because they were prevented from doing so by the brilliant and daring Confederate officer, General Thomas J. ("Stonewall") Jackson. In May and June, with a force of only 18,000 men, Jackson fought a number of engagements in the Shenandoah Valley, defeating Union forces three times the size of his army and holding a constant threat over the city of Washington.

Meanwhile, in June, the Confederate troops defending Richmond launched a series of furious counterattacks, known as the Seven Days' Battles, against McClellan's army. Led by General Robert E. Lee, General "Stonewall" Jackson, and the dashing cavalry officer, General James E. B. ("Jeb") Stuart, the Confederate troops forced McClellan to drop back to the James River and the covering fire of Union naval forces.

On August 29–30, two months after the successful defense of their capital, the Confederates won another victory at the Second Battle of Bull Run (see map 3, page 387). Union General John Pope, who had fought in successful campaigns in the western theater and was overcon-

fident, launched this new drive toward Richmond. But Lee and Jackson caught him at Bull Run and inflicted a serious defeat. The light of Pope's burning wagons and supplies could be seen in Washington, and the city was in a panic.

Encouraged by these successes, the Confederacy decided to stage three powerful offensives designed (1) to regain control of the Mississippi, (2) to recover the ground lost in Tennessee and Kentucky, and (3) to invade Maryland and draw that state into the Confederacy. All three offensives failed.

On September 4 General Lee crossed the Potomac into Maryland with 40,000 picked troops, confident of victory. On September 17, at Sharpsburg near Antietam Creek (see map 3, page 387), he engaged General McClellan and a force of 70,000 men. The Battle of Antietam, as this engagement was called, was the bloodiest of the entire war. Both sides were so exhausted that McClellan did not try to pursue the Confederate troops and win a decisive victory.

The battle of Gettysburg. The year 1863 opened with both sides war-weary and discouraged. The southern offensive in the fall of 1862 had failed, and the South had begun to despair of winning the support of Great Britain and France. The North, although victorious in the western theater, had suffered a series of defeats in the east, and the capture of Richmond seemed as remote as on the day that war broke out.

Such was the situation when, in June 1863, General Lee struck for the second time into the North, hoping to drive a wedge into the Union and deal a fatal blow to the northern war effort. By the end of the month, his army of 75,000 men was moving northward across Maryland into Pennsylvania. On June 30 advance patrols of the Confederate and Union armies met at Gettysburg, Pennsylvania (see map 4, this page), and for two days the main armies fought desperately as they maneuvered for position on the hills around the town.

On July 3 Lee staked the fate of his army and, as it turned out, of the Confederacy itself on a powerful bid for victory. Led by General George E. Pickett, 15,000 of Lee's finest troops charged up Cemetery Ridge through the devastating fire of Union troops under the command of General George G. Meade. For a brief dramatic moment the Confederate battle flag floated on the crest of the ridge. But the Union forces were too strong, and the broken remnants of Pickett's force fell back.

The next day, July 4, Lee started his sorrowful but skillful retreat back to Virginia. To the disappointment of Lincoln, the overcautious Meade did not pursue the Confederate forces. "Our army held the war in the hollow of their hand," Lincoln said, "and they would not close it. Still," he added, "I am very grateful to Meade for the great service he did at Gettysburg."

The battle for Vicksburg. On July 4, 1863, the Union won another victory with the fall of Vicksburg, Mississippi.

The campaign that resulted in the fall of Vicksburg was one of General Ulysses S. Grant's most notable achievements. Starting in March 1863, he marched his army southward from its base in Memphis, rapidly overcame Confederate opposition in five battles, and on May 22 laid siege to Vicksburg, the stronghold of Confederate forces on the Mississippi (see map 5, this page).

For six weeks Vicksburg held out, suffering terrible punishment from Grant's cannons and from the Union gunboats in the river. Finally, on July 4, reduced to starvation and with no further hope left, the Confederate defenders surrendered. Five days later Port Hudson, Louisiana, fell into Union hands. Within a week a Union steamboat from St. Louis arrived in New Orleans, which had been held by Union forces for more than a year.

With control of the Mississippi River in Union hands, the Confederacy was finally split in two along the Mississippi. Another of the North's major objectives had been accomplished, and the time was approaching for the final drive to end the war.

❺ War in the West: March–July 1863

The Union breaks through. On September 9, 1863, two months after the fall of Vicksburg, a Union army under General William S. Rosecrans occupied Chattanooga, Tennessee, a key railway center and an important gateway to the deep South (see map 6, page 390). Rosecrans then set out in pursuit of the Confederates, commanded by General Braxton Bragg, who turned on him at Chickamauga Creek and gave him a terrible beating, driving him back into Chattanooga. Indeed, if troops under General George H. Thomas had not held back the Confederates long enough to allow Rosecrans to withdraw his main forces, the battle would have ended in utter disaster for the North. For his part

389

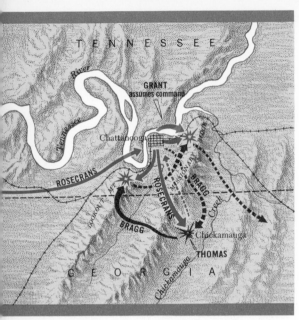

6 Fighting Around Chattanooga: September–November 1863

in the battle, General Thomas won the title of the "Rock of Chickamauga," and replaced Rosecrans in command of the Union army at Chattanooga.

The Union army remained penned up

7 Sherman's Drive East and North: May 1864–April 1865

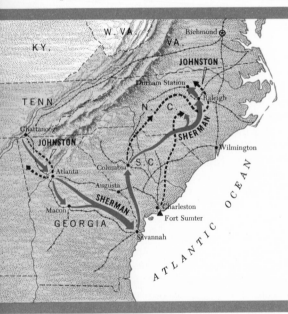

in Chattanooga until late in November. Then, reinforced with fresh troops, the army under the command of General Grant himself and with Generals Thomas, Hooker, and Sherman as his subordinates opened an offensive. In two bitterly contested engagements—Lookout Mountain and Missionary Ridge—the Union troops broke through Confederate defenses, and opened the way into the deep South.

Beginning of the end. On March 9, 1864, General Grant was given supreme command of all the Union armies. Two months later, acting on Grant's orders, General William T. Sherman set out from Chattanooga with 100,000 men to invade Georgia. The greatly outnumbered Confederate army under General Joseph E. Johnston fell back, fighting heroically and destroying railroads and bridges as it retreated. Sherman pushed on relentlessly, and on September 2 he entered Atlanta. Two months later, with some 60,000 men, he cut loose from his base of supplies at Atlanta and started toward Savannah, Georgia, on the Atlantic coast (see map 7, this page). On December 22 Sherman wired President Lincoln, "I beg to present you as a Christmas gift the city of Savannah."

Behind him on his famous "March to the Sea," Sherman left a swath of destruction 300 miles long and 60 miles wide. Railroad tracks, heated red-hot in giant bonfires, were twisted around trees and telegraph poles. Bridges lay in tumbled ruins. Crops were uprooted, livestock slaughtered, and farmhouses and outbuildings reduced to ashes. Sherman's purpose, of course, was to weaken southern resistance, but he also left a legacy of bitterness among southerners.

By the spring of 1865, Sherman's army was moving northward through the Carolinas with General Joseph E. Johnston's weary army trying to slow him down.

Meanwhile, back in Virginia, General Grant in May 1864 had been hammering away at Richmond, pushing through difficult terrain against fierce Confederate resistance (see map 8, opposite page). Grant's losses in this Wilderness Campaign were enormous, but he drove on. Despite the frightful cost in lives and the seemingly endless battles, Grant refused to abandon his objective. "I propose to fight it out along this line if it takes all summer," he wrote in May 1864 to General Halleck.

Grant's words were unhappily prophetic for the Confederate cause. He did fight all summer—and into the fall and the winter. But the superior resources and manpower of the Union were at last having a decisive effect.

Lee surrenders. In the spring of 1865, Sherman's army continued to move northward, and Grant's troops were hammering at the doors of Richmond. On April 2 General Lee withdrew from the city, and the Stars and Stripes at last flew over the former Confederate capital.

From Richmond, Lee moved swiftly westward toward Lynchburg, Virginia, with Grant close on his heels (see map 8, this page). Lee thought for a time that he might escape with his army into North Carolina and there carry on the war with General Johnston, who was as yet undefeated. But Lee was in a hopeless position. The jaws of the northern trap were beginning to close. Finally, on April 9, accepting the hopelessness of his situation, Lee surrendered.

Appomattox Court House. The two men, Lee and Grant, met in a house in the small village of Appomattox Court House in Virginia. Lee was in full dress uniform with jewel-studded sword at his side, Grant in a private's blouse, unbuttoned at the neck.

Grant offered Lee generous terms. He allowed the officers and men to return to their homes with the promise that they would not again take up arms against the Union. The troops had to surrender their weapons, but Grant permitted Lee's officers to keep their pistols and swords. When Lee mentioned the severe condition of southern agriculture, Grant said, "Let all the men who claim to own a horse or mule, take the animals home with them to work their

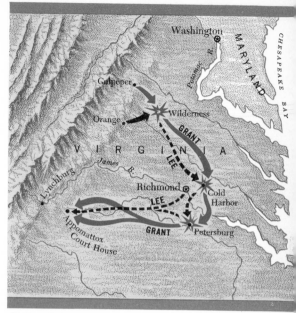

❽ Grant's Campaign Around Richmond: May 1864– April 9, 1865

little farms. This," he added, "will do much toward conciliating our people."

The meeting ended, Lee mounted his famous horse Traveler and rode off. Union troops started to cheer. Grant ordered them to be silent. "The war is over; the rebels are our countrymen again," he said.

So the long bitter conflict ended.

◢ SECTION SURVEY

1. It has been said that the Union blockade was as effective in overpowering the South as were the armies of Grant and Sherman. Discuss this point.

2. Compare the significance of the Union victories in the west with that of the Confederate victories in the east in 1862.

3. Discuss the significance of the battles of Gettysburg and Vicksburg.

4. What were the terms of surrender that Grant offered Lee?

IDENTIFY: battles of Bull Run, Army of the Potomac, gunboats, battle of Vicksburg, Sherman's "March to the Sea"; McClellan, Halleck, Forrest, Albert S. Johnston, Farragut, Pope, "Stonewall" Jackson, "Jeb" Stuart, Pickett, Meade, Joseph E. Johnston; July 3, 1863; April 9, 1865.

3 The war brings severe hardships to the southern people

The war completely transformed the lives of the people in the Confederacy. During the first few weeks there was the excitement—and the sadness—as men and boys left for the battlefields, confident and in high spirits. After a few months, as casualty lists grew longer and shortages of food and other supplies began to pinch, the war became a grim reality, relieved on occasion by news of a Confederate victory. From 1861 to 1865, the South was a nation in arms.

Manpower and the draft. During the first year of the war, the Confederacy relied entirely on voluntary enlistments. On April 16, 1862, however, it turned to *conscription*, or the draft, making every white man between the ages of eighteen and thirty-five liable for military service unless lawfully exempt.

The draft was unpopular, especially in the mountainous regions, where Confederate conscription officers were sometimes shot or driven off. In general, southerners insisted that conscription was contrary to their new constitution. Strong believers in states' rights, they refused to admit that the Confederate government had the authority to reach into a state and pull a man out of his home into military service.

Many southerners also objected to the draft on the ground that it was unfair. The original conscription law exempted workers in a long list of occupations. It also permitted a drafted man to hire a substitute. Since the "substitute" provision favored people of wealth who could afford to hire substitutes, poorer people grumbled that the conflict was "a rich man's war and a poor man's fight." Late in 1863 the Confederate government stopped the privilege of hiring substitutes, and in 1864 it reduced the exemptions and increased the draft limits to include all white men between the ages of seventeen and fifty.

During the war, by voluntary enlistment and the draft, the Confederacy maintained an army of about 400,000 men. Altogether, from 1861 to 1865, the Confederacy enlisted or drafted about 1,300,000.

Southern finances. Raising money was a far more difficult problem for the Confederacy than raising manpower, for most of the wealth of the South was in land and slaves. The Union blockade, which, as you know, cut off most of the South's trade with other countries, also prevented the Confederacy from raising money from customs duties.

During the opening year of the war, patriotic southerners lent $100,000,000 to the Confederacy in return for war bonds, but this source of income was soon exhausted. The government bor-

ARTILLERY OFFICER

GENERAL OFFICER

INFANTRY PRIVATE

NORTH CAROLINA MILITIAMAN

CAVALRY COLONEL

CAVALRY CORP

Southern uniforms—War Between the States

rowed another $15,000,000 from abroad, and raised about $100,000,000 from taxation. But the income from borrowing and taxation was far from adequate to pay for the war, and the Confederacy had to rely mainly on "paper money."

Before the war ended, the government printed more than $1,000,000,000 in Confederate bank notes. The only value these bank notes had was the promise of the Confederate government to redeem them—that is, exchange them for gold or silver—"after the ratification of a treaty of peace between the Confederate States and the United States of America." As the prospect of a southern victory became increasingly remote, the Confederate currency steadily declined in value. By 1865 each dollar bill was worth only 1.6 cents in gold. With northern victory the Confederate war bonds and bank notes became worthless.

Meanwhile, prices soared during the war. People who had goods to sell demanded more and more of the Confederate bank notes in return for their commodities. Southerners used to say that a woman could take money to market in a basket and bring her purchases home in a pocketbook.

Southern industry. But paper money was only one of the reasons for skyrocketing prices. Another reason was the shortage of goods. The Union blockade deprived southerners of practically all luxuries, such as tea and coffee, as well as many of the most essential products —clothing, hardware, medicines and soap. As one historian put it, "The blockade was the real destroyer of the South."

Despite heroic efforts manufacturing establishments in the Confederacy could not supply all the needs of either the army or the civilian population. Confederate soldiers often marched without shoes, slept without blankets, and lived in ragged clothing. Fortunately for the Confederate troops, they won many battles and captured large supplies of Yankee food, clothing, and munitions.

Agriculture and transportation. Civilians felt the pinch of hard times even more than the soldiers. City people suf-

NATHAN BEDFORD FORREST

When the war broke out, Nathan Bedford Forrest (1821–77) was a successful planter and businessman and an influential citizen of Memphis, Tennessee. He promptly enlisted as a private in the Tennessee Mounted Riflers. A few weeks later, however, the governor of the state sent for him, gave him a colonel's commission, and authorized him to raise and command a regiment of cavalry. One of the ablest military leaders in the Confederacy, before the war ended Forrest rose to the rank of lieutenant general.

During the last two years of the war, Forrest carried out long, daring raids behind enemy lines. Union General Sherman once called Forrest's raiders "the most dangerous set of men which this war has turned loose on the world. They are splendid shots," Sherman added, "and utterly reckless."

Actually, Forrest was a highly intelligent commander who never discounted the odds against him. His simple but effective rule was to "get there first with the most men"—a principle often misquoted as "git there fustest with the mostest."

Forrest led a charmed life. During the course of the war, twenty-nine horses were shot from under him, and on many occasions he escaped almost miraculously from encircling enemy forces.

In a farewell message to his troops, written on May 9, 1865, Nathan Bedford Forrest demonstrated that he could be as honorable in defeat as he had been courageous in war: "I have never on the field of battle," he wrote to his men, "sent you where I was unwilling to go myself; nor would I now advise you to a course which I felt myself unwilling to pursue. You have been good soldiers; you can be good citizens. Obey the laws, preserve your honor, and the government to which you have surrendered can afford to be and will be magnanimous."

fered most of all from the shortage of goods and the soaring prices. By 1863 many southerners faced starvation.

This tragic situation was not caused by lack of food in the Confederacy, for the South was an agricultural region. In addition, there was plenty of labor to work the farms and plantations, for the slaves, on the whole, remained loyal to their masters. The serious problem was lack of transportation.

When the war started, the Confederacy had only about a third of the railroad mileage then in existence—about 9000 miles out of a total of more than 30,000 miles for the entire country. Southern planters had depended largely on the rivers to send their cotton to the seaports. As the war continued, the Confederacy had difficulty keeping even its limited railroad mileage in operation. Because they had no way to replace worn-out equipment, southerners tore up branch lines and used branch line engines, cars, and rails to keep main lines in operation.

The transportation problem in the South was so severe that, before the war ended, people in Richmond rioted for food while barns in the Shenandoah Valley were filled with wheat. So it was throughout much of the South.

During the last few months of the war, the food shortage became so desperate that many Confederate soldiers deserted to get back home and help feed their families. For four long years the war brought sorrow and suffering to rich and poor alike in the South.

ℯ **SECTION SURVEY**

1. On what grounds did many southerners object to military conscription?
2. What methods did the Confederate government use to raise money for the war?
3. Why was the issuance of huge amounts of paper money harmful to the southern people?
4. Show how lack of industry helped to defeat the South.
5. Explain why lack of transportation helped to defeat the South.

4 Life behind Union lines undergoes important changes

The North, with its superiority in material resources, never experienced the hardship and suffering that southerners had to endure. Nevertheless, the war created problems and brought many changes in the everyday affairs of life in the northern states.

Manpower and the draft. The North, like the South, at first recruited its troops by volunteer enlistments. On March 3, 1863, however, Congress passed a conscription law making all able-bodied male citizens between the ages of twenty and forty-five liable for military service. As in the South the law allowed a drafted man to hire a substitute. The federal law also permitted a drafted man to buy exemption by the payment of $300 to the government.

The Conscription Act aroused violent opposition. Riots occurred in a number of cities. The most serious riot broke out in New York City on July 13, 1863, and lasted for four days. Mobs roamed the streets, broke into shops, burned homes, and killed and plundered in an orgy of violence. Seventy-six people were killed before troops, rushed to New York from General Meade's army at Gettysburg, could restore order.

Of more than 2,000,000 men who served in the Union armies during the four years of warfare, the draft provided only a small fraction. Much more effective as a means of raising troops was the "bounty system." In an effort to attract volunteers, the federal, state, and local governments each paid a "bounty" to all who volunteered for service. When the federal, state, and local bounties were totaled, a man might receive as much as $1000 for enlisting.

While the bounty system was effective as a means of recruitment, it did give rise to the dishonest practice of "bounty jumping." A man would enlist in one locality and collect his bounties, then desert and re-enlist under another name in another locality and collect additional bounties. Some "bounty jumpers" enlisted and deserted twenty or thirty times before they were caught.

Northern finances. In its efforts to raise money for the war, the North relied on the tariff, war bonds, an income tax, and issuance of paper money.

From 1832 to 1861, southern planters and many farmers in the West continued to oppose high tariffs. In 1861, however, with several southern states out of the Union, the Republicans in Congress promptly passed the Morrill Tariff Act, raising import duties to an average of 25 per cent of the value of the imported goods. The Morrill Tariff Act was designed to protect manufacturers from the competition of European rivals. After war broke out, Congress revised the rates upward until by 1864 they reached an average of 47 per cent, the highest up to that time.

Southern planters and midwestern farmers had also favored a decentralized banking system. In such a system, state and local banks were free to issue their own bank notes and to make loans with little if any control from the federal government. After 1861, however, the Republican Congress adopted a law that did away with state bank notes and established a system of national banks.

In 1863 Congress passed the National Banking Act. The new law permitted five or more individuals with a capital of $50,000 to secure a charter and organize a national bank. The directors of the bank were required to invest at least one third of the bank's capital in United States bonds. When the bank had deposited these bonds with the Secretary of the Treasury, it was allowed to issue national bank notes up to 90 per cent of the value of the bonds. This provision had two important effects. First, it encouraged banks to buy government bonds (that is, to lend the government money). Second, it provided a sound and uniform currency for the entire country.

Neither the tariff nor the sale of government bonds to banks and to individuals provided enough money to finance northern war costs. In an effort to secure the necessary money, Congress passed an income tax. By the end of the war, incomes between $600, and $5000 were being taxed 5 per cent, incomes of $5000 or more were being taxed 10 per cent.

Congress also issued paper money, known as *greenbacks* because the back of the money was usually printed in green. The value of the "greenbacks," like the value of the Confederate paper money, depended upon the government's ability to redeem them in gold or silver at some future date. As a result, their value rose with every northern victory and fell when the North suffered defeats. At one point, the "greenbacks" were worth only 35 cents of a dollar's worth of gold, but by the end of the war their value had risen to 78 cents. Paper money helped to drive prices up-

Northern uniforms—War Between the States

THE GATLING GUN

In 1862 Dr. Richard J. Gatling took out a patent on a weapon which was destined to revolutionize warfare. The Gatling gun had six barrels, which were loaded and fired by a hand crank. It could be swung in any direction and, therefore, could be highly effective against advancing troops. In spite of its value, the Gatling gun met with only limited use during the War Between the States. In 1866, however, it was officially adopted by the United States Army and by the armies of a number of foreign countries. In 1893 Dr. Gatling added an electric motor drive with which he was able to fire 3000 rounds a minute.

In the meantime, in 1884, Hiram Stevens Maxim had invented a single-barrel machine gun which used the recoil of the barrel to do the loading and firing. The Maxim machine gun and, a decade later, the Browning machine gun, which used the discharge gases to operate itself, were the first truly automatic weapons. As a result, in 1911 the War Department declared the Gatling gun obsolete. For more than forty years, machine guns based on the Maxim or the Browning principles had the field to themselves.

And yet, had Dr. Gatling lived, he would have seen his idea revived. In 1956 a new weapon, the Vulcan, was demonstrated at Maryland's Aberdeen Proving Ground. Like the first Gatling gun of 1862, the Vulcan is a multi-barreled weapon. It fires so rapidly that the individual explosions merge into a steady drone.

ward, but inflation never got out of hand as it did in the South.

Northern industry booms. Inflation did not get out of hand in the North partly because of the ability of northern industry to produce all the materials the armed services and the civilian population needed. With the tariff to protect them from foreign competition and huge war orders to meet, manufacturers did not hesitate to build new factories. For example, in Philadelphia alone 180 new factories opened between 1862 and 1864.

The war also stimulated the development and use of laborsaving machines. Elias Howe's sewing machine, first patented in 1846, made it possible for clothing manufacturers to produce uniforms more rapidly for the Union armies. A machine for sewing uppers to the soles of shoes, an improved version of which was patented by Gordon McKay in 1862, put shoe manufacturing on a mass production basis.

There was a great deal of "profiteering" during the war as greedy businessmen took unfair profits at a time of national necessity. Even worse, there were cases of outright business deceit. Some manufacturers sold the government blankets and uniforms of such poor quality that they fell apart in the first heavy rains. As stories of these practices got around, the Michigan legislature charged that "traitors in the disguise of patriots have plundered our treasury."

But "profiteers" were a by-product of a development far more enduring—the enormous expansion of American industry. During the war years the United States took a long step forward on the road that was to lead it to the position of the world's greatest industrial power.

Agricultural expansion. Northeastern and midwestern agriculture, as well as industry, was greatly stimulated during the war years by government aid, war orders, and the development of laborsaving machines.

The Republican Party, as you have seen, represented a combination of midwestern farmers and northeastern businessmen. It is not surprising, therefore, to find that the Republican Congress passed legislation favorable to farmers.

The Homestead Act of 1862 gave 160 acres of land to any man or woman who paid a small registration fee and lived on his *homestead*° for five years. Under this act, between 1862 and the end of the war, the United States government gave about 2,500,000 acres of land to some 15,000 settlers. Most of the new farms were in the Middle West.

In 1862 the government also adopted two other measures to aid agriculture, as well as industry: (1) It created the United States Department of Agriculture, and (2) with the Morrill Act of 1862, it launched the United States upon a huge program of agricultural and industrial education. The Morrill Act gave each state 30,000 acres of land for each Senator and Representative it had in Congress under the 1860 census. The income from the sale or rental of this land was to be used for purposes of education—a special kind of education. Each state was to create at least one college in which agriculture and the "mechanic arts," like engineering, were to be emphasized. These colleges came to be called "land-grant colleges."

Farmers of the northeastern and midwestern states prospered with rising prices and a ready market for all they could produce. With money in their pockets, thousands of farmers were able to buy laborsaving machinery, such as mechanical reapers, which had been invented by Obed Hussey and Cyrus H. McCormick in the early 1830's. The reaper, improved plows, and other farm machinery helped to speed the revolution in agriculture that was gaining momentum during the war years.

Growth of the railroads. Railroads, no less than industry and agriculture, also prospered during the war. For example, the value of Erie Railroad stock increased sevenfold in three years. New lines were also built, many of them with

---

° *homestead:* a farm, including the farmhouse and other buildings.

Lincoln's Gettysburg Address (1863)

*F*our score and seven years ago our fathers brought forth on this continent a new nation, conceived in liberty, and dedicated to the proposition that all men are created equal.

Now we are engaged in a great civil war, testing whether that nation, or any nation so conceived and so dedicated, can long endure. We are met on a great battlefield of that war. We have come to dedicate a portion of that field as a final resting place for those who here gave their lives that that nation might live. It is altogether fitting and proper that we should do this.

But, in a larger sense, we cannot dedicate—we cannot consecrate—we cannot hallow—this ground. The brave men, living and dead, who struggled here, have consecrated it far above our poor power to add or detract. The world will little note nor long remember what we say here, but it can never forget what they did here. It is for us, the living, rather, to be dedicated here to the unfinished work which they who fought here have thus far so nobly advanced. It is rather for us to be here dedicated to the great task remaining before us—that from these honored dead we take increased devotion to that cause for which they gave the last full measure of devotion; that we here highly resolve that these dead shall not have died in vain; that this nation, under God, shall have a new birth of freedom; and that government of the people, by the people, for the people, shall not perish from the earth.

---

the help of government *subsidies,* or financial aids, and land grants. As you have seen, these lines helped to unite the Northeast and the Middle West.

One of the most important railroad developments during the war was the decision of the Republican Congress to build a transcontinental railroad, which people had been talking about for a long time. In 1862 Congress granted a charter to the Union Pacific and the Central Pacific Railroads, authorizing them to build a railway from Omaha, in Nebraska Territory, to California. Congress also promised the railroads liberal cash subsidies and generous gifts of land along the right of way. Although actual construction did not begin until after the war (page 448), the subsidies and land grants showed how far the new Republican government was prepared to go in providing federal aid for business and industry.

The changes that took place behind the Union lines during the years from 1861 to 1865 were of great importance to the future of the nation. As you will see, the growth of industry, stimulated by the war, gained momentum in the years following the war.

✔ SECTION SURVEY

1. What methods did the North use to raise an army?
2. (a) Describe the methods used by the North to finance the war. (b) Explain the National Banking Act of 1863.
3. Give the reasons for the boom in northern industry during the war.
4. What conditions stimulated agricultural prosperity in the North?
5. Indicate the steps taken by Congress during the war to encourage railroad building.

IDENTIFY: New York Draft Riots, "bounty jumpers," Morrill Tariff Act, "greenbacks," "profiteering," Homestead Act, Morrill Act of 1862, subsidies; Elias Howe, Gordon McKay, Hussey, McCormick; 1862, 1863.

5 The Union deals with political problems at home and abroad

The war thrust an almost unbearable burden on the shoulders of President Lincoln. Even while he was occupied with the conduct of the fighting itself, he had to deal with a host of problems, including the conduct of foreign affairs.

Great Britain and France. During the first two years of the war, the governments of Great Britain and France were friendly to the Confederate States of America. This friendship deeply concerned President Lincoln and the federal government.

There were strong reasons why Great Britain, France, and other European nations wanted the South to win the war. European manufacturers, particularly in Great Britain, looked forward to the creation of a new nation that would provide them with cotton and other raw materials and, at the same time, place no tariffs on the importation of their manufactured goods. European shipowners looked forward to the weakening of their business competitors in New England and the Middle Atlantic states if the North lost the war.

To be sure, millions of Europeans hoped for the destruction of slavery in the South. But Lincoln at first discouraged these people when, as you will see, he made it clear that he was not fighting the war to free the slaves, but to preserve the Union.

Strained relations. Only a few months after the war started, an incident occurred that nearly led to a disastrous break between the United States and Great Britain. The trouble started when a Union war ship commanded by Captain Charles Wilkes stopped a British steamer, the *Trent*, and seized two Confederate commissioners to Great Britain and France—James M. Mason and John Slidell. The British, furious at this violation of their rights as a neutral, talked of war with the United States and actually sent troops to Canada. But President Lincoln avoided trouble by releasing the two Confederate agents and admitting that Captain Wilkes had been wrong.

Even more serious was the problem of Confederate war ships built in British shipyards. A number of these war ships, among them the *Florida* and the *Alabama*, left Great Britain in the summer of 1862 and began to destroy large numbers of Union merchant vessels. But Great Britain stopped the construction of other Confederate war ships when the American minister to Great Britain pointedly warned the British foreign minister, "It would be superfluous in me to point out to your lordship that this is war."

Fortunately for the Union, during the closing months of 1862 northern victories on the battlefield and a proclamation by President Lincoln against slavery ended the threat of foreign intervention on the side of the South.

The Emancipation Proclamation. President Lincoln believed that slavery was wrong, but when war did come he refused to turn the war into a crusade to free the slaves. He realized that such a crusade would throw the border states into the Confederacy.

But the anti-slavery forces in Congress were not satisfied to leave matters at this point. In April 1862, therefore, Congress abolished slavery in the District of Columbia, paying the owners for the loss of their slaves. Later in the spring, Congress abolished slavery in United States Territories. Congress also suggested the possibility of providing financial aid to any of the southern states that would adopt a program freeing their slaves over a period of years.

As late as August 1862, Lincoln revealed his reluctance to turn the war into a crusade to free the slaves. "My paramount object in the struggle," he declared, "is to save the Union, and it is not either to save or to destroy slavery. If I could save the Union without freeing any slave, I would do it, and if I could save it by freeing all the slaves, I would do it. And if I could save it by freeing some and leaving others alone, I would also do that. What I do about slavery and the colored race I do because I believe it helps to save this Union. And what I forbear, I forbear because I do not believe it would help to save this Union."

By the fall of 1862, however, Lincoln was convinced that he must go much further than he had yet gone to win the support of anti-slavery people in both the United States and in other countries. He knew that a war fought, in part at least, to free the slaves would win the support of millions of Europeans and

CONFEDERATE SEA RAIDERS

Best known of the Confederate sea raiders was the *Alabama*. Built in England, she sailed from Liverpool in July 1862, and after a brief but effective career was destroyed off the French coast by the *U.S.S. Kearsarge*. Northerners, angry with the British, circulated a picture of the *Alabama* bearing the caption, "Built of English oak, in an English yard, armed with English guns, manned by an English crew, and sunk in an English Channel."

Less well known is the sequel to the *Alabama* story. Some of the officers and crew of the *Alabama* swam ashore from the sinking vessel and made their way to England. There they joined a number of other men who pretended to be ordinary citizens, but were actually officers and men of the Confederate Navy. One night in October 1864, they sailed from Liverpool for the Madeira Islands. There they boarded the vessel *Sea King*, which had been secretly purchased in England. Renaming her the *Shenandoah*, they hoisted the Confederate flag and put out to sea.

They were headed for the whaling grounds off the Alaskan coast. On the way they sank a number of Union vessels. By the time they reached the whaling grounds, Lee had surrendered at Appomattox. But the captain of the *Shenandoah*, refusing to believe the war was over, continued to sink Union ships. At one time eight whalers were burning within sight of the Confederate raider. Finally, the truth could no longer be denied, and the *Shenandoah* sailed for England. During her year at sea she had destroyed 38 ships and taken 1053 prisoners—all without fighting a battle or killing a man.

The activities of the *Shenandoah*, *Alabama*, and other Confederate cruisers built or purchased in Great Britain finally cost the British government $15½ million in gold. This was the amount an arbitration commission—which met in Geneva, Switzerland, in 1872—awarded the United States as compensation for damages to American shipping.

greatly lessen the danger of foreign intervention on the side of the Confederate States. It would also win Lincoln and his government the wholehearted support of the abolitionists in the North.

Lincoln prepared his Emancipation Proclamation, but kept it secret, waiting for a northern victory on the battlefield. On September 22, 1862, five days after Union forces stopped Lee's invasion of the North in the bloody Battle of Antietam, Lincoln issued the famous Emancipation Proclamation. In this Proclamation he declared that all slaves in states or parts of states still fighting against the United States on January 1, 1863, would from that time on be forever *emancipated*—that is, free—wherever the Union armies could liberate them or they could escape to the North.

The Thirteenth Amendment. President Lincoln used his Constitutional authority as Commander-in-Chief of the United States military forces to issue the Emancipation Proclamation. Whether this authority gave him the right to free the slaves was an unanswered question. Moreover, the mere Proclamation did not, of course, actually free any slaves either in the border states or elsewhere.

In order to settle the slavery question once and for all, as you will see, an amendment freeing the slaves everywhere throughout the United States and the Territories of the United States was introduced in Congress early in 1865. This, the Thirteenth Amendment, was finally ratified by the necessary three fourths of the states, eight months after the war ended.

The Copperheads. In the North—as well as in the South—there was from the beginning active opposition to the war. Leaders of the opposition in the North were called "Copperheads" by Union sympathizers, after the stealthy and poisonous snake of that name. The Copperheads argued that the cost of the war in lives, money, and loss of personal liberty was too great to be justified. They also argued that the South could not be defeated and that the war was therefore useless. Finally, they insisted that even if the North should win, a Union based on compulsion was a denial of the Constitution and of democracy itself.

The strength of the Copperheads, most of whom were members of the Democratic Party, varied from place to place and from month to month. The more extreme Copperheads organized secret societies such as the Knights of the Golden Circle and the Sons of Liberty. They discouraged enlistment and encouraged men to desert. They also helped Confederate prisoners to escape and smuggled war materials into the Confederacy.

■ The War Between the States has been called the first modern war, in part because it introduced the Gatling gun, balloons for aerial observation, and these forerunners of the large ironclad steamships of a later day. The *Merrimac* (left) was southern; the *Monitor* (right) was northern.

■ Mathew Brady was the first great American news photographer. Throughout the war he was everywhere behind Union lines, taking pictures that are priceless today. After the war, he took this picture of Union troops celebrating their victory in a parade at Washington, D.C.

The most influential Copperhead leader was Clement L. Vallandigham, a member of Congress from Ohio. He was finally arrested in 1863 and convicted of opposing the war effort. Lincoln banished him to the Confederacy, but Vallandigham promptly moved to Canada. While in exile he was nominated by the Democrats for the governorship of Ohio, but lost the election.

The election of 1864. Dissatisfaction over the war split the Democratic Party. In the election of 1864, large numbers of Democrats joined the Republicans to form the so-called Union Party. This party chose Lincoln for the Presidency and Andrew Johnson, a former Democratic member of Congress from Tennessee but an opponent of secession and the Confederacy, for the Vice-Presidency. The Democratic Party named General George B. McClellan as its candidate for the Presidency.

Anti-war feeling was running so high in 1864 that President Lincoln fully expected to be defeated. "We are now on the brink of destruction," he wrote to a friend. "It appears to me that the Almighty is against me, and I can hardly see a ray of hope."

But the tide of the war turned in favor of the North during the months immediately preceding the election. Sherman's capture of Atlanta in September and his march through Georgia convinced many voters that the end of the war was in sight. Moreover, Lincoln's opponent, General McClellan, refused during the campaign to support the platform of his own Democratic Party, which declared that the war was a failure and ought to be stopped immediately. As a result, Lincoln won an overwhelming victory, receiving 212 electoral votes to 21 for the Democratic candidate. The mere fact that a Presidential election was successfully held in wartime was in itself a victory for representative government.

SECTION SURVEY

1. Why did France and Great Britain sympathize with the Confederacy?

2. What was Lincoln's main reason for refusing to abolish slavery at the start of the war?

3. (a) Explain the provisions of the Emancipation Proclamation. (b) Since the Proclamation did not actually free any slaves, why did Lincoln issue it?

4. Compare, in the form of a chart, the parties, candidates, issues, and results in the election of 1864.

IDENTIFY: *Trent* affair, *Alabama* settlement, Thirteenth Amendment, Copperheads, Union Party; Captain Wilkes, Mason and Slidell, Vallandigham, Andrew Johnson; January 1, 1863; 1865.

401

■ CHAPTER SURVEY

(For review, see Section Surveys, pages 384, 391, 394, 398, 401.)

Points to Discuss: 1. (a) Why was it important that Lincoln keep the border states in the Union? (b) Discuss Lincoln's statesmanship in meeting this problem.

2. (a) Indicate the over-all military strategy of the South at the start of the war. (b) Evaluate the success of the South in carrying out this strategy.

3. (a) What were the several different plans of attack of the North at the war's beginning? (b) Which proved to be the most successful and why?

4. The blockade was the real destroyer of the South. Discuss.

5. Compare the methods used by the North and South to finance the war.

6. Contrast economic conditions in the North and South during the war.

7. Explain the difference between the Emancipation Proclamation and the Thirteenth Amendment.

8. Lincoln's leadership has often been given as a major reason for the North's victory. Do you agree? Justify your views.

9. How does the "American System" compare with the economic policies of the 1860's?

Using Maps and Charts: 1. (a) Using the map on page 383, identify the major land and sea campaigns undertaken by the North and South. (b) Check your accuracy by using the maps on pages 385–91.

2. The map on page 388 refers to the battle of Gettysburg. Reconstruct the battle by use of the map data and then check your account against the text.

3. Reconstruct the closing battles of the war by use of the map on page 391.

4. Referring to the map on page 827, compare the population of the North and South in 1860.

Consulting the Sources: See Ellis, *Docs.*, No. 110, concerning American Diplomatic Relations with the Papal States. No. 114 contains some of the poems of the Poet of the Confederacy, Father Abram Ryan.

■ TRACING THE MAIN IDEAS

In 1865 the terrible trial by fire and sword came to an end and the nation was in a position to estimate its losses. The conflict had been frightfully expensive in men and money. It cost the southern states more than a billion dollars, the northern states several times that amount. After all pensions and other costs were paid, the war probably cost the American people a total of ten billion dollars. It was also frightfully costly in life. Not counting those permanently injured, the North lost about 359,-000 men; the South lost about 258,000 men.

The war had many far-reaching results. It ended the doctrine of secession. It strengthened the Union by increasing the power of the federal government at the expense of the states. It strengthened democracy by showing that a representative form of government could operate successfully in wartime.

Not least important, the four-year trial by fire and sword helped to speed the development of American industry.

In the spring of 1865, the people of the United States stood on the threshold of a new era. New opportunities were opening before them. But of course they could not at the time know this. They could look only into the immediate future. And the big problem they faced, northerners and southerners alike, was "to bind the nation's wounds" and join hands as a reunited people.

Unit Survey (Reread "Tracing the Main Ideas," pages 379, 402.)

OUTSTANDING EVENTS

1844 James K. Polk elected President.
1848 Zachary Taylor elected President.
1850 Taylor dies; Millard Fillmore becomes President.
1850 Compromise of 1850.
1851–56 Kelly, Bessemer develop processes for making steel cheaply.
1852 Franklin Pierce elected President.
1853 Perry arrives in Japan.
1854 Ostend Manifesto is issued.
1854 Kansas-Nebraska Act.
1854 Republican Party is formed.
1856 James Buchanan elected President.
1857 Dred Scott decision.
1858 Lincoln-Douglas debates.
1859 John Brown raids Harper's Ferry.
1860 Abraham Lincoln elected President.
1860 South Carolina secedes.
1861 Morrill Tariff Act.
1861 South fires on Fort Sumter; War Between States (1861–65) begins.
1862 Battle of *Monitor* and *Merrimac.*
1862 Emancipation Proclamation.
1862 Homestead Act.
1863 Battle of Gettysburg.
1863 National Banking Act.
1864 Lincoln re-elected President.
1865 Lee surrenders to Grant.
1865 Lincoln is assassinated; Andrew Johnson becomes President.
1865 Thirteenth Amendment ratified.

THEN AND NOW

1. (a) Compare military conscription during the War Between the States with conscription today. (b) What lessons have been learned from the past?
2. Compare the major political parties, their 1860 party conventions, platforms, and choice of candidates with those of the major parties in 1960.

EXTENDING YOUR HORIZON

1. Compare the interpretation of Lincoln as given in Richard Hofstadter's *The American Political Tradition* [Knopf (Vintage)], Chapter 5, with that in Clinton Rossiter's *The American Presidency* [Harcourt, Brace; New American Library (Mentor)], pages 73–75.
2. Valuable insight into Lee's military problems and strategy can be gained

through reading Bruce Catton, "Decision at Antietam," *American Heritage,* August 1958; and Clifford Dowdey, "General Lee's Unsolved Problem," concerning his relations with Jefferson Davis, in *American Heritage,* April 1955.
3. For a comparison with the journalism of a modern war correspondent, read Sylvanus Cadwallader, "Three Years with Grant," *American Heritage,* October 1955.

INDIVIDUAL ACTIVITIES

1. Make a chart showing how each section (North, South, and West) stood on each of the following issues: (a) tariff, (b) United States Bank, (c) internal improvements at national expense, (d) cheap land, (e) slavery.
2. Prepare a short talk on "Henry Clay —the Great Compromiser." Consult Clement Eaton's *Henry Clay and the Art of American Politics* (Little, Brown), and his article, "Everybody Liked Henry Clay," in the *American Heritage,* October 1956.
3. Give a report on Clara Barton's work.

GROUP ACTIVITIES

1. Let a capable group of students undertake a more thorough investigation of the Compromise of 1850 and the events of the decade following in an effort to determine why there was no "Compromise of 1860." Helpful sources to consult include John Kennedy's essay dealing with Webster and the Compromise of 1850 in his *Profiles in Courage* (Harper: Pocket Books), the pamphlets in *Problems in American Civilization,* "Amherst Series" (Heath) entitled *The Compromise of 1850* and *Slavery as a Cause of the Civil War,* and the article by Allan Nevins, "Buchanan, Douglas, and the Imminent War," *American Heritage,* August 1956. A thoughtful reading of Howard K. Beale's essay, "What Historians Have Said about the Causes of the Civil War," in Book One of *The Making of American History* edited by Donald Sheehan (Dryden), will lead the students to realize that there are no easy answers to the problem.
2. "If, then, the student of American religious history were seeking to disprove the fallacy that all Catholics think alike, he

could hardly do better than to choose the Civil War as ground whereon to rest his case." Let a group of students endeavor to support or refute this statement of Monsignor Ellis from his book *American Catholicism,* page 98, by investigating the attitudes of Catholic immigrants and hierarchy toward slavery, secession, and the War Between the States. Consult Chapter IV of *American Catholicism* and study related documents in the same author's *Documents of American Catholic History.* See, too, Theodore Maynard, *The Story of American Catholicism,* and the *Dictionary of American Biography.*

SUGGESTED FURTHER READING

BIOGRAPHY

CAPERS, GERALD N., *Stephen A. Douglas, Defender of the Union,* Little, Brown.

CATTON, BRUCE, *Grant Moves South,* Little, Brown.

COMMAGER, HENRY STEELE, *America's Robert E. Lee,* Houghton Mifflin.

*CURRENT, RICHARD N., *The Lincoln Nobody Knows,* McGraw-Hill.

EHRLICH, LEONARD, *God's Angry Man,* Pocket Books. About John Brown.

HORAN, J. D., *Mathew Brady: Historian with a Camera,* Crown.

LORANT, STEFAN, *The Life of Abraham Lincoln: A Short Illustrated Biography,* New American Library (Signet Books).

NOLAN, JEANNETTE, *The Little Giant,* Messner. About Stephen A. Douglas.

PETRY, ANN, *Harriet Tubman: Conductor on the Underground Railroad,* Crowell.

*ROSS, ISHBEL, *Angel of the Battlefield: The Life of Clara Barton,* Harper.

SANDBURG, CARL, *Abraham Lincoln: The Prairie Years* and *The War Years,* One-volume edition, Harcourt, Brace.

——, *Storm over the Land,* Harcourt, Brace. Lincoln during the war.

STERN, PHILIP VAN DOREN, *The Man Who Killed Lincoln,* Random House.

SWANBERG, W. A., *First Blood: Story of Fort Sumter,* Scribner.

THOMAS, BENJAMIN P., *Abraham Lincoln,* Knopf.

WILSON, FORREST, *Crusader in Crinoline,* Lippincott; and others. About Harriet Beecher Stowe.

WOODWARD, W. E., *Meet General Grant,* Liveright; Tudor.

OTHER NONFICTION

ANGLE, PAUL M., ed., *The Lincoln Reader,* Rutgers Univ. Press; Pocket Books. Selections about Lincoln by sixty-five authors.

——, and EARL SCHENCK MIERS, *The Living Lincoln,* Rutgers Univ. Press.

BISHOP, JIM, *The Day Lincoln Was Shot,* Harper; Bantam.

CATTON, BRUCE, *Glory Road,* Doubleday. Nonfiction by a leading authority on the War Between the States.

——, *Mr. Lincoln's Army,* Doubleday.

——, *A Stillness at Appomattox,* Doubleday; Pocket Books.

——, *This Hallowed Ground: The Story of the Union Side of the Civil War,* Doubleday.

CRAVEN, AVERY, *The Coming of the Civil War,* Scribner.

DOWDEY, CLIFFORD, *The Land They Fought For,* Doubleday. The Confederacy.

LEECH, MARGARET, *Reveille in Washington,* Grosset & Dunlap (paper). Day-by-day account of life in the capital.

MEREDITH, ROY, *Storm over Sumter,* Simon and Schuster.

NEVINS, ALLAN, *Ordeal of the Union,* Scribner, 2 vols. The decade 1847–57.

——, *The Emergence of Lincoln,* Scribner, 2 vols.

PRATT, FLETCHER, *Civil War in Pictures,* Doubleday.

——, *Short History of the Civil War,* Pocket Books.

QUARLES, BENJAMIN, *The Negro in the Civil War,* Little, Brown.

WILEY, B. I., *The Life of Billy Yank,* Bobbs-Merrill. Union soldiers.

——, *The Life of Johnny Reb,* Bobbs-Merrill. Confederate soldiers.

HISTORICAL FICTION

BOYD, JAMES, *Marching On,* Grosset & Dunlap. A young southern farmer.

CHURCHILL, WINSTON, *The Crisis,* Macmillan. Famous novel about the war.

CRANE, STEPHEN, *The Red Badge of Courage,* Appleton-Century-Crofts; and others. Boy at battle of Chancellorsville.

DOWDEY, CLIFFORD, *Bugles Blow No More,* Rinehart. Picture of southern defeat.

STREET, JAMES, *Tap Roots,* Dial Press; Longmans, Green. Southern abolitionists.

——, *By Valour and Arms,* Dial Press, Longmans, Green. Attack on Vicksburg.

PART **3**

THE

NATION

REUNITED

The major themes in Part Two of this book were the growth of the nation from 17 to 36 states and the swift advance of the frontier from east of the Mississippi to the Pacific Ocean; the rise of sectionalism and the crisis of the War Between the States; and the changes that were taking place in everyday life as the Industrial Revolution gathered momentum. All these developments took place during the lifetime of Abraham Lincoln (1809–65).

Theodore Roosevelt was six years old when Lincoln was shot down by an assassin. During his rich and full life Roosevelt saw the reunited nation grow from 36 to 48 states, expand overseas, and fight a great war "to make the world safe for democracy." During Roosevelt's boyhood, the United States was still a predominantly agricultural country. Before he died in 1919, the United States had become one of the leading industrial powers of the world.

UNIT SIX

Rebuilding the Nation

1865–1900

The South Is Restored to the Union

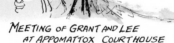

MEETING OF GRANT AND LEE
AT APPOMATTOX COURTHOUSE

Although the War Between the States came to an end at Appomattox Court House on April 9, 1865, bitterness between the North and the South continued for many years. In part this was the inevitable result of a terrible conflict in which each side was convinced that its cause was just.

But the war itself does not fully explain the bitterness that long divided these two sections of the United States. Equally important as a cause, perhaps more so, was the decade of *reconstruction*, or rebuilding the Union, that followed the end of conflict between the armed forces of the North and South.

The postwar problems facing the North and the South were formidable indeed. There were stubborn political problems involved in the task of reconstructing shattered governments and welcoming the former Confederate states back into the Union. There were complex economic problems involved in the job of rebuilding the war-devastated industries of the South and reopening normal trade relationships. There were enormously difficult social problems involved as former slaves and white people alike struggled to adjust themselves to a new way of life.

And, as you will see in this chapter and in Chapter 21, both the North and the South were confronted by a breakdown of public morality, with graft and corruption reaching into every level of government—local, state, and national. This breakdown was, in part, the inevitable consequence of a terrible war that dislocated long-established ways of life in every section of the country. But it had even deeper roots. During the latter half of the 1800's, the lives of Americans everywhere—North, South, and West—were being transformed by the rapid development of industry, a flood of immigration, and the phenomenal growth of cities.

AS THE STORY DEVELOPS

1. Presidents Lincoln and Johnson strive for lenient reconstruction.
2. The Radical Republicans destroy the work of Lincoln and Johnson.
3. The Radical Republicans enact a severe program of reconstruction.
4. After a tragic decade southern government is restored to southerners.
5. New developments in agriculture and industry create a "New South."

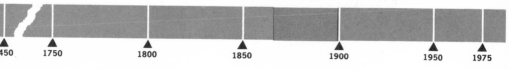

450   1750   1800   1850   1900   1950   1975

1
Presidents Lincoln and Johnson strive for lenient reconstruction

On March 4, 1865, when the end of the war was rapidly drawing near, President Lincoln stated the policy of reconstruction he intended to follow in regard to the South. The sullen roar of cannon fire in front of Richmond would soon be stilled, but the moving language of Lincoln's Second Inaugural Address was destined to live on as part of the nation's heritage.

"With malice toward none," he said; "with charity for all; with firmness in the right, as God gives us to see the right; let us strive on to finish the work we are in; to bind up the nation's wounds; to care for him who shall have borne the battle, and for his widow, and his orphan—to do all which may achieve and cherish a just and lasting peace among ourselves and with all nations."

■ As president of Washington and Lee College (later Washington and Lee University), Robert E. Lee strove to reunite the nation in spirit and in fact.

Lincoln's program. Lincoln's were not idle words. He had already taken steps to develop a program of reconstruction based upon the policy of "charity for all," and had every intention of carrying out that program.

As early as December 8, 1863, Lincoln outlined his program for restoring the South to the Union in his Proclamation of Amnesty° and Reconstruction. This program was based on Lincoln's theory that the Confederate states had never succeeded in leaving the Union. They had for a time left the family circle, so to speak, but they were still part of the family, and the immediate problem was to get them back into the family circle as rapidly as possible.

The plan Lincoln proposed for reestablishing what he called the "proper political relation" consisted of two major steps. First, he offered full pardon to all southerners who would take an oath of allegiance to the Union and promise to accept the federal laws and proclamations dealing with slavery. (The only southerners Lincoln excluded from this offer were men who had resigned civil and military positions under the federal government to serve the Confederacy, members of the Confederate government, Confederate army officers above the rank of colonel, and Confederate navy officers above the rank of lieutenant.) Second, when in any southern state 10 per cent of those who had the right to vote in 1860 took the oath of allegiance, the state could draw up a new constitution, elect new officers, and return to the Union on a basis of full equality with all other states.

In 1863 this program applied only to those areas of Virginia, Tennessee, Arkansas, and Louisiana that had been conquered by Union armies. Lincoln intended to apply it to all other Confederate areas as soon as they were in Union hands.

The Radical Republicans. The Republican Party split on the question of Lin-

• •

° *amnesty:* a broad pardon for offenses against a government.

■ After the war, southerners faced bewildering problems in creating new political, social, and economic systems. They also had the enormous job of rebuilding countless cities, towns, and farms. This picture was taken in Richmond, Virginia, as war ended.

coln's program. One group called "Radical Republicans," led by Thaddeus Stevens of Pennsylvania, wanted to punish the South. Another group, more moderate in its views, lined up with Lincoln. But many of the moderate, or conservative, Republicans felt that Congress, not the President, was responsible for laying down the terms on which the southern states could rejoin the Union.

A practical problem of politics influenced the thoughts and actions of many Republicans. They realized that the southern Senators and Representatives who returned to Congress would vote against many of the measures that the Republicans had adopted—a high tariff, the national banks, free land, federal aid to railroads (pages 395–98). The Republicans had every reason to believe that the South would be overwhelmingly Democratic once the war ended. One way for the Republicans to keep the Democrats from regaining power was to give the vote to the former slaves, now called *freedmen*, who would keep the Republicans in power. Another way to accomplish the same end was to de-

prive former Confederate leaders of the vote and of the right to hold office.

The Wade-Davis Bill. With these considerations in mind, on July 2, 1864, the Radical Republicans in both houses of Congress voted in favor of a program much more severe than the one proposed by President Lincoln.

The Wade-Davis Bill, as it was called, provided that no new state governments were to be organized in the South until at least 50 per cent of the qualified voters in the state had taken an oath of past as well as future allegiance to the Union. Moreover, no one who had fought for the Confederate States of America, regardless of rank, was to be allowed to vote.

President Lincoln refused to approve the bill on the ground that it was too severe, and the bill was not passed over his veto. Thus, even before the war ended, the Republicans were divided in their views about the problem of restoring the South to the Union, and it was apparent that Lincoln was going to have to fight hard to get Congress to adopt his constructive and compassionate policy of reconstruction.

THE DEATH OF ABRAHAM LINCOLN

Friday, April 14, 1865, was much like any other day at the White House. The usual number of visitors came to see President Lincoln about government affairs or to ask favors of him.

In the evening the President and Mrs. Lincoln went with friends to the Ford Theater to see an English play, *Our American Cousin.* Lincoln watched the play from an armchair in a box overlooking the stage. Shortly after ten o'clock, John Wilkes Booth, a former actor, entered the box and fastened the door behind him. Armed with a Derringer pistol and a dagger, he rested the pistol on the back of the chair and shot the President through the head. An officer named Major Rathbone rushed to the President's aid, but Booth slashed at him with the dagger and leaped to the stage, tripping and injuring himself as he fled.

Witnesses disagreed as to what the wild-eyed fugitive shouted as he escaped across the stage. Some thought he cried "*Sic semper tyrannus!*" (Thus be it ever to tyrants.) Others thought they heard him say "The South is avenged!"

A young army doctor came to the aid of the President, but Lincoln never regained consciousness. He was carried to a house across the street, where he died the next morning.

Booth was eventually found hiding in a barn in Virginia. He refused to give himself up, and shots were fired, but whether he died by his own hand or was killed by a Union soldier is not known.

The entire nation mourned the President's death. Carl Sandburg, poet and Lincoln biographer, has described the slowly moving funeral train that carried Lincoln's body to its final resting place at Springfield, Illinois: "There was a funeral," he wrote. "It took long to pass its many given points. Many millions of people saw it and personally moved in it and were part of its procession. The line of march ran seventeen hundred miles. As a dead march nothing like it had ever been attempted before."

Lincoln is assassinated. Whether or not Lincoln's tact and moderation could have won acceptance of his policy must remain an unanswered question, for on April 14, 1865, he was assassinated.

Sorrow and anger gripped the entire country—South as well as North—and, as one member of Lincoln's cabinet wrote, "brave men wept." Most south- erners had despised Lincoln during the war, but by now had come to feel that he was a wise and compassionate man who offered them their best hope for a workable program of reconstruction.

But Lincoln was gone. Flags throughout the nation flew at half-mast, bells tolled, and crowds of weeping citizens filed through the funeral train as it stopped in cities and towns between Washington, D.C., and Lincoln's last resting place in Springfield, Illinois. Meanwhile, the former Vice-President, Andrew Johnson, shouldered the heavy burdens of the Presidency.

Johnson becomes President. Andrew Johnson was a self-educated man. In order to achieve success, he had had to overcome handicaps as great as those that Abraham Lincoln had faced. Deprived of the opportunity of any formal schooling, he had spent his boyhood as a tailor's apprentice. Later, with the aid of his devoted wife, he learned to read and write. While still a young man, he was elected mayor of his community, a small mountain village in eastern Tennessee. This was the beginning of a political career that took him to the state legislature, to the national House of Representatives, to the governorship of Tennessee, and in 1857 to the Senate of the United States. Although he owned a few slaves, Johnson disliked the large planters who were so influential in the South, and he resisted the secession of Tennessee in 1861.

During the war Johnson's service in behalf of the Union won him an appointment as military governor of Tennessee, with the responsibility for controlling those areas of his state occupied by federal troops. When the Republicans, including Lincoln himself, despaired of winning the Presidential election in 1864 (page 401), Johnson, a Democrat, was placed on the so-called "Union" ticket in the hope that he would draw votes for Lincoln.

Andrew Johnson was a man of many virtues, among them self-assurance, a fighting spirit, and the moral courage to act according to his own convictions. Unfortunately, he lacked sufficient patience, tact, and political skill to hold his own against political opponents.

Johnson adopts Lincoln's plan. One of Johnson's first decisions as President was to offer rewards for the arrest of Jefferson Davis and other former Confederate leaders. The Radical Republicans were delighted at Johnson's action, for they saw in him, or thought they saw, a leader who would help them to carry out their own program.

Johnson soon disappointed the Radicals by adopting Abraham Lincoln's plan almost in its entirety. He officially recognized the reconstructed governments of Tennessee, Arkansas, Louisiana, and Virginia. He retained Lincoln's entire cabinet. In only two or three respects did he depart from the program previously laid down by President Lincoln. First, he excluded a few more of the Confederate leaders from the right to vote and hold office. Second, he insisted that the southern states must repeal their ordinances of secession and repudiate their war debts. Third, they must ratify the Thirteenth Amendment freeing the slaves.

The Lincoln-Johnson program is completed. Reconstruction proceeded along these lenient lines. Within a few months all of the Confederate states except Texas had adopted new constitutions and organized new governments.

When Congress assembled on December 4, 1865, Senators and Representatives from the southern states were waiting outside the doors to take their seats in the national legislature. To many observers it looked as though the long and dreadful war was finally ended and the restored nation was about to start a new chapter in its history.

 SECTION SURVEY

1. What did Lincoln mean when he said, "With malice toward none; with charity for all"?

2. By referring to the terms of Lincoln's reconstruction plan, show that he practiced what he preached in his Second Inaugural Address.

3. Why were the Republicans divided in their views about how the South was to be treated?

4. Compare the ideas of Lincoln, Johnson, and the Radical Republicans on reconstruction.

IDENTIFY: amnesty, freedmen, Wade-Davis Bill; Booth; April 14, 1865.

2

The Radical Republicans destroy the work of Lincoln and Johnson

A new chapter in American history opened when Congress assembled on December 4, 1865, but it was not the chapter that President Lincoln and President Johnson had outlined. It was instead one of the darkest chapters in the life of the nation.

Economic chaos in the South. The scene in the South at the end of the war was one of utter poverty. Crumbling chimneys rose from the ashes of once lovely mansions, grass grew in the roads, broken bridges lay in ruins, railroads were destroyed, and livestock had been driven from the farms.

The situation in the cities was especially grim. One observer commented that the business section of Richmond, one of the great manufacturing centers of the South, lay in ruins. It consisted, he said, of "beds of cinders, cellars half filled with bricks and rubbish, broken and blackened walls, impassable streets deluged with debris." Atlanta in Georgia and Columbia and Charleston in South Carolina had been burned, and the gaunt skeletons of chimneys rose above the blackened devastation. In city and country alike, wherever armies had fought, the land lay desolate.

Social chaos. The southern economy as a whole as well as southern property was torn apart by the four-year conflict. A citizen of Mississippi wrote in April 1865 that "our fields everywhere lie untilled. Naked chimneys and charred ruins all over the land mark the spots where happy homes . . . once stood. Their former inhabitants wander in poverty and exile, wherever chance or charity affords them shelter or food. Childless old age, widows, and helpless orphans beggared and hopeless, are everywhere."

Everywhere, too, were the former slaves, now freedmen, some four million of them. They were free at last, but free to do what? Most of them were un-educated. None had ever owned land, none had ever worked for his own wages. Nor could most of their former owners pay them wages, for the Confederate money was worthless and United States currency was almost nonexistent in the South. To be sure, the land remained, but seeds and agricultural tools had almost disappeared.

Disease, always the companion of hunger and lack of sanitation, swept across the South. It was especially serious in the cities and on the outskirts of the cities, where uprooted people struggled to survive in makeshift shelters. Tens of thousands of people—men and women and children—died during the summer and winter of 1865–66. In some crowded urban areas disease swept away as many as one quarter to one third of all the Negroes, and the death rate among the white population was almost as grim.

The Freedmen's Bureau. The United States Army provided some relief in the form of food and clothing for white people and Negroes alike. But the major responsibility for helping the South through the difficult period of readjustment fell upon the Freedmen's Bureau.

Congress passed a bill creating the Freedmen's Bureau on March 3, 1865, one month before Lincoln's death, as a special agency in the War Department, and gave it the responsibility for looking after "refugees, freedmen, and abandoned lands." The agents of the bureau, who were everywhere in the South, were expected to help poverty-stricken white people, but their major responsibility was to serve as guardians of the freedmen. The agents were expected to guide the freedmen in their first steps toward self-support and, if necessary, to protect them against people who might try to take advantage of them.

Northerners and southerners differed in their attitude toward the Freedmen's Bureau. Most northerners felt it an honest effort to help the South to bring order out of the social chaos. Southerners, on the other hand, resented the bureau. Southerners charged that many of the bureau agents deliberately encouraged the freedmen to look upon their former owners as enemies, and were therefore responsible for creating friction between the two races.

Southerners also charged the bureau with raising false hopes among the freedmen, thereby making the process of readjustment increasingly difficult. One of the "false hopes" to which southerners referred was the freedmen's belief that they would all receive farms. During the summer and fall of 1865, the rumor circulated that every former slave would get "forty acres and a mule" as a Christmas gift from the government in Washington. The only basis for this rumor was the vague promise in the Freedmen's Bureau bill that abandoned land would eventually be distributed among the freedmen. But the freedmen accepted the rumor as truth. Overjoyed at the prospect of soon owning farms, they refused to work for the whites.

Restrictions on Negroes. Faced with this desperate situation—economic chaos and millions of uprooted and unemployed men and women—southern leaders began to take steps of their own to restore order. One of the steps they took was the adoption of laws to regulate the conduct of Negroes.

Laws of this kind, known as "slave codes," had existed before the war, as you know. The new laws contained some, though by no means all, of the earlier provisions. In general—for the codes varied from state to state—the laws forbade Negroes to possess firearms unless licensed to do so, to appear on the streets or roads after sunset, to travel without licenses, and to assemble without the presence of white men.

Many southerners insisted that restrictions of this kind were needed to restore order in the South. As proof that they did not intend to try to force the Negro back into slavery, southerners pointed to other provisions in the codes that were improvements in the civil rights of Negroes. Included among these provisions were the rights of Negroes to own personal property, to sue in

OLIVER OTIS HOWARD

Oliver Otis Howard (1830–1909) was born in Maine. A graduate of Bowdoin College, and later of West Point, he took command of a Maine volunteer regiment in June 1861, and commanded a brigade at the First Battle of Bull Run.

During the War Between the States, Howard commanded a Union army corps at Chancellorsville, Gettysburg, Missionary Ridge, and Chattanooga, and led the right wing of Sherman's army in the march from Atlanta to the sea. In this march Howard did everything in his power to prevent looting and unnecessary violence on the part of Union troops.

After the war General Howard headed the Freedmen's Bureau in its campaign to furnish food, clothing, medical services, and education to the stricken southern states. In 1867 he founded Howard University in Washington, D.C., a nonsectarian and nonracial institution, whose primary purpose was to help Negroes secure an education.

In 1873 he was sent as a peace commissioner to the fierce Apache Indians in the Southwest, where he established a reputation for honesty and friendship because of his fair treatment of the Apaches.

General Howard retired from active army service in 1894, and died in Burlington, Vermont, in 1909.

court and be sued, and to act as witnesses in court cases involving one or more of their own race.

Such was the situation in December 1865 when the newly elected Senators and Representatives from all the former Confederate states except Texas appeared in Washington to take their seats in Congress. The former Confederate states had taken all the steps required by both President Lincoln and President Johnson for readmission to the

Union. The new Senators and Representatives therefore fully expected to take their seats in Congress and to share with northern Congressmen the task of restoring order to the South.

Congress refused to admit the southern Senators and Representatives. What motives prompted Congress to turn its back on the South's duly elected Congressmen? Why did Congress refuse to accept the Lincoln-Johnson program for restoring the South to the Union?

Why Congress rejected the Lincoln-Johnson program. As you know, the Radical Republicans never shared either Lincoln's or Johnson's constructive attitude toward the South. From the day Lincoln's program began to take shape, the Radical Republicans had argued that southern leaders could not be trusted. Now, in December 1865, they pointed to the legal restrictions placed on Negroes as evidence that southerners were unwilling to recognize the complete freedom of the Negro.

The Radical Republicans also disagreed with the Lincoln and Johnson theory about the nature of the war. Both Lincoln and Johnson had taken the point of view that the conflict was *a rebellion of individuals.* This being so, the President could use his pardoning power, granted him by the Constitution, to restore the South to the Union.

Charles Sumner, leader of the Radical Republicans in the Senate, opposed Lincoln's theory with the "state suicide" argument. According to Sumner, the southern states, *as complete political organizations,* had committed "state suicide" when they seceded from the Union. Now, with the war over, they were in the same position as any other unorganized territory of the United States. This being the case, Congress alone had the Constitutional right to lay down the terms on which they should be admitted to the Union.

Thaddeus Stevens, majority leader of the House, held an even more drastic point of view. According to Stevens, the former Confederate states were now completely outside the Union and did not exist even as territories. In Stevens' opinion, they were "conquered provinces," and should be treated as such.

The Radical Republicans were also motivated by strong economic and political interests. They were confronted with the fact that the newly elected Senators and Representatives from the South were opposed to the harsh program of the Radical Republicans. They argued, and convincingly, that if the former leaders in the South were restored to power, they might combine with northern Democrats to destroy the Republican Party. Were this to happen, much of the legislation in favor of the industrial North would be abolished. Protective tariffs would be lowered, federal aid to the railroads might be ended, and the new national banking system might be replaced by one more pleasing to agricultural interests.

There were many Republicans who shared Lincoln's and Johnson's attitude toward the South. Had these, the moderate Republicans, been willing to join with their Democratic colleagues in the House and Senate, they could have controlled Congress—and carried on a more lenient reconstruction program. But they failed to do this, and so control of both houses of Congress passed into the hands of the Radicals.

SECTION SURVEY

1. If you had been living in the South in 1865, what would have been the most important (a) economic problems and (b) social problems that you and your family would have faced?

2. (a) Describe the work of the Freedmen's Bureau. (b) Contrast northern and southern opinion of this bureau.

3. (a) List four legal restrictions placed on Negroes by southern leaders. (b) What argument did southerners use to defend these restrictions?

4. Discuss the political and economic reasons which led Congress to reject the Lincoln-Johnson program.

IDENTIFY: "forty acres and a mule," "state suicide" theory, "conquered provinces" theory; Sumner, Stevens; 1865.

3 The Radical Republicans enact a severe program of reconstruction

By refusing in December 1865 to seat the Senators and Representatives from the southern states, the Radical Republicans practically guaranteed their own control of both houses of Congress. Exercising this control, within a few months they restored military rule in the South, thereby sowing seeds of bitterness that were to live for many years.

The first steps. Congress immediately appointed a joint committee of six Senators and nine Representatives, dominated by Thaddeus Stevens, to study the entire question of reconstruction. While it waited for this committee to report, Congress proceeded to safeguard the rights of the freedmen.

As one step in this direction, Congress passed a bill enlarging the powers of the Freedmen's Bureau. The new law gave the bureau power to prosecute in military courts, rather than in civil courts, any person accused of depriving a freedman of his civil rights. President Johnson promptly vetoed the bill, pointing out (1) that trial by military courts violated the Fifth Amendment of the Constitution, and (2) that Congress had no power to pass *any* laws with 11 states unrepresented. Johnson's veto infuriated the Radical Republicans. After long debate they finally gathered enough votes to pass the bill over the President's veto.

In the meantime, Congress prepared another piece of legislation designed to protect the freedmen. The Civil Rights Bill, as it was called, was designed to give Negroes full citizenship and guarantee them complete equality of treatment with all other citizens. Johnson also vetoed this bill on the ground that it was an unconstitutional invasion of states' rights. The Radical Republicans were able to muster enough votes to pass this measure, the Civil Rights Act, over Johnson's veto.

Both of Johnson's vetoes were based

■ This laboratory picture taken in the South in the late 1880's shows that some Negroes, despite difficulties, were securing an education.

on constitutional grounds. Nevertheless, they cost him the support of a number of moderate Republicans who, without any desire to "punish" white southerners, believed that Congress should protect the rights of the freedmen.

The Fourteenth Amendment. The Radical Republicans now decided to draw up a program of reconstruction and write it into the Constitution itself, where it would be safe not only from Presidential vetoes, but also from future action by Congress itself. The Joint Committee on Reconstruction drafted the program in the form of an amendment. Congress made some changes in the original proposal, and in June sent the Fourteenth Amendment to the states for ratification. The amendment contained four major sections:

Section 1 gave Negroes citizenship by stating that "All persons born or naturalized in the United States and subject to the jurisdiction thereof, are citizens of the United States and of the state wherein they reside." Section 1 also specified that no state could limit privileges of citizenship, or deprive persons of "life, liberty, or property, without due process of law," or deny them "the equal protection" of the laws (see Constitution, page 198).

415

Section 2 clearly declared that any state which deprived Negroes or deprived any other citizens of the vote° was to lose its representation in the House of Representatives "in the proportion which the number of such male citizens shall bear to the whole number of male citizens twenty-one years of age in such state." For example, a state in which one third of all the adult males were Negroes would be deprived of one third of its Representatives in Congress if it deprived all Negroes of the right to vote.

Section 3 struck directly at all southerners who, having at some time served in state or federal government, had then played an active role in the Confederacy. Such persons were deprived of the right to hold "any office, civil or military, under the United States, or under any state."

Section 4 made it unconstitutional for the United States or "any state" to pay any part of the Confederate debt or to pay any compensation to any person for "the loss or emancipation of any slave."

Radical Republicans win control. Tennessee ratified the Fourteenth Amendment in July 1866 and was immediately readmitted to the Union. But all of the other southern states rejected the amendment by overwhelming votes. This action by the South brought the reconstruction program to a standstill.

What would Congress do next? The answer to this question depended in part on the Congressional elections in the fall of 1866. If the Democrats should win control of Congress, they would return to the Lincoln-Johnson program. If the Radical Republicans won, anything could happen.

At this point several events helped to swing the voters toward the Radical Republicans. During the spring and summer, race riots broke out in Memphis and New Orleans. In the late summer President Johnson made a trip to

° States could withhold the vote from persons who had participated in a "rebellion" or "other crime."

Chicago, stopping on the way to make a number of election speeches. When his political opponents heckled him, Johnson answered them heatedly and in plain language. His blunt talk antagonized many voters.

More important, however, as a reason for Radical Republican strength was the memory of the war itself. In this, the worst calamity that had ever fallen upon the nation, both sides had suffered immense casualties. Sorrow and bitterness provided many votes for Radical Republican candidates for office.

In the election the Radical Republicans increased their hold on both houses of Congress. With more than a two-thirds majority in both the Senate and the House, they were now free to override Presidential vetoes.

Congress "reconstructs" the South. In March 1867 the Radical Republicans passed, over Johnson's vetoes, a number of measures that, taken together, provided a complete program for reconstruction. The new program, which Congress was determined to force upon the South, may be broken down into five major provisions.

First, Congress divided the ten southern states that had rejected the Fourteenth Amendment into five military districts, each under the charge of a military governor, with federal troops to maintain law and order while the states drafted new constitutions and organized new governments.

Second, Congress deprived most of the former Confederate leaders of the right to vote and hold office. The restrictions were the same as those Congress had earlier written into the Fourteenth Amendment.

Third, Congress gave the freedmen the right to vote and hold office.

Fourth, Congress authorized the states to write new constitutions in which they guaranteed Negroes the right to vote.

Fifth, Congress required the states to ratify the Fourteenth Amendment.

Southerners now had no choice. One by one, the states held conventions, drafted new constitutions, organized new governments, and entered the Union under the terms laid down by Congress.

Congress impeaches Johnson. By the summer of 1868, all but three of the southern states had returned to the Union on the terms laid down by Congress. (Mississippi, Texas, and Virginia finally accepted all of the terms and were readmitted in 1870.) Meanwhile, the Radical Republicans determined to remove their hated "enemy," President Johnson, from office.

In order to find grounds for impeachment and to reduce the President's power of appointment, Congress in 1867 adopted the Tenure of Office° Act over Johnson's veto. Under this law the President could not dismiss important civil officers without the consent of the Senate. Believing the law unconstitutional, Johnson determined to put it to a test, and in February 1868 he demanded the resignation of Secretary of War Edwin M. Stanton, who had consistently co-operated with Johnson's enemies, the Radical Republicans.

The House immediately adopted a resolution stating, "That Andrew Johnson, President of the United States, be impeached of high crimes and misdemeanors° in office." Having passed the resolution, the Radicals then hunted for other reasons to bolster their case against the President. Among the charges finally drawn up was one that accused the President of making "with a loud voice certain intemperate, inflammatory, and scandalous harangues" against Congress!

On the basis of such dubious evidence, President Johnson was impeached. His trial before the Senate, over which Chief Justice Salmon P. Chase presided, lasted about two months. After prolonged debate it be-

came clear that Johnson was not guilty of any offense for which he could legally be removed from office. Nevertheless, when the Senate cast its vote it stood 35 to 19 against Johnson, just one vote short of the necessary two-thirds majority required for removal from office. Only the integrity of a handful of Senators had saved the President from conviction. He remained in office until the expiration of his term on March 4, 1869, almost a year after his trial, but his influence as President was at an end.

Radical Republicans lose favor. It soon became apparent, however, that the Radical Republicans had over-reached themselves by attacking the President. For two years they had run the country on their own terms. They had brushed aside the Lincoln-Johnson program of reconstruction and overridden Johnson's repeated vetoes of their own program. But when they tried to remove the President from office, public opinion finally began to turn against them.

The election of 1868. The Presidential election of 1868 revealed how far the Radical Republicans had fallen from favor. Their candidate, Ulysses S. Grant, barely squeaked through with a

■ General Ulysses S. Grant, the successful strategist of northern victory, became President in 1869 and spent eight years in the White House.

° *tenure of office:* the period during which an individual has the right to continue in office.

° *misdemeanor:* a minor violation of the law, such as disorderly conduct, contrasted with a more serious or high crime, such as murder, which is called a *felony.*

victory. Although he won by an overwhelming electoral vote of 214 to 80, capturing 24 of the 36 states, his popular majority was only 309,000 out of 5,715,000 votes. A shift of only a few thousand votes in a handful of states would have swung the election to Horatio Seymour, the Democratic candidate.

The Radical Republicans studied the election returns with sober faces. It was quite clear that only the Negro vote had given them a majority, small though it was, of the popular vote.

The Fifteenth Amendment. With this disturbing conclusion in mind, the Radicals drew up the Fifteenth Amendment and submitted it to the states for ratification. The Fifteenth Amendment was short and to the point: "The right of citizens of the United States to vote shall not be denied or abridged by the United States or any state on account of race, color, or previous condition of servitude."

The Fifteenth Amendment was ratified by the necessary three fourths of the states and became part of the Constitution in 1870. Mississippi, Texas, and Virginia—the last three southern states to return to the Union—were required to ratify the amendment as a condition for readmission.

✔ **SECTION SURVEY**

1. Give the provisions of the new Freedmen's Bureau law and the Civil Rights Act. Explain why Johnson vetoed these laws and why his veto attempts failed.

2. (a) Why did Congress propose the Fourteenth Amendment? (b) Read the Fourteenth Amendment on pages 198–99 and summarize the main ideas in each of its sections.

3. Describe the five major provisions of the Congressional plan for reconstruction.

4. What were the reasons for Johnson's impeachment?

5. Show the connection between the election of 1868 and the Fifteenth Amendment.

IDENTIFY: due process of law, equal protection of the laws, Tenure of Office Act; Stanton, Chase, Grant, Seymour; 1867.

4 After a tragic decade southern government is restored to southerners

The Radical Republican program of reconstruction forced an unwelcome revolution upon the South. "The bottom rail is now on top," southerners sometimes exclaimed. And so it was, for ten long years—from 1867 to 1877.

Help from the North. As soon as the war ended, northerners began to pour into the South. Many of the northerners, including some agents of the Freedmen's Bureau and a number of teachers and missionaries, were motivated by high ideals. They tried to carry to the war-ravaged land the healing benefits of food, clothing, medical supplies, and education. Some of these unselfish people were successful, winning from the beginning the confidence and respect of the men and women, white and Negro alike, whom they had come to help. Others, equally well-intentioned but ignorant of southern ways of life, only antagonized the people with whom they tried to work.

Carpetbaggers and scalawags. Another group of northerners, called "carpetbaggers" because they carried all their earthly possessions in suitcases made from carpeting material, also moved into the southern states. Many of the carpetbaggers were seeking legitimate business opportunities. Others were motivated largely by greed. Horace Greeley, editor of the New York *Tribune*, wrote that the carpetbaggers were "stealing and plundering, many of them with both arms around Negroes, and their hands in their rear pocket, seeing if they cannot pick a paltry dollar out of them." Southerners scorned the carpetbaggers. Some responsible Negroes tried to warn their neighbors against associating with unscrupulous carpetbaggers.

But it was upon the "scalawags," the men born in the South who co-operated with their former enemies, that white southerners heaped their greatest scorn.

Some white southern politicians were prompted by the best of motives, believing that the quickest way to restore peace and prosperity to the nation was to forgive and forget. Others were selfish individuals who seized the opportunity to advance their own fortunes at the expense of their neighbors. Whatever their motives, their fellow southerners held them in contempt and referred to them as scalawags or, in harsher terms, as "renegades" or "mangy dogs."

Carpetbag governments. Such were the men—good and bad alike—who controlled the governments of the southern states during most of the Reconstruction Period. Many of the "carpetbag governments" were inefficient, wasteful, and corrupt. The worst of the governments were dominated by dishonest adventurers whose only thought was to feather their own nests at the expense of their fellows. The freedmen, most of whom were inexperienced, were easily victimized by the carpetbaggers and scalawags. Indeed, in only two states, Louisiana and South Carolina, did the freedmen hold a majority of seats in the legislature.

Northerners held most of the important political offices, at least during the early years of reconstruction. They were able to get themselves elected because so many white southerners had been deprived of the right to vote and because they persuaded the freedmen to vote for them. Take, for example, the seven southern states that had been readmitted to the Union by 1868. As a result of the first elections held in these states, four of the seven governors, ten of the fourteen United States Senators, and twenty of the thirty-five United States Representatives were carpetbaggers. The carpetbaggers were so powerful that southern scalawags and freedmen had to be content with the less important state and federal offices.

Under such circumstances, it was not surprising to find extravagant expenditures for needless luxuries that went to the legislators themselves. The new rulers were often willing to take bribes for handing out favorable corporation charters to businessmen, often northerners, who were interested in developing southern railroads and other enterprises. Taxes multiplied 10 to 15 times as the debts of the southern states mounted after the war. Although some of this money went for worthwhile projects, much of it found its way into the pockets of unscrupulous politicians.

It is important to note, however, that graft and corruption were not confined to carpetbag governments in the South. As you will see in the next chapter, public morality sank to an extremely low level in all sections of the United States during the postwar years.

It is also worth noting that, in spite of the almost impossible situation in which they found themselves, responsible southern legislators were able to further a number of constructive developments. They protected homes and farms against arbitrary foreclosures—that is, against unjustified seizure by dishonest officials. They strengthened public education. They spread the tax bur-

■ In this Thomas Nast cartoon, a carpetbagger has before him a bag of others' faults, which he sees, while on his back are his own unseen faults.

LUCIUS LAMAR PLEADS FOR RECONCILIATION

On March 11, 1874, Senator Charles Sumner of Massachusetts, one of the leaders of the Radical Republicans, died. Representative Lucius Lamar of Mississippi delivered a speech praising Sumner and mourning his passing. The eulogy was all the more noteworthy because, in pre-war days, Lamar had been an ardent advocate of southern independence.

But Lamar's speech was more than a tribute to a departed political enemy. It was a moving plea for reconciliation between the North and the South. In his oration Lamar said that Sumner, before his death, had come to believe "that all occasion for strife and distrust between the North and South had passed away . . . ." Lamar added: "Is not that the common sentiment—or if it is not, ought it not to be—of the great mass of our people, North and South? . . .

"Would that the spirit of the illustrious dead whom we lament today could speak from the grave to both parties to this deplorable discord in tones which would reach each and every heart throughout this broad territory: 'My countrymen! know one another, and you will love one another!' "

White southerners fight back. By 1867 southern whites were striking telling blows at scalawags, carpetbaggers, and politically ambitious Negroes by organizing a number of secret societies. The best known of these secret organizations were the Knights of the White Camellia and the Ku-Klux Klan.

In the beginning, these organizations intended to restore order, especially at the local level. One of their tactics was to frighten the Negroes and their white leaders and by this means keep them out of politics. Bands of hooded men, clothed in ghostly white robes, rode abroad at night, stopping now and then at a house to issue their warning.

But the plan quickly got out of hand. Before long, terror and brutality rode with the Klansmen across the countryside. Moderate southerners, fearful of northern reaction and disgusted with the brutality, withdrew their support from the secret societies.

Congress also took steps to end the lawlessness by passing a series of Military Enforcement Acts, sometimes called the Force Acts (1870-71). These acts gave the President power to use armed forces in the South, to suspend the writ of habeas corpus, and to provide for federal supervision of southern elections.

In 1872 Congress also passed the Amnesty Act, which restored political rights—including, of course, the right to vote—to about 160,000 former Confederates. As a result of the Amnesty Act, after 1872 only about 500 of the white southerners were still barred from political activities.

The federal measures combined with the withdrawal of most southerners from membership practically ended the Ku-Klux Klan at that time. As the new federal measures went into effect, as most white southerners began to vote again, and as responsible southern leadership again made itself felt, the carpetbag governments in several states collapsed.

Radical reconstruction ends. During the opening years of the 1870's, north-

den more equally, and reorganized local government and the judicial system. And most of the state constitutions drafted during reconstruction days continued in effect for many years.

Mixed with the good, however, were widespread graft and corruption. It was this and the rule of ignorant and unscrupulous men that the former Confederate leaders refused to tolerate. And because they could not fight back with the political weapon of the ballot, they chose another means—terror and intimidation.

Clothing of the 1860's

erners began to lose interest in reconstruction. For one thing, the deaths of Thaddeus Stevens in 1868 and Charles Sumner in 1874, both ardent leaders of the Radical Republicans, greatly weakened the Radical strength. Moreover, as the years passed, more and more people began to believe that chaos would continue in the South as long as the former southern leaders were kept from power.

Many northerners who had at first championed the cause of the Negro became disillusioned at reports of the political inexperience of most Negroes in the South, having forgotten that until 1865 the Negro had been held in complete subjection as a slave and therefore had little, if any, education and no practice in government. Many people began to say that perhaps the freedmen *did* need the guidance of the southern white leaders. In any case, these northerners believed that it would be better to let the South work out the problems of government and race relations in its own way.

Moreover, a growing number of businessmen were ready to call a halt to the Radical program of reconstruction. A disorganized, poverty-ridden South was not good for business, on either side of Mason and Dixon's line.

Finally, as the years passed, more and more responsible leaders in both the North and South began to work for genuine reconciliation.

By 1877 most northerners had either lost interest in the South or had come to the conclusion that it was impossible even with armed force to impose northern ideas and practices upon the southern people. In 1877, shortly after the election of President Rutherford B. Hayes, the last federal troops were withdrawn from the southern states.

SECTION SURVEY

1. Define (a) carpetbagger and (b) scalawag.

2. Why is the period of reconstruction sometimes called "the tragic era"?

3. What were the constructive developments of the carpetbag governments during this period?

4. How did the federal government react to the secret societies and the violence that developed in the South during this period?

5. Explain why many northerners began to favor withdrawal of federal troops from the South.

IDENTIFY: Knights of the White Camellia, Ku-Klux Klan, Force Acts, writ of habeas corpus, Amnesty Act; Greeley, Hayes; 1867–77.

New developments in agriculture and industry create a "New South"

During the 1880's southerners in growing numbers began to speak of the "New South." Many of those who used this term, including Editor Henry W. Grady of the Atlanta *Constitution*, urged their fellow citizens to abandon the one-crop system of agriculture and develop all the resources of a rich land—the minerals and the forests as well as the soil which yielded cotton, tobacco, sugar, rice, corn, wheat, and other crops. Above all, Grady and others who shared his beliefs urged southerners to convert the region's raw materials into manufactured goods in southern mills and factories.

Breakup of plantations. One of the striking characteristics of the postwar South was the breakup of many large plantations. This process started in 1865, immediately after the war ended. Planters, who had little if any cash to hire farm laborers, began to sell portions of their plantations to the more prosperous independent farmers. As a result of the breakup of the large plantations and the opening of new lands, between 1865 and 1880 the number of small farms more than doubled, while the size of the average southern farm decreased.

The Negro, who had emerged from slavery without education, without land, almost without clothes to wear upon his back, also benefited from the breakup of the large plantations. As the years passed, a small but growing number of freedmen acquired small farms.

Tenant farming and sharecropping. While some poor whites and an even smaller number of Negroes became owners of small farms, many others entered into a *tenant* relationship with the large landowners. A planter usually rented portions of his land to several tenants, who supplied their own seed, mules, and provisions. The owner managed the scattered tenant holdings much as if these made up the old-time plantation, in this way retaining some of the advantages of large-scale production. Many tenants remained tenants all their lives. Others saved enough money to buy a plot of land and thus become small landowners.

Less fortunate was the *sharecropper*. He furnished nothing but his labor, getting his cabin, seed, tools, mule, and a plot of land from the owner. In return for his labor, the sharecropper received a percentage of the crop that he produced. Since the sharecropper did not get paid until harvest time, he had to buy provisions for himself and his family on credit. In order to obtain credit, he was compelled to give a "lien," or mortgage, on the crops that he expected to plant and harvest. In turn, if he could not pay all his debts with the crop of any given year, these debts were added to the bill that must be paid a year later.

When the crops were harvested, almost all of the sharecropper's share of the money usually went to pay his bills. Because he also had to pay interest on his debt, the sharecropper found it very difficult to get out of debt. And as long as he was in debt, he was practically bound to the soil, since the law forbade him to leave the state until his bills were paid. Frequently the landlord also owned the country store where the sharecropper bought his provisions. Since the sharecropper was always in debt and almost never had any cash, he had no choice but to trade at the landlord's store.

Many sharecroppers raised only cotton or tobacco since the landlord insisted on the cultivation of these crops exclusively. The landlord argued that the sharecroppers did not know anything about other crops and that cotton and tobacco had the advantage of being dependable cash crops.

Although tenant farming and sharecropping were carried on in other parts of the country, these practices were especially widespread in the South. Indeed, considering the desperate economic situation confronting southerners during the years immediately after the war, it is evident that tenant farming and sharecropping provided a workable solution to an extremely difficult problem. But it is also evident that tenant farming and sharecropping made it difficult for the South to abandon its traditional one-crop system and develop a diversified type of farming.

Agricultural progress. Despite the formidable problems confronting the southern farmer, the South made considerable progress during the postwar years. Southerners, like farmers in other parts of the United States, benefited from new developments in science and technology. During the 1870's and 1880's improved machinery for sowing, cultivating, fertilizing, and reaping was introduced. In 1872 Alabama and Virginia established agricultural colleges; by 1900 the other southern states had followed their example. As a result of the influence of these institutions and the development of scientific agriculture in other parts of the country, the cultivation of traditional crops was improved, and some new plants were introduced.

Cotton continued to be the most important single crop. Indeed, by 1871 the South was producing more cotton than it had in 1860. The older states increased their yield per acre by liberal use of commercial fertilizers and improved farming methods. Much of the total increase, however, came from the opening of new cotton lands in the western part of the South. By 1900 the production of cotton in Texas alone was one third of the nation's total.

Improved farming methods led to greatly increased production of tobacco, rice, sugar, corn, and other traditional crops. But the most important change in the agricultural life of the South was the development of truck farming and fruit growing. Because of the expansion of railroads and the invention of the refrigerator car, it was possible to ship fresh vegetables and fruit to the urban centers in the North. The long growing season in the South and an abundance of cheap labor also stimulated truck farming. As early as 1900, thousands of

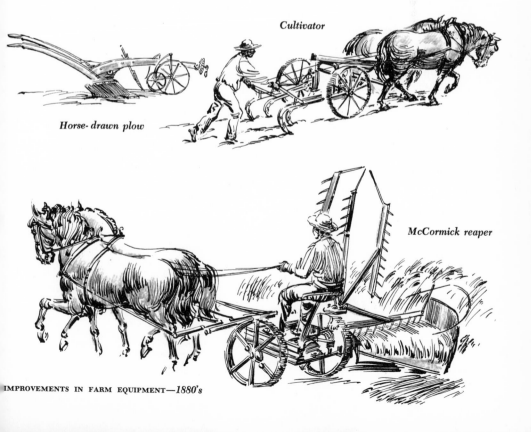

Cultivator

Horse-drawn plow

McCormick reaper

IMPROVEMENTS IN FARM EQUIPMENT—*1880's*

NUMBER OF CITIES WITH MORE THAN 100,000 POPULATION

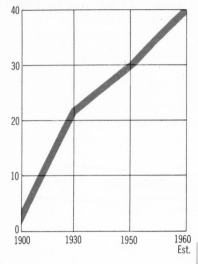

POPULATION GROWTH OF SELECTED CITIES

City	1890	1930	1960 Est.
Atlanta, Ga.	65,533	270,366	523,000
Birmingham, Ala.	26,178	259,678	450,000
Charlotte, N. C.	11,557	82,675	204,000
Columbia, S. C.	15,353	51,581	122,000
Houston, Tex.	27,557	292,352	925,000
Jackson, Miss.	5,920	48,282	155,000
Little Rock, Ark.	25,874	81,679	135,000
Louisville, Ky.	161,129	307,745	420,000
Memphis, Tenn.	64,495	253,143	510,000
Miami, Fla.	under 1,600	110,637	292,000
New Orleans, La.	242,039	458,762	606,400
Oklahoma City, Okla.	4,151	185,389	340,000
Richmond, Va.	81,388	182,929	241,000

Tennessee iron mill

GROWTH OF PIG IRON PRODUCTION

Each symbol represents 1,000,000 tons.

GROWTH OF COTTON TEXTILE INDUSTRY

Each symbol represents 2,000,000 spindles.

North Carolina textile plant

refrigerator cars were rolling northward, hauling to the rapidly growing northern cities the welcome supplies of green vegetables, watermelons, strawberries, oranges, apples, and peaches.

A dream takes shape. An even more remarkable development in the New South was the growth of industry. In this respect, as in agriculture, the South was responding to forces that were transforming the economic life of the other regions of the United States and, for that matter, of most of the nations of the Western world.

The industrial development of the South actually started before the outbreak of the War Between the States. By 1860 about 10 per cent of the manufactured wealth of the United States came from southern textile mills, iron works, lumber projects, and sugar refineries. But the economic disorganization that came with the war and reconstruction ruined many southern industries, and for nearly 20 years the South made little if any industrial progress.

By the late 1870's, however, southerners in rapidly growing numbers were reaching the conclusion that progress for the South depended upon two parallel developments—industrialization and public education. The development of industry would enable the South to take fuller advantage of its rich heritage of natural resources. The development of education would enable the South to make better use of its human resources.

"Such was the dream which began to form itself in the brain of some of the ablest and most responsible of the southern leaders," southern historian W. J. Cash wrote in *The Mind of the South*. This dream, he went on to say, was "to become in the years between 1880 and 1900 the dream of virtually the whole southern people—a crusade preached with burning zeal from platform and pulpit and editorial cell—a mighty folk movement, which already by the turn of the century would have performed the astounding feat (in a land stripped of capital) of calling into existence more than four hundred cotton mills; which already by the turn of the century would be performing the scarcely less striking feat (for this country) of beginning to build a definite public school system, pitifully inadequate, hardly more than embryonic outside the towns and villages as yet, but growing surely and steadily."

Industrial development. The money to build factories, mines, steel mills, railroads, and other industries came in part from northern investors, in still larger part from the South itself. Profits from expanding agriculture were poured into new industrial ventures. In community after community, the people themselves gathered in mass assemblies to plan a factory, often a textile mill, and to raise the necessary capital. Throughout the South farming villages were transformed into mill towns within the space of a few years.

Many of the early mills were controlled by a single family or a small group of persons, who owned the houses in which the workers lived, the stores where they bought their goods, and the other buildings in the town. The workers depended on the owners for their jobs and had to spend their wages for the rental of company-owned dwellings and for provisions bought from company-owned stores. As a result, the labor organizations that were developing so rapidly in the North during these years, as you will see, made little headway in the South at this time.

The growth of southern industry was dependent not only on local and northern capital, natural resources, and a cheap labor supply, but also on improvements and extensions of southern railroads. The War Between the States left the southern railroads in terrible condition. But the old railroads were quickly rebuilt, and new lines constructed. By 1890 the South possessed a railroad system twice as large as that of 1860.

One measure of the industrial development of the New South was the growth of cities. Between 1870 and

■ Atlanta, Georgia, had long been a trading center for cotton and other agricultural products. But when this picture was made in 1887, Atlanta was becoming an industrial center as well. Passengers waited for trains under the large shed in the background.

1890, for example, Durham, North Carolina, developed from a small village to a flourishing tobacco center. Richmond in Virginia and Nashville in Tennessee established themselves as leading urban centers of the New South. Atlanta's population increased from 37,000 to 65,000 between 1880 and 1890. Birmingham, Alabama, founded in 1871 on the site of a former cotton field, was transformed within a few years into a bustling iron and steel center, often called "the Pittsburgh of the South."

By 1900 the manufactured products of the South were worth four times as much as in 1860. With its growing industrial cities, its factories and mills and mines, its developing system of transportation, the South was beginning to be more and more like other regions of the United States. But with all its industrial progress, the New South had a long way to go to catch up industrially with other sections of the country.

Educational developments. In education, as in agriculture and industry, the South made progress during the closing years of the 1800's. But every forward step had to be accomplished in spite of formidable handicaps.

Among the outstanding contributions to southern education were the gifts of northern philanthropists. Especially noteworthy were the gifts of George Peabody and John F. Slater, both New England millionaires. The Peabody Fund was created in 1867; the Slater Fund, in 1882. Income from these funds helped to provide educational opportunities for white and Negro people alike in the years when the South was struggling to rebuild its war-shattered economy. In 1905, after the most pressing need was past, the trustees of the Peabody Fund donated one and one-half million dollars to the George Peabody College for Teachers at Nashville, Tennessee.

The gifts of northern philanthropists helped greatly to create better understanding between the North and the South. They also provided encouragement for those who were struggling with the problem of building an educational system in the southern states.

But the money provided by private sources was only a drop in the bucket. Most of the burden of rebuilding the schools and opening up educational opportunities for white people as well as for Negroes had to be shouldered by the southern states. Slowly, as the economic situation improved, the South was able to provide larger opportunities.

Political developments. Most southerners belonged to the Democratic Party. There were southern Republicans, to be sure, but they were completely outnumbered in local, state, and national elections. For example, when the Presidential elections rolled around, the former Confederate states cast all their electoral votes for the Democratic candidates. For this reason, people began to refer to the southern states as the "Solid South."

The "Solid South" was born during reconstruction days when Radical Republican governments composed largely of carpetbaggers, scalawags, and freedmen controlled the southern states. In their determination to rid themselves of Radical Republican rule, white southerners poured into the Democratic Party. After 1877, when the last federal troops were withdrawn from the South and the former Confederate states were once more free to rule themselves, southerners continued for the most part to support the Democratic Party.

The only real threat to the established party was from the Negroes, who were slowly but steadily making progress in both economics and education, and whose sympathies were for the most part with the Republican Party under which they had gained their freedom. To prevent this threat from materializing, the southern states, beginning with Mississippi in 1890, began to adopt laws and frame new constitutions designed to exclude large numbers of Negroes from the polls, or voting places, on grounds other than "race, color, or previous condition of servitude."

A number of states adopted a poll tax° and a literacy test.° Since many southern Negroes had little money and little if any education, these laws kept large numbers from voting.

But the poll tax and the literacy test also kept large numbers of poor whites from voting. In an effort to remedy this situation, several states, starting with Louisiana in 1898, wrote a "grandfather clause" into their constitutions. This clause declared that, even if a man could not pay the poll tax or pass the educational test, he could still vote if he had been eligible to do so on January 1, 1867, or if he were the son or the grandson of a man who had been eligible to vote on January 1, 1867. Under this clause many poor whites were allowed to vote, but most Negroes, whose fathers or grandfathers had been slaves, could not vote. The "grandfather clause" was declared unconstitutional by the Supreme Court in 1915.

••

° *poll tax:* a flat tax imposed on every person, used in some states as a requirement for voting.
° *literacy test:* an examination to determine whether a person can read or write or whether he possesses a certain amount of education; used in many states as a requirement for voting.

SECTION SURVEY

1. Explain why tenant farming and sharecropping were especially widespread in the postwar South.

2. Show how science and technology contributed to agricultural progress in the South during the postwar years.

3. Give three reasons for the industrial development of the South.

4. Summarize the factors which influenced the development of education in the South.

5. Show how each of the following affected the Negro's right to vote: (a) poll tax, (b) literacy test, and (c) "grandfather clause."

IDENTIFY: "New South," one-crop system of agriculture, "the Pittsburgh of the South," philanthropist, "Solid South"; Grady, Peabody, John F. Slater; 1877.

(For review, see Section Surveys, pages 411, 414, 418, 421, 427.)

Points to Discuss: 1. (a) Compare the Presidential plan of reconstruction with the Congressional plan. (b) What important motives guided the Radicals?

2. It has been said that in the South from 1867 to 1876 "the bottom rail was on top." Explain the meaning of this phrase through a discussion of the Radical reconstruction policy and southern resistance to it.

3. In your opinion, what is the historical significance of the impeachment trial of President Johnson?

4. Evaluate democratic gains resulting from the War Between the States. Consider political, economic, and social results.

5. Why was the outcome of the Congressional elections of 1866 of the utmost importance to the Radicals?

6. Explain the meaning of the terms the "New South" and the "Solid South" in describing conditions in the South following the War Between the States.

Using Maps and Charts: 1. Using the charts on page 424, answer the following questions: (a) How many southern cities had a population of more than 100,000 in 1890? in 1930? Account for the change. (b) The pictographs showing the growth of the cotton textile industry tell an interesting story. Describe the factors which led to this growth.

2. (a) Consulting the map on pages 830–31, make a list of the agricultural products produced in the South today. (b) How did southern farming change?

3. (a) Using the map on pages 834–35, make a list of the industrial products produced in the New South. (b) What historic forces led to this development?

Consulting the Sources: Commager and Nevins, *The Heritage of America*, contains enlightening contemporary accounts of conditions in the South following the War Between the States. See Nos. 184–88.

■ TRACING THE MAIN IDEAS

In 1865, just before his tragic death, President Lincoln urged the victorious North to act, "With malice toward none; with charity for all;" and in this way to build "a just and lasting peace. . . ."

President Johnson's efforts to apply Lincoln's policy by quickly restoring the Union were effectively blocked by the Radical Republicans who controlled Congress. For various reasons, the Radical Republicans wished to decide how the former Confederate states should be reconstructed. The more extreme members of the Radical group wanted to revolutionize the South by transferring political power from the white leaders to the Negroes.

White southerners were disturbed at the prospect of living in a position of political, economic, and social equality with former slaves. Without power to resist by armed force, they used every means at their command to defeat the northern program of reconstruction.

Unable to enforce their will upon the South, northerners gradually lost interest, and in 1877 the last federal troops were withdrawn from the former Confederate states.

During the 1880's and 1890's the outline of a New South began to appear. With the slow but steady development of more diversified agriculture, truck farmers began to ship growing quantities of fruit and vegetables to markets in the North. Southern mines began to supply increasing amounts of ore to southern furnaces. Textile mills and other factories began to transform southern villages into growing cities.

In 1900 the South was still basically an agricultural region. Southerners were still struggling to recover from the economic disaster of the war. But they were making progress and, like people in the North and the West, were being swept into the future by the growing forces of industry.

Democracy Undergoes Severe Trials

RAILROAD YARD - 1880's

C HANGE is often disturbing, and in no period of American history was change more disturbing than in the generation following the War Between the States. You have seen how drastic changes came to the South in "the tragic era" of reconstruction and how southerners struggled to adjust to these changes. Equally striking changes were occurring in the Northeast, the Middle West, and the West during these years.

The major cause of these changes was the rapid growth of industry after the war. New power-driven machinery was invented and installed in large factories, giant corporations were organized, and new methods of mass production were developed. These exciting developments made many new products and services available to more and more American people and helped to raise their standard of living.

But there were dark shadows in this bright picture. As industries grew, cities grew and became overcrowded, creating new problems—problems of sanitation, disease, fire, and transportation.

In order to see this dramatic and disturbing period of American history clearly, it is necessary to take several looks at it. In later chapters you will see how "big business" grew and in growing created complex problems, not only for itself, but also for farmers, miners, wage earners, and small businessmen. In this chapter you will see how graft and corruption plagued American political life during the postwar years, and how repeated efforts were made to root out this dishonesty in government.

AS THE STORY DEVELOPS

1. Graft and corruption spread in the years following the war.
2. A start is made toward restoring honesty to government.
3. The cause of political reform moves forward despite setbacks.

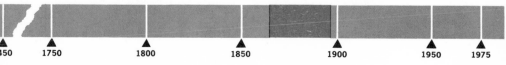

450   1750   1800   1850   1900   1950   1975

1
Graft and corruption spread in the years following the war

It was Ulysses S. Grant's unhappy destiny to occupy the White House during a period in which graft and corruption infected every level of government—federal, state, and local.

President Grant. In 1868, when he won the election for the Presidency on the Republican ticket (pages 417–18), Grant enjoyed the respect and confidence of millions of his fellow citizens. His well-earned reputation rested upon his success as commander of the Union armies during the latter years of the War Between the States. Had he turned down the honor of serving as President, he would have gone to his grave as a popular hero. Unfortunately, his lack of political experience proved too great a handicap, and his eight-year administration proved to be what one historian has called "the darkest page in the history of the Presidency."

Grant himself was an honest, upright man. His great weakness—which could have been a virtue if it had been tempered by reason—was a blind loyalty to friends. Being honest himself, he could not believe that his associates were any less honest, and he stubbornly refused to admit that some of those whom he called friends often used him and his office to advance their own fortunes.

General Grant, the brilliant commander of armies on the battlefield, was one man; President Grant, another. It was Grant, the successful general, who, at Appomattox Court House, offered generous terms to the vanquished enemy and who, when Union troops started to cheer, ordered them to be silent, softening his order with the words, "The war is over; the rebels are our countrymen again." It was Grant, the inexperienced politician, who, during the years from 1869 to 1877, failed to exercise strong leadership while the country was swept by scandals involving both Democrats and Republicans.

The Crédit Mobilier scandal. Even before Grant took office, the federal government was involved in an unsavory scandal involving construction of the first transcontinental railroad.

The building of a transcontinental railroad had been considered during the 1850's, but construction was not authorized until 1862. At that time, as you know, Congress granted a charter to the Union Pacific Railroad and to the Central Pacific Railroad. The Union Pacific was to build westward from the Missouri River at Omaha, in Nebraska Territory. Meanwhile, the Central Pacific was to build eastward from Sacramento, California.

Building such a railroad was an extremely expensive and risky undertaking. But since such a railroad would be important in the development of the nation, the federal government gave various kinds of subsidies to the railroad companies. Besides receiving a free right of way through the public lands, both companies were also given land grants on both sides of the track (see diagram, page 468). Both companies also received in the form of government bonds a grant of $16,000 for every mile of track completed on the level plains, $32,000 for every mile of track through hilly country, and $48,000 for every mile of track in the mountains.

The Union Pacific Railroad was built by a construction company chartered in Pennsylvania under the name of the Crédit Mobilier (kreh-DEE moh-bee-LYEH). Ownership of the Union Pacific and the Crédit Mobilier was held jointly by the same directors. In other words, when the Union Pacific directors met to vote on a contract for the construction of part of the railroad, they were able to vote in favor of awarding the contract to the Crédit Mobilier, of which they were also owners. By voting for enormous construction contracts, they diverted to the Crédit Mobilier and into their own pockets, in the form of profits, government bonds and land that had been granted as subsidies to the Union Pacific. When Congressional committees finally investigated, it was discovered that graft from the unsavory deal had reached the pockets of some Congressmen, who had been bribed in an effort to prevent the investigations.

The "salary grab." The Crédit Mobilier scandal was occupying the attention of Congress when the Senators and Representatives voted themselves a 50 per cent increase in salaries—from $5000 to $7500 per year. Congressmen pushed the salary bill through on the last day of the session, March 3, 1872. To make matters worse, they made the measure retroactive for two years, which meant that each Congressman would receive two years' back pay, or $5000, in addition to the future increase in salary. The public was so outraged at this "salary grab" that Congress repented and hastily repealed the act at the opening of the next session of Congress. Although the "salary grab" was perfectly legal, it does indicate the "something for nothing" philosophy which motivated many of the public figures in Washington—Democrats and Republicans alike—during these unsettled years.

The Treasury Department scandal. Hardly had public resentment died when another scandal hit the headlines of the newspapers. The Secretary of the Treasury, William A. Richardson, signed a contract with a private citizen, John D. Sanborn, giving him authority to collect some overdue federal taxes, with the right to pocket half of all he could collect. By methods resembling blackmail, Sanborn collected $427,000, retaining for his share about $213,000.

When he was called to the witness stand to explain the whole affair, Sanborn swore that he had kept only a small part of the "commission," having been forced to give $156,000 to his "assistants"! It was generally understood that these "assistants" were politicians who had influence with the Secretary of the Treasury and who had used their influence to swing the tax-collection contract to Sanborn. But the contract was legal, and the "commission" was paid in full. A new law prevented the situation

GRANT'S FIGHTING SPIRIT

Ulysses S. Grant (1822–85), General-in-Chief of the Union armies, emerged from the War Between the States in a blaze of glory. Unhappily, as President of the United States from 1869 to 1877, he seemed unable to come to grips with graft and corruption in government, and the honor that he had gained as a military leader was diminished. But, in the end, Grant redeemed his reputation.

In 1884 Grant's business partner betrayed his trust, the firm went bankrupt, and Grant, sixty-two years of age, found himself nearly penniless. Then Grant learned that he was dying of cancer.

In a final desperate effort to recover some of his fortune and leave his family secure, Grant worked day and night to complete his *Personal Memoirs*. Writing against time, working in agonizing pain and through long sleepless nights, he finished his task only four days before his death in New York on July 23, 1885.

Grant had won his last struggle. His *Memoirs* earned more than $450,000, and provided his family with the security for which he had fought so valiantly.

from recurring, however, and the head of the Treasury Department resigned.

The "Whisky Ring." The new Secretary of the Treasury, Benjamin H. Bristow, was an honest official who promptly discovered other peculiar and corrupt practices in his department. Investigation disclosed that taxes were not being collected on about seven eighths of the liquor distilled in the United States. Further investigation revealed that officials high in public life were guilty of blackmail and fraud.

According to the tax law, a distiller who failed to pay the revenue taxes on distilled liquor would be compelled, if caught, to pay a double tax. Any informer who revealed to the government the failure of a company to pay its taxes received 10 per cent of the tax penalty as a reward. The informer had a good chance of collecting more, however, by blackmailing the tax-evading company than he could get by reporting the evasion.

The Secretary of the Treasury discovered that a ring of whisky distillers and blackmailers had been defrauding the United States government of no less than a million dollars annually. The Supervisor of Internal Revenue in St. Louis, John McDonald, who was involved in the conspiracy, went to prison for a year, but not before the trail of corruption had been traced even to President Grant's private secretary.

Other scandals. Meanwhile, another overripe scandal was unearthed with the discovery that Secretary of War William W. Belknap had accepted $24,500 in bribes from a trader at Fort Sill in what is now Oklahoma. Belknap had decided to give the profitable and exclusive trading concession to a New York friend. The trader, who was making a huge profit from the Indians around Fort Sill, agreed to pay Belknap and his friend each $6000 a year if he were allowed to retain his concession.

When evidence of this bribery was presented, the House of Representatives voted unanimously to impeach Secretary Belknap. When the Senate held impeachment proceedings, Belknap hastily resigned. Despite all the evidence, the Senate failed by a close vote to convict the ex-Secretary of War. The Senators who voted "not guilty" claimed that, because Belknap had resigned, he was no longer subject to trial by the Senate.

There were other evidences of graft in the federal government. The Secretary of the Navy "sold" business to builders and suppliers of ships. The Secretary of the Interior worked hand in glove with land speculators. President Grant himself had no part in these unsavory activities, but many people felt that he was at fault for allowing his "friends" to hide behind his good name.

Corruption in state governments. Corruption was as bad, if not worse, in the state governments. In 1868 when the Erie Railroad, which was controlled by Daniel Drew, James ("Jim") Fisk, Jr., and Jay Gould, wanted to sell $10,000,000 worth of additional stock,° Gould went to the New York state capital at Albany with a trunk full of money to bribe the legislators to legalize the sale of the stock. Votes were openly bought and sold as a steady stream of greedy legislators passed through the door of Gould's hotel room. Evidence suggested that the governor of New York sold his influence for $20,000 and that state senators got $15,000.

The Tweed Ring. Perhaps worst of all was the corruption in municipal, or city, governments. William M. Tweed, an uneducated chairmaker, rose in fifteen years to be the multimillionaire "dictator" of New York City in the 1860's and 1870's. Working with Tammany Hall— the Democratic political organization and the so-called political "machine" of the city—"Boss" Tweed controlled the entire government of New York City.

How did Tweed gain control? Very simply. He or his men met immigrants when they landed, fed them, found them jobs, gave them coal, left them baskets of food at Thanksgiving and Christmas. After they secured the right to vote, the newcomers returned Tweed's "friendship" by voting for the men he favored. Moreover, when elections seemed doubtful, men packed the ballot boxes in favor of Tweed's candidates. One man might vote several times, using a different name and address each time.

How did Tweed use his power? He overloaded pay rolls. He sold jobs. He sold franchises and charters—licenses to operate, that is—to companies that provided services to the city. A courthouse, started in 1868, was to cost $250,000; three years later, still uncompleted, it had swallowed up $8,000,000. In three years Tweed and his crooked "ring" stole an estimated $20,000,000 from New

(Continued on page 434)

° *stock:* certificates of part ownership in a corporation (see page 474).

THOMAS NAST, MASTER CARTOONIST

Thomas Nast (1840–1902), one of the greatest political caricaturists of all time, was born in Germany. His family immigrated to the United States when he was only six years old. He studied art, and by the time he was twenty had demonstrated his amazing skill. In the early 1870's, when he was attacking the Tammany Hall political machine, he was offered a half million dollars to drop his work and move abroad.

It was during his anti-Tammany campaign that Nast drew one of his most famous cartoons, "The Tammany Tiger Loose." In this cartoon he showed a ravenous beast in an arena with the bodies of his victims lying around him. The beast was about to devour the "Republic," pictured in the form of a helpless young woman. The corrupt political boss, "Emperor Tweed," was seated in the stands, surrounded by his henchmen. Under the cartoon Nast asked readers the

question "What are you going to do about it?" The aroused citizens of New York took such vigorous action that Tweed and his associates fled the country. But they could not escape Nast. Several years later, in Spain, Boss Tweed was identified by a person who recognized him from one of Nast's drawings, and Tweed was returned to New York and sent to prison.

The "Tammany Tiger" is only one of many famous symbols by which Thomas Nast is remembered today. He invented the Republican elephant and the Democratic donkey. But his most popular creation was the lovable image of Santa Claus which has come to be cherished by millions of children. It was Thomas Nast who took Washington Irving's St. Nicholas, Clement Moore's "right jolly old elf," and the South German Pelze Nickel and portrayed them as the merry old gentleman with the long white beard.

York. It is further estimated that between 1868 and 1871 the "ring" and its business friends cost the city close to $100,000,000.

Reasons for the corruption. What were the reasons for the low level of public morality during the years following the War Between the States?

The war itself was partly responsible. In wartime, when national survival is at stake, the all-important consideration is to get things done quickly. Cost is secondary, and money flows freely into war industries. During the war years, with business booming, unscrupulous businessmen and legislators had a rare opportunity to engage in dishonest practices. These practices were carried into the postwar years.

A related and equally significant explanation of the postwar graft was the rapid growth of large-scale industry, about which you will read in Chapter 23. In earlier times, when factories and other business enterprises were small, the businessman was well known to the community, and if his practices were dishonest, he was apt to lose the good will of his neighbors. But the new corporations were impersonal. The men who controlled these huge enterprises were hardly known, even by many of their own stockholders. It was much easier for those who were unscrupulous to get away with questionable practices.

◢ **SECTION SURVEY**

1. Grant's administration has been called "the darkest page in the history of the Presidency." Describe four scandals that tend to support this conclusion.

2. Although Grant was not personally involved in these scandals, people blamed him for them. Why?

3. Show that graft and corruption also existed on the state and local levels.

4. What were the reasons for the low level of public morality during the years following the War Between the States?

IDENTIFY: Crédit Mobilier, "salary grab," Whisky Ring, Tammany Hall, Tweed Ring; Belknap, Drew, Fisk, Gould, "Boss" Tweed, Nast.

2 A start is made toward restoring honesty to government

Newspapers in the late 1860's and the early 1870's were filled with stories and cartoons attacking graft in government—including graft among officials at the federal, state, and local levels. The most famous American cartoonist was Thomas Nast of New York, whose powerful cartoons in *Harper's Weekly* helped to reveal to the public the infamy of "Boss" Tweed and his friends.

These revelations of corruption in high places stimulated a widespread demand for reform. Among the many reform movements of these years, none aroused greater interest than the proposal to appoint men to public jobs on the basis of merit. Under the "spoils system," which Andrew Jackson had helped to establish (page 271), government jobs were handed out to political favorites. Under the proposed "merit system," the men who received the highest grades in competitive examinations would be given the jobs, whether the men were Republicans or Democrats.

Growth of the reform movement. In 1871, in response to the demand for a reform of the *civil service,*° Congress authorized a Civil Service Commission to study the problem and to make recommendations. Although President Grant appointed able men to this commission, he was lukewarm to the idea. In 1875 the chairman resigned in disgust, and the commission was discontinued.

Meanwhile, in 1872 a group of reform Republicans, who called themselves the Liberal Republican Party, met in Cincinnati and nominated Horace Greeley, the editor of the New York *Tribune,* as their Presidential candidate to run against the Radical Republican candidate, President Grant. The Democrats, meeting two months later in Baltimore, also nominated Greeley, hoping

° *civil service:* All the employees of the government—federal, state, and local—other than the military.

by this means to benefit from the split in the Republican Party.

The Liberal Republican platform included a pledge to fight graft and dishonesty in public life, and a specific plank, or section, urging civil service reform. But Grant won by an overwhelming electoral vote—286 to 66.

The defeat at the polls in 1872 was a disheartening blow to the reformers. Within a year, however, they began to gather strength. For one thing, new scandals in public life drove an increasing number of Americans into the reform movement. As a result of growing dissatisfaction with Grant's administration, the Democrats managed to win control of the House of Representatives in the Congressional elections of 1874.

The election of 1876. The Democrats, heartened by the clear evidence of a growing demand for reform, approached the 1876 elections confident of victory. They chose as their Presidential candidate Governor Samuel J. Tilden of New York. Governor Tilden had won nation-wide attention by helping to break up the Tweed Ring in New York. Two planks in the Democratic platform were demands for civil service reform and an end to graft in public life.

The Republicans—who "were running scared," as the politicians say—nominated a man well known for his interest in reform, Governor Rutherford B. Hayes of Ohio. Hayes, who had worked for a merit system in his own state, promised to work for civil service reform in the federal government. He also promised to end the unhappy period of reconstruction.

Both Tilden and Hayes were well-to-do men. Both were closely associated with industrialists and businessmen. Both firmly opposed the money policy demanded by farmers, which you will read about in Chapter 24. The one big asset Tilden had was the fact that he was running against a party that for eight years had been identified with scandal after scandal.

Election returns are disputed. The election gave Tilden 250,000 more popular votes than Hayes received. The first count of the electoral votes, based on early returns, also gave him an advantage over Hayes—184 to 165. As a result, most newspapers at first stated that Tilden had won.

As it turned out, the papers had jumped to the wrong conclusion. Tilden with his 184 electoral votes was one vote short of the necessary majority. Ordinarily, when no Presidential candidate has a clear majority of the electoral vote, the House of Representatives chooses the President. But this was no ordinary election. Four states—South Carolina, Florida, Louisiana, and Oregon—had each sent in *two* different sets of returns. In all, 20 electoral votes from these four states were claimed by both the Republicans and the Democrats. Tilden needed only one of these disputed votes in order to win. Hayes, however, needed every one of the 20 votes.

The single disputed vote from Oregon was quickly settled in favor of Hayes, raising his total to 166 electoral votes. But the remaining 19 votes from the three southern states aroused a storm of controversy. The Republicans claimed all three states for Hayes, but the Democrats insisted that, since these states were still under carpetbag rule, the will of the majority had not been expressed. For a time the controversy threatened to plunge the nation into violence.

The dispute is settled. Unfortunately, the Constitution provided no solution for this complicated situation. According to the Constitution, after an election "The president of the Senate shall, in the presence of the Senate and House of Representatives, open all the certificates [electoral votes], and the votes shall then be counted." But counted by whom? If, in this case, the Republican-controlled Senate counted the votes, the Senators would throw out the Democratic returns and give the election to Hayes. If, on the other hand, the Democratic-controlled House counted the votes, the Representatives would throw out the Republican returns and give the election to Tilden.

In order to break the apparently hopeless deadlock, Congress created an Electoral Commission consisting of fifteen members—five Senators, five Representatives, and five Justices of the Supreme Court. By previous arrangement the Senate chose three Republicans and two Democrats; the House, two Republicans and three Democrats. Four of the Justices—two Republicans and two Democrats—were named in the act itself. These four Justices were to name a fifth —an independent voter without ties to either party.

It was generally understood that the one "independent" member of the Electoral Commission would be Justice David Davis. At the last minute, however, Davis resigned from the Supreme Court because of his election to the Senate, and the place he was to have held on the Electoral Commission went to Justice Joseph P. Bradley, a Republican. It was not surprising, therefore, that when the disputed votes were counted by the commission, the returns from South Car-

olina, Florida, and Louisiana went to the Republicans by a "straight" party vote of eight Republicans as opposed to the seven Democrats on the commission. So Hayes, who had received a minority of the popular votes, became President of the United States, and on Monday, March 5, 1877, entered the White House.

As it turned out, the controversial election of 1876 proved to be a victory for the process of orderly government. Tilden and the Democrats, although deeply disappointed, accepted the decision. Equally important, by their moderation, the American people in general saved the country from violence and bloodshed.

Hayes faces difficulties. President Hayes had four difficult years in the White House. Throughout his administration the Democrats controlled the House, and for two years, from 1879 to 1881, the Senate as well. Although the Democrats did not try to upset the decision of the Electoral Commission, they called Hayes "His Fraudulency" and "Old Eight to Seven" to remind him that they questioned his right to the Presidency.

Hayes also faced opposition from members of his own party. The election of 1876 split the Republicans into two groups—the "Stalwarts" and the "Half-Breeds." The Stalwarts, led by "Boss" Roscoe Conkling of New York, included most of the Radical Republicans who had created and enforced the severe program of southern reconstruction. The Stalwarts, sometimes called "Old Guard" Republicans, were opposed to reform and to reformers, including the President himself, whom they called "Granny Hayes." The Half-Breeds, led by James G. Blaine of Maine and John Sherman of Ohio, agreed with Hayes that at least some reform was needed.

Hayes battles for reform. The opposition he faced did not prevent President Hayes from fighting for the legislation he believed to be right and proper.

One of his first acts as President was to withdraw federal troops from the

■ In a torchlight parade of 1876, Republican "Boys in Blue" campaigned for Rutherford B. Hayes. Their costumes were meant to reawaken the wartime fervor of northern voters in support of the Republicans.

South. Southern political leaders, free once again to manage their own affairs in their own way, broke the power of the Radical Republicans who had controlled Congress during the years of reconstruction and replaced them with southern Democrats. In their own states they destroyed the carpetbag governments which had been the source of so much controversy.

In addition to bringing the tragic Reconstruction Era to an end, President Hayes has the distinction of being the first President to initiate reforms in the federal civil service. When he took office, he refused to follow the practice of many earlier Presidents of discharging thousands of officeholders and replacing them with political favorites. He also insisted that all persons recommended by Congressmen for jobs should be carefully investigated. These reforms, for such they were, angered the Stalwart Republicans. But, as far as the Stalwarts were concerned, the worst was yet to come. One of Hayes' cabinet members, Carl Schurz, a German-born Republican, introduced the merit system into the Department of the Interior. And the President himself courageously removed a prominent Republican leader, Chester A. Arthur, from his job as Collector of Customs in New York because of his undue political activity. "Boss" Conkling and other "Old Guard," or Stalwart, Republicans were furious, but Hayes stood his ground.

Hayes did nothing, however, to antagonize the Stalwarts in his reaction to new problems that were confronting the nation's farmers and wage earners. He opposed the demand of farmers for a money policy that would be favorable to them, and, as you will see, resisted their efforts to get the government to issue more paper money and silver coins.

President Hayes, like most Americans of his time, was also opposed to labor organizations. When a series of railroad strikes broke out in 1877 and disorder threatened, Hayes sent federal troops to the potential trouble spots and broke the strikes, as you will see.

The election of 1880. Well before the nominating conventions for the 1880 elections, President Hayes announced that he would not be a candidate for re-election. The Stalwart wing of the Republican Party, fed up with talk of reform and eager to return to the "good old days," tried to win the nomination for former President Ulysses S. Grant. But the Half-Breed wing of the party, led by James G. Blaine, who wanted the nomination for himself, managed to block this attempt. Finally, in order to break the deadlock, the Republican convention nominated a war veteran, General James A. Garfield of Ohio. In order to win the support of the disappointed Stalwarts, the convention chose a leading Stalwart for its Vice-Presidential candidate, Chester A. Arthur, former Collector of Customs for the Port of New York.

The Democrats also pinned their hopes for the Presidency on a war veteran, General Winfield S. Hancock of Pennsylvania.

Neither of the two major parties faced up to the real issues of the time. It was a third party, as you will see—the Greenback-Labor Party—that pointed to the basic problems of the new industrial age —labor legislation, regulation of railroads and other "big business," the money issue, and an income tax.

The election was a close one. Garfield won with an electoral vote of 214 to Hancock's 155, but the popular vote totaled 4,449,053 for the Republicans, 4,442,035 for the Democrats.

Civil service reform. On July 2, 1881, in the Washington railway station, President Garfield was shot by Charles J. Guiteau, a disappointed—and mentally unbalanced—office seeker. Garfield died in September.

The tragic death of the President shocked the country into an awareness of the evils of the old spoils system. Chester A. Arthur, the new President, rose above politics and, responding to the widespread demand for reform, supported the Pendleton Civil Service Act.

The Pendleton Act, which became

Clothing of the 1880's

law in 1883, provided for a bipartisan three-man commission (one on which both parties were represented) to give competitive examinations to candidates for public offices. The first examinations were to be for only about 12 per cent of the federal jobs, including some of the positions in the federal departments, the customhouses, and the large post offices. But the President was given authority to broaden the list of offices to be filled by examination. The Pendleton Act also forbade the party in power to ask for campaign contributions from federal office-holders. President Arthur appointed as head of the commission a well-known champion of civil service reform and extended the list of "classified" federal positions—positions for which civil service examinations had to be taken.

So it was that, after years of agitation, reformers at last managed to write into law the principle that federal jobs below the policy-making level should be filled by competitive examination. In years to come, future Presidents would greatly extend the list of classified positions. By 1883, however, an all-important principle had been established, and a long step had been taken to make government more honest and more efficient.

Presidential candidates in 1884. By the narrowest of margins, the Democrats won the election of 1884, and for the first time since 1861 a Democratic President prepared to occupy the White House. It was the split in the Republican Party that opened the way for the Democratic victory—that, and, as you will see, an ill-advised reference to the Roman Catholic religion.

When election year rolled around, Chester A. Arthur made it clear that he would like to have another four years in the Presidency. But his fellow Stalwarts had lost faith in him because of his reform activities. The leader of the Half-Breed wing of the Republican Party, James G. Blaine, won the nomination.

Blaine—handsome, colorful, and persuasive—was often called "the Plumed Knight from the state of Maine." During the course of his political career, he had managed to stir up a number of enemies, including the reform element in his own party. His enemies accused Blaine of using his political influence to secure favors for big business—at a generous profit for himself. Disgruntled at his nomination, a large group of Republicans, nicknamed "Mugwumps," bolted the party and voted for the Democratic candidate.

The Democrats made the most of Blaine's reputation as "a tool of the special interests" by choosing for their Presidential nominee a man who had a long record of reform activities. Grover

438

Cleveland, who had been mayor of Buffalo and governor of New York, was known to be thoroughly honest, courageous, independent—and stubborn almost to a fault when he believed that he was fighting for a principle. His reform activities had provoked strong opposition within his own party. This opposition proved to be an asset. "We love him for the enemies he has made," one of his admirers commented.

The Democrats win. In the campaign the big issues of the day were almost forgotten as the politicians heaped abuse upon the rival candidates. Each party diligently raked over the personal life of the opposition candidate, searching for misconduct that could be held against him.

Throughout the campaign the two candidates, Blaine and Cleveland, ran neck and neck. With only a few days remaining before the election, it became clear that the decision depended upon the vote of New York state. And then, on the very eve of the election, at a reception given for Blaine by a group of Protestant clergymen, one of the speakers called the Democrats the party of "Rum, Romanism, and Rebellion."

The speaker's use of the word "rum" was a deliberate attempt to "smear" the Democrats. His use of the word "rebellion" referred, of course, to the alliance between northern Democrats and the "Solid South" Democrats. Both of these references were indiscreet, but the speaker's reference to "Romanism"—the Roman Catholic religion—was fatal. It is generally agreed that Blaine's failure to rebuke the speaker for this insult to Roman Catholic voters cost him the election. The final count showed that Cleveland had won New York by a margin of only 1149 out of a total of 1,125,000 votes. Cleveland also won the Presidency, squeaking through with 219 electoral votes to Blaine's 182.

The election of 1884 was the first Presidential victory for the Democrats in 28 years. It was one sign that memories of the War Between the States were beginning to recede.

↙ **SECTION SURVEY**

1. Contrast the "spoils system" with the "merit system" of appointment to government jobs.
2. In what way was the election of 1876 one of the most unusual in our history?
3. What position did each of the following groups take concerning reform: (a) Liberal Republicans, (b) Stalwarts, and (c) Half-Breeds?
4. What was the Pendleton Act of 1883?
5. Describe the campaign of 1884. What was the significance in the election of the slogan "Rum, Romanism, and Rebellion"?
IDENTIFY: Electoral Commission, "Old Guard" Republicans, "Old Eight to Seven," "Mugwumps"; Greeley, Tilden, Hayes, Conkling, Blaine, Garfield, Arthur, Guiteau; 1872, 1880, 1881.

3 The cause of political reform moves forward despite setbacks

When President Cleveland entered the White House in 1885, the first Democratic President to do so since the inauguration of Buchanan in 1857, the movement for political reform entered a new phase.

Cleveland takes a firm stand. President Cleveland, who strongly believed that "a public office is a public trust," took a firm stand on important issues even though he knew that his action would antagonize influential members of his own party.

He supported civil service reform by doubling the number of federal offices on the classified list. He took a step in the direction of conserving the nation's natural resources by recovering more than 80,000,000 acres of public land illegally held by railroads, lumber companies, and cattle interests. He also signed a bill in 1887 creating a federal Division of Forestry.

One of his most courageous acts was his attempt to block pension "grabs" by veterans of the Union army. For many years the Pension Bureau had been handing out pensions with an extremely

■ In 1886, Thomas Nast, the cartoonist, showed President Cleveland turning pension seekers away from the money vault of the United States Treasury.

of 1876. The act provided that, if a state sent in more than one set of electoral returns, Congress had to accept the returns approved by the governor of the state.

The Hatch Act of 1887 was designed to help the nation's farmers. As you will see, the Hatch Act authorized annual grants of money for the creation and maintenance of experimental laboratories and demonstration farms in each of the states.

The Interstate Commerce Act of 1887 was adopted in an effort to eliminate unfair business practices of the railroads. This was by far the most important legislation adopted by Congress during Cleveland's first administration. When Congress drafted the Interstate Commerce Act, as you will see in Chapter 24, it initiated a new and far-reaching policy in regard to the relations between government and business.

Congress refused, however, to accept the President's vigorous recommendation that the tariff rates be lowered. In spite of the President's strongest urging, the high-tariff men in the Senate blocked the administration bill providing lower tariff rates.

Harrison is elected in 1888. The reform activities that President Cleveland had carried on during his term in the White House, and especially his campaign for lower tariffs, antagonized a considerable number of the political leaders of his own party. Nevertheless, in 1888 the Democrats decided to nominate him for a second term.

Although Cleveland won nearly 100,000 more popular votes than his opponent, Benjamin Harrison, he lost the election by an electoral count of 233 to 168. The Republicans won the Presidency and control of both houses of Congress.

Cleveland's policies reversed. Benjamin Harrison was a successful lawyer, a veteran of the Union army, and the grandson of former President William Henry Harrison. He was not, however, a "strong" President. In his opinion, his duty as Chief Executive was to follow

generous hand. Now and then, however, the request for a pension was based on such flimsy grounds that even the bureau balked. Frequently, when this happened, the disappointed pension seeker asked his Congressman to get the pension for him by pushing a special bill through Congress. President Cleveland vetoed more than 200 of these bills. In so doing, he antagonized many ex-soldiers, who were united in the politically powerful veterans' organization, the Grand Army of the Republic, known as the G.A.R.

Congress passes important laws. In addition to these personal accomplishments of Cleveland himself, Congress adopted several important laws during the years from 1885 to 1889.

The Presidential Succession Act of 1886 provided that, if both the President and the Vice-President died or were disabled, the Cabinet officers would succeed to the Presidency in the order in which their offices had been created.

The Electoral Count Act of 1887 was designed to prevent another disputed election similar to the one that had aroused such controversy in the election the wishes of the Senators and Representatives, who in turn had the responsibility of carrying out the wishes of the people.

During President Harrison's administration the Republicans reversed many of President Cleveland's policies. They returned to the spoils system, making a clean sweep of Democratic officeholders (except those on the classified list) and replacing them with Republicans. Congress passed the Dependent Pension Act that granted a pension to every Union veteran who had served a minimum of 90 days and who, either during or after his period of service, had become disabled. Veterans requesting these pensions needed only to prove that for either physical or mental reasons they could not earn a living by manual labor. Congress also adopted the highest protective tariff the country had seen up to that time. The McKinley Tariff of 1890, introduced by Congressman William McKinley of Ohio, raised rates from an average of about 38 per cent to an average of close to 50 per cent.

But the "Old Guard" Republicans did not have everything their own way. In an effort to appeal to farmers, laborers, miners, small businessmen, and the American public in general, Congress passed two important pieces of legislation in 1890. The Sherman Silver Purchase Act was intended to appeal to western mining interests and to increase the amount of money in circulation as a benefit to farmers, wage earners, and small businessmen. The Sherman Antitrust Act was intended to protect the public at large from monopoly practices and other abuses of free enterprise that had arisen with the growth of industry. You will read about these two important pieces of legislation in Unit Seven.

Growing dissatisfaction. Neither the Sherman Silver Purchase Act nor the Sherman Antitrust Act served to overcome the growing dissatisfaction with President Harrison's Republican administration. Wage earners, united in the newly organized American Federation of Labor (Chapter 25), had no reason to hope their demands would be met by the Republicans. Farmers, abandoning hope of help from either of the major parties, began to take steps with the support of organized labor to secure control of the government and bring about long-sought reforms. And the public in general, struggling to make ends meet in the face of rising prices for manufactured goods, blamed their troubles on the Republican-sponsored McKinley Tariff.

Of course, the problems Americans faced in the 1890's could not be explained simply in relation to a tariff act or the policies of a political party. Basic to everything else was the fact that a new industrial civilization was being born. Enterprising business leaders were creating new industries; technology was creating new jobs and opportunities—and, in the process, displacing men from older lines of work; and the entire economy was growing at an ever more rapid rate of speed. In this rapidly expanding economy, wage earners on the whole were better off than workers in industrial Europe; some wage earners were doing very well indeed; and a large middle class was beginning to emerge. But there was poverty, too, and insecurity for millions of workers. And there were large problems clamoring for attention.

The growing need for reform. Whatever the causes may have been, there was ample evidence in the early 1890's that reforms of several kinds were urgently needed.

In 1892 Henry Demarest Lloyd was gathering material for his book *Wealth Against Commonwealth*. As he looked around at the new industrial society that was transforming everyday life throughout the country, the author concluded that it left much to be desired. "Nature is rich;" he wrote, "but everywhere man, the heir of nature, is poor." It should be possible in this new age, he went on to say, for every human being to enjoy "a plenty undreamed of" in earlier times. "But between this plenty . . . and the people hungering for it step the 'cornerers' "—the giant industries and the enormous business enterprises.

Henry Demarest Lloyd's book reached a nationwide audience because it expressed the deep-seated discontent of millions of Americans. It was not industrialism that the people feared and hated. They agreed with Lloyd that the new industrial age held the promise of a brighter future for people everywhere. What concerned many Americans was that the new industrialism had created extremes of poverty and wealth. Expanding industries brought vast wealth to a few owners, while the majority of workers lived in poverty. For a solution to this problem, many thoughtful Americans turned to government—whether controlled by Republicans or Democrats.

By 1892 the demand for government action had reached clamorous proportions. Owners of small businesses and wage earners in every section of the country, and especially the western farmers, were calling for reform measures.

The election of 1892. The rising volume of discontent throughout the country turned the election of 1892 into a spirited three-way contest. Both the Republicans and the Democrats realized that they would have to do something to meet the demand for reform. They were prodded into action by the formidable strength of a new party, the Populist Party, which had been created in 1891. The Populist Party was organized, as you will see later, by farmers. But it also attracted wage earners and many other voters who were discontented with the policies of the two major parties.

The Republicans were definitely on the defensive. President Benjamin Harrison, who had led the country since 1889, and the Republican Party as a whole, were subjected to widespread criticism. As you have seen, the Republican administration had managed to antagonize a large number of voters. The President himself had abandoned civil service reform and returned to the old spoils system. Congress had opened the door to a flood of pensions for "disabled" veterans. Congress had also adopted the highest protective tariff in history—the McKinley Tariff. In spite of the criticism, the Republicans decided to stand on their record, and nominated President Harrison for a second term.

The Democrats, eager to take advantage of the demands for reform from both wage earners and farmers, nominated Grover Cleveland. As you have seen, Cleveland had already won a reputation as a champion of honest politics.

The Democrats won, with Cleveland gathering 277 electoral votes to Harrison's 145. The Democrats also won control of both houses of Congress. But the new Populist Party—an out-and-out reform party—made a remarkable showing. Although the Populist candidate, James B. Weaver, collected only 22 electoral votes, his popular vote totaled more than 1,000,000, and the party itself managed to elect three governors and send numerous representatives to state legislatures and to Congress.

Cleveland runs into trouble. From the beginning President Cleveland ran into trouble, and, as the months passed, he and his administration piled up enemies right and left. He antagonized wage earners with his labor policy, and farmers with his money policy, as you will see later. People in general blamed him and his administration for a depression that hit the country shortly after he took office. In the Congressional elections of 1894, the voters expressed their dissatisfaction with the Democratic administration by electing enough Republican Senators and Representatives to give the Republicans control of both houses of Congress.

The Wilson-Gorman Tariff Act. The McKinley Tariff had been one of the principal issues in the Presidential campaign of 1892, and Cleveland's victory stemmed in part from his promise to lower the tariff. Acting on the President's recommendations, in December 1893 William L. Wilson of West Virginia, who was chairman of the Ways and Means Committee of the House of Representatives, introduced a bill that provided substantial reductions in existing tariff rates. The bill passed the House without any great difficulty. When it reached the Senate, however, it ran into the unyielding opposition of the Republicans and a number of high-tariff Democrats. Led by Senator Gorman of Maryland, the friends of a high tariff added more than 600 amendments to the original bill.

The Wilson-Gorman bill, as it was called, provided lower average tariff rates than the act it was designed to replace—39.9 per cent to the McKinley Tariff's 48.4 per cent. But it was still a high protective tariff, and President Cleveland was furious, especially with the Democrats who had voted for the high-tariff provisions. He did not veto the bill, for in his opinion it was a better measure than the McKinley Tariff. But he refused to endorse it by adding his signature, preferring instead to allow it to become law by leaving it on his desk for ten days, when it automatically became law without his signature.

Dissatisfaction with the Wilson-Gorman Tariff. During the tariff debates in the Senate, powerful *lobbies,* or pressure groups, tried by every means in their power to influence the votes of doubtful Senators. Producers of iron, steel, wool, glass, and hundreds of other commodities demanded tariff protection.

One of the most active of these lobbies was the American Sugar Refining Company, usually called "the sugar trust."° The original House bill had completely removed the tariff on raw and refined sugar. The sugar trust, determined to get the tariff restored, immediately went to work on the Senate. During the course of the long and heated debate over the sugar tariff, the value of the sugar trust's stock rose and fell on the New York Stock Exchange. In the end, however, the trust won, and the tariff on sugar was restored.

The Wilson-Gorman Tariff cost the

....

° *trust:* a group of companies centrally controlled to regulate production, reduce expenses, and eliminate competition (see page 476).

VOTING MACHINES

The first practical voting machine, or vote recorder, was built in Rochester, New York, in 1899. Since then, voting machines have been greatly improved, and are now widely used, especially in large towns and cities. Voting machines have certain advantages. They speed up the voting process, make it easier for the voter to indicate his choices, help to prevent fraud, and provide a quick, accurate count of the votes cast.

Few people know that back in 1868 Thomas Edison, at the age of twenty-one, became interested in building a vote recorder. Then, as now, Congressmen voted by the roll call. That is, when the time came to vote on an issue, the presiding officer of the Senate or the House called upon each member to rise and say "Aye" or "No." Believing this to be a waste of time, Edison invented an electric voting machine. But to Edison's surprise, Congressmen told him they did not want such a machine. The minority was especially opposed. When they were called upon to vote, they wanted to be able to demonstrate their opposition to a bill by standing up and answering with a resounding "No!"

So Edison's electric voting machine never got any further than the Patent Office. Other inventors have made better progress with similar devices used in public elections. But to this day Congress prefers the traditional roll call when it comes time to vote.

Democrats the support of large numbers of Americans who agreed with President Cleveland that this measure was an example of "party perfidy [treachery] and party dishonor." As far as millions of voters were concerned, the Democrats had broken their campaign promise to do away with a high protective tariff.

Decision against an income tax. The original tariff bill that Representative Wilson introduced in the House of Representatives would have drastically lowered the tariff rates. With the lower rates in mind and expecting a loss in revenue to the government, the House Ways and Means Committee added a clause to the tariff bill providing for a 2 per cent tax on all incomes of more than $4000.

The income tax clause provoked violent debate, but it finally passed both houses of Congress and became law. Opponents of the income tax immediately tested the new measure in the courts, and in 1895 the Supreme Court declared it unconstitutional by a vote of five to four. The Supreme Court ruled against the income tax because it was a direct tax not apportioned among the states according to population, as required by the Constitution (page 174).

The Democratic administration could by no stretch of the imagination be held responsible for the Supreme Court's negative decision on the income tax. Nevertheless, farmers, wage earners, and the rank and file of Americans considered this decision as merely one more example of how the government favored "big business." For this reason, the Supreme Court's rejection of the income tax helped to fan the flame of protest that was sweeping the country.

Financial panic and depression. It was the financial Panic of 1893 and the subsequent depression that caused President Cleveland his greatest anxiety. On May 5, 1893, only two months after Cleveland took the oath of office, the value of stocks on the New York Stock Exchange suddenly plunged downward. As the weeks passed, the situation became rapidly worse. Thousands of businesses failed. Factories closed their doors. It is estimated that 4,000,000 workers were unemployed. The prices of farm produce dropped so low that farmers could not afford to pay the freight to market. By the end of the year, the nation was in the grip of one of the worst depressions in its history.

There were a number of reasons for the depression that hit the country in 1893, but, as the depression deepened, money became the central issue. In the Republican convention of 1896, the Republicans, favoring a money policy demanded by businessmen and industrialists, nominated William McKinley of Ohio as their candidate. The Democrats, adopting the money policy of the Populist Party, nominated William Jennings Bryan of Nebraska. You will read a full account of this dramatic Presidential election in Chapter 24. McKinley won the election, as you will see, and the Populist Party died out. But the forces of reform soon rallied, in the early 1900's, to a new and more powerful banner—the banner of the Progressive movement.

✓ SECTION SURVEY

1. What did President Grover Cleveland mean when he said that "a public office is a public trust"?

2. Explain how each of the following laws helped to solve an important national problem: (a) Presidential Succession Act of 1886, (b) Electoral Count Act of 1887, (c) Hatch Act of 1887, and (d) Interstate Commerce Act of 1887.

3. (a) Why did Cleveland allow the Wilson-Gorman Tariff bill to become a law without his signature? (b) What was the reaction of rank-and-file Americans to this law and to the Supreme Court decision on its income tax provision?

4. Describe the Panic of 1893. Discuss its effect on the election campaign of 1896.

IDENTIFY: pension "grabs," McKinley Tariff of 1890, *Wealth Against Commonwealth*, Populist Party, lobbies, trust, Panic of 1893; Henry Demarest Lloyd, Weaver; 1887, 1892.

Points to Discuss: 1. Discuss the importance of the rapid development of industry to the drastic changes which took place throughout the country following the War Between the States.

2. In what sense was the result of the election of 1876 a victory for the process of orderly government?

3. Why has the Pendleton Act been called the "Magna Carta of civil service reform"?

4. Compare the parties, candidates, issues, and results in the elections of 1880, 1884, 1888, and 1892.

5. What do you consider to be the three most significant laws relating to political democracy passed between 1865 and 1896? Discuss each.

6. Compare the position of the Republican and Democratic Parties on the issues of the tariff and of pensions in the period 1865–96. Be specific.

Using Charts: 1. Consult the Chronology of Events. Point out and explain the political, economic, and social developments during the administration of each of these Presidents: Grant, Hayes, Arthur, Cleveland, and Harrison.

2. Which of these Presidents do you think left the most impressive record?

Consulting the Sources: See Commager, *Documents*, No. 317, for Cleveland's Tariff Message of 1887 asking for tariff reduction. See No. 312 on pensions.

■ TRACING THE MAIN IDEAS

Change, unrest, new ways of living, and new problems—these were characteristics of every section of the United States during the years from 1865 to 1900. Many of the new problems that Americans faced were the inevitable result of the war that for four long years had convulsed the nation and disrupted long-established ways of living. To an even greater extent, however, the new problems were the result of the Industrial Revolution that was transforming the United States from an agricultural nation into a great industrial power.

The war itself had hastened the process of industrialization. Keyed to feverish pitch during the war years, northern industry continued to expand after 1865 —and with ever-increasing speed. Nor was the process of industrialization confined to the North. It was transforming life in the South, and, as you will see in the next chapter, it helped men to conquer the last frontiers of the West.

But the new ways of living brought serious problems as well as excitement and drama. Morality in public life sank to an all-time low as a "get-rich-quick" spirit and greed for power infected millions of Americans. The very foundations of democracy itself were imperiled as wealth and power became concentrated in the hands of a relatively few pioneers of the new industrial age. Through their control of the giant corporations that were springing up, of the railroads, and of the mines, factories, and banks, the new industrial leaders were able to exert powerful influence over government at every level.

There is, however, another side of the story. As Americans became increasingly aware of the threat to democracy, they began to take steps to correct the situation. In later chapters you will see how the American people undertook to solve the numerous problems that faced them.

CHAPTER **22** 1865–1900

Americans Conquer "The Last Frontier"

Chief JOSEPH

CHIEF Joseph, leader of the Nez Percé (neh pehr-SEH) Indians, stood proudly but sorrowfully before his conquerors. "I am tired of fighting," he said. "Our chiefs are killed. . . . It is cold and we have no blankets. The little children are freezing to death. . . . My heart is sick and sad. From where the sun now stands I will fight no more, forever."

The year was 1877. The time, sunset. The place, the plains of Montana, only a few miles from the border between Canada and the United States.

The Nez Percé Indians had lived in the Oregon country. They claimed, and truthfully, that for half a century they had dwelt in peace with the white men.

Recently, in the years after 1865, the shadow of trouble had fallen across the lands inhabited by the Nez Percé. Pioneers by the thousands had poured into the Pacific Northwest, men from the North and men from the South, many of them war veterans hardened by combat and eager to settle and build a new way of life for themselves in the fertile valleys of the Oregon Territory. As the pressure for land increased, the newcomers began to look with greedy eyes at the Nez Percé hunting grounds. And at last the order from the government in Washington arrived: The Nez Percé were to be moved from their land and sent to a reservation—a tract of land set aside by the federal government as a dwelling place for the tribe.

The Nez Percé refused to submit. Chief Joseph tried to lead his people to safety and new homes in Canada. With two hundred warriors and six hundred women and children he fled eastward across the mountains, closely pursued by United States troops. For two months, during which they traveled more than 1300 miles, Chief Joseph and his people outwitted their pursuers. They were in what is now Montana, within sight of the Canadian boundary and safety, when they were surrounded and forced to surrender.

Chief Joseph and his conquerors were actors in one of the most dramatic phases of American history. They stood in 1877 on the last frontier of the West —the Great Plains, a vast area stretching from what are now Montana and North Dakota southward to Texas. From time immemorial this land had belonged to the Indians. Now it was being claimed by people from the North and South and from distant Europe.

This is the story of the conquest of the Indians—those of the mountains as well as those of the Great Plains. It is also the story of the West itself and of new ways of life on the last frontier.

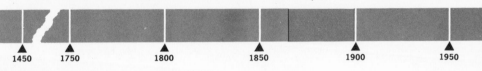

1450   1750   1800   1850   1900   1950   19

1 Land-hungry Americans conquer the Indians of the Great Plains

On their western edge the Middle Western prairies merge into the Great Plains. Although there is no sharp line separating the prairies from the Great Plains, it has been customary to accept the 100th meridian as the dividing line (see map, pages 818–19). Usually, as one travels westward from the 100th meridian to the Rocky Mountains, the rainfall decreases and the grass becomes shorter.

Obstacles to settlement. It was along the line of the 100th meridian that the westward advance of the settlers halted for at least a generation during the early years of the 1800's. The reluctance of the pioneers to settle on the Great Plains arose in part from misinformation. Earlier explorers, accustomed to wooded country with abundant rainfall, had established the idea that the Great Plains were for the most part uninhabitable desert. Maps printed at this time called the plains the "Great American Desert." By the 1850's, however, this notion was being dispelled. Traders and pioneers who crossed the plains to California and to the Pacific Northwest reported that much of the plains country was good for settlement.

But there remained a formidable obstacle to settlement—the Indian population of the Great Plains.

Bow and arrow against the long rifle. The Plains Indians had learned what the white man was going to have to learn—how to adapt himself to the plains environment. The buffalo, or bison, provided the Indians with food, clothing, and shelter.

The Indians were powerful enemies. They rode horses with superb ease. Before they secured rifles, they fought with spears and with short bows, from which they could drive their arrows with amazing rapidity and penetrating force. They were protected by shields of buffalo hide, which they coated with glue made from horses' hooves and hardened over the fire to a consistency almost like iron. One of their favorite tactics was to gallop around their enemy, hiding behind horses and shields, and deliberately drawing enemy fire. When the enemy's ammunition was exhausted, they darted in to strike him down with their arrows and long spears.

Faced with these weapons and tactics, the white man was at first under a great disadvantage. His long rifle could be reloaded and fired only with great difficulty from the back of a galloping horse.

A new weapon. The invention of the revolver in the late 1830's and its subsequent use ended the Indians' temporary superiority in weapons. A short, stubby weapon, the revolver could be reloaded easily at full gallop, and several bullets could be fired in rapid succession without reloading. Armed with this new weapon, frontiersmen in the 1850's began to move out on the plains with new confidence.

A new method of transportation. The early pioneers who crossed the plains to the Southwest, California, and the Pacific Northwest depended upon horses and oxen for transportation. A man afoot on the waterless plains was in grave danger of dying from thirst, sunstroke, or cold. The horse thief became Public Enemy No. 1.

The man on horseback, however, could not transport goods in any bulk. To fill this need, the Conestoga wagon lumbered out upon the plains in caravans that at night formed circles around a campfire for protection against Indian attack. As time passed, stagecoach lines provided speedier transportation.

But it was the railroad that finally provided an adequate system of transporta-

tion. The first transcontinental line was completed on May 10, 1869, when the Central Pacific and the Union Pacific met at Promontory Point, in what is now Utah (see map, this page).

Construction of the first transcontinental railroad to the Pacific coast began in 1866, the year after the war ended. Chinese workers were imported to do the bulk of the physical labor on the Central Pacific. The Union Pacific, building from Omaha, in Nebraska Territory, drew many of its workers from the ranks of the Irish immigrants. All work was done under the eyes of scouts, whose job it was to protect the railroad

builders from bands of hostile Indians. The first transcontinental railroad was a magnificent achievement. It contributed enormously to the economic growth of the nation, for it brought the Atlantic and the Pacific seaboards within a week's journey of each other, and opened a route to the rich resources of the West. The "wedding of the rails" at Promontory Point in Utah in 1869 was a scene of great jubilation. Surrounded by the grimy workmen, silk-hatted gentlemen drove a golden spike to hold the last rails in place while the telegraph carried the news to Americans everywhere.

The railroad linked the Atlantic and the Pacific coasts. It carried northerners and southerners alike into the still untamed West. It also split the buffalo herds in two, and the herds were split again and again as such new lines as the Atchison, Topeka, and Santa Fe crept across the grasslands. The completion of the Northern Pacific Railway in 1883 sealed the fate of the final, northern herd. (See map, opposite page.)

Destruction of the buffalo. For a few brief years there was wholesale slaughter of the buffalo. Parties of hunters debarked from trains with horses and equipment, killed the buffalo at will, and loaded the hides on trains bound for the eastern markets. It has been estimated that between 1871 and 1874 hunters killed nearly 3,000,000 buffalo each year. By 1875 hunters were selling their buffalo hides for sixty-five cents to one dollar and fifteen cents each. The waste was frightful. Buffalo carcasses were abandoned, and for every hide taken, four were left on the plains.

The disappearance of the buffalo doomed the Plains Indians, who had built their hunting culture upon the vast herd that originally roamed the plains. When they destroyed the buffalo, the white hunters destroyed the Indians' only source of food, clothing, and shelter. Almost the last of the free Indians in the United States were driven on to remote reservations, where they lived as wards—that is, under the protection and control—of the federal government.

Thus the revolver and the railroad, both products of the Industrial Revolution, helped to sweep the Indians from the Great Plains and to open the way for settlement.

The last Indian wars. Despite his advantages over the Indians, the white man had to fight long and hard to drive the Indians from their last hunting grounds on the Great Plains. Between 1865 and 1886 there was almost constant conflict between the whites and the Indians. Never in all its history had the United States conducted such a vigorous campaign on its frontiers. In all of these campaigns, men who had fought on the southern side and men who had fought on the northern side in the War Between the States now fought as comrades in arms against a common enemy.

And the Indians fought back, struggling to hold on to their lands and their distinctive way of life. The smaller the area into which they were compressed, the more savagely the Indians struck back. But the savagery was not all on one side. The whites fought with broken promises as well as with guns. It was President Hayes himself who said to Congress in 1877, the same year in which Chief Joseph made his heroic attempt to lead his people to freedom in Canada, "Many, if not most, of our Indian wars have had their origin in broken promises and acts of injustice on our part."

By the middle of the 1880's, however, the period of burning, scalping, and slaughter was over. The Indians were huddled on reservations, their power forever destroyed. The work of the War Department, which was in charge of Indian affairs, was finished.

■ Many buffalo were shot by people like Buffalo Bill Cody to feed the gangs of railroad builders. But many more were wantonly slaughtered, as shown here.

449

■ This may not resemble the powwows you see on television. But it is an actual photo of the meeting of government officials with Indian chiefs on January 16, 1891, at Pine Ridge, South Dakota. William Cody (Buffalo Bill) is shown shaking hands with two chiefs.

But an Indian problem still remained. It was a problem of assimilating into American life the 200,000 to 300,000 "original Americans," of helping them to take part in the life of the country.

"Americanizing" the Indians. The federal government made its first attack upon the problem of assimilating the Indians with the passage of the Dawes Act in 1887. In this law Congress looked forward to the time when the reservation system would be ended and the Indian would take his place as an equal among other American citizens.

The Dawes Act provided that each head of a family could, if he wished, claim as his own 160 acres of land. Bachelors, women, and children were entitled to lesser amounts. Legal ownership of the property was to be held in trust by the federal government for 25 years. During this period the Indian could neither sell his land nor use it as security for a mortgage. The Burke Act of 1906 modified this provision. It gave the Secretary of the Interior authority to reduce the 25-year period in any case in which he was convinced that the Indian was capable of handling his own affairs.

The Dawes Act and the Burke Act were designed to protect the Indians from unscrupulous speculators. These acts also provided that Indians who accepted the land and abandoned the tribal way of life were to be given citizenship, including the right to vote. Meanwhile, Congress granted larger appropriations for Indian education and made education compulsory for all Indian children.

A look ahead. Federal legislation enabled some of the Indians to adopt the white man's way of life and become American citizens. But most of the Indians remained on the reservations, clung to their tribal customs, and lived as wards of their guardian, the federal government. Between 1887 and the 1920's, a large proportion of their reservation lands was taken from them, and their lot became more desperate.

In 1924, partly as a reward for the services of their young men in World War I, the Indian population as a whole was given citizenship. But citizenship did not diminish the harsh fact that their poverty was perhaps greater than that of any other group in the United States. To be sure, the discovery of oil on some of the Indian lands, among them the Osage reservation in Oklahoma, brought unexpected riches to a few Indians. But for the Indians as a whole, conditions were hard. Their death rate, because of infant mortality and disease among adults, was so high that the Indian population was decreasing.

By the 1920's it was becoming increasingly evident that the federal policy was a failure. Nothing in the Indians' tradition had prepared them for the role of individual farmers, and those who did attempt to change their way of life were all too often forced to struggle with the poorest possible land. Moreover, the government-sponsored education failed to equip the Indian children for the new lives that they were expected to lead.

During the late 1920's and the 1930's the federal government began to adopt a new policy toward the Indians. Congress made a notable advance with the passage of the Wheeler-Howard Act of 1934. This act encouraged the Indians to practice self-government and to develop their own community life on their own reservations. It undertook to provide a more effective type of education —an education designed to teach the Indians to use their land more efficiently, by practicing soil conservation and by developing improved methods of raising and marketing their farm products and their livestock. The new educational program included adults as well as children, and made the schools a center of community life.

In 1920 the total Indian population in the United States had been reduced to only about 245,000, and, as you have seen, it was still decreasing. During the late 1920's, however, the tide was reversed, and by 1950 the Indian population had risen to nearly 350,000. Almost every state included some Indians in its population, but the great majority lived west of the Mississippi River.

In 1953 Congress passed a resolution declaring that federal supervision of Indian tribes should be ended as soon as each tribe was able to manage its own affairs.

SECTION SURVEY

1. In combat, what advantages did the Indian have at first over the frontiersman?
2. Describe how each of the following contributed to the defeat of the Indians: (a) the revolver and (b) the railroads.
3. In the wars between the whites and the Indians, "savagery was not all on one side." Explain.
4. What part did each of the following play in the Americanization of the Indians: (a) Dawes Act of 1887 and (b) citizenship law of 1924?
IDENTIFY: Indian reservation, Great Plains, prairies, buffalo, long rifle, Conestoga wagon, Burke Act, Wheeler-Howard Act of 1934; Chief Joseph; 1869.

2 Cattlemen and cowboys move out onto the Great Plains

Cattlemen began to move out onto the Great Plains in the late 1860's, long before the Indians were conquered. By the 1890's the cattle industry had become "big business," its products passing from the western ranges through the stockyards, slaughterhouses, and packing plants to become a major item of domestic and world trade.

Rise of the Cattle Kingdom. Many of the cattle for the cattle industry came from the ranches in southeastern Texas formerly operated by Spaniards and Mexicans. These ranches were occupied by the Texans, who also took over the huge herds of wild cattle, called long-horns, estimated in 1865 to number about 5 million head. The wild herds sprang from cattle lost by the Spaniards and by the American wagon trains crossing the plains in earlier days.

It was no easy task for the first Texans to learn how to handle the cattle, wild or tame. Writing in the 1870's, Colonel Richard I. Dodge warned that "the wild cattle of Texas . . . animals miscalled tame, are fifty times more dangerous to a footman than the fiercest buffalo." But with the aid of the horse, the saddle, the rope, and the revolver, the cowboys learned how to handle the longhorns on the open grasslands.

The "long drive." People in the growing cities of the nations needed enormous quantities of beef. The problem was to find a means of transporting the steers to the urban markets. Transportation was provided by the railroads, which in the 1860's were beginning to push out upon the Great Plains.

A cattleman's "gear"

As the steel rails moved westward, Texans drove enormous herds north on "long drives" to towns that grew up along the railroads. By 1870 Kansas cattle towns like Abilene, Ellsworth, and Ellis (all on the Kansas Pacific Railroad) and Dodge City and Wichita (on the Atchison, Topeka, and Santa Fe Railway) had become roaring, riotous communities (see map, page 448).

During the early years of the long drives, nearly all of the steers driven from Texas were sold in the cattle towns at good prices. In time, however, the number of cattle began to exceed the demand, and Texans who arrived in late fall were either unable to sell their steers or had to sell them at a loss.

The open range. At this point, enterprising cattlemen began to winter their surplus steers on the open range, or unfenced grazing lands, near the cattle towns. After fattening them during the winter, they sold them at high prices in the towns before the new cattle drives from Texas arrived to glut the market.

This was not the first time that cattle had been pastured on the short grass of the Great Plains. Pioneers crossing the plains to the Southwest and to the Pacific Northwest in the 1830's, 1840's, and 1850's had watched buffalo grazing. In addition, many of the wagon trains had wintered on the plains, and the pioneers had discovered that their horses and cattle grew fat on the short and thin, but nutritious, grass. The great freight carriers and stagecoach companies—like Russell, Majors & Waddell—regularly pastured their stock on the open range. The open-range cattle industry did not develop, however, until the railroads provided access to markets, and the Texans provided the huge herds of cattle.

The cattle rush. News that there was quick money to be made in the open-range cattle business soon reached the eastern seaboard and spread to Europe. The cattle rush that followed was similar in many respects to the gold rush that had populated California in 1849-50. Prices for land and steers soared as

■ A famous photographer, W. H. Jackson, took this picture of a western ranch house in 1872. The arsenal of firearms attests to the determination of these cattlemen to hold the open range against farmers and sheepherders. They were not successful.

men scrambled over the Great Plains, staking out claims that they had bought or simply taken and held at gunpoint.

Lured by the hope of quick gain, men in growing numbers rushed to the cattle country to win the longed-for riches. They built dugouts, sod huts, or simple ranch houses, pastured their herds on the open grasslands, and some, though by no means all, made fortunes.

Until the 1880's the cattlemen were the rulers of the Great Plains. This was the period of the long drive, the open range, the roundup, and the picturesque roving cowboy with his occupation and his costume adapted to the environment in which he lived.

The end of the open range. The open-range cattle industry passed, however, almost as quickly as it had come. The increased production of meat resulted in ruinously low prices. In 1885 a severe drought burned up the grasses on the overstocked range, and cattle starved by the thousands.

Even more disastrous for the cattlemen was the arrival of the sheepherders and farmers in the 1880's. Sheep cropped the grass so close that none was left for the cattle. Farmers, sometimes called "sodbusters" and "nesters," broke up the open range with their farms and barbed-wire fences (see page 456). The cattlemen fought desperately, for they were determined to keep the range

open. But they fought a hopeless battle. By the close of the 1880's the open, unfenced range on which cattlemen grazed and fattened huge herds was fast becoming a thing of the past.

For only a few years the cattlemen ruled a kingdom of their own on the unfenced plains of the West. But during these years they made a lasting impression on American life. To this day western movies, western TV programs, western novels, and western magazines provide popular entertainment for millions.

Ranches and fences. By the 1890's the western cattle industry centered in the high plains running through eastern Montana, Wyoming, Colorado, the New Mexico Territory, and western Texas. Most ranchers by now owned and fenced their property with barbed wire, leasing from the government additional grazing lands that they needed. New laws were drawn up governing water rights and other matters of concern to dwellers in the semiarid and arid regions.

Ranches varied in size from 2000 to 100,000 acres. To an easterner, accustomed to small farms of a few hundred acres at most, ranches of this size seemed enormous. But the ranches had to be large since each steer required a grazing area of from 15 to 75 acres, depending upon the amount of rainfall and the resulting growth of grass.

453

MEMORIES
OF THE WEST

In 1902, in the introduction to his novel *The Virginian*, Owen Wister wrote a glowing tribute to the cowboy and the wild, free life of the Great Plains. Producers of western movies and television shows are still trying to recapture and portray the images that Wister described:

"Had you left New York or San Francisco at ten o'clock this morning, by noon the day after tomorrow you could step out at Cheyenne. There you would stand at the heart of the world that is the subject of my picture, yet you would look around you in vain for the reality. It is a vanished world. No journeys, save those which memory can take, will bring you to it now. The mountains are there, far and shining, and the sunlight, and the infinite earth, and the air that seems forever the true fountain of youth—but where is the buffalo, and the wild antelope, and where is the horseman with his pasturing thousands? So like its old self does the sagebrush seem when revisited, that you wait for the horseman to appear. . . .

"What is become of the horseman, the cowpuncher, the last romantic figure upon our soil? For he was romantic. Whatever he did, he did with his might. The bread that he earned was earned hard, the wages that he squandered were squandered hard—half a year's pay sometimes gone in a night—'blown in' as he expressed it . . . Well, he will be here among us always, invisible, waiting his chance to live and play as he would like. His wild kind has been among us always, since the beginning: a young man with his temptations, a hero without wings. . . ."

With the invention of better instruments for drilling into the ground and the improvement of windmills for pumping water, many cattlemen watered their stock from wells scattered over their ranches. In years of abundant rainfall, cattlemen might prosper since their herds could fatten on the natural grasses, but in years of drought cattlemen were forced to feed their stock hay or cottonseed cake, a costly business that frequently wiped out all profits.

Growth and specialization. The development of the railroads revolutionized the cattle industry, which tended to become more and more specialized. Many ranchers on the plains began to concentrate on the breeding and raising of cattle. The steers were then sold to farmers in the rich corn and pasture lands of the prairie country. After being fattened for market, the cattle were shipped to nearby stockyards in Omaha, Kansas City, East St. Louis, St. Joseph, Sioux City, St. Paul–Minneapolis, and Chicago (see map, page 448). There they were slaughtered and transported in refrigerator cars to eastern cities and sometimes from there to Europe.

In the development of the livestock industry of the West, we see how men used the prairies, the semiarid plains, and the high plateaus and mountain valleys for grazing lands on which they produced a substantial part of the nation's meat and wool. By the 1890's the livestock industry in the West had become an organized, specialized business, closely tied to the economic life of the nation.

SECTION SURVEY

1. What was meant by the "long drive"?
2. Explain how cattlemen used the open range of the Great Plains.
3. Give the reason for the cattle rush of the 1870's.
4. Why did the open range disappear?
5. Show how the development of the railroads helped to bring about specialization in the cattle industry.

IDENTIFY: Cattle Kingdom, longhorns, roundup, ranch.

3 Farmers plow the tough sod of "the last frontier"

Farmers followed the cattlemen out on the prairies and plains. In about one generation, from 1870 to 1900, pioneers settled more land than all of their American forefathers combined.

In the 263 years between the first tiny settlement at Jamestown in 1607 until 1870, Americans transformed a total of 407,734,041 acres of wilderness into farm lands. Mighty though this achievement was, its pace was quite leisurely when compared to the speed with which men conquered the prairies and the plains. In the 30-year period from 1870 to 1900, pioneers settled an additional 430,000,000 acres—an area roughly equal to the combined areas of Norway, Sweden, Denmark, the Netherlands, Belgium, Germany, and France.

What was happening in America to make possible this rapid settlement of the last frontier?

Free land for settlers. One compelling attraction of the West was free land. In 1862, as you have seen (page 397), Congress enacted the Homestead Act granting 160 acres to all individuals who wished to qualify by settling a farm, or, as it was called, a "homestead."

Settlers rushed to accept the offer. Thousands of the pioneers were ex-soldiers who, uprooted by the war, sought new homes in the West. Thousands of others came from worn-out farms in the East, particularly from New England, in the hope of finding more fertile land on the prairies and the plains. Still other thousands came from Europe. In many areas of the Middle West, more than half of the pioneers were immigrants—Germans, Norwegians, Swedes, Danes, Czechs, Finns, and Russians.

The railroads encourage settlement. Without the railroad, however, the free land in the West, no matter how attractive in itself, would have remained unpopulated. During the 1870's and the 1880's four great transcontinental railroads crossed the prairies and the plains. Those railroads, and the branch lines running out from the main lines, opened up the western country for settlement.

The western railroads, as you recall, were built with the aid of large cash subsidies and grants of land from the federal government (see diagram, page 468). The railroads were allowed to sell this land and thus help raise the money needed for constructing their lines.

At the time the grants were made to the railroads, the land itself was almost worthless. Before the railroad companies could profit from their grants, they had to persuade people to move into the unsettled areas. Because the land was close to the railroads and therefore would be valuable, the railroad companies could hope to sell it, even though free land was available in more remote areas. But it was not only the initial cash

■ Advertisements such as this one of 1873 were used by the railroads to induce settlers to buy the lands they had been given by the government.

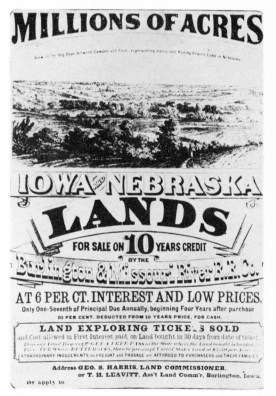

income from the sale of land that was important to the railroads. Even more important, in the long run, was the fact that once the land was settled, the railroads would gain revenue from passengers and freight. In addition, the unsold land remaining in the possession of the railroads would rise in value once settlers began to build farms and villages and towns along the right of way.

With these considerations in mind, the railroads launched extensive advertising campaigns, sending their literature and their agents even into Europe. Life on the plains was pictured in glowing colors, and as an added inducement the prospective purchaser was frequently offered free transportation to any land that he might buy from the railroad company. The transatlantic steamship lines, always eager to obtain passengers and freight, also launched advertising campaigns in Europe.

The problem of houses and fences. Despite these inducements, settlers did not at first pour out upon the plains. For one thing, they were still influenced by the old myth of the "Great American Desert." An even more important factor was the scarcity of wood.

New England stone wall with gate

Mid-western split-rail fence

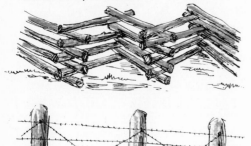

Prairie barbed-wire fence

The pioneers solved the problem of housing, as men have always done, by making use of the best available building material. On the plains this was sod. Cut out of the soil, bricklike chunks of sod formed the walls of shelters. With a few precious pieces of wood, the settlers framed the roof, finishing it with a layer of sod to keep out the wind and weather.

Fencing was even more difficult, for the pioneers could not farm without fences to protect their crops, and on the plains there was no material for fences.

During the decade of the 1870's, nearly every newspaper on the edge of the plains devoted a large portion of each issue to a discussion of the problem of fencing. The first adventurous pioneers tried everything, even mud walls, but without success. Ordinary wire strung between a few precious wooden posts was not effective, for cattle could get their heads through the smooth strands of wire and gradually work an opening in the fence.

The problem of fencing was finally solved by a New Hampshire-born Yankee, Joseph Glidden, who at the time of his invention was living in De Kalb, Illinois. The solution was barbed wire—wire, that is, with sharp, projecting points. Glidden took out his patent in 1874. Barbed-wire fences proved effective as a barrier to cattle, and within ten years the open range was crisscrossed by a network of barbed-wire fences.

The problem of water. The scarcity of water, like the scarcity of wood, was a problem that the pioneer farmers had never had to face in the eastern part of the United States or in the European countries from which they had migrated. The eastern farmers secured their water from springs bubbling to the surface or from shallow wells dug twenty to thirty feet to the water table ° underground. They hauled it to the surface in buckets or pumped it up easily by hand; later, in the twentieth century, they pumped it by gasoline-driven or electric pumps. But on the Great Plains, where

• •

° *water table:* the depth below which the ground is saturated with water.

the water table was much deeper, machinery was needed to drill deeper wells. And once the well shafts had reached the water table, the farmers needed mechanical pumps to draw the water to the surface.

In a search for oil during the 1860's, petroleum companies began to develop new drilling machinery capable of penetrating farther beneath the surface than ever before. This machinery speedily found its way to the Great Plains, where men put it to work tapping the underground supplies of water.

Meanwhile, other inventors were developing windmills capable of operating pumps to draw the water to the surface. It was another New Englander, Daniel Halladay of Connecticut, who developed the self-governing windmill that automatically adjusted itself to the pressure of the wind and thus operated at a uniform speed.

Windmills were first used, as you know, by cattlemen to secure water for their stock, then adopted by the railroads to provide water for their steam locomotives as they crossed the plains. But the windmill really came into its own when farmers began to settle on the semiarid lands. Factories producing windmills were soon doing a thriving business.

Other problems of the settlers. Railroads, barbed wire, factory-made windmills—all products of the new industrial age—helped the farmer to conquer the Great Plains. So, too, did the development of a better method for farming areas with a limited amount of rainfall. "Dry farming," as this method was called, involved deep plowing and careful cultivation to keep the surface of the soil pulverized and thus conserve as much as possible of the precious moisture. In addition, the development of improved farm machinery helped to lighten some of the farmer's work.

But there were other problems the pioneers had to solve, problems for which the inventors, the manufacturers, and the agricultural experts had no ready answer. For one thing, the cattle-

Windmill about 1870

men resented the settlers who broke up the open range with their fences. Bitter fights raged in the early days between cattlemen and farmers, and many unmarked graves soon dotted the plains. But it was an unequal struggle, for by sheer force of numbers the farmers soon won, and the herds of cattle were driven behind their own fences or forced westward to land too dry for farming.

Nature also contributed to the difficulties that pioneers faced on the plains. Until men learned to adapt themselves to the new environment, life was sometimes harsh beyond endurance. It was the unrelieved round of daily labor that impressed writers who tried to recapture in words the life of the farmers on the Great Plains. The pioneers in this region entered a land that was ready and waiting for the plow. There were no logrollings, no house-raisings. In the novels of O. E. Rölvaag (ROHL-vahg), *Giants in the Earth* and *Peder Victorious*, we have a picture of empty plains and lives spent beneath a burning sun, of grasshopper plagues, of drought, of ruined crops, of bitter cold and blind-

Settlers racing to claim Oklahoma land

THE OKLAHOMA "SOONERS"

On March 23, 1889, President Benjamin Harrison issued a proclamation that set in motion a wild rush toward the "District of Oklahoma." In his proclamation, the President announced that free homesteads of 160 acres would be available "at and after the hour of twelve o'clock noon, on the twenty-second day of April." The Army immediately established patrols along the boundaries of the district to guard against premature entry, and waited for the rush to begin.

It was a short wait. Within days, land-hungry pioneers were camping on the boundary, and all roads leading to the area were jammed with wagons and carts and men and women on horseback. By the morning of April 22, somewhere between 50,000 and 100,000 people were packed solidly along the boundary line, waiting for the signal to go.

Exactly at noon the officer in charge fired a shot, and the wild stampede began. It was a scene of utter confusion, one filled with clouds of dust, the crack-

ing of whips, and the wild cries of the drivers urging their horses to greater speed. Wagons of every shape, size, and description lumbered along hub to hub, and riders on horseback raced madly ahead of the procession.

But even the swiftest riders discovered that they were not there "soon" enough. In spite of army precautions, many "Sooners" had managed to evade the patrols, slip across the boundary, and stake out claims before the area was officially opened.

Within a few hours of the deadline, every inch of "Oklahoma District" was occupied, and the new settlers were hastily erecting temporary shelters. But there was not nearly enough land to go around, and thousands of disappointed land-seekers started back along the roads they had hopefully traveled earlier.

In 1890 Oklahoma was organized as a Territory. Later, other areas in the Territory were opened to homesteaders, and in 1907 Oklahoma was admitted to the Union as the forty-sixth state.

ing blizzards. Many pioneers gave up the struggle and moved back to the East. But others remained and forced the plains to yield their treasures.

In addition to the problems he had to face during the early period of settlement, the farmer in the 1880's and 1890's encountered many new problems created by the growth of industrialism. In the new industrial age, as you will see, the farmer became increasingly concerned with freight and shipping charges, prices established in distant markets, cost of farm machinery, interest rates on mortgages, and many other factors he could not control.

The last frontier. In spite of all obstacles, however, the farmers continued to push out upon the plains, fencing the land as they advanced, building homes and villages—and new states. The roll call of states that entered the Union in the half-century after 1865 is an impressive one—Nebraska in 1867; Colorado in 1876; North Dakota, South Dakota, Montana, and Washington in 1889; Idaho and Wyoming in 1890; Utah in 1896; Oklahoma in 1907; and New Mexico and Arizona in 1912.

In 1890 the Superintendent of the United States Census made a significant statement: "Up to and including 1880," he declared, "the country had a frontier of settlement, but at present the unsettled area has been so broken into by isolated bodies of settlement that there can hardly be said to be a frontier line."

⌐ **SECTION SURVEY**

1. Show how (a) the Homestead Act and (b) the railroads speeded the settlement of the West.
2. How did the farmers on the plains solve the problems of housing and fencing?
3. Discuss the importance of the windmill to the Great Plains farmers.
4. If you had been living on the Great Plains in the late 1800's, what problems and pleasures might you have experienced?
IDENTIFY: sod houses, "dry farming," the last frontier; Glidden, Halladay, Rölvaag; 1862, 1874, 1890.

Miners discover new treasures in the western mountains

Developments of the new industrial age—railroads, barbed wire, well-drilling machinery, better windmills, labor-saving farm machines of many kinds—all made it possible for the farmer to conquer the last frontiers in the West. But the West in turn helped to speed the course of the Industrial Revolution. From western farms came an unending supply of foodstuffs for the rapidly growing populations of the cities. From western mines came an apparently limitless supply of gold and silver to provide capital to build the nation's industries. From other western mines came a steadily swelling volume of iron and copper and other metals.

From "Forty-Niners" to "Fifty-Niners." As you have seen (page 339), the discovery of gold in California drew men by the tens of thousands to the Pacific coast in 1849–50. Some of the "Forty-Niners" made fortunes, but the majority were disappointed. Refusing to admit defeat, prospectors began to explore the valleys and slopes of the mountainous regions between the Pacific Ocean and the Great Plains.

In 1859 prospectors discovered gold near Pike's Peak in the unorganized territory of Colorado. More than 100,000 "Fifty-Niners" rushed to the scene to stake their claims. Caravans of Conestoga wagons lumbered across the plains with the slogan "Pikes Peak or bust" lettered on the white canvas. Some men shouldered packs and crossed the plains on foot. Others pulled handcarts behind them. Perhaps half of the fortune hunters returned the way they had come, but with the slogan changed to "Busted, by gosh!" Nevertheless, enough remained to organize the Territory of Colorado in 1861, and in 1876, as you know, the state of Colorado was admitted to the Union.

Even more valuable than the Colorado deposits were the discoveries of silver in 1859 in the western part of the

JAMES CARDINAL GIBBONS

From a childhood back in the days of Andrew Jackson until after World War I, James Gibbons (1834–1921) experienced the forces of growing America and observed the great increase in the Catholic part of the population. As a churchman, he believed that a good Catholic was likely to be a good American; just as firmly he believed the American Constitution was very favorable to Catholicism. So, on the occasion of receiving his "red hat" in Rome, in 1887, he declared: "I proclaim, with a deep sense of pride and gratitude . . . that I belong to a country where the civil government holds over us the aegis [shield] of its protection without interfering in the legitimate exercise of our sublime mission as ministers of the Gospel of Jesus Christ."

From the time of Grover Cleveland, Gibbons was to be the friend and confidant of Presidents, of many non-Catholic religious and lay leaders, and a lasting symbol of the blessing the Church gave to America's progress. In 1887, when the struggling labor movement was threatened by Church censure of the Knights of Labor (as a secret society), Gibbons persuaded Rome to prevent this. He urged that censure was unnecessary and might convince the working men that the Church was indifferent to their problems.

In the same year the Cardinal wrote strongly in the *North American Review* about many of the same abuses in national life which were to arouse reformers over the next three decades, particularly greed for wealth and political corruption. Always the constructive kind of critic, however, Gibbons received this tribute from former President Theodore Roosevelt in 1917: "Taking your life as a whole, I think you . . . the most respected, and venerated, and useful citizen of our country."

Territory of Utah. Within a decade nearly $150,000,000 worth of silver and gold had been extracted from the famous Comstock Lode in what is now Nevada (see map, page 448), and by 1890 the total had reached $340,000,000. Enough of the original prospectors stayed after the stampede of 1859 to organize the Territory of Nevada, which became a state in 1864.

Gold in the Black Hills. In 1874 other prospectors discovered gold in the Black Hills that rise out of the plains of South Dakota (see map, page 448), and another gold rush followed. This area was Indian territory, the Sioux Reservation, and the federal government tried to keep the prospectors out of the region. The attempt was soon abandoned, however, and in 1877 the entire area was thrown open to white occupation.

The most valuable mine in the Black Hills—and the largest producer of gold in the United States—is the Homestake Mine. First discovered in 1876, it was sold the following year for $70,000. By 1940 the mine had produced more than $440,000,000 worth of gold.

Early mining communities. During and after the War Between the States, mining communities sprang up literally overnight in these and other areas of the West. Miners, prospectors, and gold-crazed people from all parts of America were the original "settlers" in territory that is now eastern Washington and Oregon, western Montana, Idaho, New Mexico, and Arizona.

Life in the mining camps has been described vividly in *The Luck of Roaring Camp* by Bret Harte and in *Roughing It* by Mark Twain. From these and other contemporary accounts we form a picture of wild, lawless communities of tents, rough board shacks, and smoke-filled saloons strung along a muddy street.

Each mining camp passed through several distinct stages of development. At first, every man was a law unto himself, relying for his safety upon his fists or the guns in his holsters. Then the more respectable citizens began to organize their own private police force, often called "vigilantes" (vij-i-LAN-tees), in an effort to maintain order. Soon they built schools and churches—crude shacks, perhaps, but important steps toward civilized living. With the schools and churches came organized local government. Then came the appeal to Congress for recognition as an organized Territory of the United States, and eventually the adoption of a constitution and admission to the Union as a State.

Today the mountain regions, the valleys, and the high plateaus of the West are dotted with abandoned mining communities—ghost towns, as they are called. The abandoned mine shafts and the sagging, windowless cabins remain as mute testimony to the fact that the prospector and the miner once pioneered on this vast frontier.

Exploration is systematized. The early discoveries of gold and silver acted like magnets, drawing adventuresome prospectors into the unexplored mountainous regions of the West. Before long, however, the work of exploration was conducted on a more systematic basis, partly through the efforts of the federal government. Between 1865 and 1879 the government at Washington sent many expeditions into the mountains, and in 1879 the United States Geological Survey was organized. Private industry also sent out carefully organized expeditions. The picturesque prospector with his pack horse and hand tools continued to roam the mountains, but long before the end of the 1800's, an increasing number of the mineral deposits were being discovered by expeditions equipped with the latest technological devices and knowledge of geology.

Minerals for industry. The development of the nation's industries brought a growing demand for metals of all kinds. The list of minerals that have been discovered in the western mountains is impressive. Copper, needed when the electrical industry developed, was found in enormous quantities around Butte, Montana; Bingham, Utah; and in Nevada and Arizona. Lead and

Coal-mining machine—1890's

zinc, needed for various new industries, were discovered in the same area. These and other metals have helped the United States to become the leading industrial nation in the world.

Mining becomes big business. The systematic exploration for mineral wealth was paralleled by other developments that brought about great changes in mining. New methods of extracting the metal from the ore were discovered, colleges of mining engineering were opened, powerful machinery was invented, great corporations were organized, and armies of skilled technicians and engineers began to move into the mining regions. New equipment and the growing knowledge of chemistry and metallurgy enabled companies to work low-grade ores with profit.

By the 1890's mining had become "big business." Engineers, equipped with the latest tools of science and technology, were converting the West into a region of incalculable value to the industrial development of the nation.

SECTION SURVEY

1. Who were the "Fifty-Niners"?
2. Describe life in the early mining communities, and tell how it gradually improved.
3. How was the picturesque prospector replaced by systematic exploration?
4. Give the reasons why mining became a big business by 1890.

IDENTIFY: "Pikes Peak or bust," Comstock Lode, Homestake Mine, vigilantes, ghost towns; Bret Harte, Mark Twain.

Points to Discuss: 1. "The revolver and the railroad, both products of the Industrial Revolution, helped to sweep the Indians from the Great Plains and open the way for settlement." (a) Explain this statement. (b) Evaluate the justice of the treatment of the Indians.

2. Compare the cattle rush in the 1870's with the California gold rush of 1849–50, as to causes and results.

3. (a) Explain how railroads, barbed wire, and windmills (a) affected the manner in which the Cattle Kingdom developed, and (b) helped the farmer to conquer the problems of the Great Plains.

4. Summarize the problems faced by the western pioneer which were a result of forces of the new industrial age.

5. The last frontier disappeared in 1890. Explain how this happened, and indicate the importance of that disappearance.

6. (a) Do you believe that western stories and movies give an accurate picture of life in the West between 1870 and 1890? (b) Which aspects of western life seem to be overstressed and which neglected?

Using Maps and Charts: 1. Using the map on pages 818–19, locate the Great Plains and describe their characteristics and climate.

2. (a) Consulting the maps on pages 830–31 and 834–35, describe the agricultural and industrial development that has taken place in the Great Plains. (b) Name the states in this area today.

3. Using the map on page 448, answer the following: (a) How many railroads connected the Middle West with the Far West? (b) What was the significance of Promontory Point? of the Comstock Lode? (c) Where did the cattle business begin? (d) What railroads were available to cattlemen using the Chisholm Trail?

Consulting the Sources: For life on the frontier, see Commager, *The Heritage of America*, Section XXVII, "The Last West."

■ TRACING THE MAIN IDEAS

The conquest of the Plains Indians and the settlement of the land west of the Mississippi River took place, for the most part, during and immediately following the War Between the States. Although by the 1890's the process was not complete, settlers had poured into the prairies and plains in such numbers that the Superintendent of the Census was impelled to announce that the frontier no longer existed.

The development of the resources of this vast region, almost one half the total area of the present United States, called forth all the courage and intelligence that men could command. The West was not one region, but many regions, each basically different from the others. Each group of settlers—cattlemen, farmers, and miners—learned to adapt themselves to their environment and to make use of the most easily developed natural resources—the grasslands, the fertile soil, and the precious metals. As the years passed, they learned how to modify the environment and to seek out and develop other resources.

The conquest of the West was, in one sense, merely a prelude to an even larger chapter in American history—the transformation of the nation from a predominantly agricultural country to one of the great industrial giants of the modern world. That transformation is the subject of Unit Seven and of later chapters in this book.

Unit Survey (Reread "Tracing the Main Ideas," pages 428, 445, 462.)

OUTSTANDING EVENTS

1867 Congress' plan of reconstruction.
1868 Fourteenth Amendment ratified.
1868 House impeaches Johnson.
1868 Ulysses S. Grant elected President.
1869 First transcontinental railroad is completed.
1870 Fifteenth Amendment ratified.
1872 Amnesty Act.
1872 *"Alabama Claims"* are settled.
1872 Grant re-elected President.
1873 Nationwide economic depression.
1876 Rutherford B. Hayes elected President.
1877 Troops withdrawn from South.
1880 James A. Garfield elected President.
1881 Garfield assassinated and Chester A. Arthur becomes President.
1883 Pendleton Act passed.
1884 Grover Cleveland elected President.
1887 Dawes Act gives land to Indians.
1888 Benjamin Harrison elected President.
1890 McKinley Tariff.
1890 End of Frontier.
1892 Grover Cleveland elected President.
1893 Business slump; lasts until 1896.
1894 Wilson-Gorman Tariff.

THEN AND NOW

1. Compare southern industry and agriculture today with what they were before the War Between the States (consult page 425).

2. What is the origin of the term, "the Solid South"? In what Presidential elections of recent decades has this pattern deviated? How do you account for this?

EXTENDING YOUR HORIZON

1. A good picture of the "long drive" and its place in the history of the Great Plains is given in Chapter II, "The Texas Invasion," in Ernest S. Osgood's *The Day of the Cattleman* (Phoenix Books).

2. A vivid portrayal of a western mining town is given in Lucius Beebe's article, "Panamint: Suburb of Hell," *American Heritage*, December 1954.

3. Read Chapters II, III, and IV of Emerson Hough, *The Passing of the Frontier* (Yale Univ. Press). Compare this concept of the cowboy with that generally portrayed on television.

INDIVIDUAL ACTIVITIES

1. Read the chapter "This is Sure Some Cripple Creek" in Irving Stone's *Men to Match My Mountains* (Doubleday) for the story of one of Colorado's great gold fields and give a report to the class.

2. Read "The Buffalo and the Indian," pages 343–53, in *Glory, Gold and God* by Paul I. Wellman (Doubleday). Indicate for the class the connection the author reveals between the buffalo and Indian wars.

3. Summarize for the class several of the interesting episodes described in *Roughing It* by Samuel L. Clemens [Harper Modern Classics; Rinehart (paper)].

GROUP ACTIVITIES

1. Select a group of students to prepare a discussion on the conflict in the Reconstruction period between Andrew Johnson and the Radical Republicans which culminated in his impeachment trial. Worthwhile sources to consult include Claude Bowers, *The Tragic Era* (Houghton Mifflin), especially Chapter Two, "Andrew Johnson, a Portrait"; the article by Milton Lamask, "When Congress Tried to Rule," *American Heritage*, December 1959; and that by David Donald, "Why They Impeached Andrew Johnson," *American Heritage*, December 1956. Vernon Parrington's account of "The American Scene" found in Book Two, *The Making of American History*, edited by Donald Sheehan, will provide good background for the postwar setting. See also, the essay on Edmund Ross in John F. Kennedy, *Profiles in Courage* (Harper; Pocket Books); and Chapter 15, "The Conflict over Reconstruction" in Richard D. Heffner's *A Documentary History of the United States* (Mentor). Let the group choose a chairman to plan and guide the discussion.

2. Select a committee for a limited research project in the *Dictionary of American History*. Let the individuals in the group seek information on *one* of the following topics: "Solid South"; "New South"; Nast Cartoons; "Rum, Romanism, and Rebellion"; Electoral Commission. Each stu-

dent should pursue clues given in the original topic to find additional information within the *Dictionary of American History* and report to the class on the extent of their investigation.

SUGGESTED FURTHER READING

BIOGRAPHY

BURGER, NASH K., and JOHN K. BETTERSWORTH, *South of Appomattox*, Harcourt, Brace. Ten biographies of southerners.

CLEMENS, SAMUEL L., *Life on the Mississippi*, Harper; and others. Mark Twain's life as a river pilot.

FUESS, CLAUDE M., *Carl Schurz, Reformer*, Dodd, Mead.

GRAHAM, SHIRLEY, and GEORGE LIPSCOMB, *George Washington Carver, Scientist*, Messner.

°KORNGOLD, RALPH, *Thaddeus Stevens*, Harcourt, Brace.

°NEVINS, ALLAN, *Grover Cleveland: A Study in Courage*, Dodd, Mead.

SEITZ, DON CARLOS, *Horace Greeley*, Bobbs-Merrill.

STRYKER, LLOYD PAUL, *Andrew Johnson, A Study in Courage*, Macmillan.

WASHINGTON, BOOKER T., *Up from Slavery*, Houghton Mifflin; and others. Autobiographical.

WINSTON, R. W., *Andrew Johnson, Plebeian and Patriot*, Holt.

OTHER NONFICTION

BUCK, PAUL, *The Road to Reunion, 1865–1900*, Knopf (Vintage Books); Peter Smith.

DICK, EVERETT NEWTON, *Sod House Frontier, 1854–1890*, Johnsen. Social history.

FRANKLIN, JOHN HOPE, *From Slavery to Freedom: A History of American Negroes*, Knopf.

HOLBROOK, H. STEWART, *The Story of American Railroads*, Crown.

HOWARD, ROBERT WEST, ed. *This Is the West*, Rand McNally; New American Library (Signet Books). Essays.

°JOSEPHSON, MATTHEW, *The Politicos*, Harcourt, Brace.

LA FARGE, OLIVER, *A Pictorial History of the American Indian*, Crown.

MOODY, JOHN, *The Railroad Builders*, Yale Univ. Press.

RANDALL, JAMES G., *The Civil War and Reconstruction*, Heath.

SPENCER, SAMUEL REID, *Booker T. Washington and the Negro's Place in American Life*, Little, Brown.

THOMPSON, HOLLAND, *The New South*, Yale Univ. Press.

°WEBB, WALTER PRESCOTT, *The Great Plains*, Ginn; Grosset & Dunlap (paper).

WOODWARD, C. VANN, *Reunion and Reaction*, Doubleday (Anchor).

HISTORICAL FICTION

BUSCH, NIVEN, *Duel in the Sun*, Morrow; and others. Excellent western.

CATHER, WILLA, *My Ántonia*, Houghton Mifflin. Novel about the West.

——, *O Pioneers!*, Houghton Mifflin.

CHURCHILL, WINSTON, *Coniston*, Macmillan. Corrupt politics.

CLEMENS, SAMUEL L., and C. D. WARNER, *The Gilded Age*, Grosset & Dunlap. Materialism after the War Between the States.

FERBER, EDNA, *Cimarron*, Doubleday; others. Rush of settlers into Oklahoma.

FINNEY, GERTRUDE, *The Plums Hang High*, Longmans, Green. Life in Middle West.

FORD, PAUL LEICESTER, *The Honorable Peter Sterling*, Hillary House. Politics.

GARLAND, HAMLIN, *Main-Travelled Roads*, Harper Modern Classics. Short stories of life on Great Plains.

——, *Son of the Middle Border*, Macmillan.

GREY, ZANE, *The U. P. Trail*, Grosset & Dunlap; Pocket Books. Railroad building.

JACKSON, HELEN HUNT, *Ramona*, Little, Brown; Grosset & Dunlap. Plight of the Indians.

ROLVAAG, OLE EDVART, *Giants in the Earth*, Harper. Pioneers in North Dakota.

——, *Peder Victorious*, Harper. Sequel to *Giants in the Earth*.

WISTER, OWEN, *The Virginian*, Macmillan; and others. Novel with cowboy hero.

UNIT SEVEN

The Rise of Industrialism

1860's–1890's

Business Leaders Spur the Growth of American Industry

CHANGING WAYS

OF AMERICAN LIFE

I N the 1870's a large majority of Americans lived in the country or in small rural villages and towns. This was the age of dirt roads; of carriages and wagons; and of covered bridges, their wooden sides plastered with circus advertisements and notices of county fairs. It was the age of oil lamps; woodstoves; the handpump or the open well; and the Saturday-evening bath in a washtub in the center of the kitchen floor.

This was the age of sewing circles and spelling bees; the one-room schoolhouse; and the country store with its tubs of butter and pickles, its cracker barrel, and its clutter of groceries and clothing and household articles hanging from the ceiling and spilling over the

shelves. Symbols of the age were the small family-owned factory and the blacksmith shop at the crossroads with its charcoal fire, its huge bellows, and its burly smith in grimy leather apron exchanging quips with loungers while he shaped and fitted new shoes to a neighbor's horse.

But a new age was coming into being. Symbols of the new age were rapidly growing cities, large factories with smoke pouring from their towering stacks, long lines of railroad cars rumbling across the countryside, and a growing number of farm machines standing outside barns or operating in the fields. In brief, life in the new industrial age was being transformed in many ways.

This, then, is the story of how America began to change from a rural, agricultural economy to an urban, industrial way of life.

AS THE STORY DEVELOPS
1. **Transportation and communication systems bind the nation together.**
2. **Expanding business creates more products for more people.**
3. **New forms of business organization are developed as industry expands.**
4. **Business pioneers give new directions to American life.**

1 Transportation and communication systems bind the nation together

The heart of an industrial society is the city. It is here that most factories and workers are concentrated, most raw materials are fashioned into finished products, and most goods and services are bought and sold.

If the city is the heart of an industrial society, the routes of transportation are the veins and arteries. Into the city flow the vital resources gathered from farm and mine and forest and sea. Out of the city flow the unending supplies of manufactured articles, moving day and night over a vast transportation network to every corner of the land and overseas to other lands.

Just as the human body cannot function without heart and veins and arteries, so an industrial economy cannot function without its urban manufacturing centers and an efficient system of transportation and communication.

The growth of cities. One of the most striking developments during the years between 1865 and 1900 was the rise of the modern city with its busy railroad yards; its unsightly, smoking factories; its white-collar workers; and its wage earners. This development was taking place in the industrial center of Western Europe. But in the United States during these years, urban growth was even more impressive than in Europe. Scores of cities in the United States grew from sprawling towns to huge urban centers. In 1870, for example, about 75 per cent of the people lived in the country or in communities of fewer than 2500 inhabitants. By 1900 only about 60 per cent of all Americans were living on farms or in small rural communities. The urban population had skyrocketed. While in 1870 only about 10,000,000 of the nation's total population of 39,904,593 were urban dwellers, by 1900 more than 30,000,000 of America's 76,094,134 people were living in urban areas.

The amazing growth of cities was the result of a number of revolutionary developments, including the discovery of new sources of power, the application of hundreds of new inventions and new processes, and the enormous expansion of the nation's transportation and communication network.

The growth of railroads. Between 1870 and 1900 railway mileage in the United States increased from 53,000 miles to more than 190,000. During these same years the railroads improved in speed, comfort, and safety. Double sets of tracks replaced single sets, allowing steady streams of traffic to flow in two directions at once. Iron rails, which had shattered beneath heavy loads, were replaced by steel rails. Wooden bridges were replaced by bridges of iron and later of steel. Coal, a more efficient fuel, replaced wood in the tenders of locomotives. In 1869 George Westinghouse patented the air brake, a system of power braking more efficient than the old hand brake.

To control the movement of trains and to help prevent accidents, the *block system* was developed. An engineer could not take his train into a new stretch, or "block," of track until getting an all-clear signal from the newly invented semaphore, indicating that there were no other trains in the block.

Railroad passenger comfort increased. In the 1850's cars had been little more than tobacco-stained and overcrowded wooden boxes, but in the next twenty years George M. Pullman and others invented and placed in operation sleeping cars, dining cars, and parlor cars.

A nationwide network of steel. The successful building and operation of the first transcontinental line (page 448) quickly led to the construction of several others. By 1893 five major, or trunk, lines crossed the plains and mountains to the Far West, while north of the Canadian border the Canadian Pacific furnished a fifth route to the Pacific coast. Feeder, or branch, lines were also built —in the West and South as well as in the Northeast and Middle West—to link the trunk lines with surrounding areas. Pres-

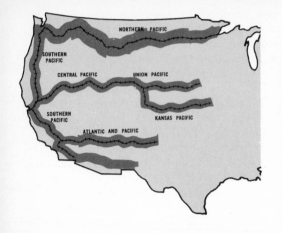

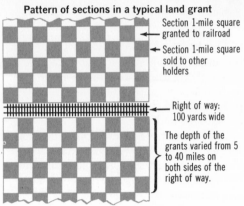

Pattern of sections in a typical land grant

Section 1-mile square granted to railroad

Section 1-mile square sold to other holders

Right of way: 100 yards wide

The depth of the grants varied from 5 to 40 miles on both sides of the right of way.

ently a network of steel served every part of the country, however remote from the major centers of industry and transportation.

Most of this railroad building was done with the aid of cash subsidies and grants of land from the federal government. Although some of the land grants were later returned to the government, before 1900 the transcontinental railroads had received about 164,000 square miles of land.

Long before 1900, thanks to individual enterprise, government aid, and new inventions, the industrial economy of the United States possessed steel arteries of transportation equal to the task of moving enormous quantities of freight and passengers.

Importance of steamships. While land transportation was being improved, traffic on the sea lanes and inland waterways was also being developed. During the latter half of the 1800's, sailing ships on the oceans and on the Great Lakes were replaced by fleets of steam-driven, steel-hulled freighters and sleek passenger liners. The ocean-going vessels carried millions of emigrants from Europe to the rest of the world, mostly to the United States. They also freighted raw materials and manufactured goods to and from the expanding world markets.

Urban transportation. Meanwhile, in the growing urban areas new methods of transportation enabled people to move quickly from one part of a crowded city to another. By the end of the 1800's, electric trolleys were rapidly replacing horse-drawn cars. Steam-driven and, later, electric-powered elevated trains rumbled along above the crowded streets. By the early 1900's subway trains were carrying passengers below the streets of New York and Boston.

As steel-framed skyscrapers climbed higher and higher into the air, elevators, powered first by steam and then by electricity, were developed to carry passengers and freight from story to story. Indeed, without the elevator, skyscrapers could not have been used.

From telegraph to telephone. Equally important in the development of America's industrial economy were improvements in the field of communications. Until the 1870's the telegraph had marked the most significant advance in the art of communicating since the invention of printing from movable type. From the 1870's on, however, new inventions appeared one after another.

The telegraph had been first successfully developed in the United States by Samuel F. B. Morse and in England by Charles Wheatstone during the late

1830's and the early 1840's—just as the new steam railroads were beginning to make their appearance. The telegraph moved across the country with the railroads—indeed, the safe operation of railroads would have been impossible without the telegraph.

In 1866, some twenty years after Morse's invention, Cyrus W. Field had finally succeeded in laying a successful transatlantic telegraph cable. During the next few years additional underwater cables connected North America with other continents, giving American businessmen—and other Americans—an almost instantaneous means of communication with the rest of the world.

In 1876 another inventor, Alexander Graham Bell, a teacher of the deaf in Boston, applied for a patent on a telephone he had invented. Bell's telephone quickly captured the public's imagination, and in 1885 the American Telephone and Telegraph Company was organized to put the new invention into widespread use. The first crude instrument was rapidly improved, benefiting from Thomas Alva Edison's work in the field of electricity. Soon there were spider webs of telephone wires throughout the nation's cities, and telephone lines began to reach out into rural areas.

Other influential inventions. The telegraph, the underwater cable, the telephone—all of these inventions were landmarks in the history of communications. But this is only part of the story. During the late 1800's other inventions and developments began to reshape American life.

There was, for instance, the all-important typewriter, developed in the 1860's by Christopher Sholes of Wisconsin, and steadily improved until it had become an essential part of all business operations. There was the improved postal system, without which modern business could not hope to function.

The improvement of machines for making cheap paper from wood pulp and for printing newspapers, books, and magazines also played a vital part in the development of more effective means of

Menlo Park, N.J.

EDISON'S INVENTION FACTORY

During the course of his long and energetic life, Thomas Alva Edison (1847–1931) was granted more than 1000 patents. Among the inventions or improvements for which he received credit are the phonograph, the incandescent lamp, the storage battery, and the mimeograph.

But perhaps his greatest invention was the "invention factory." In 1876, then twenty-nine years old and with a substantial number of successes already behind him, Edison designed and built a research laboratory at Menlo Park, New Jersey. There, under "the wizard's" direction, a team of brilliant assistants began to turn out numerous inventions.

Edison's "invention factory" was the forerunner of the great research laboratories of today. The era of the lone inventor who worked by trial and error was rapidly drawing to a close. A new era, that of organized collective research, was just coming into being. With the construction of his laboratory at Menlo Park, Edison became one of the pioneers of this new age.

communication. And then, of course, there was the camera, which, in time, provided new forms of recreation as well as new techniques for industry and research.

By 1900 the modern transportation and communication systems of the United States were beginning to take shape. Even more far-reaching developments were to come after 1900. Meanwhile, improvements in transportation and communications were binding all parts of the country into a single complex economic unit. Specialized business enterprises, both agricultural and industrial, were springing up in all parts of the land, each playing its part in the ever-expanding, interlocking economic system.

▶ SECTION SURVEY

1. "If the city is the heart of an industrial society, the routes of transportation are the veins and arteries." Explain.

2. Describe the methods used by the federal government to aid the building of railroads.

3. In your opinion, what were the most important developments in communication in the nineteenth century?

IDENTIFY: block system; Westinghouse, Morse, Field, Bell, Edison, Sholes; 1866, 1869, 1876.

2 Expanding business creates more products for more people

The old question, "Which came first, the chicken or the egg?" is a good one to keep in mind when thinking about the Industrial Revolution. For example, did improvements in transportation and communications come first, and then the big factories and mass production? Or was it the other way around?

The answer, of course, is that the Industrial Revolution was the product of a number of different developments in a number of different fields, all of which were going on at the same time, and all of which combined to transform, or "revolutionize," the older ways of life. These developments included new sources of power, new machines, new and bigger industries, and new ways of selling.

New sources of power. At the beginning of human history and for many thousands of years, man's only source of power was his own muscles. About five or six thousand years ago man learned to domesticate animals, among them the donkey, the horse, and the camel, so that he could use them in his work. Later, he learned to harness the power of falling water and the power of the wind. Less than two hundred years ago, in the late 1700's, he discovered how to put steam to work. For nearly a hundred years the steam engine was man's most important "mechanical slave." Then, in the late 1800's, man learned to use two new sources of power—oil and electricity.

New uses for oil. From the earliest times people had known about the dark, thick substance that oozed from the earth in certain places and that we now call "petroleum," or "oil." Now and then people used it as salve or as a crude fuel for lamps. By the middle of the 1800's, Americans were beginning to use increasing amounts for these purposes and as axle grease for their wagons.

In the early 1850's it was discovered that kerosene, an efficient and inexpensive fuel for lamps, could be refined from petroleum. The growing demand for kerosene prompted Edwin L. Drake, a retired railroad conductor, to try the experiment of drilling an "oil well" near Titusville, Pennsylvania. This was in 1859. While he was drilling, people thought he was crazy. When the oil began to flow, however, people quickly changed their minds. Within a matter of weeks, men were sinking wells wherever they had the slightest suspicion that there was oil.

Kerosene rapidly replaced whale oil as an efficient fuel for lamps. In every American city, peddlers carted kerosene through the streets, stopping from door to door to sell their product. And as the years passed, oil was used more and more as a lubricant for the nation's growing number of machines.

It was the development of the internal combustion engine, which burned gasoline or, later, diesel fuel, that finally boosted oil into the position of one of the nation's major sources of power. In Chapter 29 you will see how oil as a source of power virtually revolutionized the lives of country people and city dwellers alike.

Power from electricity. Electricity, like oil, was known to man long before he put it to practical use. The work of two Italians, Galvani and Volta, led in the late 1700's and early 1800's to the invention of the storage battery. The storage battery, which supplied small amounts of electric current at low "voltages," greatly aided the work of those experimenting with the uses of electricity in Europe and America. Even more far-reaching in its consequences was the discovery of the principles on which the electric motor and the dynamo are based. Although many experimenters contributed to these discoveries, a major share of the credit belongs to England's Michael Faraday and America's Joseph Henry.

Thousands of Americans first learned about the dynamo when they visited the Centennial Exhibition at Philadelphia in 1876 and saw one in operation converting mechanical energy into electrical energy. They crowded around the throbbing machine, not understanding how it worked, but realizing, many of them, that it marked a long step forward in man's quest for control of the forces of nature.

In 1882, six years after the Philadelphia Centennial Exhibition, Thomas Edison built in New York City the first large central power plant in the United States for the generation of electricity. Edison drove his dynamos with steam engines. Other steam-powered electric generating plants soon appeared in other cities. Another giant stride forward was made in 1895 with the opening at Niagara Falls of the first large hydro-

EDWIN DRAKE'S OIL WELL

Edwin L. Drake struck oil on Sunday, August 28, 1859. The first oil boom in history had started. So, too, had a brand new industry.

Edwin Drake had gone to public school in Vermont, worked on a farm, and clerked in a drygoods store. He had left his last job, that of a conductor on the New Haven Railroad, because of poor health. Such was the man who turned up in Titusville, Pennsylvania, in the spring of 1858 as "general agent" of the Seneca Oil Company at a salary of one thousand dollars a year. His job was to "raise and dispose of oil."

The stream on which the company had bought land was called Oil Creek. In places oil oozed out of the ground and discolored the water. Indians had mixed the oil with coloring matter to make glistening, waterproof war paint. Settlers had used it for liniment.

The Seneca Oil Company didn't want liniment. It wanted oil for lamps. Lots of oil. But how to get it? That was Drake's problem.

At first, he tried to dig wells, but they filled with water, and the sides caved in. Finally, he hired a blacksmith to drill a well for him. "Uncle Billy," the blacksmith, started to drill in June 1859. By Saturday, August 27, the drill was down 69 feet. Uncle Billy hauled it up and knocked off for the day. On Sunday, when he walked over to the well, just for a look, he found the pipe brimming with oil.

The word spread like wildfire. Within a few days every inch of land up and down Oil Creek had been bought or leased, and new wells were being drilled. Within a few weeks the road along Oil Creek was filled with wagons hauling barrels of oil to market.

electric plant for producing electricity from water power. In spite of these developments, by 1900 only about 2 per cent of America's manufacturing industries were powered by electricity. The revolutionary impact of this new source of power was to come in the twentieth century.

Steel for the new industries. Behind the story of new sources of power lies still another story—the discovery of new processes for producing steel.

Iron ore and coal—these were the raw materials for an industrial age. And the United States was blessed with an abundance of each. Immense deposits of iron ore lay untouched near the western shores of Lake Superior. Perhaps 500,000 square miles of coal fields, or about one half of the world's known deposits, were waiting to be tapped, the largest of them in Pennsylvania.

Steel, a hard, tough metal containing iron, carbon, and other elements, was not a new material. Men had made it for centuries and fashioned it into weapons, tools, and utensils. But until the middle of the 1800's, no one knew how to produce steel cheaply and in large quantities.

In the 1850's an Englishman, Henry Bessemer, and an American, William Kelly, discovered independently of each other a new process for making large quantities of steel cheaply by burning out impurities in molten iron with a blast of air. During the next few years the "Bessemer process," as it was called, was steadily improved, and other effective processes were developed.

The annual production of steel in the United States soared steadily upward during the last quarter of the 1800's and the opening years of the 1900's. In 1870, for example the United States produced only about 68,000 tons of steel, and railroad builders were buying their rails and structural steel largely from Great Britain. By 1900, however, Americans were producing more than 10,000,000 tons of steel annually, and would increase their production to 44,000,000 tons by the end of World War I in 1918.

Without steel—as well as copper and other metals—there would have been no Industrial Revolution as we know it in the United States. Steel, power, and rapidly growing factories—here were the keys to the new industrial age.

The growth of mass production. Much of the growing steel production at this time was going into the construction of railroads, bridges, heavy machinery, factories, mills, and other industrial enterprises. In brief, during these years, American businessmen were laying the foundations of an industrial system that would in the twentieth century make the United States the most productive country in the world and provide the American people with the highest standard of living in history.

But it takes more than power, raw materials, and factories to produce an industrial economy. It also takes skilled labor, skilled management, and the willingness of people to invest money in the development of new industries and the expansion of old. This, too, was part of the American story.

As business expanded and factories grew larger and larger, the men who owned and managed the factories continually developed more efficient methods of production. You have seen how the principle of interchangeable parts was worked out by Eli Whitney and put into practice during the first half of the 1800's (page 250). This development called for a *division of labor*. For instance, a shoemaker no longer made an entire shoe. Instead, in great shoe factories—mostly in New England—parts of the shoe were cut and shaped by men working at machines that performed only a single operation at a time. The different parts—heel, sole, lining, and so on—were then brought together at a central location in the factory and assembled into a shoe. Specialization of machines and workmen and centralization of assembly became increasingly important in all large factories. Division of labor was being adopted by meat packers and food processors as well as by manufacturers of shoes, clothing,

The Montgomery Ward catalogue for 1878 included this engraving to show customers how their orders were invoiced, packaged, and sent out from Chicago. Smaller articles were gathered in baskets to be wrapped and mailed. Heavier items (left) were crated and shipped.

stoves, and other consumer goods. Each year more and more products appeared on the shelves of the new stores that were springing up in the cities.

New ways of selling products. The small general store, as well as the small family-owned factory, became less important in America during the late 1800's. To be sure, general stores selling all kinds of merchandise continued to exist here and there, as they do today, but completely new types of establishments appeared to handle the ever-growing quantity of products that were pouring forth from the nation's factories.

The specialty store concentrated upon a single line of goods—hardware, clothing, groceries, shoes, and so forth.

The department store—really a collection of specialty stores under one roof—was a city institution. John C. Wanamaker opened one of the first department stores in the United States in Philadelphia in 1876. Marshall Field opened another in Chicago in 1881. As the years passed, other merchants opened department stores in other cities.

Chain stores with branches in many cities also began to appear during the latter half of the 1800's. Pioneers in this field of selling were the Great Atlantic and Pacific Tea Company, founded in 1859, and the F. W. Woolworth Company, founded in 1879. Chain stores and department stores could charge less for goods because, among other advantages, they could buy their goods in large quantities at lower prices.

Mail-order houses. Specialty stores, department stores, and chain stores were all part of the urban scene. In 1872, however, Aaron Montgomery Ward started in Chicago a mail-order business aimed at the rural market. A few years later, the Sears, Roebuck mail-order business was started. Montgomery Ward and Sears, Roebuck used the same business methods. Customers placed orders and paid for them by mail; goods were shipped by mail or railway express. Catalogues from these two mail-order houses were prized possessions in every rural household and in many a cattleman's or sheepherder's bunkhouse or camp. They helped to bring the outside world into isolated farms and speeded the transformation of farm life.

Raw materials poured into the great factories. Finished products poured out of the factories and into the mail-order houses and stores. Through these retail establishments the products of America's farms and industries became available to more and more people.

473

Show how each of the following created "mechanical slaves" for man: (a) steam, (b) petroleum, and (c) electricity.

2. Bessemer, Kelly, and Whitney helped America's growing industrial economy. Explain.

3. Discuss four important developments in the selling of products during the latter 1800's.

IDENTIFY: dynamo, division of labor (specialization), mass production; Drake, Faraday, Joseph Henry, Wanamaker, Marshall Field, Ward; 1859.

3 New forms of business organization are developed as industry expands

Most of America's factories in the 1860's and 1870's, like most of the retail stores, were small enterprises owned by individuals or families, called *individual proprietorships.* Just as the owner of the country store knew all of his customers, so the owner of a small factory knew all of his workmen—and often called them by their first names. Most wage earners in the 1860's lived in small towns, worked in small factories or mills, and took part in community activities with their employers.

During the next thirty years much of this small-town, friendly, personal relationship began to disappear from the American scene. It was crowded out of existence by the huge industrial plant located in or on the outskirts of a large city and employing hundreds, even thousands, of wage earners, who were often strangers to one another and even more remote from the men who owned the business.

Partnerships. As businesses grew in size, it became necessary to find ways of sharing the expanding costs and responsibilities of ownership. The *partnership* as a form of business organization began to be used more frequently. The partnership, even then, was an old, old form of business organization.

When two or more men go into partnership, they have the advantage of greater *capital°* and greater skill than one man, for as a rule each partner invests both money and time in the enterprise. But partnerships have one weakness from the businessman's point of view. Each partner is competely liable, or responsible, for anything that happens to the business.

Corporations. As industries grew larger in the 1800's, another form of business organization, the *corporation,* became more common. It gradually became the leading form of business organization in the United States.

To start a corporation, it is necessary for three or more persons to apply to a state legislature for a *charter,* or license, to start a specific business enterprise. Once granted, this charter permits the interested persons to organize a corporation and sell shares of *stock,* or certificates of ownership, to raise the capital needed to carry on the specified enterprise. The *stockholders* or *shareholders* —those who invest their money in the enterprise—may periodically receive *dividends,* that is, a share of the corporation's profits. Legally, a corporation is regarded as an individual—an "artificial person" entirely separate from its owners—possessing such rights as the right to make contracts, to buy and sell property, and to sue and be sued in court.

The corporate form of business organization has important advantages over the individual proprietorship and the partnership. Two advantages are especially important to the corporation itself. First, the corporation can draw upon very large reservoirs of capital because it can sell shares of stock to many people, either in large or small amounts. Second, the charter gives the corporation "perpetual life" that cannot be interrupted by the death or withdrawal from the business of one or several of its owners.

For the owners, or investors, the cor-

∙∙∙
° *capital:* the wealth, whether in money or property, owned or employed in a business enterprise.

poration also offers two important advantages. First, a stockholder can sell all or part of his stock whenever he chooses to. Second, the person who invests in a corporation has only "limited liability." That is, if the corporation fails, he loses only the money he has invested in its stocks; he cannot be made to pay off any debts that the bankrupt corporation may owe. This makes the corporation far safer as an investment than, for example, a partnership, in which each partner has "unlimited liability" for the debts of the enterprise, and may lose his home and everything else he owns, if the business fails.

Corporations grow after 1860. During the first half of the 1800's, only a few of the larger industries—such as the textile mills at Lawrence and Lowell in Massachusetts, and some banks and railroads—were organized as corporations. But in these cases the corporations were usually owned by only a handful of persons. By the 1860's, however, businessmen needed increasing amounts of capital to build, equip, and operate the new manufacturing enterprises that utilized the vast resources of America's forests, soils, mines, and waters. Because the corporate form of business organization proved ideal for gathering large amounts of capital, it came to be widely adopted during the latter half of the 1800's.

Business consolidation. During the latter half of the 1800's, there was also a growing trend toward business combination, or consolidation. Corporations in the same type of business joined together to create large combinations.

There were some reasons to think that these combinations would be an improved form of business organization. Several corporations when banded together could save money by eliminating competing salesmen and advertising, by making better use of by-products, by securing lower prices for larger purchases of raw materials, and by dealing mutually with transportation companies, workers, and banks. It was also thought that consolidation would put an end to "cutthroat competition," in which rival corporations kept undercutting prices until none was earning any profits.

But these large enterprises might also become a threat to important principles of freedom in the American economic system. If a group of corporations consolidated, they might gain a *monopoly*, or complete control, over a particular line of business. Monopoly control might lead to great economic evils because it could operate "in restraint of trade"—that is, it could dry up the flow of competition, which lies at the heart of a free enterprise economy.

For example, a business combination might have so much power that it could "freeze out" competitors by undercutting prices until the competitor failed, and then raise prices to make up its losses. Or when a consolidated enterprise had gained monopoly control in a given area of business, it could charge whatever it chose, denying to purchasers their right to shop around for the best bargains. These and other economic evils stemming from monopoly con-

■ In earlier times, stocks were traded under the trees along New York's Wall Street. But by 1885 stock trading was done in this ornate building.

trol of business presently became problems, as you will see, for American government, for American businessmen who wanted to safeguard the flow of competition, and for the American people as a whole.

Corporations form pools. One of the earliest ways in which corporations combined was by organizing *pools*. To form a pool, it was only necessary for several corporations to agree to divide all their business opportunities among themselves by one means or another. For example, several railroads serving the same city might agree as to the percentage of the local business each would handle. Or they might agree to charge uniform freight rates so that none would gain a price advantage over the others. Or a group of manufacturing corporations might agree to divide the country into several market areas, each of which would be reserved for the salesmen of one of the corporations in the pool and would be "off limits" to all the others.

■ In this powerful cartoon of 1887, monopolists are tearing the life out of Uncle Sam, helplessly bound by "defective laws." The viper of political corruption is about to strike. At the lower left, "the people's interests," sound asleep, are proceeding too slowly to the rescue.

"Pooling," as it was called, was never a satisfactory form of business organization. Unlike the corporation, which operated under a legal charter, a pooling agreement had no legal standing. For that reason, courts refused to judge cases in which a member of a pool had violated his agreement with the other members. Pools, then, were merely "gentlemen's agreements." In 1887 they were declared illegal in interstate commerce (page 496), and practically disappeared.

Powerful trusts are created. Meanwhile, other businessmen developed a second form of business consolidation. This new form was called the *trust*.

Businessmen who wanted to organize a trust first had to reach an agreement with the principal stockholders in the several corporations involved. Under the agreement, the promoters of the trust gained control of the stock in all the corporations and thus of the corporations themselves. In exchange, the promoters, or "trustees" as they were called, gave the stockholders of the corporations "trust certificates" on which dividends were paid out of the profits of the trust.

With control of the stock in their hands, the "trustees" could run several corporations as a single giant business enterprise. If the "trustees" could get control of enough corporations, they could secure monopoly control of an entire field of business and charge whatever prices or rates they wished to charge. They could, for example, lower prices temporarily in one area to drive a competitor out of business, while raising prices everywhere else.

During the 1870's and the 1880's giant trusts swallowed up corporations in one after another of the nation's big industries, including oil, steel, sugar refining, and whisky distilling. Whenever a trust did get control of enough corporations to secure a monopoly and eliminate competition, it then raised prices on the products it controlled. Consumers—those who purchased and used these products —complained bitterly about the prices that they had to pay. The smaller competing businesses complained even more bitterly as they saw the trusts closing in on them.

The magazines and newspapers of the time were filled with articles, letters, and editorials pointing out the evils of the "all-powerful monopolies," and pleading with the government to step in and restore freedom of enterprise. But local, state, and federal governments were powerless. There were no laws that said that trusts and monopoly practices were illegal.

The Sherman Antitrust Act. Finally, in 1890, during the administration of President Benjamin Harrison, Congress tried to destroy the roots of monopoly practices by passing the Sherman Antitrust Act. At the time this act was passed, the public assumed that it was designed to break up the giant trusts and restore a larger measure of competition. This seemed to be what Congress intended, for Section 1 of the act declared: "Every contract, combination in the form of trust or otherwise, or conspiracy, in restraint of trade or commerce among the several states or with foreign nations is hereby declared to be illegal. . . ." And Section 2 went on to state that "Every person who shall monopolize, or attempt to monopolize, or combine or conspire with any other person or persons, to monopolize any part of the trade or commerce among the several states, or with foreign nations, shall be deemed guilty of misdemeanor. . . ." The act further stated that individuals and corporations found guilty of violating the law would be liable to legal penalties.

Weakness of the Sherman Antitrust Act. Actually, few Americans, including even corporation lawyers and Congressmen who voted for the act, were able to explain precisely what the new law did and did not prohibit. When it drafted the act, Congress failed to define such words as "trust," "combination," "conspiracy," and "monopoly."

As a result of its loose wording, the Sherman Antitrust Act proved extremely difficult to enforce. In seven out of the first eight cases brought by the gov-

ROCKEFELLER AND THE OIL INDUSTRY

In 1870, when John D. Rockefeller and a number of his associates formed the Standard Oil Company of Ohio, scores of small companies were competing with one another in what had become a wild and cutthroat business. Determined to win out over his competitors, Rockefeller, in 1871, persuaded a number of his rivals to join Standard Oil in a new organization, the South Improvement Company, which was chartered in Pennsylvania.

One of the major purposes of this new organization was to secure special favors from railroads. Since the South Improvement Company controlled such a large proportion of the oil business, the railroads were willing to co-operate. They agreed to give a partial refund, or rebate, on the freight charges for every barrel of South Improvement oil they carried. Moreover, the Rockefeller interests even managed to get the railroads to pay them rebates on oil shipped by their competitors.

These competitors raised such a cry of protest that the Pennsylvania legislature repealed the charter of the South Improvement Company. But Rockefeller continued to make arrangements with the railroads, and, as his power increased, drove his weaker competitors into bankruptcy and bought them out one by one.

By 1878 the Standard Oil Company controlled 90 per cent of the American oil business. In 1882 Rockefeller and his associates organized the Standard Oil Trust, through which, for the next ten years, they dominated the oil industry. The "trust" form of organization was declared illegal by the Sherman Antitrust Act of 1890, and two years later the Standard Oil Trust was forced to dissolve. But the same men who had directed the trust continued to hold controlling ownership of the oil companies which formerly had composed the trust, and remained for a long time the undisputed leaders of one of the nation's giant industries.

ernment against giant business combinations, or trusts, the courts ruled against the government.

In 1895 the Supreme Court handed down a decision in the case of *U.S. v. E. C. Knight Company* that reduced the antitrust legislation almost to a dead letter. In this decision the Court ruled that the company, which had secured control of 98 per cent of the sugar refining business, was not guilty of violating the antitrust law because its control of the refining process alone did not involve restraint of interstate trade. A monopoly itself was not illegal, the Court stated. It became illegal only when it served in some way to restrain interstate trade.

This and other decisions by the Supreme Court convinced industrialists that they were free to consolidate. As a result, the movement to form business consolidations actually gained momentum during the years following the adoption of the Sherman Antitrust Act.

And yet, in spite of its glaring weakness, the Sherman Antitrust Act was highly significant. It marked the first attempt by the federal government to help make rules for the conduct of big business, and it established a precedent for later and more effective legislation.

Holding companies. After 1890 some of the nation's business leaders abandoned the trust form of organization and turned to another style of business consolidation—the *holding company*. From the beginning the holding company was perfectly legal. To form a holding company, it was necessary to get a charter from one of the states. The directors of the holding company then issued stock in the holding company itself. With the money raised by the sale of stock, the directors then bought controlling shares of stock in two or more corporations that were actually engaged in producing goods or services, such as manufacturing companies, mining companies, electric power companies, or transportation companies. The holding company did not itself produce either goods or services. But the company did control all the corporations whose stock it held.

After the 1890's many great consolidations in America followed this form of organization. It was legal. It was responsible for its actions because the holding company, unlike the older trust, operated under a charter that could be revoked if the terms of the charter were violated. And when a holding company threatened to monopolize an industry, it was liable, like a trust, to prosecution under the Sherman Antitrust Act, although conviction was unlikely.

Interlocking directorates. Another form of consolidation that often defied prosecution was the *interlocking directorate*. In an interlocking directorate some or all of the directors of one company served as directors of several other companies. Even without formal organization it was possible for these directors to reach secret agreements among themselves and to establish a uniform policy for an entire industry. In so doing, of course, they might create a monopoly and run the risk of prosecution under the Sherman Antitrust Act. But, as you have seen, it was not easy to prove that a monopoly existed. And its existence was especially difficult to prove when the monopoly had been created by means of interlocking directorates and secret agreements.

↙ SECTION SURVEY

1. What four advantages does the corporate form of business organization have over the partnership?

2. In the form of a four-column chart entitled "Forms of Business Consolidation," define each of the following forms, give reasons for their creation, objections of small businessmen and consumers, and methods used by government to control abuses: (a) pools, (b) trusts, (c) holding companies, and (d) interlocking directorates.

3. How did Rockefeller organize the oil industry?

4. (a) Summarize the provisions of the Sherman Antitrust Act. (b) Why was this law difficult to enforce?

IDENTIFY: capital, charter, stock, dividends, cutthroat competition, monopoly; 1890.

4 Business pioneers give new directions to American life

The men who presided over the new world of throbbing machines, noisy factories, and crowded cities were the business leaders and the financiers. The influence of the businessman was reflected in local, state, and national politics.

Growing influence of the businessman. Between 1789 and 1860 thirteen Presidents had been elected—seven of whom were from the South, six from the North. Between 1860 and 1900 each of the seven Presidents elected was from the industrial regions of the Northeast or from the Middle West. On nearly all essential issues, moreover, the major differences between the Republicans and the Democrats disappeared during these years.

The business leaders of this period do not fit into a single type. They varied greatly in their personalities, abilities, and methods of doing business. They were pioneers, possessing the virtues as well as the shortcomings of pioneers. Some were rough. Some were picturesque. Some were urbane, polished men of the world. They were all energetic, enterprising, eager to seize upon the unlimited opportunities that they saw in the new industrial world that was emerging in the late 1800's. Some were fabulously successful. Others, the "small businessmen," never amassed the fortunes or won the power necessary to gain a place in history. But all—"big" business leaders and "small" businessmen alike—shared the ideal of self-reliant individualism.

These pioneers of industrialism who appeared in increasing numbers after 1865 were heralds of a new type of leadership and of new ways of life in the machine age.

Cornelius Vanderbilt. "Commodore" Cornelius Vanderbilt was born in 1794 when George Washington, a wealthy landowner, was President of the United States. By 1865 Vanderbilt, having start-

■ "Commodore" Cornelius Vanderbilt.

ed life as a poor boy, had accumulated great wealth. In 1865 Vanderbilt, then seventy-one years of age, owned a fleet of steamships worth $10,000,000. Twelve years later, when he died at the age of eighty-two, he was worth $105,000,000.

Even in his seventies Commodore Vanderbilt was a tall, erect, powerfully built, energetic individual, with white hair, black eyes, and a defiant bearing. He could hardly write, and his spelling was impossible. His ungovernable temper won him many enemies. He seemed to act on impulse, following his own intuitions, or even consulting astrologers or fortune tellers, in his business affairs. Vain to an unusual degree, he printed his own picture on all the stock in his Lake Shore and Michigan Southern Railroad.

What did Vanderbilt contribute to American life? For one thing, he consolidated the railroad companies that provided service between New York and Chicago. Before he secured control of the different lines, passengers and freight had to be transferred 17 times between the two cities, and the trip took at least 50 hours. When he had completed the consolidation, one train made the entire trip in about 24 hours. He replaced iron rails and wooden bridges with steel rails and steel bridges.

He built double tracks to make two-way traffic safe and speedy. He constructed new locomotives and terminals. Achievements such as these made possible the rapid development of America's industrial economy and help to explain why by 1900 America was the world's leading industrial nation.

Andrew Carnegie. Andrew Carnegie was another of the fabulous business leaders who arose during the early decades of industrialism. Born in 1835 in Scotland, Carnegie came to America at the age of twelve and settled with his parents in Allegheny, now a part of Pittsburgh. At fourteen he was working 12 hours a day as a bobbin boy in a cotton mill for one dollar and twenty cents a week. He studied hard, and at sixteen was a telegraph clerk earning about four dollars a week, which was a fair salary in those days. A likable lad, he came to the attention of Thomas A. Scott, superintendent of the Pennsylvania Railroad, who struck up a friendship with Carnegie. At seventeen Carnegie became private secretary to Scott, who by then had become president of the Pennsylvania Railroad. As Scott's secretary Carnegie made many friendships that served him in good stead in later years.

In 1859 Carnegie bought an oil well, thus getting started on the ground floor of the new oil industry. He made money. But he soon turned to another new industry, that of steel, and it was in this field of enterprise that he spent the rest of his business life.

Carnegie frankly admitted that he knew nothing about steel manufacturing. The secret of his success lay in his ability as a salesman and promoter. He knew how to gather around him men who were specialists. He was a relentless driver, never satisfied with himself or with others. One day he received a telegram from one of his plant superintendents: "We broke all records for making steel last week," the telegram read. "Congratulations," Carnegie wired back, "Why not do it every week?"

Carnegie, however, was not unappreciative of the work of others. Those whom he liked and befriended were pulled rapidly up the ladder to financial success. Charles M. Schwab, for instance, who entered one of Carnegie's plants as a stake driver at a dollar a day, became president of the Carnegie Steel Company at the age of thirty-four, and his share of profits in 1896 was $1,300,000. Similar stories are told of Carnegie's friendship for Henry Phipps, Henry C. Frick, and others.

By 1900 Andrew Carnegie, who started life as a poor immigrant boy, was said to be the second richest man in the world. He owned all the types of property and equipment necessary in the mass production of steel, including deposits of iron ore, limestone, and coal; ships and railways to carry the raw material to his smelters and mills; and huge steel plants from which the finished products poured forth. Carnegie sold his steel property in 1901 for $225,-000,000. This tremendous financial deal was negotiated by J. P. Morgan, the most famous investment banker of the

(Continued on page 483)

■ Andrew Carnegie in his earlier years.

■ The powerful American steel industry had its beginnings in foundries like this one, which made cannons, rifled artillery pieces, and projectiles for the Union armies during the War Between the States.

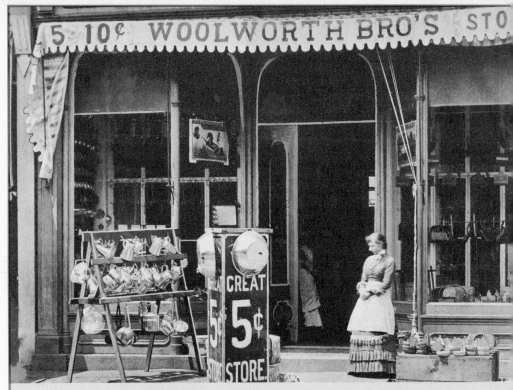

WOOLWORTH'S FIVE–AND–TEN–CENT STORES

Frank Winfield Woolworth was born in Rodman, New York, April 13, 1852. As a boy he loved to "play store," but for some reason he was not particularly successful as a clerk in the various stores in which he worked as a young man. In fact, he was a poor salesman.

In 1878 Frank heard of a store with a counter at which only five-cent articles were sold. He persuaded his own employer to try out this novel idea. It succeeded beyond all expectations, and Woolworth decided to go into business for himself.

In 1879 Frank Woolworth opened a store in which he sold only goods priced at a low figure. For a time he was barely able to keep his head above water, but as the years passed, with the help of various partners, he succeeded in building several important "chains" of stores.

In 1912 Woolworth combined these chains into a single organization, the F. W. Woolworth Company. Many of the articles the new company sold were manufactured in large quantities especially for F. W. Woolworth stores. By this means, these stores were able to sell at low prices an increasing number of articles which had always before been fairly expensive. Because of their low prices, these stores were for a long time called "five-and-ten-cent stores."

In 1913 the Woolworth Building was completed in New York. For many years this 792-foot skyscraper remained the world's tallest building. From this headquarters the firm expanded its business by adding more and more stores, not only in the United States, but in Canada as well. When Woolworth died in 1919, his personal fortune was estimated at 65 million dollars.

Frank Winfield Woolworth was one of the pioneers of modern American merchandising. His success rested in large part upon his conviction that it was better to make a small profit on many items than to try for larger profits on a smaller number of high-priced articles. This policy, adopted by Henry Ford and other American businessmen, has helped an increasing number of Americans to enjoy the products of the industrial age.

time, and his associates. Out of the negotiations was born the mighty United States Steel Corporation, then the largest corporation in the world.

Carnegie retired in 1901. He spent much of the rest of his life giving away his money to education and other causes. "I started life as a poor man," he once said, "and I wish to end it that way." Before his death he had disposed of more than $350,000,000. Public libraries in many towns and villages stand today as monuments to Carnegie's generosity, while foundations created by his money still support causes such as education, world peace, and medical research.

John D. Rockefeller. Even richer than Carnegie was John D. Rockefeller, born in 1839, who started life as a poor boy and accumulated the world's greatest fortune. One of five children, Rockefeller left high school after one year to work as a clerk for about three dollars a week. In 1858, at the age of nineteen, he went into the wholesale food business with an Englishman named M. B. Clark. The War Between the States brought large profits to the new company. Rockefeller promptly invested his money in oil refineries, and from this point on oil became his major interest.

By 1900, however, Rockefeller's interests had broadened. He owned the controlling stock in the gigantic Standard Oil Company, in railway lines, in steamship lines, in iron ore deposits in Colorado and in the Lake Superior region, in steel mills, and in numerous other enterprises. When the United States Steel Corporation was being organized by J. P. Morgan, Rockefeller sold to the newly formed corporation his iron ore deposits and Great Lakes steamers, receiving $80,000,000 for the iron ore deposits alone.

Like Carnegie, in his later life Rockefeller gave away many millions, and the foundations created with his money today foster research and promote the public welfare.

Pioneers of industrialism. These were only a few of the many pioneers of the new industrial society. Like other pioneers—cattlemen, prospectors, frontier farmers—they helped to develop the resources of a new land. They were endowed with great energy and rare ability. They were gamblers, willing to take chances in the hope of gain. They were highly competitive men in a highly competitive society, at a time when few laws had been enacted to bring order into the mad rush of business enterprise. They were absorbed in the wild excitement of building a new industrial world, of creating huge fortunes, of securing power.

They have frequently been condemned for their selfishness and for the business methods that they used to climb to power. At the same time, their critics have acknowledged that these men built new industries, introduced efficient organization, and provided opportunities that enabled many people to invest their savings profitably in the new industries that were springing up all over the nation.

Leaders of this type were the products of their time. It is unlikely that they will ever again appear in American life. But while they were on the stage, they played an important part in an important period of the nation's development, and they helped to give new directions to American life.

📖 **SECTION SURVEY**

1. What did Cornelius Vanderbilt contribute to American life?

2. How did Andrew Carnegie build up his huge fortune? What, after his retirement, did he do with this fortune?

3. State the reasons for Woolworth's success in merchandising.

4. (a) Draw up a list of characteristics which entitle Vanderbilt, Carnegie, and Rockefeller to be called "pioneers of industrial society." (b) On what grounds were these men criticized by some people?

5. What important contributions did the business pioneers make to American economic life?

IDENTIFY: United States Steel Corporation, Standard Oil Company; J. P. Morgan.

■ **CHAPTER SURVEY**   (For review, see Section Surveys, pages 470, 474, 478, 483.)

Points to Discuss: 1. Explain the statement that America has changed from a rural, agricultural economy to an urban, industrial way of life.

2. The railroad and the automobile were the most outstanding developments in the transportation field from 1870 to 1920. Why was this so?

3. Show how the telegraph, the undersea cable, the telephone, and the wireless are landmarks in the history of communications.

4. Steel, power, and machines were keys to the new Industrial Age. Discuss.

5. Describe methods used by key business leaders to consolidate and control vast areas of economic enterprise.

6. What was the significance of the passing of the Sherman Antitrust Act?

7. The business leaders of this period helped give new direction to American life. Was this good or bad? Discuss.

8. Consider the problems as well as the benefits that came to the average American as a result of industrialism.

Using Charts: 1. Using chart 1 on page 836, compare railroad mileage in 1830 with that in 1880. Explain.

2. (a) Referring to the chart on page 468, explain the federal plan for land grants to railroads. (b) What grants were made?

3. (a) Using chart 8 on page 825, compare the ratio of rural to urban population in the United States in 1790 with the ratio in 1900. (b) What caused the changes?

4. Using charts on pages 832–33, answer the following: (a) What advances in American industry between 1850 and 1900 were most significant in helping to create big business? (b) Which of these major advances help explain large-scale development of railroad transport? (c) Compare power output by sources in 1850 and in 1900 and explain the change. (d) What connection can you see among increasing output per worker, shifts in power sources, and major advances in American industry? (e) Why is the number of hours worked per week decreasing? (See also chart 4 on page 845.)

Consulting the Sources: For accounts of activities of Ford, Rockefeller, and Carnegie, see Commager and Nevins, *The Heritage of America,* Nos. 214, 218–19.

■ **TRACING THE MAIN IDEAS**

During the years between 1865 and 1900, the United States grew by leaps and bounds. By the opening years of the 1900's, the United States had become the leading industrial nation in the world. Smoking factory chimneys, the rumble of steam-driven and electric machinery, and long trains of freight cars pulling into and out of congested urban centers were symbols of the Industrial Revolution.

Particularly in the Northeast and Middle West, and to a lesser extent elsewhere in the nation, industrialism was transforming the lives of the people. Raw materials from America's vast reservoir of natural resources poured into the mills and factories. Finished products in ever-growing quantities poured from the factories.

Mass production led to specialization. Financiers raised the capital to build the railroads and the factories. Manufacturers developed more efficient methods of producing goods. Merchants developed new methods of advertising and selling. Many workers—clerks, stenographers, managers, factory workers, and others—manned the new industrial plants. New methods of business organization were developed, and great corporations and combinations of corporations increasingly replaced the earlier family-owned businesses.

Throughout America a new spirit of fierce competition drove men at a faster and faster pace. It was an exciting and a productive period in the nation's history. But some of the changes created problems for many people. Much of the nation's history since 1865 is concerned with the efforts of Americans to adjust their ways of life to the new forces of growing industrialism.

Farmers Revolt Against Big Business Practices

CHANGING WAYS

OF AMERICAN LIFE

AFTER 1865 American farmers stood on the threshold of the new industrial age. To be sure, neither the farmers nor the great majority of their fellow Americans were aware of the sweeping developments that were about to transform life in America, in Western Europe, and eventually throughout the world.

Even by 1870, however, the handwriting was on the wall. Steel rails were creeping out onto the prairies, across the plains, and through remote mountain valleys, opening up new farm lands and bringing older farm lands in closer touch with the cities. Farm machines were beginning to appear on some of the nation's more prosperous farms, enabling the farmer to produce more with less labor. The rapidly growing industrial cities were opening up ever-larger markets for farm products. As a result of these and other related developments, the farmer was becoming an increasingly important part of the new industrial economy.

In the 1870's farmers had every reason to assume that better times lay ahead for the nation's rural population. Better times did come, but not in the 1880's and 1890's. Instead, as industrialism swung into full stride, American farmers in general were confronted with a host of new problems.

AS THE STORY DEVELOPS

1. Farm life remains laborious but simple up to the 1870's.
2. Farmers face complex new problems in the industrial age.
3. Farmers organize to bring pressure on government.
4. Farmers almost win control of the national government.

485

1 Farm life remains laborious but simple up to the 1870's

Every ten years federal census takers, following the requirement laid down in the Constitution, travel up and down the highways and byways of America. They visit every household, count every individual, make note of occupations and other relevant data, and send their reports to the nation's capital, where they are compiled and published.

The farm population in 1870. The returns from the 1870 census showed that the nation's urban population was growing more rapidly than the rural population. Whereas in 1860, 80 per cent of the American people had lived in rural areas, by 1870 only about 75 per cent of all Americans lived on farms or in small towns and villages. Even so, it was clear that the United States was still predominantly a farm country.

The 2,660,000 farms that the census takers visited in 1870 varied, as one would expect, from place to place. Some were large, others small. Some farmers were prosperous; others just managed to earn a livelihood for themselves and their families. But regardless of size or degree of prosperity, the farms of 1870 shared certain characteristics.

The day of hand tools. Manual labor and a few simple hand tools characterized farm work in 1870, even as they had characterized farm work through the ages. It is easier, perhaps, to visualize the typical farm of 1870 by starting with things the farmer did not have.

On no farms, for instance, were there gasoline-driven machines or machines powered by electricity. The farmers pumped the water they used by hand, hoisted it in buckets from open wells, or, if they were fortunate, connected a pipe to a hilltop spring and allowed the water to flow into the barn and the farmhouse. There were no electric ranges; farm wives cooked on clumsy wood stoves or, rarely, on the newly developed kerosene stoves. There were no gas or electric lights; for illumination farmers used smoky kerosene lamps and lanterns. There was no central heating; there were only stoves and, in the milder climate of the South, open fireplaces. There were no mail-order catalogues from which a farmer could order ready-made clothing, tools, household equipment, and other articles he wanted. In 1870 these "modern" conveniences had not yet been developed.

On a few of the nation's larger and more prosperous farms, improved machines were becoming increasingly important. Steel plows were in general use. Horse-drawn corn planters, mowers, hayrakes, reapers, and threshers were being manufactured and bought in growing numbers. But in 1870 relatively few farmers enjoyed the advantages of this equipment.

In 1870 many farmers depended almost entirely upon hand tools—axes, saws, spades, pitchforks, sickles, scythes, and rakes. For power they relied mainly on their own muscles and on horses, mules, or oxen.

There was nothing new in this situation. For many farmers farm life in the United States in 1870 was not essentially different from American farm life in, say, 1770 or 1820.

The self-reliant workman. The farmer's lot was not an easy one. He and his sons had to get up at daybreak—and even earlier in the winter—to milk the cows, bring in firewood for the stoves, feed the hens and pigs, and fill the water trough for the livestock. When night fell—and even after dark in the winter—the farmer was still busy with the unending round of milking, feeding, and general chores.

But hard though farm life was, it had compensations. A farmer was his own boss. His land and his labor furnished most, if not all, of life's essentials—food, clothing, and shelter. The farmer who had to rely mainly on his own efforts developed a spirit of independence that no wage earner could hope to enjoy.

But not all American farmers in 1870 shared this feeling of independence.

Nearly one fourth of the families living on farms at this time did not own the land they worked. They either rented farms as tenants or operated them as sharecroppers (page 422).

Social life. Except for farmers who lived very close to a growing city or a large town, opportunities for social activities in 1870 were limited. For most farm families there were only three centers of social activity—the nearest town, the church, and the school.

The Saturday drive to town in a wagon or buggy behind "Old Dobbin" was a big weekly event. Even a five-mile drive took an hour each way, and a ten-mile trip meant about four hours on the road. As for the "town," it might be nothing more than a country store at the crossroads, with a blacksmith shop on the opposite corner. Or it might be a sizable village, or even a county seat with a courthouse, a railroad station, several stores, a bank, a doctor's office, a lawyer's office, and a considerable cluster of houses, including the homes of a handful of retired farmers.

These Saturday trips were a combination of business and pleasure. While the mother shopped for the few items she needed, and while the farmer arranged for the sale of his cash crops or settled his account at the bank or the store, the children played with their friends. But with the shopping and the business there was the opportunity to chat with neighbors, to watch or take part in some horse trading in front of the blacksmith shop, and to get the latest news of the outside world.

The Sunday trip to church was another bright spot in the week. Once again "Old Dobbin" was hitched to the wagon or buggy, and the entire family, freshly scrubbed and dressed in their best clothes, drove down the road to the church. There they sang, listened to the sermon, and when the service was over, gathered in front of the church for a few minutes of leisurely talk before they drove back home.

The local school. On weekdays the children attended a one-room elemen-

WOLVES,
CYCLONES,
AND PRAIRIE FIRES

It is difficult today to realize the hardship and dangers faced by the hardy pioneers who first settled the prairies and plains. Wolves prowled at night, hunting for stray livestock. Coyotes raided the farmyards. At times, swarms of grasshoppers darkened the sky, devoured the growing crops, and left a trail of desolation.

And often there was hostile weather to contend with—drought, a burning sun under which plants withered and died, blizzards that swept the plains with blinding force and buried livestock in great drifts, cyclones that roared out of the summer skies without warning and destroyed everything in their paths.

In some ways the most terrifying of all hazards was the prairie fire. In a volume of poems called *Prairie Songs*, Hamlin Garland described a prairie fire:

"A curving, leaping line of light,
A crackling roar from lurid lungs,
A wild flush on the skies of night—
A force that gnaws with hot red tongues,
That leaves a blackened, smoking sod—
A fiery furnace where the cattle trod."

■ By 1870, many pioneer families lived in log houses like this one in Iowa. Earlier cabins had usually been built one story high, of rounded logs notched at the corner, with oiled paper or skins for window openings. Here, the logs have been squared, with regular window openings, and a second story. Interiors (left) might have such comforts as a bed with rope springs, a gateleg table, and a clock. The cylindrical object in front of the window is a butter churn. Leaning against the outer wall of the house are a rake and a cradle scythe, used to cut grain by hand. By the 1870's, horse-drawn reapers and rakes were beginning to replace these tools.

tary school, some of the boys and girls trudging two or three miles each way along the country roads. School terms were short, for the children were needed to help with spring planting and fall harvesting. The teacher, usually a young lady, although young men often tackled the job, taught all grades, but the emphasis in 1870 as in earlier times was on "readin', 'ritin', and 'rithmetic." During the school term the teacher often boarded in the homes of the pupils, staying a month in one home, the next month in another, and so on.

The school was also a community center. Graduation day was a big occasion, and now and then during the year there were spelling bees and other events for parents as well as children.

Loneliness of farm life. For most farm families, however, farming in 1870 was a hard, lonely way of life. It was especially hard and lonely for the pioneers living on the prairies and plains.

Hamlin Garland, who spent his boyhood on farms in Wisconsin, Iowa, and the Dakotas, pictured in his books and short stories the dreary lack of social life in isolated farming communities. In his famous collection of tales, *Main-Traveled Roads*, Garland wrote:

"The main-traveled road in the West (as everywhere) is hot and dusty in summer, and desolate and drear with mud in fall and spring, and in winter the winds sweep the snow across it; but it does sometimes cross a rich meadow where the songs of the larks and bobolinks and blackbirds are tangled. Follow it far enough, it may lead past a bend in the river where the water laughs eternally over its shallows.

"Mainly it is long and wearyful, and has a dull little town at one end and a home of toil at the other. Like the main-traveled road of life it is traversed by many classes of people, but the poor and the weary predominate."

Hardest of all was the lot of immigrant farmers who, by 1870, were beginning to move out upon the newer portions of the prairies and the plains (page 455). Immigrant pioneers had to

Farm family in Sunday clothes

adjust themselves not only to the strange physical environment, but also to a very different social environment from that with which they had been familiar in their homelands. At first they did not know the language or customs of their neighbors. Churches were different, schools were different, and life in every way was different from life in the Old World.

But the farmers of 1870 were not unhappy with their lot. They expected to work hard, and they expected to live more or less apart from their neighbors.

The problems that troubled America's farmers in the late 1870's, 1880's, and 1890's were not the age-old problems of hard manual labor and the loneliness of farm life. The problems that troubled them were new problems growing out of the new industrial economy that was beginning to bring changes to every part of American life.

SECTION SURVEY

1. Explain why farm life in 1870 was not very different from farm life in 1770 or 1820. Compare with farm life in 1960.
2. Although farm life in 1870 was not easy, it had compensations. Explain.
3. If you had been living on a farm in 1870, what opportunities for social life would have been open to you?

IDENTIFY: Hamlin Garland.

2 Farmers face complex new problems in the industrial age

For American farmers in general, the last twenty-five or thirty years of the 1800's brought new problems.

Not all farmers were equally affected by these problems. Farmers who remained self-sufficient continued to live much as their parents had lived before them. And many farmers living near city markets, especially farmers concentrating on truck gardening and dairying, were fairly well off. In fact, many wheat growers and other single-crop farmers turned to dairying in the 1870's and 1880's.

The majority of the nation's farmers, however, were in serious trouble during the last quarter of the 1800's. What were the new problems the farmers faced?

Overproduction and falling prices. The most fundamental cause of agricultural discontent—overproduction and falling prices—was rarely understood by the farmers themselves.

From 1865 to about 1900, the farmers produced more food than people could afford to buy. This increase of food in the American markets was the result of (1) the rapid opening of new farm lands on the prairies and plains, and (2) the development of new farm machinery and improved methods of farming.

Why did American farmers not sell their surplus products to other countries? They did. But competing agricultural countries such as Russia, Canada, Argentina, and Australia were also seeking customers abroad, and often with the same products that the United States wanted to export. Thus there was an increased amount of certain kinds of food on the world market as well as in the United States.

Whenever there is a greater supply of any commodity than there is demand for that commodity, prices fall. Since the 1930's, as you will see later, the federal government has tried to "support" farm prices in the United States, but in the late 1800's nobody even suggested such activity on the part of government. Thus, farm prices kept falling.

Wheat, which had brought $2.50 a bushel in 1868, dropped to an average of 78 cents a bushel in the late 1880's. Because of high transportation costs and for other reasons, however, the farmers actually often got only 30 cents a bushel. Corn fell to 15 cents a bushel and, being cheaper than coal, was often used for fuel. Cotton, which in the late 1860's had sold for 65 cents a pound, declined to 5 cents a pound in 1895. As a result, growers of these important staple crops were farming at a loss.

Farm costs remain high. The situation was even more desperate than these figures indicate. To add to their difficulties, the farmers paid what seemed to them unnecessarily high prices for the shoes, clothing, kerosene, furniture, farm machinery, household equipment, and processed goods that they bought. In many instances these high prices resulted from the exclusion of cheaply made European goods by the high tariffs that were put on imports in order to protect domestic manufacturers. And in some instances the prices were high because they had been artificially raised by monopolies.

Mortgages and increased debts. To make matters worse, the farmers almost always owed money. Many of them had borrowed money in the form of mortgages to pay for their land, homes, and barns. They had added to this burden of debt by borrowing money to pay for fences, livestock, seed, and machinery. As prices for agricultural products fell with overproduction, the farmers were unable to pay their debts. To stave off disaster, they increased their mortgages by borrowing more money from local bankers or other money lenders.

The 1880's were often called "the decade of mortgages." Of the total number of farms in the country, 43 per cent were mortgaged. In Kansas the number reached 60 per cent. The popular songs of the day illustrated the frightful burden of the mortgage:

"We worked through spring and winter—
Through summer and through fall,
But the mortgage worked the hardest—
And the steadiest of them all.
It worked on nights and Sundays—
It settled down among us—
And never went away.
Till with failing crops and sickness—
We got stalled upon the grade,
And then there came a dark day on us,
When the interest wasn't paid;
And there came a sharp foreclosure,
And I kind o' lost my hold,
And grew weary and discouraged,
And the farm was cheaply sold."

There was, of course, another side to the story. By means of mortgages, men with little or no money could borrow the capital they needed to buy a farm, or purchase farm machinery and make improvements on existing farms. It was not mortgages in themselves, but the hard times and the high interest rates that they had to pay on mortgages that troubled the farmers.

High interest rates. During the late 1800's, interest rates on western farm loans ran from 8 to 20 per cent. These rates were higher than the interest rates charged to industrial and commercial enterprises. The higher rates on farm loans were explained on the ground that farming, for a number of reasons, was a riskier business than industry or commerce. In addition to these high interest rates, money brokers charged a commission for arranging farm loans.

Two hundred loan brokers in Kansas, starting with nothing, were said to have become millionaires within a few years. The manager of one loan company wrote: "During many months of 1886 and 1887 . . . My desk was piled high every morning with hundreds of letters, each enclosing a draft° and asking me to send a farm mortgage from Kansas or Nebraska." In 1889 the citizens of New Hampshire, for example, had $25,000,000 invested in mortgages on western farms.

....

° *draft:* a written order to an individual or a bank directing the payment of money.

The problem of money. The farmer blamed his troubles on the shortage of money, which was only part of the problem, but an important part. To understand the farmer's point of view and his political activities during the 1880's and 1890's, it is necessary to see how money affected his everyday life.

The first thing to remember is that money is a *medium of exchange*—that is, something of value given in exchange for goods or services. Its value is determined by the goods or services it will buy. A flour miller might say, "One dollar will buy one bushel of wheat." A farmer might say, "One bushel of wheat will buy one dollar." Both the flour miller and the farmer are saying the same thing; both are stating the value of a dollar *and* the value of a bushel of wheat.

The second thing to remember is that there are two ways to change the value of a dollar *and* the value of the bushel of wheat. All other things being equal, if we *increase the amount of wheat,* let us say double it, then "one dollar will buy two bushels of wheat" or "two bushels of wheat will buy one dollar." If we *decrease the number of dollars in circulation,* say by one half, we can accomplish the same result, for one half as many dollars will now buy just as much wheat. That is, "fifty cents will buy one bushel of wheat" and "one dollar will buy two bushels of wheat"; or again "two bushels of wheat will buy one dollar."

In actual practice, the problem of money value is not so simple as this illustration suggests. But the illustration may help to clarify the problem of the western farmer in the years between 1870 and 1900.

Falling farm prices. Between 1865 and 1900 the price, or value, of farm products fell lower and lower. Or, to state it differently, the value of money rose higher and higher. Let us take a specific example to show how this affected the farmer. In 1868 Olaf Erickson sold 1000 bushels of wheat at $2.50 a bushel. In 1868, then, his wheat brought him $2500. Since his interest payments that year amounted to $250, he could pay this debt with the income from 100 bushels of wheat, or one tenth of his income. Each year, from 1868 on, Olaf continued to raise and sell 1000 bushels of wheat. But by 1890 wheat was bringing only 75 cents a bushel. Olaf's income in 1890, therefore, was only $750. Since his interest payments were still $250, he now had to pay his debt with the income from 334 bushels of wheat, or one third of his total income.

As far as Olaf could tell, he had done nothing to bring about this state of affairs. He owned the same farm. He worked just as hard every day from sunup to sundown. Yet his income had dropped from $2500 a year to $750 a year. Something was wrong. Olaf was working as hard and raising as much wheat as ever. Clearly, Olaf reasoned, the *value of money* had changed. Money was harder to get. Money was scarce. Money was "tight" or "expensive." It had gone up in value. That is why, Olaf thought, the same amount of wheat brought him fewer dollars each year.

Olaf, of course, forgot that there were far more farmers in 1890, both in the United States and in other countries, than there had been in 1868, and that each of his fellow farmers (or most of them) was producing far more wheat than he had produced in 1868.

Although Olaf did not understand the whole complex problem, he did have his finger upon one key to his difficulties. The supply of money in the United States was not expanding rapidly enough during the late 1800's to meet the needs of the new industrial economy. The answer, as Olaf saw it, was simple enough: Let the government increase the amount of money in circulation. This would "cheapen" the dollar and therefore raise the price of farm products. Then Olaf could pay his debts, buy what he needed, and enjoy a decent standard of living.

The middlemen. Farmers also blamed many of their difficulties on the so-called *middlemen* who bought from the farmer and sold to wholesalers and retailers. The services performed by these middlemen—the brokers, produce buyers, grain-elevator operators, and stockyard owners—were important in the distribution of farm products. But farmers believed that the middlemen were taking too large a share of the wealth produced on farms and ranches.

Many of the middlemen no doubt did take advantage of the farmers. Farmers, having little cash and credit, and needing money to pay their debts, had to sell their goods at harvest time even if prices were ruinously low. The middlemen, backed by considerable capital, could afford to store what they bought from the farmer until prices went up. Of course, prices did not always go up, and middlemen were sometimes ruined when prices fell.

The railroads. Farmers, especially on the prairies and plains, reserved their chief hatred, however, for the railroads. Like other Americans, farmers had at first welcomed the coming of the railroad with enthusiasm. They believed that it would open distant markets to them. They believed that it would increase the value of their farm lands by bringing more and more farmers into the community. For these reasons, farmers who could afford to do so often bought a few shares of railroad stock. And frequently the governments of small farming communities invested in railroad stocks and bonds in return for the promise of a branch line to the community.

Unfortunately, events did not always develop as the farmers expected. In the first place, the railroad stock that farmers owned proved to be so small a part of the whole issue of stock that the farmers had little voice in determining the policies of the railroads.

In the second place, the farmers expected that competition between the railroads would keep freight rates low. In this hope they were also disappointed because the railroads charged "differential freight rates." The different

The Shelburne Museum, Vermont

THE COUNTRY STORE

For the farmer in the late 1800's, the old country store at the crossroads was an important institution. Here the farmers gathered to buy and sell, to trade horses, to get mail, to exchange gossip, and, seated around the potbellied stove, to discuss politics and swap tall stories of farming, fishing, and hunting. A reporter for an Illinois newspaper wrote, "There are more ducks killed around the stoves . . . than are slain in twenty-four hours along the Illinois River. . . ."

The country store was filled with goods of every sort. There were shelves of dry goods—bolts of cloth, ribbons, buttons, thread, hooks and eyes, shirts, shoes, suspenders, celluloid collars, and red flannel underwear. Some shelves held drugs and patent medicines, tobacco and pipes. Others were filled with china, horse medicine, coffee grinders, shoe blacking, stove polish, soap, and cartridges. One could buy lamps, lampwicks, and kerosene; hay forks, rakes, and axes; rubber boots, shaving mugs, and mustache cups. And there were the foodstuffs—packaged goods, penny candy in jars, barrels of pickles and barrels of crackers, huge blocks of cheese waiting to be cut into five-cent slices.

The old country store was characterized by its informality, its distinctive aroma, and, in summertime, its swarms of flies, most of which somehow managed to evade the streamers of sticky flypaper hanging from the ceiling. "You can kill a fly," an old country saying went, "but ten flies come to one fly's funeral."

railroads were competitors only at terminal points in the major cities, not in the towns and villages along any given stretch of track. To state it differently, railroad officials bid against each other for "long haul" shipments between two distant cities served by two or more lines, sometimes cutting their rates so low that they were operating at actual losses. They made up these losses, however, by charging much higher rates for "short haul" shipments to communities served by only one railroad.

Farmers protested, of course, against this so-called "long-haul, short-haul abuse" on the part of the railroads. But it was difficult for them to do anything about the situation.

Many of the problems that farmers faced in the 1870's, 1880's, and 1890's were new, strange, and complicated. The age-old problems of hard manual toil and isolation—these problems farmers knew and understood. But the new problems of overproduction, falling prices, "tight" money, high interest rates, middlemen, and high shipping costs—these problems most farmers did not at first understand. Like all other Americans they had to grope their way into the new industrial age.

✔ SECTION SURVEY

1. Explain the connection between overproduction and declining farm prices in the period following the War Between the States.
2. What significant factors made the prices of goods that farmers bought disproportionately high?
3. (a) The 1880's were often called "the decade of mortgages." Discuss. (b) Why were interest rates on farm loans high?
4. Describe the reasoning of farmer Olaf Erickson when he blamed the shortage of money for the decline in farm prices.
5. What were the farmers' grievances against (a) the middleman and (b) the railroads?

IDENTIFY: medium of exchange, "tight" money, differential freight rates, long-haul, short-haul shipments.

3 Farmers organize to bring pressure on government

One of the first lessons that farmers learned as they began to tackle the problems facing them in the last twenty-five or thirty years of the 1800's was the need for co-operative action.

The Grange. The first national farm organization was started in 1867, with headquarters in Washington, D.C. The Patrons of Husbandry, or the Grange, as the organization was commonly called, was the brain child of a clerk in the United States Department of Agriculture. Oliver Hudson Kelley had spent most of his adult life in Minnesota. He was familiar with the hardships and loneliness of farm life. He proposed, therefore, to establish a national organization with a local chapter in every farm community. These local chapters would provide an opportunity for farm families—men, women, and children—to meet for recreation and to listen to discussions of better ways of farming.

Kelley resigned his job with the government in order to devote full time to organizing the Grange. For a few years he fought an uphill battle. By 1872, however, farm prices were falling rapidly, and the farmers, bewildered and disturbed, began to join the Grange in growing numbers. By 1875 some million and a half farmers were enrolled as Grange members, most of them in the Middle West.

Farmers' co-operatives. Kelley had started the Grange primarily as a social organization to combat the problems of social isolation and the lack of educational opportunity. The farmers who joined in the 1870's, however, were more interested in the economic aspects of their problems and in the slogans "Co-operation" and "Down with monopoly."

Working together in the Grange and in numerous local farm organizations, farmers began to organize co-operative associations, usually called *co-operatives*. A farm co-operative could bypass middlemen (1) by selling the produce of a group of farmers directly to big city markets and (2) by purchasing farm machines and clothing and household goods in large quantities at wholesale prices. Before long, farmers began to set up not only co-operative stores but also co-operative grain elevators for storage, co-operative creameries, and even co-operative factories to manufacture their own farm machines and equipment.

Most of these early co-operative ventures failed, partly because of the farmers' lack of business experience, partly because the farmers did not have enough capital to compete successfully with already established businesses. The failures left farmers who had invested in the co-operatives worse off than before. But they did not give up, for there was still the possibility of political action.

Influence in state politics. As early as 1870, farmers in Illinois had enough political influence to force the state legislature to investigate unfair practices by the railroads. As a result, in 1871 the Illinois legislature created a commission to fix maximum freight rates, and made it illegal for a railroad to charge "differential freight rates." Encouraged by the passage of these so-called "Granger laws" in Illinois, farmers in Minnesota, Iowa, and Wisconsin were able to get their legislatures to adopt similar laws regulating railroad rates and practices.

The railroads protested these laws, of course, and in some instances refused to obey them. But in 1876 and 1877 the Supreme Court in a series of decisions known as the "Granger cases," of which the most far-reaching case was *Munn v. Illinois,* ruled that state legislatures did have the right to regulate businesses that affected the public, including grain elevators and railroads.

Unfortunately for the farmers, the railroads either found ways of evading the laws or were able to exert enough pressure on the legislators to get the laws repealed. The most serious blow for the farmers, however, came in 1886 when the Supreme Court qualified its decision in the "Granger cases" by its ruling in

the case of the *Wabash, St. Louis and Pacific Railway Company v. Illinois.* In this case the Court ruled that state legislatures had no power to regulate traffic that moved across state boundaries.

The Interstate Commerce Act. The 1886 decision by the Supreme Court led to the passage by Congress of the Interstate Commerce Act of 1887. This act was badly needed, for the railroads were guilty of a number of unfair practices.

"Pooling" arrangements were one of the practices to which farmers and the public at large objected. In many cases several railroads operating in the same area and across state borders would get together and form a pool (page 476). All members of the pool then agreed not to compete with each other, but instead to charge certain agreed-upon rates. As a result, farmers and other persons using the railroads often had no choice but to pay the exorbitant rates.

Another practice the public wanted corrected was the granting of special favors. In order to get business, competing railroads often gave large corporations especially low rates. Or instead of actually lowering the rates, the railroads sometimes agreed to return part of the shipping charges in the form of *rebates,* or refunds.

Farmers and the public also complained, as you know, that railroads sometimes charged more for a short haul than for a long haul. Because of this practice it sometimes cost more to send goods a few miles than it did to send the same goods from, say, Chicago to New York.

Provisions of the act. The Interstate Commerce Act, adopted in 1887 and applying to all railroads passing through more than one state, made it illegal for railroads (1) to make "pooling" arrangements, (2) to give special favors in the form of lower rates or rebates, (3) to charge more for a short haul than for a long haul over the same line, and (4) to charge unjust or unreasonable rates. The act also required railroads to print and display their rates, and ordered them to give a minimum of ten days' public notice before changing rates.

Finally, the Interstate Commerce Act created an Interstate Commerce Commission (ICC) of five members appointed by the President and confirmed by the Senate. The commission had authority (1) to investigate complaints against railroads, (2) to summon witnesses, (3) to examine a railroad's accounts and correspondence, and (4) to require railroads to file annual reports of operations and finances and to adopt a uniform system of accounting.

The commission, however, lacked real power since it had no authority to enforce its orders. If a railroad refused to accept the commission's recommendations, the commission had to appeal to the courts for an order compelling the railroad to obey. In some instances the courts refused to grant such orders. In other instances the courts reversed the commission's decision.

And yet, in spite of its limitations, the Interstate Commerce Act was a highly significant piece of legislation. It was the first important attempt by the federal government to regulate transportation, and it created the first "regulatory commission" in United States history. Because the act set a precedent for more sweeping measures that Congress later adopted, it marked a turning point

in the history of the relations between government and business. And this important outcome, you will recall, was a result of the efforts by American farmers to organize and to use their combined power to secure legislation favorable to their interest. Thus, although the "Granger laws" were overruled, their effect was a partial victory for the organized farmers.

Politics and paper money. While struggling with railroad legislation, farmers also turned to a more serious problem—the problem of falling prices for farm produce. Ignoring the facts of (1) overproduction and (2) competition from farmers overseas, they blamed low prices solely on the scarcity of money.

The farmers' analysis of their problem was partly right, for during the late 1860's and the 1870's money was becoming increasingly scarce. In 1865, for example, the amount of "currency," or money of all kinds, in circulation in the United States averaged $31.18 per person. By 1872 the average had dropped to $20.43; by 1878, to $16.95.

Faced with growing hardship, farmers began to demand that the government increase the supply of currency in circulation. When neither the Republicans nor the Democrats promised to help them, farmers began to leave the older political parties and join the Greenback-Labor Party, commonly called the Greenback Party.

The Greenback Party took its name from the paper money, known as "greenbacks," that the government had issued during the War Between the States (page 395). After the war the government began to *retire* the greenbacks, or withdraw them from circulation. Farmers and other "cheap money" advocates protested. The "cheap money" people wanted *more*, not fewer, greenbacks in circulation.

Greenbacks are redeemed in gold. But the "cheap money" people failed to get what they wanted. Instead, in 1875 Congress adopted the Resumption Act. This act ordered the Secretary of the Treasury to redeem *in gold* all green-

THE GREATEST SHOW ON EARTH

The coming of the circus, the Fourth-of-July celebration, and the county fair in the autumn—these were the big events of the year for farm boys and girls and for their parents. Most exciting of all was the circus, and the most famous of all circuses was the one operated by Phineas T. Barnum.

Barnum, one of the ablest showmen in American history, started his circus in 1871, billing it as "The Greatest Show on Earth." Ten years later, he joined with his major rival, J. A. Bailey, to form the famous Barnum and Bailey Circus.

Every spring the circus started its annual tour, traveling from town to town in wagon trains over the dusty country roads. Agents traveled ahead of the show, plastering colorful posters on the sides of barns, on fence posts, and in the windows of the general stores. And for weeks in advance, farm boys for miles around were crossing off the days on their calendars and saving every penny they could get their hands on in anticipation of the big event.

The coming of the circus lifted the farm youth out of the routine of their everyday life and into a strange, exciting world. Under the big tent they saw "Jumbo, the King of Elephants," trained bears, snarling tigers and roaring lions, giants and dwarfs, fat men and bearded ladies, sword swallowers and clowns, acrobats and jugglers and other entertainers who performed feats the like of which they had never seen.

And when the show was over, many a farm lad dreamed of leaving home and following the circus. A few actually did run away, but most were content to live with their memories and to begin counting off the weeks and months until the circus would appear again.

backs presented to the Treasury on or after January 1, 1879. As a result of this action, by January 1, 1879, the greenbacks were worth their full, or face, value in gold. Under these circumstances, owners of greenbacks did not bother to redeem them, and Congress decided to allow 346 million of them to remain in circulation as a permanent part of United States currency.

Meanwhile, in 1875, dismayed by Congress' decision to redeem the greenbacks in gold, the "cheap money" advocates decided to take their case to the people at the polls. That was when they organized the Greenback Party and nominated Peter Cooper of New York as their Presidential candidate in the election of 1876. Although the Greenback Party did not win a significant number of votes in the 1876 election, the Greenbackers did not cease their battle for "cheap money."

The silver issue. President Rutherford B. Hayes, who entered the White House in 1877, successfully opposed the pressure of the Greenbackers in their continued efforts to get more paper money into circulation. But he was unable to block another move by the "cheap money" people to increase the volume of currency in circulation.

Back in 1834 the government had adopted a law providing for the coinage of both gold and silver, at a ratio of about sixteen to one. That is, the government offered to buy sixteen ounces of silver for the same price it paid for one ounce of gold. At the time—and for that matter until the 1870's—silver was relatively scarce, and silver producers could sell sixteen ounces of silver to private concerns or individuals for *more than* one ounce of gold. As a result, they did not take silver to the United States Mint to be coined into silver dollars. Indeed, silversmiths often melted down silver dollars rather than pay more for the same amount of the uncoined metal, called silver *bullion*.

In the 1870's, however, this situation changed. As a result of the discovery of huge amounts of silver in Colorado and Nevada (pages 459–60), the supply of silver increased tremendously and the value of silver bullion began to fall. In 1874, for the first time in more than thirty years, sixteen ounces of silver bullion sold on the open market for *less than* one ounce of gold.

The Mint stops coining silver. Faced with falling prices, silver producers recalled the government's offer to buy at the ratio of sixteen to one. But when they tried to sell their silver bullion to the Treasury Department, they discovered that in 1873 Congress had passed a law in which silver dollars were dropped from the list of standard coins.

Silver producers were furious at the loss of a profitable market for their bullion. They turned their anger against Congress for what they called the "Crime of '73." Actually, as the record shows, Congress had passed the law because for more than thirty years the silver producers had not wanted to sell their bullion to the government.

But the "Crime of '73" became a rallying cry for those who demanded that the government buy silver. The demand for this action came mostly from the West. But the silver people also received support from other Americans, including farmers, who wanted more currency in circulation.

The Bland-Allison Act. In 1877 Richard P. Bland of Missouri introduced a bill in the House of Representatives calling for free and unlimited coinage of silver dollars at a ratio of sixteen to one. When this bill reached the Senate, it was modified by Senator William B. Allison of Iowa to become the Bland-Allison bill.

The Bland-Allison bill authorized the Treasury Department to buy and mint not less than $2,000,000 and not more than $4,000,000 worth of silver each month. President Hayes vetoed the bill, but Congress passed it over his veto in 1878. The new law was a victory for the silver interests, the Greenbackers, and other "cheap money" people.

The Greenback movement fails. The Greenback Party reached its high-water mark in the Congressional elections of 1878. When the election returns were counted, it was discovered that the Greenback Party had polled a million votes and elected members to Congress. This was a surprise and a shock to the major parties. But the triumph was short-lived. Two years later, when President James A. Garfield was elected, the Greenbackers secured only 300,000 votes for their Presidential candidate, General James B. Weaver.

Yet despite the fact that it had failed to achieve its goal, the Greenback movement, like the Granger movement, taught the farmers several valuable lessons. They learned from their experience with the Grange and with local farm organizations that they could, if united, gain influence in state legislatures. They learned from the Greenback movement that even strong influence in the national legislature might not be beyond their reach. And they learned that the secret of power lay in organization.

Farmers' alliances. Even before the Greenback Party began to break up, farmers in community after community and state after state began to form organizations called "alliances." During the early 1880's the different state alliances in the North and Northwest organized a loose federation called the Northern, or Northwestern, Farmers' Alliance. The southern groups joined in a much more tightly knit organization known as the Southern Alliance.

Both of the alliances followed the example of the Grange and experimented with co-operative buying and selling organizations. Both were prepared to take action to protect the farmers from the exploitation of manufacturers, railroads, and middlemen.

Hard times in the late 1880's transformed the alliances into formidable political organizations. By 1890, for example, the Southern Alliance membership numbered 3,000,000 white members and 1,000,000 Negroes who were enrolled in an affiliated Colored Alliance.

Conditions were especially bad on the

■ Between 1862 and 1875, silver coins were so scarce that the Treasury issued "postage currency" for use as small change.

Great Plains where, starting in 1886, a ten-year series of droughts turned farm lands into arid desert. Driven to desperation, thousands of farmers finally gave up the hopeless struggle and moved back to the East. But others remained and continued to fight the land and the men that they held responsible for much of their trouble—the owners of railroads and factories, the directors of banks and insurance companies that held farm mortgages, and the middlemen who bought and sold farm produce. They also continued their pressure, along with other "cheap money" interests, to get the government to put more money into circulation.

The Sherman Silver Purchase Act. During the administration of President Benjamin Harrison, the Republicans in Congress were eager, as you know, to increase tariff rates. They succeeded when the McKinley Tariff Act became law in 1890 (page 441). But in order to secure enough votes to pass this tariff act, the Republicans had to make a deal with the "cheap money" people.

During the years 1889 and 1890 six new states entered the Union—North Dakota, South Dakota, Montana, Washington, Idaho, and Wyoming. These states, all in the West, greatly increased the political strength of the farmers and the silver mining interests in both the House and the Senate. Congressmen representing farming and silver mining areas of the country agreed to vote for the McKinley Tariff Act provided that the high-tariff Congressmen would in turn vote for a "cheap money" bill.

As a result of this "deal," the Sherman Silver Purchase Act became law in 1890. This act required the United States Treasury to purchase 4,500,000 ounces of silver each month at the prevailing market price. The act also required the Treasury to pay for this silver with paper money that could be redeemed in either gold or silver.

The Sherman Silver Purchase Act pleased silver mining interests, for the United States Treasury was now obliged to buy almost all of the silver mined in the United States. The Act also pleased the farmers and other "cheap money" people, for it forced the government to make monthly additions to the supply of currency in circulation.

New farm leaders gain fame. Leaders of the Farmers' Alliances were active in securing passage of the Sherman Silver Purchase Act and other legislation favorable to farmers. A number of the leaders became national figures by reason of their powerful oratory, their vigor, and the depth of their convictions. Among the nationally famous leaders was Ignatius Donnelly of Minnesota, a spellbinder on the platform and a pamphleteer with a biting literary style. In Kansas, "Sockless Jerry" Simpson, who denounced the rich monopolists of the East, was a powerful force. Kansas also produced Mrs. Mary Elizabeth Lease, a colorful person who fanned the flame of

political unrest by her fervent speeches.

In the South a new group of political leaders representing the poorer farmers rose to challenge the traditional leaders of the Democratic Party. Among the most picturesque and eloquent of the new leaders were Governor James Hogg of Texas, Tom Watson of Georgia, and "Pitchfork Ben" Tillman of South Carolina. "Pitchfork Ben" Tillman's nickname came from one fiery campaign speech in which he promised, if elected to the Senate, to take his pitchfork and jab it into the "old ribs" of President Cleveland, a man whom the farmers considered their enemy.

The big question. By 1890 the farmers were facing a major question: Should they form a third party? Most northern farmers were in favor of a new party; most southern farmers were opposed. Southern farm leaders feared that a third party would divide the Democratic vote, and especially the white vote, and that as a result the Negroes might become a political power once again, as they had been during the days of reconstruction. Because of their fear of the Negro vote, most Southern Alliance leaders preferred to try to capture control of the Democratic Party, rather than start a new farm party.

 SECTION SURVEY

1. (a) What was the original purpose of the Patrons of Husbandry (the Grange)? (b) Why were farmers' co-operatives formed? (c) How successful were they?
2. How did the "Granger laws" aim to curb the abuses of the railroads?
3. Contrast the Supreme Court ruling in *Munn v. Illinois* (1877) with that in *Wabash, St. Louis and Pacific Railway Company v. Illinois* (1886).
4. Discuss the strengths and limitations of the Interstate Commerce Act of 1887.
5. Explain the reasons for the formation of (a) the Greenback Party and (b) Farmers' Alliances. What did each achieve?
IDENTIFY: rebates, "cheap money," Resumption Act, bullion, "Crime of '73," Bland-Allison Act, Sherman Silver Purchase Act; Kelley; 1867, 1875, 1878, 1890.

■ City people as well as farmers took the election of 1892 seriously. In Chicago a Republican and a Democrat each promised to pull the other through the streets in a wagon if his candidate lost. The Republican, for Harrison, is pulling the Democrat, a Cleveland backer.

4 Farmers almost win control of the national government

Should the farmers form their own national political party? This was the question that farmers faced and discussed in the light of flickering oil lamps in schoolhouses and Grange halls during the summer of 1890.

Birth of the Populist Party. The Congressional elections in the fall of 1890 drew the farmers from their homes in what seemed to be a fiery crusade. In the words of one contemporary writer of Kansas: "The dragon's teeth were sprouting in every nook and corner of the state. Women with skins tanned to parchment by the hot winds, with bony hands of toil, and clad in faded calico, could talk in meeting, and could talk right straight to the point." Led by women like Mary Elizabeth Lease, the people bluntly stated their grievances.

In a powerful speech Mrs. Lease proclaimed: "Wall Street° owns the country. It is no longer a government of the people, by the people, and for the people, but a government of Wall Street, by Wall Street, and for Wall Street. The great common people of this country are slaves, and monopoly is the master. The West and South are bound and prostrate before the manufacturing East. . . . There are thirty men in the United States whose aggregate wealth is over one and one-half billion dollars. There

° **Wall Street:** a street in New York City's financial district and the nation's principal financial center; often used as a symbol of the great financiers.

501

are half a million looking for work. . . . We want money, land, and transportation. . . . We will stand by our homes and stay by our firesides by force if necessary, and we will not pay our debts to the loan-shark companies until the government pays its debts to us. The people are at bay, let the bloodhounds of money who have dogged us thus far beware."

Fired by this new militant spirit, the farmers elected two Senators and nine Representatives in the Congressional election of 1890, and pledged double that number of Democrats and Republicans in Congress to support their demand for help. As a result of these successes, in 1891 the farmers decided to forget their differences and form a third party. A meeting made up chiefly of Farmers' Alliance leaders from the West and Middle West launched the People's Party, or the Populist Party, at Cincinnati, Ohio, in 1891. In Omaha, Nebraska, the following year, the Populists drew up a platform and nominated James B. Weaver of Iowa for President of the United States.

The farmers' "Declaration of Independence." The Populists adopted their platform on July 4, 1892. In the platform they demanded far-reaching reforms.

"We meet in the midst of a nation brought to the verge of moral, political, and material ruin," stated the platform. "The people are demoralized. . . . The newspapers are largely subsidized or muzzled; public opinion silenced; business prostrated; our homes covered with mortgages; labor impoverished; and the land concentrating in the hands of the capitalists . . . We have witnessed for more than a quarter of a century the struggles of the two great political parties for power and plunder, while grievous wrongs have been inflicted upon the suffering people. We charge that the controlling influences dominating both these parties have permitted the existing dreadful conditions to develop without serious effort to prevent or restrain them. Neither do they now promise us any substantial reform. . . . They pro-

pose to sacrifice our homes, lives, and children on the altar of Mammon.°. . . "

Specific Populist demands. The Populist platform then listed the specific demands of the farmers: (1) an increase in the currency, to be secured by the "free and unlimited coinage of silver at a ratio of sixteen to one"; (2) government ownership of railroads, telegraphs, and telephones; (3) the return to the government of all land held by railroads and other corporations in excess of their needs; (4) a graduated income tax, requiring people with higher incomes to pay a proportionally higher tax; (5) a system of national warehouses where farm produce could be stored until market conditions improved, with the government providing loans on each deposit by a farmer; (6) certain political reforms, including the direct election of United States Senators, and the adoption of the secret ballot, the initiative, and the referendum (Chapter 27).

There were also certain planks in behalf of the industrial wage earner, for the Populist Party had strong support from the ranks of labor. Among other things, the Populists demanded shorter working hours and restrictions on immigration, which they held responsible for unemployment and low wages.

The election of 1892. The Populist campaign of 1892 was even more vigorous than the campaign of 1890. In the Middle West great crowds of farmers gathered with their families at outdoor meetings and picnics to listen to Populist speakers. James B. Weaver, the Populist Presidential candidate, traveled widely, and everywhere throughout the Middle West he spoke to enthusiastic audiences. In the South, however, it was a different story. Southern whites, fearful of the Negro vote, refused to abandon the Democratic Party, and Populist speakers in the South were greeted with howls and jeers.

President Benjamin Harrison, running for re-election on the Republican ticket, was defeated, as you know, by the

° **Mammon:** an ancient god, symbol of wealth and materialism.

Democratic candidate, Grover Cleveland. Although the Democrats won a sweeping victory, the Populists polled more than 1,000,000 of the popular votes; won 22 electoral votes for their Presidential candidate; elected Populist governors in North Dakota, Kansas, and Colorado; and gained a number of seats in state legislatures and in Congress.

No third party had ever demonstrated so much strength a year after its birth. It was clear to Democrats and Republicans alike that the Populist movement was much more than the protest of a few discontented Americans.

Depression and growing resentment. For the two older political parties, however, the worst was yet to come. In 1893, as you know, the country sank into a serious economic depression. Farm prices plunged downward. Factories closed their doors, and thousands of unemployed wage earners walked the streets desperately looking for jobs.

Farmers and wage earners blamed the depression on "tight money." They demanded that the government increase the amount of currency in circulation by the "free and unlimited coinage of silver at a ratio of sixteen to one."

President Cleveland blamed the crisis on the Sherman Silver Purchase Act of 1890. He believed that it was not "tight money" that had led to the depression, but rather uncertainty over the "value of money." Cleveland insisted that the only way to end the depression was to accept gold as the single standard of value for the nation's currency. This was an oversimplified explanation, for the depression was world-wide. But there was some truth in the President's analysis. In order to understand Cleveland's point of view and to see why he took the action he did, it is necessary to review the money policy of the government from the 1870's to the 1890's.

A review of the money problem. As you have seen (pages 491–92), during the 1870's and 1880's farmers blamed their difficulties, in part at least, on the government's refusal to increase the supply of money, or currency, in circulation. Farmers and other *debtors* wanted "cheap money" with which to pay their overwhelming burden of debt. On the other hand, *creditors* and businessmen in general wanted to be paid back in dollars worth at least as much as the dollars they had lent or invested. They wanted, therefore, to restrict the amount of money in circulation. They wanted what they called "sound money."

The "cheap money" people failed in the 1870's to get the government to increase the supply of money by issuing additional greenbacks. Between 1878 and 1890, however, the "cheap money" people and the owners of silver mines managed to win two victories—one, a minor victory, the other a rather substantial victory.

In the Bland-Allison Act of 1878, as you recall, a Republican Congress ordered the Treasury Department to coin not less than $2,000,000 and not more than $4,000,000 worth of silver each month. But this small increase in the currency did not satisfy either mineowners or other "cheap money" people.

In the Sherman Silver Purchase Act of 1890, another Republican Congress ordered the Treasury Department to purchase 4,500,000 ounces of silver bullion each month. Congress also ordered the Treasury to buy the silver at the prevailing market price and to pay for it with new bank notes. Printed on these bank notes was the promise to redeem them in either gold or silver. This meant that a man could walk into a bank and exchange his silver bank notes for either silver or gold coins, whichever he preferred. The government called this policy *bimetallism*—meaning that two metals, gold and silver, furnished the security for all the nation's currency.

Acting under the authority of the Sherman Silver Purchase Act, the Treasury began in 1890 to buy silver in large quantities. The mineowners were delighted, for they now had a sure market for almost the entire output of their mines. Farmers and other "cheap money" people were pleased, but they considered the new law merely a halfway measure. What they demanded in the Populist platform of 1892 was the "free and unlimited coinage of silver at a ratio of sixteen to one."

The shrinking gold reserves. By 1893, however, the Treasury Department was becoming deeply concerned about the policy of bimetallism. The value of silver had fallen until the actual silver in a silver dollar was worth only 60 cents. Since silver as well as gold provided the "backing," or security, for the nation's currency, an increasing number of Americans began to grow uneasy about this situation. As a result, more and more people began to exchange their silver bank notes for gold coins, rather than for silver coins. By the time Cleveland entered the White House in March 1893, the gold reserves had shrunk to only a little more than $100,000,000.

The shrinkage in gold reserves created a serious crisis for the government. If the gold reserve completely disappeared, the government would no longer be able to keep its promise to redeem bank notes and government bonds with gold coins. It would, instead, have to pay with silver. And, since by midsummer of 1893 the value of the silver in a silver dollar had fallen to 49 cents, prices would soar in a runaway inflation, and the nation would plunge into a major economic disaster.

Repeal of the Sherman Silver Purchase Act. President Cleveland acted promptly. He called a special session of Congress to repeal the Sherman Silver Purchase Act. The President's recommendation provoked violent debate. Representatives of silver mines, farmers, and "cheap money" people in general refused to consider repeal. But in the late fall the administration finally secured enough votes to push the repeal bill through Congress.

Repeal of the Sherman Silver Purchase Act stopped the flow of silver into the Treasury. But the gold reserves continued to shrink, for there were still many millions of silver bank notes in circulation and the Treasury kept on redeeming them in gold. By 1895 the gold reserves had dropped to only $41,000,000. It seemed to be only a question of time before the United States would go off the gold standard—that is, would stop redeeming its paper currency with gold—and runaway inflation would start.

Cleveland is aided by bankers. At this critical point President Cleveland accepted the recommendation of a group of bankers headed by J. P. Morgan. The bankers offered to lend gold to the government, receiving government bonds as security. The bankers also agreed (1) to secure half the gold from foreign countries, (2) not to take any gold from the Treasury by exchanging bank notes for gold, and (3) to try

■ Election posters of the 1890's were often quite elaborate. Among other ideas this poster tried to persuade voters in 1896 that industry and agriculture would thrive under Republican tariff "protection," whereas workers and farmers would be reduced to poverty under Democratic "free trade."

to cut gold payments to foreign countries to an absolute minimum.°

The arrangement worked. When people heard that J. P. Morgan and other leading bankers of the country were behind the government, confidence returned and the run on the gold reserves ended. Many Americans, those with "sound money" views, felt that President Cleveland and the bankers had acted courageously and wisely, and in so doing had saved the United States from disaster. But "cheap money" Americans were furious. Pointing out that the bankers had charged a generous commission for their services, they insisted that President Cleveland had actually made a "deal with Wall Street."

The battle is joined. By 1896, when the nominating conventions opened to choose Presidential candidates, both major parties were split between the "sound money," gold-standard people and the "cheap money," silver people.

The Republicans chose William McKinley of Ohio, a veteran of the War Between the States and a champion of high protective tariffs. Although McKinley tried to straddle the money issue, during the campaign he became the leader of the people who favored the gold standard.

The Democratic convention opened with a bitter struggle between the "sound money" wing of the party and the "silver" wing. The "sound money" delegates were soon howled down, and the "cheap money" wing, now in control of the convention, promptly adopted a platform demanding "free and unlimited coinage of both gold and silver. . . ."

The battle lines were drawn, with the Republicans on the "sound money" side, the Democrats on the side of the farmers, wage earners, and others who wanted "cheap money." But the Democrats had not yet selected a Presidential candidate. Rejecting President Cleveland, the "silver" Democrats began to look for a man who could lead them to victory.

••

° Gold was the international medium of exchange.

■ The Democratic candidate lost the election of 1896 but tried again in 1900, still battling the "crown of thorns" and the "cross of gold." Familiar symbols of patriotism were enlisted in the attack on monopoly. But Bryan lost again in 1900.

William Jennings Bryan. The field was wide open when a handsome young lawyer stepped forward to address the huge assemblage of 15,000 people. Only thirty-six years old, William Jennings Bryan of Nebraska was unknown to most of the eastern delegates. Between 1891 and 1895 he had served in the House of Representatives. This was the sum of his political experience in the national capital. But when he began to speak at the convention, people listened.

"We do not come as aggressors," Bryan cried. "Our war is not a war of conquest; we are fighting in the defense of our homes, our families, and prosperity. We have petitioned, and our petitions have been scorned; we have entreated, and our entreaties have been disregarded; we have begged, and they have mocked when our calamity came. We beg no longer; we petition no more. We defy them! . . .

"You come to us and tell us that the great cities are in favor of the gold standard; we reply that the great cities rest upon our broad and fertile prairies. Burn down your cities and leave our farms, and your cities will spring up again as if by magic; but destroy our farms and the grass will grow in the streets of every city in the country. . . .

"Having behind us the producing masses of this nation and the world, supported by the commercial interests, the laboring interests, and the toilers everywhere, we will answer their demand for a gold standard by saying to them: You shall not press down upon the brow of labor this crown of thorns, you shall not crucify mankind upon a cross of gold!"

With the closing words of Bryan's "Cross of Gold" speech, wild tumult broke out on the floor of the convention. Here was the Democratic standard-bearer. Here were youth, enthusiasm, and fitting leadership for a crusade to wrest power from the big business, "sound money" groups.

The Democratic nomination of Bryan and the adoption of a platform demanding free and unlimited coinage of silver left the Populists in an awkward position. The Democrats had stolen part of their thunder. When they met in convention, the Populists decided that they had no choice but to support Bryan as their Presidential candidate, but they tried to preserve their party identity by nominating Tom Watson of Georgia for the Vice-Presidency rather than Arthur Sewall of Maine, the Democratic nominee for Vice-President.

The crusade. Bryan turned the campaign into a crusade. He took to the road, traveling 18,000 miles in twenty-seven states. In fourteen exhausting weeks Bryan accomplished the almost superhuman feat of making six hundred speeches, addressing an estimated five million people. With these speeches, Bryan roused his supporters into a frenzy of enthusiasm.

With what they regarded as ruin staring them in the face, the "sound money" people threw everything they had into the campaign to defeat Bryan. Under the leadership of "Mark" A. Hanna of Ohio, McKinley's campaign manager and a wealthy businessman, the Republicans raised at least $3,500,000 to offset the $300,000 campaign fund available to Bryan. Nearly every influential newspaper in the country backed the Republicans. Many factories paid all their workers on the Saturday before election with the warning that they would have no jobs if Bryan were elected the following Tuesday.

McKinley wins the election. Bryan lost with 176 electoral votes to McKinley's 271. But the popular vote was much closer—7,000,000 for the Republicans, 6,500,000 for the Democrats. Although the country had decided in favor of the gold standard, the farmers and other advocates of "cheap money" had come close to winning the Presidency and control of Congress.

Defeat in the 1896 election and the arrival of better times for the farmers broke the back of the Populist Party. As you will see, however, during the opening years of the twentieth century a new third party, the Progressive Party, as well as progressive Democrats and Republicans, won many of the reforms that the Populists had demanded.

⌐ **SECTION SURVEY**

1. Why was the Populist Party formed? In your opinion, which four planks in the Populist Party platform of 1892 would have aided the farmer most at that time?

2. Show how the Populist Party tried to appeal to the industrial wage earner.

3. Give the parties, candidates, issues, and results of the election of 1896.

IDENTIFY: free and unlimited coinage of silver, "sound money," bimetallism, gold standard, "Cross of Gold" speech; Mary Elizabeth Lease, Morgan, Bryan, Hanna.

Points to Discuss: 1. Evaluate the results of the Granger movement.

2. Explain the reasons for the gap between the prices the farmer received for his products and the prices he paid for goods he bought.

3. (a) Explain why farmers wanted cheap money, greenbacks, and free and unlimited coinage of silver. (b) Describe their efforts to achieve these goals.

4. How would you have felt about cheap vs. sound money if you had been (a) a debtor farmer, (b) a creditor businessman, (c) a banker, (d) a retired person living on a pension?

5. How did each of the following complicate the farm problem? (a) railroads, (b) interest on mortgages, (c) protective tariff.

6. Explain why farmers supported the (a) Greenback Party, (b) Patrons of Husbandry, (c) Populist Party.

7. Review the Populist Party program in the interests of farmers and laborers.

8. The Interstate Commerce Act marked a turning point in the history of the relations of government and business. Explain.

9. Refer to the "Cross of Gold" speech to explain why William Jennings Bryan was called "the voice of populism."

Using Charts: 1. Consult chart 1 on pages 832–33, in answering these questions: (a) What major advances in American agriculture were made between colonial times and 1900? (b) Compare these with the advances in transportation, communication, and manufacturing. (c) How would you explain the slower progress in agriculture at this same time?

2. Refer to charts 5 and 6 on page 829, in answering the following: (a) Compare the number of farms in 1850 and 1900. (b) Explain the increase. (c) Compare the average size of farms in 1850 and 1900. (d) Explain the decrease. (e) Is there any connection between the two charts?

Consulting the Sources: For life in the Great Plains area, see Commager and Nevins, *The Heritage of America,* in Section XXVII, "The Last West."

■ TRACING THE MAIN IDEAS

Machines, science, and industry transformed American life with increasing speed after 1870 and created many new problems for farmers as well as for all other Americans. Most farmers lost the individual freedom they had possessed when they were more or less self-sufficient, producing a good part of what they needed on their own land. Increasingly, farmers became dependent upon forces that they as individuals could not control—upon the railroads that carried their goods to market, upon prices fixed in distant markets, upon tariffs that sometimes raised the cost of manufactured goods, upon the supply of money made available by the federal government.

Faced with these new problems, farmers began to organize new political parties and to increase their influence in the old parties in an effort to gain influence in state and federal governments. They hoped by this means to secure laws that would regulate the railroads, the industries, and the other parts of the economic system and thus make life easier for the farm population.

But industrialism brought benefits as well as problems. Power-driven machines made life immeasurably easier. Increased production enabled the farmer to feed himself and his fellow citizens far better than men had ever been fed before. Developments in transportation and communications broke down the isolation of farm life and brought the farmer and his family into touch with the life of the world beyond the farm.

It was as difficult for the farmer as it was for all other Americans to adjust to the new industrial age. The problems were all too real. By the 1900's, however, farmers began to understand that Americans were becoming increasingly interdependent and that their best hope of realizing the bright promise of the new age was to learn to work together.

Workers Organize to Safeguard Their Interests

CHANGING WAYS

OF AMERICAN LIFE

O N April 14, 1865, when President Lincoln was shot down in Ford's Theater in the nation's capital, the United States was still a predominantly agricultural country. By 1900 it had become the leading industrial and manufacturing nation in the world.

America's amazing industrial growth was possible only because of immense improvements in transportation, notably the railroad and the steamship; the development of power-driven machines; the organization of business into large corporations; the construction of giant factories and other industrial plants; the development of more efficient production techniques; and the rapid growth in the number of wage earners.

The workers—women and children as well as men—came from the farms and the rural towns and villages. They also came from Europe, in a mighty flood of immigration numbering hundreds of thousands every year.

Both the older Americans and the newcomers entered a new world when they moved into America's growing industrial communities. In the early days of power-driven machines and mass production, they were as much pioneers as the men and women who had earlier pushed America's frontiers westward to the Pacific. And like pioneers in every age, wage earners in the late 1800's faced complex problems.

AS THE STORY DEVELOPS

1. The growth of industry brings new problems to wage earners.
2. Mounting immigration, despite problems, adds strength to the nation.
3. Wage earners begin to organize to overcome their grievances.
4. Organized labor faces opposition in its early efforts to win reforms.

508

1 The growth of industry brings new problems to wage earners

The industrial developments that were transforming the United States from 1865 to 1900 created new problems as well as new opportunities for wage earners. Like all other Americans, the wage earners had to adapt themselves to a society that was rapidly changing because of the rise of industry.

New owner-worker relations. For one thing, large corporations hiring thousands of workers changed the old-time relations between owners and employees. In earlier days when factories and mills were small, the owner knew his workers and often took a personal interest in their welfare. But in the huge factories workers seldom saw the owners, most of whom were stockholders living in widely separated parts of the country.

Nor did many owners know at first hand what conditions were like in their factories and mines. They bought shares of stock as an investment. They employed managers to run the plants.

Moreover, the workers themselves often were less interested in the factory than they had been in the old days when it was small and when they knew the owner. The worker was less interested because, as the factory grew larger and larger, he, as an individual, became less and less important. If he objected to the way the factory was run, he could easily be spared. Singlehanded, he could not hope to have much influence over the conditions under which he worked. Nor could he reasonably hope to become an owner beyond, perhaps, buying a few shares of stock. To be sure, many men did succeed in becoming foremen and managers, and some were able to climb the industrial ladder to positions of wealth and power.

Within a generation or two, most immigrant groups had adopted American ways, but had retained a few reminders of their origins. Here, in New York's Union Square, Irish-Americans celebrated Saint Patrick's day in 1874. The first such celebration in New York was in 1762.

But in general, as factories became larger and more impersonal, it became harder and harder for individual workers or small groups of workers to "bargain" with their employers over wage rates and working conditions.

Company towns. Workers in so-called "company towns" labored under the greatest disadvantages. There were mining districts in Pennsylvania and West Virginia and textile-mill regions in the South where the companies owned whole towns—all the houses, stores, and other buildings. The companies employed the teachers and the doctors. The local magistrates and the policemen owed their jobs to the company. In these towns no worker dared to protest the rent he paid for his company-owned house or the prices he paid in the company-owned store. Frequently, the worker received part of his wages, not in cash, but in credit at the company store.

Effects of mechanization. The use of power-driven machines in factories also created new problems for wage earners. Often the new machinery could do the work of several wage earners. Indeed, the new machine might produce much more than the displaced wage earners. Thus, the installation of new machines in a plant often threw workers out of jobs. This form of unemployment is known as *technological unemployment*. Of course, the new machines often created new and different jobs because workers were needed to build and repair the machines. Further, the higher output of the machines increased the nationwide production of goods, and thereby created jobs of many kinds. But it is also true that displaced workers often found it difficult to get new jobs or had to learn new skills.

Machines were also physically dangerous. Until about 1910 little was done to safeguard workers from accidents. Devices for preventing accidents were almost unknown. When an accident occurred, the worker himself was usually blamed. If he were disabled, he received no compensation to pay for doctors and hospitalization. If a worker were killed, his family was usually left without an income, for employers did not insure the lives of wage earners. That industrial hazards were a problem of primary importance is evident from the fact that between 1900 and 1910, for example, 3 per cent of all employed workers in the United States were killed or injured annually as a result of industrial accidents.

Effect of the railroads. The development of a complex and vast network of railroads also affected the industrial worker, particularly in the decades immediately following the War Between the States. Before the development of the railroad network, manufacturers tended to sell their products only in nearby market areas, without competition from other areas. With the completion of the railroads, however, a manufacturer could sell his products anywhere in the country, provided that his prices were as low as those elsewhere.

This creation of a competitive national market for goods also created a competitive national market for labor. For example, if cotton goods were being made cheaper in southern mills because of lower wage rates, then New England manufacturers of cotton goods were inclined to reduce their wage rates in order to compete with the lower-priced output of the southern mills.

The business cycle. Like other citizens, workers were greatly influenced by what economists call the *business cycle*. This means the expansion of industry during periods of prosperity and the recurring contraction during periods of depression. Businessmen and government officials had not yet learned what they now know about cushioning the effects of depression. Workers lived in constant dread of being laid off or of having their wages sharply reduced whenever business conditions took a downturn.

Even when business was good, unemployment was a harsh reality that brought hunger and misery to a large percentage of industrial workers.

Precisely how many workers were unemployed at any given time we do not know, for labor statistics of the late

1800's were not very accurate. We do know, however, that between 1870 and 1900 hundreds of thousands of jobless men walked the streets in search of work. One authority estimates that in 1889, a fairly typical year, 19 per cent of the workers in the fields of manufacturing and transportation were jobless.

Effects of the closed frontier. As long as the frontier remained open, farmers on worn-out eastern land could choose between migration to the frontier or migration to the city. Many did choose to continue farming and moved to the West. After about 1900, however, there was less and less opportunity for eastern farmers to find good cheap western land. As the shoe pinched worse and worse, farmers in the East turned increasingly to the cities for work. Thus they helped to swell the population of the cities and tended to drive down the wages of the industrial worker. In this respect the labor market was like any other market. An oversupply of workers tended to push wages down.

Low wages and long hours. During the last quarter of the 1800's, wage earners complained with increasing bitterness about the low wages they were paid. There were, as you have seen, a number of reasons why wages tended to be low: the increasing power of employers over employees; the creation of a competitive national labor market; depressions; and the flooding of the labor market by new workers.

Wage earners also complained about the long hours they were required to work. After 1865 an 11-hour day was common in American industry. By the 1880's the textile workers of Massachusetts were exceptional in enjoying a 10-hour day. In many places textile workers toiled from 12 to 14 hours daily at their looms and spindles.

From 1900 to 1920 the hours of work began to be shortened. The average working hours in factories decreased from 57 per week in 1909 to 50 per week in 1919. But even as late as this, the 12-hour day prevailed in the steel industry, for example.

It was indeed a new and rapidly changing world with which the American wage earner had to wrestle in the closing years of the 1800's. The problems wage earners faced were complex problems, and neither the workers nor the owners of the industries nor the people in general had any ready answers. And, as you will see, the immigrants who entered the country during this period searching for new opportunities encountered those same problems and others.

✓ **SECTION SURVEY**

1. Compare relations between owners and workers in the small, privately owned mills and the huge, corporation-owned factories.

2. Why were the workers alarmed at the introduction of new power-driven machines?

3. How did each of the following affect the worker: (a) railroads, (b) business cycle, and (c) end of the frontier?

4. (a) What were two of the most common complaints of workers in the 1880's and 1890's? (b) Why has fear of unemployment always been a major complaint of wage earners?

IDENTIFY: company town, technological unemployment.

2 Mounting immigration, despite problems, adds strength to the nation

The immigrant played an essential part in the amazing industrial development of the United States from 1865 to 1900. He came in the first place as a worker seeking larger opportunities than he could hope for in the Old World. As a worker and as a new citizen he stayed and helped to build "modern" America.

In his efforts to find a place for himself in his new homeland and in the industrial age, the immigrant did not always meet with sympathy and understanding. Instead, in the last part of the 1800's, the newcomer was often greeted with distrust and suspicion.

■ Many Chinese laborers, after helping build the western railroads, stayed on as track workers, or "gandy dancers." In this painting by Joseph Becker, a group is waving as a Central Pacific train puffs along between snowsheds built as a protection against avalanches.

The problem of numbers. Part of the difficulty was the overwhelming number of immigrants who poured into the country during these years. During the 29 years from 1870 to 1899, a total of more than 11,000,000 men, women, and children entered the country.

The changing character of immigration. The changing character of immigration, as well as the swelling tide, alarmed many Americans. Down to the early 1880's the largest number of immigrants came from northwestern Europe —from Great Britain, Ireland, Scandinavia, Germany, and the Netherlands. But after 1890 an increasingly large number came from southern and eastern Europe and from the Near East. The languages, customs, and ways of living of these immigrants were quite different from those of immigrants from northwestern Europe.

Effect of immigration on labor. The great numbers of immigrants had an enormous influence on American life. Although some of the newcomers settled on farms, the great majority moved

to the densely crowded slum areas of the cities. Here they competed with established residents for housing, thereby driving up rents and real estate prices.

Most immediate of all, however, was their effect upon American workers. They competed with American wage earners for jobs, thereby driving down the existing scale of wages. To be sure, immigrants helped to stimulate the economy by creating new demands for factory and farm products. But the average wage earner was more disturbed by the job competition of the immigrants than he was impressed with the stimulating effects of large-scale immigration.

Tension on the Pacific coast. Chinese workers on the Pacific coast, particularly in California, were the first victims of the rising feeling against all immigrants. In 1868 the United States had drawn up the Burlingame Treaty with China. This treaty gave the Chinese the right to immigrate to the United States. For a number of years, Chinese laborers had been welcome additions to the labor supply. They had been willing to do the hardest and least profitable jobs for very low wages. They had furnished the backbone of the construction gangs that built the western section of the first transcontinental railroad (page 448). By the 1870's, 75,000 Chinese workmen had entered the country. Most of them had settled in California, where they made up about 20 per cent of all the workers.

Such was the situation in 1873 when a depression hit the country. Unemployment mounted in California as in other parts of the United States. Men feared that the Chinese would take their jobs at low wages. Fear and insecurity were increased by the fact that the Chinese, for reasons not always of their own choosing, lived entirely to themselves, and did not learn American ways.

The Chinese are excluded. Ill feeling, already running high, was fanned into violence by crowds of unemployed workmen who gathered on street corners and sand lots. The "sand lotters" began to mutter, and presently fell upon the unfortunate Chinese, killing some, burning the property of others.

In co-operation with distressed farmers in California, the workingmen had enough strength to influence the writing of a new state constitution in 1879. California's new constitution prohibited Chinese from owning property or taking part in certain occupations.

The opponents of Chinese immigration were also influential enough to get the national Congress to adopt an "exclusion bill" in 1879. The 1879 bill prohibited all but a few Chinese from settling in the United States in any year. Because this bill violated the Burlingame Treaty of 1868 it was vetoed by President Hayes. But under pressure the Chinese government agreed to raise no objections if the United States wished to regulate immigration, and in 1882 Congress enacted a new Chinese Exclusion Act which, with several extensions, continued in effect until World War II. The Chinese Exclusion Act forbade the immigration of Chinese laborers and denied American citizenship to Chinese born in China. Only students and a few other groups of Chinese could enter the United States.

Other immigration restrictions. The Chinese Exclusion Act of 1882 was the first of a long series of restrictions on immigration, enacted mainly because of pressure from worker groups. The second was the repeal in 1885 of the Contract Labor Law.

The Contract Labor Law had been adopted by Congress in 1864, when booming wartime industries were desperate for workers. The law permitted American employers to recruit laborers in Europe. Under the law it was legal for employers to have workmen abroad sign contracts agreeing to come to the United States to work for a specified employer for specified wages for a specified period of time. It was illegal for the workers to leave the job while the contract was in force. American workers objected to the law on the grounds that (1) it came dangerously close to setting up a slave-labor system and (2) it subjected American workers to the unfair competition of cheap foreign labor.

With the repeal of the Contract Labor Law behind them, American wage earners brought pressure upon Congress to pass other restrictive measures. One bill that kept coming up for thirty years would have forbidden entry to any immigrant who could not read and write. Congress actually did pass this legislation on several occasions, but each time the President then in office vetoed the bill. In 1917, however, Congress passed a "literacy test" bill over President Woodrow Wilson's veto, and the door to immigration was shut a little further.

The role of the immigrants. From 1865 to 1900, the restrictions placed on immigration were relatively minor. And without the more than 11,000,000 immigrants who poured into the United States between 1870 and 1900, America's industrial progress would have moved at a much slower tempo. Immigrant muscles as well as brains helped to transform the United States from a predominantly agricultural country into a giant industrial power.

513

1. Describe the changing character of immigration after 1880.

2. Discuss three ways in which immigration affected the American worker.

3. Give the reasons for the passage of the Chinese Exclusion Act of 1882.

4. Why was the Contract Labor Law of 1864 repealed?

5. "Immigrant muscles as well as immigrant brains helped to transform the United States from a predominantly agricultural country into a giant industrial power." Explain.

IDENTIFY: Burlingame Treaty of 1868, "sand lotters," literacy test.

3 Wage earners begin to organize to overcome their grievances

Faced with numerous problems in the new industrial age, wage earners, like farmers, began increasingly to seek solutions for their problems through organization.

The National Labor Union. Labor organizations, as you know, were not new. During the war years 1861–65, however, industry boomed, the cost of living soared, and the labor movement gained new momentum.

In 1866 representatives of national and local unions and various reform groups met in Baltimore and launched the National Labor Union. The leader was William Sylvis, an experienced and able organizer of iron molders. The National Labor Union met annually for six years and reached a membership of 600,-000. In 1868 it helped push through Congress a law establishing an 8-hour day for laborers and mechanics employed by or in behalf of the federal government. But after unsuccessfully supporting a third-party movement in the election of 1872, the National Labor Union faded away.

The Knights of Labor. Far more important than the National Labor Union was the Knights of Labor, founded in 1869 in Philadelphia by Uriah S. Stephens, a tailor. The Knights of Labor tried to unite all American workers into one great union—skilled and unskilled workers°; men and women; white and Negro workers; foreign-born and "natives." The Knights aimed "to secure to the toilers a proper share of the wealth that they create; more of the leisure that rightfully belongs to them." Among other things, the Knights favored an 8-hour day and abolition of child labor.

The Knights of Labor also tried to organize and operate their own co-operative stores and manufacturing plants, as some farmers had done (page 494). They hoped by this means to save for themselves the profits that normally went to manufacturers and middlemen and at the same time to secure lower-priced goods. However, most of the 135 co-operative enterprises they started failed, largely because they did not

∙∙∙

° *skilled workers:* those whose jobs require a certain amount of training and education, such as electricians and carpenters.

unskilled workers: those whose jobs require little or no training and the use of only the simplest tools.

■ Steam locomotives and large factories were predominant symbols of the growth of industry. In principle, this old locomotive was no different from later ones. Fire generated steam in the long boiler; steam drove pistons attached to the rods on the big driving wheels.

have enough money to buy good machinery and to hire more qualified managers.

Reasons for the Knights' success. In most of their efforts, the Knights of Labor were more successful. They were influential in the passage by Congress of the Chinese Exclusion Act in 1882 and the repeal of the Contract Labor Law in 1885 (page 513).

The Knights of Labor officially frowned on strikes, preferring to settle disputes between managers and laborers through industrial *arbitration.*° However, it was a successful railroad strike in 1885 that did most to boost membership. For the first time in American labor history, railroad operators met strike leaders on equal terms and conceded labor's chief demands. When the strike occurred, the Knights numbered about

° *arbitration:* the hearing and judging of a dispute by an *arbitrator,* a person chosen or agreed to by both sides to act as referee. A group or board of arbitrators is sometimes used instead of a single person.

500,000 members, but by 1886 their membership had reached the high-water mark of 700,000.

The remarkable growth of the Knights of Labor was only partly the result of successful strikes. It also owed much to the idealism and enthusiasm of Terence V. Powderly, who succeeded Uriah S. Stephens as leader of the Knights of Labor.

Reasons for decline. The decline of the Knights was almost as rapid as their rise. In 1888 only 260,000 members were enrolled, and by 1890 this figure had dropped to about 100,000.

There were several reasons for this decline in membership. For one thing, the Knights lost an important railroad strike in 1886 against the system of southwestern railroads controlled by Jay Gould, the financier. This strike antagonized the public because of violence accompanying it and because of the shortages of food and coal which resulted. In the second place, the Knights were made up of too many discordant groups

THE HAYMARKET AFFAIR

On May 4, 1886, a large group of workingmen gathered in Haymarket Square in Chicago. They were there to protest an attack by police on strikers in which, on May 3, one striker had been killed and a number of others wounded.

The meeting was conducted in an orderly manner, and the crowd was beginning to leave, when a large force of policemen, nearly two hundred in all, appeared. Suddenly, without warning, a bomb burst in the midst of the policemen, killing one and wounding many others.

No one ever identified the bomb thrower. Nevertheless, eight "radicals" who, on earlier occasions, had advocated violence were arrested. Seven of the men were sentenced to death, the eighth to fifteen years in prison. Four were executed, one committed suicide, and after several years the remaining three were pardoned by Governor Altgeld of Illinois.

No evidence was ever produced to indicate that organized labor was responsible for the violence in Haymarket Square. Indeed, when Samuel Gompers, President of the A. F. of L., spoke out against what he considered the unjust action of the courts, many members of his own organization protested vigorously. In defense of his own position, Gompers said, "I abhor anarchy, but I also abhor injustice when meted out even to the most despicable being on earth."

Nothing during the 1880's did more to turn public opinion against organized labor than the tragic Haymarket affair. For many years large numbers of Americans continued to believe that organized labor was filled with anarchists and to identify the labor movement with radicalism.

to develop and maintain real strength. The skilled craftsmen especially disliked and distrusted the Knights' policy of taking in unskilled workers, with whom they felt they had little or nothing in common.

Finally, the leadership of Terence V. Powderly, while in many ways admirable, came to be too general in its aims to satisfy numerous workers. Many wage earners were beginning to reach the conclusion that a strong labor movement must avoid political crusades and concentrate upon the immediate job of improving working conditions for specific, well-organized groups of workers. It was this conviction that accounted for the rise of a rival organization of workers, the American Federation of Labor (A. F. of L.).

The rise of the A. F. of L. The American Federation of Labor was by far the most important labor organization in the United States during the late 1880's and the opening decades of the twentieth century. Started in 1881 under another name and reorganized in 1886, the A. F. of L. quickly replaced the Knights of Labor as the leading American labor organization.

Unlike the Knights of Labor, the A. F. of L. was a federation of separate national *craft unions,* each representing a group of skilled workers in a separate trade, or craft, such as carpentry, welding, or typography. It sought to organize all skilled workers by their craft rather than by the industry in which they worked. However, the A. F. of L. did include a few *industrial unions* which attempted to organize all the workers in a specific industry, unskilled as well as skilled.

Each A. F. of L. union was free to bargain collectively for all its members, to call strikes, and to manage its own affairs. The central organization of the A. F. of L. gave general leadership and aid to the national unions.

The A. F. of L. also differed from the Knights of Labor in keeping itself aloof from general reform movements and from independent or third-party political activities. The A. F. of L. was an economic organization of workers emphasizing craft unionism—"pure and simple unionism."

Program of the A. F. of L. The A. F. of L. program called for such reforms as the 8-hour working day and the 6-day working week; for legislation protecting workers on dangerous jobs and compensating them and their families in case of injury or death; for higher wages and for generally better working conditions. The A. F. of L. threw its weight in political contests to whichever party or candidate came closest to representing the aims of the labor organization.

The A. F. of L. accepted the capitalistic free-enterprise system. It did insist, however, on controlling the skilled labor market, on getting a larger share of the output of industry through higher wages and shorter hours, and on improving labor conditions.

With the exception of a single year, the president of the A. F. of L. from 1886 to 1924 was its principal founder, Samuel Gompers, who did much to instill the principle of discipline in the ranks of labor.

The A. F. of L. grew rapidly. Whereas in 1890 it numbered only 100,000 members, by 1900 membership had climbed to 500,000. The strength of the organization was its single-track devotion to its program and its determination to win as much as possible for skilled workers in the immediate present.

✔ **SECTION SURVEY**

1. Why did American workers decide to organize unions?

2. Describe the (a) purposes, (b) successes, and (c) reasons for the decline of the Knights of Labor.

3. How did the A. F. of L. differ from the Knights of Labor?

4. What is meant by the statement that the A. F. of L. was "job-conscious rather than class-conscious"?

IDENTIFY: National Labor Union, skilled worker, unskilled worker, arbitration, craft union, industrial union; Sylvis, Uriah S. Stephens, Powderly, Gompers; 1869, 1886.

4 Organized labor faces opposition in its early efforts to win reforms

When American workers began to organize during the latter half of the 1800's, they encountered numerous setbacks in their efforts to improve the conditions of their labor. Their attempts to form unions and to seek recognition of their unions' right to bargain for them met with widespread opposition.

Public opposition to unions. During the late 1800's public opinion and government usually supported employers whenever they engaged in conflicts with unions or with workers striking for the recognition of their unions.

The reasons for this opposition to unions are not hard to understand. Most Americans had grown up in the older, rural America where the individual worker had more control over his fate than he now had in the great industrial plants of giant corporations. They believed that every employer had the right to hire and fire as he pleased.

Many Americans, including large numbers of workers themselves, resented union demands for the *closed shop*—that is, for the plant in which only union members could be hired as employees. The closed shop seemed to put undue restrictions on the freedom of a worker to join a union or not, as he saw fit, and on the property rights of owners. When machines or plants were damaged in strikes, as they sometimes were, public resentment mounted.

Many Americans also believed that the rank and file of workers were quite content with their lot. The fact that only a small minority of the wage earners had joined unions seemed to support this belief. In fact, as late as 1914 only about one worker out of ten belonged to a labor organization. Many Americans held that the best workers could still climb the ladder to success to become managers and even owners. In the minds of most Americans, the entire labor problem and industrial conflict itself were blamed on "ambitious" and "power-eager" labor leaders interested primarily in personal advancement.

Immigrants distrust unions. In addition, many of the immigrants tended to resist the labor movement. It is true that some of the immigrants became union members and even union leaders. The great majority of the first generation, however, were essentially satisfied with conditions in their new homeland. They were better off in the New World than they had been in the Old. They had left Europe in part because they wanted to be as free as possible from all sorts of restrictions. Thus they did not like unions, with their dues, their rules, and their insistence that no one work for less than a certain wage.

Division in the ranks of labor. The mechanization of industrial plants also weakened the over-all power of the nation's wage earners to speak on their own behalf. When factories were small and all the workers knew one another, the skilled worker could see that the work of the unskilled worker, however minor, was an essential part of the whole process of production. But when factories grew large and workers became strangers to one another, the skilled worker came to look down on the unskilled worker.

The large number of immigrants who came during the late 1800's separated the unskilled from the skilled workers even more widely than before. Some of the newcomers had skills, but most of them did not and had to take such unskilled jobs as they could get. Because of differences in language and customs, skilled workers shunned them.

Thus the wage earners themselves were divided into two groups: (1) a small number of skilled workers who gained more and more bargaining power with employers, and (2) a great number of unskilled, unorganized laborers whose voices and interests counted very little.

Industry opposes the unions. With a majority of Americans generally distrustful of unions, huge industrial enterprises found it not too difficult to influence public opinion and government in their own favor. They hired lawyers to fight their battles in the courts. They spent a great deal of money on advertising and other types of publicity in order to win the sympathies of the public. They paid skillful lobbyists to influence legislation —men who knew how to get laws passed or to defeat bills that employers did not like. Some corporations made it a standard practice to contribute handsomely to the political party most likely to win an election, hoping by this means to secure favors from the government.

Employers also developed more direct methods to discourage workers from joining unions. One of these methods was the *black list.* Employers' associations, made up of several manufacturers, "black-listed" certain workers as undesirable—sometimes because the workers were incompetent, sometimes because they were labor organizers, sometimes merely because they belonged to a union. The black list was circulated throughout an entire industry, all over the country. No man whose name appeared on such a black list could hope to get a job in that industry, at least under his own name.

Many employers also required workers applying for a job to sign a written agreement not to join a union. The workers called these agreements *yellow-dog contracts.* A worker who violated one of these contracts promptly lost his job.

Yellow-dog contracts and black lists were only two of a number of methods by which employers tried to prevent workers from organizing. Sometimes private detectives, posing as workers, joined unions and informed the employers of any plans for strikes and reported the names of the union leaders. Sometimes when strikes broke out, unscrupulous employers actually paid agents to commit acts of violence, which were then blamed on labor. At other times, of course, the workers themselves destroyed property and resorted to violence. Such violence provided employers with a good excuse for demanding the aid of local police, the state militia, or even federal troops to restore order and break the strike.

Sometimes when a strike was called, the owner of a plant fought back with another weapon, the *lockout*. That is, he promptly closed the plant, thus "locking out" the workers. Then he brought in "strikebreakers"—non-union workers hired to do the work of those on strike—and the plant was reopened in spite of the angry strikers outside its gates. On other occasions the owner simply locked the plant and waited until the hungry, impoverished strikers were willing to come back to work on any terms.

State support of industry. With public opinion on their side, employers could and did count on the aid of government in conflicts with workers. There were, it is true, some exceptions to this general rule.

In most of the serious labor disputes, however, governors sent the state militia to the scene of the trouble, where their presence worked to the advantage of the employers. Whenever they sent the militia, the governors argued that the troops were needed in order to protect property, to prevent violence, and to maintain order. Since the governors were sworn to uphold law and order, this seemed a reasonable argument.

On the other hand, the appearance of the state militia frequently made it impossible for the workers to continue to strike. In 1892, for example, the state militia was called out during a strike of steelworkers at a Carnegie steel mill at Homestead, Pennsylvania. The strike collapsed and the power of the steelworkers' union was broken. Many years passed before steelworkers anywhere in the United States were able to form unions.

Federal support of industry. In the last quarter of the 1800's, the Presidents of the United States in general followed the example of the governors of the states in ordering troops to the scene of trouble. Thus, when in 1877 a series of railroad strikes broke out in Pennsylvania and Maryland, and state troops

■ The sleeping and parlor cars halted by the Pullman strike of 1894 were extremely ornate, with plush upholstery, inlaid paneling, and gleaming brasswork.

proved unequal to the task of restoring order, President Hayes sent federal soldiers to the trouble centers, and the strikes collapsed. Federal troops were also called out during railroad strikes in New York, New Jersey, Ohio, Indiana, Michigan, Illinois, and elsewhere.

A famous case of federal intervention occurred near Chicago in 1894 when a strike was called against the Pullman Palace Car Company by the American Railway Union under the leadership of Eugene V. Debs. The strike was supported by railway workers around Chicago and elsewhere when they refused to handle Pullman cars on trains. When Governor Altgeld of Illinois declined to use the state militia or to ask for federal help, President Cleveland sent federal troops anyway. Cleveland declared that he was justified in taking such action in order to guarantee the delivery of the mails—an argument which provoked much debate at the time and later, for mail trains were in fact running and the mails were being delivered. Whatever the merits of the arguments for and against the use of troops in the Pullman strike, the friends of organized labor were bitter about their use.

The courts support industry. The courts, no less than governors and Presidents, generally used their powers in behalf of ownership and management in the late 1800's. For example, during the famous Pullman strike of 1894, the owners asked a federal court in Chicago to issue an *injunction,* or court order, forbidding Eugene Debs and other labor leaders from continuing the strike. The court issued the injunction. It justified this action on the ground that the strikers had entered into "a conspiracy in restraint of trade," and that they were therefore violating the Sherman Antitrust Act, passed in 1890, which declared such conspiracies illegal (page 477).

Debs defied the court order. Instead of calling off the strike, he called upon the leaders of other unions to call a general strike° as a token of sympathy for the Pullman strikers. Although organized labor was firmly in sympathy with Debs and the American Railway Union, the union leaders refused to respond to Debs' call for a general strike. Debs was promptly arrested for "contempt of court."° He was sentenced to six months in jail for his refusal to obey the injunction. Labor denounced this conviction as "government by injunction." But the Supreme Court in 1895 upheld the Federal Circuit Court, Debs was placed behind bars, and the strike was broken.

President Cleveland consistently aroused the opposition of organized labor. Labor had been angered in 1893 when Cleveland appointed as Attorney General a man who had been a corpora-

tion lawyer and who was an avowed opponent of the Sherman Antitrust Act. Cleveland's role in the Pullman strike and other strikes further aroused the antagonism of organized labor. Thus organized labor vigorously supported the farmers in the Populist Party during the early 1890's. And they rallied enthusiastically to the support of William Jennings Bryan in the election of 1896.

After 1895 the injunction became a powerful weapon against organized labor since employers were often successful in securing injunctions to prevent or break up strikes. Labor complained bitterly, but the only relief it could hope for was (1) that the Supreme Court would reverse its decision of 1895 or (2) that Congress would modify the Sherman Antitrust Act so that it could not be used against labor unions.

But despite setbacks in its struggle, organized labor continued to fight for its aims and for public recognition and support. By the early 1900's, as you will see, there were signs that the lot of American workers was beginning to improve.

✔ **SECTION SURVEY**

1. Explain why public opinion in the late 1800's usually supported employers rather than labor.
2. In what way did some immigrants hold back the labor movement?
3. "The mechanization of industrial plants also weakened the over-all power of the nation's wage earners." Explain.
4. Show how employers used each of the following as weapons against organized labor: (a) publicity, (b) lobbyists, (c) contributions to political parties, (d) black list, (e) yellow-dog contract, and (f) lockout.
5. Give facts to prove that in disputes with labor, industry was often supported by (a) state governments, (b) the federal government, and (c) the courts.
IDENTIFY: closed shop, employers' associations, strikebreaker, Pullman strike, injunction, general strike, contempt of court, "government by injunction"; Debs, Altgeld; 1894.

° *general strike:* a mass strike in many industries and trades throughout a section or an entire country.
° *contempt of court:* refusal to obey or to respect the orders and procedures of a court; generally an offense punishable by fine and imprisonment.

Points to Discuss: 1. What made the United States one of the leading industrial nations of the world?

2. What problems did wage earners have to face between 1865 and 1900?

3. Discuss important effects of immigration on wage earners.

4. Why did the American workers wish to restrict immigration?

5. In the period 1870–1900, indicate the major grievances of workers against (a) employers, (b) state governments, and (c) the federal government.

6. Show how the worker used each of the following to adjust himself to life in an industrial society: (a) labor unions, and (b) federal laws.

7. In what ways did machines widen the gap between skilled and unskilled workers?

Using Charts: 1. Using charts 1, 2, and 5 on page 824, answer the following: (a) Show the connection among charts 1, 2, and 5. (b) Explain the rise in immigration between 1820 and 1914.

2. Refer to charts 1 and 4 on pages 844–45. (a) Compare the increase in total population with that in the labor force between 1850 and 1910. (b) What connection, if any, is there between these figures and the rise of organized labor? (c) Compare average number of hours per week worked in 1850 with the number in 1900. Discuss economic developments contributing to the change. (See pages 832–33.)

3. (a) Compare the number of workers in manufacturing in 1870 with that in 1900. (See chart 5 on page 833.) (b) What connection, if any, is there between these figures and the rise of organized labor?

Consulting the Sources: See the account of Cardinal Gibbons' defense of the Knights of Labor in Ellis, *Docs.,* No. 128. For the Altgeld-Cleveland controversy, see Commager, *Documents,* No. 334.

■ **TRACING THE MAIN IDEAS**

The rapid development of large-scale industry between 1865 and 1900 created new problems for wage earners. They attempted to solve these problems by organizing labor unions. Through the labor movement Samuel Gompers and other labor leaders outlined a program of democracy that differed in many respects from the traditional ideas of democracy.

Democracy in the earlier days was largely based on the ability of the individual to help himself. But the growth of great corporations made it increasingly difficult for the individual worker to meet and solve his own problems. As a result, the workers organized unions through which they could act as a united group. They also began to demand government protection in the form of laws providing maximum hours of work, minimum wages, and compensation for accidents.

By 1900 labor organizations were beginning to exert considerable influence upon government at both the state and the federal level. They were beginning to support those candidates in the major political parties who were most friendly to the progress of the workers. They also insisted that it was their democratic right to organize, to bargain as an entire group, and to strike if necessary to protect their rights.

In their demands and in their actions, wage earners were reacting to the new industrial society that was transforming the United States. Like farmers and all other Americans, they were seeking to adjust themselves to the industrial age.

26

Industrialization Transforms American Ways of Life

CHANGING WAYS

OF AMERICAN LIFE

"W E cannot all live in cities," Horace Greeley once remarked, "yet nearly all seem determined to do so." Greeley, the famous newspaper editor, was speaking of a new phenomenon in American life—the movement of many people away from the rural areas and into the great urban centers—the trend toward "urbanization" in America. From 1865 to 1900, growing numbers of young men and women and a considerable number of older people were leaving the farms and country villages and heading cityward. The majority of these people moved to the larger cities, those having populations of 25,000 to 50,000 or more.

What was the compelling attraction of the growing cities? The answer was "opportunity"—opportunity for adventure, opportunity to win fame and fortune. The city offered jobs in offices and factories, work in the building trades, employment for skilled and unskilled alike, the chance to carve out a successful career in any one of hundreds of lines of enterprise. Many young people were eager to share in the excitement of the new age and found the attractions of urban life irresistible.

For a number of years ways of life in the city and the countryside drew far apart, and terms like "city slicker" and "country hick" were often heard. As the years passed, however, the differences between life in rural and urban areas became less marked.

AS THE STORY DEVELOPS
1. **Cities grow and change under the impact of industrialism.**
2. **Education responds to the changing patterns of American life.**
3. **Journalism and literature show striking changes in the industrial age.**
4. **Important developments occur in architecture and other fine arts.**
5. **New forms of recreation enliven American ways of life.**

1 Cities grow and change under the impact of industrialism

The city had many faces. It was stores and banks and offices, museums and libraries and theaters, churches and schools. It was freight yards—and, in seaports, water fronts—ringed by drab factories, warehouses, stockyards, and wholesale markets. It was slum areas with cheerless tenement buildings crowded one against another along narrow, dirty streets and alleys littered with rubbish. It was row after row of houses arranged, in the newer cities, in a neat pattern of "blocks" or "squares." It was pretentious mansions, the costly show places of the self-appointed leaders of "society."

But mainly the city was people—rich people, people with modest incomes, poor people—all affected in more or less different ways by the new world of power-driven machines and mass production that was steadily transforming the world around them.

Concentration of wealth. One of the most obvious characteristics of the new world of industry was the concentration of wealth in relatively few hands. There were, to be sure, differences of income throughout American history, but the gap between the richest and the poorest had never been as great as it was in the late 1800's.

Many of the new, self-educated millionaires built huge mansions, filled with expensive and gaudy furnishings and art objects. They bought race horses, yachts, and summer estates. Sometimes they gave extravagant parties costing tens of thousands of dollars.

The rich as public benefactors. As time went on, however, the newly rich, and especially their children who had gone to college, smoothed off the rougher edges. Wealthy Americans traveled abroad. They increasingly gave money to build and support churches, college buildings, art galleries, opera houses, great libraries, and universities.

As time passed, many successful businessmen began to accept the responsibility for using their money to improve the community. For example, during the course of his lifetime, Andrew Carnegie, a self-made man, gave $60,000,000 to help towns and cities establish free public libraries. Men of enormous wealth, such as Ezra Cornell, Leland Stanford, John D. Rockefeller, Sr., Jonas Clark, Matthew Vassar, and Cornelius Vanderbilt, founded or gave endowments to colleges and universities. J. P. Morgan,

■ This mansion in North Carolina is one of many built by wealthy people in the late 1800's.

© *Arnold Newman*

Hull House

JANE ADDAMS

Jane Addams (1860–1935) was one of America's most influential women—a social reformer, humanitarian, and crusader in the cause of peace. On a trip to England in 1887–88, she visited the London slums, was horrified by the suffering she witnessed, and determined to dedicate her life to helping the poor. Returning to the United States, she purchased a building called Hull House in the midst of the Chicago slums and opened it to the public in 1889.

At Hull House, Miss Addams provided kindergartens for the children of working mothers, classes in child care and other activities, and recreational facilities for youth and adults. For a time she had to contend with the opposition of business and political leaders, who considered her a dangerous meddler. In time, however, even her most bitter critics came to realize that she was performing a great service. Social workers from all parts of the United States and from foreign countries visited Hull House, and then returned to their own communities to apply the lessons that they had learned.

Jane Addams did not confine her activities to Hull House. She was influential in securing child-labor legislation and appropriations for public parks. As the years passed, she became increasingly active in the cause of world peace, and in 1931 received the Nobel peace prize. But her most enduring memorial was the growing recognition by people in all walks of life that they shared a responsibility for alleviating poverty and suffering.

Henry C. Frick, Andrew W. Mellon, and dozens of others built up costly and valuable art collections, many of which were in time opened to the public. Others gave financial support to our great symphony orchestras.

Thus, the arts and education in America began to benefit from fortunes made in railroads, the stock market, and industry. Some of the new business "magnates" became the patrons of art and culture, much as the kings and princes of the Renaissance had encouraged and helped the artists of their day.

The middle-income group. Lower down on the economic ladder were the professional people, the smaller businessmen, the clerks, the managers, and the more successful skilled workers. This group raised its standard of living and took advantage of the new inventions which promoted comfort—gas and electric lighting, modern plumbing, new household appliances, and the like. They attended the theater, patronized libraries, bought magazines and books, and increasingly sent their children, not only through high school, but also to college.

Opportunities for women expand. The continuing development of coeducational universities in the Middle West and the West and the establishment in the East of such women's colleges as Mount Holyoke, Wellesley, Vassar, and Smith meant that more young women could obtain an education equal to that once enjoyed only by young men. The battle for the higher education of women was a real one, for many people still doubted the physical and mental ability of girls to do college work. But what was at first a questionable experiment proved a successful one. Women college graduates took increasingly active parts in civic affairs. Some became business executives, and others entered the professions. By 1900 there were 1000 women lawyers, 3000 women ministers, and 7500 women doctors in the United States.

For girls who did not go to college but who were eager for careers, there were new opportunities associated with business, especially stenographic jobs in offices, banks, and industrial plants. The development of a practical typewriter was a tremendous benefit to business as well as to women eager to take jobs outside the home.

In addition to these new activities, a great many women of the urban middle class became members of the women's clubs which, beginning feebly after the War Between the States, rapidly multiplied. These clubs at first concerned themselves largely with discussions of literary and cultural topics, but before the end of the 1800's they were also fighting political corruption, working for better health and recreational conditions, and in some instances taking up the battle for woman suffrage. While only a few western states had given women the right to vote in political elections by 1900, the number grew in the next decade and a half. Meanwhile, in states which gave them limited suffrage, women took part increasingly in local elections of school board members. Gradually, opposition to women's participation in public affairs began to yield to the steady and often vigorous pressure of such champions of women's rights as Elizabeth Cady Stanton, Lucy Stone, Susan B. Anthony, Anna Howard Shaw, and Carrie Chapman Catt.

The lower-income groups. On the lower rungs of the economic ladder were the very poor people, including large numbers of immigrants. The people in lower-income groups enjoyed only some of the advantages of the new urban culture. They could not afford to send their children to school beyond the elementary grades. Frequently, in fact, young boys and girls had to take jobs in factories even before they finished grammar school. Nor could most of the poorer people take advantage of the constantly improving state of medicine or send their sick to the hospitals.

Yet even the poor were in some ways touched by improvements in urban living. In the late 1880's a group of high-minded men and women, largely college trained, founded social "settlement houses," patterned after English models, in some of the worst slum areas of the major cities. These centers for recreation, education, and decent living reached only a small part of the slum population, but they were nevertheless important. Working through her many charitably supported welfare agencies, the Church offered food, shelter, and some measure of hope to many of the most poverty-stricken urban citizens. And by the opening of the twentieth century, some cities were building playgrounds in the least privileged areas.

Moreover, opportunities to climb the economic ladder existed, even for the poor, and the opportunities far surpassed those in the Old World. These opportunities drew the immigrants to the American cities in an ever-swelling volume. And it was a determination to increase the opportunities and to provide a better way of life for all Americans that motivated the numerous reform programs and the development of more and better schools in the late 1800's and the opening years of the twentieth century. Finally, it was these opportunities that caused many of the poorer people to exert strenuous efforts to acquire an education and to rise above the environment into which they were born.

⤅ **SECTION SURVEY**

1. Explain what is meant by the statement, "The city had many faces."

2. "The arts and education in America began to benefit from fortunes made in railroads, the stock market, and industry." Discuss.

3. In what ways had the middle-income group raised its standard of living by the late 1800's?

4. Show how the growth of cities was accompanied by expanding opportunities for women.

5. What measures were being taken at this time to improve the lot of the poor people?

IDENTIFY: settlement house, Salvation Army; Jane Addams.

2 Education responds to the changing patterns of American life

Like almost every other aspect of American life, education was transformed by the rising force of industrialism. Most obvious were (1) increased school enrollments, (2) new methods of teaching, and (3) new courses of study.

Expansion of the schools. In 1870 about 7,000,000 children were enrolled in American schools, most of them in the lower grades. By 1900, in the course of thirty years, the number had more than doubled. An even more important indication of the growing demand for education was the fact that during this same period the number of high schools multiplied ten times.

Between 1900 and 1920 the growth of enrollment and increase in construction of school buildings were to be even more striking. When the twentieth century opened, a total of about 16,000,000 children were attending American schools; by 1920 the number had risen to about 23,000,000. This growth reflected the increasing throngs of children in America's cities, but it also testified to the rapid accumulation of wealth that could be taxed to support education.

From old ways to new. The structure of the school system and to some extent the subject matter of education were to undergo some changes in the new industrial age. The centers of even moderately large cities could no longer rely upon anything like the "little red schoolhouse" to care for the needs of hundreds, and then thousands of new pupils. Neighborhood schools had to be constructed with separate classrooms and supplied with particular teachers for each grade. Only in the distinctly rural areas could the one-room school continue to operate. In these matters as in others, urban America was beginning to establish the standard.

The subject matter was to change very slowly from a traditional emphasis upon arithmetic, spelling, geography, and history. Also, in high schools it was taken for granted that students, even those who were not going on to college, had no other reason to be there except to learn to master difficult subjects, like mathematics and ancient languages. Only very slowly did the so-called "useful" subjects enter the curriculum. Indeed, it was at first only in separate vocational or technical schools that anything but traditional learning was made available.

Along with the public schools there came to be more parochial schools for Catholics. By the end of the century, in accordance with the decrees of the Third (1884) Plenary Council of Baltimore, it was clearly understood that every pastor had a responsibility to see to the education of the young under Church auspices. And just as America was long alone in making an ideal of a large free school system, so the Catholic Church in America was very different from the Church in other lands because the Catholic Church in America showed a determination to make a school in every parish the standard. Many of the bishops requested that the pastors erect schools before permanent churches.

Direct influence of industrialism. The needs of the new industrial society were also reflected in the courses of study of elementary and secondary schools. By the opening of the twentieth century, the educational program was being broadened to include the natural sciences and such "practical" and "useful" subjects as industrial designing and drawing, business arithmetic, bookkeeping, typing, stenography, shopwork, domestic science or home economics, and the manual arts.

Many school administrators also reflected the growing influence of business and industry. Superintendents and principals became more and more like businessmen in their emphasis upon efficiency.

New trends in higher education. The colleges and universities no less than the elementary and the secondary

■ The growth of American technical knowledge was symbolized in 1883, when the great Brooklyn Bridge at New York was opened with a showy display of fireworks. The construction of the bridge, and the making of its steel cables, required advanced engineering skill.

schools began to respond to the needs of the new age. New technical schools, such as the Columbia University School of Mines, the Massachusetts Institute of Technology, and the Case School of Applied Science, turned out growing numbers of men prepared to take important jobs in railroad building, in mining, and in other engineering projects. The state universities and land-grant colleges (page 397) in particular reflected the newer emphasis on practical training for a wide variety of fields.

Even the older colleges that emphasized classics often felt obliged to revise their courses of study to include more science and "practical" subjects. Under the influence of President Charles W. Eliot of Harvard, President Andrew D. White of Cornell, and other educational leaders, the colleges modified the old, rigid curriculum in which every student had to study Latin, Greek, and mathematics.

In an effort to provide a program of education more useful to an industrial and urban society, the colleges and universities began to enrich their courses of study with additional subjects not only in the natural sciences but in the social sciences and modern languages as well.

It was no longer possible for every student to take all the subjects in the curriculum. To meet individual differences, the "elective" system was introduced.

At the same time marked progress was made in the professional study of medicine and law. This was especially important, for the people living the congested and complex life of the urban centers needed increasingly the services of good lawyers and doctors.

In these and many other ways, education responded to the changing patterns of everyday life after 1865.

SECTION SURVEY

1. How did the rise of industrialism influence American education in the latter part of the 1800's?

2. What changes occurred in the new age in the (a) structure of the school system? (b) subject matter of education?

3. How did the Third Plenary Council of Baltimore influence the development of Catholic schools in America?

4. Describe the ways in which colleges and universities responded to the needs of the new age.

IDENTIFY: "learning by doing," elective system; Charles W. Eliot, Andrew D. White.

3 Journalism and literature show striking changes in the industrial age

Newspapers, magazines, and novels also revealed the influence of the new urban industrial way of life. Most obvious was an enormous increase in circulation of printed material. Only slightly less obvious were changes in both appearance and content.

Growth of newspapers and magazines. In the period between 1870 and 1900, the number of daily newspapers in the country increased from 600 to nearly 2500. Their circulation multiplied by six times—a jump far greater than the growth in population. This huge expansion reflected gains in the reading ability of great segments of the population. It also reflected a new trend in journalism.

Several important mechanical inventions made it possible to print newspapers as well as magazines and books in greater numbers and at lower costs. Most important of these inventions were improved printing presses, the typewriter, and the Linotype, a fast and efficient typesetting machine invented by Ottmar Mergenthaler in 1885.

Mass circulation was also stimulated by the rapidly developing art of advertising. Businessmen were ready to advertise, but they insisted that newspapers and magazines in which they advertised have a mass circulation. The desire to secure advertising stimulated publishers to capture an ever-wider reading public. Thus the publishers used more and more "popular" articles written in a "catchy" style to attract the great mass of American people.

New leaders and new trends. Three of the outstanding leaders of the new trend in journalism were Charles A. Dana, Joseph Pulitzer, and William Randolph Hearst.

Dana, publisher of the New York *Sun,* dug up sensational news and gave it prominent space on the front pages of his paper. Pulitzer, publisher of the New York *World,* followed much the same technique. His paper appealed to the general reader because it contained human-interest stories and devoted considerable space to the scandalous activities of the rich and the tragedies of the poor. Pulitzer also developed the comic strip, the sports page, and the special-feature section with its columnists, puzzles, and advice to the lovelorn.

Hearst, who was Pulitzer's chief rival, outdid Pulitzer at his own game. The son of a self-made California millionaire, Hearst bought the New York *Journal* in 1895 and ran up its circulation beyond that of any other paper. Hearst denounced the irresponsibility and selfishness of some of the well-to-do and so appealed to the masses of people. But his special success rested on his ability to hire gifted feature writers, able sports reporters, and popular comic artists. His success also rested upon his ability to get the most sensational news before anyone else and to play it up for all it was worth—frequently for far more than it was worth. The use by both Hearst and Pulitzer of a comic strip printed in color and featuring a character named the "Yellow Kid" is said to have given the name of "yellow journalism" to excessive sensationalism in newspapers.

Journalism becomes big business. Well before the turn of the century, journalism began to adopt the methods of other big business enterprises. Leading publishers began to buy up small papers and to consolidate great newspaper chains. Large chains could use the same feature articles, the same comic strips, and even the same editorials. This was especially true as the different parts of the nation and the world became increasingly interdependent, with public interest reaching out beyond the local community to national and world affairs. Moreover, the newspaper chains subscribed to great news-reporting services, such as the Associated Press (AP) and the United Press (UP), which collected news items from every corner of the earth.

Even the newspapers that remained

independent were influenced by the trend toward standardized practices in journalism. Many of them also subscribed to the big news-reporting services and bought columns, comic strips, and other features from "syndicates."

Mass circulation magazines. Magazines, like the daily newspapers, began to adapt themselves to the changing ways and changing times. To be sure, some of the older magazines, such as the *Atlantic Monthly, Harper's, Scribner's,* and others, continued to appeal to the better educated people. Even before the War Between the States, however, a new type of popular magazine began to appear. The new low-priced publications contained material aimed at mass circulation among "average" readers. One of the most successful of the newer magazines was the *Ladies' Home Journal,* established in 1883. It provided reading material that would interest millions of women, and it further ran up its circulation by lowering its price to ten cents. Under the editorship of a Dutch immigrant, Edward Bok, the *Ladies' Home Journal* sponsored many crusades to raise standards of living and improve community life.

Literature about urban life. Literature—no less than schools, newspapers, and magazines—reflected the growing influence of urban industrialism and a business-centered civilization on American life. On the most popular reading level were the success stories for boys which Horatio Alger, Jr., and W. T. Adams (under the name of Oliver Optic) turned out by the dozens. These stories in a sense glorified an urban society in which, no matter how humble a man's beginnings, there were opportunities for the hard-working boy to climb to the top of the ladder by sheer pluck and luck.

William Sydney Porter (O. Henry) struck a very different note with short stories in which he gave realistic pictures of American life, both urban and rural. Different again were the artistic novels of Edith Wharton, who pictured the conflicts in the New York of the

THE POPE SPEAKS

ON LABOR

"Some opportune remedy must be found quickly for the misery and wretchedness pressing so unjustly on the majority of the working class. . . . By degrees it has come to pass that working-men have been surrendered, isolated and helpless, to the hard-heartedness of employers and the greed of unchecked competition. The mischief has been increased by rapacious usury, which, although more than once condemned by the Church, is nevertheless, under a different guise, but with like injustice, still practiced by covetous and grasping men. To this must be added that the hiring of labor and the conduct of trade are concentrated in the hands of comparatively few; so that a small number of very rich men have been able to lay upon the teeming masses of the laboring poor a yoke little better than that of slavery itself."—From *Rerum Novarum.*

1880's between the newly rich and the older well-to-do families with established social positions. Henry James suggested the tensions of members of America's leisure class who chose to live in the sophisticated urban centers of Europe.

One of the best-known novels of the period was *The Gilded Age,* written by Samuel L. Clemens (Mark Twain) and Charles Dudley Warner. In a humorous but biting manner, the writers described the crude and corrupt activities of many politicians and get-rich-quick land speculators operating in the national capital. Edward Bellamy's *Looking Backward: 2000–1887* was another widely read book. In this book the author described an imaginary society of the future that would lack the shortcomings of the real world in which he lived.

One of the ablest writers was William Dean Howells, whose realistic stories furnished a faithful picture of middle-class life in America. Howells was espe-

■ Parents of the latter 1800's tried to keep their children from reading "dime novels" like those about Nick Carter. But they also objected to Mark Twain's *The Adventures of Tom Sawyer* when it appeared in 1876. Above, Tom talks Ben into whitewashing his fence.

cially successful in telling of the triumphs and tragedies of a self-made man in *The Rise of Silas Lapham.*

Notable exceptions. There were, of course, many authors whose work was in no way influenced by the changing ways and changing times. Emily Dickinson, for example, was one of a number of authors who were interested in literature for the sake of literature itself. Miss Dickinson, a sheltered New England writer, created many thought-provoking short poems, discovered only after her death and since recognized as poetry of great distinction.

Even many of the books written for the general public had no apparent relation to the new issues of industrialism. For instance, General Lew Wallace's *Ben Hur*, a widely read novel, dealt with the conflict between paganism and Christianity during the days of the early Roman Empire. The growing reading public also enjoyed the highly romantic and sentimental novels of Mary Jane Holmes, Bertha M. Clay, and E. P. Roe. The colorful Wild West adventure stories which enterprising publishers put out in paper covers for only ten cents—the famous "dime novels"—also appealed to millions of readers.

"Local color" writers. Partly in reaction against the more or less standardized ways of city life, another group of writers concentrated upon those regions of the United States still largely under the influence of the older, rural ways of living. The greatest of these "local color" writers was Samuel L. Clemens (Mark Twain), co-author of *The Gilded Age* (page 529) and the first important writer from west of the Atlantic seaboard states. His unforgettable *Life on the Mississippi, The Adventures of Tom Sawyer, The Adventures of Huckleberry Finn*, and *Roughing It* dealt with the raw life on the Mississippi River and in western mining camps. Edward Eggleston's *The Hoosier Schoolmaster* likewise touched a "folksy" note in describing life in rural Indiana.

The colorful and heroic verses of Joaquin (hwah-KEEN) Miller and the realistic stories of mining camps that flowed from the pen of Bret Harte made the nation aware of the Far West. Helen Hunt Jackson increased the awareness of the Far West with her romantic stories of Spanish missions and of Indian life in old California. Perhaps the best known of her novels is *Ramona*. Hamlin Garland, in *Main-Traveled Roads* (page 489) and other books, wrote of the harsh conditions suffered by pioneers on the northern prairies.

The South, too, had its share of local-color writers. Thomas Nelson Page wrote of old-time Virginia with its great plantations. George Washington Cable and Grace King brought to readers throughout the country a picture of life among the French-speaking Creoles of Louisiana. And Joel Chandler Harris of Georgia won fame for his "Uncle Remus" tales.

New England, like other regions, excited the imaginations of local-color authors. A number of writers, among them Mary E. Wilkins Freeman and Sarah Orne Jewett, pictured the decline of rural life in New England as young people abandoned the rocky, unproductive family farms to seek their fortunes in the growing cities.

■ Mark Twain built this house in Hartford, Connecticut, where he lived for many years and wrote a number of his famous works. The high porch resembles the wheelhouse of a river steamboat and reminded the author of his days as a Mississippi River pilot.

1. Describe two developments that made possible mass circulation of newspapers and magazines.

2. Indicate the contributions of each of the following to the field of journalism: (a) Dana, (b) Pulitzer, and (c) Hearst.

3. What is meant by the statement that newspaper publishing became big business?

4. Explain why the *Ladies' Home Journal* became a successful mass-circulation magazine.

5. Show how the novels of this period reflected the "growing influence of urban industrialism and a business-centered civilization."

IDENTIFY: Linotype, "yellow journalism," Associated Press, United Press, syndicates, dime novels, local color; Mergenthaler; 1885.

4 Important developments occur in architecture and other fine arts

Architecture and art, no less than journalism and literature, revealed the influence of urban life and the growth of industry after 1865.

Decline and revival of architecture. For a number of years after the War Between the States, architecture sank to the lowest level it had ever reached in American history. During the 1870's and the 1880's many of the successful manufacturers, railroad magnates, and financiers poured fortunes into mansions with fantastic turrets and overdone decorations in dreadful taste. These gaudy show places, as well as numerous public buildings and smaller houses in equally poor taste, were a far cry indeed from the dignified and beautiful structures Americans had designed and built along simple classical lines in the late 1700's and early 1800's.

Toward the end of the 1800's, however, a number of architects, notably Henry Hobson Richardson and Richard Morris Hunt, both of whom had studied in Europe, began to design more pleasing and practical houses and public buildings. They built along the sturdy and restrained lines of the Romanesque and Renaissance styles of the Old World.

The World's Columbian Exposition, or World's Fair, held in Chicago in 1893, helped to quicken public interest in good architecture. Many of the buildings that housed the exhibits were designed in the simple classical style. Thousands of visitors carried back to their home communities memories of beautiful structures with noble pillars and clean, direct lines.

New trends in architecture. One structure at the Chicago World's Fair, the Transportation Building, heralded a really new day in architecture. Its architect, Louis H. Sullivan, taught that "form follows function." By this he meant that the best-designed building is one that has a style and uses materials perfectly suited to the purposes of the building. Gradually this idea was adopted by more and more architects, among them Frank Lloyd Wright, who started to practice his profession in Chicago in 1893, and became one of the world's foremost architects.

Although private homes and church buildings failed to make much use of such new materials as steel, concrete, and plate glass, the necessities of urban life did stimulate a new type of business structure. As the business districts of metropolitan centers became more crowded and as real-estate values soared, architects sought to solve the problem by building upward rather than sideward.

The "invention" of skyscrapers. How could men erect taller buildings? Ingenious architects provided the answer by constructing huge steel frames and filling the spaces with stone, brick, concrete, and glass. The Home Insurance Building, built in Chicago in 1884, set the example for these towering structures. During the next few years, both in Chicago and New York, builders erected taller and taller skyscrapers.

But the new buildings created a new problem. They turned the narrow

■ The Flatiron Building, New York City's first skyscraper, towered above its neighbors when it was completed in 1902. It is now dwarfed by countless taller buildings, but still stands as a landmark in the skyscraper development that made modern New York City possible.

streets above which they towered into dark, gloomy canyons. In an effort to solve this problem, the governing authorities of New York City finally adopted an ordinance requiring architects to "set back" the higher stories of all tall buildings so that more light would reach the streets. This ordinance accomplished its purpose. It also relieved the rectangular lines of the box-like skyscraper and accounted for the magically beautiful and unique character of the New York sky line. Like many other activities of American life, architecture began to reveal more and more the influence of new times and new ways of living.

Painting and sculpture. The new industrial age had less influence on painters and sculptors than it did on architects. The most important development in the history of the fine arts during the years between 1865 and 1900 was the increasing skill of the artists who had studied in European art centers. The improving standards in American art also rested in part on the ability and the willingness of wealthy Americans to assemble great collections of masterpieces, to establish art schools, and to buy the works of American artists.

The themes that painters and sculptors chose often seemed to have little to do with the issues raised by the

533

■ Many American artists went to Europe to study in the latter 1800's. Some remained for the rest of their lives. One of these was Mary Cassatt, who painted "In the Box" (above) in 1897. Her work was influenced by the great French painters Degas, Manet, Monet, and others but also reflected her own individuality and, to some extent, her American background.

■ In the painting below, the American artist Thomas Eakins showed traditional interest in trees and sky and water. But he also showed his interest in the industrial age by the scrupulous detail he used in painting the steel bridge in the background.

growing urban and industrial society. Gifted sculptors created great statues of Lincoln and other national heroes. One of the outstanding creations was the "Adams Monument" in Rock Creek Cemetery in Washington, D.C., made by Augustus Saint-Gaudens (saynt-GAW-d'nz) in memory of the wife of Henry Adams, the famous historian. This monument, sometimes referred to as "The Peace of God," represents a brooding, hooded figure and suggests the mystery of life and death.

A number of painters did equally outstanding work. George Inness captured on canvas the beauties of woodland scenes. Winslow Homer's brilliantly colored seascapes suggested the strength and primitive force of the sea. Albert Ryder's mystical, legendary paintings also pictured a world remote from the market place and factory.

The influence of industrialism on art. A number of artists, however, did reveal in their work the influence of industrial and urban America. Thomas Eakins, for example, painted famous and wealthy Americans with such frank realism that they avoided him and neglected his talents. But Eakins refused to change his style for the sake of immediate popularity and profit, and continued to paint life as he saw it. In a painting designed to reveal the surgeon's scientific skill, the "Clinic of Dr. Gross," Eakins suggested very concretely the new scientific trend of his age. Other artists also portrayed urban and industrial scenes.

✔ **SECTION SURVEY**

1. What did Louis Sullivan mean by the statement that in architecture "form follows function"?

2. Why can the skyscraper be called an invention?

3. Describe the themes that inspired our noted sculptors and painters.

4. To what extent did industrialism influence art?

IDENTIFY: "set back"; Louis Sullivan, Wright, Saint-Gaudens, Inness, Homer, Ryder, Eakins.

5 New forms of recreation enliven American ways of life

Recreation, like all other aspects of everyday living, was transformed by the new urban, industrial age. The well-to-do, having time and money, went in for such new and, at first, exclusive sports as tennis and golf. Gradually, however, the middle-income groups also began to enjoy such forms of recreation.

New types of rural recreation. The development of transportation, especially the construction of railroads and, in the early twentieth century, the improvement of rural highways, helped to bring the circus and the Wild West show to even the smaller country towns.

For many thousands of American boys and girls, and for their parents as well, one of the most memorable events of the year was the arrival of the circus. P. T. Barnum's tent circus, which he had started in 1871 in Brooklyn was called "the greatest show on earth."

Equally awaited was the arrival of the Chautauqua. The Chautauqua movement was an educational enterprise started in 1874 on the shores of Chautauqua Lake in upper New York state. From the beginning the enterprise was a success. Each year thousands of Americans from all over the United States traveled to Chautauqua Lake to enjoy a summer vacation and to benefit intellectually and spiritually from the lectures and sermons provided for them. As the years passed, the Chautauqua program became increasingly varied, adding illustrated travel talks, stage presentations, and humorous acts to the more serious lectures and the religious services. Finally, following Barnum's example, other enterprising leaders began to organize traveling tent programs similar to those earlier developed on the shores of Chautauqua Lake. By the early 1900's, the traveling Chautauquas were bringing a glimpse of the outside world into many rural communities.

■ Girls well clad in bloomer costumes were playing basketball about the year 1900.

New types of urban recreation. During the 1880's the bicycle evolved from the clumsy, high-wheeled, dangerous contraption it had been into something like the machine with which we are familiar today. As a result, bicycling became a great fad, as well as a means of getting to and from work for thousands of people.

The theater also gained popularity, particularly for the middle-income groups. At its best the theater in this period offered admirable plays in which great actors, American and foreign-

■ Bicycles of the late 1800's resembled ours, but lacked mudguards. Bicycle races were common. These people were merely enjoying a ride.

born, appeared on the stage. Some of the most appealing programs, however, were the melodramas that reminded city dwellers of their own rural background. Such plays as *Shore Acres, Way Down East,* and *The Old Homestead* attracted large audiences. There was also an equally popular series of melodramas on significant urban themes, including such plays as *Bertha, the Sewing-Machine Girl.* Vaudeville shows, providing a variety of singing, dancing, and gymnastic acts, also attracted large audiences.

By the turn of the century, commercialized amusement parks were also attracting large crowds of city people and making fortunes for their owners. In many cases trolley car companies built these amusement parks just outside the city, thereby reaping the income from the parks as well as from trolley fares.

More prosperous Americans, city and rural dwellers alike, journeyed to the great expositions, such as the one held in Philadelphia in 1876 and the one held in Chicago in 1893.

Physical exercise and American sports. During the last quarter of the 1800's, an increasing number of urban dwellers became aware of the need to provide larger opportunities for physical exercise, especially for youth. One answer was gymnasiums, which began to appear in growing numbers in the cities and towns and as part of the educational plants of schools and colleges.

These same years also saw the rapid development of three major spectator sports—baseball, football, and basketball.

Baseball in various forms had been played for many years before the first professional team, the Cincinnati Red Stockings, was formed in 1869. Seven years later, in 1876, the National League was organized. In 1900 the American League was formed. Well before the turn of the century, urban dwellers in growing numbers were packing ball parks to watch what was becoming one of America's favorite spectator sports.

Football, which evolved from the English game of Rugby, was also becoming increasingly popular. The first intercollegiate football contest was played between Rutgers and Princeton in 1869, with twenty-five men on each side. Within a few years, intercollegiate contests were being held in the West as well as in the East. Played mostly by college men, football in the early days was a rough-and-tumble game, so rough, in fact, that some people protested against its "brutality" and demanded its abolition. As the years passed, however, new rules were developed, and the game became better organized.

Basketball, which also became a typically American sport, was first played in 1892 by students at the Y.M.C.A. college in Springfield, Massachusetts. Its inventor, Dr. James Naismith, then an instructor in physical education, created the game in order to provide the same opportunities for recreation in the winter that baseball provided in the spring, and football in the autumn. The game proved enormously popular and within a few years it was being played all over the country.

The older rural forms of recreation—picnics, amateur baseball, pitching horseshoes, and so forth—continued to be popular. Increasingly, however, the ways in which people relaxed and amused themselves were being transformed in the new industrial age.

FOOTBALL

IN THE 1880'S

The following report of the Yale-Princeton game of 1884 appeared in the New York *Evening Post*. Although the reporter probably exaggerated, the account does remind us that football in the 1880's was still a rough-and-tumble game with only the most rudimentary rules.

"The spectators could see the elevens hurl themselves together and build themselves in kicking, writhing heaps. They had a general vision of threatening attitudes, fists shaken before noses, dartings hither and thither, throttling, wrestling, and the pitching of individuals headlong to earth; and all this was an exceedingly animated picture which drew from them volley after volley of applause. Those inside the lines, the judges, reporters, and so on, were nearer and saw something more. They saw real fighting, savage blows that drew blood, and falls that seemed as if they must crack all the bones and drive the life from those who sustained them."

SECTION SURVEY

1. Show how the circus and the Chautauqua movement affected rural and urban recreation.

2. If you had been living in the 1880's and 1890's, what types of recreational activities would have been available to you?

3. In what ways did recreational activities in the 1880's and 1890's differ from those today?

4. What three major spectator sports were developed in the latter part of the 1800's?

IDENTIFY: vaudeville; Barnum.

■ CHAPTER SURVEY

(For review, see Section Surveys, pages 525, 527, 532, 535, 537.)

Points to Discuss: 1. The new business magnates became the patrons of art and culture, much as the princes of the Middle Ages had performed a similar function in their day. Discuss this statement.

2. Give specific examples to show that between 1870 and 1900 education on every level was transformed.

3. Describe how American journalists and novelists exposed the social problems arising out of industrialization.

4. Show how architecture and art revealed the influence of industrial life.

5. The writers of the late nineteenth and early twentieth century in this country were, in a sense, discoverers of a new America. Name the writers who fit this description, and indicate their contributions to American life by reference to their works.

6. Compare American recreation patterns of 1900 with those of 1800.

Using Charts: 1. Which major advances in American industry during the period 1850–1900 (see chart 1 on pages 832–33) made life more comfortable for people?

2. Using charts 6 and 8 on pages 824–25, (a) show how the life expectancy average changed between 1790 and 1900. (b) Summarize the shift from rural to urban population during the same period, and account for the shift.

Consulting the Sources: See Commager and Nevins, *The Heritage of America*, Nos. 215–16, for passages from the writings of John Spargo and Upton Sinclair.

■ TRACING THE MAIN IDEAS

Between 1865 and 1900 the United States was transformed from an essentially agricultural nation to a predominantly industrial nation. Growing numbers of people poured into the great urban centers which each year exerted a more and more powerful influence upon all aspects of American life, including education, journalism, literature, architecture, art, and recreation.

What had made the cities such a powerful influence?

In trying to answer this question we must remember that the cities were the centers of industry. Thus we find ourselves going back to the factories and mass production. And when we look at the factories, with their mass production, we find that they depended upon power-driven machines. And when we look at the power-driven machines— and the almost countless number of inventions and discoveries that made the new machines possible—we find ourselves face to face with science and technology—that is, with the application of science to industry. Or to put it in other terms, we come face to face with scientists, engineers, manufacturers, businessmen, and financiers. Without science and technology there would have been no thriving factories and no large industrial cities.

The world of the late 1800's was changing with bewildering speed. New leaders were appearing, and new ways of living and working, too. The American people—rich and poor, city dweller and country folk—had to adjust to the new conditions.

The new age was full of promise for a richer and fuller life for all men everywhere. But before the promise could be realized, many problems still had to be solved. You will read about some of these problems and the ways in which the American people tried to solve them in the following chapters.

Unit Survey (Reread "Tracing the Main Ideas," pages 484, 507, 521, 538.)

OUTSTANDING EVENTS

1866 Field lays transatlantic cable.
1867 Sholes develops typewriter.
1867 Grange is organized.
1869 Knights of Labor is founded.
1869 Westinghouse patents air brake.
1873 Silver dollars discontinued.
1875 Resumption Act.
1876 Patent on telephone applied for.
1876–77 "Granger cases" decided.
1877 Series of railroad strikes.
1878 Bland-Allison Act.
1882 Chinese Exclusion Act.
1886 A.F. of L. is organized.
1886 Haymarket Riot.
1886 James Gibbons, Archbishop of Baltimore, named second American Cardinal.
1887 Interstate Commerce Act.
1887 Gibbons defends Knights of Labor in Rome.
1889 Hull House is opened to public.
1889 Opening of Catholic University of America.
1890 Sherman Antitrust Act.
1890 Sherman Silver Purchase Act.
1893 Silver Purchase Act is repealed.
1894 Pullman strike.
1896 Gold discovered in Klondike.
1896 William McKinley elected President.

THEN AND NOW

1. Compare the demands of organized labor today with those in the 1870's and 1880's.

2. Compare the present attitude of the American public toward big business with the American attitudes in the period 1870–1900. Account for any differences.

3. Compare the demands and the problems of the American farmer in the 1880's and 1890's with those of today.

EXTENDING YOUR HORIZON

1. Read Bernard A. Weisberger's portrayal of the activities of Dwight Moody and Ira Sankey in "Evangelists to the Machine Age," *American Heritage*, August 1955.

2. For an interesting interpretation of a prominent political figure of the 1890's and after, read the essay "William Jennings Bryan: The Democrat as Revivalist," in Richard Hofstadter's *The American Political Tradition* [Knopf (Vintage)].

3. For a fuller understanding of the southern agrarian revolt and its relationship to the Farmers' Alliance and the Populist movement, read Chapter 3, "The Rise of the Rednecks," in Hodding Carter's *The Angry Scar* (Doubleday).

4. An interesting feature of the 1896 political campaign is seen in the account of Margaret Leech taken from her book *In the Days of McKinley*, "The Front Porch Campaign," *American Heritage*, December 1959.

5. For deeper insight into the problems of labor between 1870 and 1900 read in Part 7 of Stewart Holbrook's *Dreamers of the American Dream* (Doubleday), Chapters 1, 2, and 4 entitled respectively "War on the Monongahela," "The Noble Order of Knights," and "The Debs Rebellion."

INDIVIDUAL ACTIVITIES

1. Choose a chapter from Samuel P. Orth's *Our Foreigners* (Yale Univ. Press), and report on the immigrant group from which your forefathers came.

2. Read "Carnegie," pages 74–88 in Stewart Holbrook's *The Age of the Moguls* (Doubleday), and tell why Carnegie has been termed America's greatest taskmaster. Read his views on "Wealth" as set forth in 1889 in Richard Heffner's *A Documentary History of the United States*, pages 166–73.

3. Read pages 339–49 in O. E. Rolvaag's *Giants in the Earth* for a graphic account of the grasshopper plague on the plains. Read aloud certain more vivid paragraphs.

4. Consult the *Dictionary of American Biography* for class reports on "Sockless Jerry Simpson," agrarian reformer, and on "Pitchfork Ben Tillman," southern agrarian.

5. Ignatius Donelly was a colorful figure in the Populist movement. Read Chapter XIII, "Apostles of Protest," in Stewart Holbrook's *Lost Men of American History* (Macmillan). Prepare an oral report.

6. Read Chapter XII, "The Age of the Dinosaurs," in James Truslow Adams, *The Epic of America*, Little, Brown. What is Adams' concept of the "captains of industry"?

GROUP ACTIVITIES

1. Have a number of students read Chapter II, "The Industrial Boom in the North," in *The Emergence of Modern America, 1865–1878* by Allan Nevins (Macmillan), and prepare reports describing the development of four great industries of this period.

2. Select two committees to prepare discussions on the efforts of the farmers to solve the problems confronting them in the years between 1870 and 1896. One committee can concentrate on problems with railroads and middlemen, while the other concentrates on the farmers' difficulties involving money supply and purchasing power. Use the *Dictionary of American History* as a basic source of information to supplement your text. Look up such topics as The Grange, Munn vs. Illinois, Farmers' Alliances, Greenback Party, the "Crime of '73," etc., and then follow the clues given to additional information.

3. The role of the immigrant in shaping the character of American Catholicism as we know it has been a prominent one. Let a group of students investigate this role and present the results to the class in a panel discussion. Helpful material will be found in Monsignor Ellis' *American Catholicism*, especially pages 101–111 and 117–121, in Theodore Maynard's *The Story of American Catholicism* and in John Higham's *Strangers in the Land* (Rutgers Univ. Press) which is good on the nativist movement. Christopher Dawson provides an excellent historical backdrop on the importance of immigration influences in determining the present form of American Catholicism in "Catholic Culture in America," *The Critic*, June–July 1959.

4. Have students prepare a discussion on the advantages and disadvantages of modern industry and of corporations as a form of capitalistic organization to owners, workers, and consumers. They should utilize material in the text and investigate in the *Dictionary of American History* corporations, capitalism, trusts, specific acts of Congress, and additional related materials which will be suggested.

SUGGESTED FURTHER READING
BIOGRAPHY

ALLEN, FREDERICK LEWIS, *The Great Pierpont Morgan*, Harper; Bantam.

BEARD, ANNIE S., *Our Foreign-born Citizens*, Crowell. Famous immigrants.

GARST, SHANNON, *Buffalo Bill*, Messner.

HUGHES, RUPERT, *The Giant Wakes*, Borden. About Samuel Gompers.

NEVINS, ALLAN, *John D. Rockefeller: The Heroic Age of American Enterprise*, Scribner, 2 vols.

WINKLER, JOHN K., *Incredible Carnegie*, Doubleday.

OTHER NONFICTION

BUCK, S. J., *The Agrarian Crusade*, Yale Univ. Press. Farm problem.

°HACKER, LOUIS, *The Triumph of American Capitalism*, Columbia Univ. Press.

HANDLIN, OSCAR, *The Uprooted*, Little, Brown; Grosset & Dunlap.

HENDRICK, B. J., *Age of Big Business*, Yale Univ. Press.

HICKS, JOHN D., *The Populist Revolt*, Univ. of Minnesota Press.

KRAMER, DALE, *The Wild Jackasses: The American Farmer in Revolt*, Hastings House. Political action by farmers.

MOODY, J., *The Railroad Builders*, Yale Univ. Press.

——, *The Masters of Capital*, Yale Univ. Press.

MUMFORD, LEWIS, *The Brown Decades: A Study of the Arts in America, 1865–1895*, Dover.

ORTH, S. P., *The Armies of Labor*, Yale Univ. Press.

RIIS, JACOB A., *How the Other Half Lives*, Scribner. Slums of New York.

SCHLESINGER, ARTHUR M., *Rise of the City*, Macmillan. Development of urban life.

SHANNON, JAMES, *Catholic Colonization on the Western Frontier*, Yale Univ. Press.

HISTORICAL FICTION

BELLAMY, EDWARD, *Looking Backward*, Random House (Modern Library).

DAVENPORT, MARCIA, *The Valley of Decision*, Scribner; Grosset & Dunlap,

GARLAND, HAMLIN, *Main-Traveled Roads*, Harper Modern Classics; Rinehart.

HOWELLS, WILLIAM DEAN, *The Rise of Silas Lapham*, Houghton Mifflin; Random House (Modern Library).

LANE, ROSE WILDER, *Let the Hurricane Roar*, Longmans, Green.

NORRIS, FRANK, *The Octopus*, Doubleday.

PREBBLE, JOHN, *Buffalo Soldiers*, Harcourt, Brace.

STONE, IRVING, *Adversary in the House*, Doubleday. About Eugene Debs.

WHARTON, EDITH, *The Age of Innocence*, Random House (Modern Library).

UNIT EIGHT

The Arrival
of Reform

1897–1920

The "Square Deal" Stimulates Reform

TEDDY ROOSEVELT
AND NATURALIST
JOHN MUIR VISIT
YOSEMITE VALLEY—
1903

THE fortunes of nations as well as of individuals sometimes change with bewildering rapidity. But men have no certain way of foreseeing when change will come or of predicting its directions.

The administration of President McKinley, from 1897 to 1901, is a case in point.

Who on McKinley's inauguration day could have foreseen that within a little more than a year the nation would be at war with Spain in a conflict called the Spanish-American War, and that before McKinley's four years in office were over the United States would become a great colonial power with possessions in the Pacific and the Caribbean? (You will read about these striking international developments in Unit Nine.)

And who, looking at the solid triumph of big business in the election of 1896, would have dared to predict that with-in six years a new reform movement, the Progressive movement, would begin to sweep the country and a progressive President and Congress would draw up new rules for the conduct of business?

The reform movements of the early 1900's were really a continuation, on a broader front, of earlier efforts to preserve and strengthen democracy in the new industrial age. As you will see, however, the progressives also tackled other problems, including the increasingly serious issue of the conservation of the nation's natural resources.

AS THE STORY DEVELOPS

1. The Progressive movement brings reforms to government.
2. Theodore Roosevelt promotes a "square deal" for all people.
3. Theodore Roosevelt stimulates conservation of natural resources.

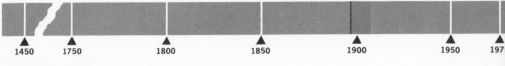

1450   1750   1800   1850   1900   1950   197?

The Progressive movement brings reforms to government

The victory of William McKinley and the Republicans in the election of 1896 (page 506) seemed to many Americans to spell the doom of the reform movement. In 1897 the conservative Republicans seemed to have a clear road to their objectives. They had defeated the joint efforts of the Democrats and the Populists to put William Jennings Bryan in the White House, and they were now free to adopt the legislation that they thought was best for the country. One of the first measures they adopted was the Dingley Tariff of 1897, which raised average tariff rates to a new high of 57 per cent.

In the meantime the depression of 1893–96 gave way to a wave of prosperity. Business flourished. New corporations sprang up almost overnight, and older corporations merged to form giant trusts and industrial concerns. The short-lived Spanish-American War of 1898 (Chapter 30) did not have much effect on the economic growth of the country.

Surrounded by signs of prosperity and caught up in the fervor of war and expansion overseas, many Americans in the late 1890's began to forget the financial panic, the depression, and the uprising of the Populists and other reform groups in the election of 1896. But by the turn of the century a new reform movement, called the Progressive movement, was in full swing.

Objectives of the progressives. The Progressive movement cut across party lines. It included many individuals from the Bryan wing of the Democratic Party. It also included a growing number of discontented Republicans who called themselves "insurgents."

Leaders of the Progressive movement had a number of objectives. (1) They were determined to restore control of the government to the rank and file of people, or, to use Lincoln's phrase, to make the government more truly one "of the people, by the people, for the people." (2) They were determined to correct the abuses and the injustices that had crept into everyday life with the development of industrialism and the growth of great urban centers. (3) They were determined to restore greater equality of opportunity in economic affairs by drawing up new rules for the conduct of business.

The progressives were optimists. They believed that the reforms they were seeking would make the United States a more prosperous and a more democratic country, and would provide an example that the whole world might wish to follow. They wanted to free business from its own monopolistic restraints and to raise new standards of honesty for both business and government.

Robert M. La Follette. Robert M. La Follette of Wisconsin, or "Fighting Bob" as he was familiarly called, was one of the outstanding leaders of the Progressive movement. La Follette graduated from the University of Wisconsin in 1879. During the next few years he fought his way upward in local and state politics. He won his political victories over the opposition of the Republican political machine that dominated the state in the interest of the railroad and lumber magnates. During the process of winning elections, he established a reputation for fearless honesty. By cultivating the art of public speaking and by making friends with farmers and working people, he became so influential in Wisconsin that in 1900 he won the governorship.

As governor, La Follette helped to break the power of the political machine that had been running the state and to restore control of the government to the majority of the people. He persuaded hesitant legislators to levy heavier taxes on the railroads and on the newer public utilities—the gas, electric, and streetcar companies. He also persuaded the legislators to create commissions to regulate the public-utility

■ In this cartoon of 1912, "Fighting Bob" La Follette displays a poster purporting to show conditions in his state before and after he became governor.

companies. The forests and water-power sites of the state had largely been secured by great industrial corporations. But La Follette, in co-operation with Charles Van Hise, president of the University of Wisconsin, inaugurated a movement for the conservation of the forests and water-power sites.

The La Follette administration also promoted good government in the state by making use of university men to help legislators find needed facts and draft laws that the courts could not easily set aside. He also appointed university men to serve on the new state regulatory commissions. The "Wisconsin Idea," as the La Follette movement was called, attracted nationwide attention.

Other progressive leaders. Emboldened by La Follette's example, other governors and men in public office began to attack corrupt government and greedy corporations. Joseph W. Folk, a Missouri circuit attorney, became governor of the state in 1906 largely as a result of his success in prosecuting a ring of corrupt politicians in St. Louis. Charles Evans Hughes became governor of New York in 1907 chiefly because of his success in bringing to light the highly questionable business practices of certain insurance companies.

Hiram Johnson of California fought the political "bosses" and the great railroads that had so powerful an influence in the state. Elected governor of California in 1910, Johnson continued his fight to make government responsible to the people rather than to corporate wealth.

By no means all of the men and women who supported the Progressive movement held public offices. For example, Jane Addams, the social worker, attacked the problem of newly arrived immigrants living in the slums of Chicago. Miss Addams, as you know, organized a community center, known as Hull House, where the people of the neighborhood could gather for schooling, entertainment, and social activities, and where they could bring their many problems and get help and counsel. Hull House became a model for numerous other social-service centers in urban areas throughout the country.

The "muckrakers." In addition to leaders in public office and to such dedicated private citizens as Jane Addams, the Progressive movement included large numbers of scholars, journalists, preachers, and novelists. Theodore Roosevelt applied the name "muckrakers" to the writers who exposed in clear, graphic terms the evils and corruption they found in politics and the business world. Although Roosevelt used the term in a disparaging manner, the writers accepted it with pride, and it came into popular use.

The "muckraking" movement as such, however, is usually dated from an article, "Tweed Days in St. Louis," written by Lincoln Steffens and Claude H. Wetmore for the October 1902 issue of *McClure's Magazine*. The following month *McClure's* began the serial publication of Ida M. Tarbell's critical *The History of the Standard Oil Company*. The public responded so enthusiastically to these pieces that *McClure's* immediately printed other articles along the same lines, and a number of other magazines followed suit. By 1904 most of the nation's periodicals were publishing attacks on abuses in American life.

Novelists as well as journalists attacked the evils of the day. Among the leading novelists who contributed to the muckraking movement were Jack London, Winston Churchill (not the British statesman), Upton Sinclair, Frank Norris, Booth Tarkington, David Graham Phillips, and William Allen White.° Upton Sinclair's sensational novel *The Jungle* exposed unsanitary practices in the meat-packing industry—and, incidentally, turned many of his readers into vegetarians. Frank Norris's novel *The Octopus* exposed the railroads' control over rural political and economic life. And Jack London in *The War of the Classes, The Iron Heel,* and *Revolution* warned of a revolution that could wipe out private capitalism.

The root of the problem. In periodicals, novels, pamphlets, and scholarly books the muckrakers brought to light many abuses in American life. It was Lincoln Steffens, however, who pinpointed the basic problem in a series of articles later published in book form with the title of *The Shame of the Cities.* Years later, in his *Autobiography,* he summarized his conclusions. The basic problem facing Americans was not the development of industrialism or of business, large or small. "It was 'privilege' that was the source of the evil." It was the demand for special privileges from government that had to be controlled, according to Steffens, or it would lead to abuses and corruption.

Millions of Americans in the late 1900's and the early twentieth century shared the views expressed by Lincoln Steffens. They also agreed that one way to combat the evils of special privilege was to restore control of government to a majority of the people.

The Australian ballot. One of the first steps in the direction of more democratic government was the adoption of the *Australian,* or *secret, ballot.* Before about 1890 voting had not been done in

secret. Each political party printed its own ballots, choosing a distinctive color, so that when a voter cast his ballot—as he did in open view of anybody who cared to watch—it was easy to determine how he had voted. The secret ballot, developed in Australia and adopted in the United States, made this open voting impossible by placing the names of all candidates for office on a single sheet of paper, printing all ballots at public expense, and requiring voters to mark and cast their ballots in secrecy.

The initiative, referendum, and recall. Another reform measure seeking to secure a more democratic, or responsive, government centered in the use of the initiative, referendum, and recall. All of these had been advocated by the Populists in the 1890's.

The *initiative* enabled voters in a state to initiate, or introduce, legislation at any time. Suppose, for instance, that a group of citizens wished to increase support for the public schools in their state. First, they would draw up a bill. To this bill they would attach a petition containing the signatures of a certain percentage of the voters in the state. (The number, usually from 5 to 15 per cent, varied from state to state, depending upon state law.) When the petition was presented to the state legislature, the representatives were required by law to debate it openly.

The *referendum* was a logical companion to the initiative. Take, for example, a bill pending before a state legislature that would give excessive privileges to a public utility company. By securing a specified number of signatures to a petition, voters could compel the legislature to place the bill before *all* the voters of the state for their approval or disapproval. In effect, the referendum made it possible for every qualified voter to act as a legislator.

The device known as the *recall* made it possible for voters to remove an elected office holder before his term expired. When a specified number of voters, usually 25 per cent, presented a petition, the officials were obliged to

---

° William Allen White also became famous as owner and editor of the Emporia (Kansas) *Gazette,* a newspaper whose editorials were read and quoted throughout the country.

call for a special election. In this election all of the voters had an opportunity to cast their ballots for or against continuing the person in office.

South Dakota, in 1898, was the first state to adopt the initiative and the referendum. Eventually, 20 states adopted initiative and referendum procedures, and 12 states adopted the recall.

The direct primary. In their effort to make government more responsive to the people's wishes, the progressives also advocated the *direct primary*.

Under the long-established system, all candidates for public office were nominated in political conventions. Since the conventions were easily controlled by professional politicians, the rank and file of voters had little if any opportunity to express a preference for one candidate over another.

The direct primary remedied this situation by providing for what might be called "a nominating election." This election was held well in advance of the regular election. A man who wanted to run for a public office could, by securing a specified number of signatures to a petition, have his name printed on the primary ballot of any one of the political parties. On the day of the primary election, the registered voters of each party then marked their ballots for their candidate.

The direct primary was first adopted

Women's clothing of the early 1900's

in Wisconsin in 1903. In time it spread in one form or another to every state.

Woman suffrage. Woman suffrage also became a part of the progressive program. By 1900 four states—Wyoming, Utah, Colorado, and Idaho—had granted full voting privileges to women. As a result of progressive agitation, between 1910 and 1914 seven other states, all west of the Mississippi, granted women the right to vote. By 1919, fifteen states had swung into line, and the next year, with the adoption of the Nineteenth Amendment, women's right to vote was written into the Constitution of the United States.

Direct election of Senators. Another reform advocated by the progressives was the direct election of United States Senators. According to the Constitution, Senators were chosen by the state legislatures. During the opening years of the 1900's, however, progressive members of the House of Representatives urged the adoption of an amendment that would allow the people to vote directly for Senators, in the same way that they voted for the President, the Vice-President, and the members of the House. But the Senate, which was often criticized as a "rich man's club" and which included in its membership many politicians who owed their jobs to political bosses and political machines, blocked every attempt to get this amendment before the states.

In the end, however, the rising power of the progressives proved too much for the machine politicians. In 1913, in the Seventeenth Amendment, as you will see, the right to choose Senators was taken from the state legislatures and given to the voters at large.

Reform of city government. While the progressives were winning victories at the state and federal level, they were also seeking to reform corrupt city governments. The older, long-established type of municipal government consisted of a mayor and a large city council, elected by the voters and given complete responsibility for running municipal affairs. This system made it relatively easy for a well-organized political machine, using corrupt election procedures, to get control of the government and to use its power in any way it saw fit.

Galveston, Texas, led the way to a new type of government in 1900 after a disastrous hurricane and tidal wave took the lives of one sixth of the people and destroyed a third of the city's property. In an effort to meet the emergency, Galveston gave a commission of five men extraordinary power to run the city. The experiment proved so successful that the *commission* form of government soon spread to other cities.

By 1912 more than 200 communities were operating under the commission form of government. People argued that it was simple, more efficient, and less expensive. They claimed, furthermore, that responsibility for the proper conduct of city affairs was more readily fixed, since the commission was much smaller than the old city council and since each elected commissioner was directly responsible for a separate function of the city government, such as the police, the fire department, sanitation, and public works.

Dayton, Ohio, in 1914 was responsible for the development of another effective innovation in city government. In Dayton the elected commissioners, acting like the board of directors of a large corporation, appointed a *city manager* to administer municipal affairs. The city manager, a specialist without political connections, was expected to run the city as efficiently and economically as possible. City manager government also spread to numerous cities.

The progressives were, indeed, a powerful force in American life in the opening years of the twentieth century. In the remaining pages of this chapter, you will see how a progressive President, Theodore Roosevelt, and a progressive-minded Congress used their power to bring about long-demanded changes in the relations between government and business.

CHIEF JUSTICE WHITE

Edward White at sixteen departed from Georgetown College to join the Confederate forces in his native Louisiana. He survived the war and became a successful lawyer and politician, and served briefly as a judge in the state court system, until, in 1891, he was elected to the United States Senate. In the midst of a bitter Senate contest over the tariff, in 1894, President Cleveland nominated him to the Supreme Court. After sixteen years as an Associate Justice, President Taft named him Chief Justice. Both Taft and Cleveland risked considerable criticism for these appointments because White was a Catholic. There was also a lingering resentment in Washington against former Confederate soldiers and the memory of a co-religionist, Chief Justice Roger B. Taney, who had been known for his southern sentiments.

Nevertheless, it became the duty of Chief Justice White, the former Confederate, to write a decision which declared unconstitutional the "grandfather clauses" in some southern state constitutions—because these provisions were in violation of the Fifteenth Amendment that guaranteed the Negro's right to vote. And during World War I, he upheld the constitutionality of Selective Service, thereby upholding the United States Army against which he had fought as a youth.

The Supreme Court, during White's service, had the difficult task of defining the powers of state governments and the national government while the regulation of big business was being worked out. The application of the Sherman Antitrust Act, and the regulation of transportation by the Interstate Commerce Commission, were established in cases before the Court in which White's reasoning powers were tested. He proved effective in his opinions and the persuasion of his associates.

1. What were the objectives of the progressives?

2. (a) Describe the qualities of "Fighting Bob" La Follette which made him a leader of the progressives. (b) List four ways in which La Follette restored control of the government to the people of Wisconsin.

3. (a) Who were the muckrakers? (b) Indicate specific abuses brought to light by individual "muckraking" writers.

4. Lincoln Steffens held that "privilege" was the basic evil in American society. Offer specific evidence from history to support his contention.

5. Show how each of the following extended political democracy: (a) Australian ballot, (b) initiative, (c) referendum, (d) recall, (e) direct primary, and (f) the Seventeenth and Nineteenth Amendments.

IDENTIFY: Dingley Tariff, "Wisconsin Idea"; Steffens; 1897.

2 Theodore Roosevelt promotes a "square deal" for all people

President McKinley and the Republicans entered the elections of 1900 confident of victory. The Democrats, who had again nominated William Jennings Bryan, tried to make free silver a major issue in the campaign. But Americans in general, including most farmers, were enjoying prosperity, and they returned McKinley to the White House with an electoral vote of 292 to 155.

But McKinley's days were numbered. Six months after his second inauguration, on September 6, 1901, he was shot by a half-crazed assassin while holding a reception at the Pan-American Exposition in Buffalo. He died a few days later and, to the dismay of the conservative Republicans, the recently elected Vice-President, Theodore Roosevelt, became the nation's Chief Executive.

Theodore Roosevelt's background. Theodore Roosevelt, who lived from 1858 to 1919, was born into a well-to-do New York family. As a boy he traveled abroad with his parents and enjoyed other advantages of great wealth. He studied at Harvard, where he acquired a taste for history and politics. After graduation he served a two-year term, from 1882 to 1884, as a member of the New York State Legislature. Part of the next two years he lived on a cattle ranch in the Dakota Territory. Returning home in 1886, he made an unsuccessful attempt to become mayor of New York City. He devoted the following three years to the study and writing of history, a task that had occupied much of his spare time since his college days.

In 1889 President Harrison appointed Roosevelt to the Civil Service Commission, where he served effectively for six years. In 1895 he became president of the New York City Police Commission, leaving this job in 1897 to become Assistant Secretary of the Navy. When war with Spain broke out in 1898, he resigned his post in the Navy Department to organize, with Leonard Wood, a volunteer cavalry regiment known as the "Rough Riders." After the war he became the Republican governor of New York, but his vigorous, independent actions so alarmed the Republican political bosses that in 1900 they decided to get him out of active politics by "kicking him upstairs" into the office of the Vice-Presidency.

Such was the man who at the age of forty-two became the youngest President the United States had ever had—and, as the conservative Republicans had rightly feared, one of the most colorful and independent.

Roosevelt as a progressive. A man of immense energy, Roosevelt had a great gift for sensing what was in the public mind, for expressing public opinion in telling phrases, and for fighting with sensational zeal for the things he believed to be right.

At the same time, Theodore Roosevelt was a good politician. That is to say, he was ready to compromise, taking half a loaf when he felt that the whole loaf could not be had. What he did for the Progressive movement was to give it dramatic national leadership.

He did not start the Progressive movement. Nor did he go as far in specific situations as many progressives felt he could and should go. But his general popularity, his enthusiasm, his ability as a speaker, and his position enabled him to promote the reform movement.

Roosevelt wins the 1904 election. Roosevelt's progressive ideas antagonized many of the leaders of the Republican Party. When election year 1904 rolled around, the Republican political leaders would have abandoned him in favor of a more conservative candidate had they dared. But by this time "Teddy" Roosevelt, as he was familiarly called, enjoyed widespread popularity. No other candidate had a chance in the nominating convention, which did not even vote, but chose Roosevelt by acclamation° to head the Republican ticket.

Roosevelt won a resounding victory at the polls—336 electoral votes to 140 for his Democratic opponent, Judge Alton B. Parker of New York. He captured every state outside the Solid South, and even won Missouri, which had not voted for a Republican President since 1868.

What was the secret of Roosevelt's popularity with the rank and file of voters? In the course of the campaign, he had announced that he was "unhampered by any pledge, promise, or understanding of any kind, save my promise, made openly to the American people, that so far as my power lies I shall see to it that every man has a square deal, no less and no more." This promise carried weight, as you will see, because Roosevelt's record during his first term in office convinced millions of voters that he meant what he said.

Roosevelt settles a coal strike. Less than a year after he followed McKinley into the office of Chief Executive,

....

° *acclamation:* In a political convention the chairman may declare that a candidate has been chosen "by acclamation" when his nomination is greeted by the delegates with such a roar of approval as to make voting unnecessary.

Theodore Roosevelt's
"The New Nationalism" (1910): EXCERPT

Our country—this great republic—means nothing unless it means the triumph of a real democracy, the triumph of popular government, and, in the long run, of an economic system under which each man shall be guaranteed the opportunity to show the best that there is in him ...

I stand for the square deal. But when I say that I am for the square deal, I mean not merely that I stand for fair play under the present rules of the game, but that I stand for having those rules changed so as to work for a more substantial equality of opportunity and of reward for equally good services ...

Roosevelt had an opportunity to show where he stood on the question of organized labor. In the spring of 1902, a strike broke out in the anthracite coal fields of Pennsylvania. The mines were owned largely by the railroad companies that served that region. The miners worked long hours, lived in company towns, had to buy from company stores, and because of low wages found it hard to make ends meet. Organized as part of the United Mine Workers Union, they had asked for a 9-hour day, a 20 per cent wage increase, improved working conditions, and recognition of their right to bargain as a union. The coal operators, headed by George F. Baer, president of the Philadelphia and Reading Railway Company, refused to negotiate with the union, whereupon the miners went out on strike.

By fall the price of anthracite coal had risen from $5 to more than $30 a ton, and the country faced a coal-less winter with factories closed and homes without heat. The mineowners demanded that the President send federal troops into the area to break the strike, as President Cleveland had done in the case of the Pullman strike of 1894 (page 519). Roosevelt refused. Instead, he

Men's clothing of the early 1900's

summoned representatives of the owners and of the union to a White House conference.

At the White House conference John Mitchell, leader of the United Mine Workers, proposed that the President appoint an impartial commission to settle the dispute by arbitration. The mineowners refused to listen to the proposal. Furious at this lack of co-operation, Roosevelt let it be known that he was considering sending the army to take over the mines and operate them in the name of the government. Faced with this prospect, the mineowners agreed to accept the decision of a board of arbitration.

After four months of study, the board gave its decision. The miners received a 9-hour day and a 10 per cent wage increase. But the board did not grant the miners the right to negotiate as a union.

Although the miners won only part of their demands, the case was a landmark in the history of organized labor. For the first time the federal government had stepped into a labor controversy with the idea of protecting the interests of all concerned—wage earners, owners, and, by no means least important, the public.

The Danbury Hatters' case. Organized labor was pleased with Roosevelt's handling of the coal strike. It was not pleased, however, with the outcome of another labor dispute that started in 1902. In that year the hatters' union started a nationwide *boycott°* of the hats produced by a hat manufacturer of Danbury, Connecticut. The hat company claimed that the boycott restrained trade and was therefore illegal under the Sherman Antitrust Act. After a long delay, in 1908 the Supreme Court decided in favor of the hat manufacturer. As a result, the members of the hatters' union became liable for three times the damages suffered by the manufacturer.°

Theodore Roosevelt was in no way responsible for the rulings of the Supreme Court. On the other hand, organized labor, thoroughly alarmed at the outcome of the Danbury Hatters' case, held the government responsible for failing to draft laws that would provide reasonable protection for labor unions.

Roosevelt as "trust buster." Even before the labor troubles of 1902 started, Roosevelt had directed his Attorney General to bring suit under the Sherman Antitrust Act against the Northern Securities Company. This was a holding company that James J. Hill, creator of the Great Northern Railway Company, Edward Harriman of the Northern Pacific and other roads, and J. P. Morgan, key New York banker, had arranged in order to bring under one control the three leading railroads serving the country between Lake Michigan and the Pacific Northwest. "We do not wish to destroy corporations," Roosevelt announced, "but we do wish to make them subserve the public good." In 1904 the Supreme Court by a vote of five to four held that the Northern Securities Com-

....

° *boycott:* refusal of workers or other groups to purchase goods from an organization or, in some cases, even to do business with the organization.
° In 1917 the case was finally settled when the union agreed to pay $234,000 damages.

pany did restrain trade and was illegal under the Sherman Antitrust Act.

Early in 1903, while the Northern Securities Company case was still pending in the courts, Congress passed two important pieces of legislation. The first measure, the Expedition Act, speeded up antitrust cases by giving them a priority over other cases in the federal courts. The second measure created the Department of Commerce and Labor, with a Secretary in the President's cabinet. The new department included a Bureau of Corporations, which was authorized to investigate and report on the activities of corporations.

After 1904, encouraged by the decision of the Supreme Court in the Northern Securities Company case and by his own victory at the polls, Roosevelt started action against a number of other trusts.° During his second term the "beef trust" and the "fertilizer trust" were dissolved by order of the Supreme Court. Altogether, 44 suits against trusts were started during Roosevelt's administration.

But even when the Supreme Court ordered a trust to dissolve, the men who controlled the various corporations often continued to run them as a unit by meeting informally and sharing in the decisions of the separate corporations. By arrangements of this kind—often called "communities of interest" or "gentlemen's agreements"—the corporations could continue to do informally what they had previously done as a trust. The possible advantages of large-scale operations, both for the consumer and for the corporations, were obviously very great. Moreover, big business was so tied together that any attempt to break up a monopoly was like trying to unscramble the eggs in an omelet. The trend of the times was toward larger and larger combinations of business, and nothing Roosevelt or anyone else was able to do reversed this trend.

••
° The term "trust," first used to describe a specific form of business combination (page 476), came to mean any large business organization that tried to secure a monopoly.

"Good" and "bad" combinations. Before he left office in 1909, Roosevelt reached the conclusion that the problem of trusts was not simply one of size. What really mattered was whether a business combination was "good" or "bad." He asked Congress to pass laws defining "good" and "bad" practices, but Congress refused.

Finally, in 1911, two years after President Roosevelt had left office, the Supreme Court adopted Roosevelt's point of view. In the cases of the Standard Oil Company of New Jersey and the American Tobacco Company, the Court ruled that the Sherman Antitrust Act's prohibition of "all combinations in restraint of trade" should mean "all *unreasonable* combinations in restraint of trade." In applying the "rule of reason," as it was called, the Supreme Court from then on decided whether a large business combination was "reasonable" or "unreasonable" by looking not merely at its size, but also at its effect upon the public.

Important railroad legislation. The Roosevelt administration had much better success in regulating railroads than it had in breaking up the giant trusts. Following the President's recommendations, Congress adopted two laws which put teeth into the Interstate Commerce Act of 1887 and strengthened the Interstate Commerce Commission (page 496).

The Elkins Act of 1903 made it illegal for a shipper to accept a rebate, just as the Interstate Commerce Act had made it illegal for a railroad company to give one.

The Hepburn Act of 1906 contained a number of even more severe regulations. It increased the number of Interstate Commerce Commissioners from five to seven and gave them authority (1) to regulate express and sleeping-car companies, oil pipelines, bridges, railroad terminals, and ferries doing business across state lines; (2) to fix "just and reasonable" rates, subject to approval by the federal courts; (3) to restrict the granting of free passes; and

■ A cartoonist of the time showed Theodore Roosevelt about to attack "monopoly." Uncle Sam is saying, "Wade in, Theodore, I'm with ye!"

(4) to require that uniform methods of accounting be used by railroads.

In 1910, after President Roosevelt had left office, Congress also passed the Mann-Elkins Act which placed telephone, telegraph, cable, and wireless companies under the control of the Interstate Commerce Commission.

Laws protecting public health. President Roosevelt also gave leadership to a movement to bring distilleries, patent-drug producers, and meat-packing houses under government regulation. Government chemists had long known that some of these enterprises were deceiving and defrauding the public and, in some cases, were actually endangering public health. Many canned foods were spoiled or were treated with poisonous preservatives. Patent medicines often contained harmful habit-forming drugs or ingredients that could not possibly relieve any ailments. Meats in the packing houses were often diseased.

Against the powerful opposition of the meat-packing interests, Roosevelt and the progressives in Congress in 1906 succeeded in getting the Meat Inspection Act passed. This act gave the federal government power to inspect all meat shipped from one state to another.

Congress also adopted the Pure Food and Drug Act of 1906. This act forbade the manufacture, sale, or transportation of adulterated or poisonous patent medicines and foods. It also required the makers of patent medicines to put labels on containers indicating the exact nature of the contents. Five years later, in 1911, Congress supplemented this law by making it illegal to use false or misleading labels.

These acts helped to strengthen the developing theory that the federal government had a responsibility for protecting the public welfare.

SECTION SURVEY

1. Describe the highlights of Roosevelt's colorful career before he became President.

2. Contrast Roosevelt's handling of the 1902 coal strike with Cleveland's handling of the Pullman strike in 1894.

3. (a) What facts support Roosevelt's claim to the title of "trust buster"? (b) How do you explain his limited success?

4. The Elkins Act, the Hepburn Act, the Meat Inspection Act, and the Pure Food and Drug Act were important steps toward a new relationship between government and industry. Discuss this statement.

IDENTIFY: "square deal," Danbury Hatters' case, Northern Securities Company case, Expedition Act, Department of Commerce and Labor, "communities of interest," "rule of reason," Mann-Elkins Act; 1903, 1906, 1910.

3 Theodore Roosevelt stimulates conservation of natural resources

"The first work I took up when I became President," Roosevelt wrote in his *Autobiography*, "was the work of reclamation." This, the job of reclaiming and conserving the nation's natural resources, proved to be one of Theodore Roosevelt's greatest contributions.

Natural resources are wasted. At the time that Theodore Roosevelt became President, almost nothing had been done to safeguard the nation's natural resources. Indeed, from the first days of settlement Americans had used the nation's resources without regard for the future. Pioneer farmers had cut and burned their way westward, with ax and fire transforming enormous areas of forest lands into farm lands. With careless generosity the federal and state governments had encouraged waste, especially during the latter half of the 1800's, handing over to private individuals and to corporations priceless resources—agricultural and grazing lands, forest regions, mineral deposits, oil fields, and water-power sites.

By 1900 only 200,000,000 of the nation's original 800,000,000 acres of virgin forest were still standing, and four fifths of the timber was privately owned. The men who controlled the nation's corporations were, in general, no more concerned about waste than the pioneer settlers had been. Lumber companies slashed their way through the forests without regard for fire protection, replanting, or the preservation of young trees. Cattlemen and sheepmen overgrazed semiarid lands, stripping them of their protective covering of grass and often converting them into dust bowls.

Coal companies worked only the richest and most accessible veins, leaving the bulk of the coal buried in abandoned mines. Oil companies allowed natural gas to escape unused into the air. The growing cities polluted rivers and streams with sewage and the waste

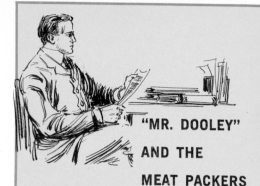

"MR. DOOLEY" AND THE MEAT PACKERS

Finley Peter Dunne was one of the most widely read humorists of the late 1890's and early 1900's. The most famous fictional character he created was "Mr. Dooley," an Irish-American of Chicago. A whole generation of Americans laughed at Mr. Dooley's comments on the news of the day. These comments, often highly critical of persons and policies, were expressed with shrewd wit and common sense.

Upton Sinclair's book *The Jungle*, which appeared in 1906 and which contained a severe attack upon the unsanitary practices of the meat packers, prompted one of Mr. Dooley's typical observations. In this instance, he described President Theodore Roosevelt's reaction to the book:

"Tiddy was toyin' with a light breakfast an' idly turnin' over th' pages iv th' new book with both hands. Suddenly he rose fr'm th' table, an' cryin': 'I'm pizened,' begun throwin' sausages out iv th' window. Th' ninth wan sthruck Sinitor Biv'ridge on th' head an' made him a blond. It bounced off, exploded, an' blew a leg off a secret service agent, an' th' scatthred fragmints destroyed a handsome row iv ol' oak trees. Sinitor Biv'ridge rushed in thinkin' that th' Prisidint was bein' assassynated be his devoted followers in th' Sinit, an' discovered Tiddy engaged in a hand-to-hand conflict with a potted ham. Th' Sinitor fr'm Injyanny, with a few well-directed wurruds, put out th' fuse an' rendered th' missile harmless. Since thin, th' Prisidint, like th' rest iv us, has become a viggytaryan, an' th' diet has so changed his disposition that he is writin' a book called *Suffer in Silence*, didycated to Sinitor Aldrich."

from factories, destroying fish and creating a menace to public health. The only excuse for these wasteful practices was that Americans had become accustomed to thinking that their natural resources were inexhaustible.

Early conservation efforts. By the late 1800's the situation was becoming increasingly serious. A rapidly growing population was making heavier and heavier demands upon the nation's resources. The growing industries were devouring raw materials in ever larger quantities. Here and there thoughtful Americans began to realize that their resources could not last forever.

Beginning as early as 1873, the American Association for the Advancement of Science began to urge Congress to take some action to prevent the waste of natural resources. As a result of their efforts and the efforts of other farsighted people, in 1887 Congress established the Forest Bureau in the Department of Agriculture. And in 1891 Congress took further action by passing a law authorizing the President to withdraw timberlands from public sale. Acting under this law, President Harrison set aside a national forest reserve of 17,000,000 acres, and Presidents Cleveland and McKinley more than doubled this area.

Such was the situation when Theodore Roosevelt entered the White House. A small beginning had been made. But the public as a whole had not yet learned to think of conservation as a serious national problem.

Roosevelt's leadership. During the course of his two administrations, President Roosevelt awakened public interest to the need for conservation, aroused Congress to action, and managed to get the federal and the state governments to adopt new policies.

Roosevelt was admirably fitted by both temperament and experience to be America's foremost champion of conservation. From his boyhood days he had been intensely interested in nature. As an avid student and keen observer, he realized early in his life that America's natural resources were being despoiled and wasted at an alarming rate, and he missed no opportunity to express himself forthrightly and vigorously on the subject of conservation.

In 1901, the year he stepped into the White House, Roosevelt warned his fellow Americans that "The forest and water problems are perhaps the most vital internal problems of the United States." And in a special message to Congress he reminded the legislators that "The mineral wealth of this country, the coal, iron, oil, gas, and the like, does not reproduce itself. . . ." If we waste our resources today, he warned, "our descendants will feel the exhaustion a generation or two before they otherwise would. . . ."

From talk to action. But President Roosevelt was never a man to be content with mere talk. In 1903 he vetoed a bill to give private interests the right to build a dam and an electric generating plant at Muscle Shoals, Alabama. During his administrations, with the enthusiastic support of the chief of the Forest Service, Gifford Pinchot (PIN-shoh), he withdrew from public sale 150,000,000 acres of forest land—an area substantially larger than France. He also withdrew millions of acres of coal and phosphate lands and potential water-power sites.

In response to his urging, Congress created a number of wildlife sanctuaries and national parks. Needless to say, in all of these activities Roosevelt ran up against strong opposition from private interests.

The Newlands Reclamation Act. For one of the most important acts of his administration, however, President Roosevelt received considerable support, especially from western Congressmen. Early in his Presidency he threw his influence behind a bill sponsored by Senator Francis G. Newlands, a Democrat from Nevada. The bill passed both houses of Congress, and in 1902 the Newlands Reclamation Act became law. This act provided that money from the sale of public lands in 16 western States and Territories was to be used to build irrigation projects which would reclaim

The Roosevelt Dam in the Tonto National Forest of Arizona was one of the first of many dams, large and small, that have been built to bring the nation's waters under control.

wasteland, that is, make it suitable for farming. Money from the sale of water to farmers who settled on the reclaimed land was to go into a revolving fund with which additional irrigation projects were to be financed.

Reclamation work started at once. Within four years 28 different irrigation projects were under way. By 1911 the Shoshone (shoh-SHOH-nee) Dam in Wyoming and the Roosevelt Dam in Arizona were in operation. Water from the enormous reservoir created by the Roosevelt Dam flowed through irrigation canals and ditches to transform 200,000 acres of desert into rich farm land. As other projects were completed, additional thousands of acres of wasteland were brought under cultivation.

The White House Conference. In 1907 Roosevelt took another important step when he appointed the Inland Waterways Commission. The commission did not confine its investigations to water transportation. Instead, it studied nearly every aspect of the conservation program. In the report that it submitted to the President, the commission urged him to organize a national conference to publicize the need for conservation.

Roosevelt immediately issued invitations for a meeting to be held at the White House in May 1908. Those invited included the governors of all the states, members of the Senate and House, justices of the Supreme Court, representatives of leading scientific associations, and scores of prominent citizens.

The White House Conservation Conference was a great success. One of the direct outgrowths of the conference was the appointment of a fifty-man National Conservation Commission headed by Gifford Pinchot and made up of roughly equal numbers of scientists, businessmen, and political leaders. This commission went to work at once on a systematic study of the country's mineral, water, forest, and soil resources. It submitted its inventory to the President in December 1908.

Another important outgrowth of the White House Conference was the appointment of state conservation agencies in 41 of the states by governors convinced of the need for action.

The North American Conservation Conference. Still another outgrowth of the 1908 meeting at the White House was the North American Conservation Conference. In February 1909, in re-

MSGR. JOHN A. RYAN,

APOSTLE OF SOCIAL JUSTICE

No American took more serious notice of *Rerum Novarum,* Leo XIII's encyclical on the rights of labor, than did John A. Ryan (1869–1945), priest of the Archdiocese of St. Paul. Ryan had been a student at Catholic University in Washington; from 1915 on, he was professor of moral theology there. In 1906 he published *A Living Wage.*

Ryan wished to convince all Americans of the importance of social justice, not just to raise the standard of living, but to support human dignity. Thus he urged state action to prevent payment of wages below the level which would support life in "frugal comfort." Some falsely accused him of being a socialist—that is, of advocating state ownership of all means of production. But he always advocated private ownership—by more of the people. Workers should own their homes, have some productive property, or own part of the industry they worked for.

In 1917 Ryan wrote a summary of his ideas for reconstructing the social order. He believed World War I would leave a great postwar reconstruction problem, and perhaps cause revolutions like the one which did occur in Russia. When a national committee of Catholic bishops accepted his ideas, the result was the publication of the "Bishops' Program of Social Reconstruction." It included high wages and government support of the nation's economy, regulation of business by government, and a measure of labor ownership and management of industry. It was, for that time, a very radical program, but some of its ideas are now given effect in law and practice.

Msgr. Ryan lived to see most of his proposals accepted as worthwhile. In 1931, Pius XI's encyclical *Quadrigesimo Anno* gave renewed and timely emphasis to social justice, and to the apostolate of social justice represented by Msgr. Ryan.

sponse to an invitation from President Roosevelt, representatives from Canada, Newfoundland, Mexico, and the United States gathered in Washington to study the conservation problems of all of North America. At this meeting, as at the earlier White House Conservation Conference, the delegates drew up a "Declaration of Principles" in which they listed a number of specific recommendations, including measures for the protection of wildlife and of "such birds as are useful to agriculture."

Before the conference ended, it approved a suggestion for calling a world conference. The President then issued invitations to the major nations to meet at The Hague in the Netherlands to consider world natural-resource problems. On March 4, 1909, however, Roosevelt's term of office ended, and his successor in the White House, President Taft, allowed the project to lapse.

In spite of this disappointment, Theodore Roosevelt could look back upon almost eight years in the White House with the assurance that he and those who shared his views had succeeded in arousing public opinion to the need for conservation. Equally important, he had established the foundations of a conservation program for the future.

SECTION SURVEY

1. Pioneers, corporations, and state and federal governments were all responsible for the waste of our natural resources. Explain.

2. Show how Theodore Roosevelt tried to arouse the nation to the need for conservation.

3. Describe the significance of the Newlands Reclamation Act of 1902.

4. Discuss the contributions of the following conferences to the conservation movement: (a) White House Conservation Conference of 1908 and (b) the North American Conservation Conference.

5. In what ways did "Teddy" Roosevelt establish "the foundations of a conservation program for the future"?

IDENTIFY: Inland Waterways Commission; Pinchot.

Points to Discuss: 1. Explain the rise of the Progressive movement at the turn of the century.

2. Evaluate the contributions of the Progressive movement to American life.

3. Give evidence of the influence exerted on American thinking by "muckrakers."

4. By reference to his domestic policies, show why Theodore Roosevelt's accession to the Presidency in 1901 can be termed a "revolution of the first magnitude."

5. What claim has Theodore Roosevelt to the title "America's foremost champion of conservation"?

6. The government's role in relation to business changed from that of a referee in the nineteenth century to that of a true regulator in the twentieth. Support this statement with concrete evidence.

Using Charts: 1. Consult the Chronology of Events (pages 850–59) under Theodore Roosevelt in answering the following: (a) Indicate and explain the events relating to conservation. (b) Indicate and explain the laws relating to railroads. (c) Which of the laws were designed specifically to help the consumer? (d) Which events were favorable to labor?

2. Referring to the Business Activity chart (pages 850–59), compare the depression of 1907 with the depression of 1873 and the Panic of 1893 in length and severity.

Consulting the Sources: Interesting excerpts from Finley Peter Dunne's inimitable character "Mr. Dooley" can be found in Ellis, *Docs.*, No. 144.

■ TRACING THE MAIN IDEAS

The victory of the Republicans in the election of 1896 broke the strength of the Populist movement. With the triumph of the Republicans and returning prosperity, many people concluded that the reform movement had lost its force.

But the reform movement was not dead. On the contrary, during the opening years of the 1900's it gained new life in the Progressive movement. Guided by the progressives, including President Theodore Roosevelt, the relationship of government and business began to change. In earlier times—until, say, the 1880's—the government's role had been, in general, that of a referee who stood on the side lines and was called in

only when one of the players disobeyed the rules. Now, in the twentieth century, the government was beginning to take a more active part, to accept more responsibility for regulating the activities of business in the interest of the public welfare. For this changing conception of the role of government in the new industrial age, both Republicans and Democrats were responsible.

As you will see in the next chapter, the reforms started under President Roosevelt were continued under the Republican administration of President Taft and, to an even greater degree, under the Democratic administration of President Wilson.

The "New Freedom" Extends Reform

PRESIDENT WILSON
IN HIS STUDY —

Ꞧ. Houkhan

Fᴙᴏᴍ 1901 to 1921, the White House opened its doors to three different Presidents. From 1901 to 1909, "Teddy" Roosevelt—colorful, dynamic, forceful—promised to give all Americans a "square deal" and, on the whole, succeeded in fulfilling his promise. From 1909 to 1913, William Howard Taft—a huge man, genial, highly intelligent, thoroughly competent, but without "Teddy's" ability to capture the public's imagination—made several contributions to the reform program. From 1913 to 1921, Woodrow Wilson—scholar, idealist, in his own quieter way sharing Theodore Roosevelt's conviction that the President's job was to lead Congress and the country—promised a "new freedom" to all Americans, and did much to fulfill this promise before World War I broke out in 1914.

The basic issue with which each of the three Presidents had to grapple was the role of government in the new industrial age. Should government try to guarantee vigorous competition by breaking up the giant industries? This is what the reformers of the 1880's and 1890's had demanded, and this is what they thought they had secured with the passage of the Sherman Antitrust Act of 1890.

Or should government accept the trend toward larger and larger industrial combinations and be content to make rules under which "good" combinations could prosper and "bad" combinations could be broken up? This was the view that Theodore Roosevelt came to accept.

AS THE STORY DEVELOPS

1. The Progressive movement gains and loses under Taft.
2. Opportunity for all is expanded under Wilson's "New Freedom" program.

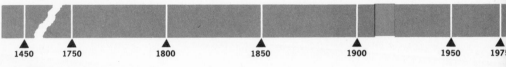

1450   1750   1800   1850   1900   1950   197

The Progressive movement gains and loses under Taft

Under President Roosevelt's leadership, as you have seen, the Progressive movement became almost a crusade. In order to insure its continued success after he left the White House, Roosevelt decided to throw his support to the Presidential candidacy of his close friend and associate, his Secretary of War, William Howard Taft.

The election of 1908. As election year 1908 rolled around, it was evident that Roosevelt could win the Republican nomination and the election itself if he chose to run for another term in the White House. Although a financial panic and depression in 1907 had given his opponents an opportunity to criticize him, his popularity with the public at large was at its peak. But Roosevelt stood by an earlier announcement that he did not intend to run again.

At the Republican convention in Chicago, Roosevelt had enough political friends among the delegates to win the nomination for William Howard Taft of Ohio on the first ballot. Roosevelt also played a leading role in the drafting of the Republican platform. The platform called for strengthening the Interstate Commerce Act of 1887 and the Sherman Antitrust Act of 1890, for conservation and the development of an improved highway system, for a postal savings system, and for a revision of the tariff.

The Democrats, meeting in convention in Denver, again chose William Jennings Bryan as their Presidential candidate. The platform they adopted condemned the Republican Party as the organization of "privileges and private monopolies." It called for a lower tariff, new antitrust legislation, and a federal income tax.

One unusual feature of the election campaign was the action taken by the American Federation of Labor. Until 1908 the A. F. of L. had followed a policy of neutrality in politics. That is to say, it had consistently refused to throw its support behind one political party, choosing instead to support friends of organized labor from both of the major parties. In 1908, however, the A. F. of L. abandoned this traditional policy and came out for Bryan and the entire Democratic ticket.

In spite of the support of organized labor, the Democrats lost by a considerable margin, with Taft receiving 321 electoral votes to Bryan's 162. The Republicans also retained control of both houses of Congress.

Taft continues reforms. William Howard Taft, a Cincinnati lawyer and judge, was a big, good-natured man who had served the Roosevelt administration in the Philippines and in the War Department. Although conservative, he nevertheless recognized the force of the Progressive movement. During his four years in the White House, he supported a number of important reform measures.

Taft's administration chalked up an impressive list of accomplishments that progressives had favored. Taft's Attorney General, George W. Wickersham, started 90 antitrust suits against big corporations compared with 44 suits started under President Roosevelt. Following Taft's recommendation, Congress strengthened the Interstate Commerce Act by passing the Mann-Elkins Act of 1910. The Mann-Elkins Act, as you have seen, placed telephone, telegraph, cable, and wireless companies under the jurisdiction of the Interstate Commerce Commission. Congress also established a Bureau of Mines in the Department of the Interior, and created a new department with cabinet rank—the Department of Labor. In an attack upon the evils of child labor, Congress established a Children's Bureau in the Department of Labor. Congress also established an 8-hour day for all workers on projects contracted for by the federal government.

In addition to its antitrust measures and efforts to improve the lot of wage earners, the Taft administration also took steps to create a healthier political climate. President Taft himself added a considerable number of federal jobs to the civil service list, and Congress adopted the Publicity Act requiring political parties to make public the sources and amounts of the money that they spent in political campaigns.

President Taft also supported legislation establishing a postal savings system and a parcel-post service. The postal savings system transformed every post office in the land into a safe and convenient savings bank. The parcel-post system provided inexpensive package delivery services for people who had previously been dependent upon private carriers for such services.

Taft's administration was also responsible for the adoption of a constitutional amendment concerning a federal income tax. The Sixteenth Amendment, which had been recommended by Taft and proposed in July 1909, was ratified by the required number of states by February 1913.

Taft's stand on the tariff antagonizes progressives. In spite of an impressive list of reform measures, President Taft early in his administration began to lose the support of the progressives in the Republican Party. As a result, he relied more and more on the conservative members of the party.

The split between President Taft and the progressives began to appear as early as April 1909, when Congress adopted the Payne-Aldrich Tariff. This was the first major revision of the tariff since the Dingley Tariff Act of 1897 (page 543). The progressives had worked for lower tariff rates. In the new act some reductions were in fact made, but rates on many of the thousands of items listed were actually increased.

Taft's conservation policy costs him support. While the tariff controversy was still going on, Taft was also violently attacked for his stand on conservation. Indeed, some of his most bitter critics charged that he had sabotaged Theodore Roosevelt's conservation program. Although this was an unfair charge, it is true that the conservation movement suffered a setback during the opening months of Taft's administration.

Taft's Secretary of the Interior, Richard A. Ballinger, was a cautious lawyer. After examining the timber law of 1891, he came to the conclusion that the President's authority to withdraw land from sale extended only to timberlands. He therefore restored to public sale valuable water-power sites that President Roosevelt had previously withdrawn. Gifford Pinchot, whom Taft had continued in office as head of the Forest Service, promptly protested. Taft sided with Pinchot, and the lands in question were returned to the forest reserve. But Pinchot, an ardent conservationist, was not satisfied. From this time on he was convinced that Ballinger was on the side of private interests and opposed to the conservation program.

Pinchot's fears were strengthened when Ballinger allowed extensive coal and timberlands in Alaska to pass into private hands. This action aroused a storm of controversy throughout the country, reaching the muckraking magazines and the headlines of the daily press and becoming in 1910 the subject of an investigation by a Congressional committee. In the midst of the storm, Taft removed Pinchot from office.

Although Ballinger resigned in 1911 and the new Secretary of the Interior restored the Alaskan lands to the federal forest reserve, the damage had been done. Taft's stand on the tariff and on the Ballinger controversy cost the Republicans large numbers of votes in the Congressional elections of 1910. For the first time in sixteen years, the Republicans lost control of the House of Representatives.

Actually, Taft did a great deal to advance the conservation program. After receiving authorization from Congress, he withdrew almost 59,000,000 acres of coal lands from public sale. He also signed the Appalachian Forest Reserve Act, which enabled the government to add about 1,250,000 acres of land in the White Mountains of New Hampshire and the Southern Appalachians to the federal reserves.

Progressives win a political victory. Early in 1910 the progressive wing of the Republican Party launched an attack upon the Speaker of the House. Since 1903, Speaker Joseph G. Cannon of Illinois, nicknamed "Uncle Joe," had been one of the most powerful officers in the government. As Speaker, he appointed all House committees and selected the chairmen. He appointed himself as chairman of the powerful Committee on Rules, which determined the order of business in the House. Acting in this capacity, he could prevent any bill to which he objected from coming out of committee for debate on the floor of the House. Moreover, as presiding officer of the House, he could determine who should speak during debate by recognizing or refusing to recognize anyone he pleased. As a result of these powers, "Uncle Joe" was able to rule the House with an iron hand.

The progressives charged that Cannon, a conservative, had used his great power to block progressive legislation. Determined to put an end to his autocratic rule, in March 1910 Representative George W. Norris of Nebraska rose on the floor of the House to propose an amendment to the House rules. He moved that in the future the Committee on Rules be elected by the members of the House instead of being chosen by the Speaker, and that the Speaker himself be excluded from membership on the Rules Committee.

Speaker Cannon, solidly supported by the conservatives, fought desperately to maintain his power. The heated debate continued through the night, lasting for almost thirty hours. About 40 progressive Republicans finally voted with the Democrats in favor of Norris's motion and stripped the Speaker of his traditional powers over the Committee on Rules. A year later the House placed still greater restrictions upon the Speaker by depriving him of his power to appoint members of the remaining committees. With this victory the progres-

■ The genial William Howard Taft addresses a crowd on a visit to an Indian memorial.

sives stripped the Speaker of the House of much of his powers. From then on, the Speaker was the presiding officer of the House, not its ruler.

The Republican Party splits. By 1912 the Republican Party was split wide open, with the "old guard" on one side, the progressives on the other. Theodore Roosevelt, by now dissatisfied with Taft's leadership, was determined to run again for the Presidency. In order to do so, Roosevelt had to brush aside the obvious candidate of the progressive forces, Robert M. La Follette of Wisconsin. Roosevelt also had to line up enough delegates to the nominating convention to insure his own nomination.

But President Taft had the advantage that the occupant of the White House always has at a political convention. When the Republican convention began to organize, the Roosevelt partisans claimed that many of their delegates were refused seats by the steam-roller methods of the Taft forces. The convention named Taft as its candidate. Disgruntled at this turn of affairs, Roosevelt's supporters left the Republican convention and called another convention, which nominated him for the Presidency and launched a new third party —the Progressive Party, sometimes called the "Bull Moose" Party.°

••

° The party adopted as its emblem the bull moose as a tribute to Roosevelt, who often used the term to describe the strength and vigor of a person.

WILSON SPEAKS

On democracy

"Democratic institutions are never done—they are, like the living tissue, always a-making. It is a strenuous thing, this, of living the life of a free people: and we cannot escape the burden of our inheritance. . . .

"It behooves us once and again to stand face to face with our ideals, to renew our enthusiasms, to reckon again our duties, to take fresh views of our aims and fresh courage for their pursuit."—from an address given at Middletown, Connecticut, April 30, 1889

On education

"The educated man is to be discovered by his point of view, by the temper of his mind, by his attitude towards life, and his fair way of thinking. He can see, he can discriminate, he can combine ideas and perceive whither they lead; he has insight and comprehension. His mind is a practiced instrument of appreciation. He is more apt to contribute light than heat to a discussion. . . ."—from an address given in Cambridge, Massachusetts, July 1, 1909

On American ideals

"My dream is that, as the years go on and the world knows more and more of America, it will also drink at these fountains of youth and renewal; that it also will turn to America for those moral inspirations which lie at the basis of all freedom; that the world will never fear America, unless it feels that it is engaged in some enterprise which is inconsistent with the rights of humanity; and that America will come into the full light of the day when all shall know that she puts human rights above all other rights and that her flag is the flag not only of America, but of humanity."—from an address given at Independence Hall, Philadelphia, July 4, 1914

The "Bull Moose" Republicans with "Teddy" Roosevelt at their head adopted a platform calling for numerous reforms. The platform favored legislation in the interest of labor; it advocated tariff reform; it endorsed the initiative and referendum; and it declared that it stood for government control over unfair business practices. In a spirited campaign, full of fight and an almost frenzied zeal, Roosevelt popularized his "New Nationalism" program. By the phrase "New Nationalism" he meant the extension of the powers of the federal government so that it might become an effective instrument in the battle for progressive measures and social reform.

The Democrats nominate Wilson. The Democrats, who had made marked gains in the Congressional elections of 1910, had every reason to believe that the split in the Republican Party would insure their own return to power. Many leading Democrats fought for the nomination, which in the end went to Governor Woodrow Wilson of New Jersey. The Democratic Party platform called for tariff reduction, banking reform, laws in behalf of labor and the farmers, and the enforcement of stronger antitrust legislation. Both the platform and the nomination of Wilson indicated that the Democratic Party was under the influence of its progressive wing.

Wilson had been nationally known for only a few brief years before his nomination. The son of a southern Presbyterian minister, he had been educated at Princeton, the University of Virginia, and Johns Hopkins University, where he had become a Doctor of Philosophy in political science. In 1902 he became president of Princeton University. His writings emphasized the idea that the President of the United States ought to be the real leader of the government, taking the initiative and interpreting the will of the people.

Not until Wilson became governor of New Jersey in 1910 did he favor what might be called the newer progressive ideas. As governor he fought the political machine bosses of his party, showing a remarkably astute independence. He also took the lead as governor in pushing through the legislature laws designed to reform the lax corporation laws of the state. Wilson also showed more and more interest in other progressive measures. Thus he became the logical choice of the progressives in the Democratic Party. The campaign proved him to be a gifted orator. He was also a moralist and an idealist. He sensed the popular discontent in the country, and his neatly turned phrases about establishing a "New Freedom" for the common man greatly appealed to those who were convinced that special privilege menaced the nation. Wilson was a man of convictions—determined, courageous, and independent.

The Democrats win. The election returns gave the Democrats a resounding victory. Wilson's electoral majority was the largest in United States Presidential history up to that time—435 electoral votes to 88 for Roosevelt and 8 for Taft.

In spite of his overwhelming electoral vote, Wilson was a "minority" President. He received only 6,286,214 popular votes out of a total of more than 15,000,-000. Nevertheless, he could count upon widespread public support for his progressive "New Freedom" program.

⌕ **SECTION SURVEY**

1. Give the parties, candidates, issues, and results of the election of 1908.

2. "Taft's administration chalked up an impressive list of accomplishments which progressives had favored." Justify this statement.

3. Show how each of the following contributed to Taft's unpopularity with the progressives: (a) Payne-Aldrich Tariff of 1909 and (b) Ballinger-Pinchot controversy.

4. (a) Explain the reasons for the revolt against "Uncle Joe" Cannon. (b) What were the results?

5. Indicate the parties, candidates, issues, and results of the election of 1912.

IDENTIFY: Department of Labor, Publicity Act, Sixteenth Amendment, "Bull Moose" Party, "New Nationalism"; 1913.

2 Opportunity for all is expanded under Wilson's "New Freedom" program

With his "New Freedom" program President Wilson hoped to restore to the people that equality of opportunity that they had enjoyed when the frontier was still open to settlers. Wilson believed that this equality of opportunity had for the most part disappeared. He believed that it had been destroyed by the closing of the frontier, by great corporations, and by the often corrupt alliance between government and business.

Wilson pleads for the "New Freedom." When President Wilson took office, he at once recommended to Congress a positive program for realizing his idea of the public welfare. Opposed by pressure groups and lobbies representing special business interests, in public addresses and in written statements he used all his oratorical skills to appeal to the people for support.

The legislation that took shape and was enacted during Wilson's first administration did not fully realize the President's ideal of economic freedom and equality for the common man. But it went fairly far in that direction.

Tariff reform. Like the majority of Democrats, Wilson held that high protective tariffs were "the mother of trusts." Such tariffs, he believed, gave special favors to big business by excluding from the country products which foreign manufacturers could make and market more cheaply. It was also true, of course, that tariffs protected jobs and helped workers maintain higher wages than European workers received.

In an effort to check the trend toward monopoly and reduce the cost of living, the Wilson administration pushed through Congress the Underwood Tariff Act of 1913. This act did not establish free trade,° but it went further to-

•••

° *free trade:* the exchange of goods between countries unhampered by regulations or high tariffs aimed to keep out foreign goods.

563

Wilson's "The New Freedom" (1913):
EXCERPT

$\mathbb{J}$ take my stand absolutely, where every progressive ought to take his stand, on the proposition that private monopoly is indefensible. And there I will fight my battle ... I am for big business, and I am against trusts. Any man who can survive by his brains, any man who can put the others out of the business by making the thing cheaper to the consumer at the same time that he is increasing its intrinsic value and quality, I take off my hat to, and I say: "You are the man who can build up the United States, and I wish there were more of you" ...

---

ward reducing tariffs than any acts adopted in more than fifty years. It lowered duties on almost a thousand items, including cotton and woolen goods, iron, steel, coal, wood, agricultural implements, and many agricultural products. The average of all duties was reduced from 41 to 29 per cent.

To make up for the revenue thus lost, the Underwood Tariff Act took advantage of the recently ratified Sixteenth Amendment to the Constitution by including a section providing for an income tax. The new law provided for a "graduated" tax ranging from 1 to 6 per cent on incomes over $3000 per year.

The Underwood Tariff was carried through against strong opposition. Its opponents claimed it would seriously harm American business. Whether these claims were justified, however, remained an unanswered question, for in 1914 war broke out in Europe and many of the normal trade relations were shattered. During World War I American business boomed, and American manufacturers did not need a tariff to protect them from foreign competition.

But the Underwood Tariff did answer the widespread cry for tariff reform. Moreover, in its income tax provision, it laid down the principle that those with more income must bear a heavier share of the expenses of government. This rule is sometimes called the "ability-to-pay" principle of taxation.

Demand for a new banking system. The second important achievement of Wilson's "New Freedom" administration was in the field of money and banking. Almost everyone was dissatisfied in some degree with the existing banking system. Many reforms were proposed. The major struggle, however, took place between those who favored a strongly centralized banking system under private control, and those who wished the government to exercise a greater amount of regulation over money and banking.

In general, the more conservative business groups wanted greater private centralization of the existing banking system. They argued that this centralization would enable the stronger banks to help the less favored banks during times of financial crisis.

On the other side were the Bryan Democrats and the progressive Republicans. They believed that the existing banking system was already too much under the control of the great bankers and financiers—the "money trust." They wanted the government, not private bankers, to have control over the banking system. This control, they argued, would enable the government to regulate the amount of currency in circulation at any given time and in this way help to stabilize prices.

The Federal Reserve System. The Federal Reserve Act of 1913 was a compromise between these two proposals. It provided for the establishment of 12 Federal Reserve districts, each with a Federal Reserve Bank. The operations of these district banks were to be supervised and co-ordinated by a Federal Reserve Board located in Washington, D.C. All national banks were to be members of a Federal Reserve Bank, and state banks meeting certain requirements were invited to join.

The Federal Reserve Banks were strictly "bankers' banks," established to provide services only for their member banks, not for business concerns or private citizens. In times of crisis, when weak banks were on the point of failing, the Federal Reserve Banks could transfer money reserves and thus help to prevent failure and the loss of people's savings.

The Federal Reserve System also provided a more "elastic" currency. At certain times in the year money is in especially great demand. Farmers, for example, need money most in the spring, when seed, fertilizer, and equipment must be bought, and in the fall, when they must pay for harvesting. Unless the amount of money in circulation can be increased in times of money shortage, money will become scarce and the interest rate on loans will rise. But if the amount of money can be temporarily increased during the times of greatest need, bank loans can be made at reasonable interest rates.

The Federal Reserve System makes it possible to put more money into circulation or to withdraw some from circulation according to the needs of the time. It provides this elastic currency by controlling the amount of lending that member banks can do.

One method of control works as follows: When a man borrows money from the bank, he signs a note promising to pay back the loan. The Federal Reserve Banks are authorized to *rediscount* these "promissory notes." That is, the Federal Reserve Banks are authorized to take the notes from the member banks and to release for each note received a certain amount of currency. When the borrower repays his loan to the member bank, and the bank repays its loan to the Federal Reserve Bank, the promissory note is returned, and the Federal Reserve currency is withdrawn from circulation. Thus, as people need money and borrow from the banks, the supply of currency expands. When the need is less great and fewer loans are being made, the supply of currency decreases.

Antitrust laws strengthened. The third great achievement of Wilson's "New Freedom" program was its effort to strengthen the antitrust laws. The Clayton Antitrust Act of 1914 helped to put teeth in the older Sherman Antitrust Act.

The Clayton Act was aimed at business practices that until then had not been illegal. (1) It prohibited business organizations from selling at lower prices to certain favored purchasers *if* such price discrimination helped to create a monopoly. (2) It prohibited "tying contracts"—that is, contracts requiring a purchaser to agree that he would not buy or sell the products of a competitor. (3) It declared interlocking directorates illegal in companies capitalized at $1,000,000 or more. (4) It prohibited corporations from acquiring the stock of another company *if* the purchase tended to create a monopoly.

The Clayton Act also attempted to protect the farmer and the wage earner. As you have seen (page 520), the Sherman Antitrust Act of 1890 had been used on a number of occasions against labor unions. The Clayton Act, on the other hand, specifically declared that "the labor of a human being is not a commodity or article of commerce. Nothing contained in the anti-trust laws shall be construed to forbid the existence and operation of labor, agricultural, or horticultural organizations . . . nor shall such organizations, or the members thereof, be held or construed to be illegal combinations or conspiracies in restraint of trade, under the anti-trust laws."

The Clayton Act also prohibited the granting of an injunction in a labor dispute *unless* the court decided that an injunction was necessary "to prevent irreparable injury to property." By no means least important, the act declared that strikes, peaceful picketing, and boycotts were legal under federal jurisdiction.

Organized labor hailed the Clayton Act as a great victory and sometimes referred to it as the wage earner's Magna Carta. From labor's point of view, it marked a long forward step. As you will see, however, the courts tended to in-

NOTHING IN THIS HAND!

INTERLOCKING DIRECTOR

$

NOTHING IN THIS HAND!

$

■ A famous cartoonist, Fitzpatrick, drew this sleight-of-hand performance in 1914 to dramatize the problems government faced in trying to regulate corporations with interlocking directorates.

terpret the act in such a way that the injunction continued to be used as a major weapon against strikes.

The Federal Trade Commission. The Federal Trade Commission, created by Congress in 1914 as part of President Wilson's "New Freedom" program, was authorized to advise and regulate industries engaged in interstate and foreign trade. The act establishing the commission stated that it should be a bipartisan body of five members.

The act authorized the commission (1) to require annual and special reports from corporations; (2) to investigate the business activities of persons and corporations (except banks and transportation companies, both of which were covered by other laws); (3) to publish reports on its findings; and (4) to order corporations to stop unfair methods of competition that were declared illegal by the act. Among the unfair practices investigated by the com-

mission were mislabeling, adulteration of products, and false claims to patents. If a corporation refused to obey an order to "cease and desist" such practices, the commission could appeal to the courts for aid in enforcing the ruling. But the law protected the corporation by providing that it could appeal to the courts if it considered the "cease and desist" order to be unfair.

The Federal Trade Commission was intended to prevent the growth of monopolies. It was also hoped that the commission would help to bring about a better understanding between big business and the government.

Other "New Freedom" measures. The tariff, money and banking, regulation of trusts—these were the major problems tackled by Congress during Wilson's first administration. Much more reform legislation might have been adopted if the outbreak of war in Europe in the summer of 1914 had not interrupted the "New Freedom" program. Even so, Congress found time to pass several other important measures.

In 1914 Congress adopted the Smith-Lever Act. Among other things, this act provided federal funds for rural education. The educational programs were to be carried on by the Department of Agriculture in co-operation with the land-grant colleges. Federal grants of money were to be matched by similar grants from the states receiving this aid.

Three years later, in 1917, just before the United States entered World War I, Congress adopted the Smith-Hughes Act. This additional measure provided federal funds for vocational education in both rural and urban areas of the country. It established a Federal Board for Vocational Education. As in the case of the earlier Smith-Lever Act, federal grants were to be matched by grants from the states receiving this aid. You will learn more about these acts in Chapter 29.

The Federal Farm Loan Act of 1916 made it easier for farmers to borrow money. This act divided the country into 12 agricultural districts. For each district, it established a Farm Loan Bank from which the farmers could secure mortgages at rates lower than those available at regular banks.

The Adamson Act, also adopted in 1916, provided that workers on railroads operating in interstate commerce were to receive the same pay for an 8-hour day as they had been receiving for a 10-hour day. This act, at Wilson's urging, was adopted by Congress in a successful effort to prevent a nationwide railway strike. Since at this time the United States was moving rapidly toward entry into World War I, such a strike would have been disastrous. President Wilson and the Democratic administration were sharply criticized for what their opponents called a "surrender" to labor, and the law itself was challenged in the courts. In 1917, however, the Supreme Court upheld its constitutionality.

Presidential candidates in 1916. By 1916 President Wilson had established himself as a vigorous, forceful leader. The delegates to the Democratic National Convention in St. Louis pointed with pride to his solid list of achievements and enthusiastically renominated him by acclamation for a second term.

The Republicans, meeting in Chicago, chose Supreme Court Justice Charles Evans Hughes, former governor of New York, as their standard bearer. The Progressive Party, also meeting in Chicago, nominated Theodore Roosevelt. But Roosevelt, unwilling to split the Republican vote again, refused the nomination and threw his support to Hughes. The Progressive Party, deprived of Roosevelt, decided not to nominate another candidate. As a result, the Republicans, once more united, entered the campaign hopeful of victory.

Wilson wins the election. During the campaign Hughes toured the country, criticizing the Democrats for the Underwood Tariff and for their conduct of foreign affairs. Wilson, on the other hand, contented himself with delivering a number of speeches from the front porch of his summer home in New Jersey. Speakers for the Democratic Party, adopting the slogan "He kept us out of war," piled up an impressive following, especially in the Middle West.

The election itself turned out to be one of the closest in American history. Early in the morning after the election, the Democrats conceded that Hughes had won. But as the votes from the West began to pour in, the tide began to turn, and the final count from California clinched the victory for Wilson. The final electoral vote was 277 for Wilson, 254 for Hughes. California proved to be the decisive state—and the Democrats won in California by a margin of only 3773 popular votes! And yet, despite the closeness of the vote, Wilson entered the White House with the knowledge that he had won against a united Republican Party, as had not been true in the election of 1912. Even more reassuring, he had collected nearly 600,000 more popular votes than Hughes.

It was not, however, the "New Freedom" program that occupied the President during his second administration. A month after he took the oath of office on March 4, 1917, as you will see later, the United States became involved in World War I.

⌐ **SECTION SURVEY**

1. In what two ways was the Underwood Tariff a progressive measure?
2. Show how the Federal Reserve Act was a compromise between those who favored a privately controlled, centralized banking system and those who favored greater government regulation over banking.
3. (a) Describe three ways in which the Clayton Antitrust Act of 1914 "put teeth in the older Sherman Antitrust Act." (b) Why did the wage earners regard this law as the Magna Carta of labor?
4. Discuss the powers of the Federal Trade Commission in curbing the growth of monopolies.
5. Indicate the parties, candidates, issues, and results of the election of 1916.
IDENTIFY: "New Freedom," promissory note, rediscount, Federal Farm Loan Act, Adamson Act; 1913, 1916.

Points to Discuss: 1. (a) Compare and contrast the personalities and theories of Taft and Roosevelt. (b) Explain why Taft, despite his progressive achievements, was considered a conservative.

2. What effect did Taft's Presidency have on the Bull Moose candidacy of Roosevelt?

3. Theodore Roosevelt, Taft, and Wilson all had to grapple with the role of government in the new industrial age. Compare the respective views of the role of government as held by Roosevelt and Wilson.

4. Discuss the successes and failures of the progressive reformers in their efforts to make government more democratic and more responsive to the people's needs.

5. In what sense was the Federal Reserve Act of 1913 a progressive victory?

6. Evaluate the results of Wilson's "New Freedom" program as an effort to restore greater economic competition.

7. Compare Theodore Roosevelt's "square deal" and Woodrow Wilson's "New Freedom" in their (a) aims, (b) legislative accomplishments, and (c) influence in history.

Using Charts: 1. Consulting the Business Activity chart (pages 850–59), compare the 1919 depression with other depressions of the twentieth century.

2. Refer to chart 4 on page 841, and (a) compare the Underwood Tariff with the Payne-Aldrich Tariff, and (b) explain the difference in import duties.

3. Using chart 1 on page 836, (a) compare railroad mileage in 1880 with that in 1920, and explain the reason for the increase. (b) What conclusions can you draw for the period 1890–1920 from charts 2 and 3 on page 836?

Consulting the Sources: See Commager, *Documents,* Nos. 380 and 389, and compare the ideas of T. Roosevelt on the New Nationalism with those in Wilson's First Inaugural.

■ TRACING THE MAIN IDEAS

In 1909, when William Howard Taft entered the White House, the Progressive movement was in full swing. His predecessor, Theodore Roosevelt, had captured the imagination of the American people and won their support for his "square deal." Taft was less forceful, less imaginative, much more conservative than "Teddy" Roosevelt. Nevertheless, during his administration Congress adopted a number of significant reform measures. But Taft did not move rapidly enough or far enough to please the progressive wing of his party, and in the election of 1912 the Republicans split, with the progressives voting for Roosevelt, and the conservatives voting for Taft. The Republicans lost the election, and Woodrow Wilson, a Democrat, became President.

President Wilson breathed new life into the Progressive movement. He shared the belief of many leaders in both parties that the rise of giant industries threatened to destroy the equality of opportunity that had for so long been an important part of the American way of life. He agreed with millions of Americans that the government had to assume the responsibility for safeguarding free enterprise and democracy.

In his "New Freedom" program President Wilson undertook to restore a larger measure of competition to the economic life of the country. He undertook to provide rules that would insure greater equality of opportunity for the American people as a whole.

Both the "New Freedom" and the earlier "square deal" were attempts by America's leaders, Democratic and Republican, to come to grips with the problems created by the transformation of the United States from an agricultural country to one of the leading industrial powers of the world.

"The Big Change" Begins in American Ways of Life

CHANGING WAYS

OF AMERICAN LIFE

As the United States approached the middle of the twentieth century, Frederick Lewis Allen wrote a book reviewing and interpreting fifty years of American history. He called his book *The Big Change,* and added the subtitle, *America Transforms Itself, 1900–1950.* Note that Allen did not say "America *was* transformed," but chose instead to emphasize that Americans were themselves responsible in large part for "the big change."

The transformation, as Allen saw it, was "in the character and quality of American life by reason of what might be called the democratization of our economic system, or the adjustment of capitalism to democratic ends." It was, he went on to say, "the way in which an incredible expansion of industrial and business activity, combined with a varied series of political, social, and economic forces, has altered the American standard of living and with it the aver-

age American's way of thinking and his status as a citizen."

In 1900 the United States was in full process of passing from a predominantly rural economy to a predominantly industrial economy. Older ways of life were being replaced by new. Americans as a whole—business leaders, politicians, farmers, wage earners, the general public—were struggling to adjust their daily lives and their institutions to the changing ways and changing times. There was little in past experience to help them with this adjustment, for the Industrial Revolution was creating a world the like of which no man had ever seen or even dreamed of. The new world was one of crowded cities, of new sources of power, of machines, of mass production. It was a world of feverish activity, of great inequalities of wealth, of an increasingly productive economy that each year was providing more and more people with more food, more clothing, more of the necessities and luxuries of life.

During the years from 1900 to 1920, a growing number of Americans, including businessmen, became increasingly aware of the need for modifying some of the attitudes and practices carried over from the early days of the Industrial Revolution. In 1920 there were still many deep shadows in the American scene. Large and difficult problems remained unsolved. But "the big change" was already beginning to have an important influence on the direction of American life.

569

1. New inventions and new ideas revolutionize American industry.
2. The life of the farmer improves in the twentieth century.
3. Conditions improve for industrial workers as productivity rises.

1 New inventions and new ideas revolutionize American industry

In 1900 America was still in the horse-and-buggy age. But that age would not last much longer. Great changes were transforming the country, and even greater changes lay immediately ahead.

Older ways of living. At the opening of the twentieth century, one could still ride in horse-drawn streetcars; hitching posts and watering troughs were common sights; livery stables and blacksmith shops were centers of activity in every town; at nightfall the lamplighter made his rounds, lighting gas lamps that still furnished illumination for most American streets.

It is easier, perhaps, to picture the America of 1900 if you realize the things that people did not have and did not know. At that time there were no jazz bands, no beauty parlors, no income tax. No one had heard of vitamins, insulin, or penicillin. Women could vote in only four states—Wyoming, Colorado, Utah, and Idaho. Parcel post did not exist. Neither did boy scouts nor 4-H clubs. There were no motion pictures, radios, or airplanes. Automobiles were still curiosities; people often called them "horseless carriages," and referred to their drivers as "engineers."

Signs of change. And yet, in 1900, Americans stood on the threshold of a new way of life. Indeed, much of the new was already apparent. By 1900 railroad builders had constructed 192,566 miles of track. All the great trunk lines had been built across the continent. Day and night, long lines of freight cars rumbled across the country loaded with products of America's farm lands, mines,

mills, and factories. New railroad lines were being constructed—by 1920 the nation's railroad mileage would reach its high mark of 260,000 miles of track.

Automobiles and highways. While railroad builders were feverishly engaged in building their network of steel rails, a number of inventors in Europe and America were experimenting with a new source of power—the "internal combustion" engine, in which the fuel, usually gasoline, was converted into a vapor and exploded within the engine walls. Among the American experimenters were Charles E. Duryea, George B. Selden, Elwood Haynes, Alexander Winton, and Henry Ford. These men and others developed the gasoline engine.

By 1900 "horseless carriages" that often surprised pedestrians and frightened horses were beginning to appear on the road. During the early years of its history, the automobile remained a plaything for wealthy people. Mass production soon lowered costs, however, bringing the automobile within reach of people with modest incomes. Whereas in 1900 there were only 8000 automobiles in the United States, by 1920 there were 1,107,639 trucks and 8,131,522 passenger cars on the roads and highways. The internal combustion engine had given the nation a new and major means of transportation.

The development of the automobile depended, of course, upon a number of other inventions and developments. One was the discovery by Charles Goodyear of the process for vulcanizing, or hardening, rubber, for which he had obtained his first patent in 1844, and upon which the development of the rubber industry was based. Other inventions led to improvements in the process of refining petroleum into gasoline, and in the development of batteries, generators, and other electrical devices.

The development of the automobile also depended upon—and helped to stimulate—the construction of paved roads. In 1904, for example, there was a total of 2,151,570 miles of rural roads in the United States. Nearly all of these roads were little better than dirt lanes, although some were "surfaced" with gravel, clay, or crushed oyster shells. By 1924, however, 472,000 miles of rural highways had paved surfaces. By 1924 older roads were being widened, graded, and paved at the rate of about 40,-000 miles a year, at an annual cost of one billion dollars.

The airplane. While engineers were building a network of paved roads across the country, other men were experimenting with another revolutionary method of transportation. At the beginning of the twentieth century, a number of inventors, including Samuel P. Langley, were experimenting with powered flight. But it was the Wright brothers, Orville and Wilbur, who on December 17, 1903, first succeeded. The first flight lasted for only about 120 feet. At the time, the achievement did not attract much attention. Within a few years, however, the first crude flying machines were being replaced by more effective planes, and men were making longer and longer flights. In 1919 a Navy seaplane crossed the Atlantic by way of the Azores, and two English fliers, John Alcock and A. W. Brown, flew nonstop from Newfoundland to Ireland.

Wired and wireless communications. Equally revolutionary were the developments in communications during the opening years of the twentieth century. Europeans and Americans were only beginning to get used to the idea of the telephone when, in 1895, a twenty-one-year-old Italian inventor, Guglielmo Marconi (goo-LYEL-moh mahr-KOH-nee), gave the first demonstration of wireless telegraphy. Eight years later, from a station on the sand dunes of Cape Cod, Massachusetts, he transmitted an entire message across the ocean to England and received a reply.

Within a few years, wireless equipment had been installed on all large vessels, and wireless messages were being sent over land and sea by powerful transmitters. Meanwhile, scientists and engineers were experimenting with the transmission of the spoken word through

Model-T Ford

DEVIL WAGONS

Until about 1905 automobiles were luxuries that only wealthy people could afford, and expensive toys for mechanically minded men. To the average person they were public nuisances, noisy contraptions that frightened horses and sometimes caused accidents. Some people called them "devil wagons." Others joked about their undependability. Typical of the jokes was this one that appeared in *Life* Magazine in 1904:

"Do you enjoy your automobile?"

"Yes, I enjoy my automobile immensely."

"But I never see you out."

"Oh, I haven't got that far yet. I am just learning to make my own repairs."

the air, as distinguished from the transmission merely of signals. But it was not until the 1920's that commercial radio broadcasting became a reality.

One of the most significant inventions in the field of communications was the three-element vacuum tube, invented by Lee De Forest in 1906. The telegraph and the telephone, as well as wireless communication, benefited from this improved vacuum tube, which could be used to relay telegraph and telephone impulses over long distances. By 1915 New York and San Francisco were linked by telephone.

The motion picture. Thomas Armat's invention of the motion picture projector, in 1895, made possible the development of a new method of communication as well as a new form of recreation.

MAN CANNOT FLY   *The Wrights' plan*

On October 22, 1903, the following prediction appeared in the *Independent*, a New York weekly periodical. The writer, Simon Newcomb, was an astronomer, head of the Nautical Almanac Office, United States Naval Observatory.

"The example of the bird does not prove that man can fly," he wrote. "There are many problems which have fascinated mankind since civilization began, which we have made little or no advance in solving.... May not our mechanicians ... be ultimately forced to admit that aerial flight is one of that great class of problems with which man can never cope, and give up all attempts to grapple with it? ... Imagine the proud possessor of the aeroplane darting through the air at a speed of several hundred feet per second! It is the speed alone that sustains him. How is he ever going to stop? ... The construction of an aerial vehicle which could carry even a single man from place to place at pleasure requires the discovery of some new metal or some new force. Even with such a discovery we could not expect one to do more than carry its owner."

On December 17, two months later, the Wright brothers made their first successful powered flight at Kitty Hawk, North Carolina.

In the early days, when films ran only a few minutes, the motion picture was used as a novelty feature of vaudeville programs. Before long, however, it began to achieve importance as a completely new and distinct form of entertainment. In 1903 a film called *The Great Train Robbery* really demonstrated the possibilities of the motion picture. This pioneer "picture story" set the pace. Within a few years directors and producers, among them D. W. Griffith, who won fame in 1914 for his film *The Birth of a Nation,* were proving to ever larger audiences that the motion picture could do a great deal that was impossible on the stage. Night after night people crowded into the "nickelodeons," as the early motion picture theaters were called, and for the usual admission of five cents watched such popular stars as Mary Pickford, Douglas Fairbanks, and Charlie Chaplin.

New methods of production. The new world that was coming into being in the opening years of the twentieth century depended upon the development of an old source of power, steam, and the even faster development of new sources of power—oil and electricity. Between 1900 and 1920 the production of oil in the United States jumped from 63 million barrels annually to about 443 million barrels. By 1914 nearly one third of the nation's factory machines were being driven by electricity, and the use of electric power was rapidly increasing. High-voltage transmission lines were carrying the pulsing energy of dynamos —steam-driven or water-driven—to widely scattered cities. Smaller transmission lines, or "feeders," were carrying electricity to small towns and villages and even to some isolated farms.

Productivity of America's factories was greatly increased, not only by the development of new sources of power, but also by the invention of the *assembly line.* On an assembly line, individual parts were not taken to a central location, but were moved up in orderly succession to stations along a slowly moving track, or "conveyer belt." At each station, workers added a new part to the product on the track. Finally, a steady succession of finished products came off the end of the assembly line. Developed in the early 1900's by Henry Ford in the manufacture of automobiles, by the time of World War I the assembly line was becoming an essential element of America's developing industrial economy.

Increasing efficiency. *Efficiency engineering* also helped to increase the productivity of America's factories. Credit for originating this development is usually given to Frederick W. Taylor.

Taylor became interested in the problem of securing greater efficiency from machines and from the men who operated the machines. In the course of his studies of this problem, he developed "time-and-motion" analyses of plant operation. With a stop watch in his hand, Taylor carefully watched a worker operating a machine and counted the number of motions the worker made to complete a particular operation. Then he worked out ways to reduce the number of movements of the worker's hands and feet. Sometimes the worker was trained to use his hands and feet more effectively. Sometimes the machine itself was redesigned, and its controls were placed in more convenient locations.

The development of Taylor's methods made great economies possible in every stage of mass production. Each process in the mechanized industrial plant was simplified and speeded up along the assembly line. Each worker performed a highly specialized task, working with the least possible effort and producing the maximum output.

The "Ford Idea." Henry Ford had made a major contribution to American industry by pioneering in the development of the assembly line. But he made what was perhaps an even more fundamental contribution by introducing a revolutionary theory of wages.

On January 5, 1914, Ford announced that he was nearly doubling the wages of the workers in his plants. Beginning immediately, he said that his 13,000 employees would receive a minimum wage of $5 for an 8-hour day. This announcement swept almost all other news off the front pages of America's newspapers. It was "a bolt out of the blue sky," the New York *Sun* declared, "flashing its way across the continent and far beyond, something unheard of in the history of business." The New York *Herald* called it "an epoch in the world's industrial history."

Ford was both warmly applauded and sharply criticized for his action. But the criticism did not prevent the "Ford idea" from spreading to other industries. Rising wages gave American workers greater purchasing power. They were then able to buy more and more of the products of America's expanding industry. As the years passed, more and more people came to understand that mass production and mass purchasing power are mutually interdependent. This understanding was an essential part of what Frederick Lewis Allen called "the big change" that was transforming America in the opening years of the twentieth century.

■ In this excerpt from the New York *Sun*, Ford's new plan was described as "profit sharing," but in effect it raised wages and shortened hours.

$10,000,000 TO MEN OF FORD MOTOR CO.

Employees Will Share Profits Annually Under Plan Devised by Ford.

$5 A DAY LOWEST WAGE

Hours Reduced From 9 to 8— Men Fight at Factory for Employment.

1

"In 1900 America was still in the horse-and-buggy stage." Explain this statement.

2. Describe three advances in transportation which helped to create modern America.

3. Show how De Forest and Marconi contributed to the revolution in communication.

4. Discuss two major contributions made by Henry Ford to our economic system.

IDENTIFY: vulcanizing rubber, nickelodeons, assembly line, efficiency engineering; Goodyear, Langley, Wright brothers, Armat, Taylor; 1844, 1903, 1906.

2 The life of the farmer improves in the twentieth century

The life of the farmer, like the lives of other Americans, was being transformed during the years between 1900 and 1920.

Growing demand for farm produce. One of the most significant ·developments in the opening years of the 1900's was the startling growth of the urban population. Between 1900 and 1920 the urban population increased by about 24,000,000, the rural population by only about 6,000,000. Between 1900 and 1920 urban dwellers increased from about 40 per cent of the total population to more than 50 per cent. Whereas in 1900 there were only 832 communities of 2500 to 5000 persons, by 1920 the number had jumped to 1255, and many of the larger cities had doubled, tripled, and quadrupled in size.

The swelling urban population came in part from the nation's farms as farm youths in growing numbers left home to seek their fortunes in the cities. But it came in much larger part from the more than 14,000,000 immigrants who poured into the United States between 1900 and 1920. Regardless of the source, however, the growing urban population meant more mouths to feed and a growing demand for farm products.

Rising prices and more money. The rapidly growing demand for farm products enabled the farmer to charge higher prices. Indeed, between 1900 and 1920 farm prices increased threefold.

"Cheaper" money, as well as the increased demand for farm products, helped to raise prices. In spite of the fact that the Republicans had firmly planted the financial system on the gold standard, new discoveries of gold in the Klondike region of Canada, and in Alaska, in 1897, and the invention of more efficient methods of extracting gold from ore greatly increased the supply of the precious metal. As the supply of gold increased, the value of gold fell. And as the value of gold fell—making money "cheaper"—the prices of all other products rose.

Moreover, the value of farm lands increased, rising on the average fourfold between 1900 and 1920. As a result, many farmers were able to sell their surplus acreage for a handsome profit and either retire or buy new farm machines.

Laborsaving machines. Although laborsaving machines were being used in growing numbers even before the War Between the States, the real Agricultural Revolution—from hand tools to power-driven machines—came after 1900. According to the census records, in 1870 the total value of all farm implements and machinery in the United States amounted to $271,000,000. By 1900 the figure had risen to $750,000,000; by 1910 to $1,265,000,000; by 1920 to $3,595,000,000.

Whereas in 1900 farmers were still carting their produce to market in wagons, by 1920 they were using trucks in rapidly growing numbers. Census figures show that in 1910 farmers spent $32,000,000 for motor vehicles; in 1920, $392,000,000.

Even more revealing as a measure of the machine age was the use of tractors. In 1910 there were only 1000 tractors on American farms; by 1920 there were 246,000.

Gasoline and electricity—these new sources of power were revolutionizing rural as well as urban life in the opening years of the twentieth century. Power-driven machinery—pumps, saws, plows, harrows, seeders, harvesters, milking machines, trucks, and tractors —began to lift the burden of labor from the farmer and made it possible for him to produce far more products with much less toil.

The growth of scientific agriculture. Growth of scientific knowledge, as well as power-driven machinery, helped to revolutionize farming. Chemists discovered new secrets of the soil, enabling farmers to check soil exhaustion and replenish worn-out land with new and cheap fertilizers and better methods of cultivation. Biologists improved the life span and the productivity of livestock, plants, grains, and fruits. Bacteriologists discovered ways to check blights and diseases in both the plant and the animal worlds.

Many scientists devoted their lives to the study of agricultural problems. They began to develop new grains and fruits resistant to disease and better adapted to varying climatic conditions. One of their most important discoveries was that of vitamins.

Federal aid to farmers. Much of the new research and experimentation was carried on by the federal government or in state institutions created with the aid of federal grants. As you have seen (page 397), in 1862 a Republican Congress adopted three measures of great importance for farmers: (1) it enacted the Homestead Act, granting farmers free land; (2) it passed the Morrill Act, granting land to the states for the establishment of so-called "land grant" colleges of agriculture and mechanical arts, thus launching the United States upon a vast program of agricultural and industrial education; and (3) it created the Department of Agriculture.

In later years the federal government greatly expanded this program of aid to farmers. The Hatch Act of 1887, for example, provided money for agricultural experiment stations and farms in each state. The Smith-Lever Act of 1914 pro-

■ A laboratory worker of the Bureau of Plant Industry (about 1905) is shown helping in the research that has aided American farming.

vided additional money for the employment of "county extension agents" who were to travel among the farmers of each county carrying to them "useful and practical information on subjects relating to agriculture and home economics." The Smith-Hughes Act of 1917 provided money for the support of vocational education in the public schools, including education in agriculture, industries, trade, home economics, and the training of teachers.

Farmers become businessmen. By the opening years of the 1900's, the farmer had become an important part of the nation's industrial economy. To be sure, on thousands of small farms tucked away in mountain valleys and in areas remote from railroads and paved highways, farm families lived much as their forefathers had lived a hundred years earlier. But these more or less self-sufficient farms were exceptions. Most of the nation's farm produce was raised by

NATIONAL CATHOLIC

WELFARE CONFERENCE

The new century would bring several new things which would change the appearance of the Catholic Church in the United States. The year 1908 saw this onetime missionary church removed by Pope Pius X from the jurisdiction of the *Congregation de Propaganda Fide*. Although this change was more symbolic than anything like a fundamental change in organization, it was a mark of maturity. Since that time American Catholics have begun themselves to support and supply overseas missioners. The first American missionary society, the Maryknoll Fathers, was founded in 1911.

The Catholic population was about twelve million Americans in 1900, less than a third of what it is today. Catholics were then about one sixth of all the people, and were still mainly thought of as immigrants. Today, Catholics are about one fifth of the population, and the immigrant stamp has disappeared.

Perhaps the most significant organization for the Catholic Church's mature position in America derived from a committee which was first set up to take care of relief work in World War I, and then was continued for peacetime affairs. The National Catholic War Council, a body which was presided over by a committee of the bishops, supported chaplains and helped the troops with all kinds of social services. It became, after the war, the National Catholic Welfare Conference. It has functioned in Washington, D.C., ever since, to provide an information service, promote social action, direct lay activities the bishops wish to encourage, and give aid and support to many activities of international importance, like refugee relief, that have required attention. Under a committee of ten bishops, the N.C.W.C. may act for the Church in America, subject to the approval by the entire hierarchy of what it does.

farmers who, whether they liked it or not, had become businessmen.

The commercial farmer specialized in one or two or three crops, or in dairy farming, or in raising livestock. He needed money, or capital, to buy his machinery and to hire labor. He found it necessary to keep careful accounts and to pay the keenest attention to market conditions. He was, in brief, one part of an abstract thing known as the "nation's economy." When the economy prospered, the farmer could hope to prosper; when the economy went into a depression, the farmer was certain to suffer.

Changing ways of living. Equally revolutionary was the impact of the new industrial age on the everyday lives of farm families. By the twentieth century loneliness and social isolation were becoming memories to an increasing number of the nation's farmers. The slender thread of telephone wires was spinning a net of communications across the countryside. The automobile—notably, Henry Ford's "Tin Lizzie"—was bringing the farm closer to the town and the city. Whereas in 1870 or even in 1900 a five-mile drive to town meant a one- or two-hour trip behind "Old Dobbin," by 1920 the same trip could be made in the family car in a matter of half an hour or less. This meant more trips to town, often for an evening at the new motion pictures.

With better communications and transportation and with more money in their pockets, farmers could provide better education for their children and better living conditions for their families. The one-room school continued to dominate the rural educational scene, but more and more farm children began to come from miles around to enjoy the advantages of "consolidated schools," and many were able to continue their education at the state university. For farm children, no less than for their fathers and mothers, life "down on the farm" in the opening years of the 1900's was far more comfortable and interesting than it had ever been before.

1. Give two reasons why farm prices increased threefold between 1900 and 1920.

2. Show how each of the following helped the farmer to produce more with less toil: (a) farm machinery, (b) trucks, (c) tractors, (d) gasoline, and (e) electricity.

3. Describe four ways in which scientific research helped to revolutionize farming.

4. Discuss four ways in which the federal government aided farmers.

IDENTIFY: Hatch Act, Smith-Lever Act, Smith-Hughes Act, "Tin Lizzie," "consolidated schools."

3 Conditions improve for industrial workers as productivity rises

For the industrial worker as well as for the farmer, conditions improved considerably during the opening years of the twentieth century. In the first place, as you have seen, wage earners benefited from the fast-increasing productivity of America's economic system. In the second place, through organization the wage earners were beginning to gain enough strength to exert real influence on state legislatures and on Congress. In the third place, a growing number of Americans, including many industrialists, were beginning to realize that the industrial age had raised numerous problems for a democratic society, problems that had to be solved if democracy itself was to survive. In the fourth place, through articles appearing in popular magazines and in the daily newspapers, the public in general was becoming increasingly aware of the need for eliminating many of the wage earners' grievances.

Early social legislation. In an effort to improve the conditions of the wage earner, legislators both in Europe and in the United States began to pass laws commonly referred to as "social legislation." These laws mainly were passed by the northern and western states; the South, with its newer industrial development and its special problems, did little during this period to promote the welfare of workers through state laws.

In general, the first state laws limited hours of work and improved working conditions. As early as 1879 Massachusetts adopted a measure prohibiting women and children from working more than 60 hours a week. Oregon enacted a similar law in 1903, and other states followed these examples.

Meanwhile, New York state initiated a series of laws protecting workers as well as consumers. One law, for example, passed in 1882, prohibited the making of cigars under unsanitary conditions in tenement houses or elsewhere.

The recognition that certain types of work involved special risk led to the passage of a Utah law in 1896 limiting the working day of miners to 8 hours. New York in 1910 broke new ground in passing the first important state law to compensate workers for accidents that took place on the job.

In 1912 Massachusetts set a precedent by passing the first "minimum-wage law." The Massachusetts act established a minimum-wage rate below which employers could not ask a wage earner to work. These early laws represented a new approach to the problems of the wage earners in the emerging industrial society.

Early objections of the Supreme Court. Much of the early social legislation was declared unconstitutional by the Supreme Court. The chief objection of the Court was that such laws deprived owners of the property rights guaranteed them by the Constitution. The Court argued that a law limiting a man's control over his business, including his policies of employment, actually deprived him of part of his property without the "due process of law" guaranteed in the Fifth and Fourteenth Amendments.

The Supreme Court also objected to social legislation on the ground that it violated an individual's right to enter

■ In this final stage of an early Ford assembly line, bodies are being lowered onto frames to be bolted down and driven away. As assembly line techniques were perfected, a problem for owners and workers arose from the monotonous nature of the simple, repetitive work.

into any contract he wished. According to the Court, when a worker accepted employment and an employer agreed to pay him, a "contract" had been made even though the terms were not written down. It was the individual worker's "right" and the individual owner's "right" to decide, for example, whether the working day should be 8, 10, 12, or 14 hours. The Constitution guaranteed both workers and owners this "right." Following this "freedom-of-contract" line of reasoning, the Supreme Court, in the case of *Lochner v. New York* (1905), declared unconstitutional a New York law which had fixed a maximum working day of 10 hours for the bakers of that state.

Changing attitude of the Court. Many people objected that such an interpretation of the Constitution was unjust to labor. These people pointed out that it was unrealistic to assume that the individual worker could actually bargain with a corporation that employed thousands of men. They insisted that the Court's interpretation of the right to enter a contract really deprived every worker of any freedom to bargain with his employers.

Supreme Court justices, like many other American citizens, gradually began to change their attitude toward social legislation. The justices found other clauses in the Constitution that enabled states to exercise the so-called "police power" and to limit the individual's right to do as he pleased with his property. The Court began to maintain that the Constitution had reserved to each state the power to enact legislation necessary to protect the health and well-being of all its citizens. On these grounds the Supreme Court, in the case of *Muller v. Oregon* (1908), upheld an Oregon law that provided a 10-hour day for women, thereby setting a precedent for the approval of other social legislation.

Federal laws aid labor. The states rather than the federal government enacted most of the early social legislation.

But this situation was unsatisfactory as far as workers were concerned since certain states, especially in the South, lagged behind others in passing social legislation. This situation prompted organized labor and its champions to seek relief by federal laws.

Except for its Constitutional power "to promote the general welfare" and "to regulate interstate commerce," the federal government had little power to control labor relations. To be sure, the federal government did have the power —and used it—to control working conditions for its own employees. In 1868, as you have seen, Congress established an 8-hour day for laborers and mechanics employed by or in behalf of the United States government. In 1892 all federal government employees were given an 8-hour day.

Later, in 1908, acting under its power "to regulate interstate commerce," Congress enacted an Employers' Liability Act protecting railroad workers from bearing all the costs of accidents that occurred on the job. And in 1916, when the unions of the railroad workers, called the Railroad Brotherhoods, threatened to strike for an 8-hour day, Congress, as you have seen, passed the Adamson Act. This act gave railroad workers the same pay for an 8-hour day that they had been getting for a 10-hour day.

During President Wilson's administration Congress also granted labor's request that it be exempt from the charge of conspiring "to restrain trade." As you have seen, the Clayton Antitrust Act of 1914 helped to clear up some of the clauses in the Sherman Antitrust Act of 1890 to which labor had objected.

By the time World War I broke out in Europe in 1914, labor still had many grievances, and it was still far from its goals. But it could look back upon a number of reforms gained through half a century of struggle. And perhaps most important of all, the organized labor movement in general enjoyed a small but steadily growing measure of support from public opinion.

THE "WOBBLIES"

The Industrial Workers of the World (I.W.W.), sometimes called the "Wobblies," was a radical labor organization that took shape about 1905. In the preamble to its constitution, the I.W.W. proclaimed that "the working class and the employing class have nothing in common."

The I.W.W. hoped to build an industrial union—one that would include all workers, skilled and unskilled alike. Its ultimate goal was a federation of industries owned by the workers. To gain its ends, the I.W.W. proposed to use strikes, boycotts, and sabotage.

The Industrial Workers of the World never included more than 75 or 100 thousand members. Most of its strength was in the western mining and lumbering areas. By 1912, however, it was strong enough to lead strikes in the eastern textile industries.

The years prior to World War I saw this radical organization at its peak of growth. After the war it was reduced to only a feeble remnant.

SECTION SURVEY

1. Give four reasons why the conditions of wage earners began to improve in the early 1900's.

2. Describe the various kinds of social legislation passed by the states to aid workers.

3. On what grounds did the Supreme Court declare this early social legislation unconstitutional?

4. How did the Supreme Court later justify these state laws?

5. Show how the federal government improved working conditions for government employees and railroad workers.

IDENTIFY: freedom of contract, *Lochner v. New York*, police power, *Muller v. Oregon*, Employers' Liability Act, Railroad Brotherhoods.

Points to Discuss: 1. (a) Compare transportation facilities in 1900 with those in 1920. (b) Show how these changes transformed American life.

2. Describe the economic and social changes in farm life as a consequence of developments between 1900 and 1920.

3. Describe the developments during these years which made possible the tremendous economic growth of the United States and its high standard of living.

4. Give evidence of how the Industrial Revolution was reflected in the Agricultural Revolution of the twentieth century.

5. (a) Summarize the provisions of the most important laws of states in social legislation. (b) Discuss the shifting views of the Supreme Court on this legislation.

Using Charts: 1. Using the charts on pages 832–33, answer the following: (a) Which of the major advances in American industry during the period 1900–20 was most influential in transform-ing transportation and communication? (b) During this same period America is said to have acquired many mechanical slaves. Explain this statement by referring to the charts. (c) Explain the enormous increase in output per worker in the period 1900–20. (d) What was the output per worker in 1910? Your answer should be stated in precise terms. (e) Explain the increase in steel production 1870–1929.

2. Referring to chart 6 on page 845, give reasons for the rise in school enrollment in the period 1910–20.

3. Consulting the charts on pages 828–29, answer the following: (a) What was our farm population during the period 1900–20? (b) How many acres were being harvested by 1920? (c) Give evidence to show increasing farm production 1900–20.

Consulting the Sources: See Commager, *Documents,* Nos. 364 and 366, and contrast Court views in *Lochner v. New York* and in *Muller v. Oregon.*

■ TRACING THE MAIN IDEAS

During the years between 1900 and 1920 the United States completed the process of passing from a predominantly agricultural economy to a predominantly industrial economy. By 1920 the United States had become the most productive industrial nation on the face of the earth.

In 1900 Americans were still living in the horse-and-buggy age. It was, however, a dying age. Old ways were rapidly giving way to new. People living during the years between 1900 and 1920 saw the emergence of automobiles, airplanes, radio, motion pictures, the assembly line, and many other developments destined to transform older ways of living.

But the rapidly increasing productivity of the nation's economy and the steadily rising standard of living were only the most obvious signs of the new America that was coming into being.

Less obvious, but equally significant, were the changes that were beginning to take place in the thinking of many Americans. More and more people were beginning to modify some of the attitudes and practices that they had carried over from the early days of the Industrial Revolution. More and more people were beginning to realize that organized labor had an important role to play in the new industrial economy. Slowly but surely, Americans were beginning to take the first halting steps toward what Frederick Lewis Allen called "the adjustment of capitalism to democratic ends."

In 1920 the American people still had a long, hard road to travel. But although they had no way of knowing it, the road down which they were beginning to move would bring them by mid-century to the highest standard of living the world had ever seen.

Unit Survey (Reread "Tracing the Main Ideas," pages 557, 568, 580.)

OUTSTANDING EVENTS

1897 Dingley Tariff.
1898 South Dakota adopts initiative and referendum.
1900 McKinley re-elected President.
1901 McKinley is assassinated; Theodore Roosevelt becomes President.
1902 Newlands Reclamation Act.
1903 Department of Commerce and Labor is created.
1903 Elkins Act.
1903 Wisconsin adopts direct primary.
1904 Theodore Roosevelt re-elected President.
1904 Founding of the National Catholic Educational Association.
1906 Pure Food and Drug Act.
1906 Meat Inspection Act.
1906 Hepburn Act.
1907 Financial panic and depression.
1907 "Gentlemen's Agreement" with Japan.
1908 White House Conservation Conference.
1908 William H. Taft elected President.
1909 Payne-Aldrich Tariff.
1910 Mann-Elkins Act.
1910–11 Speaker of the House loses power.
1912 Woodrow Wilson elected President.
1913 Sixteenth Amendment ratified.
1913 Seventeenth Amendment ratified.
1913 Underwood Tariff.
1913 Federal Reserve Act.
1914 Federal Trade Commission is created.
1914 Clayton Antitrust Act.
1915 Birth of the second Ku Klux Klan.
1916 Adamson Act.
1916 Wilson re-elected President.
1917 Smith-Hughes Act.
1919 Publication of the Bishops' Program of Social Reconstruction; founding of National Catholic Welfare Conference.
1920 Nineteenth Amendment ratified.

THEN AND NOW

1. How have Progressive efforts of the 1900's affected present-day political practices in the nation and in your state?
2. Compare the influence and effects of the development of the gasoline engine and electricity at the turn of the century with those of jet propulsion and atomic power in our day.
3. Compare attitudes in the late nineteenth century and in the present toward our natural resources and the need for their conservation. Does the need seem greater today?
4. Study the twelve-point program set forth by the American bishops in 1919, and seek to discover how much of this program has been written into our social legislation by Congress since 1919.

EXTENDING YOUR HORIZON

1. For a vivid account of a New York factory fire in 1911, read Tom Brooks, "The Terrible Triangle Fire," *American Heritage*, August 1957.
2. The role of J. P. Morgan in the Panic of 1907 is told by John A. Garraty in his interesting account "A Lion in the Street," *American Heritage*, June 1957.
3. Peter R. Levin in his book *Seven by Chance: The Accidental Presidents* (Farrar, Straus) has several interesting chapters (VIII through X) on Theodore Roosevelt. Compare his picture with that given by Richard Hofstadter in "Theodore Roosevelt: The Conservative as Progressive" in *The American Political Tradition*.
4. John A. Garraty presents a novel account of Theodore Roosevelt's telephone efforts to secure the 1916 nomination in an unpublished document, "T.R. on the Telephone," *American Heritage*, December 1957.
5. A good source on reform for the era is Chapter XV, "Muckrakers and Other Critics," in Stewart Holbrook's *Lost Men of American History* (Macmillan).

INDIVIDUAL ACTIVITIES

1. Prepare an oral report on either Susan B. Anthony or Lillian Gilbreth based on related chapters found in David K. Boynick's *Pioneers in Petticoats* (Crowell).
2. Report to the class on the story behind the passage of the Meat Inspection and the Pure Food and Drug Acts. Consult Mark Sullivan's *Our Times* (Scribner), Vol. II, and see the article by G. H. Carson, "Who Put the Borax in Dr. Wiley's Butter?" in *American Heritage*, August 1956.

3. For keener insight into the social problems of the Progressive Era, consult Richard Hofstadter's *Great Issues in American History* (Vintage), Volume II, Part V, Progressivism. Read Documents 1 and 3 by Lincoln Steffens and Walter Lippmann. Report to the class on the role of crusading journalists in the reform of government.

4. Read pages 138–44 in John Tracy Ellis' *American Catholicism* and report to the class on the development of the National Catholic Welfare Conference and the work of John A. Ryan in the movement for social justice. Include in your report the "Bishops' Program of Social Reconstruction" set forth in 1919 and the part played in its development by Monsignor Ryan. For the points of the Bishops' Program, consult Ellis, *Documents,* or *Our Bishops Speak, 1919–1951* (Bruce), edited by Raphael M. Huber.

5. Read the account of Finley Peter Dunne's inimitable "Mr. Dooley" in "The Carnegie Libraries" as found in *Democracy and the Gospel of Wealth,* in *Problems of American Civilization* (Heath).

GROUP ACTIVITIES

1. Select two or three students and let each assume that he is to be the organizing chairman of a group discussion on the careers of Albert Beveridge, Robert La Follette, and George Norris, three Senators of the Progressive Era. Let each student work individually to compile a list of available library resources to which he might send his group for help in finding material for such a discussion. Let the class decide who has the best list.

2. Select a committee to study more closely and to evaluate the New Nationalism and New Freedom programs of Theodore Roosevelt and Woodrow Wilson. Helpful sources of information include the essays on the two men in *The American Political Tradition* by Richard Hofstadter; "The Progressive Ferment," Chapter 20 of Richard Heffner's *A Documentary History of the United States;* and Documents 11 and 12 in Part V of Hofstadter's *Great Issues in American History* (Vintage), Volume II. The committee can seek to agree or disagree with the view of William A. White that the two programs offered a choice "between Tweedledum and Tweedledee."

3. Using the sources just recommended above, let several students prepare political speeches voicing the views of the major candidates in the 1912 campaign. Use other resources available in preparing the talks, and let the class members question the candidates on their views.

SUGGESTED FURTHER READING
BIOGRAPHY

BOWEN, CATHERINE DRINKER, *Yankee from Olympus: Justice Holmes and His Family,* Little, Brown; Bantam. Semifictional biography of Oliver Wendell Holmes, Jr.

BRYAN, FLORENCE H., *Susan B. Anthony, Champion of Women's Rights,* Messner.

ELLIS, ELMER, *Mr. Dooley's America: A Life of Finley Peter Dunne,* Knopf.

HARLOW, ALVIN F., *Theodore Roosevelt, Strenuous American,* Messner.

*HOOVER, HERBERT, *The Ordeal of Woodrow Wilson,* McGraw-Hill.

*LINK, ARTHUR, *Wilson: Road to the White House,* Princeton Univ. Press.

——, *Wilson: The New Freedom,* Princeton Univ. Press.

LORANT, STEFAN, *The Life and Times of Theodore Roosevelt,* Doubleday.

MC KINLEY, SILAS B., *Woodrow Wilson,* Praeger.

MOWRY, GEORGE E., *Theodore Roosevelt and the Progressive Movement,* Univ. of Wisconsin Press.

PRINGLE, HENRY F., *Theodore Roosevelt: A Biography,* Harcourt, Brace (Harvest Books).

STEFFENS, LINCOLN, *Autobiography of Lincoln Steffens,* Grosset & Dunlap; Harcourt, Brace (text ed.).

WHITE, WILLIAM A., *The Autobiography of William Allen White,* Macmillan.

OTHER NONFICTION

BOWERS, CLAUDE, *Beveridge and the Progressive Era,* Houghton Mifflin.

DUNNE, F. P., *Mr. Dooley at His Best,* Scribner. Satirical humor.

*FAULKNER, HAROLD U., *The Quest for Social Justice: 1898–1914,* Macmillan.

*GOLDMAN, ERIC, *Rendezvous with Destiny: A History of Modern American Reform,* Knopf (Vintage Books).

*HOFSTADTER, RICHARD, *The Age of Reform: From Bryan to F.D.R.,* Knopf (text ed.).

REGIER, C. C., *The Era of Muckrakers,* Peter Smith.

STEFFENS, LINCOLN, *Shame of the Cities,* Peter Smith. Corruption in city politics.

PART 4

THE NATION AS
A WORLD LEADER

How thirteen colonies on the fringe of a vast, untamed wilderness eventually became a nation holding a position of world leadership—such is the dramatic story of the United States. This story has unfolded in less than 200 years.

One way to visualize the swift rise of the American nation is to think of the three men whose names appear on the time line below. Each of these men lived through a distinct period in the rapidly developing life of the nation.

Theodore Roosevelt, the last of the three, was born before the War Between the States. He lived to see the reunited country grow from 36 to 48 states; acquire Alaska, Hawaii, Puerto Rico, and other far-flung Territories; fight in World War I to "make the world safe for democracy"; and develop from a predominantly agricultural country to the leading industrial power of the world.

Part Four of *Rise of the American Nation* begins with the emergence of the United States as a world power in the early 1900's and brings us to the present. This period of the nation's history is marked by the impressive developments that have carried the United States to the proud position of leadership in the free world.

Millions of Americans living today hold vivid memories of World War I; the "Golden Twenties"; the Great Depression of the 1930's; the excitement, tragedy, and overwhelming sorrow of World War II; and the years since 1945, years filled with trouble and yet so bright with promise.

In Part Four of *Rise of the American Nation* we, the living, are writing our own history and adding still another chapter to the dramatic story of the nation that now carries the heavy burden and the large opportunity of world leadership.

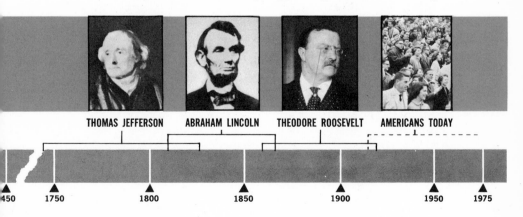

THOMAS JEFFERSON   ABRAHAM LINCOLN   THEODORE ROOSEVELT   AMERICANS TODAY

1450   1750   1800   1850   1900   1950   1975

UNIT NINE

Becoming a World Power

1898–1920

CHAPTER

30 `1898–1914`

The Nation Expands
in the Pacific

THE AMERICAN FLEET
SAILS AROUND THE WORLD —

R. Houhhm

Fᴙᴏᴍ 1823 until nearly the end of the 1800's, Americans devoted most of their energy to the settlement and development of the continental United States. To be sure, Americans traveled to Europe and Europeans traveled to America. The two-way flow of people and ideas across the Atlantic never ceased. And always, of course, there was vigorous trade between the two continents. But it was the conquest of the untamed West and, after 1865, the development of industry that engaged the major energy of the American people.

By the 1890's, however, a revolution was taking place in American opinion. With the West becoming settled and the United States rapidly becoming a major industrial power, an increasing number of Americans became interested in owning or controlling lands beyond their continental boundaries.

In this chapter you will see how Americans acquired a new interest in world affairs. You will see how they emerged from the Spanish-American War of 1898 in possession of the Philippine Islands and other islands in the Pacific Ocean. You will see how this growing Pacific empire created new problems for the United States, and how it forced America's leaders to develop new policies for dealing with the nations of the Far East.

AS THE STORY DEVELOPS

1. Americans become interested in expansion overseas.
2. The Spanish-American War makes the United States a colonial power.
3. The nation acquires the Philippines, Hawaii, and Samoa.
4. The United States exerts increasing influence in the Far East.

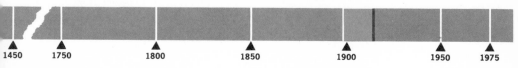

1450   1750   1800   1850   1900   1950   1975

Americans become interested in expansion overseas

Great Britain, France, the Netherlands, Spain, Portugal—these were the old colonial powers. They had started their policies of *imperialism*—of collecting colonies and building empires—back in the 1500's and 1600's. Now, in the middle of the 1800's, they owned and controlled a large portion of the world. But there were still huge areas of the earth unclaimed by any colonial nation.

The race for empire. During the latter half of the 1800's, there was a mad rush to gain ownership or control of the remainder of the underdeveloped areas of the earth. Nations previously little interested in expansion joined the race—among them Belgium, Germany, Italy, Japan, and Russia. Within a few years the rival colonial powers gobbled up almost all of the huge continent of Africa and sliced off large portions of China and other areas in the Far East. By the opening years of the 1900's, nearly all of the underdeveloped regions of the world had been divided among the rival colonial empires.

Reasons for the New Imperialism. The Industrial Revolution was to a great extent responsible for the mounting interest in colonies. Factories needed raw materials in ever-growing quantities. In order to keep their factories operating, manufacturers had to find new markets for the finished products. Improvements in transportation, especially in the steamship, made it possible for businessmen to buy and sell in a truly worldwide market. And as trade increased and profits accumulated, businessmen and bankers began to look overseas for opportunities to invest their savings. More than any other single factor, the growth of industry speeded up the race to secure colonies and to control the underdeveloped lands.

It is not surprising that Great Britain, which was the leading industrial power in the world before 1900, built the largest empire. Close on the British heels were France, Belgium, and the Netherlands—and in each of these countries the process of industrialization was in full swing by the end of the 1800's.

Nor is it surprising that the countries that were late in starting down the road of industrialism were also late in entering the race for empire. Germany, Italy, and Japan were among these countries. As a result, when they began to look around for colonial possessions, they found most of the world already divided, and they became jealous and angry.

There were still other reasons for the growth of world-wide imperialism in the latter part of the 1800's and the early 1900's. One was the invention of new instruments of warfare, notably repeating rifles and machine guns. By 1900 both the repeating rifle and the machine gun were becoming standard army equipment. Armed with these weapons, a small band of professional soldiers could easily conquer and control people living in underdeveloped regions.

Public support for imperialism. Another reason for the growth of imperialism was the attitude of people in the colonial powers. No government could have gone very far down the road of empire without the support of public opinion. There were objectors in every country, but in general the man-in-the-street was as eager for empire as the statesman or the businessman. The English factory worker, the French shopkeeper, the German farmer—these and other solid citizens of the colonial powers were all proud of their country's empires. With the support of their own citizens, the governments of the colonial nations were able to spend huge sums of money needed for armies to occupy the colonial territories and for navies to guard the ever-lengthening sea lanes to and from the colonies.

End of the American frontier. With a few exceptions the American people had never been interested in acquiring colonies. Indeed, with the American Revolution they had cast off their own colonial status and become an inde-

ALASKA AND THE GOLD RUSH

Large numbers of Americans were either amused or indignant when Secretary of State William Seward purchased Alaska from Russia in 1867 for over 7 million dollars. Many people referred to Alaska as "Seward's folly" and "Seward's icebox." Thirty years passed before Americans began to realize what a great bargain they had made.

On June 16, 1897, the steamship *Excelsior* docked in San Francisco. No one paid much attention to a number of grizzled prospectors who staggered down the gangplank carrying battered boxes and bundles. Then the prospectors began to talk, and within hours their story was being headlined from coast to coast.

Gold! The greatest discovery in history. Where? On the Klondike River, a tributary of the upper Yukon River, just east of the Alaskan-Canadian border.

A great gold rush started. From every part of the United States and Canada, and by every possible route, men headed for the gold fields. Thousands of men landed at Juneau, Alaska, and headed inland over the treacherous, snow-covered Chilkoot Pass for the Yukon. Many died on the way. Those who got through staked out claims on every creek on the Alaskan-Canadian border. Life during the winter of 1897–98 was grim. The diet for the lucky ones consisted of the "three B's"—bread, beans, and bacon. The less fortunate almost starved. But the gold was there, and when the spring thaws came and the men could work, hundreds found themselves rich.

The Klondike provided the inspiration for countless stories, including some of the novels of Rex Beach and Jack London. Not least important, the flow of gold from Alaska and Canada brought an end to the free silver controversy.

pendent nation, and their sympathies were with colonial peoples, not with the colonizing powers.

America's lack of interest in acquiring colonies is, of course, easy to understand. For three hundred years, the undeveloped West was, in a sense, an American "colony." Even as late as 1867, when Secretary of State Seward bought Alaska (see above), it was not unreasonable for people to ask, "What does the United States want with more land?"

In 1890, however, the Census Office announced that the frontier no longer existed. There was still, to be sure, plenty of good land waiting to be settled. But the best land was becoming more expensive, and an important phase of American development was ending.

American industrialism grows. Moreover, by 1890 the United States was rapidly becoming one of the leading industrial nations of the world. American manufacturers, like manufacturers in Europe, needed a continuing flow of raw materials. They also needed markets for the products of their factories.

There was, to be sure, a big difference between American and European businessmen. Europeans, lacking sufficient raw materials and markets at home, were under considerable pressure to get firm control of new sources of raw materials and new markets. American businessmen were not under this same pressure.

The United States was a young country, only partly developed. The country as a whole, and especially the great West, still offered large supplies of raw materials and almost limitless opportunities for the sale of manufactured goods and the investment of surplus money. But American businessmen realized that this situation would not last forever. For this reason, it is perhaps accurate to say that by 1890 a growing number of American businessmen were mildly interested in having the United States enter the race for colonies.

American expansionists. Until 1898, at least, American interest in colonies was stimulated not so much by businessmen as by preachers, scholars, politicians, and military leaders.

One of the most influential advocates of colonial expansion was a minister, the Reverend Josiah Strong. In 1885 the Reverend Mr. Strong, then living in Cincinnati, Ohio, wrote a book entitled *Our Country: Its Possible Future and Its Present Crisis.* This book attracted nationwide attention when it was published in 1891. The world is now entering "upon a new stage of its history," he wrote. He then urged Americans to adopt a vigorous colonial policy.

Even more influential than the book by the Reverend Mr. Strong was one written by Captain Alfred Mahan in 1890 under the title *The Influence of Sea Power upon History, 1660–1783.* Mahan's book attempted to show that the greatest nations of the world had risen largely because of their sea power

and that greatness was not possible without sea power. He argued that the United States must therefore strengthen its navy. It must also secure colonies overseas. Mahan claimed that colonies were needed as naval bases and as refueling stations, or "coaling stations." He also pointed out that colonies would provide raw materials and markets, thereby strengthening the industrial organization on which a great sea power must rely in modern times.

Strengthening the navy. Even before Captain Mahan's book appeared in print, Congress had taken steps to strengthen the navy. These steps were needed. In 1880, for example, the United States had fewer than a hundred "seagoing vessels"—and many of these were "seagoing" in name only, with rusty boilers and planking rotted beyond repair.

Starting in 1882, however, the situation began to change when Congress authorized the construction of "two steam-cruising vessels of war." Three years later, the Navy Department created the Naval War College at Newport, Rhode Island. About this time the Bethlehem Steel Corporation began to build a plant for the fabrication of "armor plate"—tough steel sheets used to protect the hulls and superstructures of war ships. By 1895 the "White Squadron," sometimes called the "Great White Fleet," was under construction.

The United States stands ready. In 1895 the United States had not yet really entered the race for empire. But the ground had been prepared. For various reasons, a growing number of Americans were becoming increasingly interested in the question of colonies. Many businessmen were beginning to become uneasy at the prospect of their European competitors gaining control of the markets of underdeveloped areas. The nation's industrial plant—its mines, factories, and transportation system—was rapidly becoming one of the most productive in the world. And a new navy, small but modern and efficient, was ready for action.

1. Explain why the Industrial Revolution was largely responsible for the mounting interest in colonies in the latter half of the nineteenth century.

2. What other factors led to the growth of the New Imperialism?

3. "For three hundred years, the undeveloped West was, in a sense, an American colony." Discuss.

4. Show how each of the following affected American interest in colonies: (a) closing of the frontier, (b) industrial development after 1865, and (c) Alfred Mahan.

IDENTIFY: imperialism, colonial empire, coaling station; Josiah Strong; 1867, 1890.

2 The Spanish-American War makes the United States a colonial power

The Spanish-American War of 1898 marked a turning point in American history. Before the war, which lasted only a few weeks in the spring and summer of 1898, Alaska and the Midway Islands° were the only lands that the United States owned beyond its immediate boundaries. Within a few years after the war ended, the American flag was flying over a number of islands in the Pacific Ocean, the United States was deeply involved in the Far East, and American influence was being strongly exerted in the lands bordering the Caribbean Sea.

Trouble in Cuba. Cuba and Puerto Rico, both in the Caribbean, were the last remnants of Spain's once mighty empire in the New World. Spaniards had once called Cuba "the Ever Faithful Isle." In 1868, however, when a violent revolution broke out, the Cubans proved to be something less than faithful to their Spanish rulers. It took Spain ten years to crush this uprising, and even then Spain did so only with a promise to provide long-awaited reforms. But

°These islands were occupied in 1867 in the name of the United States.

discontent still continued to smolder.

The trouble was that most of the people of Cuba worked at starvation wages for landowners who lived in extreme luxury. To make matters worse, the Spanish government in Madrid exploited the Cubans, antagonizing landowners as well as landless workers.

Spanish misrule plus an economic crisis finally plunged Cuba into another revolution. The United States was partly responsible for the economic crisis. In 1890, as you have seen, Congress adopted the McKinley Tariff Act. This act allowed Cuban sugar, which was the major crop of the island, to enter the United States free of duty. As a result, trade between the United States and Cuba prospered, reaching a total of over $100,000,000 a year. However, in 1894 the United States adopted the Wilson-Gorman Tariff Act, which placed a 40 per cent duty on all the raw sugar imported into the United States. As soon as the 1894 tariff went into effect, sugar began to pile up in Cuban warehouses, plantations closed down, and thousands of Cuban workers lost their jobs. Driven to desperation by the economic crisis and angry at Spain's failure to provide the reforms promised in 1878, the Cubans rose in revolution.

Revolution in Cuba. The revolution started in 1895 under the leadership of General Máximo Gómez. Bands of revolutionists roamed the countryside, killing, burning, and plundering.

The Spaniards, led by General Valeriano Weyler, nicknamed "The Butcher," retaliated with a policy of savage repression. General Weyler ordered all people living in territory controlled by the revolutionists into concentration camps, or prison camps, run by the Spaniards. Spanish soldiers then marched through the abandoned countryside, destroying buildings and putting to death all persons found in the area without permission. What the revolutionists had not destroyed, the Spaniards did. Large areas of Cuba were reduced to utter ruin. Starvation and disease plagued the land.

The revolution affects America. In a strictly legal sense, the revolution in Cuba was no concern of the United States. Spain was a sovereign, independent nation, free to do as it pleased with its own colonies. This was freely admitted by the American government, which officially adopted a policy of neutrality.

But the effects of the revolution could not be confined to Cuba. The revolutionists themselves did everything within their power to win the sympathy and support of the United States. In spite of protests from Spain, the revolutionists waged a vigorous propaganda campaign in America. They also bought arms and ammunition in the United States which they smuggled into Cuba.

The revolution also affected American pocketbooks. Before the uprising began, Americans had invested a total of more than $50,000,000 in Cuban plantations, in the transportation system, and in business establishments. Moreover, trade between Cuba and the United States was crippled by the revolution.

As the months passed, more and more American citizens began to express their sympathy for the revolutionists. They recalled their own efforts to win independence from the British back in the days of the American Revolution.

The press whips up sympathy. American newspapers helped to inflame public opinion. Two New York papers—William Randolph Hearst's New York *Journal* and Joseph Pulitzer's New York *World*—were especially active in support of the revolutionists. The owners of these papers discovered that sales skyrocketed when they published sensational stories and pictures of Spanish atrocities in Cuba.

The methods of the "yellow press," as these sensational newspapers have been called (page 528), were highly successful—at least from a financial point of view. For instance, when Hearst bought the *Journal* in 1895 it had a circulation of 30,000. Two years later, sales had jumped to 400,000. By 1898 the figure had passed the million mark.

Newspapers in other towns and cities quickly copied the methods of Hearst and Pulitzer. Before long, the public, feeding on the sensational stories and pictures, began to clamor for United States intervention in Cuba.

By 1898 even the more conservative newspapers, including weekly religious journals such as the *Congregationalist* of Boston, insisted that the United States had a moral responsibility to restore order to the war-ravaged island of Cuba.

McKinley tries to avoid war. When President William McKinley entered the White House on March 4, 1897, he was strongly opposed to war. Many of his close advisers as well as most businessmen firmly supported the President's position. The United States was just emerging from the depression that had started in 1893, and businessmen in general were fearful that a war, or even the threat of a war, would throw the country back into a depression.

For nearly a year the President managed to maintain the official policy of neutrality. But early in 1898 several events forced his hand.

On February 9, 1898, American newspapers headlined a letter written by the Spanish minister to the United States, Enrique Dupuy de Lôme (en-REE-keh doo-PWEE duh LOHM). In the letter Señor De Lôme characterized President McKinley as a "would-be politician." The Spanish minister had written the letter to a friend in Havana. It was not intended for publication. Indeed, it had been stolen from the mails and sold to the press. But the harm was done. Unthinking Americans at once concluded that the uncomplimentary remark reflected the attitude of all Spaniards.

A few days later, on February 16, Americans read even more startling news in their papers. The night before, the United States battleship *Maine* had gone down in Havana harbor with the loss of more than 250 American lives. Captain Charles D. Sigsbee, commander of the *Maine,* stated that the disaster followed an explosion of unknown origin and urged that "public opinion should be suspended until further report." In Havana flags were flown at half-mast, theaters and places of business were closed, and expressions of sorrow and sympathy were forwarded to Washington. All of this was brushed aside by the public. People jumped to the conclusion that the Spaniards had destroyed the ship. "Remember the *Maine!*" became a national slogan.

In spite of these incidents, President McKinley refused to give in to the clamor for war. Angered at his refusal to act, Assistant Secretary of the Navy Theodore Roosevelt declared that the President "has no more backbone than a chocolate éclair." But McKinley still hoped for a peaceable solution.

Spain meets American demands. Late in March, with the President's approval, the Department of State sent an ultimatum° to Spain. In the ultimatum the United States demanded (1) that Spain immediately cease all fighting in Cuba and grant an armistice to the revolutionists, and (2) that the Spanish forces in Cuba immediately abolish the concentration camps.

On April 9 the Spanish government accepted the ultimatum. The American mininster to Madrid promptly cabled the good news to President McKinley and added, "I hope that nothing will now be done to humiliate Spain. . . ."

Congress declares war. Despite this surrender by the Spaniards, on April 11, 1898, President McKinley asked Congress to intervene in Cuba. Why?

The only explanation seems to be that the war spirit had proved too much for the President to resist.

On April 19, after a week of debate, Congress by large majorities voted to use the land and naval forces of the United States to secure the full independence of Cuba. But Congress also adopted the Teller Resolution. This resolution stated that the United States claimed no "sovereignty, jurisdiction, or control over said island, except for the

⸱⸱⸱

° **ultimatum:** in diplomatic language, a final statement of terms whose rejection may lead to the breaking off of diplomatic relations or to war.

pacification thereof," and promised that once Cuba was free the United States would "leave the government and control of the island to its people."

Victory in the Pacific. Curiously enough, the "war for Cuban liberty" started not in Cuba but in the Pacific. For weeks before Congress declared war, the Navy Department had been preparing for action. Commodore George Dewey, commanding a fleet in the Far East, had been sent to Hong Kong with orders to stand by. When he received word that war had been declared, Dewey promptly headed for the Philippine Islands, the center of Spanish power in the Pacific.

On the night of April 30, Dewey's six ships slipped past the fortress of Corregidor and into the harbor of Manila, capital of the Philippines (see map, this page). At daybreak on May 1, the American war ships opened fire. Their guns outranged those on the Spanish vessels, and by noon the one-sided battle was over. The Spaniards lost nearly 170 men and all their vessels. The

591

Americans lost only one man—who died of heatstroke.

Although Commodore Dewey controlled Manila harbor, he did not have enough men to land and seize the city. While he waited for a landing force to arrive from the United States, he sent arms and ammunition to a band of Filipinos led by Emilio Aguinaldo (eh-MEE-lyo ah-gee-NAHL-doh). The Filipinos, eager to throw off Spanish rule and win their independence, began to organize for an attack on Manila.

Two months passed. Then, early in August, American transports arrived with a strong landing party. The position of the Spanish garrison was hopeless. Cut off by Dewey's war ships from all hope of relief, surrounded on the land side by the Filipino revolutionists, and faced with an attack by an American army, Manila surrendered on August 13, 1898.

Victory in the Atlantic. On May 1, while Commodore Dewey was destroying Spanish sea power in the Pacific, Spain's Atlantic fleet was gathering at the Cape Verde Islands off the west coast of Africa. On April 29 the Atlantic fleet under Admiral Cervera (sehr-VEH-ra) started westward.

News that Admiral Cervera's fleet was steaming toward America threw Americans living in coastal areas into a panic. One coastal town after another begged for naval protection.

The alarm was unwarranted. Cervera's fleet was hopelessly inadequate for the task assigned to it, and the gallant admiral sailed only with the thought of saving the honor of Spain, not with the hope of victory. Instead of attacking, the Spaniards slipped into the harbor at Santiago, Cuba, for refueling. Here they were bottled up by an American squadron commanded by Admiral William T. Sampson and Commodore W. S. Schley (see map, opposite page).

On Sunday morning, July 3, Cervera's force made a wild dash for the open sea. But the American ships were waiting, and as the Spanish fleet raced out of the harbor and steamed along the coast, it was met by murderous fire. Within four hours the battle was over. Not a single Spanish vessel escaped.

Land fighting in Cuba. In contrast to the United States Navy, which moved swiftly and efficiently, the War Department was quite unprepared. When the war began, the regular army numbered fewer than 30,000 officers and men, scattered in small contingents over the entire country. More than 200,000 men immediately volunteered for war service, among them Theodore Roosevelt, who resigned his post as Assistant Secretary of the Navy to become lieutenant colonel of a volunteer regiment of cavalry known as the "Rough Riders."

The volunteers swamped the army, which had neither officers nor equipment to provide the necessary training. The port of departure in Tampa, Florida, at the end of a single-track railroad, was a scene of chaos. Although Secretary of War Russell A. Alger had boasted that he would land an army in Cuba within twenty-four hours after the outbreak of hostilities, it was actually two months before the first troop transports left the United States for Cuba.

This force of 17,000 men was poorly trained and equipped. Many of them carried antiquated rifles. The food was poor, and the army was without adequate hospital and sanitary facilities. It

"ROUGH RIDER" OFFICER

NAVAL GUNNER'S MATE

INFANTRYMAN

American uniforms—Spanish-American War

is no wonder that hundreds of American soldiers died needlessly, most of them from dysentery, typhoid, malaria, and yellow fever.

On June 24 the two armies clashed. Slowly, by hard fighting, the Americans under General William Shafter pushed the enemy back through the fortified village of El Caney and across San Juan Hill (see map, this page). By July 2 American forces had advanced to within a mile and a half of Santiago. It was this fact that led Admiral Cervera to make his desperate attempt to escape with the Spanish fleet. The destruction of the Spanish navy was the final blow. General Ramón Blanco, commander at Santiago, surrendered his forces on July 17.

Meanwhile, another American army, under General Nelson A. Miles, landed on the Spanish island of Puerto Rico, east of Cuba. The Americans encountered no opposition, and by the last days of July were in control of the island.

The fruits of victory. The United States entered the war with the argument that it was fighting merely to free the oppressed Cubans. It ended the war with an empire on its hands.

American and Spanish commissioners met in Paris in October 1898 to negotiate a peace treaty. By the terms of the treaty, Spain agreed to surrender all claim to Cuba. In addition, Spain agreed to cede to the United States the following territories: (1) Puerto Rico; (2) the Pacific island of Guam (see map, pages 842-43); and (3) the Philippines—in exchange for which the United States agreed to pay Spain $20,000,000.

As a result of the war, the United States also acquired Wake Island in the Pacific (see map, pages 842-43). American armed forces had landed on Wake on July 4, 1898, and raised the American flag. Congress later annexed Wake.

Until 1898, except for the two square miles of the Midway Islands, the United States owned no overseas possessions. When the Senate ratified the peace treaty, however, the United States became a colonial power.

The expansionists—followers of Josiah Strong, Alfred Mahan, and others—were delighted at this turn of events. But many Americans were deeply troubled. Was it wise and proper for the United States to join the European powers in the race for empire? Did the United States want to assume responsibility for a colonial empire scattered over the Pacific Ocean and the Caribbean Sea?

SECTION SURVEY

1. What were the causes of the Cuban revolt against Spain in 1895?

2. To what extent did each of the following help bring about the Spanish-American War: (a) the "yellow press," (b) the De Lôme letter, (c) destruction of the *Maine,* and (d) American investments and trade with Cuba?

3. The Teller Resolution aroused much respect for the United States. Why?

4. Describe briefly the highlights of the fighting in (a) the Pacific and (b) Cuba.

5. (a) Give the terms of the Treaty of Paris of 1898. (b) In what sense can the Spanish-American War be said to mark a "turning point in American history"?

IDENTIFY: ultimatum, "Rough Riders"; Pulitzer, Hearst, Commodore Dewey, Aguinaldo, Cervera.

3 The nation acquires the Philippines, Hawaii, and Samoa

The Philippine Islands presented Americans with an immediate and difficult problem: Should the United States set them free, just as it was prepared to set Cuba free? Or should it now turn on Emilio Aguinaldo and his followers and force them to accept American rule?

American dilemma. President McKinley was one of countless Americans who wrestled with his problem. After much thought McKinley decided to establish American rule in the Philippine Islands.

As he later explained to a group of fellow Americans, the United States could not return the Philippines to Spain, for "that would be cowardly and dishonorable." It could not give them to France, Germany, or Great Britain, for "that would be bad business and discreditable." It could not turn them over to the Filipinos, for they were "unfit for self-government."

"I walked the floor of the White House night after night," McKinley explained, "and I am not ashamed to tell you, gentlemen, that I went down on my knees and prayed Almighty God for light and guidance more than one night. And one night late it came to me this way . . . There was nothing left for us to do but to take them all, and to educate the Filipinos, and uplift and civilize and Christianize them . . . "

President McKinley's motives were good, but his knowledge of the facts was incomplete. Indeed, he later confessed that when the news of Dewey's victory had reached him, he had had to look for the islands on the map. As for "Christianizing" the Filipinos, all but the Mohammedan Moros had long since been converted to Catholicism.

Public opinion is divided. Many Americans agreed with McKinley that it was America's duty to assume what the British poet Rudyard Kipling had called "the white man's burden." Others hoped to profit economically by following the path of world empire. Still others, mostly army and navy leaders, believed that the United States needed the islands as strategic bases.

But opponents of imperialism viewed the decision with serious misgivings. "It will be only the old tale of a free people seduced by false ambitions and running headlong after riches and luxuries and military glory," Carl Schurz, a prominent Republican, warned.

Conquest and early rule. Events that followed seemed to lend support to Schurz's dire prophecy. The conquest of the Philippines turned out to be more difficult than the defeat of Spain. The Filipinos were no more willing to accept American rule than they had been to endure Spanish rule. For three years 70,000 American troops fought in the islands at a cost of $175,000,000 and a casualty list as high as that of the Spanish-American War. By 1902, however, American arms were victorious.

Despite this unhappy beginning the United States lived up to McKinley's solemn promise "not to exploit, but to develop; to civilize, to educate, to train in the science of self-government." In the Philippine Government Act of 1902, Congress created a system of government for the islands, under which they were to be ruled by a governor and a small legislative body—an elected assembly and an appointed upper house. The United States Congress was to retain veto power over all legislation. The plan did not go into effect until 1907. Meanwhile, William Howard Taft, the first governor, ruled wisely and well. He co-operated closely with the Filipinos, including as many of them as possible in the new government.

Filipino dissatisfaction. But the Filipinos were not satisfied. Many of them wanted full self-government. Their dissatisfaction became apparent in 1907 when the elected lower house met for the first time. Three quarters of the representatives in this body were pledged to work for independence. Their hopes rose high in 1913 when Woodrow Wilson became President of the United

States. Leading Democrats had opposed the conquest of the Philippines, and the Democratic Party had pledged itself to grant independence at the earliest possible date.

These hopes, however, were soon dashed. Although the Jones Act of 1916 did give the Filipinos the right to elect the members of both the upper and lower houses of the legislature, Congress did not grant the coveted gift of independence. The act merely promised independence "as soon as a stable government can be established."

America keeps its promise. Meanwhile, the islands prospered. Highways, railroads, telegraph and telephone lines were built. Education reduced illiteracy from 85 per cent in 1898 to 37 per cent in 1921. Disease was greatly reduced and Filipino health steadily improved. Exports and imports swelled in volume as the result of an American tariff policy which, in 1902, gave a 25 per cent tariff reduction to products from the Philippines and, in 1913, established free trade on many articles traded between the islands and the United States.

Most important of all, as you will see, the United States finally kept its promise to set the islands free.

Early relations with Hawaii. In 1898 Hawaii (see map, page 842), as well as Cuba and the Philippines, occupied the attention of Congress and the American people. American interest in the Hawaiian Islands went back many years.

Before 1865 about the only relations that the United States had with these central Pacific islands were through traders and missionaries. But after 1865 American businessmen began to develop the resources of Hawaii—chiefly sugar cane and pineapples. The Hawaiians became increasingly alarmed as the wealth and power of the islands passed into the hands of foreigners. Finally, led by Queen Liliuokalani (lee-LEE-woh-kah-LAH-nee), they announced they intended to end foreign influence.

Foreigners seize control. Foreign businessmen, including Americans, aided by a number of influential Hawaiians, met this challenge with prompt action. They started a revolution.

At this critical moment the American minister to Hawaii intervened. Claiming that he was acting only to protect American lives and property, he requested the aid of the marines who were conveniently at hand on a nearby war ship. The Hawaiian soldiers, concluding that the marines had come to the assistance of the revolutionists, refused to fight. The new government, controlled by the foreign business interests and missionaries, asked to be annexed to the United States. The American minister promptly raised the Stars and Stripes, and on February 1, 1893, marines began to patrol the islands.

Congress refuses to annex Hawaii. When the news of these events reached the United States, furious protests poured into Congress from all sections of the country. Many people did not want island territory. They were indignant at the manner in which American marines had been used. They were afraid that overseas expansion would lead to heavy military expenditures.

President Cleveland sent a commission to Hawaii to investigate. The commission ordered the American flag

■ The University of Santo Tomás in Manila marks the cultural development of the Philippines. Its history is one of heroism.

hauled down and heard evidence from both sides. In its report to President Cleveland, the commission stated that the revolution had been started largely by American businessmen, aided by the American minister and the marines.

After studying the report, Cleveland concluded that the only way to make amends was to apologize to Queen Liliuokalani and to restore her to her throne. But to do this would have required the exercise of force against the new government. By now Congress was fed up with the whole affair, and in 1894 it adopted a resolution refusing to interfere further in Hawaii.

Annexation of Hawaii. Then came the Spanish-American War which, as you have seen, generated a new spirit in America. The question of Hawaii once again was brought up on the floor of Congress. This time, in 1898, by an overwhelming vote, the islands were annexed to the United States and given Territorial status.

Samoa is acquired. As in Hawaii, American interests in the Samoan Islands were of long standing. In 1878 the United States secured from a Samoan chief the right to use the harbor of Pago Pago (PAHN-goh PAHN-goh) on the island of Tutuila (too-too-EE-lah) as a naval base. The Samoans granted similar privileges to Germany and Great Britain.

The three countries—Great Britain, Germany, and the United States—then became involved in a lively scramble for control of the islands. At one point, in the year 1889, a naval clash among the three powers was narrowly averted, largely because of a typhoon which blew the rival squadrons out to sea.

Finally, in 1899, the British withdrew and the islands were divided between Germany and the United States. Germany lost control of its share of the islands when it was defeated in World War I. But Tutuila with its excellent anchorage in the harbor of Pago Pago remained in the hands of the United States, which developed it into a major naval base in the Pacific.

✔ **SECTION SURVEY**

1. (a) Give three reasons why the United States decided to take over the Philippines as a colony. (b) What was the main argument of the opponents of imperialism?

2. Evaluate the record of the United States in the Philippines as a case study in the history of imperialism.

3. (a) Why were Americans interested in Hawaii? (b) Trace the story of United States acquisition of Hawaii.

4. Summarize the events leading to America's acquisition of part of Samoa.

IDENTIFY: "White man's burden," Jones Act; William Howard Taft, Liliuokalani; 1898, 1899.

4 The United States exerts increasing influence in the Far East

By 1900 the United States held, in the area of the Pacific, Hawaii, Midway, Guam, Wake, the Philippine Islands, and part of Samoa. With this new territory the American people assumed heavy responsibilities. These new responsibilities, plus events that were taking place in the Far East, led the United States in 1899–1900 to proclaim the *Open Door policy* for China. This policy formed the basis for American action in the Far East, and involved the United States in the affairs of Russia and Japan. To understand the Open Door policy adopted by the United States, it is necessary to review American relations with China during the 1800's.

The China trade. America's interest in China began back in 1784 when the *Empress of China* sailed from New York with a cargo for Canton, a Chinese seaport. The venture proved profitable, and enterprising Yankees were quick to seize the new trading opportunity.

Most of the Orient trade started in Philadelphia, New York, and New England ports. After a long voyage around South America, the ships anchored in the Pacific Northwest. There they traded with the Indians, exchanging blankets, axes, guns, and other goods for furs.

When they had a full cargo, the Yankee skippers then headed out across the Pacific Ocean for China (see map, pages 296–97).

As Samuel Eliot Morison stated in his *Maritime History of Massachusetts,* "Many a Boston family owes its rise to fame and fortune to the old Northwest and Chinese trade. . . . Salem became the American and for a time the world emporium° for pepper. . . . Tinware that itinerant Yankees peddled throughout the eastern states was made from Banka° tin. . . . This commerce with the Far East, in pursuit of which early discoverers had scorned the barren coast of Massachusetts, was a primary factor in restoring the commonwealth to prosperity and power."

Early diplomatic relations. In spite of this growing trade, it was not until 1831 that the word "China" appeared in a public or Presidential message or paper. In the 1840's, however, relations between the United States and China became closer.

At first, the Chinese had admitted foreign traders, but as time passed China's rulers began to fear the influence that foreigners were exerting in their country. When China placed restrictions on traders from Great Britain, British troops, between 1839 and 1842, fought a series of battles with Chinese forces. The British won and forced the Chinese to open several ports, called "treaty ports," to British trade.

Americans demanded and secured similar privileges when the American envoy to China, Caleb Cushing, negotiated a treaty which gave the United States all trading privileges granted by China to other nations and extended to Americans the right of *extraterritoriality*. This meant that American citizens in China who were charged with violations of China's civil or criminal laws had the right to be tried in American courts. Other foreign nations, in addi-

. . . .

° *emporium:* a principal center of trade.
° *Banka:* an island in Indonesia with important tin mines.

tion to Great Britain and the United States, also secured trading privileges and extraterritorial rights in China.

These concessions from China encouraged foreign businessmen to settle in the Far East. As the years passed, outsiders began to exercise more and more influence in China. Many of China's leaders resented this development, but they were powerless to prevent the growing influence of the Western World.

Among all the imperialistic powers interested in the Far East, the United States seemed least eager to grab Chinese territory. As a result, relations between the two countries remained friendly through the 1800's.

Crisis in China. In the 1890's, however, a major crisis developed. Japan, itching for empire, entered the race for colonies with an attack upon China in the Sino-Japanese War of 1894–95. In this war Japan won the large island of Formosa, certain territory on the Shantung Peninsula, and control of Korea (see map, page 768).

While China was helpless as a result of the Japanese attack, Germany, Russia, Great Britain, and France rushed in to secure their share of the booty. It appeared for a time as though China would soon be carved up and divided among the imperial powers.

The crisis in China posed a problem for the United States. Americans did not want Chinese territory. On the other hand, Americans did not intend to be squeezed out of the Chinese markets.

Announcing the Open Door policy. John Hay, who became Secretary of State in 1898, had a solution for the problem. He sent a note to all the powers concerned asking them to assure the United States (1) that they would keep open all "treaty ports"; and (2) that they would guarantee to all nations engaged in trade with China equal railroad, harbor, and tariff rates. In short, Hay asked for an Open Door policy that would insure American businessmen the opportunity to compete on equal terms with other traders in China. Although the response to his note was not encouraging, Hay announced on March 20, 1900, that the Open Door policy was in effect and would be maintained.

The Boxer Rebellion. Naturally enough, the Chinese deeply resented the efforts by Japan, Russia, and the European powers to get control of their country. On the rising tide of resentment, the Chinese launched a movement to drive all "foreign devils" from their country. The movement was led by a band of Chinese whom westerners called "the Boxers."

In the spring of 1900, the Boxers suddenly attacked. They killed about 300 foreigners in northern China. Then they surrounded the foreign settlement in Tientsin (TYEN-TSIN) and the British legation in Peking (now Peiping), where men and women from many nations had gathered for protection.

The foreign powers promptly rushed troops to the relief of the besieged people. The joint expeditionary force included 2500 American troops from the Philippines as well as units of fighting men from Japan and several European nations. By August 14 the expeditionary force had relieved the foreigners in Tientsin and Peking, but not before 65 of the besieged had been killed.

■ American military forces, part of the relief expedition sent to China in 1900, are shown plodding through the muddy streets of Peking.

The Boxer Rebellion provided the colonial powers with an excellent excuse to seize additional territory from China. But John Hay took a firm stand in opposition. On July 3, even while the expeditionary force was fighting its way inland to Peking, Hay announced that the United States wanted to "preserve Chinese territorial and administrative entity . . . and safeguard for the world the principle of equal and impartial trade with all parts of the Chinese Empire."

Largely because of American influence, China did not lose any territory as a result of the Boxer Rebellion. China did, however, have to pay an indemnity° of $333,000,000. The American share of the indemnity amounted to about $24,000,000, half of which the United States government turned over to American citizens to compensate them for losses of personal property in China. The American government then returned the remainder of the money.

Grateful for this generous action, the Chinese government put the money into an educational fund to send Chinese students to the United States. This fund enabled thousands of China's ablest youth to study in American colleges and universities. These students helped to build closer understanding between the two countries.

The Open Door policy in China had other far-reaching consequences. It immediately involved the United States in the affairs of Russia and Japan, both of whom were expanding in the Far East.

Japan opens its doors. Before 1853 the Japanese had lived on their islands in almost complete isolation from the rest of the world. Japan's rulers forbade foreigners to enter Japan; only the Dutch had been able to win the right to carry on a limited amount of trade through one small Japanese port. In 1853, however, Japan's isolation was abruptly shattered when Commodore Matthew C. Perry arrived in Japanese

· ·

° *indemnity:* compensation for loss, damage, or injury.

PERRY'S VISIT TO JAPAN

Commodore Matthew C. Perry landed in a small village at the mouth of Tokyo Bay on July 14, 1853. The Japanese received the Americans as though they were visitors from another planet. They had never seen a steamship, which they called a "fire wheel ship," and of which one of them wrote, "she runs as quick as a dragon in swimming." Nor had they seen or heard of the telegraph. Perry set up instruments in buildings about a half-mile apart and connected them with wires. Japanese runners tried to outrace the messages, but always, to their astonishment, without success.

But none of the gifts Perry brought with him astonished the Japanese more than the model steam railroad. It was a quarter-scale model, complete with engine, tender, passenger car, and 370 feet of track laid in a circle. The car was too small for the Japanese to ride in. Not to be cheated out of a ride, however, they took turns riding on the roof. As Perry wrote in his official report, "It was a spectacle not a little ludicrous, to behold a dignified mandarin whirling around the circular road at the rate of twenty miles an hour, with his loose robes flying in the wind."

waters with a squadron of American naval vessels and demanded an audience with Japan's governing authorities.

The exchange of presents that took place between the Americans and Japanese during a conference in 1854 symbolized the difference between the two countries. The United States received gifts of silk, brocades, lacquer ware, and other fine handmade articles; the Japanese received tokens of the new industrial world—a telegraph set, guns, and model railroad trains.

As a result of this conference and a later one, the United States and Japan signed the Treaty of Kanagawa. With this treaty both countries expressed a desire for peace, friendship, and developing trade. Japan also agreed to open two ports to United States trading vessels. Later, Japan opened other ports.

Japan enters the race for empire. Few events in modern history have had such far-reaching effects as the opening by the United States of the doors of Japan. Two major developments followed at once. In the first place, Americans and other traders started a lively commerce with Japan that grew to large proportions in the 1900's. Second, Japanese leaders were convinced that they should adopt the industrial techniques of the western nations.

Not all Japanese were immediately convinced of the need for industrializing and westernizing Japan. But a group of younger men were determined to modernize their country. These younger men started and successfully completed a revolution in 1868. Once they were in power, the process of modernization went on at an astonishingly rapid rate.

Japanese students traveled and studied in the major countries of Western Europe and the Americas, particularly the United States, borrowing from each country those techniques and developments that they found most promising. Japan borrowed ideas about governmental institutions from Great Britain, army organization from Germany, industrial techniques and educational organization from the United States.

By the end of the 1800's, Japan was a transformed country. But the "new" Japan faced new problems. Knowledge of science, medicine, and sanitation had reduced the death rate. This was a welcome development. But the lower death rate also meant a larger population—and this created difficulties, for Japan was a small country without enough farm land to feed all of its people adequately. The Japanese also needed raw materials for their new factories and markets for their products.

Faced with these problems, Japan started upon a program of imperialism similar to that being followed by the other industrial nations of the world. Japan needed colonies to secure food for its surplus population and to provide raw materials and markets for its growing industries. So it was that Japan entered the race for empire and became one of the rivals for control of strategic areas in the Far East.

As you have seen, Japan started its career as an imperial power with an attack upon China in the Sino-Japanese War of 1894–95. Ten years later, Japan plunged into war with Russia.

United States involvement. Although the Russo-Japanese War of 1904–05 took place on the western shores of the Pacific, nearly half a world away from the continental boundaries of the United States, Americans were immediately concerned. The new commitments of the United States in the Pacific had given Americans a direct interest in the affairs of the Far East. The war between Russia and Japan, fought on Chinese soil and in Pacific waters, threatened to interfere with the prospects of

American business in China. It also threatened to weaken, if not to destroy, the Open Door policy.

Acting on his own authority, President Theodore Roosevelt warned Germany and France that the United States would side with Japan if they gave aid to Russia. With Roosevelt acting as mediator, representatives from Russia and Japan met at Portsmouth, New Hampshire, during the summer of 1905 and worked out terms for the settlement of the conflict. In 1906, as a result of his efforts, Roosevelt received the Nobel peace prize.

The Treaty of Portsmouth transferred Russia's interests in Korea and Manchuria to Japan. The treaty also gave Japan the southern half of Sakhalin Island (see map, page 768). But the Russians refused to grant Japan's demand for a cash indemnity, and Roosevelt persuaded the Japanese, against their will, to waive this demand.

Roosevelt was delighted with the results of his efforts to end the Russo-Japanese War. The Treaty of Portsmouth left the Open Door policy intact. It maintained for a time the balance of power in the Far East. Neither Japan nor Russia nor any other colonial power had a dominant position in China. The doors of China remained open on equal terms to American business and trade.

↙ SECTION SURVEY

1. Trace American interest in Chinese trade from origins in 1784 to 1840.

2. Give the reasons for Chinese-American friendship 1840–1900.

3. (a) Describe the circumstances which led to the Open Door policy. (b) State the provisions of this policy.

4. What problems of modern Japan pointed it toward a program of imperialism?

5. Discuss the part played by Theodore Roosevelt in the Russo-Japanese War of 1904–05.

IDENTIFY: extraterritoriality, Boxer Rebellion, Treaty of Portsmouth, Nobel peace prize; Cushing, John Hay, Commodore Perry; 1853, 1900.

Points to Discuss: 1. What factors account for renewed American interest in colonies in the 1890's?

2. Discuss the reasons for American concern over the Cuban revolt of 1895.

3. What do you consider to be the key factors leading to the outbreak of the Spanish-American War? Justify your views.

4. In what sense do you think the conflict might have been avoided?

5. "The United States entered the war . . . to free the oppressed Cubans. It ended the war with an empire on its hands." Explain.

6. Contrast the arguments of those who favored American acquisition of the Philippines with those opposing acquisition.

7. Compare and contrast the Open Door policy for the Far East with the Monroe Doctrine for the Western Hemisphere.

8. What have proved to be far-reaching consequences of the opening of Japan in the mid-nineteenth century?

Using Maps: 1. (a) Since the war against Spain was designed to free Cuba, why was Dewey's fleet ordered to the Philippine Islands? (See the map on page 591.) (b) What was the significance of Dewey's victory?

2. The map on page 593 shows the naval strategy in the Caribbean Sea. (a) Identify the role played by each of the persons named in the map. (b) Describe the naval strategy of the Americans. (c) Locate the scenes of American victories.

3. Using the map on pages 842–43, point out the possessions the United States acquired as a result of the Treaty of Paris of 1898.

Consulting the Sources: On America's Open Door policy see correspondence of John Hay in Commager, *Documents*, No. 350. Nos. 372 and 420 add further information concerning United States-Japanese relations.

■ TRACING THE MAIN IDEAS

During the latter half of the 1800's, the major colonial powers of Europe were engaged in a lively race for empire. The United States, however, was not especially interested in entering the race. To be sure, in 1867–68 Secretary of State Seward persuaded Congress to annex the Midway Islands and to purchase Alaska, but Congress did so reluctantly and Americans on the whole were indifferent.

Toward the end of the 1800's, American sentiment began to change. It was the Spanish-American War, however, that finally started the United States down the road of imperialism.

The Spanish-American War of 1898 was begun in protest against Spanish policy in Cuba. It ended with a treaty in which Spain agreed to give up its claim to Cuba and in which the United States gained the Philippine Islands, as well as Guam and Puerto Rico. In addition to the Philippines and Guam, the United States acquired other territories in the Pacific area. Hawaii was annexed in 1898, and a portion of Samoa was acquired in 1899. To protect its growing interests, the United States insisted upon an equal opportunity to share in the business and trade of the Far East. This policy, known as the Open Door policy, involved Americans in the troubled affairs of eastern Asia, and committed the United States to a role of power politics in the Pacific.

But America's interest in colonies was not confined to the Pacific area. As you will see in the next chapter, the Caribbean offered even larger and more inviting opportunities for the development of American interests.

31

The Nation Expands in the Caribbean

BUILDING THE PANAMA CANAL –

O N August 12, 1898, the Spaniards signed the armistice that brought the Spanish-American War to an end. For both the United States and Spain this was a turning point in history.

By the terms of the armistice, Spain agreed (1) to leave Cuba, (2) to cede Puerto Rico and Guam to the United States, and (3) to allow American troops to occupy the Philippine Islands until a formal peace treaty could be drawn up and signed.

August 12, 1898, was a sad day for the Spanish nation. The Spaniards had reason for sorrow, for the Spanish-American War did indeed strike the final telling blow to the once mighty Spanish empire.

For the American people, however, the Spanish-American War marked an important milestone on the path of empire and world power. After 1898, as you have seen, the United States rapidly became a major power in the Pacific and in the Far East. And, as you will see in this chapter, between 1898 and 1914 the United States turned the Caribbean Sea into what was sometimes called "an American lake."

AS THE STORY DEVELOPS

1. Americans begin to build an empire in the Caribbean.
2. The United States modifies and strengthens the Monroe Doctrine.
3. The nation becomes involved in difficulties with Mexico.

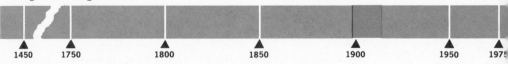

1450 1750 1800 1850 1900 1950 1975

1 Americans begin to build an empire in the Caribbean

The United States began to move into the area of the Caribbean Sea with the Spanish-American War in 1898. In less than twenty years, as you will see, the American flag was flying not only over Puerto Rico, but also over the Panama Canal Zone and the Virgin Islands; American advisers were helping to govern a number of small countries in and around the Caribbean; and the United States had developed a foreign policy for the Western Hemisphere.

"Does the Constitution follow the flag"? The acquisition of Puerto Rico, the Philippines, and other overseas possessions brought the American government face to face with an extremely important question: Were the people who lived in these areas entitled to all the rights guaranteed by the Constitution to citizens of the United States? Or, as the question was often stated, "Does the Constitution follow the flag?"

This question gave Congressmen reason for pause. Living in the newly acquired territories, for example, were savage tribes of Philippine head-hunters, as well as millions of Spanish-speaking people who had little understanding of the word "democracy." But if the Constitution did indeed "follow the flag," all of these people were entitled to all of the rights of American citizenship. Congressmen refused to accept this as an answer.

The Supreme Court's answer. The Supreme Court gave the answer in the so-called Insular Cases—a series of decisions handed down in 1901 and reaffirmed in other decisions between 1901 and 1922. The Supreme Court decided that there are two kinds of possessions —"incorporated" and "unincorporated." The "incorporated" possessions—Hawaii and Alaska—were destined for statehood, and the citizens of these possessions were therefore entitled to all the Constitutional rights guaranteed to United States citizens. The "unincorporated" possessions—Puerto Rico, the Philippines, Samoa, and others—were not destined for statehood, and the people of these areas were not, therefore, entitled to *all* of the Constitutional guarantees. The people of the "unincorporated" possessions were, however, entitled to certain fundamental rights, such as the guarantee that they would not be deprived of life, liberty, or property without due process of law.

With the Insular Cases the Supreme Court helped to develop a colonial policy for the United States. What the Court actually did was to turn America's growing colonial empire over to Congress to rule as it saw fit.

A government for Puerto Rico. In 1900, with the Foraker Act, Congress provided for the government of Puerto Rico. The new government consisted of a governor and an executive council appointed by the President of the United States. It also provided for a lower house elected by the Puerto Ricans.

Puerto Ricans were discontented, however, and continued to demand a larger voice in their own government. In 1917, shortly after the Filipinos won a similar victory in the Jones Act of 1916, the United States adopted a second Jones Act making Puerto Rico a United States Territory and giving the Puerto Ricans American citizenship. Puerto Ricans were also granted the right to elect both the lower and the upper houses of their legislature. Finally, in 1950, Congress gave Puerto Ricans their complete freedom. In 1952, they formed the Commonwealth of Puerto Rico. Today, Puerto Rico is, as one of its statesmen said, "associated with the American Union by bonds of affection, common citizenship, and free choice."

Strings on Cuban independence. Although Cuba has never been considered an American colony, American influence over Cuban affairs has been strong ever since the Spanish-American War.

The Teller Resolution, which Congress adopted at the same time that it declared war on Spain, pledged the

Cubans their independence (page 591). But the Cubans did not secure their freedom as soon as the war ended. For more than three years after the war, while Congress was deciding what to do about the island, Cuba was ruled by an American army of occupation under General Leonard Wood.

In 1901 Congress finally reached a decision. Cuba was to be returned to its own people, subject, however, to certain conditions that were incorporated in the Army Act of 1901 as the Platt Amendment: (1) The Cuban government must never enter into any agreements with foreign governments that might endanger Cuban independence. (2) The Cuban government must never incur debts that it could not hope to repay in a reasonable time. (3) The Cuban government must give the United States "The right to intervene for the preservation of Cuban independence, the maintenance of a government adequate for the protection of life, property, and individual liberty." (4) The Cuban government must place naval bases at the disposal of the United States. Congress also announced that the United States would not withdraw its military forces until the Platt Amendment had been written into the Cuban constitution.

This was not the "independence" that many Cubans had expected, yet they had to agree to the American demands. Accordingly, they accepted the Platt Amendment, and in 1902 the American forces were withdrawn.

A protectorate is established. Actually, Cuba became a "protectorate" of the United States. Webster's *New International Dictionary* defines "protectorate" as "A relation of superior authority assumed by one power or state over an inferior or a dependent one, whereby the former protects the latter from domestic or foreign disturbance or dictation . . . also . . . the country so protected." Cubans were not happy with this relationship because of their previous experience under Spanish rule.

On three different occasions between 1906 and 1920, American troops landed in Cuba to maintain order and to protect American business and property. Moreover, American diplomatic pressure frequently forced the Cubans to accept policies that were formulated in the United States.

In 1934, as you will see, Congress abolished the Platt Amendment. By so doing, Congress officially ended America's role of "protector" of Cuba.

Growing interest in a canal. During the years following the Spanish-American War, the United States was being pulled along a path of empire it had not foreseen. As the empire continued to grow in the Atlantic and the Pacific, people began to say that the United States needed two navies—one to protect its interests in the Pacific, the other to safeguard the Atlantic and the Caribbean.

But there was an alternative to a two-ocean navy. That was a canal across the narrow Isthmus of Panama separating the Atlantic and Pacific Oceans or, as another possible route, through Nicaragua (see map, opposite page). A canal would enable a fleet to pass easily and quickly from one ocean to another. It would also be of enormous commercial value to the United States, as well as to the merchant fleets of the entire world. Indeed, as early as 1878 a French company, the Panama Canal Company, had secured from Colombia the right to build a canal across the Isthmus of Panama, which was then a province of Colombia. But French efforts failed because of tropical diseases, lack of finances, engineering problems, and graft.

When the Spanish-American War broke out, the U.S. battleship *Oregon*, then in California waters, started a run around South America in an effort to reach and strengthen the Atlantic fleet. Public imagination was stirred, and for six weeks daily reports of the ship's progress appeared in every newspaper. The voyage of the *Oregon* convinced many Americans that a canal was needed and that the canal must be controlled by the United States.

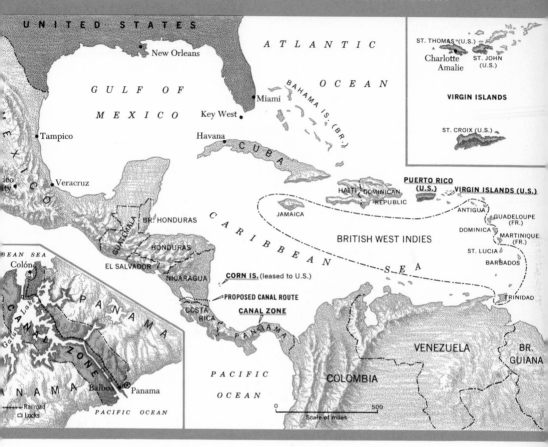

Great Britain withdraws its canal rights. Talk about building a canal through the Isthmus of Panama had gone on for a good many years. In fact, as early as 1850, the United States and Great Britain agreed in the Clayton-Bulwer Treaty that, if a canal were built, they would together control it and guarantee that it be unfortified and remain open to all nations in wartime.

By 1898, however, the United States government had changed its thinking about the canal project. Americans had concluded that the canal was so important to the United States that this country must have exclusive control over it. Negotiations were therefore opened with Great Britain, and in 1901 the Hay-Pauncefote Treaty was signed. In this treaty Great Britain abandoned all rights to share in the building and the management of the canal.

As a result of the Hay-Pauncefote Treaty, the United States was free to build and operate the canal. But it was understood that the canal would be open to all nations and that it would remain neutral in time of war.

Difficulties are encountered. The next step was to secure a right of way either through Nicaragua or across the Isthmus of Panama. The United States government decided in favor of the Isthmian route, and Secretary of State John Hay immediately opened negotiations with the foreign minister of the Colombian government, Señor Herrán. Soon the details were worked out and the Hay-Herrán treaty was ready for ratification. In return for a 99-year lease to a six-mile strip of land across the province of Panama, the United States agreed to pay Colombia $10,000,000 and a yearly rental of $250,000.

THE CONQUEST OF YELLOW FEVER

Dr. Walter Reed checked the time. It was 11:50 P.M., on the night of December 31, 1900. He was seated in the Columbia Barracks at Quemados, Cuba, writing to his wife back in the States. "Only ten minutes of the old century remain..." he wrote. "The prayer that has been mine for twenty years, that I might be permitted in some way or at some time to do something to alleviate human suffering has been granted. A thousand Happy New Years!"

Late in the summer of 1899, an epidemic of yellow fever had broken out in Cuba. Yellow fever is a disease that used to kill thousands of people each year in tropical and coastal cities. Dr. Walter Reed, an army surgeon, and three other doctors had been sent to Havana to investigate the situation. The other men were James Carroll, Jesse W. Lazear, and Aristides Agramonte. Their first important clue came from a Cuban doctor, Carlos J. Finlay, who had long suspected that yellow fever was transmitted by a certain mosquito, the *Stegomyia*. Dr. Reed and his fellow surgeons, impressed with this theory, began to carry on their own experiments. This took great courage, for they were constantly exposed to the dread disease.

Carroll, Lazear, and several other volunteers allowed themselves to be bitten by infected mosquitoes. All contracted the fever. All recovered, except Lazear, who died within a few days. He had given his life that others might live.

By their heroic work Dr. Reed and his associates had finally discovered the cause of yellow fever. Armed with the new knowledge, Major William Crawford Gorgas, son of a Confederate soldier, and Chief Surgeon of American Forces in Cuba, immediately took steps to eradicate the *Stegomyia* mosquito. Later, he also cleaned up the Canal Zone, making it possible for the United States to build the Panama Canal.

Matters stood at this promising point when the legislators of Colombia adjourned without taking action. They hoped that through further negotiations they would be able to secure better terms. But many Americans, including President Theodore Roosevelt, were furious, for as a result of Colombia's delay in ratifying the treaty the canal project was effectively blocked.

Revolution in Panama. Fortunately for the United States, many leaders in the province of Panama were also indignant at Colombia's delay in granting the right of way. These leaders had also dreamed of a canal that would place the province of Panama at a crossroads of world commerce. For years the people of Panama had resented control by Colombia. Colombia's delay was the last straw.

In Panama a group of men secretly met and began to organize a revolution. They were encouraged by representatives of the French company that had attempted in the 1880's to build a canal and now wanted to recover as much as it could of its investment.

One of the Panamanian leaders journeyed to Washington—secretly, of course—and asked the American government for assistance. Although open aid was refused, the Panamanian left Washington with the conviction that the United States would not interfere when the revolution started.

According to rumors, the revolution was to begin on November 4, 1903. On November 2 an American gunboat, the *Nashville,* arrived at Colón (see inset map, page 605). Hardly had it dropped anchor before a Colombian transport arrived with Colombian soldiers. The Colombian generals in command of the expedition immediately proceeded to the city of Panama, leaving orders for the troops to follow. Shortly after they arrived in Panama, however, the Colombian generals were seized and thrown into jail.

The seizure of the Colombian generals was a signal for the outbreak of the revolution. Two Colombian gunboats in the harbor hastily weighed anchor and fled, their commanders having been bribed by the revolutionists. A third gunboat fired one shot that killed a Chinese bystander, after which it, too, steamed away. So, with a minimum of violence, the city of Panama fell into the hands of the revolutionists.

Meanwhile, in Colón a dispute broke out, in the course of which Colombian soldiers and naval officers threatened to kill every American in the city. At this point United States marines landed. Colombian authorities demanded to know by what right Americans dared to interfere. The Americans replied that back in 1846 the United States had signed a treaty with Colombia in which the United States had guaranteed the free transit of the Isthmus. The United States government also added that no Colombian troops would be permitted to land within fifty miles of Panama. By this time other United States war ships had appeared off both Colón and Panama, and the United States had more than enough naval strength on hand to make its warning effective.

Panama grants the right of way. Largely because of American aid the revolution of Panama was a success. On November 4, 1903, the new government of Panama was installed in office. Two days later, on November 6, the United States recognized the independence of Panama.

Two weeks later, on November 18, Panama granted the United States the long-sought right of way across the Isthmus. The Hay–Bunau-Varilla (boo-NOH va-ree-YAH) Treaty, as it was called, gave the United States a perpetual lease to a ten-mile strip of land joining the Atlantic and the Pacific. In return, the United States agreed to pay Panama $10,000,000 and a yearly rental of $250,000.

Did the United States help to start the revolution in Panama? On one occasion President Theodore Roosevelt boastfully remarked, "I took Panama." On other occasions he denied that the United States had in any way helped to carry out the revolution. But irrespective of how the revolution was started, one fact is certain: It was a stroke of good fortune for the United States, and President Theodore Roosevelt did not lose a minute in making the most of the situation to advance American interests in Central America and the Caribbean.

Compensation for Colombia. Colombia was furious, of course, and the affair did much to stimulate the fear and distrust of the "Yankee" that was already strong throughout Latin America. In later years the United States attempted to conciliate the Colombian people. President Woodrow Wilson's Secretary of State, William Jennings Bryan, negotiated a treaty offering Colombia $25,000,000 by way of partial compensation, but the Senate of the United States refused to ratify the agreement. In 1921, however, the Senate ratified a similar agreement, and Colombia received $25,000,000 as partial compensation for the loss of the province of Panama.

■ This picture, which was taken in 1913, shows construction in progress on the enormous gates of the Miraflores lower locks of the Panama Canal.

Building the canal. Meanwhile, work on the canal progressed under the direct supervision of the United States Army Corps of Engineers. One of the first and most difficult tasks was the conquest of malaria, yellow fever, and other tropical diseases. Until these conditions were brought under control, workmen from the United States found it almost impossible to live in the Canal Zone.

Using medical discoveries made by Dr. Walter Reed and his colleagues in Cuba, Dr. William C. Gorgas, the surgeon in charge of the health problem in Panama, was able to turn a deadly, steaming tropical jungle into a relatively healthy region.

By 1914 the canal was completed (see inset map, page 605) at a cost of approximately $400,000,000. Its completion was a major triumph of engineering and a personal triumph for the engineer in charge, Colonel George W. Goethals (GOH-thalz).

The first traffic moved through the canal just as World War I broke out in Europe. During both of the great world wars, the canal added immeasurably to the naval strength of the United States, while its value as a peacetime artery of trade and commerce has been almost incalculable.

✔ SECTION SURVEY

1. How did the Supreme Court answer the question, "Does the Constitution follow the flag?" What were the insular cases?

2. What provisions did Congress make for the government of Puerto Rico?

3. (a) Give the provisions of the Platt Amendment. (b) How can it be said that this made Cuba an American protectorate?

4. Give the economic and military reasons for American interest in a canal through Central America.

5. (a) Discuss the problems involved in acquiring the Canal area and in building the canal. (b) Indicate the role played by Theodore Roosevelt.

IDENTIFY: Clayton-Bulwer Treaty, Hay-Pauncefote Treaty, recognition of a country, Hay–Bunau-Varilla Treaty; Reed; 1850, 1903.

2

The United States modifies and strengthens the Monroe Doctrine

During the opening years of the 1900's, as you have seen, the United States on a number of occasions intervened in the internal affairs of the smaller countries around the Caribbean Sea.

On what grounds did the United States justify this interference?

Reasons for interference. Intervention was necessary, Americans argued, to maintain law and order not only in the United States, but also in the countries that lay near the borders of the United States. In the first place, the United States government had an obligation to protect the lives and properties of its own citizens living in other countries. In the second place, the United States was determined as a matter of self-interest and self-defense to prevent European countries from intervening in the political affairs of the Western Hemisphere, and there would be less temptation for such intervention where law and order prevailed.

Americans developed the argument of self-defense into a well-defined foreign policy. This foreign policy consisted of the Monroe Doctrine strengthened, as you will see, by Theodore Roosevelt's interpretation of the doctrine, called the Roosevelt Corollary.

The original Doctrine of 1823. As you have learned (pages 261–62), the Monroe Doctrine was proclaimed at a time when European colonial powers were threatening to extend their political systems to the Western Hemisphere. In brief, President Monroe warned Europe in 1823 (1) not to attempt any further colonization in the Americas, and (2) not to interfere with existing independent governments in the Western Hemisphere.

When this warning was first issued and for many years thereafter, the United States did not have the necessary naval strength to enforce the policy. But the support of Latin Americans and the backing of the British Royal Navy gave weight to Monroe's words.

The first major test. The first major test of the Monroe Doctrine came during the 1860's when Napoleon III of France attempted to establish a French empire in Mexico. He could not have hoped for a more opportune time. Many French people were discontented with his rule, and a successful adventure in Mexico might stir their imaginations and distract them from their domestic troubles. Mexico, disturbed by revolution, had suspended payment on foreign bonds. The United States, torn by war between North and South, was in no position to prevent France from doing what it pleased in Mexico.

Napoleon's desire to seize control of Mexico had the support of numerous Frenchmen—of militarists and others seeking adventure and of businessmen seeking trade. So he acted. Together with Great Britain and Spain he sent an expedition to Mexico, supposedly to secure repayment of Mexico's debts. After Mexico repaid its debt, Great Britain and Spain withdrew. But Napoleon refused to pull out his troops. Instead, aided by Mexicans opposed to President Benito Juárez (beh-NEE-toh HWAH-rehs), Maximilian of Austria was installed as emperor. Juárez retired to El Paso del Norte near the United States border.

The United States immediately protested France's action, pointing out that French occupation of Mexico was a clear violation of the Monroe Doctrine. The United States also gave Juárez what aid it could without making a definite break with France. Not until 1865, however, was the American government in a position to take firm action. Then, with the war between the North and South ended, the United States prepared to send an American army to the Mexican border—farther, if necessary.

But the American army was not needed. Napoleon, faced with the danger of war in Europe and realizing that he could not hope to hold Mexico, withdrew his forces. Juárez and his followers destroyed Maximilian's army, and executed Maximilian in 1867.

It was a sorry affair all around. However, by upholding the Monroe Doctrine, Americans greatly increased their standing in the eyes of the rest of the world.

A second major test. A second major test of the Monroe Doctrine came in 1895. The immediate issue was a boundary dispute between Venezuela and British Guiana (see map, page 605).

This dispute had been going on ever since Great Britain acquired British Guiana back in 1814. Despite the protests of Venezuela, Great Britain had time and again pushed the western boundary of British Guiana on to territory claimed by Venezuela. Finally, in 1882, Venezuela demanded that Great Britain submit the controversy to arbitration. In a case involving arbitration, the nations engaged in the dispute agree in advance to accept the decision of a neutral party, known as the arbitrator.

The British refused to submit the boundary controversy to arbitration. In 1895 the Venezuelan government asked the United States to intervene. President Cleveland decided to act. In a message so blunt that it has few parallels in diplomatic history, Secretary of State Richard Olney warned Great Britain that the United States would not tolerate any further interference with Venezuela and demanded an immediate settlement of the affair by arbitration.

"Today the United States is practically sovereign on this continent," Olney boldly declared, "and its fiat° is law upon the subjects to which it confines its interposition. Why? . . . It is not because of the pure friendship or good will felt for it. It is not simply by reason of its high character as a civilized state, nor because wisdom and justice and equity are the invariable characteristics of the dealings of the United States. It is because, in addition to all other grounds, its infinite resources combined with its isolated position render it master of the

- -

° *fiat:* an authoritative order or decree.

situation and practically invulnerable against any or all other powers."

Great Britain indignantly rejected Olney's blunt demands. In the first place, the British retorted, the Monroe Doctrine had not been violated. In the second place, the Monroe Doctrine was not a recognized part of international law. In the third place, the United States had no business interfering.

President Cleveland refused to take no for an answer. When the British refusal to arbitrate reached him, he appointed an American commission and ordered it to investigate the controversy and reach a decision. This was a direct challenge to British imperial power.

Realizing that war between Great Britain and the United States was a real possibility, responsible men in both countries began to urge moderation. Partly because of their efforts and partly because of British difficulties in South Africa at the time, the British government suddenly reversed its position and agreed to arbitrate the boundary dispute. It even offered to help the American commission with its investigation.

Once more the Monroe Doctrine had been successfully upheld by the United States. And on this occasion the United States could maintain that its foreign policy had been used to protect a weak state against the power of a great empire. Even more important, perhaps, was the fact that the British, desiring American friendship, now in effect recognized that the United States had special interests in the Caribbean area.

A third major test. In 1902, seven years later, Venezuela again became involved in a dispute with European countries. Venezuela was unable to repay debts owed to Great Britain, Germany, and Italy. After their demands for repayment produced no results, the three countries took joint action. They withdrew their diplomatic representatives, blockaded the Venezuelan coast, and seized several small gunboats.

At this point President Theodore Roosevelt warned the European powers that any attempt to seize territory in the Western Hemisphere would be a violation of the Monroe Doctrine. Then he urged the countries involved to submit the dispute to arbitration. They did so, and the matter was settled.

The Drago Doctrine. In the case of Mexico and in both of the Venezuelan controversies, the United States had intervened in the name of the Monroe Doctrine to warn European nations to keep out of the politics of the Western Hemisphere. In all of these controversies, the United States had helped to protect its weaker neighbors.

By 1902, however, it was becoming clear that many Americans were eager to promote their own interests in Latin America. The United States had gone into the Spanish-American War in 1898 with the announced purpose of helping the oppressed Cubans, and it had come out of the war in control of Cuba and owning Puerto Rico. Moreover, by the opening years of the 1900's, Americans in growing numbers were investing money in the Caribbean countries.

Latin-American leaders began to become alarmed at the growing interest and influence of the United States. In 1902 one of these leaders, Luis M. Drago, Argentine Minister of Foreign Affairs, announced a policy for Latin America that came to be known as the Drago Doctrine.

Señor Drago declared that Argentina would not admit the right of any country, European or American, to use force to collect debts from a Latin-American nation. He took the position that, when individuals or nations lent money, they did so at their own risk.

Nearly all of Latin America's leaders, as well as many citizens of the United States, agreed with Luis M. Drago. But in 1904 President Roosevelt announced a policy that was in complete opposition to the Drago Doctrine. The immediate occasion for the announcement was trouble in the Dominican Republic.

The Roosevelt Corollary. The Dominican Republic (see map, page 605) owed long-overdue debts to several European countries as well as to American investors. When the European countries threatened to use armed force to collect the money, President Roosevelt at once intervened.

In his annual message to Congress in 1904, Roosevelt boldly announced that, if it became necessary for any nation to interfere in the affairs of a Latin-American country, it would be the United States that interfered, not a European government. "Chronic wrongdoing, or an impotence which results in a general loosening of the ties of civilized society, may in America, as elsewhere, ultimately require intervention by some civilized nation," Roosevelt declared, "and in the Western Hemisphere the adherence of the United States to the Monroe Doctrine may force the United States, however reluctantly, in flagrant cases of such wrongdoing or impotence, to the exercise of an international police power."

The new policy laid down in 1904 by President Roosevelt came to be known as the Roosevelt Corollary to the Monroe Doctrine. With this policy, the United States assumed the role of "big policeman" in the Western Hemisphere. On a number of occasions during the next two decades, the United States used the Roosevelt Corollary as justification for intervening in the affairs of its neighbors south of the Rio Grande.

There was, of course, another side to the Roosevelt Corollary. It aimed to make conditions in the Latin-American countries such that European governments would have no excuse for intervention. In this sense, the Roosevelt Corollary helped all of the American countries. But Latin Americans could not forget that it was also a weapon that could be used against them and was an insult to their national pride.

A protectorate over the Dominican Republic. The United States first exercised its "international police power" by intervening in the affairs of the Dominican Republic. In 1905 President Roosevelt reached an agreement with the Dominican government. As part of the agreement, he promised to guarantee

RIFLEMAN   OFFICER

United States Marine uniforms

the *territorial integrity* of the Republic. That is, he promised to use American armed forces, if this were necessary, to prevent any European country from seizing Dominican territory. In exchange for this guarantee, the Dominican government agreed to allow an American agent to collect the customs duties, to turn over 45 per cent of the duties to the Dominican government, and to apportion the remainder of the money among its foreign creditors.

President Roosevelt asked the Senate to convert this agreement into a formal treaty. When the Senate refused, Roosevelt proceeded to put the agreement into effect without Senate approval. In 1907, however, the Senate ratified a treaty containing a slightly revised version of the original agreement.

Although customs duties doubled under American supervision and the financial position of the Dominican Republic improved, the Dominican people as a whole resented this control by the United States. Finally, in 1916 the Dominican government announced that it intended to end the protectorate.

The United States answered this challenge by landing marines and suspending the Dominican legislature. For eight years, until 1924, the Dominican Republic was ruled by a military dictatorship under the American government. The United States withdrew its military forces in 1924, but did not give up its role of "protector" until 1940.

A protectorate over Haiti. The same general methods used to secure control of the Dominican Republic were applied to the Republic of Haiti, which lies at the western end of the same island occupied by the Dominican Republic (see map, page 605).

When revolutions shook the debt-ridden Haitian republic in 1914, the United States landed marines. The marines marched to the National Bank of Haiti, seized $500,000 of government gold from the vaults, and loaded it on an American cruiser, which carried it to New York for deposit. Although the Haitian republic retained title to this gold and received interest from the United States, control of the money was taken out of Haitian hands.

The Haitians were then asked to ratify a treaty prepared by the United States Department of State. This treaty gave the United States (1) supervision over Haiti's finances, (2) the right to intervene to maintain order, and (3) control over the Haitian police force. After considerable pressure from the United States, the legislature of Haiti ratified the treaty, which went into effect early in 1916.

Unfortunately, neither the ratification of the treaty by the puppet legislature nor the continued presence of an American military force was sufficient to restore law and order completely. During the next four or five years nearly 2000 Haitians were killed in riots and other outbreaks of violence.

Nevertheless, some improvements did come to the republic during the years that the United States was in control. Some Americans, however, shared the viewpoint of many Haitians, who argued that better sanitation, health, education, and increased prosperity were not worth the loss of freedom.

Despite continued resentment in Haiti and growing pressure from the American public to end military occupation of the island, the treaty permitting American control was renewed in 1926, as you will see. But in 1930 President Herbert Hoover announced that all American troops would be withdrawn at the expiration of the treaty in 1936. Two years before that date, in 1934, President Franklin D. Roosevelt withdrew all military forces and gave the Haitian government a greater share of authority over the finances of the republic.

American interference in Central America. Twice during the first two decades of the 1900's, American military forces were used in Nicaragua and Honduras to get control of these republics. And in addition to this, the United States exercised a large amount of influence over the governments of Colombia, Costa Rica, and Guatemala (see map, page 605). This influence was secured by means of a policy that came to be called "dollar diplomacy."

Under the so-called "dollar diplomacy," American bankers, sometimes by invitation of the Department of State, lent money to Caribbean governments. When the debtors failed to repay their debts or the interest on their loans, the United States government intervened to protect American investments. This intervention took various forms, including the landing of marines, the supervision of elections, and support to the political group that favored the United States.

Purchase of the Virgin Islands. By purchase of three of the Virgin Islands from Denmark, the United States completed its colonial holdings in the Caribbean (see map, page 605).

Back in 1868 Secretary of State Seward had tried to get Congress to buy the Virgin Islands. Congress had refused then, and refused again in 1902.

In 1917, however, with World War I raging in Europe, the United States was fearful that Germany might secure control of these strategic bases, and it renewed the offer to buy the islands. This time negotiations were completed. With the payment of $25,000,000 to Denmark, the islands became outposts of America's Caribbean empire.

Like Puerto Rico the Virgin Islands are poor and have required considerable expenditures of American money for relief. But their value to the United States cannot be measured in terms of dollars and cents. As the map on page 605 shows, the Virgin Islands lie at the eastern edge of the West Indies. United States naval bases on the islands, and on Puerto Rico, help to guarantee American control over the Caribbean Sea and the approaches to the Panama Canal.

✎ SECTION SURVEY

1. (a) How did Americans justify intervention in the Caribbean area around 1900? (b) Review key provisions of the Monroe Doctrine.

2. Describe the Maximilian affair as the first major test of the Monroe Doctrine.

3. (a) Relate the facts and the outcome of the Venezuela boundary dispute. (b) How did Olney's interpretation in this matter broaden the Monroe Doctrine?

4. (a) How did the Roosevelt Corollary conflict with the Drago Doctrine? (b) How did it modify the Monroe Doctrine? (c) Give examples of its application.

5. Describe the reaction of the Latin Americans to the Roosevelt Corollary.

IDENTIFY: territorial integrity, dollar diplomacy, purchase of Virgin Islands; Napoleon III, Juárez; 1895, 1902, 1904, 1917.

3 The nation becomes involved in difficulties with Mexico

American investments south of the Rio Grande in time involved the United States in conflict with Mexico.

By the time Woodrow Wilson became President in 1913, American citizens had invested a total of nearly one billion dollars in Mexican oil wells, mines, railroads, and ranches. Most of Mexico's trade was with the United States.

Dictatorship and revolution. Mexico's President Porfirio Diaz was in large part responsible for the fact that his country was closely tied to the United States. Although Diaz had the title of "President," he was actually a dictator who had ruled Mexico since 1877. During the course of his long rule, he had brought peace and order to the country. He had also done a great deal to develop Mexico's material resources. But, in order to develop the country's resources, he had encouraged foreign investors to finance and operate mines, factories, and other industries by offering them special privileges. Given this encouragement, foreign capital, much of it from American investors, had poured into Mexico. As a result, however, foreign investors and the privileged friends of dictator Diaz enjoyed most of the material benefits of Mexico's developing economy.

Finally, in 1910, the Mexicans staged a successful revolution. Diaz resigned and left for Europe. A sincere reformer, Francisco Madero, then became president. But President Madero did not remain in office long. Early in 1913 he was assassinated and Victoriano Huerta (WEHR-tah) seized the government.

But Huerta had many enemies, including the friends of the late President Madero. The struggle between Huerta and his enemies, led by Venustiano Carranza, plunged Mexico into more violence and bloodshed.

Wilson's policy of "watchful waiting." Needless to say, Americans with investments in Mexico were deeply troubled by the situation. Not only investors were troubled. Millions of people throughout the Americas were dismayed that Huerta had risen to power as the result of a cold-blooded murder.

Under the circumstances, a number of Americans hoped that President Wilson would send an armed force into Mexico to protect the American investments and to restore law and order. Wilson chose, instead, to follow a policy that he hoped would preserve the independence of the Mexican people.

Wilson outlined his policy in a speech that he gave in Mobile, Alabama, shortly after he had been elected. "The United States will never again seek one ad-

A FEW "FIRSTS"

During the years that Mexico was being shaken by revolution, Americans chalked up a number of "firsts" in transportation and communication.

The first airmail delivery in America took place in the autumn of 1911 when Postmaster General Frank H. Hitchcock and Captain Paul Beck flew a sack of mail in a Curtiss biplane a distance of a few miles between two points near New York City.

In that same year C. P. Rogers made the first transcontinental airplane flight. His total time in the air between New York and Pasadena, California, was 82 hours and 4 minutes.

On January 7, 1912, the New York *Sun* carried an advertisement of "The Disco Self-Starter"—"the most marked advance shown for motor cars for 1912 . . . Safe—Sure—Simple. We can make your car self-starting and up-to-date in three hours. . . ."

On January 1, 1913, the Parcel Post Service was inaugurated in the United States.

On June 17, 1914, work on the first transcontinental telephone line connecting the Atlantic and Pacific coasts was completed when the last pole was set in place on the Nevada-Utah state line.

On August 15, 1914, the Panama Canal was opened to traffic.

In October 1914 work began on the Lincoln Highway, which was eventually to carry automobile traffic from coast to coast.

powers, not only within their borders but from outside their borders also." He then urged the Latin-American countries to settle the Mexican problem in their own way.

Although a number of European countries promptly recognized the Huerta government, Wilson refused to do so. He pointed out that Huerta had come to power, not by the will of the Mexican people, but by means of force and murder. Moreover, he was convinced that the Mexicans themselves would soon get rid of Huerta. Meanwhile, Wilson announced that the United States would follow a policy of "watchful waiting."

Wilson's refusal to intervene pleased most Latin Americans, who could hardly believe their ears. But many American businessmen with Mexican investments were furious as they saw life and property destroyed in Mexico, and they savagely attacked the President.

Wilson decides to intervene. As the months passed, however, even President Wilson began to lose patience. Hundreds of small revolutionary bands roamed Mexico, but they were not organized, and Huerta remained in power. More disturbing was the fact that Huerta seemed to take delight in taunting the United States. Nor did he stop with taunts. American citizens were killed in Mexico, and there were rumors that Huerta might try to *confiscate*, or seize, American property.

The final crisis came in April 1914 when a Mexican official arbitrarily arrested several American sailors who had landed in a zone of Tampico, Mexico, then under martial law, to buy gasoline. The sailors were soon released, but Huerta refused to apologize for the incident. To make matters worse, a German ship arrived at Veracruz with a cargo of machine guns and other military supplies for Huerta. President Wilson then ordered the United States marines to seize Veracruz. Emboldened by America's action, the anti-Huerta forces in Mexico began to gain strength, and Huerta fled the country.

ditional foot of territory by conquest," he declared. "We have seen material interests threaten constitutional freedom in the United States," he went on to say. "Therefore we will now know how to sympathize with those in the rest of America who have to contend with such

The "ABC mediation." The United States was now in a position to dictate the choice of the new Mexican president. But Wilson would have none of this. Instead, he accepted an invitation from Argentina, Brazil, and Chile—sometimes called the "ABC powers"—for United States representatives to meet with Mexican leaders and other interested parties and try to reach a solution agreeable to all concerned. Huerta could not afford to ignore a similar invitation, and the conference was held at Niagara Falls, Canada. As a result of the "ABC mediation," Huerta resigned and left for Europe.

Venustiano Carranza then established himself in power in Mexico, and American forces were withdrawn from Veracruz. And in 1915, after Carranza guaranteed that Mexico would respect the lives and property of foreigners, the United States recognized him as the head of the Mexican government.

Wilson sends troops to Mexico. But trouble still continued, for the victors in Mexico began to quarrel among themselves. One of the men who turned against Carranza was Francisco (Pancho) Villa (VEE-lyah). Angry at the United States for helping Carranza and hoping at the same time to force American interference in Mexico, Villa and his followers in 1916 seized 18 Americans in northern Mexico and cold-bloodedly put them to death. Later, he crossed the border and raided Columbus, New Mexico, killing 17 Americans. President Wilson immediately declared that he intended to send an expedition into Mexico to capture Villa, "dead or alive." Carranza agreed, although with understandable reluctance, and General John J. Pershing led an initial force of some 5000 men across the border. But the deeper Pershing penetrated Mexican territory, the more hostile the Mexicans became. For a time the shadow of full-scale war hung over both countries. More than 100,000 troops of the United States National Guard were camped at the Mexican border. Finally, in January 1917, American

■ "Pancho" Villa, a brilliant horseman, was thought of by many Mexicans as a modern Robin Hood. In Mexico his memory still lives in ballads and tales.

troops withdrew from Mexico, with Villa still at large.

President Woodrow Wilson had tried, and tried sincerely, to respect the independence and freedom of the Mexican people. In the end, however, he had to use force to maintain law and order and respect for the United States. In the course of this troubled chapter in Mexican–United States relations, Wilson learned that it was not easy for the United States to keep aloof from a nearby country where disorder threatened Americans.

⮕ **SECTION SURVEY**

1. Show how the economic interests of the United States and Mexico were closely interwoven.

2. (a) Describe the circumstances that led to Wilson's policy of "watchful waiting." (b) Explain this policy.

3. Why did Wilson abandon "watchful waiting"?

4. What important lesson did Americans learn from their experiences with Mexico during the years 1910–17?

IDENTIFY: confiscate, ABC powers; Diaz, Madero, Huerta, Carranza, Villa, Pershing; 1914, 1916.

■ CHAPTER SURVEY (For review, see Section Surveys, pages 608, 613, 615.)

Points to Discuss: 1. For the American people the Spanish-American War marked an important milestone on the path of empire and world power. Explain this statement as it applied to (a) the Pacific, (b) the Caribbean.

2. In what sense does the Platt Amendment seem out of tune with the Teller Resolution?

3. Theodore Roosevelt said: "I took Panama and left Congress to debate about it." What did he mean?

4. Why did the United States pay Colombia $25,000,000 in 1921?

5. How did American aid contribute to the success of the Panama revolution?

6. How was the meaning of the Monroe Doctrine broadened by (a) the Olney interpretation in the Venezuela boundary dispute and (b) in the Venezuela debt controversy, (c) the Roosevelt Corollary in the Dominican debt controversy?

7. Discuss historical highlights of Mexican-American relations, 1900–17.

Using Maps: Use the map on page 605 for the following questions:

1. Indicate why the Caribbean Sea was once called an "American Lake."

2. (a) In traveling from the Caribbean to the Pacific through the Panama Canal, at which cities would you enter and leave the Canal? (b) How many locks are shown?

3. Identify the major islands of the Virgin Islands.

4. What is the approximate distance from Miami, Florida, to each of the following: (a) Puerto Rico, (b) Havana, Cuba, and (c) the Virgin Islands?

5. (a) Identify the countries in Central America. (b) What are their chief products? (Consult an encyclopedia.)

6. Describe briefly the Mexican-American crisis which occurred in 1914 at Tampico and Vera Cruz.

7. Do you think a second canal should be built at the place indicated on the map? Justify your point of view.

Consulting the Sources: See A. B. Hart, ed., *American History Told by Contemporaries*, Vol. 5, Nos. 38 and 50, for the humorous but critical poems of Wallace Irwin concerning America's foreign relations. No. 40 gives Wilson's message to Congress relative to our Mexican relations in 1913.

■ TRACING THE MAIN IDEAS

The Spanish-American War of 1898 marked a turning point in America's position in the world. During the opening decade of the 1900's, the United States embarked upon a program of imperialism similar in many ways to that being followed by the powers of the Western world, as well as by Japan.

Driven by complex forces that were reshaping the pattern of life throughout the world, the United States began at the turn of the century to extend its influence in the Pacific and the Caribbean. The Panama Canal provided a connecting link between the various parts of America's rapidly growing empire. To protect that vital artery of trade, the United States took steps to bring the Caribbean countries under its influence. Each new step the United States government took, each new commitment it

assumed, led to additional steps and additional commitments.

By 1914 the United States had formulated two basic foreign policies. The Open Door policy aimed to secure equality of opportunity for Americans in the Far East. The Monroe Doctrine, to which new teeth had been added by the Roosevelt Corollary, aimed to safeguard United States interests in the Western Hemisphere.

During the opening years of the 1900's, the United States became a world power. But the position of world power brought with it new problems and new responsibilities.

In the next chapter you will see why and how the United States was drawn into World War I, and how the nation emerged from that conflict as a great world power.

32

The Nation Fights a War in Europe

AMERICANS ADVANCE IN ARGONNE OFFENSIVE

THE summer of 1914 ushered in a new age—an age characterized by violence and revolution. Within the course of a few fateful months, the fabric of peace went up in flames, and the world was plunged into what until then was the most terrible war in history.

On the morning of July 28, Americans opened their newspapers with shocked surprise. In screaming headlines the New York *Tribune* reported, "AUSTRIA DECLARES WAR, RUSHES VAST ARMY INTO SERBIA; RUSSIA MASSES 80,000 MEN ON BORDER." Other papers carried the same news.

In general, the reaction of the American public was one of both stunned disbelief and withdrawal. Europeans could not be so reckless. But if they were, well, let them reap the consequences. Americans wanted no part of this uncivilized behavior.

The conflict that started in the summer of 1914 spread rapidly. Before it ended four years later, 30 nations on 6 continents were involved; more than 8 million fighting men had been killed; an equal number of civilians had lost their lives; and property worth countless billions of dollars had gone up in smoke and flames.

But before looking at the war itself, it is necessary to find answers to several important questions: Why did the news of war come as such a surprise to the American public? Why did Americans think that the war was no concern of theirs? And, finally, what at last drew the United States into the conflict?

AS THE STORY DEVELOPS

1. Americans become active in the development of international co-operation.
2. Despite efforts at peace, World War I breaks out in Europe.
3. The United States tries to remain neutral in World War I.
4. The United States declares war and mobilizes its strength.
5. American troops and ideals help the Allies win the war.

1750   1800   1850   1900   1950   1975
450

1

Americans become active in the development of international co-operation

During the late 1800's and the opening years of the 1900's, the great nations of the world had made strong strides along the road of international co-operation. By 1914 millions of men and women in both Europe and America were convinced that major wars were a thing of the past.

The peace movement. For nearly a hundred years a strong peace movement had been steadily gaining strength (page 345). During the early 1900's antiwar societies in both Europe and America stepped up their activities. These societies printed and distributed numerous pamphlets containing arguments against war. The pamphlets pointed out that war was wasteful and failed to solve the problems it was intended to solve— that even the victors paid too high a price for victory.

But the advocates of peace did not rest their case on these more or less general arguments. They reminded people of the growing interdependence of nations, and they listed the many steps men had taken along the road of international co-operation.

Growing interdependence. It was obvious to everyone that science and technology were rapidly breaking down the barriers of space and time and bringing the peoples of the earth closer together. Railway trains rumbled across national boundaries carrying freight and passengers. Luxurious liners steamed back and forth across the oceans, and freighters loaded and unloaded cargoes in all the ports of the world. The telegraph, the telephone, and underwater cables enabled men to carry on almost instantaneous communication from one end of the earth to the other.

These and other technological developments greatly increased the number, variety, and importance of activities that people of different nations could and did carry on together. Businessmen

bought and sold in truly world-wide markets and built industries in countries other than their own. Humanitarian associations, among them the Red Cross, organized on an international basis. Professional groups—scientists, engineers, medical men, scholars in many fields—formed international societies and pooled their knowledge for the benefit of all peoples.

International agencies. Governments as well as individual citizens were also engaged in a growing number of activities requiring the co-operation of a number of different nations. Among the first international agencies were the International Telegraph Union (ITU), organized in 1865; the Universal Postal Union (UPU), organized in 1874; and the International Meteorological Organization (IMO), organized in 1878. By 1914, 30 different international agencies of government had been organized to deal with problems common to many nations —and, in some cases, common to all nations. Included in the problems were those of transportation, communications, disease and sanitation, weights and measures, postal regulations, and maritime rules.

Although the international administrative agencies were not organized specifically to prevent war, they did help to promote the cause of peace. By the very process of bringing the peoples of the world together in co-operative attacks upon common problems, all of these agencies helped to strengthen international understanding.

The Pan-American Union. Meanwhile, the governments of the leading nations of the world had been taking direct steps to prevent war. On several occasions during the late 1800's and the opening years of the 1900's, delegates from many different nations met to discuss the issues of war and peace.

The Pan-American Conference of 1889–90 was one of the early meetings. Delegates from the Latin-American countries and the United States met in Washington where, with Secretary of State James G. Blaine serving as chairman, they organized the International Union of American Republics.

In his farewell speech to the delegates, Secretary of State Blaine said, "If, in this closing hour, the conference had but one deed to celebrate, we should dare call the world's attention to the deliberate, confident, solemn dedication of two great continents to peace, and to the prosperity which has peace for its foundation. We hold up this new Magna Carta, which abolishes war and substitutes arbitration between the American republics, as the first and great fruit of the International American Conference."

Since 1890 the International Union of American Republics—known today as the Organization of American States or, more simply, as the Pan-American Union—has held periodic meetings to discuss common problems. In 1908 President Theodore Roosevelt laid the cornerstone of the Pan-American Union building in Washington, D.C., on land given by the United States. The building itself was constructed with funds contributed by each of the 21 American republics plus a substantial grant from Andrew Carnegie.

In the opening years of the 1900's, as you know, United States expansion and interference in the Caribbean area aroused the antagonism of a number of Latin-American countries. These were the same years in which the Pan-American Union was seeking to weld the 21 American republics into a co-operative community of nations. United States action in the Caribbean greatly weakened the influence of the Pan-American Union. Nevertheless, to people throughout the Americas, the Pan-American Union was the symbol of a new, more peaceful world that was coming into being, and a bright promise for the future.

The Hague Conferences. Millions of men and women in both Europe and the Americas had also taken hope from two conferences held in Europe.

The First Hague Conference, called at the request of the tsar of Russia, met at The Hague in the Netherlands in 1899. Twenty-six nations sent delegates. After long and careful deliberation the delegates strongly urged nations to try to settle disputes by means of mediation or arbitration. In cases involving mediation, two or more nations engaged in a dispute would ask a disinterested third party or nation to "recommend" a solution. In cases involving arbitration, as you know, two or more nations engaged in a dispute would agree in advance to accept the decision of a neutral party. In order to encourage nations to submit their disputes to arbitration, the First Hague Conference organized the Permanent Court of Arbitration with headquarters at The Hague. The conference also tried to lessen the horrors of warfare by outlawing certain weapons and by drawing up rules for the conduct of land and sea forces.

The Second Hague Conference, called by the tsar of Russia and President Theodore Roosevelt, met at The Hague in 1907. This time 44 nations sent delegates. The conference drafted additional "rules" for the conduct of war. It also adopted the Drago Doctrine (page 610), which stated that no nation should use force to collect debts "unless the debtor country refused arbitration, or having accepted arbitration, failed to submit to the award."

The results of the first two Hague Conferences greatly encouraged men who were working to promote peace. Plans were under way for a third conference when war broke out in Europe.

Individual efforts to promote peace. American citizens, both in public office and in private life, took an active part in the search for ways to prevent war. Edward Ginn, well-known Boston publisher, provided a grant of money to establish the World Peace Foundation. Andrew Carnegie set up the Carnegie Endowment for International Peace; donated money to construct the "peace palace," the building for the Permanent Court of Arbitration at The Hague; and, as you know, gave a grant to help construct the Pan-American Union building in Washington, D.C.

Although President Theodore Roosevelt believed that some wars were necessary, he played a leading role in the peace movement. He was responsible, as you know, for the 1905 peace conference held at Portsmouth, New Hampshire, at which Japan and Russia reached an agreement ending the Russo-Japanese War. The following year Roosevelt took the lead in urging France and Germany to meet at the Algeciras (al-juh-SEER-uhs) Conference in Spain to settle a dispute over control of Morocco in North Africa. Roosevelt and his successor, President Taft, played an active part in other international negotiations.

President Wilson, who entered the White House in 1913, was an even stronger champion of international understanding. He vigorously supported his Secretary of State, William Jennings Bryan, who successfully negotiated antiwar treaties with 21 nations in 1913 and 1914. These treaties declared that every controversy, without exception, must be submitted to a joint commission for investigation and recommendation. The nations that signed these treaties promised not to go to war until the commissions had made their reports.

By 1914 men had built what seemed to be a solid and enduring structure of peace. Why, then, did war break out?

SECTION SURVEY

1. Describe the factors which contributed to the peace movement in the early 1900's.
2. In what ways did international administrative agencies help to promote peace?
3. Trace the history of Pan-American co-operation efforts from 1889 to 1908.
4. (a) Evaluate the results of the first two Hague Peace Conferences. (b) What interrupted plans for a third conference?
5. Summarize briefly the contributions of two American Presidents and two private citizens to international understanding.

IDENTIFY: mediation, arbitration, Permanent Court of Arbitration; 1889–90, 1899.

2 Despite efforts at peace, World War I breaks out in Europe

War broke out in 1914 because the elaborate safeguards men had built to prevent war were not so powerful as the divisive forces that were pulling nations apart. Despite the many efforts being made to preserve peace in the early 1900's, the nations of Europe during these years were, so to speak, standing on a powder keg. In the summer of 1914, someone struck a spark to the powder, and all men's hopes and plans for peace suddenly exploded.

The "spark" that began the war. The spark was struck in the Balkan Peninsula of Europe (see map, page 623).° The man who struck the spark was a young Serbian student named Gavrilo Prinzip. The members of a Serbian secret society to which Prinzip belonged had pledged themselves to work—and fight, if need be—to free all Slavs° of the Balkan Peninsula who were under the rule of the Austro-Hungarian empire. One of their most hated enemies was the Archduke Francis Ferdinand, heir to the throne of Austria-Hungary.

Early in the summer of 1914, news reached Prinzip and his fellow conspirators that the archduke planned to visit the city of Sarajevo (SAH-rah-yeh-voh), capital of the province of Bosnia, then under Austrian rule, now a part of Yugoslavia. The conspirators slipped across the borders of Serbia into Bosnia and were waiting on the streets of Sarajevo on Sunday, June 28, when the archduke drove by in his carriage with his wife, the Duchess of Hohenberg, at his side. Prinzip fired his Browning pistol into the carriage, killing both Archduke Francis Ferdinand and his wife.

° Countries occupying the Balkan Peninsula included Montenegro, Serbia, Albania, Bulgaria, Rumania, Greece, and Turkey.
° *Slavs:* a race of people widely spread over central, eastern, and southeastern Europe. The Slavs under Austro-Hungarian rule were called South Slavs.

POPE BENEDICT XV AND WORLD WAR I

The start of the great war in 1914 is believed to have hastened the dying of Pope St. Pius X. When asked by the Austrians to bless their cause, he refused, saying that he blessed peace, not war.

For his successor, Pope Benedict XV, the next four years were difficult ones. Italy was neutral for a year, but had political ties with Germany and Austria (in the Triple Alliance). While seeking to prevent the spread of the war, although the Italian government paid little attention to him, Benedict was accused by both sets of belligerents of unneutral meddling. The accusations continued after Italy entered the war on the side of Britain, France, and Russia.

By 1917, when the United States declared war on Germany, Europe's people were war weary. President Wilson had declared, in January, that there must be a "peace without victory." It was with

great reluctance that, in April, he asked Congress to declare war on Germany to make the world safe for democracy.

In August, however, Wilson was somewhat embarrassed by proposals for stopping the war which came to all the belligerents from Pope Benedict. To prevent further bloodshed and secure a just peace, at a time when some important statesmen on both sides had declared it was futile to continue hostilities, the Pope offered reasonable proposals for a settlement. These resembled in some respects Wilson's own peace plan of the year following, the famous Fourteen Points of 1918: freedom of the seas, arbitration of disputed frontiers, disarmament, and the substitution of the moral force of right for material force. To these proposals, Wilson replied for the United States and the Allies that no peace could be made with the existing German government.

Gavrilo Prinzip and a number of his companions were caught and brought to trial. But Francis Joseph, the 83-year-old emperor of Austria-Hungary, and his associates were not content merely to punish the men who had murdered the archduke. They decided to use this opportunity to put an end once and for all to plots and schemes for Slavic independence. What better way to do this, they asked themselves, than to destroy

the power of Serbia, the country they held responsible for most of the activities directed against Austro-Hungarian rule of the Slavs? Accordingly, Austria made certain severe demands against Serbia, which Serbia refused to meet.

As tension mounted, European diplomats struggled to solve the differences between Austria-Hungary and Serbia. But Austria lined up the support of its main ally, Germany, and prepared for war. And so, Austria-Hungary declared war on Serbia on July 28, and the Austrian armies began to move southward across the border.

The war spreads. The action of Austria-Hungary set in motion a chain of explosive events. Russia, a Slavic country sometimes called the "Protector of the Slavs," immediately ordered a general mobilization of its armies and prepared to aid Serbia. Germany promptly declared war on Russia on August 1. When France, an ally of Russia, refused to declare its neutrality, Germany declared war on France on August 3. Great Britain, an ally of France, then declared war on Germany on August 4 and on Austria on August 12.

A week after Austria-Hungary's attack on Serbia, then, five of the major nations of Europe were at war. During the following weeks and months the conflict widened. Before it ended, the war had engulfed 30 nations on 6 continents. The nations siding with Austria-Hungary and Germany came to be known as the Central Powers. Those allying themselves with Russia, France, and Great Britain were commonly referred to as the Allied Powers, or simply as the Allies.

Did the tragic incident at Sarajevo really start World War I? Yes and no. It was the immediate cause, the spark that touched off the explosion. But there were deep, underlying causes which help to explain why the war came and why it spread so rapidly and so widely.

Nationalism as a cause. An intense spirit of nationalism was one of the underlying sources of tension. The term *nationalism* often refers to the strong feeling people have for their own country, but it may also refer to the desire of a subjugated people to throw off foreign rule and create their own nation. As you have seen, it was a desire to free certain Slavs from Austro-Hungarian rule that prompted Gavrilo Prinzip and his fellow conspirators to assassinate the heir to the throne of Austria-Hungary. As for Austria-Hungary, it was the determination to crush the rising spirit of nationalism among the Slavic people and to hold the Austro-Hungarian empire together that prompted that nation to declare war on Serbia. But the spirit of nationalism was not confined to the Balkan Peninsula. In almost every country of Europe, as well as in the colonies overseas, there were subjugated people who longed to win their independence.

Imperialism as a cause. Another disruptive force was imperialism—the struggle for colonies. As you have seen (pages 586–88), during the late 1800's and the early 1900's the major powers of the world were engaged in a race for empire. By 1914, so far as colonies were concerned, the nations of Europe could be grouped into two classes: the "have" nations and the "have-not" nations.

Great Britain and France, each with huge colonial empires, were among the "have" powers. Although Russia owned no colonies, it did possess immense areas of underdeveloped land, and for this reason was also in the "have" category.

Germany, on the other hand, was among the "have-not" nations. It did own colonies in Africa and in the Pacific, but its colonial empire was relatively small, and the nation was eager to secure additional territory. Italy was in a similar situation—and one of the reasons that finally brought Italy into the war on the Allied side was a promise of colonies when the war ended.

International rivalries. Rivalry between nations was not, however, confined to the race for colonies. Austria-Hungary's attack on Serbia was prompted in part by its desire to strengthen its hold on the Slavic peoples and its influence in the Balkan Peninsula. Russia, on the other hand, came to Serbia's aid because Russia wanted to prevent Austria-Hungary from increasing its influence.

France supported Russia, not only because it was Russia's ally, but also because it saw a chance to recover Alsace-Lorraine, a former French area which the Germans had secured in 1871. Italy desired nearby territories within the Austro-Hungarian empire. Every Balkan country looked greedily at some ter-

ritory belonging to one or more of its neighbors. Russia longed for ice-free harbors in the Baltic Sea and for an outlet through the Dardanelles and the Bosporus into the Mediterranean Sea. Germany, the major Baltic Sea power, and Turkey, which controlled the Dardanelles, feared and distrusted Russia.

Search for a "balance of power." The mounting tensions with their accompanying series of plots and intrigues led inevitably to an armament race. Long before 1914 the relative sizes of naval forces and armies were occupying a major part of the attention of every European government.

In addition to building up their military forces, European governments tried to gain security with the *balance-of-power system*. This meant, in the simplest terms, that every country tried to increase its own strength by securing as many allies as possible. Thus Germany, Austria-Hungary, and Italy joined in what came to be known as the Triple Alliance. In an effort to maintain a balance of power, Great Britain, France, and Russia formed what came to be known as the "Triple Entente" (ahn-TAHNT).° Both of these rival alliances had been completed by 1907.

Austria's declaration of war on Serbia immediately set the whole system of

. . . .

° *Entente* is the French word for "understanding."

power alliances into motion. Of all the powers, only Italy failed to live up to its obligations under the treaties binding it to Austria-Hungary and Germany. Holding out to see which side would promise the most, Italy did not enter the war until 1915, and then on the Allied side.

Peace or war? During the opening years of the 1900's, strong forces pulled men and nations in both directions at the same time. With one hand, governments joined in the efforts to strengthen the bonds between nations and build a solid structure of peace. With the other hand, governments plotted and schemed against one another and desperately planned for war.

✔ **SECTION SURVEY**

1. (a) How did the assassination of Francis Ferdinand at Sarajevo ignite World War I? (b) Distinguish between an *immediate* cause and an *underlying* cause.

2. (a) Describe ways in which intense nationalism was an underlying source of tension. (b) How were imperialism and international rivalries contributing factors?

3. To what extent did militarism and the search for a "balance of power" contribute to the war fever?

IDENTIFY: Slavs, Balkan Peninsula, "have" and "have-not" nations, Central Powers, Allied Powers, Triple Alliance, Triple Entente; 1914.

3 The United States tries to remain neutral in World War I

America's first reaction to the outbreak of war in Europe, as you have seen, was one of shocked surprise and withdrawal. The war seemed unreal, a nightmare that would not last.

Wilson urges neutrality. But the war was all too real, and on August 19, 1914, President Wilson urged his fellow Americans to be "neutral in fact as well as in name" and "impartial in thought as well as in action."

Americans did not find it easy to follow President Wilson's advice. From the beginning they were torn between the desire to avoid war and sympathy for one or the other of the two sides.

Millions of recently naturalized Americans had friends and relations in Europe. Men and women of German origin —or of Austrian or Turkish origin— hoped for the victory of the Central Powers. Those of Irish origin saw in the war a chance for Ireland to win independence from Great Britain.

On the other hand, the majority of Americans were obviously sympathetic with the Allied Powers. The ties of language, a democratic type of government, and deep-rooted traditions bound Americans to Great Britain. The ties with France were also strong. After all, it was the French who, back in 1778, had come to the aid of Americans fighting for their independence. As World War I went on, this sympathy for the Allies led thousands of young Americans to enlist in the British, Canadian, and French armies. A special unit of volunteer American fliers, called the Lafayette Escadrille, was created as part of the new French flying force.

Although in 1914 American sympathies were divided, there is no doubt that the great majority of Americans hoped for an Allied victory. On the other hand, most Americans supported the President's policy of neutrality and prayed for an early end of the war.

The German plan of attack. The Central Powers, under the leadership of the German High Command, had every intention of ending the war quickly. Following carefully worked out plans, the Germans intended to conquer France before the French armies were fully mobilized, and then turn against the Russians.

Before looking at the German plan to conquer France, it is important to have in mind a picture of the French defenses. Long before the war the French, fearful of German attack, had built powerful fortifications along the entire Franco-German frontier. Indeed, the "anchor points" of this defense line, the fortresses of Sedan and Verdun, were considered impregnable (see map, this page). The German High Command was fully aware that these fortresses could be captured only at tremendous cost. But the French had not fortified the border between France and Belgium. The French counted on an international agreement, which the Germans had signed, that in the event of war Belgium would be respected as a neutral nation.

The German Chancellor, Bethmann Hollweg, however, called the international agreement to neutralize Belgium "a scrap of paper," and the German High Command launched its offensive against neutral Belgium and against Luxembourg as well, intending to reach the borders of France in six days. As the map on this page shows, five powerful German armies were to strike in a great wheeling motion at northern France. The German armies on the left flank were to be the pivot of this attack. Their job was to prevent the French from launching a counteroffensive across Alsace-Lorraine and deep into Germany. Meanwhile, according to plan, the armies on the right flank were to sweep through neutral Belgium in six days, crush the disorganized French armies in northern France, and, after capturing Paris, wheel back toward the Franco-German frontier and squeeze the bulk of the French forces in a giant vise.

The German plan fails. The German plan failed, largely because Belgium resisted. Fighting gallantly, the small Belgian army compelled the Germans to take eighteen days to cross Belgium, not the six called for in the timetable. This delay gave General Joffre, commander of the French armies, time to rush troops to the Belgian border. It also gave the British time to transport an army of about 90,000 men to northern France.

The French and the British arrived too late to save Belgium. Nor were they able to stop the Germans at the Belgian frontier. Crushed by the superior might of the Germans, the French and British retreated to the Marne River, where Joffre had prepared his main defense.

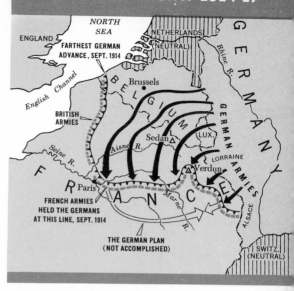

WESTERN FRONT: 1914-17

Fighting against seemingly hopeless odds, the French and British stopped the German offensive early in September 1914 at the Marne River in the First Battle of the Marne. The Germans then fell back to the Aisne (EHN) River, where they dug a line of trenches and checked an Allied counteroffensive.

Stalemate on the Western Front. The First Battle of the Marne was one of the most decisive of the entire war. If the Germans had won the battle, they might have crushed all remaining French and British resistance in a matter of weeks.

By 1915 the war in Western Europe had reached a stalemate. Both sides were entrenched along a 600-mile line that reached from the Swiss border to the English Channel. During the next three years both the Germans and the Allies mounted a number of offensives across "no man's land," a thin strip of land separating the German and Allied trenches, in an effort to break through the enemy line and end the trench warfare. Many thousands of men died in these offensives, but until the spring of 1918 neither side was able to make any significant gains. Day after day, the newspapers carried the terse notice, "All quiet on the Western Front."

HENRY FORD'S PEACE SHIP

On December 4, 1915, the Scandinavian steamship *Oscar II*, known to the public as "Ford's Peace Ship," sailed from New York. Its destination was Europe; its mission, to bring an end to the war that had already taken hundreds of thousands of lives.

From the opening day of the conflict, Henry Ford had publicly called the war sheer madness. One day in the fall of 1915, after reading that 20,000 men had been killed in the previous twenty-four hours, he exclaimed that he would spend half his fortune if he could shorten the war by even a single day. A newspaper reporter overheard him, and the statement made headlines. More than that, it attracted the attention of a number of peace enthusiasts, who persuaded Ford that determined mediation efforts on the part of neutral nations had a good chance of ending the war.

Ford's enthusiasm soared. He visited President Wilson and urged him to send an official mediation commission to Europe. Wilson had no faith in the proposal and said so. Ford then chartered a steamship and issued invitations to American leaders to travel with him to Europe as an unofficial peace delegation. When the ship sailed, its passenger list included over 60 delegates and almost as many newspaper and magazine correspondents.

The expedition failed to accomplish its purpose of neutral mediation. The opposing forces unleashed in Europe were too strong and too bitter to give way before such efforts. Ford himself spent a week in Norway, then returned home. The other delegates soon followed. Ford later stated, "I wanted to see peace. I at least tried to bring it about. Most men did not even try."

There were, to be sure, other fronts —and on all of them, as well as in Western Europe, men were fighting and dying. The Central Powers and Russia were locked in combat along the entire Eastern Front. Turkish troops defended a precarious line that reached southward through Palestine as far as Medina, in Arabia, against the British and French and their allies. Fighting men of Austria-Hungary and Italy faced each other in the area of their common boundary north of the Adriatic Sea (see map, page 623).

British interference with American trade. The prospect of a long war was bad news indeed for Americans who hoped to remain neutral. It meant, among other things, that warfare on the high seas would be intensified as Great Britain and Germany each redoubled its efforts to prevent supplies from the United States and other neutral countries from reaching the other side.

The British fleet, which controlled the seas, at least during the opening months of war, blockaded the German coast (see map, page 623) and laid explosive mines in the North Sea. To the astonishment and anger of Americans, the British navy also blockaded neutral countries, such as Norway, Sweden, Denmark, and the Netherlands, through which American goods flowed into Germany. American anger increased when the British began to examine American mail bound for Europe and ordered all neutral ships to stop at British ports, where their cargoes were searched.

The United States protested vigorously, arguing that Great Britain's actions were "illegal" and a flagrant violation of the "rights of neutrals," who had the right to travel the high seas provided they were not carrying war materials.

Submarine warfare. American anger at Great Britain subsided, however, in the face of German submarine warfare. This new type of warfare raised serious problems.

According to international law, naval vessels of countries at war had the right to stop and search a neutral ship. If the neutral ship carried arms, munitions, and other materials useful in war, known as *contraband,* the naval vessel had the right to seize the neutral ship and take it into port as a prize of war. If it were impossible to take the neutral vessel into port, the war ship was required to take passengers and crew to a safe place before sinking the prize.

Submarines could not take prizes into port because they were not armed to defend themselves against enemy war ships while on the surface. Nor could they take the passengers and crew of a large vessel on board. Least of all was it possible for them to surface and search neutral ships, for the moment that they rose to the surface they were "sitting ducks" for even one well-aimed shot from a naval gun. By their very nature, submarines were instruments of stealth. They were designed to lurk in the deeps, to strike suddenly without warning at the vitals of an enemy ship, and to get away before a counterattack.

Germany unleashes its submarines. Although the Germans had a powerful surface fleet, it was no match for the British Royal Navy. The Germans, therefore, had decided to concentrate on the construction of submarines, called U-boats. Early in the war the Germans notified President Wilson that they intended to turn their submarines loose in the Atlantic.

Angered by this announcement, President Wilson promptly replied on February 10, 1915, that the United States would hold Germany responsible for any acts that endangered American property and lives on the high seas.

Sinking of the Lusitania. The Germans were convinced that their submarine blockade would ruin Great Britain. They therefore ignored President Wilson's warning and turned their U-boats loose in the Atlantic shipping lanes. On March 28, 1915, the British steamer *Falaba* was torpedoed and sunk near Ireland, carrying to death more than 100 persons, including an American.

This and other incidents were the prelude to the destruction of the British liner *Lusitania* off the southern coast of Ireland on May 7, 1915, with the loss of 1198 lives, including 128 Americans. Since the *Lusitania* was carrying war materials bound for England, the Germans held that they were not responsible.

In three vigorous messages to the German government in Berlin, the American State Department protested against the sinking of the *Lusitania* and warned that any repetition of such action would lead to serious consequences.

American anger at the *Lusitania* affair was still at the boiling point when on August 19, 1915, another U-boat sank the *Arabic,* a British liner, with the loss of two American lives.

Alarmed at the furious indignation of the American people, Germany on September 1 gave a written promise that in the future "Liners will not be sunk by our submarines without warning . . . provided that the liners do not try to escape or offer resistance." With this promise Americans had to be content.

The sinking of the *Lusitania* marked a turning point in American feeling about the war. Increasing numbers of Americans began to realize that the conflict was not far off in Europe alone, but was close at hand. They were beginning to understand that neutrality might become impossible. Nevertheless, in 1915, most Americans continued to hope the United States could avoid war.

✔ **SECTION SURVEY**

1. Show why Americans found it difficult to remain neutral in World War I.

2. (a) Describe the German plan of attack. (b) What events checked a quick German victory? (c) What was the significance of the First Battle of the Marne?

3. (a) Discuss British interference with American trade. (b) Why were Americans more angered by German submarine warfare?

4. (a) Why did the sinking of the *Lusitania* mark "a turning point in American feeling about the war"? (b) How did Germany modify its submarine activity as a result?

4 The United States declares war and mobilizes its strength

From the summer of 1914 to the spring of 1917, the United States moved slowly but steadily toward war. As the months passed, it became apparent to an increasing number of Americans that neutrality was impossible.

More sinkings and more promises. In March 1916 the Germans broke their promise and attacked a French passenger vessel, the *Sussex*. Lives were lost and several Americans were injured. President Wilson promptly threatened to break diplomatic relations with Germany unless the German government gave immediate and firm assurance that it would abandon its present methods of submarine warfare.

In what came to be known as the "*Sussex* pledge," Germany renewed its earlier promise not to sink liners without warning and without providing for the safety of the passengers. To this promise, however, the Germans added an important reservation. They would keep the promise on condition that the United States would persuade the Allies to modify the food blockade of Germany, which, according to Berlin, was inflicting hunger and starvation on German women and children. The Washington government replied that the British blockade had nothing to do with German violation of American neutral rights on the high seas.

A rising war spirit. American opinion was divided over the efforts of the Wilson administration to enforce neutrality. Some people, including former President Theodore Roosevelt, felt that the United States was not firm enough. Others believed that the American government was unwisely going too far in its threatening demands on Berlin. Secretary of State Bryan, for example, resigned during the *Lusitania* crisis because he feared that Wilson's stand would lead to war against Germany. In Bryan's opinion, the United States should forbid American citizens to travel on British and French ships. Bryan also believed that Congress should stop all Americans from selling war materials to the belligerents.

Preparing for war. President Wilson refused to follow the advice of Bryan and others who shared Bryan's views. Instead, Wilson helped to arouse the public to the support of a program for greatly increasing the size of both the army and the navy. The National Defense Act, passed in June 1916, increased the regular army from 106,000 to 175,000 men and provided for officers' training camps. A three-year naval program, begun in 1916, was carried out vigorously. In 1916 the government also created the Council of National Defense and the United States Shipping Board. These agencies planned for the mobilization of the country's resources in case of war and launched a huge shipbuilding program.

The war preparations did not mean that either the administration or the American public in general had abandoned all hope of remaining neutral. Indeed, many Americans, as you know, voted for the re-election of Wilson in November 1916 on the ground that "he kept us out of war."

But six months later, under the leadership of the President and Congress, the American people entered the conflict, millions of them with considerable enthusiasm. What happened in these six months to lead the administration to take this momentous step?

Diplomatic relations are broken. On February 1, 1917, Germany renewed its unrestricted submarine warfare, thus going back on the "*Sussex* pledge." A German proposal to permit only one American passenger ship to sail to England each week added insult to injury.

The German High Command reached the momentous decision to renew unrestricted submarine warfare fully aware that this decision would almost certainly bring the United States into the war against Germany. The High Command took the calculated risk that submarines would be able to destroy Great Britain's power and will to fight before the United States could provide effective help.

Wilson met the new challenge promptly. On February 3 he broke off diplomatic relations with the German government at Berlin.

Moving toward war. During February and March several developments contributed to the mounting war feeling in the United States.

On February 24, British naval intelligence agents handed to the American ambassador to Great Britain a German message they had intercepted and decoded. The message had been sent from Germany by Foreign Secretary Alfred Zimmerman to the German minister in Mexico, Von Eckhardt. It contained instructions about what to do in case war broke out between Germany and the United States. In this event, Von Eckhardt was to offer Mexico an alliance with Germany. With German support Mexico was to attack the United States and "reconquer the lost territory in New Mexico, Texas, and Arizona." President Wilson released the Zimmerman note to the Associated Press on March 1. The American people received it with shocked surprise and rising anger.

On March 12 President Wilson, through the State Department, announced that all American merchant vessels operating through war zones would be armed for defense against German submarines. The public received this announcement with mixed reactions, but in general approved.

There were other and deeper forces moving American sympathies toward the Allies and toward war with Germany. For one thing, American ties with Great Britain and France were traditionally closer than those with Germany. Not least important, American shipments of munitions to the Allied Powers had risen from six million dollars in 1914 to nearly a half billion dollars in 1916, and by April 1917 American bankers had lent more than two billion dollars to the Allies. Naturally, Americans who had invested money in the Allied cause hoped to see the Allies win. But historians have found no evidence to indicate that economic interests in any way influenced President Wilson's conduct in the critical weeks before the war.

The President's "War Message." As the weeks passed, President Wilson came to the reluctant conclusion that America's entrance into the war was inevitable. On March 20 he called an emergency cabinet meeting. At that meeting he and his official advisers gravely considered the entire situation, from the deep-rooted and long-standing grievances against Germany to the recent series of disturbing incidents. Supported by his entire cabinet, the President on March 21 called a special session of Congress to meet on April 2. On the evening of April 2, 1917, the Senators, Representatives, and a number of distinguished guests gathered at the Capitol to hear President Wilson present his "War Message." Every seat was filled, and the galleries were packed with a solemn, hushed group of America's leaders.

■ Before a joint session of Congress, President Wilson at this dramatic moment delivered the address which led the United States into World War I.

In ringing words the President condemned Germany's submarine warfare as "the wanton and wholesale destruction of the lives of noncombatants, men, women, and children, engaged in pursuits which have always, even in the darkest periods of modern history, been deemed innocent and legitimate. Property can be paid for; the lives of peaceful and innocent people cannot be. . . . The challenge is to all mankind. . . . We will not choose the path of submission and suffer the most sacred rights of our Nation and our people to be ignored or violated," the President declared. "The wrongs against which we now array ourselves are no common wrongs; they cut to the very roots of human life."

But Wilson was too great an idealist to rest his case upon the evils of unrestricted submarine warfare alone. Our ultimate purpose, he insisted, "is to vindicate the principles of peace and justice in the life of the world as against selfish and autocratic power and to set up amongst the really free and self-governed peoples of the world such a concert of purpose and of action as will henceforth ensure the observance of those principles." Then, in measured words, came the call to Americans to rise in a crusade for a better world:

"We are glad, now that we see the facts with no veil of false pretense about them, to fight thus for the ultimate peace of the world and for the liberation of its peoples, the German peoples included: for the rights of nations great and small and the privilege of men everywhere to choose their way of life and of obedience. The world must be made safe for democracy. Its peace must be planted upon the tested foundations of political liberty. We have no selfish ends to serve. We desire no conquest, no dominion. We seek no indemnities for ourselves, no material compensation for the sacrifices we shall freely make."

Congress declares war. Congress promptly declared war. On April 4 the Senate voted a war resolution by a count of 82 to 6. Two days later, on April 6, the House voted 373 to 50 to support the President's recommendation.

America's entry into the conflict had an immediate effect upon other neutral countries. During the months between April 1917 and July 1918, a number of Latin-American states declared war—Panama, Cuba, Brazil, Guatemala, Nicaragua, Costa Rica, Haiti, and Honduras. Most of the other American countries, although unwilling to enter the conflict, severed diplomatic relations with Germany.

Raising an army. Meanwhile, as soon as war was declared, the United States began to mobilize its manpower and its natural resources. On May 18 Congress adopted the Selective Service Act, which provided for the registration of all men between the ages of twenty-one and thirty. The act was amended on August 31, 1918, to include all men between the ages of eighteen and forty-five. Before the war ended, more than 24,000,000 men were registered by their local draft boards, and 2,810,296 of this group were drafted into the army.

Even before the draft began to operate, construction had been started on training camps. This in itself was an enormous undertaking, for each camp was in effect a small city complete with barracks, mess halls, and other facilities capable of handling thousands of men. During the summer and fall of 1917, nearly 2,000,000 Americans poured into these camps to begin military training.

Financing the war. Equally pressing was the need to raise the huge sums of money required to finance the war. Congress decided to raise approximately two thirds by borrowing, the remaining one third by taxing current income.

The government borrowed money by the sale of war bonds, many of which were issued in denominations as low as $50. Through four "Liberty Loan Drives" and a "Victory Loan Drive," the government borrowed a total of more than 21 billion dollars.

The government also raised money to finance the war by boosting income-tax rates and by levying excise taxes on railroad tickets, telegraph and telephone messages, alcoholic beverages, tobacco, and certain amusements.

Mobilizing industry. Materials were as important as manpower and money. The big problem was to stimulate production and prevent waste.

In an effort to achieve this goal, Congress gave the President sweeping wartime powers. He was, for example, authorized to set the prices of many commodities, including food and fuels. He was also authorized to regulate, or even to take possession of, factories, mines, meat-packing houses, food-processing plants, and all transportation and communication facilities. The President exercised these vast powers through a number of wartime agencies, or boards.

The War Industries Board, established in July 1917, became the virtual dictator of manufacturing. It developed new industries needed in the war effort. It regulated business in order to eliminate waste and nonessential goods. It made purchases both for the Allies and for the American government. It established "priorities"; that is, it determined which manufacturers were entitled to first claim to vital war materials. Before the end of the conflict, the War Industries Board was regulating the production of some 30,000 commodities.

Other federal agencies also took an active part in planning the war program. The War Finance Corporation lent public funds to businesses needing aid in manufacturing war materials.

The Emergency Fleet Corporation built ships faster than German submarines could destroy them, increasing American tonnage from some 2 million to more than 11 million tons. The Railroad Administration, headed by the Secretary of the Treasury, William G. McAdoo, took over the operation of the railroads. As director general, McAdoo reorganized the lines and controlled rates and wages in the interest of war efficiency. The Postmaster General was placed in charge of the telegraph, telephone, and cable lines. The Fuel Administration stimulated a larger output of coal and oil, and encouraged economies in their use.

Mobilizing labor. The successful mobilization of industry depended, of course, upon the complete co-operation of labor. In an effort to deal with labor disputes, President Wilson in April 1918 appointed the National War Labor Board with Frank P. Walsh and ex-President Taft as co-chairmen. This board was authorized to arbitrate disputes between workers and employers. In June, Wilson appointed the War Labor Policies Board. This board was authorized to establish general policies affecting wages, hours, and working conditions. As a result of these measures and of the co-operation of organized labor, labor disputes were reduced to a minimum during the war years.

Conserving food. The problem of food was equally critical. Late in 1917, in part to help conserve grain, which is

AIRPLANE PILOT

INFANTRY OFFICERS

LEWIS MACHINE GUN

INFANTRYMAN

BROWNING MACHINE GUN

LIGHT BROWNING AUTOMATIC RIFLE

HAND GRENADE

American uniforms and weapons—World War I

used in making alcohol, Congress adopted and submitted to the states an amendment to the Constitution prohibiting the manufacture, sale, or transportation of alcoholic liquors. This amendment, the Eighteenth, was declared ratified by the necessary three fourths of the states in 1919, and went into effect on January 16, 1920.

The measure to conserve grain was only one of the moves that the government made in order to guarantee food for the American people and for the other peoples associated with the United States in the war effort. Herbert Hoover, an able engineer who had successfully managed food relief in war-stricken Belgium, was placed in charge of the Food Administration. Hoover brought about a vast expansion of agriculture, forbade the hoarding or willful waste of food, and encouraged the people to observe "wheatless" and "meatless" days. The sale of sugar and other commodities was limited. All this took place without actual rationing.° The Food Administration depended on publicity and persuasion to get people to co-operate-in conserving food.

Mobilizing public opinion. In addition to mobilizing material resources and manpower, the government undertook to gain the co-operation of the American people for the war effort.

The Committee on Public Information circulated millions of leaflets describing in glowing language America's official war aims and denouncing the German government. The colleges, the schools, the press, churches, fraternal lodges, women's organizations, and civic groups all co-operated with the government's campaign "to sell the war to the American people." In all sorts of public gatherings, the war aims were publicized in brief speeches delivered by well-known people called "Four-Minute Men." Never before had the government tried to influence the minds of the people on so vast a scale.

••
° *rationing:* a method of limiting the sale of scarce goods which insures equal distribution among the civilian population.

Controlling dissent. From the beginning the great majority of Americans enthusiastically supported the war effort. There were, however, a number of dissenters who, in greater or lesser measure, were not in sympathy with the government's war effort.

To deal with these people, Congress in June 1917 adopted the Espionage Act. This act was aimed at treasonable and disloyal activities.

In May 1918 Congress strengthened the Espionage Act by an amendment, often called the Sedition Act. This act provided penalties of up to $10,000 in fines and 20 years' imprisonment, or both, for anyone found guilty of interfering with the sale of war bonds, attempting in any way to curtail production, or using "disloyal, profane, scurrilous, or abusive language" about the American form of government or any of its agencies.

Operating under these laws, the Department of Justice arrested at least 1597 persons. Of these, 41 received prison sentences of from 10 to 20 years. Among those convicted were Eugene V. Debs, four times the Socialist candidate for the Presidency; Congressman Victor Berger of Milwaukee; and "Big Bill" Haywood, leader of the Industrial Workers of the World (I.W.W.). In addition, newspapers and periodicals that ventured to criticize the government in its conduct of the war were deprived of their mailing privileges.

Many loyal Americans, themselves thoroughly in sympathy with the war effort, objected to the Espionage Act and the Sedition Act. They based their objections on the ground that the government should not interfere so drastically, even in wartime, with the Constitutional rights of citizens.

For the most part, however, Americans did not need persuasive arguments or restrictive laws to secure their loyalty. Americans entered the war on a great wave of enthusiasm, convinced, as Wilson had put it, that this was indeed a crusade "to make the world safe for democracy."

1. What were the reasons for America's entrance into World War I?
2. In your opinion, which one of these reasons was most important? Explain.
3. Describe the methods used (a) to raise an army and (b) to finance the war.
4. (a) Show how industry and labor were mobilized. (b) What measures were used to conserve food?
5. Discuss the purpose of the Espionage Act of 1917 and the Sedition Act of 1918.
IDENTIFY: *"Sussex* pledge," unrestricted submarine warfare, Zimmerman note, Selective Service Act, rationing; April 6, 1917; 1919.

5 American troops and ideals help the Allies win the war

America's declaration of war came none too soon. In the spring of 1917, the Allies were facing a grim situation, and by the end of the year their position was desperate.

The military situation in 1917. By 1917 the Allies, who had suffered enormous losses, were war-weary and discouraged. In March they were further disheartened by news that the tsar of Russia had been deposed and a new revolutionary government established.

America's entry into the conflict in April was one of the few bright spots in a year during which Allied fortunes sank lower and lower.

In the fall Germany threw a number of crack divisions into the Austrian campaign, and on October 24 a combined force of Austrians and Germans crashed through the Italian lines at Caporetto (see map, page 623). Before the Italians could make a stand in mid-November, they had lost more than 600,000 men and 6000 square miles of territory. French and British troops, rushed from the Western Front, helped to stop the rout and saved Italy from collapse.

Most serious of all, however, was the news from Russia. On November 7 the Bolsheviks, a party of radical communists, seized power. A month later they signed an armistice with Germany. Almost three months later, in March 1918, they concluded the peace treaty of Brest-Litovsk (BREST lee-TOFSK). Meanwhile, Rumania, unable to stand alone against the Central Powers in eastern Europe, had sued for peace and in 1918 signed a peace treaty at Bucharest.

As a result of these developments, by the end of 1917 the Germans were free to concentrate most of their forces on the Western Front. General Ludendorff, commander of the German armies, prepared for an offensive intended to end the war before United States troops could play an important role.

American naval forces. Meanwhile, the United States Navy, which had been rapidly building its strength since 1916, went into action. Before the war ended, Admiral William S. Sims, Commander of the United States Naval Forces Operating in European Waters, had established 45 naval bases located as far north as Murmansk, in Russia, and as far south as Greece.

French Renault tank used by American troops

In co-operation with the British navy, American naval forces patrolled the North Sea and effectively bottled up the German fleet. They also laid most of a 230-mile barrier of mines that stretched across the North Sea from Norway to the Orkney Islands (see map, page 623). This barrier greatly increased the hazards for German submarines seeking to reach the open waters of the Atlantic Ocean or to return to their bases in Germany.

Meanwhile, other naval vessels helped to convoy merchant ships and troop transports through the submarine-infested waters of the Atlantic Ocean. The Anglo-American convoy system was so effective that 2,000,000 men or more were transported to Europe with the loss of only a few hundred lives. It was a remarkable record and an enduring tribute to the efficiency of the naval forces. It was also a severe blow to the German High Command, which had counted on the submarine warfare to prevent American troops and supplies from reaching Europe in time to play a decisive part in the war.

The A.E.F. arrives in France. While the United States Navy was carrying out its job, or jobs, on the high seas, the land forces were being organized.

One of President Wilson's first moves was the appointment of General John J. Pershing as Commander of the American Expeditionary Forces (the A.E.F.). General Pershing was one of the few United States generals who had previously commanded any sizable body of troops in actual warfare. A graduate of West Point, he had served in Cuba, in the Philippines, and in 1916 as commander of the expedition sent into Mexico to capture Pancho Villa.

Pershing landed in France early in June 1917, with a staff of fewer than three hundred men, and immediately established A.E.F. headquarters. By the end of June, the first regiments of the First Division arrived, and on July 4 several thousand "Yanks" marched through Paris amid the heartfelt cheers of the French people.

During the next few months American troops, or "doughboys," arrived in ever-swelling numbers. By May 1918 they were pouring in at the rate of 10,000 a day. By the fall of 1918 more than 2,000,000 had landed in France.

In order to supply and maintain this huge army, the Americans built docks, 1000 miles of railroad, and thousands of miles of telephone and telegraph lines in Europe. They landed 17,000 freight cars and more than 40,000 trucks. They also built training camps, hospitals, and storage houses and ammunition dumps.

Germany's last bid for victory. On March 21, 1918, the Western Front exploded into violent action as the Germans, reinforced by seasoned troops released from the Russian front, launched a powerful campaign, or "peace offensive." The Germans hoped to end the war with this final mighty effort. In an almost continuous series of battles, the German armies thrust first at one part of the Allied lines, then at another, hoping for a conclusive breakthrough. At the end of two weeks, they had gained 1500 square miles of territory and inflicted 160,000 casualties. By the end of May, they were at the River Marne, only 37 miles from Paris.

Pershing's original plans had called for a period of training behind the lines before his troops went into action. Also, from the beginning of America's participation in the war, he had insisted that American troops should fight as a separate army under their own top command. But in the spring of 1918, he temporarily abandoned both of these objectives and consented to putting every available man into the lines immediately. French, British, and American troops fought under a unified Allied command directed by the French military leader, Marshal Foch (FOHSH).

The German advance is stopped. Fighting desperately, French, British, Belgian and American troops finally stopped the Germans. On May 28 the First Division of the United States Army took Cantigny (kahn-tee-NYEE). Three days later the Third Division, in

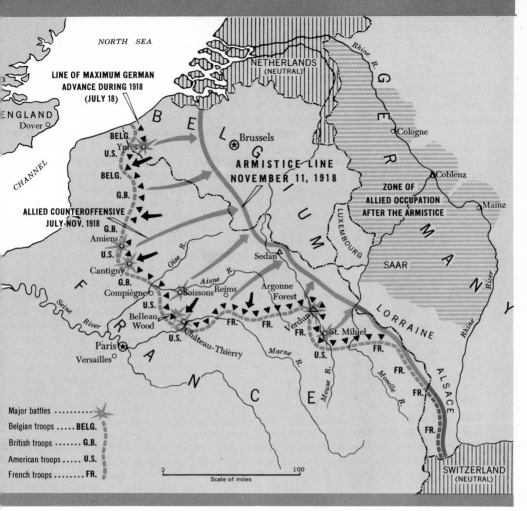

NORTH SEA

LINE OF MAXIMUM GERMAN
ADVANCE DURING 1918
(JULY 18)

ENGLAND
Dover

CHANNEL

BELGIUM

NETHERLANDS
(NEUTRAL)

Rhine R.

Brussels

ARMISTICE LINE
NOVEMBER 11, 1918

ZONE OF
ALLIED OCCUPATION
AFTER THE ARMISTICE

Cologne

Coblenz

Mainz

BELG.
Ypres
U.S.

BELG.

G.B.

ALLIED COUNTEROFFENSIVE
JULY-NOV. 1918
G.B.
Amiens

U.S.

Cantigny

G.B.
Compiègne
U.S.

Belleau
Wood
U.S.

Paris
Versailles

FRANCE

Seine River

Oise R.

Soissons
Aisne R.
Reims

Château-Thierry

Marne R.

Sedan

Argonne
Forest

FR.   FR.
Verdun
FR.

St. Mihiel
U.S.

Meuse R.

Moselle R.

FR.

GERMANY

SAAR

LUXEMBOURG

LORRAINE

ALSACE

Rhine River

FR.

FR.

SWITZERLAND
(NEUTRAL)

Major battles ....
Belgian troops ..... BELG.
British troops .... G.B.
American troops ..... U.S.
French troops .... FR.

0   100
Scale of miles

---

a last-ditch defense of Paris, only 40 miles away, helped the French hold the Germans at Château-Thierry (shah-TOH tyeh-REE). At Belleau (BEL-loh) Wood the Second Division, including marines, held back the Germans in six days of fighting (see map, this page).

Then, on July 15, the Germans made a desperate bid for victory and threw everything they could into one final ferocious assault around Reims (REEMZ). In this, the beginning of the Second Battle of the Marne, the Allied lines held, and on July 18 Marshal Foch ordered a counterattack spearheaded by the First and Second American Divisions and the First French Morocco Division. The Germans began to fall back. The tide had at last turned.

The Allied victory drive. With the last great German offensive checked, the Allies now took the initiative. In July Foch launched a terrific offensive along the entire length of the line. The Germans were driven back.

Fighting as a separate American army under the command of General Pershing, the "doughboys," 500,000 strong and supported by French troops and British planes, launched a powerful attack on the area around St. Mihiel (SAN mee-YEL) in September 1918. Three days of savage fighting put this section of the southern front under American control.

Then, against withering artillery and machine-gun fire, the Americans drove toward Sedan, the highly fortified posi-

635

tion that the Germans had seized from the French in 1914 and held ever since. In one of the most spectacular battles Americans had ever fought, United States troops pushed for 47 days toward their objective. The fighting in this tremendous Meuse-Argonne (MYOOZ AHR-gun) offensive involved 1,200,000 combatants. The Americans alone suffered 120,000 casualties, including the killed and wounded. But they pushed the German line back 30 miles, and captured 28,000 prisoners and large supplies of war materials.

Important though they were, the American victories represented only part of the tremendous offensive against the crumbling German lines. The Belgians, British, and French, confident now of victory, were fighting fiercely along the entire front.

Under these hammer blows German morale began to sag, and Germany's allies lost heart. In September the Turkish armies in Palestine and Arabia suffered crushing blows, and Bulgaria surrendered unconditionally. On November 3 the crews of the German ships at Kiel, a German naval base, mutinied rather than put to sea. Army units also mutinied, and riots broke out in German cities. On November 3, Austria signed an armistice with the Italians.

Convinced at last that the war was lost, Kaiser Wilhelm Hohenzollern, ruler of Germany, fled to the Netherlands, leaving his country in the hands of revolutionists, who signed an armistice with the Allies on November 11, 1918.

The armistice terms. The armistice itself was signed in a railroad car on a siding in the forest of Compiègne (kohn-PYEN[y]) on the eleventh hour of the eleventh day of the eleventh month of 1918. The Germans signed grimly, for the terms were severe.

The Germans agreed to evacuate France, Belgium, Luxembourg, and Alsace-Lorraine without delay. They agreed to surrender to the Allies an enormous amount of war materials, including most of Germany's naval vessels, and to return prisoners, money, and all valuables taken from the occupied countries. They agreed to renounce the Treaty of Brest-Litovsk with Russia and the Treaty of Bucharest with Rumania.

In addition, the Allies reserved the right to occupy all German territory west of the Rhine, and a strip of territory about 18 miles wide on the east bank of the Rhine (see map, page 635).

Wilson's Fourteen Points. An American expression of idealism, as well as American fighting strength, played a

■ In this famous railroad car, German representatives met Marshal Foch and his Allied associates to arrange Germany's surrender. Just 22 years later, in World War II, Adolf Hitler humiliated the French by forcing them to surrender to the Germans in the same railroad car.

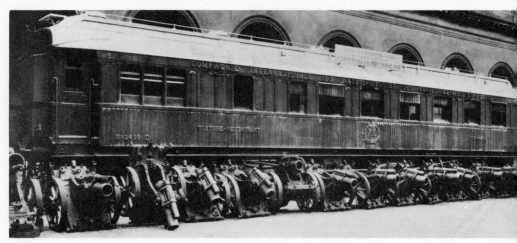

large part in breaking the Central Powers' will to fight. This important part of the story of World War I goes back to the early winter of 1917-18.

As you recall, in November 1917 the Bolsheviks seized control of Russia and shortly thereafter signed a peace treaty with Germany. At this time the Bolsheviks published a number of secret treaties that the Allies had drawn up at the beginning of the war. These secret treaties outlined in detail how the Allies planned to divide the spoils of war if they were successful in defeating the Central Powers.

President Wilson chose this opportunity to lay before the world what he firmly believed was "the only possible program for world peace." Wilson's program, which he presented to Congress on January 8, 1918, included fourteen principles, or "points."

The first group of points aimed to end the causes of modern war, as Wilson understood these causes. Specifically, he called for open diplomacy instead of secret diplomacy; for freedom of the seas instead of their control by a superior naval power; for the removal of tariffs and other economic barriers between nations; for the reduction of land armaments; and for the temporary international control of colonies in place of the existing imperialism.

President Wilson also called for the liberation of peoples long held in bondage by Russia, Austria-Hungary, Germany, and Turkey. Among these peoples were the Poles, Czechs, Slovaks, and South Slavs. Wilson's proposal also included the people living in the German-held region of Alsace-Lorraine. These and other groups were to have the right of "self-determination." That is, they were to decide for themselves the country in which they wished to live.

But the "Fourteenth Point" was the heart of President Wilson's program. With this famous point Wilson urged the creation of a "general association of nations" to give "mutual guarantees of political independence and territorial integrity to great and small states alike."

Influence of Wilson's program. The Fourteen Points and statements explaining them were printed during the war in the languages of the peoples of central Europe and dropped by plane into the heart of the enemy country. All this publicity encouraged the Slavic peoples within Germany and Austria-Hungary to boycott the war effort of their masters and to speed up their own liberation. Even the German people found in the Fourteen Points hope for a just and lasting peace, rather than a continued regime of autocracy° and militarism under the Kaiser and his associates.

Moreover, as defeat pressed closer upon them, the German and Austrian peoples saw in Wilson's program an escape from the harsh penalties that the Allies would otherwise impose upon them. Thus, when the great German military offensives failed in the summer of 1918, and when Wilson made it clear that he would not negotiate with any German authority not representative of the people, the Germans and Austrians took steps to overthrow their rulers.

President Wilson and millions of Americans had entered the conflict with the burning conviction that they were waging a crusade "to make the world safe for democracy." In the winter of 1918-19, they believed that this goal was at last in sight.

••
° *autocracy:* a government in which all or nearly all power is held by a single ruler.

📖 **SECTION SURVEY**

1. Explain why the military situation was desperate for the Allies in 1917.
2. Describe the contributions of the United States Navy to winning the war.
3. Discuss the part played by the A.E.F. in defeating the German army.
4. What were the armistice terms of November 11, 1918?
5. Discuss the part of Wilson's Fourteen Points in bringing an end to the war.
IDENTIFY: Bolsheviks, Treaty of Brest-Litovsk, convoy, "doughboys," secret treaties, self-determination; Sims, Pershing, Foch; November 11, 1918.

■ CHAPTER SURVEY

(For review, see Section Surveys, pages 620, 624, 627, 633, 637.)

Points to Discuss: 1. By 1914, men had built what seemed to be a solid and enduring structure of peace. Explain the basis of this statement.

2. Evaluate the role of (a) imperialism, (b) nationalism, (c) militarism, (d) the balance of power, and (e) international anarchy in contributing to World War I.

3. Explain the factors that prevented America from realizing its desire to remain neutral in the war.

4. How was American idealism embodied in these slogans: "a war to end all wars" and "a war to make the world safe for democracy"?

5. Evaluate with specific evidence the importance of American aid to Allied victory in World War I.

6. According to Wilson's war message, what were the reasons for American entrance into the war?

7. Describe the methods used by the American government to (a) raise an army, (b) pay for the war, (c) mobilize industry and labor, (d) secure the support of public opinion, and (e) control dissent.

8. Was the peace of the armistice an objective of the League of Nations?

Using Maps: 1. Using the map on page 623, identify (a) the Allied Powers, (b) the Central Powers, and (c) the major neutral nations.

2. Using the same map, compare British and German naval strategy.

3. Using the map on page 625 and consulting the text, (a) show why the Germans violated the neutrality of Belgium, and (b) explain why the Germans failed to conquer the French armies in 1914.

4. Referring to the map on page 635, (a) locate the positions held by American troops, (b) identify American victories, and (c) indicate the area which the Allied armies occupied after the war.

Consulting the Sources: See Paul M. Angle (ed.), *By These Words*, pp. 428–437, for the text of Wilson's "peace without victory" address to the Senate in January, 1917. See also "A Reluctant President Asks for War," p. 439.

■ TRACING THE MAIN IDEAS

The outbreak of World War I in the summer of 1914 came as a blow to millions of Americans and other peoples throughout the world. During the opening years of the 1900's great strides had been made in the direction of international co-operation. Suddenly, in 1914, all men's hopes for peace were blown to bits.

Despite America's desire to remain neutral, the United States was drawn closer and closer to the conflict. As the months passed, President Wilson and a growing number of Americans began to believe that the war was essentially a conflict between autocracy on the one hand and democracy on the other. On this high note of idealism, the United States entered the conflict.

Hundreds of millions of people throughout the Americas, Europe, the Near East, and the Far East rejoiced when the armistice was signed on November 11, 1918. These people believed that they had won "the war to end wars," one "to make the world safe for democracy." Many of these people looked to the United States for leadership in the difficult task of building a peaceful world.

In the winter of 1918–19, it was clear to Americans and to people in other lands that the United States had become a major world power. It was also clear that with Europe in ruins the United States had the opportunity of becoming the most influential nation on the face of the earth.

Unit Survey (Reread "Tracing the Main Ideas," pages 601, 616, 638.)

OUTSTANDING EVENTS

1850 Clayton-Bulwer Treaty.
1853 Perry arrives in Japan.
1867 U.S. buys Alaska.
1867 French forces leave Mexico.
1889–90 Pan-American Conference.
1895 Venezuela boundary dispute.
1898 Spanish-American War.
1898 U.S. annexes Hawaiian Islands.
1899 First Hague Conference.
1899–1900 Open Door policy proclaimed.
1900 Boxer Rebellion.
1901 Insular Cases are decided.
1901 Hay-Pauncefote Treaty.
1905 Treaty of Portsmouth.
1907 Second Hague Conference.
1913 Policy of "watchful waiting."
1914 Panama Canal opened to traffic.
1914 World War I starts.
1916 "*Sussex* pledge."
1917 U.S. buys Virgin Islands.
1917 U.S. enters World War I.
1918 World War I ends.
1918 Wilson presents his Fourteen Points.

THEN AND NOW

1. How has the celebration of November 11 been changed since it was first established as Armistice Day?
2. Compare the influence of the press today in shaping American attitudes toward foreign affairs with press influence at the time of the Spanish-American War.
3. Compare the terms of the Alien and Sedition Acts of 1798 with the Espionage Act of 1917 and Sedition Act of 1918.

EXTENDING YOUR HORIZON

1. One of the early advocates of American imperialism was Alfred T. Mahan. Read the excerpt from his book *The Interest of America in Sea Power* in Richard Heffner's *A Documentary History of the United States*, Chapter 19, "Imperial America."
2. The role of General Shafter in the Spanish-American War is highlighted by Stewart Holbrook in Chapter XIV, "War in the Mauve Decade," of *Lost Men of American History* (Macmillan).
3. George Kennan has a thought-provoking Chapter (IV) entitled "World War I" in *American Diplomacy 1900–1950*

[Univ. of Chicago Press; New American Library (Mentor)]. See also Laurence Stallings, "The War to End War," *American Heritage*, October 1959.

INDIVIDUAL ACTIVITIES

1. On an outline map of the world indicate all the possessions the United States has ever owned in the Atlantic and Pacific Oceans. Circle those which it still owns.
2. Prepare a chart of United States possessions. List their names, date acquired, and present-day importance.
3. Prepare an oral report comparing the original Monroe Doctrine, the Olney interpretation, and the Roosevelt Corollary in the following respects: reasons for issuance of the document, important principles involved, significance of the statement originally and with the passage of time. Consult Dexter Perkins, *A History of the Monroe Doctrine*, Little, Brown; and Thomas A. Bailey, *Diplomatic History of the American People* (Appleton-Century-Crofts).
4. For more information about the role of newspapers during the Spanish-American War, see Bailey's *Diplomatic History of the American People* and John Kennedy Winkler's *William Randolph Hearst* (Hastings House).
5. Study the cartoons dealing with the Spanish-American War in Roger Place Butterfield's *The American Past* (Simon and Schuster). Then, draw an original cartoon illustrating some aspect of the war.
6. List the popular songs at the time of World War I.

GROUP ACTIVITIES

1. Select a group of students to prepare a round-table discussion on this topic: The Spanish-American War: Causes and Consequences. A good basic source for evaluating these is the pamphlet *American Imperialism in 1898* in *Problems of American Civilization*, "Amherst Series," with special attention given to the articles by Julius Pratt, Joseph E. Wisan, and Richard Hofstadter. See, also, the article by William Leuchtenberg, "The Needless War with Spain," *American Heritage*, February 1957; and Chapter 1 of Kennan's *American Di-*

plomacy 1900–1950; as well as Walter Millis' *The Martial Spirit* (Houghton Mifflin); and Frank Freidel's *The Splendid Little War* (Little, Brown). The discussion ought to include an evaluation of the wisdom and justice of American acquisition of the Philippines.

2. Students interested in military history may work together to produce reports dealing with the war on land and sea in the Spanish-American War and World War I. Comparisons may be drawn.

3. The causes presented by historians for American entrance into World War I are varied. Let a group of more ambitious students seek to explore those views and present them to the class together with their own evaluation. Sidney Fay's *Origins of World War I* (Macmillan) will afford a good beginning, and Chapter 21, "The Great Crusade and After," in Richard Heffner's *A Documentary History of the United States* can be consulted with profit. Some articles in *Wilson at Versailles* in *Problems of American Civilization* are also good for differing views.

4. Let two or three students examine carefully the key messages of Wilson between 1914 and 1917 with relation to the war in Europe up to the point of our entrance. Included among numerous sources for these documents are Documents 6, 7, and 8 in Richard Hofstadter's *Great Issues in American History* (Vintage), Volume II. Then, for contrast, let them examine Document 9, Senator Norris' "Speech Against the Declaration of War," given just two days after Wilson's War Message to Congress. It is an expression of isolationist sentiment.

SUGGESTED FURTHER READING

BIOGRAPHY

BLUM, JOHN MORTON, *Woodrow Wilson and the Politics of Morality*, Little, Brown.

GORGAS, M. D., and B. J. HENDRICK, *William Crawford Gorgas: His Life and Work*, Doubleday.

JUDSON, CLARA I., *Soldier Doctor: Story of William Gorgas*, Scribner.

LUTZ, ALMA, *Susan B. Anthony*, Beacon.

RICKENBACKER, EDWARD V., *Fighting the Flying Circus*, Lippincott. About World War I pilot; autobiographical.

ROOSEVELT, THEODORE, *Rough Riders*, Scribner.

WOOD, L. N., *Walter Reed: Doctor in Uniform*, Messner.

OTHER NONFICTION

°BAILEY, THOMAS A., *Wilson and the Peacemakers*, Macmillan.

°BEALE, HOWARD K., *Theodore Roosevelt and the Rise of America to World Power*, Johns Hopkins Univ. Press.

°BEMIS, SAMUEL FLAGG, *A Short History of American Foreign Policy*, Holt.

°——, *The Latin-American Policy of the United States: An Historical Interpretation*, Harcourt, Brace.

°DULLES, RHEA FOSTER, *America's Rise to World Power 1898–1954*, Harper.

°GRISWOLD, A. WHITNEY, *The Far Eastern Policy of the United States*, Harcourt, Brace.

°LIPPMANN, WALTER, *United States Foreign Policy: Shield of the Republic*, Little, Brown.

MILLIS, WALTER, *The Road to War*, Houghton Mifflin. Why America entered World War I.

°PRATT, JULIUS W., *America's Colonial Experiment*, Prentice-Hall (text ed.).

°SLOSSON, PRESTON W., *The Great Crusade and After, 1914–1928*, Macmillan.

°TANSILL, CHARLES C., *America Goes to War*, Little, Brown. World War I.

WEEMS, JOHN E., *The Fate of the Maine*, Holt.

HISTORICAL FICTION

BOYD, THOMAS, *Through the Wheat*, Scribner. Novel about American soldier.

DUNNE, FINLEY PETER, *Mr. Dooley in Peace and War*, Small, Maynard.

HETH, EDWARD H., *Told with a Drum*, Harper. German-American city in World War I.

NASON, LEONARD H., *Chevrons*, Doubleday; Grosset & Dunlap. Soldiers in World War I.

——, *The Fighting Livingstones*, Doubleday; Grosset and Dunlap. World War I.

REMARQUE, ERICH MARIA, *All Quiet on the Western Front*, Little, Brown; Fawcett (Crest). Novel about German soldier in World War I.

SCANLON, W. T., *God Have Mercy on Us!*, Houghton Mifflin. A story of 1918.

STALLINGS, LAURENCE, *Plumes*, Harcourt, Brace; Grosset & Dunlap. A family that fights in all the American wars.

UNIT TEN

The "Golden Twenties"

1920–1932

Years of Prosperity End in a Crash

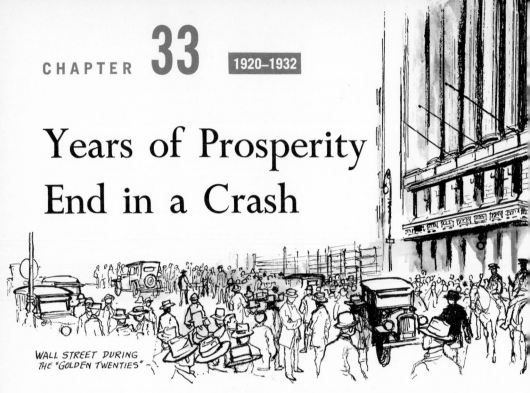

WALL STREET DURING THE "GOLDEN TWENTIES"

ON December 4, 1918, President Wilson and many of his official advisers left New York harbor on the army transport *George Washington* bound for Europe and the peace conference at Versailles (vehr-SIGH) near Paris. The vessel docked at Brest, France, on December 13. While waiting for the conference to open, President Wilson visited Paris, London, Rome, and other European cities. Everywhere he went people gave him a tumultuous welcome.

But Wilson's triumph was short-lived. At the peace conference all the bitterness of four long years of warfare burst into the open. Wilson did win acceptance of his proposal for a League of Nations designed to safeguard the peace. But in order to do so, he had to compromise many of his principles.

By 1920 it was clear that the American people had rejected Wilson's leadership. As you will see in Chapter 34, the United States refused to join the League of Nations and, in a sense, turned its back upon Europe. And, as you will see in the following pages, Americans also turned their backs upon Wilson's domestic policies. In the elections of 1920, they restored the Republicans to a position of leadership.

During the decade of the 1920's, three Republican Presidents—Warren G. Harding, Calvin Coolidge, and Herbert Hoover—presided over a country that on the whole enjoyed a period of prosperity unparalleled before that time. But the era of the "Golden Twenties" ended with an economic collapse and the most shattering depression in American history.

AS THE STORY DEVELOPS

1. Woodrow Wilson and the Democratic Party lose popularity.
2. Republicans assume responsibility for governing the country.
3. The Great Depression shatters the prosperity of the "Golden Twenties."

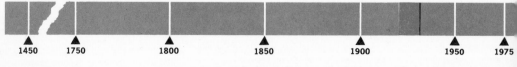

1450 1750 1800 1850 1900 1950 1975

1

Woodrow Wilson and the Democratic Party lose popularity

Before America's entry into the war, President Wilson had concentrated on his program of domestic reform. As you have seen, his first administration from 1913 to 1917 reduced tariffs, strengthened the antitrust laws, and established the Federal Reserve System. In these and other ways, Wilson worked to restore competition in American business and to protect the consumer.

The war, however, interrupted Wilson's "New Freedom" program. And after the war he became deeply involved in the task of organizing world peace. As a result, he had little time left to deal with such pressing domestic problems as a postwar business slump, a decline of farm prices, and widespread unemployment.

Wilson loses support at home. As for the American people, they were growing tired of international issues. They were more interested in their personal affairs than in a peace treaty or a League of Nations.

The Congressional elections of 1918, held just a few days before the armistice, showed the direction in which the political winds were blowing. President Wilson appealed to the voters to return a Democratic Congress. Ignoring his appeal, they elected a Republican majority of both the Senate and the House.

During the next two years a number of developments combined to speed up this trend away from the Democratic Party.

Wilson's illness. When President Wilson returned from the Versailles Conference in the summer of 1919, he found many Senators critical of the Covenant, or constitution, of the League of Nations. But the President refused to compromise on the basic points of the Covenant. Instead, he tried to win the American public to his point of view.

Late in the summer of 1919, Wilson set out by special train on a grueling nationwide speaking tour. After three weeks of continuous speechmaking, he suffered a stroke which paralyzed his whole left side from jaw to foot. He was rushed back to Washington, where his condition improved somewhat. But he remained an invalid for the rest of his term, indeed until his death in 1924.

The postwar depression brings problems. Wilson's illness came at a time when the country was suffering from a severe postwar depression. With the signing of the armistice, the government immediately began to cancel its wartime contracts. Businessmen in industries producing munitions and other products for the armed forces suddenly found themselves faced with the problem of reconverting their plants to peacetime production. New machinery had to be installed, new customers lined up. During the period of reconversion, factories closed down or operated with greatly reduced labor forces.

Farmers also suffered as a result of the transition from war to peace. For a short period, while Europe was recovering from the destruction of war, the American farmer could still sell nearly all that he produced at good prices. But as European farm lands began to swing back to normal production, the American farmer's wartime markets began to disappear. Farm prices, which had soared during the war years, dropped as competition increased. Wheat, for example, which had sold as high as $2.26 a bushel, dropped to less than $1.00 a bushel in 1922. Almost half a million American farmers lost their farms during this troubled period.

Meanwhile, wage earners were also facing problems during the period of the postwar depression. Large numbers of government employees who had been working in wartime agencies lost their jobs when the war ended. Hundreds of thousands of industrial wage earners were thrown out of work when factories closed down or curtailed operations. Many of the 4,500,000 returning servicemen were unable to find work.

As the depression deepened, as wages

During the Boston police strike of 1919, a few policemen remained on duty. One is shown here talking to a mounted member of the state guard.

fell lower and lower, and as more men and women lost their jobs, discontent swelled alarmingly. During 1919 more than 4,000,000 workers were at one time or another out on strike. Three of the strikes were especially serious.

The Boston police strike. On September 9 the police force of the city of Boston left their posts in a strike against what they claimed was unfair treatment. In defense of their action, they pointed out that (1) they were still working at pre-war wages, (2) they had to buy their own uniforms, (3) they were forced to work in inadequate and overcrowded station houses, and (4) the police commissioner had refused to permit them to affiliate with the American Federation of Labor.

The strike left Boston without police protection. When rioting and looting broke out, the mayor immediately called out that portion of the state guard over which he shared authority with the governor. On the third day Governor Calvin Coolidge himself ordered the rest of the state guard to Boston. The policemen, realizing that the strike

was lost, announced that they were prepared to return to work.

At this point, however, the police commissioner refused to allow the strikers to return to their jobs. He announced that he intended to employ a new police force. Governor Coolidge supported the commissioner. "There is no right," Coolidge flatly stated, "to strike against the public safety by anybody, anywhere, any time." Coolidge's statement was widely applauded all over the country. It brought him to public attention and helped him to win the Vice-Presidential nomination on the Republican ticket in 1920.

The coal strike. Less than two months after this police strike, on November 1, 1919, the United Mine Workers (U.M.W.) went out on strike. Led by their newly elected president, John L. Lewis, they demanded higher wages and a shorter work week. On November 9, United States Attorney General A. Mitchell Palmer secured an injunction against the union. The injunction ordered the officers of the U.M.W. to stop all activities tending to encourage the strikers. This injunction was based on a wartime law that had given the federal government emergency powers over food and fuel. "We cannot fight the government," John L. Lewis declared, and the strike was called off.

But the coal miners refused to return to work. Finally, following President Wilson's suggestion, the problem was submitted to a board of arbitration. The board gave the miners a 27 per cent wage increase, but refused to consider a reduction in the weekly hours of work.

The steel strike. Meanwhile, discontent among workers in the steel industry led to a strike involving more than 300,000 workers. The steelworkers had been dissatisfied for a long time with their working conditions. In some plants they worked as long as 12 hours a day and 7 days a week. Moreover, they had not been able to form a union to speak for them. During the summer of 1919, however, a number of A.F. of L. unions formed a committee which launched a vigorous organizing campaign in the steel towns. The strike started on September 22, 1919, after management had refused to recognize the right of this committee to speak for all the steelworkers.

As the weeks passed, violence erupted around some of the steel mills. At Gary, Indiana, martial law was declared, and federal troops moved in to limit picketing and to keep order. Finally, with public opinion running against the steelworkers, the strike was called off, and in January 1920 the men returned to their jobs. Three years later, however, the steel companies agreed to establish an 8-hour day.

Declining strength of organized labor. The postwar depression did not last long. By the opening months of 1920, American export trade was soaring as orders for goods began to pour in from the war-devastated countries. The value of United States exports rose to three times the 1913 level.

As economic conditions improved and jobs became more plentiful, many workers lost their interest in unions. Membership in the A.F. of L., which had reached a peak of more than 4,000,000 early in 1920, began to decline.

There were, of course, other reasons for the decline of the labor movement. The failure of the steel strike and of other strikes during 1919 discouraged workers. The use of the injunction, as in the strike of the United Mine Workers, was another discouraging factor. Moreover, a "Red scare" that swept the country in 1919–20 caused large numbers of citizens, including many workers, to turn against organized labor.

The "Red scare." During the years immediately following the war, federal and state governments conducted a vigorous drive against anarchists, communists, and socialists. The Espionage Act (page 632), passed in wartime to punish treasonable or disloyal activities, remained in effect after the war. Under this law, revolutionists and suspected revolutionists continued to be arrested and fined. Some of the people who were

arrested and who lacked American citizenship were deported to the countries from which they had come.

One important reason for the postwar concern with radicals was the Bolshevik Revolution which had erupted in Russia in November 1917 (page 633). This event frightened many Americans who feared that radicals in the United States might try to follow the Bolshevik example. Rumors of revolutionary plots circulated widely during the years from 1917 through 1920.

But there was more than rumor to arouse alarm. During the spring and summer of 1919, more than thirty bombs were discovered by postal authorities in packages addressed to prominent citizens, including three members of Wilson's Cabinet and a Supreme Court justice. And matters reached a terrible climax in New York City on September 16, 1920, when at noontime a bomb exploded in crowded Wall Street killing 38 persons, injuring hundreds, and causing property damage variously estimated from $500,000 to $2,500,000.

Meanwhile, Attorney General Palmer had been active. In the fall of 1919, he instructed his agents in the Department of Justice to arrest radical agitators throughout the country. Of those arrested as a result of the so-called "Palmer raids," 249 were deported.

Criticism of the "Palmer raids." A number of Americans, both Democrats and Republicans, criticized certain illegal aspects of this drive against radical movements. In many cases the raids were conducted without search warrants. Critics claimed that, in his zeal to round up dangerous radicals, the Attorney General sometimes ignored Constitutional rights of free citizens.

But it was not just against Attorney General Palmer that the critics directed their fire. By 1920 about one third of the states had passed laws to punish advocates of revolutionary change. The New York State Assembly even expelled five duly elected Socialist members on the ground that their ideas were against the best interests of the country.

President Warren G. Harding, advocate of "normalcy," was a man of distinguished appearance.

Election of 1920. In the Presidential election of 1920, the unsettled condition of the country gave the Republican candidate for the Presidency, Senator Warren G. Harding of Ohio, a decided advantage over his Democratic opponent, Governor James M. Cox of Ohio. Farmers, workers, and businessmen naturally blamed the administration in office for the troubled times.

In the face of this dissatisfaction, the Republican candidate's plea for a return to "normalcy" proved attractive to many Americans. At this point they were tired of Europe and its wars, tired of Wilson's attempts to "save the world for democracy." Businessmen regarded the few remaining regulations of business that were held over from wartime as unnecessary government interference. Workers and farmers felt that their problems, among them unemployment and falling prices, were being neglected.

All of these reasons combined to defeat the Democratic candidates. Harding won 61 per cent of the popular vote, or approximately 16,000,000 votes to Cox's 9,000,000. The electoral vote was even more sweeping, giving Harding 404 to Cox's 127. Eugene V. Debs, still in prison for violating the Espionage Act during the war, received nearly a million votes on the Socialist ticket.

The election of 1920 was the first Presidential contest in which all eligible women could vote. The long struggle for woman suffrage had been won in August 1920, when the Nineteenth Amendment went into effect.

An interesting side light of the 1920 campaign is the identity of the Vice-Presidential candidates. Calvin Coolidge, who was to succeed Harding as Republican President, was to set the political tone of the "Golden Twenties." Franklin D. Roosevelt, the youthful Democratic Vice-Presidential candidate, was to become one of the most controversial Presidents in American history.

Party differences fade. In the decade that followed their defeat in 1920, the Democrats failed to work out a clear-cut program to challenge the Republicans. They turned away from the spirit of reform that had characterized Wilson's first administration. More and more, the Democratic Party accepted the conservative principles of its rival. Democrats as well as Republicans supported high tariffs and believed that big business should be let alone. It was for this reason, as you will see, that in 1924 the Democrats chose as their Presidential candidate a Wall Street corporation lawyer who was as conservative in economic matters as his Republican opponent. As the years passed, it became increasingly difficult to distinguish between the viewpoints of the two parties.

SECTION SURVEY

1. What were some of the problems facing Americans in the postwar depression?

2. (a) Indicate the reasons for labor unrest after the war. (b) Summarize facts in the police, coal, and steel strikes of 1919.

3. Why did organized labor decline?

4. (a) Indicate the conditions that gave rise to the "Red scare." (b) On what grounds were the "Palmer raids" criticized?

5. Give the parties, candidates, issues, and results of the election of 1920.

IDENTIFY: Bolshevik Revolution, a return to "normalcy," Nineteenth Amendment; Coolidge, John L. Lewis.

2 Republicans assume responsibility for governing the country

Warren G. Harding, who took the oath of office and became President on March 4, 1921, was a genial, small-town Ohio newspaperman who had climbed to the top of the political ladder in his own state. Before his elevation to the Presidency, he had served as United States Senator in Washington. Handsome and distinguished in appearance, with a warm, easygoing manner, he had numerous friends in every walk of life.

Farm relief and financial reform. It was not an easy job that Harding took over when he entered the White House. During the latter months of 1920, a second postwar depression had hit the country. Farmers, wage earners, businessmen, and the public in general were clamoring for governmental action, and for the fulfillment of the President's campaign promise of a return to "normalcy."

In response to widespread demand for help, Congress adopted the Emergency Tariff of May 27, 1921. This tariff measure raised rates on some agricultural products, but failed to raise farm prices generally.

The following month, in June, Congress adopted the Budget and Accounting Act. This act created a Bureau of the Budget in the Treasury Department, with a director appointed by the President. The new measure was designed to reduce extravagance and waste in government, and to provide a more efficient and economical method of handling government expenditures.

Up to this time Congress had made annual appropriations on a piecemeal basis, with no great concern for matching income and expenditures—that is, for "balancing the budget." Under the new system all government agencies and departments were required to submit their annual requests for funds to the Director of the Budget. The director then had the responsibility of drawing up a detailed budget in which he listed estimated income and expenditures for the coming fiscal year.° Once the budget was prepared, the President submitted it to Congress, which could, if it chose, raise or lower the director's estimates.

Charles G. Dawes, the first director of the budget, proved himself an extremely capable administrator. Under his leadership and that of the Secretary of the Treasury, Andrew W. Mellon, the government began to use surplus revenues to reduce the national debt. At the end of World War I, the debt totaled more than 25 billion dollars. During the 1920's it was cut by about one third, but it still totaled more than 16 billion dollars when, as you will see, the United States entered the Great Depression in the closing months of 1929.

The Veterans' Bureau and the bonus. Meanwhile, Congress tackled another problem that the Harding administration had inherited—the problem of the war veterans. Many veterans, as well as many other Americans who had not served in the armed forces during the war, felt that the government should provide "adjusted compensation" for ex-servicemen. Those who argued for adjusted compensation pointed out that during the war the servicemen had received low pay while workers at home were reaping high wartime wages in more or less safe occupations.

In August 1921 Congress created the Veterans' Bureau. President Harding then appointed Charles R. Forbes as its first director. The Veterans' Bureau was authorized to handle veterans' claims for compensation and hospitalization, to provide medical care for sick veterans, and to administer the government program of veterans' insurance.

The Veterans' Bureau was only a partial answer to the demands of the veterans. The American Legion, the Veterans of Foreign Wars, and other vet-

....
° **fiscal year:** the twelve-month period considered as a year for general accounting, budgeting, and planning purposes. The fiscal year of the United States government begins on July 1.

ALFRED E. SMITH

In 1918, Alfred E. ("Al") Smith became governor of New York, the first Catholic to hold such political office.

Al Smith, at thirty, had been but one of the machine politicians chosen to go to the state legislature at Albany from New York's east side. There, from 1914 to 1918, he grew to be a capable and social-minded legislator. He lacked a formal education and spoke with a crude accent, but he was honest, learned rapidly, and gained a state-wide reputation. As a governor in the 1920's, he earned national prominence.

The period was one of general failure for Governor Smith's party, the Democrats, in national elections. In part, this was because rural Democrats disliked city Democrats, especially Catholics. Also, rural America was in favor of Prohibition, while urban workingmen were against it. Yet, in 1928, the party nominated Al Smith for President. He lost to Republican Herbert Hoover, who would probably have won against any opponent, but to Smith and most Catholics it appeared that rural, small town Democrats had made a switch to the Republicans out of prejudice.

The Fordney-McCumber Tariff. On September 21, 1922, the Harding administration adopted another important measure, the Fordney-McCumber Tariff Act. Congress had been working on this measure for months. Wiping out the reductions made in the Underwood Tariff of 1913 (page 563), the new tariff law established rates that were considerably higher. The limited protection for farmers in the Emergency Tariff of 1921 was continued by this act. Rates on hundreds of manufactured products were revised sharply upward.

The Fordney-McCumber Tariff also authorized the President to raise or lower any of the tariff rates by as much as 50 per cent. The President was to act only if investigation by a Tariff Commission revealed that a particular tariff, or duty, did not equalize the cost of production at home and abroad. As it turned out, most of the adjustments made under this clause in the law were upward rather than downward.

Public scandals. In spite of a number of solid accomplishments, the Harding administration left behind it a long record of corruption.

President Harding was not himself involved in the corruption. His mistake was in appointing undeserving men to office. Harding found it hard to distinguish good from evil in the men who surrounded him in political life. For instance, his Cabinet contained such able and respected men as Charles Evans Hughes, who became Secretary of State; Andrew W. Mellon, who headed the Treasury Department; and Herbert Hoover, who remained Secretary of Commerce until he was elected President in 1928. But Harding's administration also contained several irresponsible and dishonest politicians who betrayed their leader and brought disgrace upon his administration.

One group of self-seeking politicians from Harding's home state, known as the "Ohio Gang," succeeded in having one of its number, Harry M. Daugherty, placed in the Cabinet as Attorney General. An investigation later revealed that

erans' organizations continued to press Congress for adjusted compensation. Congress responded in 1922 with a bonus bill. President Harding vetoed the bill because it did not include any provision for raising the necessary money.

Finally—to glance ahead—in 1924 Congress passed another bonus bill over President Coolidge's veto. The bill provided adjusted compensation for all veterans except those with ranks above that of captain. Each man was to receive $1.25 a day for overseas service and $1.00 a day for service in the United States. But the payments were not to be given in cash. They were, instead, given in the form of a paid-up twenty-year life insurance policy. Veterans who held the policy for twenty years would receive full compensation. Those who wished could borrow money against the policy up to 25 per cent of its value.

Daugherty had used his position as head of the Department of Justice to protect violators of the prohibition amendment. Another Harding official, Thomas W. Miller, defrauded the government in the sale of alien properties—that is, foreign-owned properties that had been seized by the American government during World War I. Charles R. Forbes, who headed the Veterans' Bureau, could not satisfactorily account for 200 million dollars spent by his organization.

The most famous scandal took its name from the naval oil reserve lands at Teapot Dome in Wyoming. Secretary of the Interior Albert B. Fall persuaded the Secretary of the Navy, Edwin C. Denby, secretly to transfer to his (Fall's) jurisdiction the Teapot Dome reserve and another oil reserve at Elk Hills, California. In return for bribes, Fall leased the Elk Hills fields to an oil speculator, Edward Doheny, and the Teapot Dome reserve to another oil speculator, Harry F. Sinclair.

These scandals did not become publicly known until Coolidge took office, when Fall, Forbes, and Miller were each prosecuted and imprisoned. Some hint of what was going on reached Harding in 1923, however, and his health broke under the worry and strain. He died suddenly in the summer of 1923.

Calvin Coolidge. Vice-President Calvin Coolidge, who rose to the Presidency left vacant by Harding's death, was a man of unquestioned honesty.

Coolidge had built his political career in Massachusetts, advancing from state legislator to governor. He became to millions of Americans a symbol of the thrifty, old-fashioned, simple, country American. In a period of extravagance and "big money," his simplicity also helped to regain for the Republican Party the public confidence that had been lost as a result of the scandals of the Harding administration.

The election of 1924. Only once during the 1920's did the Republican program face any serious opposition. Curiously enough, the opposition came in part from within Republican ranks.

The revolt broke out in 1924 when the staunchly conservative Calvin Coolidge was nominated by his party for the Presidency. Coolidge had made clear his belief that government should encourage, but not regulate, business. He also disapproved of special legislation to help workers or farmers.

Resisting these conservative policies, a group of progressive Republicans broke away from the Republican Party and formed a new Progressive Party. They nominated as their standard bearer Senator Robert M. La Follette of Wisconsin. The Progressive Party received the backing of three important groups of Americans who were dissatisfied with both major parties—western farmers, organized labor, and the Socialists. The Progressive program called for government action on a number of fronts. It urged federal credit and other assistance for farmers, social legislation and additional laws to protect the rights of labor, and government ownership of railroads and water power resources.

La Follette received almost five million votes, the largest number any third party has ever mustered. With La Follette's death shortly after the campaign, however, the Progressive Party lost its strength and faded into insignificance.

The Democrats in 1924 nominated John W. Davis, a conservative corporation lawyer. During his campaign Davis concentrated on the corruption in the Harding administration. But the Republicans met this challenge by claiming credit for the prevailing prosperity. The argument of prosperity proved effective. In spite of the Progressive revolt, which split the Republicans into two factions, Coolidge won by a landslide, piling up 382 electoral votes to 136 for Davis and 13 for La Follette.

Coolidge and thrifty government. Endorsed by an overwhelming vote, President Coolidge continued to conduct government on a frugal basis. On the grounds of economy, he vetoed a bill providing bonus payments to veterans of World War I. As you have seen (page 648), Congress passed this bill over his veto. Coolidge also vetoed the McNary-Haugen Bill which was designed to stabilize farm prices by allowing the government to buy up agricultural surpluses and sell them abroad.

In other matters, too, Congress and the President did not see eye to eye. But the President remained popular. "Keep cool with Coolidge" was a slogan of the day. He could have been re-elected in 1928 had he wished. But a year before the election he distributed to the press a short statement, "I do not choose to run for President in 1928."

The election of 1928. With Coolidge out of the Presidential race, the Republicans nominated Herbert C. Hoover of

■ When this picture was taken in 1926, Calvin Coolidge (left) was President. His frugality and honesty were doing much to restore Republican prestige. With him is Herbert Hoover, then Secretary of Commerce, but destined to succeed Coolidge in the Presidency.

California. Hoover was a successful mining engineer with a notable record as an administrator of relief in Europe during and after the war and as Secretary of Commerce since 1921. Hoover's running mate was Senator Charles Curtis of Kansas.

The Democrats nominated New York's Governor Alfred E. Smith, who had sponsored social legislation in his state. Smith advocated a federal farm relief program along the lines of the McNary-Haugen Bill, which Coolidge had vetoed. Smith also urged stricter regulation of public utilities. These planks in the Democratic platform had strong appeal for many Americans. But Smith had political handicaps that cost him support within his own party. He was opposed to prohibition, he was a Roman Catholic, and he was connected with the Tammany political machine in New York City—all of which made him unpopular with large groups of voters, especially in the South and West.

Hoover carried the country with more popular votes than any Presidential candidate had ever accumulated up to that time. In the Electoral College he received 444 votes to Smith's 87. Smith lost his own state of New York. He also lost the traditionally Democratic states of Virginia, Florida, North Carolina, Tennessee, and Texas, which for the first time since the War Between the States gave their votes to a Republican.

Herbert C. Hoover. President Herbert Hoover summed up his political beliefs in the phrase "rugged individualism." His general point of view was very close to Harding's idea of "normalcy" and to Coolidge's belief that government should encourage business but not give special assistance to individuals. Hoover, however, displayed more initiative and imagination than his Republican predecessors. Having been an engineer and businessman, he saw an important role for the "expert" in government, and advocated a moderate amount of social and economic planning.

When Hoover took office, he looked forward to a prolonged period of increasing prosperity. He believed that Americans now expected more than the necessities of life. "The slogan of progress," he declared, "is changing from the full dinner pail to the full garage." For about six months, booming business and heavy consumer buying seemed to bear out this prediction.

The Hawley-Smoot Tariff. In 1929, with most Americans enjoying an unprecedented wave of prosperity, Hoover called Congress into special session to consider farm relief and a "limited revision" of tariffs.

The Hawley-Smoot Tariff bill, calling for the highest tariff in American history, came to Hoover for his signature in the spring of 1930. The President felt that some of the rates were too high. He also pondered a petition signed by 1000 leading economists who argued that such high tariffs would raise prices, create hardships for American consumers, seriously interfere with world trade, and invite economic reprisals from other countries. But, believing that protective tariffs encouraged business prosperity, Hoover put aside his doubts and signed the bill. In less than two years, some 25 countries took steps to cut down imports of American products.

The Agricultural Marketing Act. Hoover did depart from the policies of his Republican predecessors, however, in supporting the Agricultural Marketing Act. This act created a Federal Farm Board consisting of eight members and the Secretary of Agriculture. Under the law, this board was authorized to lend up to $500,000,000 to co-operative farm groups to help them store or market crops and to keep prices stable.

In his support of federal legislation providing financial assistance to farmers, Hoover was taking a modest turn away from the "rugged individualism" that he favored in theory. As you will see later, the stock market crash in the autumn of 1929 and the Great Depression that followed brought new and ever heavier pressures for government action to aid farmers, wage earners, businessmen, and consumers in general.

✓ **SECTION SURVEY**

1. Describe changes in government financing resulting from the Budget and Accounting Act.
2. Evaluate Republican tariff policies as shown by Fordney-McCumber and Hawley-Smoot tariff measures of 1922 and 1930.
3. "In spite of a number of solid accomplishments, the Harding administration left behind it a long record of corruption." Reveal the record.
4. Indicate the parties, candidates, issues, and results of the elections of 1924 and 1928.
IDENTIFY: adjusted compensation, Veterans' Bureau, "Ohio Gang," Teapot Dome scandal, McNary-Haugen Bill, rugged individualism, Agricultural Marketing Act, Progressive Party; Hoover, Alfred E. Smith.

3 The Great Depression shatters the prosperity of the "Golden Twenties"

Flourishing business conditions and a rising standard of living contributed to the political success of the Republican Party during the 1920's. Between 1922 and 1929 factories hummed and jobs were plentiful. Americans were, on the whole, better fed, clothed, and housed than they had ever been before.

Easy money. The most conspicuous evidence of prosperity during the so-called "Golden Twenties" was the ease with which many Americans made and spent money. Millions of workmen were receiving relatively high wages, many businessmen earned large profits, and an ever-growing number of stockholders received substantial dividends.

A good part of the money that Americans made went to buy consumer goods, and the retail trade began to report huge annual sales. Some of the profits of successful business enterprises went back into industry, to expand and improve the plants and to support industrial research. Some paid for workers' recreational facilities, some for welfare programs providing insurance and pensions for employees. Large sums flowed into philanthropies, such as medical research, education, and the welfare of the poor.

As surplus income piled higher and higher, more and more Americans from all walks of life were tempted to invest their savings or their profits in the stock market with the hope of big returns.

The limits of prosperity. Not all Americans shared in the widespread prosperity of the "Golden Twenties." Many workers lost their jobs when new machines were introduced in mills and factories. Some craftsmen, such as blacksmiths and harness makers, whose skills were no longer needed, found it difficult or impossible to adapt to the monotonous work on assembly lines. Furthermore, some industries—such as coal, textiles, and leather—never fully recovered from the postwar slump of the early 1920's. Finally, many farmers did not share in the prosperity that other Americans were enjoying.

The plight of the farmers. After the war, as you have seen, American farmers lost many of their European markets. Also, as you will see, laws passed in the early 1920's virtually put an end to immigration. So this traditional source of new customers was now also lost to the farmer. But, although markets were shrinking, farm production—with the help of new machines and new techniques—jumped more than 20 per cent between 1919 and 1929.

When supply is high and demand is low, when more people want to sell goods and fewer people want to or are able to buy them, prices inevitably drop. And while farm prices were falling, the prices of the industrial goods that the farmer needed rose higher and higher. As a result, many farmers found it increasingly difficult to meet their mortgage payments or the installments on their farm machinery. Thus, during the industrial prosperity of the 1920's, large numbers of American farmers were sinking deeper into debt, and many of them lost their farms.

The belief in prosperity. But relatively few people in the "Golden Twenties" paid much attention to these limitations of prosperity. Most Americans believed, with Herbert Hoover, that "we in America are nearer to the final triumph over poverty than ever before in the history of any land."

Such optimistic statements crowded out those few that warned of difficulties ahead. As a result, the depression that started late in 1929 came as a stunning blow to most Americans.

The stock market crash. On October 24, 1929, a panic of selling broke out on the New York Stock Exchange as frantic orders to sell stock came pouring in. The causes of this panic were chiefly overproduction and overspeculation. More goods had been produced than could be profitably sold. And a great many stocks that had been bought by Americans were either worthless or overinflated. That is, the businesses behind such stocks either existed on paper only, or their actual value was far less than the market value of the stock.

Overproduction and overspeculation had caught up with the American people. The overinflated prices of stocks tumbled downward. On October 29 prices sank to a shattering new low when over 16 million shares of stock were dumped on the market. By the middle of November, the average value of leading stocks had been cut in half, and stockholders had lost 30 billion dollars. With this "crash" of the stock market, the Great Depression started.

At first, business and government leaders tried to reassure the American people. "There is nothing to worry about," said Charles E. Mitchell of the National City Bank. "Business is fundamentally sound," announced Secretary of the Treasury Andrew Mellon. But such words, no matter how reassuring, could not stem the tide of economic disaster that was racing across the country.

The Great Depression spreads. Before the year 1929 was over, banks all over the country were closing their doors. Businesses everywhere cut back production, and many concerns, finding themselves without customers, were forced out of business. Factories and mines were shut down. Empty railroad cars began to pile up on the sidings. By 1930 there were between 6 and 7 million unemployed Americans. The result was a chain reaction. Unemployment meant fewer customers; a decrease in customers brought on further cutbacks in production; these, in turn, resulted in more unemployment. By 1932 nearly 12 million Americans were out of work.

The depression struck at all classes. Many well-to-do Americans saw their fortunes, invested in stocks or businesses, melt away before their eyes. But it was the industrial workers and the farmers who suffered most severely, for most of them had no savings to tide them over a period of unemployment. In every city thousands of unfortunate men and women stood in lines to get free meals of bread and soup. Families forced out of their homes moved to villages that sprang up on the unused land at the edge of the cities.

For the farmers the depression came as a final blow. As you have seen, most farmers had never shared fully in the prosperity of the twenties. But bad as conditions were before, they became steadily worse between 1929 and 1932. Farm prices fell lower and lower. As their incomes shrank, more and more farmers saw their farms pass into the possession of the mortgage holders. In some midwestern states desperate farmers joined hands and used force to prevent sheriffs from foreclosing mortgages on the farms which were their homes and their means of livelihood.

Many thousands of men from cities and farms wandered over the land seeking jobs at any wages, traveling by foot or on the brake rods of trains, sleeping on park benches or wherever else they could lay their heads. Never had America known such widespread suffering.

What caused the Great Depression? There is no simple way to explain what caused the Great Depression. Econo-

■ As depression deepened, private agencies, like St. Peter's mission, donated food to the jobless. The big man is Heywood Broun, famous newspaperman.

mists agree that there were many causes, but they disagree about which was the most important.

President Hoover insisted that the major cause of the depression was the world-wide economic disorder that followed World War I. Many economists agreed with Hoover. They pointed to the vast destruction of property during the war and the world-wide dislocation of trade during and after the war.

Other economists argued that America's high tariff policies helped to stifle world trade and hurt American business. High tariffs, they claimed, prevented other countries from selling their goods in the United States. This in turn prevented them from securing the dollars that they needed to buy American products.

Still other economists blamed the depression on the excessive borrowing of money—for stocks, for comforts purchased on the installment plan, or for the expansion of businesses. These critics also claimed that the federal government failed to control bank loans and to protect the public against the sale of worthless stocks.

Some economists have argued that depressions are an inevitable part of our economic system. According to this view, business expands during periods of prosperity in order to obtain the largest possible profits. But when factories produce more goods than the people can buy, the factories have to contract and cut down on production, at least until their surpluses are consumed. For this reason, these economists have argued, prosperity and depression are inevitable parts of the business cycle.

Finally, a number of students of the Great Depression have traced that calamity to uneven distribution of income. These economists have argued that, if farmers had received better prices for their products and if workers had received higher wages, the American people would have been able to buy a larger proportion of the surplus goods. Had this happened, these economists claim, the factories would have kept busy and the depression could have been avoided.

Hoover and the depression. Whatever its causes, the depression confronted the Hoover administration with two emergencies. First, there was the widespread misery of people without jobs or farms, without money to buy enough food or clothing, and increasingly without hope. Some Americans urged the federal government to extend direct relief to those in need. President Hoover, however, believed that direct aid was a responsibility of the local communities. Direct federal relief, he said, would undermine the self-respect of the persons receiving it.

To the second emergency, the collapse of business and agriculture, Hoover responded more actively. He instructed the Federal Farm Board to buy up agricultural surpluses in an effort to raise falling farm prices. With the support of Congress, he started a number of public works programs, among them Boulder Dam (later called Hoover Dam) on the Colorado River. By means of these projects, he hoped to stimulate business and provide some employment.

Also at Hoover's urging, Congress created the Reconstruction Finance Corporation (RFC) in February 1932. The Reconstruction Finance Corporation was authorized to lend large sums of money to banks, life insurance companies, railroads, farm mortgage associations, and other enterprises. President Hoover and his associates hoped that this method of pumping money into key businesses would stop the downward spiral of the depression.

In response to Hoover's recommendation, Congress also passed the Home Loan Bank Act in July 1932. This act created a series of special banks designed to provide financial assistance to savings banks, building and loan associations, and insurance companies—all of which lent money on mortgages. By providing financial aid to these key mortgage institutions, Hoover hoped to reduce foreclosures on homes and farms and to stimulate construction of residential buildings.

In adopting these measures, the President and Congress were accepting, for the first time, the idea that the federal government must assume certain responsibilities when the nation's economy becomes disordered. Unfortunately, the measures that they adopted did not succeed in stopping the downward trend of the depression.

The election campaign of 1932. Although several issues, among them prohibition, entered into the Presidential campaign of 1932, there was really only one important issue—the depression. The Republicans renominated Herbert Hoover, expressing their faith that the policies of his administration would presently pull the country out of the depression. During the campaign Hoover continued to blame the depression on international conditions. He declared that his policies were beginning to bring recovery.

Both of these claims were vigorously rejected by the Democratic Presidential candidate, Franklin Delano Roosevelt, who was governor of New York at the time of his nomination. Roosevelt maintained that Republican policies, not international conditions, were to blame for the depression. In opposition to these policies, he argued that the federal government should help provide direct relief to the needy and direct aid to the farmers. He called for a broad program of public works. And he demanded that safeguards be set up to prevent wild speculation and fraudulent issues of stock. To this end he proposed laws that would protect the bank depositor, the purchaser of stocks, and the home owner. Referring to unemployed workers, desperate farmers, and others, Roosevelt stated that the "forgotten man" must have a "new deal."

Roosevelt wins. Franklin D. Roosevelt and his running mate, John Nance Garner of Texas, swept the country in the Presidential election of 1932. When the count was in, Roosevelt had 23 million popular votes to Hoover's 16 million. Roosevelt carried 42 states and piled up 472 electoral votes to Hoover's 59. Moreover, the Democrats secured decisive majorities in both houses of Congress. Not since the War Between the States had the Democratic Party won such a sweeping victory.

A majority of voters throughout the 1920's had given the Republicans credit for the prosperity of those years. Now a great many Americans seemed to be saying that the Republicans should take the blame for the depression. Many who voted for the Democrats were really voting against Hoover rather than for Roosevelt. But many more saw in Franklin Delano Roosevelt the kind of dynamic personality that they believed was needed to lead the country out of its troubles.

Roosevelt had promised the American people a "new deal." During the four months between Election Day and Inauguration Day—March 4, 1933—workers, farmers, and even many businessmen waited impatiently and hopefully to see how the new President would carry out his pledge. You will read about the New Deal in Chapters 36 and 37.

■ Trying to stimulate the economy, President Hoover authorized public works like this great dam, now called Hoover Dam, near Las Vegas, Nevada.

SECTION SURVEY

1. (a) What were signs of prosperity in the "Golden Twenties"? (b) What groups failed to share in this prosperity? (c) Account for the farm depression in the midst of this prosperity.

2. Describe the hardships suffered by many during the Great Depression. What do economists consider to have been major causes of this depression?

3. Describe and evaluate Hoover's efforts to combat the depression.

4. Give the parties, candidates, issues, and results of the election of 1932.

5. Economic conditions are often attributed to the party in power. Republicans were credited with the prosperity of the 1920's and blamed for the Great Depression. Give other examples.

IDENTIFY: stock exchange, Reconstruction Finance Corporation, "the forgotten man"; Franklin D. Roosevelt, John Nance Garner; October 1929.

■ CHAPTER SURVEY (For review, see Section Surveys, pages 646, 651, 655.)

Points to Discuss: 1. Indicate the connection between World War I and the depression of 1920–21.

2. What were some reasons for the defeat of the Democratic Party in 1920?

3. Describe the constructive achievements of the Republican administrations during 1920–32. Would you include their tariff program? Explain.

4. What evidence can you offer that the tariff acts of 1921 and 1922 hurt the farmer more than they helped him?

5. Speaking in the 1920's, Hoover said: "We in America are nearer to the final triumph over poverty than ever before in the history of our land." (a) What evidence tended to support his statement? (b) Why were some Americans inclined to be critical of this view?

6. There would have been a depression in 1929 even without the stock market crash. Defend or refute this statement.

Using Charts: 1. Using chart 1 on page 844, calculate the approximate percentage of the population which was included in the labor force in 1920, and compare this percentage with earlier figures.

2. Consulting charts 3 and 4 on pages 840–41, answer the following: (a) Compare the rates of the Fordney-McCumber Tariff with those tariffs that preceded and followed it. (b) In 1920 what was the relation of our exports to our imports? (c) How do you reconcile this relationship with the passage of the Fordney-McCumber Tariff? (d) Explain the change in the export-import picture by 1930. Was it connected with the Hawley-Smoot Tariff?

3. Using the Business Activity chart on pages 850–59, compare the duration and intensity of the depression of 1929 with those that preceded it.

Consulting the Sources: For a contemporary account of how Coolidge received the news of Harding's death and of Coolidge's inauguration, see A. B. Hart (ed.), *American History Told by Contemporaries*, Vol. 5, No. 196. See Ellis, *Documents*, No. 160, for Alfred E. Smith's Oklahoma City campaign address of September 28, 1928.

■ TRACING THE MAIN IDEAS

After three years of unrest and readjustment following World War I, Americans enjoyed a decade of enormous prosperity. During the "Golden Twenties" business prospered, wages were high, and relatively few persons were unemployed.

Here and there warning voices called attention to the difficulties faced by large numbers of farmers and to other weaknesses of the economic system. Most Americans, however, believed that prosperity had come to stay.

And then, toward the end of 1929, the great industrial machine that the United States had built up, particularly during World War I and the 1920's, began to grind to a halt. At first, people could not believe that the situation was serious. But as the months passed and conditions became steadily worse, it became increasingly evident that the nation was confronted with a major crisis.

What was wrong? Americans did not agree on all the answers to this question. But they did agree that something must be done to save the country from complete economic collapse.

In such an atmosphere the election campaign of 1932 was fought. With the victory of Franklin D. Roosevelt and the Democratic Party, Congress began a series of experiments collectively referred to as the "New Deal."

But the shock and disillusionment that swept across the United States in the opening months and years of the 1930's were not confined to domestic affairs. As you will see, by the time Franklin D. Roosevelt entered the White House in 1933, the structure of peace that men had been building since World War I was beginning to crumble. At home and abroad Americans were confronted with the most serious problems they had ever faced.

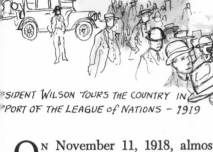

CHAPTER **34** 1920–1932

The Nation Spurns World Leadership

PRESIDENT WILSON TOURS THE COUNTRY IN SUPPORT OF THE LEAGUE of NATIONS – 1919

O N November 11, 1918, almost everyone in America took the day off from work. Factories, offices, stores, and schools closed their doors while Americans, old and young, poured into the streets of every city and town and village across the land to celebrate the armistice that had brought an end to World War I. In an exultant statement to the press, President Wilson announced, "Everything for which America fought has been accomplished." So it seemed to him, and so it seemed to Americans in general on November 11, 1918.

But Wilson realized, as millions of Americans did not, that it is easier to win a victory on the battlefield than it is to build a lasting peace. He warned his fellow Americans of the formidable problems that remained to be solved and challenged them to assume the responsibility of world leadership. Americans, however, were tired of wartime restrictions, and eager to return to the everyday business of living. And when, as the months passed, the European nations with whom the United States had fought on the battlefield began to quarrel over the spoils of war, Americans became increasingly disillusioned.

President Wilson struggled hard to hold his fellow Americans in line. But, by the opening years of the 1920's, the American people had repudiated Wilson, rejected the League of Nations, and turned their backs upon Europe and the opportunity to assume the challenging role of world leadership.

AS THE STORY DEVELOPS
1. The United States refuses to join the League of Nations.
2. The United States keeps out Europe's people and goods.
3. The United States moves toward the Good Neighbor policy.
4. The United States works with other nations to prevent war.

450   1750   1800   1850   1900   1950   1975

657

1 The United States refuses to join the League of Nations

On December 4, 1918, the army transport *George Washington* threaded its way out of New York harbor and steamed toward Europe. Its most distinguished passenger was Woodrow Wilson, President of the United States. He was bound, as you know, for the peace conference to be held at Versailles, near Paris.

Wilson was the first President ever to leave the United States during his term of office. He hoped to persuade the other representatives at the conference to adopt the Fourteen Points, or principles, that he had earlier outlined as "the only possible program for world peace" (pages 636–37).

The "Big Four." The peace conference, which opened at Versailles on January 18, 1919, had much of the tension and excitement of a melodrama played on the stage. But in this case the stage was the world; the principal characters were the chief officials of the four leading powers—Great Britain, France, Italy, and the United States; and the outcome of the drama would affect the lives of millions of people.

Woodrow Wilson arrived at the conference after a triumphal journey through Great Britain, Italy, and France. Masses of people in all three countries turned out to greet the American President, who symbolized their hope for a new and better postwar world. Encouraged by this reception, Wilson felt that he could use his great popularity to bring about a just peace based on his Fourteen Points. But the three other leading delegates at Paris wanted a very different kind of peace.

David Lloyd George, the British Prime Minister, had just won a general election by using the vindictive slogans "Hang the Kaiser" and "Make Germany Pay." He had no intention of becoming unpopular with the British voters by showing generosity toward the Germans, or by giving up England's naval supremacy and accepting Wilson's idea of "freedom of the seas."

The "Tiger" of French politics, Premier Georges Clemenceau (ZHORZH kl'mahn-SOH), believed that the only way to defend France was to crush Germany. He was cynical about President Wilson's idealism.

The last of the "Big Four" delegates, Italy's Vittorio Orlando, wanted to acquire the Austrian territory that had been secretly promised to Italy when Italy joined the Allies in 1915.

The problem of secret treaties. The united opposition of Lloyd George, Clemenceau, and Orlando was not the only problem Wilson faced. There was also the problem of secret treaties.

As you have seen (page 637), shortly after the Bolsheviks seized power in November 1917 and took Russia out of the war, they published certain secret treaties that the Allies had made with the Russian tsar and with one another before the United States entered the war. The new Communist rulers of Russia hoped to discredit the Allied cause by exposing these treaties as "imperialist diplomacy," and to some extent they succeeded.

Under the terms of these treaties, the Allies were to divide the spoils of victory. Great Britain was to take over Germany's colonies, except for certain territories in the Pacific Ocean which were to go to Japan.° France, Russia, Serbia, and Italy were to enlarge their national boundaries at the expense of Germany and Austria-Hungary. And, finally, Germany was to make huge payments, called *reparations*, to the Allies to compensate them for damages resulting from the war. These secret arrangements obviously contradicted several of Wilson's Fourteen Points, such as open diplomacy, national self-determination, and the end of colonialism.

Wilson's dilemma. Faced with these secret treaties and with the united opposition of Lloyd George, Clemenceau,

----
° Japan had declared war on Germany in 1914.

and Orlando, Wilson could take one of two paths. He could compromise, or he could walk out of the Paris Peace Conference. Indeed, at one point he almost did give up and go home. But he realized that such a step might be taken as a confession of failure. He was also afraid that Communism might spread from Russia into Central Europe if a peace treaty were delayed and conditions remained unstable. His strongest reason for staying, however, was his faith in a League of Nations. Such a League, he was convinced, would in time remedy any injustices that the peace treaty might contain.

The Treaty of Versailles. The final peace treaty, called the Treaty of Versailles, was completed and signed late in June 1919. The treaty showed the results of bargaining between Wilson on one side and Lloyd George, Clemenceau, and Orlando on the other.

The Treaty of Versailles and related treaties made important changes in the map of the world, and especially in the map of Europe. They gave Germany's colonies to the Allied victors, but under a *mandate system* which required the new owners to account for their colonial administration to the League of Nations.

Certain border areas of pre-war Germany were lopped off. One important area, Alsace-Lorraine, was assigned to France. Other areas were included in a new country, Czechoslovakia, and in a re-created Poland. In an effort to satisfy the nationalist desires of various peoples in eastern Europe, several other independent states were created, including Finland, Estonia, Latvia, Lithuania, and Yugoslavia. Certain border changes were made for Italy, Greece, Rumania, and Belgium (see maps, pages 660–61).

Under the Treaty of Versailles, the German government reluctantly accepted full responsibility for starting the war, and agreed to remain disarmed. Germany also agreed to pay large reparations for war damage.

Wilson failed to convince the other Allied representatives that vengeance and greed were weak foundations for a

Wilson (center) and other dignitaries

WILSON'S EUROPEAN TOUR

On Friday, December 13, 1918, the *George Washington* steamed cautiously through a heavy mist into the harbor of Brest, France. President and Mrs. Wilson left the ship immediately and traveled to Paris. They were overwhelmed by the reception they received. Cheering crowds lined the flag-draped boulevards. "Long live Wilson!" they cried. "Long live the United States!" To millions of French men and women, the American war leader and author of the Fourteen Points was the symbol of a new day in which war and injustice would be banished from the earth, and peace and fair play would reign supreme.

In Italy and Great Britain, Wilson received the same tumultuous welcome. The streets of Rome were jammed with cheering crowds. And Britishers greeted the President with shouts of welcome and tear-filled eyes.

Wilson was too shrewd a man to be blind to the hatreds and jealousies of the European nations and to the determination of national leaders to maintain the old power system. He realized that it would be hard to write a peace treaty based on ideas of justice and peace. When, at a formal dinner in Buckingham Palace, the English king toasted the power of the American military establishment, Wilson gently replied that governments must obey "the great moral tide running in the hearts of men."

Before he left for Europe, President Wilson had said to his secretary that the trip would be either "the greatest success or the supremest tragedy in all history." It turned out to include a measure of both.

The "Big Four" at Versailles included, from left to right, Vittorio Orlando of Italy, David Lloyd George of Great Britain, Georges Clemenceau of France, and President Woodrow Wilson. In an effort to satisfy some national groups,

lasting peace. But he did successfully oppose some of the more unreasonable demands of the Allies. And he had the great personal satisfaction of seeing the Covenant of the League of Nations written into the Treaty of Versailles.

The League of Nations. The League of Nations, with headquarters at Geneva, Switzerland, provided international machinery to make war less likely. The machinery consisted of (1) a permanent Secretariat, or administrative and secretarial staff; (2) an Assembly in which each member nation had one vote; and (3) a Council, the all-important executive body. The Council mainly represented the five great powers, who were to be permanent Council members—France, Great Britain, Italy, Japan, and the United States—although other nations were also represented by means of rotating membership. Germany was excluded from League membership although, with the overthrow of the Kaiser, Germany had become a

democratic republic. Closely related to the League were the Permanent Court of International Justice, the International Labor Organization, and a number of other international agencies.

War was not outlawed by the Covenant of the League of Nations. But each League member agreed, before going to war, to make every effort to solve its difficulties in a friendly way, and even then to wait during a "cooling off" period before striking a blow. Any member failing to do this was to be regarded as an "aggressor." The other members might then decide, through the Council, to refuse to trade with the offender. When such a policy was adopted, it was known as applying "economic sanctions" against the offender. Moreover, the Council might go further and recommend to the member nations the use of force against the aggressor state. To forestall efforts to change the new map of the world by force, Article Ten of the Covenant provided that each member

1914 boundaries

1919 boundaries

New nations

they remade the map of Europe, as shown on these two pages. But in so doing they antagonized other national groups, whose dissatisfactions later arose to be included among the causes leading to World War II.

of the League was to guarantee the territorial integrity and political independence of every other member.

The Covenant of the League also created agencies for many worthwhile causes: improving conditions of labor and health throughout the world, working for the reduction of armaments, and trying to abolish slavery and the narcotic trade. These were important achievements in international co-operation.

Weaknesses of the League. The League of Nations was not, of course, a perfect organization. It had several serious weaknesses. For one thing, taking action against an aggressor was almost impossible for a number of reasons. First, the term "aggressor" was not defined. Second, the Council could only recommend that nations take action, and no member could be compelled to act upon these recommendations. Third, any member of the Council could block the wishes of the other members because all important decisions of the

Council had to be reached by unanimous vote. In brief, the work of the League depended upon the willingness of its members to co-operate.

Another basic weakness of the League was its guarantee of existing political boundaries. When the map of the world was redrawn, some peoples found themselves living in the country of their choice, but others did not. Those who did not had no way to secure further changes in their national boundaries.

A third weakness was the League's failure to provide adequate machinery for recommending solutions to economic problems that might lead to war. Trade rivalries and tariff barriers still existed, as did imperialism, yet the League was not equipped to do much more than study such problems. Finally, the League was in no position to tackle the problem of reducing armaments.

Despite its shortcomings, however, the League of Nations was a promising beginning in the difficult task of creating a new co-operative world order, dedicated to international peace and justice. In the 1930's, about 60 nations belonged to the League, which was bringing an important new ingredient into international affairs: the organized moral judgment of a majority of the nations of the world.

The Senate rejects the League. Early in July 1919 President Wilson returned confidently from Paris to ask the Senate to approve the Treaty of Versailles, and thereby to bring the United States into the League. The Senate shattered his high hopes by rejecting the treaty.

Senator Henry Cabot Lodge of Massachusetts, chairman of the important Committee on Foreign Relations, and other Republican Senators were annoyed that Wilson had not invited any of them to participate in the peace negotiations at Versailles. They pointed out that a problem as important as the creation of a world organization should have been considered by Republicans as well as by Democrats.

But opposition to the League was based on more than such partisan considerations. Many Americans thought that the Treaty of Versailles was unjust, and they were unwilling to have the United States join a League which pledged its members to carry out the provisions of the treaty. Others were afraid that Great Britain, supported by the votes of its five self-governing dominions,° might control the League.

But the greatest opposition to the League of Nations arose out of a general postwar reaction against American involvement in the affairs of Europe. Many Americans who were influenced by this reaction pointed with alarm to Article Ten of the League Covenant, which pledged each member to guarantee the existing political boundaries of the other members. Those who opposed the League of Nations for this reason argued that such a pledge might involve the United States in war.

°°°

° Canada, Newfoundland, South Africa, Australia, and New Zealand.

Wilson refuses to compromise. Despite the opposition to the League of Nations in the Senate and throughout the country, the Senate might have voted for it if President Wilson had been willing to accept certain changes.

But Wilson refused to compromise. He traveled across the country making speeches in defense of the League, until his health broke in the fall of 1919. He then hoped for a Democratic victory in the Presidential election of 1920 to demonstrate that the public supported his cause. But the Republican landslide of that year and the election of President Harding (page 646) indicated that the American people preferred to forget all about the League of Nations and world problems in general. They paid no heed to Wilson when he warned, "Arrangements of the present peace cannot stand a generation unless they are guaranteed by the united forces of the civilized world."

The rise of Japanese, Italian, and German expansionism in the 1930's proved Wilson's words to have been prophetic. But by that time, as you will see, the League, without the United States as a member, had become too weak to take actions which might have prevented the outbreak of World War II.

SECTION SURVEY

1. Compare the views of Wilson, Lloyd George, Clemenceau, and Orlando concerning the treaty of peace.

2. Give four ways in which the Treaty of Versailles changed the map of the world.

3. (a) Describe the structure of the League of Nations. (b) What machinery did the League set up for the prevention of war?

4. Summarize the weaknesses of the League.

5. (a) List four arguments presented by Americans who rejected the League. (b) To what extent would you blame Wilson for the failure of the treaty?

IDENTIFY: reparations, mandate system, economic sanctions, Article Ten of the League Covenant; Lodge.

2 The United States keeps out Europe's people and goods

The United States' refusal to join the League of Nations was based in part upon a desire to avoid becoming involved again in Europe's troubles and quarrels. But this impulse to cut off ties with the Old World led much further than the rejection of the League.

The United States also tried, with considerable success, to keep out the people and products of Europe and Asia. The immigration and tariff laws passed during this period were the most restrictive in American history and were bitterly resented by Europeans and Japanese. European resentment was aroused even further by America's efforts to collect the money that it had lent to its European allies during and immediately after the war.

Closing the gates to immigration. During the 1920's the United States reversed one of its oldest traditions by closing its gates to immigration almost completely. Earlier, it is true, the United States had excluded Chinese and most other Asiatics by specific laws. And, in 1907, President Theodore Roosevelt had negotiated a "Gentlemen's Agreement" with Japan, by which the Japanese agreed to forbid the emigration of laborers to the United States.

With these exceptions, however, the historic role of the United States as a haven of refuge and a land of opportunity for immigrants had never been seriously questioned by most Americans before the war. Indeed, during the decade before World War I, more Europeans settled in the United States than in any previous ten-year period.

Reasons for closing the gates. Why did a nation of immigrants and descendants of immigrants suddenly decide to bar its doors to newcomers? One reason was the general anti-European feeling that swept over America after the war. But certain groups in the population had special reasons of their own.

Organized labor, for example, argued that new immigrants were willing to work for lower wages and thus pulled down the standard of living of American workingmen. Industrialists who had formerly favored immigration as a source of cheap, plentiful unskilled labor no longer needed masses of unskilled workers, for by 1920 the railroads had been built and the basic industries such as steel were well developed. Finally, there were many established Americans who felt that the newer immigrants, mainly from eastern and southern Europe, did not easily become "Americanized." These Americans thought that it was harmful to the country to admit settlers whose languages and customs were so different from those of older inhabitants.

The immigration laws. Responding to all of these arguments, Congress passed three laws in the 1920's that progressively restricted immigration from Europe. The Emergency Quota Act of 1921 introduced a *quota system* which limited the number of Europeans and others who could be admitted to 3 per cent of the total number of persons of their nationality residing in the United States in the year 1910. The 1921 act also set a total yearly limit of about 350,000 immigrants.

In 1924 an even more severe law was passed which reduced the annual quota from 3 to 2 per cent, and changed the base year from 1910 to 1890. This change in the base year discriminated against Italian, Austrian, Russian, and other eastern and southern Europeans because people of those nationalities had immigrated to the United States mainly after 1890. Some exceptions were made to the quota restrictions for students, the wives and children of resident American citizens, and immigrants from Canada and the Latin-American countries. But immigrants who were barred from American citizenship for any reason were excluded under the law of 1924.

Finally, the National Origins Act of 1929 shifted the base year of immigration to 1920, but counterbalanced this more liberal provision by reducing to 150,000 the total number of immigrants to be admitted during any one year.

Effects of the quota system. The new immigration policies aroused a great deal of bitterness, especially among those eastern and southern European nationalities that were discriminated against under the quota system. The Japanese were also aroused because the immigration act of 1924 ended the Gentlemen's Agreement of 1907, which Japan had faithfully observed, and closed the doors completely to Japanese immigrants.

America's new immigration policies also affected economic and political conditions in Europe. In former years many Europeans who were out of work or discontented could migrate to the United States. But now, with America's gates closed, there was no place for them to go. Many of these discontented people, as you will see, turned in desperation to demagogues° such as Mussolini and Hitler who promised to solve their problems by setting up dictatorships.

The war of tariffs. While closing its doors to immigrants, the United States was also, like other nations, raising tariff barriers to keep out foreign products. As you have seen, the Fordney-McCumber Tariff of 1922 increased the import duties on hundreds of items. About eight years later, the Hawley-Smoot Tariff of 1930 lifted tariff rates to the highest level in American history.

America's high tariff policy proved a cruel blow to many countries in Latin America and in Europe. The prosperity of the countries affected depended in large part upon the sale of products to the United States. When America's high tariffs deprived them of their best markets, their economic situation became desperate. Factories closed, men were thrown out of work, and the surplus of farm products mounted steadily.

....

° *demagogue:* an unprincipled political leader who inflames the prejudices of his followers to advance his own interests.

Some countries struck back by raising their own tariff barriers against American goods. And so the high tariffs that Congress hoped would aid American industry helped in the end to deprive many American businessmen and farmers of the foreign markets they badly needed. Thus the ink was hardly dry on the peace treaties before the nations of the world were engaged in another war, a trade war fought with tariffs.

War debts and high tariffs. America's high tariff policy created still another problem. How were European countries to pay their war debts to the United States if they could not sell their goods in this country?

The war had changed America's relation to Europe from debtor to creditor. Before the war American businessmen had borrowed money from Europeans to finance new industries. Indeed, America's amazing industrial development between 1865 and 1914 would have been impossible had it not been for the investment of European capital. During the period of American neutrality, however, before the United States entered the war in 1917, Europeans began to sell their American stocks and bonds in order to buy war goods. And, as the war progressed, the American government lent huge sums to the warring countries. As a result, by 1918, nearly all the European countries owed money to the United States. The total amounted to about 10 billion dollars.

The American government granted reduced interest rates to the debtor nations and arranged for repayment of the loans over a long period of years. Yet, despite the generous terms, the bankrupt European countries emerged from the war with no clear idea as to how they could repay their debts.

President Wilson reminded the American Congress of one possible solution to Europe's problems when in 1921 he declared, "If we wish to have Europe settle her debts, we must be prepared to buy from her." But this solution became impossible when the United States adopted a high-tariff policy.

War debts and reparations. The only other solution open to the European Allies was to collect war damages, or reparations, from Germany, and to use this money to repay their war debts to the United States. In 1921 a Reparations Commission fixed the total of German reparations at 33 billion dollars. Unfortunately for the victorious European countries, Germany was in the midst of severe economic troubles, and was in no position to pay such a huge sum. In an effort to secure the money, Germany borrowed heavily from bankers in the United States and in Europe.

But there was a limit to the amount that the German government could borrow, and, as the years passed, it became increasingly clear that the reparations would have to be reduced. They were reduced twice—once in 1924 and again in 1929. In spite of this relief, however, Germany's economic situation grew steadily worse. By 1930 it looked as though the Germans could make no further reparations payments.

War debts create ill feeling. Faced with this situation, the debtor countries notified the United States that they could no longer meet their payments on the war debts. After all, they argued, they had contributed far more to victory in blood and sacrifice than had America and it would be only fair of the United States to cancel all war debts.

The American government, supported by the majority of Americans, refused to admit such a claim. It insisted that the war debts to the United States and German reparation payments to the Allies were two entirely separate matters. Americans pointed out that some of the loans—perhaps as much as a third of the total amount—had, in fact, been made after the armistice. Americans also reminded the European countries that they were not too poor to spend large sums for armaments.

The arguments pro and con were thrown overboard in 1931 when the debtors, with the exception of Finland, refused to make even a token payment. President Hoover then declared

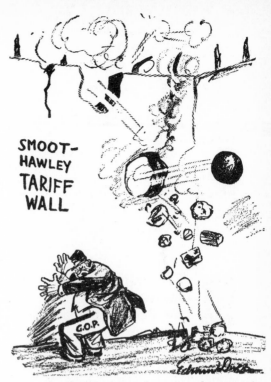

■ As the election of 1932 drew near, the cartoonist Edmund Duffy pictured Republicans trying to hold the tariff wall against Democratic onslaught.

a year's resting period, or *moratorium*, on the payment of war debts. But since Germany did not make any further reparation payments, the whole question of war debts was left permanently unsolved.

In the end, most of the war debts and most of Germany's reparations remained unpaid. But America's unsuccessful attempt to collect the war debts increased Europe's resentment against the United States. And the European victors' attempt to collect reparations from Germany, though equally unsuccessful, created a feeling of bitterness among the German people, which, as you will see, contributed to the rise of Adolf Hitler and of Nazism° and the Nazi Party in the early 1930's.

°°

° *Nazism:* a German fascist social and political movement; its name derived from the National Socialist German Workers Party founded about 1920 by Hitler and others.

665

1. Give four reasons why the United States closed its gates to immigrants after World War I.

2. Compare the provisions of the immigration laws of 1921, 1924, and 1929.

3. Describe three important results of this restrictive immigration policy.

4. In what ways did America's high-tariff policies backfire?

5. The war changed America from a debtor nation to a creditor nation. Explain.

6. (a) What reasons did the European allies give for stopping payments on their war debts? (b) Evaluate American answers to these arguments.

3 The United States moves toward the Good Neighbor policy

During the opening years of the twentieth century, as you have seen, Presidents Theodore Roosevelt, William Howard Taft, and Woodrow Wilson had all intervened at one time or another in the affairs of Latin-American countries. They had justified their intervention on the grounds that it was necessary (1) to safeguard the Panama Canal, (2) to prevent European countries from extending their influence in the Caribbean, and (3) to protect American investments in Latin America.

This Caribbean policy, as it was called, was continued by Presidents Warren G. Harding and Calvin Coolidge. Critics of the policy—and there were many of them on both sides of the border—referred to it as "dollar diplomacy." Many Latin Americans called it "Yankee imperialism."

Investments in Latin America. The rising tide of criticism of America's Caribbean policy did not, however, stop the flow of American money into the countries south of the Rio Grande. During the "Golden Twenties," as you have seen, many Americans had money to invest. The rich yet economically underdeveloped countries of Latin Amer-

ica offered inviting opportunities for investment, and American dollars financed the construction of factories, railroads, mines, and ranches in the lands to the south. Whereas in 1913 United States investments in Latin America totaled $1,300,000,000, by 1928 they totaled more than $5,000,000,000.

American intervention continues. American interest in Latin America grew in proportion to the amount of American money invested in the region. President Coolidge frankly admitted that the policy of the United States government was to protect the property and lives of American citizens wherever they went.

During these years many Latin-American countries were passing through a social and economic revolution. Frequently two groups in a country struggled to gain control, and each group claimed that it alone represented the people and the legal government. When this happened, the United States tended to recognize the group that was most friendly to American interests.

In some instances the United States played a more active part in the struggle for power. On occasions it forbade the sale of arms to the group it disliked and armed the group it supported. Worst of all from the Latin-American point of view, the United States government sometimes sent armed forces to protect American lives and property.

Relations with Nicaragua. American policy toward Nicaragua offers an example of the kind of intervention that Latin Americans fiercely resented. The United States was particularly concerned about Nicaragua because Americans had invested substantial sums of money in the country. Moreover, Nicaragua was close to the vital Panama Canal. Finally, there was the prospect that a new canal might eventually be built through Nicaragua itself. President Taft had sent marines into the country during an internal conflict in order to protect American investments and the nearby Panama Canal. President Coolidge withdrew the marines in 1925, but sent them back the following year when new disturbances broke out.

This policy was unpopular throughout Latin America. It was also unpopular with large numbers of Americans who claimed that the United States government was really making war. President Coolidge denied this and spoke of the American occupation as a police duty. But criticism was so strong that the administration took measures to solve the problem by peaceable means.

In 1927 President Coolidge sent Henry L. Stimson, an able and experienced administrator, to Nicaragua. After a period of negotiations, Stimson finally brought peace between the Nicaraguan factions. President Coolidge then withdrew most of the United States marines, leaving only enough to assure the protection of American property if violence again broke out.

The withdrawal of most of the marines helped to relieve the tension between the United States and Nicaragua. But the Nicaraguans were still not satisfied. They demanded the withdrawal of all the marines and the end of American interference. In 1933 President Hoover finally withdrew all United States troops.

Strained relations with Mexico. United States relations with Mexico also reflected the determination of the government in Washington to protect American interests below the Rio Grande. As you will recall (page 613), during Wilson's administration a sweeping social revolution in Mexico raised new problems in the traditionally uneasy relations between the two countries. American lives and property suffered in the upheaval. But far more threatening to Americans who had invested in Mexican property was the Mexican constitution of 1917.

The Mexican constitution of 1917 launched Mexico on a bold new policy. Some of its provisions antagonized certain groups of Americans. Article 27 declared that "only Mexicans . . . have the right to acquire ownership [of, or] . . . to develop mines, waters, or mineral fuels in the Republic of Mexico. The nation may grant the same right to foreigners, provided they agree to be considered Mexicans in respect of such property, and accordingly not to involve the protection of their government in respect of the same." Because this provision was retroactive, it canceled concessions made to foreigners by earlier governments. Foreign businessmen and investors were quick to protest.

The same article also alarmed Catholics, in Mexico and in other countries. It decreed that "Churches shall have no legal capacity to acquire, hold, or administer real property or loans on real property." The new constitution also placed other restrictions upon the Church. Foreign priests were no longer permitted to live and work in Mexico, and the number of priests within each Mexican state was to be determined by the state legislature. Equally disturbing were Articles 3 and 130, forbidding the Catholic Church to engage in any but elementary education.

During 1917 and 1918 the United States was too involved in the European war to take any action in regard to Mexico. Moreover, not all of the provisions of the constitution were at once applied. But immediately after the armistice in 1918, oil investors and other American owners of property in Mexico clamored for intervention. These businessmen were joined by many Catholics who were greatly disturbed over the policies of the Mexican government. The situation grew worse when the Mexicans supported the anti-American faction in Nicaragua. By 1927 relations between the United States and Mexico were close to the breaking point.

Relations with Mexico improve. In 1927, however, the United States began slowly to modify its policy. President Coolidge took the first step by sending Dwight W. Morrow, a successful banker, as ambassador to Mexico.

Instead of threatening Mexico with the United States' might, Morrow tried to understand the Mexican point of view. His sincerity, intelligence, and charm quickly won him many friends in Mexico. He was helped in his mission by Charles A. Lindbergh, the young

WILL ROGERS

Will Rogers (1879–1935) was one of America's greatest humorists. "Give me the truth," he once said. "I'll exaggerate it and make it funny." In thirty years as an actor, writer, and radio commentator, he won millions of devoted followers among the American people.

Born in 1879 in Oklahoma (then known as Indian Territory), he was proud of his partly Indian ancestry. "My ancestors didn't come over on the *Mayflower*," he told a Boston audience. "They met the boat."

He had learned to use the lasso during his youthful days as a cowboy, and he began his vaudeville career in New York with a lasso act. But it was Rogers' homely, dry comments about leading public figures and recent events—often delivered while he twirled a rope—that endeared him to his audiences and won him his great reputation on the stage, in the movies, over the radio, and as a newspaper columnist.

He had numerous friends in all walks of life, but his humor spared none of them. Once, referring to President Coolidge's quality of reserve, he said: "Cairo's a great place. I was the only tourist there who never went out to see the Sphinx—well, I've seen Cal Coolidge." Speaking of the government's efforts to help the farmers, he commented, "One thing about farmers' relief. It can't last long, for the farmers ain't got much to be relieved of."

It was a great shock to the entire nation when, in 1935, on the start of an around-the-world flight with his friend Wiley Post, their plane crashed into the sea near Point Barrow, Alaska, and both men were killed.

aviator-hero who had recently completed the first solo, nonstop transatlantic flight. Will Rogers, the famous humorist, lent his talents to the cause of better Mexican-American relations.

The skillful work of America's "ambassadors of good will" repaired much of the damage done in the past. The Mexicans agreed to recognize American titles to subsoil minerals, such as petroleum, that had been in effect before the constitution of 1917.

Moving toward a new policy. The Morrow mission marked a turning point in our relations with Mexico and with other Latin-American countries. From 1927 on, both Calvin Coolidge and his successor, Herbert Hoover, went out of their way to cultivate more agreeable relations with the Caribbean republics and with the nations of South America. Coolidge went to Havana, Cuba, in 1928 and personally opened a Pan-American Conference. Hoover toured South America in the months between his election and inauguration.

The people of Latin America were honored and pleased by the friendly attention of an American President and a President-elect. Their governments encouraged American investments and gave those investments greater protection than in the past. The United States, in turn, stopped intervening by force in the internal affairs of any Latin-American nation.

The Monroe Doctrine is modified. But America's southern neighbors still resented the 1904 Roosevelt Corollary to the Monroe Doctrine. As you have seen (page 611), the Roosevelt Corollary stated that the United States had the right to act as policeman of the Western Hemisphere.

In the hope of improving still further our relations with Latin America, the Department of State declared in 1930 that the Monroe Doctrine no longer would be used to justify United States intervention in Latin-American domestic affairs. Thus, by the end of the 1920's, relations with Latin America had been considerably improved.

1. Why did America's Caribbean policy arouse resentment in Latin America and criticisms in the United States?

2. Describe our relations with Nicaragua from Wilson's administration to that of President Hoover.

3. Indicate the principal reasons for growing American hostility toward Mexico after 1917.

4. Trace the course of improved relations between the United States and Mexico.

IDENTIFY: "Yankee imperialism," "dollar diplomacy," Mexican constitution of 1917; Henry Stimson, Dwight Morrow, Charles Lindbergh, Will Rogers.

4 The United States works with other nations to prevent war

While the United States was taking its first halting steps toward improved relations with Latin America, it also began to move toward international cooperation. In 1920, it is true, the Department of State completely ignored communications from the newly established League of Nations in Geneva. But as the months passed, American experts in international law, public health, and finance became important advisers in League activities. During President Harding's administration the United States began to send "observers" to Geneva to take unofficial parts in the work of League committees dealing with epidemics, slavery, and the narcotic trade. By 1924 American delegates were attending League conferences.

America and the World Court. Both Harding and Coolidge recommended that the United States join the Permanent Court of International Justice, popularly known as the World Court, which had been created in 1920 to arbitrate international disputes. But the Senate, jealous of its right to make treaties and influenced by Americans who were fearful of "entangling alliances," agreed to join only on its own terms. The nations already belonging to the World Court refused to accept the Senate's terms, and the matter was dropped.

The armaments race. The government was more successful in its efforts to stop the naval armaments race in which it was engaged with Great Britain and Japan. Relations between the United States and Japan were particularly strained after World War I. Americans resented the Japanese occupation of the Shantung Peninsula in China. This occupation, begun in 1914, violated America's Open Door policy, which was designed to keep China's territory intact and to prevent any single power from dominating China. Americans were concerned because Japan was allied with Great Britain.

As a result of the tension created by this situation, each of the three powers was rapidly building up its naval strength. Many people in all three countries were afraid that the naval arms race might lead to war.

■ While it did not join the League of Nations, the United States sent unofficial delegates to this Assembly Building of the League, at Geneva.

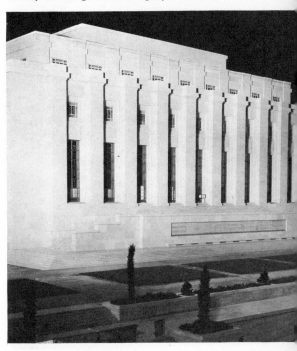

BILLY MITCHELL

The German dreadnought *Ostfriesland* was considered unsinkable. With her triple hull, her 85 watertight compartments, and her heavy armor plating, she had survived 18 direct hits from 12- and 14-inch guns in the Battle of Jutland in 1916. Now, on Thursday, July 21, 1921, she was anchored off the Atlantic coast, not far from Washington, D.C. Seized by the Allies at the end of the war, by international agreement the battleship was to be sunk, and the deadline for the sinking had been set at Sunday, July 24. The American navy was prepared to do the job. The Atlantic fleet stood ready to blast the captured vessel to pieces, and, if gunfire failed, to rip her apart with demolition charges placed inside her hull.

But a different method was to be tried first. General Billy Mitchell of the Army Air Service, a pioneer in the development of modern air power, had rashly promised to sink the unsinkable *Ostfriesland* with bombs. Many high-ranking naval officers ridiculed the idea that planes could sink a powerful battleship, but General Mitchell had won the opportunity to try.

Shortly after noon Mitchell's bombers appeared in the distance, small specks on the horizon that grew rapidly in size as they roared toward their target. Then the bombs fell. Great columns of water were hurled high into the air, and the ships of the Atlantic fleet, standing off at a safe distance, were shaken by the explosions.

Slowly the *Ostfriesland* began to sink. The observers watched in silence as her bow came up. They could see the enormous holes torn in her sides by the bombs. Her stern went under water. She rolled over completely, and within half an hour after the first bomb was dropped, the supposedly unsinkable dreadnought disappeared beneath the waves.

Billy Mitchell had demonstrated that a new era in military history had begun.

The Washington Conference. It was against this disturbing background that nine powers with interests in Asia met in the American capital on November 12, 1921. Secretary of State Charles Evans Hughes opened the Washington Naval Conference with a dramatic proposal. In his opening remarks he boldly proposed a ten-year "naval holiday" during which no new war ships were to be built. Specifically, he suggested that the United States, Great Britain, and Japan each scrap enough of its own war ships to bring the naval strength of the three great sea powers into a ratio of 5:5:3. These limitations applied only to "capital ships," that is, to battleships and heavy cruisers of 10,000 tons or more.

According to this plan, Great Britain and the United States would be equal in naval strength while Japan would have three fifths as much tonnage in capital ships as each of the other two countries. France and Italy, moreover, were to have fleets of equal size, with a ratio of 1.75 to the other powers. That is, if Great Britain and the United States each had 500,000 tons of capital ships, Japan would be allowed 300,000 tons, and France and Italy 175,000 tons each.

At first Hughes's suggestion was received in silence. But when its full significance became clear, a tremendous cheer rose from the galleries and the floor of the convention. Here was a concrete, significant proposal to end the naval race. In the discussion that followed, Japan objected to taking an inferior place. But, eager to make economies at home, the Japanese delegates finally accepted the proposal on one condition. They insisted that Great Britain and the United States should not further fortify any of their Pacific colonies, except Hawaii. These agreements were included in what came to be called the Five-Power Treaty.

Other agreements are reached. The Five-Power Treaty was only one of several agreements reached at the Washington Conference. Among the others were the Four-Power Pact and the Nine-Power Treaty.

In the Four-Power Pact, Japan, Great Britain, France, and the United States agreed to respect one another's rights in the Pacific. They also agreed to consult with one another in the event of any act of aggression in the Pacific area.

The Nine-Power Treaty was signed by all the nations represented at the conference. The treaty powers guaranteed the territorial integrity of China and promised to uphold the Open Door policy by promoting trade and other relations "between China and the other powers upon the basis of equality of opportunity."

Developments in the Pacific area following the Washington Conference seemed to justify the widespread belief that a major step toward peace had been taken. Japan withdrew, at least partially, from the Shantung Peninsula. Japan also withdrew troops that had occupied parts of Siberia during the Russian Revolution. Later, at a London Naval Conference held in 1930, Japan agreed to extend the naval holiday. As you will see, however, this agreement marked the high tide of Japanese co-operation with the Western powers.

The attempt to "outlaw war." In addition to favoring disarmament, the United States tried to prevent war by what has been called a policy of "wishful thinking." In 1928 Secretary of State Frank B. Kellogg joined with the French foreign minister, Aristide Briand (ah-rees-TEED bree-AHN), in asking all nations to sign a pledge outlawing war "as an instrument of foreign policy." The signers were also to agree to settle all disputes by peaceful methods.

Eventually 62 nations initialed the document, but the Kellogg-Briand Pact, or the Pact of Paris as the agreement was called, proved to be little more than a statement of good intentions. In signing, each nation added its own reservations. None was willing to outlaw war waged in self-defense. Since nearly every nation going to war justifies its action by the plea of self-defense, this reservation destroyed any effectiveness the pact might have had.

Finally, the document said nothing about enforcement. Those who signed it were not even bound to consult with one another in case some government acted aggressively. At best, the Kellogg-Briand Pact represented little more than an agreement that war was evil.

The peace structure begins to crumble. The opening act in the tragedy that later engulfed the entire world began in 1931, although at the time its full significance was not understood. Without warning, the Japanese army rolled across the frontiers of Manchuria (see map, page 741). China, large but helpless, could do little to defend its great northern province. Within a few months the Japanese had torn the province away from the Chinese. A Japanese program to sweep "foreign" influence out of the Far East and to build an Asia for the Asiatics was under way.

Japan's aggression was a violation of the Covenant of the League of Nations and an outright challenge to the Open Door policy of the United States. Japan was bluntly reminded of such facts by Secretary of State Henry L. Stimson.

■ Secretary of State Charles Evans Hughes labored to prevent war in the early 1920's, later became Chief Justice of the United States.

In their 1931 invasion of Manchuria, the Japanese forces met little opposition from the ill-equipped Chinese troops. Within a year, this large, rich Chinese province carried the flag of the Rising Sun. The peace had been broken, and the movement toward world conflict was under way. Japan renamed the province Manchukuo and established puppet rulers.

In a formal note issued in 1932, Stimson called Japan's attention to its flagrant violation of the Nine-Power Treaty (1922) and of the Kellogg-Briand Pact (1928), both of which Japan had signed. The United States "does not intend," Stimson wrote, "to recognize any situation, treaty, or agreement which may be brought about by means contrary to the covenants and obligations of the Pact of Paris."

Meanwhile, the League of Nations was summoned to consider what action, if any, should be taken. To this meeting President Hoover sent an American representative. The League debated. It sent a commission to Manchuria to investigate and to report its findings. But beyond a statement of its agreement with the so-called Stimson Doctrine, the League failed to act. Confident that the nations of the world would not act collectively to preserve peace, the Japanese withdrew from the League and prepared to conquer China and Southeast Asia.

The structure of peace had begun to crumble. As you will see, Fascist Italy and, after 1933, the rising Nazi regime in Germany realized that they too could safely embark upon a program of ag-

gression. The peace structure that rested upon the Paris Peace Conference (1919), the Washington Conference (1921–22), and the Kellogg-Briand Pact (1928) was not firm enough to stand a heavy blow. And the powers of the world, which by collective action might have bolstered the crumbling structure of peace, were unwilling and unable to act together.

✓ SECTION SURVEY

1. What conditions led to the Washington Naval Conference of 1921–22?
2. (a) Summarize the provisions of the Five-Power Treaty. (b) Indicate the reason for the Four-Power Pact.
3. Discuss the significance of the Nine-Power Treaty for (a) China, (b) the United States, and (c) Japan.
4. Why did the Kellogg-Briand Pact (Pact of Paris) of 1928 prove "to be little more than a statement of good intentions"?
5. (a) How did the United States react to the Japanese invasion of Manchuria? (b) Describe the reaction of the League of Nations.

IDENTIFY: capital ships, "naval holiday," Stimson Doctrine; Hughes, Kellogg, Briand; 1922, 1932.

■ CHAPTER SURVEY

(For review, see Section Surveys, pages 662, 666, 669, 672.)

Points to Discuss: 1. Explain the reasons why the secret treaties made it difficult to frame a peace on the basis of Wilson's Fourteen Points.

2. Despite its shortcomings, the League of Nations was a promising beginning in the difficult task of creating a new cooperative world order. (a) Relate its chief weaknesses. (b) Why did its future look promising?

3. (a) In what ways do you believe Wilson made important contributions to the Versailles peace? (b) Did he share any responsibility for its weaknesses?

4. Explain the connection between high American tariffs, Allied war debts, and German reparations payments.

5. American initiative was responsible for work undertaken at the Washington Conference (1921–22). Evaluate the results.

6. The feeble peace structure which rested upon the Paris Peace Conference (1919), the Washington Conference (1921–22), and the Kellogg Pact (1928) was not firm enough to stand a heavy blow. (a) Identify each international negotiation. (b) Do you agree or disagree with the statement? Justify your position.

Using Maps and Charts: 1. Comparing the maps on pages 660 and 661, (a) identify the new nations that appeared after World War I. (b) Which nations lost territory as a result of World War I? (c) Locate the Balkans and the Baltic states.

2. Using chart 2 on page 824, (a) compare the immigration into the United States in 1914 with that in 1940. (b) Explain this radical change. (c) What effect did it have on the composition of our population?

3. Using charts 3 and 4 on pages 840–41, (a) indicate what happened to American exports and imports between 1920 and 1940. (b) Explain the change.

Consulting the Sources: For Wilson's address on the League of Nations at Versailles, see A. B. Hart, *American History Told by Contemporaries,* Vol. 5, No. 201. For Senator William Borah's speech against the Versailles Treaty, see No. 193.

■ TRACING THE MAIN IDEAS

In the United States and in other countries, war-weary people hailed the armistice of November 11, 1918, as a turning point in history. Men and women everywhere were filled with faith in the future. They looked forward to a far better world than any they had ever known. They were prepared to co-operate in a mighty effort "to make the world safe for democracy."

President Wilson reminded American citizens that they had a major responsibility in the building of a lasting peace. "It will now be our fortunate duty," he declared, "to assist by example, by sober friendly counsel, and by material aid in the establishment of just democracy throughout the world." But Wilson's advice went unheeded.

In the immediate postwar years the United States did help Europe by supplying food, clothing, medical supplies, and huge loans of money. And during the 1920's the United States worked closely with the League of Nations in efforts to remove sources of international friction, and took steps to establish better relations with Latin America. But the fact that the United States refused to join the League, that it barred its doors to immigration, and that it raised tariff barriers to a new high did not win friends for America abroad.

By 1932 the faith and good will that had been so widespread throughout the world in 1918 were rapidly evaporating. In place of the prosperity of the 1920's, the world was faced with a deepening economic depression. In place of faith and good will the world was confronted by intense international rivalry and a growing feeling of suspicion and distrust. Japan had already begun its program of aggression, the Italians were threatening their neighbors, the Nazi movement was gathering strength in Germany, and the structure of peace was breaking into fragments.

CHAPTER **35** `1920–1932`

The Pace of Living Accelerates in the "Golden Twenties"

CHANGING WAYS

OF AMERICAN LIFE

Every age, or period, in history has certain characteristics that distinguish it from every other age. The decade of the 1920's was no exception. Writers, combing the records and in many cases searching their personal memories, have pinned various labels on the 1920's—among them the "Golden Twenties," the "Roaring Twenties," the "Age of Disillusionment," the "Decade of Wonderful Nonsense," the "Jazz Age," and the "Ballyhoo Years."

These labels suggest that the period of the 1920's was characterized by widespread prosperity, by an unusual outpouring of energy, by a sharp increase in the productivity of American industry, by disillusionment with the outcome of the crusade to make the world safe for democracy, by an emphasis on the material aspects of life, and by the desire "to get rich quick" and to have a good time. All of this was true.

But people's ideas, beliefs, and everyday habits did not suddenly change as though by some stroke of magic on Armistice Day in 1918. Neither did their ideas, beliefs, and habits suddenly change when the shadow of the Great Depression fell over the land in the opening years of the 1930's.

The forces that gave new directions to American life in the 1920's were deeply rooted in American history and, for that matter, in the history of the Western world. Stimulated in part by World War I, the Industrial Revolution gathered new momentum in the 1920's. Power-driven machines, new sources of energy, more efficient factories, better methods of marketing goods—all of these helped to bring prosperity to the American people.

But the influence of industrialization reached far beyond the economic life of the nation. It continued to transform everyday life in town and country alike. It gave new directions to science and education. It affected literature, art, architecture, and recreation.

AS THE STORY DEVELOPS
1. The Industrial Revolution moves with increasing momentum.
2. New ways of living develop in country, town, and city.
3. Education, literature, and the arts reflect new ways of living.
4. Striking changes occur in the daily life of Americans.

The Industrial Revolution moves with increasing momentum

By 1920 the power-driven machine had become one of the dominant symbols of America. There were machines in the factories, machines on farms, machines in the home—and the number and variety of machines were multiplying at an ever more rapid rate. The development of the machine depended, however, upon other developments, including new sources of energy, increased production of metals, and more efficient methods of business organization.

New sources of energy. Energy to drive the machines—this is the first requirement of an industrial nation. And the United States had sources of energy in abundance. It had enormous deposits of coal, huge underground pockets of oil and natural gas, water-power sites, and the technological "know-how" needed to generate electric power in almost unlimited amounts.

By the 1920's coal, the traditional source of energy for the Industrial Revolution, was meeting stiff competition from petroleum, natural gas, and electricity. Between 1920 and 1930 the annual consumption of coal actually dropped by about 20 per cent. During these same years the production of petroleum more than doubled. Natural gas made even greater gains, with production increasing 150 per cent.

But the most phenomenal development was in the production and use of electricity. In 1900 this new source of energy had hardly been tapped. By 1920 Americans were producing 56 billion kilowatt-hours annually; by 1930, 114 billion. In brief, the United States was using more electricity than all the other countries of the world combined.

The assembly line. As energy to drive machines became increasingly abundant, businessmen and engineers tackled the problem of using it most efficiently. Older types of machinery were improved and new machines were developed for factory, farm, and home. But it was the organization of production within industrial plants—the organization of machines on a conveyer-belt assembly line—that provided one of the striking characteristics of the American economy in the 1920's.

As you have seen, mass production was an essential element of American industry long before the 1920's. Standardized interchangeable parts had been used by manufacturers in growing numbers ever since Eli Whitney had developed this technique in his gun factory more than a century earlier (page 250). But the conveyer-belt assembly line was relatively new. First used on a large scale by Henry Ford in 1914, it was soon adopted by other industries.

Behind the final assembly line in some industries were the subassembly lines, and yet smaller assembly lines that supplied the subassembly lines. Feeding parts to the assembly lines were automatic machines, that is, machines requiring only semi-skilled labor for their operation.

Bigger and bigger industries. Mass production could be carried on only by large, highly organized industrial concerns. During the "Golden Twenties" there was plenty of surplus capital to finance the development of industry. As a result, older industries grew by leaps and bounds, and new industries began to climb into the ranks of the giants.

Most of the growth of industry was the result of *mergers*—that is, the combining of two or more independent companies into one larger company. Between 1919 and 1929, for example, more than a thousand mergers took place in manufacturing and mining. By 1930, two hundred corporations owned nearly half of the country's corporate wealth and one fifth of the total national wealth.

Industrial efficiency. As industries continued to grow in size, they also continued to move toward greater efficiency. Efficiency engineering was not, of course, a product of the 1920's. As you have seen (page 573), around the beginning of the twentieth century, Frederick W. Taylor pioneered in studies of machines and the workmen who operated them. During the 1920's "time-and-motion" studies, as they were called, were generally undertaken before a new machine or process was installed in an industrial plant.

Businessmen also applied efficiency engineering, or "scientific management," to the problems of business planning and office bookkeeping. This new approach to industrial efficiency was called "cost accounting." Cost accountants found out the cost of every item of machinery, materials, and labor that went into the total cost of producing or selling a product. They could then show businessmen how to cut costs and thus gain greater production at lower prices.

Herbert C. Hoover, as Secretary of Commerce under Presidents Harding and Coolidge, helped to spread the idea of scientific management. He encouraged industry to use fewer and simpler standardized parts and models as a way of achieving economy and efficiency.

In his effort to promote economy and efficiency, Hoover did not stop at standardization. He also tried to minimize the waste involved in competition. He urged business organizations to share information, to work out common policies, and to draw up codes of fair practices.

This attitude of the government naturally encouraged the growth of large-scale industry. During these years the government did not make any great effort to enforce the Sherman Antitrust Act and the Clayton Antitrust Act. In the 1920's both business and government were more interested in industrial efficiency than in industrial competition.

Advertising and marketing. Marketing techniques also became increasingly effective during the 1920's. Advertising, installment buying, and the growth of mail-order houses, department stores, and chain stores all helped to move the products of farm and factory into the homes of consumers.

Manufacturers spent large sums of money on advertising in an effort to get the public to choose their products instead of those of their competitors. Advertising firms devoted an increasing amount of time to the study of public psychology in order to discover how to appeal to consumers most effectively. Advertising firms also urged Americans to abandon the deeply rooted American ideal of thrift. In "an age of abundance," they said, continued prosperity depended upon spending, not upon saving.

Mail-order houses, department stores, and chain stores continued to grow in number and in size. The companies that had pioneered in new methods of marketing during the latter half of the 1800's —Montgomery Ward; Sears, Roebuck; the Great Atlantic and Pacific Tea Company; F. W. Woolworth; Marshall Field; John Wanamaker—were still among the leaders in their fields. These companies and many others that had been organized by the 1920's were getting a big portion of the nation's retail business.

Two new developments, both destined to contribute to a future revolution in the packaging of goods, first emerged in the 1920's. In 1923 Clarence Birdseye developed a method of quick-freezing for preserving perishable foods. In this same year the Du Pont company bought the American patent rights to cellophane, a transparent wrapping material invented by a Swiss chemist, Dr. Jacques Edwin Brandenberger.

By the closing years of the 1920's, frozen foods were beginning to be sold in stores, and cellophane was beginning to attract attention.

The automobile industry. New sources of power, mass production, more efficient methods of producing and marketing goods—these were only part of the

Clothing of the early 1920's

story of America's economic expansion in the 1920's. Equally important was the development of the automobile.

In 1920 about 8,000,000 passenger cars and about 1,000,000 trucks were registered in the United States. By 1930 about 23,000,000 passenger cars—an average of one car for every six citizens—and 3,500,000 trucks were traveling the nation's streets, roads, and highways. The "automobile revolution," as it has been called, was in full swing.

This revolution had far-reaching consequences. By 1930, cars, trucks, and buses had almost completely replaced horse-drawn vehicles, and even the railroads and trolley cars were beginning to suffer from the formidable competition of the gasoline-driven vehicles.

By the end of the "Roaring Twenties," the automobile industry had become the nation's biggest business, with an annual product valued at $3,500,000,000 in 1929. Moreover, this new industrial giant used huge quantities of steel, glass, rubber, and other materials. It created a rising demand for materials to build paved roads, garages, and service stations. It is estimated that 5,000,000 persons, or one in every nine workers in the United States, were employed in the automobile industry or in one of the related businesses by 1930.

New industries. Garages, service stations, and trucking firms were only a few of the new industries that emerged during the 1920's. The increasing availability of electricity stimulated production of numerous laborsaving devices for the home—among them refrigerators, vacuum cleaners, toasters, electric irons, electric fans, and electric ranges.

The chemical industry, in which Germany had led the world before World War I, became in the 1920's one of America's most rapidly growing enterprises. By 1929 several American chemical companies were larger than any of their European competitors. In 1930 Du Pont, the giant among chemical companies, was producing 1100 different products in 80 different factories in the United States. Among the products pouring out of the chemical plants were rayon, synthetic resins, and a growing variety of plastics.

Later in this chapter you will see how radio and motion pictures provided new sources of entertainment for millions of Americans. These industries also created new demands for materials and provided job opportunities for thousands.

✔ SECTION SURVEY

1. Show why the United States in the 1920's had almost unlimited sources of energy for its machines.

2. Describe the importance of the conveyer-belt assembly line in mass production.

3. What evidence can you cite to show that American industry was growing bigger and bigger during this period?

4. Indicate four new industries that emerged during the 1920's.

5. Show how life today has been influenced by developments that took place in the 1920's.

IDENTIFY: merger, scientific management, cost accounting; Ford, Birdseye.

2 New ways of living develop in country, town, and city

During the 1920's the onward march of industrialization continued to affect the lives of the American people—urban and rural, men and women, rich and poor alike. The nation was growing in industrial power and in population.

Facts and figures. The 1920 census revealed that the population of the United States was almost 106,000,000. It also revealed that, for the first time in American history, town and city folk outnumbered country dwellers. In round numbers the urban population then totaled 54,000,000; the rural population was 51,500,000.

The onward march of urbanization and industrialization was even more apparent by the end of the decade. The census of 1930 showed that the population of the United States had increased by 17,000,000, climbing to a grand total of almost 123,000,000. Most of the increase was in the urban areas, which could boast of almost 69,000,000 inhabitants by the end of the decade. The rural population, on the other hand, totaled only about 54,000,000.

But many of the people listed under the heading of "rural" lived in small towns and villages. Between 1920 and 1930 the actual farm population of the country decreased from 31,614,269 to 30,445,350, as youth in growing numbers left the farms for larger opportunities in the booming cities.

Changing ways on the farm. By the 1920's farm life was being transformed at an ever more rapid pace.

There was visible evidence that the isolation and loneliness of farm life were a thing of the past. Paved roads were reaching out across the countryside. Telephone and electric wires stretched up and down roads and across the fields to the farmhouses. Single-wire antennas, called "aerials" in the 1920's, strung between peak of house and peak of barn, carried music, news, and entertainment by way of one of the new radio sets into living rooms and kitchens. Henry Ford's "Tin Lizzies" were parked beside barns and houses.

Visible, too, was evidence that the machine had lifted much of the burden of toil from the farmer. Where electricity was available, it was used for lighting, for pumping water, and for operating refrigerators, vacuum cleaners, sewing machines, and other laborsaving devices for the home. Milking machines could be found on many dairy farms. And trucks, tractors, and power-driven farm implements of many kinds were being used in rapidly growing numbers.

Power-driven machines made it possible for a farmer to do much more work in much less time and with much less physical effort. More efficient farming methods and better plants and breeds of livestock also helped to increase productivity on the farms.

Farm problems. But increased productivity also created problems. A surplus of farm products drove farm prices downward. To be sure, not all farmers were hit equally hard by the related problems of agricultural surpluses and falling prices. Dairy and truck farmers

■ Farmers in the early 1920's carefully studied advertisements like this one, for tractors were beginning to replace horses on American farms. Notice that this tractor's top speed was 4 miles an hour.

1921

4 CYLINDER (VERTICAL)	McC.—D. 15—30
ENGINE SPEED	1,000 R.P.M.
ROAD SPEEDS	2,3,4 M.P.H.
WEIGHT	5,750 LBS.

profited from the shift in American eating habits away from cereals toward more milk, butter, vegetables, and fruit. Indeed, the citrus fruit industries of California, Texas, and Florida enjoyed a spectacular development as a result of the rising demand for their products and the organization of co-operative advertising and marketing organizations. Tobacco growers also enjoyed a "seller's market"° as cigarette smoking became increasingly popular. The large mechanized farms continued to prosper, principally because they could afford the best machines and equipment and could market their products most economically.

But although some farmers prospered, many others suffered. Hardest hit were the owners of small farms. Many of them, handicapped by lack of money to buy expensive equipment and by limited acreage, found it increasingly difficult to make a living. And when the shadow of the Great Depression began to reach across the land in 1929 and 1930, it was the small farmer who first lost his home and the land that he depended upon for a livelihood.

Changing ways in town and city. Meanwhile, towns and cities across the land were undergoing a spectacular growth. Between 1920 and 1930, for example, the rapidly growing population pushed 25 of America's older cities above the 100,000 figure, and raised the total number of urban centers with inhabitants of 100,000 or more from 68 to 93. Some urban areas more than doubled their populations during the decade following World War I.

The very appearance of urban centers began to change rapidly. Huge new apartment houses appeared on what had once been vacant lots or on the sites of former one-family houses. New skyscrapers pierced the sky line as builders undertook to provide modern office space for the growing industries.

Less spectacular but no less signifi-

••
° *seller's market:* a market in which the seller is at an advantage because demand for his goods exceeds the supply.

FLORIDA'S REAL ESTATE BOOM

In 1920 the population of Miami, Florida, was 30,000. By 1925 it had soared to 75,000—and this was only the beginning. As Frederick Lewis Allen put it in his book *Only Yesterday,* "The whole city had become one frenzied real estate exchange. There were said to be 2000 real estate offices and 25,000 agents marketing house lots or acreage." For miles around, the land was divided into building lots. Speculators and promoters from every state in the Union were jammed into every available living accommodation, even into tents.

It was the same story in scores of other Florida cities. Prices skyrocketed. Land bought in the early 1900's for as little as $25 sold in 1925 for $150,000. People bought anything and everything, picking their lots from blueprints spread out on the tables of real estate offices in New York, Cleveland, Chicago, Denver, and other cities and towns throughout the country. Most of the buyers were speculators who paid only 10 per cent of the purchase price and who hoped to resell their land in a matter of days or weeks at a huge profit. Who cared that many of the developments outlined on the blueprints were still under water or in impassable swamps? Anything was possible, and tomorrow the swamp *might* be converted into a twentieth-century Venice, complete with canals, lagoons, and luxurious villas.

Some of the dreams of quick riches did indeed come true. Most didn't. And by the summer of 1926, it was becoming clear that the madness had run its course. By 1927 Miami and a number of other Florida cities were having difficulty collecting their taxes, and throughout the country thousands of speculators were ruefully counting their losses.

But Florida still had a pleasant climate, sun-swept beaches, abundant natural resources. In later years and happier times the state capitalized upon these assets to become one of the nation's leading resort areas.

cant was the changing appearance of the shopping areas. From one end of the city to another—and it was the same in all the towns and cities—merchants remodeled older stores or built new stores to provide for the needs of the growing population.

Streets built in earlier times for horse-drawn vehicles and for a more leisurely way of life became increasingly crowded and noisy as automobiles and trucks multiplied. And during the 1920's a new method of transportation, the bus, began to compete with the older electric trolleys. Although in the census of 1920 not a single bus was registered in the United States, by 1930 there were 40,507 registered.

Perhaps most spectacular of all was the development of suburban areas. Streetcar lines and paved roads pushed out from the cities into the surrounding countryside. Farms in outlying areas were divided and subdivided into building lots, and row after row of houses appeared in developments called by such fanciful names as "Sunset Acres," "Grand View," and "American Venice."

New opportunities for women. The changing appearance of the cities reflected larger and deeper transformations in the character of American life. One of the most striking developments was the growing freedom and opportunity enjoyed by women.

For a hundred years prior to the 1920's, women had been winning for themselves a growing measure of equality with men. They had been winning larger opportunities in political, economic, and social affairs. But their greatest gains came in the 1920's.

With the adoption of the Nineteenth Amendment in 1920, women won the right to vote in national elections. This was a landmark in women's long struggle to win equality with men.

Equally important were the gains made by women in social and economic activities. Countless housewives were released from long hours of drudgery by the new laborsaving devices—electric washing machines and irons, new types

of cooking stoves, vacuum cleaners, and electric refrigerators. Ready-made garments and inexpensive sewing machines also relieved women of much of their labor. Packaged foods and canned goods helped to lighten the task of preparing meals.

Women who benefited from these new services found new uses for their leisure time. Many read more books and magazines, went to more art exhibits, heard more lectures. Others worked for civic improvements by promoting playgrounds, by taking part in political affairs, and by influencing public opinion through such organizations as the League of Women Voters. Still others took active parts in parent-teacher associations. Never before had so many American women found time and opportunity to develop their interests and hobbies.

The rapidly multiplying machines in mills, plants, and factories created new jobs for women, who could work on some assembly lines just as efficiently as men. This was especially true in the textile and tobacco factories that were springing up in the South. It was also true of the canning industry, and of many other types of factory production. Moreover, women were finding increasing opportunities to work at selling jobs and as clerks and stenographers.

Wage earners' gains and losses. The surge of women into offices and factories was only one phase of the revolution that was transforming the lives of wage earners. The ever more rapid development of power-driven machinery continued to free many workers from backbreaking toil. Increased productivity brought generally higher wages, with which workers could buy products they had never before been able to afford.

Wage earners also benefited from studies undertaken to find ways of lessening fatigue and eliminating accidents on the job. From these studies businessmen learned that workers were happier and actually produced more when their employers showed an interest in them as human beings. Profiting from this les-

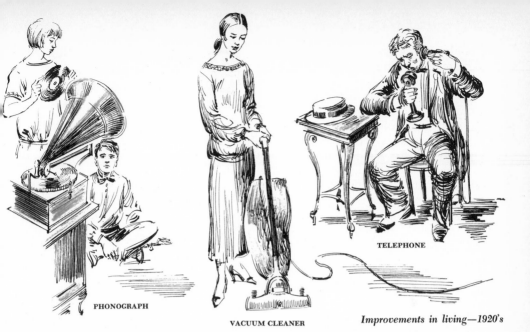

PHONOGRAPH

VACUUM CLEANER

TELEPHONE

Improvements in living—1920's

son, a growing number of employers introduced profit sharing and retirement plans and provided cafeterias, game rooms, and ball parks for employees.

But although employers as a whole showed increasing interest in working conditions, they opposed labor unions even more vigorously than before the war. A growing number of corporations in the 1920's organized "company unions." These unions received their name from the fact that they were organized inside the plants, often by the employers or their representatives, and were dominated by the employers rather than the workers. Company unions, as well as the higher standard of living of the workers, contributed to the decline in strength of organized labor during the 1920's.

Negroes encounter new problems. The rapid growth of industry during World War I and the 1920's provided Negroes with new opportunities as well as with new problems. In response to the demand for labor during the war years, nearly half a million Negroes from the South poured into the northern industrial centers. They went to work in the coal mines of West Virginia and Illinois, the meat-packing plants of Chicago, the steel mills of Pittsburgh, the automobile factories of Detroit, and in the industries of other large cities. This large-scale migration continued through the 1920's when more than half a million southern Negroes moved northward. The Negro population of the northern states more than doubled between 1910 and 1930, increasing from 1,027,674 to 2,409,219.

But Negroes in the North did not find the equality of opportunity that they sought so eagerly. They got the hardest jobs and the lowest pay in the mines, mills, and factories. Northern wage earners sometimes staged protest strikes against the Negro—not always without reason, however, for some industrialists on occasions imported Negroes as strikebreakers. Race riots broke out in Chicago, Tulsa, Omaha, and other cities. Despite their enjoyment of greater political and legal rights, northern Negroes were faced with discrimination in employment, housing, and social life.

And one of the severest blows of all came when the Negroes—who had furnished their full quota of soldiers to the armed forces—returned from World War I to find a new Ku Klux Klan operating in the North as well as in the South. The new Klan, founded in Atlanta, Georgia, in 1915, recruited much of its strength in the North. It operated on a broader front than the original Klan, causing trouble for Negroes, Jews, Catholics, and any other group that it chose to call "un-American."

New opportunities for Negroes. But although the Negroes who moved north found new problems, they also found new opportunities. The number of Negroes in industry almost doubled, rising from about 600,000 to more than a million between 1910 and 1930. During these same years the number of Negroes employed in clerical occupations more than doubled, jumping from 19,000 to nearly 41,000, and the number employed in civil service jobs rose from about 22,000 to about 50,000, most of them among the postal employees. By 1930 some 70,000 Negroes owned their own businesses.

Negroes in rapidly growing numbers were securing higher education and contributing to American life in music, art, and the sciences. Before the decade of the 1920's ended, some 15,000 Negroes held college degrees, and high school enrollments in both the North and the South were rising sharply.

Marian Anderson was just beginning her triumphant career as one of the world's great singers. Countee Cullen, a gifted writer, was on the threshold of a distinguished career. George Washington Carver, in his late sixties, was still actively engaged in the scientific research that made him one of the nation's most productive scientists and teachers.

⮑ **SECTION SURVEY**

1. In what ways was farm life in the 1920's different from farm life in 1870?
2. Show how increased productivity on the farms had both good and bad effects.
3. Describe the changes that were taking place in city life.
4. In the 1920's women enjoyed greater freedom and opportunity than ever before. Justify this statement.
5. "Although the Negroes who moved north found new problems, they also found new opportunities." Explain.

IDENTIFY: suburban, company union, Ku Klux Klan; Marian Anderson, Countee Cullen, George Washington Carver.

3 Education, literature, and the arts reflect new ways of living

The influence of industrialism penetrated ever more deeply into the schoolhouse and the classroom during the 1920's. As the industrial society began to expand, it became increasingly clear that people needed a far more extensive program of education than that which had been considered adequate in earlier times. Under the impact of the machine, the educational system continued to change.

Growth of enrollment. One important development was the increase in school enrollment. In 1900, for instance, the total high school enrollment had numbered fewer than 700,000. During the next two decades this number had risen steadily until by 1920 it had reached a total of about 2,500,000. Then the enrollment soared, reaching by 1930 a figure of approximately 4,800,000.

The colleges showed similar gains. Between 1900 and 1920 enrollments in institutions of higher education had jumped from about 237,000 to 597,000. During the 1920's this figure almost doubled, climbing to 1,100,000 by 1930.

To meet the needs of the enormous increase in students, American states and communities were called upon to spend huge sums for new school buildings, teachers, and equipment. The wealth created by the growing industrialism provided taxes for education. There were, of course, many youths who still could not afford to go beyond elementary school. But after 1920 a larger proportion than ever before enjoyed the advantages of a high school education.

Changes in the curriculum. The growing complexity of the industrial society with its emphasis upon highly specialized skills called for men and women trained in mathematics, engineering, science, and the skilled trades. Confronted with these striking changes in society and with the rapidly growing enrollment in the schools, educators began to enlarge the curriculum to include an increasing amount of work in vocational training, home economics, commercial courses, health, sanitation, physical education, modern foreign languages, and civic education. Special trade schools, technical schools, and commercial schools were built in an effort to adapt the educational system to the machine age.

Changes in organization and administration. The machine age was also leaving its mark upon the organization and administration of the schools. The development of the automobile, for example, made it possible to bring students from widely scattered areas to centrally located school buildings. As a result, in rural regions, consolidated schools of good quality serving an area of many square miles replaced the scattered, one-room "little red schoolhouses." In the cities a few high schools were built to accommodate as many as 5000 to 10,000 students. Many people, however, began to feel that the schools and colleges of America were too much influenced by the techniques of organization and administration found in the industrial plant—speed-up, efficiency methods, and standardization.

Toward a more effective education. Education during these years was not, however, entirely given over to mass production methods. Students of education were beginning to reach new conclusions about how people actually learn and about the purposes of education. Educators, following in the path earlier marked out by the psychologists William James and G. Stanley Hall, were proving that a child's mind can be molded—within limits. Other scholars, among them John Dewey, continued to emphasize that life itself is an education, and that the way to produce effective citizens is to give boys and girls actual experience in the art of democratic living. Still another group of scholars, led by psychologists like Edward L. Thorndike, began to work out tests for the measurement of intelligence and the evaluation of the educational

■ In this high school classroom of the 1920's, students are conducting their own study of government. Earlier, such student participation was uncommon.

process. Commissions of educators met more and more often to lay plans for adapting schools to a changing society.

Gaining momentum during the opening decades of the twentieth century, all of these educational developments were in full swing by the 1920's.

Journalism. Schools and colleges are only one source of education. Among others newspapers and magazines are noteworthy. Both reflected the influence of the machine age. By the 1920's journalism had become big business, highly organized and highly standardized. The *Reader's Digest*, started in 1922, quickly won nationwide circulation with its digests of articles from other journals. *Time* Magazine, started in 1923, also won a wide circle of readers with its terse comments on current affairs.

Many of the older newspapers, individually owned and individually operated, were being bought up one by one by the great newspaper chains. Chain newspapers ran the same syndicated columns, the same editorials, the same comics, the same sports news, the same advertisements, and subscribed to the same news services—the Associated Press, the United Press, and the International News Service. The newspapers, like the magazines, reflected the ideals, interests, and problems of industrial America.

683

HIGHLIGHTS OF AMERICAN WRITING

EDGAR LEE MASTERS (1869–1950): *Spoon River Anthology,* verse epitaphs for inhabitants of an imaginary town.

AMY LOWELL (1874–1925): "Patterns" and "Lilacs," pictures in verse

ROBERT FROST (1874–): "Mending Wall," "The Death of the Hired Man," and many other plain poems about New England that show deep insight and feeling

H. L. MENCKEN (1880–1956): Numerous witty essays; *The American Language,* discussion of the development of English in the United States

EUGENE O'NEILL (1888–1953): America's first important dramatist: long dramas involving psychological studies of character; shorter plays such as *In the Zone* and *Beyond the Horizon;* and one comedy, *Ah, Wilderness*

EDNA ST. VINCENT MILLAY (1892–1950): *Renascence, Second April,* and other collections of short, romantic poems including sonnets

PEARL BUCK (1892–): *The Good Earth,* novel about the fortunes of a Chinese family, and other novels about China

THORNTON WILDER (1897–): *The Bridge of San Luis Rey,* novel based on the theme that love links the living with the dead; *Our Town,* play that has become an American classic

STEPHEN VINCENT BENÉT (1898–1943): "The Devil and Daniel Webster," short story; *John Brown's Body,* long narrative poem about the War Between the States

Literature. Much of the literature of the 1920's dealt with ever-popular themes such as love, personal conflicts, and adventure. Many authors, however, wrote about the conflicts and the confusions of the machine age. In his poem *The Waste Land* T. S. Eliot pictured society in the machine age as grim, barren, standardized, commercialized, cheap, and vulgar. Edwin Arlington Robinson echoed the emptiness and futility of a society which found its deepest satisfaction in a materialistic world of money and mechanical gadgets. Carl Sandburg, who found much to admire in the new industrialized society, also showed how terrible life could be when man glorified the machine and neglected himself.

The fiction of the 1920's also reflected the influence of the machine age. *This Side of Paradise,* a popular novel by F. Scott Fitzgerald, revealed the tragic confusion into which America's youth had been plunged in a society all too often characterized by fast living and hard drinking. In *Main Street, Babbitt,* and other novels, Sinclair Lewis portrayed the hypocrisy and the shallowness of men who worshiped the dollar and the material comforts with which the machine provided them. The short stories of Sherwood Anderson poignantly reflected the loss of the old craft skills. Ernest Hemingway, one of the so-called "hard-boiled realists," told of the tragic plight of Americans who lived abroad in order to escape the standardized culture of machine-dominated America.

Theodore Dreiser, in the novel *An American Tragedy,* pictured youth caught in the mad drive for power and wealth, and condemned a society whose ideals and morals were materialistic and grasping. Willa Cather's *The Professor's House* dealt with the contrasting values of an older world that had time for poetry and the newer world that was so much concerned with the material aspects of life. In several novels, John Dos Passos wrote of the crushing effect the machine had upon the ideals and aspirations of the individual.

Music. Music, too, reflected the influence of the new industrial age. Many people believed that the syncopated jazz that became popular in the 1920's expressed the rhythms and the accelerated speed and energy of the machine. Informed music critics found much to praise in the expressive scores of composers like George Gershwin.

Music also became increasingly available to all the people through the radio, the phonograph, and musical instruments manufactured at lower and lower costs. Moreover, wealth created by the new industrial age supported symphony orchestras and opera companies.

Painting and design. In painting and design Americans were more and more influenced by Europeans like Cézanne, Manet, Monet, Degas, Matisse, and Picasso. Some modernists boldly experimented with geometric designs that often resembled machines in their emphasis on hard angles, masses, and abstract form. Many American artists continued to paint the more conventional themes, but they painted them in new ways. Other native painters tried to reveal the meaning of the machine age in their paintings of factories, warehouses, slums, and railroads.

New art forms. The machine age was also opening up entirely new forms of art. In the hands of artists, the camera was able to capture the spirit and meaning of the new age. New methods of reproduction made it possible for most people to own inexpensive yet excellent copies of the world's outstanding works of art. These techniques of reproduction were adopted by even the inexpensive magazines, with the result that millions of Americans had the opportunity to see the work of the world's greatest photographers, illustrators, and artists.

Aided by commercial artists and industrial designers, manufacturers began to produce telephones, furniture, fabrics, clothing, typewriters, glassware, refrigerators, stoves, automobiles, and a host of other articles that showed that machines and machine products might be beautiful in design and structure.

■ The revival of the Liturgical Movement and the accent in modern art of the strong line and simplicity of design were mutually beneficial. St. Patrick's Church combines both.

Architecture. Inspired by outstanding architects like Louis Sullivan and Frank Lloyd Wright (page 532), other architects began to promote the idea that a building ought to use the materials and follow the forms most suitable to the purposes for which it was to be used.

For many people the skyscraper became a symbol of the influence of the machine upon architecture. Built of steel, glass, and concrete, it towered into the sky in order to use as little expensive ground space as possible, with its upper stories set back to prevent the streets from being darkened. In its emphasis upon clear-cut vertical lines and its massing of windows, the skyscraper was an excellent example of how purpose and materials dictated design. Outstanding examples were the New York Telephone Company Building and the Empire State Building in New York City, the State Capitol at Lincoln, Nebraska, and the Los Angeles Public Library.

1. Describe three ways in which the educational system was changed to meet the demands of the machine age.

2. What is meant by the statement, "Journalism had become big business"?

3. Referring to the works of four writers, show how the problems of the machine age were reflected in the literature of the 1920's.

4. Jazz has been called "the folk music of the machine age." Do you agree? Justify your opinion.

5. In what ways were American artists and architects influenced by the ideas of the machine age?

 Striking changes occur in the daily life of Americans

With money in their pockets and more leisure time than they had ever enjoyed before, Americans in the 1920's turned to recreation and entertainment in a big way. They poured into the countryside, packed stadiums, and jammed motion picture theaters. Indeed, it was this vigorous pursuit of entertainment that led historians to refer to the 1920's as the "Jazz Age" and the "Age of Wonderful Nonsense."

The automobile. For millions of American families, the automobile was a major source of recreation. Entire families piled into the car for an evening's ride or for a week-end trip.

By the 1920's the automobile was no longer the exclusive possession of the well-to-do. Of 123 working-class families interviewed in a typical midwestern city in 1923, 60 owned cars.

Another development of the 1920's was the swing from the open to the closed car. Also during the latter half of the twenties, the design of cars became an endless topic of conversation.

But although the automobile made travel comfortable and private, it also created new problems. The number of people killed in traffic accidents kept rising. Young people asserted their independence by driving off in the family car, free from the supervision of parents. Many Americans believed that the automobile was disrupting the family and helping to break down the established moral code of the nation.

These were by no means the only ways in which the automobile affected American life and created new problems. It also increased the difficulties of law enforcement by providing a convenient means of escape for criminals. And it played a major role in the breakdown of prohibition by providing a means for transporting illegal liquor.

National prohibition of liquor. As you have seen (page 632), the Eighteenth Amendment was ratified by the necessary three fourths of the states by January 1919. This amendment gave the federal government power to prohibit "the manufacture, sale, or transportation of intoxicating liquors within, the importation thereof into, or the exportation thereof from the United States and all territory subject to the jurisdiction thereof. . . ."

In October 1919 Congress passed the Prohibition Enforcement Act, usually called the Volstead Act, over President Wilson's veto. This act defined as "intoxicating liquor" any beverage containing more than one half of one per cent of alcohol. The Volstead Act turned enforcement of the law over to the Bureau of Internal Revenue, and created the special office of Commissioner of Prohibition.

Prohibition creates problems. Before the 1920's were far advanced, however, the prohibition experiment created serious problems in American life. Long coastlines in the east and west and unguarded frontiers to the north and south made it impossible to stop the flow of illegal liquor into the country.

Bootlegging became big business controlled by criminal elements in the large cities. The gangster Al Capone, who ruled Chicago with an iron hand, traveled about in an armored car, owned an estate in Florida, and commanded a small "army" of gangsters equipped with revolvers, sawed-off shotguns, and submachine guns. Gang wars and other violence became common in many American cities during the "Roaring Twenties." Moreover, the gangs branched out to seize control of gambling establishments and dance halls. By the end of the decade, they had begun to develop the so-called "rackets." The racketeers collected "protection" money from businessmen, threatening violence if their victims failed to pay.

For this open and widespread violation of the law, the people themselves were in part to blame. Many Americans, who were otherwise law-abiding, refused to take prohibition seriously. Finally, in 1933, the prohibition era came to an end when the necessary number of states ratified the Twenty-first Amendment. This amendment repealed the Eighteenth Amendment, and returned the power to control the sale of intoxicating drinks to the states themselves.

Radio. Meanwhile, another development was transforming the lives of millions of Americans, young and old alike. The new development was radio.

KDKA, the first commercial broadcasting station, began to operate in Pittsburgh on November 2, 1920. Radio immediately became a craze. By 1922 sales of receiving sets and radio parts totaled more than $60,000,000. By 1929 sales amounted to almost $400,000,000, more than 600 broadcasting stations had been licensed, and one third of all the homes in the nation owned radio receivers.

Radio brought an enormous variety of information and entertainment directly into the home. The most popular programs featured "crooners," jazz musicians, comedians, sports announcers, and newscasters.

But many Americans felt that radio was not fulfilling its great promise as an instrument of education and culture. They criticized the dominant role of the advertiser who paid the broadcasting companies and entertainers, and therefore in many cases determined what programs would be presented.

Despite the trivial content of many programs, however, radio served the American people in a variety of ways. By providing common experiences simultaneously all over the country, it increased the feeling of national consciousness and unity. Like the automobile, radio helped to break down the isolation and monotony of rural life. It encouraged popular interest in current events, including sports, and offered useful information on health, home economics, and techniques of farming. It made serious music available to more Americans than ever before. Finally, outside the home, radio provided greater safety for airplanes and ships.

Movies. The motion picture industry also enjoyed a spectacular growth during the 1920's. As you have seen (page 572), during the opening years of the twentieth century Americans packed the nickelodeons, as the first motion picture houses were called, to enjoy this new source of entertainment. By the 1920's, however, the nickelodeons had

■ Early movies were made to appeal to American humor. Many of them, as the comedy pictured here, became the steady diet of entertainment.

been replaced by huge and lavish motion picture "palaces." By 1927 more than 20,000 motion picture theaters were operating with a combined seating capacity of 18,000,000 people. By the end of the decade, weekly audiences approached the 100,000,000 mark, and the industry itself had become big business, the fourth largest in the nation.

A major step forward was made in 1927 when Warner Brothers released *The Jazz Singer*, featuring Al Jolson. This was the first successful "talkie." For years the industry had been working on the problem of using sound with pictures. Within a year of the first success, the old silent films were being replaced by the even more popular sound pictures.

During the 1920's the movie industry turned out great numbers of films which were more polished in technique and more sophisticated in content than the pre-war films. These new films emphasized such popular themes as social advancement, the reckless enjoyment of life, and the independence of women. In the prosperity of the "Golden Twenties," many Americans who hoped to become rich learned from the films produced by Cecil B. de Mille and Ernst Lubitsch how the rich behaved, or were thought to behave, how they dressed, and how they amused themselves.

Not all the films of this period, however, were concerned with such frivolous matters. Erich von Stroheim's *Greed* transformed a naturalist novel by Frank Norris into a film which described with great power how greed for money warped the character and finally destroyed the lives of a working-class couple. Lewis Milestone's *All Quiet on the Western Front*, based on a novel about World War I by Erich Remarque, expressed very movingly the widespread anti-war feeling of the 1920's. Other films, like Robert J. Flaherty's *Nanook of the North*, successfully captured the grandeur of nature in distant places.

Sports. During the postwar period the interest in traditional spectator sports rose markedly. Baseball remained the most popular professional game, with an average yearly attendance of between 9 and 10 million at major league games. Babe Ruth replaced Ty Cobb as the idol of fans and in 1927 astounded the baseball world by hitting a record number of sixty home runs. College football drew some 30,000,000 spectators in the same year. Red Grange, a halfback for the University of Illinois, became a national hero and won a movie contract. Prize fighting continued to enjoy tremendous popularity, and in 1927 ardent boxing fans spent $2,658,660 to see the famous Dempsey-Tunney match. Professional golf and tennis matches also increased their audiences during the 1920's.

Some critics claimed that the United States had become a nation of spectators, satisfied to watch passively while a small group of professionals played for money or glory. Others denied that this was true and pointed to the active participation of Americans in golf, tennis, sand-lot baseball, swimming, camping, skating, bowling, and other sports.

Feats and fads. Americans in the postwar period were unusually responsive to new fads and fashions and dramatic public events. This period has been called the "Jazz Age" with some justice, for the rhythmic music of jazz was perhaps the most consistently popular of the new fashions. Most of the other fads of the period shifted rapidly from year to year: from the Chinese-originated game of mah-jongg to crossword puzzles, to vigorous dances like the Charleston, to eccentric activities like flagpole sitting and marathon dances.

But in some instances the objects of the nation's sudden enthusiasm were individuals of character and accomplishment. By far the most glorified hero of the 1920's was Charles A. Lindbergh, who in May 1927 made the first nonstop flight from New York to Paris in his plane, *The Spirit of St. Louis*. Another fearless voyager was Commander (later Admiral) Richard E. Byrd, who made the first flights to both the North and the

THE MIRACLE OF "THE LONE EAGLE"

Shortly before eight o'clock on the morning of May 20, 1927, Charles Augustus Lindbergh climbed into the cockpit of his single-engine plane and started down the runway of New York's Roosevelt Field. The plane, heavily loaded with gasoline, seemed reluctant to leave the ground, but finally rose sluggishly into the air and disappeared into the skies, headed for Paris, France.

The twenty-seven-year-old Lindbergh had been flying for three years. A passion for aviation, as well as the offer of a $25,000 prize to the first man to fly nonstop between New York and Paris, prompted Lindbergh to try his great venture. As a result of his modesty, his quiet confidence, and his skill as a flier, he had won the financial support of a group of St. Louis businessmen. He acknowledged this support by calling his plane *The Spirit of St. Louis.*

The flight of 3600 miles took 33 hours and 39 minutes. During all this time Lindbergh, who had no radio, was out of touch with the world, a lone figure in a small single-engine plane flying across the vast emptiness of the North Atlantic. And while he battled fog and wind and the deadliest enemy of all, sleep, the entire nation prayed for his success and waited anxiously for word. When he landed in the early evening at Le Bourget Airport near Paris, the shy young man was unprepared for the enthusiastic crowd of 100,000 people waiting to greet him. There followed a triumphant reception in several European countries and in the United States. Overnight "Lindy," or "The Lone Eagle," had become a national hero.

After he became a public figure, Lindbergh did much in writing and in public lectures to popularize aviation and contribute to its development. But he will always be remembered chiefly for the heroic solo flight across the Atlantic that was a triumph of skill and courage.

South Pole. Other Americans who followed the example of Lindbergh and Byrd proved that the postwar period was an age of authentic feats as well as eccentric fads.

SECTION SURVEY

1. In what ways has the automobile revolutionized American family life?

2. Show the connection between prohibition and racketeering in the 1920's.

3. Discuss the role of (a) radio and (b) the movies as forms of education and recreation.

4. "Some critics claimed that the United States had become a nation of spectators." What is your opinion?

5. To what extent have developments that took place during this period affected your life today?

IDENTIFY: Volstead Act, KDKA, *The Spirit of St. Louis;* Babe Ruth, Lindbergh, Commander Byrd; 1927.

■ **CHAPTER SURVEY**   (For review, see Section Surveys, pages 677, 682, 686, 689.)

Points to Discuss: 1. By 1920 the power-driven machine had become one of the dominant symbols of industrial America. Describe the factors that contributed to this development.

2. Justify the use of each of the following terms to describe the tempo of the 1920's: (a) "Golden Twenties," (b) "Roaring Twenties," (c) "Age of Disillusionment," (d) "Jazz Age," (e) "Decade of Wonderful Nonsense," and (f) "Ballyhoo Years." Which do you think is the best description of the twenties? Explain.

3. In the 1920's both business and government were more interested in industrial efficiency than in industrial competition. Give evidence.

4. Show how the progress of industrialization affected the lives of people (a) on the farms and (b) in the cities.

5. In your opinion, what was the most significant influence of the machine age on (a) education, (b) journalism, (c) music, (d) art, and (e) architecture?

6. The principal critics of American life during the years between World War I and World War II condemned the growing importance of the machine in the lives of men. (a) Summarize the arguments of these critics. (b) How were these arguments answered?

Using Maps and Charts: 1. Using chart 7 on page 825, (a) make a list of the ten largest cities in 1890 and in 1930. (b) Explain the changes that you note.

2. Using the data in the charts on pages 836–37, write a brief statement on the revolution in American transportation and communication that occurred in the 1920's.

3. Basing your answer on the charts on pages 832–33, indicate the change in the power output by sources between 1900 and 1920. Show the effect on manufacturing, agriculture, transportation.

4. Referring to the map on pages 842–43, (a) identify the possessions of the United States in 1930 and (b) the areas of heavy American investments.

Consulting the Sources: For a contemporary account of President Harding and his friends, see Commager and Nevins, *The Heritage of America*, No. 246.

■ **TRACING THE MAIN IDEAS**

Many critics of American life during the 1920's claimed that modern technology was standardizing people's lives. They pointed out that every night all over America people tuned their radios to the same programs, becoming as passive and uncreative as the machine itself. The critics also were disturbed because the machine which had given men such vast power was being used largely to make money, to provide more or less meaningless recreation, and to bring about destruction in wartime. The machine, they insisted, might ultimately spell the ruin of man unless he could learn to use it for beneficial human and social ends.

Other students of American civilization, however, defended the machine. They insisted that it relieved men of backbreaking toil and that it made possible higher standards of living, more leisure, more consumer goods, more comforts, more time for education and pleasure. As evidence of the machine's contribution to better living, they pointed out, for example, that good music was available to nearly all Americans who cared to tune their radios to the proper station. Education in the machine age, also argued its defenders, did not need to lead to standardization; rather, it might use motion pictures, radio, and the growing knowledge of psychology to break away from binding traditions and to enlarge the freedom and strengthen the personality of the individual.

As the 1920's drew to a close, however, arguments about the advantages and disadvantages of modern technology were suddenly pushed into the background. As you will see in the next chapter, during the 1930's the American people struggled through the greatest economic depression in their history.

Unit Survey (Reread "Tracing the Main Ideas," pages 656, 673, 690.)

OUTSTANDING EVENTS

1914 Ford's conveyer-belt assembly.
1919 Eighteenth Amendment ratified.
1920 KDKA begins operation.
1920 Warren G. Harding elected President.
1921–29 Laws restricting immigration.
1921–22 Washington Naval Conference.
1921 Bureau of the Budget is created.
1922 Fordney-McCumber Tariff.
1923 Harding dies, and Calvin Coolidge becomes President.
1924 Teapot Dome scandal.
1924 Coolidge elected President.
1928 Kellogg-Briand Pact.
1928 Herbert Hoover elected President.
1929 Stock Market crash; beginning of Great Depression.
1931 Moratorium on war debts declared.
1932 RFC is created.
1932 Stimson Doctrine is announced.
1932 Franklin D. Roosevelt elected President.

THEN AND NOW

1. Compare problems of corruption and racketeering which followed upon passage of the Eighteenth Amendment with such problems today.

2. Compare the "Red Scare" following World War I with the threat of Communism in our own day.

3. Compare the condition and problems of farmers in the prosperous "Twenties" with those of today.

4. How do possible consequences flowing from development of automation compare with economic and social consequences of assembly-line mass production in earlier days?

EXTENDING YOUR HORIZON

1. For interesting light on the Sacco-Vanzetti trial of 1921, read the article by Francis Russell "Tragedy in Dedham," *American Heritage*, October 1958; then, see the reply to this view as expressed by Mrs. Dorothy G. Wayman in a letter to Russell, "Sacco-Vanzetti: the unfinished debate," *American Heritage,* December 1959.

2. Andrew Mellon was an influential conservative of the Twenties. Read the account of Mellon in Stewart Holbrook's *The Age of the Moguls,* and contrast this with Holbrook's portrayal of Carnegie.

3. Read the view of Coolidge by Peter Levin in *Seven by Chance* (Farrar, Straus), Chapter X, "An American Primitive."

4. Historians considering the Harding era tend to highlight the scandals. For a less traditional treatment, read Chapter XVI, "In Praise of the Harding Era," in Holbrook's *Lost Men of American History.*

INDIVIDUAL ACTIVITIES

1. Read and report on newspaper accounts and actual case histories of individual suffering during the 1929 depression period in David A. Shannon's *The Great Depression* [Prentice-Hall (Spectrum Books: paper)].

2. Plan to report to the class on the role of government in the Red Scare following World War I. Base your report on the chapters "The New Enemy—Communism," and "Palmer's Red Raids" from Don Whitehead's book *The FBI Story* (Random House).

3. For the early career of FBI chief J. Edgar Hoover, read the chapter "The Roaring Twenties," in Whitehead's book.

4. Draw a chart showing the fluctuations in tariff rates from 1789 to 1930 (consult the chart "The Rise and Fall of U.S. Tariffs" on page 841). Indicate on your chart the apparent reasons for each increase or decrease.

5. Consult Chapter 22 of Heffner's *A Documentary History of the United States,* and study the text of Hoover's 1928 speech setting forth his doctrine of "Rugged Individualism." Then compare this expression of conservatism with that reflected by Carnegie on "Wealth" (pages 166–73 of the same book).

6. Two interesting documents on the Ku Klux Klan in the 1920's can be found in Hofstadter, *Great Issues of American History,* II, Part VI. One is "The Klan's Fight for Americanism," by Hiram Evans (Imperial Wizard of Klan), and the other is William A. White's "Letter on the Ku Klux Klan." Compare this movement in the 1920's with that of the Know-Nothing Party in the 1850's. Consult the *Dictionary of American History.*

GROUP ACTIVITIES

1. Let a group of students investigate views as to causes of the Great Depression, and analyze and evaluate them for the class. Good sources include J. K. Galbraith, *The Great Crash* (Houghton Mifflin); Dixon Wecter, *The Age of the Great Depression, 1929–1941* (Macmillan); and Herbert Hoover, *Memoirs* (Macmillan). See too, articles by Galbraith, "The Days of Boom and Bust," *American Heritage*, August 1958, and "Coolidge, Hoover, and the Great Crash" in *Times of Trial* edited by Allan Nevins.

2. The question is often raised by historians whether the failure of the United States to ratify the Versailles Treaty and to join the League was due more to Senator Lodge and his followers or to Wilson himself. Select a committee to study the matter carefully for a panel report to the class. The Amherst Series pamphlet *Wilson at Versailles* will offer a variety of views for consideration. See, too, T. A. Bailey's article, "Woodrow Wilson Wouldn't Yield," *American Heritage*, June 1957, and the chapter, "The Supreme Infanticide" in Volume II of Sheehan's *The Making of American History*.

3. Let several students listen to the Edward R. Murrow record on the period of the Twenties in his "I Can Hear It Now" Series (CBS). They should prepare questions for discussion by the class the day after the record is played in class.

4. Select a committee to collaborate with the school's art department in preparing an exhibit of American art between the two World Wars to be supplemented by a lecture by a member of the art department.

SUGGESTED FURTHER READING

BIOGRAPHY

BARUCH, BERNARD M., *My Own Story*, Holt.

GARWOOD, DARRELL, *Artist in Iowa: the Life of Grant Wood*, Norton.

HANDLIN, OSCAR, *Al Smith and His America*, Little, Brown.

LINDBERGH, CHARLES, *We*, Grosset & Dunlap; Putnam.

MERZ, CHARLES, *And Then Came Ford*, Doubleday.

MORRISON, HUGH, *Louis Sullivan, Prophet of Modern Architecture*, Norton.

REYNOLDS, QUENTIN, *The Wright Brothers*, Random House.

STONE, IRVING, *Clarence Darrow for the Defense*, Doubleday.

°WHITE, WILLIAM ALLEN, *A Puritan in Babylon*, Macmillan. Calvin Coolidge.

WISE, W. E., *Jane Addams of Hull House*, Harcourt, Brace.

OTHER NONFICTION

ALLEN, FREDERICK LEWIS, *Only Yesterday*, Harper; Bantam.

FAULKNER, HAROLD U., *From Versailles to the New Deal*, Yale Univ. Press.

FRAZIER, FRANKLIN E., *The Negro in the United States*, Macmillan.

HOOVER, HERBERT, *The Great Depression*, Macmillan.

JOHNSON, GERALD W., *The Lines Are Drawn*, Lippincott. Pulitizer Prize cartoons.

LEIGHTON, ISABEL, ed. *The Aspirin Age*, Simon and Schuster. Light essays.

MELLQUIST, JEROME, *The Emergence of an American Art*, Scribner. Art at the turn of the century.

NEVINS, ALLAN, *The United States in a Chaotic World*, Yale Univ. Press. International affairs 1918–33.

SOULE, GEORGE, *Prosperity Decade*, Rinehart. From 1917 to 1929.

HISTORICAL FICTION

ADAMS, SAMUEL HOPKINS, *Revelry*, Liveright. Scandals during Harding's administration.

BACHELLER, IRVING, *Uncle Peel*, Grosset & Dunlap; Lippincott. The 1920's.

BAKER, DOROTHY, *Young Man with a Horn*, Houghton Mifflin. Jazz trumpeter who lived in the 1920's.

BARNES, MARGARET, A., *Years of Grace*, Houghton Mifflin. Jazz Age in Chicago.

CATHER, WILLA, *The Professor's House*, Knopf. Culture vs. materialism.

FITZGERALD, F. SCOTT, *The Great Gatsby*, Scribner (paper).

LAWRENCE, JOSEPHINE, *If I Have Four Apples*, Grosset & Dunlap. Novel about Great Depression.

LEWIS, SINCLAIR, *Arrowsmith*, Harcourt, Brace. Novel about idealistic doctor.

——, *Babbitt*, Harcourt, Brace. Satirical novel about businessman.

——, *Main Street*, Harcourt, Brace. Novel about pettiness of small-town life.

MARQUAND, JOHN P., *The Late George Apley*, Little, Brown; Pocket Books. Story of a Boston aristocrat.

SINCLAIR, UPTON, *Between Two Worlds*, Viking. The decade 1919–29.

——, *Oil!*, Laurie [London]. Oil scandals.

UNIT ELEVEN

Years of the New Deal

1932–1941

The Nation Undertakes a Great Experiment

YOUNG MEN OF CIVILIAN CONSERVATION CORPS CLEARING A FOREST OF FIRE-HAZARDS —

PRESIDENT Franklin Delano Roosevelt took office on March 4, 1933, in the midst of the Great Depression. He began his administration with a ringing summons to the American people to face the future with courage and faith. "The only thing we have to fear is fear itself," he confidently stated. His calm words helped to lift the burden of despair and rallied the people behind the government.

The President outlined his New Deal program in a crisp, dramatic Inaugural Address. He presented it with recommendations for immediate action to a special session of Congress that he promptly called upon taking office.

The New Deal had in general three aims—relief, recovery, and reform. Because people everywhere were clamoring for action, the three aims were often mixed together as objectives of a single act of Congress. Sometimes measures that were adopted to realize one of the aims interfered with other measures designed to achieve the other aims.

But for purposes of analysis, it is convenient to divide the New Deal into its three essential parts: (1) measures to provide relief for the unemployed; (2) measures to speed the recovery of agriculture, industry, commerce, and labor; and (3) measures to remedy certain weaknesses in the economic system.

Such was the general nature of the Great Experiment that President Roosevelt and Congress launched in the spring of 1933.

AS THE STORY DEVELOPS

1. The New Deal provides relief and work for the unemployed.
2. Recovery measures are launched to stimulate agriculture.
3. Recovery measures aid banking, building, and transportation.
4. Recovery measures help industry and encourage labor.
5. The New Deal carries out various reform measures.

1450   1750   1800   1850   1900   1950   1975

1

The New Deal provides relief and work for the unemployed

The most urgent task that Roosevelt faced when he took office was to provide food, clothing, and shelter for millions of jobless, hungry, cold, despairing Americans. By 1933 nearly 14 million people were out of work.

Direct relief. To meet the need, the Roosevelt administration immediately launched what seemed at the time to be a colossal program of direct relief. In two years the Federal Emergency Relief Administration (FERA), created in 1933, and other federal agencies distributed 3 billion dollars to needy Americans. Money was distributed to the states, leaving state and local administrators free to use the money as they saw fit—for direct relief or to provide jobs. At one time nearly 8 million families were on direct relief.

But few liked this kind of relief. The unemployed did not want charity; they wanted jobs. And so plans were made to replace direct relief with a program that would provide work.

Work relief. The federal government attacked the problem of providing jobs in several different ways. For instance, during 1933–34 it paid nearly one billion dollars in wages to men and women whom it had drawn from the relief rolls and to whom it had given jobs or "made work" projects. Many of the "made work" projects had relatively little value. Critics of the New Deal called this type of work "boondoggling."

President Roosevelt and the other New Dealers were aware that federal charity and "made work" were at best necessary evils. What men and women needed and what the New Deal administration wished to provide was socially useful work. A new agency, the Works Progress Administration (WPA), was created in 1935 to accomplish this purpose. Harry L. Hopkins, who had been administrator of the FERA since 1933, was made head of the WPA. This new agency co-operated with state and local governments, which shared in both the cost and the administration of the work relief program.

The WPA program helped people in many walks of life. By 1936 more than 6000 schoolhouses had been constructed or repaired; new sewage plants had been built in 5000 communities; approximately 128,000 miles of secondary roads had been constructed or improved; and other permanent public improvements had been made. Unemployed actors, musicians, and writers enriched the lives of their fellow Americans by providing plays, concerts, and other types of recreation.

At the peak of its activity, in March 1936, nearly 4 million Americans were working for the WPA. Congress voted about $6,300,000,000 during 1935 and 1936 for the Works Progress Administration.

Work for youth. Perhaps the greatest tragedy of the depression was its effect upon millions of America's young people. Many could not continue in school —elementary school, secondary school, or college—because they lacked adequate food and clothing or were homeless. Those who graduated during the depression years faced the bleak prospect of unemployment. Thousands of jobless young people roamed the country in search of work, lounged on street corners and in poolrooms, or turned to crime.

Two agencies were created to bring immediate work relief to the youth of the nation. One of the early acts of the Roosevelt administration was the organization in 1933 of the Civilian Conservation Corps (CCC). At times as many as 500,000 young men between the ages of 18 and 25 were enrolled in the CCC. Nearly all of them were unmarried; most of them were drawn from poverty-stricken families. These youths were scattered across the land in 2600 work camps. They were provided with food, clothing, and shelter; they were paid wages which they were expected to share with their families; and they were

ROOTS OF THE NEW DEAL

President Roosevelt had a knack of explaining New Deal ideas clearly. He explained many of these ideas over radio in what he called "fireside chats." But he had not originated all these concepts.

The New Deal was the product of ideas drawn from widely different sources. In the first place, it leaned upon earlier movements—the Granger and Populist movements, Theodore Roosevelt's "square deal," Robert M. La Follette's Progressive movement, and Woodrow Wilson's "New Freedom."

Roosevelt giving a fireside chat

In the second place, the New Deal drew upon experience gained in World War I. Using in some instances the same officials who had served during 1917 and 1918, the New Deal set up an elaborate network of federal agencies. These agencies greatly increased the power of the Presidency. They also increased the power of the federal government at the expense of the states.

In the third place, the laws and the administrative machinery of the New Deal were characterized by the American instinct for trial and error. President Roosevelt frankly confessed that many of the New Deal measures were experiments and promised that if they proved unworkable, they would be abandoned. This promise was not always kept. Like other political regimes, the Roosevelt administration could not afford to admit that it made mistakes.

In the fourth place, the New Deal was in part influenced by experiments undertaken in other countries to break the world-wide depression. The Scandinavian countries and Great Britain had brought private banking under a considerable measure of government control, and had carried out housing projects for low-income groups. Denmark, France, and Brazil had tried to raise agricultural prices by limiting production of farm produce and by paying outright grants of money to farmers. These and other experiments were familiar to the experts who surrounded President Roosevelt and who, called the "brain trust," served as his advisers.

offered opportunities for recreation and education.

Moreover, the work done by those enrolled in the CCC was socially useful. They built fire trails in the forests, cleared swamps, planted trees, constructed small dams for flood control, cleared land for public parks, and in other ways helped to conserve the nation's natural resources.

A second New Deal work relief measure aided young people still in school. The National Youth Administration (NYA), created in 1935, distributed federal money to needy students, who were paid regular wages for tasks which the local educational authorities arranged in and around the schools. During its first year the NYA gave jobs to more than 400,000 students.

The New Deal youth program accomplished three purposes: (1) It saved hundreds of thousands of youths from idleness. (2) It enabled hundreds of thousands of young people to get an education. (3) It kept many young Americans out of the overcrowded private labor market.

Evaluating the relief program. The New Deal relief projects aroused much criticism, not only from Republicans, but also from members of the President's own party. It is true that many mistakes were made. There was incompetence. There was waste. Now and then some of the vast sums of money appropriated for work relief were used to bring undue pressure on workers at election time.

Some of the New Dealers admitted the truth of these criticisms. They insisted, however, that there had been no precedents for the gigantic task they had been forced to undertake. They also pointed out that they had been handicapped by lack of adequately trained personnel to carry out some of their programs.

But, despite admitted weaknesses in the work relief program, all New Dealers claimed that it had fully justified itself. Work provided by the federal government, they insisted, had saved millions of Americans from hunger, and had given them an opportunity to retain some measure of self-respect.

◢ **SECTION SURVEY**

1. What were the immediate problems confronting Roosevelt when he took office in 1933?

2. Which of these problems were solved by the activities of the WPA?

3. "Perhaps the greatest tragedy of the depression was its effect upon millions of America's young people." (a) Explain this statement. (b) Show how the New Deal tried to solve this problem.

4. (a) Summarize the criticisms that were made of the New Deal relief program. (b) How did New Dealers answer?

IDENTIFY: direct relief, FERA, work relief, "boondoggling," CCC, NYA.

2 Recovery measures are launched to stimulate agriculture

The New Deal measures to provide direct relief and work relief were rushed through Congress in an effort to meet the urgent needs of millions of suffering Americans. Simultaneously, the New Deal administration put into effect a recovery program designed to restore the health of the nation's economic system.

Saving the farmers' homes. One of the first efforts of the New Deal government was to save the land and homes of farmers. When Roosevelt became President, two out of every five farms were mortgaged. Moreover, farmers all over the country were faced with mounting debts—back taxes, interest payments, and payments on the principal of their loans. Unable to pay their debts, farmers in growing numbers were forced to watch their farms pass into the hands of banks, insurance companies, and private mortgage holders. The farmers then rented their former land as tenants or were left homeless and jobless.

To relieve this desperate situation, the federal government made available a huge sum of money to be lent to farmers at a low interest rate. The loans served several purposes. Some farmers borrowed money to buy seed, fertilizer, and equipment necessary to continue operations. Others borrowed money to buy back their farms or pay their taxes.

Still others borrowed money from the government to refinance loans that they could not repay at the time. Suppose, for instance, that Mr. Grumman, a farmer, owed $5000 that he had to repay over a 20-year period with interest at 5 per cent. The depression made it difficult if not impossible for Mr. Grumman to meet his yearly payments on this debt. He was faced with the foreclosure of his mortgage and the loss of his farm and home. But under the new government program he could borrow $5000 from Federal Land Banks in order to pay off his debt to the mortgage holder.

The new debt could run for as long as 50 years, with interest at 2.25 per cent.

This liberal system of federal credit enabled hundreds of thousands of farmers to protect their lands and their homes. The farm credit programs were administered by the Farm Credit Administration (FCA), created in 1933.

Higher incomes for farmers. In a second major attack upon the farm problem, the New Dealers tried to increase the income of farmers. The basic government formula for farm recovery was simple. The first step was to raise the prices of farm products. With more dollars in their pockets, the farmers—then about one fourth of the nation's population—would buy more manufactured goods. This new demand would help to reopen many factories. These factories would hire more workers. Industrial unemployment would be reduced. The industrial workers, in turn, would spend more money, which in time would help to reopen still more factories. So the demand for goods of all sorts, from farm and factory, would spiral upward. The key to the situation, as the New Dealers saw it, was higher farm prices.

The government set out to increase farm prices by utilizing the law of sup-

■ Tom Howard, a political cartoonist, satirized the New Deal by showing Uncle Sam trying to cope with calls from too many of the new agencies.

ply and demand. An illustration may serve to explain the government's procedure. Take the case of a grocery store which has bought more oranges than it can sell to its customers. The surplus oranges lie in the bins. They are about to rot. What does the storekeeper do? He reduces the price of the oranges. Next time, of course, he will know better and will order fewer oranges, hoping that by reducing the available supply he can sell all the oranges at a good price. This is essentially the policy that the New Deal applied to farm goods in the Agricultural Adjustment Act of 1933.

Limiting farm production. The government reduced the supply of farm products by several methods. In the first place, agents from the Department of Agriculture, acting under the authority of the Agricultural Adjustment Administration (AAA), went among the farmers urging them to sign agreements not to use one quarter to one half of their land. By thus limiting the amount of farm produce, the government hoped to raise prices. But even with higher prices the farmer had less income because he had fewer products to sell. The government therefore paid each farmer a certain sum of money for each acre that he took out of production. The money for these subsidies, or "benefit payments," was secured by collecting taxes from the food processors—from meat packers, canners, flour millers, and others who prepared, or "processed," farm products.

Under this crop restriction program, millions of acres of farm land were taken out of production. In 1933 a million cotton planters plowed under cotton, and did not plant about 10 million acres ordinarily under production.

As a result, the 1933 cotton crop was reduced by about 4 million bales and the price of cotton almost doubled, while the planters received almost 200 million dollars in federal subsidies. Producers of wheat, corn, hogs, rice, tobacco, dairy products, cattle, rye, barley, peanuts, flax, grain, sorghum, and sugar signed similar agreements to limit production.

Evaluating the agricultural program.
The New Dealers were pleased with the success of the agricultural recovery program. They pointed out that, as a result of the program, the prices of farm products had risen and farmers were earning more money. They also pointed out that with this increased purchasing power the farm population was spending more money and thus helping to get the wheels of industry rolling once again. These favorable results, the New Dealers said, were the outcome of a sound program of federal planning.

But there was also severe criticism of the New Deal agricultural program. In the first place, critics pointed out, it was necessary to levy taxes on the food processors in order to get money for the subsidy payments. These taxes were passed along to the consumer in the form of higher prices. In other words, money was being taken from the urban consumer and given to the farmer. While the one quarter of the population that lived on farms was getting more money, the three quarters of the population that lived in urban areas was experiencing an actual decline of purchasing power.

In the second place, the larger farmers benefited far more from the program than did small farmers, tenant farmers, and sharecroppers. Poorer farmers felt that the benefit payments seldom filtered down to them in amounts to which their toil and their needs entitled them. In the third place, many critics considered the program bureaucratic,° full of red tape, confusion, and inefficiency. Finally, millions of Americans condemned a program which deliberately produced scarcities at a time when hunger and suffering were widespread.

The program is declared unconstitutional. It was the Supreme Court, however, that brought the Agricultural Adjustment Act of 1933 to an end by declaring it unconstitutional. In a decision handed down early in 1936 in the case of *United States v. Butler,* the Supreme

••
° **bureaucratic:** concentrating too much power in an unnecessary number of administrative bureaus.

THE DUST BOWL

The year 1934 brought a long, drawn-out nightmare to thousands of farmers living in western Kansas, southeastern Colorado, the Oklahoma Panhandle, northeastern New Mexico, and the semi-arid plains of Texas. Relentless winds swept over drought-ridden land, burying fields, fences, and houses under thousands of tons of drifting dust. Cattle and poultry died. A young boy on his way home from school was found buried in the dust only a quarter of a mile from his home. Farmers were driven to despair. Millions of acres were abandoned by poverty-stricken families, who, in their desperation, piled their possessions in trucks and moved to the cities or to California.

What caused this dreadful situation? The plains had experienced drought and dust storms even when buffalo and cattle grazed on their long grasses. But as farmers moved in and plowed more than a third of the area, partly as a result of pressure to grow more wheat during World War I, they destroyed the protecting cover of grass, and the soil lay bare beneath the burning sun, defenseless against the driving wind. Only a prolonged drought was required to bring disaster. In 1934 the drought came.

After this disaster, the Soil Conservation Service encouraged farmers to use contour plowing, to plant soil-saving crops, and to set out trees in shelter-belt strips to break the force of the wind. By the late 1930's, the farmers in the Dust Bowl were beginning to win their battle against drought, wind, and dust.

Court stated that Congress had no constitutional right to use its taxing power to divert money to a specific group of Americans—in this case, the farmers. The Court also ruled that the power to regulate agriculture belonged to the states, and that the federal government had no authority to interfere.

The adverse Supreme Court decision did not, however, end New Deal efforts to help the farmer. As you will see in the next chapter, the Roosevelt administration finally found other ways to aid farmers.

✔ **SECTION SURVEY**

1. What measures did the New Dealers introduce to help farmers retain their land and homes?
2. Show how the Agricultural Adjustment Act of 1933 aimed to raise farm income.
3. Give the arguments for and against the New Deal agricultural recovery program.
4. Why did the Supreme Court declare the Agricultural Adjustment Act of 1933 unconstitutional?

IDENTIFY: FCA, AAA, subsidy, *United States v. Butler,* dust bowl.

Recovery measures aid banking, building, and transportation

While trying to bring recovery to agriculture, the New Deal was also attempting to restore the health of the country's banks and currency. When Roosevelt took office on March 4, 1933, the entire nation was in the grip of an unprecedented financial collapse.

Bank failures mount. For months crowds of panic-stricken people had been selling stocks and rushing to banks in an effort to withdraw their deposits before the banks failed. By March 1933 nearly every stock exchange and numerous banks in the United States had closed. Many of the states, in a belated effort to save their financial institutions, had ordered all banks to suspend activities until further notice. From one end of the country to the other, many people hid money in mattresses, under carpets, or in any place they considered safe.

With so many banks closed, it was almost impossible for the everyday business life of the nation to be carried on. People could not pay their bills by check, and there was not enough currency in circulation to meet the needs of even a depressed economy.

The bank holiday. One of Roosevelt's first acts was a proclamation effective on March 6, 1933, closing every bank in the country for an indefinite period. Congress then enacted a series of laws that forbade any bank to reopen until it gave proof to the Department of the Treasury of its soundness and its ability to carry on business without endangering the deposits of its customers. Most banks were able to satisfy the financial experts in the Treasury Department and quickly reopened.

Abandoning the gold standard. Shortly after Roosevelt ordered the "bank holiday," Congress authorized the Secretary of the Treasury to call in all gold coins and gold certificates then in circulation, and provided a maximum penalty of a $10,000 fine and ten years in jail for any person found guilty of hoarding gold. With this action Congress abandoned the gold standard, which in the past had meant that all paper currency was redeemable in gold on request.

Later, in October 1933, President Roosevelt announced that he had authorized the Reconstruction Finance Corporation (page 654) to buy and sell gold in the world market in order that the United States would be able to take "in its own hands the control of the gold value of our dollar." Still later, at the end of January 1934, Roosevelt announced that under the new policy the gold value of the dollar would be only 59.06 cents in relation to the old "gold" dollar, whose value had been 100 cents in gold.

■ In 1935 this PWA project was under way at Dubuque, Iowa. It is a lock being built in order to help keep the upper Mississippi River navigable. Besides providing needed jobs, PWA work on waterways and highways added considerably to the national strength.

By "devaluing" the dollar, the New Deal administration hoped to force prices upward and in this way help the farmers. In this respect, however, the measure was a disappointment.

"Pump priming." In its effort to revive the industrial life of the nation, the New Deal followed a procedure called "pump priming." When the pump in a well does not draw water, it is sometimes necessary to "prime the pump" by pouring a little water down the well shaft. This water seals the crack around a washer in the shaft and thus helps to create a vacuum into which the well water rises so that it can be pumped up.

One of the major "pump priming" agencies was the Reconstruction Finance Corporation, which, as you know, had been started under the Hoover administration. By October 1936 the RFC had lent 11 billion dollars to railroads, banks, insurance companies, and industrial enterprises. Much of this money was quickly repaid.

But the New Deal also "primed the pump" in other ways. It undertook a building program of a magnitude that would have staggered Americans of an earlier generation. The New Dealers recognized that the building industry is one of the major keys to the economic life of the nation. It draws materials from many sources, and when construction work is going on men are busy in forests, mines, and factories throughout the land. The building industry employs hundreds of thousands of workers in normal times. The construction of houses, schools, churches, factories, and other buildings is thus a matter of concern to all Americans.

Construction of public works. The building program of the New Deal started in June 1933, when the Public Works Administration (PWA), headed by Harold L. Ickes, Secretary of the Interior, began to contract with private firms for the construction of public works such as bridges, government buildings, power plants, conservation projects, and dams. The federal government also encouraged states and municipalities to carry on their own building programs, offering them loans and outright gifts amounting to from 30 to 45 per cent of the total cost of the projects.

By the summer of 1936, public projects completed under this program included about 70 municipal power plants; several hundred schools and hospitals; nearly 1500 waterworks; and numerous federal, state, county, and municipal buildings. The program also included expenditures of 8 million dollars on public health work and of more than 250 million dollars for naval construction.

Repair and building of homes. The New Dealers also sought to revive the key building industry by a program designed to stimulate residential construction. Like so many of the New Deal measures, however, this program was double-barreled. It had as a second goal the relief of home owners.

When President Roosevelt took office, many homeowners were desperate. Every day an average of 1000 Americans stood by while their homes, representing their life earnings, were foreclosed by the mortgage holders and sold at public auction. In June 1933 Congress came to the aid of these needy Americans with the creation of the Home Owners' Loan Corporation (HOLC). With money borrowed at low interest rates from this government agency, many homeowners paid off their old mortgages. At the same time, they arranged with the HOLC to pay off their new mortgages over a long period with much smaller monthly payments. Between 1933 and 1936, the homes of more than a million American families were saved by the HOLC.

To provide further aid to the owners of homes and businesses, as well as to stimulate the building industry, the Federal Housing Administration (FHA) was established in 1934. Acting through the FHA, the government encouraged banks to lend money to individuals for repairing houses and business properties and for constructing new buildings by insuring the banks against losses on such commercial loans. Yet so desperate was the financial position of most Americans that up until 1936 relatively few individuals were able to take advantage of the FHA loans, and little residential construction was started.

A federal housing program to provide homes for the very poor was no more successful. Although the PWA lent and gave money to some 27 cities for slum clearance and for the erection of "low cost" apartment houses, results were disappointing. For one thing, the government's attempt to provide model living quarters ran building costs up so high that rents for the finished apartments were usually beyond the reach of the poor families.

Aid to transportation. Equally as important as the building industry to the economic life of the United States is its transportation system. Even before the depression the railroads had lost business as a result of the increasing competition of motor, water, and air traffic. The depression hit the railroads a stunning blow. Between 1929 and 1933 their income was cut in half, with the result that almost one third of all the railway companies in the United States went bankrupt. Others were saved from complete collapse only by loans from the Reconstruction Finance Corporation.

To recover lost business, some of the western railways lowered their passenger rates from 3.2 cents to 2 cents per mile. The experiment proved so successful that the Interstate Commerce Commission ordered all lines to adopt the same rate. Government loans also made it possible for the railroads to install modern equipment, such as diesel engines and streamline trains. Moreover, in 1935 buses and trucks engaged in interstate commerce were placed under the regulation of the Interstate Commerce Commission.

All of these measures helped the railways. But at the same time that the government was aiding the railroads, it was also spending huge sums of money for the improvement of the nation's highways and waterways, thereby giving a boost to the competitors of rail traffic.

SECTION SURVEY

1. Explain the purpose of (a) the bank holiday, (b) abandonment of the gold standard, and (c) devaluing the dollar.

2. Describe the various ways in which the New Deal "primed the pump."

3. Evaluate the importance of (a) the Home Owners' Loan Corporation and (b) the Federal Housing Administration as recovery measures.

4. What steps were taken at this time to help the transportation industry?

5. In your opinion, in which area of activity was the New Deal recovery program most effective? Explain.

IDENTIFY: PWA; Ickes.

4 Recovery measures help industry and encourage labor

All of the New Deal's recovery measures were intended to stimulate industry in one way or another. Money that first went into the pocket of the farmer was likely to find its way into the pocket of a factory worker, who in turn was likely to spend it for food, clothing, and other essentials. Building projects, whether public works or homes, provided jobs—and money—not only for construction workers, but also for the almost endless line of wage earners who in mine, forest, and factory supplied the necessary materials.

But the New Deal did not stop with these more or less indirect methods of reviving the nation's industrial machine. It tackled the problem head on with the National Industrial Recovery Act, usually referred to as the NIRA.

The NIRA. The National Industrial Recovery Act went into effect in June 1933 as an emergency measure to last for two years. It was intended to revive industry by enabling American employers to co-operate in a great planned effort for the re-employment of the jobless and the raising of wages. Co-operation was to replace competition as one of the major driving forces behind American industry. Antitrust legislation, such as the Sherman Antitrust Act and the Clayton Antitrust Act, were disregarded. Instead, the government now officially encouraged businessmen to forego competition and form co-operative trade associations.

The NIRA provided that each industry should, with the aid of the National Recovery Administration (NRA), adopt a "code of fair practices." Once these codes had been approved by the President, they became binding upon the entire industry.

Under the vigorous leadership of General Hugh S. Johnson, administrative head of the NRA, some 95 per cent of American industries adopted such fair practice codes within a few months. The codes differed a great deal. But, in general, they limited production and provided for the common control of prices and sales practices. In addition, most codes outlawed child labor and stipulated that hours of labor for adults should not exceed 40 hours a week and that wages should not be less than $12 or $15 a week. General Johnson, a picturesque personality often called "Ironpants" Johnson, attempted to capture patriotic sentiment in a great crusade to arouse the enthusiasms of the whole country in support of the co-operative program of the NRA.

Labor under the NIRA. Perhaps the most important provisions in the National Industrial Recovery Act, and certainly the most controversial provisions, were those contained in the famous Section 7a. This section guaranteed certain powers to organized labor. It guaranteed workers the right to bargain

■ Consumers who bought only NRA-produced goods could display the NRA blue eagle. General Johnson here finds his eagle on White House doors.

MOTHER KATHERINE DREXEL

After the discouraging events in the years following Reconstruction, there was little hope that the government would continue its aid to Negroes. At the same time, the western Indians were being confined to reservations. Until private agencies began to take an interest, it appeared that these two groups of people were to be left to suffer in poverty and exclusion from the normal social process. The Church, concerned about the reservation Indians, founded the Catholic Indian Bureau in 1874. Then, in 1884, the Third Plenary Council made a formal plea for aid to Indian and Negro missions.

The most striking response to this plea came from Katherine Drexel (1858–1955). She was the heiress grand-daughter of Francis Drexel, one of America's richest, most successful private bankers. With a complete dedication of what she was, a strong character and perhaps the richest woman of her time, she founded the Sisters of the Blessed Sacrament. Her sisters continue to work with the needy.

collectively with their employers. Employers were forbidden to exercise any pressure upon a worker to join a particular union or to remain a non-union worker. Employers were also forbidden to refuse work to a man simply because he belonged to a union.

Arguments in favor of the NIRA. President Roosevelt defended the NIRA on the grounds that it gave labor an opportunity to organize in order to get a share of profits in the form of higher wages, that it abolished child labor, and that it put an end to many unfair trade practices. He also maintained that it was responsible for putting 4 million people to work and for raising the total annual wages of the nation by 3 billion dollars.

Criticisms of the NIRA. But the NIRA also had its critics. As the months passed, these critics became increasingly outspoken.

In the first place, owners of small businesses charged that the NRA codes of fair practices had mostly been made by and for large corporations. They claimed that some codes, in assigning quotas of production to particular factories in an industry, gave unfairly small quotas to the smaller plants. They also insisted that the minimum-wage provisions in the codes gave an advantage to the highly mechanized factories, whose owners could afford to pay higher wages.

In the second place, it was difficult to enforce the codes. "Chiselers" ignored codes they had helped to draw up and had promised to obey. As a result, honest manufacturers and dealers suffered from unfair competition.

In the third place, the courts for the most part refused to enforce the "fair practices" provisions of the codes.

And finally, while a major purpose of the NRA was to aid recovery by increasing the purchasing power of consumers, many manufacturers defeated this purpose by raising prices to cover the increase in wages. In fact, the NRA did not maintain a steady policy toward prices. At one time it aimed to keep prices up; at another it demanded that they be brought down.

The main objection to the NIRA, from a large number of businessmen, was that it stimulated unionization and collective bargaining. Moreover, certain provisions in Section 7a of the act were not clear. For instance, did company unions, under the influence of managers and owners, have the right to engage in collective bargaining? Labor, fearful of the domination of management, said that company unions could not honestly represent the workers and should be outlawed. Management disagreed. Another source of confusion concerned the rights of the minority of workers in a factory. Did the representatives of a union that included the majority of the workers in a plant have the right to speak also for the minority which belonged to another union or which did not belong to any union?

The National Labor Board. In an effort to settle these confused points of the law, Congress established the National Labor Board (NLB), which later became the National Labor Relations Board (NLRB). The National Labor Board was given the power to conduct elections in plants and to determine which labor organization had the right to bargain for all the workers in that particular plant. It also served as a board of arbitration to settle labor disputes that were brought before it by labor and management.

But the NLB was unpopular with businessmen, who claimed that it usually settled disputes in favor of labor.

As a result, business began more and more openly to oppose the entire NRA program. When management refused to grant the demands of the unions, a wave of strikes broke out and the country was torn by dissension. Yet, despite these criticisms of the National Labor Board, prior to the summer of 1935 the board settled more than four fifths of the 3755 disputes referred to it and averted nearly 500 strikes.

The NIRA declared unconstitutional. The NIRA lasted less than two years. In May 1935, in the case of *Schechter v. United States,* the Supreme Court declared the NIRA unconstitutional. The judges stated unanimously that Congress had delegated too much of its legislative power to the President, that the President had no power to approve or disapprove of industry codes, and that such codes were not legally binding upon industry. The Court also insisted that, in giving the federal government the right to regulate interstate commerce, the Constitution did not give the government the power to regulate every aspect of business.

The Wagner Act. One important idea in the NIRA was quickly reborn. In 1935 Congress passed the famous Na-

■ For many years, American steelworkers were not organized, but in the late 1920's a start toward organization was made. Here, in the 1930's, the National Labor Relations Board is holding an election to decide which union shall represent the steelworkers.

tional Labor Relations Act, often called the Wagner Act after one of its sponsors, Senator Robert F. Wagner of New York. Workers hailed the Wagner Act as the "Magna Carta of Labor."

The Wagner Act, like the equally famous Section 7a of the NIRA, guaranteed to labor the right to organize, to bargain collectively with employers for better wages and working conditions, and to engage in "concerted activities . . . for other mutual aid." The Wagner Act specifically condemned certain employer practices as unfair to labor. It also declared that the majority of the workers in any plant or industry could select representatives for bargaining with management.

A permanent National Labor Relations Board was set up to administer the Wagner Act, which was openly prolabor. Under the Wagner Act the organization of labor proceeded rapidly. While the Wagner Act was in a sense a reform measure, it was also intended to promote industrial recovery by guaranteeing to organized labor a better chance of raising its wages and of thus increasing its purchasing power. No single measure of the New Deal aroused a greater amount of controversy than Senator Wagner's National Labor Relations Act.

SECTION SURVEY

1. Show how the NIRA aimed to help (a) industry and (b) labor.

2. In your opinion, what were the two most effective arguments in favor of the NIRA?

3. Discuss the two most important criticisms of the NIRA. Do you agree with them? Explain.

4. Why did the Supreme Court declare the NIRA unconstitutional?

5. Workers hailed the National Labor Relations Act as the "Magna Carta of Labor." Cite reasons.

IDENTIFY: NRA, Section 7a of the NIRA, *Schechter v. United States*, National Labor Relations Board; General Hugh Johnson, Wagner; 1935.

5 The New Deal carries out various reform measures

Relief and recovery measures were urgently needed in the 1930's, but only fundamental reforms could protect the nation against another depression. So, at least, the New Dealers reasoned.

Savings are protected. In one of its major reform acts, the New Deal administration in 1933 established the Federal Deposit Insurance Corporation (FDIC), which guaranteed the savings of bank depositors. At first set at $2500, the guarantee was raised in 1934 to $5000, and later to $10,000.

The New Deal also strengthened the banks in other ways. For example, it increased the power of the Federal Reserve System. Industrial and savings banks were brought into it, thus placing them under the supervision of a national authority. The Federal Reserve Board was given additional power to regulate credit as a check upon reckless speculation.

Another series of laws was designed to protect the public against worthless stocks. Any salesman—bank, brokerage house, or individual—who failed to give full and honest information about the true value of the stocks and bonds that he sold was subject to a severe penalty. In 1934 the Securities and Exchange Commission (SEC) was created to administer these laws and to regulate the stock exchanges.

Social security for the people. In another of its fundamental reform measures, the New Deal boldly attacked the problem of individual security.

The Social Security Act of 1935 had three major goals. First, it provided unemployment insurance for individuals who lost their jobs. The money for this purpose was raised by a payroll tax on employers in businesses employing more than 8 workers. The unemployment insurance fund was administered by state insurance systems, in co-operation with the federal government.

A second goal of the Social Security Act was to provide old-age pensions ranging from $10 to $85 a month for persons over sixty-five. The money for this purpose was raised by a payroll tax on employers and a social security tax on the wages of employees.

A third goal of the Social Security Act was to help the handicapped—the blind, the deaf-mutes, the crippled, the aged, and dependent children. Federal pensions up to $20 a month were available for needy persons over sixty-five, provided that the states appropriated an equal amount. Federal funds were also available for those states which sought to protect the welfare of needy children, the blind, the crippled, and other handicapped people. All of the provisions of the Social Security Act were administered by the Social Security Board.

President Roosevelt considered the Social Security Act "a cornerstone in a structure which is being built." It was admittedly only a beginning; excluded from its provisions were public employees, farm laborers, domestic servants, and employees of religious, charitable, and nonprofit educational institutions. Nevertheless, by 1937 nearly 21 million workers were entitled to unemployment benefits, and 36 million workers to old-age pensions.

Providing electricity for homes. Another reform movement sought to bring the benefits of electric power to an increasing number of people. Despite widespread development of electric power up to the 1930's, only one third of America's homes had electricity; in rural areas only fifteen out of every hundred houses were wired.

In an effort to solve this problem, the President by an Executive Order in 1935 created the Rural Electrification Administration (REA). The REA was given the responsibility for developing a program for generating and distributing electricity in isolated rural areas.

Regulation of utility companies. Several months later Congress passed the Public Utility Holding Company Act, al-so called the Wheeler-Rayburn Act. The purpose of this measure was to give the federal government greater power to regulate the nation's gas and electric industries. The act gave the Federal Power Commission authority to regulate the interstate production, transmission, and sale of electricity. It gave the Federal Trade Commission similar authority over gas. It gave the Securities and Exchange Commission authority to regulate the financial practices of public utility holding companies.

By regulating the financial operations of the public utility holding companies, the New Deal administration hoped to break up a trend toward monopoly in public utilities that had been gaining momentum in the 1920's and early 1930's. The measure was designed to prevent any holding company from controlling more than a "single integrated public utility system" operating in a single area of the country. Under the law utility companies were forbidden to engage in any business other than the production and distribution of gas or electric power. They were also forbidden to issue new stocks and bonds without first getting the approval of the Securities and Exchange Commission.

Finally, in a "death sentence" clause the Public Utility Holding Company Act gave the public utility holding companies five years to readjust their financial affairs. At the end of five years, any company that could not prove that it was actually distributing gas or electricity in a given localized area would be dissolved.

The TVA and its objectives. With the creation of the Tennessee Valley Authority (TVA), Congress in 1933 launched the United States upon an experiment which had no parallel in American history. The scene of the experiment was the region drained by the Tennessee River and its tributaries (see map, page 708). This region, including parts of seven states, was larger than England and Scotland combined.

The Tennessee Valley Authority moved into this region with a plan for

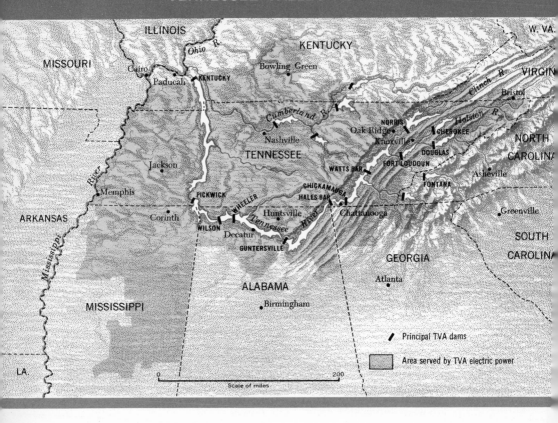

Principal TVA dams

Area served by TVA electric power

the unified development of all its resources. The purpose of the plan was to improve economic and social conditions; that is, the resources were to be developed for the benefit of the people who lived in the valley, as well as for the benefit of all the people of the United States. After a decade of trial and error, New Dealers justified their enthusiasm over the TVA program by pointing to several accomplishments.

Power development. High on the list of achievements of which the TVA enthusiasts were especially proud was the construction of 21 large dams on the Tennessee River and its major tributaries (see map, this page) and thousands of smaller dams on creeks and brooks. Power plants had been erected to convert the "white coal" of the river into vast quantities of electricity. From these federally owned power plants, high-voltage transmission lines fanned

out to cover the region with a network of wires leading into farmhouses in even the most remote valleys. Whereas in 1935 only one in every hundred homes in the state of Mississippi had electricity, by 1945 twenty homes out of a hundred were wired. The per capita consumption of electric power in the TVA region was 50 per cent higher than the average for the entire United States. Moreover, rates for electric power had been cut by about one third.

Flood control. The TVA dams were also planned as part of a system of flood control. Into a central control room now come daily reports from thousands of observers all over the valley, as well as radio reports from automatic rain gauges located in inaccessible spots. These reports tell of the amount of rainfall and the volume of water flowing in each brook, creek, and river. Buttons are pushed, sluice gates in great dams open or close, and millions of tons of water are released or stored for future use.

Prevention of soil erosion. Hand in hand with flood control has gone a program to prevent soil erosion and restore the fertility of the land. Millions of trees have been planted. Their roots hold the soil in place, and their leaves pile up year after year and absorb and hold the rain and melted snow. Fertilizer produced by the electric power of TVA dams has been sold at cost to the farmers of the Tennessee Valley. Agents from the Department of Agriculture have helped the farmers by teaching them the value of fertilizers, contour plowing, crop rotation, and the planting of soil-restoring crops.

Other purposes. The TVA program includes numerous other features. River transportation has been improved. New roads have been built. Factories have sprung up, providing jobs for thousands of workers. Hundreds of thousands of acres of land have been converted into public parks for Americans to enjoy. Lakes have been stocked with fish for the pleasure of vacationists and the profit of commercial fishermen. Schools, libraries, and hospitals have been constructed.

Criticisms of the TVA. This is one side of the story. There is also another side. The private power companies, representing a 12-billion-dollar industry, bitterly fought the TVA. Spokesmen for the private power interests declared that the TVA was an unwarranted intervention by the federal government in private industry. They declared that it helped to swell the growing ranks of public officeholders. And they insisted that the lower rates charged by the TVA for its electric power were not the result of more efficient production. If the TVA paid taxes like all private industries, critics insisted, it would have to charge much more for its electricity. Advocates of the TVA believed that its rates should be used as a "yardstick" to govern the rates charged by private power producers. But, the private pow-

Fort Loudoun Dam extended navigation on the Tennessee River to Knoxville. TVA power was used by the nearby Oak Ridge atomic-energy center during and after World War II.

er companies insisted, the TVA was an unfair, "16-inch yardstick," and the cheap electricity that it generated was a gift from the taxpayers of the entire nation to the people of one region.

SECTION SURVEY

1. Show how the savings of Americans are protected by the (a) FDIC, (b) Federal Reserve Board, and (c) SEC.

2. Discuss the three main purposes of the Social Security Act of 1935.

3. The New Dealers hoped "to break up a trend toward monopoly in public utilities." Explain this by referring to the provisions of the Public Utility Holding Company Act.

4. The TVA has been described as "an experiment which had no parallel in American history." Give four reasons that support this statement.

5. What arguments have been advanced against the TVA?

IDENTIFY: payroll tax, Rural Electrification Administration, "white coal," TVA "yardstick."

■ CHAPTER SURVEY

(For review, see Section Surveys, pages 697, 700, 702, 706, 709.)

Points to Discuss: 1. In his first Inaugural Address (March 4, 1933), Franklin Delano Roosevelt said: "The only thing we have to fear is fear itself." What did he mean?

2. Describe the relief program of the New Deal in the following areas: (a) food and clothing, and (b) work.

3. Show how the New Deal helped the farmer to (a) retain his home and (b) obtain a higher income.

4. Discuss the methods used by Roosevelt to restore the stability of the country's banks and currency. How effective were they?

5. The National Industrial Recovery Act became a "storm center." Why?

6. (a) List the economic reforms made by the New Deal. (b) Next to each, state briefly what it was intended to accomplish.

7. (a) List the social reforms undertaken by the New Deal. (b) Next to each, state briefly what it tried to do.

8. Why did the New Deal create so much controversy? Refer specifically to measures dealing with labor, farming, and the TVA.

Using Maps and Charts: 1. Use the chart on page 718 to answer the following: (a) Explain the increase in labor-union membership between 1900 and 1920. (b) Explain the decrease between 1920 and 1930.

2. Using the section on Franklin D. Roosevelt in the Chronology of Events (page 858), indicate the legislation designed to aid (a) young people, (b) organized labor, (c) bank depositors, (d) home owners, (e) the unemployed, (f) businessmen, and (g) investors.

3. Using charts 2 and 6 on pages 844–45, answer the following: (a) Explain the effects of the Great Depression on the distribution of income after 1929. (b) Explain the drop in elementary school enrollment and the rise in high school enrollment between 1930 and 1940.

4. Consulting chart 4 on page 828, (a) compare farm acres harvested and production per acre between 1920 and 1935, and (b) account for the ups and downs.

5. Using the map on page 708, (a) identify the states included in the TVA project, (b) indicate the areas where TVA electricity is used, and (c) indicate the significance of Oak Ridge.

6. Using charts 3 and 4 on pages 840–41, answer the following: (a) Compare the rates of the Reciprocal Trade Agreements Act of 1934 with the tariffs that preceded it. (b) Do you see a relationship between the relatively low rates under the reciprocal trade agreements and the increase in exports and imports beginning in 1940? (c) Did other factors promote an increase?

Consulting the Sources: F. D. Roosevelt's First Inaugural, Commager and Nevins, *The Heritage of America*, No. 250.

■ TRACING THE MAIN IDEAS

When Franklin D. Roosevelt became President of the United States in 1933, the nation was in the depths of the worst depression it had ever experienced. Roosevelt, a person of great energy and overwhelming enthusiasm, took, at least publicly, an optimistic view of the situation.

Surrounding himself with people who for the most part shared his own views about the nation's problems, Roosevelt immediately opened a three-pronged attack upon the depression. In a series of relief measures, Congress, led by the administration, tried to provide adequate food, clothing, and shelter for the millions of unemployed and needy Americans. In a second series of recovery measures, Congress attempted to revive the nation's industrial machine and replace the nation's economy on a solid foundation. In a third series of reform measures, Congress undertook to strengthen the economic system by correcting what the New Dealers believed to be basic weaknesses.

The Great Experiment Goes on Trial

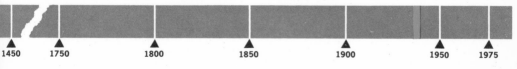

PRESIDENT ROOSEVELT CAMPAIGNING - 1936

By 1936 the United States was beginning to recover from the Great Depression. National income had risen sharply since 1932, having jumped from a low of less than 47 billion dollars to almost 70 billion. Industrial production, once again on the rise, was double that of 1932. These and other figures gave convincing proof that in four years the nation had made considerable progress in its battle against the depression.

How much this progress could be attributed to the New Deal was, however, an open question. Some Americans, including large numbers of Republicans, argued that progress had been made in spite of the New Deal. Others, including many Democrats, argued that the New Deal had saved the country from complete catastrophe and had started it on the road to recovery.

But the depression was far from conquered. In 1936 three and one half million people were still working on government relief projects. Nine million men and women were still unemployed. Many factories and mines were still closed or were working at far less than full capacity. Although the country was on the road to recovery, the American people still faced many problems.

Such was the situation when in 1936 the voters entered another Presidential election year. Should Roosevelt be reelected? Should the New Deal be continued? These were the big questions facing the voters.

As you will see, Roosevelt won by an overwhelming majority. But, as you will also see, during his second term in office he faced mounting problems. In a real sense the New Deal was on trial.

AS THE STORY DEVELOPS

1. The New Deal battles against mounting opposition.
2. The reform program of the New Deal moves forward.
3. The momentum of the New Deal begins to slow down.

1450   1750   1800   1850   1900   1950   1975

The New Deal battles against mounting opposition

During 1936 and 1937 President Roosevelt and the supporters of the New Deal ran into growing difficulties. They fought back vigorously and successfully in the 1936 Presidential election campaign, struggled to "reform" the Supreme Court, and ran head on into a business slump.

Roosevelt campaign promises. Meeting in Philadelphia in June 1936, the Democratic National Convention enthusiastically renominated Roosevelt for a second term, and again chose John Nance Garner of Texas as his running mate. The delegates also drafted a platform that contained strong endorsement of the New Deal.

During the campaign Roosevelt again showed his great skill in rallying widespread support. He emphasized the gains made in production and employment during his first term. Business activity, he declared, was almost normal again, thanks to "pump priming." He promised to balance the budget and, at the same time, warned that it was even more important "to balance the human budget." Great steps, he repeated, had been taken toward that goal. But, he added, the New Deal still had a long, hard road to follow. "We have only just begun to fight," he promised.

Roosevelt's supporters. Lined up behind the President were not only most members of his own party, but also countless rank-and-file Republicans. Most of the progressive Republican leaders who had supported him in 1932 continued to do so. Labor was overwhelmingly for the President who had done so much to advance its interests. Many farmers, remembering the benefits that they had received during the past four years, backed the President. One sixth of the people had received federal money, directly or indirectly, for relief; they, too, supported Roosevelt. The local Democratic political ma-chines, some of which had used relief money to strengthen their own power, stood solidly for the re-election of the entire Democratic ticket.

Roosevelt's critics. But the President and the New Deal also had many critics, including a number of influential members of the President's own party, who "took a walk" from the party and supported the Republican candidate. Roosevelt's Democratic opponents included such leading political figures as John W. Davis, the Democratic Presidential candidate in 1924; John J. Raskob, chairman of the Democratic National Committee in 1928; and "Al" Smith, the Democratic candidate for the Presidency in 1928. Roosevelt's Republican critics included most big business leaders, many small businessmen who had suffered under the NRA, bankers, private power companies, great newspapers, and many professional men.

Opponents of President Roosevelt sometimes referred to him as "that man in the White House" and likened him to a dictator. Maintaining that he was undermining the Constitution, they pointed out that the Supreme Court had declared unconstitutional seven out of nine important New Deal measures. They insisted that the American way of life —individualism, free enterprise, and private property—was being thrown overboard for socialism and regimentation. Roosevelt's critics denied that the New Deal had restored prosperity. They pointed to continued unemployment. They made much of the fact that the administration had piled up a huge national debt of over 33 billion dollars and had failed to balance the budget.

The Republican candidate and promises. The Republican leaders, however, could not hope to win the election of 1936 merely by opposing the New Deal. Their only chance to win was to secure the votes of a great many people who had actually been helped by the New Deal. In an effort to secure these votes, they nominated friendly, thrifty Governor Alfred M. Landon of Kansas for President.

Governor Landon was considered a "liberal" Republican. Although he was in the oil business, he had the support of many farmers who knew him and trusted his judgment. Moreover, in a period when most states and the federal government had been piling up huge debts, Governor Landon had been able to balance the Kansas budget.

The Republican platform promised to continue agricultural benefits to farmers, to befriend labor, and to keep the controls on the stock markets and on reckless speculation. The Republicans admitted that these were all New Deal measures, but they insisted that the Republican Party could carry them out more effectively and more economically than the Democrats. The Republicans also promised to balance the budget and to restore to the states certain powers that the federal government had seized in order to carry out the New Deal program. Thus the Republicans adopted what had traditionally been the Democratic states' rights position.

Roosevelt wins. The election campaign was filled with angry charges and countercharges. Into the campaign the Republicans poured more than 9 million dollars, the Democrats somewhat more than half that amount. Keen popular interest was reflected in the vote, which totaled more than 45 million.

Roosevelt and Garner swept the country with an electoral vote of 523 to 8 in their favor. Only Maine and Vermont cast electoral ballots for Landon. Roosevelt's popular vote was also impressive —27,476,673 to Landon's 16,679,583. Moreover, the Democrats won or kept control of all but six governorships and maintained their leadership of both houses of Congress. Not since the re-election of President Monroe in 1820 had a Presidential candidate won such overwhelming backing from voters.

Roosevelt criticizes the Court. In 1937, early in his second term,° President

....
° Under the Twentieth Amendment to the Constitution, adopted in 1933, the beginning of the Presidential term of office was advanced from March 4 to January 20.

■ Governor Alfred Landon of Kansas is here concluding his bid for the Presidency on the Republican ticket. He was popular, but he lost the election.

Roosevelt opened an attack upon the Supreme Court. Roosevelt was upset because the Court had set aside as unconstitutional the National Industrial Recovery Act (page 703), the Agricultural Adjustment Act (page 698), and five other important New Deal laws. He was also disturbed because the Court had declared unconstitutional a number of important state laws, among them a New York state measure providing minimum wages for women and children. Moreover, the federal courts had used the power of the injunction to block federal agencies from carrying out a number of New Deal measures.

Roosevelt declared that all too often certain members of the Supreme Court thought in terms of the "horse and buggy" era. He concluded that the advanced age of most of the justices kept them from thinking about problems in terms of modern needs. "A dead hand was being laid upon this whole program of progress," the President later declared. It was, he said, the hand of the Supreme Court of the United States.

Roosevelt seeks Court "reform." On February 5, 1937, in a special message to Congress, President Roosevelt submitted a plan for reorganizing the federal judiciary. He asked Congress for the power to appoint an extra justice

THE "HINDENBURG" DISASTER

Early in May 1936, the German dirigible *Hindenburg* captured the imagination of people throughout the world when it began to carry passengers on the first commercial transatlantic air route in history. The giant craft, 803 feet long and 135 feet high, was sustained in the air by 7 million cubic feet of highly inflammable hydrogen gas. It contained a luxurious dining room, a lounge bar, shower baths, and cabins with berths and running water. Its first flight established a transatlantic record by crossing from Germany to Lakehurst, New Jersey, in 61 hours and 38 seconds.

For a year the *Hindenburg* carried passengers back and forth across the Atlantic. Then, in one flaming moment on May 17, 1937, disaster struck. The huge craft was approaching the mooring mast at Lakehurst. Crowds of spectators lined the edge of the landing field as the giant silver-colored ship slowly settled toward the earth. Suddenly the airship burst into flames which shot 500 feet in the sky; the metal framework, stripped of its covering, twisted and buckled; and, while the spectators watched in horror, passengers leaped from windows, dropping through the flames to the ground, where many of them were dragged to safety by heroic rescuers.

In 32 seconds it was all over. Thirty-six passengers had perished. A pile of twisted metal and smoking ruins was all that remained of the airship.

Helium gas, which the Germans did not possess, would have prevented the catastrophe, for helium would not have exploded. But the damage was done, and the pictures of the disaster, caught by newsreel cameras and shown to millions on movie screens, turned the public against this type of air transportation. May 17, 1937, marked the final transition from gas-borne airships to the heavier-than-air craft now flying.

to the Supreme Court for each existing justice who did not retire upon reaching the age of seventy. In this way, the Court might be increased from nine to a maximum of fifteen members. When Roosevelt made this proposal, six of the nine justices were seventy years of age or older. Roosevelt's proposal, therefore, would have let him appoint six new justices more favorable to the New Deal point of view.

Changes in the Supreme Court. Although the President fought vigorously for his "reform" proposal, he lost the battle. His own party refused to support him in Congress, and public opinion ran strongly against him. In general, people did not want to run the danger of destroying the delicate balance of legislative, executive, and judicial powers that the Founding Fathers had written into the Constitution.

But although Roosevelt lost the battle for Court reform, in the end he gained most of the things for which he had fought. In the first place, the Court began to approve important New Deal measures. The National Labor Relations Act (page 706) and the Social Security Act (same page) were tested and found constitutional. Moreover, the Court gave its blessing to an act passed by the state of Washington establishing minimum pay for women and children. This act was almost identical to the one of New York state that the Court had earlier declared unconstitutional.

Had the Court suddenly come to realize that it might be well to approve certain popular legislation in order to prevent a drastic reform of the Court itself? Many Americans believed that such was the case.

Moreover, during Roosevelt's second administration the membership of the Court changed almost completely. A whole series of vacancies occurred through death and retirement. By 1941 Roosevelt had been given the opportunity to replace all but two of the original members with justices who appeared to be more sympathetic to New Deal legislation.

The business slump of 1937–38. Early in 1937, while the issue of the Supreme Court was being argued in villages, towns, and cities across the land, the nation's industrial machinery once again began to slow down. By the autumn of 1937, factories in growing numbers were closing down. Unemployment was rising. It began to look as if the gains of the past four years had been lost.

The Democrats spoke of what was taking place as a *recession,* a term meaning a business slump not as severe as a "depression." The Republicans, on the other hand, called it the "Roosevelt depression." Roosevelt's opponents blamed the Democrats and their New Deal program for the business slump, just as the Democrats in 1931 had blamed the Republicans for the Great Depression.

Politics aside, there was fairly widespread agreement on the major cause of the slump. Back in 1932, when he was first running for election, Roosevelt had promised to balance the budget. Instead of doing this, however, his administration had piled up the largest national debt in history. The Republicans, as you have seen, had made the most of this fact in the election campaign of 1936. But it was not only the Republicans who had attacked Roosevelt for his failure to balance the budget. Many Democrats and friends of the New Deal had become increasingly uneasy about the mounting debt.

Mindful of the growing criticism, the New Deal administration had seized the first chance to reduce expenditures. In 1936, with business conditions steadily improving, the administration had begun to cut expenditures for relief and public works. Unfortunately, at the time private industry was not yet strong enough to give jobs to the men and women dropped from relief projects. Once again, therefore, the nation's economic system started on a downward spiral.

New "pump priming." Fortunately, measures adopted to fight the Great Depression automatically began to act as brakes against the 1937–38 recession. More than 2,000,000 wage earners in 25 states, protected by the Social Security Act, began to collect unemployment insurance. The new banking laws protected the savings of depositors. And numerous government agencies were ready to lend money to business, to construct public works, and thus to create new jobs.

President Roosevelt and Congress began once again to "prime the economic pump" by increasing government lending and spending. The Reconstruction Finance Corporation again came to the rescue of business enterprises in distress. The WPA doubled the number of people at work on its projects, increasing the number of workers on its payroll from 1,500,000 to 3,000,000. As the months passed, it began to be clear that the downward spiral of the recession had been reversed. By the end of 1938, the nation's economic machinery was once again beginning to pick up speed.

The Democrats were quick to claim another victory for the New Deal. The Republicans, on the other hand, insisted again that recovery had come in spite of the New Deal. And many Americans, Democrats and Republicans alike, continued to express alarm at the ever-growing national debt.

✔ **SECTION SURVEY**

1. (a) Contrast the views of Roosevelt's friends and critics in 1936. (b) Indicate the parties, candidates, issues, and results of the 1936 election.

2. (a) What reasons did Roosevelt give in calling for a reorganization of the Supreme Court? (b) In what sense might he have been said to have achieved his goal even though he apparently lost?

3. Show how the measures adopted to combat the Great Depression acted as brakes against the recession which occurred in 1937–38.

IDENTIFY: "Roosevelt depression"; John Raskob, Alfred E. Landon.

2 The reform program of the New Deal moves forward

During the 1936 election campaign President Roosevelt had promised the voters that, if re-elected, he would continue the New Deal. Neither the business recession of 1937–38 nor the mounting criticism of his policies prevented Roosevelt from continuing his program.

Growth of the A.F. of L. As you have seen (page 706), the Wagner Act of 1935 guaranteed to workers the right of collective bargaining and forbade employers to discriminate in any way against organized labor. Under the protection of this law, the American Federation of Labor launched a vigorous campaign to recruit new members. During its recruiting campaign the A.F. of L. began to show a lively interest in organizing unskilled workers in the mass production industries—steel, automobiles, aluminum, aircraft, utilities. But the A.F. of L. drive to organize unskilled workers did not move rapidly enough to please many labor leaders.

Organization of the CIO. Growing impatience with the A.F. of L. finally led John L. Lewis, powerful head of the United Mine Workers, and a group of like-minded labor leaders to organize

the Committee for Industrial Organization in 1935. The CIO, as it was called, immediately launched a great drive to organize workers in the automobile, steel, rubber, oil, radio, and other industries in industrial unions. The new industrial unions, sometimes called *vertical* unions, included all workers, skilled and unskilled, in an industry. The United Automobile Workers (UAW), for example, represented all the workers in the automotive plants. Whereas, in earlier times, workers in the automobile industry had negotiated contracts through many separate unions—electrical, welding, metalworking, and the like—now they negotiated as a single powerful organization.

Within a few months the CIO had become a lively rival of the older A.F. of L. Disturbed by the growing influence of this new organization, A.F. of L. leaders ordered the CIO to disband. When John L. Lewis and other CIO leaders refused to obey this order, the A.F. of L. expelled them for "insurrection." But the CIO continued to operate, and in May 1938 it reorganized as a separate body, the Congress of Industrial Organizations (still called CIO), with John L. Lewis as its first president. By 1940, when Philip Murray succeeded Lewis as president, the CIO had a membership of 3,625,000, a figure roughly equal to that of the older A.F. of L.

The sit-down strike. Meanwhile, spirited organizational campaigns by both the A.F. of L. and the CIO resulted in a wave of strikes that reached a peak in 1937 and 1938.

In November 1936 several hundred workers in the General Motors plants at Flint, Michigan, staged a *sit-down strike*. Instead of leaving the plant and organizing picket lines in the traditional method of strike operations, the workers simply sat down in front of their machines and announced that they would not leave until management granted them the contract that they demanded.

The sit-down strike, which made it impossible for management to bring in

■ John L. Lewis worked long toward many goals, including greater safety in mines. In 1957 he soberly inspected results of an Illinois coal-mine disaster.

strikebreakers, proved extremely effective. Within a few months this relatively new labor weapon spread to steel, oil refining, textile, and shipbuilding plants and involved more than half a million workers. All of the leading automobile manufacturers except Ford now recognized the United Automobile Workers, the powerful new CIO union, as bargaining agent for the automobile industry. The United States Steel Corporation, long a foe of unions, finally accepted the CIO steelworkers' union as the bargaining agent of the steelworkers. The CIO also organized the workers in farm machinery plants and in many other industries and made some headway in persuading agricultural laborers to join a CIO union.

Effective though it was, the sit-down strike was only one of the reasons for the rapid growth of the CIO. After the Supreme Court in 1939 ruled that sit-down strikes were illegal, the CIO—as well as the A.F. of L.—continued to forge ahead. In general, it was the Wagner Act of 1935 with its guarantee of the right to collective bargaining that gave organized labor its great opportunity.

Jurisdictional strikes. Much of the labor unrest during the late 1930's sprang from bitter rivalry between the A.F. of L. and the CIO. In many instances representatives of both organizations tried to unionize the same workers in the same plant. Disputes arose over which one had the "jurisdiction," or right, to enroll a particular group of workers, and sometimes these disputes led to *jurisdictional strikes*. Management thus was put in a difficult spot, for if it recognized the CIO union, the A.F. of L. workers would go out on strike; if it recognized the A.F. of L. union, the CIO workers would go out on strike; and if it refused to recognize either union, it would run the risk of violating the Wagner Act!

The New Deal administration in general followed a "hands-off" policy in the conflicts between the A.F. of L. and the CIO unions, though many people felt that the National Labor Relations Board favored the CIO. As the problem of jurisdictional strikes became increasingly serious, however, the NLRB, with the support of President Roosevelt, tried with increasing success to settle disputes between the two rival labor organizations, to prevent strikes, and to mediate strikes. The great wave of strikes that reached its peak in 1937 and 1938 diminished in the following years as both labor and management reluctantly came to accept the intervention of the federal government.

The Fair Labor Standards Act. Largely as a result of the labor policies and legislation of the New Deal, organized labor became a powerful force in the country during the 1930's. But the New Deal did not merely encourage and support organized workers. In the special session of Congress that the President called in the autumn of 1937 to check the business recession, he proposed among other measures the Fair Labor Standards Act, sometimes called the Wages and Hours Law.

This act was to promote re-employment and to increase the purchasing power of all workers, organized and unorganized. The bill proposed a vast extension of federal control over industry. In the President's words, it would put "a floor below which wages shall not fall, and a ceiling beyond which the hours of industrial labor shall not rise."

Stubborn opposition quickly developed to the Fair Labor Standards Act. Many employers opposed the bill on the ground that it was unwarranted and unwise interference by the government. But the bill was pushed through Congress with the support of friends of labor and of northern industrialists. The latter believed that they would find it easier to meet the competition of southern manufacturers, with their low wage rates, if a nationwide minimum wage scale existed.

The Fair Labor Standards Act went into effect in October 1938. It provided that a legal maximum work week of 44 hours in 1938 be decreased to 40 hours

Labor Union Membership

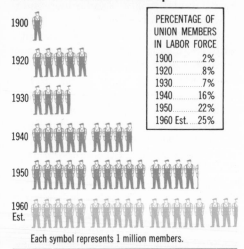

1900

1920

1930

1940

1950

1960
Est.

PERCENTAGE OF UNION MEMBERS IN LABOR FORCE	
1900	2%
1920	8%
1930	7%
1940	16%
1950	22%
1960 Est.	25%

Each symbol represents 1 million members.

by 1940, with time-and-a-half pay for overtime. It also provided that minimum wages of 25 cents an hour in 1938 be increased to 40 cents an hour by 1945. It prohibited the employment of children under sixteen in industries producing goods for interstate commerce. The Department of Labor was charged with enforcing the act.

Importance of the act. The Fair Labor Standards Act was important for several reasons. First, it marked a great extension of the federal government's control over industry. Second, it aimed not only to stimulate employment by providing for a shorter working day, but also to increase the purchasing power of a large part of labor. Third, the act made it unnecessary for the country to amend the Constitution in order to prohibit child labor. Fourth, it encouraged social legislation by the states, since it removed some of the most marked differences in hours and wages between the North and the South. Fifth, it brought the benefit of federal support to the unorganized as well as to the organized workers of the nation.

Although the Fair Labor Standards Act affected only workers employed in interstate industries, by 1940 about 13 million men and women were benefiting

from the law. The Wagner Act of 1935 and the Fair Labor Standards Act of 1938 were the underpinning of the New Deal's program to reform the conditions of labor in the United States. Roosevelt hailed the new law as being, after the Social Security Act, "the most far-sighted program for the benefit of workers ever adopted in this or in any other country."

The Soil Conservation and Domestic Allotment Act. Equally far-reaching were New Deal measures to improve the economic position of the nation's farmers. When in 1936 the Supreme Court ruled against the Agricultural Adjustment Act of 1933 (page 698), Congress promptly passed another law.

The Soil Conservation and Domestic Allotment Act of 1936 gave benefit payments to farmers who co-operated with the government in a soil conservation program. Farmers who agreed to participate in the program leased part of their acreage to the government. Under the supervision of state farm agencies, the farmers then undertook to restore the fertility of the leased land by practicing the best conservation measures, by liberal use of fertilizer, and by sowing soil-restoring plants, such as clover. In return for these efforts, the farmers received a certain sum of money for every acre they withdrew from production.

By this means the government hoped to develop nationwide knowledge of sound conservation practices. Equally important, by limiting production the government hoped to raise the prices of farm products.

The Bankhead-Jones Act. With the Bankhead-Jones Farm Tenant Act of 1937, the New Deal administration undertook to help tenant farmers, sharecroppers, and migratory farm workers, who moved from place to place in search of jobs. The new law created the Farm Security Administration (FSA). It authorized the FSA to lend money at low interest rates to tenant farmers, sharecroppers, and farm laborers who wished to buy farms. Applications for these loans had to be approved by committees of local farmers. Farmers who received the loans had 40 years to repay them. By 1940, 13,000 farmers were buying land through the FSA.

In addition, the FSA gave relief to needy farm families. It also built self-managed camps for migratory workers.

The Agricultural Adjustment Act of 1938. But the heart of the New Deal agricultural reform program was the second Agricultural Adjustment Act, passed in 1938. This act contained a number of important provisions:

(1) It provided benefit payments to farmers in proportion to the number of acres that they withdrew from production and planted in soil-conserving crops.

(2) The government was authorized to decide the amount of corn, wheat, rice, cotton, tobacco, and other staple crops that could be marketed each year. With the approval of two thirds of the producers of these commodities in each locality, the government then assigned a certain allotment to each farmer. If he exceeded this allotment, he had to pay a fine when he marketed such crops during a time of surplus.

(3) When, in spite of restricted planting, there were large harvests, the surpluses were stored by the government for eventual release in "lean" years. But the farmer did not lose his income from the surplus crops. The government, operating through the Commodity Credit Corporation, gave him "commodity loans" on all the produce he placed in storage.

The amount of these loans was fixed at slightly below *parity*—that is, below a figure based on average prices of each of the commodities for the period from August 1909 to July 1914. When the market price of a commodity rose to the "parity" level, the farmer was to sell the stored crop and repay the loan. If the market price remained below "parity," the farmer kept the money and the government kept his crop. By this method—called the "ever-normal granary plan"—the government attempted to keep the price of agricultural products at a steady level, thus benefiting both farmers and consumers. It was a program of "price supports based on parity."

(4) The act also authorized the government to insure wheat crops against drought, flood, hail, and plant diseases.

Evaluating the farm program. In 1932, in the depths of the Great Depression, farm income had sunk to a low of less than 5 billion dollars. By 1938 it had risen to more than 8 billion. By 1940 it totaled more than 9 billion.

But critics were quick to point out that the increased income came from higher prices paid by consumers and from subsidies paid by the government—with taxpayers' money. These critics continued to charge that "money had been taken from Peter to pay Paul."

Critics, including many farmers, also resented increasing government controls over production. They were also fearful that continued grants and subsidies would destroy the farmer's independence.

Critics also charged that, as a result of the government's price support program, America's agricultural products were losing out in foreign markets. This decrease in exports, the critics declared, was a matter of serious concern for the entire nation.

All of these criticisms vanished, at least temporarily, when in 1941 the United States was plunged into World War II. Then, as friends of the New Deal were quick to point out, the country owed much to the farm legislation of the 1930's. This legislation had improved the economic condition of a large group of Americans. It had increased the fertility of millions of acres of land. It had made it possible for the United States to feed a large portion of the war-devastated world.

Shelter for low-income groups. During his second term in office, President Roosevelt also continued his attack upon the housing problem. The National Housing Act of 1937, usually called the Wagner-Steagall Act, had two aims: (1) to stimulate business revival

THE WORLD OF TOMORROW

In the early summer of 1939, a great World's Fair opened on what had recently been marshland on the outskirts of New York City. The flags of almost all the nations on the face of the earth waved above "The World of Tomorrow," and visitors, approaching the fair, saw great structures of glass and metal with vaulted roofs glittering in the sunlight.

Sixty nations had erected pavilions and sent exhibits valued at more than 100 million dollars. Among the great nations, only Germany and China were not represented. Exhibits were devoted to industry, labor, health, medicine, the arts, education, government, and recreation. Where, only a few months before, cattails had swayed in the breeze and frogs had claimed the marshland as their own, there was a city of marvels, a monument to man's ingenuity.

Shortly after the fair opened, Hitler's armored divisions rolled across Poland, and World War II began. Thus, "The World of Tomorrow" became to some a mockery of man's hopes and aspirations. But to others the fair stood as a symbol and a promise of what the world might yet achieve.

by government spending for the construction of houses; and (2) to "remedy the unsafe and unsatisfactory housing conditions and the acute shortage of decent, safe, and sanitary dwellings for families of low income in rural and urban communities."

The National Housing Act created the United States Housing Authority (USHA), which took over the 51 low-cost housing projects that the PWA had sponsored. It also embarked on a far more ambitious program of housing construction. By 1941 the USHA had lent $750,000,000 for the construction of 161,162 housing units.

Other New Deal reforms. In 1938 Congress passed the Food, Drug, and Cosmetic Act, which replaced the earlier Pure Food and Drug Act of 1906 (page 553). The 1938 act required an adequate testing of new drugs before they were offered for sale. It also required manufacturers to list on the labels of their products the ingredients that the products contained. In addition, the Wheeler-Lea Act, also passed in 1938, prohibited manufacturers from making false or misleading claims in their advertising.

The following year, in 1939, Congress also tackled the thorny problem of improper political practices. The Hatch Act placed restrictions upon federal officeholders below the policy-making level in the executive branch of the government. Such officeholders were prohibited (1) from taking an active part in political campaigns, (2) from soliciting or accepting political contributions from workers on relief, and (3) from using their official positions to influence the course of Presidential or Congressional elections. In 1940 the Hatch Act was amended to include state and local government employees whose pay came completely or even partially from federal funds. The 1940 amendment also limited the amount of money a political party could spend in any one year to a maximum of $3,000,000, and the amount any individual could contribute to $5000 annually.

1. What conditions prompted the organization of the CIO?

2. Discuss three important ways in which the Fair Labor Standards Act has influenced labor conditions in the United States.

3. Show how each of the following aimed to improve the economic condition of farmers: (a) Soil Conservation and Domestic Allotment Act, (b) Bankhead-Jones Farm Tenant Act, and (c) Agricultural Adjustment Act of 1938.

4. Evaluate the New Deal farm program by writing a list of the arguments for and against it.

5. What steps did the New Dealers take to (a) provide homes for low-income families and (b) aid consumers?

IDENTIFY: vertical union, sit-down strike, jurisdictional strike, UAW, FSA, commodity loans, parity, "ever-normal granary plan," price supports, Hatch Act; John L. Lewis, Philip Murray.

3 The momentum of the New Deal begins to slow down

By the middle of President Roosevelt's second term, it was becoming evident that the President's influence was beginning to decline. In 1937, as you have seen, he had suffered a major defeat when he failed to push through Congress his bill for the reorganization of the Supreme Court. In the Congressional elections in the fall of 1938, he suffered an even more serious defeat.

Roosevelt fails to "purge" the Democratic Party. As the elections approached, Roosevelt decided to "liberalize" the Democratic Party and to "purge," or rid, Congress of those conservative Democrats who had voted against his reform program. Singling out by name several Democrats, he urged voters to defeat them at the polls.

Roosevelt's campaign to liberalize the Democratic Party failed. With only one exception all of the Congressmen whom Roosevelt had asked the people to retire from office were re-elected. Moreover, a great many new Democratic Congressmen who were opposed to the New Deal were chosen by the voters. To add to Roosevelt's dismay, the Republicans won additional seats in Congress, with the result that the Democrats barely kept their majority.

New Deal activities suspended. President Roosevelt, a shrewd politician, was quick to see the meaning of the 1938 elections. Realizing that the tide of public opinion was beginning to run against him, he began to suspend earlier New Deal activities. By 1939 Congress was cutting appropriations for many of the New Deal agencies, such as the WPA and the CCC.

As a result of the threatening world situation (Chapter 38), the PWA and the WPA were shifting their attention from public works to projects involving national defense, such as the building of airports, military highways, and barracks. Other New Deal agencies, such as the Civilian Conservation Corps and the National Youth Administration, brought their operations to an end when Congress cut off further appropriations. Although the Tennessee Valley Authority weathered attacks within and without Congress, the President's recommendation that similar projects be developed in six other areas of the country received little support. Nor did the efforts of Senator Wagner to advance a vast national health program fare any better.

The driving impulse of the New Deal to move forward had spent itself. Those who maintained that the reform objectives of the New Deal were still far from being realized faced stiffer and stiffer opposition and growing indifference from the public in general. This changed attitude toward the New Deal can be explained, in part at least, by recovery from the business recession of 1937–38 and by growing concern over the problem of national defense.

Roosevelt's financial policies opposed. Much of the opposition to the New Deal came from men and women who were convinced that Roosevelt's

financial policies were undermining the nation's economic system. With the return of better times, this group became increasingly large and outspoken.

The New Dealers supplied three different methods for their relief, recovery, and reform programs.

One method was inflation. Although Congress authorized President Roosevelt to print paper money, he never did so. He did, however, decrease the gold content of the dollar (page 700).

A second way was *deficit spending.* This meant that the government spent more than it received in taxes, with the result that the budget was unbalanced, or showed a deficit. President Hoover's administration had spent almost 3 billion dollars more than it received in income; and President Roosevelt had continued and greatly enlarged the na-

tional debt. In the 1930's the national debt increased from about 16 billion dollars to more than 40 billion dollars.

Men and women in both parties were highly critical of the failure of the Roosevelt administration to balance the budget. Businessmen in particular lost confidence in an administration that piled up a larger and larger national debt.

Another method by which the New Deal had financed its operations was by raising taxes. In 1935 the administration asked Congress to increase taxes on corporations and to levy taxes on gifts and inheritances. Critics called this a "soak the rich" proposal because it put a new tax burden upon the well-to-do. Despite strong opposition, however, Congress passed the Revenue Act of 1935, often called the Wealth Tax Act. With this measure Congress increased the income tax for individuals and large corporations and levied taxes on gifts and estates. Congress also imposed an "excess-profits tax" on corporations, with a maximum tax rate of 12 per cent on profits exceeding 15 per cent. But the revenue thus obtained did not balance the budget, and the national debt continued to grow.

In the Revenue Act of 1936, called the Undistributed Profits Tax Act, Congress moved still further in the direction of taxing corporation profits. It laid a steeply graduated tax on the undistributed profits of corporations; that is, on those profits which were not distributed to stockholders. Business bitterly complained that the new taxes would discourage new investments in business expansion and prevent the accumulation of surpluses for use in depression years.

In 1938, however, as a result of growing opposition to the New Deal, Congress began to reverse the taxation policy of earlier years. The Revenue Act of 1938 provided for a sharp reduction of corporation taxes. And in 1939 Congress abolished the undistributed profits tax. At the same time, however, it raised the corporation income tax to a maximum of 19 per cent. In addition, for the first time in history, Congress required employees of cities and states to pay taxes to the federal government.

Roosevelt runs for a third term. Despite the fact that Roosevelt's influence was weakening, and despite the fact that the two-term tradition for Presidents was widely accepted as part of the unwritten Constitution (page 171), Roosevelt decided to run for a third term. The President did not at first announce his decision, although he hinted that the critical foreign situation might compel him to be a candidate. But behind the scenes he quietly arranged matters so that it would have been almost impossible for anyone in the Democratic Party to run against him without his consent.

As a result of Roosevelt's influence in his own party, the Democratic convention chose him on the first ballot at Chicago in July 1940. It also, without general enthusiasm, accepted his Secretary of Agriculture, Henry A. Wallace of Iowa, formerly a Republican, as his running mate.

The Democratic platform promised to extend social security, to stress the low-cost housing program, and to advance government ownership of public utilities. It also promised to keep the country out of war and to send no armies abroad unless the nation were attacked.

Republicans nominate Willkie. The Republicans chose as their candidate Wendell L. Willkie, a New York lawyer who was president of the Commonwealth and Southern Utilities Company. Willkie had a long record of progressive sympathies. For instance, in 1932 he had voted for the Democratic candidate for the Presidency, Franklin D. Roosevelt. He favored many of the principles of the New Deal. But he believed that the New Deal had been administered in such a way as to endanger individualism, free enterprise, and democracy. On the other hand, Willkie had been the chief spokesman of the power companies in their fight against the TVA.

Warmhearted, engaging, and informal, Willkie proved a strong candidate.

The Republican platform condemned the New Deal for its "shifting, contradictory, and overlapping administrations and policies." It promised to revise the tax system in order to stimulate private enterprise and to promote prosperity. It also promised to keep the major New Deal reforms, but to administer the laws with greater efficiency and less waste. The Republicans also demanded a Constitutional Amendment that would limit Presidents to a maximum of two terms. Like the Democrats, the Republicans promised to keep America out of war unless the nation were attacked.

The campaign of 1940. The ominous threat of a second World War hung over the election campaign of 1940. In 1937, as you will see, Japan invaded China, and in the fall of 1939 Hitler plunged Europe into war. In the fall of 1940, while the American people were arguing domestic policies and preparing to cast their ballots in a peaceful election, Great Britain was fighting desperately for sheer survival.

Both Roosevelt and Willkie advocated a vigorous program of national defense. Both urged all aid to Great Britain short of war. In general, there was no great difference in their attitude toward the conflict raging abroad.

■ On the way to deliver his speech accepting the Republican nomination in 1940, Wendell Willkie was cheered in his home town of Elwood, Indiana.

INVASION FROM MARS

At eight o'clock on the evening of October 30, 1938, millions of radio listeners throughout the country heard the following announcement: "The Columbia Broadcasting System and its affiliated stations present Orson Welles and the Mercury Theater of the Air in *The War of the Worlds*, by H. G. Wells."

There was a brief pause, followed by a weather report. Then an announcer declared that the program would be continued from a New York hotel. A jazz band came on the air. Suddenly the music stopped. An announcer, his voice tense and anxious, broke in to declare that a professor had just observed a series of explosions on Mars. Other announcements followed in rapid order. A meteor had landed near Princeton, New Jersey. Fifteen hundred people had been killed. No, it wasn't a meteor. It was a spaceship from Mars. Martian creatures were emerging. They were armed with death rays. They had come to wage war against the people living on earth.

An untold number of listeners were seized with panic. Some fell to their knees and began to pray. Others gathered their families, rushed from their homes, and fled on foot or by car into the night.

And yet it was only a radio play. CBS stated this fact clearly at four different spots in the hour-long program. Numerous explanations were advanced for this outburst of mass hysteria. But one thing was clear—the extraordinary power of radio broadcasting.

The election returns. Roosevelt won a sweeping victory in an election in which more Americans voted than in any previous contest in American history. But the returns clearly showed that the President had lost some of his earlier popularity. In general, the Democrats lost more heavily in the Middle West, where Willkie showed his chief strength. But the Democrats made up for these losses by strengthening their support in the cities of the East, where the labor vote counted heavily. Roosevelt's 60 per cent popular majority in the election of 1936 was reduced to just under 55 per cent in the 1940 election. In round numbers this meant that 27 million Americans voted for Roosevelt, and 22 million for Willkie. The popular vote was, therefore, much closer than was indicated by the vote in the Electoral College, where Willkie polled only 82 electoral votes to Roosevelt's 449. Although the Democrats retained their control of Congress, the Republicans increased their strength in both the national and state legislatures.

During Roosevelt's third term, domestic issues, especially the New Deal program of relief, recovery, and reform, received less attention as foreign problems and war itself absorbed the energies of both the government and the people. So a great period of reform in American history came to an end. Whether this suspension of reform activities was the result of war, or whether the reform impulse had spent itself, remains an unanswered question.

On domestic issues, however, they differed sharply, with Willkie attacking Roosevelt for irresponsibility and Roosevelt attacking Willkie for "unwitting falsifications of fact." Willkie traveled 30,000 miles through 34 states in a whirlwind campaign that, toward the end, left him hoarse and almost voiceless. Roosevelt, on the other hand, limited himself to a few addresses.

SECTION SURVEY

1. By 1938 "The driving impulse of the New Deal to move forward had spent itself." Explain.

2. (a) Describe the three methods used by the New Dealers to raise money. (b) Why were these methods criticized?

3. Discuss the historical significance of Roosevelt's decision to run for a third term.

4. Give the parties, candidates, issues, and results of the election of 1940.

IDENTIFY: purge, deficit spending, national debt; Wallace, Willkie.

Points to Discuss: 1. Discuss the reasons for Roosevelt's victory in the Presidential election of 1936.

2. (a) Why did Roosevelt try to reform the Supreme Court? (b) Give reasons for the failure of his plan. (c) What position would you have taken on the issue? Give arguments to support your opinion on this matter.

3. It was the Wagner Act of 1935 (pages 705–06) with its guarantee of the right to collective bargaining that gave organized labor its great opportunity. Explain why this was so.

4. The Wagner Act of 1935 and Fair Labor Standards Act of 1938 were the underpinning of the New Deal's program to improve conditions of labor. Discuss the significance of this statement.

5. (a) How did the Agricultural Adjustment Act of 1938 aim to improve the economic position of the farmer? (b) What is your opinion of this law as a permanent solution of the farm problem?

6. Summarize the various ways in which the New Deal tried to help the following groups: (a) the consumer, (b) the low-income families on farms and in the cities,

(c) young people, (d) the aged, and (e) workingmen.

7. Compare (a) the parties, (b) the candidates, (c) the issues, and (d) the results in the elections of 1936 and 1940.

8. Why was the New Deal largely suspended after 1938?

9. Why were so many Americans critical of the way that the New Deal was being financed?

10. Should the federal government engage in "pump priming"? Justify your position.

Using Charts: 1. Answer the following questions based on the chart on page 718: (a) Explain the increase in labor-union membership between 1930 and 1940. (b) Why is it that in 1940 only 16% of the labor force belonged to unions?

Consulting the Sources: For Roosevelt's Court Message and editorial comment on his plan, see *Problems in American Civilization*, "Franklin D. Roosevelt and the Supreme Court," Heath History Series, pp. 17–34.

■ TRACING THE MAIN IDEAS

By 1936 the New Deal program faced a large and growing body of opposition, some of which came from within the Democratic Party itself. Despite this opposition President Franklin D. Roosevelt was re-elected by an even larger majority than he had won in 1932.

In his Inaugural Address the President admitted that the New Deal had not yet accomplished many of its objectives. As he said, the New Deal had not yet reached "the promised land."

The major New Deal reforms during Roosevelt's second administration were designed to improve the lot of the wage earner and the farmer and to provide better housing for middle-income and lower-income families. These and other measures were extremely unpopular with large numbers of Americans.

As the years passed, opposition to the New Deal program began to mount. Many critics felt that the government was interfering too much with the long-established rights of free enterprise and, in so doing, was threatening individualism and democracy.

By the end of 1938, the opposition had become so strong that President Roosevelt decided to postpone other far-reaching reforms that he had been considering. Indeed, during 1939, 1940, and 1941 the administration began to suspend the activities of several New Deal agencies.

Another reason for the President's decision to postpone the reform program was his growing concern over international affairs. This concern, as you will see, was well founded.

The Nation Moves from Isolationism into War

ROOSEVELT AND CHURCHILL MEET AT SEA FOR ATLANTIC CHARTER CONFERENCE

I N 1933, when Franklin Delano Roosevelt became President for the first time, it was clear that few Presidents had entered office under more unfavorable circumstances.

The Great Depression, the worst depression the country has ever experienced, was becoming worse week by week, not only in the United States but throughout the world.

Equally disturbing was the growth of warlike dictatorships in Asia and Europe. To American dismay, the Japanese war machine had already rolled across the borders of Manchuria and, as you have seen, wrested that province from the Chinese. But there was no way for President-elect Roosevelt or anyone else to foresee that in 1933 Hitler would win control of Germany; that by 1936 a powerful German army would move into the Rhineland in outright defiance of the Versailles Treaty; and that by 1940 Hitler's Nazis, Mussolini's Fascists,

and the Japanese war lords would have plunged the world into the most devastating conflict in history.

During the 1930's the United States took an increasingly active interest in foreign affairs. It recognized the Soviet Union. It made provisions to grant independence to the Filipinos. It expanded the Good Neighbor policy. And, although the United States tried desperately to remain neutral in a war-torn world, by the end of 1941 the American people found themselves playing a leading role in the struggle against the dictator nations.

AS THE STORY DEVELOPS

1. The United States broadens its relations with other countries.
2. The United States tries to follow a policy of isolationism.
3. The United States finds isolationism difficult to maintain.
4. The United States becomes involved in World War II.

1450   1750   1800   1850   1900   1950   1975

1 The United States broadens its relations with other countries

American foreign policy in the 1930's was influenced by two basic considerations: (1) the Great Depression at home and abroad and (2) the rising threat of dictatorships in Europe and Asia. Both of these developments played a part in nearly every decision made in Washington during these troubled years.

Recognition of the Soviet Union. In 1933, during the first year of the New Deal administration, the United States recognized the Soviet Union. Those who favored this move gave a number of reasons for reversing America's long-established policy toward the Soviet Union. They argued that it was only realistic to recognize a regime that had maintained itself in power for 16 years. They pointed out that an increased flow of trade between the two countries would be advantageous to the United States and might help, at least in a small way, to revive American business. They reminded their fellow Americans that the Soviet Union and the United States shared a common concern about the threat of Japanese aggression.

In reply to these arguments, the opponents of recognition pointed out that the Communists made no secret of their dream of world conquest. But this objection was met when the Soviet Union promised to stop all propaganda activities in the United States. As it turned out, the Soviet rulers did not keep their promise. Moreover, United States recognition of the Soviet Union did not result in a substantial increase in trade between the two countries.

Steps toward Philippine independence. Much happier in its outcome was America's policy in regard to the Philippines. In the Jones Act of 1916, as you have seen (page 595), the Woodrow Wilson administration promised to give the Philippines their independence. During the 1920's one administration after another postponed this action, claiming that the Filipinos were not yet prepared for independence. In 1933, however, late in President Hoover's administration, a Democratic majority in Congress passed an independence act, called the Hawes-Cutting Act, over the President's veto.

The Philippine legislature rejected this measure. Many Filipinos were fearful that one of the provisions of the act, giving the United States the right to retain military and naval bases on the islands, would enable Americans to continue their control. Other Filipinos argued that once they were free, the United States would raise tariff barriers against Philippine products.

In an effort to overcome these fears, Congress in 1934 passed a second Philippine Independence Act, the Tydings-McDuffie Act. This measure proved to be more acceptable to the Filipinos. It provided for the establishment of a Philippine Commonwealth and outlined a transitional ten-year program during which tariffs were to be gradually increased on Philippine goods imported into the United States. This would give the Filipinos an opportunity to adjust to an independent economy. Ten years after the establishment of a commonwealth—on July 4, 1946, as it turned out—the Philippines were to become entirely independent, save for the retention of naval bases by the United States.

The Good Neighbor policy. During the 1930's the United States also redoubled earlier efforts to improve its relations with Latin America. The Good Neighbor policy, as it came to be called, had been started by Presidents Coolidge and Hoover (page 667). President Roosevelt carried it a step further.

Self-interest as well as a genuine desire for friendship and understanding motivated the Good Neighbor policy. During the 1920's Americans in growing numbers began to realize that the United States could not afford to continue antagonizing its Latin-American neighbors. When the Great Depression came in the opening years of the 1930's, this realization began to harden into

Proclamation of Philippine Independence (1946): EXCERPT

Whereas it has been the repeated declaration of the ... government of the United States of America that full independence would be granted the Philippines as soon as the people of the Philippines were prepared to assume this obligation; and

Whereas the people of the Philippines have clearly demonstrated their capacity for self-government; ...

Now, therefore, I, Harry S. Truman, ... do hereby recognize the independence of the Philippines as a self-governing nation ...

---

firm conviction. The United States needed the trade of the peoples south of the Rio Grande. The rise of dictatorships in both Europe and Asia further strengthened the conviction that it was important for the United States to establish friendlier relations with its Latin-American neighbors.

Proof of the Good Neighbor policy. In 1933 President Roosevelt expressed a widely shared feeling when in his Inaugural Address he declared, "In the field of foreign policy, I would dedicate this nation to the policy of the good neighbor—the neighbor who resolutely respects himself and, because he does so, respects the rights of others." Later that year, in a conference held in Montevideo, Uruguay, the United States joined the other American countries in a pledge not to interfere in the affairs of their neighbors. "No state," the pledge declared, "has the right to intervene in the internal or external affairs of another state."

The Montevideo Pact marked a turning point in United States relations with its Latin-American neighbors. As President Roosevelt stated a few days after the pact had been signed, "The definite policy of the United States from now on is one opposed to armed intervention." During 1934 the United States took

several steps to demonstrate that it intended to honor the pledge embodied in the Montevideo Pact. In the spring, in a treaty with Cuba, it canceled the Platt Amendment (page 604), which for 33 years had given the United States the right to intervene in Cuban affairs. In August it completed a process started earlier by President Hoover and withdrew its troops from Haiti. In 1936 it signed a new treaty with Panama in which the United States surrendered its rights to intervene in the affairs of the tiny republic of the Isthmus. And gradually it gave up its control over the customhouses of the Dominican Republic, a control established in 1905.

The Good Neighbor policy tested. The Good Neighbor policy was put to a severe test in 1938 when President Lázaro Cárdenas (LAH-sah-roh KAHR-dehnahs) of Mexico issued an order confiscating the properties of all foreign oil companies. Foreign investors, including Americans, protested vigorously and demanded action from their governments. In response to such demands, Great Britain broke off diplomatic relations with Mexico. President Roosevelt, however, refused to intervene on behalf of American investors. Instead, he urged the United States oil companies to negotiate directly with the Mexican government. As a result of these negotiations, the problem was settled in 1941, and by 1949 the Mexican government had completed all of its payments on the American oil claims.

International trade agreements. In renouncing its earlier policy of imperialism, the United States tried to improve economic, political, and cultural relations among the nations of the Western Hemisphere. The Roosevelt administration also tried to promote an international revival of trade by offering to negotiate with any country special trade agreements for lowering tariffs.

Secretary of State Cordell Hull was especially interested in developing a program of *reciprocal tariffs*. In the Trade Agreements Act of 1934, Congress authorized such a program. This act permitted the President to raise or lower existing tariffs by as much as 50 per cent without Senate approval. As a result, the Roosevelt administration could bargain, or "reciprocate," with other countries. A nation that lowered its tariffs against the United States would, in turn, receive more favorable tariffs on the goods that it sent to the United States. By 1940 Hull had signed 22 reciprocal trade agreements.

Equally important was the provision of the Trade Agreements Act that the benefits of each reciprocal trade agreement were also to extend to every nation that did not discriminate in its tariffs against the United States. This provision was known as the "most-favored nation" clause because it offered any country the opportunity to be treated as well as the nation seemingly "most favored" in a specific agreement. Since some 380 special tariff discriminations against the United States existed prior to the Trade Agreements Act, this provision was extremely important. It gave the Roosevelt administration an effective instrument for stimulating American business by improving trade relations with other nations of the world.

New tariff agreements worked out with Canada and Great Britain under the Trade Agreements Act became especially significant. They stimulated a great increase of trade between these countries and the United States, providing an economic foundation for the political co-operation that became so important as World War II drew near.

SECTION SURVEY

1. What were the arguments for and against recognition of the Soviet Union?
2. (a) State the provisions of the Tydings-McDuffie Act. (b) Indicate its significance.
3. Cite four examples of the Good Neighbor policy.
4. Discuss the importance of the Trade Agreements Act.

IDENTIFY: Montevideo Pact, reciprocal tariff, "most-favored nation" clause; Cárdenas, Hull.

2 The United States tries to follow a policy of isolationism

While the United States was strengthening the Good Neighbor policy in the opening years of the 1930's, the threat of war became increasingly ominous. In Asia and Europe war clouds gathered as the militaristic leaders of Japan, Italy, and Germany started their armies down the road of aggression.

The rise of dictatorships. As the years passed, the Roosevelt administration was compelled to deal with a growing number of totalitarian° rulers. Benito Mussolini, who seized power as the leader of Italian Fascism in 1922, was a swaggering, domineering ruler with unlimited ambition. He dreamed of controlling the Mediterranean and the Middle East. The Japanese war lords, who in the late 1920's managed to secure control of their own country, were equally ruthless. Their seizure of Manchuria in 1931 (page 671) was only one step in a program to win control of the Far East and the Pacific. Adolf Hitler, the Austrian-born fanatic who climbed to power in Germany in 1933, was a reckless, impulsive ruler, a schemer, and a liar who gloried in his lies. Joseph Stalin, who in the 1920's succeeded Nikolai Lenin as the strong man of the Soviet Union, made no secret of his intention to spread Communism throughout the world.

There were other dictators, including General Francisco Franco, who came to power in Spain in 1939 after a bloody civil war. But it was Japanese, Italian, and German dictatorships that in the 1930's proved to be most aggressive.

The totalitarian threat to democracy. Hitler, Mussolini, and the Japanese war lords openly expressed their contempt for democracy. It was, in Mussolini's

••

° *totalitarian:* referring to a form of government that suppresses the freedom of the individual citizen and uses the nation's total resources to further the plans of a dictator or a small ruling group.

■ These German troops, well equipped despite the provisions of the Versailles Treaty, occupied the Rhineland in 1936. Onlookers with outstretched hands are giving the Nazi salute. Many Americans tried to ignore this evidence that militarism was loose in Europe again.

words, "a rotting corpse" that must in time be replaced by what he considered a more efficient form of government and a "superior" way of life.

All of the dictatorships scorned the democratic rights of free speech and a free press. In the eyes of the totalitarian rulers, the individual existed to serve the state and had no rights except those that the state chose to give him.

All of the dictatorships glorified force. Compelling the people to work for "bullets rather than butter," they converted their industries to war production and devoted their major efforts to building increasingly powerful armies, navies, and air forces.

Aggression and mounting tension. By the middle of the 1930's, while President Roosevelt and Congress were struggling with the Great Depression, the dictators were ready to move. In 1935 Mussolini's blackshirted Fascists attacked the African nation of Ethiopia (see map, pages 740–41), using bombing planes and poison gas against a virtually defenseless people.

Meanwhile, Japan was insisting upon its right to build a navy equal in size to that of any other power. In 1934 and 1935 the Japanese tried to get the other powers to agree to the principle of equality in naval armaments. When the other powers refused, Japan withdrew from agreements reached at the Washington Naval Conference of 1921–22 (page 670) and in subsequent treaties, and began a rapid build-up of its naval forces.

Then, in March 1936, German troops moved into the Rhineland (see map, page 735) in clear violation of the Treaty of Versailles. With this move, Hitler also revealed that for some time he had been secretly rearming Germany, which, under the terms of the Versailles Treaty, had been limited to hardly more than token armed forces. In July civil war broke out in Spain. In October Germany and Italy signed a military alliance and began to call themselves the Axis° Powers. In November 1936 Germany, Italy, and Japan announced that

• •

° *Axis:* a name made up by Mussolini, who said the line from Rome to Berlin formed the "axis" on which the world would turn thereafter. Eventually Japan was included among the Axis Powers.

they were joining in an Anti-Comintern° Pact, thus hiding their aggressive designs under the pretense of resisting Communism.

And on the night of July 7, 1937, Japanese and Chinese troops clashed at the Marco Polo Bridge near Peiping on the Chinese-Manchurian border (see map, page 768). This border "incident" developed into a full-scale war. In time, historians referred to it as the beginning of World War II in the Far East.

Roots of American isolationism. Despite the growing threat to peace, the great majority of Americans clung to their determination to avoid becoming involved in war. They believed that it was possible as well as desirable for the United States to remain isolated. Why did Americans feel this way?

In the first place, most Americans were disillusioned about the results of World War I. The war had not brought the peace, disarmament, and democracy which millions of people had hoped to see established across the face of the earth. Instead, it had been followed by constant quarreling among the European powers, by tariff wars, and by failures to reduce armaments.

Most important of all, the war had been followed by an unwillingness or an inability to make the League of Nations an effective instrument of peace. The isolationists refused to accept the argument that the League of Nations might have been more successful had the United States joined. They argued that the weakness of the League was the best possible evidence that the United States had been wise in its refusal to become a member. This widespread disillusionment with the results of World War I and with the League of Nations became increasingly intense when the League failed to check the aggressions of Italy, Germany, and Japan in 1935–37.

Disillusionment of Americans over

••

° *Comintern:* an international organization, dominated by the Russian Communist Party, whose aim was to spread Communism throughout the world.

World War I was intensified in 1934 when the Senate Munitions Investigating Committee, under the chairmanship of Senator Gerald P. Nye of North Dakota, started to investigate war profits. Figures released by the Nye committee suggested that many American bankers and munitions makers had reaped rich profits from World War I. Many people concluded that America's loans to the Allies had been largely responsible for drawing the United States into what later appeared to be a futile conflict.

But disillusionment about World War I was not the only basis for American isolationism. Most Americans believed that the Atlantic and Pacific Oceans would protect the United States from attack even if totalitarian aggressors succeeded in crushing all opposition in Europe and Asia. Those who shared this view also argued that improved relations with Latin America gave the United States another safeguard against attack.

The ranks of the isolationists were strengthened by two other groups. Many Americans believed that the government's first responsibility was to combat the Great Depression. Many others, deeply convinced pacifists, believed that all wars were unjustifiable and that the United States should avoid being drawn into another conflict, no matter what the cost. Pacifism was strong, especially among young people, in both the United States and Great Britain during the 1930's.

Isolationism in practice. In 1934 American isolationists won the first of a series of victories when Congress passed the Johnson Debt Default Act. This act prohibited the American government and private citizens from lending money to any country that had defaulted, or failed to repay, its war debts.

The Johnson Debt Default Act revealed the deep and widespread annoyance of Americans with the failure of the European nations to repay their war debts. By 1934 only Finland continued to maintain its debt payments. Americans were especially annoyed because some of the defaulting nations were pouring increasing amounts of money into armaments. Americans by and large did not intend to provide any more money for armaments, or to risk becoming involved in another war because of entangling investments.

The isolationists won another victory in 1935 when the Senate refused to vote in favor of the United States' joining the World Court (page 669). Early in January 1935, President Roosevelt had urged the Senate to vote in favor of membership. "I hope," he said, "that at an early date the Senate will advise and consent to the adherence by the United States" to the World Court "to make international justice practicable and serviceable." But the Senate refused to provide the necessary votes, largely because of isolationist opposition.

Congress passes neutrality acts. Taking advantage of the widespread sentiment against war, the isolationists in 1935–37 pushed through Congress a series of neutrality acts. Congress passed the first Neutrality Act in 1935, largely as a result of Mussolini's unprovoked attack upon Ethiopia. Congress passed additional neutrality acts in 1936 and 1937 when civil war broke out in Spain and the aggressive actions of Germany and Japan threatened world peace.

In general, the neutrality legislation (1) prohibited the shipment of arms and munitions to "belligerents," or warring nations; (2) authorized the President to list commodities other than munitions that could be sold to belligerents only on a "cash-and-carry" basis; and (3) made it unlawful for American citizens to travel on the vessels of the belligerent nations.

The aim of the neutrality laws was to keep Americans out of war. With these laws the United States abandoned its long-established doctrine of freedom of the seas. The government withdrew the traditional rights of citizens to travel where they wished. The government also limited the rights of citizens to trade with warring countries.

Dissatisfaction toward neutrality. Strong though it was, isolationism by no means represented the unanimous thinking of the American people. Many Americans were dismayed by the abandonment of individual rights that earlier generations of Americans had fought so hard to establish.

Still other Americans regretted that the neutrality laws made it difficult for the United States to help the victims of aggression. They feared that Italy, Germany, Japan, and other possible aggressors would become bolder if the United States refused to aid weaker nations. In their view, if the United States allowed aggressors to crush their weaker neighbors, the United States might one day find itself truly isolated and surrounded by powerful enemies.

Finally, many of the international-minded citizens argued that the United States had a moral responsibility to aid the victims of unprovoked aggression. This attitude cut across party lines. There were internationalists as well as isolationists in both the Democratic and the Republican Parties.

Roosevelt's policy changes. Between 1933 and 1937 President Roosevelt did not take a firm stand concerning America's responsibility in a troubled world. On occasions he seemed to side with the isolationists; on other occasions, with the internationalists.

In 1933, only three months after Roosevelt first took office, he failed to support the work of an important conference called by the League of Nations. The delegates to the London Economic Conference, as it was called, hoped to agree upon a way to stabilize the currencies of the world. Stable currencies would boost trade and help to bring about world-wide economic recovery. Although the United States was not a member of the League of Nations, President Hoover had pledged support for the London Economic Conference. But President Roosevelt refused to give wholehearted support. During the conference he ordered the United States delegates to limit their discussions to a consideration of tariffs. As a result, the conference failed.

During the next three or four years Roosevelt also ceased to press for United States entrance into the League of Nations. And he approved the Neutrality Act of 1935 because, in his own words, "It was intended as an expression of the fixed desire of the government and the people of the United States to avoid any action which might involve us in war."

By 1937, however, Roosevelt was becoming impressed with the seriousness of the world situation and with the need for the United States to take a positive stand against aggression. In a speech that he gave in Chicago on October 5, 1937, the President said:

"If we are to have a world in which we can breathe freely and live in amity without fear—the peace-loving nations must make a concerted effort to uphold laws and principles on which alone peace can rest secure. . . .

"When an epidemic of physical disease starts to spread, the community approves and joins in a quarantine of the patients in order to protect the health of the community against the spread of the disease. . . ."

The majority remains isolationist. In his famous "quarantine" speech President Roosevelt expressed views that the majority of Americans were not yet ready to accept. Proof of this came with the *"Panay* incident." On December 12, 1937, Japanese planes bombed and strafed a United States gunboat, the *Panay,* and three American oil tankers on the Yangtze River near Nanking, China (see map, page 768). Several Americans were killed and numerous others were wounded.

Secretary of State Hull immediately sent a sharp note to the Japanese government. He demanded full apologies, compensation, and a promise that no such incident would recur. The Japanese met all of Hull's demands.

During the course of this "incident," which might have led to serious international consequences, the American public revealed how strongly it favored keeping out of war. While the *Panay* matter was still headline news, Representative Louis Ludlow of Indiana proposed an amendment to the Constitution. This amendment would have required a national referendum to ratify a declaration of war except in case of actual attack. Largely because of pressure from the President, the proposal was rejected. Meanwhile, a public opinion poll revealed that 54 per cent of the American people thought that the United States should completely withdraw from China.

By the end of 1937, the tide of aggression was rising rapidly in Asia as well as Europe. Many Americans, including President Roosevelt, were becoming increasingly alarmed. But the American people as a whole clung to the belief that it was possible for the United States to remain isolated.

■ Soon after Japanese aircraft struck the American gunboat *Panay,* someone snapped this picture along her decks. The ship is sinking, and the crew line up to abandon her. But the unprovoked and unexplained attack failed to alert Americans to Japan's aggressive intentions.

1. Discuss the ideas that the totalitarian dictators shared in common.
2. List the events of 1935–37 which posed a threat to peace.
3. What were the roots of the widespread feeling of isolationism among Americans in the period 1920–37?
4. (a) Summarize the main provisions of the Neutrality Acts passed between 1935 and 1937. (b) State the arguments that were raised against these laws.
IDENTIFY: Axis Powers, Anti-Comintern Pact, Nye Senate Munitions Investigating Committee, Johnson Debt Default Act, World Court, London Economic Conference, "quarantine" speech, *Panay;* Mussolini, Hitler, Lenin, Stalin, Franco; 1934, 1937.

3 The United States finds isolationism difficult to maintain

By 1938 the dictators were becoming more and more ruthless. Time after time during 1938 and 1939, headlines of new aggressions and new crises crowded other news off the front pages of America's newspapers.

Spreading warfare. The situation was serious enough when the year 1938 opened. Japan's land, sea, and air forces were attacking along the length of the Chinese coast and pushing inland up the river valleys. Hundreds of thousands of Chinese, uprooted by war, were fleeing into the interior. Meanwhile, halfway around the world, the Spanish Civil War was bringing misery to hundreds of thousands of other people.

Spain had become an international battleground. Hitler and Mussolini were helping Franco, making the most of the opportunity to test their latest military equipment and to give picked "volunteers" actual battle experience. Soviet "volunteers" in considerable numbers were fighting against Franco and his Nazi and Fascist allies. Franco's foes in the "International Brigade" also included volunteers from numerous other countries, including the United States. Among the volunteers were large numbers of men who hated all dictatorships, Communist no less than Fascist.

New aggressions—and Munich. Such was the situation when on March 11, 1938, mechanized units of Hitler's powerful army rolled across the frontier into Austria (see map, page 735). Two days later Hitler announced the union of Austria and Germany.

With Austria under his control, Hitler turned greedy eyes toward the western territory of Czechoslovakia. This territory, known as the Sudetenland (soo-DAYT'n-land), contained a large proportion of German-speaking people. Hitler demanded that Czechoslovakia turn over the Sudeten region to Germany. As the summer wore on, Hitler became increasingly belligerent, threatening to seize the territory by force if Czechoslovakia did not meet his demands. By the end of the summer, a major crisis was at hand, for Czechoslovakia, with one of the best trained armies in Europe and with the sympathy of other democratic nations overwhelmingly on its side, resolutely refused to bow to Hitler.

Tension was at the breaking point when British Prime Minister Neville Chamberlain, French Premier Édouard Daladier, Mussolini, and Hitler met at Munich. There on September 30, 1938, the four men signed a pact in which they agreed to accept nearly all of Hitler's demands. The Czechs, forsaken by their friends, turned over most of the Sudeten region to Germany. In the meantime Prime Minister Chamberlain, whose intense desire for peace blinded him to Hitler's true nature, returned to England confident that the Munich Agreement had put an end to the threat of aggression in Europe. "I believe," he said, "it is peace for our time."

Other leaders did not share Chamberlain's confidence. They believed his policy of "appeasement" would only lead Hitler to make further demands. Throughout Europe nation after nation began to rearm with redoubled speed.

Axis Powers

Axis-controlled lands
Sept. 1, 1939

NORWAY

SWEDEN

FINLAND

ESTONIA

LATVIA

LITHUANIA

U.S.S.R.

NORTH SEA

GREAT BRITAIN

N. IRELAND

EIRE

DENMARK

GER.

GERMAN INVASION OF POLAND
STARTS WAR, SEPT. 1, 1939

London

English Channel

NETH.

BELG.

LUX.

RHINELAND
MAR. 1936

Berlin

GERMANY

SUDETENLAND
SEPT. 1938

Warsaw

POLAND

CZECHOSLOVAKIA
MAR. 1939

BESSARABIA

Paris

Munich

AUSTRIA
MAR. 1938

HUNGARY

RUMANIA

BLACK SEA

FRANCE

SWITZ.

YUGOSLAVIA

BULGARIA

Adriatic Sea

ITALY

Rome

APRIL 1939

ALBANIA

TURKEY

CIVIL WAR, JULY 1936

SPAIN

PORTUGAL

GREECE

TO ETHIOPIA
MAY 1935

CRETE

MEDITERRANEAN SEA

BALTIC SEA

Growing concern in the United States. President Roosevelt was one of a growing number of American leaders who viewed the events of 1938 with deepening concern. As early as January 28, in a special message to Congress, he coupled a promise to continue to work for peace with a warning that it was time for the United States to build up its own defenses. Congress responded to Roosevelt's request by increasing appropriations for the armed forces and, in May, by authorizing more than a billion dollars for a "two-ocean navy."

In private conversations Roosevelt referred to the aggressions of Japan, Italy, and Germany as "armed banditry," and Roosevelt's Secretary of the Interi-

or, Harold L. Ickes, called Hitler a "maniac." Officially, however, the President contented himself with personal notes to the heads of foreign governments, including Mussolini and Hitler, pleading with them to settle their differences by negotiation and international co-operation. But since the United States was committed to the hands-off policy of isolationism, no one paid much attention to the President's words.

Hemispheric defense. As the Sudeten crisis approached the breaking point, however, President Roosevelt did make one commitment. In August 1938, in a speech at Queen's University in Ontario, Canada, he extended the protection of the Monroe Doctrine to Canada. Sol-

Franklin D. Roosevelt's
"Four Freedoms" Speech (1941): EXCERPT

In the future days which we seek to make secure, we look forward to a world founded upon four essential human freedoms.

The first is freedom of speech and expression—everywhere in the world.

The second is freedom of every person to worship God in his own way—everywhere in the world.

The third is freedom from want—which, translated into world terms, means economic understandings which will secure to every nation a healthy peacetime life for its inhabitants—everywhere in the world.

The fourth is freedom from fear—which, translated into world terms, means a world-wide reduction of armaments to such a point and in such a thorough fashion that no nation will be in a position to commit an act of physical aggression against any neighbor—anywhere in the world . . .

---

emnly, in measured words, he promised Canadians that "the people of the United States will not stand idly by if domination of Canadian soil is threatened by any other Empire."

Roosevelt's promise to Canada represented only one of several steps the United States was taking to develop a hemispheric defense policy. Earlier, in the Buenos Aires Conference of 1936, the United States and the 20 other republics belonging to the Pan-American Union had established the foundation of a Western Hemisphere security system. At Buenos Aires the delegates had agreed to look upon a threat to the security of any one American country as a threat to the security of all American countries. They had also agreed to consult together when and if such a threat developed.

In December 1938, with the war clouds rapidly gathering, the members of the Pan-American Union met again,

this time in Lima, Peru, for the eighth regular Pan-American Conference. At Lima the delegates repeated their pledge of solid opposition to any threat of foreign intervention in the affairs of the Western Hemisphere. But the Declaration of Lima, as it was called, went a step further. It provided that at the first sign of trouble the foreign ministers of the Western Hemisphere would meet to decide what action their countries should take.

Roosevelt's promise to Canada and the Declaration of Lima provided additional assurance that the Monroe Doctrine had become a "multilateral," or many-sided, policy, rather than a "unilateral," or one-sided, policy. By 1938 it was clear, as Roosevelt said, "that national defense has now become a problem of continental defense."

More crises—and World War II. In 1939 events moved swiftly toward a climax. On January 4, in his annual message to Congress, President Roosevelt warned that the world situation had become extremely grave. He urged greatly increased appropriations for the armed services. He also urged Congress to reconsider the neutrality legislation adopted during 1935–37.

The President's worst fears were soon confirmed. On March 15, 1939, Hitler's armies moved into the rest of Czechoslovakia. On April 7 Mussolini's troops invaded Albania (see map, page 735).

Awakening at long last to their common peril, Great Britain and France stated that an attack upon Poland would mean war. Great Britain and France also tried to get the Soviet Union to join them in an agreement to oppose by armed force any further aggression by either Hitler or Mussolini. It was with shock, therefore, that the democratic nations learned on August 23, 1939, that the U.S.S.R. had just signed a nonaggression pact with Germany.

Seemingly freed by the Soviet pact from the danger of a two-front war, Hitler struck swiftly. On September 1, without warning, he sent his bombers and his powerful mechanized divisions across the border into Poland (see map, page 735). Two days later, on September 3, Great Britain and France declared war on Germany.

While Great Britain and France were mobilizing, troops of the Soviet Union invaded Poland from the east. By the end of September, all organized Polish resistance had been crushed, and Germany and the U.S.S.R. divided Poland between them. The Soviets then demanded and won the right to establish military and naval bases in Estonia, Latvia, and Lithuania (see map, page 735).° And on November 30, after Finland refused to grant Soviet demands to establish military bases on Finnish soil, the U.S.S.R. launched an attack against its small neighbor.

And so, in 1939, World War II started and began to spread across Europe.

••

° In June 1940 the U.S.S.R. also seized the Rumanian province of Bessarabia.

SECTION SURVEY

1. (a) Give the terms of the Munich Agreement of 1938. (b) Indicate its significance.
2. What steps did the United States take to strengthen the defenses of the Western Hemisphere?
3. Summarize the events that led to the outbreak of World War II.
    IDENTIFY: Declaration of Lima, appeasement, nonaggression pact; Chamberlain, Daladier; 1938, 1939.

4 The United States becomes involved in World War II

American sympathies in 1939 were overwhelmingly in favor of the nations fighting against Germany. At the same time, however, Americans clung to their determination to stay out of war. President Roosevelt was merely voicing a widely shared feeling when, in a "fireside chat" over radio on September 3, he said, "As long as it remains in my power to prevent, there will be no blackout of peace in the United States."

Congress amends neutrality laws. On September 21, 1939, however, Roosevelt urged a special session of Congress to amend the Neutrality Act of 1937. "I regret that Congress passed the Act. I regret equally that I signed the Act," he declared. As Roosevelt pointed out, the existing embargo on the export of arms and munitions to belligerent nations actually favored Germany. If it were not for the embargo, Great Britain and France could use their control of the seas to secure from the United States the arms that they desperately needed. Hitler, on the other hand, did not need military equipment, for he had been preparing for war for years.

The debate lasted for six weeks, with many Congressmen demanding outright repeal of the neutrality legislation, and many others insisting on retaining every provision of the existing laws. Congress finally agreed on a compromise proposal. The most important change in the new law was the abolition of the arms embargo. This change permitted any country to buy arms and munitions from the United States provided that the goods were transported to Europe on foreign ships. Roosevelt signed the measure and proclaimed it in effect on November 4, 1939.

The new law greatly helped the nations resisting Hitler. Between November 1939 and August 1940 the British took almost half of all United States exports. During the summer of 1940, the proportion jumped to two thirds.

Declaration of Panama. While Congress was debating the problem of neutrality, the members of the Pan-American Union met at Panama to consider problems of hemispheric defense.

On October 3, 1939, the delegates to the Panama Conference issued a declaration warning all belligerent war vessels to stay out of a "safety zone" around the Americas roughly 300 to 1000 miles

Stukas in flight

"BLITZKRIEG"

With the *blitzkrieg*, Hitler unleashed a new type of warfare. Before the war started, he had assembled a number of highly mobile, highly mechanized units, including tanks and mounted artillery. These units, known as *Panzer* divisions, were supported by a new type of specially designed aircraft, the *Stukas*, or dive bombers. Concentrating intense fire power upon a single section of the enemy line, the *Panzers* and *Stukas* drove through and fanned out in the rear. Then they raced over the countryside, overrunning command posts and supply depots, and paralyzing lines of transportation and communication. When the enemy was completely disorganized, the infantry moved in and "mopped up" all remaining resistance.

Using the *blitzkrieg*, Hitler was invincible in the early days of the war. But, in time, the Allies organized their own mobile units and their own clouds of fighters and bombers. Then it was a different story. They, too, could use the methods of the *blitzkrieg*. Sometimes, when it suited their purposes, they allowed Hitler's *Panzers* to pierce their own lines, then sealed off the gap, shot down the *Stukas*, and destroyed the Nazi tanks and armored equipment with their own mechanized units.

eration among the nations of the Western Hemisphere.

The fall of France. While Hitler was carrying on his *blitzkrieg*, or "lightning war," against Poland in 1939, the French rapidly mobilized. They braced themselves for an attack against the Maginot (ma-zhee-NOH) Line—the formidable chain of forts guarding their eastern frontier. But Hitler did not attack. As the weeks of inaction lengthened into months, people began to joke about the "phony war," which some referred to as a *sitzkrieg*.

On April 9, 1940, the joking ceased. On that date Hitler began to demonstrate the true meaning of blitzkrieg. In rapid order in the weeks that followed, his powerful *Panzer*, or armored, divisions, supported by fighters and bombers, overran Denmark, Norway, the Netherlands, Belgium, Luxembourg, and northern France (see map, page 754). On May 26 the British began a heroic evacuation of their expeditionary forces from the beaches of Dunkirk, a seaport in northern France on the Strait of Dover. Although they were forced to leave much of their equipment, they succeeded in saving most of their men. On June 10 Italy, sensing that France was doomed, declared war on France and Great Britain.

Hitler's blitzkrieg came to a halt when on June 22, 1940, France signed an armistice with Germany. The revengeful Hitler forced the French to sign in the same railway car on the very spot in the forest of Compiègne where almost 22 years earlier, on November 11, 1918, the French and their allies had accepted Germany's surrender at the close of World War I. In London the French National Committee pledged continued resistance by the "Free French" under General Charles de Gaulle (sharl duh GOHL), and began to rally part of the French colonial empire against the Nazis. Meanwhile, Marshal Pétain (peh-TAN) became the leader of a German-controlled French government with headquarters at Vichy (vee-SHEE) in central France (see map, page 754).

wide. Germany, Great Britain, and France challenged this declaration on the ground that no nation or group of nations had the right to close any part of the high seas to their ships. The declaration was important, however, as an additional indication of genuine co-operation

The Battle of Britain. With the fall of France, Great Britain stood alone—alone and almost defenseless, for the British had left most of their war equipment on the beaches of Dunkirk, and their armies were disorganized.

On May 10, 1940, Winston Churchill replaced Neville Chamberlain as Prime Minister of Great Britain. With a gift for leadership given to few men, Churchill rallied the British people, strengthening their determination to fight and their hope of ultimate victory. Shortly after taking office he promised that the British would never surrender. If by any chance Great Britain itself were to fall, he declared, "Then our Empire beyond the seas, armed and guarded by the British fleet, would carry on the struggle until, in God's good time, the New World, with all its power and might, steps forth to the rescue and liberation of the Old."

By the end of June, with France under complete control of the Nazis, Churchill was preparing his people for the coming "Battle of Britain." "Hitler knows that he will have to break us in this island or lose the war," Churchill said. "If we can stand up to him, all Europe may be free and the life of the world may move forward into broad, sunlit uplands. But if we fail, then the whole world, including the United States, including all that we have known and cared for, will sink into the abyss of a new Dark Age. . . .

"Let us therefore brace ourselves to our duties, and so bear ourselves that, if the British Empire and its Commonwealth last for a thousand years, men will still say, 'This was their finest hour.'"

The supreme test for which Churchill had been preparing the British came in the late summer of 1940. In August, Hitler hurled a swarm of fighters and bombers against Great Britain in an all-out effort to sweep the Royal Navy from the English Channel and the Royal Air Force from the skies. The Royal Navy fought back furiously, and the Royal Air Force, though almost hopelessly outnumbered, flew day and night, sometimes shooting down as many as 100 Nazi bombers in a single 24-hour period. In October, advised by his naval and air chiefs that an attempt to invade Great Britain would be suicidal, Hitler postponed his invasion plan, "Operation Sea Lion," until spring.

"Never in the field of human conflict," Churchill declared, referring to the record of the Royal Air Force, "was so much owed by so many to so few."

The destroyer deal. Meanwhile, President Roosevelt had been scraping together every piece of military equip-

■ During the "Battle of Britain," Hitler's Luftwaffe (aircraft) rained bombs on most of England's great cities. This picture shows fires raging around St. Paul's Cathedral in London.

GREENLAND

ICELAND

CANADA

SIGNING OF THE ATLANTIC
CHARTER, AUG. 1941

NEWFOUNDLAND

NORWAY

SWEDEN

FINLAND

Murmansk

GREAT
BRITAIN
London

FRANCE

GERMANY

EUROPE

Leningrad

Moscow

SOVIE

P E

YALTA CONFERENCE
FEB. 1945

UNITED
STATES

New
York

Washington 1889-90

NORTH AMERICA

BERMUDA

BAHAMA IS.

Havana—1928,1940

MEXICO

Mexico City
1901-02

PANAMA
CANAL

Panama
1939

TRINIDAD

PERU

Lima
1938

SOUTH

BRAZIL

Rio de Janeiro
1906, 1942

AMERICA

Santiago
1923

CHILE

URUGUAY

Buenos Aires
1910, 1936

ARGENTINA

Montevideo
1933

ATLANTIC

OCEAN

SPAIN

ITALY

Casablanca
MOROCCO

ALGERIA

Yalta

TURKEY

Teheran

IRAQ
IRAN

LIBYA

Cairo
EGYPT

SUEZ
CANAL

SAUDI
ARABIA

FRENCH WEST AFRICA

AFRICA

ETHIOPIA

UNION OF
SOUTH AFRICA

INDIA

The following nations, neutral throughout most of the war, joined the Allies after 1944:

ARGENTINA	PERU	LEBANON
CHILE	URUGUAY	SAUDI ARABIA
ECUADOR	VENEZUELA	SYRIA
PARAGUAY	EGYPT	TURKEY

ment the American armed forces could spare—rifles, machine guns, artillery— and making it available to the British. But mostly the British needed destroyers to block the expected invasion across the English Channel.

On September 3, 1940, with the Battle of Britain raging to a climax, President Roosevelt announced that he had transferred to the British 50 over-age American destroyers. In exchange the British government gave the United States the right to lease naval and air bases in Newfoundland and in Bermuda, the Bahamas, Jamaica, Trinidad, and other British possessions in the Caribbean (see map, pages 740–41). The two most important bases in Newfoundland and Bermuda, however, were not part of "the deal." These were "gifts

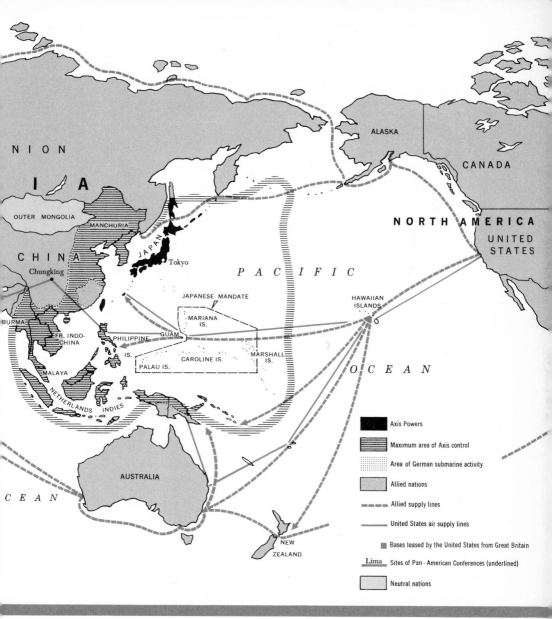

N I O N

I A

OUTER MONGOLIA

MANCHURIA

JAPAN

Tokyo

CHINA

Chungking

BURMA

FR. INDO-CHINA

PHILIPPINE IS.

MALAYA

NETHERLANDS INDIES

AUSTRALIA

OCEAN

NEW ZEALAND

ALASKA

CANADA

NORTH AMERICA
UNITED STATES

PACIFIC

JAPANESE MANDATE

MARIANA IS.

GUAM

CAROLINE IS.

PALAU IS.

MARSHALL IS.

HAWAIIAN ISLANDS

OCEAN

Axis Powers

Maximum area of Axis control

Area of German submarine activity

Allied nations

Allied supply lines

United States air supply lines

Bases leased by the United States from Great Britain

Lima Sites of Pan-American Conferences (underlined)

Neutral nations

generously given and gladly received."

United States defense measures. During the summer and fall of 1940, the United States was also taking steps to strengthen its own defenses.

In June, in an effort to check subversive activities, Congress passed the Alien Registration Act, best known as the Smith Act. This law made it illegal for any person in the United States to ad-

vocate the overthrow of the government by force or violence, or to belong to an organization that advocated the violent overthrow of government.

In July, Secretary of State Hull and the foreign ministers of the other American nations gathered in Havana, Cuba, to make plans for meeting the world crisis. The uppermost problem on the minds of the delegates was the fear that

Germany would attempt to seize the Western Hemisphere colonies of the countries it had conquered. In order to prevent this from happening, the conference adopted the Act of Havana. This act stated that the moment the territorial integrity of any colony was in danger, the American republics, acting singly or collectively, would take control of the colony. From then until the end of the war, the colony would be governed by a group of trustees from the American republics.

Two weeks later President Roosevelt met with Prime Minister Mackenzie King of Canada. At this meeting in New York state, the leaders of Canada and the United States created a Permanent Joint Board on Defense to plan for the "defense of the north half of the Western Hemisphere."

In the meantime Congress was furiously debating the pro's and con's of the first peacetime draft in American history. The Burke-Wadsworth Act finally passed and was signed by President Roosevelt on September 16, 1940. The law required all men between the ages of twenty-one and thirty-five to register for the draft, and made them liable for one year of military training.

Roosevelt's Lend-Lease proposal. By the end of 1940, American supplies were flowing to Great Britain, and America's defense program was gathering momentum. But President Roosevelt was not satisfied that the government was doing all it could "to keep war away from our country and our people."

What worried Roosevelt most was the fact that the British were approaching financial exhaustion and could not much longer afford to pay cash for the war materials that they so desperately needed. In a fireside chat and a week later in his annual message to Congress, Roosevelt warned that "Our country is going to be what our people have proclaimed it to be—the arsenal of democracy." Roosevelt proposed that the United States increase greatly its production of military equipment of all kinds so that it could lend or lease to the British

and to the other governments resisting Hitler any materials that they needed.

Roosevelt's Lend-Lease proposal provoked a storm of controversy in Congress and throughout the country. Many people agreed with the President that the Lend-Lease proposal offered America its best hope of avoiding full-fledged participation in the war. Others, including, of course, the isolationists, took a directly opposite position. They argued that Lend-Lease would surely involve America in a shooting war.

Overriding all objections, Congress passed the Lend-Lease Act in March 1941 and appropriated an initial sum of 7 billion dollars for ships, planes, tanks, and anything else that the Allies° needed. When on June 22, 1941, Hitler's armies invaded the Soviet Union despite the German-Russian nonaggression pact, the United States made Lend-Lease materials available to the U.S.S.R.

The Battle of the Atlantic. Just as the isolationists had predicted, the Lend-Lease arrangement inevitably drew the United States closer to a shooting war. By the spring of 1941, German and Italian submarines were turning the North Atlantic into a graveyard of ships. In April United States naval vessels began to "trail" enemy submarines, radioing their location to British war ships. In July American troops occupied Iceland (see map, page 754) in order to prevent its occupation by Germany.

In September President Roosevelt issued "shoot on sight" orders to American war ships operating in the "safety zone" established back in 1939 at the Panama Conference (page 737). Later in September American war ships began to convoy merchant vessels as far as Iceland. And in November Congress removed the last remnants of the neutrality legislation by voting to allow American merchant vessels to enter combat areas. Roosevelt promptly armed the merchant vessels and provided them with navy gun crews.

° *Allies:* the nations united in fighting the Axis Powers, including the governments-in-exile of conquered countries.

The U.S.S. *Zane*, a destroyer which was used in Atlantic convoys during the Lend-Lease period. Beginning in September 1941, these convoys escorted, as far as Iceland, American merchant vessels which were carrying military equipment of all kinds to Great Britain.

The Atlantic Charter. In August 1941, while the United States was moving rapidly toward an undeclared shooting war with Germany, President Roosevelt and Prime Minister Churchill met to discuss the larger issues involved in the conflict. The two men held their conference on a heavily guarded war ship off the Newfoundland coast. At this meeting, the first of several similar conferences, the two leaders drew up a broad statement of war aims that came to be called the Atlantic Charter.

Like Woodrow Wilson's Fourteen Points (page 637), the Atlantic Charter listed a number of "common principles" upon which men of good will could build a lasting peace and a better world. In the Atlantic Charter, Roosevelt and Churchill pledged themselves to work for a world free of aggression, a world in which every nation, large or small, would have the right to adopt its own form of government. Once the aggressors were crushed, the Charter declared, all nations must work together to free all men everywhere from the burden of fear and want.

Rising threat from Japan. While most American eyes were focused on the European theater of war, Japan was pushing its conquests in the Far East. In July 1941 Japanese troops occupied French Indo-China (see map, page 768). Thoroughly alarmed, President Roosevelt immediately "froze" all Japanese assets in the United States.° He also placed an embargo on the shipment of gasoline, machine tools, scrap iron, and steel to Japan. Japan promptly retaliated by freezing all American assets in areas under its control.

As a result, trade between the United States and Japan practically ended. And then in August the United States sent a Lend-Lease mission to China.

The Japanese, convinced that American resistance was stiffening, began to shape up plans for an attack upon the United States. Even as the war leaders were making final preparations, however, the Japanese government sent a

° Bank balances in this country belonging to Japanese were blocked, preventing withdrawal of funds or even expenditure within the United States.

■ Shocked and grim, Americans learned of the devastation wrought by the Japanese at Pearl Harbor. From left to right, the battleships *Arizona, Tennessee,* and *West Virginia* are afire.

"peace" mission to Washington. On November 20, 1941, this mission demanded that the United States (1) unfreeze Japanese assets, (2) supply Japan with aṣ much gasoline as it needed, and (3) cease all aid to China. The United States refused to meet these demands, but offered several counterproposals.

The negotiations continued for more than two weeks. Finally, on December 7, 1941, the Japanese mission announced that further negotiations were useless because the United States clung to "impractical principles" and had failed "to display in the slightest degree a spirit of conciliation."

The attack on Pearl Harbor. On Sunday morning, December 7, 1941—even before Japan's reply had been delivered to the American government—carrier-borne Japanese planes roared down without warning upon the United States fleet in the great American naval and air base at Pearl Harbor, in Hawaii (see map, page 769). Taken unaware, the Americans lost almost all of their planes and eight battleships and suffered the partial destruction of several other naval units. More than 2000 soldiers, sailors, and civilians were killed, and almost 2000 more were wounded. The same day the Japanese also attacked Wake, Midway, Guam, the Philippine Islands, and other American bases.

The United States declares war. Americans were shocked beyond words as the radio announced what had happened on the morning of December 7,

1941. The United States was not prepared for such an unprovoked attack. And with almost complete unanimity, the American people supported President Roosevelt the next day when he asked Congress for a declaration of war against Japan. The Senate declared war unanimously; the House, with only one dissenting vote. Great Britain and the governments-in-exile that had fled their countries when Hitler conquered them also immediately declared war against Japan. Three days later, on December 11, Germany and Italy declared that a state of war with the United States existed, whereupon Congress declared war upon these two countries.

⮞ **SECTION SURVEY**

1. (a) Why did Roosevelt favor amending the neutrality laws of 1935–37? (b) Summarize the changes that were made.

2. What was the significance of each of the following to hemispheric defense: (a) Declaration of Panama and (b) Act of Havana?

3. Describe the steps taken by the United States to (a) strengthen its own defenses and (b) help the Allies.

4. "The Atlantic Charter was a statement of high idealism." Explain.

5. Summarize the events that led to the Japanese attack on Pearl Harbor.

IDENTIFY: blitzkrieg, "phony war," Dunkirk, Battle of Britain, destroyer deal, Smith Act, Burke-Wadsworth Act, "arsenal of democracy," Battle of the Atlantic; De Gaulle, Pétain, Churchill.

744

(For review, see Section Surveys, pages 729, 734, 737, 744.)

Points to Discuss: 1. Few Presidents, it has been said, had entered office under more unfavorable circumstances than did Franklin D. Roosevelt. Describe the national and international crises which he had to face.

2. Do you think it was a wise move for the United States to recognize the Soviet Union in 1933? Justify your answer.

3. Evaluate the significance of the grant of independence to the Filipinos.

4. (a) Explain how the Monroe Doctrine was transformed into a multilateral principle by Franklin D. Roosevelt's Good Neighbor policy. (b) Trace the steps which led to the change.

5. During the 1930's, while the European dictators were becoming increasingly ruthless, the American people were becoming more isolationist. Offer evidence to support this statement.

6. Despite a determination to remain neutral in World Wars I and II, the United States finally entered each conflict. Describe events which led to a reversal of traditional policy in each of these wars.

7. Isolationism and neutrality in the twentieth century have been difficult policies to maintain when powerful nations engage in war. Oppose or defend this statement with evidence. (See map, pages 842–43.)

Using Maps and Charts: 1. Consulting the map on page 735, (a) identify the Axis powers, (b) point out the lands seized by Germany, (c) tell which of Mussolini's conquests are shown, (d) identify the lands controlled by the Axis powers on September 1, 1939.

2. Using the charts on pages 824–45, draw up an inventory of American military strength and resources for war in 1941.

3. What conclusions about the "shrinking globe" can you draw from a study of the map on pages 842–43?

Consulting the Sources: See Angle, *By These Words*, pages 473–83, for Roosevelt's "quarantine speech" at Chicago. For the text of the Atlantic Charter, see pages 510–11. See also, "Roosevelt Accepts the Challenge of Japan," pages 513–22.

■ TRACING THE MAIN IDEAS

During the 1930's the curtain began to rise upon one of the greatest tragedies of the modern world. The tragedy started with the Great Depression, which plunged millions of people all over the world into unemployment, confusion, and unrest. Then, in the middle 1930's, the armies of Japan, Italy, and Germany began to march across the troubled face of the earth, following the bidding of their power-mad leaders and leaving death and destruction behind them as they marched. Before 1941 drew to a close, most of the nations of the world were involved in the most terrible conflict in human history.

The overwhelming majority of the American people were at first determined to remain aloof from the war. They supported Congress when it enacted neutrality legislation in 1935, 1936, and 1937. But as the dictators crushed their weaker neighbors, Americans began to realize that the democratic way of life and free people everywhere were in grave danger. More and more Americans began to realize that, by helping other nations to resist aggression, the United States would strengthen democracy and protect itself.

By 1939, when World War II broke out in Europe, the United States had begun to reverse its traditional policy of isolationism. During the next two years neutrality was abandoned as the United States became "the arsenal of democracy." American ships carried cargoes of war materials to Great Britain, the Soviet Union, and China. America's navy, air force, and army were strengthened with feverish speed. On December 7, 1941, the Japanese struck at Pearl Harbor. The curtain had finally risen. The United States was at war.

Unit Survey (Reread "Tracing the Main Ideas," pages 710, 725, 745.)

OUTSTANDING EVENTS

1933 Twentieth Amendment ratified.
1933 Agricultural Adjustment Act.
1933 Roosevelt declares bank holiday.
1933 Congress abandons gold standard.
1933 Twenty-first Amendment ratified.
1933 U.S. recognizes Soviet Union.
1933 NIRA goes into effect.
1933 TVA is created.
1934 SEC is created.
1934 Reciprocal Trade Agreements Act.
1934 Platt Amendment canceled.
1935–37 Neutrality Acts.
1935 NIRA declared unconstitutional.
1935 Social Security Act.
1935 Wheeler-Rayburn Act.
1935 National Labor Relations Act.
1936 AAA ruled unconstitutional.
1936 Soil Conservation and Domestic Allotment Act.
1936 Franklin D. Roosevelt re-elected President.
1938 Fair Labor Standards Act.
1938 New Agricultural Adjustment Act.
1938 CIO separates from A.F. of L.
1939 Sit-down strikes ruled illegal.
1939 Germany invades Poland; World War II begins.
1939 Neutrality Act of 1937 amended.
1940 Alien Registration Act.
1940 Franklin D. Roosevelt re-elected President.
1941 "Four Freedoms" speech.
1941 Lend-Lease Act.
1941 Atlantic Charter states war aims.
1941 Japanese attack Pearl Harbor; U.S. enters World War II.

THEN AND NOW

1. Compare New Deal methods of dealing with the Great Depression with the traditional laissez-faire attitude toward economic depressions in 1873 and 1893.

2. Compare isolationist attitudes of the 1930's with those prior to World War I.

3. Look for common difficulties in action faced by the United Nations and by our government under the Articles of Confederation.

EXTENDING YOUR HORIZON

1. National conventions for choosing party candidates for President are a long-standing tradition. Read the interesting article by Roy F. Nichols "It Happens Every Four Years," *American Heritage,* June 1956.

2. For elaboration on the theory that World War II was rooted in World War I, read Chapter V of Kennan, *American Diplomacy.*

3. Marquis Childs presents results of an interview with President Roosevelt in "I've Got This Thing Simplified," *American Heritage,* April 1957.

4. Hofstadter offers an objective analysis of Roosevelt in his essay "Franklin D. Roosevelt, Patrician as Opportunist," in *The American Political Tradition.*

INDIVIDUAL ACTIVITIES

1. Read the text of Roosevelt's broadcast to the nation on December 9, 1941, as given in Paul Angle, *By These Words,* pages 515–22. Select passages to read in class.

2. Draw a time-line of the years 1933–40. Above the line, list the major New Deal laws. Under the line, list the Supreme Court decisions which declared some of the legislation unconstitutional.

3. Compare America's attempts to maintain neutrality before the War of 1812, before World War I, and before World War II. (a) What were the similarities and the differences? (b) Why did these attempts fail?

4. Consult Hofstadter's *Great Issues in American History,* II, Part VII, "World War II and the Post-War World"—Documents 1–5. Read Roosevelt's "Quarantine the Aggressor" speech and his Lend-Lease press conference. For contrast, see Burton Wheeler's speech opposing Lend-Lease and Lindbergh's speech on America and the war. Report to class.

GROUP ACTIVITIES

1. Several able students should prepare a panel offering comparisons and contrasts in the political philosophies of Woodrow Wilson, Theodore Roosevelt, Herbert Hoover, and Franklin Roosevelt after investigating available source material. (See specifically Hofstadter, *Great Issues in American History,* II, Part V, Documents 11 and

12, and Part VI, Documents 8 and 9.)

2. Plan a debate based on the Amherst Series pamphlet *The New Deal: Revolution or Evolution.* Varied views are given which will aid both sides in the debate.

3. Roosevelt's efforts at Court reform in the 1930's spotlighted public attention on the Supreme Court. Encourage a group of able students to prepare a discussion for the class which will provide a better understanding of the historic role of the Court and of the specific issues involved in Roosevelt's time. Students can utilize the pamphlet *Franklin D. Roosevelt and the Supreme Court* (Amherst Series). For the historical background, articles by Carl B. Swisher, Charles Warren, and Robert Cushman are valuable. They should also consult the article by Merlo J. Pusey, "F. D. R. and the Supreme Court," in *Times of Trial* edited by Allan Nevins (Knopf).

SUGGESTED FURTHER READING
BIOGRAPHY
BURNS, J. M., *Roosevelt: The Lion and the Fox,* Harcourt, Brace.

DAVIS, KENNETH S., *Eisenhower: Soldier of Democracy,* Doubleday.

*MOLEY, RAYMOND, *After Seven Years,* Harper. Critical of New Deal.

NICOLAY, HELEN, *MacArthur of Bataan,* Appleton-Century-Crofts.

PERKINS, FRANCES, *The Roosevelt I Knew,* Viking.

SHERWOOD, ROBERT E., *Roosevelt and Hopkins: An Intimate History,* Harper.

TUGWELL, REXFORD G., *The Democratic Roosevelt,* Doubleday. Early New Deal.

WEINGAST, DAVID E., *Franklin D. Roosevelt: Man of Destiny,* Messner.

OTHER NONFICTION
*BAILEY, THOMAS A., *The Man in the Street,* Macmillan. Impact of American public opinion on foreign policy.

*BEARD, CHARLES A., *American Foreign Policy in the Making, 1932–1940,* Yale Univ. Press.

BLIVEN, BRUCE, *Story of D-Day: June 6, 1944,* Random House (Landmark Books).

BROGAN, DENIS W., *The Era of Franklin D. Roosevelt,* Yale Univ. Press.

COMMAGER, HENRY STEELE, ed., *The Pocket History of the Second World War,* Pocket Books.

EISENHOWER, DWIGHT D., *Crusade in Europe,* Doubleday.

*FAIRBANK, JOHN D., *The United States and China,* Harvard Univ. Press.

JANEWAY, ELIOT, *The Struggle for Survival,* Yale Univ. Press. United States mobilizing for World War II.

*LANGER, WILLIAM L., and S. EVERETT GLEASON, *The Challenge to Isolation: 1937–1940,* Harper.

——, *The Undeclared War: September 1940–December 1941,* Harper.

*LATOURETTE, KENNETH SCOTT, *The American Record in the Far East, 1945–1951,* Macmillan.

Life's Picture History of World War II, by the Editors of *Life,* Simon and Schuster.

LORD, WALTER, *Day of Infamy,* Holt. Attack on Pearl Harbor.

MILLIS, WALTER, *This is Pearl! The United States and Japan–1941,* Morrow.

NEVINS, ALLAN, *The New Deal in World Affairs,* Yale Univ. Press.

PRATT, FLETCHER, *War for the World,* Yale Univ. Press. American armed forces in World War II.

PYLE, ERNIE, *Brave Men,* Holt. Reporter describes soldiers in Italy and France.

*SCHLESINGER, ARTHUR M., JR., *The Age of Roosevelt,* Houghton Mifflin, 2 vols.

*TANSILL, CHARLES C., *Back Door to War: The Roosevelt Foreign Policy, 1933–1941,* Regnery. A critical view.

HISTORICAL FICTION
BROWN, HARRY, *A Walk in the Sun,* New American Library (Signet Books). United States army in Italy, World War II.

DRURY, ALLEN, *Advise and Consent,* Doubleday. Description of machinery of government in action.

HARGROVE, MARION, *See Here, Private Hargrove,* Oxford; Holt. Humorous view of life in the army.

LEWIS, SINCLAIR, *It Can't Happen Here!,* Doubleday. Prediction of events if United States were ruled by dictator.

MICHENER, JAMES A., *Tales of the South Pacific,* Macmillan; Pocket Books.

O'CONNOR, EDWIN, *The Last Hurrah,* Little, Brown.

SINCLAIR, UPTON, *Between Two Worlds,* Viking. Novel dealing with 1920's.

——, *Dragon Harvest,* Viking. Novel tracing events from Munich to fall of France.

——, *Dragon's Teeth,* Viking. Novel discussing road to Hitlerism.

——, *A World to Win,* Viking, Novel about events from fall of France to Pearl Harbor.

UNIT TWELVE

Challenges
of War
and of Peace

1941–1960's

Americans Fight a Second World War

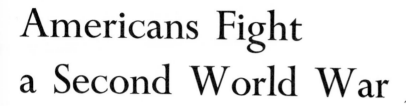

AMERICAN
ARMORED FORCES
IN NORTH AFRICA
– 1942

WORLD War II had been under way a little more than two years when on December 7, 1941, Japan's savage blow at Pearl Harbor plunged America into the global conflict.

America's enemies had the great advantage of what military men call "interior lines of supply and communication." Germany, Italy, and Japan were so situated geographically that the supply lines from their farms and factories to the fighting fronts were relatively short. The United States and its allies, on the other hand, had to establish and protect supply lines that often stretched thousands of miles across sea and land to fighting men in far-off areas of the earth.

America's enemies had an even greater advantage. They had been preparing for war for many years. During these years they had trained huge armies; they had converted their factories to war production; and they had accumu-

lated vast stores of rifles, machine guns, tanks, planes, and hundreds of other instruments of modern warfare. The United States, on the other hand, had not really begun to prepare for war until the summer of 1940, and even then preparations had been limited. Indeed, it was America's lack of preparation that led Hitler, Mussolini, and the Japanese war lords to believe that they could win the war before the United States could mobilize its enormous resources and man power.

Faced by such overwhelming odds, the American people grimly entered the conflict.

AS THE STORY DEVELOPS

1. Surviving disasters on all fronts, the Allies begin to take the offensive.
2. Americans accept government controls and win the "battle of production."
3. The Allies gradually fight their way to victory in Europe.
4. Allied victories in the Pacific bring an end to World War II.

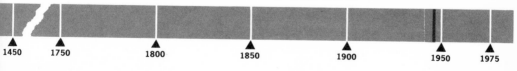

1450   1750   1800   1850   1900   1950   1975

Surviving disasters on all fronts, the Allies begin to take the offensive

During most of 1942, while the Americans were converting to a wartime economy, the United States and its allies suffered a series of almost unrelieved disasters in every theater of the war.

Japan's early gains in the Pacific. The scene at Pearl Harbor on the evening of December 7, 1941, was one of utter destruction. America's offensive power in the Pacific had been wiped out by the Japanese surprise attack. The shattered remnants of a once-powerful fleet put out to sea to avoid further attack, or were towed to naval bases on the Pacific coast for repairs.

Three days later Japan struck again, destroying two of Great Britain's most powerful war ships, the *Repulse* and the *Prince of Wales,* which had left the British naval base of Singapore without air cover in search of a Japanese convoy. By the end of December, Japan had seized the American islands of Guam and Wake; had captured the British colony of Hong Kong; and had launched attacks upon Thailand, British Malaya, and the American-controlled Philippines and Midway.

Disaster in the Pacific. The new year brought with it a mounting fury of destruction, with Japanese naval and land forces moving swiftly over a widening area of conquest in the Pacific and Far East (see map, pages 768–69). On January 2, 1942, Japanese troops poured into Manila, capital of the Philippines. On January 11 the Japanese invaded Borneo and the Dutch colony of Celebes (SEL-uh-beez) in the Netherlands Indies. On February 15 the advancing tide of Japanese troops, having swept down the Malay Peninsula, overran the British naval base at Singapore. Later in the month a Japanese naval force operating in the Java Sea met an Allied fleet composed of United States, British, Dutch, and Australian war ships. In

the engagement that followed, known as the Battle of the Java Sea, the Japanese administered a crushing blow to the Allies, sinking a number of cruisers and destroyers.

By the end of March, the Japanese had conquered most of the Netherlands Indies and their rich supplies of oil, tin, rubber, quinine, and other vital war materials; they had seized Rangoon, Burma; and they were relentlessly driving British, Indian, and Chinese troops from Burma.

Meanwhile, on the Philippines a small force of Americans and Filipinos under General Douglas MacArthur continued their heroic but hopeless resistance against the invading Japanese. Enemy submarines and planes sank two out of every three vessels bringing supplies and reinforcements. Defeat was only a matter of time. In January 1942 Manila surrendered, and MacArthur's forces retired to the Bataan Peninsula. In March MacArthur himself was ordered to Australia to take command of the Allied forces in the South Pacific. Fighting against overwhelming odds, the hungry, sick, exhausted survivors on Bataan were captured on April 9. On May 6 the outnumbered and starving troops on the fortress of Corregidor guarding Manila Bay were forced to surrender. During these days the Japanese also cut the Burma Road, destroying the last land route between the outside world and China (see map, pages 768–69).

Thus, by the end of May 1942, almost six months after their attack on Pearl Harbor, the Japanese had brushed aside all opposition and were poised to strike westward at British-dominated India; southward at the vast continent of Australia; and eastward through Hawaii at the Pacific coast of the United States. These were black days for Americans and their weary allies. But by the end of May, Japan had reached the peak of its success.

Japan is checked in the Pacific. Japan suffered its first serious reverse early in May 1942. Carrier-based planes from a British-American naval force caught

■ In the early days of the war, Americans had much to learn about jungle fighting, at which the Japanese were already experts. But the Americans learned quickly. Here, trees and vines have been leveled and American troops are cautiously wiping out Japanese resistance.

a Japanese fleet moving southward in the Coral Sea, which laps the northeastern coast of Australia, and sank or severely damaged more than 30 Japanese war ships.

Japanese forces received another setback early in June 1942 when they launched a two-pronged sea-borne attack on the Aleutian Islands and Hawaii. The ultimate objective of this two-pronged drive was an invasion of the United States. American forces stopped the northern campaign, but only after Japanese troops had occupied the Aleutian islands of Attu and Kiska (see map, pages 768–69). United States naval forces blocked the southern campaign by victory over the Japanese in a major battle off the island of Midway.

There are several reasons why the United States was at last beginning to stem the tide of Japanese aggression. First, early in 1942 the United States and Great Britain had pooled their resources, as yet meager, and created a unified command in the Pacific. Second,

the American people were beginning to win the important "battle of production" on the home front. The products of the nation's farms and factories were pouring into supply depots and forward bases on Midway, in Hawaii, in New Caledonia, in Samoa, and in Australia. Finally, time had been gained by the courageous resistance of Americans and Filipinos on Bataan and Corregidor.

The tide turns in the Pacific. On August 7, 1942, the United States undertook its first major offensive action when marines stormed ashore at Guadalcanal in the Solomon Islands (see map, pages 768–69). Two days after the Americans landed, the Japanese sank four heavy cruisers supporting the invasion, three American and one Australian. Loss of these ships was a major catastrophe. For four desperate months marines and army troops clung to a toehold around Guadalcanal's airport, renamed Henderson Field, repelling savage attacks from the air, the sea, and the surrounding jungle.

In November the Japanese made a desperate effort to regain their former bases in the Solomons, without which they could not move southward to invade Australia. But Admiral William F. Halsey intercepted the huge fleet of war ships and transports, and in a furious battle, November 12–15, completely routed the Japanese. Guadalcanal was at last secure. The tide had turned. From then on, the United States held the initiative in the Pacific.

Disaster in Europe. The situation in the Atlantic and in Europe during the winter and spring of 1942 was as forbidding as the situation in the Pacific had been early in 1942. German and Italian submarines lurked off the east coast of the United States and along the sea routes to England, turning the Atlantic into a vast area of flaming wreckage. During most of 1942, the Axis sank ships more rapidly than the United States and Great Britain could build new ones. England, a solitary fortress in the Atlantic, could not hope to hold out much longer unless reinforcements arrived, and unless something could be done to break the air supremacy which permitted the Nazis to rain down destruction upon British industrial areas.

On the continent of Europe, as in the Pacific, the tide of Axis conquest was rolling with terrifying speed. Yugoslavia lay beneath the Axis yoke. The Greeks had been reduced to near starvation. The Soviet Union had lost its rich grainfields in the Ukraine region, and a large number of its major industrial centers had been turned into smoking rubble. Part of the destruction was done by the Russians themselves, for, as they retreated before the Germans, they applied a "scorched earth" policy to their land, destroying everything that they could not carry with them.

Despite Russian resistance the Nazi *Panzer* divisions rolled on, in the summer offensive of 1942, overrunning the oil fields of the Caucasus and rumbling into the outskirts of Stalingrad on the Volga River (see map, pages 754–55).

Beyond lay the Ural Mountains, to which the Russians had moved many factories they had snatched from the path of the Germans, and where they were feverishly building new industries.

In the Mediterranean, as on the continent of Europe, the Axis forces were triumphant everywhere. German and Italian aircraft with bases in Italy, Greece, the Greek island of Crete, and North Africa virtually forced British naval craft out of the Mediterranean, and thus denied the British the use of the Suez Canal route to the Indian Ocean. Long mistress of the seas, Great Britain was compelled to send its ships thousands of miles around Africa to reach Egypt, the Middle East, and India. By the autumn of 1942, the German *Afrika Korps* under General Erwin Rommel had advanced to the frontiers of Egypt, where it stood poised for a final thrust at the Suez Canal and the oil fields of the Middle East.

Allied November victories. November 1942 marked a turning point of the war. In the Pacific, as you have seen, the three-day naval battle of Guadalcanal, on November 12–15, started the Allies on their long island-hopping drive to Tokyo. In North Africa the British General Bernard Law Montgomery · caught Rommel by surprise late in October, driving him back across the desert toward eventual and complete defeat. "For three years we have been trying to plug holes all over the world," Montgomery said to his men as they entered battle at El Alamein, in Egypt. "Now, thank God, that period is over."

Montgomery's words were prophetic. A few days later, on November 8, a mighty invasion armada led by General Dwight D. Eisenhower landed thousands of British, Canadian, and American troops on the northern coast of Africa (see map, pages 754–55). On November 19 the Russians, with the Volga River at their backs, began an encircling movement around the Nazis at Stalingrad. Within several weeks, after a heroic defense of their city, the Russians forced the Germans at Stalingrad to surrender. The siege had been lifted, and Hitler's boastful "supermen" had suffered an immense disaster.

"This is not the end," Winston Churchill said in November 1942. "It is not even the beginning of the end. But it is, perhaps, the end of the beginning." Subsequent events justified Churchill's prediction. Before 1942 drew to a close, the Allies held the initiative in Europe, as in the Pacific. From then until the end of the war, they exerted a steady pressure on the enemy until, in their gathering strength, they pierced the Axis defenses and plunged their armored forces into the heart of the aggressor nations.

Wartime co-operation. How had the Allies been able to survive the disasters of the period from December 7, 1941, to the fall of 1942? Why were they able in November to begin to seize the initiative? One answer is that the tremendous strength of America's manpower and war materials was beginning to have its effect. Another answer is that in their struggle for survival the Allied Powers worked as a team.

On January 1, 1942, the 26 Allied nations at war with the Axis Powers issued a joint declaration. In this declaration the 26 countries, calling themselves the United Nations,° (1) promised full co-operation in the war effort, (2) agreed not to make a separate peace, and (3) endorsed the war aims outlined in the Atlantic Charter (page 743).

Lend-Lease. Early in 1941, as you recall, even before the United States entered the conflict, Congress had laid the basis for large-scale co-operation with the Lend-Lease program (page 742).

After the attack on Pearl Harbor, the program went into high gear. The United States shipped immense quantities of war materials across the submarine-infested sea routes to its allies in the

••
° Eventually additional countries joined the ranks of the nations united in fighting the Axis. In 1945 the term "United Nations" (UN) was adopted as the official name of the permanent international organization that these nations formed.

INFANTRYMAN WITH BAZOOKA
COLD-WEATHER OUTFIT
FIGHTER PILOT
OFFICER
INFANTRYMAN WITH GARAND RIFLE

American uniforms and weapons—World War II

Pacific and to Great Britain, Russia, and the British armies stationed in Egypt and in the Middle East. The victories at Stalingrad and El Alamein owed much to American war materials. Before the war ended, the amount of Lend-Lease aid reached a total cost of more than 50 billion dollars, of which 69 per cent went to Great Britain, somewhat less than 25 per cent to the U.S.S.R., and smaller quantities to other Allies.

But Lend-Lease was not a one-way arrangement. During the war the United States received, in exchange, goods and services valued at nearly 8 billion dollars, most of which came from Great Britain. For example, when the first 600,000 American troops reached Northern Ireland after America's entry into the war, and when the American air forces began to arrive in England, the British provided bases, housing, and equipment. The Lend-Lease program was an outstanding example of wartime co-operation.

Co-operative planning. But without joint planning of strategy, all other co-operative efforts would have had very

(Continued on page 756)

753

ICELAND

ATLANTIC

GREAT

NORTH SEA

N. IRELAND

EIRE

BRITAIN

DENMARK

NORWAY

SWEDEN

FINLAND

BALTIC SEA

ESTONIA

Lenin

LATVIA

LITHUANIA

GER.

SO

1942-45

1940-44

London

Dunkirk

NETH.

Berlin

1945

Warsaw

1945

POLAND

1944

Kiev

English Channel

JUNE 6, 1944

BEL.

GERMANY

NORMANDY

Paris

LUX.

1944

1945

CZECHOSLOVAKIA

FRANCE

Vienna

AUSTRIA

HUNGARY

1945

RUMANIA

1944

Vichy

SWITZ.

"VICHY FRANCE"

PORTUGAL

SPAIN

ITALY

ADRIATIC SEA

YUGOSLAVIA

1944

1944

Rome

1944

BULGARIA

SARDINIA

Anzio

Cassino

Naples

Salerno

ALBANIA

Strait of Gibraltar

1942

Algiers

1943

Palermo

GREECE

SP. MOROCCO

Bizerte

1944

1943

Casablanca

1942

1943

Tunis

SICILY

CRETE

MOROCCO (Fr.)

ALGERIA (Fr.)

TUNISIA (Fr.)

MALTA

MEDITERRANEAN

El Ala

1943

1942

0   1000

Scale of miles

LIBYA

OCEAN

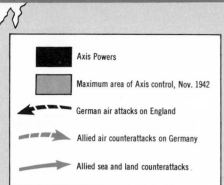

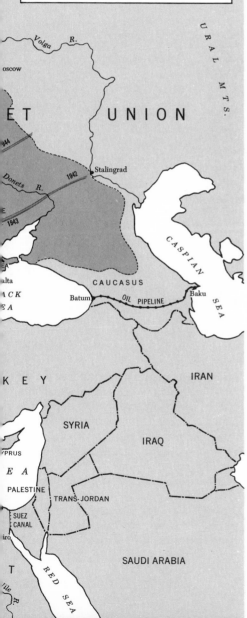

■	Axis Powers
▨	Maximum area of Axis control, Nov. 1942
◄╌╌	German air attacks on England
╌╌►	Allied air counterattacks on Germany
━━►	Allied sea and land counterattacks

Dark days for the Allies

1939 *Sept.–Oct.:* German invasion and conquest of Poland.

1940 *Apr.–June:* German invasion of Denmark, Norway, Luxembourg, Belgium, Netherlands, France.
May: British evacuation from Dunkirk.
June–July: Fall of France; establishment of Vichy government.
Aug.–Oct.: Battle of Britain (German air attacks).
Oct.: Axis aggressions in Balkans.
Nov.–Feb. 1941: British offensive in Mediterranean and North Africa.

1941 *Feb.–May:* Battle of the Atlantic begins.
Mar.–Apr.: Axis counteroffensive in North Africa.
Apr.–June: German invasion of Greece, Yugoslavia, Crete.
June: German invasion of U.S.S.R. begins.

Allied gains: the tide turns

1942 *May–Aug.:* Allied air attacks on Germany begin.
Oct.–Nov.: Allied counteroffensive in North Africa begins.
Nov.–Mar. 1943: Russian counteroffensives in U.S.S.R.; German surrender of Stalingrad (in February).

1943 *May:* Allied victory in North Africa; end of African campaign.
July–Aug.: Allied invasion of Sicily.
July–Jan. 1944: Russians drive Germans back in U.S.S.R. and enter Poland.
Sept.: Allies begin Italian campaigns.
Sept. 8: Italy surrenders.

1944 *June 6:* Allied invasion along Normandy coast (Operation Overlord).
Aug.: Allied forces land in southern France.
Aug. 25: Allies liberate Paris.
Sept.: Allies liberate Belgium, Luxembourg.
Sept.: Battle for Germany begins.
Sept.–Dec.: Russians conquer Yugoslavia and Hungary.
Dec.: Battle of the Bulge (last German counteroffensive).

Allied victory in Germany

1945 *Feb.–Apr.:* Allied invasion of Germany.
May 7: Germany surrenders.
May 8: V–E Day (end of war in Europe).

755

little effect. Shortly after the attack on Pearl Harbor, Prime Minister Churchill and a group of military, naval, and technical aides visited Washington to help plan the conduct of the war. In Washington they met with General George C. Marshall, Chief of Staff of the Army, and leaders of the air, land, and sea forces. This meeting was the first of a series held by the military leaders of the countries fighting the Axis Powers.

From the beginning, however, the larger military strategy was worked out by the combined Chiefs of Staff of Great Britain and the United States and submitted to President Roosevelt and Prime Minister Churchill for final approval. When Russian troops were involved, Stalin and his military staff were, of course, drawn into the planning. Similarly, the Chiefs of Staff of China, Australia, New Zealand, Canada, and other members of the United Nations were consulted before action involving their military forces was undertaken.

These conferences required a spirit of give and take. Final decisions were not always popular with all of the parties concerned. For example, the decision made in the summer of 1942 to concentrate American forces against Germany, and to send a minimum of support to the Pacific, was extremely unpopular with the desperate Chinese, the Australians, the New Zealanders, and many Americans on the Pacific coast. Another major decision reached at this same time displeased the Russians. Hard-pressed in the summer of 1942, they urged their allies to relieve the pressure on the Soviet Union in eastern Europe by opening a "second front" in western Europe. British and American military leaders did not feel that they were sufficiently prepared to do this. As a result, Roosevelt and Churchill, as you have seen, decided to land troops in North Africa instead, from where they could strike at southern Europe, or what Churchill called the "soft underbelly" of the Axis.

✓ SECTION SURVEY

1. The period from December 1941 to May 1942 constituted "black days for Americans and their weary allies." Explain.
2. What conditions and events helped the Americans to stem the tide of Japanese aggression?
3. "November 1942 marked a turning point of the war." Justify this statement by referring to events that occurred in the European and Pacific theaters of war.
4. Show how the Lend-Lease program helped the United States and its allies.
5. Give examples of joint planning of strategy which helped to win the war.

IDENTIFY: Bataan, Guadalcanal, "scorched earth" policy, *Afrika Korps*, United Nations, "second front"; MacArthur, Halsey, Rommel, Montgomery, Eisenhower, Marshall.

2 Americans accept government controls and win the "battle of production"

The Allied landings in North Africa in November 1942, and the victories at Guadalcanal, El Alamein, and Stalingrad—all within a few months of one another—were won on the farms and in the factories of the United Nations, as well as on the fighting fronts. By the end of 1942, the United States in particular had become "the arsenal of democracy."

Hitler underestimates Allied Powers. When he declared war upon the United States on December 11, 1941, Hitler had already made two grave mistakes. First, he had failed to invade England. Had he launched an invasion across the English Channel immediately after the British armies lost most of their equipment at Dunkirk, he might have conquered Great Britain.

Hitler's second mistake was his surprise attack upon the U.S.S.R. on June 22, 1941. Despite his phenomenal successes, his failure to take Moscow before Christmas 1941 should have been a warning to him. He had ignored this warning. The following spring, as you recall, he sent his armies even farther across the vast plains of the Soviet Union. He wanted the wheat of the Ukraine, the oil of the Caucasus, and the industrial resources of the Donets region and the area along the Volga River. Instead, his troops eventually met disaster in front of Stalingrad.

On December 11, 1941, Hitler made his third major mistake by declaring war upon the United States. He miscalculated the speed with which the American people could convert their peacetime industries to war production.

America's production soars. One of the amazing demonstrations of America's productivity was staged on the nation's farm lands. Despite the fact that 2,000,000 agricultural workers enlisted or were drafted into the armed forces, the farmers managed to raise record-breaking crops. They raised enough food to supply the American people as well as their allies.

The output of America's mines and factories was equally impressive. For example, between July 1, 1940, and July 31, 1945, United States manufacturing plants produced 296,601 military planes, including 97,000 bombers; 86,388 tanks; 88,077 scout cars and carriers; 16,438 armored cars; 2,434,553 trucks; 991,299 light vehicles, such as jeeps; 123,707 tractors; 17,400,000 rifles and side arms; 2,724,897 machine guns; 315,000 pieces of artillery; and 41,400,000,000 rounds of ammunition.

In addition, America's shipbuilders launched 71,060 naval vessels and 45,000,000 tons of merchant ships, creating the greatest navy and merchant marine that the world had ever seen. By 1943 five ocean-going vessels were being launched every twenty-four hours to join the growing fleet that was linking America's farms and factories with the far-flung battle fronts.

All in all, production during the war years was 75 per cent greater than in peacetime. According to Donald M. Nelson, first chief of the War Production Board (WPB), created in January 1942, America's production was "a remarkable demonstration of power. . . .

Women in the Labor Force

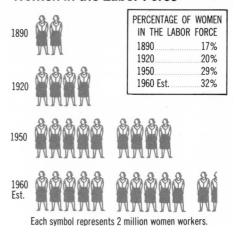

PERCENTAGE OF WOMEN IN THE LABOR FORCE	
1890	17%
1920	20%
1950	29%
1960 Est.	32%

Each symbol represents 2 million women workers.

American industry turned out more goods for war than we ever produced for our peacetime needs—yet had enough power left over to keep civilian standards of living at an astonishingly high level."

Financing the war. Where did the money come from to finance the war? A little more than one third of the money came from taxes, which were raised to the highest level in American history. The government borrowed the remainder, chiefly by selling huge issues of bonds. Because of this borrowing, the national debt shot upward. In 1941 it had totaled not quite 49 billion dollars. By the spring of 1945, it reached nearly 259 billion dollars.

The dollar cost of the war was staggering. During World War II the government spent far more per month for military purposes than it had spent for the entire War Between the States! By 1945 military expenditures totaled 400 billion dollars—twice the sum that the federal government had spent for all of its activities, including all wars, between 1789 and 1940!

Government control of production. The task of mobilizing the nation's manpower and resources required a tremendous amount of planning. This was the job of the federal government, which created a complicated network of agencies to organize the war effort.

At the top there was a policy-making board called the Office of War Mobilization (OWM), headed until 1945 by James F. Byrnes, formerly Senator from South Carolina and until 1942 a justice of the Supreme Court. The job of the OWM was to unify the activities of the many war agencies.

Just below the OWM was the War Production Board, which affected the daily lives of nearly every man, woman, and child in the United States. It controlled the allocations of raw materials to industrial plants. It searched the country for scrap iron and canvassed the nation's kitchens for fats, tin, and aluminum. It directed the conversion of factories making peacetime goods into units producing war materials. It stimulated the construction of new industrial plants, including 60 synthetic rubber centers to provide substitutes for the natural rubber formerly secured from the Malay Peninsula and the Netherlands Indies.

In addition, the WPB restricted the production of consumer goods, including automobiles, refrigerators, radios, electric appliances, garden tools, typewriters, plumbing fixtures, metal toys, and almost all civilian goods requiring materials necessary to the war effort. It rationed gasoline in order to conserve oil and rubber. It even controlled styles of clothing in order to save wool, cotton, rayon, and other vital materials.

Mobilizing resources. Under the leadership of Paul V. McNutt of Indiana, the War Manpower Commission (WMC) was another agency that closely touched the lives of numerous Americans. It operated the Selective Service System, which by the end of the war had drafted nearly 10,000,000 of the more than 15,000,000 Americans who served in the armed forces. It discouraged men and women from working in non-essential occupations, and by 1945 had helped to channel nearly 30,000,000 workers into war industries.

In its effort to mobilize the nation's resources and to direct America's wartime activities, the federal government created numerous other agencies, among them the War Shipping Administration and the Office of Defense Transportation. These agencies closely supervised the railroads, express services, and shipping, with the result that freight and troops were moved efficiently in vast quantities over land and sea. Another agency, the Office of War Information, bolstered the morale not only of the armed forces but also of the civilians by publicizing the achievements of war production. It also presented the war aims of the United Nations, constantly broadcasting them in dozens of languages to the whole world.

By 1944, more than 3,000,000 men and women were employed by the federal government—2,168,366 in war agencies; 1,037,755 in non-war agencies. These figures did not, of course, include members of the armed forces. In addition, hundreds of thousands of other Americans served voluntarily on local selective service and rationing boards and in positions of civilian defense as air raid wardens and airplane spotters.

Government control of prices. One of the ways in which the government most closely regulated the lives of civilians was through price controls. It was evident from the beginning of the war that the shortage of consumer goods and the increased purchasing power of the industrial and agricultural workers would drive prices skyward, bringing on inflation. This had happened in World War I, causing much suffering among the poorer people. The government was determined to prevent prices from skyrocketing again. In its first step against inflation, the government raised income taxes, by this means draining off dollars that would otherwise have competed for goods in the stores. As a second step, the government encouraged the public to buy war bonds, arguing that such purchases were both a patriotic duty and a sound investment. But it was clear that these measures alone would not prevent inflation.

In 1942, following the example of the European governments, Congress authorized the Office of Price Administration (OPA) to establish ceilings, or top limits, on prices and to set up a rationing system. The OPA issued ration books° for gasoline, fuel, shoes, coffee, sugar, fats and oils, meat, butter, and canned foods. It also established rent controls. By these measures it protected consumers from price increases and unfair distribution as the available supply of goods dwindled and as the housing shortage became acute.

Despite all of these efforts, the prices of consumer goods rose, especially those of food. By 1944 the cost of living had risen 30 per cent above that prevailing in 1941 before the attack on Pearl Harbor. There was some grumbling from Americans who resented government controls over their daily lives, and there was some violation of the rationing system by people willing to buy in the "black market."° On the whole, however, the public accepted price controls and rationing as a wartime necessity.

Government control of wages. Shortly after the attack on Pearl Harbor, the union leaders of the A.F. of L., the CIO, and the Railroad Brotherhoods promised President Roosevelt that the organized workers of the country would not strike for the duration of the war. At the same time they insisted that it was the government's responsibility to see that, in return for the "no-strike pledge," the workers would receive fair treatment. By the spring of 1942, however, the cost of living had risen, and the workers were becoming restless.

In July 1942, the National War Labor Board (WLB), which was created to deal with labor problems, attempted to

....

° *ration book:* a book of coupons received by each civilian from the government; when buying a rationed product, the purchaser had to give the seller a designated number of coupons in addition to the money price.
° *black market:* a term used to describe business transactions carried on in violation of price controls, in which purchasers often paid exorbitant prices in order to obtain more than their share of rationed products.

WOMEN IN WORLD WAR II

During World War II, many more women than ever before disregarded the old saying that "woman's place is in the home." By 1943 more than 2 million women were working in war plants, replacing men who had left for the armed services. And, for the first time, the American armed forces, which had previously used women only as nurses, now organized corps of women to substitute for men in non-combatant jobs. More than 250,000 women entered the Army (as Wacs), the Coast Guard (as Spars), the Navy (as Waves), and the Marine Corps. In the services, women worked as machinists, storekeepers, and office workers; they operated radios, and drove jeeps and trucks.

When people recovered from their surprise at seeing women in these new roles, they began to speak of "the girl behind the man behind the gun."

work out a compromise. It granted a 15 per cent wage increase to readjust the workers' incomes to the rise in living costs since January 1, 1941. Several months later Congress and President Roosevelt authorized the WLB to "freeze" the wages and salaries of all workers at the newly established levels.

For a time there was relatively little trouble. But as prices continued to rise, labor again became restless, and here and there, in local situations, strikes broke out. In such instances the government usually intervened, and for the most part succeeded in settling the disputes quickly.

Many critics claimed that the War Labor Board was biased in favor of labor, and they insisted that any man-hours lost in strikes endangered the whole war effort. To this charge President Roosevelt replied that the actual number of man-hours lost through strikes was an insignificant part of the total man-hours worked. "The production necessary to equip and maintain our vast forces of fighting men on global battle fronts is without parallel . . ." he stated in October 1944. "The production which has flowed from this country to all the battle fronts of the world has been due to the efforts of American business, American labor, and American farmers, working together as a patriotic team."

Government control of profits. Paralleling its efforts to control prices and wages, the government undertook to regulate profits. This was done principally by means of taxation. Personal income taxes were greatly increased for people in the higher income brackets. But the most drastic means of controlling profits was the excess profits tax, levied in 1940, which obliged corporations to pay to the government as much as 90 per cent of all excess profits.

Americans did not like government controls, but accepted them with the understanding that they would be removed when the emergency was over.

⌙ **SECTION SURVEY**

1. Cite three mistakes made by Hitler.
2. Show how America's agricultural and industrial production made the United States "the arsenal of democracy."
3. What methods were used by the federal government to finance the war?
4. The federal government created "a network of wartime agencies to organize and carry on the war effort." Explain by giving five examples.
5. Describe the measures taken by the federal government to control (a) prices, (b) wages, and (c) profits.

IDENTIFY: Office of War Mobilization, War Production Board, War Manpower Commission, Selective Service System, Office of War Information, Office of Price Administration, ration books, "black market," National War Labor Board; Byrnes.

3 The Allies gradually fight their way to victory in Europe

In the summer of 1942, while the United States was beginning to win the battle of production at home, President Roosevelt and Prime Minister Churchill of Great Britain decided to strike at what Churchill called the "soft underbelly" of the Axis.

Victory in North Africa. The opening blow, as you have seen, fell late in October 1942, when the British under General Montgomery broke through Rommel's lines at El Alamein and began to drive the Germans back toward Tunisia and Algeria. Meanwhile, on November 8, a force of 500 troop transports and 350 war ships under the command of General Eisenhower landed British, Canadian, and American troops on the coasts of French Morocco and Algeria. It was the greatest combination of land, sea, and air forces assembled up to that time.

The loss of French areas in North Africa was a serious blow to the Germans. Nevertheless, they continued to fight with great skill. But their efforts were hopeless. Allied planes and naval units cut their supply lines from Italy. General Montgomery's British Eighth Army drove steadily westward, while American forces moved eastward. Outnumbered and caught between the jaws of two enemy forces in Tunisia (see map, pages 754–55), the Germans and the Italians surrendered early in May 1943.

As a result of the victory in North Africa, the Allies captured more than 250,000 Axis troops. Far more important, the victory gave the United Nations control of the Mediterranean. Allied war ships could now operate in the Mediterranean as they pleased, protected by planes based at airfields along the North African coast. The Allies could ship supplies through the Suez Canal to India and Russia by way of Iran.

■ Allied forces were landed on the Anzio beaches in an effort to cut off the Germans at Cassino and open the road to Rome. Here, American and Canadian soldiers are firing from a rock barricade to provide cover for a patrol sent out to probe the approaches to Cassino.

Invasion of Italy. From their newly won North African bases the United Nations subjected Sicily and Italy to merciless bombing. Then, early in July 1943, British, Canadian, and American troops landed in Sicily. The Sicilians offered little resistance, and the crack German troops were greatly outnumbered by the invaders, who swiftly overran the island.

Americans and other peoples of the United Nations were thrilled at the rapid conquest of Sicily and the good news that came over the radio during the months of July, August, and September 1943. Late in July Mussolini fell from power. Before dawn on September 3, exactly four years after Great Britain had entered the conflict, the British Eighth Army landed on the southern coast of the Italian mainland. On September 8 the Italian government surrendered unconditionally, and the following day an Allied invasion force landed at Salerno.

Despite these great successes the campaign for control of Italy turned out to be one of the longest and most difficult of the entire war. Veteran German troops were rushed in to fill the gaps left by the Italians. Difficult mountain terrain and bad weather helped the Germans. On October 1 Naples fell to an American army under General Mark W. Clark, but for several months the Allies were unable to advance beyond Cassino (see map, pages 754–55). In an effort to outflank the German lines, Allied troops landed on January 22, 1944, on the Anzio beaches. Anzio was behind the Germans at Cassino and only 25 miles from Rome. But the Nazis fought desperately, and it was not until June 4, 1944, that the Allied armies entered Rome.

From Rome they moved northward. Progress was slow, and every inch of soil was won at great cost by fighting men of the United Nations—Americans, British, Canadians, Indians, New Zealanders, South Africans, French, Moroccans, Algerians, Senegalese, Italians, Poles, Greeks, Arabs, Brazilians, and a Jewish brigade from Palestine.

Although the Nazis were pressed steadily northward through the mountains, fighting continued in Italy until the last few months of the war in Europe.

Importance of the gains in Italy. The victories in Italy during 1943–44 were immensely important. Through them the Allies strengthened their control of the Mediterranean. The loss of Italy deprived Germany of desperately needed manpower. Moreover, from Italian bases Allied airmen were able to bomb southern Germany and the German-held Balkans, including the rich oil fields in Rumania.

Finally, in their efforts to check the Allies in North Africa and Italy, the Germans had been forced to withdraw many divisions from the Russian Front. This had helped the Russians to regain great stretches of valuable agricultural land in the Ukraine. Despite the Italian campaign, however, the Nazis continued to concentrate most of their military forces against the Soviet Union, and the Russians continued to call for a "second front" in Western Europe.

Victory in the Atlantic. The victories in Italy were possible only because the Allies were able to win control of the Atlantic Ocean. During the early months of the war, German submarines waged a mighty battle against ships carrying supplies to Europe. On April 23, 1942, Winston Churchill reported secretly to Parliament:

"I will begin with the gravest matter; namely, the enormous losses and destruction of shipping by German U-boats off the east coast of the United States. In a period of less than sixty days, more tonnage was sunk in this one stretch than we had lost all over the world during the last five months of the Battle of the Atlantic before America entered the war. . . ."

Gradually, however, the Allies began to gain the upper hand. Radar and other devices for detecting planes and submarines were developed. New war ships began to slide down the ways of American and British shipyards, among them small aircraft carriers called "baby flattops." During 1942 the Axis sank 585 Allied and neutral vessels in the Atlantic. During 1943, while the Allies were invading North Africa and Italy, the Axis sank only 110 ships. By the end of 1943, the Battle of the Atlantic was won.

Over the sea lanes great convoys carried the urgently needed military supplies to the Mediterranean war fronts. Other convoys carried an enormous volume of war materials and hundreds of thousands of troops to Great Britain, which by 1943 had been converted into a vast base for the invasion of Western Europe.

Victory in the air. While the United Nations were winning the Battle of the Atlantic, Allied planes began their offensive against Germany and German-occupied Europe. In 1942, American airmen began taking part in Royal Air Force raids. By the early months of 1943, the combined Anglo-American air assault had become a major factor in the war. As the months passed, the number and weight of bombs dropped on Axis territory became increasingly significant until, during the last year of the war, fleets of as many as 2000 heavy bombers were dropping tons of bombs on a single target area.

In general, United States bombers worked by day. Equipped with the new Norden bombsight, they undertook the job of pinpoint bombing, concentrating on a single factory or group of factories. Royal Air Force bombers continued the offensive by night, making blanket attacks upon industrial cities.

The destruction was immense. The incessant blows against German transportation centers, industrial plants, and military installations weakened German morale and power to resist. The Allied air raids brought relief to Great Britain, which had suffered tremendous damage from German air attacks. They also helped Russian armies seeking to drive the Nazis from Russian soil.

Liberation of Western Europe. The terrific air assault on Germany was merely part of a larger strategy—the invasion and conquest of Germany. While the Allied air forces continued their attacks with ever-growing fury, Allied convoys carried millions of tons of war materials and vast forces of men and planes to Great Britain. By June 1944 General Dwight D. Eisenhower, who had been named Supreme Commander of the Allied invasion armies in Western Europe, was satisfied that it was time to launch the attack.

"Operation Overlord," as the invasion was called, began before dawn on the morning of June 6, 1944 (D–Day). More than 11,000 planes roared into the air. Some dropped air-borne troops at key points a few miles inland from the German-occupied French coast. Others bombed roads, bridges, railway junctions, and German troop concentrations. Others formed a mighty umbrella under which a huge invasion fleet of nearly 4000 troop transports, landing craft, and war ships moved across the English Channel to the Normandy beaches (see map, pages 754–55).

The Germans had worked for years to make these beaches impregnable. Heavy artillery and machine guns were located in reinforced concrete pillboxes. Barbed wire and tank traps lined the shores. Other tangles of barbed wire were strung on steel and concrete piles sunk just below the surface of the water for hundreds of feet offshore.

Despite the years of preparation, the Germans were powerless to prevent the invasion. "Terrific air power broke up all bridges and pinned me down completely, and the terrific power of the naval guns made it absolutely impossible for reserves to come up," Field Marshal Karl von Rundstedt later explained. The Nazis resisted fiercely, but they had been outplanned, and they were outnumbered and outfought.

Allied tank forces ripped through the German defenses, and fanned out behind the lines. Aided by the French resistance, or underground movement, they quickly overran the countryside. On August 25, 1944, Paris fell. By this time the Allies had landed more than 2,000,000 men, nearly 500,000 motor

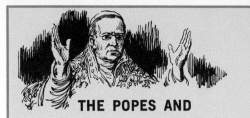

THE POPES AND
THE BACKGROUND OF WAR

Pius XI was the first Pope who had to deal with the modern totalitarian rulers. His policy was to recognize them if they would agree to *concordats*, solemn guarantees for the liberties of the Church, but he reserved every right to criticize them on moral issues. He resented the fact that a dictator's motive for signing such a treaty might be to gain a prestige that strengthened his hold on the people, but the Pope's purpose was to have a legal standard by which to judge the regime. So Pius signed the Lateran Treaty of 1929 with Mussolini, and a concordat with Hitler in 1933. Had the Russian Communists been willing to offer terms, he might have made a treaty with Stalin.

Needless to say, the treaties with Mussolini and Hitler were interpreted by them in a manner most offensive to the Pope. This in turn caused Pius XI to condemn their principles in strong terms. In 1931 he denounced Italian fascism as a heresy for its principle: "Everything for the state, nothing outside the state." Despite the concordat with Hitler, it was obvious by 1937 that "only a few times previously has there been a persecution so terrible." That year Pius XI denounced the Nazi creed of race as anti-Christian, and deplored Hitler's complete disregard for the terms of the concordat. Then, lest any Catholic be deceived by Russian maneuvers, he condemned any ideas of cooperating with atheistic Communism.

Pius XII, who became Pope in 1939, had to see his warnings against war go for nothing. But in the course of the awful conflict it was clear to many, as it had not been clear in 1914–18, that great numbers of people were looking more to the successors of Peter for moral guidance than they were to any self-appointed political saviors. President Franklin D. Roosevelt was aware of this when he sent a personal representative to the Vatican in 1939.

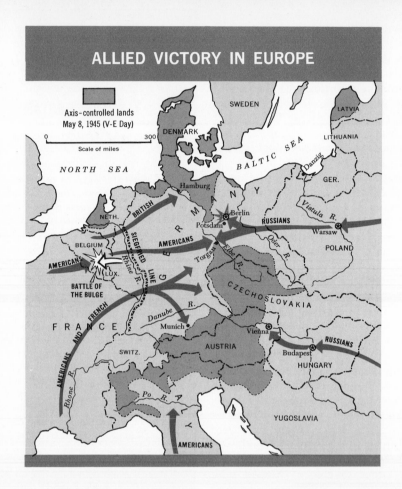

ALLIED VICTORY IN EUROPE

Axis-controlled lands
May 8, 1945 (V-E Day)

0   300
Scale of miles

SWEDEN

LATVIA

DENMARK

LITHUANIA

NORTH SEA

BALTIC SEA

Danzig

GER.

Hamburg

G E R M A N Y

Vistula R.

NETH.

BRITISH

Berlin

Potsdam

RUSSIANS

Warsaw

BELGIUM

SIEGFRIED LINE

AMERICANS

Oder R.

Elbe R.

POLAND

Torgau

AMERICANS

Rhine R.

LUX.

BATTLE OF
THE BULGE

C Z E C H O S L O V A K I A

FRANCE

AMERICANS AND FRENCH

Danube R.

Munich

Vienna

RUSSIANS

SWITZ.

AUSTRIA

Budapest

HUNGARY

Rhone R.

Po R.

I T A L Y

YUGOSLAVIA

AMERICANS

vehicles, and millions of tons of munitions and supplies.

Meanwhile, early in August, the United States Seventh Army landed on the southern coast of France and pushed rapidly up the Rhone Valley to join the Allied troops pouring in from Normandy. The combined forces then plunged onward across the battlefields of World War I and the scenes of Anglo-French disaster in the spring of 1940, but this time it was the Germans who retreated. Within six months after D–Day, France had been liberated, and the Allies had swept into the outer defenses of Germany's famous Siegfried Line (see map, this page). Here the attack at last ground to a halt, and the Allied armies paused while new ports were opened, supplies were brought up, and military units were regrouped.

Germany's last counterattack. Field Marshal Von Rundstedt chose this moment to launch a counterattack. On December 16 he struck with 24 German divisions at a weakly held point in the Allied lines. His armored forces broke through, creating a dangerous "bulge" at a weak point in the Allied lines. Christmas 1944 found the Allies fighting with desperation in the Battle of the Bulge, trying to prevent the Germans from plunging onward to the sea. Reinforcements were rushed up. The Allied lines held. Rundstedt's divisions were shattered and thrown back behind the Siegfried Line. This was the final major counterattack by the Nazis. Their defeat cost them dearly in men and equipment. Even more important, as General Eisenhower pointed out, "was the widespread disillusionment within the German army and Germany itself."

Allied victory in Germany. By February 1945 Allied preparations had been completed for the invasion of Germany itself. The air forces continued to blast industrial areas, military bases, and transportation lines. Then, in March, the Allies crossed the Rhine, encircled Nazi troop concentrations, and raced toward the heart of Germany.

Meanwhile, the Russians had been driving the Germans out of the Ukraine, had conquered Rumania and Hungary, and were closing in upon the Nazis from the south and east. On April 25, Russian and American forces met at Torgau on the Elbe River (see map, page 764). Here, by orders of the Allied Supreme Command, the advance halted.

Events that ended the war in Europe then followed in rapid order. On May 1 Hitler reportedly took his own life in the burning ruins of Berlin. On May 2 the Russians hammered their way into the last Nazi strongholds of the city, and nearly 1,000,000 German soldiers in Italy and Austria surrendered. Germany was in chaos. Within a week the Nazis in the Netherlands, Denmark, and Germany stopped fighting. And on the night of May 7, the German High Command surrendered unconditionally. May 8, 1945 (V–E Day) marked the formal end of the war in Europe.

The election of 1944. Meanwhile, in November 1944, elections were held as usual. The Republican candidate, Thomas E. Dewey, governor of New York, had attracted national attention when, as a district attorney, he had successfully prosecuted racketeers in New York. The Republicans considered Dewey a strong candidate, and, having made gains in the Congressional elections of 1942, were hopeful of victory. But the war was going well, and the Democrats argued that it would be unwise to replace experienced leaders with new men. This argument proved convincing. Roosevelt, running for a fourth term, won with an electoral vote of 432 to Dewey's 99. The new Vice-President was Harry S. Truman of Missouri.

Death of President Roosevelt. President Roosevelt did not live to see the Allied victory for which he had devoted his every effort during nearly four years of warfare. Worn out by the vast responsibilities he had assumed, he died suddenly on April 12 in the "Little White House" at Warm Springs, Georgia. The people of the United Nations were stunned at the news of his death. For three days radio stations in the United States canceled programs in order to devote time to his memory. And

■ Throngs of Americans gathered in jubilation as the news of Germany's surrender was spread by the newspapers and radio. You can be sure that the message heralded by these headlines had personal implications to many of the people shown in the picture.

Vice-President Harry S. Truman, who now became President Truman, declared, "His fellow countrymen will sorely miss his fortitude and faith and courage in the time to come. The peoples of the earth who love the ways of freedom and hope will mourn for him."

✔ SECTION SURVEY

1. Discuss the military significance of the Allied victories in (a) North Africa and (b) Italy.
2. Give two reasons why the Allies began to win the Battle of the Atlantic.
3. What conditions made possible the successful invasion of Normandy?
4. Describe the events of 1945 that led to the fall of Germany and to the end of the war in Europe.
IDENTIFY: "Operation Overlord," D–Day, Siegfried Line, Battle of the Bulge, V–E Day; Clark, Von Rundstedt, Dewey, Truman; June 6, 1944; May 8, 1945.

4 Allied victories in the Pacific bring an end to World War II

President Roosevelt died in April 1945, only a month before the Allied victory in Europe and only four months before the defeat of the Japanese brought World War II to an end.

By 1943, as you have seen, the United States and its allies felt strong enough to take the offensive in the Pacific. The over-all strategy directed by Admiral Chester W. Nimitz called for air, land, and naval forces to strike westward at the Japanese-held islands in the Central Pacific; for a fleet under Admiral Halsey to drive the Japanese from the Solomon Islands; and for General MacArthur to advance with troops along the New Guinea coast and on to the Philippines. The ultimate objective was Japan.

Preliminary victories. During 1943 American, Australian, and New Zealand fighting men pushed doggedly forward through the steaming jungles and across the vast stretches of the Central and South Pacific. The struggle was grim, for the Japanese clung to every foot of land. Few prisoners were taken.

Driving the Japanese from their threatening position before Port Moresby, which defended Australia, American and Australian troops fought their way up the New Guinea coast. Before the end of 1943, they had captured the coastal towns of Salamaua, Lae, and Finschhafen, and much of New Guinea had been recovered. American and New Zealand forces won victories in the Solomons, notably at Bougainville (boo-gan-VEEL).

Meanwhile, in the Central Pacific, Admiral Nimitz's powerful fleet moved into the Gilbert Islands and put marines ashore on Tarawa and Makin (see map, pages 768–69). Marines seized both of these islands, the former only after terrible fighting. Far to the north Japan's troops were dislodged from the Aleutian strongholds of Attu and Kiska, and the threat to Alaska was ended.

Despite these successes, won at extreme cost in lives after ferocious fighting, the Allied gains in 1943 were limited. The major Japanese positions remained untouched.

Island hopping to the Philippines. By 1944 a growing volume of men and supplies was arriving in the Pacific, and many of the areas conquered by the Allies in 1943 were being converted into great staging bases from which new advances could be made. Powerful new war ships and aircraft carriers, grouped into swift task forces,° were sweeping through the outer screen of protecting islands to blast Japanese installations and shipping routes. Carrier planes were raining explosives on the Japanese-held islands prior to invasion.

Suddenly, on January 31, 1944, the United Nations struck again, this time against the Marshall Islands (see map, pages 768–69). Three days later they seized Kwajalein (KWAH-jah-layn), one of the keys to Japanese control of the

••
° *task force:* a naval unit temporarily grouped under one commander and formed for carrying out a specific mission.

Marshalls. Kwajalein was the first Japanese possession occupied by the Allies. Three weeks later Eniwetok (eh-NEE-weh-tok) was stormed successfully. From these two newly acquired bases, strong fleets of B–24 bombers began to blast Truk (TROOK), major stronghold in the Carolines and key to Japanese control of the Southwest and Central Pacific. Meanwhile, General MacArthur, continuing his methodical advance up the New Guinea coast, seized Hollandia. By July all of New Guinea was in his hands, with only bypassed pockets of Japanese troops left to surrender or to starve.

A month earlier, in June 1944, the Pacific war erupted with extreme violence. Task-force raids and swift strikes by carrier-based planes pinned down Japanese air and naval forces and hammered the defenses of Saipan and Guam in the Mariana Islands (see map, pages 768–69). Then, under cover of intense air and naval bombardment, landing craft swept in upon the beaches. From fleet concentrations near the Philippines, the Japanese sent out swarms of planes, only to lose more than 400 in a few hours. The following day hundreds of American planes roared from the decks of carriers to strike a severe blow at the retreating Japanese fleet.

Shocked and saddened though they were by the appalling loss of life, the American people were thrilled at the victories on Guam and Saipan. They had long dreaded the thought of a slow, bloody, island-by-island advance to Japan. Now, as they saw the larger strategy unfolding, Americans realized that America's tremendous sea and air power enabled it to seize the key positions in the Pacific, leaving Japanese forces isolated and helpless on numerous islands far behind the line of battle.

Victory in the Philippines. But among the most gratifying news from the Pacific in 1944 was the reconquest of the Philippines. In October a vast armada of war ships, carriers, transports, and landing craft moved up from the New Guinea–Solomons theater of war and in from Saipan and Guam. Under naval

THE ATOMIC BOMB

On August 6, 1945, the first atomic bomb used in warfare was dropped from an American airplane onto the city of Hiroshima in Japan. Three days later, a second bomb fell on Nagasaki, another Japanese city. More than 150,000 Japanese died in the resulting holocausts. Thousands of others suffered dreadful aftereffects.

In February 1947, in *Harper's Magazine,* Secretary of War Henry L. Stimson wrote about the decision to use the bombs:

"The face of war is the face of death; death is an inevitable part of any order that a wartime leader gives... War in the twentieth century has grown steadily more barbarous, more destructive, more debased in all its aspects. Now, with the release of atomic energy, man's ability to destroy himself is very nearly complete. The bombs dropped on Hiroshima and Nagasaki ended a war. They also made it wholly clear that we must never have another war. This is the lesson men and leaders everywhere must learn, and I believe that when they learn it they will find a way to lasting peace. There is no other choice."

and air cover the converging forces poured upon the beaches of Leyte (LAY-teh) in the central Philippines (see map, pages 768–69) and eventually captured the island. Meanwhile, in one of the greatest naval engagements of the war, the Battle of Leyte Gulf, American naval forces struck a shattering blow at Japan's remaining sea power.

(Continued on page 770)

SIBERIA (U.S.S.R.)

OUTER
MONGOLIA

MANCHUKUO
(MANCHURIA)

SAKHALIN

ATTU KISKA ALEU

1943

Hwang R.

Peiping

Tientsin

KURILE IS.

"THE HUMP"

INDIA   C H I N A

SHANTUNG
PENIN.

KOREA

Hiroshima

Tokyo

STILWELL ROAD

Chungking

Yangtze R.

J A P A N

MIDWAY
IS.

19

BURMA   BURMA ROAD

Nanking

Nagasaki

Shanghai

WAR ENDS, SEPT. 2, 1945

Rangoon

Hong
Kong

OKINAWA

FR. INDO-CHINA

FORMOSA

1945

IWO JIMA

1945

1945

THAILAND
(SIAM)

Manila

PHILIPPINE IS.

MARIANA
ISLANDS

WAKE I.

P A C I F I C

MALAY PENINSULA

LEYTE

1944

SAIPAN

GUAM

1944

ENIWETOK

MARSHALL
IS.

BRITISH
MALAYA

1944-45

TRUK

KWAJALEIN

1944

SUMATRA

Singapore

BORNEO

CAROLINE ISLANDS

MAKIN

TARAWA

GILBERT
IS.

CELEBES

1943

SOLOMON
IS.

1943

N E T H E R L A N D S

Hollandia

NEW
GUINEA

JAVA SEA

I N D I E S

JAVA

Port Moresby

GUADALCANAL

SAMOA

1942-43

C O R A L   S E A

1942

NEW
CALEDONIA

I N D I A N

O C E A N

A U S T R A L I A

N E W

Z E A L A N D

0   2000
Scale of miles

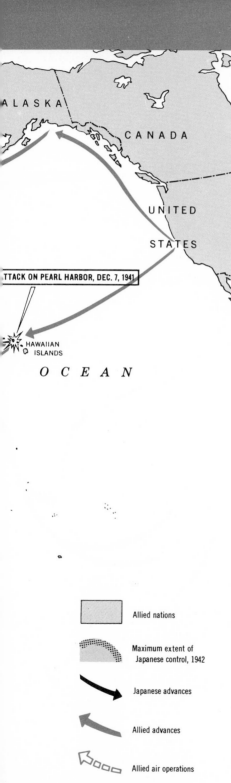

ALASKA

CANADA

UNITED

STATES

TTACK ON PEARL HARBOR, DEC. 7, 1941

HAWAIIAN
ISLANDS

O C E A N

Allied nations

Maximum extent of
Japanese control, 1942

Japanese advances

Allied advances

Allied air operations

WORLD WAR II IN THE PACIFIC

Dark days for the Allies

1941 *July:* Japanese invasion of French Indo-China.

Dec. 7: Japanese attack Pearl Harbor.

Dec. 8–11: United States declares war against the Axis.

Dec.: Japanese invasion of Thailand and Br. Malaya; capture of Wake, Guam, Hong Kong; invasion of Philippines, Midway.

1942 *Jan.:* Fall of Manila.

Jan.–May: Japanese occupy Netherlands Indies and Burma.

Feb.: Singapore surrenders to Japanese.

Feb.–Mar.: Battle of the Java Sea.

Apr.–May: Fall of Bataan and Corregidor.

May: Battle of the Coral Sea.

June: Battle of Midway.

June: Japanese occupy Attu and Kiska in Aleutians.

Allied gains: the tide turns

Aug.: U.S. marines land on Guadalcanal.

Nov.: Allied victory in naval battle of Guadalcanal.

1943 *Jan.–Sept.:* Allied gains in New Guinea.

Mar.–Aug.: Allies force Japanese from Aleutians.

June–Dec.: Allied offensive in South Pacific: Solomon Is.

Nov.–Feb. 1944: Allied offensive in Central Pacific: Gilbert Is., Marshall Is., Kwajalein, Eniwetok.

1944 *Apr.–July:* Allies seize Hollandia and regain New Guinea.

June–Aug.: Allies capture Saipan and Guam in Mariana Is.

Oct.: Allied campaign to reconquer Philippines begins.

1945 *Feb.:* Allies liberate Manila; end of Philippines campaign.

Feb.–Mar.: U.S. marines conquer Iwo Jima.

Apr.–June: U.S. marines conquer Okinawa.

May–Aug.: Allied air offensive against Japanese home islands.

Allied victory in the Pacific

Aug. 6: Atomic bomb dropped on Hiroshima.

Aug. 9: Atomic bomb dropped on Nagasaki.

Aug. 10: Japan surrenders.

Aug. 14: V–J Day (end of war in Pacific).

Sept. 2: Japan signs formal surrender on U.S.S. *Missouri*.

769

■ President Roosevelt was already showing the strains of the war when he met with Prime Minister Churchill and Premier Stalin at Yalta. About two months later, he died at Warm Springs, Georgia.

Overcoming bitter resistance on land, the conquering troops then spread over the Philippines, and early in February 1945 Manila fell to the Americans. "I shall return," MacArthur had promised when, following orders, he had left Corregidor in March 1942. "I'm a little late, but we finally came," he said in Manila in 1945 as the American and Filipino flags were raised above the city.

The Yalta Conference. Long before the Allied victories in 1945, leaders of the great powers had met at a series of conferences to develop a common strategy for defeating the Axis and to formulate plans for a lasting peace. President Roosevelt and Prime Minister Churchill met early in 1943 at Casablanca, Morocco, and again later at Cairo, Egypt, where they were joined by Generalissimo Chiang Kai-shek (chyahng KAI-SHEK) of China. From Cairo, Roosevelt and Churchill flew to Teheran, the capital of Iran, in order to confer with Premier Stalin.

Early in February 1945, President Roosevelt, Prime Minister Churchill, and Premier Stalin met again, this time at Yalta in the Crimea in southern Russia (see map, pages 740–41) to make plans for the final stages of the war. At Yalta they agreed that Great Britain, the Soviet Union, and the United States—the "Big Three"—together with France, would occupy Germany after the war. They also agreed that the "Big Three" would support free elections throughout Europe, thereby guaranteeing the right of Europeans to choose their own governments. These and other agreements were announced to the public.

But the "Big Three" also reached several agreements which they did not reveal to the public. In one of the secret agreements, Roosevelt and Churchill promised the Soviet Union that in exchange for its entrance into the war against Japan, the U.S.S.R. would receive the Kurile Islands, the southern half of Sakhalin Island, an occupation zone in Korea, and the right to dominate Outer Mongolia and Manchuria (see map, pages 768–69).

The road to victory. On February 19, 1945, a week after the Yalta Conference ended, United States marines landed on the murderous beaches of Iwo Jima (EE-wo JEE-mah). The battle will long live in history. Nearly 20,000 American marines were killed or wounded in the successful effort to gain control of the airfields on this barren volcanic island, only 750 miles from Tokyo (see map, pages 768–69).

A few weeks later the largest landing force in Pacific history began the invasion of Okinawa (o-kee-NAH-wah), some 300 miles from the Japanese homeland. The fanaticism of Japanese troops showed no signs of weakening. Japanese "suicide planes," manned by pilots who were pledged to die by diving bomb-laden planes into their targets, struck at the American fleet as it closed in on the inner defenses of Japan. Despite bitter Japanese resistance, Okinawa was taken in June.

Japan's air and sea power were broken. But Japan still had many well-trained and well-equipped divisions of soldiers. It still controlled large areas of China, although badly needed American supplies were being flown across "The Hump"° and transported by trucks over the newly opened Stilwell Road (see map, pages 768–69) to Chiang Kai-shek's embattled troops. But these supplies were only a fraction of what China needed, and Chinese troops were in no position to undertake a major offensive. Moreover, the inner defenses on the Japanese homeland were strong. On the other hand, Japan was blockaded, and, after the fall of the Nazis in the spring of 1945, the full weight of the United Nations was available for the final struggle in the Pacific.

Day by day the American task forces grew bolder, driving the remaining Japanese ships from the seas and sweeping in to shell shore installations on the Japanese mainland. Day by day huge fleets of bombers, now within easier striking distance of Japan, dropped torrents of fire bombs and high explosives in devastating raids upon transportation, industrial, and military centers of the Japanese home islands. By the early summer of 1945, it was clear that the blockade and the relentless bombings were destroying Japan's power to resist. How long could Japan hold out?

The Potsdam Ultimatum. With President Roosevelt's death in April 1945, the responsibility for making decisions that would bring about the defeat of Japan fell upon his successor, President Harry S. Truman. In July President Truman met with Stalin and Clement Attlee, the new British Prime Minister, at Potsdam, Germany. At this meeting the leaders of the great powers discussed, among other questions, plans for the control and occupation of Germany. They also issued an ultimatum to Japan, calling for unconditional surrender. Japan formally rejected the ultimatum on July 29.

∎∎∎∎∎∎∎∎∎∎∎∎∎∎∎∎∎∎∎∎∎∎∎∎∎∎∎∎∎
° *"The Hump"*: the name given to the mountain ranges at the eastern end of the Himalayas.

World War II ends. On August 6, 1945, at eight-fifteen in the morning, a solitary plane crossed over the Japanese city of Hiroshima (hee-ro-SHEE-mah). It flew very high. A few people looked up. No alarm was sounded. Then, suddenly, the city disintegrated in a single searing atomic blast. Nearly 100,000 of the 245,000 men, women, and children in Hiroshima were killed instantly or died soon after. A new force had been added to warfare, a force that would enormously complicate relations among nations in postwar years.

In authorizing the bombing of Hiroshima, President Truman knew that he had made a momentous decision. He had given the order only after days of conferring with his key military and political advisers. His decision was made as a last resort to force Japan to surrender, and thus to save the lives of hundreds of thousands of American fighting men. But despite the devastation of Hiroshima, the Japanese failed to surrender.

On August 8 the Soviet Union declared war on Japan.

On August 9 a second atom bomb destroyed Nagasaki.

On August 10 the Japanese government finally asked for peace.

On August 14, 1945 (V–J Day), President Truman announced by radio that Japan had accepted the Allied peace terms. The formal surrender was signed on September 2, 1945. World War II had come to an end.

⌐ SECTION SURVEY

1. Describe briefly the "island-hopping" strategy of the Americans in the Pacific.

2. What was the significance of the reconquest of the Philippines?

3. Summarize the agreements reached at the Yalta Conference in 1945.

4. Discuss the victories that led to the final destruction of Japanese air and sea power.

IDENTIFY: "Big Three," "suicide planes," Potsdam Ultimatum, V–J Day; Nimitz, Chiang Kai-shek; August 14, 1945.

■ CHAPTER SURVEY   (For review, see Section Surveys, pages 756, 760, 766, 771.)

Points to Discuss: 1. Indicate the factors which enabled the Allies to survive the military disasters of 1941–42.

2. Show that the Lend-Lease program was not just a one-way arrangement.

3. Victory in World War II was made possible by the teamwork of American business, American labor, and American farmers. Give evidence to support this statement.

4. Seek to account for general American acceptance of government controls during the war despite the deeply rooted belief in individualism and free enterprise.

5. Describe briefly the work of five wartime government agencies.

6. Indicate what you consider to be the key reasons for Allied victory in Europe.

7. In your opinion, to what extent did President Roosevelt contribute to the Allied victory?

8. Summarize the important steps to Allied success in the Pacific.

9. In what way did the Yalta Conference sow seeds of trouble for the future?

Using Maps: 1. Using the map on pages 754–55, answer the following: (a) Explain the objectives of the Allied land attacks. (b) How was Allied naval strategy co-ordinated with Allied land attacks? (c) In November 1942, which countries were under Axis control? (d) By the end of 1944, which military objectives had the Allies attained? (e) Explain the purpose of invading Italy.

2. Base your answers to the following on the map on page 764: (a) What was the objective of each of the four Allied drives into Germany from the West and the South? (b) Indicate the strategy of the Russian drives from the East. (c) Why was the Battle of the Bulge a critical military event?

3. Use the map on pages 768–69 for the following questions: (a) By 1942 which countries had been conquered by Japan? (b) Approximately how far did the Japanese fleet have to travel to attack Pearl Harbor? (c) When the Japanese were at Pearl Harbor, how far were they from the continental United States? (d) Identify the Allied nations which are shown on the map. (e) By 1944 how far had Allied forces advanced?

Consulting the Sources: For text of agreements reached at Yalta, see Commager, *Documents*, No. 557.

■ TRACING THE MAIN IDEAS

The cost of World War II in human lives, money, and property was enormous. In the United States alone the federal government spent more money than it had during the entire period from 1789 to 1940, including the cost of all earlier wars. Billions of dollars of property went up in smoke and flames. Parts of many of the world's major cities were reduced to rubble.

The loss of human life was staggering. According to General Marshall's final report, 201,367 Americans had been killed by the end of June 1945, about 600,000 had been wounded, and 57,000 were missing. Other nations lost even more heavily. It has been estimated that more than 3,000,000 Germans, more than 3,000,000 Russians, more than 1,500,000 Japanese, and more than 375,000 British troops were killed in battle. Civilian deaths resulting from bombs, starvation, disease, and concentration camps ran into the millions. The exact number can never be known, for vast numbers of people simply disappeared from the face of the earth. Many other millions were uprooted and left homeless as death and destruction raged across the face of the earth.

These were only some of the immediate and terrible effects of the most devastating war in history.

The Nation Faces Postwar Problems

HARRY S. TRUMAN TAKING THE
OATH OF OFFICE AS PRESIDENT—

P RESIDENT Roosevelt did not live to see the victorious conclusion of World War II or the organization of the United Nations. Worn out from more than twelve years of struggling, first with the depression and then with war, he died suddenly on April 12, 1945.

With Roosevelt's death the burden of present and future problems fell upon his successor, President Harry S. Truman. The new leader was almost sixty-one years old, lean, gray-haired, plain and folksy, with a winning grin and a liking for mixing with ordinary people. Born and raised on a farm in Missouri, Truman had served overseas in World War I. After a successful career in local politics, he had been elected to the United States Senate. In the Senate he had supported the New Deal program, and had come to public attention during the early years of World War II when he served as chairman of a key Senate committee—the Special Committee to investigate the National Defense Program. In 1945, after only a few months in the Vice-Presidency, he was suddenly elevated to the highest office in the land.

At the simple oath-taking ceremony in which he assumed the Presidency, Truman spoke humbly. He pledged to the American people that he would carry on Roosevelt's policies, both domestic and foreign. And so, led by a new President, the United States prepared to enter the postwar world.

AS THE STORY DEVELOPS

1. President Truman meets postwar problems and offers a "Fair Deal."
2. The United States joins in the effort to organize the United Nations.
3. The United States and the Soviet Union carry on a "Cold War" in Europe.
4. Communist aggression threatens peace and leads to a "Hot War" in Asia.

1450   1750   1800   1850   1900   1950   1975

President Truman meets postwar problems and offers a "Fair Deal"

With the defeat of Japan in August 1945, the American people were eager to return immediately to the ways of peace. They wanted their sons and daughters, their brothers and sisters, their husbands and their friends home again—and the servicemen and women were just as eager to return.

Demobilization. American military and naval leaders, faced with the problem of stationing occupation troops in Germany, Italy, and Japan, warned that hasty demobilization would be dangerous for the United States. Their warnings went unheeded. Reluctantly, the military authorities gave in to public pressure. Within two years the air force had been reduced from 85,000 to 9000 planes, the navy had withdrawn hundreds of ships from active service, and the army had reduced its forces from 89 to 12 divisions.

Aid to veterans. After World War II the government did far more to help the veterans adjust to civilian life than had ever been done before. Government assistance came through the Servicemen's Readjustment Act, which Congress had passed in 1944.

The "GI° Bill of Rights," as it was called, provided for (1) government loans to enable ex-servicemen to set themselves up in business or on farms, (2) government loans to buy homes, (3) pensions and hospital care, (4) educational opportunities for ex-servicemen and women who wished to continue their schooling. Taking advantage of these educational opportunities, hundreds of thousands of veterans received money for tuition, books, and part of their living expenses while they attended school or college.

Reconversion of industry. While the veterans were returning to civilian life,

....
° **GI:** a nickname used in World War II to refer to enlisted men. The initials stand for "Government Issue."

industry was rapidly shifting from wartime to peacetime production. As a result, there was no serious unemployment during the postwar years. On the contrary, from 1945 to 1948 the number of employed workers rose from about 54 million to more than 61 million. Instead of the postwar depression that many Americans had feared would come, the nation enjoyed a high degree of prosperity. One rough measure of the prosperity was the national income, which climbed from about 181 billion dollars in 1945 to more than 223 billion in 1948, soared to nearly 240 billion by 1950, and gave signs of continuing to rise.

Postwar inflation. But prosperity brought problems, including the danger of runaway inflation. For more than a year after the war ended, President Truman, supported by like-minded members of Congress, managed to continue the price controls established during the war years (page 758). But the demand for an end of wartime controls and regulations grew increasingly insistent, and Truman's position on this matter became increasingly unpopular.

Not until November 1946 did President Truman yield to the growing pressure. In the Congressional elections of that year, the Republicans won control of both houses of Congress. Widespread dissatisfaction with wartime regulations was only part of the reason for the Republican victory. Nevertheless, four days later the President issued an Executive Order ending all controls on both prices and wages. He did, however, continue the controls on rent.

Prices immediately started to rise. High wartime wages, plus savings accumulated during the war years when many goods were scarce or simply not available, had created an enormous reservoir of purchasing power. With money to spend and a mounting demand for goods of all kinds, men and women jammed the stores and shops in a wild buying splurge. It was a "seller's market," and prices soared higher and higher. By the spring of 1947, wholesale prices had risen almost 32 per cent.

Shortage of housing. Although rent controls kept rents from climbing to ruinous levels, they did not solve the problem of the postwar housing shortage. New houses were desperately needed, for relatively few had been built during the depression of the 1930's and almost none during the war years. Meanwhile, the population had been growing—from nearly 123,000,000 in 1930 to more than 140,000,000 by the end of the war. The housing situation, already acute by 1945, became increasingly desperate as millions of veterans returned to civilian life.

During 1945 and 1946 President Truman led a drive to provide federal subsidies for the construction of new housing. But even members of his own party refused to support him, and there was widespread opposition throughout the country to any proposal that would increase the already swollen national debt. As a result, Truman failed to secure the housing legislation he wanted. By 1947, however, the private building industry was beginning to roll into high gear, and the housing situation, though still serious, began to improve.

Labor unrest. Rising prices inevitably led to demands for higher wages. In many cases industry met the demands —but promptly raised prices still higher in an effort to recover the increased costs of production. The rise in prices, in turn, spurred labor to demand additional wage boosts. So inflation continued its upward spiral, with workers blaming industry, industry blaming wage earners, and the consumer caught in the middle.

Labor unrest led to a large number of strikes. Two of the most serious of these involved the railroads and the coal-mining industry. President Truman, whose views in general were sympathetic to organized labor, finally ended the railroad strike when he threatened to declare a national emergency and draft the strikers into the army. The federal government also intervened in the United Mine Workers' coal strike. It seized the mines and issued a federal injunction that left the miners no choice but to return to work.

The Taft-Hartley Act of 1947. The postwar labor unrest and strikes alarmed the public and led to a demand for stronger federal controls over organized labor. When the Republicans won control of both houses of Congress in 1946, they attributed their victory in part to the rising demand for new labor legislation. In June 1947, following five months of bitter debate, Congress passed the Labor-Management Relations Act, better known as the Taft-Hartley Act, over President Truman's veto.

In general, the new law aimed to reduce the power that organized labor had come to enjoy as a result of the New Deal. The Taft-Hartley Act required at least a 60-day notice—a "cooling off" period—before either an employer or a union could end a contract. It prohibited unions from making contributions to political campaigns. It took from the unions the privilege of having management deduct union dues of members from their wages without the written consent of the members concerned. This is the so-called "check-off" system.

The new law also permitted management to seek injunctions in times of strikes; to talk directly with the workers about labor issues, rather than to deal with them through unions; and to sue union officials for violation of contract, or for engaging in strikes arising from jurisdictional disputes with rival unions. The law also forbade "closed shop" agreements, which in the past had prohibited employers from hiring workers who did not belong to a union.

The Taft-Hartley Act proved to be a highly controversial measure. Those who favored the law argued that it restored equality of bargaining power between employers and workers. They insisted that it merely corrected a number of unfair advantages that had been granted by the Wagner Act of 1935 to organized labor (page 705). But organized labor indignantly protested that the new law deprived the workers of many of the benefits that they had rightfully won over a long period.

Gains for organized labor. During the postwar years, however, organized labor did make several notable gains. Workers in general secured substantial wage increases. More significant in the long run were certain techniques adopted by management and labor to protect wage earners against inflation and ill health, and to offer them a larger measure of security for their old age.

An industry-wide trend was stimulated in 1948 with a contract signed by the United Automobile Workers and the General Motors Corporation. This contract included three noteworthy provisions. (1) It contained a two-way *escalator clause.* This clause provided that every three months wages should be adjusted upward or downward to keep pace with the rise or fall in the cost of living. (2) The contract contained an *annual improvement provision.* This clause provided automatic wage increases of from 2 to 2½ per cent to compensate workers for steadily increasing productivity resulting from improvements in machines and processes. (3) The contract contained several *welfare provisions,* including retirement pensions and health insurance.

The UAW–GM contract of 1948 was only one of an increasing number of contracts based on similar principles and negotiated by labor and management in the postwar years. Even more important than the contracts was the fact that both labor and management were becoming increasingly aware of the need to avoid friction. Both labor and management were seeking agreements that would provide fair returns to both workers and owners.

Candidates in the 1948 election. Despite the unsettled conditions during the shift from war to peace, by 1948 the country as a whole was enjoying a high degree of prosperity. With this in their favor, the Democrats met in convention to choose their Presidential candidate for the November elections.

The delegates to the Democratic con-

vention nominated President Truman on the first ballot. Senator Alben W. Barkley of Kentucky was chosen as his running mate. Then, largely at the insistence of President Truman and Mayor Hubert H. Humphrey, Jr., of Minneapolis, the delegates wrote into the platform a strong civil rights plank. This plank urged Congress to support the President in guaranteeing the following fundamental rights: (1) the right of every adult to vote and to participate in politics, (2) the right of everyone to an equal opportunity to work at a job of his own choosing, (3) the right of everyone to have personal security, and (4) the right of equal treatment in the armed services. The Democratic platform also contained planks calling for repeal of the Taft-Hartley Act; for federal legislation in support of housing, education, and farm prices; and for a broadening of social security benefits.

The Democratic platform split the party wide open. Southern delegates vigorously objected to a number of provisions, especially the civil rights program. A number of southern Democrats, calling themselves "Dixiecrats," formed a separate States' Rights Party and met in another convention. They nominated Governor J. Strom Thurmond of South Carolina for President.

Former Vice-President Henry A. Wallace also left the Democrats to head a new Progressive Party. The Progressive Party criticized the Truman policy toward the Soviet Union, which you will presently read about. It tried to win the support of labor and of liberal Democrats by adopting planks that suggested the more extreme aspects of the New Deal.

The Republicans were jubilant. Having won control of both houses of Congress in 1946, and with the Democratic Party split into three segments, the Republicans did not see how they could lose the election. After again nominating Governor Thomas E. Dewey of New York as their standard bearer, they adopted a platform that praised the system of American free enterprise and called for a minimum of government control over business. The Republican platform also promised to protect "both workers and employers against coercion and exploitation," and urged that the states be given greater responsibility for housing, public health, and social security.

Truman is re-elected. The public opinion polls, the majority of the newspapers, and many Americans, including leading Democrats, assumed that Dewey would win. But President Truman, who did not share this belief, carried on his campaign with vigorous confidence. He called a special session of the Republican-dominated Congress and asked it to live up to its 1946 campaign promises and do something to halt rising prices and to meet the housing crisis. Congress, however, could not reach agreement on any of the major issues. When it adjourned, President Truman toured the country, denouncing Congress for its failure to act upon important issues. Although he received only lukewarm support from his own party, the President stubbornly waged a vigorous campaign.

But few Americans expected Truman to win. The election returns therefore came as a stunning surprise to almost everyone. Truman polled 49.4 per cent of all popular votes cast; Dewey, 45 per cent; and the other candidates divided the remaining 5.6 per cent. In the Electoral College Truman won 303 votes, Dewey 189, and Thurmond 39. Wallace failed to win a single electoral vote. The Democrats regained control of Congress and won many state and city elections as well.

The "Fair Deal." Heartened by his success in the 1948 elections, President Truman decided to undertake a broad range of reforms during his second term in office. In his State of the Union Message in January 1949, he urged Congress to adopt a "Fair Deal" program. With his Fair Deal program Truman hoped to extend some of the reforms started by President Roosevelt in the New Deal days.

■ When Harry S. Truman succeeded to the Presidency in 1945, he took firm control of the office, and was elected President in 1948.

Politically wise observers greeted Truman's proposal with considerable skepticism. They doubted whether the President would be able to win support for the program from the various wings of his own party.

This skepticism proved to be well founded. Time after time during Truman's second term, many southern Democrats and a number of northern Democrats joined the Republicans to block Fair Deal measures. They blocked administration efforts to secure passage of civil rights legislation. They rejected a proposal to establish a new Department of Public Welfare—partly because many people feared such a department would open the doors to compulsory medical insurance or "socialized medicine." The President was also defeated in his drive to get Congress to repeal the Taft-Hartley Act. And although a bill providing federal aid to education received Senate approval, it was defeated in the House.

President Truman did, however, have some success with his Fair Deal program. Between 1949 and 1952, Congress (1) extended social security ben-

HERBERT HOOVER
CHIDES THE "FAIR DEALERS"

Former President Herbert Hoover was not impressed with much of the talk about the New Deal or the Fair Deal, nor with the term "the Century of the Common Man"—a term that Henry A. Wallace, among others, frequently used. "It is dinned into us that this is the Century of the Common Man," Hoover remarked on November 11, 1948. "The idea seems to be that the common man has come into his own at last. . . .

"I have not been able to find any definition of who this common man is. Most American men, and especially women, will fight if called common. . . .

"Let us remember that the great human advances have not been brought about by mediocre men and women. They were brought about by distinctly uncommon men and women with vital sparks of leadership. . . .

"It is a curious fact that when we get sick we want an uncommon doctor; if we have a construction job, we want an uncommon engineer; when we get into war, we dreadfully want an uncommon admiral and an uncommon general. Only when we get into politics are we content with the common man."

efits to approximately 10 million more persons; (2) revised the Fair Labor Standards Act of 1938 (page 717) to raise the minimum wage for workers in interstate industries from 40 to 75 cents an hour; (3) authorized the federal government to undertake a program of slum clearance and to build for rental to low-income families as many as 810,000 housing units during a six-year period; (4) continued rent controls to March 31, 1951; (5) adopted a new Agricultural Act in 1949 that established farm price supports at 90 per cent of parity through 1950, then on a sliding scale of 75 to 90 per cent as needed; (6) brought more employees of the Internal Revenue Service under civil service; (7) expanded the activities of the Reclamation Bureau in the development of flood control, hydroelectric plants, and irrigation projects; and (8) increased federal expenditures for the Rural Electrification Administration, the Farmers Home Adminstration (formerly the Farm Security Administration), and the TVA.

Other laws passed under Truman. During Truman's two terms in office, Congress also adopted a number of other important measures.

The Atomic Energy Act, signed by the President on August 1, 1946, gave the government a monopoly of the production of all fissionable materials.° The act placed the control of research and production under a five-man civilian Atomic Energy Commission (AEC).

The National Security Act of 1947 was intended to unify the three branches of the armed services and to centralize the responsibility for military research and planning. It created a new Cabinet department—the Department of Defense—to be headed by a civilian Secretary of Defense. The act provided the new Secretary with three assistants —the Secretaries of the Army, Navy, and Air Force, who were not to be members of the Cabinet.

The Presidential Succession Act of 1947, like the earlier act of 1886 (page 440), provided for the succession to the Presidency in the event that both the President and the Vice-President died while in office. The new law changed the line of succession, placing it first in the Speaker of the House, then in the President *pro tempore* of the Senate— both elected officers—and finally in the

••

° *fissionable materials:* elements such as uranium that can be split more easily than other elements to produce atomic energy.

Secretary of State, and other appointed Cabinet officers in order of rank.

In 1947 Congress also proposed the Twenty-second Amendment to the Constitution (page 202). This measure limited a President's tenure to two terms in office. By February 26, 1951, having been ratified by the necessary 36 states, the amendment had become part of the Constitution.°

The Reorganization Act of June 20, 1949, was also a product of work started in 1947. In an effort to bring greater efficiency into the vast, sprawling structure of government, President Truman had asked former President Herbert Hoover to head a commission to study the problem of governmental reorganization. In 1949 Congress wrote many of Hoover's recommendations into law.

Concern over internal security. The year 1947 also saw a sharp increase in the drive against subversive elements in government. The stepped-up drive began in March when President Truman issued an Executive Order calling for an investigation by the Federal Bureau of Investigation (FBI) and the Civil Service Commission of the loyalty of all federal employees. As a result of this order, by the end of 1951 more than 3,000,000 employees had been investigated and cleared, 2000 had resigned, and 212 had been dismissed on the ground that they were "security risks." No federal employee was brought before the courts on charges of treason or subversion.

Meanwhile, in 1948 the FBI and the Department of Justice launched an intensive general investigation into the activities of Communists in the United States. Before the year ended, 11 Communist leaders were indicted under the Smith Act of 1940 (page 742), tried, and sentenced to prison for conspiracy to advocate the violent overthrow of the government.

Finally, Congress passed the Internal Security Act of 1950, popularly known

••
° The two-term limitation did not apply to President Truman, who was in office in 1951 when the amendment was ratified.

as the McCarran Act. This law required all Communist organizations to file their membership lists with the Attorney General and to give him a statement of their financial operations.

In its deepening concern over the problem of internal security, Congress was reacting not only to the possibility of Communist subversion at home, but also to the international situation, which was rapidly becoming more and more serious.

✔ **SECTION SURVEY**

1. (a) Describe three important problems that faced Americans after World War II. (b) How was each of these problems handled?

2. What were the reasons for the passage of the Taft-Hartley Act?

3. Show four ways in which the Taft-Hartley Act limited the power of organized labor.

4. Discuss two gains made by organized labor during the postwar years.

5. Give the parties, candidates, issues, and results of the election of 1948.

6. Describe four important achievements of Truman's Fair Deal program.

IDENTIFY: GI Bill of Rights, escalator clause, "Dixiecrats," Atomic Energy Act, National Security Act, Presidential Succession Act, Twenty-second Amendment, Reorganization Act, Internal Security Act (McCarran Act); Barkley, Thurmond.

2 The United States joins in the effort to organize the United Nations

Domestic problems occupied only part of the attention of President Truman and other government officials during the years from 1945 to 1952. Even more demanding were our relations with other countries.

Roots of the United Nations. Long before World War II ended, many of the world's statesmen were soberly considering ways to build an enduring peace. As early as January 1, 1942, as you have seen (page 753), the Allies—

or United Nations, as they were called —pledged themselves to fight as a team for the defeat of Italy, Germany, and Japan. The United Nations was at first merely a wartime association of nations, but many leaders—among them Roosevelt, Churchill, and Stalin— agreed that it would be wise to convert the wartime United Nations into a permanent organization for peace.

Many Americans shared this point of view. In the Presidential election campaign of 1944, Thomas E. Dewey, the Republican candidate, Senator Arthur H. Vandenberg of Michigan, and other Republican leaders pledged their support to an international organization of nations. Thus, both Democrats and Republicans agreed to abandon isolationism and to co-operate in a bipartisan, or nonpolitical, program of international co-operation. By working together on foreign policy, the leaders of the two political parties hoped to avoid the misunderstandings that had contributed to America's refusal to join the League of Nations in 1919–20.

Dumbarton Oaks. Encouraged by the enthusiastic support of the United States, delegates from the United States, Great Britain, U.S.S.R., and China met in the summer and early fall of 1944 at Dumbarton Oaks, an estate in Washington, D.C., to prepare a rough plan for a postwar United Nations organization. On most questions of procedure, the delegates quickly reached agreement. On a number of issues, however, they could not agree.

What, for instance, were they to do with the demand of Soviet Ambassador Andrei Gromyko (gro-MEE-ko) that the U.S.S.R. be represented in the United Nations organization not by one delegation but by sixteen, one for each of "the sixteen Soviet Republics"?

And what were they to do with the thorny problem of voting in the Security Council, the body in which the great powers would hold permanent seats and which was to be mainly charged with keeping peace in the world? The United States, Great Brit-

ain, and the U.S.S.R. agreed that on matters regarding peace and security the permanent members would have to cast a unanimous vote before any action could be taken. On such matters any one of the permanent members would therefore have the right to veto any decision and thus prevent action. But should the permanent members have the right to exercise the veto on affairs of lesser importance—on what the delegates referred to as "nonprocedural matters"? On this question the delegates were deadlocked.

The Yalta Conference. Meeting at Yalta early in February 1945 (page 770), Roosevelt, Churchill, and Stalin managed to reach agreements on a number of the issues that had deadlocked the Dumbarton Oaks Conference. They agreed that two of the Soviet Union's sixteen republics—the Ukrainian and Byelorussian—would be admitted to the United Nations under the fiction that they were independent nations. The leaders also worked out a compromise proposal for voting in the Security Council and agreed to support this proposal when the time came to draft the United Nations Charter, or constitution. Finally, they agreed to call a United Nations Conference in San Francisco on April 25, 1945, to draw up the Charter of a permanent organization.

The San Francisco Conference. Delegates from 50 nations took part in the San Francisco Conference. They represented three fourths of the peoples of the earth. They adopted five working languages for the conference—English, Russian, French, Spanish, and Chinese. Despite differences in speech, dress, physical characteristics, religious ideas, and modes of living, the delegates were all working for one objective—the formation of a world organization.

Many people were disappointed when the delegates sharply disagreed on certain issues. Other people felt that such disagreements were to be expected in a conference composed of so many delegates from so many different

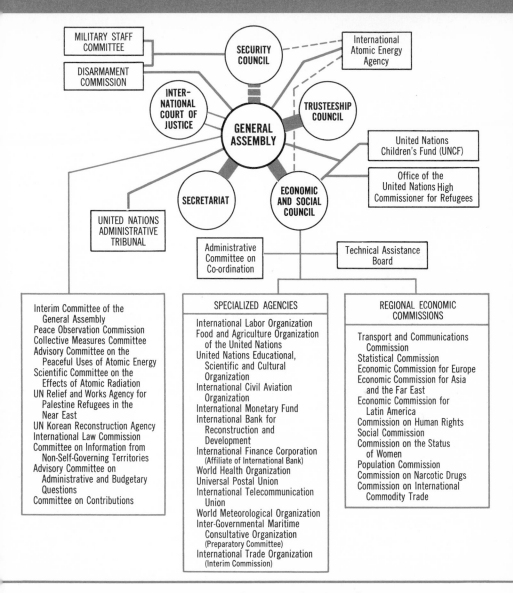

nations. The controversies were settled by compromise, however, and in the surprisingly short time of eight weeks the conference reshaped the Dumbarton Oaks and the Yalta proposals into the Charter of the United Nations.

With only two dissenting votes the United States Senate agreed to join the new world organization, and on August 9, 1945—three days after the bombing of Hiroshima—President Truman signed the Charter. On October 24 —now celebrated as United Nations Day—the United Nations organization came into existence, its charter having been ratified by the required number of countries.

Purposes and organization. The purposes of the United Nations are clearly stated in the Preamble to the Charter: "We the peoples of the United Nations, determined to save succeeding generations from the scourge of war . . . to promote social progress and better standards of life in larger freedom . . . have resolved to combine our efforts to

In a New York City building of striking modern architecture, the United Nations does its work.

be the "town meeting" of the world, in which all members of the United Nations were to be equally represented. It was to make recommendations for the peaceful settlement of disputes. It was to elect the six nonpermanent members of the Security Council, certain members of the Trusteeship Council, and all members of the Economic and Social Council.

(III) The Economic and Social Council, composed of eighteen members, was to study economic, social, cultural, and health problems of the world, and to make recommendations to the General Assembly or to individual member countries of the United Nations.

(IV) The International Court of Justice, modeled after the World Court (page 669), was to decide legal disputes referred to it by the disputing nations themselves. It was to give advisory opinions when asked to do so. But it could not enforce its decisions.

(V) The Secretariat was to handle the administrative work of the United Nations.

(VI) The Trusteeship Council was to look after the welfare of the peoples in colonial areas.

Early days of the United Nations. The United Nations, like the former League of Nations, was not a world government. Rather, it was an organization of independent nations. It could not in any way interfere with the domestic affairs of any of the member nations unless the "Big Five" and two other members of the Security Council agreed that such intervention was necessary to preserve peace.

In the 1940's many critics of the United Nations insisted that the organization was doomed to fail because the member nations refused to give up any of their national sovereignty. Other people shared the opinion expressed by President Truman when in 1945 he presented the Charter to the Senate for approval: "This Charter," he stated, "points down the only road to enduring peace. There is no other."

accomplish these aims . . ." In general, the United Nations seeks to maintain peace, provide security, promote justice, increase the general welfare, and establish human rights.

Six major organs and numerous related agencies were created to carry on the work of the United Nations.

(I) The Security Council was to be the police authority of the world, charged with the task of preventing war. It was to consist of eleven members. Five of these, the so-called "Big Five" powers—the United States, China, France, the Soviet Union, and Great Britain—were to hold permanent seats. The six nonpermanent members were to be elected for two-year terms. The Security Council was to meet in continuous session, and to be ready to go into action at a moment's notice. It was to have at its command an international military force to check aggression. But it could act on matters of peace and security only by an affirmative vote of at least seven members— and any one of the five permanent members could prevent all action by a single negative vote, or veto.

(II) The General Assembly was to

Within a matter of months, Truman's warning that there was no other road to enduring peace took on new meaning for millions of people in the United States and in other lands. By 1948 the world situation had become so tense that Trygve H. Lie (TRIG-vuh LEE), the first Secretary-General of the United Nations, felt it his duty to issue a pointed warning. "The trouble," he declared, "lies in the intense conflict over the settlement of the last war between East and West, and, especially, between the two most powerful single nations in the world today—the United States and the Soviet Union."

⤤ SECTION SURVEY

1. What were the major problems that had to be solved before a United Nations organization could be created?
2. Which of these conflicts were settled at the Yalta Conference?
3. Describe the purposes of the United Nations.
4. Indicate the chief functions of the (a) Security Council, (b) General Assembly, (c) Economic and Social Council, (d) International Court of Justice, (e) Secretariat, and (f) Trusteeship Council.
5. "The United Nations is not a world government." Explain.

IDENTIFY: Dumbarton Oaks, San Francisco Conference, "Big Five"; Gromyko, Trygve H. Lie; October 24, 1945.

The United States and the Soviet Union carry on a "Cold War" in Europe

At the end of World War II, millions of people suffered from lack of food, clothing, shelter, and medical attention. Never in human history had suffering been so widespread nor the need for help so desperate.

America's new role in the world. The United States responded generously to the need for assistance. During and immediately after the war, the United States played an active role in creating three important United Nations agencies: (1) the United Nations Relief and Rehabilitation Administration (UNRRA), (2) the International Bank for Reconstruction and Development, and (3) the International Monetary Fund. These UN agencies began to operate at once. They supplied food, clothing, shelter, and medical care to many millions of needy persons in the war-torn areas of Europe, Asia, and Africa, and provided money for the reconstruction of ruined industries. A large part of the money for these activities came from the United States.

After the war ended, an increasing volume of American dollars and supplies flowed directly to the war-devastated areas. A major contribution came from private organizations—churches, schools, fraternal societies, and civic associations. Even larger was the direct contribution of the United States government. This contribution took the form of supplies, equipment, loans, and the assistance of specialists and experts.

In their foreign aid programs Americans were motivated by generosity, self-interest, and considerations of military strategy. Large numbers of people believed that it was their duty to share their products and technical skills with others less fortunate. An increasing number began to realize that America's high standard of living could be maintained only if the peoples of other nations were also in a position to buy and to sell. And many Americans, including leaders of both major political parties, had learned from World War II the value of controlling strategic areas of the earth as military bases and as sources of vital raw materials.

Expanding Soviet influence. America's new role of world leadership brought it into conflict with the Soviet Union, which also emerged from the war as a major power. Even before the war ended, the Soviets began to move aggressively against their weaker neighbors, and to send their Moscow-trained Communists into nearly every country on the face of the earth.

In 1940, the countries of Latvia, Lithuania, and Estonia were incorporated into the Soviet Union, The U.S.S.R. also acquired large portions of Poland and Rumania, as a consequence of World War II. Through Communist governments that they helped to establish, the Soviets had, by 1948, secured control of the "free" governments of Poland, Rumania, the eastern portion of Germany, Hungary, and Czechoslovakia (see map, pages 806–07).

Soviet influence reached beyond Eastern Europe into the Mediterranean. Moscow-trained Communists were especially active and powerful in war-torn Greece and Italy.

In the Far East, as well as in Europe, the U.S.S.R. was deeply entrenched. As a result of the Yalta agreements (page 770) and because of Russia's last-minute entry into the war against Japan, the Soviet Union secured control of large areas of former Chinese and Japanese territory.

Growing conflict. The Communist rulers defended their aggressive actions on the ground of self-defense. They feared, they said, that the United States would lead the "capitalist nations" in an attack against the U.S.S.R. They claimed that the possibility of such an attack required them to maintain powerful military forces and to exercise control over bordering countries from which an attack against the U.S.S.R. could be launched.

The United States, on the other hand, objected bitterly to the Soviet Union's aggression against its weaker neighbors. Americans resented the Soviet policy of maintaining huge military forces since the United States and other countries had demobilized most of their armed forces. Moreover, Americans loathed the ruthless methods used by the Communists to crush all opposition. Most Americans regarded the Soviet Union as the world's newest aggressor, the heir to Nazi methods of expansion. The American people were convinced that Communism was the mortal enemy of democracy and human rights.

As friction increased, the Soviet press and radio, rigidly controlled by the government, pictured the United States in the most unfavorable light. The Soviet government forbade its citizens to listen to the American "Voice of America" radio broadcasts. It refused to become a member of the United Nations Educational, Scientific, and Cultural Organization (UNESCO), which had been established to promote understanding among the peoples of the world. It permitted very few Americans to visit the U.S.S.R. or its "satellite" nations.°

As tension mounted, growing numbers of Americans began to wonder why the Soviets were hiding their activities from the free world behind an "iron curtain."

Deadlock over the atomic energy issue. Inability to reach agreement on international control of the atom bomb greatly increased the fear and suspicion that were rapidly widening the gap between the Communist countries and much of the rest of the world. Early in 1946, acting on the initiative of the United States, the United Nations created an Atomic Energy Commission. On June 14, 1946, at the first meeting of this Commission, the United States Representative, Bernard M. Baruch (buh-ROOK), presented America's proposal for international control. "We are here," Baruch said to his fellow members of the Commission, "to make a choice between the quick and the dead. . . . Let us not deceive ourselves: We must elect world peace or world destruction. . . ."

Baruch proposed that complete control of atomic energy be turned over to an international agency responsible to the United Nations. This agency would have full authority to enter any country to inspect atomic energy installations. The United States—at that time the

••

° *satellite nation:* a country under the domination of a more powerful country. The satellite nations of the U.S.S.R. operate under governments imposed upon them by the U.S.S.R., and are controlled by communists.

only nation that had atom bombs—was ready, Baruch announced, to give up its secrets to the new world authority. But, he warned, the United States would not reveal any secrets until the United Nations provided for "immediate, swift, and sure punishment for those who violate the agreements that are reached by the nations." Baruch insisted that each of the "Big Five" on the Security Council give up its right to the veto on all matters involving atomic energy.

When the United States proposal reached the Security Council, nine nations, including the United States, voted for it. But the Soviet Union killed the proposal by a veto.

The Soviets then advanced a counterproposal. They opposed any system of genuine international inspection and control. Instead, they insisted that the United States immediately destroy its atom bombs, that the United Nations declare atomic warfare to be illegal, and that all nations promise not to manufacture atom bombs. But the Soviets flatly refused to accept Baruch's proposal to abandon the veto right in the Security Council. This meant that, if any nation, including the U.S.S.R., violated its promise not to make atom bombs, the Soviet Union or any of the other permanent members of the Security Council could by a single veto block all action on the part of the United Nations.

As months passed and the United Nations failed to find an acceptable compromise, more and more people began to share the opinion of General Frederick Osborn, deputy United States representative to the Atomic Energy Commission, who on July 1, 1948, declared, "Apparently the rulers of the Soviet Union do not desire—perhaps do not dare—to raise the iron curtain at this time."

The Truman Doctrine. Faced with the menace of Communist aggression, the United States began to formulate a policy of "containment." This policy aimed to "contain," or restrict, Soviet

The Marshall Plan (1947): EXCERPT

𝕴t is logical that the United States should do whatever it is able to do to assist in the return of normal economic health in the world, without which there can be no political stability and no assured peace. Our policy is directed, not against any country or doctrine, but against hunger, poverty, desperation, and chaos. Its purpose should be the revival of a working economy in the world, so as to permit the emergence of political and social conditions in which free institutions can exist . . .

Any government that is willing to assist in the task of recovery will find full cooperation, I am sure, on the part of the United States Government. Any government which maneuvers to block the recovery of other countries cannot expect help from us. Furthermore, governments, political parties, or groups which seek to perpetuate human misery in order to profit therefrom politically or otherwise will encounter the opposition of the United States . . .

expansion and to check the spread of Communism. The new policy was first applied to Greece and Turkey. In 1947 Greek Communists, supported by the Russians, were about to seize control of the Greek government. At the same time the Soviet Union was trying to force Turkey to give up control of the Dardanelles, the strait between European and Asiatic Turkey. Soviet control of Greece and of the Dardanelles would enable the U.S.S.R. to dominate the northeastern Mediterranean and the vital sea lane that runs through the Suez Canal (see map, pages 842–43).

Such was the situation that prompted President Truman on March 12, 1947, to announce to Congress the so-called "Truman Doctrine." This doctrine stated that the United States must "help free people to maintain their free institutions and their national integrity." He then asked Congress for authority to help the Greeks and Turks to strengthen their armed forces and to check the spread of Communism. Congress responded with an initial appropriation of 400 million dollars.

The Marshall Plan. It soon became apparent that aid to Greece and Turkey was not enough to prevent the spread of Communism. All of war-torn Europe was in economic difficulties, and Communists, some of them trained in Moscow, were winning many converts among hungry, disillusioned people.

Early in June 1947, in a speech at Harvard University, Secretary of State George C. Marshall suggested a solution to Europe's economic problems. The "Marshall Plan," as his recommended program came to be called, proposed to help European countries to help themselves to get their farms, factories, and transportation systems operating efficiently again. The United States would provide money, supplies, and machinery to any nation, including the Soviet Union and its satellites, that agreed to co-operate in the program.

For almost ten months Congress argued the pro's and con's of the Marshall Plan, officially known as the European Recovery Program (ERP). Those who favored the proposal insisted that the best way to block the spread of Communism and strengthen our own economic system was to restore the economic health of Europe. Opponents de-clared that the United States could not afford to "carry Europe on its back."

In the spring of 1948, however, Congress passed the European Recovery Program by large majorities in both houses. The President then appointed Paul Hoffman, an experienced business-man, to head the Economic Cooperation Administration (ECA), which was set up to carry out the program. Mr. Hoffman tackled the job with enthusiasm. "I think," he declared, "that America, in helping the free peoples of the world to remain free and gain in strength, is living up to its best traditions and will, itself, gain in strength by so doing."

Despite the opposition of Russia and its satellites, all of whom denounced the plan as "Yankee imperialism," the European Recovery Program proved to be an outstanding success. Slowly but steadily Europe began to recover from the most devastating war in history.

The Berlin "airlift." Meanwhile, tension increased almost to the breaking point in Germany. In 1945 the great powers had agreed to a joint occupation of Germany. Great Britain, France, and the United States occupied western and southern Germany, and Russia occupied eastern Germany. Berlin, within the Russian-controlled zone, was also divided into four sections, each controlled by one of the four powers.

■ The Berlin airlift was an effective and dramatic answer to Soviet pressure. Here, German workmen are unloading a shipment of flour from the cargo deck of a huge U.S. Air Force C–74.

On June 24, 1948, the Russians suddenly blocked all roads, canals, and railways connecting Berlin and the Western Zone of Germany. By this move they apparently hoped to force the three Western powers out of Berlin.

The British-American answer to the Soviet challenge was the Berlin airlift. Starting in the summer of 1948 and continuing for nearly a year, British and American planes flew a total of more than 100 million miles and transported more than 2 million tons of food and supplies, including coal, to Berlin. This crisis in East-West relations was resolved in 1949 with the aid of the United Nations.

North Atlantic Treaty Organization. The Russian blockade of Berlin and Communist efforts to wreck the Economic Recovery Program aroused growing alarm throughout Western Europe. In April 1949, determined to meet the threat of Soviet aggression, nine Western European countries joined the United States, Canada, and Iceland in an alliance known as the North Atlantic Treaty Organization (NATO).°

In the Atlantic Pact—the treaty proposing such an alliance—each member country agreed ". . . that an armed attack against one or more of them in Europe or North America shall be considered an attack against them all . . ." They also agreed to resist such an attack with armed force, if necessary.

Since the Atlantic Pact was a treaty, it had to be approved by the United States Senate before the United States could join in the agreement. The debate extended over a period of more than three months. The chief issue was whether or not the Atlantic Pact would compel the United States to go to war to assist another country without an act of Congress. This, as you recall, was the very issue that had been largely responsible for keeping the United States out

• •

° The nine European countries were Great Britain, France, Belgium, the Netherlands, Luxembourg, Italy, Denmark, Norway, and Portugal. West Germany, Turkey, and Greece joined later. (See map, pages 806–07.)

of the League of Nations in 1919. In the end, however, the Senate ratified the agreement in July 1949. Eventually General Eisenhower was appointed Supreme Commander of the NATO forces.

Thus, by the end of 1949 the United States policy of "containment" had begun to take shape, at least as far as Europe was concerned. NATO strengthened the military defenses of Western Europe. The European Recovery Program strengthened its economic structure and, by so doing, eliminated much of the discontent that had so often led people into Communism.

Meanwhile, however, trouble was brewing in the Middle East and in Asia.

✔ **SECTION SURVEY**

1. Describe the various ways in which the United States helped the peoples of the world after World War II.
2. Show how the Soviet Union expanded its influence during the period following World War II.
3. Discuss the reasons for the growing hostility between the United States and the U.S.S.R.
4. Compare the American and Soviet plans for control of atomic energy.
5. How did each of the following help to "contain" the spread of Communism: (a) Truman Doctrine, (b) Marshall Plan (European Recovery Program), (c) Berlin airlift, and (d) NATO?
IDENTIFY: UNESCO, satellite nations, iron curtain, Atomic Energy Commission, containment, ECA; Baruch, Hoffman.

4 Communist aggression threatens peace and leads to a "Hot War" in Asia

Postwar troubles were not confined to Europe. During President Truman's administration they seriously threatened peace in the Middle East and in Asia.

Tensions in the Middle East. During the war the United States had managed to transport Lend-Lease supplies from the head of the Persian Gulf across Iran into Russia. Both Soviet and American troops were stationed in Iran during these years. After the war the United States pulled out its troops. But the Russians, eager to control the oil-rich land adjoining their borders, ignored their earlier promise to withdraw troops. Tension mounted, but after the United Nations intervened in 1946, the Russians withdrew their military forces.

In the meantime, shadows were gathering over Palestine on the eastern shores of the Mediterranean. Since the end of World War I, Great Britain had ruled Palestine under a mandate from the League of Nations. On May 14, 1948, when Great Britain voluntarily gave up this mandate, the Jews in Palestine proclaimed the independence of the new state of Israel. This action plunged Israel into war with the neighboring Arab countries of Egypt, Transjordan, Lebanon, Syria, Iraq, and Saudi Arabia (see map, pages 806–07). The United Nations at once took steps to put an end to the fighting. Finally, a United Nations mission under the leadership of Dr. Ralph J. Bunche, the grandson of an American slave, managed to get both sides to agree to an armistice. As a result of his energetic and able services, Dr. Bunche received the Nobel peace prize.

Communists win control of China. While an uneasy peace was being restored in the Middle East, Chinese Communists, backed by their Soviet allies, were rapidly winning control of China, the most populous country in Asia. The struggle for control of China began long before World War II.

In 1927, four years before the Japanese moved into Manchuria (page 671), Chiang Kai-shek, leader of the Chinese Nationalist forces, opened war on the Chinese Communists. For a time China was torn by civil conflict. But after Japan attacked China, the two opposing Chinese factions joined forces against their common enemy. During World War II Chinese troops, for the most part poorly armed, heroically resisted the invading armies of Japan. In 1945, in recognition of its valiant efforts, China was admitted to the United Nations as one of the "Big Five."

But China's troubles were not over. With the end of World War II, the struggle between Chiang's Nationalist forces and the Chinese Communists for control of China once again erupted in armed conflict. The Russians supported the Chinese Communists, led by Mao Tse-tung (MAU DZUH-DOONG), supplying them with arms and munitions. The United States, on the other hand, provided military and other assistance to Chiang's Nationalist government. Meanwhile, however, General George C. Marshall, who served as Truman's ambassador to China from 1945 to 1947, tried to get the two sides to reach an agreement and end the conflict. But in 1947 Marshall abandoned the attempt. He reported that Chiang's government was riddled with corruption and inefficiency, and recommended that the United States abandon its policy of military aid to the Nationalists.

By 1949 the Communists had conquered most of China. Completely defeated on the mainland, Chiang and his Nationalist government, together with a small army, retreated to the island of Formosa, or Taiwan (see map, pages 806–07).

The United States continued to recognize the Nationalists as the legal government of China, and the Nationalists continued to represent China in the Security Council of the United Nations. Nevertheless, it was generally agreed that the Communist victory was a major triumph for the U.S.S.R., and a disaster for the United States and its allies.

Korea is divided. In the meantime, trouble was brewing in Korea. Between 1910 and 1945 the Koreans had been ruled by Japan. During the closing days of World War II, however, Russian and American troops swept the Japanese out of Korea. After the war General Douglas MacArthur was appointed Supreme Commander of the Allied Powers, and placed in charge of the occupation forces in Japan. His responsibilities also included the southern portion of Korea.°

At the end of the war, a line drawn across the Korean peninsula at the 38th parallel (see map, page 791) separated American occupation forces in the south from Russian occupation forces in the north. Americans and most other peoples considered this a temporary arrangement, and looked forward to the time when the two halves of Korea would be re-united and Russian and American troops would be withdrawn.

But despite United Nations efforts to unite the country, Korea remained divided, and Soviet and American troops continued to occupy their respective parts of the country. Then in 1948 North Korea and South Korea set up separate governments, both of which claimed authority to rule the entire country. The North Korean government, controlled by Communists and supported by the Russians, called itself the "People's Republic." The South Korean government, of which Syngman Rhee (SING-man REE) had been chosen president in an election sponsored by the United Nations, called itself the "Republic of Korea" (ROK). The United States and 30 members of the United Nations, not including the Soviet Union, recognized the Republic of Korea as the lawful government.

Finally, the United States and the Soviet Union withdrew their troops. They left behind them two Korean armies that they had helped to train—one in the north, another in the south. These two armies glared at each other across the 38th parallel. Now and then the North Koreans sent raiding parties across the border into South Korea.

The Korean challenge. Such was the unhappy Korean situation when, on June 25, 1950, the North Korean army

....

° In 1951 Japan received independence in a treaty signed at San Francisco. During the occupation period the Japanese had adopted a number of reforms, and relations between Japan and the Western powers had been restored to a friendly basis.

TRYGVE LIE ON WORLD PEACE

Late in 1952, after serving for seven years as Secretary-General of the United Nations, Trygve Lie (TRIG-vuh LEE) resigned and returned to his native Norway. During the next few months he put into writing some of his thoughts about the future of the United Nations and the possibility of world peace. In the final chapter of his book *In the Cause of Peace* he expressed his belief that "The victory of democracy over world communism in our time is possible if we win the trust of the billion and one-half underprivileged persons now living in Asia, Africa, and several parts of South America. If, on the other hand, these millions—or a great part of them—are lost to democracy, our basic principles and our very way of life, even our prospects for peace and freedom, will be exposed to the greatest of pressures."

"How long," he asked, "can political democracy in the underdeveloped areas last without the economic underpinnings which a true democracy requires before it can function? ...

"At this very moment," he went on to say, "democracy as a form of government and a way of life is on trial in an area including a majority of the world's people: If, in the short time available, it can build an economic foundation under its political promises, by expanding programs like that of United Nations technical assistance, the future of our way of life is assured."

suddenly launched a full-scale invasion of South Korea. News of the invasion reached the United States late that evening. Long distance telephone lines began to hum as calls were put through to President Truman visiting at his home in Independence, Missouri; to high officials on week-end vacations; and to Secretary-General Trygve Lie at the temporary headquarters of the United Nations at Lake Success, near New York City.

On the following day the UN Security Council, meeting in an emergency session, adopted a resolution branding the invasion as an "armed attack" and ordering an immediate "cease fire." The Soviet delegate, Jacob A. Malik, did not attend this meeting. Six months earlier, the Soviet Union, angered by the refusal of the Security Council to admit a delegate from Communist China, had decided to boycott the Security Council by recalling Malik to Russia. Not even the Korean crisis could make the Russians change their minds and end the boycott. Had Malik been present, he could have used his veto power to block all UN action. His absence enabled the UN to act vigorously, not only on that historic Sunday, but also later in the week.

The challenge is answered. Meanwhile, President Truman had flown to Washington and was busy conferring with the heads of the State and Defense Departments. On Tuesday, at noon, the big news broke: The President of the United States had pledged American arms to the defense of Korea. That same evening the Security Council adopted a second resolution in which it used the term "aggressor" to describe North Korea and called upon the members of the UN to furnish all possible assistance to the South Koreans.

By Friday, June 30, six days after the North Koreans had crossed the 38th parallel, the United Nations was firmly committed to action. In response to the call for help, President Truman had ordered the United States Seventh Fleet to prevent any attack upon Formosa

and to blockade the Korean coast. Truman had also ordered United States air and ground forces into Korea.

In Congress, at UN headquarters, and throughout the free nations of the world, the decisions made during this fateful week in 1950 brought new hope. For the first time in history, the members of a world organization had dared to challenge aggression.

The Korean War. Unfortunately, the UN itself had no troops to throw into action. Soviet vetoes in the Security Council had blocked every effort to create a United Nations military force. Although 19 members of the UN finally contributed assistance, the major burden of defending South Korea fell upon the United States.°

For a time it looked as though the North Koreans would overrun all of Korea. The South Koreans, or "ROK's," were hopelessly outnumbered. Neither they nor the first American troops, hastily rushed from the occupation forces in Japan, had the equipment to stand up against the enormous, heavily armored, Soviet-made tanks of the North Korean army. By early August the ROK's and the UN troops under General MacArthur were desperately defending a small area around the port of Pusan in southeast Korea (see map, page 791).

Then the tide suddenly turned. On September 15, 1950, General MacArthur staged an amphibious attack against Inchon and then swept eastward across the peninsula, recapturing Seoul (SOHL), the capital of South Korea. At the same time a strongly reinforced United Nations army, now well equipped and powerfully supported from the air, launched a counteroffensive from southeastern Korea. The North Korean forces, caught in a huge trap, began to break up. Thousands surrendered. The rest fled northward across the 38th parallel with MacArthur's troops in hot pursuit. By Novem-

•••

° Later, the UN established a United Nations command and invited the United States to name the commanding general. General Douglas MacArthur was chosen.

ber advance units of the UN forces were at the Yalu River, the boundary between North Korea and Communist China. MacArthur was convinced the war would end soon.

Then, suddenly, the tide turned again. Late in November hundreds of thousands of Chinese Communist "volunteers"° swarmed across the Yalu River to reinforce the North Korean troops. In a conference at Wake Island on October 15, General MacArthur had assured President Truman that the Chinese Communists would not enter the war and that, if they did, the UN forces could handle them. But now the worst had happened. UN troops, their lines extended, and outnumbered in many cases by hundreds to one, fought desperately to keep from being wiped out. Finally, after weeks of the most desperate fighting, MacArthur's forces managed to stabilize their defense line near the 38th parallel.

The "Great Debate." The entry of Chinese Communist troops—"volunteers" or otherwise—completely changed the nature of the war. The United Nations now faced a problem of the utmost gravity. Should it heed MacArthur's request and give him permission to blockade the China coast, bomb the Chinese mainland, and help Chiang Kai-shek's Nationalist forces to launch an invasion of China?

MacArthur's proposal provoked a heated debate that shook the administration, the Congress, the American public, the delegates to the UN, and millions of people in the free world. Those who agreed with MacArthur argued that quick, decisive action would bring a speedy end to the Korean conflict and restore peace to the Far East. Those who disagreed argued that an attack upon Communist China might bring the U.S.S.R. openly and in full strength to the aid of its Communist ally and start another world war.

••

° By claiming that the Chinese troops were "volunteers," Mao Tse-tung hoped to prevent the UN from interfering in China or attacking it as an aggressor nation.

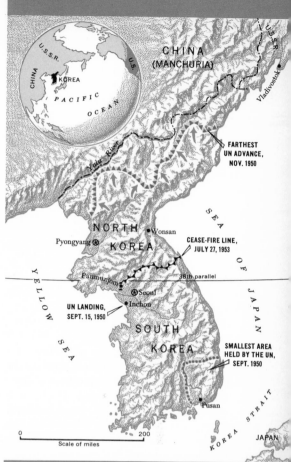

CHINA
(MANCHURIA)

U.S.S.R.

U.S.

CHINA

KOREA

PACIFIC

OCEAN

Vladivostok

FARTHEST
UN ADVANCE,
NOV. 1950

Yalu River

NORTH
KOREA

Pyongyang

Wonsan

SEA

CEASE-FIRE LINE,
JULY 27, 1953

Panmunjom

38th parallel

OF

YELLOW

Seoul

Inchon

UN LANDING,
SEPT. 15, 1950

JAPAN

SEA

SOUTH
KOREA

SMALLEST AREA
HELD BY THE UN,
SEPT. 1950

Pusan

KOREA STRAIT

JAPAN

0   200

Scale of miles

The opponents of MacArthur also pointed to another danger. If the United States committed its military forces to a major war in Asia, the Soviet Union would be free to do as it pleased in Europe. General Omar Bradley, Chairman of the Joint Chiefs of Staff, summed up this point of view clearly when he said that an attack upon Communist China "would involve us in the wrong war, at the wrong place, at the wrong time, and with the wrong enemy."

Stalemate in Korea. By January 1951 President Truman had reached his decision. He ordered General MacArthur to establish the strongest possible defense line near the 38th parallel, but forbade a blockade of the China coast, the bombing of China, and the use of

Chiang's troops to invade China. The war in Korea was to remain strictly a "police action" intended only to protect South Korea.

In 1951, therefore, the Korean War reached a stalemate. The North Koreans and the Chinese Communist "volunteers" from time to time hurled themselves against the UN defenses, only to be killed by the thousands. United Nations planes continued to bomb and strafe North Korean lines of communication as far as the Yalu River. And UN troops, mostly Americans, continued to fight—and many to die—in a war for which there seemed to be no solution.

Meanwhile, General MacArthur, refusing to accept Truman's decision as final, tried to carry his case over the President's head to prominent leaders in Congress. In April 1951 President Truman relieved MacArthur of his command. "I could do nothing else and still be President," Truman explained, defending his action. General Matthew B. Ridgway replaced MacArthur as Commander of the UN forces.

American policy and "Point Four." During 1951 and 1952, while the United Nations worked to bring about peace in Korea, the United States continued the rapid build-up of its land, sea, and air forces. It strengthened NATO with a continuing flow of military equipment. It enlarged and expanded its chain of air bases in Western Europe, around the Mediterranean, and in the Pacific.

The military build-up, however, was only part of America's response to the challenge of Communism. Through economic aid and technical assistance, the United States assumed a major responsibility for helping less fortunate areas of the world to combat poverty and disease and to raise their standards of living. The Marshall Plan, as you have seen, was intended primarily for Europe. A new plan, the "Point Four" program, was aimed at underdeveloped areas anywhere in the world.

President Truman first announced the Point Four program, also called the Technical Assistance Program, in his Inaugural Address in January 1949. "The United States," he said, "is embarking on a bold new program for making the benefits of our scientific advances and industrial progress available for the improvement and growth of underdeveloped areas." To be sure, private business as well as the government had been assisting underdeveloped countries for many years. The "new" part of the program, and the "bold" part, consisted of bringing the many scattered activities into a carefully planned, co-ordinated program. As the President warned, the United States would have to carry the major financial burden of the Point Four program. But, he promised, much of the work would be conducted by and through the United Nations.

The Point Four program got off to a slow start. But the outbreak of the Korean War convinced even the most optimistic—those who felt that peace had come to stay—that the world was facing a grave crisis. By 1952 most Americans were persuaded that United States policy should include provision for foreign aid and the strengthening of military defenses throughout the free world. However, the question of how much aid and to whom it should be granted remained a subject for debate.

SECTION SURVEY

1. What were the events that created tension during the postwar years in (a) the Middle East and (b) the Far East?

2. (a) Discuss the events leading to the Korean War. (b) How did the United States answer the challenge involved?

3. (a) What provoked the "Great Debate" during the Korean War? (b) Indicate the position you would have taken during this debate. Give reasons for your opinion.

4. Describe the importance of the Point Four program.

IDENTIFY: Chinese Nationalists, 38th parallel, People's Republic, Republic of Korea, ROK's; Bunche, Mao Tse-tung, Marshall, Rhee, Malik, MacArthur, Ridgway; June 25, 1950.

■ CHAPTER SURVEY (For review, see Section Surveys, pages 779, 783, 787, 792.)

Points to Discuss: 1. What were some of the highly controversial aspects of the Taft-Hartley Act?

2. Give the provisions of the Democratic civil rights plank in 1948.

3. Discuss reasons why Truman's Fair Deal met with only limited success.

4. Summarize and evaluate the measures taken by the Truman administration to strengthen internal security.

5. The preamble of the United Nations Charter lists the aims of the organization as peace, security, justice, social progress, and human rights. Show how the important UN organs and agencies seek to achieve these objectives.

6. (a) Explain what is meant by the "Cold War." (b) By 1949 the United States policy of containment had begun to take shape in Europe. Give evidence.

Using Maps and Charts: 1. Use the United Nations chart on page 781 and the text to answer these questions: (a) Which are the major UN organs? Give the specific function of each. (b) Which organ has the largest number of agencies?

2. Using the map on page 791, answer these questions: (a) Why was UN morale in the Korean War at its lowest ebb in the early part of September 1950? (b) What event in that same month bolstered UN morale? Why? (c) Compare the cease-fire line of July 1953 with the 38th parallel. (d) What is the distance from the 38th parallel to the Yalu River? to the Soviet Union?

Consulting the Sources: For Truman's own account of his inauguration, see Paul M. Angle, *The American Reader,* Chapter XXIV, No. 1, page 642.

■ TRACING THE MAIN IDEAS

During the years from 1945 to 1953, the United States entered a new era in man's long history. Both on the home front and in the field of international relations, America's leaders had to grapple with new and formidable problems.

The big problem on the home front was conversion from a wartime to a peacetime economy. Americans met this problem in full stride, made the necessary postwar adjustments, and entered a period of great prosperity.

The big problem in the field of international relations was the world-wide challenge of Communism. During Truman's administration the United States developed a foreign policy designed to "contain" the Soviet Union and to check the spread of Communism.

Through economic and technical assistance, notably in the Marshall Plan and the Point Four program, the United States undertook to help less fortunate countries achieve a richer and more rewarding way of life.

Through the United Nations and collective defense arrangements such as the North Atlantic Treaty Organization, the United States undertook to build a shield of military might around the "free world."

Both of these programs—(1) economic aid and (2) military defense—were taking shape when in June 1950 the North Korean Communists, with support from Communist China and the Soviet Union, launched a full-scale attack upon South Korea. The Korean War stiffened the resolve of America's leaders—and the public—to continue the policy of "containment" with redoubled vigor on economic and military fronts.

Such was the situation when, in November 1952, the American people went to the polls to cast their votes in another Presidential election.

The Nation Prospers in an Uneasy World

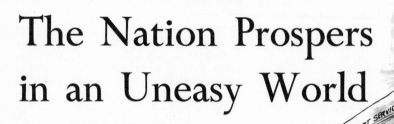

PRESIDENT EISENHOWER
RETURNING FROM GOODWILL TRIP

O N November 4, 1952, Americans
filed into polling booths and voted
to end the twenty-year period of Democratic leadership. For twenty years the
burdens of high office had been carried
by only two Presidents—Franklin D.
Roosevelt (1933–45) and Harry S. Truman (1945–53). Now the burdens were
to be transferred to the shoulders of a
new leader, Dwight D. Eisenhower.
Millions of Americans hoped that under
his leadership the new Republican administration could relieve international
tensions and restore a larger measure of
stability to the American scene.

As you will see, however, the years
following 1952 brought no lasting relief
from the tensions of the Cold War.
During his two terms, President Eisenhower dealt with a series of grave international crises. And although during
the 1950's the nation's standard of living rose steadily, the government faced
problems inherited from earlier days
and new problems that few Americans
in 1952 foresaw.

AS THE STORY DEVELOPS

1. Eisenhower encourages business, but main-
   tains popular programs.
2. The government struggles with other
   domestic problems.
3. The nation continues to meet the challenge
   of Communism.
4. The nation faces recurring world crises.

1450   1750   1800   1850   1900   1950   1975

Eisenhower encourages business, but maintains popular programs

In the 1952 campaign, the Republicans adopted the slogan "It's time for a change." But they did not agree among themselves as to the nature of the change they wanted. Like the Democrats, they were split into a conservative wing and a liberal wing.

The election of 1952. Confident of a Republican victory, each wing of the Republican Party fought vigorously to control the nominating convention. The conservatives failed to gain the nomination for their candidate, Senator Robert A. Taft of Ohio. The liberals won, nominating General Dwight D. Eisenhower for the Presidency and Richard M. Nixon of California for the Vice-Presidency.

The Democrats also entered their 1952 nominating convention as a divided party. In general, conservative Democrats had little liking for the New Deal and the Fair Deal. Moreover, southern Democrats differed sharply with many of their colleagues on the issue of civil rights. Faced with this party split, the Democrats finally chose Governor Adlai E. Stevenson of Illinois for their Presidential candidate, and Senator John Sparkman of Alabama as their Vice-Presidential nominee.

Both parties waged hard-fought campaigns. The Republicans charged the Democrats with "political corruption" and promised to "clean up the mess in Washington." The Republicans condemned their opponents for steadily enlarging the powers of the federal government over the states. Further, Eisenhower charged the Truman administration with "bungling" in the Korean War.

Stevenson was an effective campaigner. He defended the Fair Deal and the foreign policies of the Truman administration. And he insisted that there was no easy road to the "peace, prosperity, and progress" that the Republicans were promising the voters.

On November 4, 1952, voters in record numbers cast their ballots. Eisenhower won 57 per cent of the popular vote—33,824,351 to Stevenson's 27,314,987. His majority in the electoral count was overwhelming, 442 to 89, and he carried even the traditionally Democratic states of Virginia, Tennessee, Florida, and Texas. But the Republicans managed to control Congress by only bare majorities in both houses.

Elections of 1954, '56, and '58. The Republicans held their slender majority in Congress for only two years. In the 1954 Congressional elections the Democrats won control of the legislative branch of the government by majorities of 27 seats in the House and 2 in the Senate. Eisenhower's popularity appeared to be undiminished, however, and as the months passed it became increasingly clear that Republican chances for victory in the 1956 elections depended in large measure upon his willingness to run for a second term.

Then, in September 1955, the nation learned that the Chief Executive had suffered a heart attack. Even after his recovery was certain, the public wondered whether he would run for re-election. Eisenhower himself answered this question on February 29, 1956, with the declaration that he was willing to be a candidate.

Both of the major parties held nominating conventions in August. The Republicans enthusiastically renominated Eisenhower and Nixon. The Democrats renominated Adlai Stevenson and chose for his running mate Senator Estes Kefauver of Tennessee.

In the campaign the Republicans reminded voters that the country was enjoying the highest standard of living in American history. The Democrats blamed the Republicans for the continuing high cost of living, and for falling farm prices. They also charged that the Republicans had failed to develop an effective foreign policy.

Eisenhower's popularity returned him to the White House with a popular vote of more than 35,000,000 to Stevenson's

THE FORD FOUNDATION

During the twentieth century, many of America's great fortunes were turned over to private foundations to be used for public welfare. On December 13, 1955, the Ford Foundation, established by Henry Ford II in 1950, announced that it was giving 500 million dollars to 4157 privately supported colleges, universities, and hospitals throughout the United States and its possessions. The Ford Foundation grant was the largest gift in the history of philanthropy.

The funds provided were to be distributed within the next 18 months. The largest portion, 210 million dollars, was to provide salary increases for teachers in 615 liberal arts and science colleges and universities; 200 million dollars was to be used to improve and extend services of 3500 nonprofit hospitals; and the remaining 90 million dollars was to supply better instruction in 42 privately supported medical schools.

The dramatic announcement of this enormous gift served to point out to Americans and to the world at large the readiness of private enterprise to contribute to the public welfare. The Ford Foundation also has supported various projects designed to improve the economic well-being of people in all countries and to promote freedom, democracy, and world peace.

nearly 26,000,000, and an electoral count of 457 to 73. But the voters returned a Democratic majority to Congress, substantially increasing the lead the Democratic Party had won in 1954.

In the 1958 Congressional elections, the Democrats won by a landslide, piling up large majorities in both houses. As a result, in his last six years in office, Eisenhower had to work with a Congress controlled by the Democrats.

Encouraging private business. The Eisenhower administration generally tried to reduce government interference in the affairs of states and of private business. For many years there had been controversy over the ownership of oil fields lying off the coasts of Florida, Louisiana, Texas, and California. Who owned these oil fields, the federal government or the states? With the approval of the Eisenhower administration, Congress settled this offshore oil controversy with the Submerged Lands Act of 1953, which gave the states control of the underwater oil deposits.

The Tennessee Valley Authority again became an issue in 1954 when the Atomic Energy Commission required additional electricity. Opposing a TVA proposal to build steam plants to generate electricity for the AEC, the administration awarded the contract to the Dixon-Yates group of private utility companies. But the Dixon-Yates contract aroused such a storm of controversy that it was canceled.

The Eisenhower administration made other determined efforts to encourage private enterprise. (1) Shortly after taking office, the President abandoned the wage and price controls imposed during the Korean War. (2) Former President Hoover agreed to head a new commission to recommend ways of securing greater efficiency in government and removing government competition with private business. (3) In 1954 Congress amended the Atomic Energy Act, giving private industry a larger opportunity to develop atomic energy for peaceful uses. (4) The federal government reduced or completely ended its participation in business activities including the manufacture of synthetic rubber, the operation of railroads, ships, and hotels, and the production of motion pictures.

Balancing the budget. Many of the measures taken to reduce competition with private business were also designed to lower the cost of government. Once in office, Eisenhower made government economy and a balanced budget "the first order of business." Appropriations for defense and foreign aid were reduced in spite of arguments from some Democrats that the administration was weakening national security. In 1956, for the first time in eight years the government ended its fiscal year with a surplus.

"Modern Republicanism." The Eisenhower administration did not attempt to repeal the basic social and economic legislation developed during the New Deal–Fair Deal era. President Eisenhower was personally in sympathy with much of this legislation. He favored a moderate extension of some of the New Deal–Fair Deal programs—an expansion of social security and of federal support for education, housing, slum clearance, and public health activities. This policy—together with support for the United Nations, military aid for American allies, and economic and military help for underdeveloped countries —was called "Modern Republicanism."

Social legislation. Shortly after he took office in 1953, President Eisenhower moved to promote the welfare of his fellow citizens. Early in April, he signed a joint resolution of Congress, transforming the Federal Security Agency into the Department of Health, Education, and Welfare. In January 1954, in his State of the Union message, he urged Congress to expand the social security program and consider ways of providing additional federal aid for housing, education, and health.

Congress responded by extending social security to an additional 10½ million persons and by increasing benefits. By 1955 about 90 per cent of the nation's workers were covered by social security.

Congress also set aside additional money for the construction of hospitals and for medical research. And in 1955 it authorized 500 million dollars for slum clearance and urban redevelopment.

But Congress refused to appropriate money to build schools and raise teachers' salaries. Many members of both political parties feared that federal support of education might lead to federal control. In 1958, however, after the Rus-

sians had successfully launched several earth satellites, Congress adopted legislation providing loans for able students, principally for students of science.

Gains for organized labor. During the Eisenhower administration Congress raised the hourly minimum wage under the Fair Labor Standards Act from 75 cents to $1.00. In June 1955, the Ford Motor Company and the General Motors Corporation signed contracts (renewed in 1958) which moved the United Automobile Workers toward a guaranteed annual wage. The contracts provided, among other things, for the companies to pay unemployment benefits.

During the 1950's a growing number of unions set up welfare funds to take care of their members. Some of the unions used surplus capital to buy stocks, bonds, and real estate.

In December 1955, the AF of L and the CIO met in New York and voted to combine. The new organization, called the AFL–CIO, with George Meany as president and Walter Reuther as vice-president, had 15 million members.

The Labor Act of 1959. There were also problems for organized labor. In 1957–58 a Congressional committee headed by Senator John L. McClellan revealed corrupt leadership in certain unions, notably in the powerful Teamsters Union. Several labor officials were brought into court and given jail sentences. The leaders of the AFL–CIO insisted that the corrupt practices were confined to only a small segment of organized labor. They took steps, however, to put their own house in order. In the meantime, Congress adopted the Labor-Management Reporting and Disclosure Act of 1959. This law contained a number of important provisions: (1) It prohibited Communists or persons convicted of felonies within the five previous years from serving as officials or employees of labor unions. (2) It prohibited secondary boycotts and the picketing of parties other than those directly involved in the strike. (3) It required labor unions to file with the Secretary of Labor annual reports giving

Hemingway

HIGHLIGHTS OF AMERICAN WRITING

In 1954 the Nobel prize for literature was awarded to an American—Ernest Hemingway. The citation read "For his powerful, style-forming mastery of the art of modern narration, as most recently evinced in *The Old Man and the Sea*."

Hemingway was thus recognized in the 1950's as one of the giants of world literature. But he was not the first American to be so honored. The Nobel prize for literature had been given in 1930 to Sinclair Lewis, in 1936 to Eugene O'Neill, in 1938 to Pearl Buck, and in 1949 to William Faulkner. (See page 684 for discussion of the work of most of these writers.)

The steel strike of 1959. In 1959, the contract between the steel industry and the United Steel Workers of America came up for renegotiation. The workers asked for a wage increase and other benefits, claiming that the steel industry could afford to meet these requests without raising the price of steel. The industry refused to discuss a wage increase unless the union would agree to changes in work rules that would eliminate "featherbedding," or the assignment of more men to a piece of work than management felt were needed.

On July 15, the union called a strike involving 500,000 steel workers and plants that produced 85 per cent of the nation's steel. Negotiations dragged on for week after week. Finally, President Eisenhower, using powers granted him in the Taft-Hartley Act, asked for an 80-day anti-strike injunction. On November 7, the injunction went into effect and the workers returned to their jobs.

The injunction did not, of course, settle any of the issues. It was not until January 4, 1960, that the union and the industry reached an agreement. The new agreement provided for step-by-step wage increases over a period of 30 months. In the dispute over work rules, the union maintained the right to place its own workers.

complete information about their financial activities and other matters. (4) It required employers to report any loans or payments made to unions, as well as any payments made to labor relations consultants. (5) It required national labor organizations to hold elections at least every five years. (6) It provided a "bill of rights" guaranteeing members of labor unions the right to attend meetings, nominate candidates for office, and vote in elections.

The new labor legislation went into effect in September. In the meantime, President Eisenhower and Congress had been facing another difficult problem of labor-management relations.

✔ **SECTION SURVEY**

1. Compare the elections of 1952 and 1956 with respect to (a) parties, (b) candidates, (c) issues, and (d) results.

2. Describe the steps taken by the Eisenhower administration to encourage private enterprise.

3. Summarize the important social legislation passed at this time.

4. (a) Give your opinion of the Labor-Management Reporting and Disclosing Act of 1959 and (b) support your position.

5. (a) State the issues in the steel strike of 1959 and (b) explain how it was settled.

IDENTIFY: Submerged Lands Act of 1953, Dixon-Yates, "Modern Republicanism," Department of Health, Education, and Welfare, AFL–CIO; Taft, Nixon, Stevenson, Meany, Reuther, McClellan.

2 The government struggles with other domestic problems

While dealing successfully with a number of domestic problems, the Eisenhower administration also grappled with others for which there appeared to be no ready solutions.

The farm problem. With the exception of large commercial producers, farmers in the 1950's did not share as fully as the rest of the population in the "Eisenhower prosperity." Between 1952 and 1956, farm income dropped 26 per cent.

There were a number of reasons for this situation, including the loss of foreign markets, and growing competition from farmers in other countries. Basically, however, the problem was overproduction in relation to national demand. It was not a new problem. Since the early 1930's the productivity of the farm worker had almost doubled, largely because of advances in technology.

From 1942 to 1954, the government tried to guarantee the farmer a *fixed* or *rigid* price support of 90 per cent of parity. When prices dropped below this 90 per cent level, the government bought surplus commodities at the fixed price.

Under this policy, grain elevators, warehouses, and other storage facilities were presently bursting, and storage charges alone were costing the government nearly a million dollars a day. But surpluses continued to pile up, and prices continued to fall.

Secretary of Agriculture Ezra Taft Benson persuaded the Eisenhower administration to abandon rigid price supports and adopt a flexible scale of 82½ per cent to 90 per cent. This, he maintained, would discourage farmers from growing crops that were glutting the market. It would encourage them to grow those crops not in surplus.

Despite considerable opposition the Eisenhower administration backed up the Benson program of flexible price supports. In 1956, however, the govern-ment made a major change in the farm program. The "soil bank," as it was called, was designed to encourage the use of more land for providing forage, for growing trees, and for reservoirs. Farmers were to be paid for their withdrawing land from commercial cultivation. By the end of 1958, the "soil bank" had paid 1.6 billion dollars to farmers for withdrawing land previously used for growing wheat, corn, cotton, tobacco, and rice.

Internal security and Constitutional rights. The Eisenhower administration also inherited the problem of protecting the country against subversion, without, at the same time, denying Americans their constitutional rights to freedom of criticism and association. Congressional committees were sometimes charged with handling individuals accused of subversion without proper regard for fair judicial practices. Among the most controversial of these committees was the one headed by Senator Joseph McCarthy of Wisconsin.

During the first two years of the Eisenhower administration, Senator McCarthy carried on intensive investigations of possible Communist influence in the government. He brought charges against leading Americans no longer in government service, against the Department of State, and against the army. Many Americans applauded McCarthy for his efforts, but others criticized him for what they called his recklessness and his disregard of constitutional rights. In 1954 McCarthy's influence declined, partly as a result of a Senate resolution censuring him for some of his actions.

During this troubled period the Supreme Court undertook to protect the constitutional rights of individuals without risking national security. Among its most significant decisions, the court ruled that under the Fifth Amendment a person could be required to answer questions which might lead to prosecution if he was first granted immunity from prosecution in the courts.

Civil rights laws. Equally thorny was the problem of civil rights. During the

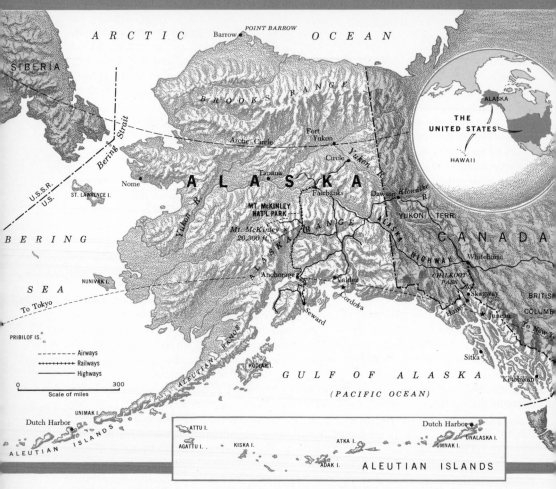

■ In June 1958, Congress passed a bill admitting Alaska to the Union as the forty-ninth state. Purchased from Russia in 1867, Alaska had begun its struggle for statehood in 1916, and had continued the struggle for 42 years. When it actually became a state in 1959, Alaska succeeded Texas as the largest state in the Union.

1930's and the years of World War II, Negro Americans had made marked progress toward fuller political, legal, and social rights. Almost each year saw less discrimination in the government service, business, education, and sports. President Truman took steps to insure equal opportunities for Negroes, and many barriers were broken down, especially in the armed services. President Eisenhower continued this policy.

In 1957, Congress passed a modified version of a civil rights bill proposed by the President. The new law (1) created

a Civil Rights Commission composed of members of both political parties, (2) authorized the government to secure court orders against anyone interfering with an individual's right to vote, and (3) provided for jury trials in certain cases involving persons charged with failure to obey court orders.

Two years later, the Civil Rights Commission reported that many Negroes were still being denied the right to vote. Early in 1960, acting on the Commission's general recommendations, the Eisenhower administration proposed a more sweeping civil rights bill. In the spring, Congress adopted a greatly modified version of the administration's proposal. The 1960 law (1) authorized the federal courts to appoint referees with power to grant voting certificates, (2) declared that *any* person who obstructed a court order of any kind by "threats or force" was guilty of a federal crime, (3) required state election officials to hold all voting records for at least 22 months after each primary or general election, and (4) declared that any person who crossed a state line while fleeing from prosecution for "hate bombing," arson, or any other destructive action was guilty of a federal crime.

The issue of integration. The most consequential development in civil rights during the Eisenhower administration was the Supreme Court decision of 1954. In *Brown v. Board of Education of Topeka,* the Court unanimously ruled that state or local laws requiring Negroes to send their children to separate schools violated the Fourteenth Amendment of the Constitution.

Several months after the momentous 1954 decision, the Supreme Court placed on local school authorities the responsibility for working out plans for gradually integrating the separate school systems. The Supreme Court also instructed federal district courts to require local school authorities to "make a prompt and reasonable start toward full compliance" and to move "with all deliberate speed."

Although considerable progress was made toward integration in the District of Columbia and some of the border states, Virginia and parts of the deep South opposed the entire policy. In March 1956 a number of southern Congressmen voiced their opposition to the new policy in a "Declaration" in which they declared that the Supreme Court decision was a "clear abuse of judicial power." And in the autumn of 1957, President Eisenhower ordered federal troops to Little Rock, Arkansas, where violence had broken out when the

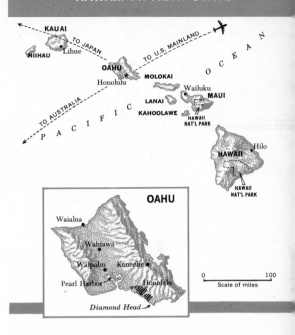

■ In March 1959, only nine months after the vote to admit Alaska to the Union, Congress voted to admit Hawaii as the fiftieth state. The state of Hawaii consists of eight volcanic islands in the Pacific Ocean, about 2400 miles from the American mainland.

school board permitted a few Negro boys and girls to attend a high school previously reserved for white students. The problem of integration was still far from a solution when the Eisenhower administration drew to an end.

Continuing prosperity. Although in 1960 Americans were still faced with stubborn domestic and international problems, they continued to enjoy a rising standard of living. To be sure, during the 1950's economic progress had been slowed down twice by recessions—the first in 1953–54, the second in 1957–58. The 1957–58 recession was the more severe of the two. Unemployment climbed to more than 5,500,000, the stock market slumped, and many Americans feared the country was entering another depression. But by 1959 unemployed workers were returning to their jobs, the stock market had reached record high levels, business was gaining momentum, and a spirit of optimism prevailed. Whereas in 1950 the gross

■ President Eisenhower and Queen Elizabeth II of England in 1959 dedicated the newly opened St. Lawrence Seaway. The seaway permits ocean-going vessels to penetrate North America.

national product° had been 264.7 billion dollars, by 1960 it had risen to about 510 billion dollars. Never before had so many Americans enjoyed such prosperity. The enjoyment of "Eisenhower prosperity," was tempered, however, by the continuing struggle with Communism and growing tensions throughout the world.

....

° *gross national product:* the total money value of all goods and services produced in the nation.

✔ SECTION SURVEY

1. Which plan—*rigid* or *flexible* price supports—would you have supported as a solution to the farm problem? Discuss your opinion.

2. Summarize and compare the key provisions of the civil rights laws of 1957 and 1960.

3. Explain how the case of *Brown v. Board of Education of Topeka* was related to the problem of civil rights.

IDENTIFY: parity, "soil bank," Civil Rights Commission, gross national product; Benson, McCarthy.

The nation continues to meet the challenge of Communism

Throughout President Truman's administration the Republicans had sharply criticized his conduct of foreign affairs. After the election of 1952, the American public waited with keen interest to learn how President Eisenhower would handle foreign affairs.

From the beginning, President Eisenhower and his Secretary of State, John Foster Dulles, continued the bipartisanship in foreign affairs that had been followed by the Democrats since American entrance into World War II. As a result of this policy and because Eisenhower made no sudden changes in his conduct of foreign affairs, the Democratic members of Congress often supported administration measures.

Ending the Korean War. During the election campaign of 1952, Eisenhower had promised to do everything within his power to end the Korean War. In December 1952, true to his promise, he visited the battle area for talks with political and military leaders. Peace talks between the warring powers were being carried on at this time in Panmunjom (PAN-MUHN-JUM) in Korea (see map, pages 806–07). These talks had dragged on and on.

On March 5, 1953, only a few weeks after Eisenhower took office, Joseph Stalin died in Moscow. The new leaders of the Soviet Union seemed to be more conciliatory toward the United States and the free world, and the North Korean Communists were now willing to negotiate. Finally, on July 27, 1953, representatives of North Korea and the United Nations signed an armistice agreement. This agreement provided for the exchange of prisoners. It also recognized the division of Korea into two countries—North Korea (Communist) and the Republic of South Korea.

In a formal treaty the United States promised to defend South Korea against attack. The United States also undertook to help the South Koreans improve their economic and social conditions.

Crisis in Indo-China. Only a few months after the Korean armistice, world peace was threatened by another Far Eastern crisis. Ever since the end of World War II, Indo-China, a French colony, had been torn by armed conflict. The Vietminh (VYET-meen), a Communist group, had been fighting to win control of the entire country from the French and their loyal, anti-Communist allies, the Vietnamese. When it became clear that Communist China was actively aiding the Vietminh, the United States began to send military equipment to the Vietnamese and French armies.

Early in 1954, the Vietminh, supported by the Chinese, launched a powerful drive against the French and Vietnamese forces. On May 7, 1954, the key French fortress of Dienbienphu (dyen-byen-FOO) (see map, pages 806–07) fell to the Communists.

In July a meeting was held in Geneva, Switzerland, to discuss the fate of Indo-China. Representatives of France, Indo-China, Communist China, the Soviet Union, and Great Britain attended the conference. There the decision was reached to divide Indo-China into two parts. The area north of the 17th parallel was recognized as the Communist state of Vietminh, later North Vietnam. The remainder of the country was divided into three non-Communist states —Laos, Cambodia, and South Vietnam (see map, pages 806–07).

Organization of SEATO. With an uneasy peace established in Southeast Asia, the Southeast Asia Treaty Organization, known as SEATO, came into being on September 8, 1954, at a conference in Manila. SEATO membership included the United States, Great Britain, France, Australia, New Zealand, Pakistan, Thailand, and the Philippines.

The Southeast Asia Treaty Organization was much weaker than its European counterpart, NATO. For one thing, important Asian countries such as India, Burma, Ceylon, and Indonesia refused to join. Moreover, unlike NATO, SEATO

did not provide for an armed force to resist aggression. The members of SEATO agreed, however, to consider an attack upon any of their number as a threat to the peace and safety of all the others. They also pledged themselves to resist attacks on Laos, Cambodia, and South Vietnam.

Strengthening Western Europe. The United States also continued its efforts to strengthen the defenses of Western Europe. In October 1954 the United States and its allies in Western Europe agreed to give the Federal Republic of West Germany full sovereign powers. They also agreed to admit West Germany to NATO, and to allow the new state to build an army of 500,000 men to serve under the NATO command. The United States, Great Britain, and France also agreed to regard an attack upon West Germany as an attack upon themselves.

The inclusion of West Germany greatly increased the military potential

■ The Nobel peace prize was awarded in 1950 to an American, Ralph Bunche (right), for his work as a UN mediator in ending the Israeli-Arab war in 1948. Shown on the left is Dag Hammarskjöld, Secretary-General of the United Nations.

Eisenhower's Disarmament Proposals at Geneva Summit Meeting (1955):
EXCERPT

I should address myself for a moment principally to the delegates from the Soviet Union, because our two great countries admittedly possess new and terrible weapons in quantities which do give rise in other parts of the world, or reciprocally, to the fear and danger of surprise attack.

I propose, therefore, that we take a practical step, that we begin an arrangement quickly; as between ourselves— immediately. These steps would include:

To give each other a complete blueprint of our military establishments . . .

Next, to provide within our countries facilities for aerial photography to the other country . . .

Likewise, we will make more easily attainable a comprehensive and effective system of inspection and disarmament . . .

of NATO. The United States continued, however, to hold the key to the defensive system of Western Europe. American supplies, equipment, and armed forces provided an essential part of NATO's power.

Atomic and hydrogen weapons. By 1954 both the United States and the Soviet Union possessed hydrogen bombs. In the face of this fearsome development, the United States made every effort to work out an agreement with the Soviet Union to end the arms race. But the Russians steadfastly refused to accept any kind of international inspection within their own borders. Without such a system of inspection, the United States refused to consider any agreement to destroy stockpiles of existing weapons, to abandon the testing of atomic and hydrogen bombs, or to stop the manufacture of nuclear weapons.

Eisenhower's proposal. In 1955, however, President Eisenhower seized an opportunity to advance a bold proposal for ending the armaments race. At a Big Four "summit conference" in Geneva in

June, President Eisenhower proposed that the Soviet Union and the United States exchange blueprints of their military establishments and permit mutual aerial observation of military installations. Eisenhower also declared that Americans were ready to make concessions to enable the two great powers to live peacefully side by side.

Although the Geneva Conference was carried on in a spirit of cordiality, it produced no tangible results. The four powers could not agree, for example, to reunite East and West Germany. Nor could they agree on the even more fateful question of disarmament.

Hopes for a change. Early in 1956 startling news came out of the Soviet Union. On February 25, Communist Party leader Nikita Khrushchev suddenly lashed out against the dead dictator, Stalin, calling him a cruel tyrant.

What was behind this attack? Was Khrushchev about to adopt a more friendly attitude toward the free world? Was he about to loosen the tight grip Stalin had held on the Russian satellite countries in Eastern Europe? Hope began to stir, and in the satellite countries people began to demand greater freedom from Soviet control.

Revolt in Poland. In October 1956 the leaders of the Communist Party in Poland elected an ardent Polish nationalist, Wladyslaw Gomulka (VLAH-dee-slaf go-MUL-ka) to be first secretary of their party. Although he was a devoted Communist, Gomulka promised the Poles freedom of speech, press, and religion.

Encouraged by Gomulka's stand, Poles staged anti-Soviet demonstrations in the streets. On a number of occasions, they exchanged shots with Soviet troops.

The Polish revolt attracted the attention of the entire world. What would Khrushchev do? Would he crush the uprising with overwhelming force? Or would he allow the Poles to have the freedom they demanded?

Khrushchev chose the latter course. He withdrew a portion of the Soviet troops from Poland. And he permitted Gomulka to remain in power.

The Hungarian tragedy. Inspired by the example of the Poles, the Hungarians also rebelled against the Soviets. On October 23, 1956, students and workers rioted in the streets of Budapest (see map, pages 806–07). They demanded the immediate withdrawal of all Soviet troops from the country and the formation of a new government under the more liberal leadership of Imre Nagy (IM-reh NAHZH).

On the following morning, Soviet tanks, artillery, and armored cars supported by jet planes moved into Budapest to put down the revolt. Violent fighting broke out as the heroic "freedom fighters" resisted with improvised weapons. The rebellion spread as entire units of the Hungarian army joined the rebels.

For four days the desperate fighting continued. And then, on October 28, the U.S.S.R. agreed to pull its troops out of Budapest. Two days later, Nagy, who was now premier, promised the Hungarians free elections and an early end to the one-party dictatorship. At the same time, the Soviet Union declared that it was willing to consider withdrawing all its troops from Hungary, Poland, and Rumania.

But even while the victorious Hungarians were celebrating their newly won freedom, the Soviet Army was bringing up reinforcements for another assault. On November 4 powerful Soviet forces launched a massive attack upon Budapest. "All Budapest is under fire," the Budapest radio reported. "The Russian gangsters have betrayed us."

In the meantime, Premier Nagy had called upon the United Nations for help. The General Assembly adopted a resolution condemning the Soviet action and demanding the immediate withdrawal of all Soviet troops from Hungary. But the U.S.S.R. paid no attention to this resolution, insisting that the Soviet government was merely helping the lawful government of Hungary to suppress gangs of bandits and restore order. And when the United Nations asked for permission to send observers to see for themselves what was going on, the Soviet Union refused permission.

Within a few days the Hungarian fight for freedom came to a tragic end. With all organized resistance ruthlessly crushed, a new Hungarian government, a puppet of the U.S.S.R., began to round up the rebels and throw them into prison or deport them to the Soviet Union. Refugees by the thousands fled across the frontier into Austria, seeking in exile the freedom denied to them in their own country.

SECTION SURVEY

1. Show how each of the following indicated the continuing challenge of Communism: (a) Korean armistice, (b) crisis in Indo-China, (c) SEATO, and (d) West Germany's admission to NATO.

2. Explain the reason for Eisenhower's bold proposal at the 1955 Geneva Conference.

3. (a) Why did the revolt in Poland attract world-wide attention? (b) What was the outcome of the Hungarian revolution?

IDENTIFY: bipartisan policy, summit conference of 1955; Dulles, Khrushchev, Gomulka, Nagy, Vietminh.

4   The nation faces recurring world crises

In the same week that the gallant Hungarians rebelled, another crisis developed, one concerning the Suez Canal. For a few tense days the world hovered on the brink of another war.

Egypt and the Suez Canal. The Canal, connecting the Mediterranean with the Red Sea, and running entirely through Egyptian territory (see map, pages 806–07), had been completed in 1869. Owned and operated by an international company with headquarters in Paris, the Canal was open on equal terms to the ships of all nations. The right to use the Canal was guaranteed by an inter-

EUROPE

NORWAY FINLAND

SWEDEN

UNION OF SOVIET

Moscow

N. IRELAND DEN.

GREAT

EIRE BRITAIN E.GER.

London Berlin POLAND

NETH.

BELG. W.GER.

Bonn

CZECH.

Paris

FRANCE SWITZ. AUS. HUNG.

Geneva Budapest

RUM.

YUGO.

BULG. Black Sea

Caspian Sea

ITALY

ALB.

PORT. SPAIN GREECE Dardanelles TURKEY

OCEAN Mediterranean Sea

TUNISIA U.A.R. (Syria)

LEB. Beirut

ALGERIA ISRAEL IRAQ IRAN

MOROCCO SUEZ CANAL

JORDAN Persian Gulf

Cairo

SAUDI ARABIA

Red Sea OMAN

YEMEN ADEN

MIDDLE EAST

ETHIOPIA INDIA

SOMALIA

KENYA

TANGANYIKA

IMPORTANT EVENTS OF THE POSTWAR PERIOD

1946 United Nations intervention in Iran.
1947 Truman Doctrine is announced (aid sent to Greece and Turkey).
       Marshall Plan is announced.
1948 Berlin blockade and airlift.
       United Nations intervention in Israeli-Arab war.
1949 Point Four program is announced.
       NATO is formed.
       Nationalist Chinese retreat to Formosa (Communists control China).
1950 Korean War begins.
1953 Korean War ends.
1954 Fighting in Indo-China (Indo-China is divided).
       SEATO is formed.
       West Germany is admitted to NATO.
1955 Summit Conference at Geneva, Switzerland.
1956 Revolt in Poland.
       Egypt seizes Suez Canal.
       Hungarian Revolution.
1957 Eisenhower Doctrine is announced.
1958 Crisis in Middle East.
       Crisis in Far East.
       Rising tension over Berlin.
1959 Big Four foreign ministers' conference;
          Khrushchev visits United States.
1960 Summit Conference fails to materialize.
       Organization of American States meets.
       World leaders meet at United Nations.

national treaty ratified in 1888. By arrangement with Egypt, British troops were stationed in the Canal Zone to safeguard the Canal and to protect British interests.

As the years passed, and especially after World War II, the Egyptians became increasingly dissatisfied with British military occupation of the Canal Zone. Finally, in 1954 the British government agreed to withdraw its forces.

Eighteen months later, in June 1956, the last British troops did withdraw.

In the meantime, Colonel Gamal Abdel Nasser, recently elected President of the Republic of Egypt, had been negotiating for a loan to build a great irrigation dam at Aswan on the Nile River. On July 19, the United States announced that it withdrew its offer of a $56 million loan for the Aswan project. Great Britain and the World

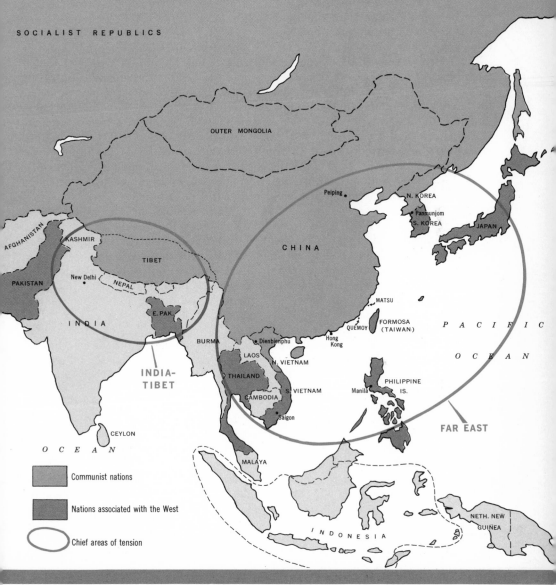

SOCIALIST REPUBLICS

OUTER MONGOLIA

Peiping

N. KOREA

Panmunjom

S. KOREA

JAPAN

AFGHANISTAN

KASHMIR

TIBET

CHINA

PAKISTAN

New Delhi

NEPAL

INDIA

E. PAK.

MATSU

FORMOSA
(TAIWAN)

QUEMOY

P A C I F I C

BURMA

Dienbienphu

Hong
Kong

INDIA-
TIBET

LAOS

N. VIETNAM

O C E A N

THAILAND

CAMBODIA

S. VIETNAM

Manila

PHILIPPINE
IS.

Saigon

FAR EAST

CEYLON

O C E A N

MALAYA

NETH. NEW
GUINEA

Communist nations

Nations associated with the West

Chief areas of tension

I N D O N E S I A

Bank immediately withdrew similar offers. Nasser, furious at this blow to his plans, announced that Egypt was going to nationalize the Canal.

The Suez Crisis. Nasser's action plunged the world into another crisis. The Western powers tried in vain to persuade the Egyptian ruler to agree to international control by the eighteen nations that regularly used the Canal.

Such was the tense situation when, on October 29, 1956, the Israeli Army moved rapidly westward through the Sinai Peninsula toward the Suez Canal. The Israeli government announced that its troops had invaded Egyptian territory in order to forestall a carefully planned attack upon Israel by Egypt.

On October 30, the British and French issued a twelve-hour *ultimatum,* or final warning. They demanded that Egypt and Israel cease fighting and allow

807

French and British troops temporarily to occupy key points in the Canal Zone. When Egypt refused, the British and French bombed Egyptian airfields and moved troops into the northern part of the Canal Zone.

Then, denouncing Israel, France, and Great Britain as aggressors, the Soviet Union threatened to intervene with force if the three nations did not immediately withdraw.

The United States now found itself in an embarrassing position. Great Britain and France, its allies in NATO, had ignored the United Nations, and, by their action, had created a situation that could easily lead to a general war. Reluctantly, the United States delegates to the United Nations voted in favor of a General Assembly resolution calling for an immediate cease-fire and the withdrawal of British, French, and Israeli troops. Great Britain, France, and Israel accepted these terms.

The Eisenhower Doctrine. As an immediate result of the Suez crisis, the United States adopted what came to be known as the Eisenhower Doctrine. Early in January 1957, President Eisenhower asked Congress (1) to authorize him to use military force if this were requested by any Middle Eastern nation to check Communist aggression, and (2) to set aside a sum of 200 million dollars to help those Middle Eastern countries that desired such aid from the United States. Congress granted both requests.

The race into space. The Eisenhower Doctrine was not the really big news of 1957. The big news, which broke on October 4, was compressed into a single word: *Sputnik*. The Russians had succeeded in hurling an artificial satellite into orbit around the earth.

The American public, long convinced that the United States had no superior in science and technology, heard the news with stunned surprise. Without attempting to belittle the Soviet achievements, President Eisenhower assured the American people that the United States was not neglecting its own program of rocket and missile develop-

ment, and that they would soon see concrete results. On January 31, 1958, the United States launched its first satellite, Explorer I, into orbit.

Rockets powerful enough to carry artificial satellites into space could also be used to hurl atomic and hydrogen bombs into the heart of an enemy country. By 1960, both the Soviet Union and the United States were building stockpiles of increasingly effective Intercontinental Ballistic Missiles (ICBM's) equipped with nuclear warheads. Push-button war that could destroy millions of lives in a single blinding instant had become a dreadful possibility.

More trouble in the Middle East. Meanwhile, the Middle East was once again in turmoil. Early in February 1958, Egypt and Syria joined to form the United Arab Republic (U.A.R.) with Egypt's Gamal Abdel Nasser as President. Nasser immediately urged the other Arab states to join the U.A.R.

In the spring, rebellion broke out in Lebanon. Charles Malik, Prime Minister of the pro-Western Lebanese government, accused Nasser of provoking the rebellion, and asked the United Nations to intervene.

In response to Malik's request, the Security Council sent observers to Lebanon. The observers found no evidence that the rebels were receiving any large quantities of arms from the U.A.R. But the fighting was still going on when, on July 14, trouble broke out in Iraq. In a pre-dawn revolution, a group of Iraqian army officers killed the pro-Western leaders and seized control of the government.

The next day, President Eisenhower ordered United States marines into Lebanon. In a special message to Congress, Eisenhower said he had sent the troops in response to an urgent request for help from the President of Lebanon. Two days later, in response to a similar request from King Hussein, Great Britain flew 2,000 crack paratroopers into Jordan.

For several weeks, American and British forces remained poised for any emergency. Meanwhile, the Secretary-General of the United Nations visited the Middle East. Late in September, after he reported that the situation in Lebanon was improving, Great Britain and the United States withdrew their troops.

Another crisis in the Far East. In the summer of 1958, while the Middle East was still boiling with unrest, a new crisis developed in the Far East. Reports from Nationalist forces on Formosa (Taiwan) revealed that Communist China was pouring shells into the Nationalist-held islands of Quemoy and Matsu as though in preparation for an invasion.

Secretary of State Dulles responded to this threat with a declaration that the United States would take "timely and effective" action to repel any invasion of Quemoy and Matsu and to defend Formosa. The Soviet Union immediately declared that it considered Red China's claims to the islands "lawful and just." Eisenhower, in a nation-wide broadcast, warned that the United States would not "retreat in the face of armed aggression, which is part and parcel of a continuing program of using armed force to conquer new regions."

By October, the crisis was beginning to ease. In an effort to clarify America's position, Dulles announced that the United States had no commitment to help the Nationalists recover the mainland. At the same time he promised that, if the Communists issued a cease-fire order, the United States would urge Nationalist China to reduce its forces on Quemoy and Matsu.

Although the immediate crisis was past, the major issue remained unsettled. Red China's Foreign Minister made this clear when, on November 1, he declared: "The Americans must pull away their hand from the Taiwan Strait. . . . We are determined to liberate Formosa and the offshore islands. . . ."

Rising tension over Berlin. The Far East crisis was hardly past when, on November 27, the Soviet Premier issued an ultimatum concerning Berlin. Khrushchev gave the Western powers six months to agree to withdraw from Berlin and make it a free, demilitarized city. If, by May 27, 1959, the Western powers had not agreed, the Soviet Union would turn over to the Communist government of East Germany complete control of all lines of communication to West Berlin, and the Western powers would have access to West Berlin only by permission of the East German government. If they tried to cross East German territory without this permission, the Soviet Union would help the East Germans to meet force with force. The United States, Great Britain, and France replied to this ultimatum by firmly repeating their determination to remain in West Berlin.

The temporary easing of tension. During 1959, however, the situation began to improve. Instead of insisting that the Western powers get out of Berlin by May 27, the Soviet Union met with the Western leaders in a Big Four foreign ministers' conference. The conference lasted for nearly three months. Although it failed to reach any important agreements, it did open the door to further negotiations.

Premier Khrushchev himself seemed to be opening the door a bit wider when, in September, he visited the United States. At the end of this visit, he and Eisenhower issued a joint declaration, stating that the most serious issue facing the world was that of general disarmament. They also expressed agreement that the problem of Berlin and "all outstanding international questions should be settled, not by the application of force, but by peaceful means through negotiation."

Encouraged by Khrushchev's apparent willingness to negotiate, the Western powers agreed to meet with the Soviet Premier at a Summit Conference. During the next few months, leaders of both East and West engaged in an extensive series of preliminary conferences.

The Summit Conference fails to materialize. As it turned out, the preparations for the Summit Conference proved to be fruitless. Early in May 1960, shortly before the conference was scheduled to open in Paris, Premier Khrushchev charged the United States with "aggression." He announced that, on May 1, Soviet troops had shot down a United States plane over the heart of the Soviet Union.

United States officials at first insisted that the U-2, as the plane was called, was engaged in weather research and had strayed off its course. Later, the United States admitted that the U-2 had indeed been engaged in aerial reconnaissance.

The Soviet Premier was in an angry mood when the heads of state gathered in Paris for the Summit Conference. He refused to take part in the conference unless Eisenhower (1) agreed to stop all future overflights; (2) apologized for the past acts of "aggression"; and (3) promised to punish those responsible for the flights.

Hoping against hope that the conference could still be held, President Eisenhower announced that the overflights had been stopped and would not be resumed. He refused, however, to apologize. Khrushchev, refusing to accept anything less than an apology, left for home. As a result, all plans for the conference had to be abandoned.

Revolution in Cuba. During the months following the failure of the Summit Conference, Soviet leaders became increasingly belligerent, and redoubled their interest in Cuba.

Early in 1959, after battling for several years, Cuba's Fidel Castro succeeded in overthrowing the government of Cuban dictator Fulgencio Batista. Mindful of Batista's cruel record of repression, the United States government and the public in general welcomed Castro's rise to power as a victory for democracy.

American sympathy rapidly evaporated, however, when Castro began to act and sound like another power-crazed dictator. He failed to hold the elections he had promised the Cuban people. He put to death hundreds of his former political enemies and jailed thousands unsympathetic to his regime. He expropri-

ated foreign-owned property.

Most serious of all, as far as the United States was concerned, Castro and other Cuban leaders began to lash out at the "Yankees" and to turn increasingly to the Communist powers for support. Castro went so far as to accept the Soviet offer of military aid if the United States "interfered" in Cuba.

In the face of rising provocations, the United States adopted a policy of patient waiting. During the summer of 1960, however, American policy hardened. The United States (1) placed a temporary embargo on the purchase of Cuban sugar; (2) announced that it was developing a sweeping program of economic aid to Latin America; and (3) urged the Organization of American States (O.A.S.), formerly Pan-American Union, to condemn Cuba's actions.

Late in August, the 21 members of the O.A.S. met in San José, Costa Rica. The conference refused to make any direct criticism of the Castro regime. It did, however, adopt a resolution condemning Communist interference in the Western Hemisphere, and urging the American countries to negotiate their differences through the Organization of American States.

World leaders gather at the United Nations. Shortly after the O.A.S. conference ended, the General Assembly of the United Nations met in New York for its fifteenth regular session. This meeting was a landmark in United Nations history. For one thing, 16 new countries, all but one in Africa, joined the world organization, bringing the total to 99. For another thing, many heads of state, as well as regular delegates, took part in the discussions. Never before in history had so many world leaders gathered in the same place at the same time.

One by one, the heads of state and the delegates rose to present their views. Spokesmen for the so-called "neutral" nations called upon the leaders of East and West to negotiate their differences and reach an agreement on disarmament.

In a widely applauded address, President Eisenhower promised the delegates that the United States would continue to seek a workable program of world disarmament based on an effective system of inspection and controls. He appealed for increased aid for underdeveloped areas and new African nations. He reaffirmed United States support of the U.N.

Any hopes the delegates might have had for a lessening of world tensions were dashed by Premier Khrushchev. He shocked the Assembly by rudely interrupting speakers and by pounding his desk with his fists, and even with a shoe, to express displeasure. In his own speeches, he abused President Eisenhower and the United States; called for a revolt against the Western powers in the remaining colonial areas; and insisted that disarmament must come first, inspection and controls later. As one Indian delegate put it, Eisenhower opened the door and Khrushchev slammed it shut.

The election of 1960. Meanwhile, with world tensions close to the snapping point, the American people prepared to elect a new President. The Democrats, meeting in Los Angeles in June, nominated Senator John F. Kennedy of Massachusetts, with Senator Lyndon Johnson of Texas as his running mate. The Republicans, meeting in Chicago in July, nominated Vice-President Richard M. Nixon of California as their Presidential candidate. For their Vice-Presidential nominee, the Republicans chose Henry Cabot Lodge of Massachusetts, Ambassador to the U.N.

In an extremely vigorous campaign, the Presidential aspirants established a precedent by appearing together on television in a series of debates. Nixon emphasized the experience he had gained as Vice-President during the "Eisenhower-Nixon administration," and reminded voters of "peace and prosperity" achieved under Republican leadership. Kennedy charged that American prestige in the world had declined in recent years, and stressed the need for new, forward-looking leadership and the realization of the nation's potentialities.

■ John F. Kennedy is shown here as he participated in a TV debate with Richard M. Nixon.

The returns from the November election gave the victory to the Democratic candidate by a narrow margin. The Democrats retained control of both houses of Congress.

Other American leaders had entered the White House in times of grave national crisis, but none had carried heavier responsibilities than those that faced John F. Kennedy as he prepared to assume the high office of the Presidency of the United States.

⌙ **SECTION SURVEY**

1. (a) What were the causes and results of the Suez crisis? (b) Explain the position taken by the United States.

2. The year 1958 was one of many international crises. Cite evidence by reference to (a) Europe, (b) the Middle East, (c) the Far East.

3. Why did the Summit Conference of May 1959 fail to materialize?

4. What actions did the United States take to counteract Castro's hostility?

5. Why was the fifteenth regular session of the General Assembly regarded as "a landmark in U.N. history"?

6. Give the parties, candidates, issues, and results of the 1960 election.

IDENTIFY: ultimatum, Eisenhower Doctrine, Sputnik, Explorer I, ICBM, push-button war, O.A.S., San José Conference (1960); Nasser, Khrushchev; 1956, 1957, January 31, 1958.

Points to Discuss: 1. Although Eisenhower won the Presidential elections of 1952 and 1956, the Democrats won control of Congress in 1954, 1956, and 1958. How do you interpret these results?

2. "The Eisenhower administration did not attempt to repeal the basic social and economic legislation developed during the New Deal–Fair Deal era." Explain and give evidence.

3. Why did Congress pass the Labor-Management Reporting and Disclosure Act of 1959?

4. "The Eisenhower administration also inherited the problem of protecting the country against subversion, without, at the same time, denying Americans their constitutional rights to freedom of criticism and association." Discuss.

5. Summarize steps taken by the President, Congress, and the Supreme Court during 1954–60 in the field of civil rights.

6. Compare SEATO and NATO with respect to (a) member nations, (b) aims, and (c) effectiveness.

7. (a) Give specific evidence to show that Communism has challenged the United States in Europe and in Asia. (b) What steps did the Eisenhower administration take to meet the challenge?

8. The Eisenhower Doctrine was actually an extension of the old containment policy first developed during the Truman administration. Discuss this statement.

9. The launching of Sputnik I led to much self-examination and self-criticism on the part of the American people. (a) Explain. (b) Indicate specific results.

10. The election of 1960 has been described by some as one of the most important in American history. Discuss.

Using Maps and Charts: 1. Base your answers on the map on page 800: (a) Locate the capital of Alaska. (b) What is the distance between Soviet Siberia and Alaska? (c) Which is now the northernmost point of the United States? (d) Explain the strategic significance of Alaska.

2. Using the map on page 801, answer the following: (a) How many of the Hawaiian Islands are shown? (b) Where are Pearl Harbor and Honolulu?

3. Using the map on pages 806–07, locate Lebanon, U.A.R., Iraq, Quemoy, Matsu, and Formosa.

Consulting the Sources: In *Vital Speeches*, November 15, 1960, see "Principles Guiding United Nations Activities," and June 1, 1960, "Collective Bargaining at the Crossroads." For Kennedy's key ideas, see John F. Kennedy, *Strategy of Peace*, Harper.

■ TRACING THE MAIN IDEAS

"Peace and prosperity!" This was one of the slogans of the Republican Party in the election campaign of 1960.

It was true, as the Republicans were quick to point out, that during the Eisenhower administration the American people had continued to enjoy a steadily rising standard of living. It was true that, during the years from 1952 to 1960, the government had ended the Korean War and brought the country safely through a series of world crises.

But it was also true, as both the Republicans and the Democrats agreed, that the decade of the 1960's promised to be the most critical the nation had ever faced. Both at home and on the international stage, Americans were confronted with the challenge of unsolved problems of the utmost complexity.

Peace there was, to be sure, but it hung by a fragile thread. The American people, faced with the responsibility of leadership of the free world, would need all the courage, resolution, and creative intelligence they could command if they were to help men everywhere build a world order which could and would guarantee an enduring peace.

Nor was continued prosperity a sure and certain thing. In an increasingly interdependent world, the well-being of the American people depended more and more upon the well-being of others.

"Peace and prosperity!" In growing numbers, the American people were beginning to realize that the two were indivisible. It was, therefore, with a sense of destiny that John F. Kennedy entered the White House in January 1961.

The Nation Faces Its Future

CHANGING WAYS

OF AMERICAN LIFE

THE material basis of civilization in the United States has been its soil, climate, minerals, forests, and the natural waterways that first gave access to a rich continent. From the time the first settlers began to penetrate the area, while America was the frontier of a European civilization, this great land of abundant natural resources has been a treasure lode. The exploitation of the natural endowment could not have been fulfilled, however, if there had not been people to work here, people who had some notion of the good life and an idea of human progress, people who have been endowed by a generous Creator. Of all of our natural resources, therefore, the human element—discoverers, pioneers, missionaries, planters and town builders, educators and statesmen —has been the greatest. They made our civilization in a rich land by co-operating with Divine Providence. By the end of the eighteenth century, Americans had discovered their identity as a nation and won independence. Then over the years they fashioned a social order and a constitutional government suitable for tremendous expansion and progress. Recognizing that people, men, women, and children, willing to work were of primary importance, our legislatures made it easy for others to become Americans, and so attracted a great many immigrants to our shores. The principal requirements for success in America have been self-reliance, modified by the habit of generosity to others in need, and tolerance which respects individual and group differences, modified only by an insistence that everyone respect fundamental human liberties. Despite the testing of a great civil conflict, 1861–1865, the United States survived in the nineteenth century with a single political framework and a sense of national destiny that was to make it a most important factor in twentieth-century world history.

Having built upon strong foundations a thriving industrial order, and with an agriculture keyed to abundance, Americans today are demonstrating their capacity to produce and consume more than one third of the goods and services of the entire world. But they accomplish all this within only seven per cent of the world's land area, and they are but six per cent of the world's population. This century has been, however, not only a time when Americans have attained a fullness of producing and consuming capacities; it has brought as well four major changes in their condition:

(1) People no longer come here in large numbers as immigrants. Instead,

they generally remain in their own lands, but look to the American example, and frequently look for American help, in order to bring about in their countries the kind of material abundance enjoyed in the United States. On the other hand, this change has not had the effect of reducing our own population growth, for in recent years the United States has had an *annual* growth greater than the total population of the entire country on the eve of the American Revolution.

(2) The United States is now forced to look beyond what once appeared to be limitless natural resources at home in order to find sufficient minerals, some varieties of food, and certain items necessary to national defense. At the same time, we seek to build up standards of living everywhere in order to provide markets for our goods. Some idea of the problem of conservation of important resources at home is suggested in a 1952 government report: "More coal, oil, and natural gas have been burned up in the last fifty years than in all previous history. It took nature over 500 million years to store in the ground these stockpiles of 'fossil fuels' which civilization is now consuming in a flash of geologic time." More economical use of our existing resources, and the development of nuclear power have become necessary.

(3) Having made the irrevocable decision to keep freedom alive, and having thereby committed ourselves to maintain a military capacity that the founders of the Republic never dreamed of, the United States has undertaken a world policy—rather than a mere foreign policy—which combines the objectives of self-defense and the common good of the United Nations.

(4) Pending the recovery, and the possible unification of Europe in the twentieth century, only America can speak now in behalf of those traditional standards, those ideals and objectives which we associate with all that is best in western civilization. It has become the role of America, in the providential order of things, to support with all of its power those ideas of the good life and of true human progress which were the heritage of Christendom, that great society which produced, among other things, the explorers, missionaries, and settlers who, literally, first put America on the map.

Americans will have to sustain the ideas that have made the United States great and powerful, and at the same time find the means and the intelligence to measure up to the new conditions. They have never lacked either moral earnestness or confidence in the face of obstacles; they have been singularly blessed with success. The claim was made in 1776 that Americans were entitled to an equal station among the nations of the world and it was based upon the idea of natural rights. Subsequently, it was the common belief in America that God was sovereign over all, and that all men were included in His moral order, and, despite a diversity of religious beliefs, that His moral order was made known to man both through reason and through revelation. The fundamental moral order is now being challenged by the cynical directors of the international Marxist conspiracy, so that America's ideals along with its material resources have been marked for destruction. The challenge to America, and to our western civilization, has been made on two levels; it can be met on these. To the rest of mankind the United States has to be an example of ordered liberty—not just of a high standard of living; an example of a nation of real people—not a collection of standardized masses. And this freedom, so ordered in the American people through the products of their economy and through the strength of their laws, challenges them by its supernatural demand for fulfillment. It will have to display to the rest of the world decency and justice given effect at home and supported abroad, rather than show licentiousness and greed. America will have to show concern and charity for the peoples of its own nation as well as the peoples of the world, who watch and wait, hoping the concepts of our councils are not vacuous, and that the source of our strength is dependable. Such is the potential moral strength of America. At the same time, Americans will have to meet the challenge of the Soviet Union and the Marxists generally on the level of military and economic power in world politics, to be strong in order to thwart aggression. It is the greatest test for America so far.

Yet whatever, spiritual or material, must enter into the response America makes to the new conditions, there will always be the requirement of the trained intelligence to make it effective. There can be no trained intelligence without formal education, its discipline and its culture. Student laziness, academic inertia, or the misdirection of youth in its formative stages could undermine one of democracy's greatest guarantees to its people. Dedication must begin early, education must produce results, if the mind is to govern the means, if the soul is to exercise its faculties, and if America is to meet its "rendezvous with destiny."

HISTORICAL ATLAS

THE PHYSICAL GEOGRAPHY OF THE UNITED STATES

Not quite a century has passed since Jules Verne drew from his fertile imagination a fantastic story of man's first flight to the moon. What was then pure science fiction may soon become exciting fact, for today man stands on the threshold of the Space Age, tomorrow he may be exploring the surface of the moon, and the day after tomorrow the infinite reaches of outer space.

It may well be that the exploration of outer space will be, as some predict, "the greatest adventure man has ever dared to take." But we do violence to the record when we ignore other great adventures, one of which was the discovery, exploration, and settlement of what is now the United States.

The first small band of Englishmen who landed at Jamestown in the spring of 1607 knew less about the North American continent than we know today about the moon and the more distant planets. They stood, a mere handful of men, on the fringe of a vast, unexplored wilderness that reached, as we now know, from sea to sea. They were the first of many thousands of pi-

oneers who through the next three centuries moved steadily westward to win one of the richest and most varied lands on earth.

The elevation profile below gives a generalized view of the country that the pioneers crossed. It does not show Daniel Boone's first group of settlers struggling over the Wilderness Road on their way to "the dark and bloody ground" west of the Appalachian Mountains. It does not show the covered wagons of the Mormons crawling across the apparently endless plains toward their final destination on the shores of the Great Salt Lake. It does not show the Donner Party caught in a blizzard in the high Sierras when within a few days' journey of their goal, the sun-drenched valleys of California. To the uninformed reader, the elevation profile means little. But to those who know something of the geography of the United States and the great drama of American history, the elevation profile is rich in meaning.

Turning the page, we come to a landforms map which gives another gen-

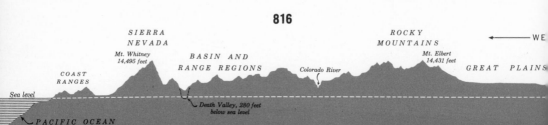

OF THE UNITED STATES

eralized view of the country. The men and women who explored this continent would have given a great deal for such a map. They could not have it so. The map had to be drawn fragment by tiny fragment and fitted together like the pieces of a jigsaw puzzle. If the history of this map could ever be told, it would include the records of surveyors and map makers as well as the stories of thousands of pioneers who fought their way across the land.

Like the elevation profile, the landforms map gives only part of the total picture. It gives an over-all view of the stage on which the great adventure which is American history has been carried on, and is being carried on today. The stage embraces half a continent; there is room on it for coastal plains, masses of mountain ranges, the broad expanse of high plateaus, and the immense sweep of the central lowlands and the Great Plains.

But the landforms map shows us only the stage. It is a stage bare of both scenery and actors. There is no hint of the dark and brooding forest that once covered so much of the continent, no hint of the immense grasslands or the

fertile valleys, no hint of the buried mineral wealth that has provided the raw material for the most productive industrial economy the world has ever known.

It takes many maps and many different charts and graphs to reveal even partially what the American people have built on this part of the North American continent that they claim as their own. In this Atlas, the 8 double-page maps and the 55 charts, graphs, and graphic summaries of significant developments give a much larger concept of the variety of the natural and human resources that help to explain the rise of the American nation.

Using the pages that follow, you can review, by way of charts, maps, and text, some major strands of American history and speculate on where these continuing strands may lead in the future. No one can tell you exactly what the challenges and opportunities of the future will be, either for you personally, or for the nation as a whole. But using the background of American history, it is possible to speculate on certain *areas* of opportunity and challenge that seem sure to arise.

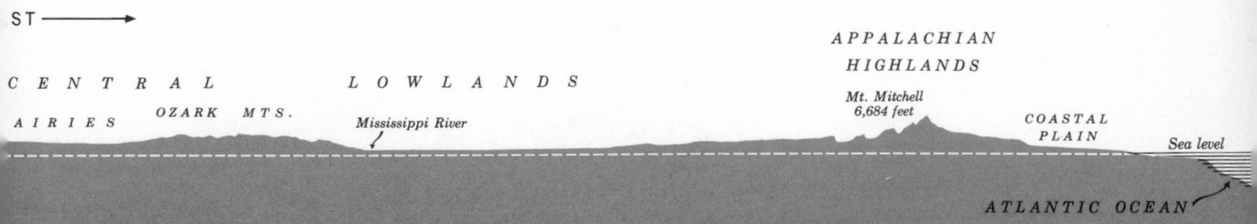

ST ——→

CENTRAL   LOWLANDS

AIRIES   OZARK MTS.   Mississippi River

APPALACHIAN
HIGHLANDS

Mt. Mitchell
6,684 feet

COASTAL
PLAIN

Sea level

ATLANTIC OCEAN

TO ALASKA

125°   120°   115°   110°   105°

C A N A D A

100°

Mt. Rainier
14,408 ft.

PACIFIC

45°

125°

OCEAN

40°

35°

30°

TO HAWAII

COAST   RANGES

CASCADE   RANGE

COLUMBIA   PLATEAUS

Columbia   R.

Snake   R.

Humboldt   R.

CENTRAL   VALLEY

Sacramento R.

SIERRA   NEVADA

BASIN   AND   RANGE   REGIONS

Great Salt
Lake

N O R T H E R N   R O C K Y   M O U N T A I N S

WYOMING
BASIN

COLORADO

PLATEAUS

Green   R.

Colorado   R.

Colorado R.

Gila   R.

S O U T H E R N   R O C K Y   M O U N T A I N S

Mt. Whitney
14,495 ft.

Mt. Whitney
14,495 ft.

Pike's Peak
14,110 ft.

G R E A T

Missouri   River

Yellowstone   R.

BLACK
HILLS

Niobrara   R.

Platte   R.

Arkansas   R.

P L A I N S

Red   R.

Brazos   R.

Colorado   R.

GU

Rio   Grande

Rio   Grande

Pecos   R.

M E X I C O

GREAT

ALASKA

170°   160°   150°   140°   130°

70°

ARCTIC   OCEAN

ARCTIC COASTAL PLAINS

BROOKS   RANGE

SIBERIA
(U.S.S.R.)

C E N T R A L

Arctic Circle

65°

Yukon   R.

P L A T E A U S

Delta Flats

ALASKA   RANGE

Mt. McKinley
20,320 ft.

CANADA

BERING

Mt. St. Elias
18,008 ft.

60°

SEA

Aleutian Range

COAST   RANGE

PACIFIC

OCEAN

ALASKA

0   500
Miles

HAWAII

158°

KAUAI

NIIHAU   OAHU

MOLOKAI

PACIFIC   OCEAN   LANAI   MAUI

HAWAII

0   100
Miles

Mauna Loa
13,680 ft.

20°

HAWAII

105°   100°

LANDFORMS OF THE UNITED STATES

CANADA

Lake Superior

SUPERIOR HIGHLAND

Mississippi River

Lake Michigan

Lake Huron

Lake Erie

L. Ontario

St. Lawrence River

ADIRONDACK MTS.

GREEN MTS.

WHITE MTS.

COASTAL HILLS

Hudson R.

Connecticut R.

CENTRAL LOWLANDS

Des Moines R.

Missouri River

Illinois R.

Wabash R.

Ohio River

APPALACHIAN HIGHLANDS

Potomac R.

BLUE RIDGE MTS.

James

PIEDMONT

ATLANTIC COASTAL PLAIN

TIDEWATER

OZARK MTS.

Arkansas R.

OUACHITA MTS.

Cumberland R.

Tennessee R.

Mt. Mitchell 6,684 ft.

Cape Fear R.

Susquehanna R.

ATLANTIC OCEAN

Sabine R.

Red R.

Mississippi R.

Alabama R.

COASTAL PLAIN

North latitude

West longitude

Lake Okeechobee

GULF OF MEXICO

Prairies

0   100   200   300   400   500
Miles

Within the overlapping life spans of three Presidents—Jefferson, Lincoln, and "Teddy" Roosevelt—the United States grew from a relatively narrow strip along the Atlantic seaboard to a nation embracing half a continent. And by 1959, the United States included Alaska to the north and the faraway islands of Hawaii. The basic data of this story appear here and on pages 822–23.

1 GROWTH IN SQUARE MILES

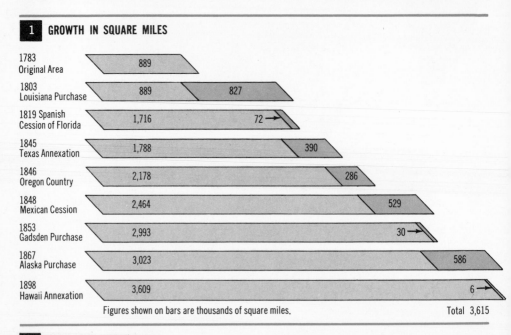

Year / Acquisition		
1783 Original Area	889	
1803 Louisiana Purchase	889	827
1819 Spanish Cession of Florida	1,716	72 →
1845 Texas Annexation	1,788	390
1846 Oregon Country	2,178	286
1848 Mexican Cession	2,464	529
1853 Gadsden Purchase	2,993	30 →
1867 Alaska Purchase	3,023	586
1898 Hawaii Annexation	3,609	6 →

Figures shown on bars are thousands of square miles.   Total 3,615

2 TERRITORIAL ACQUISITIONS

Name	Date	How Acquired	Area (sq. mi.)	Per Cent of Present Area	Present States
Original Area	1783	Won from Great Britain; established by Treaty of Paris	888,811	24%	Original 13 states, plus Illinois, Indiana, Kentucky, Maine, Michigan, Ohio, Tennessee, Vermont, West Virginia, Wisconsin, and part of Alabama, Minnesota, Mississippi
Louisiana Purchase	1803	Purchased from France	827,192	23%	Arkansas, Iowa, Missouri, Nebraska, North Dakota, South Dakota, and part of Colorado, Kansas, Louisiana, Minnesota, Montana, Oklahoma, Wyoming
Florida	1819	Treaty with Spain	72,003	2%	Florida, and part of Alabama, Louisiana, Mississippi
Texas	1845	Annexed	390,144	11%	Texas, and part of Colorado, Kansas, New Mexico, Oklahoma, Wyoming
Oregon Country	1846	Treaty with Great Britain	285,580	8%	Idaho, Oregon, Washington, and part of Montana, Wyoming
Mexican Cession	1848	Treaty with Mexico	529,017	15%	California, Nevada, Utah, and part of Arizona, Colorado, New Mexico, Wyoming
Gadsden Purchase	1853	Purchased from Mexico	29,640	1%	Part of Arizona, New Mexico
Alaska	1867	Purchased from Russia	586,400	16%	Alaska
Hawaii	1898	Annexed	6,451	Less than 1/10th%	Hawaii
		Total Present Area	3,615,238		

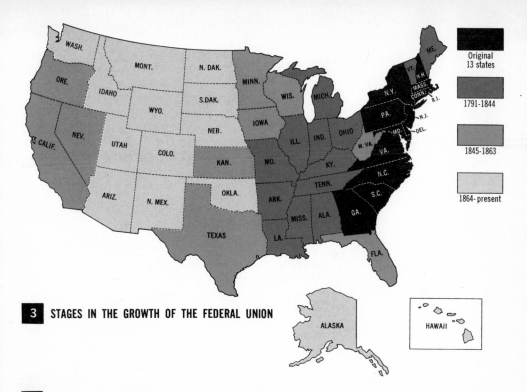

3 STAGES IN THE GROWTH OF THE FEDERAL UNION

Original 13 states

1791-1844

1845-1863

1864-present

ALASKA

HAWAII

4 DATE OF ENTRY, AREA, AND CAPITAL OF STATES

Order of Entry	State	Date of Entry	Area (in sq. mi.)	Capital	Order of Entry	State	Date of Entry	Area (in sq. mi.)	Capital
1	Delaware	1787	2,057	Dover	27	Florida	1845	58,560	Tallahassee
2	Pennsylvania	1787	45,333	Harrisburg	28	Texas	1845	267,339	Austin
3	New Jersey	1787	7,836	Trenton	29	Iowa	1846	56,290	Des Moines
4	Georgia	1788	58,876	Atlanta	30	Wisconsin	1848	56,154	Madison
5	Connecticut	1788	5,009	Hartford	31	California	1850	158,693	Sacramento
6	Massachusetts	1788	8,257	Boston	32	Minnesota	1858	84,068	St. Paul
7	Maryland	1788	10,577	Annapolis	33	Oregon	1859	96,981	Salem
8	South Carolina	1788	31,055	Columbia	34	Kansas	1861	82,276	Topeka
9	New Hampshire	1788	9,304	Concord	35	West Virginia	1863	24,181	Charleston
10	Virginia	1788	40,815	Richmond	36	Nevada	1864	110,540	Carson City
11	New York	1788	49,576	Albany	37	Nebraska	1867	77,227	Lincoln
12	North Carolina	1789	52,712	Raleigh	38	Colorado	1876	104,247	Denver
13	Rhode Island	1790	1,214	Providence	39	North Dakota	1889	70,665	Bismarck
14	Vermont	1791	9,609	Montpelier	40	South Dakota	1889	77,047	Pierre
15	Kentucky	1792	40,395	Frankfort	41	Montana	1889	147,138	Helena
16	Tennessee	1796	42,244	Nashville	42	Washington	1889	68,192	Olympia
17	Ohio	1803	41,222	Columbus	43	Idaho	1890	83,557	Boise
18	Louisiana	1812	48,523	Baton Rouge	44	Wyoming	1890	97,914	Cheyenne
19	Indiana	1816	36,291	Indianapolis	45	Utah	1896	84,916	Salt Lake City
20	Mississippi	1817	47,716	Jackson	46	Oklahoma	1907	69,919	Oklahoma City
21	Illinois	1818	56,400	Springfield	47	New Mexico	1912	121,666	Santa Fe
22	Alabama	1819	51,609	Montgomery	48	Arizona	1912	113,909	Phoenix
23	Maine	1820	33,215	Augusta	49	Alaska	1959	586,400	Juneau
24	Missouri	1821	69,674	Jefferson City	50	Hawaii	1959	6,423	Honolulu
25	Arkansas	1836	53,104	Little Rock		District of Columbia	(1791)	69	
26	Michigan	1837	58,216	Lansing					

It was not just a nation that grew from "sea to shining sea"; it was a federal union. Each new state has been admitted by act of Congress as a full and equal partner in the Union. The achievement recorded on the map (pages 822–23) and in the table above is a tribute to the men who drafted a Constitution that provided for the orderly admission of new states.

See map next page ➡

CANADA

TO ALASKA

Joint occupation by U.S. and GREAT BRITAIN, 1818-46
(Claim abandoned by RUSSIA, 1824)

Line of Treaty of 1846

Line of Treaty of 1818

Ceded to GR. BRIT.

Ceded to U.

WASH.

MONT.

N. DAK.

49°

OREGON COUNTRY, 1846

ORE.

IDAHO

42°

Spanish treaty line of 1819

S. DAK.

WYO.

NEB.

LOUISIANA PURCHASE FROM

NEV.

UTAH

COLO.

KAN.

CALIF.

MEXICAN CESSION, 1848
Acquired from Mexico by Treaty of Guadalupe Hidalgo, 1848

Colorado River

Arkansas River

Ceded by TEXAS to U.S., 1850

Granted to TEXAS, 1850

Spanish trea line of 181

TO HAWAII

ARIZ.

N. MEX.

Disputed between U.S. and MEXICO, 1845-48 (Claimed by TEXAS, 1836-50)

Red

TEXAS ANNEXATION 1845

Gila River

GADSDEN PURCHASE, 1853
(From MEXICO)

Rio

Grande

Granted to TEXAS, 1850

TEXAS

PACIFIC OCEAN

M

E

X

I

C

O

Nueces R.

ARCTIC OCEAN

SIBERIA

ALASKA
Purchased from
RUSSIA, 1867

CANADA

BERING

SEA

54° 40'

PACIFIC OCEAN

0   500
Miles

KAUAI

NIIHAU

OAHU

OCEAN

MOLOKAI

PACIFIC

LANAI

MAUI

HAWAII
Annexed, 1898

0   100
Miles

HAWAII

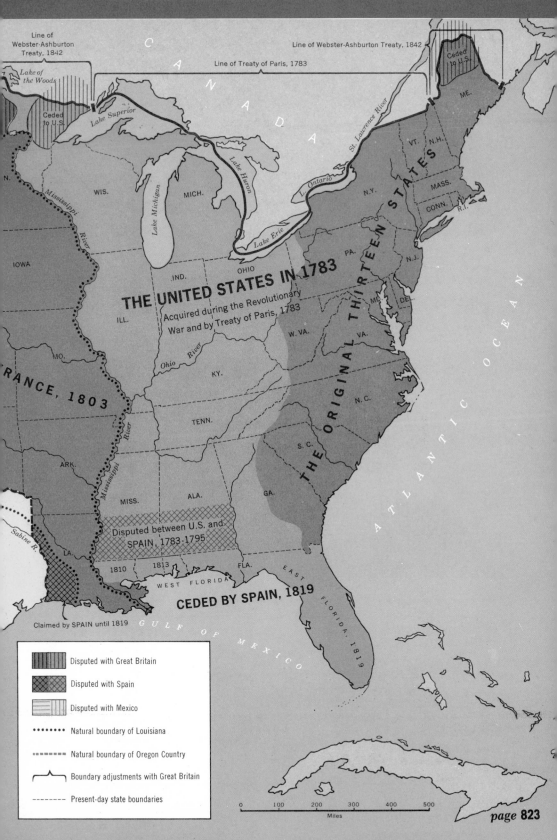

People! They came from many lands to work in the growing cities and to build a new way of life in the rapidly expanding nation. Whereas in 1790 there were only about 4 million people, by 1960 there were about 180 million. In earlier times, immigration accounted for much of the increase; today, a sharp rise in life expectancy helps to swell the population.

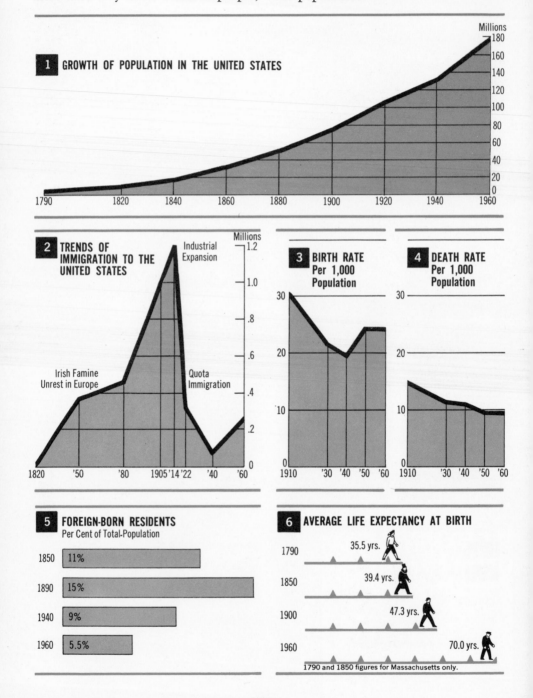

1 GROWTH OF POPULATION IN THE UNITED STATES

Millions

180, 160, 140, 120, 100, 80, 60, 40, 20, 0

1790 1820 1840 1860 1880 1900 1920 1940 1960

2 TRENDS OF IMMIGRATION TO THE UNITED STATES

Millions

1.2, 1.0, .8, .6, .4, .2, 0

Industrial Expansion

Irish Famine Unrest in Europe

Quota Immigration

1820 '50 '80 1905 '14 '22 '40 '60

3 BIRTH RATE Per 1,000 Population

30, 20, 10, 0

1910 '30 '40 '50 '60

4 DEATH RATE Per 1,000 Population

30, 20, 10, 0

1910 '30 '40 '50 '60

5 FOREIGN-BORN RESIDENTS
Per Cent of Total-Population

1850 — 11%
1890 — 15%
1940 — 9%
1960 — 5.5%

6 AVERAGE LIFE EXPECTANCY AT BIRTH

1790 — 35.5 yrs.
1850 — 39.4 yrs.
1900 — 47.3 yrs.
1960 — 70.0 yrs.

1790 and 1850 figures for Massachusetts only.

	State	Population at First Census After Entry	State Population 1960	Representatives in Congress	Largest City in 1960	City Population 1890	City Population 1930	City Population 1960 (Pre-final)
1	Delaware	59,000	446,292	1	Wilmington	61,431	106,597	95,827
2	Pennsylvania	434,000	11,319,366	27	Philadelphia	1,046,964	1,950,961	1,971,239
3	New Jersey	184,000	6,066,782	15	Newark	181,830	442,337	402,815
4	Georgia	83,000	3,943,116	10	Atlanta	65,533	270,366	484,825
5	Connecticut	238,000	2,535,234	6	Hartford	53,230	164,072	161,077
6	Massachusetts	379,000	5,148,578	12	Boston	448,477	781,188	682,303
7	Maryland	320,000	3,100,689	8	Baltimore	434,439	804,874	922,244
8	South Carolina	249,000	2,382,594	6	Columbia	15,353	51,581	95,786
9	New Hampshire	142,000	606,921	2	Manchester	44,126	76,834	88,282
10	Virginia	692,000	3,966,949	10	Norfolk	34,871	129,710	276,897
11	New York	340,000	16,782,304	41	New York	2,507,414	6,930,446	7,710,346
12	North Carolina	394,000	4,556,155	11	Charlotte	11,557	82,675	200,882
13	Rhode Island	69,000	859,488	2	Providence	132,146	252,981	206,352
14	Vermont	154,000	389,881	1	Burlington	14,500	24,789	35,531
15	Kentucky	221,000	3,038,156	7	Louisville	161,129	307,745	383,329
16	Tennessee	106,000	3,567,089	9	Memphis	64,495	253,143	491,710
17	Ohio	230,760	9,706,397	24	Cleveland	261,353	900,429	869,728
18	Louisiana	153,000	3,257,022	8	New Orleans	242,039	458,762	621,259
19	Indiana	147,000	4,662,498	11	Indianapolis	105,436	364,161	469,037
20	Mississippi	75,000	2,178,141	5	Jackson	5,920	48,282	143,962
21	Illinois	55,000	10,081,158	24	Chicago	1,099,850	3,376,438	3,511,648
22	Alabama	128,000	3,266,740	8	Birmingham	26,178	259,678	339,211
23	Maine	298,000	969,265	2	Portland	36,425	70,810	71,787
24	Missouri	140,455	4,319,813	10	St. Louis	451,770	821,960	747,127
25	Arkansas	98,000	1,786,272	4	Little Rock	25,874	81,679	105,737
26	Michigan	212,000	7,823,194	19	Detroit	205,876	1,568,662	1,654,125
27	Florida	87,455	4,951,560	12	Miami	over 1600	110,637	284,492
28	Texas	212,592	9,579,677	23	Houston	27,557	292,352	932,630
29	Iowa	192,214	2,757,537	7	Des Moines	50,093	142,559	207,823
30	Wisconsin	305,391	3,951,777	10	Milwaukee	204,468	578,249	732,637
31	California	92,597	15,717,204	38	Los Angeles	50,395	1,238,048	2,450,068
32	Minnesota	172,000	3,413,864	8	Minneapolis	164,738	464,356	477,884
33	Oregon	52,000	1,768,687	4	Portland	46,385	301,815	371,042
34	Kansas	364,000	2,178,611	5	Wichita	23,853	111,110	254,059
35	West Virginia	442,000	1,860,421	5	Charleston	6,742	60,408	84,550
36	Nevada	42,000	285,278	1	Las Vegas	0	5,165	64,405
37	Nebraska	123,000	1,411,330	3	Omaha	148,514	214,006	300,050
38	Colorado	194,000	1,753,947	4	Denver	106,713	287,861	490,969
39	North Dakota	191,000	632,446	2	Fargo	5,664	28,619	46,662
40	South Dakota	349,000	680,514	2	Sioux Falls	7,205	33,362	65,466
41	Montana	143,000	674,767	2	Great Falls	3,979	28,822	55,357
42	Washington	357,000	2,853,214	7	Seattle	42,837	365,583	551,589
43	Idaho	89,000	667,191	2	Boise	2,311	21,544	34,481
44	Wyoming	63,000	330,066	1	Cheyenne	11,690	17,361	43,505
45	Utah	277,000	890,627	2	Salt Lake City	44,843	140,267	189,454
46	Oklahoma	1,657,000	2,328,284	6	Oklahoma City	4,151	185,389	321,599
47	New Mexico	360,000	951,023	2	Albuquerque	3,785	26,570	198,711
48	Arizona	334,000	1,302,161	3	Phoenix	3,152	48,118	434,277
49	Alaska	224,094	226,167	1	Anchorage	0	2,500	43,753
50	Hawaii	620,346	632,772	2	Honolulu	22,907	138,445	290,030
	District of Columbia	14,093 (1800)	763,956	—	Washington	188,932	486,869	745,603

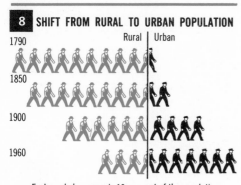

Rural | Urban

1790

1850

1900

1960

Each symbol represents 10 per cent of the population.

The maps on pages 826–27 give a graphic summary of the Westward Movement. In 1790, all but a few hardy pioneers lived in the 13 original states along the Atlantic seaboard. Then, as the nation grew, people poured westward. By 1960, the second most heavily populated state was California.

Equally striking has been the shift of population from rural to urban areas. In 1790 more than 90 per cent of Americans lived in rural areas; by 1960 only about one third.

See next page ➡

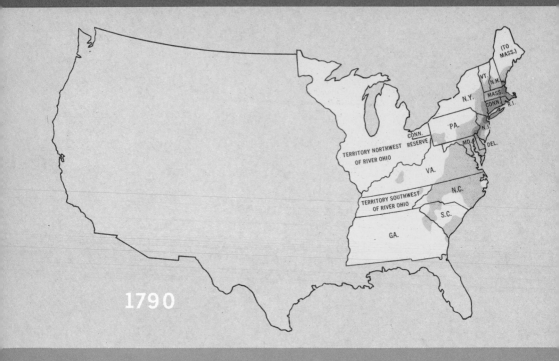

1790

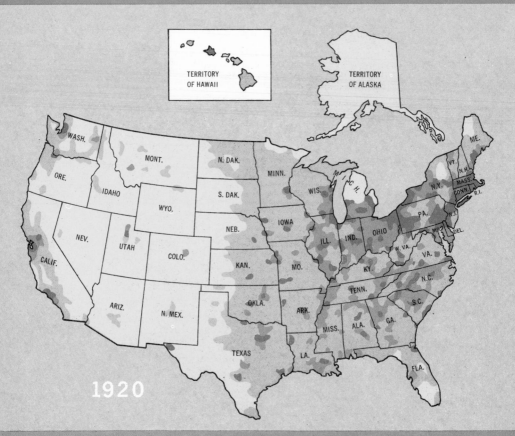

1920

PERSONS PER SQUARE MILE | Fewer than 5 | 5 to 45

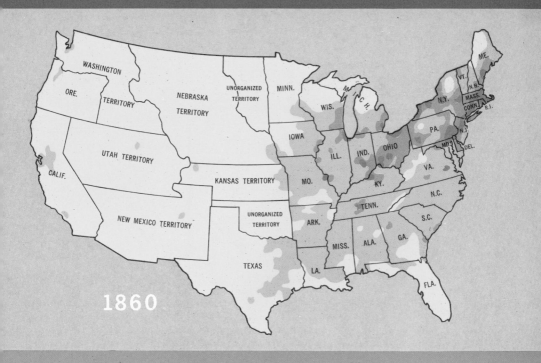

WASHINGTON

ORE.
TERRITORY

NEBRASKA
TERRITORY

UNORGANIZED
TERRITORY

MINN.

WIS.

M I C H.

ME.

VT.

N.H.

N.Y.

MASS.
CONN.
R.I.

UTAH TERRITORY

CALIF.

KANSAS TERRITORY

PA.

N.J.

IOWA

ILL.

IND.

OHIO

MD.?

DEL.

NEW MEXICO TERRITORY

UNORGANIZED
TERRITORY

MO.

KY.

VA.

ARK.

TENN.

N.C.

S.C.

TEXAS

MISS.

ALA.

GA.

LA.

FLA.

1860

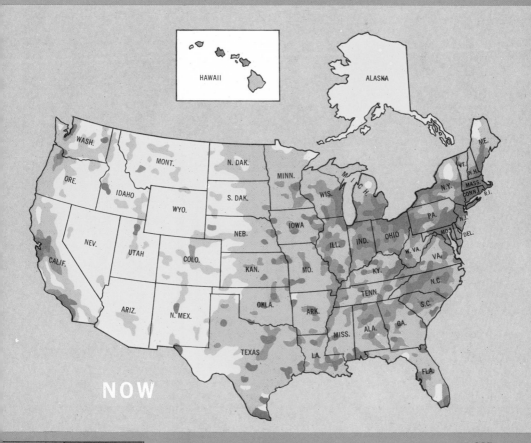

HAWAII

ALASKA

WASH.

MONT.

N. DAK.

MINN.

ME.

VT.

N.H.

ORE.

IDAHO

S. DAK.

WIS.

M I C H.

N.Y.

MASS.
CONN.
R.I.

NEV.

UTAH

WYO.

NEB.

IOWA

ILL.

IND.

OHIO

PA.

N.J.

MD.?

DEL.

CALIF.

COLO.

KAN.

MO.

KY.

W. VA.

VA.

N.C.

ARIZ.

N. MEX.

OKLA.

ARK.

TENN.

S.C.

TEXAS

MISS.

ALA.

GA.

LA.

FLA.

NOW

46 to 90	More than 90

The conquest of hunger! This is the dramatic story summarized in bare outline in the graphs on these pages and on the map on pages 830–31.

Through most of their long history, men have lived in the shadow of starvation. When, for any reason, their crops failed, famine swept the land and people died. Today, two thirds of the world's people have barely enough to eat.

Famine has never been part of the American story. From the days of the first settlements, America's fertile soil has yielded food in abundance for the swelling population. In recent times, American farmers have produced more than the American people could consume. Even though the number of farmers has declined, and even though fewer acres are being harvested, through the application of science, productivity of each farm acre has risen greatly.

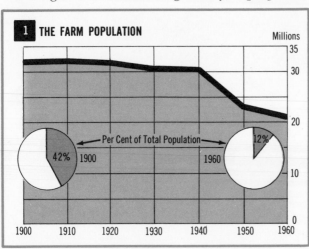

1 THE FARM POPULATION

Millions

← Per Cent of Total Population →

42% 1900   1960   12%

2 NUMBER OF PEOPLE FED BY ONE FARM WORKER

1900

1960

3 TRACTORS REPLACE HORSES AND MULES

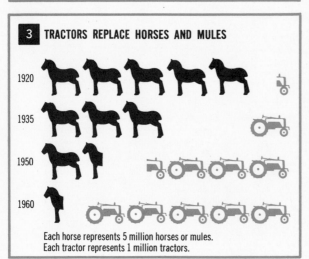

1920

1935

1950

1960

Each horse represents 5 million horses or mules.
Each tractor represents 1 million tractors.

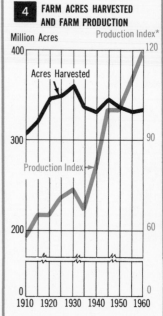

4 FARM ACRES HARVESTED AND FARM PRODUCTION

Million Acres   Production Index*

400   120

Acres Harvested

300   90

Production Index →

200   60

0   0

1910 1920 1930 1940 1950 1960

*The production index is a standard of measurement which indicates the increase or decrease of total farm production. Farm production for 1947-49 = 100.

5 NUMBER OF FARMS

1850
1900
1935
1960

Each unit represents 1 million farms.

6 AVERAGE SIZE OF FARMS

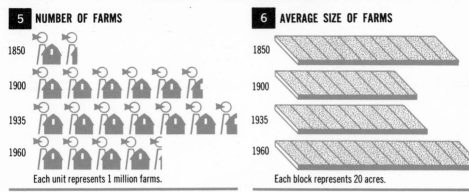

1850
1900
1935
1960

Each block represents 20 acres.

Today, with power-driven farm machines, improved breeds of livestock, hardier plants, and more effective use of fertilizers, fewer farmers are producing more food on less land than they ever produced before.

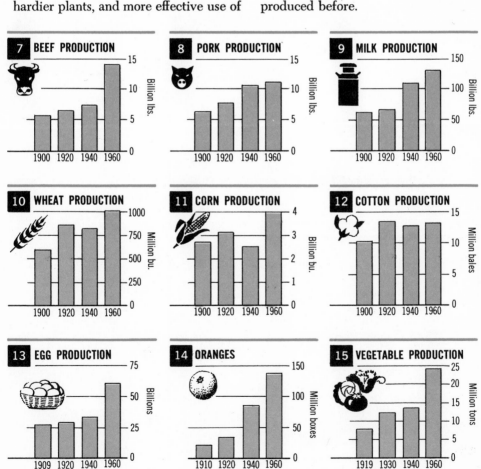

7 BEEF PRODUCTION

Billion lbs.
15
10
5
0
1900 1920 1940 1960

8 PORK PRODUCTION

Billion lbs.
15
10
5
0
1900 1920 1940 1960

9 MILK PRODUCTION

Billion lbs.
150
100
50
0
1900 1920 1940 1960

10 WHEAT PRODUCTION

Million bu.
1000
750
500
250
0
1900 1920 1940 1960

11 CORN PRODUCTION

Billion bu.
4
3
2
1
0
1900 1920 1940 1960

12 COTTON PRODUCTION

Million bales
15
10
5
0
1900 1920 1940 1960

13 EGG PRODUCTION

Billions
75
50
25
0
1909 1920 1940 1960

14 ORANGES

Million boxes
150
100
50
0
1910 1920 1940 1960

15 VEGETABLE PRODUCTION

Million tons
25
20
15
10
5
0
1919 1930 1940 1960

See map next page ➡

TO ALASKA

SALMON

P A C I F I C

SALMON

SARDINES

TO HAWAII

SARDINES

C A N A D A

Seattle

DAIRY
FRUIT

WASHINGTON
Spokane

WHEAT

Portland

POULTRY,
FRUIT

Pendleton

GRAZING

OREGON

POTATOES

Klamath Falls

GRAZING

GRAZING

GRAZING

Great Falls

MONTANA

GRAZING,
DAIRY

WHEAT,
GRAZING

WHEAT

WHEAT,
GRAZING

Minot

NORTH DAKOTA

WHEAT

GRAZING

Bismarck

CORN, LIVESTO

Billings

GRAZING

SUGAR BEETS

IDAHO

Boise

POTATOES,
BEANS

GRAZING

WYOMING

WHEAT,
GRAZING

SOUTH DAKOTA

GRAZING

Rapid City

Pierre

CORN, LIVESTOCK

Redding

Reno

NEVADA

Winnemucca

GRAZING

Ogden

Salt Lake
City

UTAH

GRAZING

GRAZING

Casper

Scottsbluff

CORN, LIVESTO

NEBRASKA

Cheyenne

San Francisco

DAIRY

CALIFORNIA

FRUIT, TRUCK
FARMING

Fresno

FRUIT
GRAZING

FRUIT, TRUCK
FARMING

Cedar City

Las Vegas

GRAZING

GRAZING

Denver

Grand Junction

COLORADO

FRUIT

SUGAR BEETS

CORN, LIVESTOCK

Linco

Salina

KANSAS

Wichit

Pueblo

WHEAT

WHEAT

COTTON

Los Angeles

CITRUS FRUIT
TRUCK FARMING

San Diego

El Centro

FRUIT,
TRUCK FARMING

Yuma

Flagstaff

ARIZONA

FRUIT, TRUCK FARMING

Phoenix

Tucson

COTTON

GRAZING

Albuquerque

NEW MEXICO

Santa Fe

BEANS

Roswell

GRAZING

Amarillo

OKLAHO

Oklahoma
City

COTTON

WHEAT

COTTON,
WHEAT

GRAZING
WHEAT

Fort Wort

El Paso

COTTON

M E X I C O

San Angelo

TEXAS

LIVESTO

San Antonio

GRAZING

FRUIT, TRUCK
FARMING

Alaska inset

ARCTIC   OCEAN

GRAZING (CARIBOU)

SIBERIA
(U.S.S.R.)

FURS

FURS

GRAZING (CARIBOU)

ALASKA

FURS

Fairbanks

FURS

CANADA

GRAIN,
TRUCK FARMING

Anchorage

FURS

B E R I N G
S E A

PACIFIC
OCEAN

SALMON

Juneau

Ketchikan

FURS

SHELLFISH

0   500
Miles

Hawaii inset

SUGAR CANE, PINEAPPLES, LIVESTOCK

OCEAN

Honolulu

PACIFIC

H A W A I I

TUNA

Hilo

0   100
Miles

AGRICULTURAL DEVELOPMENT OF THE UNITED STATES

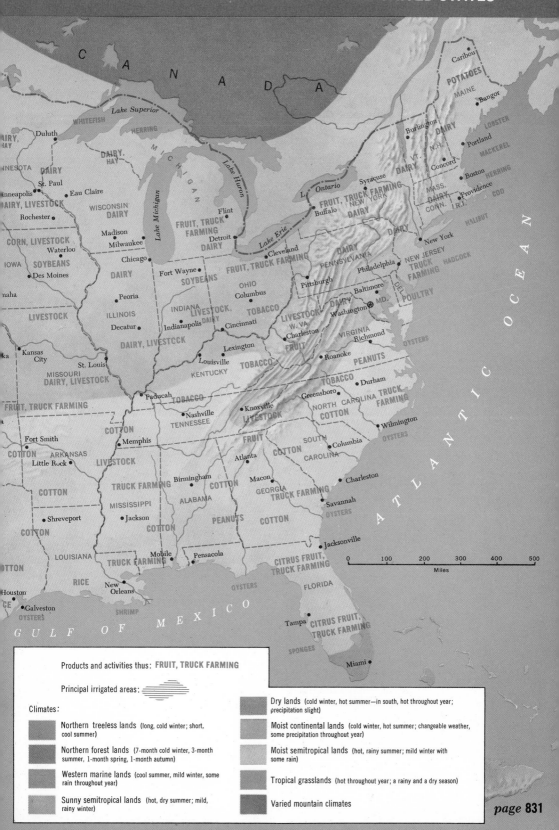

C A N A D A

Caribou
POTATOES
MAINE
Bangor

Lake Superior
WHITEFISH
DULUTH
HERRING
Burlington
DAIRY
Portland
LOBSTER

DAIRY,
HAY
DAIRY,
HAY
VT. N.H.
Concord
MACKEREL
Boston

MICHIGAN
Lake Huron
Syracuse
DAIRY
MASS.
Providence
HERRING

MINNESOTA
DAIRY
St. Paul
Eau Claire
L. Ontario
FRUIT, TRUCK FARMING
NEW YORK
Buffalo
DAIRY
CONN. R.I.
COD

Minneapolis
DAIRY, LIVESTOCK
Rochester
WISCONSIN
DAIRY
Madison
Milwaukee
Flint
FRUIT, TRUCK FARMING
Detroit
Cleveland
Lake Erie
DAIRY
New York
HALIBUT

CORN, LIVESTOCK
Waterloo
Chicago
DAIRY
Fort Wayne
SOYBEANS
FRUIT, TRUCK FARMING
Pittsburgh
DAIRY
PENNSYLVANIA
Philadelphia
NEW JERSEY
TRUCK FARMING
HADDOCK

IOWA
SOYBEANS
Des Moines
Peoria
OHIO
Columbus
Baltimore
POULTRY

omaha
ILLINOIS
INDIANA
LIVESTOCK,
DAIRY
Cincinnati
LIVESTOCK
W. VA
Washington
MD.
DEL.

LIVESTOCK
Decatur
Indianapolis
DAIRY, LIVESTOCK
Lexington
Charleston
FRUIT
VIRGINIA
Richmond
OYSTERS

Kansas
City
St. Louis
Paducah
Louisville
KENTUCKY
TOBACCO
TOBACCO
Roanoke
PEANUTS

MISSOURI
DAIRY, LIVESTOCK
COTTON
Nashville
TENNESSEE
LIVESTOCK
TOBACCO
Greensboro
Durham
NORTH CAROLINA
TRUCK FARMING

FRUIT, TRUCK FARMING
Memphis
Knoxville
FRUIT
COTTON
Wilmington

Fort Smith
COTTON
ARKANSAS
Little Rock
LIVESTOCK
Atlanta
SOUTH
CAROLINA
Columbia
OYSTERS

COTTON
TRUCK FARMING
Birmingham
COTTON
Macon
Charleston

COTTON
MISSISSIPPI
Jackson
ALABAMA
GEORGIA
TRUCK FARMING
Savannah
OYSTERS

Shreveport
COTTON
PEANUTS
COTTON

COTTON
LOUISIANA
TRUCK FARMING
Mobile
Pensacola
Jacksonville

Houston
RICE
New
Orleans
OYSTERS
FLORIDA
CITRUS FRUIT,
TRUCK FARMING

RICE
Galveston
OYSTERS
SHRIMP
Tampa
CITRUS FRUIT,
TRUCK FARMING

G U L F   O F   M E X I C O
SPONGES
Miami

A T L A N T I C   O C E A N

0   100   200   300   400   500
Miles

Legend

Products and activities thus: **FRUIT, TRUCK FARMING**

Principal irrigated areas:

Climates:

Northern treeless lands (long, cold winter; short, cool summer)

Northern forest lands (7-month cold winter, 3-month summer, 1-month spring, 1-month autumn)

Western marine lands (cool summer, mild winter, some rain throughout year)

Sunny semitropical lands (hot, dry summer; mild, rainy winter)

Dry lands (cold winter, hot summer—in south, hot throughout year; precipitation slight)

Moist continental lands (cold winter, hot summer; changeable weather, some precipitation throughout year)

Moist semitropical lands (hot, rainy summer; mild winter with some rain)

Tropical grasslands (hot throughout year; a rainy and a dry season)

Varied mountain climates

Industry and agriculture have advanced side by side to produce today in the United States the highest standard of living man has ever known. Behind the amazing advance of American industry stand the scientists and engineers who invented new machines, discovered new sources of power, and learned to tap the wealth of natural resources buried in the earth (see map, pages 834–35).

But scientists and engineers are only one part of the story. Marching by their side have been the businessmen—the owners and managers of the nation's industries—who have contributed their ingenuity and their organizing ability to the creation of America's great industrial economy.

And beside the owners and managers have marched the armies of workers, men and women whose energy, skill, and creative efforts have opened up mines, built factories, dug canals, laid railroad tracks, strung telegraph and telephone wires, and supplied the manpower to produce and distribute the almost endless variety of products that

keep pouring out in ever-mounting volume. A remarkable part of this development has been the use of inanimate power from coal, oil, gas, and water.

1 MAJOR ADVANCES OF AMERICAN INDUSTRY	
	The Colonists Had
POWER	Human Muscles Animal Muscles Wind and Water Power
PHYSICAL MATERIALS	Copper and Bronze Iron Wood and Clay Plant and Animal Fibers
MANUFACTURING	Hand Forges and Tools Man-powered Spinning Wheels and Looms
AGRICULTURE	Wooden Plow Spade Ax and Other Hand Tools
TRANSPORTATION	Horses Animal-drawn Vehicles Sailing Vessels
COMMUNICATION	Hand Printing Presses Local Newspapers

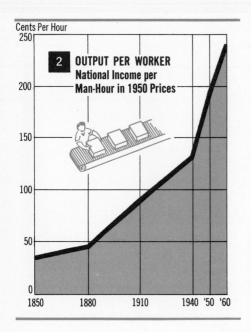

2 OUTPUT PER WORKER
National Income per Man-Hour in 1950 Prices

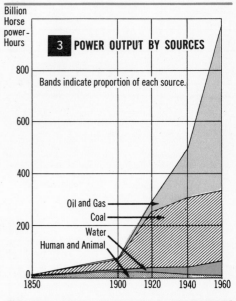

3 POWER OUTPUT BY SOURCES

Bands indicate proportion of each source.

Oil and Gas
Coal
Water
Human and Animal

1783-1850	1850 — 1900	1900 — 1920	1920 — Present
Steam Power	Hydraulic-turbine Engines Internal-combustion Engines Steam Turbines Dynamos, Electric Motors		Atomic Energy Solar Energy

Large-scale Production of Iron	Large-scale Production of Steel
	Development of Combustion
	  Fuels: Coal, Oil, Gas
	Development of Light Metals
	  and Alloys
		Large-scale Production of
		  Light Metals and Alloys
		Development of Plastics
		  and Synthetics
			Large-scale Production
			  of Plastics and Synthetics
			Development of Atomic Fuels

Water- and Steam-powered
  Factories
Interchangeable Parts
	Mass Production with
	  Centralized Assembly of
	  Interchangeable Parts
		Conveyer-belt Assembly Line	Automation

New Iron and Steel Tools
Early Agricultural Machines:
  Cotton Gin, Reaper, Harvester
	Steam Power	Genetics and Soil Science
		Gasoline and Electric Power
			Large-scale Mechanized
			  Farming

Development of Steamships
Development of Railroads
Development of Canals
	Large-scale Transport
	  by Steamship and Rail
	Early Development of
	  Internal Combustion Engines
		Automobiles, Trucks, Buses
		Development of
		  Propeller-driven Aircraft
			Development of
			  Jet Propulsion

Large-scale Printing Presses
Telegraph
Development of Magazine
  and Book Printing
	Transoceanic Cable
	Telephone
	Wireless Telegraphy
	Phonograph
		Motion Pictures
		Radio
		  Transcontinental Telephone
			Frequency Modulation
			Television

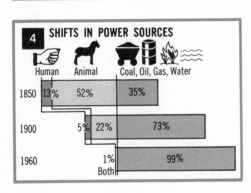

4 SHIFTS IN POWER SOURCES

Human   Animal   Coal, Oil, Gas, Water

1850   13%   52%   35%

1900   5%   22%   73%

1960   1% Both   99%

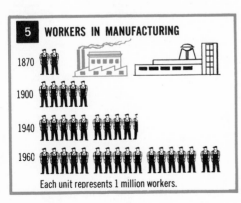

5 WORKERS IN MANUFACTURING

1870

1900

1940

1960

Each unit represents 1 million workers.

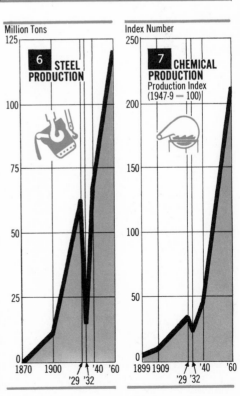

Million Tons
125

6 STEEL PRODUCTION

100

75

50

25

0
1870   1900   '40 '60
'29 '32

Index Number
250

7 CHEMICAL PRODUCTION
Production Index
(1947-9 = 100)

200

150

100

50

0
1899 1909   '40 '60
'29 '32

See map next page ➡

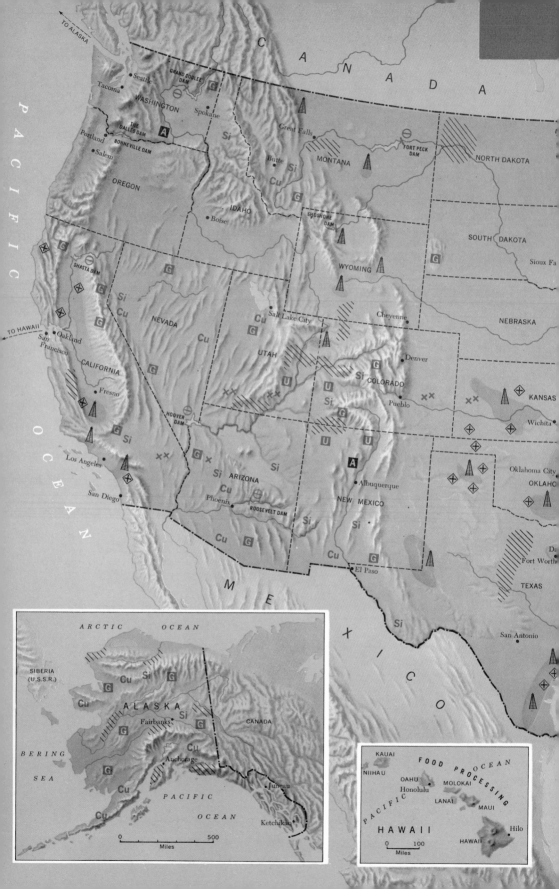

TO ALASKA

C A N A D A

PACIFIC

Seattle
Tacoma
WASHINGTON
GRAND COULEE DAM
Spokane
Si
Great Falls
FORT PECK DAM
NORTH DAKOTA
THE DALLES DAM
A
Portland
BONNEVILLE DAM
Salem
OREGON
Butte
MONTANA
Si
Cu
G
IDAHO
Boise
SHOSHONE DAM
SOUTH DAKOTA
Sioux Fa
WYOMING
SHASTA DAM
G
Si
Cu
NEVADA
Cu
Salt Lake City
Cu
G
UTAH
Cheyenne
NEBRASKA
Oakland
San Francisco
CALIFORNIA
Fresno
HOOVER DAM
Si
G
Los Angeles
San Diego
U
Si
G
U
G
U
U
Si
G
Denver
COLORADO
Pueblo
KANSAS
Wichita
ARIZONA
Si
Cu
Phoenix
ROOSEVELT DAM
Si
Cu
G
Si
A
Albuquerque
NEW MEXICO
Si
Cu
G
El Paso
Oklahoma City
OKLAHO
Da
Fort Worth
TEXAS
Si
San Antonio

TO HAWAII

OCEAN

M E X I C O

FOOD PROCESSING

ARCTIC OCEAN
SIBERIA (U.S.S.R.)
Cu
Si
G
ALASKA
Cu
Fairbanks
Si
G
CANADA
G
Anchorage
Cu
BERING SEA
G
Cu
Juneau
PACIFIC OCEAN
Cu
Ketchikan
0   500
Miles

KAUAI
NIIHAU
OAHU
Honolulu
MOLOKAI
LANAI
MAUI
HAWAII
Hilo
HAWAII
PACIFIC OCEAN
0   100
Miles

INDUSTRIAL DEVELOPMENT OF THE UNITED STATES

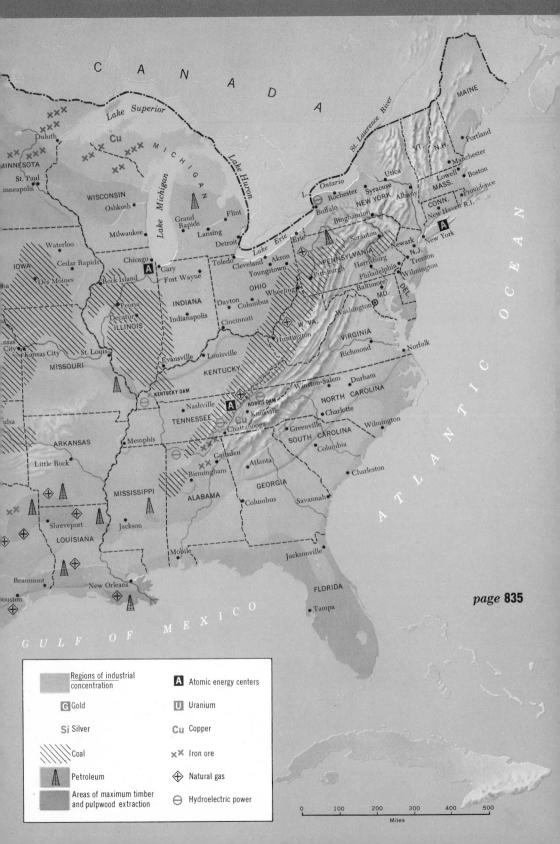

page 835

Legend:

- Regions of industrial concentration
- **G** Gold
- **Si** Silver
- Coal
- Petroleum
- Areas of maximum timber and pulpwood extraction
- **A** Atomic energy centers
- **U** Uranium
- **Cu** Copper
- ×× Iron ore
- Natural gas
- Hydroelectric power

0 100 200 300 400 500
Miles

During the early 1800's, when a great wave of pioneers was rolling westward, many Americans feared that the far reaches of the country would eventually break away from the Union. The distances were too great for government officials to travel in a reasonable length of time, the means of communication too slow and uncertain. These early fears proved groundless. The charts on these pages and the map on pages 838–39 reveal the developments that conquered time and space and made the Union possible.

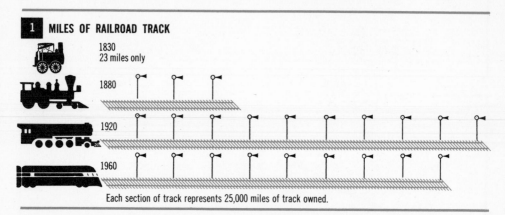

1 MILES OF RAILROAD TRACK

1830
23 miles only

1880

1920

1960

Each section of track represents 25,000 miles of track owned.

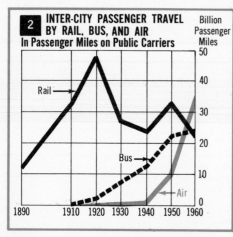

2 INTER-CITY PASSENGER TRAVEL BY RAIL, BUS, AND AIR
In Passenger Miles on Public Carriers

Billion Passenger Miles

50
40
30
20
10
0

Rail

Bus

Air

1890 1910 1920 1930 1940 1950 1960

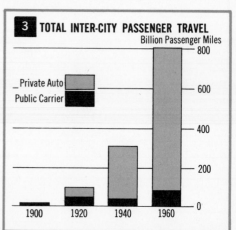

3 TOTAL INTER-CITY PASSENGER TRAVEL

Billion Passenger Miles

800
600
400
200
0

Private Auto
Public Carrier

1900 1920 1940 1960

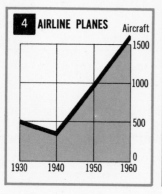

4 AIRLINE PLANES

Aircraft

1500
1000
500
0

1930 1940 1950 1960

5 AIRLINE PASSENGERS

Million Passengers

60
40
20
0

1930 1940 1950 1960

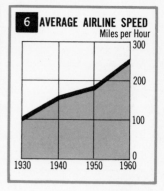

6 AVERAGE AIRLINE SPEED

Miles per Hour

300
200
100
0

1930 1940 1950 1960

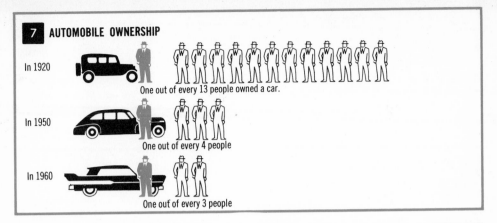

7 AUTOMOBILE OWNERSHIP

In 1920 — One out of every 13 people owned a car.

In 1950 — One out of every 4 people

In 1960 — One out of every 3 people

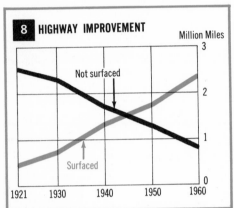

8 HIGHWAY IMPROVEMENT

Million Miles

Not surfaced

Surfaced

1921 1930 1940 1950 1960

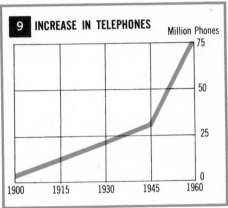

9 INCREASE IN TELEPHONES

Million Phones

75

50

25

0

1900 1915 1930 1945 1960

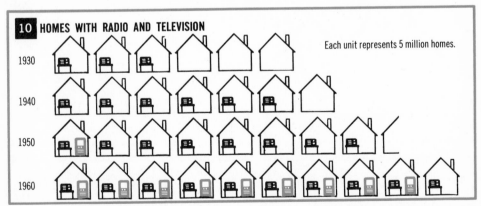

10 HOMES WITH RADIO AND TELEVISION

Each unit represents 5 million homes.

1930

1940

1950

1960

Settlers carried west by the spreading network of railroads turned virgin lands into rich farms, built cities in what had once been wilderness, and took long-buried mineral wealth from the earth for the benefit of all the people. Improved highways and mass production of automobiles, buses, and trucks put the nation on wheels. The telephone, radio, and television gave the people eyes and ears that could see and hear across the continent—and beyond. These inventions, along with the airplane, made the whole world neighbors. And this is only the beginning, for now men are looking forward to the day when they can travel through the mysterious distances of outer space.

See map next page ➡

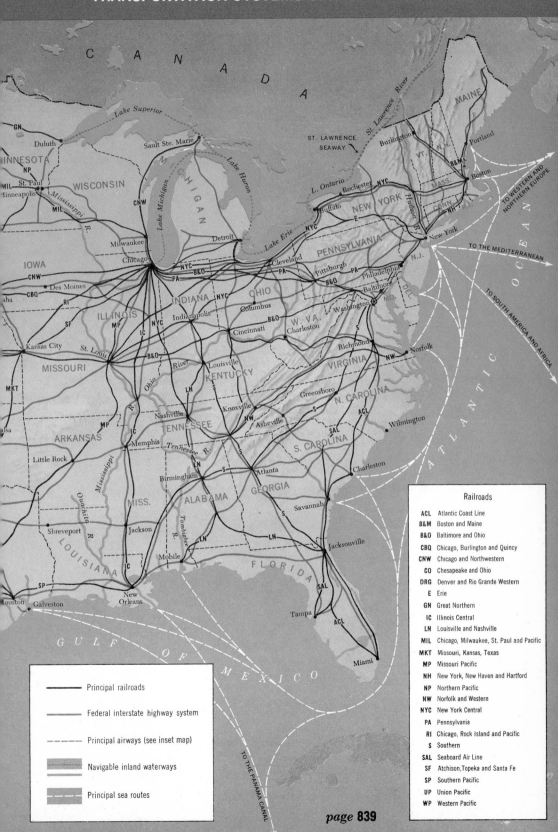

TRANSPORTATION SYSTEMS OF THE UNITED STATES

Railroads

ACL	Atlantic Coast Line
B&M	Boston and Maine
B&O	Baltimore and Ohio
CBQ	Chicago, Burlington and Quincy
CNW	Chicago and Northwestern
CO	Chesapeake and Ohio
DRG	Denver and Rio Grande Western
E	Erie
GN	Great Northern
IC	Illinois Central
LN	Louisville and Nashville
MIL	Chicago, Milwaukee, St. Paul and Pacific
MKT	Missouri, Kansas, Texas
MP	Missouri Pacific
NH	New York, New Haven and Hartford
NP	Northern Pacific
NW	Norfolk and Western
NYC	New York Central
PA	Pennsylvania
RI	Chicago, Rock Island and Pacific
S	Southern
SAL	Seaboard Air Line
SF	Atchison, Topeka and Santa Fe
SP	Southern Pacific
UP	Union Pacific
WP	Western Pacific

Legend:
- Principal railroads
- Federal interstate highway system
- Principal airways (see inset map)
- Navigable inland waterways
- Principal sea routes

page 839

In the early 1800's, when the nation was young, the bulk of its exports consisted of raw materials—such as lumber and cotton—and foodstuffs (chart 2, below). Such products continued to form most of America's exports until well into the twentieth century. By that time, the American economic system had become so productive that the total export of American manufactured goods considerably exceeded that of raw materials and foodstuffs.

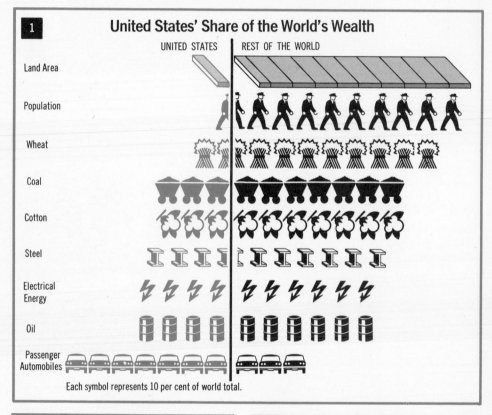

1 United States' Share of the World's Wealth

UNITED STATES | REST OF THE WORLD

Land Area
Population
Wheat
Coal
Cotton
Steel
Electrical Energy
Oil
Passenger Automobiles

Each symbol represents 10 per cent of world total.

2 RISE OF MANUFACTURED EXPORTS

Raw Materials and Foodstuffs | Manufactured Goods

1821
1850
1880
1910
1940
1960

Each unit represents 10 per cent of total exports.

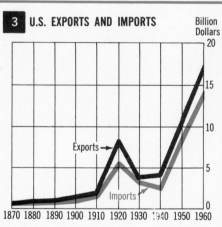

3 U.S. EXPORTS AND IMPORTS

Billion Dollars

Exports →

Imports

1870 1880 1890 1900 1910 1920 1930 1940 1950 1960

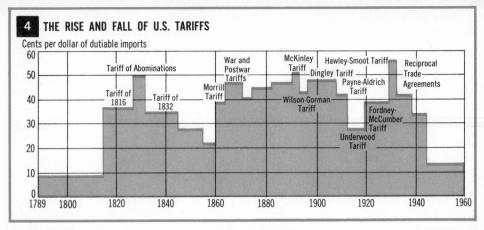

4 THE RISE AND FALL OF U.S. TARIFFS

Cents per dollar of dutiable imports

Tariff of Abominations

War and Postwar Tariffs

McKinley Tariff

Hawley-Smoot Tariff

Reciprocal Trade Agreements

Dingley Tariff

Payne-Aldrich Tariff

Tariff of 1816

Tariff of 1832

Morrill Tariff

Wilson-Gorman Tariff

Fordney-McCumber Tariff

Underwood Tariff

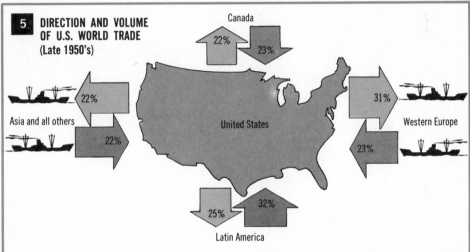

5 DIRECTION AND VOLUME OF U.S. WORLD TRADE (Late 1950's)

Canada 22% 23%

Asia and all others 22% 22%

United States

Western Europe 31% 23%

Latin America 25% 32%

America's industries and its complex transportation and communication system—the arteries of the economy—developed behind a high wall of protective tariffs (chart 4, above).

During the 1800's, Americans neither bought a great deal from other countries nor sold much to them (chart 3, left). They were pouring their money into capital goods. These were the formative years when the pioneers were moving westward across the continent, and the industrial economy was developing from an infant to a giant. In the 1800's Americans needed for their own use most of what they could produce. They needed steel for railroads, for bridges across rivers and canyons, for the framework of factory and office build-ings, for machines in factories and on farms. They needed copper for telegraph and telephone wires and for power lines to carry electricity. They needed tools, utensils, and household equipment to furnish the homes of a population that was growing rapidly.

By the early 1900's, however, America's giant industrial economy was rolling in high gear. Americans were producing more than enough for their own needs and were creating surpluses of both foodstuffs and manufactured goods for export to other countries of the world (charts 2 and 3, left). But trade has always been and must always be a two-way street (chart 5, above). Today Americans are carrying on an ever-swelling volume of world trade.

See map next page →

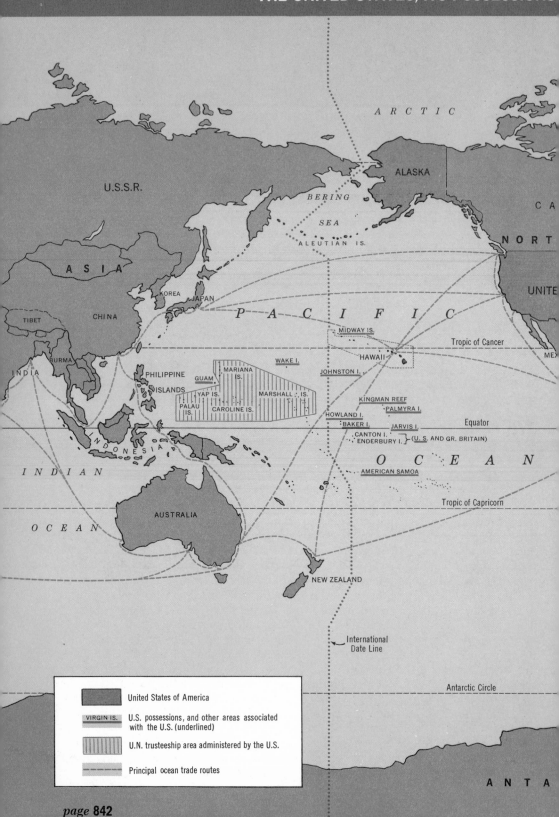

ARCTIC

ALASKA

U.S.S.R.

BERING

SEA

ALEUTIAN IS.

NORT

CA

ASIA

KOREA
JAPAN

P A C I F I C

UNITE

TIBET
CHINA

BURMA
INDIA

MIDWAY IS.

Tropic of Cancer

MEX

HAWAII

WAKE I.
PHILIPPINE
ISLANDS

GUAM

MARIANA
IS.

JOHNSTON I.

YAP IS.

MARSHALL IS.

PALAU
IS.

CAROLINE IS.

KINGMAN REEF

PALMYRA I.

INDONESIA

HOWLAND I.
BAKER I.

JARVIS I.

Equator

CANTON I.
ENDERBURY I.

(U.S. AND GR. BRITAIN)

INDIAN

O C E A N

AMERICAN SAMOA

OCEAN

Tropic of Capricorn

AUSTRALIA

NEW ZEALAND

International
Date Line

Antarctic Circle

United States of America

VIRGIN IS.   U.S. possessions, and other areas associated
with the U.S. (underlined)

U.N. trusteeship area administered by the U.S.

Principal ocean trade routes

ANTA

PRINCIPAL WORLD AIRWAYS

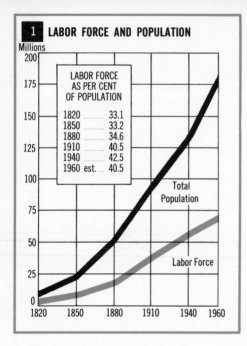

1 LABOR FORCE AND POPULATION

Millions

LABOR FORCE
AS PER CENT
OF POPULATION

1820	33.1
1850	33.2
1880	34.6
1910	40.5
1940	42.5
1960 est.	40.5

Total Population

Labor Force

1820 1850 1880 1910 1940 1960

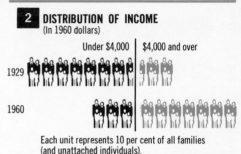

2 DISTRIBUTION OF INCOME
(In 1960 dollars)

Under $4,000 | $4,000 and over

1929

1960

Each unit represents 10 per cent of all families
(and unattached individuals).

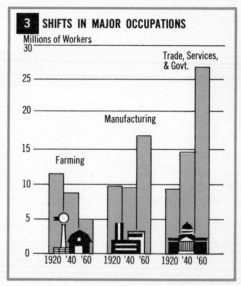

3 SHIFTS IN MAJOR OCCUPATIONS

Millions of Workers

Trade, Services,
& Govt.

Manufacturing

Farming

1920 '40 '60   1920 '40 '60   1920 '40 '60

When, in May 1790, Rhode Island ratified the Constitution and entered the Union as the thirteenth state, the total population of the United States was only about 4 million. More than nine out of every ten Americans lived on farms or in small villages. Most Europeans who gave the United States even a second thought looked down upon the infant republic with mingled scorn and amusement and predicted that it would last only a few years. Although President Washington was more optimistic, he reminded his fellow citizens that the new nation was an "experiment" entrusted to the hands of the American people.

The experiment succeeded beyond even the most daring dreams of the Founding Fathers. By the opening years of the twentieth century, the United States had become a world power. By mid-twentieth century it had become the leader of the free world.

Measured by material things—by the things men could see and touch—the United States of 1960 bore little resemblance to the infant republic of 1790. As you have seen throughout this book, the country has grown and changed through the years. Today, science and technology are transforming the face of the nation—and for that matter, the whole earth—with bewildering speed.

As the charts on these pages remind you, however, it is not just the material aspects of life that are being transformed in this swiftly moving age. One of the most striking aspects of Ameri-

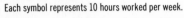

4 AVERAGE NUMBER OF HOURS WORKED PER WEEK

1850

1900

1960

Each symbol represents 10 hours worked per week.

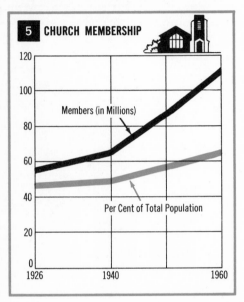

5 CHURCH MEMBERSHIP

120

100

Members (in Millions)

80

60

40

Per Cent of Total Population

20

0
1926   1940   1960

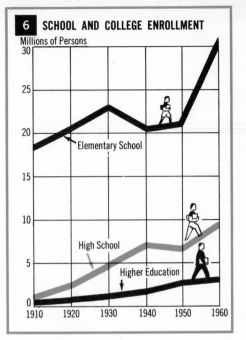

6 SCHOOL AND COLLEGE ENROLLMENT

Millions of Persons
30

25

20
Elementary School

15

10

High School

5
Higher Education

0
1910   1920   1930   1940   1950   1960

In the charts and tables in this Atlas, some figures for the year 1960 are estimates based upon normal rates of growth or decline.

can life today is the amazing variety of occupations open to the rapidly growing army of workers. Whereas in 1790 more than 90 per cent of all Americans worked on the land, by 1960 a young person had the opportunity to choose from many thousands of types of jobs.

Equally striking is the steadily rising standard of living and the growing amount of leisure time enjoyed by the American people. What are Americans doing with their leisure?

More and more Americans are joining the church of their choice. Many of the country's leaders believe that above all Americans need rededication to the values that have from the beginning sustained the growing nation.

Enrollments in schools and colleges are rising rapidly. "If a nation expects to be ignorant and free," Thomas Jefferson warned, "it expects what never was and never will be." The American people as a whole have come to share this faith in education.

Despite a growing concern for matters of the spirit, Americans are still confronted with disturbing questions. Are the American people developing the attitudes, understanding, and skills they need to meet the formidable challenges of a fast-changing world? Are they developing their minds and strengthening their understanding of the moral principles upon which the nation was founded?

These are extremely important questions—as important, perhaps, as any the American people can ask themselves as they face the future.

845

See map next page ➡

POLITICAL MAP OF THE UNITED STATES

CENTRAL TIME

EASTERN TIME

CANADA

ONTARIO
QUEBEC

NEW BRUNSWICK

NOVA SCOTIA

Lake Superior

*Hibbing
*Duluth
*Superior
Sault Ste. Marie

Caribou
Bangor
MAINE
Augusta
Lewiston
Portland

MINNESOTA
*St. Paul
*Minneapolis
*Rochester
*Mason City

WISCONSIN
*Eau Claire
*Green Bay
*Oshkosh
*Madison
*Milwaukee
*Racine

MICHIGAN
Lake Michigan
*Grand Rapids
*Flint
*Lansing
*Detroit

Lake Huron

Montpelier
VT. N.H.
Burlington
Concord
Manchester
Boston
Providence
MASS.
CONN. R.I.

L. Ontario
Rochester
Syracuse
NEW YORK
Buffalo
Binghamton
Albany
Worcester
Hartford
New York

40°

IOWA
*Des Moines
*Cedar Rapids
*Davenport
*Dubuque
*Rockford
*Rock Island
*Peoria

Chicago
Gary
Fort Wayne

Toledo
Cleveland
Akron
Youngstown

Scranton
PENNSYLVANIA
Erie
Pittsburgh
Harrisburg
Wheeling
Newark
Trenton
Camden
N.J.
Philadelphia
Dover
DEL.

ILLINOIS
*Springfield

INDIANA
*Indianapolis

OHIO
*Columbus
*Dayton
*Cincinnati
Covington

W.VA.
Huntington
Charleston

Baltimore
MD.
Washington
Annapolis

VIRGINIA
Richmond
Roanoke
Norfolk

35°
70°

St. Joseph
Hannibal
Kansas City
Jefferson City
St. Louis
East St. Louis
Evansville
Louisville
Frankfort
Lexington

MISSOURI
*Springfield

Cape Girardeau
Cairo
Paducah
Owensboro
KENTUCKY
Middlesboro

Greensboro
Raleigh
NORTH CAROLINA
Charlotte
Wilmington

ATLANTIC OCEAN

Jonesboro
Nashville
Oak Ridge
Knoxville
Asheville

Greenville

ARKANSAS
*Fort Smith
*Hot Springs
*Little Rock
*Pine Bluff
*El Dorado

Jackson
TENNESSEE
Memphis
Chattanooga

SOUTH CAROLINA
*Columbia
Charleston

MISSISSIPPI
*Columbus
*Jackson
*Meridian
Natchez

Birmingham
ALABAMA
Montgomery

Atlanta
GEORGIA
Macon
Columbus
Albany
Savannah

30°

LOUISIANA
*Alexandria
*Shreveport

Mobile
Biloxi
Pensacola

Tallahassee
Valdosta
Jacksonville
Gainesville

Baton Rouge
New Orleans

Beaumont
Lake Charles
Galveston

FLORIDA
Orlando
Tampa
St. Petersburg

25°

GULF OF MEXICO

Miami

West longitude
North latitude

0 100 200 300 400 500
Miles

Key West

20°

⊗ National capital

★ State capital

United States standard time zones are indicated by clocks:
(When it is 12:00 noon in western Alaska, it is 6:00 p.m. along the eastern coast of the United States.)

Boundaries of time zones ·······························

page 847

95°   90°   85°   80°   75°

Unit Survey (Reread "Tracing the Main Ideas," pages 772, 793, 812.)

OUTSTANDING EVENTS

1942 Corregidor surrenders to Japanese.
1942 Marines invade Guadalcanal.
1942 Allied invasion of North Africa.
1942 Pan-American Conference.
1943 Allied invasion of Italy.
1943 Cairo and Teheran Conferences.
1944 Allies invade Western Europe.
1944 Dumbarton Oaks Conference.
1945 Yalta Conference.
1945 Roosevelt dies, and Harry S. Truman becomes President.
1945 War ends in Europe.
1945 Atomic bombs dropped on Hiroshima and Nagasaki.
1945 Truman signs UN Charter.
1945 World War II ends.
1947 Truman Doctrine is announced.
1947 Marshall Plan is proposed.
1947 Taft-Hartley Act.
1948 Truman elected President.
1949 Point Four Program is announced.
1949 NATO is formed.
1950 Korean War starts.
1952 U.S. tests hydrogen bomb.
1952 Dwight D. Eisenhower elected President.
1953 Korean armistice signed.
1954 SEATO is formed.
1955 Summit conference at Geneva.
1956 Eisenhower re-elected President.
1957 Eisenhower Doctrine is announced.
1958 First U.S. satellite in orbit.
1958 Central-station atomic power plant.
1958 Marines land in Lebanon.
1960 Summit conference at Paris.

THEN AND NOW

1. What long-standing American tradition, first challenged unsuccessfully in 1928, was again challenged in 1960? How successful was the challenge?

2. The U.S.S.R. challenged the validity of the Monroe Doctrine in 1960. What was the role of Russia in our original declaration of the Monroe Doctrine?

3. Compare the risks and courage of today's pioneers of the space age with those of the early explorers.

EXTENDING YOUR HORIZON

1. For the story of an American who would become a disillusioned communist, read Bertram D. Wolfe, "The Harvard Man in the Kremlin Wall," *American Heritage,* February 1960.

2. The chapters on "The Sources of Soviet Conduct" and "America and the Russian Future" in Kennan's *American Diplomacy* will prove thought-provoking.

INDIVIDUAL ACTIVITIES

1. Report on the contents of the article by Dean Acheson, former Secretary of State, dealing with Senator Vandenberg, "Journey into Our Times," in *American Heritage,* February 1960.

2. Individuals may choose to prepare oral reports on one of the accounts such as "Captain Kelly's Last Flight" given in Stewart Holbrook's book *None More Courageous* (Macmillan).

3. Read the essays on Robert Taft and George Norris in John F. Kennedy's *Profiles in Courage,* and contrast and compare the two men in their political philosophies and the difficult choices they had to make.

4. Prepare a short biographical report on either Dwight D. Eisenhower or Harry S. Truman.

5. On an outline map of the world, indicate the areas in which communism and democracy stand opposed to each other.

6. Study the map on pages 818–19, and then make a list of the geographic factors which have influenced the economic development (agricultural, industrial, and commercial) of the area in which you live. Check your answer against the maps on pages 830–31 and pages 834–35.

7. Study the maps and charts on pages 820–23, and indicate the different methods used by the United States to acquire more territory.

8. (a) What seems to be the trend in farm population, farm production, number of farms, farm acres harvested, and use of machinery on farms? (b) Does it seem likely that the farm surplus will continue to accumulate? Base your answers on the charts on pages 828–29.

9. Using the charts on pages 844–45, summarize the trends in major occupations, distribution of income, leisure time, church membership, school and college enrollment, and in the relation of the labor force

to the total population. What is the significance of these developments?

GROUP ACTIVITIES

1. The pamphlets in the Foreign Relations Project of the North Central Association of Colleges and Secondary Schools can be used in round-table discussion of United States foreign policy toward Germany, the Soviet Union, Europe generally, the Middle East, and the Far East.

2. Farm price supports can be studied by a committee of three. One member relates the history and explains the meaning of terms; the two others present the arguments for and against this kind of aid.

3. A round-table discussion of the problems of testing A-bombs and H-bombs can be based upon these two books: *Our Nuclear Future* by Edward Teller and Albert L. Latter, Criterion; and *No More War* by Linus Pauling, Dodd, Mead. If these are not available, consult weekly news magazines for articles.

4. Choose a group of students to investigate and compare the Presidential nominations and election campaigns of Alfred E. Smith in 1928 and John F. Kennedy in 1960. They might consider the backgrounds and careers of the two men, the circumstances of their nomination in the respective political conventions, general attitudes prevailing in the country toward their candidacy. Then, let them evaluate and compare the results of the two campaigns. (If possible, consult article by Richard Hofstadter, "Could a Protestant Have Beaten Hoover in 1928?" in the *Reporter*, March 17, 1960.)

5. Let a group study and evaluate for the class the causes of America's entry into World War II on the basis of the material in *Pearl Harbor—Roosevelt and the Coming of War*, "Amherst Series" (Heath).

SUGGESTED FURTHER READING

BIOGRAPHY

BEAL, JOHN R., *John Foster Dulles: A Biography*, Harper.

DAVIS, KENNETH S., *A Prophet in His Own Country*, Doubleday. About Adlai Stevenson.

——, *General Eisenhower, Soldier of Democracy*, Doubleday (text ed.).

PUSEY, MERLO J., *Eisenhower, the President*, Macmillan.

ST. JOHN, ROBERT, *Foreign Correspondent*, Doubleday.

*TRUMAN, HARRY S., *Year of Decisions*, Doubleday. Volume I of *Memoirs*, covering his first year in office.

OTHER NONFICTION

*AGAR, HERBERT, *The Price of Power*, Univ. of Chicago Press.

BECKEL, GRAHAM, *Workshops of the World*, Abelard-Schuman. Specialized UN agencies.

*DEAN, VERA MICHELES, *The United States and Russia*, Harvard Univ. Press.

EISENHOWER, DWIGHT D., *Crusade in Europe*, Doubleday.

*GOLDMAN, ERIC, *The Crucial Decade*, Knopf. America 1945–55.

HERSEY, JOHN, *Hiroshima*, Knopf; Bantam.

HIGGINS, MARGUERITE, *War in Korea*, Doubleday.

HOOVER, J. EDGAR, *Masters of Deceit*, Holt. Communism in the United States.

*HUGHES, EMMET JOHN, *America the Vincible*, Doubleday. Concerns the decade of the 50's and the present and future.

JOHNSON, GERALD, *The Incredible Tale*, Harper. American thinking, 1900–50.

*KENNAN, GEORGE F., *Realities of American Foreign Policy*, Princeton Univ. Press.

*KISSINGER, HENRY A., *Nuclear Weapons and Foreign Policy*, Harper (text ed.).

LAURENCE, WILLIAM, *Men and Atoms*, Simon and Schuster.

LEY, WILLY, *Rockets, Missiles, and Space Travel*, Viking.

Life's Picture History of World War II, by the Editors of *Life*, Simon and Schuster.

LIPPMANN, WALTER, *The Communist World and Ours*, Little, Brown.

*LUBELL, SAMUEL, *The Future of American Politics*, Harper; Doubleday (Anchor Books).

MILLIS, WALTER, *Arms and Men*, New American Library. Modern warfare.

REDDING, SAUNDERS, *The Lonesome Road*, Doubleday. An appraisal of the Negro's part in America.

*ROVERE, RICHARD H., *Affairs of State: The Eisenhower Years*, Farrar, Straus & Cudahy.

HISTORICAL FICTION

HERSEY, JOHN, *A Bell for Adano*, Knopf. United States military government in Italy.

MASTERS, DEXTER, *The Accident*, Knopf. Scientist is killed by radiation.

MICHENER, JAMES, *The Bridges at Tokori*, Random House, Korean War.

CHRONOLOGY OF EVENTS IN AMERICAN HISTORY

(The state given after each President's name was the state of residence at time of election.)

1096 Crusades to Holy Land start.
1271–95 Marco Polo's travels in Far East.
1492 Columbus discovers America.
1494 Line of demarcation.
1497–98 John Cabot's explorations.
1498 Vasco da Gama reaches India.
1500 Cabral claims Brazil.
1513 Balboa discovers Pacific Ocean.
1519 Cortez lands in Mexico.
1519–22 Magellan's men circle earth.
1531–35 Pizarro conquers Incas.
1534 Cartier makes first voyage.
1539–42 De Soto explores Southeast.
1588 English defeat Spanish Armada.
1603 Champlain makes first voyage.
1607 Jamestown is founded.
1609 Hudson explores Hudson River.
1619 House of Burgesses meets.
1619 First slaves brought to Virginia.
1620 Pilgrims reach Cape Cod.
1620 Mayflower Compact.
1624 Virginia becomes royal colony.
1630 Massachusetts Bay Colony founded.
1632 Maryland is chartered.
1636 Roger Williams founds Providence.
1636 Hartford (Connecticut) settled.
1636 Harvard University founded.
1639 Fundamental Orders of Connecticut.
1643 New England Confederation formed.
1647 Massachusetts passes school law.
1649 Maryland Toleration Act.
1651–63 Principal Navigation Acts.
1663 Carolina is chartered.
1664 English take over Dutch colonies.
1664 New Netherland becomes New Jersey and New York.
1673 Exploration by Marquette, Joliet.
1675–76 Bacon's Rebellion.
1679 New Hampshire is chartered.
1681 Pennsylvania is chartered.
1681–82 Exploration by La Salle.
1682 Delaware granted to Penn.
1686 Dominion of New England created.
1689–1748 France and Great Britain intermittently at war.
1693 College of William and Mary founded.
1699 Woolens Act.
1701 Yale University founded.

1732 Georgia is chartered.
1732 Hat Act.
1733 Molasses Act.
1735 Zenger trial.
1740 University of Pennsylvania founded.
1746 Princeton University founded.
1750 Iron Act.
1754 French and Indian War starts.
1754 Albany Plan of Union proposed.
1754 Columbia University founded.
1755 Braddock defeated disastrously.
1756 Pitt heads British government.
1759 British capture Quebec.
1763 Treaty of Paris.
1763 Proclamation of 1763.
1764 Sugar Act, Currency Act.
1764 Brown University founded.
1765 Stamp Act.
1765 Stamp Act Congress meets.
1766 Stamp Act repealed.
1766 Rutgers University founded.
1767 Townshend Acts.
1769 Dartmouth College founded.
1770 Boston Massacre.
1772 Committees of Correspondence.
1773 Boston Tea Party.
1774 Intolerable Acts.
1774 First Continental Congress.
1775 Fighting at Lexington, Concord.
1775 Second Continental Congress.
1775 Battle of Bunker Hill.
1776 Paine's *Common Sense* appears.
1776 Declaration of Independence.
1776 American victory at Trenton.
1777–78 Howe occupies Philadelphia.
1777 Burgoyne surrenders at Saratoga.
1778 Treaty of alliance with France.
1778–79 Clark takes the Northwest.
1781 Cornwallis surrenders.
1781 Articles of Confederation go into effect.
1783 Treaty of Paris; United States independence recognized.
1785 Land Ordinance.
1786 Virginia Statute for Religious Freedom.
1786–87 Shays' Rebellion.
1787 Northwest Ordinance.
1787 Constitution drafted.

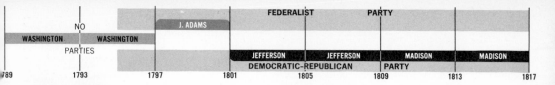

|---|---|---|---|---|---|---|---|---|
				FEDERALIST	PARTY			
		J. ADAMS						
NO								
WASHINGTON	WASHINGTON							
PARTIES								
				JEFFERSON	JEFFERSON	MADISON	MADISON	
				DEMOCRATIC-REPUBLICAN	PARTY			
1789	1793	1797	1801	1805	1809	1813	1817

1
George Washington
1732–1799; Virginia
In office: 1789–1797

1789 Congress creates Departments of State, Treasury, and War.
1789 United States courts are organized.
1789 French Revolution begins.
1789 Slater brings knowledge of power-driven machines to U.S.
1790 Assumption Bill provides for federal payment of states' war debt.
1790 Patent and copyright law.
1791 Bill of Rights ratified.
1791 Vermont enters Union.
1791 Bank of United States chartered.
1791 Lancaster Turnpike is begun.
1792 Kentucky enters Union.
1792 Gray discovers Columbia River.
1793 Genêt visit.
1793 Proclamation of Neutrality.
1793 Eli Whitney invents cotton gin.
1794 "Whisky Rebellion" is crushed.
1794 Battle of Fallen Timbers.
1794 Jay Treaty.
1795 Pinckney Treaty.
1796 Tennessee enters Union.
1797 XYZ Affair angers Americans.
1798 Eleventh Amendment ratified.

2
John Adams
1735–1826; Massachusetts
Federalist
In office: 1797–1801

1798 Navy Department is created.
1798 Alien and Sedition Acts.
1798–99 Kentucky and Virginia Resolutions outline states' rights theory.
1800 Interchangeable parts demonstrated.
1801 Marshall becomes Chief Justice.

3
Thomas Jefferson
1743–1826; Virginia
Democratic-Republican
In office: 1801–1809

1803 Ohio enters Union.
1803 *Marbury v. Madison*.
1803 Louisiana Purchase adds immense area to United States.
1804 Twelfth Amendment ratified.
1804–06 Lewis and Clark expedition.
1805–07 Pike explores western regions.
1805 War with Barbary pirates ends.
1807 Embargo Act.
1807 Steamboat *Clermont* demonstrated.
1808 Astor builds fort and trading post in Oregon country.
1809 Non-Intercourse Act.

4
James Madison
1751–1836; Virginia
Democratic-Republican
In office: 1809–1817

1811 Indian fight at Tippecanoe.
1811 National Road is begun.
1811 Fulton builds steamboat *New Orleans*.
1812 Louisiana enters Union.
1812–14 War of 1812 is fought between United States and Great Britain.
1813 Waltham experiment begins—attempt to help factory workers.
1814 Hartford Convention meets; restates Kentucky and Virginia Resolutions.
1814 Treaty of Ghent restores peace.
1815 Battle of New Orleans.
1816 Second Bank of United States chartered.
1816 Protective tariff adopted.
1816 Indiana enters Union.

BUSINESS ACTIVITY CHART

NAPOLEONIC WARS

POSTWAR PROSPERITY

EMBARGO DEPRESSION

WAR OF 1812

1789 1793 1797 1801 1805 1809 1813 1817

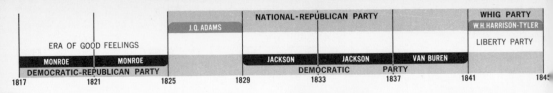

NATIONAL-REPUBLICAN PARTY

WHIG PARTY
W.H.HARRISON-TYLER

J.Q. ADAMS

LIBERTY PARTY

ERA OF GOOD FEELINGS

MONROE | MONROE
DEMOCRATIC-REPUBLICAN PARTY

JACKSON | JACKSON | VAN BUREN
DEMOCRATIC PARTY

1817 | 1821 | 1825 | 1829 | 1833 | 1837 | 1841 | 1845

5
James Monroe
1758–1831; Virginia
Democratic-Republican
In office: 1817–1825

1817–25 "Era of Good Feelings."
1817 Mississippi enters Union.
1818 Rush-Bagot Agreement approved.
1818 Illinois enters Union.
1818 Treaty settles Canadian boundary.
1818 Philadelphia-Pittsburgh Turnpike is completed.
1819 *McCulloch v. Maryland*.
1819 *Dartmouth College v. Woodward*.
1819 Financial panic.
1819 Alabama enters Union.
1819 Tallmadge Amendment introduced.
1819 Treaty gives Florida to U.S.
1820 Missouri Compromise.
1820 Maine enters Union.
1821 Missouri enters Union.
1821 Austin starts colony in Texas.
1821 First public high school opens.
1822 U.S. recognizes revolutionary governments of Latin America.
1823 Monroe Doctrine proclaimed.
1824 *Gibbons v. Ogden*.
1825 Utopian community started by Robert Owen at New Harmony.

6
John Quincy Adams
1767–1848; Massachusetts
National-Republican
In office: 1825–1829

1825 Erie Canal opens.
1828 "Tariff of Abominations."
1828 "South Carolina Exposition and Protest."
1828 Work begun on Baltimore and Ohio Railroad.
1828 Webster publishes his dictionary.

7
Andrew Jackson
1767–1845; Tennessee
Democrat
In office: 1829–1837

1830 Webster-Hayne debate.
1831 First nominating conventions.
1831 Slave uprising in Virginia.
1831 First issue of the *Liberator*.
1832 Tariff of 1832.
1832 Ordinance of Nullification.
1832 Telegraph is developed.
1832 Jackson vetoes renewal of charter for Bank of United States.
1833 Jackson withdraws deposits from Bank of United States.
1833 Compromise tariff act.
1834 National Trades Union formed.
1836 Texas declares its independence.
1836 Arkansas enters Union.
1836 Jackson issues "Specie Circular."
1837 Michigan enters Union.

8
Martin Van Buren
1782–1862; New York
Democrat
In office: 1837–1841

1837 Panic; economic depression begins.
1837 Horace Mann starts school reform.
1838 Oberlin admits women.
1841 Jacksonian era ends.

9
William Henry Harrison
1773–1841; Ohio
Whig
In office: March 4–April 4, 1841

1841 Harrison dies.

BUSINESS ACTIVITY CHART

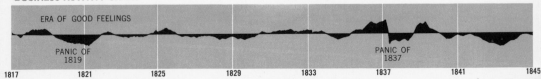

ERA OF GOOD FEELINGS

PANIC OF 1819

PANIC OF 1837

1817 | 1821 | 1825 | 1829 | 1833 | 1837 | 1841 | 1845

WHIG PARTY			REPUBLICAN PARTY	
	TAYLOR-FILLMORE			
FREE SOIL PARTY			AMERICAN PARTY	CONSTITUTIONAL UNION PARTY
POLK			PIERCE	BUCHANAN
		DEMOCRATIC PARTY		

1845 | 1849 | 1853 | 1857 | 1861

10
John Tyler
1790–1862; Virginia
Whig
In office: 1841–1845

1842 Massachusetts recognizes legal right of labor unions to exist.
1842 Webster-Ashburton Treaty.
1844 Vulcanizing process patented.
1844 Telegraph put into operation.
1845 Florida enters Union.

11
James K. Polk
1795–1849; Tennessee
Democrat
In office: 1845–1849

1845 Texas enters Union.
1846 Irish Potato Famine.
1846 Treaty settles Oregon boundary.
1846 Sewing machine is patented.
1846 Iowa enters Union.
1846 Congress declares war on Mexico.
1846 Wilmot Proviso is presented.
1846 Ether used as anesthetic.
1847 Mormons settle at Great Salt Lake.
1848 Treaty ends Mexican War; gives U.S. Mexican Cession.
1848 Polk tries to buy Cuba.
1848 Women's rights convention.
1848 Wisconsin enters Union.

12
Zachary Taylor
1784–1850; Louisiana
Whig
In office: 1849–1850

1849 Gold rush to California.
1850 Taylor dies.

13
Millard Fillmore
1800–1874; New York
Whig
In office: 1850–1853

1850 Compromise of 1850.
1850 California admitted to Union.
1851–56 Kelly, Bessemer develop processes for making steel cheaply.
1852 *Uncle Tom's Cabin* is published.

14
Franklin Pierce
1804–1869; New Hampshire
Democrat
In office: 1853–1857

1853 Gadsden Purchase approved.
1853 Perry arrives in Japan.
1854 Kansas-Nebraska Act.
1854 Republican Party is formed.
1855 *Leaves of Grass* is published.
1856 Violence breaks out in Kansas.

15
James Buchanan
1791–1868; Pennsylvania
Democrat
In office: 1857–1861

1857 Dred Scott decision.
1858 Lincoln-Douglas debates.
1858 Minnesota enters Union.
1859 John Brown raids Harper's Ferry.
1859 Drake drills first oil well.
1859 Oregon enters Union.
1860 South Carolina secedes.
1861 Kansas enters Union.
1861 Confederacy is formed.
1861 Morrill Tariff Act.

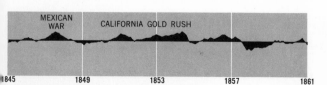

MEXICAN WAR   CALIFORNIA GOLD RUSH

1845 | 1849 | 1853 | 1857 | 1861

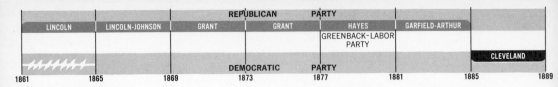

			REPUBLICAN PARTY			
LINCOLN	LINCOLN-JOHNSON	GRANT	GRANT	HAYES	GARFIELD-ARTHUR	
				GREENBACK-LABOR PARTY		
						CLEVELAND
			DEMOCRATIC PARTY			

1861   1865   1869   1873   1877   1881   1885   1889

16
Abraham Lincoln
1809–1865; Illinois
Republican
In office: 1861–1865

1861 South fires on Fort Sumter; War Between States (1861–65) begins.
1861 First Battle of Bull Run.
1861 *Trent* affair.
1862 Battle of *Monitor* and *Merrimac*.
1862 Farragut captures New Orleans.
1862 Seven Days' Battles.
1862 Second Battle of Bull Run.
1862 Battle of Antietam.
1862 Emancipation Proclamation.
1862 Union forces reach Vicksburg.
1862 Homestead Act.
1862 Morrill Act for agricultural and industrial education.
1862 Department of Agriculture formed.
1862 McKay patents shoe machine.
1863 Battle of Gettysburg.
1863 Grant takes Vicksburg.
1863 West Virginia enters Union.
1863 National Banking Act.
1864 Sherman takes Atlanta, Savannah.
1864 Nevada enters Union.
1864 Contract Labor Law permits importation of workers from Europe.
1864 Railroad sleeping car developed.
1865 Freedmen's Bureau is created.
1865 Lee withdraws from Richmond.
1865 Lee surrenders to Grant.
1865 Lincoln is assassinated.

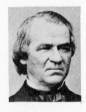

17
Andrew Johnson
1808–1875; Tennessee
Republican
In office: 1865–1869

1865 Johnson recognizes four reconstructed governments.

1865 Thirteenth Amendment ratified.
1865–86 Almost constant conflict between Indians and whites.
1866 Field lays transatlantic cable.
1866 National Labor Union is formed.
1867 Nebraska enters Union.
1867 U.S. buys Alaska.
1867 French forces leave Mexico.
1867 Congressional plan of reconstruction is set up.
1867 Sholes develops typewriter.
1867 Grange is organized.
1867 Howard University is founded.
1868 Fourteenth Amendment ratified.
1868 House impeaches Johnson.
1868 Senate acquits Johnson.

18
Ulysses S. Grant
1822–1885; Illinois
Republican
In office: 1869–1877

1869 First transcontinental railroad is completed.
1869 Westinghouse patents air brake.
1869 Knights of Labor is founded.
1870 Fifteenth Amendment ratified.
1870–71 Force Acts.
1871 Birmingham, Alabama, founded.
1872 Amnesty Act.
1872 "*Alabama* Claims" are settled.
1872 Crédit Mobilier scandal.
1873 Silver dollars dropped from list of standard coins.
1873 Nationwide economic depression.
1874 Glidden patents barbed wire.
1874 Chautauqua movement is started.
1875 Resumption Act.
1876 Colorado enters Union.
1876 Centennial Exhibition.
1876 Patent on telephone applied for.
1876 National League (of baseball teams) is organized.
1876 Presidential election disputed.
1876–77 "Granger cases" decided.

BUSINESS ACTIVITY CHART

WAR BETWEEN THE STATES   INDUSTRIAL EXPANSION   GROWTH OF RAILROADS

DEPRESSION OF 1873

REPUBLICAN PARTY
B.HARRISON
POPULIST PARTY
CLEVELAND
DEMOCRATIC PARTY
1889   1893   1897

19
Rutherford B. Hayes
1822–1893; Ohio
Republican
In office: 1877–1881

1877 Troops withdrawn from South.
1877 Series of railroad strikes.
1878 Bland-Allison Act.
1879 U.S. Geological Survey organized.
1880–90 Immigration swells.

20
James A. Garfield
1831–1881; Ohio
Republican
In office: 1881–1881

1881 Garfield is assassinated.

21
Chester A. Arthur
1830–1886; New York
Republican
In office: 1881–1885

1882 First large central electric-power plant in U.S.
1882 Chinese Exclusion Act.
1882 Standard Oil Trust organized.
1883 Civil Service Commission set up.

22
Grover Cleveland
1837–1908; New York
Democrat
In office: 1885–1889

1885 Severe drought in Cattle Kingdom.
1885 Linotype is invented.

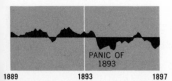

PANIC OF 1893

1889   1893   1897

1886 Presidential Succession Act.
1886 Knights of Labor number 700,000.
1886 A. F. of L. is organized.
1886 Haymarket Riot.
1886 Supreme Court qualifies 1876–77 decisions in "Granger cases."
1887 Electoral Count Act.
1887 Interstate Commerce Act.
1887 Hatch Act.
1887 Division of Forestry created.
1887 Dawes Act.

23
Benjamin Harrison
1833–1901; Indiana
Republican
In office: 1889–1893

1889 Washington, Montana, North Dakota, South Dakota enter Union.
1889 Hull House is opened to public.
1889–90 Pan-American Conference.
1890 Wyoming, Idaho enter Union.
1890 McKinley Tariff.
1890 Sherman Antitrust Act.
1890 Sherman Silver Purchase Act.
1890 End of frontier.
1891 Populist Party is organized.
1891 Congress authorizes President to withdraw timberlands from sale.
1892 Homestead steel strike.

24
Grover Cleveland
1837–1908; New York
Democrat
In office: 1893–1897

1893 Silver Purchase Act is repealed.
1893 Business slump; lasts until 1896.
1893 World's Fair held in Chicago.
1894 Wilson-Gorman Tariff.
1894 Pullman strike.
1895 First large plant for producing electricity from water power.
1895 Banks lend gold to government.
1895 Cubans revolt against Spain.
1895 Venezuelan boundary dispute.
1895 Armat invents movie projector.
1896 Bryan is free silver candidate.
1896 Utah enters Union.
1896 Gold discovered on Klondike.

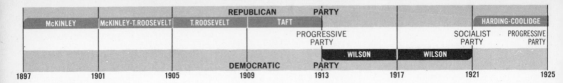

| REPUBLICAN PARTY | | | | | | | HARDING-COOLIDGE |
| McKINLEY | McKINLEY-T.ROOSEVELT | T.ROOSEVELT | TAFT | | | | |

PROGRESSIVE PARTY | SOCIALIST PARTY | PROGRESSIVE PARTY

WILSON | WILSON

DEMOCRATIC PARTY

1897   1901   1905   1909   1913   1917   1921   1925

25
William McKinley
1843–1901; Ohio
Republican
In office: 1897–1901

1897 Dingley Tariff.
1898 Spanish-American War.
1898 Treaty of Paris gives U.S. Puerto Rico, Guam, Philippines.
1898 U.S. annexes Hawaiian Islands.
1898 South Dakota adopts initiative and referendum.
1899 U.S. controls American Samoa.
1899 First Hague Conference.
1899–1900 Open Door policy proclaimed.
1900 Boxer Rebellion.
1900 Galveston, Texas, adopts commission government.
1901 Platt Amendment.
1901 Insular Cases are decided.
1901 McKinley is assassinated.

26
Theodore Roosevelt
1858–1919; New York
Republican
In office: 1901–1909

1901 Hay-Pauncefote Treaty.
1901 United States Steel is formed.
1901–02 Pan-American Conference.
1902 Newlands Reclamation Act.
1902 Coal strike in Pennsylvania.
1902 *The History of the Standard Oil Company* is published.
1902 Drago Doctrine is announced.
1902 American forces withdrawn from Cuba.
1903 Department of Commerce and Labor is created.
1903 Elkins Act.
1903 Wisconsin adopts direct primary.
1903 Radio message is sent from U.S. to England.

1903 First powered flight.
1903 Canal Zone is acquired by U.S.
1904 Northern Securities Company ruling.
1904 Roosevelt Corollary to Monroe Doctrine is announced.
1905 Treaty of Portsmouth.
1905 *Lochner v. New York.*
1905 I.W.W. is formed.
1906 Pure Food and Drug Act.
1906 Meat Inspection Act.
1906 Hepburn Act.
1906 Burke Act modifies provisions of Dawes Act.
1906 Upton Sinclair's *The Jungle* is published.
1906 Three-element vacuum tube invented.
1906 Pan-American Conference.
1907 Oklahoma enters Union.
1907 Financial panic and depression.
1907 "Gentlemen's Agreement" with Japan.
1907 Second Hague Conference.
1908 State ten-hour-day law is upheld.
1908 White House Conservation Conference.
1908 Supreme Court rules against union in Danbury Hatters' case.

27
William H. Taft
1857–1930; Ohio
Republican
In office: 1909–1913

1909 Payne-Aldrich Tariff.
1910 Mann-Elkins Act.
1910 Postal savings system started.
1910 Pan-American Conference.
1910–11 Speaker of the House loses power.
1911 "Rule of reason" is adopted.
1911 Roosevelt, Shoshone Dams opened.
1911 Transcontinental plane flight.
1912 New Mexico, Arizona enter Union.
1912 Progressive Party is formed.
1912 First state minimum-wage law.
1913 Sixteenth Amendment ratified.

BUSINESS ACTIVITY CHART

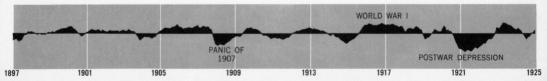

WORLD WAR I

PANIC OF 1907

POSTWAR DEPRESSION

1897   1901   1905   1909   1913   1917   1921   1925

28
Woodrow Wilson
1856–1924; New Jersey
Democrat
In office: 1913–1921

1913 Seventeenth Amendment ratified.
1913 Underwood Tariff.
1913 Federal Reserve Act.
1914 World War I starts.
1914 Panama Canal opened to traffic.
1914 Ford's conveyer-belt assembly.
1914 FTC is created.
1914 Clayton Antitrust Act.
1914 Smith-Lever Act.
1915 New York and San Francisco are linked by telephone.
1916 Jones Act.
1916 "Sussex pledge."
1917 Russian Revolution.
1917 U.S. enters World War I.
1917 Smith-Hughes Act.
1917 Government takes over railroads.
1917 U.S. buys Virgin Islands.
1918 Fighting at Château-Thierry.
1918 Fighting at St. Mihiel.
1918 Meuse-Argonne offensive.
1918 World War I ends.
1918 Wilson presents Fourteen Points.
1919 Eighteenth Amendment ratified.
1919 "Palmer raids."
1919 Treaty of Versailles (includes provision for League of Nations).
1920 Nineteenth Amendment ratified.
1920 World Court is created.
1920 KDKA begins operation.

29
Warren G. Harding
1865–1923; Ohio
Republican
In office: 1921–1923

1921 Bureau of the Budget is created.
1921 Veterans' Bureau is created.

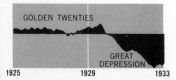

GOLDEN TWENTIES

GREAT DEPRESSION

1925   1929   1933

1921–22 Washington Naval Conference.
1921–29 Laws restricting immigration are enacted.
1922 Mussolini seizes power in Italy.
1922 Fordney-McCumber Tariff.
1923 Harding dies suddenly.

30
Calvin Coolidge
1872–1933; Massachusetts
Republican
In office: 1923–1929

1923 Du Pont buys cellophane rights.
1923 Quick-frozen foods developed.
1923 Pan-American Conference.
1924 Teapot Dome scandal, involving oil-reserve lands.
1924 Veterans' bonus bill passed.
1924 All Indians given citizenship.
1924 New Progressive Party formed.
1927 McNary-Haugen Bill vetoed.
1927 First talking movie.
1927 Lindbergh flies Atlantic.
1927 International Health Service reports that hookworm has almost disappeared from U.S.
1928 Kellogg-Briand Pact attempts to outlaw war.
1928 Pan-American Conference.

31
Herbert Hoover
1874–   ; California
Republican
In office: 1929–1933

1929 Agricultural Marketing Act.
1929 Stock market crash; beginning of Great Depression.
1930 Public-works programs started; Boulder (later Hoover) Dam begun.
1930 London Naval Conference.
1930 Hawley-Smoot Tariff.
1931 Moratorium declared on war debts owed to U.S. by European nations.
1931 Japan invades Manchuria.
1932 RFC is created.
1932 Home Loan Bank Act.
1932 Stimson Doctrine is announced.
1932–33 Federal Reserve powers enlarged.
1933 Hitler comes to power in Germany.
1933 Twentieth Amendment ratified.

857

32
Franklin D. Roosevelt
1882–1945; New York
Democrat
In office: 1933–1945

1933 CCC is created.
1933 Agricultural Adjustment Act.
1933 FCA is created.
1933 Roosevelt declares bank holiday.
1933 Congress abandons gold standard.
1933 NIRA goes into effect.
1933 NLB (later NLRB) is created.
1933 FDIC is established.
1933 TVA is created.
1933 U.S. recognizes Soviet Union.
1933 Good Neighbor policy announced.
1933 Twenty-first Amendment ratified.
1934 Roosevelt "devalues" dollar.
1934 SEC is created.
1934 Trade Agreements Act.
1934 Drought creates Dust Bowl.
1934 Platt Amendment canceled.
1935 WPA is created.
1935 Buses, trucks placed under ICC.
1935 NIRA declared unconstitutional.
1935 National Labor Relations Act.
1935 Social Security Act.
1935–37 Neutrality Acts.
1936 AAA ruled unconstitutional.
1936 Pan-American Conference.
1937 Plan to reorganize Supreme Court
1937 *Panay* incident.
1937–38 Business slump.
1938 CIO separates from A. F. of L.
1938 Fair Labor Standards Act.
1938 New Agricultural Adjustment Act.
1938 Food, Drug, and Cosmetic Act.
1938 Munich Agreement.
1938 Declaration of Lima.
1939 Germany invades Poland; World War II begins.
1939 Neutrality Act of 1937 amended.
1940 Alien Registration Act.
1940 France signs armistice.
1940 Act of Havana.

1940 Excess profits tax levied.
1941 "Four Freedoms" speech.
1941 Lend-Lease Act.
1941 Hitler attacks U.S.S.R.
1941 Atlantic Charter states war aims.
1941 Japanese attack Pearl Harbor; U.S. enters World War II.
1942 Corregidor surrenders to Japanese.
1942 Marines invade Guadalcanal.
1942 Allied invasion of North Africa.
1942 Pan-American Conference.
1942 OPA is established.
1943 Allied invasion of Italy.
1943 Cairo and Teheran Conferences.
1944 Allies attack Marshall Islands.
1944 Invasion of Marianas.
1944 Allies invade Western Europe.
1944 France is liberated.
1944 Dumbarton Oaks Conference.
1945 Yalta Conference.
1945 Roosevelt dies suddenly.

33
Harry S. Truman
1884–   ; Missouri
Democrat
In office: 1945–1953

1945 San Francisco Conference.
1945 War ends in Europe.
1945 Atomic bombs dropped on Hiroshima and Nagasaki.
1945 Truman signs UN Charter.
1945 World War II ends.
1945 Beginning of commercial TV.
1946 Coal strike by U.M.W.
1946 Philippines become independent.
1946 End to wage and price controls.
1947 Truman Doctrine is announced.
1947 Marshall Plan is proposed.
1947 Taft-Hartley Act.
1947 Presidential Succession Act.
1947 Truman calls for loyalty check.
1948 Religious exercises in schools ruled unconstitutional.
1948 UAW-GM contract with "escalator."

BUSINESS ACTIVITY CHART   Data up to March 1960 courtesy of Cleveland Trust Co.

WORLD WAR II   KOREAN WAR

GREAT DEPRESSION

| 1933 | 1937 | 1941 | 1945 | 1949 | 1953 | 1957 | 196 |

1948 Communists control Czechoslovakia.
1948–49 Berlin airlift.
1949 Point Four program is announced.
1949 NATO is formed.
1949 Communists control China.
1949 Reorganization Act.
1949 Agricultural Act.
1950 Internal Security Act.
1950 Korean War starts.
1951 Twenty-second Amendment ratified.
1952 U.S. tests hydrogen bomb.

34
Dwight D. Eisenhower
1890–   ; New York, Penna.

Republican

In office: 1953–1961

1953 Department of Health, Education, and Welfare is set up.
1953 States get title to offshore oil.
1953 Korean armistice signed.
1953 Wage, price controls abandoned.
1953 Stalin dies.
1954 Atomic Energy Act is amended.
1954 Supreme Court rules segregated public schools unconstitutional.
1954 Indo-China is divided.
1954 SEATO is formed.
1954 West Germany is admitted to NATO.
1954 Both U.S. and U.S.S.R. have H–bombs.
1955 Congress authorizes $500 million for urban redevelopment.
1955 UAW contracts move toward guaranteed annual wage.
1955 Summit conference.
1955 A. F. of L. and CIO combine.
1956 "Soil bank" is set up.
1956 Revolts in Poland and Hungary.

1956 Suez crisis.
1957 Eisenhower Doctrine announced.
1957 Civil Rights Commission created.
1957 *Sputnik* in orbit.
1958 First U.S. satellite in orbit.
1958 Congress provides for federal loans to students.
1958 Marines land in Lebanon.
1958 Matsu and Quemoy are shelled.
1958 Congress admits Alaska to the Union.
1958–59 Berlin crisis.
1959 Labor-Management Reporting and Disclosure Act.
1959 St. Lawrence Seaway is opened.
1959 Congress admits Hawaii to the Union.
1959 Steel strike.
1959 Foreign ministers' conference.
1960 Summit Conference called off.
1960 O.A.S. meeting.
1960 World leaders gather at UN.

35
John F. Kennedy
1917–   ; Massachusetts

Democrat

In office: 1961–

Index

Italicized page numbers preceded by *c*, *m*, or *p* refer to a chart (*c*), map (*m*), or picture (*p*) on the page.

Boldface page numbers are pages on which a definition or explanation is given.

For list of Special Features, see p. xiv.

For list of Maps and Charts, see p. xii.

862

Stock dividends, **474**
Stock market, 652, 801
Stockton, Robert F., 333, *m 331*
Stone, Lucy, 525
Stowe, Calvin E., 347
Stowe, Harriet B., 344, 351, 369
Strikes: development, 302; under Knights of Labor, 515–16; ended by troops, 519–20; opposed by courts, 520; first arbitration, 549–50; and Clayton Act, 565; following World War I, 644–45, *p 644;* under New Deal, 716–17; following World War II, 775, 798; and Taft-Hartley Act, 775–76, 798
Strong, Josiah, 588, 593
Stuart, Gilbert, 264–65, *p 265*
Stuart, "Jeb," 388, *m 387*
Stuyvesant, Peter, 36
Submarine warfare, 626–27, 762
Submerged Lands Act, 796
Subsistence farms, **308**
Suburban growth, 814
Subversion, 779, 799
Subways, 468
Sudetenland, 734, *m 735*
Suez Canal, 805–08, *m 755*
Suffrage, **31**; colonial limits, 31, 32, 85–86; in 1800's, 269, 427; women's, 546, 646
Sugar Act, 99
Sullivan, Louis H., 532, 685
Sumatra, 296, *m 768*
Summit Conference, (1955), 804; (1960), 809–10
Sumner, Charles, 370, 414, 420, 421
Sumter, Thomas, 131
Superior, Wis., *m 847*
Supreme Court: established by Constitution, 167, 189–90, *c 175;* powers, 167–68, 171, 189–90, *c 188;* under Marshall, 226–27, 257–58; Dred Scott, 373–74; antitrust legislation, 478, 550–51; Granger cases, 495; on social legislation, 577–78; New Deal legislation, 699, 705, 713–14; Fifth Amendment, 799; integration, 801
Sussex pledge, 628
Sutter's Fort, 339, *m 323*
Sweden, 626, *m 623*
Sylvis, William, 514
Synthetics, *c (#1) 833*
Syracuse, N.Y., 290, *m 847*
Syria (**U.A.R.**), 788, 808, *m 806*

Tacoma, Wash., *m 846*
Taft, Robert A., 795
Taft, William Howard: elected President, 559; antitrust activities, 559, *p 561;* reform measures, 559–60; on tariff, 560; and conservation, 560–61; in election of 1912, 561, 563; governor of Philippines, 594; and peace movement, 620; in World War I, 631; and "dollar diplomacy," 666
Taft-Hartley Act, 775, 798
Tallahassee, Fla., *m 847*
Tallmadge, James, 361
Tallmadge Amendment, 361
Tammany Hall, 432, 433, *p 433*
Tampa, Fla., 592, *m 847*
Tampico, Mexico, 614, *m 605*
Tanana, Alaska, *m 800*
Taney, Roger B., 373, 547
Tarawa, Gilbert Is., 766, *m 768*
Tarbell, Ida M., 544
Tariff, **57**; protective, **212**; revenue, **212**; reciprocal, **728–29**; under Confederation, 151; under Hamilton, 212; opposed by South, 158–59, 276–78, 362, 395; under American System, 253; "Tariff

of Abominations," 276–77; Compromise, 278; during War Between the States, 395, 398; McKinley, 441, 442; Wilson-Gorman, 442–43; Dingley, 543; Payne-Aldrich, 560; Underwood, 563–64; and Open Door policy, 597; Emergency, 647; Fordney-McCumber, 648; Hawley-Smoot, 651, *p 665;* and European war debts, 663–64; international trade agreements, 728–29; rise and fall of, 1789–1960, *c (#4) 841*
Tarkington, Booth, 545
Tarleton, Banastre, 131, 132, *m 131*
Taxation: direct, **100**; indirect, **100**; excise, **212**; excess profits, **722**; under British rule, 57, 59, 99–106, 107–08, *p 100;* and Continental Congress, 134; under Confederation, 151, 152–54; and three-fifths compromise, 158; under Constitution, 165, 183, 199–200, *c 185;* under Hamilton, 212–13; under Jefferson, 230; and Supreme Court, 257; and the War Between the States, 393, 395, 419; income, 395, 502, 560, 630, 722; collection scandals, 431–32; in World War I, 630–31; under New Deal, 722; in World War II, 757
Taylor, Frederick W., 573, 676
Taylor, Zachary: in Mexican War, 330–31, 333, *m 331;* elected President, 365; death, 367
Tea Act, 107–08
Teamsters Union, 797
Teapot Dome scandal, 649
Technical Assistance Program, 792
Technological unemployment, **510**
Tecumseh, 215, 239, 242
Teheran, Iran, 770, *m 740*
Tekakwitha, Katherine, 30
Telegraph, 468–69, 571, *p 295*
Telephone, 469, *c (#9) 837*
Television, 815, *c (#10) 837*
Teller Resolution, 591, 603–04
Temperance movement, 345
Tenant farming, **422**
Tennessee: settlement, 147, 149; becomes a state, 254; secession, 381; in War Between the States, *m 383, m 386, m 390;* power development, 707–10, 796, *m 708, m 847*
Tennessee River, 707, 708, *m 819, m 839*
Tennessee Valley Authority (TVA), 707–10, 796, *m 708, p 709*
Tenth Amendment, 165, 196
Tenure of Office Act, 417
Territorial growth, U.S., *m 822–23*
Texas, *m 846–47;* in Louisiana Purchase, *m 822–23;* surrendered to Spain, 260; cotton growing in, 310, 423, *m 309;* migration to, 326–27; independence, 327–28, *m 327;* annexation, 328, 330; Mexican War, 330–33, *m 822–23;* admitted as state, 363; secession, 381; cattle industry, 452, *m 448;* citrus fruit industry, 679; dust storms, 699; offshore oil, 796
Textile industry, 248–49, 299–300, 308–10, 396, 424 *See also* Cotton.
Thailand (Siam), 296, 750, *m 768, m 807*
Thames, battle, 242, *m 243*
Theater, 536. *See also* Recreation.
Third Plenary Council of Baltimore, 526, 704
Thirteenth Amendment, 198, 400
Thirty-eighth parallel, 789, *m 791*
Thomas, George H., 389–90, *m 390*

Thoreau, Henry David, 353, 355
Thorndike, Edward L., 683
Thornton, William, 264
Three-fifths compromise, 158
Thurmond, J. Strom, 776, 777
Tibet, *m 807*
Tidewater, *m 819;* river, **40**
Tientsin, China, 598, *m 768*
Tierra del Fuego, 11, *m 7*
Tilden, Samuel J., 435
Tillman, "Pitchfork Ben," 500
Time Magazine, 683
Tippecanoe, battle, 239, *m 243, p 239*
Tituba, 75
Titusville, Pa., 470, 471
Tobacco production: colonial, 21–22, 42–43, 62, 63, *p 42;* in 1800's, 308, 423, *m 309;* in 1900's, 679
Tocqueville, Alexis de, 270
Toledo, Ohio, *m 847*
Toleration Act, 41, 76
Topeka, Kan., 371, *m 847*
Torgau, Germany, 765, *m 764*
Tories, **119**; 131, 136, 137, 152. *See also* Loyalists.
Toussaint L'Ouverture, Pierre, 233
Town meeting, **87**
Townshend, Charles, 103
Townshend Acts, 103–04, 106
Township, **146**, *c 147*
Trade, foreign: pre-colonial, 8–9, 15–16, *m 6–7, p 9;* early colonial, 22, 30, 35–36, 42, 48; under British mercantile system, 56–59, 63, 64, 99–100, *m 58;* under Confederation, 151–52; as regulated by Constitution, 158–60; during Napoleonic Wars, 235–36; in 1800's, 253, 297; and merchant marine, 296–99, *m 296–97;* regulated by Federal Trade Commission, 566; under Open Door policy, 597, 599; international trade agreements, 729; rise of manufactured exports, 1821–1960, *c (#2) 840;* exports and imports, 1870–1950, *c (#3) 840;* direction and volume of, late 1950's, *c (#5) 841;* world trade routes, *m 842–43*
Trade, retail, 473, 482, 493, 676
Trade Agreements Act, 728–29
Trails, western, *m 448*
Transcontinental railroads, 397–98, 430, 447–49, *m 448*
Transjordan, 788, *m 755*
Transportation: before War of 1812, 254, *p 256;* improvements, 1800–60, 254–56, 288–94, 308, *m 289, m 293, p 288, p 291, p 294, p 298;* improvements, 1870–1900, 322, 447–49, 467–68, *m 323, m 448, p 336–37;* in twentieth century, 570–71, 614, 680, 814, *p 571, p 572;* major advances, 1607–1960, *c (#1) 832–33;* growth, 1830–1960, *c 836–37;* U.S. system, 1960, *m 838–39*
Travis, William B., 328
Treasury Department, 209, 431
Treaties: Paris (1763), 55, *m 53;* with France (1778), 129–30; Paris (1783), 137–38, *m 823;* Jay, 216; Pinckney, 216, *m 823;* Ghent, 244; Rush-Bagot, 245; Webster-Ashburton (1842) 245, *m 823;* with Spain (1819), 260, *m 822;* with Great Britain (1818), 325, *m 822–23;* with Great Britain (1846), 325, *m 822;* Guadalupe Hidalgo, 333, *m 822;* Burlingame, 513; Paris (1898), 593, *m 605;* Kanagawa, 599; Portsmouth, 600;

ACKNOWLEDGMENTS

TITLE PAGE PHOTOGRAPH: Photograph by Arnold Newman. Reprinted by special permission from *Holiday*, copyright 1959 by The Curtis Publishing Company.

INTRODUCTORY PHOTOGRAPH, p. 1: Howard Hammersley.

PART-OPENING PHOTOGRAPHS: p. 93, The Bettmann Archive; p. 285, Mathew Brady from the National Archives; p. 405, Brown Brothers; p. 583, *left to right*, The Bettmann Archive, Mathew Brady from The National Archives, Brown Brothers, Calvin D. Campbell from Black Star.

TEXT PHOTOGRAPHS: PART I: p. 9, Frick Art Reference Library photo of painting by George Catlin, courtesy of Kennedy Galleries; p. 11, Metropolitan Museum of Art, gift of J. Pierpont Morgan, 1900; p. 20, Flournoy from the Virginia Chamber of Commerce; p. 27, The Bettmann Archive; p. 31, Pioneer Village, Salem; p. 35, Library of Congress; p. 39, New York Public Library, Prints Division; p. 41, Brown Brothers; p. 46, The New York Historical Society, New York City; p. 47, The Chase Manhattan Bank Museum of Moneys of the World; p. 51, Washington and Lee University; p. 54, The Bettmann Archive; p. 55, Office Provincial de Publicité, Quebec; p. 67, The Bettmann Archive; p. 78, Dartmouth College; p. 82, The Bettmann Archive; p. 84, Aubrey P. Janion from Cushing; p. 100, The Massachusetts Historical Society, Boston; p. 106, Culver Service; p. 117, The Bettmann Archive; p. 118, Library of Congress; p. 119, Culver Service; p. 120, Standard Oil Co., N. J.; p. 127, Charles Phelps Cushing; p. 129: *top*, NYSPIX–Commerce, *bottom*, Charles Phelps Cushing; p. 134, Culver Service; p. 149, Culver Service; p. 150, Chase Manhattan Bank Museum of Moneys of the World; p. 153, Brown Brothers; p. 159, The National Archives from Cushing; p. 166, Devaney; p. 208: *top*, The Bettmann Archive, *bottom*, Brown Brothers; p. 210, Culver Service; pp. 211, 213, 218, Brown Brothers; p. 221, The Bettmann Archive; p. 225: *top*, Culver Service, *bottom*, The Bettmann Archive; p. 226, Library of Congress; p. 239, Culver Service; p. 241, NYSPIX–Commerce; p. 244, The Bettmann Archive; p. 252, Culver Service; p. 256, The Bettmann Archive; p. 265, Boston Athenaeum and Museum of Fine Arts, Boston; p. 269, Culver Service; p. 281, The Bettmann Archive.

PART II: p. 291, Tulane University; p. 294, American Steel Foundries; p. 295, National Academy of Design; p. 298, Mariners' Museum, Newport News, Va.; p. 303, Museum of the City of New York; p. 311, The Bettmann Archive; p. 315: *top*, Ragsdale from FPG, *bottom left*, Thorne American Rooms in Miniature, The Art Institute of Chicago, *bottom right*, Bradley Smith from Rapho Guillumette; p. 321, courtesy Mrs. Clyde Porter, Taos, N. Mex., from *Life* Magazine; p. 324, Gjon Mili; p. 329, Norris B. McClaugherty from Shostal; p. 332, Pennsylvania Academy of Fine Arts; pp. 336–37, *across top*, Hall Park McCollough Collection; p. 336, *middle right*, State Street Bank & Trust Co., Boston, *bottom right*, Rare Book Division, New York Public Library, *bottom left*, The Bettmann Archive; p. 337, *bottom*, Gjon Mili; p. 338, Brown Brothers; p. 345, Religious News Service; p. 348: *top*, Eliot Elisofon, courtesy *Life*, © 1953, Time Inc., *bottom*, The Butler Institute of American Art; p. 352, The Ohio State Archeological and Historical Society; p. 355, The Bettmann Archive; p. 366, Library of Congress; p. 369, The Frederick Hill Meserve Collection; p. 375, Culver Service; p. 400, The National Archives; p. 401, Library of Congress.

PART III: p. 408, Library of Congress; p. 409, Library of Congress; p. 415, Culver Service; p. 417, Library of Congress; p. 419, The Bettmann Archive; p. 425, both Devaney; p. 426, Culver Service; p. 435, Culver Service; p. 436, Culver Service; p. 440, The Bettmann Archive; p. 449, Culver Service; p. 453, The National Archives; p. 455, The Bettmann Archive; p. 458, Oklahoma Historical Society; p. 469, New York *Daily Graphic;* p. 473, The Bettmann Archive; p. 475, Culver Service; p. 476, *Puck;* p. 477, Brown Brothers; p. 479, Ewing Galloway; p. 480, Bettmann Archive; p. 481, Putnam County Historical Society; p. 482, Brown Brothers; p. 488, both Gjon Mili; p. 493, Eliot Elisofon, courtesy *Life*, © 1953 Time Inc.; p. 499, Chase Manhattan Bank Museum of Moneys of the World; p. 501, Chicago Historical Society; p. 504, Library of Congress; p. 505, The Bettmann Archive; p. 509, The J. Clarence Davie Collection, Museum of The City of New York; p. 512, Thomas Gilcrease, Institute of History and Art, Tulsa, Okla.; p. 516, The National Archives; p. 519, National Gallery of Art, Index of American Design; p. 524, Ewing Galloway; p. 527, *Steelways*, from American Iron and Steel Institute; p. 530: *left*, Seidman Americana Collection, *right*, Illustration by Worth Brehm from *The Adventures of Tom Sawyer*, reprinted by permission of Harper & Brothers; p. 531, Courtesy of Mark Twain Library & Memorial Commission; p. 533, Courtesy of the New York Times Studio; p. 534: *top*, *Life*, © 1954 Time Inc.; p. 534, *bottom*, The Metropolitan Museum of Art, Alfred N. Pfernnett Fund, Gift of George D. Pratt, 1934; p. 536: *top*, The Bettmann Archive, *bottom*, Brown Brothers; p. 537, Library of Congress; p. 544, American Monthly Review of Reviews, Feb. 1912, from the Chicago *Tribune;* p. 552, Culver Service; p. 555, U.S. Forest Service; p. 561, Underwood & Underwood; p. 562, Harris & Ewing; p. 566, Fitzpatrick, in Cartoons, Mar. 1914, from the St. Louis *Post-Dispatch;* p. 571, Ford Motor Company; p. 572, Smithsonian Institution; p. 573, New York Historical Society; p. 575, The National Archives; p. 578, Ford News Bureau and Automobile Manufacturers' Association.

PART IV: p.587, The Bettmann Archive; p. 595, Fenno Jacobs from Three Lions; p. 598, The National Archives; p. 607, Panama Canal Photograph; p. 615, The National Archives; p. 621, Wide World; p. 629, Culver Service; p. 636, Brown Brothers; p. 644, Brown Brothers; p. 646, Culver Service; p. 650, Wide World; p. 653, The Bettmann Archive; p. 655, Union Pacific Railroad; p. 659, National Archives; p. 660, United Press; p. 665, Brown Brothers; p. 669, C. E. Boesch; p. 671, Culver Service; p. 672, United Press International; p. 678, International Harvester Co.; p. 683, Brown Brothers; p. 685, Roy Clark from Black Star; p. 687, Culver Service; p. 689, Culver Service; p. 696, Franklin D. Roosevelt Library; p. 698, Brown Brothers; p. 699, Culver Service; p. 701, Wide World; p. 703, Brown Brothers; p. 704, Wide World; p. 705, Acme Photo; p. 709, T.V.A.; p. 714, Wide World; p. 716, Wide World; p. 720, Brown Brothers; p. 723, Wide World; p. 730, Brown Brothers; p. 733, Wide World; p. 738, Wide World; p. 739, From Underwood & Underwood; p. 744, Official U.S. Navy Photo; p. 751, U.S. Army; p. 761, Wide World; p. 764, Wide World; p. 765, Brown Brothers; p. 767, U.S. Air Force; p. 770, Wide World; p. 777, Culver Service; p. 778, Wide World; p. 782, Devaney; p. 786, Wide World; p. 789, Wide World; p. 798, United Press International Photo; p. 802, United Press International Photo; p. 803, United Press International Photo.

CHRONOLOGY PHOTOGRAPHS: All from the Library of Congress except the following: p. 851: *left*, The Metropolitan Museum of Art, *right*, C. P. Cushing, Brown Brothers; p. 852, *right*, C. P. Cushing; p. 854, *top left*, G. A. Douglas from Gendreau; p. 857, *bottom right*, F.P.G.; p. 858: *left*, Franklin D. Roosevelt Library, Hyde Park, N. Y., *right*, U.S. Army Photo; p. 859, Chase News Photo, Washington, D. C.